SAINT THOMAS AQUINAS

COMMENTARY ON THE SENTENCES
BOOK IV, DISTINCTIONS 1–13

Translated by Beth Mortensen, STD

COMMENTARY ON THE SENTENCES

Volume 7
Latin/English Edition of the Works of St. Thomas Aquinas

AQUINAS INSTITUTE | EMMAUS ACADEMIC
GREEN BAY, WI | STEUBENVILLE, OH

We would like to thank Kevin Bergdorf, Patricia Lynch, Josh and Holly Harnisch, Fr. Brian McMaster, Dr. Brian Cutter, and the Studentate Community of the Dominican Province of St. Albert the Great, USA, for their support. This series is dedicated to Marcus Berquist, Rose Johanna Trumbull, John and Mary Deignan, Thomas and Eleanor Sullivan, Ann C. Arcidi, the Very Rev. Romanus Cessario, OP, STM, and Fr. John T. Feeney and his sister Mary.

Published with the ecclesiastical approval of
The Most Reverend David L. Ricken, DD, JCL
Bishop of Green Bay
Given on July 16, 2017

Printed in the United States of America

Second Printing 2020

LIBRARY OF CONGRESS CATALOGING-IN-PUBLICATION DATA

Names: Thomas, Aquinas, Saint, 1225?-1274, author. | Mortensen, Beth, translator. |
Thomas, Aquinas, Saint, 1225?-1274. Commentary on the Sentences, Book IV, 1-13 |
Thomas, Aquinas, Saint, 1225?-1274. Commentary on the Sentences, Book IV, 1-13. English

Title: Commentary on the Sentences, Book IV, 1-13 / Thomas Aquinas ; translated by Beth Mortensen, STD.

Description: Steubenville : Emmaus Academic, 2019. |
Series: Latin/English edition of the works of St. Thomas Aquinas ; Volume 7

Identifiers: LCCN 2017937985 | ISBN 9781623400385 (hard cover)

Classification: LCC BX1749.T512 2015 | DDC 230'.2--dc23 LC record available at https://lccn.loc.gov/2017937985

Notes on the Text

Latin Text of St. Thomas

The Latin text used in this volume is originally based on the 1858 Parma Edition, transcribed by Roberto Busa. It was subsequently revised by The Aquinas Institute according to the 1947 M. F. Moos Edition. Certain key passages have been footnoted as having a text corrected according to the Provisional Leonine Edition (PLE). We would like to express our gratitude to the Leonine Commission for their help in the correction of these passages.

English Translation of St. Thomas

The English translation of the *Commentary on the Sentences* in this volume was prepared by Beth Mortensen, STD. It has been edited and annotated by Michael Bolin, PHD, Jeremy Holmes, PHD, and Peter Kwasniewski, PHD. Translations of the *Sentences* of Peter Lombard are taken from *The Sentences, Book 4: On the Doctrine of Signs*, Toronto: Pontifical Institute of Mediaeval Studies, 2009, translated by Giulio Silano. Used with permission.

This translation of the *Commentary on the Sentences, Book IV*, has been made possible in part by a major grant from the National Endowment for the Humanities: Exploring the human endeavor. Any views, findings, conclusions, or recommendations expressed in these volumes do not necessarily represent those of the National Endowment for the Humanities.

DEDICATED WITH LOVE TO
OUR LADY OF MT. CARMEL

Contents

INTRODUCTION

Thomas Aquinas was a towering intellect of the Middle Ages, whose influence has extended across the centuries and spanned academic disciplines. Living at a time when Greek philosophy and Roman jurisprudence were being transformed into the theology and philosophy of the new universities, Aquinas integrated the Platonist tradition at its height with a bold use of Aristotle. He did not hesitate to engage the work of Islamic scholars, such as Avicenna and Averroes, as well as Jewish commentators like Rabbi Moses Maimonides. While naturally subject to the prejudices of his day, Aquinas nevertheless managed a remarkable degree of objectivity when evaluating even the authorities he most revered, such as Aristotle and Augustine. Much of Aquinas's enduring importance comes from his ability to sift all these sources and meld a coherent structure from them.[1]

While Aquinas's best-known work, the *Summa theologiae*, has existed in English for decades, his first major work, the *Commentary on the Sentences* of Peter Lombard (often called the *Scriptum* for *Scriptum super libros Sententiarum*[2]) has been translated only in small portions.[3] In this present set of volumes, the Aquinas Institute makes the entirety of Book IV of the *Scriptum* available in English for the first time in history. This translation could not have been accomplished without a 2013 Scholarly Editions and Translations grant from the National Endowment for the Humanities.

The *Sentences* of Peter Lombard was the standard theological text from the twelfth through the fifteenth century.[4] Producing a commentary on Lombard's text served as the equivalent of today's doctoral dissertation, since it qualified the commentator to teach at the university. Accordingly, all of Aquinas's contemporaries, from Albert the Great to William of

---

[1] Of the biographies written about St. Thomas, several enter into the details of how the *Commentary on the Sentences* came to be written and comment on its structure, content, and characteristics as well as the place it occupies in Aquinas's corpus of writings. The best and most up-to-date account is that of Jean-Pierre Torrell, *Saint Thomas Aquinas,* vol. 1: *The Person and His Work,* trans. Robert Royal (Washington, DC: The Catholic University of America Press, 1996; rev. ed. 2005), 36–53, although still very useful is James A. Weisheipl, *Friar Thomas d'Aquino: His Life, Thought, and Works,* with corrigenda (Washington, DC: The Catholic University of America Press, 1983), 53–92. For further discussion see M.-D. Chenu, *Toward Understanding St. Thomas,* trans. Albert M. Landry and Dominic Hughes (Chicago: Regnery, 1964), 226–37; E. M. Macierowski, *Thomas Aquinas's Earliest Treatment of the Divine Essence* (Binghamton, NY: Global Publications, 1998), 1–16; Simon Tugwell, *Albert and Thomas, Selected Writings* (New York: Paulist Press, 1988), 363–418.

[2] Also called Scriptum super Sententiis or Scriptum super Sententias. In citations, it is typical to find In IV Sent. for Book IV of Aquinas's Commentary on the Sentences.

[3] The largest translation of Aquinas's *Commentary on the Sentences* to be published until now is Peter Kwasniewski's *On Love and Charity: Readings from the Commentary on the Sentences of Peter Lombard* (Thomas in Translation series. Washington DC: Catholic University Press, 2008), which translates, in whole or in part, twelve Distinctions from the *Scriptum*, including one Distinction from Book IV.

[4] It remained in use in some schools even to the end of the eighteenth century. See Romanus Cessario, *A Short History of Thomism* (Washington, DC: The Catholic University of America Press, 2005), 62. For a more comprehensive history of the *Sentences* and its commentaries through the centuries (including one by Martin Luther), see Philipp W. Rosemann, *The Story of a Great Medieval Book: Peter Lombard's "Sentences"* (Peterborough, Ont.: Broadview Press, 2007). Although here we are compelled to focus on the *Sentences* in relation to Thomas Aquinas's opus, readers who wish to investigate the massive historical significance of Peter Lombard and his *Sentences* should see Marcia L. Colish, *Peter Lombard,* 2 vols. (Leiden: E. J. Brill, 1994) and Philipp W. Rosemann, *Peter Lombard* (Oxford: Oxford University Press, 2004).

Ockham to John Duns Scotus and beyond, produced their own commentaries on the *Sentences*, yet none of these have fully appeared in English to date. As Peter Kwasniewski points out in his book *On Love and Charity: Readings from the Commentary on the Sentences of Peter Lombard*,

> Manuscripts of Aquinas's *Scriptum* were considerably more diffused and studied in the centuries after Thomas's death than either of his *Summae* tended to be, largely because of the fact that Lombard's *Sentences* retained its status as a standard textbook. (A budding student of theology in the middle of the fourteenth century could readily find out what a whole sequence of great masters—e.g., Albert, Bonaventure, Thomas, Scotus—had to say about the Holy Spirit as charity by just looking up Book I, Distinction 17. Surely this common set of reference points must have been a major factor in the remarkable pedagogical endurance of the *Sentences*.)[5]

The *Sentences* commentary tradition in general is important to every aspect of medieval studies, and Aquinas's work is a high point in the genre. There is scarcely any issue facing the medieval mind that Thomas did not address in this first demonstration of his mastery of the knowledge of his time. Political philosophy and law, Church authority, language and linguistics, semiotics and sign theory, philosophical anthropology, marital relations and mysticism all have a *locus classicus* in Aquinas's *Commentary on the Sentences*. Thus its translation will be helpful not only to medievalists and theologians, but to anyone with an interest in influential philosophical systems, religious themes, or even the history of education.

Indeed, Aquinas's *Commentary on the Sentences* is much more than a commentary. It is the only one of his works that is comparable to the *Summa* in size and scope: 1,501,918 words as compared to the *Summa's* 1,657,689 words; no other work of Aquinas even attempts to be so comprehensive and detailed. Moreover, it includes topics that Aquinas never treated in the *Summa Theologiae* or anywhere else in his opus.[6] On the other hand, the *Commentary on the Sentences* often contains explicit and in-depth accounts of arguments or positions that Aquinas refers to only implicitly or as subtext in his later works. And of course, the *Commentary on the Sentences* is crucial to any consideration of developments in Aquinas's thought over the course of his career.

However, the *Commentary on the Sentences* is not a commentary in the sense of Thomas's later commentaries on Scripture or works of Aristotle. The format of the *Scriptum* was not a careful, line-by-line analysis of Peter Lombard's work, but the product of a lively classroom discussion in which Aquinas enjoyed the liberty to take up any inquiry the Lombard's text inspired. As Tugwell observes, "The lectures on the *Sentences,* which preceded graduation as a Master, gave scope for the exploration of isolated topics, since the lecturer was quite free to take up any point he wanted and tease it out with little reference to the actual text of the Lombard."[7] In many Distinctions, the Prologue containing the *divisio textus* and the Exposition that closes

---

[5] Peter Kwasniewski, *On Love and Charity: Readings from the Commentary on the Sentences of Peter Lombard* (Thomas in Translation series. Washington DC: Catholic University Press, 2008), 6.

[6] An example of the latter would be *In IV Sent.* d. 49, q. 1, a. 2, qa 5, "Whether beatitude is the same thing as the kingdom of God." There is no query quite like it elsewhere.

[7] *Albert and Thomas*, 249.

the Distinction are the only points in the discussion where Thomas explicitly refers to the *Sentences*. Torrell notes:

> Between these two markers [the *proemium* and the *expositio textus*] we can see the vestiges of the literal commentary, which was honored less and less. If we wish to get an idea of the proportions of the young professor's text compared with that of the Master, we can consider the example Father Chenu once gave: the two pages of distinction 33 of Book III provide Thomas with the occasion to pose 41 questions, which he develops over 88 pages.[8]

Thomas's apparent tangents and departures from the Lombard's discussions suggest that an incipient vision of an order, conciseness, and pedagogical tightness was forming in his mind during this academic exercise, to attain its maturity in his *Summa theologiae*. Yet the format of the *Commentary on the Sentences* also afforded a certain quality of expansiveness and exploration that the later *Summae* could not accommodate.

The Text

The *Commentary on the Sentences* follows the structure of Peter Lombard's *Sentences*,[9] which is divided into four books; each book is subdivided into topics called "Distinctions".[10] This set of volumes represents Book IV of this monumental work.

Within each Book of the *Commentary on the Sentences*, St. Thomas follows the division of Distinctions set down by Peter Lombard, and further divides each Distinction into questions, and then articles, and finally *quaestiunculae* or "sub-questions." We have preserved Thomas's own system of posing questions and objections in the series of quaestiunculae, then listing the responses and replies to all the quaestiunculae together.

The Latin text with which we began was our own corrected and revised version of Robert Busa's digital text. Until now, Renaissance and medieval scholars have been relying on the 1944 edition of Moos, which covers Distinctions 1–22.[11] The second half of Book IV is available in the

---

[8] *The Person and His Work*, 41.

[9] On the overall structure of Lombard's *Sentences,* see Rosemann, *Lombard,* 54–70; Colish, *Lombard,* passim; W. J. Hankey, *God in Himself: Aquinas' Doctrine of God as Expounded in the* Summa Theologiae (Oxford: Oxford University Press, 1987), 19–35; see also Vincent McNabb's analysis of the contents of classic summaries of theology: "Saint Thomas and Moral Theology," in *Xenia Thomistica,* ed. Sadoc Szabó (Rome: Vatican Press, 1925), 2:187–202. In an immensely useful publication from 1932, "Plan des Sentences de Pierre Lombard d'après S. Thomas" (*Bulletin Thomiste* 3 [1930–1933], Notes et communications, 131*–154*), Paul Philippe offered a complete structural overview of the *Sentences* from the perspective of Aquinas, a kind of aerial map for the would-be explorer of either the base text or the commentary. St. Thomas's own ingenious *divisio textus* of the four books may be found in the Prologue to Book I, which Ralph McInerny has translated in *Thomas Aquinas: Selected Writings* (London/New York: Penguin, 1998), 51–54; cf. Torrell, *Person and Work,* 42–44, for a brief discussion of the plan offered in this Prologue, and references to secondary literature.

[10] The division of Peter Lombard's *Sententiae* into Distinctions is attributed to Alexander of Hales (cf. Torrell, *Person and Work,* 40).

[11] *Scriptum super libros Sententiarum,* vols. 3 and 4 (containing Books III and IV, dd. 1–22), ed. Maria Fabianus Moos (Paris: Lethielleux, 1933 and 1947).

Parma edition (1858).[12] It is standard procedure to cross-check problematic texts and lacunae with the older "Piana" edition, revised and reprinted by Vives in 1879.[13] The Aquinas Institute has followed this procedure in refining the quality of our Latin text and correcting some inconsistencies that had crept in over time, particularly in digital transfers of these older editions. However, we owe an enormous debt of gratitude to Adriano Oliva and the Leonine Commission for allowing the Aquinas Institute access to the provisional version of the forthcoming critical edition of Book IV of the *Scriptum*. Since its founding 1870 to provide definitive editions of Aquinas's works, the Leonine Commission has become the standard for the editing of medieval texts. At this writing, the Leonine's critical edition of the Latin text of Book IV of the *Scriptum* is nearing completion. This generous collaboration has allowed us to correct our translation at certain key points, which are indicated by footnotes to the Latin text under the abbreviation PLE (Provisional Leonine Edition).

For the references Aquinas makes to other authors, we have provided sufficient data to locate the texts in a modern edition. Critical editions of Patristic authors have been used where available, substituting CCSL citations for the PL and PG citations in Moos. All quotations from authorities, especially from Scripture, have been translated directly from Thomas's text, not taken from modern translations. As is well known, Thomas cites from memory and so his quotations are not always exact; he occasionally elides different texts or ascribes to one author or book what is to be found in another. (The same is true for his rather frequent citations from "the Gloss," a notoriously complicated tangle of sources found in many forms and variants.[14]) These discrepancies are duly noted. It is all the more necessary to pay attention to *his* take on Scripture passages, since modern translations can fail to capture just the point that Thomas discerns in a particular verse as he knew it in Latin. Since Thomas cites Scripture by book and chapter, we have taken the liberty of inserting verse numbers. When Thomas refers to Psalms by number, he follows the numbering of the Vulgate. Because many people in modern times follow the Hebrew numbering (which is, in most cases, one ahead of the Vulgate's), we have used this numbering in the English translation.

At the beginning of many articles, the reader will find a note indicating *loca parallela* or "parallel texts," for readers who wish to consult other places in St. Thomas's works where he deals with the same or similar topics. However, scholars such as Chenu have warned against the danger of using parallel texts to forge an artificial structure in a systemization that overlooks the object, method, and development of each passage in context.[15] As Peter Kwasniewski advises:

---

[12] For Book IV, dd. 23–50: Sancti Thomae Aquinatis *Opera omnia*, vol. 7/2: *Commentum in quartum librum Sententiarum magistri Petri Lombardi* (Parma: Typis Petri Fiaccadori, 1858), pp. 872–1259.

[13] For the story of the revisions of this text and the Leonine Commission's progress in producing its edition, see Adriano Oliva, OP: "The Leonine Commission, 125 Years after its founding, Settles in Paris" at http://dspace.unav.es/dspace/bitstream/10171/16171/1/9.%20OLIVA.pdf.

[14] We do not enter into the exquisite minutiae of *Gloss* composition but are content, with a nod to the convenient PL edition, to refer in our notes to "Strabo's *Gloss*"—aware that it is not really Strabo's. See M. T. Gibson, "The Place of the *Glossa ordinaria* in Medieval Exegesis," in Ad litteram: *Authoritative Texts and Their Medieval Readers,* ed. Mark D. Jordan and Kent Emery, Jr. (Notre Dame: University of Notre Dame Press, 1992), 5–27.

[15] See Chenu, Toward Understanding St. Thomas, 272-73 and 276.

Dedicated students of St. Thomas know they should handle with care . . . the variety of overlapping treatments he left behind: one pays close attention to the genre of the work, the exact question being investigated, the resources brought to bear on it, the purpose of the inquiry, and, of course, its place in the overall life and writings of its author. One treats an earlier text as, *ceteris paribus,* less definitive than a later text; one treats a disputed question or a *quodlibet* differently from a theological *summa. . .* One may say, in short, that the notion of a parallel text is valid provided one does not entertain false expectations of the completeness or exactness of any parallelism.[16]

For these reasons, our efforts to cross-reference *loca parallela* in other works of Aquinas have focused on including all *extensive* parallels on a given subject (bearing in mind that in many cases looser or broader parallels abound); hence, more oblique or generic ones are not mentioned.

Our thanks also go out to the Pontifical Institute for Mediaeval Studies (Toronto), for permission to use Giulio Silano's translation of Book IV of Peter Lombard's *Sentences* wherever Aquinas quotes the Lombard's words in the prologue and exposition of each Distinction.[17] Silano's translation should allow students to locate the original passages Aquinas comments upon with much more ease and speed, illuminating references that would otherwise be completely abstruse. For efficiency, quotations from Peter Lombard's *Sentences* are marked only with their reference within the *Sentences*; British spelling in these quotations has been brought into conformity with American standards for consistency within the text.

Book IV

Book IV, as St. Thomas sets forth in his prologue to the whole Book, is the study of the "medicine" for the infirmity that is sin. This medicine was bestowed on humankind in the form of the Incarnation: "From this universal medicine," that is, the Word of God made flesh in Christ, "come forth other particular medicines resembling the universal medicine, and by these intermediaries the power of the universal medicine reaches the sick: and these are the sacraments."[18]

Thus Book IV treats the seven sacraments of the Christian church: efficacious signs that are offered to the faithful to give them the grace to reach the goal of human life. Each of the sacraments are investigated in turn in Distinctions 1-42; Distinctions 43-40 deal with the sacraments' aim in "beatitude," the blessedness or happiness that awaits the human soul in heaven.

When Aquinas died before finishing his master-work, the *Summa theologiae,* his followers filled in the missing sections on penance, marriage, and beatitude with passages copied and re-shuffled from Book IV of the *Scriptum,* using an order presumably handed down to them

---

[16] Peter Kwasniewski, *On Love and Charity: Readings from the Commentary on the Sentences of Peter Lombard* (Washington, DC: The Catholic University of America Press, 2008), Full Introduction (available at http://cuapress.cua.edu/res/docs/thomasaquinas-suppmaterials.pdf), p.18-19.

[17] Peter Lombard and Giulio Silano. *The Sentences, Book 4: On the Doctrine of Signs.* (Toronto: Pontifical Institute of Mediaeval Studies, 2010).

[18] *In IV Sent.,* Proemium.

from St. Thomas. This translation will make these passages available in English for the first time within the context of the work to which they belong organically.

The treatise on matrimony (Distinctions 26–42) is of special note, since it is the only place in Aquinas's work where he gives an extensive treatment to marriage as a natural institution and a sacrament. In the midst of a careful legal analysis of marriage as a contract with the consequent "debt" it incurs, moments of unlooked-for sensitivity arise, such as St. Thomas's mild admonition that

> a wife is not subject to the power of her husband like a slave girl; rather there is a certain partnership between man and wife, which is terminated by the death of one of them, so that a dying man cannot leave his wife to another in his will. And so it is clear that wives do not have the same nature as possessions.[19]

A poetic conclusion (popularly attributed to 17th century Bible commentator Matthew Henry) drawn from the creation of woman in Genesis makes some of its earliest appearances in Book IV of the *Scriptum*:[20]

> *She was not formed either from the highest part, nor from the lowest, but from the side of man.* She seems to have been taken from the most excellent place: for the heart is the most important of the members, and the ribs are right beside it. And it must be said that the heart is the most noble as regards the origin of life, but the head as to the full complement of virtues, in which occur movement and sense, which the sensitive life consists in.

Book IV also boasts two of Aquinas's little-known meditations on the Mass in the Expositions to Distinctions 8 and 12.[21] Here he departs for a moment from the text of the Sentences to delve into the meaning of the rich manifold signs that enfold the sign that is the sacrament of the Eucharist. Distinction 8's Exposition gives a *divisio* of the Mass that focuses on the effect on the congregation of each step in the liturgy. The Exposition to Distinction 12 opens the significance of every gesture of the priest in representing Christ's Passion during the Canon of the Mass.

A Note on the Translation

In 2012, when the Aquinas Institute launched its project to publish Aquinas's *Opera Omnia* in bilingual Latin-English editions, we did not imagine we would be making Thomas's works available to the largest and broadest readership that he has ever enjoyed in history. Yet the

---

[19] *In IV Sent.,* d. 38. q. 1. a. 1. qa. 1.

[20] Peter Lombard writes in *Sentences*, Book II, d. 18, q. 2 (104), 1 that "[Woman] was formed not from just any part of [man's] body, but from his side, so that it should be shown that she was created for the partnership of love, lest, if perhaps she had been made from his head, she should be perceived as set over man in domination; or if from his feet, as if subject to him in servitude." He raises this image again in Book IV, d. 28, q. 4 (176), 1, where Aquinas takes it up in this passage from his exposition to Distinction 28. Aquinas uses the argument also in *In IV Sent.*, d. 15, q. 2, a. 5, qa 1, in conjunction with a reference to the conjugal partnership in Augustine's opening to *De Bono Conjugii*. Aquinas's linking of these two texts seems to be the reason that the comparison is found vaguely attributed to Augustine in much modern literature, though its provenance has been traced no earlier than Hugh of St. Victor, (*De Sacramentis*, Book 1, VI, XXXV) and the Lombard himself.

[21] See also http://www.newliturgicalmovement.org/2015/07/st-thomas-aquinass-early-commentary-on.html#.WUWzRZBuJnJ

bilingual format of our books means that they are useful to uninitiated students of Aquinas as well as seasoned scholars and everyone in between. The English translation has opened these works to readers in Russia and the Far East and has reached beyond universities and seminaries to the intellectually curious in every state of life.

This new and varied readership has emboldened us to depart somewhat from the revered ideal of translation handed down to us from William of Moerbeke, whose medieval translations of Aristotle from Greek to Latin preserved so nearly a one-to-one correspondence between key terms that they enabled Aquinas to penetrate the Philosopher's works despite little knowledge of Greek. Many of our readers come to Aquinas's works without the formation in Aristotelian expressions or medieval thought that were for centuries the normal preparation for reading Aquinas. While preserving most of the customary translations of technical terms, we have striven to avoid renderings whose only justification was their currency among Thomists in the last century, in favor of a translation in as plain English as possible. While it is obviously beyond our power to supply the background that would enable every reader to understand St. Thomas, we have offered the occasional glossary footnotes for key expressions that may seem misleadingly familiar to the new student of Aquinas (e.g. *species,* and *sacramentum et res*). We hope in this way to make Aquinas at least somewhat accessible to the neophyte while allowing his words to speak for themselves to his old friends.

COMMENTARY ON THE SENTENCES
BOOK IV, DISTINCTIONS 1-13

PROLOGUE

Misit verbum suum, et sanavit eos, et eripuit eos de interitionibus eorum. Psal. 106, 20.

Ex peccato primi hominis humanum genus duo incurrerat, scilicet mortem, et infirmitatem. Mortem propter separationem a vitae principio, de quo in Psalm. 35, 10, dicitur: *apud te est fons vitae*; et qui separatur ab hoc principio, de necessitate moritur: et hoc factum est per primum hominem. Unde dicitur Rom. 5, 12: *per unum hominem peccatum in mundum intravit, et per peccatum mors.* Infirmitatem vero propter destitutionem gratiae, quae est hominis sanitas, quae petitur Hierem. 17, 14: *sana me Domine, et sanabor*; et ideo in Psalm. 6, 3, dicitur: *miserere mei Domine, quoniam infirmus sum.*

Ad hoc autem sufficiens remedium haberi non poterat, nisi ex verbo Dei, quod est *fons sapientiae in excelsis*, Eccli. 1, et per consequens vitae: quia sapientia vitam tribuit possessori, Eccli. 7; unde dicitur Joan. 5, 21: *sicut pater suscitat mortuos et vivificat; sic filius quos vult, vivificat.*

Ipsum etiam est virtus Dei, quo omnia portantur; Hebr. 1, 3: *portans omnia verbo virtutis suae*; et ideo est efficax ad infirmitatem tollendam. Unde in Psalm. 32, 6, dicitur: *verbo Domini caeli firmati sunt*; et Sap. 16, 12: *neque herba neque malagma sanavit eos, sed sermo tuus, Domine, qui sanat omnia.* Sed quia *vivus est sermo Dei et efficax, et penetrabilior omni gladio ancipiti*, ut dicitur Heb. 4, 12, necessarium fuit ad hoc quod nobis medicina tam violenta proficeret, quod ei carnis nostrae infirmitas adjungeretur, ut nobis magis congrueret. Hebr. 11, 17: *debuit per omnia fratribus assimilari, ut misericors fieret.* Et propter hoc, *verbum caro factum est, et habitavit in nobis*; Joan. 1, 14. Sed quia haec medicina tantae est efficaciae ut omnes sanare possit (*virtus enim exibat de illo, et sanabat omnes*, ut dicitur Luc. 6, 19), ideo ab hac universali medicina et prima aliae particulares medicinae procedunt universali medicinae conformes, quibus mediantibus virtus universalis medicinae proveniat ad infirmos: et haec sunt sacramenta, *in quibus sub tegumento rerum visibilium divina virtus secretius operatur salutem*, ut Augustinus dicit.

He sent his Word and healed them, and delivered them from all their destructions (Ps 107 [106]:20).

By the sin of the first man, the human race incurred two things, namely, death and infirmity. Death, because of its separation from the principle of life, of which it is said, *with you is the font of life* (Ps 36 [35]:9); whoever is separated from this principle necessarily dies, and this happened through the first man. Hence it is said, *by one man sin entered the world, and by sin, death* (Rom 5:12). But the human race incurred infirmity because it forsook grace, which is man's health. Jeremiah seeks this health when he says: *heal me, Lord, and I shall be healed* (Jer 17:14); and similarly the Psalm says, *have mercy on me, Lord, for I am weak* (Ps 6:2).

But a sufficient remedy could be obtained for this only from the word of God, which is the *font of wisdom on high* (Sir 1:5) and, accordingly, the source of life: for wisdom endows its possessor with life (cf. Sir 7). Thus it is said, *as the Father raises up the dead and gives life, so the Son also gives life to whom he will* (Jn 5:20).

The word is the power of God, by which all things are upheld: *upholding all things by the word of his power* (Heb 1:3). And this is why it is efficacious for removing infirmity. Thus it is said, *by the word of the Lord the heavens were established* (Ps 33 [32]:6); and *neither herb nor poultice cured them, but your word, O Lord, which heals all things* (Wis 16:12). But because *the word of God is living and effectual, and more piercing than any two-edged sword* (Heb 4:12), for a treatment so violent to be effective for us it was necessary that the infirmity of our flesh might be joined to it, so that it might be more suited to us; therefore, *he had to become like his brethren in all things, so that he could be a merciful and faithful high priest* (Heb 2:17). And for this reason, *the Word became flesh and dwelt among us* (Jn 1:14). But because this treatment is so powerful that it can cure all men (*for power went out from him and he cured all*, as it says in Luke 6:19), therefore from this universal medicine come forth other particular medicines resembling the universal medicine, and by these intermediaries the power of the universal medicine reaches the sick: and these are the sacraments, *in which, under the cover of visible things, divine power works our healing in a hidden way*, as Augustine says.[1]

---

1. This definition is not found verbatim in Augustine; cf. Isidore, *Etymologiarum* (ed. Lindsay), Bk. 6, ch. 19, par. 40: "Quae ob id sacramenta dicuntur, quia sub tegumento corporalium rerum uirtus diuina secretius salutem eorundem sacramentorum operatur; unde et a secretis uirtutibus uel a sacris sacramenta dicuntur"; and Gratian, *Decretum*, Pt. 2, causa 1, qu. 1, can. 84: "Sunt autem sacramenta: baptisma, crisma, corpus et sanguis, que ob id sacramenta dicuntur, quia sub tegumento corporalium rerum diuina uirtus secretius salutem eorundem sacramentorum operatur" (ed. E. Friedberg, 388).

Sic ergo in verbis propositis tria tanguntur: scilicet confectio medicinae, sanatio ab infirmitate, et liberatio a morte.

Confectio medicinae tangitur in hoc quod dicit: *misit verbum suum*; quod quidem referendum est et ad Verbi incarnationem, quod dicitur a Deo missum, quia caro factum; Gal. 4, 4: *misit Deus filium suum factum ex muliere*; et ad sacramentorum institutionem, in quibus *accedit verbum ad elementum, et fit sacramentum*, ut sic sit conformitas sacramenti ad Verbum incarnatum. Sanctificatur enim creatura sensibilis per Verbum Dei et orationem; 1 Timoth., 4.

Sanatio autem ab infirmitate peccati et reliquiarum ejus, tangitur in hoc quod dicitur: *et sanavit eos*; quae quidem sanatio per sacramenta fit: unde ipsa sunt unguenta sanitatis, quae Christus quasi unguentarius confecit; unde et in Psalm. 102, 3, dicitur: *qui propitiatur omnibus iniquitatibus tuis*, quantum ad peccata; *qui sanat omnes infirmitates tuas*, quantum ad peccatorum reliquias.

Liberatio autem a morte tangitur in hoc quod dicitur: *et eripuit eos de interitionibus eorum*. Et quia interitus in mortem violentam sonare videtur, ideo congrue ad poenalem mortem referri potest: quia ratio poenae est ut contra voluntatem sit, sicut ratio culpae ut sit voluntaria; et ideo culpa ad infirmitatem reducitur, poena ad mortem: quia via ad poenam est culpa, sicut infirmitas ad mortem. Non solum autem separatio animae a corpore mors dici potest, sed etiam omnes praesentis vitae poenalitates: et ideo pluraliter *interitiones* nominantur, sicut et 2 Cor. 11, 23: *in mortibus frequenter*. A morte ergo corruptionis naturae eripiet Verbum incarnatum per resurrectionem: quia *in Christo omnes vivificabuntur*; 1 Corinth. 25, 22, Isai. 26, 19: *vivent interfecti mei* etc.; sed a mortibus poenalitatum per gloriam: tunc enim absorpta erit mors per victoriam; 1 Corinth. 25; et de his in Psalm. 102, 4, dicitur: *qui redimit de interitu vitam tuam*, quantum ad primum: *qui coronat te in misericordia*, quantum ad secundum.

Sic ergo ex verbis propositis tria possumus accipere circa hunc quartum librum, qui prae manibus habetur, scilicet materiam: quia in eo agitur de sacramentis, et de resurrectione et gloria resurgentium.

Item continuationem ad tertium librum: quia in tertio agebatur de missione Verbi in carnem, in hoc autem libro de effectibus Verbi incarnati; ut quartus respondeat tertio, sicut secundus primo.

Item divisionem istius libri. Dividitur enim in partes duas: in prima determinat de sacramentis; in secunda

Therefore in this way three things are touched upon in the words above: namely, the preparation of this medicine, healing from infirmity, and liberation from death.

The preparation of the medicine is touched upon when it says, *he sent his word*. This should be understood as referring to the Incarnation of the Word, who is said to be sent by God because he became flesh: *God sent his Son, born of a woman* (Gal 4:4). It should also be understood as referring to the institution of the sacraments, in which *the word is combined with the element and the sacrament is made*;[2] so that in this way a sacrament is similar to the Incarnate Word. For sensible creation is sanctified by the Word of God and prayer (1 Tim 4:5).

But healing from the infirmity of sin and all it leaves behind is referred to when it says, *and healed them*. This healing happens indeed through the sacraments, and so they are themselves the ointments of healing, which Christ, like an apothecary, prepared. Hence it also says, *who forgives all your iniquities*, as to sin, and *who heals all your infirmities*, as to the effects of sin (Ps 103 [102]:3).

But deliverance from death is referred to when it says, *and delivered them from all their destructions*. And since 'destruction' suggests violent death, this text can be taken as referring to penal death, for the notion of punishment is that it is against one's will, just as the notion of fault is that it is voluntary; and thus fault is related to infirmity and punishment to death, for fault is the way to punishment just as infirmity is the way to death. But besides the separation of the soul from the body all the punishments of this present life can also be called death, and therefore it says *destructions* in the plural, just as it says in 2 Cor 11:23, *often in deaths*. Therefore, from the death of nature's corruption the Incarnate Word will deliver us by his resurrection: *for in Christ all will be made alive* (1 Cor 15:22); and *my slain shall rise again* (Isa 26:19). But from deaths of punishment the Incarnate Word will deliver us through glory, for then death will be swallowed up by victory (cf. 1 Cor 15); and concerning this the Psalm says, *who redeems your life from destruction*, with regard to the first (Ps 103 [102]:4); *who crowns you with mercy*, with regard to the second.

And so from the words quoted we can gather three things concerning this fourth book, which is now at hand. First, the matter: for it is about the sacraments, the resurrection, and the glory of those rising again.

Next, that it is a continuation of the third book: for the third was about the sending forth of the Word in flesh, but this book is about the effects of the Incarnate Word, so that the fourth book corresponds to the third just as the second does to the first.

Lastly, the division of this book, for it is divided into two parts: in the first, the sacraments are examined; in the sec-

---

2. Augustine, *In Iohannis euangelium tractatus* (CCSL 36), Tract. 80, par. 3.

determinat de resurrectione, et gloria resurgentium, 43 distinct., ibi: *postremo de conditione resurrectionis et modo resurgentium . . . breviter disserendum est.* Item prima dividitur in duas. In prima determinat de sacramentis in generali; in secunda descendit ad sacramenta novae legis, 2 dist., ibi: *jam ad sacramenta novae legis accedamus.*

ond, the resurrection and the glory of the resurrected, as it says at Distinction 43: *lastly, we must briefly discuss the condition of the resurrection and the manner of the risen.*[3] Likewise, the first part is divided into two parts. In the first, he defines the sacraments in general; in the second, he moves to the sacraments of the New Law at Distinction 2: *let us now proceed to the sacraments of the New Law.*[4]

3. *Sent.* IV, 43.1 (244), 1.
4. *Sent.* IV, 2.1 (11), 1.

DISTINCTION 1

SACRAMENTS IN GENERAL

Prima in duas: in prima dicitur de quo est intentio: in secunda prosequitur, ibi: *sacramentum est sacrae rei signum*. Circa primum duo facit: primo proponit materiam de qua agendum est. Secundo ostendit quid de ea primo dicendum sit, ibi: *de quibus quattuor primo consideranda sunt*.

Sacramentum est sacrae rei signum. Hic determinare incipit de sacramentis in communi; et dividitur in partes duas: in prima determinat de sacramentis secundum se; in secunda de divisione sacramenti in suas partes, ibi: *duo autem sunt in quibus sacramentum consistit*. Prima in duas: in prima ostendit quid est sacramentum; in secunda necessitatem institutionis sacramentorum, ibi, *triplici autem ex causa sacramenta instituta sunt*. Prima in duas: in prima venatur genus sacramenti; in secunda differentias, ibi: *signorum vero alia sunt naturalia . . . alia data*. Circa primum duo facit: primo ponit sacramentum in genere signi; secundo definit signum, ibi: *signum vero est res praeter speciem quam ingerit sensibus, aliquid aliud ex se faciens in cognitionem venire*.

Signorum vero alia sunt naturalia . . . alia data. Hic venatur differentias: et primo unam differentiam communem omnibus sacramentis, quae est ut imaginem gerat; secundo aliam quae est propria sacramentorum novae legis, in quibus est perfecta ratio sacramenti, scilicet ut causa existat, ibi: *sacramentum enim proprie dicitur, quod ita signum est gratiae Dei, et invisibilis gratiae forma, ut ipsius imaginem gerat et causa existat*.

Duo autem sunt in quibus sacramentum consistit. Hic dividit sacramentum in duas partes: et primo in partes integrales; secundo in partes subjectivas, ibi: *jam videre restat differentiam sacramentorum veterum, et novorum*. Et circa haec, duo facit: primo ostendit differentiam inter sacramenta veteris et novae legis; secundo determinat de quodam sacramento veteris legis, quod maxime cum sacramentis novae legis communicat, ibi: *fuit autem inter illa sacramenta sacramentum quoddam, scilicet circumcisionis, idem conferens remedium contra peccatum quod*

The first part is divided into two: in the first, the intention is stated; in the second, it is pursued, at "*a sacrament is a sign of a sacred thing*".[1] Concerning this he does two things. First, he proposes the matter to be discussed. Second, he shows what will be said about it: first, at *concerning which, four things must first be considered*.[2]

"*A sacrament is a sign of a sacred thing*". Here he begins to define the sacraments in general, and it is divided into two parts: in the first, he defines the sacraments in themselves; in the second, he divides the sacraments into their parts, at *a sacrament consists of two elements*.[3] The first is in two parts: in the first, he shows what a sacrament is; in the second, the necessity of the institution of the sacraments, at *The sacraments were instituted for a threefold cause*.[4] The first is in two parts: in the first, he seeks out the genus of sacraments; in the second, the differences, at "*But some signs are natural . . . others are conventional*".[5] Concerning the first point he does two things: first, he places the sacrament in the genus of signs; second, he defines signs, at "*A sign is a thing which, over and above the form which it impresses on the senses, causes something else to come into the mind through itself*".[6]

"*But some signs are natural . . . others are conventional*". Here he delineates the differences: first, one difference common to every sacrament, which is that it bears an image; second, another difference which is proper to sacraments of the New Law, in which the nature of a sacrament is perfectly realized, namely, that it acts as a cause, at *For a sacrament is properly so called because it is a sign of God's grace and a form of invisible grace in such a manner that it bears its image and is its cause*.[7]

A sacrament consists of two elements. Here he divides a sacrament into two parts: the first is essential parts, and the second, subjective parts, at *it now remains to note the difference between the old and new sacraments*.[8] And concerning these, he does two things: first, he shows the difference between the sacraments of the Old Law and of the New Law; second, he examines a certain sacrament of the Old Law which shares the most with the sacraments of the New Law, at *And yet there was one among those sacraments, namely circumcision, which conferred the same remedy against sin as*

---

1. *Sent.* IV, 1.2.1, citing Augustine, *De civitate Dei*, Bk. 10, ch. 5.
2. Peter Lombard, *Sententiae* IV, 1.1.2.
3. *Sent.* IV, 1.5.6.
4. *Sent.* IV, 1.5.1.
5. *Sent.* IV, 1.4.1, citing Augustine, *De doctrina christiana*, Bk. 2, ch. 1, n. 2.
6. *Sent.* IV, 1.3.1, citing Augustine, *De doctrina christiana*, Bk. 2, ch. 1, n. 1.
7. *Sent.* IV, 1.4.2.
8. *Sent.* IV, 1.6.1.

nunc baptismus praestat. Quarum prima pars cum praecedentibus est de lectione praesenti.

baptism does now.[9] The first of these parts with everything preceding it is the topic of the present lecture.

---

9. *Sent.* IV, 1.7.1.

QUESTION 1

THE ESSENCE OF THE SACRAMENTS

Hic quaeruntur quinque:
Primo, quid sit sacramentum;
secundo, de necessitate sacramentorum;
tertio, ex quibus consistat sacramentum;
quarto, de efficacia sacramentorum novae legis;

quinto, de efficacia sacramentorum veteris legis.

Here five questions arise:
first, what is a sacrament;
second, on the necessity of the sacraments;
third, what a sacrament consists of;
fourth, on the efficacy of the sacraments of the New Law;
fifth, on the efficacy of the sacraments of the Old Law.

ARTICLE 1

What is a sacrament[10]

Quaestiuncula 1

AD PRIMUM SIC PROCEDITUR. Videtur quod inconvenienter definiatur sacramentum per hoc quod dicitur: *sacramentum est sacrae rei signum.* Sacramenta enim sunt alligamenta sanitatis, ut dicitur in Glossa super illud Psalm. 146, 3: *qui sanat contritos corde.* Sed de ratione medicamenti non est ut aliquid significet, sed solum ut efficiat sanitatem. Ergo sacramentum non est signum.

PRAETEREA, omnes creaturae sensibiles sunt signa invisibilium divinorum, ut patet Rom. 1, nec tamen dici possunt sacramenta. Ergo male definitur sacramentum *sacrae rei signum.*

PRAETEREA, serpens aeneus, de quo dicitur Num. 21, signum fuit sacrae rei, scilicet crucis Christi: nec tamen fuit sacramentum. Ergo definitio praedicta est male data.

PRAETEREA, triplex est signum; scilicet demonstrativum, quod est de praesenti; rememorativum, quod est de praeterito; prognosticum, quod est de futuro. Sed nullum istorum competit sacramento, cum quandoque recipiens sacramentum, gratiam non habeat, nec habuit, nec in posterum habiturus sit. Ergo non omne sacramentum est signum.

TO THE FIRST WE PROCEED THUS. It seems that 'sacrament' is unfittingly defined by saying *a sacrament is a sign of a sacred thing.*[11] For sacraments are bonds of health, as it says in the Gloss on the Psalm: *who heals the broken-hearted* (Ps 147 [146]:3).[12] But the idea of medicine is not that it signifies something, but only that it brings about health. Therefore, a sacrament is not a sign.

OBJ. 2: Furthermore, all sensible creatures are signs of invisible divine things, as is clear from Romans 1:20, but nevertheless they cannot be called sacraments. Therefore, sacrament is wrongly defined as *a sign of a sacred thing.*

OBJ. 3: Furthermore, the brass serpent that is spoken of in Numbers 21 was a sign of a sacred thing, namely, the cross of Christ, but it was still not a sacrament. Therefore, the definition mentioned is badly written.

OBJ. 4: Furthermore, there are three kinds of sign, namely the demonstrative, which concerns the present; the commemorative, which concerns the past; and the prognostic, which concerns the future. But none of these corresponds to a sacrament, since sometimes the person receiving the sacrament does not have grace, nor has had it, nor ever will have it afterward. Therefore, not every sacrament is a sign.

---

10. Parallels: ST III, q. 60, aa. 1, 2, 3.

11. Lombard attributes this definition to Augustine; it seems to be based on phrases in Book 10 of *De civitate Dei* (CCSL 47), especially ch. 5, l. 15: "sacrificium ergo uisibile inuisibilis sacrificii sacramentum, id est sacrum signum est."

12. For the Gloss, see PL 113:1073.

PRAETEREA, signum contra causam dividitur. Sed aliquod sacramentum est causa. Ergo non omne sacramentum est signum.

OBJ. 5: Furthermore, sign is not in the same genus as cause. But some sacraments are causes. Therefore, not every sacrament is a sign.

Quaestiuncula 2

ULTERIUS. Videtur quod male definiatur signum, cum dicitur: *signum est res praeter speciem quam ingerit sensibus, aliquid aliud ex se faciens in cognitionem venire.* Unum enim oppositorum non debet poni in definitione alterius. Sed res et signa ex opposito dividuntur, ut patuit in 1 dist. primi libri. Ergo res non debet poni in definitione signi.

PRAETEREA, secundum Philosophum in libro *Priorum*, omnis effectus suae causae signum esse potest. Sed quidam effectus sunt spirituales, qui nullam speciem ingerunt sensibus. Ergo non omne signum aliquam speciem sensibus ingerit.

PRAETEREA, omnis locutio fit per aliqua signa. Sed angeli loquuntur non prolato aliquo sensibili sermone, ut in 2 Lib., dist. 2, dictum est. Ergo non omne signum est sensibile.

OBJ. 1: Moreover, it seems that a sign is wrongly defined when it is said, *a sign is a reality that conveys something else to the mind, besides the appearance it presents to the senses.*[13] For one of two opposites cannot be included in the definition of the other. But reality and sign are divided as opposites, as is clear in Distinction 1 of Book I. Therefore, 'reality' should not be included in the definition of sign.

OBJ. 2: Furthermore, according to the Philosopher in the *Prior Analytics*, every effect can be a sign of its cause.[14] But some effects are spiritual, and so they present no appearance to the senses. Therefore, not every sign presents some appearance to the senses.

OBJ. 3: Furthermore, every utterance is made by certain signs. But angels speak without uttering sensible words, as was said in Distinction 2 of Book II.[15] Therefore, not every sign is sensible.

Quaestiuncula 3

ULTERIUS. Videtur quod haec definitio male detur: *sacramentum est invisibilis gratiae visibilis forma, ut imaginem gerat, et causa existat.* Sicut enim in littera dicitur, in duobus sacramenta consistunt, scilicet in rebus et verbis. Sed sicut res sunt visibiles, ita verba sunt audibilia. Ergo debuit dicere: visibilis et audibilis forma.

PRAETEREA, omnis forma est intrinseca vel exemplaris. Sed sacramenta non sunt formae intrinsecae invisibilis gratiae, ut per se patet: nec iterum formae exemplares, cum gratia invisibilis non imitetur rem visibilem, sed e converso. Ergo sacramentum nullo modo est forma invisibilis gratiae.

PRAETEREA, character baptismalis est sacramentum et res, ut infra, dist. 4, quaest. 1, dicetur, et similiter corpus Christi verum existens in altari. Sed neutrum istorum est forma visibilis. Ergo definitio non est bene data.

OBJ. 1: Moreover, it seems that this definition is badly written: *a sacrament is the visible form of invisible grace, so that it bears an image and becomes a cause.*[16] For just as it says in the text, sacraments consist of two things, namely, things and words. But just as things are visible, so words are audible. Therefore, it should have said: "visible and audible form."

OBJ. 2: Furthermore, every form is either intrinsic or exemplar. But it is self-evident that sacraments are not intrinsic forms of invisible grace; nor, on the other hand are they exemplar forms, since invisible grace does not imitate visible reality, but vice versa. Therefore, a sacrament is in no way a form of invisible grace.

OBJ. 3: Furthermore, the baptismal character is a sacrament-and-reality, as will be said below, in Distinction 4, Question 1. And similarly the body of Christ is a real thing existing on the altar. But neither of these is a visible form. Therefore, the definition is not well written.

---

13. Augustine, *De doctrina Christiana*, Bk. 2, ch. 1: "signum est enim res praeter speciem, quam ingerit sensibus, aliud aliquid ex se faciens in cogitationem uenire" (CCSL 32).

14. See *Prior Analytics*, Bk. 2, ch. 27: "Anything such that when it is another thing is, or when it has come into being the other has come into being before or after, is a sign of the other's being or having come into being . . . For example the proof that a woman is with child because she has milk" (70a7–14).

15. See *In II Sent.*, d. 2, q. 2, a. 3.

16. *Summa Sent.* tract. 4, ch. 1 (PL 176:177). Elsewhere Lombard attributes this definition to Augustine's *De civitate Dei*, where it does not appear verbatim. In *Sic et Non*, Qu. 117, sent. 109, l. 818, Peter Abelard cites "a certain epistle" of Augustine's as stating: "Sacramentum est invisibilis gratiae visibilis forma" (ed. Boyer/McKeon, 407)—a phrase frequently quoted by medieval authors such as Gratian, Berengarius, and Augustine of Dacia.

PRAETEREA, imago est quod ad imitationem alterius fit; forma autem exemplaris est ad cujus imitationem aliquid fit. Ergo non est idem forma et imago respectu ejusdem. Sed sacramentum est forma invisibilis gratiae. Ergo non est imago respectu ejusdem.

PRAETEREA, in definitione generis non debet poni differentia constitutiva alicujus specierum in quas dividitur genus. Sed esse causam ejus quod figurat, est differentia sacramentorum novae legis. Ergo non debet poni in definitione communi sacramenti.

OBJ. 4: Furthermore, an image is what is made in imitation of something else, while an exemplar form is what something is made in imitation of. Therefore, one thing cannot be a form and an image with regard to the same thing. But a sacrament is a form of invisible grace. Therefore it is not an image with regard to the same thing.

OBJ. 5: Furthermore, the definition of a genus should not include the constitutive difference of one of the species into which the genus is divided. But to be the cause of what it represents is the constitutive difference of sacraments of the New Law. Therefore, it should not be included in the general definition of sacraments.

Quaestiuncula 4

ULTERIUS. Videtur quod definitio quam ponit Augustinus, sit incompetens; scilicet: *sacramentum est in quo sub tegumento rerum visibilium divina virtus secretius operatur salutem.* Occultatio enim manifestationi opponitur. Sed signum instituitur ad manifestandum. Cum ergo tegumentum occultationem importet, videtur quod male ponatur in definitione sacramenti.

PRAETEREA, frequenter accipientes sacramenta, salutem non consequuntur. Ergo operatio salutis non debet poni in definitione sacramenti.

PRAETEREA, in sanctis hominibus divina virtus operatur ad salutem ipsorum, ut dicitur Isai. 26, 12: *omnia opera nostra operatus es in nobis,* nec tamen sancti homines dicuntur sacramenta. Ergo idem quod prius.

OBJ. 1: Moreover, it seems that the definition that Augustine sets down, namely, *a sacrament is that in which, under the cover of visible things, divine power works our salvation in a hidden way,*[17] is unfitting. For secrecy is opposed to manifestation. But a sign is instituted to make something manifest. Since, therefore, a cover implies secrecy, it seems that it is wrongly included in the definition of sacrament.

OBJ. 2: Furthermore, often those receiving the sacraments do not obtain salvation. Therefore, working salvation should not be included in the definition of sacrament.

OBJ. 3: Furthermore, in holy men divine power is working for their salvation, as it says, *You worked all our works in us* (Isa 26:12). But holy men are not called sacraments. Therefore, the same as before.

Quaestiuncula 5

ULTERIUS. Videtur quod definitio Hugonis a sancto Victore, sit incompetens, quae talis est: *sacramentum est corporale vel materiale elementum, extrinsecus oculis suppositum, ex institutione signans, ex similitudine repraesentans, et ex sanctificatione invisibilem gratiam continens.* Materia enim non praedicatur de toto. Sed materiale elementum est materia sacramenti. Ergo male ponitur in definitione sacramenti ut genus.

PRAETEREA, in quibusdam sacramentis non est elementum, sed elementatum, sicut in extrema unctione est oleum. Ergo definitio non est communis omnibus sacramentis.

PRAETEREA, similitudo est rerum differentium eadem qualitas. Sed non potest esse eadem qualitas re-

OBJ. 1: Moreover, it seems that the definition of Hugh of St. Victor is inadequate.[18] It goes like this: *A sacrament is a corporeal or material element set externally before the eyes, signifying something by its institution, representing something by its likeness, and containing invisible grace by its sanctification.*[19] For matter is not said of the whole, but the material element is the matter of a sacrament. Therefore, it is wrongly set down as the genus in the definition of sacrament.

OBJ. 2: Furthermore, in certain sacraments there is no element, but rather something made from elements, such as the oil in extreme unction. Therefore, this definition is not common to all the sacraments.

OBJ. 3: Furthermore, a likeness is the same quality in different things. But the same quality cannot exist in spir-

---

17. See earlier note.

18. Parallel: *ST* III, q. 64, a. 2, ad 2.

19. Hugh of St. Victor, *De sacramentis fidei,* Bk. 1, pt. 9, ch. 2: "Sacramentum est corporale vel materiale elementum foris sensibiliter propositum ex similitudine repraesentans, et ex institutione significans, et ex sanctificatione continens aliquam invisibilem et spiritalem gratiam" (PL 176:317). Part of this text is cited as the sed contra of *ST* q. 62, a. 3: "sacramentum ex sanctificatione invisibilem gratiam continet."

rum spiritualium ad corporalia. Ergo nec similitudo; ergo male dicitur: *ex similitudine repraesentans*.

PRAETEREA, si est aliqua similitudo, illa est ex naturali proprietate materialis elementi. Si ergo ex similitudine repraesentat, et idem est repraesentare quod significare, ut potest patere per definitionem signi in littera positam; ergo sacramentum non significat ex institutione.

itual and corporeal things; therefore, there is no likeness. Therefore, it is wrong to say *representing something by a likeness*.

OBJ. 4: Furthermore, if there is any similitude, then it is from the natural properties of the material element. Therefore, if it represents something by similitude (and to represent is the same thing as to signify, as can be seen clearly by the definition of sign set forth in the text), then a sacrament does not signify anything by its institution.

Response to Quaestiuncula 1

RESPONDEO dicendum ad primam quaestionem, quod sacramentum secundum proprietatem vocabuli videtur importare sanctitatem active, ut dicatur sacramentum quo aliquid sacratur, sicut ornamentum quo aliquid ornatur. Sed quia actiones activorum dicuntur esse proportionatae conditionibus passivorum, ideo in sanctificatione qua homo sanctificatur, debet esse talis sanctificandi modus qui homini competat secundum quod rationalis est, quia ex hoc est homo. Inquantum autem est rationalis, habet cognitionem a sensibilibus ortam; unde oportet quod sanctificetur hoc modo quod sua sanctificatio sibi innotescat per similitudines sensibilium rerum; et secundum hoc invenitur diversa acceptio sacramenti. Aliquando enim sacramentum importat rem qua fit consecratio; et sic passio Christi dicitur sacramentum; et haec est prima acceptio quam Magister ponit.

Aliquando vero includit modum consecrationis, qui homini competit secundum quod causae sanctificantes et sua sanctificatio per similitudines sensibilium sibi notificantur; et sic sacramenta novae legis sacramenta dicuntur: quia et consecrant, et sanctitatem significant modo praedicto, et etiam primas sanctificationis causas significant; sicut baptismus et[20] puritatem designat, et mortis Christi signum est.

Aliquando etiam includit tantum significationem praedictarum consecrationum, sicut signum sanitatis dicitur sanum; et hoc modo sacramenta veteris legis, sacramenta dicuntur, inquantum significant ea quae in Christo sunt gesta, et etiam sacramenta novae legis.

Relicto ergo primo modo dicendi sacramentum (quia de hujusmodi sacramentis dictum est in 3 libro), de sacramentis secundo et tertio modo dictis non poterit alia communis definitio assignari nisi dicatur: *sacramentum est sacrae rei signum*; nisi quod oportet ut subintelligatur talis modus significandi, qui est per similitudinem

I ANSWER THAT, 'sacrament,' according to the proper meaning of the word, seems to convey 'sanctity' in an active sense, so that anything that renders something sacred is called a sacrament, just as whatever renders something ornate is called an ornament. But since the actions of the things acting should be proportionate to the condition of the things acted upon, for this reason in the sanctification of man there should be a mode of sanctification befitting man according as he is rational, for this is what makes him a man. But insofar as he is rational, his knowledge arises from his senses. Thus it is necessary that he be sanctified in such a way that his sanctification also becomes known to him through the likenesses of sensible things. And in keeping with this one finds diverse ways of taking the word 'sacrament.' For sometimes 'sacrament' conveys the thing by which a consecration happens; in this way the Passion of Christ is called a sacrament. And this is the first way of taking the word that the Master mentions.

But sometimes it includes the mode of consecration that befits a man according as both the sanctifying causes and his own sanctification are made known to him through sensible likenesses. And in this way the sacraments of the New Law are called sacraments, for they not only consecrate but also signify sanctity in the way mentioned and signify the first causes of sanctification as well: for example, baptism both sanctifies, and designates purity and is a sign of the death of Christ.

However, sometimes it includes only the signification of the consecrations mentioned, as a sign of health is called healthy. And in this way the sacraments of the Old Law are called sacraments, inasmuch as they represent those things that were accomplished in Christ, including the sacraments of the New Law.

Therefore, leaving behind the first way of saying 'sacrament,' (since this kind of sacrament was discussed in Book III), the only way to give another common definition to 'sacraments' said in the second and third ways is to say: *A sacrament is a sign of a sacred thing*, although one must understand behind the word 'sign' that manner of signifying

---

20. *baptismus et.—baptismus sanctificat et* PLE.

rei sensibilis quod Magister addit quod est id ut scilicet ejus similitudinem gerat.

AD PRIMUM ergo dicendum, quod quamvis significatio non sit de ratione curationis simpliciter, est tamen de ratione curationis talis quae fit per sacramenta, ut ex dictis patet.

AD SECUNDUM dicendum, quod res sensibiles non sunt signa divinorum ut sunt sacrantia, sed ut sunt in seipsis sacra. Sacramentum autem debet intelligi signum rei sacrae ut est sacrans; et ideo non oportet quod omnes res sensibiles sint sacramenta.

AD TERTIUM dicendum, quod quamvis serpens aeneus esset signum rei sacrae sacrantis, non tamen inquantum sacrans est actu: quia non ad hoc adhibebatur ut aliquis sanctificationis effectus perciperetur; sed solum effectus exterioris curationis; et similis est ratio de imagine crucis, quae ponitur tantum ad repraesentandum.

AD QUARTUM dicendum, quod sacramenta novae legis tria significant; scilicet causam primam sanctificantem, sicut baptismus mortem Christi; et quantum ad hoc sunt signa rememorativa. Item significant effectum sanctificationis quam faciunt; et haec significatio est eis principalis; et sic sunt signa demonstrativa. Nec obstat, si aliquis sanctitatem non recipit: quia non est ex defectu sacramenti, quod, quantum in se est, natum est gratiam conferre. Item significant finem sanctificationis, scilicet aeternam gloriam; et quantum ad hoc sunt signa prognostica. Sacramenta vero veteris legis erant totaliter signa prognostica.

AD QUINTUM dicendum, quod signum, quantum est in se, importat aliquid manifestum quo ad nos, quo manuducimur in cognitionem alicujus occulti. Et quia ut frequentius effectus sunt nobis manifestiores causis; ideo signum quandoque contra causam dividitur, sicut demonstratio quia est quae dicitur esse per signum a communi, ut in 1 *Physicor.* dicitur; demonstratio autem propter quid est per causam. Quandoque autem causa est manifesta quo ad nos, utpote cadens sub sensu; effectus autem occultus, ut si expectatur in futurum; et tunc nihil prohibet causam signum sui effectus dici.

which is through the likeness of a sensible thing. The Master adds this where he says that *it bears an image.*

REPLY OBJ. 1: Although signification does not belong to the notion of healing simply speaking, it does belong to the notion of the kind of healing accomplished through the sacraments, as is clear from what has been said.

REPLY OBJ. 2: Sensible things are not signs of divine things as things that sanctify, but as things that are sacred in themselves. But a sacrament should be understood as a sign of a sacred thing as sanctifying. And thus it is not necessary that all sensible things be sacraments.

REPLY OBJ. 3: Although the bronze serpent was a sign of a sacred thing sanctifying, nonetheless it was not the sign of a sacred thing actually then sanctifying; for it was not employed for the sake of reaping some effect of sanctification, but only the effect of exterior healing. And the same argument would apply to an image of a cross that is set up only as a representation.

REPLY OBJ. 4: Sacraments of the New Law signify three things. They signify the first sanctifying cause, as baptism signifies the death of Christ; and in this regard they are commemorative signs. They also signify the effect of sanctification that they cause, and this is their principal signification; and in this way they are demonstrative signs. Nor is it any obstacle if someone does not receive sanctity, since this is not due to anything lacking in the sacrament, which, considered in itself, is such as to confer grace. Finally, they signify the goal of sanctification, namely eternal glory, and in this regard they are prognostic signs. The sacraments of the Old Law, however, were completely prognostic signs.

REPLY OBJ. 5: A sign, in itself, conveys something manifest with respect to us, by which we are led to the understanding of something hidden. And since quite often effects are more manifest to us than causes, for this reason sign is sometimes divided against cause, just as a 'quia' demonstration is said to be through a sign of what is common, as is said in *Physics* 1;[21] but a 'propter quid' demonstration is made through the cause. However, sometimes a cause is manifest to us inasmuch as it falls under our senses while the effect is hidden, as when it is expected in the future. And then nothing prevents a cause from being called the sign of its effect.

Response to Quaestiuncula 2

AD SECUNDAM QUAESTIONEM dicendum, quod, sicut dictum est, signum importat aliquod notum quo ad nos, quo manuducimur in alterius cognitionem. Res autem primo notae nobis, sunt res cadentes sub sensu, a quo omnis nostra cognitio ortum habet; et ideo signum quantum ad primam sui institutionem significat

TO THE SECOND QUESTION, it should be said that, as has been said, a sign conveys something recognized by us, which leads us to the understanding of something else. However, the first things we recognize are the things that fall under our senses, from which our every understanding arises; and thus 'sign,' as regards its first institution, signi-

---

21. Aristotle, *Physics*, Bk. 1, ch. 1, 184a17–21.

aliquam rem sensibilem, prout per eam manuducimur in cognitionem alicujus occulti; et sic Magister accipit hic signum. Contingit autem aliquando quod aliquod magis notum quo ad nos, etiam si non sit res cadens sub sensu, quasi secundaria significatione dicatur signum; sicut dicit Philosophus in 2 *Ethic.*, quod signum generati habitus in nobis oportet accipere fientem in opere delectationem, quae non est delectatio sensibilis, cum sit rationis.

AD PRIMUM ergo dicendum, quod definitio[23] illa non est per oppositas res, sed per oppositas rationes; unde etiam ibidem dictum est, quod omne signum est res.

AD SECUNDUM dicendum, quod in rebus intelligibilibus fit processus ab his quae sunt notiora simpliciter, sicut patet in mathematicis; unde ibi effectus non sunt signa causarum; sed in rebus sensibilibus.

AD TERTIUM DICENDUM similiter de locutione angelorum, quod fit per ea quae sunt notiora simpliciter: unde non possunt proprie dici signa, sed quasi transumptive.

fies some sensible thing insofar as it leads us to understand something hidden; and this is the way that the Master takes 'sign' here. But it sometimes happens that something more known to us, even if it is not a sensible thing, is called a 'sign' by a kind of secondary meaning; as the Philosopher says in *Ethics* 2, that *one must take as the sign of a habit existing in us the pleasure which follows on action,*[22] which is not a sensible pleasure, since it is rational.

REPLY OBJ. 1: That division is not through opposite things, but through opposite notions; hence it says in the same place that every sign is a thing.

REPLY OBJ. 2: Among intelligible things there can be a progression that begins from things that are more known simply, as is clear in the case of mathematics. The effects are not signs of the causes in cases like this, but only among sensible things.

REPLY OBJ. 3: The response concerning the speech of the angels is similar: it works through things that are more known simply, and so they cannot be called signs properly, but metaphorically, as it were.

Response to Quaestiuncula 3

AD TERTIAM QUAESTIONEM dicendum, quod illa definitio Magistri completissime rationem sacramenti designat, prout nunc de sacramentis loquimur. Ponitur enim efficientia sanctitatis in hoc quod dicitur: *ut causa existat*; et modus competens homini quantum ad cognitionem, in hoc quod dicitur: *invisibilis gratiae visibilis forma*; et modus significationis homini connaturalis, scilicet ex similitudine sensibilium, in hoc quod dicitur: *ut imaginem gerat*.

AD PRIMUM ergo dicendum, quod quia visus est nobilior inter alios sensus, et plures differentias rerum ostendit, ut dicitur in 1 *Metaphysica*; ideo, ut Augustinus dicit, nomen visus ad omnes alios sensus extenditur; et ideo visibilis ponitur hic pro sensibili communiter.

AD SECUNDUM dicendum, quod forma sumitur hic communiter pro figura, secundum quod est in quarta specie qualitatis, et non pro forma exemplari: quia per mutationem figurae imaginibus aliquid repraesentamus. Vel si sumatur pro forma exemplari, hoc est inquantum sacramenta sunt quodammodo causae invisibilis gratiae; et ita in via generationis praecedunt, quamvis quantum ad institutionem imitentur.

TO THE THIRD QUESTION, it should be said that the Master's definition quite thoroughly conveys the notion of sacrament, as we are speaking about sacraments now. For that they effect holiness is referred to in *exists as a cause*, and the mode befitting man as to his understanding is indicated when he says, *in the visible form of invisible grace*, and the mode of signification connatural to man where he says, *as it bears an image*.

REPLY OBJ. 1: Sight is more noble than the other senses, and shows more the differences between things, as is said in the beginning of the *Metaphysics*.[24] Consequently, as Augustine says, the name 'sight' is extended to the other senses.[25] And thus *visible* is set down here for the sensible generally.

REPLY OBJ. 2: Form is here taken generally for figure, according as it is in the fourth species of quality, and not for exemplar form; for we represent something in images by the changing of a figure. Or if it is taken for exemplar form, this would be inasmuch as sacraments are in a certain way causes of invisible grace. And in this way they come before invisible grace in the order of generation, even though they are patterned after it as regards their institution.

---

22. Aristotle, *Nicomachean Ethics*, Bk. 2, ch. 3, 1104b4.
23. *definitio.—divisio* PLE.
24. Aristotle, *Metaphysics*, Bk. 1, ch. 1, 980a26–27.
25. Augustine, *Confessions* (CCSL 27), Bk. 10, ch. 35: "Ad oculos enim proprie uidere pertinet. Utimur autem hoc uerbo etiam in ceteris sensibus, cum eos ad cognoscendum intendimus."

AD TERTIUM dicendum, quod character baptismalis et corpus Christi verum non dicuntur sacramenta nisi secundum quod conjunguntur[26] signis sensibilibus.

AD QUARTUM dicendum, sicut ad secundum, quod forma quae est figura, non habet oppositionem ad imaginem, cum figura imago dicatur.

AD QUINTUM dicendum, quod sacramentum non dividitur per sacramenta veteris et novae legis sicut genus per species, sed sicut analogum in suas partes, ut sanum in habens sanitatem, et significans eam. Sacramentum autem simpliciter est quod causat sanctitatem. Quod autem significat tantum, non est sacramentum nisi secundum quid. Et ideo esse causam potest poni in definitione sacramenti, sicut habens sanitatem in definitione sani.

REPLY OBJ. 3: The baptismal character and the true body of Christ are only called sacraments insofar as they are joined to external sensible signs.

REPLY OBJ. 4: As was said in the response to the second objection, the form that is a figure is not opposed to image, since a figure is called an image.

REPLY OBJ. 5: 'Sacrament' is not divided into sacraments of the Old Law and of the New Law as genus is divided into species, but as an analogous term is divided into its parts, as healthy is divided into those things having health and those things signifying it. But a sacrament is, simply speaking, what causes sanctity, while something that merely signifies is a sacrament only in a certain respect. And therefore to be a cause can be included in the definition of sacrament, just as having health can be included in the definition of what is healthy.

Response to Quaestiuncula 4

AD QUARTAM QUAESTIONEM dicendum, quod definitio illa Augustini, si tamen in verbis illis sacramentum definire intendit, datur de sacramento quantum ad id quod est principale in ratione ipsius, scilicet causare sanctitatem. Et quia sacramenta non sunt primae[27] causae sanctitatis, sed quasi causae secundariae et instrumentales; ideo definiuntur sacramenta, sanctificationis instrumenta. Actio autem non attribuitur instrumento, sed principali agenti, cujus virtute instrumenta ad opus applicantur, prout sunt mota ab ipso; et ideo sacramenta non dicit esse sanctificantia, sed quod in eis divina virtus occulta existens sanctificat.

AD PRIMUM ergo dicendum, quod sacramentum est causa et signum. Est quidem causa instrumentalis; et ideo virtus agentis principalis occulte in ipso operatur, sicut virtus artis vel artificis in serra. Sed inquantum est signum, est ad manifestandum hujusmodi occultationem; ut sic ante significationem sit occultum; sed postquam significatio facta est actu, sit manifestum.

AD SECUNDUM dicendum, quod hoc contingit per accidens ex defectu recipientium. Definitiones autem respiciunt hoc quod per se est, sicut quod ignis calefacit, quantum in se est, quamvis ex parte passivi impediri posset.

AD TERTIUM dicendum, quod in sacramentis Deus operatur salutem sicut in instrumentis, quibus mediantibus salus causatur; sed in hominibus sicut in subjectis recipientibus salutem; et ideo ratio non sequitur.

TO THE FOURTH QUESTION, it should be said that this definition from Augustine, if in fact he intended to define 'sacrament' in those words, considers a sacrament with regard to what is principal in its account, namely, to cause holiness. And since sacraments are not the proper causes of holiness but secondary and instrumental causes, as it were, therefore sacraments are defined as instruments of sanctification. But an action is not attributed to an instrument, but to a principal agent, by whose power the instruments are applied to their work inasmuch as they are moved by it. And thus he does not say that sacraments are 'things that sanctify,' but that the hidden divine power existing in them sanctifies.

REPLY OBJ. 1: A sacrament is a cause and sign. It is, of course, an instrumental cause; thus the power of the principal agent works in it in a hidden way, as the power of an art or craftsman works in a saw. But inasmuch as it is a sign, it is for the manifestation of this kind of hidden thing in such a way that before the signification it is hidden, but after the signification has been accomplished it is manifest.

REPLY OBJ. 2: This happens incidentally through a defect in the one receiving the sacrament. But definitions have to do with what is essential, like the fact that fire heats considered in itself, although it could be prevented on the part of what is heated.

REPLY OBJ. 3: God works salvation in the sacraments as in instruments through whose mediation he causes salvation; but he works salvation in men as in subjects receiving salvation, and thus the argument does not follow.

---

26. *conjunguntur signis.—coniunguntur exterioribus signis* PLE.
27. *primae.—propriae* PLE.

Response to Quaestiuncula 5

AD QUINTAM QUAESTIONEM dicendum, quod definitio Hugonis de sancto Victore eadem est cum definitione quam Magister in littera ponit, hoc excepto quod addit causam significationis, quae est institutio, et causam efficientiae, quae est sanctificatio: idem enim est dictum *materiale elementum exterius oculis suppositum, et ex institutione significans,* quod *invisibilis gratiae visibilis forma*; et *ex similitudine repraesentans,* idem est ei quod dicitur, *ut imaginem gerat*; et *ex sanctificatione invisibilem gratiam continens,* idem est ei quod dicitur: *ut causa existat.*

AD PRIMUM ergo dicendum, quod sicut formae artificiales sunt accidentales, tamen in artificialibus tota substantia est materia, et propter hoc praedicatur, ut dicatur, phiala est aurum; ita etiam cum in sacramentis forma non det esse substantiale, sed accidentale in genere causae et signi, non est inconveniens ut materia sacramenti de ipso praedicetur, et in ejus definitione sicut genus ponatur; hoc enim etiam in aliis accidentibus contingit, ut dicitur in 7 *Metaphysica,* ut cum dicitur: *simum est nasus curvus.*

AD SECUNDUM dicendum, quod elementum accipitur communiter pro quolibet corporali visibili, sive sit elementum simplex, sive elementatum; et utimur tali modo loquendi propter verbum Augustini, qui dicit: *accedit verbum ad elementum, et fit sacramentum.* In baptismo enim, qui est sacramentorum janua, materia est elementum simplex.

AD TERTIUM dicendum, quod inter corporalia et spiritualia non attenditur similitudo per participationem ejusdem qualitatis, sed per proportionalitatem, quae est similitudo proportionatorum; ut sicut se habet aqua ad delendas maculas corporales, ita gratia ad abluendum spirituales; et secundum hunc modum similitudinis transferuntur etiam corporalia ad spiritualia.

AD QUARTUM dicendum, quod res sensibilis secundum praedictam similitudinem ex naturali proprietate pluribus est conformis; et ideo quantum est de se aequaliter potest quodlibet illorum significare. Ad hoc ergo quod ad unum determinetur, et sic sua significatio sit certa, oportet quod accedat institutio, quae ad unum determinet; quia etsi repraesentatio quae est ex similitudine naturalis proprietatis, importet aptitudinem quamdam ad significandum, attamen determinatio et complementum significationis ex institutione est.

TO THE FIFTH QUESTION, it should be said that Hugh of St. Victor's definition is the same as the definition the Master includes in the text, except that he adds the cause of a sacrament's signification, which is its institution, and the cause of a sacrament's efficacy, which is its sanctification: for it is the same thing to say *material element externally set before the eyes, signifying something by its institution* and *visible form of invisible grace*; and *representing something by a likeness* is the same as *so that it bears an image*; and *containing invisible grace by its sanctification* is the same as *so that it exists as a cause.*

REPLY OBJ. 1: Artificial forms are accidental, and so in artificial things the whole substance is matter, and this is the basis on which it is named, as when one says, *the cup is a gold thing*. In the same way, since in the sacraments the form does not give the substantial being but an accidental being in the genus of cause and sign, it is not unfitting that the matter of the sacrament be predicated of it, and be included as the genus in its definition. For this happens in other accidentals as well, as is said in *Metaphysics* 7,[28] as when it is said, *a curved nose is a snub thing.*

REPLY OBJ. 2: 'Element' here is taken generally for any corporeal visible thing, whether it be a simple element or something made from elements; and we speak this way because of Augustine, who says, *the word is combined with the element and the sacrament is made.*[29] For in baptism, which is the gateway of the sacraments, the matter is a simple element.

REPLY OBJ. 3: Between corporeal and spiritual things we do not look for a likeness by participation in the same quality, but for a likeness by proportion, which is a likeness of proportionate things; for example, just as water is for removing corporeal stains, so grace is for cleansing spiritual ones. According to this mode of likeness, even corporeal things are applied to spiritual things.

REPLY OBJ. 4: A sensible thing according to the likeness mentioned is similar to many other things by its natural property; and thus in itself it can signify any of those things equally. Therefore, for it to be determined to one thing, and for its meaning to be certain, it is necessary for it to be brought together with its institution which determines it to one meaning. For, although the representation from the likeness of its natural property carries an aptitude for a certain signification, nevertheless the determination and completion of its signification are from the institution.

---

28. Aristotle, *Metaphysics,* Bk. 7, ch. 5, 1030b14.
29. Augustine, *In Iohannis euangelium tractatus* (CCSL 36), Tract. 80, par. 3.

ARTICLE 2

On the necessity of the sacraments

Quaestiuncula 1

AD SECUNDUM SIC PROCEDITUR. Videtur quod sacramentis humanum genus etiam post lapsum non indigeat. Per gratiam enim et virtutes peccati vulnera sanantur in nobis: quia gratia a sanctis dicitur sanitas et decor animae. Philosophus etiam in 2 *Ethic.* comparat virtutem sanitati corporali. Cum ergo sacramenta sint instituta ut medicinae peccati, ut Hugo de sancto Victore dicit, videtur quod eis non indigeamus.

PRAETEREA, contraria contrariis curantur. Sed homo morbum peccati incurrerat, se per affectum rebus temporalibus subjiciendo. Ergo videtur inconveniens modus curationis ut sub rebus sensibilibus humilietur, sicut Magister dicit.

PRAETEREA, id quod est causa occultationis et erroris, non prodest ad eruditionem. Sed tradere spiritualia sub signis corporalibus est occultatio quaedam spiritualium; unde et pluribus est causa erroris, sicut patet de illis qui Deum credebant per lineamenta corporalia distingui propter modum loquendi symbolicum in Scripturis. Ergo non facit ad eruditionem nostram sacramentorum exhibitio, ut Magister dicit.

PRAETEREA, 1 Tim. 6, 8: *corporalis exercitatio ad modicum utilis est*. Sed exercitatio quae fit in sacramentis, est corporalis: quia res quae in usum veniunt, corporales sunt. Ergo eis non indigemus propter exercitationem, ut iterum Magister dicit.

SED CONTRA, Augustinus dicit contra Faustum, quod omnis religio habuit aliqua signa exteriora, in quibus conveniebant ad Deum colendum. Sed in ecclesia Dei, post peccatum in hoc mundo peregrinante, est verissima religio. Ergo oportet in ea esse hujusmodi signa: et haec sunt sacramenta; ergo indigemus eis.

PRAETEREA, medicina vulneri debet esse proportionata. Sed vulnus peccati devenerat in humano genere usque ad corpus, in quo habitat lex peccati, ut dicitur Rom. 7. Ergo debuit medicina etiam per aliqua corporalia ei

OBJ. 1: To the second we proceed thus. It seems that the human race did not need the sacraments even after the fall of man.[30] For grace and the virtues heal the wounds of sin in us, since the saints call grace the health and the beauty of the soul. Also, the Philosopher in *Ethics* 2 compares virtue to bodily health.[31] Since, therefore the sacraments were instituted as medicine for sin, as Hugh of St. Victor says,[32] it seems that we do not need them.

OBJ. 2: Furthermore, contraries are healed by contraries. But man incurred the disease of sin by subjecting himself to temporal things through affection. Therefore, it seems an unfitting mode of treatment that he be humbled under sensible things, as the Master says.

OBJ. 3: Furthermore, nothing that causes concealment and error is beneficial for instruction. But to hand on spiritual things under the sign of physical things is a kind of concealment of spiritual things; hence it also causes many to err, as is evident with those who believed that God was delineated by physical features because of the symbolic mode of speaking found in the Scriptures. Therefore, experiencing the sacraments does not facilitate our instruction, as the Master says.

OBJ. 4: Furthermore, *physical activity is profitable only a little* (1 Tim 4:8). But the activity that happens in the sacraments is physical, because the things that come into use are physical. Therefore, we do not need them for the sake of the activity, as the Master says again.

ON THE CONTRARY, Augustine says against Faustus that every religion had some external signs, in which people came together for the worship of God.[33] But in the church of God, wayfaring in this world after sin, there is the truest religion. Therefore, it is necessary that there be signs of this kind in it, and these are the sacraments. Therefore we need them.

FURTHERMORE, medicine should be proportionate to the wound. But the wound of sin had affected the human race even as far as the body, where the law of sin lodges, as is said in Romans 7:23. Therefore, the medicine also has to be

---

30. Parallels: *ST* III, q. 61, a. 1; *SCG* III, ch. 119; *SCG* IV, chs. 55–56.

31. Aristotle, *Nicomachean Ethics*, Bk. 2, ch. 2, 1104a11.

32. Hugh of St. Victor, *De sacramentis fidei*, Bk. 1, pt. 8, ch. 12 (PL 176:313).

33. Augustine, *Contra Faustum*, Bk. 19, par. 11: "in nullum autem nomen religionis, seu uerum, seu falsum, coagulari homines possunt, nisi aliquo signaculorum uel sacramentorum uisibilium consortio conligentur: quorum sacramentorum uis inenarrabiliter ualet plurimum et ideo contempta sacrilegos facit" (CSEL 25:510).

parari. Sed hujusmodi sunt sacramenta. Ergo sacramentis homo in statu naturae lapsae indiget.

prepared for it through bodily things. But the sacraments are this kind of thing. Therefore man needs the sacraments in his fallen state.

Quaestiuncula 2

ULTERIUS. Videtur quod etiam ante peccatum homo eis indiguisset. Homo enim etiam ante peccatum gratia indigebat, ut in 2 Lib., dist. 24, art. 4 ad 2, dictum est. Sed sacramenta sunt instituta ad gratiae collationem. Ergo homo eis in statu innocentiae indiguisset.

PRAETEREA, Dionysius assignat hanc causam institutionis hujusmodi sensibilium figurarum in sacramentis: quia per hujusmodi sensibiles figuras materiale nostrum melius reducitur ad spiritualia, propter connaturalitatem cognitionis nostrae ad sensibilia. Sed homo in statu innocentiae materialis erat, et ex sensibilibus cognitionem accipiens, propter quod etiam in paradiso dicitur positus ad operandum, ut naturales vires rerum experiretur. Ergo et hunc indiguit hujusmodi sacramentis.

PRAETEREA, matrimonium sacramentum quoddam est. Hoc autem in paradiso fuit institutum in statu innocentiae, ut patet Gen. 2. Ergo in statu innocentiae homo sacramentis indiguisset.

SED CONTRA, Matth. 9, 12: *non opus est sanis medico, nec etiam medicina*. Sed Hugo de sancto Victore dicit, quod sacramenta sunt vasa medicinalia. Ergo non erant in statu innocentiae necessaria, cum morbus non erat.

PRAETEREA, sacramenta virtutem sortiuntur ex passione Christi: unde et de latere ipsius in cruce pendentis fluxisse dicuntur. Sed si homo non peccasset, Christi passio non fuisset. Ergo nec sacramenta.

OBJ. 1: Moreover, it seems that even before sin man needed them.[34] For man also needed grace before sin, as was said in Book II, Distinction 24, Article 4, Reply to the 2nd Objection. But the sacraments were instituted to confer grace. Therefore, man needed them in his state of innocence.

OBJ. 2: Furthermore, Dionysius gives this reason for the institution of these kinds of sensible figures in the sacraments: namely, that through sensible figures our material selves are better drawn on to spiritual things, due to the connaturality of our understanding with sensible things.[35] But man in the state of innocence was a material being, coming to understand by his senses, which is why even in paradise he was set to work, so that his natural powers would experience things. Therefore, he also needed sacraments like these in paradise.

OBJ. 3: Furthermore, marriage is a sacrament. But it was instituted in paradise in the state of innocence, as is clear from Genesis 2. Therefore, in the state of innocence man needed sacraments.

ON THE CONTRARY, *those who are healthy do not need a doctor* (Matt 9:12), nor medicine either. But Hugh of St. Victor says that sacraments are vessels of medicine.[36] Therefore, they were not necessary in the state of innocence, since there was no sickness.

FURTHERMORE, sacraments draw their power from the Passion of Christ; hence they are also said to have flowed from his side when he was hanging on the Cross. But if man had not sinned, Christ's Passion would not have happened. Therefore, neither would the sacraments have existed.

Quaestiuncula 3

ULTERIUS. Videtur quod in statu legis naturae sacramenta non fuerunt necessaria. Non minus enim est necessaria eruditio quae fit per praecepta quam illa quae fit per sacramenta. Sed praecepta non fuerunt alia data ad bene vivendum, praeter ea quibus naturali ratione ad bene vivendum informabantur. Ergo videtur quod nec sacramenta debuerunt pro tempore illo institui, cum ea lex

OBJ. 1: Moreover, it seems that in the state of the law of nature, sacraments were not necessary.[37] For the instruction that happens through commandments is just as necessary as that which happens through sacraments. But there were no other commandments given for living well beyond those by which people were taught to live well by natural reason. Therefore, it seems that neither did the sacraments

---

34. Parallels: *In II Sent.* d. 23, q. 2, a. 1, ad 1; *ST* III, q. 61, a. 2.
35. Pseudo-Dionysius, *Ecclesiastical Hierarchy*, ch. 1, n. 2 (PG 3:374).
36. Hugh of St. Victor, *De sacramentis fidei*, Bk. 1, pt. 9, ch. 3 (PL 176:319).
37. Parallels: *ST* III, q. 61, a. 3.

naturalis non dictet: quod patet ex hoc quod non sunt eadem apud omnes et secundum omne tempus.

PRAETEREA, sacramenta, quando instituta sunt, necessaria sunt ad salutem, ut patet Joan. 3, 5: *nisi quis renatus fuerit ex aqua et Spiritu Sancto, non potest introire in regnum Dei.* Sed ea quae ante legem scriptam videntur esse sacramenta, erant voto celebrata, et non necessitate, ut Hugo de sancto Victore dicit. Ergo non erant sacramenta, et per consequens nec necessaria.

SED CONTRA, secundum Hugonem, quandocumque fuit morbus, fuit et medicina morbi. Sed in statu legis naturae erat morbus peccati. Ergo necessaria erat sacramentorum medicina.

need to be instituted for that time, since natural law did not dictate them, which is clear from the fact that they are not the same for all men and in every age.

OBJ. 2: Furthermore, sacraments, when they were instituted, were necessary for salvation, as is clear from John 3:5: *Unless you are born again from water and the Holy Spirit, you cannot enter into the kingdom of God.* But the things which appear to have been sacraments before the written law were celebrated by choice and not out of necessity, as Hugh of St. Victor says.[38] Therefore, they were not sacraments, and accordingly they were not necessary.

ON THE CONTRARY, according to Hugh, anytime there was a sickness, there was also a medicine for the sickness.[39] But the sickness of sin existed in the state of the law of nature. Therefore, the medicine of the sacraments was necessary.

Quaestiuncula 4

ULTERIUS. Videtur quod nec debuerunt supra illa sacramenta legis naturae alia superaddi in lege Moysi. Quod enim superadditur alteri, debet esse magis ad perfectionem accedens. Sed sacramenta quae fuerunt in lege naturae, erant propinquissima perfectis sacramentis, quae sunt in lege nova, ut patet de oblatione Melchisedech. Ergo non debuit fieri superadditio per legem Moysi.

PRAETEREA, superadditio ad id quod bonum erat, vel mutatio ejus, non debet fieri nisi propter meliorationem. Sed sacramenta veteris legis non habebant alium effectum meliorem effectu sacramentorum legis naturae: quia utraque sacramenta significabant tantum. Ergo non debuit fieri aliqua mutatio ipsorum, vel superadditio ad ea.

SED CONTRA, sacramenta, ut Magister in littera dicit, ad eruditionem instituta sunt. Sed secundum Gregorium, per incrementum temporum crevit scientia sanctorum patrum, et fides etiam magis explicata est, ut in 3, dist. 25, quaest. 3, art. 2, quaestiunc. 1, dictum est. Ergo oportuit in lege Moysi alia sacramenta addi sacramentis legis naturae.

OBJ. 1: Moreover, it seems that the other sacraments of the law of Moses need not have been added to the sacraments of the law of nature.[40] For what is added to something else should be closer to perfection. But the sacraments that existed in the law of nature were the closest to the perfect sacraments that are found in the New Law, as we see in the offering of Melchizedek.[41] Therefore, it needed no addition from the law of Moses.

OBJ. 2: Furthermore, one should only add to what is good, or change it, if it brings improvement. But sacraments of the Old Law did not have any effect that was better than the effect of the sacraments of the law of nature, for both sacraments merely signified. Therefore, they should not have been changed or added to.

ON THE CONTRARY, sacraments, as the Master says in the text, were instituted for instruction. But according to Gregory, the knowledge of the holy patriarchs grew with the passing of time,[42] and faith also became more explicit, as was said in Book III, Distinction 25, Question 3, Article 2, Subquestion 1. Therefore, it was necessary in the law of Moses that other sacraments be added to the sacraments of the law of nature.

---

38. Hugh of St. Victor, *De sacramentis fidei*, Bk. 1, pt. 11, ch. 5 (PL 176:345).
39. Hugh of St. Victor, *De sacramentis fidei*, Bk. 1, pt. 8, ch. 12 (PL 176:313).
40. Parallels: *ST* III, q. 61, a. 3.
41. See Genesis 14.
42. Gregory the Great, *Homiliae in Hiezechihelem prophetam* (CCSL 142), Bk. 2, hom. 4, n. 12: "Qua in re hoc quoque nobis sciendum est quia et per incrementa temporum creuit scientia spiritalium patrum."

Quaestiuncula 5

ULTERIUS. Videtur quod in lege nova non debuerunt aliqua sacramenta remanere. Veniente enim veritate cessat figura. Sed gratia et veritas jam per Christum Jesum facta est, Joan. 1. Non ergo indigemus sacramentis gratiam ipsius et veritatem signantibus.

PRAETEREA, apostolus Galat. 3, dicit, quod antiqui patres erant sub elementis mundi servientes, sicut pueri sub paedagogo usque ad praefinitum tempus a patre. Sed tempus plenitudinis est tempus incarnationis, ut ibidem dicitur. Ergo cum sacramentum sit materiale elementum, videtur quod ex tunc non debuerimus sub sacramentis salutem quaerere.

SED CONTRA, quando est tempus medicandi, tunc magis necessariae sunt medicinae. Sed tempus aptissimum spirituali medicationi est tempus gratiae; unde in Psal. 101, tempus miserendi, annus benignitatis Dei dicitur. Ergo in statu gratiae maxime necessaria sunt sacramenta, quae sunt medicinae quaedam.

OBJ. 1: Moreover, it does not seem that some sacraments needed to remain in the New Law.[43] For with the coming of truth, figures cease. But grace and truth have now come through Jesus Christ, as it says in John 1:17. Therefore, we do not need sacraments representing his grace and truth.

OBJ. 2: Furthermore, the Apostle says in Galatians 4:2–3 that the ancient patriarchs were serving under the elements of the world, like boys under a disciplinarian, until the time determined by the Father. But the time of fullness is the time of the Incarnation, as said in the same place. Therefore, since a sacrament is a material element, it seems that since that time we should not have had to look for salvation under sacraments.

ON THE CONTRARY, when it is time to medicate, then medicines are more necessary. But the most appropriate time for spiritual medication is the time of grace. Hence it is called a time of mercy, a year of favor (Ps 101:14). Therefore, in the state of grace, the sacraments, which are a kind of medicine, are especially necessary.

Response to Quaestiuncula 1

RESPONDEO dicendum, ad primam quaestionem, quod sacramenta non erant necessaria necessitate absoluta, sicut necessarium est Deum esse, cum ex sola divina bonitate instituta sint, sed de necessitate quae est ex suppositione finis; non ita tamen quod sine his Deus hominem sanare non posset, quia sacramentis virtutem suam non alligavit, ut in littera dicitur (sicut cibus necessarius est ad vitam humanam), sed quia per sacramenta magis congrue fit hominis reparatio; sicut equus dicitur necessarius ad iter, quia in equo facilius homo vadit.

Hujusmodi autem congruitatis causa potest accipi ex hoc quod homo per peccatum praecipue circa sensibilia corruptus erat, eis detentus ne in Deum surgere posset. Erat autem praedicta corruptio quantum ad cognitionem: quia humana mens circa sensibilia tantum occupari noverat, intantum ut quidam nihil extra sensibilia crederent; et si qui ad cognitionem intelligibilium pervenirent, ea secundum modum rerum sensibilium judicabant. Similiter quantum ad affectionem: quia eis quasi summis bonis inhaerebant, Deo postposito. Similiter etiam quantum ad actionem: quia homo eis inordinate utebatur.

TO THE FIRST QUESTION, I answer that the sacraments were not necessary by an absolute necessity, as it is necessary that God exist, since they were instituted out of divine goodness alone; but rather they are of the necessity that comes from supposing the end. Yet they are not necessary in such a way that God could not heal man without them, since he has not chained his power to the sacraments, as it says in the text (in the way that food is necessary to human life), but they are necessary because man is more fittingly restored through the sacraments, as a horse is said to be necessary for a journey because man travels more easily on a horse.

But the reason for this sort of fittingness can be found in the fact that man's corruption through sin had especially to do with sensible things, and they held him back from being able to rise up to God. Moreover, this corruption happened with respect to the understanding: for the human mind came to be captivated by sensible things alone, to the extent that some people believed nothing but what was sensible; and even if some attained to an understanding of intelligible things, they judged them according to the mode of sensible realities. Likewise with respect to the affections: for, neglecting God, they clung to sensible things as if they were the highest goods. Likewise again with respect to their actions: for man made use of sensible things inordinately.

---

43. Parallels: below, d. 2, q. 1, a. 4, qa. 1; *ST* III, q. 61, a. 4; *SCG* IV, ch. 57.

Necessarium ergo fuit ad curationem peccatorum ut homo ex sensibilibus in spiritualia cognoscenda proficeret, et ut affectum quem circa ea habebat, in Deum referret, et ut eis ordinate et secundum divinam institutionem uteretur; et ideo necessaria fuit sacramentorum institutio, per quae homo ex sensibilibus de spiritualibus eruditur; et haec est secunda causa quam Magister ponit: per quae etiam affectum, qui sensibilibus subjicitur, in Dei reverentiam referret; et haec est prima causa: per quae etiam circa ea in honorem Dei excitaretur; et haec est tertia causa.

Ad primum ergo dicendum, quod gratia et virtutes sanant formaliter, sicut sanitas; sed sacramenta quodammodo effective, sicut medicinae quaedam. Unde sicut non sequitur: sanitas sanat; ergo medicinae non sunt necessariae; ita nec haec: gratia sanat; ergo sacramenta non sunt necessaria: sed magis posset contrarium concludi.

Ad secundum dicendum, quod per eadem contrario modo fit virtus et corrumpitur, ut in 2 *Ethic.* Unde sicut corruptio virtutis facta est in homine per hoc quod se sub sensibilibus rebus humiliavit propter ipsa sensibilia; ita reparatio virtutis convenienter fit per hoc quod homo sub eis humiliatur propter Dei reverentiam; et sic contraria contrariis curantur: quia contraria debent accipi circa idem.

Ad tertium dicendum, quod remanentibus in sensibilibus praedictus modus tradendi spiritualia est occulti erroris occasio; a quibus etiam congruum est sancta occultare, ut Dionysius dicit. Sed eis qui instruuntur ex sensibilibus in spiritualem intellectum consurgere, est valde congruus: quia est conformis naturali cognitioni, qua ex sensibilibus cognitionem intellectus accipit.

Ad quartum dicendum, quod corporalis exercitatio secundum se accepta ad modicum utilis est in comparatione ad pietatem, ut ibi apostolus intendit; sed si ei pietas adjungatur, sicut fit in sacramentis, quae ad religionis pietatem pertinent, est valde utilis.

Therefore, it was necessary for the healing of sins that man should advance in understanding spiritual things through sensible things, and that he should transfer the affection that he had for them to God, and that he should use them ordinately and according to divine institution. And thus it was necessary that the sacraments be instituted, which instruct man about spiritual things through sensible things; and this is the second reason the Master mentions. The sacraments also redirect the affections, which are subject to sensible things, to reverence for God; and this is the first reason the Master mentions. Finally, by using them one is aroused to act for the honor of God; and this is the third reason.

Reply Obj. 1: Grace and virtues are the form of man's healing, like health, but sacraments are its effective source, in a way, like a medicine. Hence, just as it does not follow that since health heals, medicines are therefore unnecessary, so neither does it follow that since grace heals, sacraments are therefore unnecessary; rather, the opposite could be concluded.

Reply Obj. 2: Virtue is formed and corrupted by the same things working in opposite ways, as is said in *Ethics* 2.[44] Hence just as the corruption of virtue happened in man by the fact that he subjected himself to sensible things for the sake of sensible things themselves, so also the restoration of virtue happens fittingly by the fact that man is subjected to them out of reverence for God. This is how contraries are remedied by contraries, for contraries should be applied concerning the same thing.

Reply Obj. 3: Handing over spiritual things in the manner described to those stuck in sensible things is an occasion of hidden error; it is even appropriate to hide holy things from them, as Dionysius says.[45] But for those who are instructed by sensible things to raise their intellects to the spiritual, it is extremely appropriate, for it befits the natural process of understanding, in which the intellect receives understanding through sensible things.

Reply Obj. 4: Physical activity for its own sake is of little use compared to piety, as the Apostle means in that text; but if it is joined to piety, as happens in the sacraments, which pertain to the piety of religion, then it is extremely useful.

Response to Quaestiuncula 2

Ad secundam quaestionem dicendum, quod utilitas sacramentorum est eruditio et curatio. Quantum autem ad curationem omnibus patet quod non erant necessaria sacramenta in statu innocentiae, cum tunc morbus non esset. Sed quidam dicunt, quod erant necessaria

To the second question, it should be said that the benefit of the sacraments is instruction and healing. Now as regards healing, it is clear to everyone that the sacraments were not necessary in the state of innocence, since the sickness did not exist at that time. But some people say they

---

44. Aristotle, *Nicomachean Ethics*, Bk. 2, ch. 7, 1107a29.
45. Pseudo-Dionysius, *Ecclesiastical Hierarchy*, ch. 1 (PG 3:370).

quantum ad eruditionem: quia homo in statu etiam illo sensibilibus utebatur, et ita ex sensibilibus spiritualia significari congruebat. Sed hoc non videtur conveniens: quia significatio fit ad acquirendum cognitionem de eo quod significatur. Quamvis autem in primo statu sensibilia cognosceret, et in eis etiam spiritualium similitudines inspiceret, non tamen ex sensibilibus spiritualium cognitionem accepit, sed magis ex influentia divini luminis; et ideo sacramentis ad eruditionem non indigebat. Et hoc etiam in littera Magister videtur significare: quia refert hoc quod de eruditione dicit, ad defectum cognitionis qui est in statu peccati. Et ideo dicendum est cum aliis, quod in statu innocentiae sacramenta non fuissent necessaria.

AD PRIMUM ergo dicendum, quod sacramenta non sunt instituta ad gratiam conferendam, nisi prout gratia est sanans formaliter morbum peccati; et sic in statu innocentiae homo gratia non indigebat.

AD SECUNDUM dicendum, quod in statu innocentiae superiores partes hominis omnino inferioribus dominabantur; et ideo quamvis homo haberet sensus, et materialis esset, non tamen intellectus ex sensibilibus cognitionem accipiebat, sed ex influentia divini luminis habebat. Sed quia experientia etiam eorum quae prius sciebamus, delectabilis est, ideo operabatur ad experiendum naturae vires, non ut ex hoc habitum scientiae acciperet, sed ut ex visione experimentali eorum quae sciebat, delectaretur.

AD TERTIUM dicendum, quod matrimonium non fuisset in statu innocentiae in remedium, sed in officium. Et quia sacramenta remedia sunt, ideo proprie loquendo, non fuisset sacramentum, nisi forte inquantum rem sacram significabat; et non quidem illius sacrae rei, scilicet conjunctionis Christi et ecclesiae, per hujusmodi matrimonium homo in statu illo cognitionem accepisset; sed magis e converso ex cognitione praedictae conjunctionis convenientiam et sanctitatem matrimonii cognovisset.

were necessary as regards the instruction they give; for man made use of sensible things in that state as well, and so it was appropriate that spiritual things be represented to him by sensible things. But this does not seem fitting, for signification happens for the sake of understanding what is signified. Now although he would have understood sensible things in the original state, and he would have seen in them the likenesses of spiritual things, nevertheless he did not receive knowledge of spiritual things through sensible things, but rather from the influx of divine light; and so he did not need the sacraments for his instruction. And the Master even seems to indicate this in the text, for he relates what he says about instruction to the lack of understanding present in the state of sin. And thus one should say, with others, that in the state of innocence the sacraments were not necessary.

REPLY OBJ. 1: The sacraments were only instituted to confer grace insofar as grace is formally what heals the disease of sin; and this is not how man needed grace in the state of innocence.

REPLY OBJ. 2: In the state of innocence the higher parts of man had mastery over the lower parts; and thus although man always had senses, and was a material being, nevertheless his intellect did not receive knowledge from sensible things, but rather through the influx of divine light. But since the experience of things that we already know is delightful, he used his senses for the sake of experiencing the powers of nature, not so that he would gain knowledge from it but so that he would be delighted by experiencing the vision of things he already knew.

REPLY OBJ. 3: Marriage did not exist in the state of innocence as a remedy but as an office. And because sacraments are remedies, therefore properly speaking it was not a sacrament, except perhaps inasmuch as it represented a sacred thing. And of course in that state, man did not gain understanding of that sacred thing, namely, the union of Christ and the Church, through this kind of marriage; but rather vice versa: he understood the harmoniousness and holiness of marriage by his knowledge of that union.

Response to Quaestiuncula 3

AD TERTIAM QUAESTIONEM dicendum, quod ea quae ab homine fiunt, a cognitione ortum oportet habere; alias non essent humana opera; unde oportet quod operatio cognitioni respondeat, sicut effectus causae. In statu autem legis naturae non sufficiebat ad salutem sola naturalis cognitio, sed exigebatur fides aliquorum quae supra rationem sunt; et post lapsum exigebatur fides de reparatore, per quem erat medicina morbi; et ideo in statu illo non tantum erant necessaria opera quae sunt de dictamine legis naturalis, sed etiam alia quae essent protestationes et signa eorum quae ad reparationem perti-

TO THE THIRD QUESTION, it should be said that what a man does should arise from his understanding; otherwise, his acts would not be human acts. Hence it is necessary that action correspond to understanding as effect to cause. But in the state of the law of nature merely natural understanding was not enough for salvation, but it required faith in some things that were above reason; and after the fall of man it required faith in a restorer, through whom there would come medicine for the disease. And so in that state not only were the works arising from the dictates of the law of nature necessary, but other things that were protestations

nebant; et haec erant illius temporis sacramenta, sicut sacrificia, decimae, oblationes, et hujusmodi.

AD PRIMUM ergo dicendum, quod praecepta quae ordinant ad bene vivendum, sunt praecepta legis naturae, quae respondent cognitioni naturali. Et quia cognitio naturalis sufficienter ea dictabat, nondum per contrariam consuetudinem omnino obtenebrata, ideo non erat tanta necessitas ut eorum expressio fieret, sicut sacramentorum, quae supernaturali cognitioni respondent.

AD SECUNDUM dicendum, quod ante legem scriptam erant quaedam sacramenta necessitatis, sicut illud fidei sacramentum quod ordinabatur ad deletionem originalis peccati; et similiter poenitentia, quae ordinabatur ad deletionem actualis; et similiter matrimonium, quod ordinabatur ad multiplicationem humani generis. Sed sacrificia et oblationes et hujusmodi erant necessitatis[46] in communi, ut scilicet aliquid facerent in protestationem fidei suae, qua Deo per latriae religionem subjecti erant; sed in speciali erant voluntatis, utrum scilicet deberent sacrificia exhibere, vel oblationes, vel aliquid hujusmodi.

and signs of things related to the restoration were necessary as well. These were the sacraments of that period, such as sacrifices, tithes, offerings, and things like that.

REPLY OBJ. 1: The precepts that are ordered to living well are precepts of the law of nature, which correspond to natural understanding. And because natural understanding dictated them sufficiently since it had not yet been darkened by contrary habits, it was not necessary to make them explicit, as it was with the sacraments, which correspond to supernatural understanding.

REPLY OBJ. 2: Before the written law there were certain sacraments of necessity, like that sacrament of faith which was ordered to the removal of original sin; and likewise penance, which was ordered to the removal of actual sin; and likewise marriage, which was ordered to the multiplication of the human race. But sacrifices and offerings and things of this sort were voluntary and necessary in general, that is, it was necessary that one do something to profess one's faith, by which one was subject to God by a religious act of worship. But as regards what to do specifically they were voluntary; for example, whether one should offer sacrifices, or offerings, or anything like that.

Response to Quaestiuncula 4

AD QUARTAM QUAESTIONEM dicendum, quod cum sacramentorum usus fidei proportionaliter respondeat, sicut dictum est, oportuit quod secundum diversum statum fidei diversimode sacramenta traderentur. Fides autem quantum ad articulorum explicationem semper magis et magis crevit secundum propinquitatem temporis gratiae, ut 3 Lib., dist. 25, dictum est; et secundum hoc oportuit sacramenta magis ac magis determinari.

Et propter hoc, quia in Abraham fides primo habuit quasi notabilem quantitatem, ut propter fidei religionem ab aliis separaretur (unde et pater fidei dicitur), ideo sibi signaculum, sive sacramentum fidei, determinatum fuit, scilicet circumcisio.

Et quia tempore Moysi jam fides ad tantam quantitatem devenerat ut non solum in uno homine refulgeret, vel in familia; sed in una tota gente, populo Dei multiplicato; ideo oportuit et legem dari, quae non nisi populo ferri potest (unde legis positio est pars politicae, non oeconomicae vel monasticae) et sacramenta in speciali determinari et multiplicari; et propter hoc necessarium fuit in lege Moysi determinari sacrificia, oblationes, et decimas, quantum ad omnes singulares circumstantias,

TO THE FOURTH QUESTION, it should be said that since the use of the sacraments corresponds proportionally to faith, as was said, it was necessary that the sacraments be handed on in different ways according to the different states of the faith. Now, as regards the explication of its articles, the faith was always growing more and more according as the time of grace drew nearer, as was said in Book III, Distinction 25.[47] And it was correspondingly necessary that the sacraments be more and more determined.

Consequently, since in Abraham faith first had, as it were, a noticeable size—such that he was separated from others because of the religion of the faith (for which reason he is also called the father of faith)—for this reason a kind of sign (or sacrament of faith) was determined for him, namely circumcision.

And since at the time of Moses the faith had already attained such a magnitude that it no longer shone only in one man or family but in an entire nation since the people of God had multiplied, it was fitting both that they be given a law, which can only be borne by a nation (for which reason the laying down of law is a political function, not that of a household or individual), and also that sacraments be more specifically determined and multiplied. For this reason it was necessary in the law of Moses that sacrifices, offerings,

---

46. *erant necessitatis.*—*erant voluntatis et necessitatis* PLE
47. See q. 2, a. 2, qa. 1.

et matrimonia ordinari, et poenitentiae satisfactiones distingui.

AD PRIMUM ergo dicendum, quod quamvis oblatio Melchisedech perfectissime repraesentaret nostrum sacrificium quantum ad materiam, tamen etiam oportuit multas alias circumstantias repraesentari, sicut modum sumendi, et passionem Christi, cujus est memoriale, quae explicite significantur per agnum paschalem, et per alia legis sacramenta.

AD SECUNDUM dicendum, quod quamvis non sit facta melioratio per sacramenta veteris legis quantum ad alium effectum in genere, scilicet causare; facta est tamen quantum ad eumdem effectum qui est significare, inquantum expressius et pluribus modis futura gratiae significabantur sacramenta.

and tithes be determined for every particular circumstance, that marriage be set in order, and that distinctions be made among the various satisfactions of penance.

REPLY OBJ. 1: Although the offering of Melchizedek perfectly represented our sacrifice as regards its matter, nevertheless it was also necessary that many other circumstances be represented, like the mode of consuming it, and the Passion of Christ, whose memorial it is, which things are explicitly signified by the paschal lamb and by other sacraments of the law.

REPLY OBJ. 2: Although the Old Law did not improve anything by having a new kind of effect, namely, by being a cause, nonetheless it did make an improvement with regard to the same effect, which is to signify, inasmuch as it signified the future sacraments of grace more expressly and in more ways.

Response to Quaestiuncula 5

AD QUINTAM QUAESTIONEM dicendum, quod eadem fides est modernorum et antiquorum, ut Augustinus dicit, quia quem illi credebant venturum, nos credimus jam venisse; et ideo cum sacramenta fidei correspondeant, sicut protestationes ipsius, et ab ea virtutem habentia, oportet quod sicut antiqui patres redemptionis Christi participes effecti sunt per sacramenta quae erant signa futuri ita et in nos redemptio ejus perveniat mediantibus aliquibus sacramentis significantibus quod jam factum est, quae sunt sacramenta novae legis.

AD PRIMUM ergo dicendum, quod, sicut dicit Dionysius in Eccles. Hier., status novae legis medius est inter statum veteris legis et statum caelestis patriae; et ideo etiam ea quae sunt novae legis, et sunt veritas respectu signorum[50] veteris legis, et sunt figurae respectu manifestae et plenae cognitionis veritatis, quae erit in patria; et ideo adhuc oportet in nova lege quod maneant aliquae figurae, quae scilicet in patria, ubi erit plenaria perceptio veritatis, omnes[51] cessabunt.

AD SECUNDUM dicendum, quod sacramenta legalia gratiam non continebant; et ideo apostolus ibidem nominat ea egena et vacua; et propter hoc qui eis subdebantur, erant sub elementis pure corporalibus. Sed non est simile de sacramentis quae gratiam invisibilem continent.

TO THE FIFTH QUESTION, it should be said that the faith of modern men and of the ancients is the same, as Augustine says, because the one whom the ancients believed was coming, we believe now to have come.[48] And thus, since sacraments correspond to faith, as protestations of it and having power from it, it is fitting that just as the ancient patriarchs were made partakers of the redemption of Christ by sacraments which were signs of the future, so also among us his redemption is accomplished by the mediation of certain sacraments that signify what has already happened, which are the sacraments of the New Law.

REPLY OBJ. 1: As Dionysius says in the Ecclesiastical Hierarchy, the state of the New Law is a middle one between the state of the Old Law and the state of the heavenly fatherland;[49] and therefore also those things that are of the New Law are both the truth in relation to the significations of the Old Law and figures in relation to the manifest and full understanding of truth that will be in heaven; and thus for now it is necessary that certain figures remain in the New Law, but in heaven, where there will be an absolute perception of truth, all figures will cease.

REPLY OBJ. 2: The sacraments of the Law did not contain grace; and thus the Apostle in the same place[52] calls them impoverished and empty; and because of this, all those who were subjected to them were under purely corporeal elements. But it is not the same with sacraments that contain invisible grace.

48. See Augustine, In Iohannis evangelium tractatus (CCSL 36), Tr. 45, par. 9: "Ante aduentum Domini nostri Iesu Christi, quo humilis uenit in carne, praecesserunt iusti, sic in eum credentes uenturum, quomodo nos credimus in eum qui uenit. Tempora uariata sunt, non fides. . . . Diuersis quidem temporibus, sed utrosque per unum fidei ostium, hoc est per Christum, uidemus ingressos. . . . In signis diuersis eadem fides . . . Videte ergo, fide manente, signa uariata."

49. Pseudo-Dionysius, Ecclesiastical Hierarchy, ch. 5, n. 2 (PG 3:502).

50. signorum.—significationum PLE.

51. omnes cessabunt.—omnes figurae cessabunt PLE.

52. Galatians 4:9.

ARTICLE 3

What a sacrament consists of[53]

AD TERTIUM SIC PROCEDITUR. Videtur quod sacramenta non consistant in verbis et rebus. Sacramentum enim est aliquid unum. Sed ex duobus quae non sunt conjuncta, non potest aliquid unum fieri, nec unum potest esse forma alterius. Cum ergo verba et res sint omnino separata, videtur quod ex eis non possit constare sacramentum, ut habeat pro forma verba, et res pro materia.

PRAETEREA, sicut in sacramentis requiruntur verba, ita et facta quaedam, ut dicit Hugo de sancto Victore. Sed facta non ponuntur de integritate sacramenti. Ergo nec verba.

PRAETEREA, sacramenta sunt ad significandum et causandum. Sed utrumque horum potest fieri per res sine verbis. Ergo sacramenta non consistunt in his duobus.

PRAETEREA, sacramenta veteris legis erant signa nostrorum sacramentorum. Sed in illis non erant aliqua verba determinata. Ergo nec in nostris esse debent.

PRAETEREA, poenitentia et matrimonium sunt quaedam sacramenta. Sed de integritate eorum non sunt verba aliqua. Ergo hoc quod Magister dicit, non est verum de omnibus sacramentis.

SED CONTRA, sacramenta ex similitudine repraesentant ea quae circa Christum sunt gesta. Ergo cum in Christo fuerit verbum rei sensibili adjunctum, oportet quod hoc etiam sit in sacramentis.

PRAETEREA, medicina debet proportionari morbo. Sed morbus peccati hominem quantum ad animam et corpus infecerat. Ergo oportet in sacramentis esse verba quae respondeant animae, et res quae respondeant corpori.

PRAETEREA, secundum Hugonem, sacramenta ex sanctificatione invisibilem gratiam continent. Sed creatura sanctificatur per verbum Dei; 2 Tim., 3. Ergo oportet in sacramentis non solum res sed etiam verba esse.

RESPONDEO dicendum, quod hoc est commune in omnibus sacramentis quod consistant in rebus sensibilibus invisibilem gratiam significantibus. Sed hoc est speciale in sacramentis novae legis quod rebus verba addantur, propter tres rationes. Prima est, quia haec sacramenta non solum significant opus redemptionis quae

OBJ. 1: To the third we proceed thus. It seems that sacraments do not consist of words and things. For a sacrament is one thing. But one thing cannot be made from two things that are not united, nor can one be the form of the other. Since, then, the words and things are entirely separate, it seems that a sacrament could not be composed from them, such that it would have words for its form and things for its matter.

OBJ. 2: Furthermore, just as words are required in the sacraments, so also are certain actions, as Hugh of St. Victor says.[54] But actions are not set down as necessary for the integrity of the sacrament. Therefore, neither should words.

OBJ. 3: Furthermore, sacraments are for signifying and causing. But both of these can be done by things without words. Therefore, sacraments do not consist of these two things.

OBJ. 4: Furthermore, the sacraments of the Old Law were signs of our sacraments. But in them there were no certain determined words. Therefore, there should not be in ours.

OBJ. 5: Furthermore, penance and marriage are sacraments. But there are no particular words required for their integrity. Therefore, what the Master says is not true of all the sacraments.

ON THE CONTRARY, sacraments represent by a likeness the things that were done concerning Christ. Therefore, since in Christ the Word was joined to a sensible thing, it is fitting that this also be the case in the sacraments.

FURTHERMORE, medicine must be proportioned to the disease. But the disease of sin infected man in his soul and body. Therefore, it is fitting that there be words in the sacraments that correspond to the soul, and things that correspond to the body.

FURTHERMORE, according to Hugh of St. Victor, sacraments contain invisible grace by their sanctification.[55] But creation is sanctified by the Word of God.[56] Therefore, it is necessary that in the sacraments there be not only things but also words.

I ANSWER THAT, it is common to all sacraments that they consist in sensible things signifying invisible grace. But this is particular to the sacraments of the New Law, that they have words added to the things, for three reasons. The first is because these sacraments not only signify the work of redemption that was done by Christ, as the other sacra-

---

53. Parallels: below, d. 13, q. 1, a. 2, qa. 6, ad 2; *ST* III, q. 60, aa. 6–7; *De veritate*, q. 27, a. 4, ad 10.
54. Hugh of St. Victor, *De sacramentis fidei*, Bk. 1, pt. 9, ch. 6 (PL 176:326).
55. Hugh of St. Victor, *De sacramentis fidei*, Bk. 1, pt. 9, ch. 2 (PL 176:317).
56. See 1 Timothy 4:5: "Everything created by God is good, and nothing is to be rejected if it is received with thanksgiving; for then it is consecrated by the word of God and prayer."

per Christum est facta, sicut alia sacramenta, sed etiam ab ipsa Christi passione fluxerunt; et ideo sicut effectus proximi, habent suae causae imaginem quantum possunt, ut scilicet ex rebus et verbis consistant, sicut Christus ex Verbo et carne. Secunda ratio est, quia non solum sunt signa futurorum, sicut sacramenta veteris legis, sed praesentium et praeteritorum, ut prius dictum est, quae possunt expressius significari quam futura, sicut et certius cognosci; et ideo, significatio verborum, quae est expressissima, adjungitur significationi rerum. Tertia ratio est, quia gratiam continent ex sanctificatione quae fit per Verbum Dei, ut dictum est.

AD PRIMUM ergo dicendum, quod sacramentum est aliquid unum in genere signi vel causae, quorum utrumque relationem importat. Non est autem inconveniens ut quae sunt in se distincta uniantur in relatione ad aliquid unum, sicut accidit de multis trahentibus navim qui sunt una causa tractus navis. Et sicut pater et mater sunt unum in generatione; sic etiam verba et res sunt unum in causando et significando, et per consequens efficiunt unum sacramentum. Et quia virtus causandi est in rebus ex verbis significantibus, ut dictum est, ideo verba sunt formalia, et res materiales, per modum quo omne completivum forma dicitur.

AD SECUNDUM dicendum, quod, sicut Hugo de sancto Victore dicit, ad sacramenta concurrunt verba et res et facta: sed facta pertinent ad usum vel dispensationem sacramentorum; verba autem et res sunt de essentia sacramenti. Et ideo Magister in his duobus dicit constare sacramenta, et non in factis. Vel dicendum, quod facta ad res reducuntur.

AD TERTIUM dicendum, quod nec efficacia causandi nec expressio significandi poterat esse in rebus, nisi verba adjungerentur, ut dictum est.

AD QUARTUM dicendum, quod non est similis ratio de sacramentis veteris et novae legis, ut ex dictis patet.

AD QUINTUM dicendum, quod matrimonium secundum quod est in officium, et poenitentia secundum quod est virtus, non habent aliquam formam verborum; sed secundum quod utrumque est sacramentum in dispensatione ministrorum ecclesiae consistens, utrumque habet aliqua verba; sicut in matrimonio sunt verba exprimentia consensum, et iterum benedictiones ab ecclesia institutae; in poenitentia autem est absolutio sacerdotis verbotenus facta.

ments do, but they also flowed from the Passion of Christ itself. And therefore, as the closest effects, they have the image of their cause as much as possible, so that namely they consist of words and things, as Christ consists of the Word and flesh. The second reason is that they are signs not only of future things, like the sacraments of the Old Law, but of present and past things, as was said before, which can be more explicitly signified than future things, just as they can be known with more certainty. And therefore, the signification of words, which is most explicit, is added to the signification of things. The third reason is that they contain grace by the sanctification that happens through the Word of God, as was said.

REPLY OBJ. 1: A sacrament is something one in the genus of sign or cause, both of which imply relation. For it is not unfitting that things that are distinct in themselves be united in relation to something else, as happens when many men rowing a ship are one cause of the ship's being rowed. And just as a father and mother are one in generation, so also words and things are one in causing and signifying, and as a result they bring about one sacrament. And because the power of causing is in the things by the words signifying, as was said, therefore words are the formal component and things are the material component, in the way that everything completive is called a form.

REPLY OBJ. 2: As Hugh of St. Victor says, for sacraments words and things and actions must converge; but actions pertain to the use or administering of the sacraments, while words and things are of the essence of the sacrament. And thus the Master says that sacraments consist in these two things, and not in actions. Or it could be said that actions fall under the heading of things.

REPLY OBJ. 3: Things can have neither effectiveness in causing nor explicitness in signifying unless words are added to them, as has been said.

REPLY OBJ. 4: The nature of the sacraments of the Old Law and of the New Law is not the same, as is clear from what has been said.

REPLY OBJ. 5: Marriage as an office and penance as a virtue do not have any form of words, but according as each is a sacrament to be administered by the ministry of the Church, they both have particular words; as in marriage there are words expressing consent, as well as blessings instituted by the Church, while in penance there is the absolution given verbally by the priest.

ARTICLE 4

On the efficacy of the sacraments of the New Law

Quaestiuncula 1

AD QUARTUM SIC PROCEDITUR. Videtur quod sacramenta novae legis non sint causa gratiae. Dicit enim Bernardus: *sicut investitur canonicus per librum, abbas per baculum, episcopus per anulum; sic divisiones gratiarum diversis sunt tradita sacramentis.* Sed liber non est causa canonicatus, nec anulus episcopatus. Ergo nec sacramenta gratiae.

PRAETEREA, si sunt causae gratiae, oportet quod sint secundum aliquod genus causae. Sed constat quod non sunt materiales nec formales, cum sint extra essentiam gratiae; nec iterum sunt causae finales, quia magis sacramenta propter gratiam habendam quaeruntur quam e converso: nec iterum causae efficientes, quia solus Deus efficit gratiam, adeo quod nec angelis, qui sunt nobiliores sensibilibus creaturis, hoc communicatur. Ergo nullo modo sacramenta sunt causa gratiae.

PRAETEREA, nobilius est agens patiente, secundum Augustinum in 12 super Gen.; et secundum Philosophum, in 3 *de Anima*; et iterum causa dignior est effectu. Sed tam anima rationalis quam gratia praevalent sensibilibus elementis. Ergo sacramentum, quod est materiale elementum, ut prius dictum est, non potest agere in animam ad causandum gratiam in ipsa.

PRAETEREA, omnis causa vel est univoca vel aequivoca. In causa autem aequivoca est aliquid nobiliori modo quam in causatis, sicut calor in sole quam in aere; in causa autem univoca est aliquid eodem modo. Sed gratia non est in sacramentis neque eodem modo ut in anima, neque nobiliori modo. Ergo non sunt causa gratiae nec univoce nec aequivoce; et ita nullo modo.

PRAETEREA, sacramenta non causant gratiam in anima per modum influentiae, quia sic crearent ipsam, nec iterum educunt eam de potentia materiae, quia gra-

OBJ. 1: To the fourth we proceed thus. It seems that sacraments of the New Law are not a cause of grace.[57] For Bernard says: *Just as the canon is invested with a book, an abbot with a crozier, a bishop by a ring, so also divisions of different graces are handed on in the sacraments.*[58] But a book is not a cause of someone becoming a canon, nor is a ring the cause of someone becoming bishop. Therefore, neither are the sacraments causes of grace.

OBJ. 2: Furthermore, if they are causes of grace, they must belong to some genus of causes. But it is clear that they are neither material causes nor formal causes, since they are outside the essence of grace. Nor are they the final cause of grace, for sacraments are sought for the sake of having grace, rather than vice versa. Nor are they efficient causes of grace, for only God causes grace, as evident from the fact that this causality is not even shared with the angels, who are more noble than sensible creatures. Therefore, in no way are sacraments the cause of grace.

OBJ. 3: Furthermore, the one acting is nobler than the one acted upon, according to Augustine in Book 12 of the *Commentary on Genesis*,[59] and according to the Philosopher in Book 3 of *On the Soul*,[60] and a cause is more worthy than an effect. But both the rational soul and grace itself have greater worth than sensible elements. Therefore, a sacrament, which is a material element, as was previously said, cannot act in the soul to cause grace in it.

OBJ. 4: Furthermore, every cause is either univocal or equivocal. Now in an equivocal cause something exists in a nobler way than in the things caused, as heat exists in the sun in a nobler way than in the air; in a univocal cause, something exists in the same way as in the thing caused. But grace is not in the sacraments in the same way as it is in the soul, nor is it in them in a nobler way. Therefore, they are neither univocal causes of grace nor equivocal ones, and thus they they are not causes of grace in any way.

OBJ. 5: Furthermore, sacraments do not cause grace in the soul by pouring it in, for in that way they would create it; nor do they draw it forth from the potency of matter, for

---

57. Parallels: below, d. 18, q. 1, a. 3, qa. 1, ad 1; *ST* I-II, q. 112, a. 1, ad 2; *ST* III, q. 62, aa. 1 & 6; *SCG* IV, ch. 57; *De veritate*, q. 27, a. 4; *Quodl.* XII, q. 10; *De eccles. sacram.*; *Super Gal.* 2, lec. 4.

58. See St. Bernard of Clairvaux, *Sermo de coena Domini*, n. 2: "Sicut enim in exterioribus sunt diversa signa et, ut coepto immoremur exemplo, variae sunt investiturae secundum ea de quibus investimur,—verbi gratia, investitur canonicus per librum, abbas per baculum, episcopus per baculum et anulum simul—, sicut, inquam, in huiusmodi rebus est, sic et divisiones gratiarum diversis traditae sunt sacramentis" (*Bernardi Opera*, ed. J. Leclercq et H.M. Rochais [1968], 5:68).

59. See Augustine, *De Genesi ad litteram*, Bk. 12, ch. 16.

60. *De anima*, Bk. 3, ch. 5, 430a18–19.

tia non est in potentia naturali materiae. Ergo nullo modo gratiam causant.

Praeterea, in sacramento altaris transubstantiatur panis in corpus Christi; quod non potest fieri nisi virtute infinita, qualis non est virtus formae illius sacramenti. Ergo virtus illa non causat dictam transubstantiationem, et eadem ratione nec alia sacramenta causant quod significant.

Sed contra, haec differentia assignatur communiter inter sacramenta novae legis et veteris, quod sacramenta novae legis efficiunt quod figurant, quod sacramentis veteris legis non competit. Figurant autem sacramenta invisibilem gratiam. Si ergo sacramenta novae legis gratiam non causant, non differunt in aliquo a sacramentis veteris legis.

Praeterea, Augustinus dicit, quod aqua baptismi *corpus tangit, et cor abluit*. Sed cor non abluitur nisi per gratiam. Ergo sacramenta novae legis gratiam causant.

grace is not in the natural potency of matter. Therefore, in no way do they cause grace.

Obj. 6: Furthermore, in the sacrament of the altar, bread is transubstantiated into the body of Christ, which could only happen by an infinite power, such a power as this sacrament's form does not have. Therefore, that power does not cause the transubstantiation, and by the same reasoning neither do other sacraments cause what they signify.

On the contrary, this difference is commonly drawn between the sacraments of the New Law and of the Old Law, that the sacraments of the New Law effect what they represent, which the sacraments of the Old Law are not capable of doing. But sacraments represent invisible grace. If, therefore, sacraments of the New Law do not cause grace, then they are no different from the sacraments of the Old Law.

Furthermore, Augustine says that the water of baptism *touches the body and cleanses the heart*.[61] But the heart is only cleansed by grace. Therefore, sacraments of the New Law cause grace.

Quaestiuncula 2

Ulterius. Videtur quod in sacramentis non sit aliqua virtus specialis[62] ad gratiam inducendam. Quod enim non est in aliquo genere entium, non est ens. Sed hujusmodi virtus non potest reduci ad aliquod decem generum: quia non est forma substantialis, ut per se patet: neque in aliquod aliorum generum praeter qualitatem, nec etiam in qualitatem, ut patet discurrenti per quattuor species qualitatis. Ergo non est ens.

Praeterea, constat quod sacramenta non habent a seipsis hujusmodi virtutem. Si ergo est in eis, oportet quod a Deo habeant eam: nec est assignare, ut videtur, quando eis data sit. Non enim in ista institutione sacramentorum dari eis potuit: quia res istae et haec verba tunc non erant, et non enti nihil datur: nec iterum quotidie eis dat hanc virtutem: quia creatio dicitur esse hoc tempore solum quantum ad animas rationales et quantum ad gratiam: nec alio modo potest eis dari, nisi in eis creetur: nec iterum est probabile quod tam nobilis virtus creetur in verbis, quae statim esse desinunt; et res etiam in brevi corrumpuntur. Ergo nullo modo hujusmodi virtus est in sacramentis.

Praeterea, dicta virtus non potest computari inter minima bona: quia sic ad gratiam inducendam, quae est de maximis bonis, efficaciam non haberet: nec ite-

Obj. 1: Moreover, it seems that in the sacraments there is no spiritual power for instilling grace.[63] For anything that is not in a certain genus of being is not a being. But this power cannot be reduced to any of the ten categories of being: for it is not a substantial form, as is self-evident; nor is it in any of the categories outside of quality, nor is it in quality, as is clear to anyone considering the four species of quality. Therefore, it is not a being.

Obj. 2: Furthermore, it is apparent that sacraments do not have this power from themselves. Therefore, if it exists in them, they must have it from God; nor is it possible to specify, as it seems, when they were given it. For he could not have given it to them in the sacraments' institution, for those things and these words did not exist at that time, and nothing is given to a non-being; nor again does he give this power to them daily, for creation is said to be occurring at this moment only with respect to rational souls and grace. Nor can it be given to them in another way, unless it were created in them. Nor again is it probable that such a noble power was created in words, which immediately stop existing; and things likewise are quickly corrupted. Therefore there is no way for a power like this to exist in the sacraments.

Obj. 3: Furthermore, the power mentioned cannot be counted among lesser goods, for then it would not have efficacy for instilling grace, which is among the greatest goods.

---

61. Augustine, *In Iohannis evangelium tractatus* (CCSL 36), Tr. 80, par. 3: "unde ista tanta uirtus aquae, ut corpus tangat et cor abluat, nisi faciente uerbo, non quia dicitur, sed quia creditur? Nam et in ipso uerbo, aliud est sonus transiens, aliud uirtus manens."

62. *specialis.—spiritualis* PLE.

63. Parallels: below, d. 8, q. 2, a. 3; *ST* III, q. 62, a. 4; q. 78, a. 4; *De veritate*, q. 27, a. 4, ad 4; *Quodl.* XII, q. 10.

rum inter media, cujusmodi sunt animae potentiae, quibus homo bene et male utitur: eadem ratione nec iterum inter maxima, cum neque sit gratia, neque virtus mentis. Ergo non est aliquod bonum, et ita nihil est.

Praeterea, omne quod recipitur in aliquo, est in eo per modum recipientis; et inde est quod virtus spiritualis non potest esse in re corporali. Sed haec virtus, quae ordinatur ad gratiam inducendam, est maxime spiritualis. Ergo non potest esse in rebus corporalibus.

Praeterea, unius sacramenti non potest esse nisi una virtus, cum sit ad unum effectum. Sed una virtus non potest esse in diversis. Ergo cum in sacramento sint plura, scilicet verba et res, videtur quod non possit in sacramento esse aliqua virtus ad gratiam inducendam.

Sed contra est quod Augustinus dicit: *quae est vis aquae ut corpus tangat et cor abluat?* Ergo habet aliquam virtutem. Similiter etiam Beda dicit, quod Christus tactu mundissimae suae carnis vim regenerativam contulit aquis.

Praeterea, sacramenta medicinae quaedam sunt. Sed omnis medicina habet aliquam virtutem per quam fit efficax. Ergo et in sacramentis est aliqua virtus.

Nor again among neutral things, like the powers of the soul, which man can use well or ill; and by the same reasoning, neither is it counted among the greatest goods, since it is neither grace nor a power of the mind. Therefore, it is not something good, and so it is nothing.

Obj. 4: Furthermore, everything that is received by another is in it according to the mode of the receiver; and hence it is that spiritual power cannot exist in a corporeal thing. But the power of the sacraments, which is ordered toward instilling grace, is extremely spiritual. Therefore, it cannot exist in corporeal things.

Obj. 5: Furthermore, there can be only one power in one sacrament, since it has one effect. But a single power cannot reside in different things. Therefore, since there is more than one element in a sacrament, namely, words and things, it seems that there could not be any power in a sacrament for instilling grace.

On the contrary, Augustine says: *what is the power of water that it touches the body and cleanses the heart?*[64] Therefore, it has a certain power. Similarly, Bede also says that by the touch of his most immaculate flesh, Christ conferred a regenerative power on the waters.[65]

Furthermore, sacraments are a certain medicine. But every medicine has a certain power by which it becomes effective. Therefore, this power is also in the sacraments.

Quaestiuncula 3

Ulterius. Videtur quod haec virtus non sit in sacramentis a passione Christi. Christus enim, secundum quod homo, non dat Spiritum Sanctum, neque gratiam causat, ut in 1 Lib., dist. 14, qu. 3, art. unic., dictum est. Sed passio convenit ei secundum quod homo. Ergo efficacia virtutis quae est in sacramentis ad gratiam causandam, non potest esse a Christi passione, sed ab ejus divinitate.

Praeterea, Rom. 4, 25, dicitur, quod *resurrexit propter justificationem nostram.* Sed justificatio fit per infusionem gratiae. Ergo magis a resurrectione sacramenta praedictam virtutem habent.

Praeterea, sacramenta dicuntur a fide efficaciam habere. Sed fides non solum est de passione sed etiam de aliis articulis. Ergo non solum a passione efficaciam habent.

Sed contra, Rom. 5, super illud: *similitudinem praevaricationis Adae*, dicit Glossa: *ex latere Christi profluxerunt sacramenta per quae salvata est ecclesia.* Hoc

Obj. 1: Moreover, it seems that the sacraments do not get this power from the Passion of Christ.[66] For Christ as man did not give the Holy Spirit, nor does he cause grace, as was said in Book I, Distinction 14, Question 3, Article 1. But the Passion belongs to him as man. Therefore, the efficacy of the sacraments' power for causing grace cannot be from Christ's Passion but from his divinity.

Obj. 2: Furthermore, it is said that *he rose again for our justification* (Rom 4:25). But justification happens by the infusion of grace. Therefore, the sacraments obtain the power mentioned rather from his resurrection.

Obj. 3: Furthermore, the sacraments are said to have efficacy from faith. But one has faith not only concerning the Passion, but also concerning the other articles. Therefore, they do not only have efficacy from the Passion.

On the contrary, Concerning Romans 5:14, *death exercised dominion . . . even over those whose sins were not like the transgression of Adam, who is a type of the one who*

---

64. See the text cited in the preceding note.

65. Cf. St. Bede, *In Lucae euangelium expositio* (CCSL 120), ch. 3: "Baptizatus est dominus non ipse aquis mundari sed ipsas mundare cupiens aquas quae ablutae per carnem eius peccati utique nesciam baptismi ius induerent et quod tam innumera sub lege baptismata non poterant contra praeuaricationis malum uim regeneratiuae sanctificationis conciperent."

66. Parallels: *ST* III, q. 62, a. 5; q. 64, a. 2, ad 2.

autem factum est in passione. Ergo ex passione efficaciam habent.

PRAETEREA, sacramenta sunt medicinae contra peccata. Sed peccata sunt ablata per Christi passionem; quia mortuus est *propter delicta nostra*: Rom. 5. Ergo a passione efficaciam habent.

was to come, the Gloss says: *from the side of Christ flowed the sacraments by which the Church is saved.*[67] But this happened during the Passion. Therefore, they have their efficacy from the Passion.

FURTHERMORE, sacraments are medicine against sins. But sins are taken away by Christ's Passion, for he died *for our trespasses* (Rom 4:25). Therefore, they have efficacy from his Passion.

Quaestiuncula 4

ULTERIUS. Videtur quod sacramenta novae legis non contineant gratiam. Idem enim est subjectum gratiae et gloriae. Sed nihil potest esse subjectum gloriae nisi creatura rationalis. Ergo nec in sacramento, quod est materiale elementum, potest esse gratia.

SI DICATUR quod gratia non est in sacramentis sicut in subjecto, sed sicut in vase; contra. Esse in vase significat esse in loco, secundum Philosophum in 4 *Physic*. Sed accidenti non competit esse in loco. Ergo non potest esse verum quod dictum est.

PRAETEREA, si Deus in sacramentis gratiam posuit, hoc non est nisi propter animam, in quam gratia transfundi debet. Sed non potest eadem gratia quae est in sacramentis, in animam transfundi, quia accidens non transit de subjecto in subjectum. Ergo frustra esset ibi; et ita non est ibi: quia in operibus gratiae minus est aliquid frustra quam in operibus naturae.

PRAETEREA, secundum Philosophum in 1 *de Anima*, spiritualia, etiamsi sint in corporalibus, non dicuntur ab eis contineri, sed magis continere, sicut anima est in corpore, et continet ipsum. Sed gratia est res spiritualis. Ergo etsi sit in sacramentis corporalibus, non debet dici contineri ab eis.

SED CONTRA est quod dicitur in Glossa, Gal. 3, quod sacramenta veteris legis dicebantur egena et inania, quia gratiam non continebant. Sed hoc non potest dici de sacramentis novae legis. Ergo gratiam continent.

PRAETEREA hoc patet per definitionem Hugonis de sancto Victore supra positam.

OBJ. 1: Moreover, it seems that sacraments of the New Law do not contain grace.[68] For the same thing is the subject of grace and of glory. But nothing but a rational creature can be the subject of glory. Therefore, neither can there be grace in a sacrament, which is a material element.

OBJ. 2: If it were said that grace is not in the sacraments as in a subject, but as in a vessel, to the contrary: to be in a vessel is to be in a place, according to the Philosopher in *Physics* 4.[69] But an accident is not capable of being in a place. Therefore, what was said cannot be true.

OBJ. 3: Furthermore, if God put grace in the sacraments, he did so only for the sake of the soul, into which grace must be transfused. But the same grace that is in the sacraments cannot be transfused into the soul, for an accident does not cross over from one subject into another. Therefore, it would be there in vain; and so it is not there, for in the workings of grace less happens in vain than in the workings of nature.

OBJ. 4: Furthermore, according to the Philosopher in *On the Soul* 1, spiritual things, even if they exist in corporeal ones, are not said to be contained by them, but rather to contain them, as the soul is in the body and contains it.[70] But grace is a spiritual thing. Therefore, although it is in corporeal sacraments, it cannot be said to be contained by them.

ON THE CONTRARY, is what is said in the Gloss on Galatians 3, that sacraments of the Old Law were called impoverished and empty because they did not contain grace.[71] But this cannot be said of the sacraments of the New Law. Therefore, they contain grace.

FURTHERMORE, this is clear from the definition of Hugh of St. Victor quoted above.

---

67. See *Glossa ordinaria* on Romans 5:14 (PL 114:486).
68. Parallels: *In I Sent.*, d. 15, q. 5, a. 1, qa. 1, ad 2; *ST* I, q. 43, a. 6, ad 4; *ST* III, q. 62, a. 3; *De veritate*, q. 27, a. 7.
69. Aristotle, *Physics*, Bk. 4, ch. 3, 210a24.
70. Aristotle, *De Anima*, Bk. 1, ch. 5, 411a7.
71. See the *Glossa ordinaria* on Galatians 4:9; some MSS have Thomas referring to Galatians 3.

Quaestiuncula 5

Ulterius. Videtur quod gratia quae est in sacramentis, non differat ab illa quae est in virtutibus et donis. Gratia enim quae est in sacramentis, est gratia gratum faciens, quia facit dignum vita aeterna, ut patet de baptismo. Sed gratia gratum faciens est una tantum, quod patet ex unitate subjecti, quod est essentia animae, et ex unitate effectus, quod est Deo acceptum facere. Ergo cum gratia quae est in virtutibus et donis, sit gratia gratum faciens, videtur quod eadem gratia sit hic et ibi.

Praeterea, unum uni opponitur. Sed tam gratia quae est in sacramentis quam illa quae est in virtutibus, opponitur peccato, quia utraque peccatum destruit. Ergo est una tantum gratia.

Praeterea, idem est motus in natura a termino et ad terminum. Sed gratia sacramentalis ordinatur contra peccatum, gratia autem virtutum ad perficiendum animam, et Deo conjungendum. Ergo est una gratia in sacramento.

Sed contra, gratia in sacramento non datur nisi ei qui non ficte accedit. Sed talis habet gratiam virtutum. Cum ergo nulli detur quod jam habet, videtur quod gratia quam accipit in sacramento, sit alia.

Praeterea, virtutes et dona sunt connexa propter gratiam, ut in 3 Lib., dist. 36, quaest. unic., art. 2, et 3, dictum est, non autem sacramenta. Ergo non est eadem gratia hic et ibi.

Obj. 1: Moreover, it seems that the grace that is in the sacraments does not differ from that which is in the virtues and gifts.[72] For the grace that is in the sacraments is the grace that makes pleasing, which makes one worthy of eternal life, as is clear in baptism. But the grace that makes pleasing is only one reality, which is clear from the oneness of the subject, which is the essence of the soul, and from the oneness of the effect, which is to make it accepted by God. Therefore, since the grace that is in the virtues and gifts is the grace that makes pleasing, it seems that it is the same grace in both.

Obj. 2: Furthermore, one thing can only be opposed to one other thing. But the grace that is in the sacraments is opposed to sin just as much as the grace in the virtues, for both of them destroy sin. Therefore, there is only one grace.

Obj. 3: Furthermore, the same thing is moved in nature from an originating terminus to a terminus of destination. But sacramental grace is directed against sin, while the grace of virtue is ordered to perfecting the soul and uniting it with God. Therefore, there is one grace in a sacrament.

On the contrary, in a sacrament grace is only given to someone who does not receive it falsely. But someone like that has the grace of the virtues. Since therefore it would be given to no one who already had it, it seems that the grace that is received in the sacraments is another kind of grace.

Furthermore, virtues and gifts are interdependent because of grace, as was said in Book III, Distinction 36, Articles 2 and 3, but the sacraments are not. Therefore, it is not the same grace in both.

Response to Quaestiuncula 1

Respondeo dicendum, ad primam quaestionem, quod omnes coguntur ponere, sacramenta novae legis aliquo modo causas gratiae esse, propter auctoritates quae hoc expresse dicunt.

Sed diversi diversimode eas causas ponunt. Quidam enim dicunt, quod non sunt causae quasi facientes aliquid in anima, sed causae sine quibus non: quia increata virtus, quae sola effectus ad gratiam pertinentes in anima facit, sacramentis assistit per quamdam Dei ordinationem, et quasi pactionem. Sic enim ordinavit et quasi pepigit Deus, ut qui sacramenta accipiunt, simul ab iis gratiam recipiant, non quasi sacramenta aliquid faciant ad hoc. Et est simile de illo qui accipit denarium plumbeum facta tali ordinatione, ut qui habuerit unum de illis denariis, habeat centum libras a rege: qui quidem denarius non dat illas centum libras, sed solus rex accipienti

The first question I answer by saying that all are forced to consider sacraments of the New Law causes of grace in some way, because of the authorities who expressly say so.

But different ones claim they are causes in different ways. For certain people say that they are not causes as though they did anything in the soul, but are causes in the manner of guaranteed conditions, for the uncreated power—that is, God's—which alone causes the effects pertaining to grace in the soul, assists the sacraments through a certain ordination and agreement, as it were, from God. For thus he has ordained and agreed, as it were, that whoever receives the sacraments will receive grace from them at the same time, not as though the sacraments did anything for that. And it is the same with someone who receives a lead nickel made according to an ordination such that whoever

---

72. Parallels: below, d. 7, q. 2, a. 2, qa. 3; *In II Sent.*, d. 26, a. 6, ad 5; *ST* III, q. 62, a. 2; q. 72, a. 7, ad 3; *De veritate*, q. 27, a. 5, ad 12.

ipsum. Et quia pactio talis non erat facta in sacramentis veteris legis, ut accedentes ad ipsa gratiam acciperent, ideo dicuntur gratiam non conferre, sed promittebant tantum.

Sed hoc non videtur sufficere ad salvandum dicta sanctorum. Causa enim sine qua non, si nihil omnino faciat ad inducendum effectum vel disponendo vel meliorando, quantum ad rationem causandi, nihil habebit supra causas per accidens; sicut album est causa domus, si aedificator sit albus; et secundum hoc sacramenta essent causae per accidens tantum sanctificationis. Illa enim ordinatio quam dicunt, sive pactio, nihil dat eis de ratione causae, sed solum de ratione signi; sicut etiam denarius plumbeus est solum signum indicans quis debet accipere. Quod autem est per accidens, omittitur ab arte, nec ponitur in definitione; unde in definitione sacramenti non poneretur causalitas praedicta, nec sancti multum curassent de ea dicere.

Nec iterum sacramenta novae legis, quae differunt a sacramentis veteris legis secundum ordinationem praedictam, differrent ab eis secundum rationem causae, sed solum quantum ad modum significandi, inquantum haec significant gratiam ut statim dandam, illa vero non.

Et ideo alii dicunt, quod ex sacramentis duo consequuntur in anima. Unum quod est sacramentum et res, sicut character, vel aliquis ornatus animae in sacramentis in quibus non imprimitur character, aliud quod est res tantum, sicut gratia. Respectu ergo primi effectus sunt sacramenta causae aliquo modo efficientes; sed respectu secundi sunt causae disponentes tali dispositione quae est necessitas, nisi sit impedimentum ex parte recipientis; et hoc videtur magis theologis et dictis sanctorum conveniens.

Ad cujus evidentiam sciendum est, quod causa efficiens dupliciter potest dividi. Uno modo ex parte effectus; scilicet in disponentem, quae causat dispositionem ad formam ultimam; et perficientem, quae inducit ultimam perfectionem. Alio modo ex parte ipsius causae in agens principale, et instrumentale. Agens enim principale est primum movens, agens autem instrumentale

had one of those nickels would have one hundred pounds from the king: for indeed, the nickel itself does not give those hundred pounds, but only the king accepting it. And since no such agreement was made in the sacraments of the Old Law that those approaching them would receive graces, for this reason they are said not to confer grace, but only to promise it.

But this does not seem sufficient to do justice to the sayings of the saints. For causes in the manner of guaranteed conditions, if nothing whatsoever were done to bring about the effect either by disposing or improving, will have, as to the nature of causing, no more effect than accidental causes have, as white is the cause of a house if the builder is white; and according to this, the sacraments were only accidental causes of sanctification. For that ordination or agreement which they speak of gives them nothing of the nature of a cause, but only of the nature of a sign, as also a lead nickel is only a sign indicating who should receive it. But what is accidental is ignored by art[73] nor is it included in a definition; hence in the definition of a sacrament no causality would be included, nor would holy men have taken the trouble to say much about it.

Nor on the other hand would the sacraments of the New Law, which differ from the sacraments of the Old Law according to the ordination mentioned, differ from them according to the nature of the cause, but only as to the mode of signifying, inasmuch as these signify grace as something to be given immediately, while the others do not.

And thus other men say that two things result in the soul from the sacraments. The first is a sacrament-and-reality,[74] like a character, or some adornment of the soul in sacraments in which no character is imprinted; the other is a reality alone, like grace. Therefore, with respect to the first the sacraments are causes bringing about effects in some way; but with respect to the second they are causes disposing with such a disposition that it is a necessity, unless there were an impediment on the part of the person receiving; and this seems more consistent with the theologians and sayings of the saints.

For the evidence of which it should be known that an efficient cause can be divided in two ways. In one way, on the part of the effect, that is, in the disposing cause, which causes a disposition to the final form; and in a perfecting cause, which introduces the final perfection. In another way, on the part of the very cause in the principal agent, and in the instrumental agent. For the principal agent is the

---

73. The axiom that "no art takes notice of what is accidental" is based on Aristotle, *Metaphysics*, Bk. 6, ch. 2; cf. *ST* I-II, q. 7, a. 2, ad 2: "Accidents which are altogether accidental are neglected by every art, by reason of their uncertainty and infinity."

74. A *sacramentum* is a sign of a sacred thing, while a *res* is the sacred thing signified. *Sacramentum tantum*, "sacrament alone," means that which signifies a sacred thing but is not itself signified by anything else; it is a *sacramentum* and not a *res*. Necessarily, the *sacramentum tantum* is the first sign encountered, and consequently it is the sensible sign consisting of the form (words) and matter in each sacrament. *Res tantum*, "reality alone" or "thing alone" means a sacred thing that is signified but does not itself signify anything else; it is a *res* and not a *sacramentum*. Generally, the *res tantum* is the effect of the sacrament, and it may be *contenta* ("contained") in the sacrament, e.g., grace; or *non contenta*, ("uncontained") like union of Christ and the Church signified but not caused by marriage. *Sacramentum-et-res*, "sacrament-and-reality," means a sacred thing signified that itself signifies something further, e.g., the character in baptism.

est movens motum. Instrumento autem competit duplex actio: una quam habet ex propria natura, alia quam habet prout est motum a primo agente; sicut calor ignis, qui est instrumentum virtutis nutritivae, ut dicitur in 2 de Anima, ex natura propria habet dissolvere, et consumere, et hujusmodi effectus: sed inquantum est instrumentum animae vegetabilis, generat carnem. Sed sciendum, quod actio instrumenti quandoque pertingit ad ultimam perfectionem, quam principale agens inducit, aliquando autem non; semper tamen pertingit ad aliquid ultra id quod competit sibi secundum suam naturam, sive illud sit ultima forma, sive dispositio, alias non ageret ut instrumentum: sic qualitates activae et passivae elementorum pertingunt instrumentaliter ad formas materiales educendas de materia, non autem ad productionem animae humanae, quae est ab extrinseco.

Dicendum est ergo, quod principale agens respectu justificationis Deus est, nec indiget ad hoc aliquibus instrumentis ex parte sua; sed propter congruitatem ex parte hominis justificandi, ut supra dictum est, utitur sacramentis quasi quibusdam instrumentis justificationis. Hujusmodi autem materialibus instrumentis competit aliqua actio ex natura propria, sicut aquae abluere, et oleo facere nitidum corpus; sed ulterius, inquantum sunt instrumenta divinae misericordiae justificantis, pertingunt instrumentaliter ad aliquem effectum in ipsa anima, quod primo correspondet sacramentis, sicut est character, vel aliquid hujusmodi. Ad ultimum autem effectum, quod est gratia, non pertingunt etiam instrumentaliter, nisi dispositive, inquantum hoc ad quod instrumentaliter effective pertingunt, est dispositio, quae est necessitas, quantum in se est, ad gratiae susceptionem. Et quia omne instrumentum agendo actionem naturalem, quae competit sibi inquantum est res quaedam, pertingit ad effectum qui competit sibi inquantum est instrumentum, sicut dolabrum dividendo suo acumine pertingit instrumentaliter ad formam scamni: ideo etiam materiale elementum exercendo actionem naturalem, secundum quam est signum interioris effectus, pertingit ad interiorem effectum instrumentaliter. Et hoc est quod Augustinus dicit, quod aqua baptismi *corpus tangit, et cor abluit*; et ideo dicitur, quod sacramenta efficiunt quod figurant. Et hunc modum justificandi videtur Magister tangere in littera: dicit enim, quod homo non quaerit salutem in sacramentis quasi ab eis, sed per illa a Deo. Haec enim praepositio a denotat principale agens: sed haec praepositio per denotat causam instrumentalem.

first mover, but an instrumental agent is a moved mover. Now two kinds of action apply to an instrument: one that it has from its own nature, and another that it has to the extent that it is moved by a prior agent; as the heat of fire, which is the instrument of nutritive power, as is said in *On the Soul* II, has from its proper nature the power to dissolve and consume, and effects of that kind; but as it is the instrument of the vegetative soul, it generates flesh.[75] But it should be known that the action of an instrument sometimes attains to the final perfection that the principal agent intends, and sometimes it does not. Nevertheless, it always attains to something beyond what it is capable of according to its own nature, whether that be the final form, or a disposition; otherwise it would not work as an instrument. And in this way the active and passive qualities of elements extend instrumentally to drawing material forms from matter, but not to the production of a human soul, which is from the outside.[76]

It should be said therefore that the principal agent with respect to justification is God, nor does he need any instruments for this on his part; but on account of the fittingness for the man being justified, as was said above, he uses the sacraments as certain instruments of justification. Now a certain action befits material instruments like this by their own nature, as water cleanses and oil makes the body sleek; but furthermore, as they are instruments of divine mercy justifying us, they attain instrumentally to a certain effect in the soul itself, which corresponds first to the sacraments, like a character or something of that sort. But to the final effect, which is grace, they do not attain even instrumentally, except dispositively, inasmuch as what they attain to as efficacious instruments is a disposition, which is necessary in itself for the reception of grace. And because every instrument, in performing a natural action of which it is capable by being that particular kind of thing, attains to the effect of which it is capable as an instrument (as an axe splitting something in its sharpness attains instrumentally to the form of a stool), thus also a material element exercising a natural action in which it is a sign of an interior effect, instrumentally accomplishes an interior effect. And this is what Augustine says, that the water of baptism *touches the body and cleanses the heart*; and therefore it is said that the sacraments bring about what they represent. And the Master seems to touch on this mode of justifying in the text: for he says that man does not seek salvation in sacraments as though from them, but rather through them from God. For this preposition 'from' denotes the principal agent: but this preposition 'through' denotes instrumental cause.

---

75. Aristotle, *De anima*, Bk. II, ch. 4, 416b25.
76. See Aristotle, *On the Generation of Animals*, Bk. 3, ch. 2.

AD PRIMUM ergo dicendum, quod Bernardus, ut ex praecedentibus ibidem patet, non intendit ostendere similitudinem sacramentorum ad illa, nisi quantum ad significationem: quia anulus est signum et baculus, et similiter sacramenta; sed sacramenta ulterius sunt causae.

AD SECUNDUM dicendum, quod reducuntur ad genus efficientis causae, non principalis, sed instrumentalis. Deus autem solus est causa gratiae quasi principale agens, sed sacramenta quasi instrumentaliter et dispositive, ut dictum est, agentia sunt.

AD TERTIUM dicendum, quod agens non semper est nobilius patiente simpliciter loquendo, sed inquantum est agens. Agit enim ignis vel ferrum in corpus humanum, quod est simpliciter nobilius, quo tamen ignis est nobilior inquantum est actu calidus, et secundum hoc agit in corpus humanum; et sic non oportet quod res illae materiales quae sunt in sacramentis, sint simpliciter anima nobiliores, sed secundum quid, scilicet inquantum sunt instrumenta divinae misericordiae operantis ad justificationem. Nec iterum oportet quod instrumentaliter agens sit simpliciter nobilius effectu; quia effectus non proportionatur instrumento, sed principali agenti, qui quandoque per vilia instrumenta nobiliores effectus inducit, sicut medicus perducit ad sanitatem per clysterem.

AD QUARTUM dicendum, quod causa univoca vel non univoca, proprie loquendo et simpliciter sunt divisiones illius causae cujus est similitudinem habere cum effectu; haec autem est principalis agentis et non instrumentalis, ut dicit Alexander, secundum quod narrat Commentator. Et ideo proprie loquendo, neque instrumentum est causa univoca neque aequivoca. Posset tamen reduci ad utrumlibet, secundum quod principale agens, in cujus virtute instrumentum agit, est causa univoca, vel non univoca.

AD QUINTUM dicendum, quod ex sacramentis causatur per modum influentiae gratia: nec tamen sacramenta sunt quae influunt gratiam, sed per quae Deus sicut per instrumenta animae gratiam influit.

AD SEXTUM dicendum, quod in transubstantiatione, cum sit quasi quidam motus vel mutatio, duo sunt, scilicet recessus a termino, et accessus ad terminum. Verba ergo sacramentalia pertingunt instrumentaliter ad transubstantiationem quantum ad recessum a termino a quo; sed quantum ad accessum ad terminum ad quem non pertingunt instrumentaliter, nisi dispositive, sicut in aliis sacramentis accidit.

REPLY OBJ. 1: Bernard, as is clear in the same place as the foregoing, does not intend to show the likeness of sacraments to those, except as to their signification: for a ring and a crozier are signs, and so are sacraments; but sacraments are causes as well.

REPLY OBJ. 2: They are reducible to the genus of efficient causes, not as principal causes but as instrumental ones. For God alone is the cause of grace as principal agent, but sacraments are agents instrumentally and dispositively, as has been said.

REPLY OBJ. 3: An agent is not always more noble than what it acts upon simply speaking, but only as it is an agent. For fire or iron work upon a human body, which is simply speaking nobler, but fire is nobler inasmuch as it is heat in act, and according to this it acts on the human body. And thus it is not necessary that those material things that are in the sacraments be simply nobler than the soul, but only nobler in a certain respect, namely, as instruments of divine mercy acting for our justification. Nor again is it necessary that an instrumental agent be simply nobler than its effect, for an effect is not proportioned to the instrument, but to the principal agent, who sometimes through lowly instruments accomplishes nobler effects, as a doctor induces health through an enema.

REPLY OBJ. 4: Univocal cause and non-univocal cause, properly speaking and simply, are divisions of that cause to which it pertains to have a likeness with its effect; but this is a principal agent and not an instrumental one, as Alexander says according to what the Commentator tells us.[77] And thus properly speaking an instrument is neither a univocal cause nor an equivocal one. But it could be reduced to either kind of cause, depending on whether the principal agent, in whose power an instrument acts, is a univocal cause or a non-univocal cause.

REPLY OBJ. 5: Grace is caused by the sacraments through the mode of inflowing; but nevertheless, the sacraments are not what instill grace, but God pours grace into the soul through them as through an instrument.

REPLY OBJ. 6: Since transubstantiation is, as it were, a certain movement or change, there are two things in it: namely, movement away from a terminus and movement toward a terminus. Therefore, sacramental words attains to transubstantiation instrumentally as concerns the movement from the terminus of origin; but as to the movement toward the destination they do not attain instrumentally, except dispositively, as happens in the other sacraments.

---

77. Averroes, *Commentary on Metaphysics 11*, text 24, giving the position of Alexander of Aphrodisias.

Response to Quaestiuncula 2

AD SECUNDAM QUAESTIONEM dicendum, quod propter auctoritates inductas necesse est ponere aliquam virtutem supernaturalem in sacramentis. Sustinentes autem primam opinionem dicunt, quod illa virtus non est nisi quidam ordo ad aliquid. Sed hoc nihil est dictu: quia semper virtus nominat principium alicujus, praecipue prout sumitur hic pro virtute causae. Ad aliquid autem, sive relatio, non potest esse principium actionis, vel terminus, ut probatur in 5 Physic.; et ideo nullo modo ille ordo potest habere nomen virtutis neque rationem.

Et propter hoc dicendum aliter, quod virtus agendi proportionatur agenti. Unde alio modo oportet ponere virtutem agendi in agente principali; alio modo in agente instrumentali. Agens enim principale agit secundum exigentiam suae formae; et ideo virtus activa in ipso est aliqua forma vel qualitas habens completum esse in natura. Instrumentum autem agit ut motum ab alio; et ideo competit sibi virtus proportionata motui: motus autem non est ens completum sed est via in ens quasi medium quid inter potentiam puram et actum purum, ut dicitur in 3 Physic. Et ideo virtus instrumenti inquantum hujusmodi, secundum quod agit ad effectum ultra id quod competit sibi secundum suam naturam, non est ens completum habens esse fixum in natura, sed quoddam ens incompletum, sicut est virtus immutandi visum in aere, inquantum est instrumentum motum ab exteriori visibili; et hujusmodi entia consueverunt intentiones nominari, et habent aliquid simile cum ente, quod est in anima quod est ens diminutum, ut dicitur in 6 *Metaphysica*. Et quia sacramenta non faciunt effectum spiritualem nisi inquantum sunt instrumenta; ideo virtus spiritualis est in eis non quasi ens fixum, sed sicut ens incompletum.

AD PRIMUM ergo dicendum, quod ens incompletum quod est in anima, dividitur contra ens distinctum per decem genera, ut patet in 6 *Metaphysica*; et ideo talia entia incompleta, per se loquendo, non sunt in aliquo genere nisi per reductionem, sicut motus quantum ad suam substantiam reducitur ad illud genus in quo sunt termini motus, sicut imperfectum ad perfectum, quamvis ponatur in praedicamento passionis secundum quod importat ordinationem moventis ad motum, ut dicit Commentator. Unde et virtus haec quae est in sacramentis reducitur ad id genus in quo est virtus completa principalis agentis, quae est qualitas, vel in qua esset, si in

TO THE SECOND QUESTION, it should be said that on account of the authorities cited it is necessary to consider a certain supernatural power to be in the sacraments. But those who hold the first opinion say that this power is nothing but a certain ordering to something. But this is to say nothing: for power always refers to the principle of something, particularly as it is taken here, for a cause's power. But an ordering to something, or a relation, cannot be the beginning of an action or the terminus, as is proved in *Physics* 5;[78] and thus in no way can that order have the name of power, or the nature of it.

And because of this we must say rather that the power of acting is proportionate to the one acting. Hence it is necessary to consider the power of acting in the chief agent in one way and in the instrumental agent in another way. For a principal agent acts according to the requirements of its own form; and thus the active power in it is a certain form or quality possessing complete being in its nature. But an instrument acts as moved by another; and thus its power is proportionate to the motion. Now motion is not a complete being but is a way towards being, like something between pure potency and pure act, as is said in *Physics* 3.[79] And thus the power of an instrument as such, according to which it acts for an effect beyond what it is capable of according to its own nature, is not a complete being having being fixed in nature, but a certain incomplete being, like the air's power of acting upon sight, inasmuch as air is the instrument moved by the external visible object. And beings like this are commonly called intentions, and have a certain likeness to the being that is in the soul, which is a diminished being, as is said in *Metaphysics* 6.[80] And since sacraments do not cause a spiritual effect except as instruments, thus spiritual power is in them not like a fixed being, but like an incomplete being.

REPLY OBJ. 1: The incomplete being that is in the soul is divided against the being that is defined by the ten categories, as is clear in *Metaphysics* 6;[81] and thus such incomplete beings, speaking *per se*, are not in any category except by reduction, as motion can be reduced in its own substance to whatever category the ends of the motion are in, as the imperfect can be reduced to the perfect, although it may be placed in the category of passion according as it conveys the ordering of a mover to that which is moved, as the Commentator says.[82] Hence also this power that is in the sacraments is reduced to that genus in which the complete power of the chief agent is, which is quality, or

---

78. Aristotle, *Physics*, Bk. 5, ch. 2, 225b11.

79. Aristotle, *Physics*, Bk. 3, ch. 1, 201a10.

80. While Moos in his edition of the *Scriptum* (p. 35, n. 1) says the location cannot be determined, it seems Thomas is referring to Aristotle, *Metaphysics*, Bk. 6, ch. 4, 1027b25–35.

81. Aristotle, *Metaphysics*, Bk. 6, ch. 2, 1026a35.

82. Averroes, *Commentary on Physics 3*, text 4.

genere esset: quia virtus increata non est in aliquo genere.

Ad secundum dicendum, quod instrumento datur virtus agendi instrumentaliter dupliciter. Uno modo quasi inchoative, quando instituitur in specie instrumenti; et ideo dicit Hugo, quod continet gratiam ex sanctificatione. Alio modo datur complete, quando actu movetur a principali agente, sicut quando carpentarius utitur serra; et similiter complete datur virtus sacramentis in ipso usu sacramentorum. Nec est inconveniens, si virtus quae motui proportionatur, datur rei statim vel post modicum desiturae.

Ad tertium dicendum, quod sicut virtus praedicta non potest poni in aliquo genere entis nisi per reductionem; ita nec constitui in aliquo gradu boni, nisi per reductionem. Reducitur autem ad bona maxima, in quibus est gratia, quae quodammodo est complementum ipsius virtutis, quasi finis ejus.

Ad quartum dicendum, quod in re corporali non potest esse virtus spiritualis secundum esse completum; potest tamen ibi esse per modum intentionis, sicut in instrumentis motis ab artifice est virtus artis, et sermo audibilis existens causa disciplinae, ut dicitur in Lib. de Sensu et sensato continet intentiones animae quodammodo: etiam in motu est virtus substantiae separatae moventis, secundum philosophos, et semen agit in virtute animae, ut dicitur in 1 *de Generat. animalium.*

Ad quintum dicendum, quod sicut virtus absoluta non est complete in quolibet congregatorum ad unam actionem quam nullus per se perficere potest, sicut est de tractu navis, sed est in omnibus simul, inquantum sunt omnes loco unius agentis, et sic virtus in eis existens suam retinet unitatem; ita etiam est de instrumentis, quando unum non sufficit; et sic etiam est in aliis multis quae exiguntur ad sacramentum: quia in omnibus est illa virtus simul acceptis complete, in singulis autem incomplete.

in which it would be if it were in any genus; for uncreated power is not in any genus of being.

Reply Obj. 2: The power of acting instrumentally is given to an instrument in two ways. In one way inchoatively, as it were, when it is established as belonging to the species 'instrument'; and thus Hugh says that it contains grace by its sanctification.[83] In another way, it is given completely, when it is actually moved by a principal agent, as when a carpenter uses a saw; and similarly power is completely given to sacraments in the very use of the sacraments. Nor is this unfitting, if a power which is proportioned to a motion is given to a thing immediately or after a pause.

Reply Obj. 3: Just as the power discussed cannot be included in any genus of being except by reduction, so also it cannot be established in any level of good except by reduction. However, it is reduced to the greatest goods, among which is grace, which is in a certain way the fulfillment of the power itself, as its end.

Reply Obj. 4: In a corporeal thing there cannot be spiritual power according to complete being; but there can be being in the mode of intention, just as the power of an art is in the instruments moved by that art's skill, and the cause of instruction existing in the audible word (as is said in the book *On Sense and Sensation*[84]) contains the intentions of the soul in a certain way; even in motion there is the power of the separated substance that is causing the motion, according to the philosophers, and the seed acts in virtue of soul, as is said in *On the Generation of Animals* 1.[85]

Reply Obj. 5: Just as a power does not exist completely and absolute in every one of the things brought together for one action which none of them can complete on its own, like in the rowing of a ship, but it is in all of them together, inasmuch as all are in the place of one agent, and in this way the power existing in them retains its own unity, so also is it with instruments when one thing is not sufficient. And in this way it is also in the many other things that are required for the sacrament: for in all of them taken together that power exists completely, but in each individual part it exists incompletely.

Response to Quaestiuncula 3

Ad tertiam quaestionem dicendum, quod instrumentum praedicto modo virtutem non accipit nisi secundum quod principali agenti continuatur, ut virtus ejus quodammodo in instrumentum transfundatur. Principale autem et per se agens ad justificationem est Deus sicut causa efficiens, et passio Christi sicut meri-

To the third question, it should be said that an instrument does not receive power in the mode mentioned except when it is joined with a principal agent, so that his power is in a way poured out into the instrument. But the principal agent acting *per se* for justification is God as efficient cause, and Christ's Passion as the meritorious cause. A

---

83. See reference above.

84. Aristotle, *Sense and Sensibilia*, ch. 1, 437a12: "Rational discourse is a cause of instruction in virtue of its being audible, which it is, not in its own right, but incidentally, since it is composed of words, and each word is a symbol."

85. Aristotle, *Generation of Animals*, in fact Bk. II, ch. 1, esp. 735a5–25.

toria. Huic autem causae continuatur sacramentum per fidem ecclesiae, quae et instrumentum refert ad principalem causam, et signum ad signatum; et ideo efficacia instrumentorum, sive sacramentorum, vel virtus, est ex tribus: scilicet ex institutione divina sicut ex principali causa agente, ex passione Christi sicut ex causa prima meritoria, ex fide ecclesiae sicut ex continuante instrumento principali agenti.

AD PRIMUM ergo dicendum, quod Christus, secundum quod homo, est causa meritoria nostrae justificationis; sed secundum quod Deus, est causa influens gratiam.

AD SECUNDUM dicendum, quod resurrectio est causa justificationis quantum ad terminum ad quem; sed sacramenta magis respiciunt terminum a quo; et ideo directius respiciunt passionem, quae ad peccati deletionem principaliter quasi satisfactio quaedam ordinatur.

AD TERTIUM dicendum, quod fides dat efficaciam sacramentis, inquantum causae principali ea quodammodo continuat, ut dictum est; et ideo fides passionis, a qua immediate et directe sacramenta efficaciam habent, sacramentis efficaciam largitur.

sacrament is joined to this cause by the faith of the Church, which both refers this instrument to the principal cause, and refers the sign to the signified. And thus the efficacy or power of instruments or of sacraments is from three things: namely, from divine institution as from the principal agent cause, from the Passion of Christ as from the first meritorious cause, and from the faith of the Church as from the one joining the instrument to the principal agent.

REPLY OBJ. 1: Christ as man is the meritorious cause of our justification, but as God, he is the cause instilling grace.

REPLY OBJ. 2: The resurrection is the cause of justification as the final terminus; but the sacraments rather regard the originating terminus; and thus they more directly regard the Passion, which is ordered chiefly to the blotting-out of sin as a certain satisfaction.

REPLY OBJ. 3: Faith gives efficacy to the sacraments inasmuch as in a way it joins them to the principal cause, as was said. And thus faith in the Passion, from which the sacraments have efficacy directly and immediately, gives abundant efficacy to the sacraments.

Response to Quaestiuncula 4

AD QUARTAM QUAESTIONEM dicendum, quod, quia omne agens agit sibi simile, ideo effectus agentis oportet quod aliquo modo sit in agente. In quibusdam enim est idem secundum speciem; et ista dicuntur agentia univoca, sicut calor est in igne calefaciente. In quibusdam vero est idem secundum proportionem sive analogiam, sicut cum sol calefacit. Est enim in sole aliquid quod ita facit eum calefacientem sicut calor facit ignem calidum; et secundum hoc calor dicitur esse in sole aequivoce, ut dicitur in libro *de Substantia orbis*. Ex quo patet quod illud quod est in effectu ut forma dans esse, est in agente, inquantum hujusmodi, ut virtus activa; et ideo sicut se habet agens ad virtutem activam, ita se habet ad continendam formam effectus. Et quia agens instrumentale non habet virtutem agendi ad aliquod ens completum, sed per modum intentionis, ut dictum est, et forma introducta continetur in eo per modum intentionis, sicut sunt species colorum in aere, a quibus aer non denominatur coloratus; etiam hoc modo gratia est in sacramentis sicut in instrumento, non complete, sed incomplete quantum ad quattuor. Primo, quia in instrumento non est forma effectus secundum completam rationem speciei, sicut est in effectu jam completo, et in causa univoca. Secundo, quia est in eo per modum intentionis, et non secundum completum esse in natura, sicut forma effectus est in causa principali non univoca secundum

TO THE FOURTH QUESTION, it should be said that because every agent makes something like itself, thus it is necessary that the effect of an agent be in the agent in some way. For in some things it is the same according to species; and these things are called univocal agents, as heat is in a fire that heats another. But in certain ones it is the same according to proportion or analogy, as when the sun heats something. For there is something in the sun that makes it heat just as heat makes fire hot; and accordingly heat is said to be in the sun equivocally, as is said in the book *On the Substance of the World*.[86] From this it is clear that whatever is in the effect as a form giving being, is in the agent precisely as such, as an active power; and thus as an agent stands with regard to the active power, so it stands with regard to containing the effect. And because an instrumental agent does not have the power of acting toward something as a complete being, but only by the mode of intention, as was said, the form introduced is also contained in it by the mode of intention, as there are species of color in the air, from which the air is said to be colored. In this way, too, grace is in the sacraments as in an instrument, not completely, but incompletely, in four respects. First, because in an instrument the form of an effect does not exist according to the complete nature of the species, as it is in the effect once completed, and in a univocal cause. Second, because it is in it by the mode of intention and not according to be-

---

86. Averroes, *De substantia orbis*, ch. 2.

esse perfectum in natura, quamvis non secundum completam rationem illius speciei sive formae quam inducit in effectu, ut calor est in sole. Tertio, quia non est in eo per modum intentionis quiescentis, sicut sunt intentiones rerum in anima, sed per modum intentionis fluentis duplici fluxu: quorum unus est de potentia in actum, sicut etiam in mobili est forma, quae est terminus motus, dum movetur ut fluens de potentia in actum; et inter haec cadit medium motus, cujus virtute instrumentum agit: alius de agente in patiens, inter quae cadit medium instrumentum, prout unum est movens, et alterum motum. Quarto, quia sacramentum etiam instrumentaliter non attingit directe ad ipsam gratiam, ut dictum est, sed dispositive.

AD PRIMUM ergo dicendum, quod gratia non est in sacramentis sicut in subjecto, sed sicut in causa dispositiva instrumentali; sed intentio illa quae et virtus dicitur, est in sacramento sicut in subjecto.

AD SECUNDUM dicendum, quod pulcherrime dictum est, gratiam contineri in sacramentis sicut in vase per quamdam similitudinem. Sicut enim quod est in vase, non denominat vas, sed in eo conservatur, ut possit inde accipi cum libet; ita gratia quae continetur in sacramentis, non denominat ipsa, nec qualificat ea secundum aliquod esse completum, sed gratiam in eis accipere poterit qui eis uti voluerit.

AD TERTIUM dicendum, quod forma effectus quae est in agente principali vel instrumentali, non fit eadem numero in effectu. Nec propter hoc frustra est: quia non ad hoc ordinatur ut ipsamet in effectum fluat, sed ut ab ea vel per eam similis fiat in effectu. Causa enim efficiens non reducitur in idem numero cum forma generati, sed in idem specie, ut patet in 2 *Physic.*

AD QUARTUM dicendum, quod continere dicuntur, inquantum aliquo modo sunt causa ipsius.

ing that is complete in nature, as the form of an effect is in a non-univocal principal cause according to being that is perfect in nature, although not according to the complete account of that species or form that it instills in its effect, as heat is in the sun. Third, because it is not in it in the manner of a reposing intention, as there are intentions of things in the soul, but by the mode of intention flowing with a twofold flow: one of which is from potency into act, as also in a moving thing there is a form that is the terminus of motion, provided that it is moved so that it flows from potency into act, and between these things there falls the middle of motion, in the power of which an instrument acts. The other is from the agent to the thing acted upon, between which there falls the medium of the instrument, as one is moving and the other is moved. Fourth, because a sacrament does not attain even instrumentally directly to grace itself, as was said, but only dispositively.

REPLY OBJ. 1: Grace is not in the sacraments as in a subject, but as in a dispositive instrumental cause; but that intention which is also called power is in the sacrament as in a subject.

REPLY OBJ. 2: It has been said quite beautifully that grace is contained in sacraments as in a vessel, by a certain likeness. For just as what is in a vessel does not give a name to the vessel but is preserved in it, so that it could be taken from there whenever one likes, so also the grace that is contained in the sacraments does not give them a name, nor does it endow them with a quality as with some complete being, but whoever wishes to benefit from them can receive the grace in them.

REPLY OBJ. 3: The form of an effect either in the principal agent or in an instrument is not numerically the same form as that which is in the effect. Nor is it to no purpose on account of this fact: for its purpose is not that its very self should flow into the effect, but rather that from it or through it, something like it comes to be in the effect. For an efficient cause does not have numerically the same form as the generated, but the same form in kind, as is clear from *Physics* 2.[87]

REPLY OBJ. 4: They are said to contain in the sense that in some way they are the cause of it.

Response to Quaestiuncula 5

AD QUINTAM QUAESTIONEM dicendum, quod, sicut in 2 Lib., 26 dist., quaest. unic., art. 3, et 4, dictum est, gratia gratum faciens est una, et est in essentia animae sicut in subjecto, et ab ipsa fluunt virtutes et dona ad perficiendum potentias animae, sicut etiam potentiae fluunt ab essentia; et distinguuntur istae virtutes secun-

TO THE FIFTH QUESTION, it should be said that, as was said in Book 2, Distinction 26, Question 1, Articles 3 and 4, sanctifying grace[88] is one thing, and it is in the essence of the soul as in a subject, and from it flow the virtues and gifts for perfecting the powers of the soul, just as also the powers flow from the essence. And these powers are distin-

87. Aristotle, *Physics*, Bk. 2, ch. 7, 198a26.
88. Literally, "grace that makes pleasing."

dum diversos actus, ad quos oportet potentias animae perfici. Similiter etiam a gratia illa quae est in essentia animae, effluit aliquid ad reparandum defectus qui ex peccato inciderunt; et hoc diversificatur secundum diversitatem defectuum. Sed quia hujusmodi defectus non sunt ita noti sicut actus ad quos virtutes perficiunt; ideo hic effectus ad reparandum defectum non habet speciale nomen, sicut virtus, sed retinet nomen suae causae, et dicitur gratia sacramentalis, ad quam directe sacramenta ordinantur: quae quidem non potest esse sine gratia quae respicit essentiam animae, sicut nec virtus. Sed tamen gratia quae est in essentia animae, non potest esse sine virtutibus; et ideo virtutes in ea habent connexionem. Potest autem esse sine gratia sacramentali; et ideo gratiae sacramentales connexionem non habent. Et ita patet quod gratia quam sacramentum directe continet, differt a gratia quae est in virtutibus, et donis; quamvis etiam illam gratiam per quamdam continuationem contineant.

AD PRIMUM ergo dicendum, quod gratia gratum faciens, prout est in essentia animae, est una, sed secundum quod fluit ad defectus potentiarum tollendos, et potentias perficiendas multiplicatur.

AD SECUNDUM dicendum, quod gratia virtutum opponitur peccato, secundum quod peccatum continet inordinationem actus; sed gratia sacramentalis opponitur ei secundum quod vulnerat naturale bonum potentiarum.

AD TERTIUM dicendum, quod recessus a peccato, prout opponitur virtuti, et accessus ad perfectionem virtutis pertinent ad eamdem gratiam, non autem recessus a peccato secundum quod vulnerat naturam: quia requirit specialem medicinam, sicut in morbo corporali etiam patet.

guished according to their diverse acts, for which the powers of the soul must be perfected. Similarly also from that grace which is in the essence of the soul, something issues to repair the defect that occurred by sin; and this varies according to the various defects. But since defects like this are not so well known as the acts which virtues perfect, for this reason this effect for repairing does not have a special name, like virtue, but keeps the name of its cause, and is called sacramental grace, and sacraments are directly ordered to it; and indeed it could not exist without the grace that affects the essence of the soul, as neither could virtue. But nevertheless, the grace that is in the essence of the soul cannot exist without virtues, and in this way the virtues are interconnected through it. But it can exist without sacramental grace; and so sacramental graces are not connected to one another through it. And so it is clear that the grace that a sacrament contains directly differs from the grace that is in the virtues and gifts, although they may contain that grace as well by a certain connection.

REPLY OBJ. 1: Sanctifying grace, as it exists in the essence of the soul, is one, but it is manifold according as it proceeds to removing defects from powers and perfecting powers.

REPLY OBJ. 2: The grace of the virtues is opposed to sin inasmuch as sin contains a disordered act; but the grace of the sacraments is opposed to it inasmuch as it injures the natural good of the powers.

REPLY OBJ. 3: Withdrawal from sin as something opposed to virtue belongs to the same grace as progress in the perfection of virtue. But withdrawal from sin as something injuring nature does not: for it requires a special medicine, as is evident also in diseases of the body.

Article 5

On the efficacy of the sacraments of the Old Law

Quaestiuncula 1

Ad quintum sic proceditur. Videtur quod sacramenta veteris legis gratiam conferebant. Ut enim supra dictum est, sacramenta a sacrando dicuntur, sicut ornatus ab ornando, et munimenta a muniendo. Sed sine gratia non potest aliquid sacrari. Ergo sacramenta veteris legis gratiam conferebant.

Praeterea, in canone Missae fit oratio, ut sacrificium ecclesiae Deo sit acceptum, sicut sacrificia antiquorum accepta fuerunt; et Dan. 3, petitur ut sacrificium humiliati et contriti spiritus suscipiatur a Deo, sicut holocaustum arietum et taurorum. Sed sacrificium ecclesiae et sacrificium contriti spiritus gratiam conferunt. Ergo et sacramenta veteris legis gratiam conferebant.

Praeterea, Hugo de sancto Victore dicit, quod ex quo homo aegrotare coepit, Deus in sacramentis suis medicinam paravit. Sed medicina non potest exhiberi contra morbum peccati nisi per gratiam. Ergo sacramenta antiquorum gratiam conferebant.

Praeterea, homo periculosius infirmabatur in affectu per concupiscentiam quam in intellectu per ignorantiam. Sed sacramenta contra ignorantiam figurabant futuram salutem. Ergo multo amplius contra concupiscentiam gratiam conferebant.

Praeterea, impossibile est sine gratia satisfacere. Sed sacramenta veteris legis erant satisfactoria; unde pro diversis peccatis diversa sacrificia injungebantur in lege, ut patet Levit. 16 et 17. Ergo gratiam conferebant.

Sed contra, Hebr. 10, 4: *impossibile est sanguine hircorum et taurorum auferri peccata.* Sed gratia tollit peccatum. Ergo antiqua sacramenta gratiam non conferebant.

Praeterea, per gratiam est vita animae. Sed de praeceptis veterum sacramentorum dicitur Ezech. 20, 25: *dedi eis praecepta non bona, et judicia in quibus non vivent.* Ergo gratiam non conferebant.

Obj. 1: To the fifth we proceed thus. It seems that sacraments of the Old Law conferred grace.[89] For, as was said above, sacraments are called from 'making holy', as ornaments from 'making ornate', and fortifications from 'fortifying'. But without grace nothing can be made holy. Therefore, the sacraments of the Old Law conferred grace.

Obj. 2: Furthermore, a prayer is made in the canon of the Mass, that the sacrifice of the Church may be accepted by God just as the sacrifices of the ancients were accepted.[90] And in Daniel 3 it is asked that the sacrifice of a humble and contrite spirit be received by God, like the burnt offering of rams and bulls.[91] But the sacrifice of the Church and the sacrifice of a contrite spirit confer grace. Therefore, also the sacraments of the Old Law conferred grace.

Obj. 3: Furthermore, Hugh of St. Victor says that from the time man began to ail, God prepared a medicine in his sacraments.[92] But a medicine can only be applied against the disease of sin by grace. Therefore, the sacraments of the ancients conferred grace.

Obj. 4: Furthermore, man was weakened more dangerously by concupiscence in his emotions than in his intellect by ignorance. But sacraments acted against ignorance as figures of future salvation. Therefore, much more did they confer grace against concupiscence.

Obj. 5: Furthermore, it is impossible to make satisfaction without grace. But the sacraments of the Old Law made satisfaction; hence different sacrifices were enjoined in the law for different sins, as is clear from Leviticus 16 and 17. Therefore, they conferred grace.

On the contrary, *It is impossible for the blood of goats and bulls to take away sins* (Heb 10:4). But grace takes away sins. Therefore, the ancient sacraments did not confer grace.

Furthermore, The soul has life by grace. But concerning the precepts of the old sacraments it is said, *I gave them precepts that were not good, and judgments by which they could not live* (Ezek 20:25). Therefore, they did not confer grace.

---

89. Parallels: below, d. 18, a. 3, qa. 1, ad 1; *ST* I-II, q. 103, a. 2; *ST* III, q. 62, a. 6; q. 72, a. 5, ad 3; *SCG* IV, ch. 57; *De veritate*, q. 27, a. 3, ad 20; q. 28, a. 2, ad 12; *Super Gal.* 2, lec. 4.

90. In the Roman Canon, shortly after the consecration of the chalice, the priest prays: "Supra quæ propítio ac seréno vultu respícere dignéris: et accépta habére, sícuti accépta habére dignátus es múnera púeri tui justi Abel, et sacrifícium Patriárchæ nostri Abrahæ, et quod tibi óbtulit summus sacérdos tuus Melchísedech, sanctum sacrifícium, immaculátam hóstiam."

91. Daniel 3:39–40.

92. Hugh of St. Victor, *De sacramentis fidei*, Bk. I, pt. 8, ch. 12 (PL 176:314).

Quaestiuncula 2

ULTERIUS. Videtur quod eorum usus non erat meritorius. Nihil enim est meritorium nisi sit Deo acceptum. Sed sacramenta illa non erant Deo accepta; super illud enim Isaiae 1: *sanguinem hircorum nolui,* dicit Glossa: *praeterito utens tempore, ostendit se nunquam sacrificia Judaeorum amasse.* Ergo eorum usus non erat meritorius.

PRAETEREA, nullum opus inutile est meritorium. Sed occisio tot animalium erat omnino inutilis. Ergo non erat meritoria.

PRAETEREA, nihil efficit nisi hoc quod a Deo institutum est. Sed illa sacramenta imposuit Deus in onus; sicut in littera dicitur. Ergo eorum exercitium meritorium non erat.

PRAETEREA, Origenes dicit quod illa ratione permisit Deus hoc sibi fieri qua permisit libellum repudii. Sed libellus repudii semper malus fuit, et nunquam meritorius. Ergo nec praedictorum sacramentorum usus.

SED CONTRA, dicit Beda, quod sacramenta veteris legis suo tempore custodita vitam conferebant aeternam. Sed nihil perducit ad vitam aeternam, nisi sit meritorium. Ergo erant meritoria.

PRAETEREA, omnis actus virtutis formatae est meritorius. Sed usus sacramentorum veteris legis erat actus latriae, quae in sanctis viris caritate formata erat. Ergo erat meritorius.

OBJ. 1: Moreover, it seems that their use was not meritorious. For nothing is meritorious unless it is accepted by God. But those sacraments were not accepted by God; for about this verse: *I did not wish the blood of . . . goats* (Isa 1:11), the Gloss says, *using the past tense, he shows that he never loved the sacrifices of the Jews.*[93] Therefore, their use was not meritorious.

OBJ. 2: Furthermore, no useless work is meritorious. But the killing of so many animals was completely useless. Therefore, it was not meritorious.

OBJ. 3: Furthermore, any given thing effects only what God has established. But God imposed those sacraments as a burden, as is said in the text. Therefore, their exercise was not meritorious.

OBJ. 4: Furthermore, Origen says that God allowed this for the same reason he allowed the bill of divorce.[94] But a bill of divorce was always bad and never meritorious. Therefore, neither was the use of the aforementioned sacraments.

ON THE CONTRARY, Bede says that the sacraments of the Old Law, kept in their own time, conferred eternal life.[95] But nothing leads to eternal life unless it is meritorious. Therefore, they were meritorious.

FURTHERMORE, every act of formed virtue is meritorious. But the use of the sacraments of the Old Law was an act of adoration, which, in holy men, was with formed charity. Therefore, it was meritorious.

Quaestiuncula 3

ULTERIUS. Videtur quod non purgabant ab immunditiis carnis. Aut enim illae immunditiae sunt pure corporales, aut spirituales. A corporalibus pure non mundabant, immo magis inquinare videbantur. Similiter nec a spiritualibus, quia spirituales ab anima in corpus fiunt: quia secundum Augustinum, non inquinatur corpus, nisi prius anima inquinata fuerit. Dicta autem sacramenta animam non mundabant, cum gratiam non conferrent. Ergo neque carnem.

PRAETEREA, inter omnia sacramenta veteris legis magis erat purgativum cinis vitulae aspersus. Sed hic magis immundabat quam purgaret: quia sacerdos, qui

OBJ. 1: Moreover, it seems that they did not purge one from impurities of the flesh. For either those impurities are purely bodily, or they are spiritual. They did not cleanse from purely bodily things, but rather they seemed to soil the body more. Likewise, neither did they cleanse from spiritual impurities, for spiritual impurities proceed from the soul to the body: for according to Augustine, the body is not soiled unless the soul has been soiled first.[96] However, the sacraments mentioned did not cleanse, since they did not confer grace. Therefore, neither did they cleanse the flesh.

OBJ. 2: Furthermore, among all the sacraments of the Old Law, none was more purgative than the sprinkling of calf ashes. But this rendered one unclean rather than purg-

---

93. *Glossa ordinaria*, PL 113:1234.

94. Origen, *Homilies on Numbers*, hom. 17, n. 1 (PG 12:703).

95. See Bede, *In Marci euangelium expositio* (CCSL 120), Bk. 3, ch. 10, l. 722: "Notandum sane quia iustitia legis suo tempore custodita non solum bona terrae uerum etiam suis cultoribus uitam conferebat aeternam."

96. Augustine, *De continentia*, ch. 2, throughout.

vitulum immolaverat, immundus efficiebatur, ut patet Num. 19. Ergo nec alia sacramenta purgabant.

Praeterea, sacramenta novae legis sunt majoris efficaciae quam sacramenta veteris legis. Sacramenta autem novae legis non purgant ab irregularitatibus. Ergo nec sacramenta veteris legis ab eis purgabant; quas irregularitates Magister hic exponit immunditias carnis.

Sed contra est quod dicitur Hebr. 9, 13: *Sanguis hircorum, et cinis vitulae aspersus inquinatos sanctificat ad emundationem carnis.*

Praeterea, sicut sacramenta nostra dicuntur spiritualia, ita et illa carnalia dicebantur; Heb. 9, 1: *habuit prius testamentum justificationes culturae.* Glossa: *non veras et spirituales, sed pro modo culturae carnalis.* Sed sacramenta novae legis purgant ab immunditiis spiritualibus. Ergo illa purgabant ab immunditiis carnis.

ing him: for the priest, who sacrificed the calf, was made unclean, as is clear from Numbers 19. Therefore, neither did the other sacraments purge.

Obj. 3: Furthermore, sacraments of the New Law are more efficacious than sacraments of the Old Law. But sacraments of the New Law do not purge one from irregularities. Therefore, neither did sacraments of the Old Law purge from them; which irregularities the Master here explains as impurities of the flesh.[97]

On the contrary, is what is said: *the blood of goats and the sprinkling with the ashes of a heifer sanctifies for the purification of the flesh* (Heb 9:13).[98]

Furthermore, just as our sacraments are called spiritual, so also those were called carnal: *the first covenant had justifications of divine worship* (Heb 9:1), on which the Gloss comments: *not true and spiritual, but in the mode of fleshly worship.* But the sacraments of the New Law purge from spiritual impurities. Therefore, those sacraments purged from carnal impurities.

Response to Quaestiuncula 1

Respondeo dicendum, ad primam quaestionem, quod in sacramento est duo considerare; scilicet ipsum sacramentum, et usum sacramenti. Ipsum sacramentum dicitur a quibusdam opus operatum; usus autem sacramenti est ipsa operatio, quae a quibusdam opus operans dicitur. Cum ergo dicitur sacramentum, per se loquendo, gratiam conferre vel non conferre, justificare vel non justificare, referendum est ad opus operatum. De opere autem operato in sacramentis veteris legis duplex est opinio. Quidam enim dicunt, quod in illis sacramentis opus operatum erat signum sacramentorum novae legis, et passionis Christi, a quo efficaciam habent; et ideo illud opus operatum erat cum quadam protestatione fidei; et ideo indirecte et ex consequenti habebant justificare, quasi mediantibus nostris sacramentis per ea significatis a Deo significationem[99] habentia, ut dicit Hugo de sancto Victore. Nostra autem sacramenta directe et immediate justificant, quia ad hoc directe sunt instituta. Sed haec opinio non videtur convenire dictis sanctorum: dicunt enim, quod lex erat occasio mortis, inquantum ostendebat peccatum, et gratiam adjutricem non conferebat. Nec differt quantum ad hoc qualitercumque vel directe vel indirecte gratiam conferrent. Et praeterea secundum hoc nulla esset vel valde modica praeeminentia

The first question I answer by saying that in a sacrament there are two things to consider: namely, the sacrament itself and the use of the sacrament. The sacrament itself is called by some people a work performed; but the use of the sacrament is its actual performance, which is called by some people a work working. Therefore, when it is called a sacrament, speaking *per se*, conferring grace or not, justifying or not, is to be referred to the work performed. But about the work performed in the sacraments of the Old Law, there are two opinions. For some people say that in those sacraments the work performed was a sign of the sacraments of the New Law, and of the Passion of Christ, from which they have efficacy; and thus, that work was performed with a certain declaration of faith; and thus, as a result and indirectly they were able to justify, as though our sacraments were in the middle, having been signified by those having a sanctification from God, as Hugh of St. Victor says.[100] But our sacraments justify directly and immediately, since they were instituted directly for this. But this opinion does not seem to fit with the words of the saints: for they say that the law was an occasion of death, inasmuch as it displayed sin, and did not confer a helping grace. Nor does it make any difference however directly or indirectly they might confer grace. And furthermore, accord-

---

97. In the time of the New Law, 'irregularities' refer to canonical impediments that bar a man from either receiving or licitly exercising some order or office in the Church.

98. The verse reads in full: "For if the sprinkling of defiled persons with the blood of goats and bulls and with the ashes of a heifer sanctifies for the purification of the flesh, how much more shall the blood of Christ, who through the eternal Spirit offered himself without blemish to God, purify your conscience from dead works to serve the living God (Heb 9:13–14).

99. *significationem.—sanctificationem* PLE.

100. Hugh of St. Victor, *De sacramentis fidei*, Bk. 1, pt. 9, chs. 1–2 (PL 176:343).

sacramentorum novae legis ad sacramenta veteris legis: quia etiam sacramenta novae legis a fide et significatione causandi efficaciam habent, ut dictum est. Et ideo alii dicunt, et melius, quod nullo modo sacramenta ipsa veteris legis, idest opus operatum in eis, gratiam conferebant, excepta circumcisione, de qua post dicetur.

AD PRIMUM dicendum ergo secundum hoc quod sanctificatio quandoque importat emundationem et confirmationem spiritualem, quae fit per gratiam; et sic sacramenta veteris legis non dicebantur sacramenta, nisi quasi signa sanctificantium, ut dictum est. Alio modo sanctificatio importat mancipationem alicujus ad aliquod sacrum; et sic dicebantur sacramenta, et quasi sanctificantia, quia per ea fiebat quaedam idoneitas ad sacros usus et in templo et in vasis et in ministris et in populo. Et per hunc etiam modum apud gentiles dicebantur sacramenta militaria, quibus homo mancipabatur officio militari, quod sacramentum[101] reputabant, sicut et omnia quae ad communitatem pertinebant.

AD SECUNDUM dicendum, quod illa oratio[102] in canone Missae non attenditur quantum ad ipsa operata, quia hoc sacrificium magis placet quam illa; sed petitur ut devotio istius offerentis placeat, sicut illorum placuit: et similiter Daniel comparat sacrificium, quale tunc poterat offerre, ad devotionem illorum qui sacrificia in lege praecepta in Hierusalem cum magna devotione obtulerant.

AD TERTIUM dicendum, quod sacramenta veteris legis dicebantur medicinae quantum ad significationem, et non quantum ad collationem gratiae.

AD QUARTUM dicendum, quod homo tempore legis naturae relictus est sibi quantum ad cognitionem; et per ignorantiam erravit in idolatriam lapsus: unde ut quantum ad omnia se infirmum inveniret, oportebat ut instructus per legem et sacramentorum ejus significationem, se impotentem cognosceret sine auxilio gratiae; et ideo congruum fuit ut illa sacramenta gratiam non conferrent, ut sic salus a solo Christo expectaretur.

AD QUINTUM dicendum, quod quamvis illa sacramenta peccata non diluerent quantum ad maculam, quia gratiam non conferebant, diminuebant tamen reatum, inquantum onerosa erant; et ideo satisfactoria esse poterant, praesupposita gratia ex fide mediatoris eis collata.

ing to this view, the preeminence of the sacraments of the New Law over the sacraments of the Old Law would be either extremely little or nothing at all, for even sacraments of the New Law derive their causal efficacy from faith and from their signification, as was said. And thus others say, and better, that in no way did the sacraments of the Old Law, that is, the work performed in them, confer grace, except in circumcision, of which we will speak later.

REPLY OBJ. 1: 'Sanctification' sometimes conveys a cleansing and spiritual strengthening, which happens through grace; and in that way the sacraments of the Old Law were not called sacraments, except as signs of things that sanctify, as was said. In another way, 'sanctification' conveys the dedication of someone to something sacred; and thus they were called sacraments, and things that sanctify, as it were, since a certain fittingness for sacred use, in the temple and in the vessels and in the ministers and in the people, came to be by them. And in this way, among pagans, too, 'military sacraments' were designated, by which a man was set apart for military office, which they considered a sacred thing, as they considered all those things that pertained to the community.

REPLY OBJ. 2: That prayer in the canon of the Mass is not intended as to those things enacted in the Mass, for this sacrifice is more pleasing than those; but it asks that the devotion of the one offering it should be pleasing, just as the devotion of the ancients did please. And likewise Daniel compares the sacrifice, such as he could offer at that time, to the devotion of those who had offered the sacrifices prescribed in the law in Jerusalem with great devotion.

REPLY OBJ. 3: The sacraments of the Old Law were called medicines as to their signification, and not as to the conferral of grace.

REPLY OBJ. 4: Man at the time of the law of nature was left to his own devices as to knowledge; and having fallen, he erred by ignorance into idolatry: hence, as with all things he found himself weak, it was necessary that, being instructed by the law and the signification of its sacraments, he should realize that he was powerless without the help of grace; and thus it was appropriate that those sacraments not confer grace, so that in this way salvation would be looked for from Christ alone.

REPLY OBJ. 5: Although those sacraments did not wash away sin as to the stain, since they did not confer grace, nevertheless they did diminish the guilt, since they were burdensome; and thus they were able to make satisfaction, presupposing the grace conferred on them by means of faith in the mediator.

---

101. *sacramentum.—sacrum* PLE.
102. *oratio.—comparatio* PLE.

Response to Quaestiuncula 2

AD SECUNDAM QUAESTIONEM dicendum, quod de usu sacramentorum, qui opus operans a quibusdam dicitur, est etiam duplex opinio. Quidam enim dixerunt, quod usus ipse non erat meritorius, etiamsi in fide et caritate fierent: et hoc videtur Magister in littera dicere. Sed hoc videtur absurdum, quod labores sanctorum patrum in hujusmodi sacramentis Deo accepti non fuerint, et quod opus virtutis possit esse non meritorium. Et ideo communiter tenetur, quod usus eorum meritorius esse poterat, si ex caritate fieret. Aliqui tamen excusant Magistrum, dicentes, quod ipse intellexerit ipsa opera operata non justificare quantumcumque in caritate fierent, quamvis ipsa operatio ex caritate facta possit esse meritoria in eo qui est in statu merendi.

AD PRIMUM ergo dicendum, quod sacrificia illa per se loquendo nunquam fuerunt Deo accepta, quia gratiam non continebant, per quam Deo aliquid est acceptum; sed per accidens erant et accepta et non accepta. Accepta quidem propter significationem et devotionem offerentium; sed non accepta et abominabilia propter peccata et abusum offerentium, et quia eadem idolis immolabantur, et sic inquantum erant Deo accepta, poterant esse meritoria.

AD SECUNDUM dicendum, quod quamvis occisio animalium esset secundum se inutilis, tamen inquantum ordinabatur ad cultum Dei, ex divina institutione utilis erat, et ejus utilitates tanguntur in Glossa, Rom. 5: *lex data est ad domandum superbum*, ut scilicet Deo offerret potius quam idolis; *ad flagellandum durum*, inquantum erat ad satisfactionem; *ad instruendum insipientem*, ratione significationis, *ad ostensionem delicti, et humanae infirmitatis*; et hoc respondet primis duobus; *ad manifestationem et testimonium gratiae, et futurorum significationem*; et hoc exponit tertium.

AD TERTIUM dicendum, quod lex secundum Augustinum data est quantum ad hujusmodi sacramenta duris et superbis in flagellum et onus, ut oneratis divinis sacrificiis non liberet eis ad idolatriam declinare; sed perfectis in signum, et parvulis in paedagogum: et quantum ad hoc poterat esse eorum usus meritorius.

AD QUARTUM dicendum, quod Origenes loquitur de illis sacrificiis, secundum quod habebant aliquam rationem displicentiae ex hoc quod idolis immolabantur; et quantum ad hoc non habebant rationem meriti.

TO THE SECOND QUESTION, it should be said that concerning the use of the sacraments, which is called by some a work being performed, there are two opinions. For some people have said that the use itself was not meritorious, even if they were done in faith and charity: and the Master seems to say this in the text. But this seems absurd, because if it were true, the labors of the holy patriarchs in sacraments of this kind would not have been accepted by God, and the work of virtue could be non-meritorious. And thus it is commonly held that their use could have been meritorious, if it were done out of charity. Some people, however, excuse the Master by saying that he understood that those works performed did not justify, however much they were done in charity, although the performance itself done out of charity could be meritorious in someone who is in a state of meriting.

REPLY OBJ. 1: Those sacrifices, strictly speaking, were never accepted by God, because they did not contain grace, by which anything is acceptable to God. But they were accepted or not accepted incidentally: the ones accepted were accepted on account of their signification and the devotion of their offerers, while the ones not accepted and abominable were such on account of the sins and abuse of their offerers, and because the very same things were sacrificed to idols. And so, to the extent that they were accepted by God, they could have been meritorious.

REPLY OBJ. 2: Although the killing of animals is useless in itself, nevertheless, it was useful as directed to the worship of God by divine institution, and its benefits are touched upon in the Gloss[103] on Romans 5: *the law was given for conquering the proud man*, namely, so that he would offer to God rather than to idols; *for scourging the hard-hearted*, as it was for a satisfaction; *for instructing the foolish man*, by reason of its signification; *for displaying offenses and human weakness*; and this corresponds to the first two; *for the manifestation and witness of grace, and the signification of future things*; and this explains the third.

REPLY OBJ. 3: According to Augustine, the law concerning such sacraments was given for the hard-hearted and proud as a scourge and a burden, so that, burdened by divine sacrifices, they would not be free to slip into idolatry. But it was given to the perfect as a sign, and to the little as a teacher: and in this respect, their use could be meritorious.

REPLY OBJ. 4: Origen speaks of those sacrifices according as they had a certain account of distaste from the fact that they were sacrificed to idols; and as to this they did not have the account of merit.

---

103. *Glossa ordinaria*, PL 117:487.

Response to Quaestiuncula 3

AD TERTIAM QUAESTIONEM dicendum, quod veteris legis intentio erat homines ad timorem et reverentiam Dei inducere, et a carnalibus ad spiritualia trahere paulatim; et ideo instituit multa impedimenta, quibus homines ab usu illorum sacramentorum frequenter impedirentur, ut sic magis in reverentia haberentur, quia omne rarum carum; et sic etiam paulatim a carnalibus observantiis dissuescerent, quandoque totaliter abstrahendi in tempore gratiae. Et haec impedimenta immunditiae carnis dicebantur, quibus homo corporaliter accedere ad sancta inidoneus efficiebatur; et ab his carnis immunditiis sacramenta legis purgabant.

AD PRIMUM ergo dicendum, quod immunditiae illae non erant spirituales, quasi a peccato causatae semper, sed quasi a sacramentis[104] prohibentes.

AD SECUNDUM dicendum, quod sacerdos lavabat manus et vestimenta, ne cum manibus sanguinolentis et cinerosis alia tangeret; et quia sacrorum ad communia non debet esse commixtio; unde etiam uncti chrismate manus lavant, et abstergunt. Immundus autem reputabatur propter tria. Primo ut sacerdotes essent sub onere, sicut et alii. Secundo ad tollendum superbiam sacerdotum de hoc quod alios sanctificabant. Tertio ad significandum quod sacerdos novi testamenti propter maximam sanctitatem sacrificii semper debet se inidoneum reputare.

AD TERTIUM dicendum, quod in nova lege non sunt irregularitates tot sicut in veteri lege, nec sunt nisi in ministris ecclesiae, in quibus requiritur maxima idoneitas propter sacramentorum sanctitatem; ideo tales irregularitates non ita facile absterguntur.

TO THE THIRD QUESTION, it should be said that the intention of the Old Law was to lead men to fear and reverence for God, and to draw them from carnal things to spiritual ones little by little. And thus it established many impediments by which men were often impeded from the use of these sacraments, so that in this way they would hold them more in reverence, because anything rare is valued; and in this way also they were little by little dishabituated from their carnal observances, ultimately to be completely drawn away from them in the time of grace. And these impediments were called impurities of the flesh, by which man was made unfit for approaching the holy things bodily; and the sacraments of the law cleansed one from these impurities of the flesh.

REPLY OBJ. 1: Those impurities were not spiritual in the sense that they were always caused by sin, but in the sense that they prevented one from approaching the sacred things.

REPLY OBJ. 2: A priest washed his hands and vestments so that he would not touch other things with bloody and sooty hands; and because there should not be a commingling of sacred things with common things; hence they even wash their hands anointed with holy oil and wipe them clean. But he was considered unclean for three reasons. First, so that priests would be under the same burden as all others. Second, to take away from the priests their pride in sanctifying the others. Third, to signify that the priest of the new covenant should always consider himself unworthy because of the extreme holiness of that sacrifice.

REPLY OBJ. 3: In the New Law there are not so many irregularities as in the Old Law, and they are only in the ministers of the church, in whom the greatest fittingness is required because of the holiness of the sacraments; so these irregularities are not as easily wiped away.

---

104. *sacramentis.—sacris* PLE.

Exposition of the text

Observantiae caeremoniales. Caeremonialia dicuntur quae secundum se non habent causam manifestam ipsorum factorum, quamvis possint habere causam manifestam suae institutionis. Dicitur autem caeremonia, quasi munia Cereris; quae erat dea frugum, quia ei prius sacrificia instituta sunt, et exinde translatum est nomen ad omnem divinum cultum. Vel, sicut dicit Valerius Maximus, dicuntur a Caere oppido, in quo prius Romani suos ritus instituerunt.

Mundabant etiam interdum a corporali lepra; idest, mundatum ostendebant, quando signa quae apparuerant, cessabant.

Sine medio Deum videbant; idest, divinorum cognitionem non ex sensibilibus signis accipiebant, sed per infusionem. Et de hoc in 2 Lib., dist. 23, q. 2, a. 1, ad 1, dictum est.

Ceremonial observances. They are called ceremonial which do not have an obvious reason in themselves for the actions performed, although they might have a clear reason for their institution. But the word 'ceremony' comes from the office of Ceres, who was the goddess of grain, because previously sacrifices to her were instituted and afterward the name was transferred to every divine cult. Or, as Valerius Maximus says, they are called from the town of Caere, in which formerly the Romans instituted their rites.[105]

They also occasionally cleansed leprosy from the flesh; that is, they pointed out the one who had been cleansed, when the signs of leprosy that had appeared were stopping.

They saw God without mediation; that is, they used to receive knowledge of divine things not from sensible signs, but by infusion. And we spoke of this in Book II, Distinction 23, Question 2, Article 1, ad 1.

---

105. See Valerius Maximus, *Facta et dicta memorabilia* (LLA 314), Bk. I, ch. 1, n. 10.

QUESTION 2

CIRCUMCISION

Postquam determinavit Magister differentiam sacramentorum veteris et novae legis, hic determinat de quodam sacramento veteris legis, scilicet circumcisione, quod cum sacramentis novae legis aliquam convenientiam habet; et dividitur in partes duas: in prima determinat de circumcisione; in secunda movet quamdam quaestionem circa praedeterminata, ibi: *si vero quaeritur*, etc. Prima in tres: in prima determinat efficaciam circumcisionis; in secunda institutionem ipsius, ibi: *hic dicendum est in quo instituta fuerit circumcisio*; in tertia determinat de mutatione ipsius per baptismum, ibi: *ideo autem mutata est*, etc. Circa primum duo facit: primo ostendit quam efficaciam circumcisio habeat; secundo ostendit quod eamdem efficaciam contra originale habebant quaedam remedia ante praeceptum de circumcisione datum, ibi: *quaeritur autem de viris qui fuerunt ante circumcisionem*.

Hic quaeruntur sex:

primo, de necessitate circumcisionis;

secundo, quibus competeret;

terio, de his quae ad circumcisionem requirebantur;

quarto, de efficacia circumcisionis;

quinto, de mutatione ipsius;

sexto, de remedio quod circumcisionem praecessit.

After the Master has defined the difference between the sacraments of the Old and New Law, here he considers a certain sacrament of the Old Law, namely, circumcision, which has some affinity with the sacraments of the New Law; and it is divided into two parts: in the first, he examines circumcision; in the second, he raises a certain question about his findings, at *But if it is asked*, etc. The first is in three parts: in the first, he considers the efficacy of circumcision; in the second, its institution, at: *here it must be said how circumcision was instituted*; in the third, he examines its transformation through baptism, at: *thus however it was changed*, etc. Concerning the first he does two things: first, he shows what kind of efficacy circumcision could have; second, he shows that certain remedies had the same efficacy against original sin before circumcision was commanded, at: *but it is asked about the men who lived before circumcision*.

Here six questions arise:

first, about the necessity of circumcision;

second, to whom it applied;

third, about the things that were required for circumcision;

fourth, about the efficacy of circumcision;

fifth, its transformation;

sixth, about the remedy that preceded circumcision.

ARTICLE 1

About the necessity of circumcision

Quaestiuncula 1

AD PRIMUM SIC PROCEDITUR. Videtur quod non fuerit necessarium circumcisionem dari. Sapientis est enim facere aliquid quanto brevius potest. Sed per fidem et sacramenta legis naturae sufficienter originale purgabatur. Ergo, non oportebat in remedium originalis circumcisionem dari.

PRAETEREA, peccato originali, quia ex alio contractum est, non debetur poena sensibilis, nec expiatio per satisfactionem. Sed circumcisio poenam sensibilem ha-

OBJ. 1: To the first we proceed thus. It seems that it was not necessary for circumcision to be given.[106] For it belongs to the wise man to do something as briefly as he can. But by faith and the sacraments of the law of nature, original sin was sufficiently purged. Therefore, it was not necessary for circumcision to be given as a remedy for original sin.

OBJ. 2: Furthermore, no sensible penalty is owed to original sin, since it is contracted from another; nor is there any expiation through satisfaction. But circumcision car-

---

106. Parallels: above, q. 1, a. 2, qa. 4; below, a. 2, qa. 1–2; *ST* I-II, q. 102, a. 5, ad 1.

bebat. Ergo non erat conveniens remedium contra originale.

SED CONTRA, circumcisio est signaculum fidei, quae est in praeputio patris nostri Abrahae, Rom. 4. Sed conveniens fuit illam fidem significari, cujus oportet nos omnes imitatores existere. Ergo congruum fuit circumcisionem dari.

ries a sensible penalty. Therefore, it was not a fitting remedy against original sin.

ON THE CONTRARY, circumcision is a seal of faith, a seal which is in the foreskin of our father Abraham (Rom 4:11). But it was fitting to represent that faith, of which we all had to become imitators. Therefore, it was appropriate for circumcision to be given.

Quaestiuncula 2

ULTERIUS. Videtur quod non debuerit dari ante legem scriptam. Quia in lege naturae non erat aliqua distinctio, cum lex communis omnibus esset. Sed circumcisio signum distinctivum est: quia secundum Damascenum, est signum determinans Israel a gentibus. Ergo non debebat dari ante legem scriptam.

PRAETEREA, praecepta quae non sunt indita rationi naturali, debent ad populum per ministrorum officium tradi. Sed circumcisio non erat de dictamine legis naturalis. Ergo cum ante legem scriptam non esset ministrorum distinctio, videtur quod tunc dari non debuerit.

SED CONTRA, circumcisio, secundum apostolum, est signum fidei. Sed etiam ante legem scriptam erat distinctio fidelium a non fidelibus. Ergo tunc oportebat eis dari.

OBJ. 1: Moreover, it seems that it should not have been given before the written law.[107] For under the law of nature there was no distinction, since that law was common to everyone. But circumcision is a distinctive sign, for, according to Damascene, it is the sign distinguishing Israel from the gentiles.[108] Therefore, it should not have been given before the written law.

OBJ. 2: Furthermore, precepts that do not arise from natural reason should be delivered to the people through the office of ministers. But circumcision was not among the dictates of natural law. Therefore, since there was no distinction of ministers before the written law, it seems that it should not have been given at that time.

ON THE CONTRARY, circumcision, according to the Apostle, is a sign of faith.[109] But even before the written law there was a distinction between the faithful and unbelievers. Therefore, it was fitting for it to be given to them then.

Quaestiuncula 3

ULTERIUS. Videtur quod non debuerit differri usque ad tempus Abrahae. Quia etiam ante ipsum erant fideles ab infidelibus distincti. Sed circumcisio est signum fidei. Ergo ante tempus Abrahae dari debuit.

PRAETEREA, circumcisio majorem habet efficaciam quam sacramenta legis naturae; alias postea instituta non fuisset. Sed non minor erat necessitas efficacis remedii ante Abraham quam post. Ergo etiam ante eum dari debuit.

SED CONTRA, fides quae sacramentis efficaciam significandi dat, est fides mediatoris, ut supra dictum est. Sed Abrahae primo dictae sunt repromissiones de mediatore ex semine ejus nascendo. Ergo ei primo signum fidei distinctum dari debuit in generationis membro.

OBJ. 1: Moreover, it seems that it did not need to be delayed until the time of Abraham.[110] For even before him faithful men were distinguished from unbelievers. But circumcision is a sign of faith. Therefore, it should have been given before the time of Abraham.

OBJ. 2: Furthermore, circumcision has a greater efficacy than sacraments of the law of nature; otherwise it would not have been instituted after them. But the need for an efficacious remedy was not less before Abraham than after him. Therefore, it should have been given also before him.

ON THE CONTRARY, the faith that gives sacraments the efficacy of signifying is faith in the mediator, as was said above. But it was to Abraham that promises of a mediator to be born from his seed were first made.[111] To him first, therefore, a distinct sign of faith ought to have been given, in the member of generation.

---

107. Parallel: *ST* I-II, q. 103, a. 1, ad 3.
108. John Damascene, *De fide orthodoxa*, Bk. 4, ch. 25 (PG 94:1214.
109. See Romans 4:11.
110. Parallels: *ST* I-II, q. 102, a. 5, ad 1; *ST* III, q. 70, a. 2; *Super Rom.* 4, lec. 2; *Super Gal.* 3, lec. 6.
111. See Galatians 3:16.

Response to Quaestiuncula 1

RESPONDEO dicendum ad primam quaestionem, quod circumcisio primo et principaliter necessaria fuit ad expressiorem significationem, quam sacramenta praecedentia fuissent. Oportuit enim quod secundum processum temporis, sicut explicatio fidei crescebat, ita cresceret distinctio signorum sacramentalium. Habet autem circumcisio expressam similitudinem ablationis originalis peccati quantum ad quatuor. Primo quantum ad membrum generationis, per quam originale transfunditur. Secundo quantum ad figuram circularem, in qua significatur circulus, qui est in processu originalis infectionis, secundum quod persona corrumpit naturam, et natura personam. Tertio quantum ad poenam, quae erat in circumcisione contra delectationem concupiscentiae, in qua praecipue viget fomitis virtus. Quarto quantum ad sanguinis effusionem, in quo significatur passio Christi, per quam pro originali satisfaciendum erat. Et quantum ad hanc utilitatem definitur circumcisio, quod est signaculum curationis ab originali. Sed ex consequenti fuit alia utilitas circumcisionis scilicet distinctio fidelis populi ab infideli propter fidem ejus cui data fuit circumcisio; et quantum ad hoc definit Damascenus, circumcisionem sic: *circumcisio est signum determinans Israel a gentibus, cum quibus conversabatur.* Habuit etiam mysticam significationem; et moralem, quia erat signum castitatis servandae; et allegoricam, inquantum significabat purgationem per Christum futuram; et quasi anagogicam, inquantum significabat depositionem corruptibilitatis carnis et sanguinis in resurrectione.

AD PRIMUM ergo dicendum, quod has utilitates habuit circumcisio prae sacramentis legis naturae; et ideo post illa institui debuit.

AD SECUNDUM dicendum, quod poena illa non erat ad satisfactionem, sed tantum ad significationem.

TO THE FIRST QUESTION, I answer that circumcision first and principally was necessary for a more explicit signification than the preceding sacraments had. For it was necessary that with the passing of time, as faith became more explicit, so the sacramental signs should become more distinct. Now circumcision has an express likeness to the removal of original sin in four ways. First, as regards the member of generation, through which original sin is transmitted. Second, in its circular figure, in which is represented the cycle that is in the process of original infection, according to which a person corrupts a nature, and a nature a person. Third, as to the pain involved in circumcision, which was opposed to the pleasure of concupiscence, in which the power of kindling sin particularly thrives. Fourth, as to the shedding of blood, in which the Passion of Christ is signified, by which satisfaction would be made for original sin. And it is in regard to this benefit that circumcision, which is the seal of the cure from original sin, is defined. But as a consequence, circumcisions had another benefit, namely, the distinction of a faithful nation from unbelievers, on account of the faith for which circumcision was given; and in relation to this Damascene defines circumcision thus: *circumcision is the sign determining Israel from the gentiles among whom it dwelt.*[112] It also had mystic signification: a moral signification, because it was a sign of the chastity to be kept; an allegorical signification, inasmuch as it signified future purgation by Christ; and an anagogical signification, as it were, inasmuch as it signified the laying aside of corruptible flesh and blood in the resurrection.

REPLY OBJ. 1: Circumcision had these benefits beyond the sacraments of the law of nature; and so it had to be instituted after them.

REPLY OBJ. 2: That pain was not for satisfaction but only for signification.

Response to Quaestiuncula 2

AD SECUNDAM QUAESTIONEM dicendum, quod lex scripta non debuit dari divinitus nisi populo fideli; et ideo oportuit populum fidelem prius congregari, et ab aliis distingui, quam lex divinitus ei daretur. Hoc autem non poterat fieri nisi per aliquod signum in quo fideles ad invicem convenirent, et ab aliis distinguerentur, quod ad circumcisionem pertinet; et ideo ante legislationem debuit circumcisio dari.

AD PRIMUM ergo dicendum, quod circumcisio erat quodammodo legis naturae, inquantum tempore legis

TO THE SECOND QUESTION, it should be said that God could only have given the written law to a faithful nation; and so it was necessary that a faithful nation first be brought together, and distinguished from others, before the law was given to them. But this could only happen through a certain sign by which the faithful resembled each other and by which they were distinguished from others, which pertains to circumcision; and thus circumcision had to be given before the giving of the law.

REPLY OBJ. 1: Circumcision belonged, in a way, to the law of nature, inasmuch as it was given during the time of

112. See the citation above.

naturae data fuit, et quodammodo legis scriptae, inquantum ad ipsam praeparabat. Dispositiones autem distinctionem habent penes ea ad quae disponunt.

AD SECUNDUM dicendum, quod peccatum originale a nobis non habemus, sed aliunde; et ideo aliunde totaliter remedium habet, nobis non cooperantibus, scilicet a Deo. Et propter hoc, sacramentum quod in remedium originalis erat, a Deo immediate praecipi debuit, sicut circumcisio et baptismus. Secus autem est de sacramentis legalibus, quae erant instituta ad satisfaciendum pro actualibus.

the law of nature, and belonged, in a way, to the written law, inasmuch as it prepared for it. But dispositions have distinction belonging to those things to which they dispose.

REPLY OBJ. 2: We do not have original sin from ourselves but from someone else, and so it has a remedy completely from someone else, namely from God, without our contributing. And on account of this, any sacrament that was a remedy for original sin had to be commanded by God immediately, like circumcision and baptism. It is different with legal sacraments, however, which were instituted to satisfy for actual sins.

Response to Quaestiuncula 3

AD TERTIAM QUAESTIONEM dicendum, quod ex corruptione peccati originalis humanum genus circa tempora Abrahae usque ad profundissima peccatorum venerat, scilicet in infidelitatem, et turpissimum vitium contra naturam; et ideo tunc temporis primo conveniebat promissionem fieri manifestam de semine nascituro, in quo omnes gentes benedicerentur, et a peccatis mundarentur. Tunc etiam oportebat in significationem aliquod exemplum fidei hominibus proponi contra infidelitatem; tunc signa castitatis dari contra corruptissimam concupiscentiam; et ideo Abrahae primo data est circumcisio in signum paternitatis, ut ex quo nasciturus erat peccatorum destructor et in signum fidei, et distinctionis ab infidelibus, et in signum castitatis et munditiae.

AD PRIMUM ergo dicendum, quod ante Abraham fere omnes fideles erant: circa tempora enim ejus dicitur idolatria incepisse.

AD SECUNDUM dicendum, quod quia tunc temporis corruptio magis invaluerat, ideo etiam tunc oportebat efficacius remedium dari.

TO THE THIRD QUESTION it should be said that by the corruption of original sin, the human race around the time of Abraham had arrived at the deepest of sins, namely, infidelity, and the most shameful vices against nature; and so at that point in time it became fitting for the promise to be first made about the offspring to be born, in whom all nations would be blessed and cleansed from their sins. It was also fitting for a certain example of faith to be set down at that time in signification for men against infidelity, and also at that time, for a sign of chastity to be given against the most corrupt concupiscence; and thus circumcision was given first to Abraham as a sign of fatherhood, as the one out of whom the destroyer of sin was to be born, and as a sign of faith and of distinction from unbelievers, and as a sign of chastity and purity.

REPLY OBJ. 1: Before Abraham nearly all were faithful; for idolatry is said to have begun around his days.

REPLY OBJ. 2: Since at that point in time the corruption had gathered more strength, it was also fitting for an efficacious remedy to be given then.

ARTICLE 2

To whom circumcision applied

Quaestiuncula 1

AD SECUNDUM SIC PROCEDITUR. Videtur quod omnibus populis circumcisio dari debuerit. Data est enim in remedium contra originale. Sed morbus iste communis omnibus erat. Ergo et medicina debuit esse communis.

PRAETEREA, circumcisio data est in signum fidei. Sed Abrahae fidem imitari omnes tenebantur: ac fides semper fuit de necessitate salutis. Ergo omnibus circumcisio dari debuit.

PRAETEREA, Genes. 17, 10, dicitur: *hoc est pactum quod observabitis inter me et vos, et semen tuum post te. Circumcidetur in vobis omne masculinum.* Sed de semine Abrahae multi populi processerunt praeter filios Israel, sicut Ismaelitae, Idumaei, etc. Ergo non solum filiis Israel circumcisio competebat.

SED CONTRA, circumcisio erat signum fidei. Sed unus tantum populus erat in quo fides, et cultus Dei remansit, ceteris per idolatriam depravatis. Ergo eis tantum circumcisio competebat.

PRAETEREA, circumcisio significabat medicinam futuram per Christum. Sed tantum ex uno populo scilicet Israel, Christus nasciturus erat. Ergo tantum illi populo circumcisio competebat.

OBJ. 1: To the second we proceed thus. It seems that circumcision should have been given to all peoples.[113] For it was given as a remedy against original sin. But that disease was common to all men. Therefore, also the medicine should have been common.

OBJ. 2: Furthermore, circumcision was given as a sign of faith. But all men were bound to imitate Abraham's faith; and besides, faith was always of necessity for salvation. Therefore, circumcision should have been given to all men.

OBJ. 3: Furthermore, it says in Genesis: *This is the covenant that you will observe between me and you, and your seed after you. Every male among you shall be circumcised* (Gen 17:10). But from the seed of Abraham many nations came forth besides the sons of Israel, like the Ishmaelites, the Idumaeans, etc. Therefore, circumcision did not apply just to the sons of Israel.

ON THE CONTRARY, circumcision was a sign of faith. But there was only one people in which faith and the worship of God remained, once the rest were corrupted by idolatry. Therefore, circumcision applied to them alone.

FURTHERMORE, circumcision represented a future medicine through Christ. But Christ was to be born from only one nation, namely, Israel. Therefore, circumcision applied only to that nation.

Quaestiuncula 2

ULTERIUS. Videtur quod debuit hoc remedium etiam mulieribus communiter dari. Circumcisio enim data erat in medicinam contra primam transgressionem. Sed prima transgressio incepit a femina. Ergo et feminis remedium dari debuit.

PRAETEREA, ubi eadem causa, et idem effectus. Sed eadem causa in viris est, ut circumcisio eis daretur, et in mulieribus: quia et ipsae ad populum Dei pertinent, et in eis corruptio originalis est. Ergo eis remedium dari debuit.

SED CONTRA, Hugo de sancto Victore dicit, quod *solis masculis data est circumcisio carnis, quia sacra Scriptura per masculinum sexum animam, per feminam vero carnem significare consueverit, ut scilicet ostenderetur quod*

OBJ. 1: Moreover, it seems that this remedy should have been given to women as well.[114] For circumcision was given as a medicine against the first transgression. But the first transgression began with a woman. Therefore, the remedy should have been given also to women.

OBJ. 2: Furthermore, where the same cause exists, there is the same effect. But in men the same cause for giving circumcision exists as in women: for they too belong to the people of God, and the corruption of original sin is in them. Therefore, the remedy should have been given to them.

ON THE CONTRARY, Hugh of St. Victor says that *the circumcision of the flesh was given to men alone, for the sacred scriptures customarily represented the soul by the masculine sex, but the flesh by the feminine, so that it would be man-*

---

113. Parallel: *Super Rom.* 4, lec. 2.
114. Parallel: *ST* III, q. 70, a. 2, ad 4.

illa circumcisio animabus sanctificationem contulit, non abstulit carni corruptionem.

ifest that circumcision conferred sanctification on souls, but did not remove the corruption of the flesh.[115]

Quaestiuncula 3

ULTERIUS. Videtur quod Christo circumcidi non competebat. Sabbati enim observatio vicinior erat praeceptis moralibus, inter quae etiam computatur, quam circumcisio. Sed Christus sabbatum litteraliter non observabat; unde dicebant de ipso, Joan. 9, 16: *non est hic homo a Deo, qui sabbatum non custodit.* Ergo nec circumcisionem servare debuit.

PRAETEREA, Hebr. 7, dicit Glossa, quod Christus in lumbis Abrahae decimatus non fuit, quia decima figurabat medicinam originalis, quod in Christo non fuit. Sed similiter circumcisio, ut dictum est, significat emundationem ab originali. Ergo Christo non competebat.

SED CONTRA, Gal. 4, 4: *misit Deus filium suum, natum de muliere, factum sub lege.* Sed illis qui sub lege erant, competit circumcisio. Ergo et Christo.

OBJ. 1: Moreover, it seems that it did not apply to Christ to be circumcised.[116] For the observance of the Sabbath was closer to the moral precepts, among which it is even counted, than circumcision is. But Christ did not observe the Sabbath according to the letter; hence they said of him, *This is not a man from God, who does not keep the Sabbath* (John 9:16). Therefore neither should he have observed circumcision.

OBJ. 2: Furthermore, the Gloss on Hebrews 7 says that Christ did not pay tithes in the loins of Abraham, for a tithe represented the medicine for original sin, which was not in Christ. But similarly circumcision, as has been said, signified cleansing from original sin. Therefore, it did not apply to Christ.

ON THE CONTRARY, *God sent his son, born of a woman, made under the law* (Gal 4:4). But to those who were under the law, circumcision applied. Therefore, also to Christ.

Response to Quaestiuncula 1

RESPONDEO dicendum ad primam quaestionem, quod sicut peccatum per Adam in omnes transierat, ita oportebat per Christum in omnes sanctificationem a peccato transire; unde ad praerogativam sanctitatis ejus insinuandam oportebat quidquid ad Christum pertinebat, speciali sanctitate pollere. Et ideo in populo de quo Christus nasciturus erat, oportebat specialiter cultum Dei esse, et ipsum apud eos significari. Et quia circumcisio est signum distinguens populum Dei ab aliis, ideo oportebat populo Israel specialiter circumcisionem datam esse non solum quantum ad illos qui de stirpe Jacob erant, sed quantum ad omnes qui ad populum illum qualitercumque pertinebant.

AD PRIMUM ergo dicendum, quod circumcisio erat remedium contra originale cum significatione sanctificationis nascituri seminis, propter quod erat in membro generationis; et ideo hoc remedium illi tantum populo competebat ex quo Christus nasciturus erat. Apud alios autem manebant adhuc eadem remedia quae fuerant ante circumcisionem data, quia eis non oportebat specialia sanctitatis documenta et remedia dare.

AD SECUNDUM dicendum, quod quamvis omnes tenerentur ad habendum fidem quam habuit Abraham, non tamen omnes tenebantur imitari Abraham in fide:

TO THE FIRST QUESTION, I answer that just as through Adam sin had passed into all men, so it was necessary that through Christ sanctification from sin should pass into all men; hence, to point out his sanctity's prerogative, it was necessary that everything pertaining to Christ exert power by a special sanctity. And thus in the nation from which Christ was to be born, it was especially fitting for the worship of God to exist, and for him to be represented among them. And since circumcision is a sign distinguishing the people of God from others, it was fitting that circumcision be given particularly to the nation of Israel—not only as to those who were of the shoot of Jacob, but as to all who belonged to that people in any way.

REPLY OBJ. 1: Circumcision was a remedy against original sin together with the signification of the sanctification of an offspring to be born, on account of which it was in the generative member; and thus this remedy applied only to that nation from which Christ was to be born. But among others there still remained the same remedies that existed before circumcision was given, because to them it was not necessary to give special remedies and lessons of holiness.

REPLY OBJ. 2: Although all men were bound to holding the faith that Abraham held, nevertheless not all were bound to imitate Abraham in faith: for neither did the

---

115. Hugh of St. Victor, *De sacramentis fidei*, Bk. 1, pt. 12, ch. 2 (PL 176:350).
116. Parallels: *ST* III, q. 37, a. 1; q. 40, a. 4.

quia nec ad omnes notitia Abrahae venerat, nec omnibus erat datus ut exemplum imitabile nisi mediante semine, in quo omnes gentes benedictionem Abrahae consecuturae erant; et ideo circumcisio, quae erat signum fidei Abrahae, non omnibus populis competebat.

AD TERTIUM dicendum, quod quantum ad promissionem factam Abrahae, separatus est per electionem Dei Isaac ab Ismaele, et Jacob ab Esau, ut patet Rom. 9, non autem aliqua segregatio facta est in filiis Israel; et ideo omnes filii Israel pertinebant ad populum Dei peculiarem; et propter hoc illis solis circumcisio competebat, quasi nunquam a familia Abrahae separatis. Ismael autem et Esau tenebantur ad circumcisionem quamdiu erant in familia parentum, non autem post recessum ab eis.

knowledge of Abraham come to all, nor was he given to all as an example to be imitated, except by means of his seed, in whom all the nations were to attain the blessing of Abraham. And thus circumcision, which was a sign of the faith of Abraham, did not apply to all people.

REPLY OBJ. 3: As for the promise made to Abraham, Isaac was set aside from Ishmael by God's choice, as was Jacob from Esau, as is clear from Romans 9, while no such segregation was made among the sons of Israel; and thus, all the sons of Israel belonged to God's own particular people. And because of this, circumcision applied only to those who had never been separated, as it were, from the family of Abraham. But Ishmael and Esau were bound to circumcision as long as they were in the family of their forefathers, but not after departing from them.

Response to Quaestiuncula 2

AD SECUNDAM QUAESTIONEM dicendum, quod peccatum originale, ut 2 Lib., dist. 31, quaest. 1, art. 1, dictum est, quantum ad culpam et reatum descendit a patre in filios; quantum ad poenalitates descendit a femina: quia pater est efficiens in generatione, et mater materiam ministrat. Circumcisio autem data est contra originale ad tollendum culpam, non autem ad tollendum carnis corruptionem; et ideo viris, et non mulieribus data est: et haec est causa quae in objectione tacta est. Per hoc etiam ostenditur sacramentum imperfectum, et sua imperfectio in expectationem perfectionis ducit.

TO THE SECOND QUESTION, it should be said that original sin, as was said in Book II, Distinction 31, Question 1, Article 1, descends from father to sons as far as fault and culpability are concerned; but as concerns the penalties, it descends from the woman: for the father is the efficient cause in generation, and the mother contributes the matter. But circumcision was given against original sin in order to take away fault, but not for taking away the corruption of the flesh; and thus it was given to men and not to women: and this is the reason that is touched upon in the objection. By this it is also shown to be an imperfect sacrament, and its imperfection draws us to look forward to the perfect.

AD PRIMUM ergo dicendum, quod quamvis transgressio a femina inceperit, tamen transfusionis originalis peccati causa non fuit femina, sed vir: quia si vir non peccasset originale transfusum non fuisset; ideo dicit apostolus Rom. 5, 12, quod: *per hominem peccatum intravit in mundum.*

REPLY OBJ. 1: Although transgression began from a woman, nevertheless the cause of the transmitting of original sin was not the woman, but the man: for if the man had not sinned, original sin would not have been transmitted; and so the Apostle says: *by man sin entered the world* (Rom 5:12).

AD SECUNDUM dicendum, quod jam patet quod non est eadem causa et viris et mulieribus quantum ad hoc quod circumcisio contra originale ordinatur; similiter etiam nec quantum ad hoc quod est distinctivum et signum populi fidelis ab infideli: quia principaliter populi distinctio est ex parte virorum, quia mulieres viris subjectae sunt; et ideo etiam apud Hebraeos non computabantur genealogiae ex parte mulierum, sed ex parte virorum.

REPLY OBJ. 2: It is already clear that there is not the same cause in both men and women as regards the fact that circumcision is directed against original sin; likewise also not as regards the fact that it is a sign of the nation of the faithful and distinguishes them from unbelievers. For the distinction of this nation is chiefly on the part of the men, for the women are subject to the men; and therefore among the Hebrews genealogies were not reckoned from the woman's side, but from the man's side.

Response to Quaestiuncula 3

AD TERTIAM QUAESTIONEM dicendum, quod Christo circumcisio competebat non propter indigentiam, sed propter decentiam: cujus potest in Christo multiplex

TO THE THIRD QUESTION, it should be said that circumcision applied to Christ not because of his need, but because of its becomingness: for which many reasons can be

ratio assignari. Prima est, ut ipse se ostenderet filium Abrahae, cui praeceptum circumcisionis erat factum, et promissio nascituri seminis; et sic Dei promissionem impletam insinuaret. Secunda, ut circumcisionem, sicut et alia legalia, suscipiens, ab onere legis nos liberaret. Tertia, ut fratrem Judaeorum se ostenderet, ne haberent justam occasionem ipsum repellendi.

AD PRIMUM ergo dicendum, quod Christus in pueritia in nullo ab aliis pueris segregatus fuit quantum ad exteriorem conversationem; et ideo omnia quae ad pueros pertinebant in veteri lege, in se implere voluit. Sed quando jam ad perfectam aetatem pervenit, ostendere debuit se dominum legis esse, et legem usque ad ipsum impositam fuisse; et ideo in quibusdam supra legem operatus est, sicut de observatione sabbati, et in tactu leprosi.

AD SECUNDUM dicendum, quod decimatio erat actus tantum figuralis quantum ad illos qui in lumbis Abrahae decimabantur; et ideo Christo non competebat, quia ab originali immunis fuit: sed circumcisio etiam habet alias causas praeter significationem in illis qui circumciduntur; et ideo non est similis ratio de utroque.

assigned in Christ. The first is that he might show himself to be a son of Abraham, to whom the precept of circumcision was given as well as the promise of offspring to be born; and in this way, he implied the fulfilment of God's promise. Second, so that by undergoing circumcision, as with all the other legal prescriptions, he would free us from the burden of the law. Third, so that he would show himself to be a brother of the Jews, lest they have just occasion to reject him.

REPLY OBJ. 1: Christ was set apart from others in no way during his childhood as far as external behavior went; and thus all those things that pertained to boys in the Old Law, he wished to fulfill in himself. But when he had arrived at the age of adulthood, he had to show that he was master of the law, and that the law had been imposed up until he came. And thus in some matters he worked above the law, as in the observance of the Sabbath and in touching lepers.

REPLY OBJ. 2: Paying tithes was a purely figurative act as concerned those who paid tithes in the loins of Abraham; and thus it did not apply to Christ, for he was immune from original sin. But circumcision also has other reasons besides signification in those who are circumcised; and thus the two things do not have the same account.

Article 3

About the things that were required for circumcision

Quaestiuncula 1

Ad tertium sic proceditur. Videtur quod octavus dies non requireretur ad circumcisionem. Alia enim remedia contra originale data sive in lege naturae sive in lege gratiae, tempus determinatum non habent. Ergo nec circumcisio habere debuit ad idem data.

Praeterea, poterat contingere quod dies octavus erat dies sabbati. Sed in die illo praecepta erat quies ab exterioribus operibus. Ergo non erat de necessitate circumcisionis quod octavo die fieret.

Praeterea, illi qui vagati sunt in deserto, non fuerunt octavo die circumcisi, sed postea tempore Josue in Galgala, Josue 5; et profuit illis circumcisio, nec illis obfuit ad transgressionem, ut videtur, qui in deserto mortui sunt incircumcisi. Ergo determinatio temporis non est de necessitate circumcisionis.

Praeterea, sicut praetermittitur determinatum tempus, si praeveniatur, ita et si tardetur. Sed proseliti circumcidebantur post octavum diem, et eis valebat. Ergo et pueri poterant ante octavum diem circumcidi, et eis valere.

Sed contra, circumcisio non habebat efficaciam nec obligationem nisi ex praecepto divino. Sed circumcisio fuit in praecepto secundum determinatum tempus. Gen. 17, 12: *infans octo dierum circumcidetur in vobis.* Ergo et determinatum tempus erat de necessitate circumcisionis.

Praeterea, significatio est de necessitate sacramenti. Sed octava dies facit ad significationem. Ergo est de necessitate ipsius.

Obj. 1: To the third we proceed thus. It seems that the eighth day was not required for circumcision.[117] For other remedies given against original sin, whether in the law of nature or in the law of grace, did not have a determinate time. Therefore, neither did circumcision have to take place at the time given.

Obj. 2: Furthermore, it could happen that the eighth day was the day of the Sabbath. But on that day it was commanded to rest from external works. Therefore, there was no necessity that circumcision happen on the eighth day.

Obj. 3: Furthermore, those who wandered in the desert were not circumcised on the eighth day, but afterwards, in the time of Joshua in Gilgal (cf. Joshua 5); and the circumcision counted for those men, nor does it seem to count as a transgression for those who died in the desert uncircumcised. Therefore, the determination of time is not a necessary part of circumcision.

Obj. 4: Furthermore, just as a determinate time is missed if it is forestalled, so also if it is delayed. But proselytes were circumcised after the eighth day, and it was valid for them. Therefore also, boys could be circumcised before the eighth day, and it would be valid for them.

On the contrary, circumcision only had efficacy or obligation by God's command. But he commanded circumcision according to a determinate time: *every male infant of eight days among you shall be circumcised* (Gen 17:12). Therefore also, a determinate time was a necessary part of circumcision.

Furthermore, signification is a necessary part of a sacrament. But the eighth day contributes to the signification. Therefore, it is a necessary part of it.

Quaestiuncula 2

Ulterius. Videtur quod determinatio membri non fuerit de necessitate circumcisionis. In sacramentis enim signum debet respondere signato. Sed purgatio originalis quae significatur per circumcisionem, non est secundum aliquam partem determinatam, sed secundum totum. Ergo nec circumcisio debet aliquam partem determinatam habere.

Obj. 1: Moreover, it seems that the determination of the member was not a necessary part of circumcision.[118] For in the sacraments the sign must correspond to the thing represented. But the cleansing of original sin that is represented by circumcision is not according to any determinate part of the body, but according to the whole. Therefore, neither should circumcision have any determinate part.

---

117. Parallels: *ST* I-II, q. 102, a. 5, ad 1; *ST* III, q. 70, a. 3, ad 3; *Super Rom.* 4, lec. 2.
118. Parallels: above, a. 2, qa. 1, ad 1; *ST* I-II, q. 102, a. 5, ad 1; *ST* III, q. 66, a. 7, ad 3; q. 70, a. 3, ad 1; *Super Ioan.* 7, lec. 2; *Super Rom.* 4, lec. 2.

PRAETEREA, sacramenta maximam honestatem in se habere debent. Sed membra generationis videntur esse turpia et verecunda. Ergo non decuit ut in illo membro determinate aliquod sacramentum daretur.

SED CONTRA est quod dicitur Gen. 17, 2: *circumcidetis carnem praeputii vestri.*

OBJ. 2: Furthermore, sacraments should have the greatest propriety in them. But generative members seem to be base and shameful. Therefore, it was not becoming that some sacrament be given determinately in that member.

ON THE CONTRARY, it is said: *you shall circumcise the flesh of your foreskins* (Gen 17:11).

Quaestiuncula 3

ULTERIUS. Videtur quod cultellus lapideus sit de necessitate circumcisionis. Circumcisioni enim baptismus successit. Sed determinatum instrumentum ablutionis, scilicet aqua, est de necessitate baptismi. Ergo et determinatum instrumentum incisionis esse debuit de necessitate circumcisionis, et praecipue propter significationem quae in littera ponitur; significatio enim est de ratione sacramenti.

PRAETEREA, Gregorius dicit super Ezech.: *in sanctorum vita cognoscimus quid in Scriptura intelligere debeamus.* Sed sancti et praecipue legislatores, lapideo instrumento fecerunt circumcisionem, sicut legimus Josue 5 et Exod. 4 de Moyse. Ergo lapideum instrumentum erat de necessitate praecepti.

SED CONTRA, circumcisio non habebat vim nisi ex divina institutione. Sed in ejus institutione quae tangitur, Gen. 17, nulla fit mentio de instrumento lapideo. Ergo non fuit de necessitate circumcisionis.

OBJ. 1: Moreover, it seems that a stone knife would be necessary for circumcision.[119] For baptism is the successor to circumcision. But a determinate instrument of washing, namely water, is of necessity for baptism. Therefore, a determinate instrument of incision should be also of necessity for circumcision, and particularly because of the signification that is set down in the text; for signification is of the account of a sacrament.

OBJ. 2: Furthermore, Gregory comments on Ezechiel: *in the lives of the saints we recognize what we should understand in Scripture.*[120] But the saints and particularly the lawgivers did circumcision with a stone knife, as we read in Joshua 5 and of Moses in Exodus 4.[121] Therefore, a stone instrument was a necessary part of the command.

ON THE CONTRARY, circumcision only had force except by divine institution. But in its institution, which is touched upon in Genesis 17, no mention is made of a stone knife. Therefore, it was not a necessary part of circumcision.

Response to Quaestiuncula 1

RESPONDEO dicendum ad primam quaestionem, quod circumcisio et erat in praecepto, et erat sacramentum. Octava ergo dies erat de necessitate circumcisionis quantum ad obligationem praecepti, ita quod reus transgressionis erat qui illud tempus non observabat. Sed non erat de necessitate ejus quantum ad efficaciam sacramenti: quia etiam in alio tempore circumcisio facta suum effectum sacramentalem habebat. Sicut etiam accidit de ministrantibus nostra sacramenta, qui servant materiam et formam debitam, et omittunt aliquid de ritu ad solemnitatem sacramenti ab ecclesia instituto. Determinationis autem hujus temporis causa est et mystica, quae tangitur in littera, et litteralis quae tangitur a Rabbi Moyse: quia puer ante octavum diem est ita tener quasi in ventre matris; et ideo sicut animalia non offerebantur propter praedictam causam ante octavum diem, ita nec puer circumcidebatur.

THE FIRST QUESTION I answer by saying that circumcision was both a precept and a sacrament. Therefore, the eighth day was a necessary part of it as to the obligation of the precept, so that whoever did not observe that time was guilty of transgression. But it was not of necessity as regards the efficacy of the sacrament: for circumcision done at another time also had its own sacramental effect. Something similar happens with the ministers of our sacraments, who keep the due form and matter, and omit something of the rite instituted by the Church for the solemnity of the sacrament. Now the reason for the determination of this time is both mystical, which is touched upon in the text, and literal, which is touched upon by Rabbi Moses: for a boy before the eighth day is as tender as he was in his mother's womb; and thus as animals were not offered before the eighth day for the reason given, so neither was a boy circumcised.

---

119. Parallels: below, in the exposition of the text; *ST* III, q. 70, a. 3, ad 2; *Super Rom.* 4, lec. 2.

120. See Gregory, *Homiliae in Hiezechihelem prophetam* (CCSL 142), Bk. 1, hom. 10, l. 684: "Vel certe rotae animalia sequuntur, quia in sanctorum patrum uita cognoscimus quid in sacrae scripturae uolumine intellegere debeamus."

121. See Joshua 5:2–3; Exodus 4:24–26.

AD PRIMUM ergo dicendum, quod remedium quod praecessit circumcisionem, computatur simpliciter inter sacramenta legis naturae, quae non habebant tantam determinationem secundum Hugonem de sancto Victore, quantam habent sacramenta legis scriptae, ad quam quodammodo pertinet circumcisio. Remedium autem quod circumcisionem sequitur, scilicet baptismus, est magis generale et perfectius, nec debuit ita restringi. Et ideo non est similis ratio de circumcisione et aliis.

AD SECUNDUM dicendum, quod dies sabbati non impediebat circumcisionem: non enim erat opus pure corporale, sed sacramentale; sicut et sacrificia, quae in sabbato offerri licebat; et ideo dicitur Joan. 7, 23: *circumcisionem accipit homo in sabbato, et non solvitur lex Moysi.*

AD TERTIUM dicendum, quod illis qui in deserto vagabantur dispensatio praecepti facta est propter necessitatem, quae tangitur Josue 5: quia scilicet nesciebant quando castra movenda essent. Et iterum quia non erat necesse eos tunc aliquod signum distinctionis habere, ut Damascenus dicit, quando seorsum ab aliis hominibus habitabant; et tamen quantum ad aliquos qui ex negligentia vel contemptu praetermittebant, dicit Augustinus, quod inobedientiam incurrebant. Non autem constat quod aliqui de illis qui in deserto nati sunt, in deserto mortui sint; et videtur probabile quod non: quia dicitur in Psal. 104, 37: *Non erat in tribubus eorum infirmus.* Unde illi qui de Aegypto egressi sunt, qui circumcisi erant, mortui sunt. Et ita nullus est ibi mortuus incircumcisus. Si tamen aliqui incircumcisi mortui sunt, idem dicendum est de eis, et de illis qui ante circumcisionis institutionem moriebantur.

AD QUARTUM dicendum, quod Magister videtur sentire in littera, quod licebat imminente mortis articulo idem praevenire. Quidam vero dicunt, Hugonem de sancto Victore sequentes, quod non erat necessitas idem praeveniendi: quia illis qui ante octavum diem moriebantur, valebat ad salutem remedium quod ante circumcisionem fuerat, quod adhuc efficaciam habebat; et hoc confirmant per Judaeos qui nunc sunt, qui nunquam ante octavum diem circumciduntur, et per Glossam, Prover. 4, super illud: *unigenitus eram coram matre mea*; quae dicit, quod alius filius Bersabee parvulus non computatur, quia ante octavum diem mortuus, nominatus non fuit, et per consequens nec circumcisus. Similiter etiam confirmant per simile: quia nullum animal offerebatur Domino ante octavum diem. Secundum hanc er-

REPLY OBJ. 1: The remedy that preceded circumcision is counted simply among the sacraments of the law of nature, which, according to Hugh of St. Victor,[122] were not as fully determined as the sacraments of the written law, among which circumcision belongs in a certain way. But the remedy that follows circumcision, namely baptism, is more general and perfect, nor ought it to be so restricted. And thus there is not a similar argument for circumcision as for the others.

REPLY OBJ. 2: The Sabbath day did not prevent circumcision, for it was not a purely bodily work, but a sacramental one, as also were sacrifices, which were permitted to be offered on the Sabbath; and thus it is said, *a man receives circumcision on the Sabbath, and the law of Moses is not broken* (John 7:23).

REPLY OBJ. 3: For those who were wandering in the desert a dispensation from the precept was made on account of necessity, which is touched upon in Joshua 5— namely, they did not know when the camp would be moving. And again, because it was not necessary for them to have any sign of distinction at that time, as Damascene says, when they were living far away from any other people;[123] and yet, as regards those who omitted it from negligence or contempt, Augustine says that they were guilty of disobedience.[124] But it is not certain that any of those who were born in the desert died there, and it seems probable that they did not: for it is said: *there was no sick one among the tribes* (Ps 105[104]:37). Hence those who left from Egypt, who were circumcised, died. And thus there was no one there who died uncircumcised. But if some did die uncircumcised, the same thing is to be said about them as of those who died before the institution of circumcision.

REPLY OBJ. 4: In the text, the Master seems to hold that it was permitted to circumcise in advance when there was a danger of imminent death. But certain people say, following Hugh of St. Victor,[125] that there was no need for circumcising early: since the remedy that existed before circumcision, which had efficacy up until then, availed for the salvation of those who died before the eighth day; and they confirm this by the Jews who live today, who are never circumcised before the eighth day, and by the Gloss on Proverbs 4: *as an only son in the sight of my mother* (Prov 4:3), which says, the little one is not counted as another son of Beersheba, for since he died before the eighth day, he was not named, and as a result he was not circumcised.[126] They likewise confirm it by this likeness: no animal was offered to God before the eighth day. Therefore, accord-

---

122. Hugh of St. Victor, *De sacramentis fidei*, Bk. 1, pt. 11, ch. 3 (PL 176:343).

123. John Damascene, *De fide orthodoxa*, Bk. 4, ch. 25 (PG 94:1211).

124. Augustine, *Quaestionum in heptateuchum libri septem* (CCSL 33), Bk. 6, *Quaest. Iesu Naue*, qu. 6, l. 101: "quidam enim de aegypto exeuntium filii in illo populo incircumcisi erant, quos potuit circumcidere iesus; illorum scilicet filios, qui genuerunt in deserto et contempserunt eos circumcidere, quod inoboedientes erant legi dei."

125. Hugh of St. Victor, *De sacramentis fidei*, Bk. 1, pt. 12, ch. 3 (PL 176:350).

126. See the *Glossa ordinaria*, PL 113:1086.

go opinionem dicendum, quod non est simile de praeveniendo et differendo: quia praeceptum nullo modo quis transgredi debet, ut praeveniat; sed si transgressus fuerit differendo, debet, quantum potest, illud implere in quocumque tempore.

ing to this opinion it should be said that acting early and delaying are not the same thing: for no one should transgress a precept, as one would do by acting too early; but if he has transgressed by delaying it, he should, as much as he can, fulfill it whenever he can.

Response to Quaestiuncula 2

AD SECUNDAM QUAESTIONEM dicendum, quod circumcisio erat in signum purgationis originalis peccati, et in signum distinctionis populi, ex quo Christus propagandus erat, et in signum castitatis servandae, ut dictum est; et quantum ad omnia haec decuit ut in membro generationis fieret, quia per actum generationis et originale contrahitur, et Christus ab illo populo descendit, et in illo actu castitas consistit; et ideo membrum generationis erat de necessitate circumcisionis et quantum ad efficaciam sacramenti, et quantum ad obligationem praecepti.

AD PRIMUM ergo dicendum, quod quamvis originale peccatum quantum ad essentiam non determinet aliquam partem corporis, neque quantum ad effectum; tamen quantum ad causam determinat, ut dictum est.

AD SECUNDUM dicendum, quod membrum generationis, quod de se nobile erat, propter concupiscentiam, quae praecipue in parte illa viget, ignobile redditum est; et ideo oportebat quod in illo membro praecipue medicina apponeretur: quia *quae inhonesta sunt nostra, abundantiorem honestatem habent*, ut dicitur 1 Corinth. 12, 23.

TO THE SECOND QUESTION, it should be said that circumcision was a sign of cleansing from original sin, and a sign of the distinction of the people from whom Christ was to be brought forth, and a sign of preserving chastity, as was said. And regarding all these things, it was fitting that it be done to the generative member, for by the act of generation both original sin is contracted and Christ descended from that nation; and in that act chastity consists. And thus the generative member was a necessary element of circumcision, both as to the efficacy of the sacrament and as to the obligation of the precept.

REPLY OBJ. 1: Although original sin is not attached to any particular part of the body in its essence, nor in its effect, nevertheless it is as to its cause, as was said.

REPLY OBJ. 2: The generative member, which was noble of itself, was made ignoble because of concupiscence, which is especially strong in that part. And so it was fitting that especially in that member the medicine should be administered: for *our less respectable members are treated with greater respect*, as it says in 1 Corinthians 12:23.

Response to Quaestiuncula 3

AD TERTIAM QUAESTIONEM dicendum, quod sacramentum quod est signum et causa, efficit quod figurat; et ideo illa significatio est de necessitate sacramenti quae ad effectum sacramenti refertur, non autem illa quae refertur ad causam principalem effectus, sed est de bene esse ipsius. Cultellus autem lapideus non est de necessitate incisionis, per quam significat circumcisio suum effectum, scilicet purgationem originalis; sed habet aliquam similitudinem ad causam principalem meritoriam remissionis originalis, scilicet Christum; et ideo non erat de necessitate circumcisionis neque quantum ad obligationem praecepti, neque quantum ad efficaciam sacramenti, quod fieret cultello lapideo, quod ritus Judaeorum usque hodie ostendit: sed in principalibus circumcisionibus, in quibus Christum significari oportebat, tale instrumentum adhibitum est.

TO THE THIRD QUESTION, it should be said that a sacrament that is a sign and cause brings about what it represents; and so that signification which points to the effect of the sacrament is necessary to the sacrament; however, that signification that points to the principal cause of the effect is not necessary, but concerns rather its optimal being. Now a stone knife is not necessary for the incision by which circumcision signifies its effect, namely, the cleansing of original sin; but it has a certain likeness to the principal meritorious cause of the remission of original sin, namely, Christ.[127] And thus it was not necessary to circumcision, neither in its obligation as a precept, nor in its efficacy as a sacrament, that it be done with a stone knife, which the rite of the Jews, even to the present, shows. But in the principal circumcisions, in which it was necessary that Christ be represented, such an instrument was employed.

---

127. Since Christ is the "stone rejected by the builders" (Ps 118:22; Acts 4:11; 1 Peter 2:4; etc.) and is also the "rock" (1 Cor 10:4).

Ad primum ergo dicendum, quod aqua de se habet maximam convenientiam ad ablutionem, per quam baptismus significat quod efficit, non autem lapis ad incisionem; et ideo non est simile.

Ad secundum dicendum, quod hoc intelligendum est de illis quae sancti observant quasi ex lege obligati; sic autem non est in proposito; et ideo ratio non sequitur.

Reply Obj. 1: Water, of itself, has the greatest usefulness for washing, by which baptism signifies what it effects; but stone is not the most useful for cutting; and thus it is not the same.

Reply Obj. 2: This is to be understood concerning those things that the saints observe as though obligated by the law; however, it is not this way in the case mentioned, and thus the argument does not follow.

ARTICLE 4

About the efficacy of circumcision

Quaestiuncula 1

AD QUARTUM SIC PROCEDITUR. Videtur quod circumcisio characterem imprimebat in anima. In sacramentis enim effectus figurae respondet. Sed circumcisio exterius erat signum distinctivum, non solum purgativum. Ergo et interius characterem distinguentem imprimebat.

PRAETEREA, omne sacramentum quod non reiteratur in nova lege, characterem imprimit. Sed circumcisio in veteri lege non reiterabatur. Ergo characterem imprimebat.

PRAETEREA, aliquis adultus circumcisus poterat fictus accedere; et sic tunc effectum circumcisionis non suscipiebat; postmodum autem deposita fictione circumcisio ei valebat: alias enim non fuisset via salutis, cum iterari non posset. Ergo habebat aliquem effectum manentem in anima, ratione cujus postea effectum ultimum circumcisionis consequebatur; et hoc est character. Ergo imprimebat characterem.

SED CONTRA, in sacramentis novae legis perfectissima tantum sunt illa quae characterem imprimunt. Sed circumcisio erat longe inferior sacramentis novae legis. Ergo characterem non imprimebat.

PRAETEREA, character nos Trinitati configurat. Sed hoc indifferenter competit viris et mulieribus. Cum ergo circumcisio mulieribus non competeret, videtur quod in ea character non imprimeretur.

OBJ. 1: To the fourth we proceed thus. It seems that circumcision imprinted a character on the soul.[128] For in the sacraments the effect corresponds to the figure. But external circumcision was a distinguishing sign, not only a cleansing one. Therefore, it also imprinted a distinguishing character interiorly.

OBJ. 2: Furthermore, in the New Law, every sacrament that cannot be received more than once imprints a character. But in the Old Law circumcision could not be received more than once. Therefore, it imprinted a character.

OBJ. 3: Furthermore, some adults could have received circumcision deceitfully, and if they did, then they did not receive the effect of circumcision; but after they had relinquished their deception, circumcision availed them: for otherwise it would not have been a way of salvation, since it could not be received again. Therefore, it had some effect remaining in the soul, by reason of which the ultimate effect of circumcision came about, and this is a character. Therefore it imprinted a character.

ON THE CONTRARY, in sacraments of the New Law, only the most perfect ones imprint a character. But circumcision was inferior by far to the sacraments of the New Law. Therefore, it did not imprint a character.

FURTHERMORE, a character configures us to the Trinity. But this applies indifferently to men or women. Therefore, since circumcision did not apply to women, it seems that a character was not imprinted in it.

Quaestiuncula 2

ULTERIUS. Videtur quod circumcisio a peccato non purgaret. Rom. 3, 20: *ex operibus legis non justificatur omnis caro coram illo.* Sed alia opera legis, ut sacrificia, non videntur minus honesta fuisse quam circumcisio. Ergo nec circumcisio a peccato justificabat.

PRAETEREA, si ab aliquo peccato purgabat, praecipue videtur quod ab originali. Sed ab originali non purgabat, quod patet per hoc quod Joannes circumcisus octava die, ut dicitur Luc. 1, dixit ad Jesum Matth. 3, 14:

OBJ. 1: Moreover, it seems that circumcision did not cleanse from sin: *by the works of the law no flesh shall be justified before him* (Rom 3:20).[129] But other works of the law, like sacrifices, do not seem to have been less honorable than circumcision. Therefore, neither did circumcision justify from sin.

OBJ. 2: Furthermore, if it cleansed from any sin, it seems it would particularly cleanse from original sin. But it did not cleanse original sin, which is evident from the fact that John the Baptist, who was circumcised on the eighth

---

128. Parallels: *ST* III, q. 63, a. 1, ad 3; q. 70, a. 4; q. 72, a. 5, ad 3.
129. Parallels: below, d. 8, q. 1, a. 2, qa. 2, ad 5; *ST* III, q. 33, a. 3, ad 3; q. 62, a. 6, ad 3; q. 70, a. 4; *De veritate*, q. 28, a. 2, ad 12; *Super Rom.* 4, lec. 2.

ergo a te debeo baptizari; Glossa: *a peccato originali mundari*. Ergo nullo modo a peccato mundabat.

Praeterea, nihil impedit vitae aeternae introitum nisi peccatum. Sed circumcisio januam vitae aeternae non aperiebat, ut in littera dicitur. Ergo neque peccata purgabat.

Praeterea, quidquid tollit unum peccatum, tollit omnia: quia impium est a Deo dimidiam sperare veniam. Sed nunquam invenitur a sanctis dictum, quod circumcisio tolleret peccatum actuale. Ergo nec originale tollebat.

Sed in contrarium sunt auctoritates in littera positae.

day, as it says in Luke 1, said to Jesus, *therefore I should be baptized by you* (Matt 3:14). And the Gloss on this says, *to be cleansed from original sin.*[130] Therefore, in no way did it cleanse from sin.

Obj. 3: Furthermore, nothing prevents the entrance into eternal life except sin. But circumcision did not open the gate to eternal life, as it says in the text. Therefore, neither did it cleanse sins.

Obj. 4: Furthermore, whatever takes away one sin, takes away all: for it is impious to hope for half forgiveness from God. But it is never found among the sayings of the saints that circumcision took away actual sin. Therefore, neither did it take away original sin.

On the contrary stand the authorities cited in the text.

Quaestiuncula 3

Ulterius. Videtur quod circumcisio gratiam non conferret. Sacramentum enim non efficit nisi quod figurat. Sed circumcisio non significat gratiae collationem, sed solum culpae ablationem. Ergo gratiam non confert.

Praeterea, baptismus non amplius facit, nisi quod aufert culpam, et confert gratiam. Si ergo hoc ipsum circumcisio faciebat, baptismus in nullo circumcisionem excedit.

Praeterea, propter hoc lex vetus dicebatur occidere, quia gratiam contra concupiscentiam non conferebat. Hoc autem non esset, si circumcisio, quae erat quodammodo legis sacramentum, gratiam conferret. Ergo gratiam non conferebat.

Sed contra, in littera dicitur, quod idem remedium praebebat circumcisio quod baptismus, excepto quod januam regni caelestis non aperiebat. Sed baptismus gratiam confert, non solum culpam aufert. Ergo et circumcisio idem facit.

Praeterea, tenebra non expellitur nisi per praesentiam lucis. Sed gratia opponitur culpae, sicut lux tenebrae. Cum ergo circumcisio expelleret culpam, videtur quod gratiam conferret.

Obj. 1: Moreover, it seems that circumcision did not confer grace.[131] For a sacrament effects only what it figures. But circumcision does not signify the conferral of grace, but only removal of guilt. Therefore, it does not confer grace.

Obj. 2: Furthermore, baptism does more than circumcision only by taking away guilt and conferring grace. If, then, circumcision did these very things, baptism would not surpass circumcision in any way.

Obj. 3: Furthermore, the Old Law was said to kill because it did not confer grace against concupiscence. But this would not have been the case if circumcision, which was in a certain way a sacrament of the law, conferred grace. Therefore, it did not confer grace.

On the contrary, it says in the text that circumcision furnished the same remedy as baptism, except that it did not open the gates of heaven. But baptism confers grace; it does not merely take away sin. Therefore, circumcision also did the same.

Furthermore, darkness is not expelled except by the presence of light. But grace is opposed to fault, just as light is to darkness. Therefore, since circumcision expelled guilt, it seems that it conferred grace.

Response to Quaestiuncula 1

Respondeo ad primam quaestionem dicendum, quod character spiritualis est quoddam signum distinctivum per hoc quod hominem in aliquo statu perfectionis constituit, sicut in baptismo, confirmatione, et ordine, ut magis infra patebit. Circumcisio autem prin-

The first question I answer by saying that a spiritual character is a certain distinctive sign—distinctive in that it constitutes man in some state of perfection, as in baptism, confirmation, and holy orders, as will be clearer further on. Circumcision, however, was chiefly a sign established for

---

130. See Bede, *Homeliarum euangelii* (CCSL 122), Bk. 1, hom. 12, l. 46: "Ab illo debuit ipse iohannes baptizari, id est a peccati originalis contagione mundari, qui quamuis nullo inter natos mulierum minor tamen quasi natus ex muliere culpae naeuo non carebat ideo que cum ceteris mulierum natis ab eo qui natus ex uirgine Deus in carne apparuit opus habebat ablui."

131. Parallels: *ST* III, q. 62, a. 6, ad 3; q. 70, a. 4; *De veritate*, q. 28, a. 2, ad 12; *Super Rom.* 4, lec. 2.

cipaliter erat signum ad purgandum constitutum; et ideo in ipsa non ponebatur homo in aliquo alio statu, et sic non competebat quod in ipsa character spiritualis conferretur.

Ad primum ergo dicendum, quod circumcisio principaliter significat per se ablationem, sed distinctionem ex consequenti et per accidens, inquantum aliqui circumcidebantur, et aliqui non; et ideo oportebat quod responderet ei effectus quantum ad principalem significationem, non autem quantum ad secundariam.

Ad secundum dicendum, quod circumcisio non iterabatur: quia causa ejus, scilicet originale peccatum, iterari non poterat; et non propter hoc quod character spiritualis in ipsa imprimeretur.

Ad tertium dicendum, quod sicut in baptismo manet character spiritualis, ratione cujus fictus deposita fictione effectum baptismi recipit; ita manebat character exterior in circumcisione, quae hoc idem efficiebat.

cleansing; and therefore in it man was not placed in any other state, and in this way it did not belong to it to confer a spiritual character.

Reply Obj. 1: In itself, circumcision chiefly signifies removal, but consequently and incidentally it signifies distinction, inasmuch as some were circumcised and others were not; and thus it was necessary that the effect correspond to it as to its principal signification, but not as to its secondary one.

Reply Obj. 2: Circumcision cannot be repeated because its cause, namely, original sin, could not be repeated; and not because a spiritual character is imprinted in it.

Reply Obj. 3: As in baptism a spiritual character remains, by reason of which someone who has falsely received it receives the effect of baptism once he has relinquished his deception, so also the external character remained in circumcision, which effected the same thing.

Response to Quaestiuncula 2

Ad secundam quaestionem dicendum, quod peccatum quod ex alio contrahitur, conveniens est ut per alium tollatur; et ideo in quolibet statu post peccatum fuit aliquod remedium per quod originale peccatum ex virtute passionis Christi tolleretur. Et iterum quia non poterat puer natus, antequam haberet usum liberi arbitrii, se ad gratiam praeparare, ne omnino sine remedio relinqueretur, oportuit aliquod remedium dari quod ex ipso opere operato peccatum aboleret; et tale remedium fuit circumcisio; et ideo ab omnibus conceditur, quod peccatum auferebat, sicut significabat ablationem; et in hoc cum sacramentis novae legis quodammodo conveniebat, quia efficiebat hoc quod figurabat. Operabatur autem circumcisio peccati dimissionem a posteriori. In peccato enim originali tria sunt, scilicet culpa, reatus carentiae visionis divinae, et fomes. Prima duo totaliter tolluntur; sed tertium per sacramentum diminuitur; et ideo circumcisio, quae erat particularis abscissio, directe significabat et causabat diminutionem fomitis, et per consequens auferebat reatum visionis aeternae, et per consequens culpam. In baptismo autem e contrario est: quia prius destruit culpam, cujus ablationem significat ablutio exterior et etiam causat, et per consequens destruit alia.

Ad primum ergo dicendum, quod sacrificia erant instituta ad satisfaciendum pro peccatis actualibus, quae

To the second question, it should be said that the sin that is contracted from another is fittingly taken away by another; and thus in every state after sin there was some remedy by which original sin would be taken away by virtue of the Passion of Christ. And again, because no child born could prepare himself for grace before he had the use of his free will, lest he be left without any remedy at all, it was necessary for some remedy to be given which would obliterate sin by the very act having been done; and circumcision was this kind of remedy. And thus it is conceded by all that it took away sin, just as it signified removal; and in this, it agrees with the sacraments of the New Law, because it brought about what it represented. But circumcision worked the forgiveness of sins retroactively. For there are three things in original sin, namely, the fault, the sentence of losing the divine vision, and the kindling of sin. The first two are totally taken away, but the third is diminished by the sacrament. And thus circumcision, which was a particular cutting-away, directly signified and caused the diminishment of the kindling of sin, and as a result it took away the sentence of losing eternal vision, and, as a result, the guilt.[132] In baptism, though, it is the opposite: for first it destroys guilt, whose removal the external cleansing signifies and also causes, and as a result it destroys the other two.

Reply Obj. 1: Sacrifices were instituted to satisfy for actual sins, which man perpetrated on his own; and thus it

---

132. In his edition of the *Scriptum*, Moos offers the following note: "Here St. Thomas appears to grant that circumcision conferred grace even *ex opere operato*, but this opinion he withdrew later on, in *ST* III, q. 62, a. 6, ad 3, where the holy Doctor expressly says of this opinion: 'And so at one time it seemed to me. But if the matter be considered carefully, this too appears to be untrue,' and adds: 'And therefore it seems better to say . . .' See also *ST* III, q. 70, a. 4, and *Super Rom.* 4, lec. 2.

homo ex se perpetravit; et ideo non oportebat quod peccata tollerentur per sacrificia, sicut peccatum originale per circumcisionem.

Ad secundum dicendum, quod circumcisio quamvis a peccato originali liberaret, non tamen per eam aliquis perfecte fructum liberationis consequi poterat, quia januam non aperiebat; et secundum hoc Joannes circumcisus, a peccato originali mundari indigebat, scilicet per baptismum.

Ad tertium dicendum, quod per circumcisionem auferebatur impedimentum quod erat ex parte personae, ablato peccato originali, prout erat infectio hujus personae; adhuc tamen manebat impedimentum ex parte naturae, nondum soluto pretio; et ideo per accidens erat quod januam regni caelestis non aperiebat: quia si etiam baptismus, eamdem quantum in se est gratiam conferens quam modo confert, eo tempore fuisset, januam non aperuisset; et si modo circumcisio locum haberet, januam aperiret.

Ad quartum dicendum, quod circumcisio directe contra originale ordinata fuit, sed ex consequenti etiam actuale tollebat ubi inveniebat. Sed tamen sancti de hoc non loquuntur, quia ad hoc non erat circumcisio principaliter instituta.

was not necessary that sins be taken away by sacrifices, as original sin was by circumcision.

Reply Obj. 2: Although circumcision freed one from original sin, nevertheless one could not perfectly attain the fruit of liberation through it, because the gate was not opened; and according to this aspect, John the Baptist, though circumcised, still needed to be cleansed from original sin, namely by baptism.

Reply Obj. 3: By circumcision the impediment on the part of the person was withdrawn, for original sin was removed, inasmuch as it was the infection of this person. Nevertheless there still remained the impediment on the part of the nature, for the price had not yet been paid. And thus it was incidental that it did not open the gate of heaven; for even if baptism had existed at that time, conferring the same grace in itself that it presently confers, it would not have opened the gate; and if circumcision had any place now, it would open the gate.

Reply Obj. 4: Circumcision was directly ordained against original sin, but as a result it also removed actual sin wherever it was found. But nevertheless the saints do not speak about this, for circumcision was not chiefly instituted for this.

Response to Quaestiuncula 3

Ad tertiam quaestionem dicendum, quod circa hoc est multiplex opinio. Quidam enim dixerunt, quod circumcisio, quantum est de se, culpam tollebat, sed gratiam non conferebat, innitentes cuidam Glossae quae habetur Rom. 4, quae dicit: *in circumcisione peccata remittebantur, sed non gratia per eam praestabatur.* Dicebant enim, quod cum originale nihil aliud sit quam concupiscentia intensa cum carentia debitae justitiae, circumcisio sine hoc quod gratia conferretur, poterat auferre debitum, non auferendo reatum, ut patet per hoc quod si homo illam justitiam non habebat, non ei imputaretur ad poenam. Sed hoc non potest esse: quia manente inordinatione culpae, nullo modo potest non imputari a Deo ad poenam, cum culpae inordinatio per poenam ordinetur. Et ideo oportet, si imputatio ad poenam tollitur, quod inordinatio tollatur; quod sine gratia fieri non potest.

Et ideo alii dicunt, quod circumcisio ex sua virtute culpam tollebat, et gratia circumcisione conferebatur, non ex vi circumcisionis, sed ex divina liberalitate ablato gratiae impedimento. Sed hoc non potest esse: quia quamvis ex parte recipientis prius sit expulsio contrarii quam introductio formae, tamen ex parte causae agentis est prius introductio formae: quia non expellitur contrarium nisi introducendo formam; et ideo nisi circumcisio

I answer the third question by saying that concerning this matter there are several opinions. For some people have said that circumcision, such as it is, took away fault, but did not confer grace, drawing on a certain Gloss on Romans 4 which says: *in circumcision sins were forgiven, but grace was not supplied by it.* For they said that since original sin is nothing other than intense concupiscence with a lack of due justice, circumcision without the ability to confer grace could take away the debt, though not the culpability, as is evident from the fact that if a man did not have that justice, it would not be imputed to him for penalty. But this cannot be: for as long as the disordering of fault remains, in no way can it not be imputed by God for penalty, since the disordering of fault is put in order by the penalty. And thus it is necessary, if the imputation for penalty is removed, that the disorder is removed; which cannot happen without grace.

And therefore others say that circumcision took away fault by its own power, and grace was conferred by the circumcision, not by the force of the circumcision, but by divine generosity once the impediment to grace had been removed. But this cannot be: for although on the part of the recipient the expulsion of the contrary comes before the introduction of the form, nevertheless on the part of the agent cause the introduction of the form comes first. For

aliquo modo gratiam conferret, nullo modo culpam tolleret.

Et ideo alii dicunt, quod circumcisio conferebat gratiam quantum ad effectus privativos, qui scilicet sunt auferre culpam, sed non quantum ad effectus positivos. Sed hoc nihil est: quia effectus ultimus gratiae positivus, est facere dignum vita aeterna; quod fiebat per circumcisionem, sicut et modo fit per baptismum.

Et ideo alii dicunt probabilius ut videtur, quod dabat gratiam quantum ad effectus privativos culpae et reatus, et quantum ad quosdam effectus positivos, sicut ordinare animam et facere dignum vita aeterna; non tamen quantum ad omnes quos habet gratia baptismalis; quia illa sufficit ad totaliter concupiscentiam reprimendam, et meritorie agendum, ad quod gratia in circumcisione data sufficere non valebat; et secundum hoc intelligitur Glossa inducta.

AD PRIMUM ergo dicendum, quod sicut in sacramento altaris est aliquid ex vi sacramenti, aliquid autem ex naturali concomitantia, ut infra dicetur, ita circumcisio principaliter ordinata erat ad ablationem culpae, sed ex consequenti ad collationem gratiae.

AD SECUNDUM dicendum, quod in baptismo amplior gratia datur, ut dictum est.

AD TERTIUM dicendum, quod gratia circumcisionis non sufficienter reprimebat concupiscentiam, sicut facit gratia novi testamenti; et ideo ratio non sequitur.

a contrary cannot be expelled except by the introduction of a form; and thus unless circumcision conferred grace in some way, it would in no way remove guilt.

And so others say that circumcision conferred grace as to its privative effect, which is precisely to remove guilt, but not as to its positive effect. But this is no answer: for the final positive effect of grace is to make one worthy of eternal life; which happened by circumcision, just as now it happens by baptism.

And thus others say, more probably as it seems, that it gave grace as to the privative effect of removing guilt and culpability, and as to certain positive effects, like ordering the soul and making one worthy of eternal life, but not as to all the things that baptismal grace does. For baptismal grace is sufficient for completely repressing concupiscence and acting meritoriously, things that the grace given in circumcision was not strong enough to do; and according to this reading the Gloss cited should be understood.[133]

REPLY OBJ. 1: Just as in the sacrament of the altar there is something from the power of the sacrament, but something of natural concomitance, as will be said later,[134] so also circumcision was principally ordered to the removal of guilt, but as a result to the conferral of grace.

REPLY OBJ. 2: In baptism grace is given more fully, as has been said.

REPLY OBJ. 3: The grace of circumcision did not sufficiently repress concupiscence, as grace of the New Testament does; and thus the argument does not follow.

---

133. Moos again furnishes a note at this point: "Here St. Thomas admits that circumcision conferred grace solely as to its privative effect, namely, the demerit of eternal life. But, weighing this matter more maturely afterwards, in *ST* III, q. 62, a. 6, ad 3, and q. 70, a. 4, and *Super Rom.* 4, lec. 2, he repudiated that opinion, and said that circumcision is a solely a sign of justifying faith."

134. See d. 10, q. 1, a. 2, qa. 1.

ARTICLE 5

The transformation of circumcision

Quaestiuncula 1

AD QUINTUM SIC PROCEDITUR. Videtur quod circumcisio cessare non debuerit. Gen. 17, dicitur, quod circumcisio datur in foedus aeternum. Sed aeternum est quod nullo fine clauditur. Ergo circumcisio cessare non debuit.

PRAETEREA, illud quod cum lege non incipit, cum lege cessare non debet. Sed circumcisio ante legem incepit: non enim est ex lege, sed ex patribus, ut dicitur Joan. 7. Ergo cum lege cessare non debuit.

PRAETEREA, figuralia quae significant id quod semper faciendum est, non debet cessare, sicut de thurificatione, quae significat devotionem, patet. Sed *circumcisio cordis, cujus laus ex Deo est*, ut dicitur Rom. 2, semper facienda est; et hanc significat exterior circumcisio. Ergo cessare non debuit.

SED CONTRA, Gal. 5, 2: *si circumcidimini, Christus vobis nihil proderit.*

PRAETEREA, veniente perfecto frustra imperfectum remaneret ad idem ordinatum. Sed baptismus perfectius facit hoc ad quod circumcisio ordinata erat, quam circumcisio faceret. Ergo veniente baptismo circumcisio cessare debuit.

OBJ. 1: To the fifth we proceed thus. It seems that circumcision should not have ended.[135] For in Genesis 17:13 it says that circumcision is given as an eternal covenant. But the eternal is what is never closed by an ending. Therefore, circumcision should not have ended.

OBJ. 2: Furthermore, something that did not begin with the law need not end with the law. But circumcision began before the law: for it is not from the law but from the patriarchs, as is clear from John 7:22. Therefore, it did not need to end with the law.

OBJ. 3: Furthermore, figures that signify what should always be done should not end, as is clear in the example of using incense, which signifies devotion. But *circumcision of the heart . . . whose praise is not of men but of God*, is always to be done, as it says in Romans 2:29; and this is what external circumcision signifies. Therefore, it should not have ended.

ON THE CONTRARY, *If you let yourselves be circumcised, Christ will be of no benefit to you* (Gal 5:2).

FURTHERMORE, once the perfect comes, the imperfect that is ordered to the same thing would remain in vain. But baptism does more perfectly what circumcision was ordered to than circumcision does. Therefore, once baptism comes, circumcision had to end.

Quaestiuncula 2

ULTERIUS. Videtur quod nec alia legalia cessare debuerint. Christus enim, ut dicitur Matth. 5, non venit legem solvere, sed implere. Sed lex consistebat non tantum in moralibus, sed etiam in sacramentis legalibus. Ergo non venit ea solvere.

PRAETEREA, apud Deum non est transmutatio. Sed signum mutationis voluntatis est ut praeceptum quod prius datum est, postea revocetur. Cum ergo Deus haec sacramenta praeceperit, videtur quod cessare non debuerant.

PRAETEREA, praeceptum non potest revocari nisi per aequalem, vel superiorem. Sed Deus nunquam revocasse legitur praeceptum de sacramentis legalibus in nova lege. Ergo adhuc durant.

OBJ. 1: Moreover, it seems that also the other legal prescriptions should not have ended.[136] For Christ, as it says in Matthew 5, did not come to abolish the law but to fulfill it. But the law consisted not only in moral prescriptions, but also in the sacraments of the law. Therefore, he did not come to abolish them.

OBJ. 2: Furthermore, *there is no change in God* (Jas 1:17). But it is a sign of a change of will if a precept that was formerly given is afterward revoked. Therefore, since God commanded these sacraments, it seems they should not have ended.

OBJ. 3: Furthermore, a precept can only be revoked by an equal or superior. But we never read that God in the New Law revoked a precept of the sacraments of the law. Therefore, they are still in effect.

---

135. Parallels: *ST* I-II, q. 103, a. 3; *SCG* IV, ch. 57; *Super Rom.* 2, lec. 4; ibid., ch. 4, lec. 2.
136. Parallels: *ST* I-II, q. 103, a. 3.

SED CONTRA est quod dicitur Heb. 10, 1: *umbram habet lex futurorum bonorum.* Sed veniente veritate cessat figura. Ergo veniente Christo legalia cessare debuerunt.

PRAETEREA, Hebr. 7, 12: *translato sacerdotio necesse est ut et legis translatio fiat.* Sed in Christo translatum fuit sacerdotium, ut ibidem apostolus probat. Ergo et legalia cessare debuerunt.

ON THE CONTRARY, *The law has only a shadow of the good things to come* (Heb 10:1). But once the truth comes, the figure ceases. Therefore, with Christ having come, the legal prescriptions had to cease.

FURTHERMORE, *When there is a change in the priesthood, there is necessarily a change in the law as well* (Heb 7:12). But in Christ there was a change of priests, as the Apostle proves in the very same place. Therefore, the legal prescriptions had to end.

Quaestiuncula 3

ULTERIUS. Videtur quod tempore gratiae poterant sine peccato observari. Omnis enim Christi actio nostra est instructio. Sed Christus tempore gratiae ea observavit, sicut in multis patet. Ergo licitum est tempore gratiae ea servare.

PRAETEREA, tempore apostolorum etiam observabantur, sicut patet Act. 16, de Paulo, qui circumcidit Timotheum, et de eodem Act. 21, *qui purificatus per legem, templum intravit,* et hostias obtulit: quod non fecisset ad vitandum scandalum, si peccatum fuisset; quia veritas vitae non est dimittenda propter scandalum. Ergo sine peccato tempore gratiae observari poterant.

PRAETEREA, omnis actus qui non est de se malus, potest sine peccato fieri, et meritorie, si recta intentione fiat. Sed sacrificare et circumcidi non sunt de se mala, alias nunquam licita fuissent. Ergo si bona intentione fiant, erunt meritoria etiam modo, nedum ut sint peccata.

SED CONTRA est quod dicitur Gal. 5, 2: *si circumcidimini, Christus nihil vobis proderit.* Sed omne quod impedit profectum qui provenit ex Christi redemptione, est peccatum. Ergo circumcisio tempore gratiae non poterat fieri sine peccato, et pari ratione nec alia sacramenta.

PRAETEREA, Gal. 4, super illud: *quomodo convertimini rursus ad egena et infirma elementa?* Dicit Glossa: *ideo dicit, denuo, ut ostendat quod non distat modo lex post Christum ab antiqua idolatria.* Sed idolatria nunquam poterat observari sine peccato. Ergo nec legalia post Christum.

OBJ. 1: Moreover, it seems that in the time of grace the prescriptions of the law could be observed without sinning.[137] For every deed of Christ was for our instruction. But Christ observed them in the time of grace, as is seen in many examples. Therefore, it is permitted to keep them during the time of grace.

OBJ. 2: Furthermore, they were also observed at the time of the apostles, as is clear in the case of Paul, who in Acts 16 circumcised Timothy, and also in Acts 21, *who having purified himself according to the law, entered the temple* and offered sacrifices (Acts 21:29)—which he would not have done to avoid scandal if it were a sin; because the truth of life is not to be set aside because of scandal. Therefore, the legal prescriptions could be observed without sin in the time of grace.

OBJ. 3: Furthermore, every act that is not in itself evil can be done without sin, and even meritoriously, if it is done with the right intention. But to sacrifice and be circumcised are not evil in themselves, otherwise they would never have been allowed. Therefore, if they are done with good intentions, they will even be meritorious now, let alone without sin.

ON THE CONTRARY, *If you let yourselves be circumcised, Christ will be of no benefit to you* (Gal 5:2). But everything that impedes the benefit that comes from the redemption of Christ is a sin. Therefore, circumcision in the time of grace could not be done without sinning, and by the same argument, neither could the other sacraments of the law.

FURTHERMORE, concerning the verse: *now that you have come to know God . . . how can you turn back again to the weak and needy elements, whose slaves you want to be once more?* (Gal 4:9), the Gloss says: *therefore he says "once more," to show that now the law, after Christ, is not far from ancient idolatry.* But idolatry could never be observed without sin. Therefore, neither can the legal prescripts after Christ.

---

137. Parallels: *ST* I-II, q. 103, a. 4; q. 107, a. 2, ad 2; *ST* II-II, q. 93, a. 1; *Super Rom.* 14, lec. 1; *Super Gal.* 2, lec. 3; *Super Col.* 2, lec. 4.

Quaestiuncula 4

ULTERIUS. Videtur quod usque modo teneamur aliqua legalia observare. Tenemur enim ad observanda praecepta novi testamenti, et statuta ecclesiae. Sed praeceptum apostolorum in novo testamento fuit de quibusdam legalibus observandis. Act. 15, 28: *visum est Spiritui Sancto et nobis nihil ultra imponere vobis oneris quam ut abstineatis vos ab immolatis simulacrorum, et sanguine, et suffocato, et fornicatione*. Ergo adhuc tenemur ad haec legalia servanda.

PRAETEREA, sed si dicatur, quod fuit permissio apostolorum pro tempore illo; contra. Glossa ibidem dicit, haec esse necessaria. Sed necessaria sunt sine quibus non est salus, et de quibus non est permissio, sed praeceptum. Ergo adhuc observare tenemur.

PRAETEREA, si dicatur, quod per Paulum revocatum est, ut cum dicitur 1 Timoth. 4, 4: *nihil rejiciendum quod cum gratiarum actione percipitur*; contra. Inferior non potest praeceptum superioris revocare. Sed Paulus fuit inferior quam totum apostolorum Concilium in Hierusalem congregatum. Ergo non potuit revocare.

SED CONTRA, Petrus ibidem dicit, Act. 15, quod per gratiam Christi salvamur in lege nova sine onere legis, sicut et patres nostri; unde hoc jugum non est fidelibus imponendum. Sed onus praedictum est observatio caeremonialium. Ergo ad ea servanda non tenemur.

OBJ. 1: Moreover, it seems that we are bound even still to observe some legal prescriptions.[138] For we are bound to observe the precepts of the New Testament and the statutes of the Church. But the precept of the apostles in the New Testament was about certain legal prescriptions to be observed: *It has seemed good to the Holy Spirit and to us to impose on you no further burden beyond that you abstain from things sacrificed to idols, and from blood, and from things strangled, and from fornication* (Acts 15:28). Therefore, we are bound to keep these prescriptions of the law still.

OBJ. 2: But if it were said in reply that the permission of the apostles was only for that time, one may argue to the contrary: the Gloss says in the same place that these things were necessary.[139] But necessary things are those without which there is no salvation, and no permission is given about those things, but rather a precept. Therefore, we are bound to observe them still.

OBJ. 3: If it were said that it was revoked by Paul, as when it says: *nothing is to be rejected that is received with thanksgiving* (1 Tim 4:4); to the contrary, someone lower in rank cannot revoke the precept of the superior. But Paul was below the whole council of apostles congregated in Jerusalem. Therefore, he could not revoke it.

ON THE CONTRARY, Peter says in the same place that in the New Law *we are saved by the grace of Christ* without the burden of the law, *just as also our fathers were* (Acts 15:11). Hence this yoke is not to be imposed on the faithful. But the yoke he refers to is the observance of the ceremonial laws. Therefore, we are not bound to keep them.

Response to Quaestiuncula 1

RESPONDEO dicendum ad primam quaestionem, quod cum venit quod perfectum est, evacuari debet quod ex parte est, si ad idem ordinetur: quia gratia non facit per duo quod per unum potest facere, sicut nec natura. Circumcisio autem imperfecta erat respectu baptismi tripliciter. Primo quantum ad significationem: quia non ita significabat expresse emundationem totius hominis ab immunditia totius culpae originalis, sicut ablutio baptismalis. Secundo quantum ad efficaciam: quia non tam abundans gratia ad operandum et reprimendum fomitem in circumcisione dabatur sicut in baptismo. Tertio quantum ad utilitatem: quia non erat ejus utilitas ita communis sicut baptismi, cum haberet determinatum populum, determinatum sexum, et determinatum tempus, quod in baptismo non accidit; et ideo ad-

THE FIRST QUESTION I answer by saying that when what is perfect has come, what is partial should be discarded, if it is ordered to the same thing: for grace does not accomplish by two things that which can be done by one, just as neither does nature. Now in comparison with baptism, circumcision was imperfect in three ways. First, as to its signification, for it did not signify so explicitly the cleansing of the whole man from the uncleanness of all of original sin, as the washing of baptism does. Second, as to its efficacy, for the grace that was given in circumcision was not so abundant for working virtuously and for repressing the kindling of sin as it is in baptism. Third, as to benefit, for its benefit was not as widespread as baptism's, since it had a particular people, a particular sex, and a particular time, which does not happen in baptism; and thus, once the time

---

138. Parallels: *Super Col.* 2, lec. 4.
139. The Gloss of Rabanus Maurus, PL 114:458.

veniente tempore plenitudinis debuit cessare, baptismo substituto.

Ad primum ergo dicendum, quod aeternum hic accipitur pro saeculo; quod habet quidem finem, sed non est determinatus nobis. Vel etiam dicendum, quod circumcisio corporalis potuit esse in foedus aeternum quantum ad suum significatum, et quantum ad id quod ei succedit; sicut etiam fides potest dici semper manere ratione visionis, quae ei succedit in patria.

Ad secundum dicendum, quod quamvis cum lege non inceperit circumcisio, tamen propter legem incepit quasi legis praeparatorium; et ideo cessante lege cessare debuit.

Ad tertium dicendum, quod principalis significatio ad quam circumcisio instituta est, est ablatio originalis culpae, quia sacramentalis significatio refertur ad effectum. Hoc autem non semper faciendum erat per circumcisionem; et ideo non oportebat quod circumcisio semper remaneret. Alia autem significatio est ex consequenti, et secundum illam non oportet accipi judicium de duratione circumcisionis. Thurificationis autem significatio nunquam fuit ad significandum aliquid ut effectum ejus; et ideo non est similis ratio.

of fullness arrived, circumcision had to end, to be replaced by baptism.

Reply Obj. 1: Here 'eternal' is taken as an era, which does indeed have an end, but not one that is determined by us. Or it may be said that physical circumcision could be an eternal covenant as to its meaning, and as to what succeeds it; just as also faith can be said to remain always by reason of the vision that will succeed it in the fatherland.

Reply Obj. 2: Although circumcision did not begin with the law, nevertheless it did begin because of the law, as a sort of preparation for the law; and thus it had to end when the law ended.

Reply Obj. 3: The principal signification for which circumcision was instituted is the removal of original sin, for a sacramental signification is referred to the effect. But this did not always need to be done by circumcision, and thus it was not necessary that circumcision always remain. Moreover, the other signification was a result of the first, and considering it does not lead one to a definite judgment about the duration of circumcision. But the use of incense was never for signifying something as an effect of that something; and so the argument is not the same.

Response to Quaestiuncula 2

Ad secundam quaestionem dicendum, quod triplex erat praecipua ratio cessationis legalium. Una est, quia lex instituta fuit ad significandum gratiam novi testamenti, quae per Christum facta est; et ideo veniente Christo cessare debuerunt, sicut veniente corpore cessat umbra; et hanc causam tangit apostolus Hebr. 10, 1: *umbram habens lex futurorum bonorum.*

Alia ratio est ex imperfectione: quia in legalibus gratia non conferebatur quantam oportebat in novo testamento dari. Sicut enim virtus naturalis rei naturali proportionatur, ita virtus sacramentalis sacramento; unde oportuit alia sacramenta institui, in quibus amplior gratia conferretur; et hanc causam tangit apostolus Heb. 7, 18: *reprobatio quidem fit prioris mandati propter infirmitatem et inutilitatem.*

Tertia accipitur ex parte eorum quibus lex data est, qui erant parvuli; et ideo erant paulatim a pristina consuetudine idolatriae abstrahendi, ut sic eis concederetur eadem Deo offerre quae prius idolis obtulerunt, vel offerri viderant, sicut Rabbi Moyses dicit. Sed postmodum quando ad perfectam aetatem humanum genus pervenit, debuit ab his observantiis liber esse. Et hanc causam

To the second question, it should be said that there were three main reasons for the cessation of the legal prescriptions. The first is that the law was instituted to signify the grace of the New Testament, which came about through Christ. Thus, when Christ came, they had to end, just as a shadow ends when a body comes; and the Apostle touches on this reason: *the law having the shadow of good things to come* (Heb 10:1).

Another reason is from its imperfection: for in the legal prescriptions grace was not conferred to the extent that it was fitting for it to be given in the New Testament. For just as a natural power is proportionate to a natural thing, so also sacramental power is proportionate to a sacrament. Hence it was necessary for other sacraments to be instituted in which a more ample grace was conferred; and the Apostle touches on this reason: *there is indeed a setting aside of the earlier commandment because it was weak and ineffectual* (Heb 7:18).

The third reason is taken on the part of those to whom the law was given, who were little ones; and so they needed to be withdrawn gradually from their former custom of idolatry, so that in this way it would be granted to them to offer to God the same things that they had once sacrificed to idols or had seen offered, as Rabbi Moses says. But afterward, when human race had reached maturity, it had to

tangit apostolus Gal. 3 et 4, et Petrus Act. 15, ostendens illa legalia in onus populo rudi imposita esse.

AD PRIMUM ergo dicendum, quod Christus in hoc legem implevit quod moralibus praeceptis consilia apposuit, et praecepta magis elucidavit: sed figuris caeremonialium veritatem apposuit, et ea in seipso suscepit.

AD SECUNDUM dicendum, quod non ex mutabilitate praecipientis, sed ex prudenti dispensatione contingit quod diversa praecepta diversis temporibus accommoda proponit, sicut est in proposito.

AD TERTIUM dicendum, quod Dominus ipso facto revocavit, adimplens in se quod in figura praeceperat observandum; et ideo in sua passione dixit: *consummatum est.* Joan. 19, 30.

be free from these observances. And the Apostle touches on this reason in Galatians 3 and 4, and Peter touches on it in Acts 15, where he shows that those legal requirements were imposed as a burden on an unschooled people.

REPLY OBJ. 1: Christ fulfilled the law inasmuch as he added to the moral precepts and elucidated those precepts more. But he displayed the very truth that was in the figures of the ceremonies and assumed them in himself.

REPLY OBJ. 2: That a lawgiver sets down different precepts suited to different times, as is the case here, is not owing to the changeability of the one giving the precepts, but rather to their prudent dispensation.

REPLY OBJ. 3: The Lord revoked it by the fact that he fulfilled in himself what he had commanded to be observed in figure; and thus during his Passion he said: *it is consummated* (Jn 19:30).

Response to Quaestiuncula 3

AD TERTIAM QUAESTIONEM dicendum, quod haec quaestio videtur habere difficultatem ex quibusdam contrarietatibus quae super hoc inveniuntur tam in canone, quam in dictis sanctorum. Quandoque enim inveniuntur observata legalia tempore gratiae, quandoque autem prohibita; et de hoc etiam Petrus a Paulo redargutus videtur Gal. 2.

Et ideo super hoc Hieronymus et Augustinus diversa sensisse videntur. Volebat enim Hieronymus quod legalia statim post passionem Christi quantum ad hos ad quos gratia novi testamenti manifeste divulgata erat, fuerunt mortifera; sed apostolos quadam pia dispensatione his usos fuisse ad vitandum scandalum Judaeorum; et ideo Petrus judaizans non peccavit, dispensatorie id faciens, secundum quod etiam dicitur 1 Corinth. 9, 22: *omnibus omnia factus sum*; et similiter Paulus dispensatorie eum redarguit, ne gentiles exemplo Petri, quorum ipse apostolus erat, veteris legis sacramenta quasi necessaria quaererent: quia et ipse invenitur eadem pia simulatione servasse; et sic uterque excusatur, et Petrus a culpa, et Paulus a procaci reprehensione.

Sed quia non videtur conveniens quod apostoli aliquid contra veritatem doctrinae fecissent ad vitandum scandalum Judaeorum, nec iterum videtur conveniens quod Paulus in epistola ad Galatas aliquid simulate diceret, ubi dicit Petrum reprehensibilem fuisse; ideo Augu-

TO THE THIRD QUESTION, it should be said that this question seems to pose a difficulty due to certain contrary statements that are found concerning it both in the canon of scripture and in the words of the saints. For sometimes the legal prescripts are found to be observed in the time of grace, but sometimes they are prohibited; and even Peter and Paul seemed to argue back and forth about this (cf. Gal 2).

And as a result Jerome and Augustine seemed to have reached different opinions. For Jerome contended that for those to whom the grace of the New Testament had been plainly disseminated, the legal prescriptions were deadly, immediately after the Passion of Christ; yet the apostles, as a kind of pious exception to the rule, observed them in order to avoid scandalizing the Jews. And thus Peter did not sin by living like a Jew, doing it as an exception, according to which it is also said: *I have become all things to all men* (1 Cor 9:22).[140] And likewise Paul's rebuke of Peter was an exception to Paul's own practice, lest by Peter's example, the gentiles of whom he himself was the apostle might seek the sacraments of the Old Law as though they were necessary; for Paul himself is found to have observed the same things by a pious pretense. And in this way, according to Jerome, both are excused—Peter from fault and Paul from impudent criticizing.[141]

But since it does not seem fitting for the apostles to have done something against the truth of doctrine to avoid scandalizing the Jews, nor again does it seem fitting that Paul would have said something disingenuous in his letter to the Galatians, where he says that Peter was blameworthy.

---

140. *Dispensatorie* could also be rendered "economically," that is, in the manner of the divine economy, which adapts universal truths to particular circumstances.

141. See Jerome, *Epist.* 112 *ad Augustinum* (PL 22:921); *In Gal.*, Bk. 1, on Galatians 2:11 (PL 26:364ff.).

stinus aliter dicit, et melius, quod ante Christi passionem legalia fuerunt observanda ex necessitate divinae jussionis, et habuerunt adhuc effectum; sed post Christi passionem ante divulgationem Evangelii observari poterant a Judaeis ad fidem conversis, non spem in ipsis ponentibus, quasi alicujus virtutis essent, aut quasi sine eis gratia Christi non sufficeret ad salutem, sed ne omnino videretur lex vetus reprobanda, si statim quasi idolatria fugeretur; et ideo hoc modo erat mater synagoga deducenda ad tumulum cum honore. Sed post divulgationem Evangelii non solum non sunt salutifera, sed mortifera. Medio ergo tempore Petrus et Paulus et alii apostoli legalia observabant non simulatorie, sed vere. Petrus tamen incaute se habuit in observatione legalium, nimis condescendens Judaeis illis qui legalia observanda esse dicebant, ita ut aliqui ejus exemplo inducerentur ad ea observanda quasi necessaria; et ideo vere reprehensibilis erat, et aliquam levem incurrit culpam; et Paulus vere et non dispensative ipsum reprehendit.

ET PER HOC patet solutio ad primum et secundum: quia ante Christi passionem, quando Christus ea servavit, non erant mortua nec mortifera, sed salutifera; tempore vero apostolorum ante divulgationem Evangelii erant quidem mortua, quasi nullius existentia utilitatis, sed non mortifera.

AD TERTIUM dicendum, quod una circumstantia mutata facit actum bonum in genere, vel malum; et ideo legalia, quae absque consideratione alicujus temporis sunt indifferentia, suo tempore facta fuerunt bona, tempore autem non suo observata, sunt facta mala; et ideo bona intentione fieri non possunt bene.

So Augustine says something else, and better,[142] that before the Passion of Christ the legal prescripts were to be observed out of the necessity of divine command, and they had an effect until then. But after the Passion of Christ, yet before the dissemination of the Gospel, they could be observed by Jews converted to the faith—not placing any hope in them, as though they had some power, or as if the grace of Christ would not suffice for salvation without them, but lest the Old Law would seem to be altogether rejected, if all of a sudden it were shunned like idolatry. And thus, in this way, mother synagogue was to be led to her tomb with honor. But after the dissemination of the Gospel, the legal practices were not only not salutary, but deadly. Therefore, in the meantime Peter and Paul and the other apostles observed the legal prescriptions not in a dissimulating way, but truly. Nevertheless, Peter behaved incautiously in his observance of the legal prescriptions, catering too much to those Jews who said the legal prescriptions were to be observed, so that others were led by his example to observe them as though they were necessary. And in this way he was indeed to be criticized, and he incurred some light fault; and Paul reprimanded him truly and not as an exception.

AND FROM THIS the solution to the first and second objections becomes clear: for before the Passion of Christ, when Christ kept these laws, they were neither dead nor deadly, but salutary; while in the time of the apostles, before the dissemination of the Gospel, they were indeed dead, like things having no benefit, but not deadly.

REPLY OBJ. 3: One changed circumstance makes an act good in its genus or bad; and thus the legal prescriptions, which are indifferent apart from the consideration of the time of their observance, were made good in their own time, but when they were observed not in their own time, they became bad; and thus they cannot be made good by a good intention.

Response to Quaestiuncula 4

AD QUARTAM QUAESTIONEM dicendum, quod circa hoc tres sunt opiniones.

Una opinio dixit, quod ad litteram intelligendum est illud praeceptum quod legitur in actibus, et ejus obligatio usque nunc manet. Sed hoc manifeste contrariatur dictis Pauli, qui dixit nihil esse commune, idest immundum, per Christum, nisi ei qui aestimat aliquid esse commune, Rom. 14; et iterum est contra rationem: quia cum hoc praeceptum non sit morale, quia naturalis ratio illud non dictat, oportet quod sit caeremoniale; et ideo ejus obligatio non manet magis quam aliorum.

Et ideo alii dixerunt, quod non est intelligendum ad litteram de sanguine animalis, et suffocato animali, sed

TO THE FOURTH QUESTION, it should be said that concerning this matter there are three opinions.

One opinion has said that that precept which is written in Acts is to be understood literally, and its obligation remains until now. But this plainly goes against the words of Paul, who said that nothing was common, that is, unclean, through Christ, except to someone who considers something to be common (cf. Rom 14). Then again, it is against reason: for since this precept is not moral, because natural reason does not dictate it, it must be ceremonial; and thus its obligation does not remain any more than the others'.

And thus, others have said that it is not to be understood literally of the blood of animals and strangled ani-

142. See Augustine, *Epist.* 82 *ad Hieron.*, ch. 2 (PL 33:280–1).

de effusione sanguinis quae fit per homicidium, et de suffocatione pauperum. Sed hoc non potest stare: quia Hieronymus Ezech. 18, post illam expositionem mysticam, expositionem ponit litteralem, quam dicit apostolos etiam intendisse.

Et ideo alii dicunt, quod epistola apostolorum non erat praeceptoria quantum ad hoc quod abstinerent se ab immolatitiis, et sanguine, et suffocato; sed erat quaedam provisio ad conservandam pacem, et communem vitam gentilium et Judaeorum fidelium; et ideo fornicationem prohibuerunt quasi per se malum, quod apud gentiles non reputabatur pro peccato. Immolatitium autem prohibuerunt quasi illud quod posset suspicionem idolatriae adhuc retentae generare de gentilibus in cordibus Judaeorum; sanguinem autem suffocatum sicut quod Judaei abominabantur propter dissuetudinem: sicut etiam usque hodie si aliquis socialiter vult alii convivere, oportet quod abstineat ab his quae alter abominatur.

ET PER HOC patet responsio ad primum.

AD SECUNDUM dicendum, quod dicuntur esse necessaria quantum ad sensum mysticum praetactum, vel quantum ad observandum communitatem vitae inter Judaeos et gentiles.

AD TERTIUM dicendum, quod Paulus non revocavit, sed exposuit apostolorum intentionem, sicut qui praesens fuerat quando sententia data erat. Unde dicitur 1 Corinth. 8, 1: *de his autem quae idolis immolantur, non omnes habemus scientiam*: quia non omnes intelligebant qualiter essent prohibita.

mals, but of the shedding of blood that happens in murder, and the strangling of the poor.[143] But this cannot stand: for in Jerome's commentary on Ezekiel 18, after that mystical explanation he sets down the literal explanation, which he says the apostles also intended.[144]

And thus others say that the letter of the apostles was not preceptory regarding abstaining from sacrificed animals, and blood, and strangled animals; but it was a certain warning to preserve the peace and the shared life of gentile and Jewish members of the faithful. And thus they prohibited fornication as something evil in itself, which among the gentiles was not considered a sin. But they prohibited sacrificed animals as something that could arouse, in the hearts of the Jews, a suspicion of idolatry on the part of the gentiles; while blood and strangled animals were held in abomination by the Jews because they had a contrary custom—just as even today if someone wants to live sociably together with others, he has to abstain from those things that the other abominates.

AND BY THIS the response to the first is clear.

REPLY OBJ. 2: They are said to be necessary either with respect to the mystical sense already mentioned or with respect to the common life that had to be observed among Jews and gentiles.

REPLY OBJ. 3: Paul did not revoke it but rather explained the intention of the apostles, as someone who was present when the judgment was handed down. Hence it is said, *now concerning those things that are sacrificed to idols, we do not all have knowledge* (1 Cor 8:1): for not all were understanding in what respects they were prohibited.

---

143. See Guilelmus Altissiodorensis, *Summa aurea*, pt. 4, tr. 1, q. 2.
144. This is found rather in Jerome's comments on Ezekiel 44:31; see *Commentarii in Ezechielem* (CCSL 75), Bk. 13, ch. 44, l. 1875.

Article 6

About the remedy that preceded circumcision

Quaestiuncula 1

Ad sextum sic proceditur. Videtur quod ante circumcisionem non valebat ad remissionem originalis peccati pro parvulis sola fides. Efficacior enim est caritas quam fides. Sed caritas aliena nunquam suffecit ad meritum. Ergo nec fides ad justificationem.

Praeterea, si fides aliena valebat, ergo eadem ratione etiam infidelitas nocebat; et ita ex peccato actuali parentum puer puniretur; quod est inconveniens.

Praeterea, fides non magis juvat alium quam habentem. Sed illi qui habebant fidem, non semper juvabantur a fide: quia poterat esse quod haberent fidem informem. Ergo nec puero valebat fides parentum ad delendum originale peccatum.

Sed contra est quod dicit Gregorius in littera.

Praeterea, peccatum quod ex altero contrahitur, ex altero potest habere medicinam. Sed peccatum originale parvuli ex altero contrahebatur. Ergo poterat ex fide aliena ab ipso mundari.

Obj. 1: To the sixth we proceed thus. It seems that before circumcision existed, faith alone was not sufficient for remitting the original sin of children.[145] For charity is more efficacious than faith. But another person's charity was never enough for someone to merit. Therefore, neither would faith suffice for justification.

Obj. 2: Furthermore, if someone else's faith sufficed, then by the same argument their unbelief would also harm—and so a child would be punished for the actual sin of his parents, which is unfitting.

Obj. 3: Furthermore, faith does not help someone else more than it helps the one who has it. But those who had faith were not always helped by it: for it could be that their faith was unformed. Therefore, neither would the faith of the parents benefit the child by removing his original sin.

On the contrary, is what Gregory says in the text.[146]

Furthermore, sin which was contracted from another can have treatment by another. But the original sin of a child was contracted from another. Therefore, he could be cleansed from it by another's faith.

Quaestiuncula 2

Ulterius. Videtur quod fides non suffecerit sine aliquo exteriori signo. Dicit enim Augustinus contra Faustum, quod in nullum nomen religionis, sive verum, sive falsum, poterant homines sine aliquo signo visibili adunari. Sed per illud quo originale deletur, homines in religionem verae fidei adunantur: quia oportet hujusmodi remedium esse intrantium. Ergo oportebat quod fieret aliquo visibili signo.

Praeterea, actus mentis potest se extendere ad natos et non natos, sed conceptos, aequaliter. Si ergo fides sine exteriori signo sufficiebat ad deletionem originalis, videtur quod poterant etiam nondum nati ab originali peccato per fidem mundari.

Praeterea, modo non valet fides ad salutem sine aliquo signo exteriori. Si ergo tunc valuisset, videtur quod fuisset majoris efficaciae quam modo.

Obj. 1: Moreover, it seems that faith was not sufficient without some external sign.[147] For Augustine says against Faustus that in no religion, whether true or false, could men be united together without any visible sign.[148] But men are united in the true religion through that by which original sin is removed, since there has to be a remedy like this for those entering. Therefore, it had to happen by some visible sign.

Obj. 2: Furthermore, an act of the mind can extend equally to children born and to those conceived but unborn. Therefore, if faith sufficed for the removal of original sin without an external sign, it seems that even children yet unborn could be cleansed from original sin by faith.

Obj. 3: Furthermore, today faith is not sufficient for salvation without any external sign. Therefore, if it was sufficient back then, it seems that it would have had greater efficacy then than now.

---

145. Parallels: below, d. 4, q. 3, a. 3, qa. 2, ad 3; *ST* III, q. 70, a. 4, ad 2; *De Malo*, q. 4, a. 8, ad 12.
146. The text—from Gregory, *Moralia in Iob* (CCSL 143), Bk. 4, preface, l. 69—is given in Lombard's *Sentences*.
147. Parallels: below, d. 4, q. 3, a. 3, qa. 2, ad 3; *ST* III, q. 68, a. 1, ad 1; q. 70, a. 4, ad 2.
148. Augustine, *Contra Faustum*, Bk. 19, par. 11 (CSEL 25:510).

SED CONTRA est quia secundum hoc non esset differentia inter parvulos et adultos, quam tamen Gregorius assignat.

PRAETEREA, omnia sacramenta illius temporis habebant totam efficaciam suam ex fide. Ergo tantum faciebat fides sine exteriori signo, quantum cum eo; et ita exteriora signa non requirebantur, ut videtur.

ON THE CONTRARY, according to this there would be no difference between children and adults, which nevertheless Gregory asserts.

FURTHERMORE, all the sacraments of that age had their whole efficacy from faith. Therefore, faith worked as much without external signs as with them; and in this way external signs were not required, as it seems.

Quaestiuncula 3

ULTERIUS. Videtur quod in adultis non requireretur sacrificium, vel aliud hujusmodi. Non minus enim valet alicui fides propria quam alteri fides aliena. Sed pueris sufficiebat fides aliena sine exteriori signo, ut probatum est. Ergo et adultis.

PRAETEREA, Hugo de sancto Victore dicit, quod nullus obligabatur ad sacramenta illius temporis, sed voto celebrabantur. Sed quod est hujusmodi, non est de necessitate salutis. Ergo absque sacrificiis poterat emundari ab originali.

SED CONTRA est quod Gregorius in littera dicit, quod pro parvulis sola fides, pro adultis sacrificia et oblationes valebant.

OBJ. 1: Moreover, it seems that in adults a sacrifice would not be required, or anything like it.[149] For someone's own faith is not less beneficial to him than someone else's faith. But someone else's faith was sufficient for children without any external sign, as was proved. Therefore, also for adults.

OBJ. 2: Furthermore, Hugh of St. Victor says that no one was obligated to the sacraments of that age, but they were celebrated by choice.[150] But something like that is not necessary for salvation. Therefore, without sacrifices someone could have been cleansed of original sin.

ON THE CONTRARY, is what Gregory says in the text, that for small children faith alone sufficed, but for adults sacrifices and oblations were needed.

Response to Quaestiuncula 1

RESPONDEO dicendum, quod peccatum originale est peccatum naturae: natura autem reparari non poterat nisi per Christum; et ideo nunquam poterat remitti peccatum originale alicujus nisi facta relatione, et quadam continuatione illius qui curari debebat, ad Christum, quod per fidem fiebat; et ideo fides mediatoris semper fuit efficax ad curandum ab originali: in illis quidem qui usum liberi arbitrii habebant, propria; in aliis vero aliena, ut nec eis omnino deesset divinum remedium.

AD PRIMUM ergo dicendum, quod fides in cognitione est, caritas autem in affectione. Affectio autem est ejus quod est sibi bonum; sed cognitio est ejus quod est verum simpliciter; et ideo fides poterat magis respicere mediatorem, prout erat causa salutis alteri, quam caritas; et propter hoc magis justificatio quae fit in sacramentis, attribuitur fidei quam caritati.

AD SECUNDUM dicendum, quod fides aliena non juvabat inquantum erat actus personae, sed ex parte illa qua respiciebat objectum suum, scilicet Christum, quod erat medicina totius naturae; in quo habebat quamdam similitudinem cum sacramentis nostris, inquantum ju-

I ANSWER THAT, original sin is a sin of nature, but nature could not be repaired except through Christ. And thus, someone's original sin could only be remitted if the one to be cured were brought into relation to Christ and in a certain way joined to him, which happened through faith. And thus, faith in the Mediator was always efficacious for curing original sin—among those who had the use of free will, their own faith; for others, someone else's faith, so that they would not be lacking the divine remedy entirely.

REPLY OBJ. 1: Faith is in the intellect, but charity is in the affections. Now affection pertains to what is good for one, while knowledge pertains to what is true simply. And for this reason, faith, more than charity, could look towards the Mediator as the cause of salvation for another; and because of this, the justification that happens in the sacraments is attributed more to faith than to charity.

REPLY OBJ. 2: Someone else's faith did not help inasmuch as it was an act of that person, but rather, on the side of that by which it regarded its object, Christ, who was the medicine of the whole of nature. In this, it had a certain likeness to our sacraments, inasmuch as it justified by its

149. Parallels: *ST* I-II, q. 103, a. 1, ad 1; *ST* III, q. 68, a. 1, ad 1.
150. Hugh of St. Victor, *De sacramentis fidei*, Bk. 1, pt. 11, ch. 3 (PL 176:343).

stificabat ex objecto, quasi ex opere operato, non autem ex opere operante.

ET PER HOC patet solutio ad tertium: quia formatio et informitas fidei sunt conditiones ejus ex parte operantis, non autem ex parte objecti; et ideo informitas fidei in parente non impediebat effectum salutis in filio; impediebat autem in ipso, quia informitas illa proveniebat ex aliquo quod erat contrarium saluti, scilicet ex peccato mortali.

object, as if by the work performed, but not by the act of the one doing it.

REPLY OBJ. 3: And from this, the solution to the third is clear: for whether faith is formed or unformed is a condition on the part of the one acting, not on the part of the object; and thus, unformed faith in a parent did not impede the effect of salvation in the son, but it did impede it in himself, for its unformedness arose from something that was contrary to salvation, namely, from mortal sin.

Response to Quaestiuncula 2

AD SECUNDAM QUAESTIONEM dicendum, quod circa hoc est duplex opinio. Quidam enim dicunt, quod non sufficiebat fides sine protestatione fidei facta per aliquod exterius signum; et erat differentia inter parvulos et adultos quantum ad hoc tantum quod parvulis sufficiebat fides aliena cum exteriori signo ab aliis facto, sed adultis fides propria cum signo ab eis facto. Sed quia hoc non videtur consonare cum verbis Gregorii in littera positis, ideo alii probabilius dicunt, quod parvulis sufficiebat sola fides sine omni exteriori signo; non autem habitus fidei solum, sed motus ejus relatus ad salutem pueri in vi cujusdam intensionis[151] interioris fidei, quicumque esset ille qui quoquomodo professionem fidei suae ad puerum referret; magis tamen pertinebat hoc ad parentes, qui pueri curam habere debebant, et per quos originale contraxerat.

AD PRIMUM ergo dicendum secundum hoc, quod illud per quod homines tempore legis naturae in veram religionem congregabantur, non habebat virtutem nisi ex fide; et ideo non erat necessitatis, sed pro voto celebrabatur, ut unus alii innotesceret.

AD SECUNDUM dicendum, quod puer adhuc in utero matris existens, quantum ad humanam cognitionem pertinet, non habet esse distinctum a matre, et ideo per actum hominis consequi non potest nec nunc ut mundetur ab originali per baptismum, nec tunc ut mundaretur per fidem parentum: sed divinitus mundari potest, sicut de sanctificatis in utero apparet.

AD TERTIUM dicendum, quod fidei efficacia non est diminuta, cum omnia sacramenta ex fide efficaciam habeant; sed est ei aliquid adjunctum quod necesse est observari; sicut non est minoris efficaciae lex moris in religioso quam in saeculari; quamvis praecepta moralia sufficiant ad salutem in saeculari, sed in religioso requirantur consilia, ad quae se ex voto obligavit.

TO THE SECOND QUESTION, it should be said that concerning this there are two opinions. For certain people say that faith was not sufficient without a profession of faith made by some external sign; and there was a difference between children and adults only in that for children the faith of another was sufficient with an external sign made by another, but for adults their own faith was necessary with a sign made by themselves. But since this does not seem to agree with the words of Gregory quoted in the text, others say, with greater likelihood, that faith alone was sufficient for children, without any external sign; but not just the habit of faith, but a movement of it related to the salvation of the child by the force of some profession of interior faith, no matter who it was who, in whatever way, referred his profession of faith to the child. However, this pertained more to the parents, who should have had care of the child, and from whom he had contracted original sin.

REPLY OBJ. 1: What brought men together in true religion in the time of the law of nature only had power through faith; and thus it was not of necessity, but it was celebrated by choice, so that one man would become known to another.

REPLY OBJ. 2: The child still in the womb of his mother, as far as he pertains to human understanding, does not have being distinct from his mother, and thus it cannot happen by an act of man that he is either cleansed from original sin by baptism today, nor that he was cleansed by the faith of his parents back then: but he can be cleansed by divine power, as appears among those sanctified in the womb.

REPLY OBJ. 3: The efficacy of faith is not diminished, since all sacraments have their efficacy from faith, but there is something added to it that must be observed, even as the moral law is not of less efficacy for a religious than for someone living in the world (although the moral precepts are sufficient for salvation to the one living in the world), but in a religious there may be required counsels to which he obligated himself by his own choice.

---

151. *intensionis.—professionis* PLE.

Response to Quaestiuncula 3

AD TERTIAM QUAESTIONEM dicendum, quod illa sacramenta legis naturae non erant ex praecepto divino obligantia, sed ex voto celebrabantur, secundum quod unicuique dictabat sua mens, ut fidem suam aliis exteriori signo profiteretur ad honorem Dei, secundum quod habitus caritatis inclinabat ad exteriores actus; et sic dicimus de caritate quod sufficit motus interior. Quando autem tempus habet operandi, requiruntur etiam exteriores actus. Ita etiam quantum ad adultos in lege naturae sufficiebat sola fides, cum etiam modo sufficiat ei qui non ex contemptu sacramenta dimittit; sed ipsa fides, quando tempus habebatur, instigabat ut se aliquibus signis exterioribus demonstraret. Quando autem illa signa adhibebantur, non erat efficacia remissionis culpae ex illis exterioribus, sed ex interiori fide; et sic intelligenda sunt verba Gregorii.

ET PER HOC patet solutio ad objecta.

TO THE THIRD QUESTION, it should be said that those sacraments of the law of nature did not oblige by divine command, but were celebrated by choice, according as the mind of each dictated, so that each might profess his faith to others by external signs and do so for God's honor, according as the habit of charity inclined to external acts. And in this way we say of charity that an interior movement suffices. When, however, it has the opportunity to act, external acts are also required. So, too, for adults under the law of nature, faith alone sufficed, since also nowadays it would suffice for someone who, through no contempt, lacked the sacraments. But faith itself, when the opportunity arose, would agitate to demonstrate itself by some external signs. When those signs were displayed, however, the efficacy of the remission of fault was not from those exterior things, but from the interior faith; and this is how the words of Gregory are to be understood.

AND BY THIS the answers to the objections are clear.

EXPOSITION OF THE TEXT

In sinu Abrahae, sinus Abrahae dicitur limbus patrum, in quo distincti erant sancti ab aliis; et quia Abraham primus ab infidelibus loco et ritu se separasse legitur, ideo dicitur Abrahae sinus.

Lapideo cultro, intelligendum est non semper, sed in quibusdam notabilibus circumcisionibus, sicut legitur Exod. 4, et Josue 5.

In carne vero praeputii ideo jussa est fieri circumcisio, quia in remedium instituta est originalis peccati. Caro praeputii dicitur pellicula contegens carnem: quia in ipsa carne, ubi concupiscentia magis est, non poterat abscissio fieri sine periculo.

Tamen sub lege, ingruente necessitate mortis, ante octavum diem circumcidebant sine peccato filios. Magister hic loquitur secundum opinionem suam; tamen alia opinio quae supra posita est, videtur esse magis probabilis.

In the bosom of Abraham.[152] The bosom of Abraham is called the limbo of the fathers, in which the saints were set apart from all others; and because Abraham is said to have first separated himself from unbelievers by place and practice, it is called the bosom of Abraham.

With a stone knife[153] is to be understood not always as an element of the rite of circumcision but in certain notable circumcisions, as is read in Exodus 4 and Joshua 5.

And so circumcision was commanded to be done in the flesh of the prepuce because it was instituted as a remedy against original sin.[154] The flesh of the foreskin is called the skin protecting the flesh: for in flesh where concupiscence most resides no amputation could happen without danger.

But perhaps under the Law, if the necessity of death was pressing, they circumcised their sons before the eighth day without sin.[155] The Master here speaks according to his own opinion; however, the other opinion, which was set down above, seems to be more probable.

---

152. Peter Lombard, *Sententiae* IV, 1.7. 1 citing Bede, *Homeliarum evangelii libri duo*, bk1 hom.11.
153. *Sent.* IV, 1.9.4.
154. *Sent.* IV, 1.9. 3.
155. *Sent.* IV, 1.10.1.

DISTINCTION 2

SACRAMENTS OF THE NEW LAW

Postquam determinavit Magister de sacramentis in communi, hic descendit ad sacramenta novae legis, de quibus principaliter intendit; et dividitur in partes duas: in prima determinat de quibusdam quae praeexiguntur ad sacramenta novae legis; in secunda prosequitur de eis, 3 dist., ibi: *post hoc videndum est quid sit baptismus*. Prima dividitur in duas: in prima determinat quaedam quae praeexiguntur ad sacramenta novae legis ordine doctrinae; in secunda determinat de baptismo Joannis, quod praeexigebatur ad ea ut dispositio, sive praeparatio, ibi: *nunc autem de baptismi sacramento videamus*. Circa primum duo facit: primo ponit distinctionem sacramentorum novae legis et quantum ad numerum et quantum ad effectum; secundo ponit eorum institutionem, ibi: *si vero quaeratur*, etc. Ubi primo ponit communem sacramentorum novae legis institutionem; secundo excipit matrimonium quantum ad aliquid, ibi: *fuit tamen conjugium ante peccatum institutum*.

Nunc autem de baptismi sacramento videamus. Hic determinat de baptismo Joannis; et circa hoc duo facit: primo determinat de ipso baptismo secundum se; secundo de eo quantum ad suscipientes, ibi: *hic considerandum est*, etc. Circa primum duo facit: primo ostendit differentiam baptismi Joannis ad baptismum Christi; secundo ostendit quasdam conditiones baptismi Joannis; et primo utilitatem, ibi: *ad quid ergo utilis erat baptismus Joannis?* Secundo nomen, ibi: *sed quaeritur quare dictus est baptismus Joannis*; tertio genus, ibi: *si vero quaeritur an sacramentum fuerit, satis potest concedi*, etc. Hic est duplex quaestio. Primo de sacramentis novae legis in generali. Secundo de baptismo Joannis.

After having defined the sacraments in general, here the Master moves to the sacraments of the New Law, about which he is mainly concerned. And his treatment is divided into two parts: in the first, he examines certain prerequisites for the sacraments of the New Law; in the second, he pursues these, at: *after these matters, we must see what Baptism is*[1] (Dist. 3). The first is divided in two: in the first, he defines certain things that are prerequisites in the order of teaching the sacraments of the New Law; in the second, he examines the baptism of John, which was needed to dispose or prepare for them: *Now let us examine the sacrament of baptism.*[2] Concerning the first he does two things: first, he gives the distinction of the sacraments of the New Law both as to their number and as to their effect; second, he defines their institution, at: *If it is asked*, etc.[3] There, he first sets down the general institution of the sacraments of the New Law; second, he excepts matrimony in a certain respect, at: *Marriage, however, was instituted before sin.*[4]

But now let us examine the sacrament of baptism.[5] Here he examines the baptism of John; and about this he does two things: first, he considers that baptism in itself; second, in regard to those who received it, at: *Here it is to be considered*, etc.[6] Concerning the first he does two things: first, he shows the difference between the baptism of John and the baptism of Christ; second, he shows certain conditions of the baptism of John; and first, its benefit, at: *And so what was useful about John's baptism?*[7] Second, its name, at: *But it is asked why it is called John's baptism*;[8] third, its genus, at: *But if it is asked whether it was a sacrament, it may well be granted that it was*, etc.[9] Here there are two questions. First, concerning the sacraments of the New Law in general. Second, concerning the baptism of John.

---

1. Peter Lombard, *Sententiae* IV, 3.1 (17), 1.
2. *Sent.* IV, 2.2 (12), 1.
3. *Sent.* IV, 2.1 (11), 2.
4. *Sent.* IV, 2.1 (11), 3.
5. *Sent.* IV, 2.2 (12), 1.
6. *Sent.* IV, 2.6 (16), 1.
7. *Sent.* IV, 2.4 (14), 1.
8. *Sent.* IV, 2.4 (14), 2.
9. *Sent.* IV, 2.5 (15), 1.

QUESTION 1

SACRAMENTS OF THE NEW LAW

Circa primum quaeruntur quatuor:

primo, de distinctione sacramentorum quantum ad effectum;

secundo, de distinctione eorum quantum ad numerum;

tertio, de ordine ipsorum;

quarto, de institutione eorum.

About the first, four questions arise:

first, the distinction of the sacraments as to effect;

second, their distinction as to number;

third, their order;

fourth, their institution.

ARTICLE 1

The distinction of the sacraments as to effect

Quaestiuncula 1

AD PRIMUM SIC PROCEDITUR. Videtur quod non omnia sacramenta sint instituta in remedium contra aliquem animae defectum. Sacramentum enim a sanctitate dicitur. Sed sanctitas non semper importat remedium contra defectum, sed etiam confirmationem in bono. Ergo non omne sacramentum est ad remedium institutum.

PRAETEREA, omne remedium contra aliquem defectum ad purgationem pertinet. Sed Dionysius, distinguit sacramenta quae pertinent ad perfectionem, scilicet confirmationem et Eucharistiam, ab illis quae pertinent ad purgationem, sicut est baptismus. Ergo non omne sacramentum est ad remedium.

PRAETEREA, hoc videtur ex definitione quam Magister ponit in littera. Quibusdam enim attribuit remedium conferre et gratiam, sicut baptismo; quibusdam gratiam tantum, sicut confirmationi et ordini; matrimonio autem remedii collationem tantum. Ergo non omne sacramentum est ad remedium institutum.

SED CONTRA est quod Hugo de sancto Victore dicit, quod sacramenta sunt vasa medicinalia. Sed omnis medicina est in remedium alicujus morbi. Ergo et omne sacramentum est in remedium alicujus defectus spiritualis.

PRAETEREA, sacramenta, ut dictum est, dist. 1, quaest. 1, art. 4, quaestiunc. 1, habent efficaciam a passione Christi. Sed passio Christi directe ordinatur ad tol-

OBJ. 1: To the first we proceed thus. It seems that not all sacraments were instituted as a remedy against some defect of the soul.[10] For a sacrament is named from sanctity. But sanctity does not always convey a remedy against a defect, but also confirmation in good. Therefore, not every sacrament was instituted as a remedy.

OBJ. 2: Furthermore, every remedy against a certain defect pertains to purgation. But Dionysius distinguishes sacraments that pertain to perfection, namely confirmation and Eucharist, from those that pertain to purgation, such as baptism.[11] Therefore, not every sacrament is a remedy.

OBJ. 3: Furthermore, this is seen in the definition that the Master gives in the text. For he attributes to certain sacraments, like baptism, the conferral of a remedy as well as grace; to others, like confirmation and holy orders, only the conferral of grace; while to marriage, only the conferral of a remedy. Therefore, not every sacrament was instituted as a remedy.

ON THE CONTRARY, is what Hugh of St. Victor says, that sacraments are vessels of medicine.[12] But every medicine is a remedy for some sickness. Therefore, every sacrament, too, is a remedy for some spiritual defect.

FURTHERMORE, as was said in Distinction 1, Question 1, Article 4, Subquestion 1, sacraments have efficacy from the Passion of Christ. But the Passion of Christ is ordered

---

10. Parallels: *ST* III, q. 65, a. 1, corp. and ad 3.
11. Pseudo-Dionysius, *Ecclesiastical Hierarchy*, ch. 1, pt. 1, n. 3 (PG 3:503).
12. Hugh of St. Victor, *De sacramentis fidei*, Bk. 1, pt. 9, ch. 3 (PL 176:319).

lendos defectus nostros. Ergo et sacramenta in remedium ordinata sunt.

directly to taking away our defects. Therefore, the sacraments are also ordered to being a remedy.

Quaestiuncula 2

ULTERIUS. Videtur quod aliquod sacramentum sit tantum in remedium, scilicet matrimonium. Solus enim consensus mutuus matrimonium facit. Sed consensus non potest esse causa gratiae, quia gratia non est ex actibus nostris. Ergo in matrimonio gratia non confertur; et sic est in remedium tantum.

PRAETEREA, secundum Hugonem, sacramenta ex sanctificatione invisibilem gratiam continent. Sed sanctificatio quae fit per ministros ecclesiae, non est de essentia matrimonii quantum ad sacramenti necessitatem, sed solum est de solemnitate ipsius. Ergo non confertur ibi gratia; et sic idem quod prius.

PRAETEREA, hoc Magister expresse in littera dicit.

SED CONTRA, definitio generis debet omnibus speciebus convenire. Sed in definitione sacramenti novae legis ponitur: *ut causa gratiae existat.* Ergo convenit matrimonio; et sic non est tantum in remedium.

OBJ. 1: Moreover, it seems that one sacrament is a remedy only, namely, marriage.[13] For mutual consent alone makes a marriage. But consent cannot be a cause of grace, for grace is not from our acts. Therefore, in marriage grace is not conferred, and so it is only a remedy.

OBJ. 2: Furthermore, according to Hugh, sacraments, by their sanctification, contain invisible grace.[14] But the sanctification done by the ministers of the Church is not of the essence of marriage as necessary for the sacrament, but belongs only to its solemnity.[15] Therefore, no grace is conferred there, and so the same as above.

OBJ. 3: Furthermore, the Master expressly says this in the text.

ON THE CONTRARY, the definition of the genus must apply to all species. But in the definition of sacrament of the New Law is included *that it exists as a cause of grace.* Therefore, it belongs to marriage; and so it is not a remedy only.

Quaestiuncula 3

ULTERIUS. Videtur quod sacramenta non sint in remedium contra poenam, sed solum contra culpam. Sacramenta enim efficaciam habent ex hoc quod gratiam continent. Sed gratia non opponitur poenae, sed culpae. Ergo sacramenta non ordinantur in remedium contra poenam.

PRAETEREA, sapientis medici est per causam curare effectum. Sed causa poenae est culpa. Ergo cum Christus sit sapientissimus medicus, non instituit aliqua sacramenta ad curandum poenam, nisi ea quae curant et culpam.

SED CONTRA, extrema unctio contra infirmitatem videtur ordinari, ut patet Jac. ult. Sed infirmitas poena est. Cum ergo extrema unctio sit sacramentum, aliquod sacramentum ordinabitur contra poenam, et non tantum contra culpam.

OBJ. 1: Moreover, it seems that sacraments are not a remedy against punishment, but only against the fault itself. For sacraments have efficacy from the fact that they contain grace. But grace is not opposed to punishment, but to fault. Therefore, sacraments are not ordained as a remedy against punishment.

OBJ. 2: Furthermore, the effect of a wise physician is to cure something through its cause. But the cause of punishment is fault. Therefore, since Christ is the wisest physician, he did not institute certain sacraments to cure punishment, except those that also cure the fault.

ON THE CONTRARY, extreme unction seems to be ordained against illness, as is clear from the end of the letter of James.[16] But illness is a punishment. Therefore, since extreme unction is a sacrament, there is a sacrament that is ordained against a punishment, and not only against fault.

---

13. Parallels: below, d. 26, q. 2, a. 3, corp. and ad 4.
14. Hugh of St. Victor, *De sacramentis fidei*, Bk. 1, pt. 9, ch. 2 (PL 176:317).
15. The *sanctificatio* referred to here is the nuptial blessing given by the priest during the ceremony.
16. See James 5:14.

Quaestiuncula 4

Ulterius. Videtur quod aliquod sacramentum ordinetur contra culpam venialem. Quaedam enim sacramenta sunt nociva, nisi deposito mortali accipiantur, sicut patet de Eucharistia et de ordine. Sed dantur in remedium alicujus culpae. Ergo dantur contra venialem.

Praeterea, medicina spiritualis magis debet apponi contra culpam quam contra poenam. Sed peccatum veniale culpa aliqua est. Cum ergo aliqua sacramenta ordinentur contra poenam, multo fortius videtur quod aliquod possit ordinari contra culpam venialem.

Sed contra, poenitentia ordinatur contra mortale et veniale peccatum; quod patet per Magistrum qui infra, dist. 6, determinat de poenitentia venialium, et Augustinum in Lib. de Poenitentia. Sed poenitentia sufficit contra mortale nec aliud sacramentum contra mortale ordinatur. Ergo multo magis sufficit contra veniale; nec oportet aliquod sacramentum speciale contra veniale ordinari.

Obj. 1: Moreover, it seems that there is a sacrament ordained against venial sin.[17] For certain sacraments are harmful unless they are received by someone free from mortal sin, as is evident in the Eucharist and holy orders. But these are given to remedy some fault. Therefore, they are given against venial sin.

Obj. 2: Furthermore, spiritual medicine should be applied against fault rather than against punishment. But venial sin is a certain fault. Since, then, certain sacraments are ordered against punishment, it seems that much more should some sacrament be ordered against venial sin.

On the contrary, penance is ordered against mortal and venial sin, which is clear from what the Master says below (Dist. 6), where he discusses the confession of venial sins, and from Augustine in the book *On Penance*.[18] But penance suffices against mortal sin, nor is there any other sacrament ordained against mortal sin. Therefore, much more does it suffice against venial sin; nor is it necessary for any special sacrament to be ordained against venial sin.

Response to Quaestiuncula 1

Respondeo dicendum, ad primam quaestionem, quod quandocumque ad perfectionem alicujus rei oportet aliquid apponere ultra id quod requirit ordo illius naturae secundum se consideratae hoc accidit ad subveniendum alicui defectui illius rei; sicut quando ad sustentationem corporis non sufficit cibum ministrare, nisi addantur aliqua digestiva, signum est defectus in virtute digerente. Ex ordine autem humanae naturae nihil aliud requiritur ad ejus perfectionem spiritualem, nisi Deus influens, et gratia, et virtutes influxae. Unde cum aliquae res corporales adhibentur ad hominis sanctificationem ex quibus secundum ordinem naturae sanctificatio hominis non dependet, signum est quod hoc sit ad subveniendum alicui defectui ipsius; et ideo cum hoc inveniatur in omnibus sacramentis, omnia sacramenta in remedium alicujus spiritualis defectus instituta sunt.

Ad primum ergo dicendum, quod ex hoc ipso quod ad sanctitatem homo perducitur per ea quae naturae secundum se consideratae ordo non requirit, signum est quod alicui defectui remedium adhibetur. Unde quamvis sacramenta ex ratione sanctificationis non habeant quod sint in remedium, habent tamen hoc ex officio, sive ex modo sanctificandi.

Ad secundum dicendum, quod defectus spiritualis dupliciter contingit, sicut et corporalis. Uno modo ex positione contrarii, sicut quando corpus est aegrum,

To the first question, I answer that whenever the perfection of some thing necessitates applying something beyond what the order of its nature requires, considered in itself, this happens to supply some defect of the thing; as when, for the sustenance of the body, it is insufficient to administer food unless some kind of digestives are added, this is a sign of a defect in the power of digestion. But by the order of human nature nothing else is required for its spiritual perfection, except God flowing in, and grace, and the infused virtues. Hence when certain corporeal things are applied for man's sanctification on which, according to the order of nature, man's sanctification does not depend, it is a sign that this is for the repairing of some defect in him; and thus, since this is found in all the sacraments, all the sacraments were instituted as a remedy for some spiritual defect.

Reply Obj. 1: The very fact that man is led to sanctity by things that the order of nature considered in itself does not require is a sign that a remedy is applied for some defect. Hence although sacraments are not considered remedies under the account of sanctification, they are nevertheless considered such *ex officio*, or in their mode of sanctifying.

Reply Obj. 2: A spiritual defect happens in two ways, just as a physical one does. One way is by the intrusion of a contrary, as when a body is sick, and when there is sin

---

17. Parallels: below, d. 16, q. 1, a. 2, qa. 3, ad 1; d. 17, q. 3, a. 3, qa. 3, ad 2; *ST* III, q. 65, a. 1, ad 8; *De Malo*, q. 7, a. 11, ad 14.
18. Augustine, *Sermon* 352, ch. 2 (PL 39:1556).

et quando in anima est peccatum. Alio modo ex subtractione ejus quod ad perfectionem necessarium erat vel corporis vel animae; sicut quando corpus est debile ad exercenda corporalia opera, et similiter quando spiritus ad exequenda spiritualia. Remedia ergo quae dantur contra primum defectum, aliquid realiter tollunt; et ideo purgationis rationem habent. Remedia autem quae sunt contra defectum secundum, non tollunt aliquid secundum rem, sed solum aliquid adjiciunt ad perfectionem; et ideo talia remedia non dicuntur purgare, sed perficere. Et haec eadem sunt quae Magister dicit nos gratia et virtute fulcire inquantum perfectiva sunt; nihilominus tamen in remedium alicujus defectus sunt.

UNDE PATET solutio ad tertium.

in the soul. The other way is by the removal of something that was necessary for the perfection of either the body or the soul; as when a body is weak in carrying out physical work, and likewise when the spirit is weak in accomplishing spiritual things. Therefore, the remedies that are given against the first kind of defect remove something in reality; and thus they have the account of purgation. But the remedies that are against the second defect do not remove anything according to reality, but only contribute something toward perfection; and so remedies like this are not said to purge but to perfect. And these are the same that the Master says bolster us in grace and virtue, as they are perfective; but they are a remedy for some defect nevertheless.

AND THUS the solution to the third objection is clear.

Response to Quaestiuncula 2

AD SECUNDAM QUAESTIONEM dicendum, quod circa hoc sunt duae opiniones. Una est quod in matrimonio gratia aliqua non confertur; sed tantummodo sit in remedium contra concupiscentiam.

Hoc autem non videtur convenienter dictum: quia aut intelligitur esse in remedium concupiscentiae, quasi concupiscentiam reprimens, quod sine gratia esse non potest: aut quasi concupiscentiae in parte satisfaciens, quod quidem facit ex ipsa natura actus, non intellecta etiam ratione sacramenti; et praeterea concupiscentia non reprimitur per hoc quod ei satisfit, sed magis augetur, ut Philosophus dicit in 3 *Ethic.*: aut inquantum excusat concupiscentiae actum; quod sine matrimonio deformis esset; et hoc quidem facit per bona matrimonii quae ei conveniunt etiam inquantum est in officium, et ratione suae sanctificationis,[20] cum qua communicat cum sacramentis veteris legis; et ita per hoc non haberet aliquid prae illis, ut cum sacramentis novae legis computari debeat.

Et propter hoc alii dicunt, quod matrimonium consideratur in triplici statu. Primo ante peccatum et tunc erat tantum in officium. Secundo sub lege, ubi ex ipsa sanctificatione sua excusabilem reddebat matrimonii actum, qui absque hoc turpis fuisset. Tertio sub statu gratiae, ubi ulterius gratiam confert ad concupiscentiam reprimendam, ut scilicet unusquisque possideat vas suum in honorem, et non in contumeliam, sicut et gentes quae ignorant Deum, 1 Thessal. 4, et Tob. 6, dicitur, quod in illis qui in timore Dei uxores accipiunt et amore filiorum ad cultum Dei magis quam amore libidinis, daemon potestatem non habet.

TO THE SECOND QUESTION, it should be said that concerning this there are two opinions. One is that in marriage no grace is conferred, but it is merely a remedy against concupiscence.

But this does not seem to be fittingly said: for it is understood to be a remedy against concupiscence either by repressing it, which cannot happen without grace; or by satisfying concupiscence in part, which the act does indeed by its very nature, even when not understood under the account of sacrament (and furthermore, concupiscence is not repressed by satisfying it, but rather it is increased, as the Philosopher says in *Ethics* 3[19]); or else it excuses the act of concupiscence, which would be deformed without marriage; and this it does indeed through the goods of marriage which belong to it even as it is an office of nature, as well as under the account of its signification, which it shares with the sacraments of the Old Law. And in this way it would not have anything above those sacraments so that it should be counted among the sacraments of the New Law.

And because of this, others say that marriage is considered in three states. The first was before sin, and at that time it was only an office. The second was under the law, when by its own sanctification it rendered the marriage act excusable, which would have been disgraceful otherwise. The third is under the state of grace, where, moreover, it confers the grace to repress concupiscence so that each one may possess his own vessel in honor, not in reproach, like the gentiles who do not know God (cf. 1 Thess 4); and it is said (cf. Tob 6:17) that among those who, in the fear of God, take wives from the desire for children to raise to the worship of God rather than the love of sexual pleasure, the devil does not have power.

---

19. Aristotle, *Nicomachean Ethics*, Bk. 3, ch. 15, 1119b8–10.
20. *sanctificationis.—significationis* PLE.

AD PRIMUM ergo dicendum, quod sicut res corporales quae sunt in aliis sacramentis non habent ut propria virtute gratiam conferre possint, sed ex institutione divina, ita etiam est de illis quae matrimonium causant, quae ex ipsa institutione divina habent quod ad gratiam instrumentaliter disponant, nisi sit defectus ex parte nostra.

AD SECUNDUM dicendum, quod quaedam sacramenta sunt ad quorum efficaciam praeexigitur sanctificatio materiae, ut patet in confirmatione vel extrema unctione; quaedam vero non praeexigunt praedictam sanctificationem, sicut patet in baptismo. Unde benedictio materiae quae fit a ministro, non est de necessitate, sed de solemnitate sacramenti; et similiter est etiam de matrimonio.

AD TERTIUM dicendum, quod unumquodque denominatur ab eo ad quod est. Gratia autem quae in matrimonio confertur, secundum quod est sacramentum ecclesiae in fide Christi celebratum, ordinatur directe ad reprimendum concupiscentiam, quae concurrit ad actum matrimonii; et ideo Magister dicit, quod matrimonium est tantum in remedium; sed hoc est per gratiam quae in eo confertur.

REPLY OBJ. 1: Just as the physical things that are in the other sacraments do not have the power to confer grace by their own strength, but by divine institution, so it is also with those that cause marriage, which have from that very divine institution the ability to distribute grace instrumentally, unless there is a defect on our part.

REPLY OBJ. 2: There are certain sacraments whose efficacy requires a prior sanctification of the matter, as is evident in confirmation and extreme unction; but certain ones do not require such a sanctification, as is evident in baptism. Hence the blessing of the matter done by the minister is not of necessity for the sacrament, but is rather for the sacrament's solemnity; and it is the same way with marriage.

REPLY OBJ. 3: Each thing is named from what it is for. But the grace that is conferred in marriage, according as it is a sacrament of the Church celebrated in the faith of Christ, is ordered directly to repressing concupiscence, which coincides with the marital act; and this is why the Master says that marriage is a remedy only, but this through the grace that is conferred in it.

Response to Quaestiuncula 3

AD TERTIAM QUAESTIONEM dicendum, quod duplex est poena peccati. Quaedam quae pro peccato infligitur, sicut poena inferni, et flagella quibus a Deo temporaliter punimur; quaedam ex ipso peccato consequens immediate, et per consequens ad peccatum ordinans, sicut est debilitatio naturae ad resistendum peccato, et hujusmodi. Contra primam ergo poenam non datur sacramentum in remedium directe, sed ex consequenti, ut scilicet curata causa, scilicet peccato, cesset effectus, scilicet poena; sed contra secundam poenam datur directe aliquod sacramentum, illa scilicet quae in remedium sunt contra defectum contingentem ex subtractione necessarii, non ex positione contrarii.

AD PRIMUM ergo dicendum, quod poenae contra quas dictum est sacramentum ordinari, etiam ad gratiam contrarietatem habent: quia ex subtractione contingunt, et in contrarium gratiae ordinant.

AD SECUNDUM dicendum, quod sicut est in medicina corporali, quod curato morbo adhuc remanent aliquae reliquiae morbi ex morbo causatae, contra quas oportet specialia medicamenta dari, ita etiam est in medicina spirituali; et propter hoc contra praedictas poenas oportet esse aliqua sacramenta.

TO THE THIRD QUESTION, it should be said that suffering for sin is twofold. Some is imposed for sin, such as the suffering of hell and the scourges by which we are temporally punished by God; some following immediately upon the sin itself, and ordering to sin as a result, such as the weakening of nature in resisting sin, and things like that. Therefore, a sacrament is not given as a remedy against the first kind directly, but by way of consequence—namely, so that by having cured the cause, which is sin, the effect would cease, which is suffering. But against the second kind of suffering a certain sacrament is given directly, namely those that are remedies against defects occurring when something necessary is taken away, not those that introduce a contrary.

REPLY OBJ. 1: The sufferings against which a sacrament was said to be ordained are also contrary to grace: for they occur by taking something away and they are ordered to the contrary of grace.

REPLY OBJ. 2: Just as in bodily medicine, where once a disease is cured certain vestiges of the disease caused by it remain, against which special medicaments must be given, so also is it in spiritual medicine; and because of this there must be certain sacraments against the sufferings mentioned.

Response to Quaestiuncula 4

AD QUARTAM QUAESTIONEM dicendum, quod circa hoc est duplex opinio. Quidam enim dicunt, aliqua sacramenta in remedium venialis dari, sicut Eucharistiam, et extremam unctionem.

Sed hoc non videtur convenienter dictum: quia poenitentia purgativa est universaliter omnis peccati actualis, mortalis et venialis; unde ad hoc non oportebat aliquod sacramentum institui. Et praeterea etiam non existentibus venialibus, adhuc necessitas illorum sacramentorum esset ad consummandum in bonum, secundum doctrinam Dionysii.

Et ideo aliter dicendum, quod contra veniale non ordinatur aliquod sacramentum ad curationem ipsius principaliter institutum, quamvis ex consequenti multa sacramenta, contra venialia valeant. Veniale enim et culpa est, et dispositio ad culpam, imperfectam tamen rationem habens culpae, ita quod gratiam non excludit. Et ideo inquantum culpa est, potest tolli per omnia sacramenta quae contra culpam tollendam ordinantur; inquantum vero est dispositio ad culpam, ex ablata mortali culpa remanens, potest tolli etiam per sacramenta illa quae contra poenam ex culpa relictam et ad culpam inclinantem ordinantur.

AD PRIMUM ergo dicendum, quod illa sacramenta quae gratiam in suscipiente praeexigunt, non ordinantur directe contra culpam: quia non sunt ad tollendum contrarium, sed ad supplendum defectum.

AD SECUNDUM dicendum, quod sacramentum quod tollit mortalem culpam, sufficit etiam ad tollendum venialem; et ideo contra veniale non oportet aliquod sacramentum dari, sicut contra reliquias culpae, ad quarum ablationem poenitentia non ex toto sufficit sine aliis sacramentis.

TO THE FOURTH QUESTION, it should be said that concerning this there are two opinions. For some people say that certain sacraments are given as a remedy for venial sin, like the Eucharist, and extreme unction.

But this does not seem to be fittingly said: for penance is purgative of all actual sin, mortal and venial; hence for this end [viz., to purge venial sin], it was not necessary that a sacrament be instituted. And furthermore, even were there no venial sins, still those sacraments would be necessary for consummation in good, according to the doctrine of Dionysius.[21]

And thus it should be said otherwise that against venial sin there is not ordained any sacrament instituted chiefly for its cure, although many sacraments avail against venial sins by way of result. For venial sin is both a fault and a disposition to fault—though having an incomplete account of fault, so that it does not exclude grace. And thus, to the extent that it is a fault, it can be taken away by all the sacraments that are ordered to the removal of fault; but to the extent that it is a disposition to fault remaining from the mortal fault that has been taken away, it can be removed also by those sacraments that are ordered against the punishment left behind by fault and inclining one to fault.

REPLY OBJ. 1: Those sacraments that require grace to exist in the recipient are not ordered directly against fault; for they are not for removing a contrary, but for supplying a lack.

REPLY OBJ. 2: The sacrament that takes away mortal fault suffices also for removing venial sin; and thus no sacrament needed to be given against venial sin in the way that one needed to be given against the vestiges of fault, for whose removal penance does not entirely suffice without other sacraments.

---

21. See Pseudo-Dionysius, *Ecclesiastical Hierarchy*, ch. 3.

ARTICLE 2

The distinction of the sacraments as to number[22]

AD SECUNDUM SIC PROCEDITUR. Videtur quod non debeant esse septem sacramenta. Sicut enim supra dictum est, omnia sacramenta efficaciam habent a passione Christi. Sed unum est sacramentum quod directe est repraesentativum passionis Christi, et ipsum totum Christum continet, scilicet Eucharistia. Ergo illud sacramentum sufficeret.

PRAETEREA, quod potest fieri per unum, non debet fieri per plura. Sed per baptismum tolluntur omnia peccata. Ergo non oportebat quod aliquod aliud sacramentum contra culpam ordinaretur.

PRAETEREA, sacramenta in remedium contra defectum ordinantur. Sed duplex est defectus, scilicet culpae, quae est quasi contrarium, et poenae, quae ex defectu gratiae accidit, ut dictum est. Ergo duo sacramenta sufficerent.

PRAETEREA, in lege nova, ubi manifestior est veritas, minimum debet esse de figuris. Sed in lege naturae, secundum Hugonem, erant tantum tria sacramenta, scilicet oblationes, decimae et sacrificia. Ergo non debent esse plura sacramenta in lege nova quam tria.

PRAETEREA, sacramenta legalia nostrorum sacramentorum figurae fuerunt. Sed ipsi non habuerunt aliqua sacramenta respondentia confirmationi et extremae unctioni. Ergo nec nos hujusmodi sacramenta habere debemus.

PRAETEREA, Dionysius in *Eccl. Hierar.*, ubi de sacramentis tractat, matrimonium et poenitentiam omittit. Ergo videtur quod non sint nisi quinque sacramenta.

SED CONTRA, videtur quod sint plura. Omne enim illud quod in remedium peccati datur, videtur esse sacramentum. Sed aqua benedicta est hujusmodi, quia per eam venialia tolluntur. Ergo est sacramentum.

PRAETEREA, sicut circa concupiscentiam quae est in venereis, contingit esse peccatum intemperantiae; ita circa concupiscentiam quae est in cibis et potibus. Sed contra primam concupiscentiam habemus unum sacramentum. Ergo et contra secundam habere debemus.

PRAETEREA, Dionysius, inter sacramenta nominat monasticam consummationem, sive consecrationem. Sed non computatur inter septem sacramenta hic enumerata. Ergo sunt plura quam septem.

OBJ. 1: It seems that there should not be seven sacraments. For as was said above, all sacraments have efficacy from the Passion of Christ. But there is one sacrament which is directly representative of the Passion of Christ, and which contains the whole Christ, namely, the Eucharist. Therefore, that sacrament would suffice.

OBJ. 2: Furthermore, what can be done by one thing should not be done by many. But by baptism all sins are taken away. Therefore, it was not necessary that any other sacrament be ordered against fault.

OBJ. 3: Furthermore, sacraments are ordered as a remedy against a defect. But there are two kinds of defect, namely fault, which is a sort of contrary, and punishment, which happens from a defect of grace, as has been said. Therefore, two sacraments would suffice.

OBJ. 4: Furthermore, in the New Law, where truth is more manifest, there should be a minimum of figures. But in the law of nature, according to Hugh of St. Victor,[23] there were only three sacraments, namely offerings, tithes, and sacrifices. Therefore, there should not be more than three sacraments in the New Law.

OBJ. 5: Furthermore, sacraments of the law were figures of our sacraments. But they did not have any sacraments corresponding to confirmation and extreme unction. Therefore, neither should we have those sacraments.

OBJ. 6: Furthermore, Dionysius, when he treats the sacraments in the *Ecclesiastical Hierarchy*, omits marriage and penance.[24] Therefore, it seems that there are only five sacraments.

ON THE CONTRARY, it seems that there are more than seven. For everything that is given in remedy for sin seems to be a sacrament. But holy water is this kind of thing, since venial sins are taken away by it. Therefore, it is a sacrament.

FURTHERMORE, just as from concupiscence in sexual matters the sin of intemperance arises, so also from concupiscence in food and drink. But against the first concupiscence we have one sacrament. Therefore, we should also have one against the second.

FURTHERMORE, Dionysius[25] names among the sacraments monastic consummation or consecration. But that is not counted among the seven sacraments enumerated here. Therefore, there are more than seven.

---

22. Parallels: *ST* III, q. 65, a. 1; *SCG* IV, ch. 58; *De eccles. sacram.*

23. Hugh of St. Victor, *De sacramentis fidei*, Bk. 1, pt. 11, ch. 3 (PL 176:343).

24. This is evident simply by looking at what the chapters of the *Ecclesiastical Hierarchy* cover: 1. church hierarchy; 2. baptism; 3. the Eucharist; 4. anointing; 5. holy orders; 6. the orders of those being initiated; 7. the rite for the dead.

25. Pseudo-Dionysius, *Ecclesiastical Hierarchy*, ch. 6, p. 3 (PG 3:534).

PRAETEREA, oblationes et decimae in lege naturae erant sacramenta, secundum Hugonem. Cum ergo modo sint oblationes et decimae, videtur quod sint sacramenta; et sic idem quod prius.

PRAETEREA, sacramenta ex sanctificatione invisibilem gratiam continent, secundum Hugonem. Sed multae sunt sanctificationes per ministros ecclesiae factae quae hic non numerantur, sicut consecratio templi et altaris et sacrarum vestium, et hujusmodi. Ergo sunt plura sacramenta.

RESPONDEO dicendum, quod sacramenta ex hoc quod sunt sacramenta, habent quod sint in remedium contra defectum aliquem; ex hoc autem quod sacramenta ecclesiae, habent per ministros ecclesiae dispensari, et in membra ecclesiae transfundi. Et ideo dupliciter potest accipi numerus sacramentorum proprie.

Primo ex defectibus contra quos sacramenta ordinantur. Ordinantur autem sacramenta, ut ex dictis patet, ad tollendum contrarium, et ad supplendum defectum. Contrarium autem sanctitati est culpa: quae quidem dupliciter tollitur. Uno modo, impediendo ne fiat; et hoc modo in remedium culpae matrimonium ordinatur. Alio modo subtrahendo jam existentem; et sic contra originalem culpam ordinatur baptismus, contra actualem poenitentia.

Secundum remedium praebent supplendo quod deficit, et ea quae perfectionis sunt effectiva. Est autem duplex perfectio. Una formae ad actum; et hanc quidem perfectionem facit ordo quantum ad executionem bonorum, quia reddit hominem idoneum ad dispensationem sacramentorum; sed quantum ad perpessionem difficilium facit dictam perfectionem confirmatio, quae hominem fortem reddit, ut nomen Christi propter pressuras mundi confiteri non refugiat. Alia autem perfectio est in ordine ad finem, ad quem per actus pervenitur; et hanc quidem perfectionem quantum ad finem intra facit extrema unctio, quae est quaedam delibutio praeparans in gloriam resurrectionis; quantum vero ad finem extra facit Eucharistia, quae membra capiti conjungit. Et quia hic est ultimus terminus nostrae sanctificationis, ideo dicit Dionysius, quod omnis alia sanctificatio in Eucharistiam terminatur: quia et ordinati et baptizati Eucharistiam sumunt.

Si autem considerantur sacramenta ut sunt ecclesiae sacramenta, scilicet per ministros ecclesiae dispensanda, sic potest secundum doctrinam Dionysii, hoc modo numerus eorum accipi. In qualibet enim hierarchia oportet esse actionem hierarchicam, et exercentes eam, et recipientes. Recipientes autem per ipsas actiones superio-

FURTHERMORE, offerings and tithes were sacraments under the law of nature, according to Hugh.[26] Therefore, since there are offerings and tithes today, it seems that these are sacraments; and so, the same conclusion as above.

FURTHERMORE, sacraments contain invisible grace by their sanctification, according to Hugh.[27] But there are many sanctifications done by the ministers of the Church that are not numbered here, like the consecration of a temple and an altar and of sacred vestments, and the like. Therefore, there are more sacraments.

I ANSWER THAT, sacraments, considered as sacraments, can be a remedy against a certain defect; but considered as sacraments of the Church, they can be dispensed by the ministers of the Church, and passed on to the members of the Church. And thus the number of the sacraments can be taken properly in two ways.

First, from the defects against which the sacraments are ordered. But the sacraments are ordered, as is clear from what has been said, to the removal of a contrary and to the supplying of a lack. Now the contrary to holiness is fault, which is taken away in two ways. In one way, by preventing it from happening; and in this way matrimony is ordered to the remedy of fault. In another way, by taking away what already exists, and so baptism is ordered against original sin while penance is ordered against actual sin.

They provide the second kind of remedy by supplying what is lacking, and those things that are effective of perfection. But there are two kinds of perfection. One is the perfection of form to act, and holy orders causes this kind of perfection with respect to the execution of goods, for it renders a man suited to dispensing the sacraments; but as to withstanding difficulties, confirmation causes this perfection, for it makes a man strong, so that he may not shirk from confessing the name of Christ because of the pressures of the world. But the other perfection is in the order to the end, at which one arrives by acts; and extreme unction, which is a certain anointing preparing one for the glory of resurrection, works this perfection toward the end within; but the Eucharist, which joins members to the head, does this with respect to the external end. And because this is the last end of our sanctification, for this reason Dionysius says that all other sanctification finds its end in the Eucharist— for both ordained ministers and the baptized consume the Eucharist.[28]

But if the sacraments are considered as sacraments of the Church—namely, to be dispensed by ministers of the Church—then this is how their number can be taken according to the teaching of Dionysius.[29] For in any hierarchy there must be hierarchical action, both those doing it and those receiving it. But those receiving are perfected

---

26. Hugh of St. Victor, *De sacramentis fidei*, Bk. 1, pt. 11, ch. 3 (PL 176:343).
27. Hugh of St. Victor, *De sacramentis fidei*, Bk. 1, pt. 9, ch. 2 (PL 176:317).
28. Pseudo-Dionysius, *Ecclesiastical Hierarchy*, chs. 2 and 3 (PG:391ff.).
29. Pseudo-Dionysius, *Ecclesiastical Hierarchy*, ch. 5, n. 3 (PG 3:503).

rum in suis gradibus perficiuntur; et ideo ex parte eorum non debet esse aliquod speciale sacramentum, per quod receptivi sacramentorum fiant. Actio autem hierarchica est triplex scilicet purgare, illuminare, perficere. Sed quia nullum sacramentum novae legis purgat sine gratiae infusione, quae illuminatio dicitur; ideo Dionysius in sacramentis conjungit purgationem illuminationi. Potest autem esse in sacramentis purgatio vel a culpa; et sic habet purgativam et illuminativam vim quantum ad originale baptismus, quantum ad actuale poenitentia; vel a reliquiis culpae, et sic extrema unctio purgare habet; vel a causa culpae, quae est concupiscentia, et sic matrimonium, quod eam reprimit et ordinat, vim purgativam habet. Perfectio autem est duplex scilicet perfectio formae, et ad hanc est confirmatio, quae hominem in seipso consistere facit, ut a contrariis non facile solvatur; et perfectio finis, et ad hanc est Eucharistia, quae nos fini conjungit. Ex parte autem exercentium actiones hierarchicas accipitur unum sacramentum, scilicet ordo, per quem ministri ecclesiae ponuntur in statu exercendi hierarchicas actiones.

Potest et aliter accipi numerus sacramentorum secundum conditionem eorum quibus per sacramenta subvenitur. Sunt enim sacramenta in remedium data. Aut igitur in remedium unius personae, aut totius ecclesiae. Si primo modo, aut quantum ad ingressum, et sic est baptismus; aut quantum ad egressum, et sic est extrema unctio; aut quantum ad progressum, et hoc est dupliciter. Uno modo quantum ad executionem virtutis, vel ut a malis non superemur, et quantum ad hoc est confirmatio, vel ut bonis adhaereamus, et quantum ad hoc est Eucharistia. Alio modo quantum ad reparationem virtutis, si ipsam in pugna spirituali aliquo modo laedi contingit, et sic est poenitentia. Si in remedium totius ecclesiae, aut in regimen et multiplicationem ipsius spiritualem, et sic est ordo, quia principatus bonum multitudinis est secundum Philosophum in 5 *Ethic.*, aut quantum ad multiplicationem materialem fidelium, et sic est matrimonium.

Quidam autem accipiunt numerum sacramentorum secundum adaptationem ad virtutes, ut fidei respondeat baptismus, quod sacramentum fidei dicitur; spei extrema unctio, per quam homo praeparatur quodammodo ad futuram gloriam; caritati Eucharistia; prudentiae ordo; justitiae poenitentia; temperantiae matrimonium; fortitudini confirmatio.

Quidam vero adaptant diversis generibus culparum et poenarum; ut baptismus sit contra culpam originalem, poenitentia contra actualem mortalem, extrema unctio contra venialem, ordo contra ignorantiam, matrimonium contra concupiscentiam, confirmatio contra infirmitatem, Eucharistia contra malitiam, quia est

through the very actions of those higher up; and thus on their part there need be no special sacrament by which they become receptive of the sacraments. Now hierarchical action is threefold, namely, to purify, to illuminate, and to perfect. But because no sacrament of the New Law purifies without the infusion of grace, which is called illumination, for this reason Dionysius joins purification to illumination in the sacraments. But purification in the sacraments can either be from fault, and thus baptism has purgative and illuminative force against original sin, while penance has it against actual sin; or it can be from the vestiges of fault, and extreme unction can purify from this; or it can be from the cause of fault, which is concupiscence, and then marriage, which represses and orders it, has purgative force. But there are two kinds of perfection, namely perfection of form, and for this there is confirmation, which makes a man stand fast in himself, so that he is not easily undone by adversaries; and perfection of end, and for this there is the Eucharist, which joins us to our end. But on the part of those performing hierarchical actions, one sacrament is taken, namely, holy orders, by which the ministers of the Church are placed in a state to perform hierarchical actions.

The number of the sacraments can also be taken according to the condition of those who are helped by the sacraments. For there are sacraments given as remedies—either a remedy for one person, or for the whole Church. If the first, then either for entering, and this is baptism, or for departing, and this is extreme unction, or for progressing, and this is twofold. One way, for the execution of virtue, or so that we are not overcome by evils, and for this there is confirmation; or that we adhere to good things, and for this there is the Eucharist. Another way, to repair virtue, if it happens to be injured somehow in the spiritual fight, and so there is penance. If as a remedy for the whole Church, either it is for its direction and spiritual multiplication, and so there is holy orders, for rulership is the good of the multitude, according to the Philosopher in *Ethics* 5;[30] or it is for the material multiplication of the faithful, and so there is marriage.

But some take the number of the sacraments according to their correspondence to the virtues, so that baptism corresponds to faith, since it is called the sacrament of faith; extreme unction to hope, since through it man is prepared in a certain sense for future glory; the Eucharist to charity; holy orders to prudence; penance to justice; marriage to temperance; and confirmation to fortitude.

Still others relate the sacraments to different kinds of fault and punishment, so that baptism is against original sin, penance against actual mortal sin, extreme unction against venial sin, holy orders against ignorance, marriage against concupiscence, confirmation against weakness, Eucharist against malice (for it is the sacrament of charity,

---

30. Aristotle, *Nicomachean Ethics*, Bk. 5, ch. 3, 1130a2.

sacramentum caritatis, quae per se opponitur malitiae. Haec enim quatuor dicit Beda ex peccato consecuta.

AD PRIMUM ergo dicendum, quod quamvis Eucharistia sit memoriale ipsius Dominicae passionis, ipsum Christum continens, non tamen quantum ad omnes effectus ejus. Vel dicendum, quod propter praedictam rationem Eucharistia ordinatur ad ultimum effectum passionis Christi, quasi completissime ab ea efficaciam habens; et ideo, quantum est de se, valet contra omnes spirituales defectus; unde et cum singulis sacramentis exhibetur, quasi consummans effectum uniuscujusque; sed tamen praeexigit alia sacramenta, ut idoneus quis reddatur ad tanti perceptionem mysterii, sicut etiam in naturalibus ultima forma non datur nisi praecedentibus omnibus dispositionibus.

AD SECUNDUM dicendum, quod baptismus est sacramentum intrantium, quia facit hominem primo participem redemptionis Christi consepeliens eum in similitudinem mortis Christi; et ideo non potest iterari, sicut nec passio Christi. Et quia peccata actualia iterantur, ideo contra culpam actualem oportuit aliquod remedium adhiberi, scilicet poenitentiam, quamvis etiam baptismus ipsum deleat.

AD TERTIUM dicendum, quod defectus illi sunt generales; et non habent eamdem rationem in omnibus suis partibus; et ideo oportuit contra diversas partes eorum diversa remedia adhiberi.

AD QUARTUM dicendum, quod in lege naturae multa signa gratiae praecesserunt, sicut diluvium, occisio Abel, et hujusmodi, quae tamen non debent dici sacramenta; sed illa tantum quae ad aliquod remedium exhibebantur. Ea enim significabant rem sacram, ut actu sacrantem, quod est de ratione sacramenti, ut supra dictum est; et ideo in lege naturae Hugo, tantum ponit tria sacramenta, scilicet sacrificia, oblationes, et decimas; quia per haec, ut dicit Gregorius, remedium ante circumcisionem contra originale erat. Et quamvis tunc esset tempus figurarum magis quam modo, non oportebat esse signa determinata ad determinatos effectus gratiae, sicut modo sunt; et ideo in quadam generalitate sacramenta illa, nostra sacramenta, et ipsorum causam, scilicet passionem Christi, significabant; sicut quod per sacrificia significabatur passio, per oblationes dispositio patientis ad passionem, quia ipse se voluntarie obtulit ad passionem: Isai. 53; per decimas autem comparatio patientis ad illos pro quibus patiebatur, qui imperfecti erant, ab ipso omnem perfectionem expectantes, sicut novem per decem complentur. Horum autem duo referuntur ad Eucharistiam: scilicet sacrificium quantum ad significatum, et oblatio quantum ad materiam et usum, sed decima praefigurabat baptismum, inquantum aliquid auferebatur. Matrimonium autem et poenitentia et ordo

which is opposed *per se* to malice). For Bede says that these four things follow upon sin.[31]

REPLY OBJ. 1: Although the Eucharist is the memorial of the very Passion of the Lord, containing Christ himself, nevertheless this is not as regards all of its effects. Or it could be said that, because of the reason given, the Eucharist is ordered to the ultimate effect of the Passion of Christ, as something having efficacy completely from it; and therefore considered in itself it is effective against all spiritual defects. Hence it is also employed with individual sacraments, as something that crowns the effect of each one; but nevertheless, it presupposes other sacraments so that someone may be rendered worthy of receiving so great a mystery, just as also in natural things the final form is not given without all the prerequisite dispositions.

REPLY OBJ. 2: Baptism is the sacrament of those entering, since it makes man a participant in the redemption of Christ for the first time by burying him in the likeness of the death of Christ; and thus it cannot be repeated, just as neither could the Passion of Christ. And since actual sins are repeated, a certain remedy had to be applied against actual fault, namely, penance—although baptism also expunges it.

REPLY OBJ. 3: Those are defects in general, and they do not have the same account in each instance; and so, different remedies had to be applied against different instances.

REPLY OBJ. 4: In the law of nature many signs of grace preceded, like the flood, the killing of Abel, and such, which nevertheless should not be called sacraments, but those that presented some kind of remedy alone deserve to be called such. For they signified a sacred thing as they caused something sacred in act, which is the definition of a sacrament, as was said above; and therefore in the law of nature Hugh includes only three sacraments, namely, sacrifices, offerings, and tithes, because through these things, as Gregory says, there was a remedy against original sin before circumcision. And although back then was more a time of figures than nowadays, they did not have to be signs determined to determinate effects of grace, as they are now. And therefore, those sacraments signified, with a certain generality, our sacraments and their cause, namely the Passion of Christ, so that by sacrifices the Passion was represented, by offerings the disposition of the one suffering to his Passion, for he willingly offered himself to his Passion (cf. Isa 53); while by tithes, a comparison of the one suffering to those for whom he suffered, who were imperfect and awaiting from him all perfection, as nine are completed by the tenth. Now two of these are referred to the Eucharist—namely, sacrifice in what was signified, and offering in the matter and the use—while tithes prefigured baptism inasmuch as something was taken away. Marriage and penance

---

31. Bede, *Commentary on the Gospel of Luke*, ch. 10.

erant illo tempore, sed tamen non computantur inter sacramenta illius temporis, quia non fiebant cum aliqua consecratione. Quilibet enim primogenitus, secundum Hieronymum sacerdos erat: nec erat aliquis modus determinatus ipsorum, nisi secundum instinctum naturae, prout cuique ratio fide innata dictabat faciendum.

AD QUINTUM dicendum, quod tempore legis scriptae jam plura cum aliqua consecratione celebrabantur, quae nostris sacramentis quasi figurae respondent: quia per circumcisionem nostrum baptisma figuratur; per oblationes et sacrificia Eucharistia; per diversos ritus expiationum poenitentia; per consecrationes Aaron et filiorum ejus noster ordo; et per matrimonium jam ad aliquas certas personas determinatum et sub lege constitutum, nostrum matrimonium. Sed extremae unctionis non debuit praecedere figura: quia extrema unctio est directivum et praeparatorium in gloriam, quam tunc statim post mortem consequi non poterant, sicut modo possunt. Similiter nec confirmatio, in qua complementum Spiritus Sancti datur: tempus autem illud non erat tempus plenitudinis, sicut tempus istud.

AD SEXTUM dicendum, quod Dionysius non intendit ibi determinare de sacramentis, sed de actionibus hierarchicis, quae consistunt in consecratione per ministros ecclesiae facta. Et quia matrimonium et poenitentia possunt habere suum effectum sine tali consecratione, ideo de eis non determinavit.

AD SEPTIMUM dicendum, quod aqua benedicta non ordinatur directe ad remedium praestandum, sed ad removendum prohibens; unde datur contra daemonum nequitias et venialia, et omne quod effectum sacramentorum impedire posset: propter hoc non est sacramentum, quia removens prohibens est agens per accidens; sed sacramentale, quasi dispositio quaedam ad sacramenta.

AD OCTAVUM dicendum, quod concupiscentia quae est in actu generativae, habet specialem foeditatem ab aliis concupiscentiis: quia praeter hoc quod est infectiva personae, quod habet commune cum aliis, et idem remedium habens, scilicet poenitentiam, est etiam infectio naturae; et ideo debet habere speciale remedium, secundum quod ad purgationem naturae ordinatur.

AD NONUM dicendum, quod ad quamlibet eminentiam status datur aliqua sanctificatio, cum sit ibi necessarium speciale auxilium gratiae, sicut in consecratione regum et monachorum et monialium; et ideo sunt actiones hierarchicae; et propter hoc Dionysius de eis determinat;

and holy orders, however, existed at that time, yet nevertheless they were not counted among the sacraments of that time, for they did not happen with any certain consecration. For whoever was first-born was priest, according to Jerome: [32] nor was there any particular mode for the sacraments of that period, except according to the instinct of nature, as reason dictated to each person what was to be done by inborn faith.

REPLY OBJ. 5: In the time of the written law, many things were already being celebrated with a certain consecration, which correspond to our sacraments as figures: for our baptism is prefigured by circumcision; the Eucharist by offerings and sacrifices; penance by the diverse rites of expiation; our holy orders by the consecrations of Aaron and his sons; and our marriage in marriage then determined to certain persons and constituted under the law. But there did not need to be any pre-existing figure of extreme unction, for extreme unction is directive and preparatory for glory, which they could not attain right after death back then, as we can now. Nor likewise for confirmation, in which the completeness of the Holy Spirit is given; for at that time it was not the time of fullness, like this time.

REPLY OBJ. 6: In that passage Dionysius did not intend to define the sacraments, but the actions of the hierarchy, which consist in the consecration done by the ministers of the Church. And since marriage and penance can have their own effect without such a consecration, for this reason he did not include them.

REPLY OBJ. 7: Holy water is not directly ordered to providing a remedy but to removing a hindrance; hence it is given against the wickedness and misdemeanors of demons, and everything that could impede the effect of the sacraments. Because of this it is not a sacrament, since something that removes a hindrance is an agent *per accidens*; but it is a sacramental—a certain disposition, as it were, to the sacraments.

REPLY OBJ. 8: The concupiscence that is in the generative act has a special ugliness by comparison with other concupiscences, for besides the fact that it is infective of the person, which it shares in common with the others and for which it has the same remedy (namely, penance), there is also the infection of the nature; and therefore it should have a special remedy, according to which it is ordered to the purification of the nature.

REPLY OBJ. 9: A certain sanctification is given for any eminence of status, since the special help of grace is necessary there, as in the consecration of kings and monks and nuns. And therefore these are actions of the hierarchy, and for this reason Dionysius discusses them. But they do

---

32. Jerome, *Epistle* 73 (CSEL 55), n. 6.

non tamen habent rationem sacramenti; sed solum illa eminentia per quam homo efficitur sacrorum dispensator.

AD DECIMUM dicendum, quod oblationes et decimae erant[33] tunc inquantum erant figurales; sed quantum ad hoc nunc non manent; sed solum secundum quod sunt morales ad usum ministrorum ecclesiae et pauperum deputatae; et ideo nunc non sunt sacramenta.

AD UNDECIMUM dicendum, quod omnes illae sanctificationes ordinantur ad sacramentum Eucharistiae; et ideo non sunt sacramenta, sed sacramentalia quaedam.

not have the account of sacrament; only that eminence by which a man is made dispenser of sacred things.

REPLY OBJ. 10: Offerings and tithes existed at that time inasmuch as they were figural, but in this capacity they no longer remain. Rather, they remain only according as they are moral, assigned for the use of ministers of the Church and of the poor; and therefore nowadays they are not sacraments.

REPLY OBJ. 11: All those sanctifications are ordered to the sacrament of the Eucharist; and therefore they are not sacraments, but certain sacramentals.

---

33. *erant tunc.—erant sacramenta tunc* PLE

ARTICLE 3

The order of the sacraments[34]

AD TERTIUM SIC PROCEDITUR. Videtur quod sacramenta inconvenienter a Magistro hic ordinentur. Prius enim est quod animale est quam quod spirituale; 1 Corinth. 15. Sed matrimonium ad vitam animalem pertinet, omnia autem alia sacramenta ad vitam spiritualem. Ergo matrimonium est omnibus prius.

PRAETEREA, agens naturaliter prior est sua actione; unde et in jure prius determinatur de officiis quam de actionibus. Sed per sacramentum ordinis constituuntur dispensatores aliorum sacramentorum. Ergo ordo inter alia primo debet poni.

PRAETEREA, bonum commune est divinius quam bonum personae, ut dicitur in 1 *Ethic.* Sed matrimonium et ordo ordinantur in remedium commune, alia autem in remedium unius personae, ut dictum est. Ergo illa duo sacramenta ante alia poni debent.

PRAETEREA, Eucharistia perficit nos conjungendo fini, ut dictum est. Sed finis est ultimum in adeptione. Ergo Eucharistia post omnia debet poni.

PRAETEREA, purgatio praecedit illuminationem et perfectionem. Sed secundum Dionysium, Eucharistia pertinet ad perfectionem, similiter et confirmatio. Ergo poenitentia, quae maxime ad purgationem pertinet, videtur quod antea debet poni.

PRAETEREA, Dionysius ponit Eucharistiam ante confirmationem. Cum ergo Magister contrarium faciat, videtur quod inconvenienter ordinet.

RESPONDEO dicendum, quod prius et posterius multipliciter dicitur; sed in his quae ad actiones pertinent, prius quo ad nos est illud quod est prius in via generationis; et ideo secundum hanc viam Magister sacramenta quae sanctificationes quaedam sunt, ordinat. Prius enim in via generationis est bonum privatum quam commune, quod consurgit ex bonis singulorum, sicut homo est prior domo, et domus civitate; et ideo sacramenta quae in remedium unius personae ordinantur, prius ponuntur, inter quae primo ponitur illud quod pertinet ad intrantes, scilicet baptismus; ultimo illud quod pertinet ad exeuntes, scilicet extrema unctio; in medio illa quae pertinent ad progredientes, quae hoc modo ordinantur. Quia enim perfici bono essentialius est virtuti, et commune singulis progredientibus ad virtutem;

OBJ. 1: To the third we proceed thus. It seems that the order of sacraments is unfittingly assigned by the Master. For what is animal is prior to what is spiritual (cf. 1 Cor 15:46). But marriage pertains to animal life, while all the other sacraments pertain to spiritual life. Therefore, marriage is before all the others.

OBJ. 2: Furthermore, an agent is naturally prior to his action; hence in law, determination is made concerning offices first, and then actions. But dispensers of the other sacraments are constituted by the sacrament of orders. Therefore, holy orders should be placed first among the others.

OBJ. 3: Furthermore, the common good is more divine than the good of a person, as it says in *Ethics* 1.[35] But marriage and holy orders are appointed for a common remedy, the others as a remedy for one person, as was said. Therefore, those two sacraments should be placed before the others.

OBJ. 4: Furthermore, the Eucharist perfects us by joining us to our end, as was said. But the end is last in attainment. Therefore, the Eucharist should be placed after the others.

OBJ. 5: Furthermore, purification precedes illumination and perfection. But according to Dionysius, the Eucharist pertains to perfection just as Confirmation does.[36] Therefore, it seems that penance, which most of all pertains to purification, should be placed first.

OBJ. 6: Furthermore, Dionysius places the Eucharist before confirmation.[37] Therefore, since the Master does the opposite, it seems that he orders them unfittingly.

I ANSWER THAT, before and after are said in many ways. But in those things that pertain to actions, prior in relation to us is what is prior in the process of generation; and therefore the Master orders the sacraments, which are some kind of sanctification, according to this process. For in the process of generation, the private good comes before the common good, which arises from individual goods, just as a man is prior to a household, and a household to a city. And therefore the sacraments that are ordered to the good of one person are placed first, and among them first is what pertains to those entering, namely, baptism; last is what pertains to those departing, namely, extreme unction; in the middle are what pertain to those progressing, which are ordered in this way. For since being perfected in the good is more essential to virtue, and common to individ-

---

34. Parallel: *ST* III, q. 65, a. 3.
35. Aristotle, Nicomachean Ethics, Bk. 1, ch. 1, 1094b9–10.
36. Pseudo-Dionysius, *Ecclesiastical Hierarchy*, ch. 1, p. 1, n. 3 (PG 3:503).
37. In the same place as the preceding citation.

sed resurgere a peccato accidit huic progressui ex parte subjecti quod cecidit (unde non est omnibus commune), et quantum ad perfectionem ad bonum perfectio in forma praecedit in via generationis perfectionem in consecutione ad finem; ideo inter sacramenta quae ad progressum in bonum pertinent, primo ponitur confirmatio; quae est ad perfectionem similem perfectioni formae; secundo Eucharistia, quae est ad perfectionem in fine; tertio poenitentia quae est ad reparationem virtutis amissae. Inter sacramenta autem quae ad remedium totius ecclesiae deputantur, primo ponitur ordo: quia matrimonium, inquantum matrimonium, per ordinem dispensatur, secundum quod est sacramentum.

AD PRIMUM ergo dicendum, quod matrimonium secundum quod pertinet ad vitam animalem, non est sacramentum, sed naturae officium; sed secundum quod habet aliquid spiritualis quantum ad signum et effectum, sic sacramentum est; et quia minimum habet de spiritualitate, ideo ultimo inter sacramenta ponitur.

AD SECUNDUM dicendum, quod in sacramentorum actionibus ordo non constituit principalem agentem, sed ministrum, et instrumentum quoddam divinae operationis; in judiciis autem judex secundum formam scientiae et justitiae operatur non solum sicut instrumentum; et ideo in jure praemittuntur ea quae ad officia pertinent, sed in sacramentis non oportet.

AD TERTIUM dicendum, quod quamvis bonum commune sit divinius, tamen bonum singulare est prius in via generationis; et ideo etiam Philosophus monasticam politicae praemisit, ut patet in 10 *Ethic.*

AD QUARTUM dicendum, quod conjunctio ad finem est duplex. Una secundum plenam participationem ipsius; et ista conjunctio non efficitur per aliquod sacramentum; sed sacramenta ad eam disponunt, et inter omnia vicinius extrema unctio; et ideo ultimo ponitur inter ea quae ad remedium unius personae ordinantur. Alio modo secundum imperfectam, qualis est fruitio viae; et ad hanc ordinatur Eucharistia; et ideo non oportet quod ponatur ultima simpliciter, sed ultima in progressu ad bonum.

AD QUINTUM dicendum, quod poenitentia non dicit purgationem absolute respectu cujuslibet impuritatis spiritualis, hoc enim ad baptismum pertinet; sed purgationem in casu, scilicet quando aliquis a statu virtutis cecidit, ut iterum ad bonum redeat; et haec est secunda tabula post naufragium, secundum Hieronymum; et ideo poenitentia ponitur post illa sacramenta quae ad consummationem in bonum ordinantur.

uals progressing toward virtue; but to rise again from sin happens in this particular progress on the part of the subject who fell (hence it is not common to everyone); and as to the perfecting in the good, in the process of generation perfection in form precedes perfection in attaining the end; hence among the sacraments that pertain to advancement in good, first is placed confirmation, which stands towards perfection as perfection of form; second, the Eucharist, which is for perfection in the end; third, penance, which is for the reparation of lost virtue. But among the sacraments that are allotted to the remedy of the whole Church, holy orders is placed first; for marriage, as marriage, is dispensed by holy orders, according as it is a sacrament.

REPLY OBJ. 1: Marriage according as it pertains to animal life is not a sacrament, but an office of nature; but according as it has something spiritual in its sign and effect, to that extent it is a sacrament; and since it has the least of spirituality, for this reason it is placed last among the sacraments.

REPLY OBJ. 2: In the actions of the sacraments, holy orders does not establish a principal agent, but a minister and a certain instrument of divine operation. In judicial matters, however, a judge acts according to the form of knowledge and justice, not only as an instrument; and therefore in the courts those things that pertain to the office are brought forth first, but in sacraments this is not necessary.

REPLY OBJ. 3: Although the common good is more divine, nevertheless an individual good is prior in the order of generation; and thus even the Philosopher premised ethics to politics, as is evident in *Ethics* 10.[38]

REPLY OBJ. 4: There are two kinds of union with the end. One is according to full participation in it; and this kind of union is not brought about by any sacrament, but the sacraments dispose to it, and among all of them extreme unction is the closest; and therefore it is placed last among things ordered to the remedy of one person. The other is according to an imperfect participation in it, of which sort is the enjoyment on the way;[39] and the Eucharist is ordered to this. Therefore, it does not need to be placed last simply, but last in progress towards the good.

REPLY OBJ. 5: Penance does not bespeak purification absolutely with respect to any spiritual impurity whatsoever (for this belongs to baptism), but purification in certain cases—namely, when someone has fallen from the state of virtue, so that he might again return to the good; and this is the second plank after a shipwreck, according to Jerome.[40] And therefore penance is placed after those sacraments that are ordered to consummation in the good.

---

38. Aristotle, *Nicomachean Ethics*, Bk. 10, ch. 9, 1181b13ff. Thomas refers to the science of ethics as *monastica*, "monastics," because it deals with the individual, as "economics" deals with the family and "politics" with the state.

39. *Fruitio viae* means the possession of the end that is possible to a Christian in this life, when he is a pilgrim or *viator*, 'on the way' (*in via*).

40. This phrase occurs in many of Jerome's writings; see, for one example, *Epistle* 130, n. 9 (CSEL 56:189).

AD SEXTUM dicendum, quod Dionysius consideravit in eis ordinem magis quantum ad dispensationem eorum quam quantum ad effectum: quia Eucharistia statim baptizatis datur, si sint adulti, non autem confirmatio; ideo post baptismum immediate Eucharistiam posuit.

REPLY OBJ. 6: Dionysius considered their order more as to their dispensation than as to their effect; for the Eucharist is given to the baptized immediately, if they are adults, but confirmation is not; he therefore placed the Eucharist immediately after baptism.

ARTICLE 4

The institution of the sacraments

Quaestiuncula 1

AD QUARTUM SIC PROCEDITUR. Videtur quod non debuerint in nova lege aliqua sacramenta de novo institui. Natura enim operatur breviori via qua potest; et hoc ad ordinationem naturae pertinet. Sed gratia est magis ordinata quam natura. Cum ergo brevior via esset quod sacramenta jam in veteri lege existentia perficerentur quam aliqua de novo instituerentur, videtur quod aliqua de novo institui non debuerint.

PRAETEREA, sicut sacramenta sunt necessaria ad salutem, ita et praecepta. Sed Christus non alia praecepta moralia instituit, sed praeexistentia consiliis perfecit. Ergo nec nova sacramenta instituere debuit.

SED CONTRA, sacramenta sunt medicinae spirituales, ut prius dictum est. Sed non competit eadem medicina parvulo et adulto. Cum ergo status legis comparetur puerili aetati, status autem temporis gratiae aetati perfectae, ut patet Gal. 4, videtur quod alia sacramenta debuerunt etiam tempore gratiae instituenda.

OBJ. 1: To the fourth we proceed thus. It seems that in the New Law, no sacraments needed to be instituted anew.[41] For nature works by the shortest way it can, and this belongs to nature's order. But grace is more ordered than nature. Since therefore it would be a shorter way if the sacraments already existing in the Old Law were perfected rather than new ones being instituted, it seems that no new ones should have been instituted.

OBJ. 2: Furthermore, just as sacraments are necessary to salvation, so also are precepts. But Christ did not institute any other moral precepts, but perfected the pre-existing ones with counsels. Therefore, neither did new sacraments have to be instituted.

ON THE CONTRARY, sacraments are spiritual medicines, as was said before. But the same medicine does not suit child and adult. Since, then, the state of the law is compared to childhood, but the state of the time of grace to a perfect age, as is clear from Galatians 4, it seems that other sacraments also had to be instituted in the time of grace.

Quaestiuncula 2

ULTERIUS. Videtur quod haec eadem debuerit a principio mundi post peccatum instituere. Quia ad crudelem medicum pertinet ut efficacem medicinam non statim infirmo proponat, sed eum diu periclitari sinat. Sed a Deo omnis crudelitas relegata est. Ergo sacramenta novae legis, quae sunt efficacissimae medicinae, debuerunt statim post peccatum humano generi exhiberi.

PRAETEREA, sacramenta novae legis totam efficaciam habent ex passione Christi. Sed passio Christi operabatur etiam a principio mundi post peccatum ad reparationem, secundum quod erat credita, ut in 3 Lib., dist. 19, quaest. 1, art. 1, quaestiunc. 2 ad 2, dictum est. Ergo et tunc sacramenta institui debuerunt.

SED CONTRA, gratia perficit naturam. Sed natura procedit ex imperfectioribus ad perfectiora, sicut patet in omni motu et generatione; et similiter etiam ars. Ergo

OBJ. 1: Moreover, it seems that these same things should have been instituted at the beginning of the world, after sin.[42] For it is a cruel doctor who does not immediately give the effective medicine to a sick man, but allows him to be in danger for a long time. But all cruelty is excluded from God. Therefore, the sacraments of the New Law, which are the most effective medicine, should have been applied to the human race immediately after sin.

OBJ. 2: Furthermore, sacraments of the New Law have all their efficacy from the Passion of Christ. But the Passion of Christ was at work even from the beginning of the world for the reparation of sin, according as it was believed in (as was said in Book III, Distinction 19, Question 1, Article 1, Subquestion 2, Reply 2). Therefore, the sacraments should also have been instituted then.

ON THE CONTRARY, grace perfects nature. But nature proceeds from imperfect things to the more perfect, as is clear in every motion and generation; and art, too, acts in

---

41. Parallels: above, d. 1, q. 1, a. 2, qa. 5; *ST* III, q. 61, a. 4; *SCG* IV, ch. 57.
42. Parallels: above, d. 1, q. 1, a. 2, qa. 3 & 4; *ST* III, q. 61, a. 3.

et similiter gratia debuit prius imperfecte et postea copiose per efficaciam sacramenti dari.

the same way. In the same way, therefore, grace had to be given first imperfectly and afterward abundantly through the efficacy of the sacraments.

Quaestiuncula 3

ULTERIUS. Videtur quod statim Christo nato sacramenta institui debuerunt. Sunt enim sacramenta novae legis gratiam continentia. Sed tempus gratiae ex tunc incepit. Ergo tunc institui debuerunt.

PRAETEREA, sacramenta adjuvant ad implendum praecepta. Sed praecepta moralia omnia simul data fuerunt in ipso initio legis. Ergo et sacramenta gratiae in ipso initio gratiae omnia simul dari debuerunt.

SED CONTRA est quia quae a Deo sunt, ordinata sunt, Rom. 13, 1. Sed iste est debitus ordo, ut causa effectum praecedat, et ut illud quod prius est, primo tradatur. Ergo cum passio Christi sit causa efficaciam sacramentis praebens, et unum sacramentum sit alio prius, ut dictum est, videtur quod non debuerunt institui statim Christo nato.

OBJ. 1: Moreover, it seems that the sacraments should have been instituted immediately after the birth of Christ.[43] For it is the sacraments of the New Law that contain grace. But the time of grace began from that moment. Therefore, they should have been instituted at that moment.

OBJ. 2: Furthermore, sacraments assist us in fulfilling the precepts. But all the moral precepts had been given at the same time in the very beginning of the law. Therefore, the sacraments of grace, too, should have been given all at the same time at the very beginning of grace.

ON THE CONTRARY, whatever is from God is ordered (cf. Rom 13:1). But this is the due order, that the cause precede the effect and that what is prior is handed on first. Therefore, since the Passion of Christ is the cause supplying efficacy to the sacraments, and one sacrament is prior to another, as was said, it seems that they should not have been instituted immediately upon Christ's birth.

Quaestiuncula 4

ULTERIUS. Videtur quod sacramenta novae legis non sunt omnia a Christo instituta. Quia de confirmatione et extrema unctione non legitur aliquid dixisse. Sed extrema unctio et confirmatio sunt sacramenta novae legis. Ergo non omnia sacramenta novae legis sunt instituta a Christo.

PRAETEREA, non minoris auctoritatis est mysterium sacerdotii novae legis quam legis naturae. Sed qui sacramenta dispensabant in lege naturae, scilicet sacerdotes, pro suo libito sacramentis visibilibus suam fidem profitebantur. Ergo multo fortius hoc debet esse in lege nova, quae etiam est majoris libertatis.

SED CONTRA, sacramenta novae legis efficiunt quod significant. Sed ex institutione significant secundum Hugonem. Ergo ex institutione efficaciam habent. Sed efficacia sacramentorum non est nisi a Deo, qui solus peccata remittit. Ergo non potuit esse a puro homine sacramentorum institutio.

OBJ. 1: Moreover, it seems that the sacraments of the New Law were not all instituted by Christ.[44] For we do not read that he said anything about confirmation or extreme unction. But extreme unction and confirmation are sacraments of the New Law. Therefore, not all sacraments of the New Law were instituted by Christ.

OBJ. 2: Furthermore, the mystery of priesthood in the New Law is not of less authority than that of the law of nature. But the ones who administered the sacraments under the law of nature, namely, priests, professed their faith as they pleased, by means of visible sacraments. Therefore, much more should this be the case in the New Law, which is of even greater freedom.

ON THE CONTRARY, sacraments of the New Law effect what they signify. But they get their signification from their institution, according to Hugh of St. Victor.[45] Therefore, they have efficacy from their institution. But the efficacy of the sacraments can be from God alone, who alone remits sins. Therefore the institution of the sacraments could not be from a mere man.

---

43. Parallels: above, d. 1, a. 2, qa. 5; *ST* III, q. 61, a. 4; *SCG* IV, ch. 57.
44. Parallels: below, d. 7, q. 1, a. 1, qa. 1, ad 1; d. 13, q. 1, a. 2, qa. 6, ad 1, 3; d. 17, q. 3, a. 1, qa. 5; *ST* I-II, q. 108, a. 2; *ST* III, q. 64, a. 2; *Super Ioan.* 1, lec. 14.
45. Hugh of St. Victor, *De sacramentis fidei*, Bk. 1, pt. 9, ch.2 (PL 176:317).

Response to Quaestiuncula 1

RESPONDEO dicendum ad primam quaestionem, quod sacramenta sunt signa remedii ad quod ordinantur. Sunt autem signa repraesentantia effectus spirituales ex similitudine sensibilium rerum, quarum in sacramento est usus. Et ideo cum in nova lege oportuerit esse sacramenta majoris efficaciae propter perfectionem testamenti, debuerunt etiam esse alia signa quae expressius figurarent gratiam; et ideo oportuit nova sacramenta institui.

AD PRIMUM ergo dicendum, quod quamvis natura brevissime operetur, tamen nihil omittit de contingentibus quibus aliquid optime fieri possit et similiter gratia; et ideo in sacramentis instituendis non solum attenditur qualiter aliquid breviter fiat, sed qualiter congruenter.

AD SECUNDUM dicendum, quod praecepta moralia consequuntur naturam humanam, cum sint de dictamine rationis naturalis; et ideo permanent eadem in qualibet lege, et in quolibet statu hominis; et propter hoc non est simile de praeceptis et sacramentis, quae ex sola institutione efficaciam habent.

TO THE FIRST QUESTION, I answer that sacraments are signs of the remedy to which they are directed. Now these signs represent spiritual effects by the likeness of the sensible things used in the sacrament. And thus, since sacraments of the New Law needed to be of greater efficacy because of the perfection of this testament, there also had to be other signs beyond the old ones that more expressly figured grace; and thus it was necessary for new sacraments to be instituted.

REPLY OBJ. 1: Although nature works by the shortest way, nevertheless it omits nothing from the contingent things by which something could be best accomplished; and grace works in the same way. And thus in the sacraments that were to be instituted we should not only look for how something is done quickly, but how it is done fittingly.

REPLY OBJ. 2: Moral precepts follow human nature, since they come from the dictates of natural reason; and thus the same things remain in every law, and in every state of man whatsoever. And for this reason there is no parallel account for the precepts and the sacraments, which have efficacy from their institution alone.

Response to Quaestiuncula 2

AD SECUNDAM QUAESTIONEM dicendum, quod sacramenta novae legis, quia gratiam continent, non sunt vacua, sed plena; et ideo non competebat ea institui nisi tempore plenitudinis, quod est tempus incarnationis. Quare autem Christus suum adventum distulerit, et non statim post peccatum carnem assumpserit, in 3 Lib., dist. 1, quaest. 1, art. 4, dictum est.

AD PRIMUM ergo dicendum, quod aliter est in morbo spirituali et corporali. Non enim potest aliquis a morbo spirituali congrue curari, nisi prius morbum cognoscat, et medicinam desideret, si sit cognitionis capax; et ideo oportuit ut homo sibi relinqueretur, et sic primo tempore legis naturae infirmum se cognosceret per ignorantiam, ad idolatriam declinando; et deinde tempore legis scriptae quae auxilium contra ignorantiam praebebat, recognosceret se infirmum per concupiscentiam, ad peccata declinando, et sic salutem ab alio expectaret; qui et viam salutis docuit contra ignorantiam et sacramenta gratiae dedit contra infirmitatem concupiscentiae, ut dicitur Joan. 1, 17: *gratia et veritas per Jesum Christum facta est.* In morbo autem corporali hoc non requiritur, quia corpus non est cognitionis capax.

AD SECUNDUM dicendum, quod quamvis etiam ex tunc passio Christi efficaciam haberet, non tamen tan-

TO THE SECOND QUESTION, it should be said that the sacraments of the New Law, because they contain grace, are not empty, but full. And thus it does not befit them to be instituted in any time but the time of fullness, which is the time of the Incarnation. But the reason that Christ deferred his coming, and did not assume flesh immediately after sin, was stated in Book III, Distinction 1, Question 1, Article 4.

REPLY OBJ. 1: It is different in spiritual disease than it is in physical ones. For someone cannot be fittingly cured from a spiritual ailment unless he first recognizes the disease and desires the treatment, if he is capable of understanding; and thus it was necessary that man be left to himself, both so that in the first age of the law of nature, he would recognize that he was weak through ignorance, by sliding into idolatry; and then in the time of the written law, which was furnished to him as a help against ignorance, he would recognize that he was weak through concupiscence, by sliding into sin, and in this way he would look for his salvation from another—one who both taught him the way of salvation against ignorance and gave him the sacraments of grace against the weakness of concupiscence, as it says in John 1:17: *grace and truth came by Jesus Christ.* But in physical disease this is not required, for the body is not capable of understanding.

REPLY OBJ. 2: Although the Passion of Christ did have efficacy at that time too, nevertheless it did not have so

tam efficaciam in humana natura, pro qua nondum satisfactum erat, habebat, sicut post satisfactionem habuit, et post Christi incarnationem, quae totam naturam humanam dignificavit, ut fieret magis ad gratiam recipiendam idonea.

much efficacy in human nature, for which it had not yet made satisfaction, as it had after he had made satisfaction and after the Incarnation of Christ, which dignified all of human nature so that it was made more worthy of receiving grace.

Response to Quaestiuncula 3

AD TERTIAM QUAESTIONEM dicendum, quod sacramenta novae legis dupliciter instituta sunt. Primo ad documentum et exercitium quoddam; et sic potuerant ante passionem Christi institui. Secundo quantum ad necessitatem et obligationem, et sic eorum institutio non fuit ante passionem, quia adhuc legalia non fuerant mortua; unde a tempore praedicationis Christi usque ad passionem, sacramenta novae legis simul currebant cum legalibus, et utraque ad salutem operabantur. Sic ergo quantum ad secundum modum institutionis omnia simul in passione Christi instituta sunt; sed quantum ad primum, oportuit ut primo instituerentur illa quae sunt majoris necessitatis; unde statim in principio praedicationis suae poenitentiam praedicavit, ut legitur Matth. 4, et baptismum docuit ut legitur Joan. 3. Alia autem sacramenta processu temporis instituit et docuit.

TO THE THIRD QUESTION, it should be said that sacraments of the New Law had a twofold institution. The first was for a certain instruction and training; and in this way they could be instituted before the Passion of Christ. The second regarded necessity and obligation, and in this way their institution was not before the Passion, for the prescriptions of the law were not yet dead. Hence, from the time of Christ's preaching until the Passion, sacraments of the New Law were running at the same time as those of the Old Law, and both were working toward salvation. Accordingly, as to the second manner of institution, all the sacraments were instituted together in the Passion of Christ; but as to the first, it was necessary that there be instituted first those that were of greater necessity. Hence he preached penance right away in the beginning of his preaching, as is read in Matthew 4; and he taught baptism, as is read in John 3. Other sacraments, however, he instituted and taught over the course of time.

AD PRIMUM ergo dicendum, quod tempus gratiae dicitur quantum ad initium, et quantum ad complementum. Complementum autem ejus non fuit ante passionem, et resurrectionem Christi; unde Joan. 7, 39, dicitur: *nondum erat spiritus datus, quia nondum erat Jesus glorificatus.* Principium autem potest attendi dupliciter. Primo quantum ad praesentiam gratiae in mundo; et sic fuit in ipsa incarnatione. Secundo quantum ad ejus diffusionem in mundo, et sic fuit in praedicatione sive baptismo Christi; et ante non oportebat institui sacramenta.

REPLY OBJ. 1: The time of grace is said either as to its beginning or as to its fullness. But its fullness was not before the Passion and resurrection of Christ; hence it is said, *the Spirit was not as yet given, because Jesus was not yet glorified* (Jn 7:39). However, the beginning can be thought of in two ways. First, as to the presence of grace in the world; and this was in the Incarnation itself. Second, as to its diffusion in the world, and this was in the preaching and baptism of Christ; and before that it was not fitting for sacraments to be instituted.

AD SECUNDUM dicendum, quod praecepta moralia homini natura dictat; et ideo statim potuerunt homini simul proponi: non autem est ita de sacramentis.

REPLY OBJ. 2: Nature dictates moral precepts to man; and thus they could be proposed to man immediately. But it is not like this with sacraments.

Response to Quaestiuncula 4

AD QUARTAM QUAESTIONEM dicendum quod circa hoc est duplex opinio. Quidam enim dicunt, non omnia sacramenta a Christo immediate instituta fuisse; sed quaedam ipse per se instituit, quaedam vero apostolis instituenda commisit; scilicet confirmationem, in qua Spiritus Sanctus datur ad robur, cujus institutio esse non debuit ante plenam Spiritus Sancti missionem; et extremam unctionem, quae cum ad gloriam resurrectionis sit immediatum et proximum praeparatorium, ante resurrectionem institui non debuit. Sed quia insti-

TO THE FOURTH QUESTION, it should be said that there are two opinions about this. For some people say that not all of the sacraments were instituted directly by Christ; but he instituted certain ones himself, while he committed certain others to the apostles to be instituted—namely, confirmation, in which the Holy Spirit is given for strengthening, whose institution could not be before the full sending of the Holy Spirit; and extreme unction, which, since it was an immediate and proximate preparation for the glory of the resurrection, could not be instituted before the resurrection.

tutio sacramentorum videtur ad potestatem plenitudinis in sacramentis pertinere quam sibi Christus reservavit in sacramentis, cum ex institutione sacramenta habeant quod significent; ideo aliis probabilius videtur, quod sicut hominis puri non est sacramenta mutare, vel a sacramentis absolvere, ita nec nova sacramenta instituere; et ideo omnia sacramenta novae legis ab ipso Christo institutionem habent.

SECUNDUM HOC ERGO dicendum ad primum, quod ipse sacramentum confirmationis instituit, quando pueris sibi praesentatis manus imposuit; similiter extremam unctionem, quando apostolos ad praedicandum mittens, oleo inungere infirmos disposuit, ut sic curarentur.

AD SECUNDUM dicendum, quod sacramenta illa legis naturae non habebant aliquam efficaciam ex opere operato, sed solum ex fide; et ideo determinatio eorum ab homine puro habente fidem fieri poterat. Non autem ita est de sacramentis novae legis, quae ex opere operato gratiam conferunt.

But because the institution of the sacraments seems to belong to the power of fullness that Christ reserved to himself in the sacraments (since the sacraments get their power to signify from their institution), therefore to others it seems more probable that just as it is not for a mere man to change the sacraments, or to absolve from the sacraments, so neither is it for a mere man to institute new sacraments; and thus, all sacraments of the New Law have their institution from Christ himself.

REPLY OBJ. 1: According to this, the first objection should be answered that he himself instituted the sacrament of confirmation when he imposed his hands on the children presented to him; likewise, he instituted extreme unction when, sending the apostles to preach, he charged them to anoint the sick with oil, so that in this way they might be cured.[46]

REPLY OBJ. 2: Those sacraments of the law of nature did not have any effect by the work performed, but only by faith; and thus their determination could be done by a mere man possessing faith. However, it was not like this with the sacraments of the New Law, which confer grace by the work performed.[47]

---

46. See Mark 6:13.

47. That is, since God alone can give grace, and the sacraments of the New Law are instituted in such a way as to give grace, only God can institute them.

QUESTION 2

THE BAPTISM OF JOHN THE BAPTIST

Deinde quaeritur de baptismo Joannis, et circa hoc quaeruntur quattuor:

primo, utrum fuerit sacramentum;

secundo, de efficacia ipsius;

tertio, quibus competebat;

quarto, utrum baptizati a Joanne, essent baptismo Christi baptizandi.

Next we will consider the baptism of John, about which four questions arise:

first, whether it was a sacrament;

second, concerning its efficacy;

third, to whom it applied;

fourth, whether those who were baptized by John had to be baptized with the baptism of Christ.

ARTICLE 1

Whether the baptism of John the Baptist was a sacrament

Quaestiuncula 1

AD PRIMUM SIC PROCEDITUR. Videtur quod baptismus Joannis non fuerit sacramentum. Joan. 3, super illud: *erat Joannes baptizans* etc., dicit Glossa: *quantum catechumenis nondum baptizatis prodest doctrina fidei, tantum profuit baptismus Joannis ante baptismum Christi.* Sed catechismus non est sacramentum, sed sacramentale. Ergo baptismus Joannis non erat sacramentum sed sacramentale.

PRAETEREA, omne sacramentum est alicujus legis sacramentum. Sed baptismus Joannis non erat sacramentum legis naturae, neque legis veteris: quia, sicut Augustinus dicit, nulli praecedentium prophetarum fuit datum baptizare, nisi Joanni soli, quod non contingit de sacramentis veteris legis; similiter non est sacramentum novae legis, quia praedicationem Christi praecessit. Ergo non erat sacramentum.

SED CONTRA, sacramentum est sacrae rei signum. Sed baptismus Joannis figurabat baptismum Christi. Ergo erat sacramentum.

OBJ. 1: To the first we proceed thus. It seems that the baptism of John was not a sacrament. For commenting on the text, *John was also baptizing* (Jn 3:23), a Gloss says: *as much as the teaching of the faith benefits a catechumen who is not yet baptized, so much did the baptism of John before the baptism of Christ.*[48] But catechism is not a sacrament, but a sacramental. Therefore, the baptism of John was not a sacrament but a sacramental.

OBJ. 2: Furthermore, every sacrament is a sacrament of some law. But the baptism of John was not a sacrament of the law of nature, nor of the Old Law; for, as Augustine says,[49] it was not given to any of the preceding prophets to baptize, but to John alone, because it did not have to do with the sacraments of the Old Law; likewise, it is not a sacrament of the New Law, for it preceded the preaching of Christ. Therefore, it was not a sacrament.

ON THE CONTRARY, a sacrament is a sign of a sacred thing. But the baptism of John prefigured the baptism of Christ. Therefore, it was a sacrament.

Quaestiuncula 2

ULTERIUS. Videtur quod non baptizaverit sub hac forma: *ego baptizo te in nomine venturi.* Christus enim, in cujus nomine baptizabat, jam venerat. Ergo non competebat forma illa pro tempore illo.

OBJ. 1: Moreover, it seems that he did not baptize under this form: *I baptize you in the name of the One who is to come.* For Christ, in whose name he baptized, had already come. Therefore, that form did not befit the time.

---

48. Augustine, *In Iohannis euangelium tractatus* (CCSL 36), Tract. 4, n. 13.
49. Augustine, *In Iohannis euangelium tractatus* (CCSL 36), Tract. 5, n. 4.

PRAETEREA, eadem est fides de Christo venturo quae erat in patribus et de Christo qui jam venit, quam nos habemus. Ergo eadem est forma baptismi in nomine venturi, et in nomine Christi. Ergo baptismus idem. Sed apostoli baptizaverunt in nomine Christi, ut infra dicetur. Si ergo Joannes baptizavit in nomine venturi, idem fuit baptisma Joannis et apostolorum Christi; quod falsum est.

SED CONTRA est quod dicitur Act. 19, 4: *baptizabat Joannes populum dicens, in eum qui venturus est post ipsum, ut crederent.*

OBJ. 2: Furthermore, the patriarchs' faith in Christ to come and our faith in Christ already come is one and the same faith. Therefore, the form of baptism in the name of the One who is to come is the same as in the name of Christ. Therefore the baptism was the same. But the apostles baptized in the name of Christ, as will be said further on. If therefore John baptized in the name of the One to come, the baptism of John was the same as the baptism of the apostles of Christ, which is false.

ON THE CONTRARY, is what is said: *John baptized telling the people that they should believe in the one who was to come after him* (Acts 19:4).

Quaestiuncula 3

ULTERIUS. Videtur quod non fuit institutus a Deo. Nullum enim sacramentum a Deo institutum nominatur a ministro; non enim dicitur baptismus Petri. Sed baptismus ille dicitur baptismus Joannis. Ergo non fuit a Deo institutus.

PRAETEREA, sacramenta legis naturae, quae ad sacramenta Christi disponebant, a Deo institutionem non habuerunt, sed ex voto celebrabantur, secundum Hugonem. Sed baptismus Joannis fuit praeparatorius ad sacramenta Christi. Ergo non debuit habere institutionem a Deo.

SED CONTRA est quod dicitur Joan. 1, 33: *qui me misit baptizare in aqua, ille mihi dixit: super quem videris spiritum descendentem, et manentem super eum, hic est qui baptizat in Spiritu Sancto.*

OBJ. 1: Moreover, it seems that it was not instituted by God.[50] For no sacrament instituted by God is named from its minister; for it is not called the baptism of Peter. But that baptism is called the baptism of John. Therefore, it was not instituted by God.

OBJ. 2: Furthermore, sacraments of the law of nature which disposed people for the sacraments of Christ did not have their institution from God but were celebrated at will, according to Hugh.[51] But the baptism of John was preparatory for the sacraments of Christ. Therefore, it did not have its institution from God.

ON THE CONTRARY, is what is said: *the one who sent me to baptize with water said to me, 'He on whom you see the Spirit descend and remain is the one who baptizes with the Holy Spirit'* (Jn 1:33).

Quaestiuncula 4

ULTERIUS. Videtur quod debuit statim Christo baptizato cessare. Quia super illud Joan. 1: *vidit Joannes Jesum venientem ad se*, dicit Augustinus: *baptizatus est Dominus baptismo Joannis, et cessavit baptismus Joannis.*

PRAETEREA, baptismus Joannis erat praeparatorius ad baptismum Christi. Sed baptismus Christi incepit statim Christo baptizato: *quia tactu mundissimae suae carnis vim regenerativam contulit aquis*, ut dicit Beda. Ergo statim debuit cessare.

SED CONTRA est quod legitur Joan. 3, quod post baptismum Christi baptizabat Joannes, et discipuli ejus si-

OBJ. 1: Moreover, it seems that the baptism of John should have ceased immediately when Christ was baptized.[52] For, commenting on the text, *John saw Jesus coming to him* (Jn 1:29), Augustine says: *the Lord was baptized with the baptism of John, and the baptism of John ended.*[53]

OBJ. 2: Furthermore, the baptism of John was preparatory for the baptism of Christ. But the baptism of Christ began immediately once Christ was baptized: *for by the touch of his most pure flesh he conferred regenerative power on the waters*, as Bede says.[54] Therefore, it should have ended immediately.

ON THE CONTRARY, is what is read in John 3, that after the baptism of Christ, John was baptizing, and his dis-

---

50. Parallels: *ST* III, q. 38, a. 2; *Super Matt.* 21.

51. Hugh of St. Victor, *De sacramentis fidei*, Bk. 1, pt. 11, ch. 3 (PL 176:343).

52. Parallels: *ST* III, q. 38, a. 4; q. 39, a. 3, ad 4; *Super Ioan.* 3, lec. 4.

53. Augustine, *In Iohannis euangelium tractatus* (CCSL 36), Tract. 4, n. 14.

54. Cf. Bede, *In Lucae euangelium expositio* (CCSL 120), ch. 3.

militer baptizabant. Ergo baptismus Joannis non cessavit statim Christo baptizato.

ciples baptized in the same way. Therefore, the baptism of John did not end immediately once Christ was baptized.

Response to Quaestiuncula 1

RESPONDEO dicendum, ad primam quaestionem, quod secundum Hugonem de sancto Victore, secundum processum temporis et majorem propinquitatem ad tempus gratiae, oportuit alia et alia sacramenta institui. Unde quia in Joanne quodammodo incepit tempus gratiae (quia *lex, et prophetae usque ad Joannem*, Matth. 11, 13), non quasi ab ipso esset gratia, sed quia ad gratiam viam praeparabat; ideo ejus baptismus fuit aliquod sacramentum; quod quidem erat initiatio quaedam sacramentorum gratiae, quamvis gratia in eo non conferretur. Unde dicendum, quod baptismus Joannis sacramentum erat quodammodo medium inter sacramenta veteris et novae legis, sicut dispositio ad formam media est quodammodo inter privationem et formam. Conveniebat enim quodammodo cum sacramentis veteris legis in hoc quod erat signum tantum; cum sacramentis autem legis novae in materia, et quodammodo in forma.

AD PRIMUM ergo dicendum, quod baptismus Joannis habet aliquid simile cum sacramentalibus baptismi, inquantum erat dispositio ad baptismum Christi; sed inquantum praecessit institutionem baptismi Christi, differt a sacramentalibus, et est sacramentum per se; sicut sacramenta veteris legis, quae etiam suo modo, licet non tam de propinquo, ad sacramenta novae legis disponebant.

AD SECUNDUM dicendum, quod dispositio reducitur ad genus formae ad quam disponit; et ideo baptismus Joannis reducitur ad sacramenta novae legis, sicut incompletum in genere illo; et hoc patet ex ordine procedendi quem Magister servat.

THE FIRST QUESTION I answer by saying that according to Hugh of St. Victor,[55] it was necessary for different sacraments to be instituted at different times according to the passage of time and greater nearness to the time of grace. Hence, since the time of grace began, in a way, in John (*for the law and the prophets prophesied until John came*, Matt 11:13)—not as if grace were from him, but because he was preparing a way for grace—thus his baptism was a kind of sacrament; because indeed it was a certain initiation of the sacraments of grace, although grace was not conferred in it. Hence, it should be said that the baptism of John was a sacrament in the middle, in a way, between the sacraments of the old and of the New Law, just as the disposition to a form is in the middle, in a way, between privation and form. For in a way it agreed with the sacraments of the Old Law in the fact that it was only a sign, but with the sacraments of the New Law in its matter, and, in a way, in its form.

REPLY OBJ. 1: The baptism of John has something in common with the sacramentals of baptism, inasmuch as it was a disposition to the baptism of Christ; but inasmuch as it preceded the institution of the baptism of Christ, it differs from those sacramentals and is a sacrament in itself— like the sacraments of the Old Law, which also in their own way, although not so proximately as John's baptism, disposed people for the sacraments of the New Law.

REPLY OBJ. 2: A disposition is reduced to the genus of the form to which it disposes; and thus the baptism of John is reduced to the sacraments of the New Law, as something incomplete in that genus; and this is clear from the order of proceeding that the Master preserves.

Response to Quaestiuncula 2

AD SECUNDAM QUAESTIONEM dicendum, quod utilitas rei ex forma sua consequitur; et ideo formae sacramentorum ostendunt illud ex quo sacramenta et efficaciam et utilitatem habent. Et quia utilitas baptismi Joannis tota erat disponere ad Christum, ideo haec erat sua forma competens, ut in nomine venturi baptizaret.

AD PRIMUM ergo dicendum, quod quamvis jam venisset in carne, non tamen jam venerat ad baptizandum, et alia salutis nostrae opera exercendum.

TO THE SECOND QUESTION, it should be said that the usefulness of a thing follows from its form; and thus, the forms of the sacraments display that which gives the sacraments both efficacy and usefulness. And because the usefulness of the baptism of John was entirely to dispose people to Christ, therefore this was its appropriate form, that he baptized in the name of the One to come.

REPLY OBJ. 1: Although he had already come in the flesh, he had nevertheless not yet come to be baptized, and to perform the other works of our salvation.

---

55. Hugh of St. Victor, *De sacramentis fidei*, Bk. 1, pt. 11, ch. 6 (PL 176:345).

AD SECUNDUM dicendum, quod fides, cum sit cognitio quaedam, respicit rei veritatem; et quia diversitas temporum significatorum non diversificat veritatem, nec fides penes hoc diversificatur. Sed sacramenta respiciunt effectum; et quia non eodem modo se habet ad actum hoc quod jam est et hoc quod expectatur futurum, quia ad id quod expectatur futurum, actus ordinantur ut disponentes, ab eo autem quod jam est, effective aliquid producitur; ideo diversificatio formae per futurum et praesens designant diversitatem sacramenti.

REPLY OBJ. 2: Faith, since it is a certain understanding, looks at the truth of things; and since a difference in the times of the things signified does not change the truth, neither is the faith in this thing changed. But sacraments have to do with an effect; and because what already is and what is expected in the future are not related in the same way to an act (because for what is expected in the future, the acts are directed as things that dispose, but from what already is, something is effectively produced), therefore differentiation of form by future and present designate different sacraments.

Response to Quaestiuncula 3

AD TERTIAM QUAESTIONEM dicendum, quod Joannes suum baptismum instituit praecepto divino. Unde patet quod institutio ipsius fuit a Deo per auctoritatem, et ab ipso Joanne per ministerium.

AD PRIMUM ergo dicendum, quod propter tres rationes baptismus a Joanne nomen accepit. Primo, quia ipse fuit sui baptismi institutor aliquo modo; Petrus autem nullo modo baptismi quo baptizabat. Secundo, quia nihil in illo baptismo efficiebatur quod Joannes non faceret. Tertio, quia sibi soli erat datum illius baptismi ministerium.

AD SECUNDUM dicendum, quod fides magis determinabatur secundum appropinquationem ad Christum; et ideo etiam sacramenta, quae quaedam fidei protestationes sunt, magis a Christo remota, minus determinata esse debuerunt. Et quia baptismus Joannis de propinquo ad Christi sacramenta disponebat, ideo debuit magis habere determinationem quam sacramenta legis naturae.

TO THE THIRD QUESTION, it should be said that John instituted his baptism by divine command. Hence it is clear that its institution was from God by authority, and from John himself by ministry.

REPLY OBJ. 1: For three reasons this baptism takes its name from John. First, because he was the institutor of this baptism in a certain way, but Peter in no way instituted the baptism with which he baptized. Second, because nothing was brought about in that baptism that John did not do. Third, because the ministry of this baptism was given to him alone.

REPLY OBJ. 2: Faith became more determinate in proportion to its nearness to Christ; and thus with sacraments, too, which are certain protestations of faith: the further removed they are from Christ, the less they needed to be determined. And since the baptism of John in its nearness disposed people to the sacraments of Christ, for this reason it had more determination than the sacraments of the law of nature.

Response to Quaestiuncula 4

AD QUARTAM QUAESTIONEM dicendum, quod cessatio baptismi Joannis potest accipi dupliciter. Uno modo quando cessavit totaliter; et hoc fuit Joanne in carcerem misso, quia ministerium illud soli Joanni concessum est. Alio modo quantum ad maximum suum posse; et sic cessavit baptizato Christo: quia ex tunc ejus baptismus non fuit praecipuus, sed alius fuit eo dignior; sicut cessat officium legati domino suo superveniente, quamvis et aliqua exerceat.

ET PER HOC patet solutio.

TO THE FOURTH QUESTION, it should be said that the ceasing of the baptism of John can be taken two ways. In one way, when it ceased entirely; and this was when John was cast into prison, for that ministry had been granted to John alone. In another way, as to the height of its power, and in this way it ended once Christ was baptized; for from that time on his baptism no longer occupied the first place, but there was another, nobler than it, just as the office of a legate ceases when his superior arrives, although he also exercises it in some way.[56]

AND BY THIS the solution to the objections is clear.

---

56. That is, the legate continues to hold the position or honor of legate even when his superior has come on the scene and no longer needs to be represented by him.

ARTICLE 2

The efficacy of John's baptism[57]

Ad secundum sic proceditur. Videtur quod baptismus Joannis gratiam contulerit. Luc. 3, 3: *erat Joannes baptizans, et praedicans baptismum poenitentiae in remissionem peccatorum.* Sed remissio peccatorum non fit sine gratia. Ergo baptismus ille gratiam contulit.

Praeterea, Damascenus dicit: *purgat Joannes spiritum per aquam.* Sed purgatio spiritualis non fit sine gratia. Ergo ille baptismus gratiam contulit.

Praeterea, Augustinus dicit contra Donatistas: *ita credam Joannem baptizasse in aqua in remissionem peccatorum, ut ab eo baptizatis in spe remitterentur peccata.* Sed spes de remissione peccatorum non potest esse nisi per gratiam. Ergo baptismus ille gratiam contulit.

Praeterea, baptismus Joannis propinquior fuit baptismo Christi quam circumcisio; sed circumcisio gratiam contulit, ut dictum est, dist. 1, quaest. 2, art. 4, quaestiunc. 3. Ergo multo fortius baptismus Joannis.

Praeterea, sacramentum non instituitur, nisi ad causandum gratiam, vel significandum. Sed gratia sufficienter per sacramenta veteris legis erat significata. Si ergo baptismus Joannis gratiam non contulit, pro nihilo institutus fuit.

Sed contra, gratia non confertur sine Spiritu Sancto. Sed in baptismo Joannis non conferebatur Spiritus Sanctus, sed aqua tantum, ut patet Act. 1, 3: *Joannes quidem baptizavit aqua; vos autem baptizabimini Spiritu Sancto.* Ergo in illo baptismo non erat gratia.

Praeterea, non est idem effectus dispositionis et perfectionis. Si ergo baptismus Joannis disponebat ad baptismum Christi, cujus est gratiam conferre: quia *gratia et veritas facta est per Jesum Christum,* Joannes 1, 17, videtur quod baptismus Joannis gratiam non contulit.

Respondeo dicendum, quod hoc ab omnibus conceditur, quod non efficiebatur aliquid per baptismum Joannis quod non esset operatio hominis. Et quia gratia non potest ab homine dari, ideo patet quod baptismus Joannis gratiam non conferebat.

Ad primum ergo dicendum, quod illa auctoritas sic exponenda est, ut referatur ad diversa baptismata hoc modo. *Erat Joannes baptizans,* scilicet baptismate suo,

Obj. 1: To the second question we proceed thus. It seems that the baptism of John conferred grace: *John was baptizing, and preaching a baptism of repentance for the remission of sins* (Luke 3:3). But the remission of sins cannot occur without grace. Therefore, that baptism conferred grace.

Obj. 2: Furthermore, Damascene says: *John purifies the spirit through water.*[58] But spiritual purification does not happen without grace. Therefore, that baptism conferred grace.

Obj. 3: Furthermore, Augustine says, in his work against the Donatists: *I believe that John so baptized in water for the remission of sins, that sins might be forgiven those baptized by him in hope.*[59] But one cannot have hope for the remission of sins without grace. Therefore, that baptism conferred grace.

Obj. 4: Furthermore, the baptism of John was closer to the baptism of Christ than circumcision; but circumcision conferred grace, as has been said (Distinction 1, Question 2, Article 4, Subquestion 3). Therefore, much more did the baptism of John.

Obj. 5: Furthermore, a sacrament is instituted either for the sake of causing grace or for the sake of signifying it. But grace was sufficiently signified by the sacraments of the Old Law. If, then, the baptism of John did not confer grace, it was instituted for nothing.

On the contrary, grace is not conferred without the Holy Spirit. But in the baptism of John the Holy Spirit was not conferred, but only water, as is clear from Acts: *John indeed baptized with water, but you shall be baptized with the Holy Spirit* (Acts 1:5). Therefore, in that baptism there was no grace.

Furthermore, the effects of disposing and perfecting are not the same. If, therefore, the baptism of John disposed people for the baptism of Christ, which did confer grace (for *grace and truth came through Jesus Christ,* Jn 1:17), it seems that the baptism of John did not confer grace.

I answer that, this is granted by all, that nothing was accomplished by the baptism of John that would not be the operation of a man. And because grace cannot be given by a man, it is therefore clear that the baptism of John did not confer grace.

Reply Obj. 1: That authority is to be explained so that it is referred to the different baptisms in this way: *John was baptizing,* namely, with his own baptism, *and preaching,*

---

57. Parallel: *ST* III, q. 38, a. 3.

58. John Damascene, *On the Orthodox Faith*, Bk. 4, ch. 9 (PG 94:1123).

59. See Augustine, *De baptismo contra Donatistas* (CSEL 51:273), Bk. 5, ch. 10: "ita credam baptizasse Iohannem in aqua paenitentiae in remissionem peccatorum, ut ab eo baptizatis in spe remitterentur peccata."

et praedicans, scilicet baptismum Christi, qui est *in remissionem peccatorum*. Si autem referatur utrumque ad baptismum Joannis, sic dicitur esse in remissionem peccatorum: quia baptizatis imponebat dignos fructus poenitentiae agere, quibus peccatorum remissionem consequerentur. Unde baptismus ille erat quasi quaedam protestatio, et professio poenitentiae.

AD SECUNDUM dicendum, quod baptismus ille purgare dicitur modo praedicto: vel etiam materialiter a sordibus corporalibus in signum spiritualis purgationis per Christum futurae; vel a caecitate ignorantiae per doctrinam Joannis Christum annuntiantis.

AD TERTIUM dicendum, quod spes semper ex gratia procedit, non tamen semper ex gratia habita, sed quandoque ex gratia expectata; et sic baptismus Joannis spem faciebat remissionis peccatorum, non conferens gratiam, sed promittens eam in hoc quod praefigurabat baptismum Christi, quo gratia daretur.

AD QUARTUM dicendum, quod quamvis baptismus Joannis magis conveniret cum baptismo Christi quam circumcisio quantum ad materiam, non tamen conveniebat magis quantum ad causam institutionis: quia circumcisio ad necessitatem instituta erat ut remedium contra originale; sed baptismus Joannis, ut assuefaceret ad baptismum Christi.

AD QUINTUM dicendum, quod baptismus Joannis expressius figurabat baptismum Christi quam sacramenta veteris legis propter majorem similitudinem ad ipsum; et ideo magis de propinquo praeparabat ad ipsum in significatione, et quadam poenitentiae protestatione.

namely, the baptism of Christ, which is *for the remission of sins*. On the other hand, if both statements refer to the baptism of John, this is how it is said to be for the remission of sins: that he required the baptized to pursue the noble fruits of penance, by which they attained the remission of sins. Hence that baptism was something like a protestation and profession of repentance.

REPLY OBJ. 2: That baptism is said to purify in the way mentioned: either materially, from physical dirt, as a sign of the future spiritual purification by Christ; or from the blindness of ignorance through the teaching of John announcing Christ.

REPLY OBJ. 3: Hope always proceeds from grace, yet not always from grace possessed, but sometimes from grace awaited; and in this way the baptism of John caused hope for the remission of sins, not conferring grace but promising it in the fact that it prefigured the baptism of Christ, by which grace was given.

REPLY OBJ. 4: Although the baptism of John, as concerns its matter, had more in common with the baptism of Christ than circumcision did, nevertheless, it did not have more in common as concerns the reason for its institution—for circumcision was instituted on account of necessity, as a remedy against original sin, but the baptism of John so that it might accustom people to the baptism of Christ.

REPLY OBJ. 5: The baptism of John more expressly represented the baptism of Christ than the sacraments of the Old Law, on account of its greater resemblance to it. And therefore it prepared for it more closely in signification and in a certain protestation of repentance.

ARTICLE 3

To whom John's baptism applied

Quaestiuncula 1

AD TERTIUM SIC PROCEDITUR. Videtur quod Christo non competeret baptizari baptismo Joannis. Baptismus enim Joannis erat baptismus poenitentiae, ut dicitur Luc. 3. Sed Christo non competit poenitentia, sicut nec peccatum. Ergo nec baptizari baptismo Joannis.

PRAETEREA, omnis Christi actio nostra est instructio. Sed non instruimur baptizari baptismo Joannis. Ergo non debuit Christus illo baptismo baptizari.

SED CONTRA est quod ipse ad baptismum Joannis vadens dixit: *sic decet nos implere omnem justitiam*; Matth. 3, 15.

OBJ. 1: To the third question we proceed thus. It seems that it did not befit Christ to be baptized with the baptism of John.[60] For the baptism of John was a baptism of repentance, as is said in Luke 3.[61] But no repentance befits Christ, as he had no sin. Therefore, neither did it befit him to be baptized by the baptism of John.

OBJ. 2: Furthermore, every action of Christ is for our instruction. But we are not instructed to be baptized by the baptism of John. Therefore, Christ did not need to be baptized with that baptism.

ON THE CONTRARY, he himself said, when going to the baptism of John, *it is proper for us in this way to fulfill all righteousness* (Matt 3:15).

Quaestiuncula 2

ULTERIUS. Videtur quod nulli alii hoc baptismo debuerunt baptizari. Hoc enim est solius Christi ut a sacramentis non accipiat, sed magis eis conferat. Sed baptismus Joannis erat tale sacramentum a quo non poterat aliquid accipi. Ergo soli Christo competebat.

PRAETEREA, sacramenta eadem ratione omnibus competunt. Sed non erat necessarium quod omnes baptismo Joannis baptizarentur. Ergo nulli praeter Christum ipso baptizari debuerunt.

SED CONTRA est quod dicitur Matth. 3, 5: *egrediebantur ad illum Hierosolymitae universi, et baptizabantur ab eo.*

OBJ. 1: Moreover, it seems that no others needed to be baptized with that baptism.[62] For Christ is the only one who does not receive sacraments, but rather bestows them. But the baptism of John was a sacrament from which nothing could be received. Therefore, it was fitting only for Christ.[63]

OBJ. 2: Furthermore, sacraments are given to everyone for the same reason. But it was not necessary for all to be baptized with the baptism of John. Therefore, no one other than Christ should have been baptized with it.

ON THE CONTRARY, is what is said, *all the people of Jerusalem were going out to him, and they were baptized by him* (Matt 3:5–6).

Quaestiuncula 3

ULTERIUS. Videtur quod debuerunt illo baptismo pueri baptizari. Erat enim ille baptismus signum baptismi Christi. Sed baptismus Christi competit pueris. Ergo et ille.

OBJ. 1: Moreover, it seems that children should have been baptized with that baptism. For that baptism was a sign of the baptism of Christ. But the baptism of Christ is suited to children. Therefore, that one as well.

---

60. Parallels: *ST* III, q. 39, aa. 1 & 2; *Super Matt.* 3.

61. Luke 3:3; some MSS have a reference here to Acts 20:21, which makes little sense.

62. Parallel: *ST* III, q. 38, a. 4.

63. In *ST* III, q. 38, a. 4, obj. 2, this argument is made much clearer: "Whoever is baptized either receives something from the baptism or confers something on the baptism. But no one could receive anything from the baptism of John, because thereby grace was not conferred, as stated above. On the other hand, no one could confer anything on baptism save Christ, who *sanctified the waters by the touch of His most pure flesh*. Therefore, it seems that Christ alone should have been baptized with the baptism of John."

PRAETEREA, circumcisio dabatur etiam pueris, et eis principaliter. Sed baptismus Joannis est medium inter circumcisionem et baptismum Christi, qui datur indifferenter magnis et parvis. Ergo et baptismus Joannis parvis dari debuit.

SED CONTRA, quia baptismus ille erat ut assuescerent ad baptismum Christi. Sed hoc non poterat esse nisi ratione illorum qui discretionem habebant. Ergo pueris ille baptismus non competebat.

OBJ. 2: Furthermore, circumcision was also given to children, indeed chiefly to them. But the baptism of John is a middle between circumcision and the baptism of Christ, which is given indifferently to great and small. Therefore, the baptism of John should also have been given to little ones.

ON THE CONTRARY, that baptism was for the sake of familiarizing people with the baptism of Christ. But this could only happen through the reason of those who had discretion. Therefore, that baptism was not suited to children.

Response to Quaestiuncula 1

RESPONDEO dicendum, quod Christus pluribus de causis a Joanne baptizari voluit, quarum tres tanguntur in Glossa Marc. 1; scilicet propter humilitatem implendam (ut ipsemet dicit Matth. 3); ut baptismum Joannis approbaret, et ut aquas consecraret suae carnis tactu, et sic baptismum suum institueret. Quartam causam tangit Augustinus, ut scilicet ostenderet non interesse quis a quo baptizaretur. Quintam tangit in *Lib. quaestionum veteris et novi testamenti*, scilicet ad exemplum baptismi proponendum illis qui erant futuri filii Dei per fidem. Sextam tangit Chrysostomus, ut scilicet in baptismo miracula ostendens, evacuaret illorum errorem qui Joannem Christo majorem credebant.

AD PRIMUM ergo dicendum, quod, sicut dictum est, Christus a sacramentis nihil accepit; et ideo non dicitur baptismus Joannis baptismus poenitentiae quo ad Christum, sed quo ad alios qui ad poenitentiam per ipsum praeparabantur; sicut etiam circumcisio Christi non fuit in remedium originalis peccati, a quo Christus immunis erat.

AD SECUNDUM dicendum, quod actio Christi nostra est instructio, non ut eodem modo agamus sicut Christus fecit, sed ut pro modo nostro Christum imitemur; et ideo per baptismum suum dedit nobis exemplum, ut baptizaremur illo baptismo qui nobis competit, per quem scilicet remissionem peccatorum consequamur.

I ANSWER THAT, Christ wished to be baptized by John for many reasons, three of which are touched upon by the Gloss on Mark 1:[64] for the sake of fulfilling humility, as Christ himself says in Matthew 3; to give John's baptism his approval; and to consecrate the waters by his touch and so institute his own baptism. Augustine[65] touches on a fourth cause, namely to show that it makes no difference who is baptized by whom. Augustine gives a fifth reason in his book *Questions on the Old and New Testaments*,[66] namely to give an example of baptism to those who in the future would become children of God by faith. Chrysostom offers a sixth,[67] namely to refute the error of those who though John greater than Christ by a display of miracles at his baptism.

REPLY OBJ. 1: As has been said, Christ received nothing from the sacraments; and thus the baptism of John is not called a baptism of repentance in the case of Christ, but with regard to the others who were being prepared by it for penance; just as also the circumcision of Christ was not a remedy for original sin, from which Christ was immune.

REPLY OBJ. 2: The action of Christ is our instruction, not so that we might act in the same way as Christ did, but that we might imitate Christ after our own manner; and thus, by his baptism he gave us an example so that we might be baptized by that baptism that befits us, namely, the one resulting in the remission of sins.

Response to Quaestiuncula 2

AD SECUNDAM QUAESTIONEM dicendum, quod, sicut dicit Augustinus in Lib. *de baptismo contra Dona-*

TO THE SECOND QUESTION, it should be said that, as Augustine says in his book *On Baptism Against the Do-*

---

64. *Glossa ordinaria* (PL 114:181).
65. Augustine, *In Iohannis euangelium tractatus* (CCSL 36), Tract. 6, n. 7.
66. Augustine, *Questions on the Old and New Testaments*, q. 49 (PL 35:2249).
67. St. John Chrysostom, *Homilies on Matthew*, Homily 12, n. 2 (PG 57:446).

tistas, si Joannes solum Christum baptizasset, videretur melioris baptismi dispensator, quanto melior erat qui baptizabatur, et si omnes baptizasset videretur quod Christi baptismus non sufficeret ad salutem; et ideo quosdam alios baptizavit, sed non omnes.

AD PRIMUM ergo dicendum, quod quamvis alii a baptismo Joannis non acciperent gratiam; accipiebant tamen quoddam signum gratiae suscipiendae, et servandae poenitentiae.

AD SECUNDUM patet solutio ex dictis.

natists,[68] if John had baptized Christ alone, he would have seemed the minister of a better baptism, since the one he baptized was so much greater; and if he had baptized everyone, it would have seemed that the baptism of Christ did not suffice for salvation. And thus he baptized only some people, but not all.

REPLY OBJ. 1: Although some people did not receive grace through the baptism of John, they did receive a certain sign of the grace to be obtained, and the repentance to be observed.

THE ANSWER TO THE SECOND is clear from what has been said.

Response to Quaestiuncula 3

AD TERTIAM QUAESTIONEM dicendum, quod baptismus Joannis erat baptismus poenitentiae; et quia pueris non competit poenitentia, ideo non competebat eis ille baptismus. Nec est simile de baptismo Christi et circumcisione, quae ordinantur contra originale peccatum, quod in pueris est.

ET PER HOC patet solutio ad objecta.

TO THE THIRD QUESTION, it should be said that the baptism of John was a baptism of repentance; and since repentance does not pertain to children, that baptism did not pertain to them for the same reason. Nor is it the same with the baptism of Christ and circumcision, which are ordained against original sin, which does exist in children.

AND BY THIS the solutions to the objections are clear.

---

68. See Augustine, *De baptismo contra Donatistas* (CSEL 51), Bk. 5, ch. 9.

ARTICLE 4

Whether those who were baptized by John had to be baptized with the baptism of Christ[69]

AD QUARTUM SIC PROCEDITUR. Videtur quod baptizati baptismo Joannis, non debebant baptizari baptismo Christi. Act. enim 8 dicitur, quod apostoli in Samariam venientes, illos qui baptizati erant in nomine Jesu, non baptizabant, sed tantum manus imponebant. Cum ergo baptismus in nomine Jesu sine collatione Spiritus Sancti sit baptismus Joannis, videtur quod baptizati baptismo Joannis, non baptizabantur baptismo Christi.

PRAETEREA, Hieronymus super illud: *effundam de spiritu meo*, dicit: quod haec est causa quare quidam baptizati a Joanne, baptismo Christi iterum baptizati sunt a Paulo, Act. 20 quia fidem Trinitatis non habebant, quia neque si Spiritus Sanctus est audierant. Si ergo aliqui baptizati essent a Joanne, fidem Trinitatis habentes, videtur quod iterum baptizari non debuerint baptismo Christi.

PRAETEREA, in apostolis debuit ostendi omne illud quod est necessarium ad salutem. Sed apostolis post baptismum Joannis solus baptismus Spiritus Sancti praenuntiatur, Act. 1. Ergo non erat necessarium quod baptismo Christi iterum baptizarentur.

PRAETEREA, ad baptismum requiritur aqua et Spiritus Sanctus. Sed per baptismum Joannis erat facta ablutio aquae. Ergo non oportebat nisi quod suppleretur quod deerat, scilicet Spiritus Sanctus.

SED CONTRA est quod dicitur Joannis 3, 5: *nisi quis renatus fuerit ex aqua et Spiritu Sancto, non potest introire in regnum Dei*. Sed baptismus Joannis non regenerabat aliquo modo. Ergo necessarium erat ut iterum baptismo Christi baptizarentur.

PRAETEREA, Augustinus dicit, quod baptizabat Joannes et non est baptizatum. Sed de necessitate salutis tempore gratiae est quod homo sit baptizatus, vel saltem propositum baptismi habuerit. Ergo oportebat eos qui baptismum Joannis acceperant, iterum baptizari baptismo Christi.

PRAETEREA, impositio manuum praecedente baptismo Joannis non imprimebat characterem baptismalem. Sed character talis est de necessitate salutis vel in actu

OBJ. 1: To the fourth we proceed thus. It seems that those baptized by John the Baptist did not need to be baptized with the baptism of Christ. For in Acts 8:15–16, it is said that when the apostles went to Samaria, they did not baptize those who had been baptized in the name of Christ, but only imposed their hands upon them. Since baptism in the name of Jesus without invoking the Holy Spirit is the baptism of John, it therefore seems that those baptized by the baptism of John were not baptized with the baptism of Christ.

OBJ. 2: Furthermore, on the text, *I will pour out my spirit* (Acts 2:17), Jerome says that this is the reason why some people baptized by John were again baptized by Paul with the baptism of Christ (cf. Acts 20), because they did not have faith in the Trinity, since they had not heard if the Holy Spirit exists.[70] Therefore, if some had been baptized by John who did have faith in the Trinity, it would seem that they did not need to be baptized again with the baptism of Christ.

OBJ. 3: Furthermore, everything that was necessary for salvation had to be displayed in the apostles. But after the baptism of John, only the baptism of the Holy Spirit is foretold to the apostles (cf. Acts 1:5). Therefore, it was not necessary that they be baptized again with the baptism of Christ.

OBJ. 4: Furthermore, for baptism there is required water and the Holy Spirit. But in the baptism of John there was a pouring of water. Therefore, the only thing needed was to supply what was missing, namely, the Holy Spirit.

ON THE CONTRARY, is what is said: *unless a man is reborn from water and the Holy Spirit, he cannot enter into the kingdom of God* (John 3:5). But the baptism of John did not regenerate in that way. Therefore, it was necessary that they be baptized again with the baptism of Christ.

FURTHERMORE, Augustine says that John was baptizing and had not been baptized.[71] But it is necessary for salvation in the time of grace that a man be baptized, or at least that he have the intention of being baptized. Therefore, it was necessary for those who had received the baptism of John to be baptized again with the baptism of Christ.

FURTHERMORE, the imposition of hands preceding the baptism of John did not imprint a baptismal character. But that kind of character, either actually or in intention, is nec-

---

69. Parallels: below, in the exposition of the text; *ST* III, q. 38, a. 6; q. 66, a. 9, ad 2; *Super Matt.* 3.

70. See Jerome, *Commentary on Joel* (CCSL 76), ch. 2, l. 677: "Ergo salutare Dei uideri non potest, nisi Spiritus Sanctus effundatur. Et quicumque credere se dicit in Christum, non credens in Spiritum Sanctum, perfectae fidei oculos non habebit. Unde et in Actibus Apostolorum, qui baptizati erant baptismate Ioannis in eum qui uenturus erat, hoc est in nomine Domini Iesu, quia responderunt Paulo interroganti: Sed ne si sit quidem Spiritus Sanctus, nouimus, iterum baptizantur; immo uerum baptisma accipiunt, quia sine Spiritu Sancto et mysterio Trinitatis, quicquid in unam et alteram personam acciperis, imperfectum est."

71. Augustine, *In Iohannis euangelium tractatus* (CCSL 36), Tract. 5, par. 16.

vel in proposito. Ergo oportebat quod baptizati baptismo Joannis iterum baptizarentur baptismo Christi, et non sufficiebat eis manus impositio.

RESPONDEO dicendum, quod circa hoc est duplex opinio. Quidam enim dicunt, quod baptismus Joannis erat praeparatorius ad Christum suscipiendum; et ideo si quis baptismum Joannis suscepisset in eo sistens, non referens ad Christum, baptismus in eo frustraretur a fine suo; et ideo oportebat eum iterum baptizari baptismo Christi. Si autem non figeret spem suam in baptismo Joannis, sed ulterius referret ad Christum, sic ex gratia Christi et baptismo Joannis praeaccepto efficiebatur quasi unum quid; et ideo non oportebat quod iterum aqua baptizaretur, sed solum quod Spiritum Sanctum per manus impositionem acciperet; et haec videtur fuisse Magistri opinio in littera.

Sed quia sacramenta novae legis ex ipso opere operato efficaciam habent, ideo videtur quod spes et fides illius qui baptismum suscipit, nihil faciat ad sacramentum, quamvis posset facere ad rem sacramenti impediendam vel promovendam. Unde quantumcumque spem suam aliquis ad Christum referret baptizatus baptismo Joannis, baptismum novae legis non consequebatur; et ideo si baptismus novae legis est de necessitate salutis, oportebat quod iterum illo baptismo baptizaretur. Praeterea est generale in omnibus sacramentis, quod si omittatur quod est de substantia sacramenti, oportet id sacramentum iterari. Unde cum non esset forma debita in baptismo Joannis, oportebat quod iteraretur baptismus. Et hoc habet communior opinio, quae etiam ex verbis Augustini confirmatur, qui dicit super Joan., Hom. 5: *qui baptizati sunt baptismate Joannis, non eis sufficit: baptizandi enim sunt baptismate Christi.*

ET IDEO SECUNDUM HOC dicendum ad primum, quod ibi agitur de illis qui baptizati erant a Philippo, de quo constat quod baptismo Christi baptizaverat. Sed non erat ibi Spiritus Sanctus ad robur, sicut in confirmatione datur: quia ille non fuit Philippus apostolus, sed unus de septem diaconibus, et ideo non poterat manus imponere, quia hoc episcoporum est; et propter hoc missi sunt ad hoc Petrus et Joannes.

AD SECUNDUM dicendum, quod Hieronymus non vult tangere causam rebaptizationis, sed insufficientiam fidei ipsorum ad salutem, ut patet ex verbis praecedentibus. Praemittit enim: *qui dicit se credere in Christum, et non credit in Spiritum Sanctum, nondum habet claros oculos.* Insufficientiam autem fidei non posset esse causa

essary for salvation. Therefore, it was necessary that those baptized by John be baptized again with the baptism of Christ, and the imposition of hands was not sufficient.

I ANSWER THAT, concerning this there are two opinions. For certain people say that the baptism of John was preparatory for receiving Christ; and thus, if someone had received the baptism of John as something self-contained, not referring to Christ, baptism in that person would have been thwarted from achieving its end, and so he would have had to be baptized again with the baptism of Christ. But if he did not fix his hope in the baptism of John, but referred it further to Christ, then a single thing was made, so to speak, out of the grace of Christ and the baptism of John already received; and thus, it was not necessary that he be baptized again with water, but only that he receive the Holy Spirit by the imposition of hands. And this seems to have been the opinion of the Master in the text.

But since the sacraments of the New Law have their efficacy by the very act performed, it seems therefore that the hope and faith of the one who receives baptism does nothing for the sacrament, although it could work toward impeding or fostering the *res sacramenti*. Hence, however much someone baptized by John referred his own hope to Christ, it did not bring about the baptism of the New Law; and thus, if the baptism of the New Law is necessary for salvation, it is necessary that he be baptized again with that baptism. Furthermore, it is the case in all the sacraments that if anything of the sacrament's substance is omitted, the sacrament has to be given again. Hence, since there was not the due form in the baptism of John, baptism had to be given again. And the more common opinion holds this, which is also confirmed by the words of Augustine, who says in his *Commentary on John*, Homily 5: *Those who were baptized with the baptism of John, it was not enough for them: for they had to be baptized with the baptism of Christ.*[72]

REPLY OBJ. 1: And so, accordingly, it should be replied to the first that this text is treating of those who had been baptized by Philip, who had certainly baptized with the baptism of Christ. But the Holy Spirit was not given there for strengthening, as he is given in confirmation: for that Philip was not Philip the Apostle, but one of the seven deacons, and so he could not perform the imposition of hands, since that belongs to bishops; and for this reason, Peter and John were sent to do it.

REPLY OBJ. 2: Jerome does not mean to give a reason for rebaptizing, but to point out the insufficiency of those people's faith for salvation, as is clear from his preceding words. For he says before: *whoever says that he believes in Christ and does not believe in the Holy Spirit, does not yet have clear eyes.*[73] But insufficiency of faith could not be the

---

72. Augustine, *In Iohannis euangelium tractatus* (CCSL 36), Tract. 5, par. 6.
73. The exact text is cited in a note just above.

quare aliqui baptizarentur, sed quare instruendi essent, sicut et nunc fit.

Ad tertium dicendum, quod apostoli creduntur baptizati fuisse baptismo Christi, quamvis scriptum non inveniatur, ut dicitur in Glossa Joan. 13 super illud: *qui lotus est, non indiget nisi ut pedes lavet.* Ex quo enim ipsi alios baptizabant, ut habetur Joan. 3, videtur quod et ipsi venientes ad Christum baptizati fuerint. Si tamen Christus, qui habuit potestatem remittendi peccata, et qui virtutem suam sacramentis non alligavit, eos sine baptismo ex privilegio quodam sanctificare voluisset, non esset ad consequentiam trahendum. Ex auctoritate autem inducta non habetur quod apostoli tantum baptismo Joannis baptizati erant; sed comparatio quaedam baptismi flaminis ad baptismum Joannis.

Ad quartum dicendum, quod ad baptismum requiritur aqua cum debita forma. Joannes autem non observabat formam baptismi Christi, nec iterum erat in eo efficacia sicut in baptismo Christi; et ideo, quia omittebantur ea quae erant de necessitate sacramenti, oportebat iterum baptizari.

reason that certain people were baptized, but rather why they needed to be instructed, as is also done today.

Reply Obj. 3: The apostles are believed to have been baptized with the baptism of Christ, although it is not found written, as is said in the Gloss on John 13: *One who has bathed does not need to wash except for the feet* (John 13:10).[74] For by the fact that they were baptizing others, as John 3 relates, it seems that they, too, had been baptized when they came to Christ. But if Christ, who had the power of forgiving sins and who did not bind his own power to the sacraments, wanted to sanctify them without baptism by way of a certain privilege, such a privilege would not have been handed down to the succession.[75] It cannot be derived from the authority cited, however, that the apostles had been baptized only by the baptism of John; it is rather a certain comparison of the baptism of spirit to the baptism of John.

Reply Obj. 4: Baptism requires water with the due form. Now John did not observe the form of Christ's baptism, nor again was there an efficacy in it like there is in Christ's baptism; and thus, since things that are necessary to the sacrament were omitted, it was necessary to be baptized again.

---

74. *Glossa ordinaria*, PL 114:405.
75. That is, the bishops who were their successors.

Exposition of the Text

Quorum alia remedium contra peccatum praebent . . . alia gratia et virtute nos fulciunt. Omnia sacramenta novae legis sunt in remedium, et gratiam conferunt, ut dictum est. Ergo distinctio illa nulla videtur. Et dicendum, quod illa distinctio sacramentorum sumitur secundum id ad quod principaliter ordinantur. Quamvis ergo omnia sacramenta aliquo modo gratiam conferant, et in remedium sint, quaedam tamen principaliter ordinata sunt in remedium, contra aliquem specialem morbum, ut matrimonium contra concupiscentiam; quaedam vero de sui propria intentione sunt ordinata ad remedium morbi, et ad gratiam, sicut baptismus, qui est spiritualis regeneratio, per quam vetus homo corrumpitur, et novus generatur; quaedam autem, quia gratiam praesupponunt, ordinantur ad gratiae perfectionem sicut Eucharistia; et sic intelligenda sunt verba Magistri: *non utique propter remedium, sed ad sacramentum*; et debet accipi sacramentum large pro quolibet signo rei sacrae.

Baptismum Christi Joannes suo baptismo praenuntiavit. Ideo baptismus Christi potius quam alia sacramenta novae legis praeparatorium habuit, quia baptismus est janua sacramentorum, et ipse facit aliis viam; unde praeparatorio sacramenta alia non indigebant.

Iterum baptizabantur, immo verum baptisma accipiebant. Ex hoc patet quod praecedens baptismus non reputabatur aliquibus pro baptismo: quia qui baptisma Christi accipiebant, non iterato baptizabantur, sed verum baptisma de novo accipiebant; et ideo quasi corrigens quod dixerat: *iterum baptizabantur*, addit, *immo verum baptisma accipiebant*; et sic Magister per verba Hieronymi suam intentionem probare non potest.

Of these some offer a remedy against sin . . . others fortify us with grace and virtue.[76] All sacraments of the New Law act as a remedy and confer grace, as has been said. Therefore, that distinction seems to amount to nothing. And it should be said that that distinction between the sacraments is taken according to what they are principally ordered to. Therefore, although all sacraments confer grace in some way, and act as a remedy, nevertheless some are principally directed toward remedying a certain particular disease, as marriage is against concupiscence; while others from their proper intention are directed both toward remedying a disease and toward grace, like baptism, which is a spiritual regeneration through which the old man is destroyed and a new one generated. Some, however, since they presuppose grace, are directed toward the perfecting of grace, like the Eucharist. And this is how the words of the Master [regarding marriage] are to be understood: *not at all as a remedy, but as a sacrament*;[77] and "sacrament" should be taken broadly for any sign of a sacred thing.

John, with his baptism, foretold Christ's baptism.[78] Thus the baptism of Christ had a preparation, rather than the other sacraments of the New Law, for baptism is the gateway to the sacraments, and itself opens the way to the others. This is why the other sacraments did not need a preparation.

They are baptized again, or rather, they receive true baptism.[79] And from this it is clear that the previous baptism was not considered by some people to be a baptism: for whoever received the baptism of Christ were not baptized again, but they received the true baptism for the first time.[80] And thus, as if correcting what he had said: *they are baptized again*, he adds, *rather, they receive true baptism*; and so the Master cannot prove his point by the words of Jerome.

---

76. Peter Lombard, *Sententiae* IV, 2.1 (11). 1.

77. Giulio Silano's translation of this passage, interpreting Peter Lombard as Aquinas directs, renders *sacramentum* as "sign." *Sent* IV, 2.1 (11). 3.

78. *Sent* IV, 2.2 (12). 2.

79. *Sent* IV, 2.6 (16). 2 citing Jerome, *In Ioelem* 2, 28.

80. That is, a person who was baptized by John and later received Christian baptism cannot be said to be "rebaptized," because the baptism of John is not of the same kind as that of Christ; such a person should be said to be baptized, simply speaking, *de novo*.

DISTINCTION 3
BAPTISM IN ITSELF

Postquam determinavit Magister de his quae praeexiguntur ad sacramenta novae legis, hic incipit determinare de singulis sacramentorum novae legis; et dividitur in partes duas: in prima determinat de illis sacramentis quae sunt ordinata in remedium unius personae; in secunda de illis quae sunt ordinata in remedium totius ecclesiae; 24 dist., ibi: *nunc ad considerationem sacrae ordinationis accedamus.*

Prima dividitur in tres: in prima determinat de sacramento intrantium, scilicet baptismo, in secunda de sacramentis progredientium, 7 dist., ibi: *nunc de sacramento confirmationis addendum est*; in tertia de sacramento exeuntium, scilicet extrema unctione, 23 dist., ibi: *praeter praemissa est aliud sacramentum, scilicet unctio infirmorum.*

Prima in tres: in prima determinat de baptismo secundum se; in secunda de baptismo per comparationem ad recipientes, 4 dist., ibi: *hic dicendum est, aliquos suscipere sacramentum et rem sacramenti* etc.; in tertia secundum comparationem ad ministrantes, 5 dist., ibi: *post haec sciendum est, sacramentum baptismi a bonis et a malis ministris dari.*

Prima in duas: in prima determinat de baptismo secundum se; in secunda determinat de eo per comparationem ad circumcisionem, ibi: *solet etiam quaeri, si circumcisio amisit statim vim suam ab institutione baptismi.*

Prima in duas: in prima determinat quid est baptismus; in secunda de his quae ad baptismum requiruntur, ibi: *sed quod est illud verbum quo accedente ad elementum fit sacramentum?* Haec pars dividitur in tres secundum tria quae exiguntur ad baptismum: in prima enim determinat de forma baptismi; in secunda de materia ejus, ibi: *celebratur autem hoc sacramentum tantum in aqua*; in tertia de ipso actu ablutionis vel immersionis, ibi: *de immersione vero si quaeritur quomodo fieri debeat, praecise respondemus.*

Prima in duas: in prima determinat de forma baptismi; in secunda de institutione ipsius, ibi: *de institutione baptismi quando coepit, variae sunt aestimationes.*

After the Master has examined those things that are required for the sacraments of the New Law, here he begins to consider each individual sacrament of the New Law; and this is divided into two parts. In the first, he examines those sacraments that are directed to the remedy of one person; in the second, those that are directed to the remedy of the whole Church, at Distinction 24: *Now let us proceed to the consideration of sacred ordination.*[1]

The first part is divided into three: in the first, he examines the sacrament of those entering, namely, baptism; in the second, the sacraments of those progressing, at Distinction 7: *Now we must add something about the sacrament of confirmation*;[2] in the third, the sacrament of those departing, namely, extreme unction, at Distinction 23: *After the ones mentioned above, there is another sacrament, namely, anointing of the sick.*[3]

The first is in three parts: first, he examines baptism in itself; in the second, baptism in relation to those receiving it, at Distinction 4: *Here it is to be said that some receive the sacrament and the thing*, etc.;[4] in the third, baptism in relation to its ministers, at Distinction 5: *after these matters, it is to be known that the sacrament of baptism is given by good and wicked ministers.*[5]

The first is in two parts: in the first, he defines baptism in itself; in the second, he examines it in comparison to circumcision, at: *It is usual to ask whether circumcision lost its standing after the institution of baptism.*[6]

The first is in two parts: in the first he defines what baptism is; in the second, those things that are required for baptism, at: *but what is that word at whose addition to the element the sacrament is brought about?*[7] This part is divided into three according to the three things that are required for baptism: for in the first he defines the form of baptism; in the second, its matter, at: *And this sacrament is celebrated only in water*;[8] in the third, the act itself of washing or immersing, at: *As to the immersion, if it is asked how it ought to be done exactly, we answer.*[9]

The first is in two parts: in the first he defines the form of baptism; in the second, its institution, at: *On the institution of baptism, or when it may have begun, there are various*

---

1. Peter Lombard, *Sententiae* IV, 24.1 (131), 1.
2. *Sent.* IV, 7.1 (43), 1.
3. *Sent.* IV, 23.1 (127), 1.
4. *Sent.* IV, 4.1 (26), 1.
5. *Sent.* IV, 5.1 (33), 1.
6. *Sent.* IV, 3.8 (24), 1.
7. *Sent.* IV, 3.2 (18), 1.
8. *Sent.* IV, 3.6 (22), 1.
9. *Sent.* IV, 3.7 (23), 1.

Circa primum duo facit: primo determinat formam baptismi; secundo movet quamdam quaestionem circa formam baptismi, et determinat eam, ibi: *hic quaeritur, an baptismus esset verus, si diceretur, in nomine patris tantum*, etc.

Prima in duas: in prima determinat formam principalem baptismi; in secunda quamdam formam secundariam pro tempore observatam, ibi: *legitur tamen in actibus apostolorum, apostolos baptizasse in nomine Christi.*

Solet etiam quaeri, si circumcisio amisit statim vim suam ab institutione baptismi. Hic determinat de baptismo per comparationem ad circumcisionem, et circa hoc tria facit: primo determinat cessationem circumcisionis; secundo institutionem baptismi, ibi: *causa vero institutionis baptismi est innovatio mentis;* tertio effectum utriusque, ibi: *si quaeritur, utrum baptismus aperuerit caelum, quod non aperuit circumcisio; dicimus, quia nec baptismus nec circumcisio, regni nobis aditum aperuit, sed hostia salvatoris.*

opinions.[10] Concerning the first he does two things: first, he defines the form of baptism; second, he raises certain questions about the form of baptism, and considers them, at: *here it is asked whether it would be a true baptism if it were given only in the name of the Father,* etc.[11]

The first is in two parts: in the first he considers the principal form of baptism; in the second, a certain secondary form observed for a time, at: *And yet we read in the Acts of the Apostles that the Apostles baptized in the name of Christ.*[12]

It is usual to ask whether circumcision lost its standing after the institution of baptism.[13] Here he examines baptism by comparison with circumcision, and concerning this he does three things: first, he considers the cessation of circumcision; second, the institution of baptism, at: *but the cause of the institution of baptism is the renewal of the mind;*[14] third, the effect of each, at: *If it is asked whether baptism opened heaven, which circumcision had not done, we say that neither baptism, nor circumcision, but the Savior's sacrifice, opened up access to the kingdom for us.*[15]

---

10. *Sent.* IV, 3.5 (21), 1.
11. *Sent.* IV, 3.4 (20), 1.
12. *Sent.* IV, 3.3 (19), 1, citing Acts 18:12; 19:5; 2:38.
13. *Sent.* IV, 3.8 (24), 1.
14. *Sent.* IV, 3.9 (25), 1.
15. *Sent.* IV, 3.9 (25), 2.

QUESTION 1

THE ESSENCE OF BAPTISM

Hic quaeruntur quinque:
primo, quid sit baptismus;
secundo, de forma ipsius;
tertio, de materia ejus;
quarto, de intentione;
quinto, de institutione.

Here five questions arise:
first, what baptism is;
second, its form;
third, its matter;
fourth, its intention;
fifth, its institution.

ARTICLE 1

What baptism is

Quaestiuncula 1

AD PRIMUM SIC PROCEDITUR. Videtur quod inconvenienter sit assignata haec definitio baptismi quae in littera ponitur, scilicet: *Baptismus est ablutio corporis exterior, facta sub forma praescripta verborum.* Manente enim definito, manet definitio. Sed transeunte ablutione, quae est quaedam actio, vel passio, manet baptismus. Ergo baptismus non est ablutio.

PRAETEREA, sacramentum, secundum Hugonem, est materiale elementum. Ablutio autem non est materiale elementum, sed elementi usus. Ergo baptismus, cum sit sacramentum, non erit ablutio.

PRAETEREA, sacramentum est in genere relationis, cum sit causa, vel signum, sicut supra dictum est. Sed baptismus est sacramentum. Ergo inconvenienter ponitur in genere actionis vel passionis.

PRAETEREA, in definitione instrumenti debet poni illud ad quod est. Sed baptismus, sicut et alia sacramenta, ut prius dictum est, sunt instrumenta sanctificationis. Ergo cum in definitione ejus nulla mentio fiat de sanctificatione, videtur inconvenienter esse assignata.

OBJ. 1: To the first we proceed thus. It seems that this definition of baptism, which is set down in the text, is unfittingly assigned, namely: *Baptism is an external washing of the body, done under the prescribed form of words.*[16] For as long as the thing defined remains, the definition remains. But once a cleansing, which is a certain action or passion, has passed away, baptism still remains. Therefore, baptism is not a cleansing.

OBJ. 2: Furthermore, a sacrament, according to Hugh,[17] is a material element. Now a cleansing is not a material element but the use of an element. Therefore baptism, since it is a sacrament, will not be a cleansing.

OBJ. 3: Furthermore, a sacrament is in the genus of relation, since it is a cause or a sign, as was said above. But baptism is a sacrament. Therefore, it is unfittingly included in the genus of action or passion.

OBJ. 4: Furthermore, an instrument's definition should include what it is for. But baptism, as well as all the other sacraments, as was said before, are instruments of sanctification. Therefore, since no mention is made of sanctification in its definition, it seems to be unfittingly assigned.

Quaestiuncula 2

ULTERIUS. Videtur quod etiam inconvenienter assignetur definitio Hugonis, quae talis est: *Baptismus est*

OBJ. 1: Moreover, it seems that the definition of Hugh is also unfittingly assigned, which goes thus: *Baptism is water*

---

16. Parallels: below, exposition of the text; *ST* III, q. 61, a. 1.
17. Hugh of St. Victor, *De sacramentis fidei*, Bk. 1, pt. 9, ch. 2 (PL 176:317).

aqua diluendis criminibus sanctificata per verbum Dei. Nihil enim fit in seipso. Sed baptismus in aqua fit. Ergo baptismus non est aqua.

Praeterea, in definitione alicujus non debet poni aliquid quod non sit de essentia ejus. Sed sanctificatio materiae non est de essentia baptismi: quia in mari vel in flumine potest fieri baptismus. Ergo sanctificatio aquae non debet poni in definitione baptismi.

Praeterea, definitio debet converti cum definito. Sed potest esse aqua sanctificata verbo vitae diluendis criminibus, et tamen non erit baptismus, sicut quando non fit intinctio. Ergo haec non est competens baptismi definitio.

Praeterea, effectus qui potest impediri, non debet poni in definitione causae, quia tunc definitio esset minus quam definitum. Sed potest impediri quod per baptismum non diluantur crimina. Ergo non debet ablutio criminum in definitione baptismi poni.

sanctified by the word of God for washing away our crimes.[18] For nothing comes to be in itself. But baptism is done in water. Therefore, baptism is not water.

Obj. 2: Furthermore, nothing should be included in the definition of something that is not of its essence. But the sanctification of the matter is not of the essence of baptism: for a baptism can be done in the sea or in a river. Therefore, the sanctification of the water should not be included in the definition of baptism.

Obj. 3: Furthermore, a definition should be convertible with what it defines. But water can be sanctified by the word of life for washing away our crimes, and nevertheless there will not be a baptism, as when no one is dipped in the water. Therefore, this is not a suitable definition of baptism.

Obj. 4: Furthermore, an effect that can be prevented should not be included in the definition of a cause, because then the definition would be less than what is defined. But baptism can be prevented from washing away our crimes. Therefore, the washing away of crimes should not be included in the definition of baptism.

Quaestiuncula 3

Ulterius. Videtur quod etiam inconvenienter assignetur definitio Dionysii, quam ponit 2 cap. *Cael. Hier.*, ubi dicit: *quoddam ergo est principium sanctissimorum mandatorum sacrae actionis, ad aliorum divinorum eloquiorum et sacrarum actionum susceptivam opportunitatem, formans nostros animales habitus ad supercaelestis quietis anagogem, nostrum iter faciens, sacrae et divinissimae nostrae regenerationis traditio.* Principium enim reducitur ad genus principiatorum. Sed sacramentum non est in genere principii,[20] sed in genere sacramenti. Ergo non debet dici principium sanctissimorum mandatorum.

Praeterea, non dicitur esse principium sanctorum mandatorum nisi inquantum praeparat viam ad alia mandata. Ergo superfluum fuit postea addere: *ad susceptivam opportunitatem aliorum nos formans.*

Praeterea, nihil potest formari ad divina eloquia nisi quod est perceptivum eorum. Sed hoc quod est animale in nobis, non percipit divina eloquia, sed solum hoc quod est rationale. Ergo male dixit: *formans animales habitus ad divina eloquia.*

Obj. 1: Moreover, it seems that the definition of Dionysius, which he sets down in Chapter 2 of the *Ecclesiastical Hierarchy*, is also unfittingly assigned, where he says: *Therefore, it is a certain principle of the holiest commands of sacred action, for the opportunity receptive of other divine utterances and sacred actions, forming our animal habits toward the anagogue of supercelestial rest, making our journey, the handing over of our sacred and most divine regeneration.*[19] For a principle is traced back to the genus of the things that derive from the principle. But a sacrament is not in the genus of principle, but in the genus of sacraments. Therefore, it should not be called a principle of the holiest commands.

Obj. 2: Furthermore, it should not be said to be a principle of holy commands except insofar as it prepares a way for other commands. Therefore, it was superfluous to add afterward: *forming us for the opportunity receptive of other actions.*

Obj. 3: Furthermore, nothing can be formed for divine utterances except what is able to perceive them. But what is animal in us cannot perceive divine utterances, but only what is rational. Therefore, he said wrongly: *forming animal habits for divine utterances.*

---

18. Hugh of St. Victor, *De sacramentis fidei*, Bk. 2, pt. 6, ch. 2 (PL 176:443).
19. Pseudo-Dionysius, *Ecclesiastical Hierarchy*, ch. 2, n. 1 (PG 3:391).
20. *principii.—precepti* PLE.

Praeterea, forma et materia sunt de essentia rei. Sed ipse nullam mentionem facit de materia et forma baptismi. Ergo videtur quod insufficienter definiat.

Obj. 4: Furthermore, form and matter are of the essence of a thing. But he makes no mention of the matter and form of baptism. Therefore, it seems that he defines it insufficiently.

Quaestiuncula 4

Ulterius. Videtur quod inconvenienter assignetur definitio quam Damascenus ponit in 4 Lib. cap. 9, sic dicens: *Baptismus est per quem primitias Spiritus Sancti accipimus, et principium alterius vitae fit nobis regeneratio et sigillum et custodia et illuminatio*. Aliqui enim prius habent Spiritum Sanctum et spiritualem vitam, quam baptismum consequantur, sicut patet de Cornelio Act. 10. Ergo per baptismum non semper accipimus primitias Spiritus Sancti, nec est baptismus principium alterius vitae in nobis.

Praeterea, idem non debet poni in definitione sui ipsius. Sed regeneratio est idem quod baptismus. Ergo non debet poni in definitione baptismi.

Praeterea, illuminatio non fit nisi per virtutes intellectuales. Sed baptismus non est intellectualis virtus, sed sacramentum. Ergo non debet sibi attribui illuminatio.

Praeterea, custodia fit in nobis per divinam providentiam, de qua dicitur in Psalm. 120, 4: *ecce non dormitabit neque dormiet qui custodit Israel*. Ergo non debet hoc baptismo attribui.

Obj. 1: Moreover, it seems that the definition that Damascene gives in Book 4, Chapter 9 is unfittingly assigned, for he says: *Baptism is that by which we receive the first fruits of the Holy Spirit, and the beginning of another life happens in us: a regeneration, and seal, and safekeeping, and illumination*.[21] For some people have the Holy Spirit and spiritual life before they obtain baptism, as is clear in the case of Cornelius in Acts 10. Therefore, by baptism we do not always receive the first fruits of the Holy Spirit, nor is baptism necessarily the beginning of another life in us.

Obj. 2: Furthermore, the same thing cannot be included in its own definition. But regeneration is the same thing as baptism. Therefore, it should not be placed in the definition of baptism.

Obj. 3: Furthermore, illumination happens only by intellectual virtues. But baptism is not an intellectual virtue, but a sacrament. Therefore, illumination should not be attributed to it.

Obj. 4: Furthermore, safekeeping happens in us through divine providence, which is spoken of in Psalm 121 (120):4: *Behold, he who keeps Israel shall neither slumber nor sleep*. Therefore, this should not be attributed to baptism.

Response to Quaestiuncula 1

Respondeo ad primam quaestionem dicendum, quod secundum doctrinam Philosophi in Lib. 2 *Posteriorum*, triplex est genus definitionis. Quaedam enim sunt definitiones materiales, quas dicimus demonstrationis conclusiones: quaedam formales, quae sunt principia demonstrationis: quaedam materiales et formales simul, quae sunt demonstrationes positione differentes: quia habent medium demonstrationis, inquantum continent definitionem formalem, et conclusionem, inquantum continent materialem; sed deest solus ordo terminorum. Quia autem omne completivum quodammodo formale est respectu ejus quod completur, ideo definitio formalis non dicitur quae solum continet formam, sed illa quae continet hoc quod est completivum respectu alterius. Et quia in causis est talis ordo quod materia completur per formam, et forma per efficientem, et efficiens per finem; ideo definitio quandoque materialis

To the first question, I answer that according to the teaching of the Philosopher in Book 2 of the *Posterior Analytics*, there are three kinds of definition.[22] For some definitions are material, which we call conclusions of demonstration; some are formal, which are principles of demonstration; some are both material and formal, which are demonstrations differing in position: for they have a middle term of demonstration, inasmuch as they contain a formal definition, and a conclusion, inasmuch as they contain a material one; but only the order of terms is lacking. Since, however, everything completive is formal in a certain way with respect to whatever is completed, for this reason not only is the definition that contains the form called a formal definition, but also one that contains what is completive with respect to something else. And since the order among causes is such that matter is completed by form, and form by efficient cause, and efficient cause by final cause,

---

21. John Damascene, *On the Orthodox Faith*, Bk. 4, ch. 9 (PG 94:1122).
22. Aristotle, *Posterior Analytics*, Bk. 2, ch. 10, 94a11–14.

dicitur, quae comprehendit tantum materiam rei, formalis autem quae comprehendit formam; sicut, ira est accensio sanguinis circa cor, dicitur materialis definitio; et, ira est appetitus in vindictam, dicitur formalis. Quandoque autem materialis comprehendit formam et materiam; sed formalis causam efficientem, sicut haec dicitur materialis: tonitruum est continuus sonus in nubibus; haec autem formalis: tonitruum est extinctio ignis in nube. Quandoque autem definitio materialis comprehendit materiam et formam et efficientem, formalis autem finem: sicut, domus est coopertorium factum ex lapidibus et lignis per talem modum et talem artem, est definitio materialis respectu hujus: domus est cooperimentum prohibens nos a frigoribus et caumatibus; et hoc praecipue accidit in instrumentis, quia in eis quasi tota ratio speciei a fine sumitur.

Et quia baptismus, cum sit sacramentum, quoddam instrumentum est; ideo definitio materialis ejus erit quae comprehendit materiam et formam ejus et efficientem; et formalis quae comprehendit finem; et sic definitio quam Magister in littera ponit, est materialis. Continet enim materiam in hoc quod dicit: *ablutio exterior*; et innuit efficientem in hoc quod dicit, *facta*; et ponit formam in hoc quod dicit, *sub forma verborum praescripta*. Et sciendum, quod Augustinus, ponit eamdem definitionem, quamvis sub aliis verbis; dicit enim: *Baptismus est tinctio in aqua verbo vitae sanctificata.*

AD PRIMUM ergo dicendum, quod in sacramento baptismi sunt tria. Aliquid quod est sacramentum tantum, sicut aqua quae exterius fluit et transfluit, et non manet; et aliquid quod est sacramentum et res, et hoc semper manet, scilicet character; et aliquid quod est res tantum, quod quandoque manet quandoque transit, scilicet gratia. Magister ergo hic definit baptismum quantum ad id quod est sacramentum tantum, quia intendit ipsum materialiter definire.

AD SECUNDUM dicendum, quod sacramentum novae legis est signum et causa gratiae; unde secundum hoc est sacramentum, secundum quod habet significare, et causare. Aqua autem non habet significare et causare effectum baptismi, nisi secundum quod est abluens. Unde essentialiter baptismus est ipsa ablutio: quia ad ablutionem interiorem causandam institutus est, quam significando causat ipsa exterior ablutio: sed aqua est materia ejus remota, et ablutio ipsa est materiale baptismi; sed verbum vitae est forma completiva sacramenti. Augustinus autem et Magister definiunt baptismum per materiam proximam, quae praedicatur proprie de baptismo,

for this reason a definition is sometimes called material, when it includes only the matter of the thing, but it is called formal when it includes the form. As, for example, 'anger is the blood's racing around the heart' is called a material definition; and 'anger is an appetite for vengeance' is called a formal one. However, sometimes the material definition includes form and matter, while the formal definition includes the efficient cause, as this is called material: 'thunder is a continual sound in the clouds'; while this is formal: 'thunder is the discharge of fire in a cloud.' But sometimes the material definition includes matter and form and efficient cause, but the formal definition includes the end: as, for example, 'a house is a covering made from stones and wood in such-and-such a style with such-and-such a skill' is a material definition in comparison with this one: 'a house is a covering protecting us from cold and heat.' And this happens particularly with instruments, for with them almost the entire account of their species is taken from the end.

And because baptism, since it is a sacrament, is a certain instrument, for this reason the material definition of it will be one that comprehends its matter and form and efficient cause; and its formal definition will comprehend its end. And in this way the definition that the Master sets down in the text is material. For it contains the matter when he says: *external washing*; and it gives a nod to the efficient cause in saying, *done*; and it includes the form in saying, *under the form of words prescribed*. And it should be known that Augustine gives the same definition, although under other words, for he says: *baptism is a drenching in the water sanctified by the word of life.*

REPLY OBJ. 1: In the sacrament of baptism there are three things. There is something that is only a sacrament, like the water that flows externally and flows away, and does not remain; and something that is a sacrament-and-reality, and this remains forever, namely, the character; and something that is only a reality, which sometimes remains and sometimes passes away, namely, grace.[23] Therefore, the Master here defines baptism according as it is a sacrament only, for he intends to define it materially.

REPLY OBJ. 2: A sacrament of the New Law is a sign and a cause of grace; hence it is a sacrament according as it is able to signify and cause. But water is not able to signify and cause the effect of baptism, except insofar as it is cleansing. Hence baptism is essentially this very cleansing: for it was instituted to cause an interior cleansing, which the external cleansing itself causes by signifying it: but water is its remote matter, and the cleansing itself is the material of baptism; but the word of life is the form completive of the sacrament. Now Augustine and the Master define baptism by the proximate matter, which is properly predicated of baptism, like the matter of man-made things, as

---

23. For more about the sacrament alone, reality alone, and sacrament-and-reality, see the footnote at Dist.1, q.1, a.4, qa. 1, main response.

sicut materia de artificialibus, ut phiala est argentum; sed Hugo definivit per materiam remotam, quae non ita proprie praedicatur, nisi per causam remotam.

AD TERTIUM dicendum, quod baptismus, inquantum est sacramentum, est in genere signi vel causae; et in hoc genere constituitur per formam verborum, a qua habet significationem et efficaciam sacramentalem. Sicut autem artificialia non ponuntur in genere ex forma simpliciter, sed ex materia (non enim dicimus quod domus sit in genere qualitatis nisi inquantum artificiale figuratum, sed dicitur esse in genere substantiae), ita etiam est de sacramentis. Baptismus enim simpliciter est in genere ablutionis; sed secundum quid, scilicet inquantum est sacramentum, est in genere relationis.

AD QUARTUM dicendum, quod finis ad quem est sacramentum, est ultimum formale ipsius, a quo sumitur formalis definitio. Magister autem non intendit hic definire baptismum formaliter, sed materialiter; et ideo sanctificationem praetermisit.

a cup is silver; but Hugh defined it by the remote matter, which is not as properly predicated, except through the remote cause.

REPLY OBJ. 3: Baptism, inasmuch as it is a sacrament, is in the genus of sign or cause; and it is constituted in this genus by the form of words, from which it has its signification and sacramental efficacy. Now just as man-made things are not placed in a genus by their form, simply speaking, but rather by their matter—for we do not say that a house is in the genus of quality except insofar as it is a man-made shape, but it is rather said to be in the genus of substance—so also is it with the sacraments. For baptism, simply speaking, is in the genus of cleansing; but according to one aspect, that is, inasmuch as it is a sacrament, it is in the genus of relation.

REPLY OBJ. 4: The end for which a sacrament exists is its ultimate formal aspect, from which its formal definition is taken. However, the Master does not here intend to define baptism formally, but materially; and so he omits sanctification.

Response to Quaestiuncula 2

AD SECUNDAM QUAESTIONEM dicendum, quod definitio illa Hugonis complectitur et materiam baptismi in hoc quod dicit, *aqua*, et finem in hoc quod dicit, *diluendis criminibus*, et formam per hoc quod dicit, *per verbum vitae sanctificata*; unde est definitio composita ex materiali et formali, quasi demonstratio positione differens: et complete essentiam baptismi complectitur, excepto quod actus ablutionis intermittitur, qui facit materiam proximam baptismo; quamvis ex aliis quae ponuntur, intelligi possit.

AD PRIMUM ergo dicendum, quod haec est propria praedicatio, baptismus fit in aqua; sed haec est per causam praedicatio, baptismus est aqua.

AD SECUNDUM dicendum, quod ibi non tangitur sanctificatio, nisi illa quae fit per formam baptismi, quae consistit in invocatione Trinitatis; et haec sanctificatio est de necessitate baptismi.

AD TERTIUM dicendum, quod sacramenta non efficiunt nisi id quod figurant. Ex hoc autem ipso quod ponitur dilutio criminum, effectus baptismi potest accipi: quia baptismus materialiter non consistit in aqua nisi secundum quod est abluens; quandocumque autem est aqua sanctificata in actu ablutionis, est baptismus.

AD QUARTUM dicendum, quod idem numero quandoque est effectus alicujus et finis, sicut sanitas est effectus et finis medicantis; sed effectus, secundum quod producitur per actum medici, finis autem secundum quod est intentum a medico. Medicus autem potest impediri a productione sanitatis; sed non ab intentione; et ideo sanitas potest poni in definitione ut est finis, non autem ut

TO THE SECOND QUESTION, it should be said that that definition of Hugh encompasses both the matter of baptism by saying *water*, and the end by saying *for washing away our crimes*, and the form by saying *sanctified by the word of life*. Hence it is a definition composed of matter and form, as though a demonstration differing in position: and it completely encompasses the essence of baptism, except for leaving out the act of cleansing, which constitutes the proximate matter of baptism—although that could be understood from the other things that are included.

REPLY OBJ. 1: This is proper predication, 'baptism happens in water'; but this is predication through the cause, 'baptism is water.'

REPLY OBJ. 2: Sanctification is not touched upon there except that which happens by the form of baptism, which consists in the invocation of the Trinity; and this sanctification is of necessity for baptism.

REPLY OBJ. 3: Sacraments effect only what they represent. But by the very fact of including the washing away of crimes, the effect of baptism can be grasped: for baptism does not consist materially in water except as it cleanses; but whenever there is water sanctified in the act of cleansing, there is baptism.

REPLY OBJ. 4: Something numerically the same is sometimes an effect and sometimes an end, just as health is both an effect and an end of the one practicing medicine. But it is an effect according as it is produced by the action of the doctor, while it is an end according as it is intended by the doctor. Now a doctor can be impeded from producing health, but not from intending it; and thus health can

est effectus; et similiter dilutio criminum in definitione sacramenti.

be included in the definition as an end, but not as an effect; and similarly the washing away of crimes is included in the definition of this sacrament.

Response to Quaestiuncula 3

AD TERTIAM QUAESTIONEM dicendum, quod Dionysius ex definitione baptismi data intendit procedere ad ea quae materialiter in baptismo requiruntur: unde post hanc definitionem datam, ritum baptismi ponit; et ideo ponit eam ut demonstrationis principium: et propter hoc est definitio totaliter formalis. Et est sciendum, quod in verbis ejus aliquid ponitur quasi definitum, et aliquid ponitur tamquam definitio.

Tamquam definitum ponitur, scilicet *traditio sacrae et divinissimae regenerationis*. Ista enim est quaedam circumlocutio baptismi, qua ipse frequenter utitur; et hoc patet ex hoc quod ibi baptismum non nominat; ut sit sensus: *quoddam est principium* etc., scilicet *sacrae et divinissimae regenerationis traditio*.

Quasi definitio ponitur hic, quod dicit, *principium sanctissimorum mandatorum sacrae actionis*. Et ponit tria ad quae baptismus ordinatur, quae formaliter rationem ejus complent.

Unum est quod competit ei secundum quod est janua sacramentorum; et quantum ad hoc dicit, quod est *principium sanctissimorum mandatorum sacrae actionis*. Actiones enim sacras nominat actiones hierarchicas, scilicet purgare, illuminare, et perficere; quae praecipue in nostra hierarchia consistunt in dispensatione sacramentorum: quae quidem actiones nobis sub praecepto traditae sunt, et ad eas est principium baptismus quasi eorum janua.

Secundum competit sibi inquantum est causa, prout scilicet characterem imprimit, et gratiam confert, secundum quod homo informatur et idoneus redditur ad aliorum sacramentorum perceptionem; et quantum ad hoc dicit, quod est *formans* per characterem et gratiam *nostros animales habitus*, idest, vires animae, *ad susceptivam opportunitatem*, idest ad idoneam et opportunam susceptionem *divinorum eloquiorum* quantum ad doctrinam fidei, *et sacrarum actionum* quantum ad alia sacramenta, quae nulli non baptizato debent conferri.

Tertium competit sibi inquantum est signum et figura caelestium, et secundum hoc per baptismum manuducimur in caelestium contemplationem; et quantum ad hoc dicit, quod est *faciens iter nostrum*, idest praeparans nobis contemplationis viam ad *anagogem*, idest sursum ductionem, *supercaelestis quietis*, quae consistit in contemplatione spiritualium. Vel potest dici, quod per secundum tangit finem proximum baptismi quantum ad

TO THE THIRD QUESTION, it should be said that by the definition of baptism given, Dionysius intends to proceed to those things that are required materially in baptism. Hence, after having given this definition of baptism, he sets down the rite for baptism; and thus he includes it as a principle of demonstration; and because of this his definition is entirely formal. And it should be known that in his words something is included as the thing that is defined, and something else is included as the definition.

Something like the thing defined is set down, namely, *the handing over of a sacred and most divine regeneration*. For that is a certain circumlocution for baptism that he frequently uses, and this is clear from the fact that he does not call it baptism there—so that the sense is: *it is a certain principle*, etc., namely, *a handing on of a sacred and most divine regeneration*.

What serves as a definition is set down here where he says, *a principle of the holiest commands of sacred action*. And he sets down three things that baptism is ordered to, which formally complete its account.

One is what pertains to it as the door of the sacraments; and as to this he says that it is *the principle of the holiest commands of sacred action*. For sacred actions are what he calls the actions of the hierarchy, namely, to purify, to illuminate, and to perfect, which, in our hierarchy, principally consist in the administration of the sacraments; for certain actions were handed down to us under a precept, and baptism is a principle for them, as their door.

The second thing pertains to it as a cause, namely, as it imprints a character and confers grace, according to which man is informed and rendered apt for the reception of the other sacraments. And as to this he says that it is *forming*, through a character and grace, *our animal habits*, that is, the powers of the soul, *for the receptive opportunity*, that is, for the appropriate and opportune reception, *of divine utterances*, as to the teaching of the faith, *and sacred actions*, as to the other sacraments, none of which should be conferred on someone who has not been baptized.

The third thing pertains to it as a sign and figure of the heavens, and, according to this, through baptism we are led by the hand to the contemplation of the heavens; and as to this, he says that it is *making our journey*, that is, preparing the way of contemplation for us, for *the anagogue*, that is, for being taken upward, *of supercelestial rest*, which consists in the contemplation of spiritual things. Or it can be said that by the second he touches on the proximate end of

ea quae sunt viae; per tertium autem tangit finem remotum et ultimum, quantum ad ea quae sunt patriae; ad quam nos baptismus perducit per gratiam, quam confert, quae est res significata et non contenta.

AD PRIMUM ergo dicendum, quod Dionysius determinat de baptismo secundum quod est actio quaedam hierarchica; et ideo definit *principium mandatorum*, non quorumlibet sed illorum quibus actiones hierarchicae nobis traduntur.

AD SECUNDUM dicendum, quod per primum tangit tantum ordinem baptismi ad alia sacramenta, sed per secundum tangit effectum, quo mediante ad alia sacramenta percipienda idonee perducit, ut ex dictis patet.

AD TERTIUM dicendum, quod *animales habitus* hic dicuntur ab *anima*, et non ab animalitate, qua scilicet cum aliis animalibus communicamus; ut ostendat quod non solum baptismus corpus exterius lavat, sed etiam animam interius format.

AD QUARTUM dicendum, quod haec definitio est principium omnium quae Dionysius de baptismo tradit; unde in principio statim hanc definitionem ponit. Et quia in omnibus quae sunt propter finem, ex fine debet accipi et forma competens fini et materia competens formae et fini; ideo in hac definitione non posuit formam et materiam, sed solum ea ad quae baptismus ordinatur quasi ad finem proximum vel remotum.

baptism as regards those things that are of the way, while by the third, he touches on the remote and last end as regards those things that are of heaven, to which baptism leads us through the grace that it confers, which is the reality signified and not contained.

REPLY OBJ. 1: Dionysius examines baptism according as it is a certain hierarchical action; and thus he defines it as a *principle of commands*—not of just any commands, but of those by which the actions of the hierarchy are handed on to us.

REPLY OBJ. 2: By the first phrase he touches upon only the order of baptism to the other sacraments, but by the second phrase he refers to its effect, by means of which it leads suitably to the receiving of the other sacraments, as is clear from what has been said.

REPLY OBJ. 3: Here, the phrase *animal habits* is named from the *anima*, not from that animality that we share with the other animals. He includes this phrase so that he may show that baptism does not merely wash the body externally, but also forms the soul interiorly.

REPLY OBJ. 4: This definition is the principle of all that Dionysius delivers concerning baptism; hence he places this definition immediately at the beginning. And since in all things that are for the sake of the end one must must accept from the end both the form that befits the end and the matter befitting the form and the end, for this reason he does not place form and matter in this definition, but only those things to which baptism is ordered as proximate or remote end.

Response to Quaestiuncula 4

AD QUARTAM QUAESTIONEM dicendum, quod Damascenus praedictam definitionem venatur ex hoc ipso quod baptismus regeneratio dicitur. Cum enim generatio sit motus ad esse, constat quod baptismus est per quem nobis traditur spirituale esse. Et quia nullus potest agere actionem alicujus naturae, nisi prius habeat esse in natura illa, ideo concluditur quod baptismus est principium omnium spiritualium actionum: et secundum hoc Damascenus baptismum definivit adhuc per priora quam Dionysius, inquantum accipit primum effectum baptismi, qui est constituere in spirituali vita, ex qua habet quod regeneratio dicatur; et ideo definit baptismum ut principium spiritualis vitae in hoc quod dicit, *principium alterius vitae*, scilicet spiritualis, quae est altera a naturali; ut haec generatio sit altera a naturali, et regeneratio dicatur; et iterum ut principium eorum quae ad vitam prima consequuntur, et ideo dicit: *per quod fiunt primitiae spiritus*, idest primi spiritus effectus in nobis. Hi autem effectus vel consequuntur ipsam generationem, sicut filiatio, vel aliqua talis relatio, et sic per baptismum dicimur regenerari in filios Dei, et quantum

TO THE FOURTH QUESTION, it should be said that Damascene arrives at the definition mentioned from the fact that baptism is called a regeneration. For since generation is a movement toward being, it is clear that baptism is that by which we are granted spiritual being. And since no one can perform an action of a certain nature unless first he has being in that nature, thus it is concluded that baptism is the beginning of all spiritual actions. And according to this, Damascene defined baptism by even more basic things than Dionysius, inasmuch as he takes the first effect of baptism, which is to constitute one in spiritual life, on which basis it may be called regeneration. And thus he defines baptism as the beginning of the spiritual life in that he says, *the beginning of another life*, namely, the spiritual one, which is other than the natural one; so that this generation is different from the natural one, and is called regeneration; and again, as the beginning of the first things that follow upon life, and thus he says, *by which the first movements of the Holy Spirit happen*, that is, the first spiritual effects in us. But these effects either result from the generation itself, like sonship or some relation like that, and in this way we

ad hoc dicitur *regeneratio*, vel consequuntur formam per generationem inductam; et hoc tripliciter. Primo in ordine ad generantem, secundum quod per formam inductam genitus fit similis generanti; et quantum ad hoc dicitur *sigillum*. Secundo quantum ad esse ipsius geniti, quod per formam conservatur; et quantum ad hoc dicitur *custodia*. Tertio quantum ad actionem ejus, cujus forma est principium; et quantum ad hoc dicitur *illuminatio*.

AD PRIMUM ergo dicendum, quod primitiae spiritus dantur antequam percipiatur baptismus actu, sed non antequam percipiatur proposito habituali, sicut in Cornelio; vel actuali, sicut in aliis qui baptismi fidem habent. Vel dicendum, quod hic loquitur de vita spirituali, secundum quod homo quantum ad exteriora reputatur membrum ecclesiae, quod non fit ante baptismum, quia ad actus fidelium nullus ante baptismum admittitur.

AD SECUNDUM dicendum, quod regeneratio ponitur hic pro relatione consequente regenerationem, sicut est filiatio.

AD TERTIUM dicendum, quod etiam Dionysius, vim illuminativam baptismo attribuit, quod quidem ei competit inquantum est fidei sacramentum; unde baptizatus jam admittitur ad inspectionem sacramentorum quasi illuminatus: non autem ante debet admitti, ne sancta canibus tradantur secundum Dionysium.

Ad quartum dicendum, quod custodia conservationem importat: quae quidem est a Deo sicut a principio efficiente, a gratia autem baptismali sicut a principio formali.

are said to be regenerated by baptism as sons of God, and in this respect he says *regeneration*, or they result from the form instilled by that generation, and this happens in three ways. First, in the order to the one generating, according to which the one generated is made like the one generating by the form instilled; and this is how it is called a *seal*. The second has to do with the being of the one generated himself, which is preserved by that form; and in regard to this it is called a *safekeeping*. The third has to do with the action of whatever this form is the beginning of, and in this respect it is called *illumination*.

REPLY OBJ. 1: The first fruits of the Spirit are given before baptism is actually received, but not before the habitual intention of receiving it, as was the case with Cornelius, or the actual intention, as is the case with others who have the faith of baptism.[24] Or it could be said that here he speaks of the spiritual life, according to which man is considered a member of the Church as to externals, which does not happen before baptism, for no one is admitted to the acts of the faithful before baptism.

REPLY OBJ. 2: Regeneration here stands for the relation that follows upon regeneration, as sonship is.

REPLY OBJ. 3: Dionysius also attributed illuminative force to baptism,[25] which indeed befits it as it is the sacrament of faith; hence someone already baptized is admitted to behold the sacraments as one illuminated, but he should not be admitted before that, lest holy things be given to dogs, according to Dionysius.[26]

REPLY OBJ. 4. Safekeeping implies preservation, which indeed is from God as an efficient principle, but from baptismal grace as a formal principle.

---

24. That is, those who, as catechumens, believe the faith of which baptism is the sign.

25. Pseudo-Dionysius, *Ecclesiastical Hierarchy*, ch. 5, n. 3 (PG 3:503).

26. Reference is made here to the *disciplina arcani*, that is, the agreement of the early Christians to protect the sacred mysteries from the profanation of mockery or unbelief by keeping their content, meaning, and performance hidden from those who were not already practicing Christians. As the Byzantine prayer before communion has it: "I will not reveal your mysteries to your enemies, nor will I give you a kiss as did Judas . . . "

Article 2

The form of baptism

Quaestiuncula 1

Ad secundum sic proceditur. Videtur quod integritas formae baptismalis non contineatur in his verbis, *Ego te baptizo in nomine Patris et Flii et Spiritus Sancti.* Actio enim magis debet attribui principali agenti quam secundario. Sed principalis baptizans est Christus, ut patet Joan. 1, 33, ubi dicitur: *hic est qui baptizat*; homo autem est tantum minister baptismi. Ergo magis debuit dici, *Christus te baptizat*, etc., quam *ego te baptizo.*

Praeterea, secundum grammaticos in verbis primae et secundae personae intelligitur nominativus certus et determinatus. Sed *baptizo* est verbum primae personae. Ergo non fuit necessarium quod adderetur *ego.*

Praeterea, sacramenta habent a divina institutione efficaciam et virtutem. Sed ex forma quam Dominus tradidit Matth. ult. 19, ubi dicitur, *docete omnes gentes*, non potest haberi quod *ego te baptizo* sit de forma baptismi: quia hoc participium *baptizantes*, ponitur ibi ad designandum exercitium actus; non quasi pars formae. Ergo videtur quod non sit de necessitate formae.

Praeterea, simul Dominus praecepit actum docendi et baptizandi, Matth. ult. Sed non exigitur ad docendum quod sacerdos dicat, *ego te doceo.* Ergo similiter non exigitur ad baptismum quod dicat, *ego te baptizo.*

Praeterea, verba non debent dirigi ad eum qui non est verborum sensus perceptivus. Sed quandoque baptizatus non potest percipere sensum verborum, sicut patet quando puer baptizatur. Ergo non debet dicere, *baptizo te*, sed, *baptizo Joannem.*

Praeterea, hoc videtur ex modo loquendi quo Dominus usus est, ponens baptizandos in tertia persona dicens: *baptizantes eos.*

Praeterea, materia sacramenti non minus est de essentia sacramenti quam suscipiens illud sacramentum. Sed nulla mentio fit in forma de aqua, quae est materia sacramenti. Ergo non debet fieri mentio de recipiente, ut dicatur: *baptizo te.*

Praeterea, baptismus a passione Christi efficaciam habet, et figura est mortis Christi, ut patet Rom. 6.

Obj. 1: To the second we proceed thus. It seems that the integrity of the baptismal form is not contained in these words, *I baptize you in the name of the Father, and of the Son, and of the Holy Spirit.*[27] For an action should be attributed more to a principal agent than to a secondary one. But the principal baptizer is Christ, as is clear from the passage: *He it is who baptizes* (John 1:33); man, however, is only the minister of baptism. Therefore, it should be said *Christ baptizes you*, etc., rather than *I baptize you.*

Obj. 2: Further, according to grammarians, in verbs of the first and second person a certain and determinate subject is understood. But *baptizo* is a verb in the first person. Therefore, it was not necessary to add *ego.*

Obj. 3: Furthermore, sacraments have efficacy from divine institution and power. But on the basis of the form that the Lord handed down at the end of Matthew, where it is said, *Go therefore and teach all nations* (Matt 28:19), one cannot hold that *I baptize you* is the form of baptism: for this participle *baptizing* is set down there to designate the exercise of an act, not as part of the form. Therefore, it seems that it is not necessary to the form.

Obj. 4: Furthermore, the Lord commanded the acts of teaching and baptizing at the same time (cf. Matt 28:19). But it is not required for teaching that a priest say, *I teach you.* Therefore, in the same way it is not required for baptism that he say, *I baptize you.*

Obj. 5: Furthermore, words should not be directed to someone who is imperceptive to the meaning of words. But sometimes the baptized person cannot perceive the meaning of the words, as is clear when a child is baptized. Therefore, he should not say, *I baptize you*, but *I baptize John.*

Obj. 6: Furthermore, this seems to be the manner of speaking used by the Lord, putting the ones to be baptized in the third person, saying: *Baptizing them* (Matt 28:19).

Obj. 7: Furthermore, the matter of the sacrament is no less essential to the sacrament than the one receiving that sacrament. But in the form, no mention is made of the water, which is the matter of the sacrament. Therefore, no mention should be made of the recipient, as is said: *I baptize you.*

Obj. 8: Furthermore, baptism has efficacy from the Passion of Christ, and is a figure of Christ's death, as is clear

---

27. Parallels: *ST* III, q. 60, a. 8; q. 61, a. 5; q. 84, a. 3; *Super I ad Cor.* 1, lec. 2.

Ergo potius debuit in baptismi forma fieri mentio de fide passionis quam de fide Trinitatis.

Praeterea, omne illud in quo personae non conveniunt, debet de eis pluraliter dici. Sed personae distinguuntur quantum ad nomen: quia nomen Filii Patri non convenit, nec e converso. Ergo non debuit dici: *in nomine Patris* etc., sed: *in nominibus*.

from Romans 6. Therefore, in the form of baptism mention should have been made of faith in the Passion rather than faith in the Trinity.

Obj. 9: Furthermore, everything that the Divine Persons do not have in common should be said of them in the plural. But the Persons are distinguished by name, for the name 'Son' does not apply to the Father, nor vice versa. Therefore, it should not have been said, *In the name of the Father*, etc., but, *In the names*.

Quaestiuncula 2

Ulterius. Videtur quod liceat ea quae in hac forma ponuntur, mutare sine praejudicio baptismi. Graeci enim hanc formam baptizandi habent: *baptizatur servus Christi Nicolaus in nomine patris et filii et Spiritus Sancti*. Sed apud omnes est unum baptisma. Ergo et noster similiter baptismus fieri posset.

Praeterea, hoc quod dicit: *ego baptizo te*, ponitur in forma ad exprimendum baptismi actum. Sed actus baptismi potest effici ab uno et duobus et in unum et in duos. Ergo potest fieri mutatio formae, ut dicatur: *nos baptizamus vos*.

Praeterea, ecclesia est ejusdem potestatis nunc cujus erat primitiva ecclesia quantum ad sacramentorum dispensationem. Sed primitiva ecclesia mutavit formam baptismi: quia baptizabant *in nomine Christi*, sicut in Act. legitur. Ergo et nunc ecclesia formam mutare posset.

Praeterea, tres personae in forma baptismi ponuntur ad exprimendum fidem Trinitatis. Sed ita exprimeretur fides Trinitatis, si diceretur: *in nomine Trinitatis*, sicut si dicitur: *in nomine patris et filii et Spiritus Sancti*. Ergo potest ita mutatio fieri ut dicatur: *in nomine Trinitatis*.

Praeterea, virtus sacramentaria non consistit in verbis, nisi secundum quod ad significationem referuntur: alias non esset virtutis alicujus nisi in una lingua, quia voces non sunt eaedem apud omnes. Sed idem significat Pater quod genitor, et Filius quod genitus, et Spiritus Sanctus quod ab utroque procedens. Ergo potest hoc modo fieri mutatio, ut dicatur: *in nomine genitoris, et geniti, et procedentis ab utroque*.

Praeterea, qui corrumpit verba mutat litteras et syllabas, et per consequens dictiones. Sed infra, dist. 6,

Obj. 1: Moreover, it seems that it is permitted to change what is in this form without detriment to baptism.[28] For the Byzantines have this form for baptizing: *The servant of Christ, Nicholas, is baptized in the name of the Father, and of the Son, and of the Holy Spirit*. But there is one baptism among all men. Therefore also, our baptism could be done in a similar way.

Obj. 2: Furthermore, saying *I baptize you* is included in the form to express the act of baptism. But the act of baptism can be done by one or two people, and to one or two people. Therefore, a change of the form can be made so that it is said, *We baptize you two*.

Obj. 3: Furthermore, when it comes to administering the sacraments, the Church has the same power now that the early Church had. But the early Church changed the form of baptism: for they were baptizing *in the name of Christ*, as is read in Acts.[29] Therefore, the Church today could also change the form.

Obj. 4: Furthermore, three Persons are put in the form of baptism to express faith in the Trinity. But faith in the Trinity would be just as much expressed if one said, *in the name of the Trinity*, as when one says, *In the name of the Father and of the Son and of the Holy Spirit*. Therefore, a change can be made so that it is said, *In the name of the Trinity*.

Obj. 5: Furthermore, words hold no sacramental power unless they are referred to the signification; otherwise, they would not have any power except in one language, for vocal expressions are not the same among all. But 'father' means the same thing as the one who generates, and 'son' as the one generated, and 'Holy Spirit' as the one proceeding from both. Therefore, a change could be made in this way, so that it would be said: *In the name of the one who generates, the one generated, and the one proceeding from both*.

Obj. 6: Furthermore, someone who mangles words changes letters and syllables, and as a result, speech. But be-

---

28. Parallels: below, exposition of the text; *ST* III, q. 61, a. 5; *Super Matt.* 28; *Super I ad Cor.* 1, lec. 2.
29. See Acts 2:38 and 8:16.

dicitur, quod reputatur baptismus, quamvis aliquis verba corrupte proferat. Ergo potest fieri formae mutatio.

low, in Distinction 6, it is said that baptism is considered valid even when some of the words are uttered incorrectly. Therefore, a change can happen to the form.

Quaestiuncula 3

Ulterius. Videtur quod non possit aliquid addi vel minui. Non enim est minor necessitas in verbis quae pertinent ad formas sacramentorum, quam in verbis sacrae Scripturae. Sed in verbis sacrae Scripturae non licet addere vel minuere, ut patet Apocal. ult. Ergo nec verbis formarum in sacramentis.

Praeterea, in formis naturalibus ita est quod differentia addita vel subtracta variat speciem. Ergo et si in formis sacramentorum aliquid addatur vel subtrahatur, tolletur ratio illius sacramenti.

Praeterea, Ariani non mutabant formam istam nisi per additionem. Dicebant enim: *in nomine patris majoris et filii minoris*; et propter hoc non reputabantur baptizati. Ergo non licet addere vel diminuere in forma.

Sed contra, in littera habetur ab Ambrosio quod si fides totius Trinitatis corde teneatur et una tantum persona sit nominata, sit baptisma verum. Ergo licet aliquid de forma subtrahere.

Praeterea, actus baptizandi ponitur in forma ad excitandum attentionem. Ergo, ut videtur, licet addere verbum intentionem signans, ut dicatur: intendo te baptizare.

Obj. 1: Moreover, it seems that something could not be added or taken away. For there is no less necessity in the words that belong to the forms of the sacraments than in the words of Sacred Scripture. But it is not permitted to add to or take away from the words of Sacred Scripture, as is clear from the last chapter of the Book of Revelation.[30] Therefore, neither is it permitted with the words of the forms in the sacraments.

Obj. 2: Furthermore, among natural forms it is such that a difference added or subtracted changes the species. Therefore, also if something is added or subtracted among the forms of the sacraments, the nature of that sacrament will be destroyed.

Obj. 3: Furthermore, the Arians did not change that form except by addition. For they said, *In the name of the greater Father and of the lesser Son*; and for that reason they were not considered to have been baptized. Therefore, it is not permitted to add to or take away from the form.

On the contrary, in the text there is a statement by Ambrose that if faith in the whole Trinity is held in the heart and only one Person is named, it is a valid baptism. Therefore, it is permitted to leave something out of the form.

Furthermore, the act of baptizing is set down in the form to stir up the attention. Therefore, as it seems, it is permitted to add a word signaling the intention, as if it were said: *I intend to baptize you.*

Quaestiuncula 4

Ulterius. Videtur quod non possit fieri interpositio vel transpositio. Quia baptismus est unus actus: unus autem est actus qui est continuus, ut dicitur in 5 physicorum. Sed interruptio tollit continuitatem baptismi. Ergo tollit unitatem ejus; ergo non debet fieri aliqua interruptio.

Praeterea, sicut ad fidem Trinitatis pertinent tres personae, ita et personarum ordo. Sed in translatione[32] variatur ordo. Ergo corrumpitur forma.

Sed contra est, quia transposita nomina et verba idem significant.

Obj. 1: Moreover, it seems that there could not be an interjection or transposition. For baptism is one act, but an act is one when it is continuous, as is said in *Physics* 5.[31] An interruption, however, takes away the continuity of baptism. Therefore, it takes away its unity; therefore, there should not be any interruption.

Obj. 2: Furthermore, just as three Persons pertain to faith in the Trinity, so also does the order of Persons. But in a transposition, the order is varied. Therefore, the form is corrupted.

On the contrary, nouns and verbs that are transposed mean the same thing.

---

30. See Rev 22:18–19.
31. Aristotle, *Physics*, Bk. 5, ch. 4, 228a20.
32. *translatione.—transpositione* PLE.

Response to Quaestiuncula 1

RESPONDEO dicendum ad primam quaestionem, quod forma completiva rei media est quodammodo inter materiam quam perficit, et causam efficientem a qua producitur, ut virtus efficientis mediante forma ad materiam traducatur. Et quia medium complectitur aliquo modo utrumque extremorum, ideo forma baptismi continet et principale efficiens, unde baptismus efficaciam habet, et materiam baptismi proximam quae est actus ablutionis; et ideo ponitur: *in nomine Patris et Filii et Spiritus Sancti*, tamquam principale efficiens, a quo baptismus efficaciam habet; et ponitur actus materialis cum iis quae circumstant ipsum scilicet conferens et recipiens, in hoc quod dicitur: *Ego baptizo te*.

AD PRIMUM ergo dicendum, quod principale agens significatur in invocatione Trinitatis quae invisibiliter agit, et ideo relinquebatur ut circa actum materialem poneretur agens secundarium, scilicet minister sacramenti.

AD SECUNDUM dicendum, quod formae sacramentorum non accipiuntur ut voces significativae tantum, sed ut effectivae. Et quia nihil agit nisi secundum quod perfectum est, ideo de integritate formae baptismalis est ut ponatur totum quod ad baptismum requiritur, quamvis unum ex alio intelligi possit.

AD TERTIUM dicendum, quod in verbis illis Dominus principaliter non intendit tradere formam sacramenti, quia prius eis tradiderat, quando baptizabant etiam ante passionem; sed intendit eis praecipere actum baptizandi secundum formam prius eis traditam; et ideo ex verbis illis potest probabiliter accipi forma praedicta, quamvis non expresse ibi ponatur.

AD QUARTUM dicendum, quod quia baptismus est sacramentum necessitatis, et in sacramento requiritur intentio; ideo oportet exprimi omnia quae intentionem determinant ad actum illum; non autem sic in aliis actibus, in quibus non est tantum periculum, si intentio non adsit. Vel dicendum, quod alii actus habent efficaciam ex ipso suo exercitio tantum, sed actus baptizandi habet efficaciam ex forma verborum. Et quia talis efficacia est sacramentalis, idcirco oportet quod verba formae significando efficaciam actui praebeant; et ideo oportet baptizantem actum suum verbo significare, quamvis hoc in aliis actibus non reperiatur.

AD QUINTUM dicendum, quod ratio illa tenet de illis verbis quae proferuntur causa significationis tantum, non autem de illis quae proferuntur causa efficiendi, quae etiam oportet ad res non intelligentes proferri, ut effectus verborum determinetur ad res illas; unde etiam dicitur: *exorcizo te creatura salis*.

TO THE FIRST QUESTION, I answer that a completive form is in a certain way a middle thing between the matter that it perfects, and the efficient cause that produces it, so that efficient power is transferred to matter by means of a form. And since a middle in some way embraces both extremes, thus the form of baptism contains both the principal agent, from which baptism has efficacy, and the proximate matter of baptism, which is the act of washing; and thus it is set down: *In the name of the Father and of the Son and of the Holy Spirit*, as the principal agent from which baptism has its efficacy; and the material act is set down by the two parties to it, namely, the bestower and the recipient, by saying: *I baptize you*.

REPLY OBJ. 1: The principal agent is signified in the invocation of the Trinity, which acts invisibly; and thus it remained for the secondary agent, that is, the minister of the sacrament, to be set down in relation to the material act.

REPLY OBJ. 2: The forms of the sacraments are taken not only as significative speech, but as efficacious speech. And since nothing acts except according as it is complete, for this reason it is of the integrity of baptismal form that it set down all that is required for baptism, even if one thing could be understood from another.

REPLY OBJ. 3: In those words the Lord did not principally intend to hand down the form of the sacrament, since he had given that to them previously, when they were baptizing even before the Passion; but he intended to command the act of baptizing according to the form previously given them; and thus, from those words the aforesaid form can be probably deduced, although it is not explicitly included there.

REPLY OBJ. 4: Since baptism is a necessary sacrament, and intention is required in a sacrament, for this reason all those things needed to be expressed that determine the intention to that act; but it is not this way with other acts in which there is not such danger if the intention is not present. Or it could be said that other acts have their efficacy from the very exercise of them, but the act of baptizing has its efficacy from the form of words. And since sacramental efficacy is like this, on that account it is necessary that the words of the form supply the efficacy of the act by signifying; and thus it is necessary for the one baptizing to signify his act with words, although this may not be found in other acts.

REPLY OBJ. 5: That argument holds about those words that are uttered only for the sake of signification, but not those that are uttered for the sake of effecting, which must be uttered even toward things that do not understand, so that the effect of the words is determined to those things; hence it is also said: *I exorcize you, creature of salt*.

AD SEXTUM dicendum, quod Dominus praecipiebat actum baptismi, ut absentium; et ideo oportebat quod uteretur tertia persona: secus autem est de illis qui exercent actum illum in praesentes.

AD SEPTIMUM dicendum, quod aqua comprehenditur in definitione baptismi: quia baptismus nihil aliud est quam ablutio facta in aqua; et ideo esset nugatio, si iterum poneretur.

AD OCTAVUM dicendum, quod actio semper magis attribuitur principali agenti, quia efficacius imprimit ad agendum. Tota enim virtus mediae causae est a prima, sed non convertitur: quia prima causa a qua baptismus efficaciam habet, auctoritative est Trinitas; passio autem Christi causa secundaria et meritoria; ideo magis fit mentio de Trinitate quam de passione.

AD NONUM dicendum, quod nomen non competit voci nisi secundum quod facit notitiam de re; nomen enim dicitur quasi notamen. Notitiam autem habemus de Trinitate per fidem. Et quia est una fides Trinitatis, et una confessio Dei, quamvis sint diversae voces significantes tres personas; ideo dicitur: *in nomine*, quasi in invocatione, quae fit per professionem exteriorem interioris fidei.

REPLY OBJ. 6: The Lord was commanding the act of baptism as of those absent, and thus it was necessary that the third person be used; but it is otherwise with those who exercise this act toward those present.

REPLY OBJ. 7: Water is understood in the definition of baptism, for baptism is nothing other than a washing done in water; and thus it would be silliness if it were included again.

REPLY OBJ. 8: An action is always attributed more to the principal agent, since it more effectively propels the thing being done. For all the power of the middle cause is from the first cause and not the other way around. Since the first cause from which baptism has efficacy is, in the manner of origination, the Trinity, while the Passion of Christ is the secondary and meritorious cause, mention is better made of the Trinity than of the Passion.

REPLY OBJ. 9: A vocal expression deserves to be called a name only inasmuch as it brings about recognition of a thing; for 'name' is said as if 'designating'.[33] Now we have recognition of the Trinity by faith. And since there is one faith in the Trinity, and one confession of God, although there are various expressions signifying the three Persons, for this reason it is said, *in the name*, as in an invocation, which takes place by the outward profession of interior faith.

Response to Quaestiuncula 2

AD SECUNDAM QUAESTIONEM dicendum, quod quia sacramenta efficaciam habent ex institutione divina, et principalius est in sacramentis forma quam etiam materia; ideo sicut nulli licet mutare sacramentum, vel aliquod novum instituere, ita nulli licet mutare formam sacramenti quantum ad id quod est de essentia formae absque speciali consilio Spiritus Sancti, qui virtutem suam illis verbis non alligavit: et si mutatur, nihil agitur; et praeter hoc culpa incurritur. Si autem aliquid pertinet ad formam ex determinatione ecclesiae, si illud mutatur, nihilominus est sacramentum, sed culpa incurritur. In forma autem baptismali essentialius est quod exprimit causam agentem, a qua est tota efficacia, quam quod exprimit actum exercitum; et ideo quantum ad omnes invocatio Trinitatis est de essentia formae, nec aliqui quantum ad hoc formam mutare possunt. Quidam vero dicebant, quod actus exercitus non est de essentia formae, et quod in illa invocatione Trinitatis essentia formae consistit; quos refellit auctoritas Alexandri Papae, qui dicit, quod non est baptismus illud lavacrum quo

TO THE SECOND QUESTION, it should be said that since sacraments have their efficacy from divine institution, and the form is a more central thing in the sacraments than even the matter; therefore, just as no one is permitted to change a sacrament or to institute something new, so also no one is allowed to change the form of a sacrament in regard to what is essential to the form without the special counsel of the Holy Spirit, who did not bind his own power to those words; and if the form is changed, nothing is done;[34] and besides this, guilt is incurred. If, however, something that belongs to the form by the determination of the Church is changed, the sacrament nevertheless exists, but guilt is incurred. However, in the baptismal form the more essential thing is to express the agent cause, from which its whole efficacy comes, than to express the act exercised; and for this reason, with respect to everyone, the invocation of the Trinity is essential to the form, nor can anyone change the form with respect to this. But some people were saying that the exercise of the act is not essential to the form, and that the essence of the form consists in that invo-

---

33. There is a play on words in Latin that is impossible to translate.
34. That is, the sacrament is not perfected or confected.

aliquis in nomine patris et filii et Spiritus Sancti nihil addendo baptizatur.

AD PRIMUM ergo dicendum, quod secundum opinionem Graecorum, de necessitate formae est actus baptismi quantum ad significatum, sed non quantum ad consignificatum. Persona autem baptizans per ministerium non est de necessitate formae, quia ex eo baptismus efficaciam non habet; sed persona recipiens est de necessitate formae, quia actus ad suscipientem terminatur; et ideo differunt in forma a nobis quantum ad tria. Primo, quia personam ministri in forma non exprimunt; et hoc dicunt ad removendum errorem qui fuit in primitiva ecclesia, qui efficaciam baptismi baptizanti attribuebat, ut patet Corinth. 3. Secundo in hoc quod significant actum sub alia persona, scilicet tertia, et sub alio modo, scilicet subjunctivo vel optativo, ad significandum quod actus interior expectatur ab extra. Tertio quia personam ponunt in nominativo casu, et in tertia persona; quia quandoque baptizatus non habet intellectum ut ad eum possit dirigi sermo.

Utrum autem ipsi mutent aliquid quod sit de substantia formae, ut sic oporteat rebaptizari, quamvis quidam dicant hoc, non tamen est determinatum, sed dubium apud quosdam, quibus videtur quod sufficiat actum baptismi significare ad perfectionem sacramenti, et quod consignificationis determinatio sit ex ecclesiae institutione.

Hoc autem certum quod forma qua nos utimur, melior est: tum quia perfectior est, ut patet ex supradictis; tum quia magis consonat verbis Evangelii quod ministros baptizantes dicit; tum propter auctoritatem ecclesiae, quae hanc formam tradit, quae nunquam a vera fide legitur declinasse, hanc formam ab apostolis retinens; et ideo non licet, praecipue Latinis, in forma Graecorum baptizare: quod si praesumerent, secundum quosdam non esset baptismus, secundum quosdam autem esset, sed graviter peccarent.

AD SECUNDUM dicendum, quod unus actus qui uno agente expleri potest, non progreditur a pluribus agentibus simul, et ideo unus baptizans, cum ipse solus baptizare possit, debet significare actum suum non ut a pluribus exeuntem, sed ut a se solo; et ideo non potest dici, *nos baptizamus*; sed secundum quosdam dici potest, *ego baptizo vos*, si necessitas adsit. Nec est aliqua mutatio formae, quantum ad significationem, quia plurale non

cation of the Trinity; which the authority of Pope Alexander refuted, who said that that bath in which someone is plunged in the name of the Father and of the Son and of the Holy Spirit, without adding anything, is not baptism.[35]

REPLY OBJ. 1: According to the opinion of the Byzantines, of necessity for the form is the act of baptism as regards what is signified, but not as regards what is consignified. Now the person baptizing through his ministry is not necessary to the form, for baptism does not get its efficacy from him; but the person receiving is necessary to the form, for the act is terminated in the one receiving; and thus the Byzantines differ in form from us in three things. First, because they do not express the person of the minister in the form; and they say this to remove the error that was in the early Church which attributed the efficacy of baptism to the one baptizing, as is clear from 1 Corinthians 3. Second, in that they signify the act under a different person, the third person, and in a different mood, the subjunctive or optative, to signify that an interior act is expected from outside. Third, because they place the person in the nominative case, and in the third person; for sometimes the baptized does not have understanding such that speech could be directed to him.

However, whether they may alter something that is of the substance of the form, so that it would be necessary to be rebaptized, although some people say so, nevertheless has not been determined, but there is a doubt among some people, to whom it seems that it would be enough to signify the act of baptism for the completion of the sacrament, and that the determination of consignification would be from the Church's institution.

However, this much is certain, that the form that we use is better—both because it is more complete, as is clear from what has been said, and because it is more consonant with the words of the Gospel that asserts ministers baptizing; and because of the authority of the Church, which handed down this form and which has never been read to have declined from the true faith, having retained this form from the apostles; and therefore it is not permitted, especially to Latins, to baptize in the form of the Byzantines; and if they were to presume to do so, according to some people it would not be a valid baptism, while according to others it would be valid, but they would have sinned gravely.

REPLY OBJ. 2: One act that can be completed by one agent cannot come forth from many agents at the same time, and thus one person baptizing, since he can baptize alone, should signify his act not as going out from many but as coming from himself alone. And thus it cannot be said, *we baptize*; but according to some people it can be said, *I baptize all of you*, if there is a present necessity. Nor is this any change of the form, as to its meaning, for the plural is

---

35. Alexander III, *Decreta* (MA XXI, 1101); cf. *Decretal. Gregor. IX*, Bk. 3, tit. 42, ch. 1, "Si quis sane puerum" (RF II, 644). Thomas quotes the decretal of Alexander III in *ST* III, q. 66, a. 5, ad 2.

est nisi singulare geminatum. Potest et alia ratio assignari, quia *baptizo vos*, idem est quod *baptizo te et te*; et ideo per hoc non fit mutatio formae quantum ad sensum, sed solum quantum ad vocem. Sed nos baptizamus, idem est quod *ego et ille*; non autem *ego et ego*. Unde non omnino est idem; et ideo qui dicit, *nos baptizamus*, nihil facit; qui autem dicit, *baptizo vos*, si simul plures baptizaret, baptizatum est; sed peccat, nisi ex magna necessitate faciens.

AD TERTIUM dicendum, quod forma quam Dominus tradidit, non fuit ab apostolis mutata quantum ad intellectum: quia in Christi nomine tota Trinitas intelligitur, ut in littera habetur, sed solum quantum ad vocem: et hoc est quod quidam dicunt, quod est mutata forma sensibilis, sed non intelligibilis. Nec hoc ipsum potuissent, nisi ex familiari consilio Spiritus Sancti. Ratio autem mutationis fuit, ut nomen Christi amabile redderetur, si in ejus nomine baptismus fieret: et hoc etiam ecclesia nunc posset, si speciale praeceptum a Spiritu Sancto haberet; non autem propria auctoritate. Et quia illius mutationis causa fuit conveniens illi tempori, ideo cessante causa, cessat effectus: et modo non esset baptismus; si quis in Christi nomine baptizaret, ut communiter dicitur; quamvis quidam contrarium dicant.

AD QUARTUM dicendum, quod in nomine Trinitatis non exprimuntur ipsae personae, sed solum numerus personarum; et ideo non sufficit dicere, in nomine Trinitatis; nec esset baptismus, si diceretur.

AD QUINTUM dicendum, quod genitor non significat personam Patris sicut hypostasim subsistentem, ut hoc nomen pater, sed per modum actus; et ideo non est eadem significatio, si dicatur in nomine genitoris, et *in nomine Patris*; et similis ratio est de aliis. Quamvis autem non sit eadem vox in Graeco et Latino, tamen est eadem vocis significatio; et in qualibet lingua verba illa pertinent ad formam quae principalius sunt instituta ad signandum personas illas.

AD SEXTUM dicendum, quod qui corrupte profert verba, aut hoc facit ex industria; et sic non videtur intendere quod ecclesia intendit, unde non est baptismus: aut hoc facit ex ignorantia vel defectu linguae; et tunc dicitur quod si sit tanta corruptio quod omnino auferat sensum locutionis, non est baptismus; si autem sensus locutionis remaneat, tunc erit baptismus; et hoc praecipue accidit quod sensus non mutatur, quando fit corruptio in fine: quia ex parte finis mutatio variat consignificationem, non autem significationem, ut grammatici dicunt. Sed mutatio ex parte principii variat significationem; unde corruptio talis, maxime si sit magna, omnino sensum lo-

nothing but the singular doubled. And another reason can be brought forth: *I baptize all of you* is the same as *I baptize you and you*; and thus, by this no change of form happens as to the meaning, but only as to the expression. But *we baptize* is the same as *he and I*, but not the same as *I and I*. Therefore, it is not altogether the same; and for this reason whoever says *we baptize* does nothing; but whoever says, *I baptize all of you*, if he baptizes several at the same time, does baptize; but he sins unless doing it out of some great necessity.

REPLY OBJ. 3: The form that the Lord handed down was not changed by the apostles as to its meaning, for in the name 'Christ' the whole Trinity is understood, as is maintained in the text; but it was changed only as to the expression: and this is why some people say the sensible form was changed but not the intelligible form. Nor would they have been able to do anything like that, unless by the intimate counsel of the Holy Spirit. However, the reason for the change was in order that the name of Christ might be rendered more lovable, if baptism were done in his name; and the Church could do this even now, if it had a special command from the Holy Spirit, but not by its own authority. And because the reason for that change was befitting the time, once the cause ceases, the effect ceases; and nowadays it would not be a valid baptism if someone were to baptize in the name of Christ, as is commonly said; although some people say the contrary.

REPLY OBJ. 4: In the name 'Trinity' those Persons are not expressed, but only the number of Persons; and thus it is not enough to say, *In the name of the Trinity*, nor would it be a valid baptism, if that were said.

REPLY OBJ. 5: 'One who generates' signifies the person of the Father not as a subsisting hypostasis (as the name 'Father' does), but rather in the manner of an act. And therefore if it is said, "In the name of the One who generates," the meaning is not the same as if it is said, *In the name of the Father*. And the argument is the same with the other expressions. However, although there is not the same vocal sound in Greek and Latin, nevertheless the meaning of the vocal sound is the same; and in any language, those words pertain to the form that are instituted chiefly for indicating those Persons.

REPLY OBJ. 6: Whoever utters words incorrectly either does it deliberately, and then he does not seem to intend what the Church intends; hence it is not a valid baptism; or else he does it out of ignorance or a defect of his knowledge of the language; and then it is said that if it is such a great corruption that it completely takes away the meaning of the speech, then it is not a valid baptism; but if the meaning of the speech remains, then there will be a baptism. And it especially happens that the meaning is not changed when the corruption happens at the end of a word: for a change on the part of the end varies the consignification but not the signification, as grammarians say. But a change in the be-

cutionis auferret. Quando autem sensus locutionis aliquo modo manet, tunc quamvis mutetur forma quantum ad sonum sensibilem, non tamen mutatur quantum ad significationem: quia quamvis oratio corrupte prolata nihil significet ex veritate impositionis, significat tamen ex accommodatione usus.

ginning changes the signification; hence that kind of corruption, especially if it is a large one, takes away the entire meaning of the speech. But when the meaning of the speech remains in any way, then, although the form is changed in its sensible sound, it is nevertheless not changed as to its signification; for although prayers incorrectly spoken signify nothing by the truth of imposition, nevertheless they do signify by the accommodation of use.

Response to Quaestiuncula 3

AD TERTIAM QUAESTIONEM dicendum, quod de subtractione hoc certum est, quod si subtrahatur aliquid quod sit de essentia formae, non est baptismus, et ille qui baptizat, graviter peccat. Et quia apud omnes invocatio Trinitatis est de essentia formae ideo hoc nullo modo subtrahi potest.

Sed quidam dicunt, quod expressio actus non est de substantia formae; unde si subtrahatur, facta sola Trinitatis invocatione, erit baptismus, quamvis peccet baptizans. Sed contra hoc est decretalis Alexandri Papae tertii qui dicit, quod si quis puerum in aqua ter merserit dicendo, *in nomine patris et filii et Spiritus Sancti*, si non dicat: *ego baptizo te*, talis immersio non facit baptisma. Oportet enim quod per formam virtus Trinitatis invocatae ad materiam propositam determinetur, quod fit in expressione actus.

Similiter etiam expressio personae baptizatae est de substantia formae, quia per eam determinatur actus ad hunc baptismum; et ideo si subtrahatur, non erit baptismus.

Sed expressio personae baptizantis dicitur quod non est de forma quantum ad necessitatem sacramenti, sed ex institutione ecclesiae, ut intentio magis referatur ad actum illum; et ideo si omittatur, erit baptismus, sed peccat omittens.

De additione vero duo sunt observanda. Primum est ex parte addentis. Quia si adderet, intendens illud esse de forma, quasi volens per hoc novum ritum adducere, constat quod non intendit proferre formam qua utitur ecclesia, et ita nec facere quod ecclesia facit: quare non esset baptismus. Secus autem est, si quis ex aliqua causa adderet, ut ex devotione quadam.

Secundum est ex parte ejus quod additur: quod si est corruptivum formae, tunc non est baptismus; si autem non, est baptismus secundum quosdam; sicut si dica-

TO THE THIRD QUESTION, it should be said that concerning subtraction it is certain that if anything is subtracted that is essential to the form, it is not a valid baptism, and the one baptizing sins gravely. And since the invocation of the Trinity is essential to the form among all men, there is no way it can be taken away.

But some people say the expression of the act is not of the substance of the form; hence, if it is taken away, having only made invocation of the Trinity, there will be a baptism, although the one baptizing would sin. But against this is the decretal of Pope Alexander III,[36] who says that if someone should immerse a child in water three times while saying, *In the name of the Father, and of the Son, and of the Holy Spirit*, if he does not say, *I baptize you*, an immersion of this kind would not constitute a baptism. For it is necessary that through the form the power of the Trinity invoked is determined to the matter at hand, which is what happens in the expression of the act.

Likewise, too, the expression of the person baptized is of the substance of the form, for by it the act is determined to this baptism; and so if it were taken away, it would not be a baptism.

But it is said that the expression of the one baptizing is part of the form not as something necessary to the sacrament but as coming from the institution of the Church, so that the intention will be more referred to that act; and so if it were omitted, there would still be a valid baptism, but the one omitting it would sin.

But concerning addition, two things should be observed. The first is on the part of the one adding. For if he added something, intending it to be of the form, as though wanting by this to introduce a new rite, it is clear that he does not intend to utter the form that the Church uses, and so neither does he do what the Church does; which is why it would not be a valid baptism. It is otherwise, however, if someone added something for some other reason, say, out of a certain devotion.

The second thing to be considered is on the part of what is added; for if it is corruptive of the form, then there is no baptism, but if not, there is a valid baptism, according to

36. See reference above.

tur, *in nomine patris majoris et filii minoris*, corrumpitur fides quam forma profitetur. Si autem addatur, *et Beatae Mariae*, quidam dicunt quod non est baptismus, quia non fit baptismus in virtute Beatae Mariae: fieret autem si diceretur; *et Beata Maria juvet puerum istum*, vel aliquod hujusmodi.

Alii autem dicunt et probabilius, quod esset baptismus etiam primo modo additione facta. Quia secundum Magistrum: *in nomine patris*, idem est quod in invocatione. Potest autem in invocatione Beatae Mariae fieri baptismus, cum invocatione Trinitatis; non quasi ex virtute ejus efficaciam habeat baptismus, sicut habet ex virtute Trinitatis, sed ut ejus intercessio baptizato proficiat ad salutem. Quidam autem addunt tertium considerandum: dicunt enim, quod si fiat additio in medio vel in principio, non est baptismus; si autem in fine, est baptismus. Sed hoc nullam videtur habere rationem. Unde secundum alios qualitercumque fiat additio non refert, dummodo non sit contraria formae, et baptizans non intendat mutare ritum baptismi.

Ad primum ergo dicendum, quod illud dicitur contra haereticos qui addebant Scripturae, vel minuebant ex ea propter fidei corruptionem; et similiter in proposito additio vel subtractio corrumpens formam tollit baptisma.

Ad secundum dicendum, quod hoc est verum de differentia essentiali, non autem de accidentali. Unde si subtrahatur aliquid de essentia formae existens, vel addatur aliquid non de essentia formae, ac si sit de essentia formae, non erit baptismus.

Ad tertium dicendum, quod additio illa corrumpebat fidem Trinitatis quam exprimit forma; et ideo corrumpebat formam.

Ad quartum dicendum, quod secundum quosdam sufficiebat quantum ad invocationem Trinitatis, ut nihil minueretur de forma intelligibili, quamvis minueretur de forma sensibili, quia in una persona omnes intelliguntur. Ideo dicebant; quod una persona nominata plenus esset baptismus, si fides interius plena esset. Sed quia fides personae baptizantis vel infidelitas nihil prodest nec nocet ad baptismum, qui fit in fide ecclesiae; ideo quasi communiter modo dicitur, quod oportet omnes tres personas exprimi; et ideo ad verbum Ambrosii multipliciter respondetur. Quidam enim dicunt, quod cum dicit: *plenum fit sacramentum*, ponit sacramentum pro fide: quia qui unam tantum personam confitetur, si alias corde teneat, plenam habet fidem. Quidam vero dicunt, quod intelligitur quantum ad plenitudinem ipsius sacramenti quam habet ex fide: quod patet ex hoc quod dicit: *plenum est fidei sacramentum*; vel quod intelligatur

certain people—for example if it were said: "In the name of the Greater Father and of the Lesser Son," then the faith that the form professes is corrupted. But if what was added was, "and of the Blessed Virgin Mary," certain people say that it is not a valid baptism, because baptism does not happen in the power of the Blessed Virgin Mary; however, it would be valid if it were said, "And may the Blessed Virgin Mary help this child," or something like that.

But others say, and this is more likely, that it would be a valid baptism even in the case of the first kind of addition. For according to the Master, *in the name of the Father* is the same as in the invocation. But baptism can happen in the invocation of the Blessed Virgin together with the invocation of the Trinity—not as though the baptism would get its efficacy from her power, as it does from the power of the Trinity, but so that her intercession would assist the baptized to salvation. However, some people add a third consideration: for they say that if an addition is made in the middle or in the beginning, it is not a valid baptism; but if at the end, it is a valid baptism. But this seems to have no reason. Hence, according to others, it does not matter how the addition is done, as long as it is not contrary to the form and the one baptizing does not intend to change the rite of baptism.

Reply Obj. 1: This is said against the heretics who were adding to the Scriptures or took away from them because of the corruption of their faith; and likewise in this case, addition or subtraction corrupting the form takes away baptism.

Reply Obj. 2: This is true of essential differences, but not of accidental ones. Hence if something existing in the essence of the form were withdrawn, or if something were added that was not of the essence of the form as if it were of the essence of the form, it would not be a valid baptism.

Reply Obj. 3: That addition corrupted the faith in the Trinity which the form expresses; and thus it corrupted the form.

Reply Obj. 4: According to some people it was enough for the invocation of the Trinity that nothing be taken away from the intelligible form, although something was taken away from the sensible form, for in one Divine Person, all are understood. Therefore, they said that one Person named would be a complete baptism, if the interior faith were complete. But because the faith or unbelief of the person baptizing neither furthers nor harms the baptism, which is done in the faith of the Church, for this reason it is now said almost universally that it is necessary for all three Persons to be expressed. And so the words of Ambrose are answered in several ways. For some people say that when he says, *the sacrament is made complete*, he says 'sacrament' in place of 'faith': for whoever confesses only one Person, as long as he has the others in his heart, has complete faith. But some people say that the phrase is understood as to the completeness of that sacrament, which it has from faith; which is

secundum quosdam in casu quando una persona nominata, puer vel sacerdos moreretur (creditur enim quod invisibilis sacerdos suppleret defectum), vel in casu simili, in quo apostoli in nomine Christi baptizabant; et hoc magis consonat verbis ejus.

AD QUINTUM dicendum, quod qui intendit aliquid facere, non est consequens quod faciat illud; unde esset ad corruptionem formae: *ego intendo te baptizare*.

clear by the fact that he says, *complete is the sacrament of faith*; or that it may be understood, according to some people, in the case where the child or the priest dies when only one Person has been named (for it is believed that the invisible Priest would supply the defect), or in similar cases, in which the apostles baptized in the name of Christ; and this is more consonant with his words.

REPLY OBJ. 5: Someone who intends to do something does not necessarily do it; hence it would be a corruption of the form to say, *I intend to baptize you*.

Response to Quaestiuncula 4

AD QUARTAM QUAESTIONEM dicendum, quod cum forma verborum consistat in tribus, scilicet significatione, integritate verborum, et ordine; quidam dicunt, quod quidquid horum mutetur vel varietur, non erit baptismum. Sed quia formae sacramentorum sunt quaedam fidei professiones, fidem autem non profitentur verba formae nisi ratione suae significationis; ideo alii dicunt, quod dummodo servetur intellectus vel implicite vel explicite, etiam si non esset vocum integritas nec ordo, idem erit baptismum. Sed quia sacramentum quantum ad formam et materiam debet esse ejusdem signum, ideo alii dicunt medio modo, quod requiritur et significatio plena, et verba integra quae sunt de essentia formae. Si autem ordo, vel aliquid circa verba mutetur quod non tollit nec significationem nec integritatem verborum, erit baptismum.

ET SECUNDUM HOC ad primum dicendum, quod si fiat tanta interruptio quod intercipiat intentionem baptizantis, tunc non erit una forma; et ideo utraque per se erit imperfecta, nec sufficit ad baptismum; sicut si dicatur: *in nomine Patris*, et interponat longam fabulam, et postea dicat, *et filii*. Si autem ita fiat parva interruptio, vel verbi non corrumpentis formam, ut si dicatur: *in nomine Patris omnipotentis*; aut silentii, aut tussis, vel alicujus hujusmodi, quod intentionem non discontinuet; tunc erit ab unitate intentionis unitas formae. Constat enim quod continuitas formae ex vocibus unitatem habere non potest, cum oratio sit quantitas discreta.

AD SECUNDUM dicendum, quod quidam dicunt, quod si sit talis ordo qui mutet intellectum, non fit baptismus; ut si dicatur: *in nomine Patris baptizo te, et Filii et Spiritus Sancti*. Si autem non mutetur intellectus, erit baptismus, ut si dicatur: *in nomine Patris et Filii et Spiritus Sancti baptizo te*. Alii vero dicunt, quod qualitercumque mutetur ordo verborum, non videtur intellectus mutari; et ideo erit baptismus, quamvis peccet transponens. Et secundum hoc dicendum, quod ordo persona-

TO THE FOURTH QUESTION, it should be said that since the form of words consists in three things—namely, signification, integrity of the words, and order—some people say that if any of these are changed or altered, it will not be a valid baptism. But since the forms of the sacraments are certain professions of faith, while the words of the form only profess the faith by reason of their signification, for this reason others say that as long as the understanding is preserved, whether implicitly or explicitly, even if the integrity of expression or the order is not there, there will be a valid baptism all the same. But because a sacrament, as to form and matter, should be a sign of the same thing, for that reason others take a middle stance, saying that both the full signification and all the words that are essential to the form are required; but if the order or something about the words is changed and it does not take away the signification or the integrity of the words, the baptism will be valid.

REPLY OBJ. 1: If an interruption happens such that it disrupts the intention of the one baptizing, then there will not be one form; and thus both pieces will be incomplete in themselves, and will not suffice for baptism; for example if someone were to say, *In the name of the Father*, and then break out into a long story, and afterward say, *and of the Son*. However if a small interruption happens—either of words that do not corrupt the form, as if someone said, *In the name of the Father omnipotent*, or an interruption of silence, or a cough, or something like that, which does not disrupt the intention—then there will be unity of form from the unity of intention. For it is clear that continuity of form cannot have unity from the expressions used, since speech is a discrete quantity.

REPLY OBJ. 2: Some people say that if the order of words is such that it changes the understanding, baptism does not happen; for example, if one were to say, *In the name of the Father I baptize you, and of the Son and of the Holy Spirit*. However, if the understanding is not changed, there will be a baptism, as if were said, *In the name of the Father and of the Son and of the Holy Spirit, I baptize you*. But others say that however the order of words is changed, the understanding of them does not seem to be changed, and

rum non est quo una sit prior altera, sed quo una est ex altera; quem ordinem ipsa nomina personarum ostendunt, quocumque ordine proferantur.

thus there will be a valid baptism, although the one changing the order would sin. And according to this, it should be said that the order of the Persons is not that by which one is *before* another, but that by which one is *from* another—an order the very names of the Persons display, in whatever order they are named.

ARTICLE 3

The matter of baptism

Quaestiuncula 1

AD TERTIUM SIC PROCEDITUR. Videtur quod baptismus non debeat fieri in aqua. Ex similibus enim causis similes effectus producuntur. Sed baptismus habet similem effectum cum circumcisione. Cum ergo aqua in nullo conveniat cum instrumento circumcisionis, videtur quod non congrue fiat baptismus in aqua.

PRAETEREA, secundum Damascenum, et Dionysium, baptismus habet vim illuminativam, et in eo Spiritus Sanctus datur, et homo in filium Dei regeneratur. Sed ignis inter alia elementa plus habet de luce, et per eum ratione caloris Spiritus Sanctus, qui est caritas, significatur, et secundum Dionysium in fine Cael. Hier., ignis maxime deiformitatem significat. Ergo baptismus debet fieri in igne, et non in aqua.

PRAETEREA, secundum Damascenum, baptismus est principium vitae, et est sacramentum maximae necessitatis. Sed aer habet maximam convenientiam cum vita, quia calidus est et humidus, et est communissimum elementum, ut nulli propter ejus penuriam posset esse periculum, sicut quandoque parvulis est periculum propter defectum aquae. Ergo baptismus debuit in aere fieri, et non in aqua.

PRAETEREA, per baptismum configuramur sepulturae Christi; Rom. 6. Sed Christus in terra sepultus est. Ergo baptismus debet in terra fieri, et non in aqua.

PRAETEREA, oleum et vinum ablutiva sunt, et laetificantia, et impinguantia. Sed baptismus praeter ablutionem peccatorum, pinguedinem et laetitiam spiritualem tribuit. Ergo in his liquoribus fieri debet.

PRAETEREA, sacramenta de latere Christi fluxerunt. Sed sicut fluxit aqua, sic et sanguis. Ergo in sanguine debet fieri baptismus.

SED CONTRA est quod dicitur Joan. 3, 5: *nisi quis renatus fuerit ex aqua et Spiritu Sancto, non potest introire in regnum Dei.*

PRAETEREA, reparatio debet creationi respondere. Sed in creatione mundi Spiritus Domini commemoratur primo super aquas ferri, et ex aquis primo animam viventem produxisse, ut patet Genes. 1. Ergo et Spiritus

OBJ. 1: To the third question we proceed thus. It seems that baptism should not be done in water.[37] For like effects are produced from like causes. But baptism has an effect similar to circumcision. Since, then, water has nothing in common with the instrument of circumcision, it seems unfitting that baptism be done in water.

OBJ. 2: Furthermore, according to Damascene[38] and Dionysius,[39] baptism has an illuminative force, and in it the Holy Spirit is given, and man is regenerated as a son of God. But among all the elements, fire has the most light, and by it is represented the Holy Spirit, who is charity, by reason of its heat. And according to Dionysius in the end of the *Celestial Hierarchy*,[40] fire most of all represents what is godlike. Therefore, baptism should be done in fire and not in water.

OBJ. 3: Furthermore, according to Damascene,[41] baptism is the principle of life and the sacrament of greatest necessity. But air has most to do with life, for it is hot and wet, and it is most common element, so that its scarcity would never be a danger, as sometimes there is a danger to infants because of a lack of water. Therefore, baptism should have been done in air, not water.

OBJ. 4: Furthermore, by baptism we are configured to the burial of Christ (Rom 6:4). But Christ was buried in the earth. Therefore, baptism should happen in earth, not in water.

OBJ. 5: Furthermore, oil and wine are cleansing, and cheering, and fattening. But baptism, besides being a cleansing of sins, bestows spiritual joy and richness. Therefore, it should be done in these liquids.

OBJ. 6: Furthermore, the sacraments flowed from the side of Christ. But as water flowed, so also did blood. Therefore, baptism should be done in blood.

ON THE CONTRARY, is what is said: *unless a man is reborn of water and the Holy Spirit, he cannot enter into the kingdom of God* (John 3:5).

FURTHERMORE, the repair should correspond to the original creation. But in the creation of the world the Spirit of the Lord is recorded to have been first borne over the waters, and to have first produced living beings from the wa-

---

37. Parallels: below, exposition of the text; d. 5, q. 2, a. 1, qa. 1 & 3; d. 17, q. 3, a. 4, qa. 3; *ST* III, q. 66; q. 67, a. 3; q. 74, a. 1; *SCG* IV, ch. 69; *Quodl.* I, q. 6, a. 1; *Super Ioan.* 3, lec. 1.

38. John Damascene, *On the Orthodox Faith*, Bk. 4, ch. 9 (PG 94:1122).

39. Pseudo-Dionysius, *Ecclesiastical Hierarchy*, ch. 5, p. 1, n. 3 (PG 3:503).

40. Pseudo-Dionysius, *Celestial Hierarchy*, ch. 15, n. 2 (PG 3:327).

41. In the same passage.

Sanctus in opere reparationis primo dari debet in aqua, et per illum spiritualis vita; et sic baptismus in aqua fieri debet, quod est principium alterius vitae, et per quod primitias spiritus accepimus.

ters, as is clear from Genesis 1. Therefore, in the work of reparation, too, the Holy Spirit should be first given in water, and through him, spiritual life. And so baptism, which is the beginning of another life, and by which we receive the first fruits of the Holy Spirit, should be done in water.

Quaestiuncula 2

ULTERIUS. Videtur quod non debeat fieri in aqua simplici. Quia medicina debet esse infirmis proportionata. Sed nos, quibus medicina baptismi adhibetur, habemus corpus ex elementis mixtum. Ergo aqua baptismi non debet esse elementum simplex.

PRAETEREA, sacramenta fluxerunt de latere Christi dormientis in cruce. Sed de latere ejus non est probabile fluxisse aquam quae sit purum elementum, cum tale quid in corporibus mixtis non inveniatur. Ergo non debet in aqua simplici baptismus fieri.

PRAETEREA, pura elementa, secundum philosophos, non sunt in extremis, sed in mediis elementorum: quia in extremis alterant se invicem. Si ergo oporteret in aqua simplici baptismum fieri, non posset apud nos fieri.

PRAETEREA, constat quod aqua maris non est simplex aqua, quod ejus amaritudo et salsedo demonstrat, quae ex terrestri mixto contingit. Sed in aqua maris potest fieri baptismus. Ergo non requiritur aqua simplex.

PRAETEREA, aqua competit baptismo ratione ablutionis. Sed quaedam aqua mixta magis abluit, sicut lixivium et hujusmodi. Ergo magis baptismo competit.

SED CONTRA est quod mixtum neutrum miscibilium est. Si ergo fiat baptismus in aqua mixta, non fieret in aqua; quod esset contra doctrinam Evangelii.

OBJ. 1: Moreover, it seems that it should not be done in plain water.[42] For medicine should be proportioned to the sick. But we to whom the medicine of baptism is applied have bodies of mixed elements. Therefore, the water of baptism should not be a simple element.

OBJ. 2: Moreover, the sacraments flowed from the side of Christ sleeping on the Cross. But it is not likely that from his side flowed water as a pure element, since it is not found that way in mixed bodies. Therefore, baptism should not happen in plain water.

OBJ. 3: Furthermore, pure elements, according to the philosophers, do not exist in the extremes but in the middle of the elements, for in the extremes they change into each other. If therefore it were necessary for baptism to be done in plain water, we would not be able to do it.

OBJ. 4: Furthermore, it is clear that seawater is not plain water, as its bitterness and saltiness shows, which happen from being mixed with earth. But a baptism can be done with seawater. Therefore, plain water is not required.

OBJ. 5: Furthermore, water is used in baptism for the sake of cleansing. But certain watery mixtures cleanse better, such as lye and things of that sort. Therefore, they would suit baptism better.

ON THE CONTRARY, a mixture is neither of the things mixed to make it up. If therefore baptism happens in a watery mixture, it does not happen in water, which would be against the doctrine of the Gospel.

Quaestiuncula 3

ULTERIUS. Videtur quod non in qualibet aqua simplici possit fieri baptismus. Dominus enim tactu mundissimae suae carnis vim regenerativam contulit aquis. Sed non tetigit nisi aquas Jordanis. Ergo solae illae aquae habent vim regenerativam; et ita non in qualibet aqua potest fieri baptismus.

PRAETEREA, baptismus non potest fieri nisi in aqua verbo vitae sanctificata. Si ergo baptismus fieret in mari, vel in aliquo fluvio, tota aqua fluminis esset sanctificata; quod videtur absurdum.

OBJ. 1: Moreover, it seems that baptism cannot be done in any plain water whatsoever.[43] For the Lord conferred their regenerative power on the waters by the contact with his most immaculate flesh. But he only touched the waters of the Jordan. Therefore, those waters alone have regenerative power, and so baptism cannot be done in any water whatsoever.

OBJ. 2: Furthermore, baptism cannot be done except in water sanctified by the word of life. If, therefore, baptism happened in the sea, or in a certain river, all the water of the river would be sanctified, which seems absurd.

42. Parallel: *ST* III, q. 66, a. 4.
43. Parallel: *ST* III, q. 66, a. 4.

Praeterea, quaedam aquae non habent vim abluendi, sed magis deturpant, sicut aquae paludum. Ergo videtur quod in hujusmodi aquis non possit fieri baptismus.

Sed contra est quia materia baptismi debet esse communis: quia baptismus est sacramentum maximae necessitatis. Sed hoc non esset, nisi in qualibet aqua baptismus fieri posset. Ergo in qualibet aqua potest fieri baptismus.

Obj. 3: Furthermore, certain waters do not have the power of cleansing, but rather they soil, like swamp water. Therefore, it seems that in waters like these a baptism cannot be done.

On the contrary, the matter of baptism should be common, for baptism is the most necessary sacrament. But this would not be the case unless a baptism could be done in any water whatsoever. Therefore, baptism can be done in any water.

Response to Quaestiuncula 1

Respondeo dicendum ad primam quaestionem, quod ex institutione divina necessarium est baptismum in aqua fieri. Possunt autem institutionis accipi sex rationes. Prima est, quia aqua ratione diaphaneitatis habet aliquid de lumine, et ita competit baptismo qui habet vim illuminativam, secundum quod in eo gratia confertur. Secunda est, quia ratione humiditatis habet vim ablutivam; et ideo competit baptismo, in quo sordes culpae mundantur. Tertia est, quia ratione frigiditatis habet vim refrigerandi; et ideo competit baptismo, in quo incendium fomitis mitigatur. Quarta est, quia, ut dicitur in 17 de animalibus, aqua maxime competit generationi et augmentationi rerum viventium; unde et in principio mundi ex aqua primitus animalia producta sunt; et sic competit baptismo, inquantum est regeneratio in spiritualem vitam. Quinta est, quia in omnibus mundi partibus aqua invenitur. Sexta, quia est res quae de facili ab omnibus haberi potest sine magno pretio. Et hae duae competunt baptismo prout est sacramentum necessitatis.

Ad primum ergo dicendum, quod neque circumcisio neque baptismus tollunt originalem culpam ex virtute naturali ipsarum rerum, sed inquantum significant aliquid spirituale; et in significatione communicat aqua cum instrumento circumcisionis, quia in utroque fit ablatio alicujus.

Ad secundum dicendum, quod ignis habet lucem ex se et calorem, qui est qualitas activa; et quia Spiritus Sanctus est primum agens deiformitatem in baptismo, et primum illuminans, sed baptismus est sicut quaedam instrumentalis causa, ideo Spiritui Sancto competit figurari per ignem, sed baptismo per aquam, qua mediante transfunditur lumen a Spiritu Sancto in animam, sicut per diaphanum lumen corporale ad sensum.

Ad tertium dicendum, quod quamvis aer communicet cum vita, non tamen aer generationi viventium, sicut aqua, competit; et propter hoc magis competit aqua baptismo quam aer.

I answer that, by divine institution it is necessary for baptism to be done in water. Now six reasons can be given for this institution. The first is that water, by reason of its transparency, has something of light, and in this way it befits baptism which has illuminative power, inasmuch as grace is conferred in it. The second is that by reason of its wetness it has cleansing power; and that befits baptism, in which the soil of guilt is washed away. The third is that by reason of its coolness it has a refreshing power; and that befits baptism, in which the heat of the kindling [of sin] is mitigated. The fourth is that, as is said in *On Animals* 17, [44] water is best suited to generation and the growth of living things; hence, too, at the beginning of the world animals were produced for the first time from water; and thus it befits baptism, in which there is a regeneration to spiritual life. The fifth is that in every part of the world water can be found. The sixth is that it is a thing that can be had easily by anyone without a great cost. And these last two things befit baptism inasmuch as it is a necessary sacrament.

Reply Obj. 1: Neither circumcision nor baptism takes away original sin by the natural power of those things, but inasmuch as they represent something spiritual; and in signification, water has something in common with the instrument of circumcision, for in both, a certain removal occurs.

Reply Obj. 2: Fire has, of itself, light and heat, which is an active quality; and since the Holy Spirit is the first to make men godlike in baptism, and the first illuminator, but baptism is like a certain instrumental cause, for this reason it befits the Holy Spirit to be represented by fire, but baptism by water, by means of which light is poured out by the Holy Spirit into the soul, just as physical light passes through the transparent medium to the senses.

Reply Obj. 3: Although air has much in common with life, nevertheless it does not play the role in the generation of living things that water does; and because of this, water is more fitting for baptism than air.

---

44. In modern editions, Aristotle, *On the Generation of Animals*, Bk. 3, ch. 11, 762a10ff.; Bk. 4, ch. 2, 767a31.

Ad quartum dicendum, quod sepultura Christi est res significata, non contenta; institutio autem sacramentalis materiae attenditur principaliter quantum ad significationem rei contentae. Magis autem competit aqua tali significationi in baptismo quam terra; et ideo ratio non sequitur.

Ad quintum dicendum, quod oleum et vinum non habentur in usu ablutionis, sicut aqua, nec ita bene abluunt, quia ex eis etiam aliquae sordes contrahuntur, et desunt iterum aliae conditiones, quae aquae competunt; et ideo non ita competunt baptismo sicut aqua. Pinguedo autem devotionis et laetitia sunt quidam effectus baptismum consequentes, et non primi.

Ad sextum dicendum, quod ex latere Christi fluxit sanguis et aqua; sed sanguis ad redimendum, ut dicitur 1 Petr. 1, aqua autem ad abluendum; et ideo aqua baptismo competit, et non sanguis.

Reply Obj. 4: The burial of Christ is the thing signified but not contained; whereas the institution of the sacramental matter is chiefly directed to the signification of the thing contained. Now water is better suited to this signification in baptism than earth; and so the argument does not follow.

Reply Obj. 5: Oil and wine are not habitually used for washing, as water is, nor do they wash so well, since from them a certain soiling happens; and again, other conditions are lacking that make water suitable. And thus they are not as suitable for baptism as water. Further, the richness and joy of devotion are some of the effects consequent upon baptism, and not before it.

Reply Obj. 6: From the side of Christ flowed blood and water; but the blood was to redeem us, as is said in 1 Peter 1:18, while the water was for washing. And thus water is suited to baptism, and not blood.

Response to Quaestiuncula 2

Ad secundam quaestionem dicendum, quod permixtio aquae potest esse duplex. Una quae tollit speciem,[45] sicut quando per alterationem transit in aliam speciem, sicut per putrefactionem aliquam vel digestionem transit in vinum, aut etiam per additionem tantam alterius liquoris, quod solvatur species aquae, sicut si parum aquae multo vino admisceatur. Alia permixtio est quae non tollit speciem aquae; sicut quando alteratur aqua secundum aliquod accidens, et manet species, ut patet in aqua calefacta; vel quando additur aliquid aquae quod vel non commisceatur, sicut si aliqua solida ponantur in aqua; vel si sit commiscibile, sicut aliquod humidum, tamen est tam parvae quantitatis quod mixtionem non faciat, sed in aquam penitus convertatur. In aqua ergo primo modo permixta non potest fieri baptismus, quia jam non est aqua; in aqua autem secundo modo potest fieri. Ut autem cognoscatur quando sic vel sic permixta est aqua, sciendum est, quod sicut diversitatem speciei in animalibus judicamus ex diversitate figurarum, ita etiam diversam speciem in elementis cognoscimus ex diversitate rari et densi; et ideo si fiat tanta alteratio vel permixtio aquae quod recedatur a termino raritatis et densitatis aquae vel in actu vel in potentia, signum est quod sit species aquae transmutata; et dico in potentia, quando humor aliquis non condensatur et rarefit calido vel frigido, sicut aqua; sed aliter, sicut patet in vino, oleo, lacte, et hujusmodi.

To the second question, I answer that a mixture of water can be of two kinds. There is one that takes away the species, as when it changes into another species [of substance] by an alteration, like changing into wine by a certain fermenting or decomposition, or also by so great an addition of another liquid that the species of water disappears, as when a small amount of water is mixed into a lot of wine. There is another kind of mixture that does not destroy the species of water, as when the water is changed according to something accidental, and the species remains, as is the case with heated water; or when something is added to the water which either does not dissolve, as when something solid is put into the water—or, if it is able to be mixed in, like something moist, is nevertheless of such a small quantity that it does not constitute a new mixture, but is thoroughly converted into the water. In the first kind of watery mixture, therefore, a baptism cannot be done, for it is no longer water; but in the second kind of mixture it can be done. So that it may be recognized when this or that mixture is water, however, it should be known that just as we judge difference of species in animals from the difference of their shapes, so also we recognize different species among the elements by the difference of rare and dense; and thus, if such an alteration or mixture is made of the water that it is withdrawn from the terminus of rarity or denseness of water either in act or in potency, it is a sign that it is a kind of transformed water. And I say "in potency" to indicate when a certain fluid is not condensed and evaporated by heat or cold as water is, but differently, as we see in the instances of wine, oil, milk, and things like that.

---

45. *tollit speciem.—tollit aquae speciem* PLE.

AD PRIMUM ergo dicendum, quod non oportet quod aqua competat nobis per convenientiam in naturali proprietate, sed significando effectum qui in nobis debet fieri.

AD SECUNDUM dicendum quod de corpore Christi exivit vera aqua, sicut verus sanguis; et hoc ad probandum esse corpus Christi verum, non phantasticum, ut Manichaei ponunt. Fuit enim in eo compositio ex elementis, quod probatum fuit ex eo quod aqua, quae est elementum, prodiit ex ejus latere; et compositionem humorum probavit sanguis effluens.

AD TERTIUM dicendum, quod quamvis aqua quae est apud nos, sit aliquo modo alterata, et habens aliquid de permixtione aliorum elementorum, non tamen amisit speciem propriam.

ET SIMILITER dicendum est ad quartum de aqua maris.

AD QUINTUM dicendum, quod illae aquae quae per aliquam transmutationem speciem aquae amittunt, etsi retineant abluendi virtutem, tamen materia baptismi esse non possunt, quia prima virtus abluendi est in vera aqua; et etiam purius abluit, quia ex aliis liquoribus corpora abluta aliquo modo inficiuntur: communius etiam aqua utimur ad abluendum. De lixivio autem quidam dicunt quod speciem aquae amisit, unde baptismi materia esse non potest. Sed hoc non videtur: quia eadem ratione nec aqua transiens per mineras sulphureas et terras combustas posset esse materia baptismi; quod falsum est. Lixivium enim ab alia aqua non differt nisi in hoc quod per cineres transivit. Unde videtur aliter dicendum, quod baptismus potest fieri in lixivio, sicut et in aquis sulphureis, et in aliis aquis quae ex terra, per quam transeunt, immutantur.

REPLY OBJ. 1: Water does not need to correspond to us by sharing in our natural properties, but by signifying the effect that should happen in us.

REPLY OBJ. 2: What came from the side of Christ was true water, just as also came forth true blood; and this was to prove that the body of Christ was real, not an illusion as the Manichees maintain. For there was in him a composition of elements, which was proved by the fact that water, which is an element, went forth from his side; and the blood flowing out proved a composition of fluids.

REPLY OBJ. 3: Although the water that we have available to us may be somewhat altered and contain some mixture of other elements, nevertheless it has not lost its proper species.

REPLY OBJ. 4: And the same thing can be said to the fourth objection about seawater.

REPLY OBJ. 5: Even if they retain their power of washing, those waters that lose the species of water by some transformation cannot be the matter for baptism, since the first power of washing is in true water; and it also washes more purely, for from washing with other liquids bodies sometimes become infected; and for washing we most commonly use water. But about lye, some say that it has lost the species of water; hence it cannot be the matter for baptism. But this does not seem to be the case, for by the same argument, water passing through sulfurous channels and scorched earth could not be the matter for baptism, which is false. For lye differs from water only by the fact that it has passed through ashes. Hence, it seems that it should be said otherwise, that baptism can be done with lye, just as in sulfurous waters, and in other waters that are changed by the earth they passed through.

Response to Quaestiuncula 3

AD TERTIAM QUAESTIONEM dicendum, quod diversitas aquarum quae est per loca et situs, est differentia accidentalis, unde non mutat speciem aquae; et ideo in qualibet aqua hujusmodi, vel maris vel fluminis vel cisternae vel fontis vel stagni, potest fieri baptismus.

AD PRIMUM ergo dicendum, quod Dominus tangendo illam aquam dedit vim regenerativam in tota specie aquae, instituens eam instrumentum baptismi.

AD SECUNDUM dicendum, quod si baptizatur aliquis in mari, sola illa aqua maris pertinet ad baptismum quae potest habere aliquem effectum in baptizato vel lavando vel infrigidando, et non totum mare.

AD TERTIUM dicendum, quod si aqua paludis esset intantum ingrossata quod recederet a vera raritate aquae non esset baptismus, sicut si esset lutum, alias esset baptismus, quia adhuc species aquae manet.

TO THE THIRD QUESTION, I answer that the difference in waters that arises from place and position is an accidental difference; hence it does not change the species of water. And thus a baptism can be done in any water, whether in the sea, or a river, or a well, or a fountain, or a pool.

REPLY OBJ. 1: By touching the water, the Lord gave a regenerative power to the whole species of water, establishing it as the instrument of baptism.

REPLY OBJ. 2: If someone is baptized in the sea, the only seawater that pertains to this baptism is the seawater that has some effect on the baptized person, whether by washing or cooling, and not the whole sea.

REPLY OBJ. 3: If the marsh-water were so mucky that it departed from the true rarity of water, just as if it were mud, there would not be a baptism; otherwise it would be a baptism, for the species of water would still remain.

ARTICLE 4

The intention of baptism

Quaestiuncula 1

AD QUARTUM SIC PROCEDITUR. Videtur quod immersio sit de necessitate baptismi. Quia per baptismum configuramur sepulturae Christi, ut dicitur Rom. 6. Sed hoc non fit per baptismum nisi inquantum immergimur et occultamur in aqua, sicut Christus sub terra. Ergo immersio est de necessitate baptismi.

PRAETEREA, baptismus datur in remedium contra originale peccatum. Sed originale peccatum est in toto corpore. Ergo totum debet immergi.

PRAETEREA, si aliqua pars sufficeret ut intingeretur, praecipue videretur de membris genitalibus, in quibus praecipue originale manet, et in quibus circumcisio fiebat. Sed ablutio non potest fieri congrue in illis membris, nisi totum corpus immergatur. Ergo totum corpus debet immergi.

SED CONTRA est consuetudo in aliquibus Ecclesiis, in quibus quandoque per aspersionem et non per immersionem baptismus celebratur.

PRAETEREA, in baptismo beati Laurentii legitur quod Romanus ab eo baptizandus urceum aquae attulit, in quo constat quod immergi non poterat. Ergo immersio non est de necessitate baptismi.

OBJ. 1: To the fourth we proceed thus. It seems that immersion is necessary to baptism.[46] For by baptism we are configured to the burial of Christ, as is said in Romans 6:4. But this only happens by baptism except the extent that we are immersed and hidden in the water, as Christ was beneath the earth. Therefore, immersion is necessary to baptism.

OBJ. 2: Furthermore, baptism is given as a remedy against original sin. But original sin is in the whole body. Therefore, the whole should be immersed.

OBJ. 3: Furthermore, if dunking a certain part of the body would suffice, it would seem that this would be especially the genital members, in which original sin dwells, and in which circumcision happened. But washing cannot fittingly happen to those members without immersing the whole body. Therefore, the whole body should be immersed.

ON THE CONTRARY, is the custom in certain churches, in which baptism is sometimes celebrated by sprinkling and not by immersion.

FURTHERMORE, in the martyrdom of blessed Laurence it is read that Romanus, to be baptized by him, brought a jug of water, in which he obviously could not have been immersed.[47] Therefore, immersion is not necessary to baptism.

Quaestiuncula 2

ULTERIUS. Videtur quod non debet esse trina. Baptismus enim est tinctio in aqua verbo vitae sanctificata, ut dicit Augustinus. Sed unus est baptismus. Ergo debet esse una tinctio, sive immersio.

PRAETEREA, requiritur ad baptismum fides de unitate et de Trinitate personarum. Sed Trinitas personarum sufficienter exprimitur in forma. Ergo unitas essentiae debet exprimi in unitate immersionis.

OBJ. 1: Moreover, it seems that it does not have to be done three times.[48] For baptism is a dipping in water sanctified by the word of life, as Augustine says.[49] But there is one baptism. Therefore, there should be one dipping or immersion.

OBJ. 2: Furthermore, faith in the unity and Trinity of the Persons is required for baptism. But the Trinity of Persons is expressed sufficiently in the form. Therefore, the oneness of essence should be expressed in the oneness of immersion.

---

46. Parallel: *ST* III. q. 66, a. 7.
47. Thomas's source here is Bd. Jacobus de Voragine, *Legenda aurea*, Vita S. Laurentii, ch. 117.
48. Parallels: below, d. 28, q. 1, a. 1, qa. 2; *ST* III, q. 66, a. 8.
49. Augustine, *In Iohannis euangelium tractatus* (CCSL 36), Tract. 15, par. 4.

Praeterea, baptismus est figura passionis Christi. Sed una est passio Christi. Ergo una debet esse immersio in baptismo.

Sed contra est quod Dionysius dicit, quod debet fieri baptismus tribus immersionibus et elevationibus, ad designandum quod Christus in sepulcro jacuit tribus diebus et tribus noctibus.

Praeterea, Chrysostomus super Joan. 3: *fit immersio, ut discas quoniam virtus Patris et Filii et Spiritus Sancti omnia haec implet.* Idem dicit Hieronymus super Epist. ad Ephes. 4.

Obj. 3: Furthermore, baptism is a figure of the Passion of Christ. But there is one Passion of Christ. Therefore, there should be one immersion in baptism.

On the contrary, Dionysius[50] says that baptism should be done with three immersions and elevations, to represent that Christ lay in the tomb for three days and three nights.

Furthermore, Chrysostom comments upon John 3: *the immersion is done so that you may learn that the power of the Father and of the Son and of the Holy Spirit fulfills all these things.*[51] Jerome says the same thing in his commentary on Ephesians 4.[52]

Quaestiuncula 3

Ulterius. Videtur quod trina immersio sit de necessitate sacramenti. Legitur enim in decretis *de Consecratione*, dist. 6: *si quis presbyter vel episcopus semel immergat, et unam immersionem fecerit, deponatur.* Hoc autem non esset, nisi trina immersio esset de necessitate sacramenti. Ergo est de necessitate sacramenti.

Praeterea, sicut fides Trinitatis exprimitur per nomina trium personarum, ita per tres immersiones, ut ex dictis patet. Sed si non nominarentur tres personae non esset baptismus. Ergo similiter si non trina immersio fiat.

Praeterea, si non trina immersio est de necessitate sacramenti, statim in prima immersione baptismus habet totum effectum suum. Ergo aliae immersiones frustra adderentur, et fit injuria sacramento.

Sed contra est quod ipsa immersio non est de necessitate sacramenti. Ergo multo minus numerus immersionis.

Praeterea, auctoritas Gregorii in littera posita dicit, quod utrumque potest fieri servata ecclesiae consuetudine. Ergo non est de necessitate sacramenti neque una neque trina immersio.

Obj. 1: Moreover, it seems that a triple immersion is necessary to the sacrament.[53] For it is read in the decree *On Consecration*, Distinction 6: *if any presbyter or bishop should immerse once and do one immersion, let him be deposed.*[54] But this would not be the case unless a triple immersion were necessary to the sacrament. Therefore, it is necessary to the sacrament.

Obj. 2: Furthermore, just as faith in the Trinity is expressed by the names of the three Persons, so also by a triple immersion, as is clear from what has been said. But if the three Persons are not named it would not be a valid baptism. Therefore, it is the same if a triple immersion is not done.

Obj. 3: Furthermore, if a triple immersion is not necessary to the sacrament, the baptism will have its whole effect right after the first immersion. Therefore, other immersions would be added in vain, and injury would be done to the sacrament.

On the contrary, immersion itself is not necessary to the sacrament, much less the number of immersions.

Furthermore, the authority of Gregory cited in the text says that either way can be done in keeping with the custom of the Church. Therefore, whether there are one or three immersions is not of necessity for the sacrament.

Response to Quaestiuncula 1

Respondeo dicendum ad primam quaestionem, quod baptismus ablutionem importat. Ablutio autem per aquam potest fieri non tantum per modum immersionis, sed per modum aspersionis vel effusionis; et ideo

To the first question, I answer that baptism implies cleansing. However, cleansing by water can happen not only by immersion but also by sprinkling or pouring; and thus a baptism can be done in either way. And it seems

---

50. Pseudo-Dionysius, *Ecclesiastical Hierarchy*, ch. 2, p. 3, n. 7 (PG 3:403).
51. John Chrysostom, *Homilies on the Gospel of John*, hom. 28, n. 2 (PG 59:448).
52. Jerome, *Commentary on Ephesians*, PL 26:496.
53. Parallels: below, d. 23, q. 1, a. 1, qa. 2; *ST* III, q. 66, a. 8.
54. See the *Decretum Gratiani*, d. 6, ch. 79 (PL 187:1825).

utroque modo potest fieri baptismus. Et videtur quod apostoli hoc modo baptizarent, cum legatur quod simul una die conversi sunt quinque millia, et alia tria millia Act. 2 et 3; et ideo quando consuetudo ecclesiae patitur, vel quando necessitas incumbit propter defectum aquae, sive propter periculum pueri, de cujus morte timetur, vel etiam propter imbecillitatem sacerdotis non potentis sustentare infantem, potest sine immersione baptismus celebrari.

AD PRIMUM ergo dicendum, quod etiam in effusione aquae homo quodammodo sub aqua ponitur; et ideo quodammodo Christo per baptismum consepelitur.

AD SECUNDUM dicendum quod omnes operationes animales a capite principium habent, quia baptismus format animales habitus secundum definitionem Dionysii prius positam, art. 1, quaestiunc. 3, non autem naturales vel vitales; ideo si sit caput aspersum aqua, in totum corpus aspersio reputatur; sicut etiam juristae dicunt, quod ubi caput hominis jacet, reputatur ac si totus homo sepultus esset ibidem. Non sic autem est de aliis partibus.

AD TERTIUM dicendum, quod quamvis originale peccatum consistat praecipue in membris genitalibus quantum ad originem, tamen in operationibus animalibus consummatur quantum ad rationem culpae; et ideo potius oportet baptismum adhiberi circa caput, si necessitas incumbit, ut non totum corpus possit immergi.

that the apostles baptized in this way, when it is read in Acts 2 and 3 that five thousand were converted together on one day, and then another three thousand. And thus when the custom of the Church allows, or when necessity compels for want of water, or because of the danger to a child whose death is feared, or even because of the feebleness of the priest rendering him unable to lift the infant, a baptism may be celebrated without immersion.

REPLY OBJ. 1: In the pouring of water, too, a man is in a certain way placed under the water; and thus, by baptism he is in a certain way buried with Christ.

REPLY OBJ. 2: All animal operations have their beginning in the head—since baptism forms animal habits, according to the definition of Dionysius quoted above, Article 1, Subquestion 3—although the natural or vital operations do not. Thus, if the head is sprinkled with water, the sprinkling is considered to be for the whole body; just as also the jurists say that where the head of a man lies, it is considered as though the whole man were buried in the same place. But it is not this way with the other body parts.

REPLY OBJ. 3: Although original sin exists particularly in the genital members as to its origin, nevertheless it is completed in animal operations as far as the notion of guilt is concerned; and thus baptism must be administered to the head, if necessity prevents the whole body from being immersed.

Response to Quaestiuncula 2

AD SECUNDAM QUAESTIONEM dicendum, quod congruentissime fit trina immersio, tum ad exprimendum in factis fidem Trinitatis, tum ad significandum Christi sepulturam, cui per baptismum consepelimur, ut patet ex auctoritatibus inductis.

AD PRIMUM ergo dicendum, quod Magister exposuit tinctionem per ablutionem. Quamvis autem in trina immersione sit trina intinctio, tamen est una ablutio; sicut etiam in ablutionibus pure materialibus videmus contingere, quod aliquid pluries in aquam immergitur vel aqua perfunditur, antequam ablutio una sit perfecta.

AD SECUNDUM dicendum, quod in fide Trinitatis includitur fides unitatis; et ideo in baptismo cum fide Trinitatis expressa datur intelligi fides unitatis et in forma verborum per hoc quod singulariter dicitur: *in nomine*, et in immersione propter similitudinem immersionum. Non autem in fide unitatis includitur fides Trinitatis; et ideo congruentius est ut etiam in actu baptismi fides Trinitatis exprimatur.

AD TERTIUM dicendum, quod quamvis passio Christi sit una, tamen Christus passus triduo in sepulcro

TO THE SECOND QUESTION, it should be said that a triple immersion is the most fitting thing to do, both to express in deeds the faith in the Trinity and to signify the burial of Christ, in which we are buried together by baptism, as is clear from the authorities cited.

REPLY OBJ. 1: The Master explained dipping by washing. However, although there are three plunges in a triple immersion, there is nevertheless one washing; just as also in purely material washings we see it happen that something is immersed in water or water is poured over it several times before one washing is complete.

REPLY OBJ. 2: Faith in the Trinity includes faith in the unity; and thus in baptism, together with the faith expressed in the Trinity one is given to understand faith in the unity, both in the form of words (by the fact that *In the name* is said in the singular) and in the immersion (on account of the similarity of immersions). But faith in the Trinity is not included in faith in the unity of God; and so it is more fitting that faith in the Trinity be expressed also in the act of baptism.

REPLY OBJ. 3: Although the Passion of Christ is one, nevertheless after suffering Christ rested three days in the

quievit: et hoc baptismus significare debuit trina immersione.

tomb; and baptism had to represent this by the triple immersion.

Response to Quaestiuncula 3

Ad tertiam quaestionem dicendum, quod cum trina immersio non sit ad significandum rem in sacramento contentam, quam oportet per materiam et usum sacramenti significari, sed significet rem significatam et non contentam, quae significatio non est principalis in sacramento, trina immersio, ut in littera dicitur, non est de necessitate sacramenti. Si tamen omittatur contra consuetudinem ecclesiae, graviter aliquis peccat semel tantum immergens; et ideo per canones poena adhibetur.

Per quod patet solutio ad primum.

Ad secundum dicendum quod forma principaliter debet significare illud unde est efficacia in sacramento, cum sit medium quo quasi pervenit efficacia ad materiam quae verbo illo sanctificatur; sed materia debet principaliter significare effectum qui immediate consequitur ex usu ejus.

Ad tertium dicendum, quod unitas intentionis in tribus immersionibus facit unitatem baptismi, ut dictum est; et ideo quando aliquis intendit ter immergere, prima immersio non terminat intentionem baptizantis, et per consequens nec esse baptismi completur, nec per illam tantum habet effectum, nisi per ordinem ad alias; unde aliae non superfluunt. Si autem non intendit nisi unam facere, prima sola complet baptismum, terminans intentionem baptizantis.

To the third question, it should be said that since the triple immersion is not for signifying the reality contained in the sacrament, which has to be signified by the matter and use of the sacrament, but rather, for signifying the reality signified but not contained (a signification that is not foremost in the sacrament), it follows that the triple immersion is not necessary to the sacrament, as it says in the text. Nevertheless, were it omitted against the custom of the Church, a person would sin gravely by immersing someone only once; and thus a penalty is applied by the canons.

By this the answer to the first is clear.

Reply Obj. 2: The form should chiefly represent where the efficacy of the sacrament comes from, since it is a medium by which the efficacy contacts the matter that is sanctified by that word. But the matter should chiefly signify the effect that follows immediately upon its use.

Reply Obj. 3: Unity of intention in the triple immersion is what makes the unity of baptism, as has been said. And thus when someone intends to immerse three times, the first immersion does not complete the intention of the one baptizing, and as a result, the being of the baptism is not completed either, nor by that one immersion does it have its effect, except through its order to the others; hence the other immersions are not superfluous. But if he intends to do only one, then the first immersion alone would complete the baptism, fulfilling the intention of the one baptizing.

Article 5

The institution of baptism

Quaestiuncula 1

Ad quintum sic proceditur. Videtur quod non fuit necessarium instituere baptismum post circumcisionem. Causa enim institutionis baptismi, ut in littera dicitur, est innovatio mentis. Sed circumcisio mentem innovabat, cum peccatum auferret, et gratiam conferret, ut supra dictum est. Ergo non fuit necessarium baptismum instituere.

Praeterea, in sacramentis efficacia respondet significationi. Sed circumcisio expressius significat, ut videtur, ablationem originalis et quantum ad causam ablationis, quae est effusio sanguinis Christi et quantum ad causam traductionis, quae est generatio, in membris generationis cum sanguinis effusione facta. Ergo habuit majorem efficaciam quam baptismus; et ita non debuit post eam baptismus institui.

Sed contra, perfectum debet imperfecto succedere. Sed baptismus est perfectior circumcisione, quia communior est. Ergo debuit post circumcisionem institui.

Obj. 1: To the fifth we proceed thus. It seems that it was not necessary to institute baptism after circumcision.[55] For the reason for the institution of baptism, as is said in the text, is the renewal of the mind. But circumcision renewed the mind, since it removed sin, and conferred grace, as was said above.[56] Therefore, it was not necessary to institute baptism.

Obj. 2: Furthermore, in the sacraments efficacy corresponds to signification. But as it seems, circumcision signified more expressly the removal of original sin both as to the cause of the removal, which is the shedding of Christ's blood, and as to the cause of contracting original sin, which is generation, since it involved a shedding of blood from the member of generation. Therefore, it had greater efficacy than baptism; and thus baptism did not need to be instituted after it.

On the contrary, the perfect should succeed the imperfect. But baptism is more perfect than circumcision, because it is common to more people. Therefore, it had to be instituted after circumcision.

Quaestiuncula 2

Ulterius. Videtur quod fuerit ante passionem institutus: quia Dominus tactu carnis suae, vim regenerativam contulit aquis. Sed hoc fuit ante passionem in baptismo suo. Ergo ante passionem fuit institutus.

Praeterea, Joan. 3, 5, dixit: *nisi quis renatus fuerit ex aqua et Spiritu Sancto, non potest introire in regnum Dei.* Sed hoc fuit ante passionem. Ergo baptismus ante passionem fuit institutus.

Sed contra, causam non praecedit effectus. Sed baptismus habet efficaciam a passione Christi. Ergo non debuit ante passionem institui.

Praeterea, baptismus non fuit sine forma sua. Sed forma fuit instituta post passionem, Matth. ult. Ergo et baptismus.

Obj. 1: Moreover, it seems that it was instituted before the Passion.[57] For the Lord conferred regenerative power on the waters by the touch of his flesh. But this happened in his own baptism, before the Passion. Therefore, it had been instituted before the Passion.

Obj. 2: Furthermore, he said, *unless one is reborn of water and the Holy Spirit, he cannot enter into the kingdom of God* (John 3:5). But this was before the Passion. Therefore, baptism had been instituted before the Passion.

On the contrary, an effect does not precede its cause. But baptism has its efficacy from the Passion of Christ. Therefore, it should not have been instituted before the Passion.

Furthermore, baptism does not happen without its form. But its form was instituted after the Passion (Matt 28:19). Therefore, so was baptism.

---

55. Parallels: *ST* III, q. 62, a. 6, ad 3; q. 70, a. 4; *Super Rom.* 4, lec. 2.
56. See d. 1, q. 2, a. 2, qa. 5.
57. Parallels: *ST* III, q. 66, a. 2; q. 73, a. 5, ad 4.

Quaestiuncula 3

Ulterius. Videtur quod statim in sua institutione fuit obligatorium. Quia dicitur Joan. 3, 5, quasi in principio institutionis: *nisi quis renatus fuerit ex aqua et Spiritu Sancto, non potest introire in regnum Dei*; quod obligationem importet. Ergo statim obligatorium fuit.

Praeterea, institutio sacramentorum novae legis est per modum praecepti. Sed praeceptum statim est obligatorium. Ergo institutio baptismi statim obligabat.

Sed contra, ad idem non sunt necessaria duo remedia. Sed ante passionem, jam instituto baptismo, homines obligabantur adhuc ad circumcisionem, quae ad idem ordinatur cum baptismo. Ergo non obligabantur ad baptismum.

Obj. 1: Moreover, it seems that it was obligatory immediately upon its institution.[58] For it is said at the beginning of its institution, as it were: *unless one is reborn of water and the Holy Spirit, he cannot enter into the kingdom of God* (John 3:5)—which implies an obligation. Therefore, it was obligatory immediately.

Obj. 2: Furthermore, the institution of the sacraments of the New Law is in the manner of a precept. But a precept is obligatory immediately. Therefore, the institution of baptism obliged immediately.

On the contrary, two remedies are not needed for the same thing. But before the Passion, when baptism had just been instituted, men were still obliged to circumcision, which is ordered to the same thing as baptism. Therefore, they were not obligated to baptism.

Response to Quaestiuncula 1

Respondeo dicendum, ad primam quaestionem, quod secundum Hugonem de sancto Victore, oportuit ut secundum processionem temporum spiritualium gratiarum signa magis ac magis evidentia darentur; et ideo oportuit quod baptismus post circumcisionem institueretur; quia circumcisio significabat tantum in removendo; perfectio autem sanctificationis non est in removendo, sed in collatione gratiae, cujus effectus aqua figurat, scilicet vitam, illuminationem, et hujusmodi, de quibus dictum est; et propter hoc significat ablutionem; et iterum etiam est perfectio quantum ad usum, quia sexui utrique communis est, quod non erat de circumcisione.

Ad primum ergo dicendum, quod quamvis circumcisio auferret culpam sicut baptismus, non tamen conferebat tantam plenitudinem gratiae sicut baptismus, nec tantum diminuebat fomitem; et ideo oportuit baptismum succedere. Innovatio enim non solum consistit in remotione culpae, sed in collatione gratiae.

Ad secundum dicendum, quod illae significationes sunt rerum non contentarum; et ideo de illis nihil ad propositum.

To the first question, I answer that according to Hugh of St. Victor,[59] it was necessary that as time progressed, signs of spiritual graces be given with more and more obviousness. And thus, it was fitting that baptism be instituted after circumcision, for circumcision signified only by removing something, yet the perfection of sanctification does not consist in removing something but rather in the conferral of grace, whose effect water represents—namely, life, illumination, and the like, of which we have spoken above; and because of this, it signifies washing; and again, there is also perfection as to its use, for it is common to both sexes, which was not the case with circumcision.

Reply Obj. 1: Although circumcision removed guilt as baptism does, nevertheless it did not confer such a plenitude of grace as baptism, nor did it diminish the kindling of sin as much. And thus it was necessary for baptism to succeed it. For renewal consists not only in the removal of guilt but in the conferral of grace.

Reply Obj. 2: Those are the significations of the *res non contenta*; and so they have nothing to do with this question.

Response to Quaestiuncula 2

Ad secundam quaestionem dicendum, quod multiplex fuit baptismi institutio.

Fuit enim primo institutus quantum ad materiam in baptismo Christi; tunc enim vim regenerativam aquis contulit; et aliquo modo fuit forma figurata per praesen-

To the second question, it should be said that the institution of baptism had many phases.

For it was first instituted at Christ's baptism as to the matter, for at that time he conferred regenerative power on the waters, and in a certain way the form was represented

58. Parallels: *ST* III, q. 66, a. 2; q. 73, a. 5, ad 4.
59. Hugh of St. Victor, *De sacramentis fidei*, Bk. 2, pt. 6, ch. 3 (PL 176:448).

tiam trium personarum in signo visibili, quia Pater apparuit in voce, Filius in carne, Spiritus Sanctus in columba; et similiter fructus baptismi ibi praefiguratus fuit, quia caeli aperti sunt super eum.

Sed necessitas ejus fuit declarata Joan. 3, 5, ubi dicit: *nisi quis renatus fuerit ex aqua et Spiritu Sancto, non potest introire in regnum Dei.*

Sed usus ejus fuit inchoatus quando misit discipulos ad praedicandum et baptizandum, ut patet Matth. 10.

Sed efficaciam habuit ex passione Christi, quantum ad ultimum effectum, qui est apertio januae.

Sed divulgatio ejus quantum ad omnes nationes praecepta fuit Matth. ult., 10, ubi dixit: *euntes, docete omnes gentes,* etc.

ET PER HOC patet solutio ad objecta. Tamen sciendum, quod Matth. ult., non fuit forma instituta cum ante passionem in eadem forma baptizaverint sicut in littera dicitur, sed fuit iterata.

by the presence of the three Persons in sensible signs, since the Father appeared in the voice, the Son in the flesh, and the Holy Spirit in the dove; and in a similar way the fruit of baptism was prefigured there, for the heavens were opened above him.

Its necessity was declared when he said: *unless one is reborn of water and the Holy Spirit, he cannot enter into the kingdom of God* (John 3:5).

Its use was set in motion when he sent his disciples out preaching and baptizing, as is seen in Matthew 10.

It gained its efficacy from Christ's Passion, as to its ultimate effect, which is the opening of the gate [of heaven].

Its proclamation to all nations was commanded at the end of the Gospel of Matthew, where he said, *go therefore and teach all nations, baptizing them,* etc. (Matt 28:19).

AND BY THIS the answers to the objections are evident. Nevertheless, it should be known that the form was not instituted at the end of the Gospel of Matthew, since they had been baptizing using the same form before the Passion, as is said in the text; but there it was reiterated.

Response to Quaestiuncula 3

AD TERTIAM QUAESTIONEM dicendum, quod ante passionem nullus obligabatur ad baptismum, quia tunc non erat institutus ad obligandum, sed ad exercitandum; sed post passionem obligatorium fuit, quando circumcisio mortua fuit quantum ad omnes ad quos institutio potuit pervenire.

ET PER HOC patet solutio ad objecta. Dominus enim Joan. 3, magis praedixit obligationem futuram quam narraret praesentem nec praeceptum obligat antequam sit divulgatum.

TO THE THIRD QUESTION, it should be said that no one was obliged to baptism before the Passion, for at that time it had not been instituted in such a way as to obligate, but rather for its exercise. But after the Passion it was obligatory, when circumcision had passed away for all those whom baptism's institution could reach.

AND BY THIS, the solution to the objections becomes clear. For in John 3, the Lord foretold the future obligation rather than announcing a present one, nor did the precept obligate before it was proclaimed to all.

EXPOSITION OF THE TEXT

Baptismus dicitur corporis tinctio, etc. Sciendum est, quod *baptizare* in Graeco, idem est quod *lavare*: a lavando enim duo dicuntur, scilicet lavacrum, quod significat aquam, in qua fit lotio humano artificio praeparatam; alio modo lotio, quae significat usum lavacri. Baptismus ergo potest significare ipsam aquam, quae dicitur lavacrum; unde dicitur Tit. 3, 5: *per lavacrum regenerationis et renovationis Spiritus Sancti*; et potest significare ipsam ablutionem. Marc. 7, 8: *tenentes baptismata hominum, et calicum, et urceorum*; idest ablutiones. Et ideo Hugo de sancto Victore, definivit baptismum aquam quantum ad primam acceptionem; Magister vero ablutionem quantum ad secundam. Sed haec definitio est magis propria quia aqua non significat mundationem, neque causat, nisi secundum quod est abluens.

Unde est haec tanta virtus aquae, ut corpus tangat, et cor abluat, nisi faciente verbo? Quid sit ista virtus, et quando sit data; dictum est supra, dist. 1.

Unde nihilominus insinuare videtur verum baptisma dari posse in nomine Patris tantum, etc. Hoc est intelligendum in simili casu, sicut apostoli in nomine Christi baptizabant; alias Magister falsum diceret.

Celebratur autem hoc sacramentum tantum in aqua. Sciendum, quod aqua est materia baptismi, et potest tripliciter considerari. Quia secundum quod consideratur in sua propria natura est quasi materia remota, quia ex naturali proprietate habet aliquam convenientiam ad hoc quod sit baptismi materia ratione similitudinis. Secundum autem quod est instituta ad hoc, accipiens vim regenerativam ex tactu carnis salvatoris, sic est materia quasi disposita. Secundum autem quod consideratur sub forma verborum, est quasi materia jam informata.

Solet autem quaeri, si circumcisio amisit statim vim suam ab institutione baptismi. De hac dictum est prius distinct. 1.

Aditum nobis regni aperuit. Apertio januae non est aliud quam remotio impedimenti quod prohibebat totum humanum genus ab introitu caeli: quod quidem ab-

What we call baptism is an intinction, that is, an exterior washing of the body, etc.[60] It should be known that 'to baptize' is, in Greek, the same as 'to wash' in Latin; for by 'washing' two things are spoken of—namely, a bath, which signifies water, prepared by human skill, in which cleansing happens; or else, the very cleansing that signifies the use of the bath. Therefore, baptism can mean the water itself, which is called the bath; hence it is said, *by the bath of regeneration and renewal of the Holy Spirit* (Tit 3:5). And it can mean the washing itself: *holding to the tradition of men, the washing of cups and pots*, that is, ceremonial cleansing (Mark 7:4–8). And thus Hugh of St. Victor[61] defined baptism as water, according to the first interpretation; but the Master defined it as a cleansing, according to the second. But this latter definition is more proper, since water does not signify cleansing, nor does it cause it, except when it is washing.

"And from where does water acquire so great a power that by touching the body it cleanses the heart, except by the work of the word?"[62] What that power is, and when it is given, was discussed above in Distinction 1.[63]

It also appears to be indicated that a true baptism can be conferred in the name of the Father alone, etc.[64] This is to be understood in cases like the one where the apostles baptized in the name of Christ; otherwise, the Master would speak wrongly.

And this sacrament is celebrated only in water.[65] It should be known that water is the matter of baptism, and can be considered in three ways. For as it is considered in its own nature, it is like a remote matter, since by its natural properties it has a certain fittingness to be the matter of baptism by reason of likeness. But as it was instituted for this action, receiving regenerative power through contact with the Savior's flesh, it is like matter that has been disposed. But considered under the form of the words, it is like matter now informed.

But it is usual to ask whether circumcision lost its standing after the institution of baptism.[66] This was discussed before in Distinction 1.[67]

The Savior's sacrifice opened up access to the kingdom for us.[68] The opening of the gate is nothing but the removal of the impediment that kept the entire human race from the

---

60. *Sent* IV, 3.1 (17). 2.
61. Hugh of St. Victor, *De sacramentis fidei*, Bk. 2, pt. 6, ch. 2 (PL 176:443).
62. *Sent.* IV, 3.1 (17), 2, citing Augustine, *In Ioannem*, Tract. 80, n. 3.
63. See q. 1, a. 4, qa. 2.
64. *Sent.* IV, 3.4 (20), 3.
65. *Sent.* IV, 3.6 (22), 1.
66. *Sent.* IV, 3.8 (24), 1.
67. See q. 2, a. 5, qa. 1.
68. *Sent.* IV, 3.9 (25), 2; see Bk. 3, dist. 18, ch. 5.

latum est per passionem Christi, ut dictum est in 3 Lib., dist. 18.

entrance to heaven, an impediment that was indeed taken away by Christ's Passion, as was said in Book III, Distinction 18.[69]

69. See q. 1, a. 6, qa. 3.

DISTINCTION 4
THE EFFECTS OF BAPTISM

Postquam determinavit Magister de baptismo quantum ad ea quae conveniunt ei secundum se considerato, hic determinat de effectu baptismi per comparationem ad accipientes; et dividitur in partes duas: in prima determinat de effectu baptismi communiter quantum ad omnes; in secunda specialiter quantum ad parvulos, ibi: *solet etiam quaeri, si parvulis in baptismo datur gratia.*

Prima dividitur in partes tres: in prima ostendit quomodo quidam recipiunt sacramentum et rem sacramenti; in secunda quomodo quidam sacramentum recipiunt, et non rem, ibi: *qui vero sine fide vel ficte accedunt, sacramentum, non rem suscipiunt;* in tertia quomodo quidam accipiunt rem, et non sacramentum, ibi: *sunt et alii, ut supra posuimus, qui suscipiunt rem, et non sacramentum.*

Circa secundum duo facit: primo determinat veritatem; secundo objicit in contrarium, ibi: *videtur tamen Augustinus dicere, quod etiam ficte accedenti . . . omnia condonentur peccata, et post baptismum mox redeant.* Et circa hoc duo facit: primo objicit per auctoritatem Augustini, qui contrarium ex auctoritate apostoli probare videtur; secundo solvit: et primo ad auctoritatem Augustini, ibi: *hoc tamen, ut supra diximus, non sub assertione dixit;* secundo ad auctoritatem apostoli, ibi: *quaeritur ergo quomodo illud accipiatur. Quotquot in Christo baptizati estis, Christum induistis.*

Sunt et alii, ut supra posuimus, qui suscipiunt rem, et non sacramentum. Hic determinat de illis qui recipiunt rem sine sacramento, et circa hoc duo facit: primo ostendit quod quidam accipiunt rem sine sacramento; secundo inquirit, quid postmodum per hujusmodi sacramentum addatur, quando sacramentum susceperint, ibi: *solet etiam quaeri de illis qui jam sanctificati Spiritu, cum fide et caritate ad baptismum accedunt.*

Circa primum duo facit: primo ostendit veritatem; secundo excludit errorem, ibi: *sed dicunt aliqui nullum adultum in Christum credere, vel caritatem habere sine*

After the Master has considered baptism in what pertains to it in itself, here he considers its effect on those receiving it. And this is divided into two parts: in the first, he considers the effect of baptism commonly on all men; in the second, on infants in particular, at: *it is also usual to ask whether a grace is given to children in baptism.*[1]

The first is divided into three parts: in the first of these he shows how some people receive the sacrament and the reality of the sacrament; in the second how some people receive the sacrament but not the reality, at: *But those who approach without faith or under false pretenses, receive the sacrament, but not the thing;*[2] in the third, how some people receive the reality, but not the sacrament, at: *there are also others, as we said earlier, who receive the thing and not the sacrament.*[3]

Concerning the second he does two things: first, he determines the truth; second, he objects to the contrary, at: *And yet Augustine appears to say that in the case of one who approaches under false pretenses . . . all sins are forgiven at the very moment of baptism, but they return immediately after baptism.*[4] And about this he does two things: first, he objects by the authority of Augustine, who seems to prove the contrary from the Apostle's authority; second, he resolves it: first, as to the authority of Augustine, at: *But as we said earlier, Augustine does not say this by way of assertion;*[5] second, as to the authority of the Apostle, at: *and so it is asked how that text may be taken: "As many of you as have been baptized in Christ have put on Christ".*[6]

There are also others, as we said earlier, who receive the thing and not the sacrament. Here he considers those who receive the reality without the sacrament, and concerning this he does two things: first, he shows that some people receive the reality without the sacrament; second, he inquires what may be added afterward by a sacrament like this, when they receive the sacrament, at: *it is usual to ask regarding those who are already sanctified by the Spirit, what does Baptism confer on them when they come to baptism in fiath and charity.*[7]

Concerning the first he does two things: first, he shows the truth; second, he excludes error, at: *but some say that no unbaptized adult can believe in Christ or have charity, unless*

---

1. Peter Lombard, *Sententiae* IV, 4.7 (32), 3.
2. *Sent.* IV, 4.2 (27), 1.
3. *Sent.* IV, 4.4 (29), 1.
4. *Sent.* IV, 4.2 (27), 4.
5. *Sent.* IV, 4.2 (27), 5.
6. *Sent.* IV, 4.3 (28), 1 citing Gal 3:27.
7. *Sent.* IV, 4.5 (30), 1.

baptismo, nisi sanguinem fundat pro Domino. Circa primum duo facit: primo ostendit propositum; secundo respondet cuidam objectioni, ibi: *his autem videntur obviare,* etc. Circa primum duo facit: primo ostendit quod patientes pro Christo, si non sunt baptizati, recipiunt rem sacramenti sine sacramento; secundo ostendit idem de illis qui fidem et contritionem habent, ibi: *nec tamen passio vicem baptismi implet, sed etiam fides et contritio, ubi necessitas excludit sacramentum.*

Sed dicunt aliqui nullum adultum in Christum credere, etc. Hic excludit errorem dicentium, non posse aliquem salvari per fidem et contritionem sine baptismo; et circa hoc duo facit: primo ostendit hoc esse falsum quantum ad adultos; secundo ostendit hoc esse verum quantum ad parvulos, ibi: *parvulis non sufficit fides ecclesiae sine sacramento.*

Solet quaeri de illis qui jam sanctificati spiritu, cum fide et caritate ad baptismum accedunt. Hic determinat de baptismo eorum qui prius rem sacramenti acceperant; et circa hoc duo facit: primo ostendit effectum baptismi in eis; secundo significationem, ibi: *si quaeritur cujus rei baptismus ille sit sacramentum qui datur jam justo; dicimus,* etc.

Hic est triplex quaestio. Primo de effectu qui est in baptismo sacramentum et res, scilicet de charactere. Secundo de eo quod est res tantum, scilicet effectu ultimo baptismi. Tertio de suscipientibus alterum vel utrumque: quia de eo quod est sacramentum tantum, in praecedenti[13] dictum est.

he shed his blood for the Lord.[8] Concerning the first he does two things: first, he proves his conclusion; second, he answers a certain objection, at: *but it seems to contradict the above,* etc.[9] Concerning the first he does two things: first, he shows that those suffering for Christ, if they are not baptized, receive the reality of the sacrament without the sacrament; second, he shows the same of those who have faith and contrition, at: *nor is it suffering alone which fills the role of baptism, but also faith and contrition, where necessity precludes the sacrament.*[10]

But some say that no unbaptized adult can believe in Christ, etc. Here he excludes the error of those who say that no one can be saved by faith and contrition without baptism; and concerning this he does two things: first, he shows that this is false regarding adults; second, he shows it to be true regarding children, at: *the faith of the Church is not sufficient for children without the sacrament.*[11]

It is usual to ask regarding those who are already sanctified by the Spirit, what does Baptism confer on them when they come to baptism in faith and charity. Here he examines the baptism of those who had previously received the reality of the sacrament; and concerning this he does two things: first, he shows the effect of baptism in them; second, its signification, at: *if it is asked of what thing is that baptism a sacrament, which is given to one who is already justified, we say,* etc.[12]

Here there are three questions. First, about the effect that is the sacrament-and-reality in baptism; namely, the character. Second, about what is the reality alone, namely, the ultimate effect of baptism. Third, of those receiving either one or both: for the sacrament alone has been discussed in the previous distinction.

---

8. *Sent.* IV, 4.4 (29), 9.
9. *Sent.* IV, 4.4 (29), 6.
10. *Sent.* IV, 4.4 (29), 3.
11. *Sent.* IV, 4.4 (29), 12.
12. *Sent.* IV, 4.7 (32), 1.
13. *praecedenti.—praecedenti distinctione* PLE.

QUESTION 1

THE BAPTISMAL CHARACTER

Circa primum quaeruntur quatuor:
primo, an sit character;
secundo, quid sit;
tertio, in quo sit;
quarto, a quo sit.

Concerning the first, four questions arise:
first, if there is a character;
second, what it is;
third, in what it is;
fourth, whence it comes.

ARTICLE 1

If there is a baptismal character[14]

AD PRIMUM SIC PROCEDITUR. Videtur quod character non sit in anima. Quia, ut in 2 *Ethic.*, Philosophus dicit, omne quod est in anima, est potentia, vel passio, vel habitus. Sed character non est potentia, quia potentiae omnibus hominibus communes sunt; character autem non, cum sit distinctivum signum, sicut ipsum nomen ostendit; et praeterea potentiae sunt a natura, non autem character. Nec iterum est passio, quia passiones animae contingunt cum aliqua transmutatione corporali, ut dicitur in 1 de Anima, et pertinent ad sensitivam partem, ut dicitur 7 Physicor. Nec iterum est habitus, quia habitus ordinantur ad agendum, ut patet per definitionem Augustini: *habitus est quo quis agit, cum opus fuerit.* Ergo character collatus in baptismo, non est aliquid in anima.

PRAETEREA, omne quod est, reducitur ad aliquod genus entis. Sed character non videtur posse reduci ad aliquod genus entis, nisi forte ad qualitatem. Qualitas autem esse non potest, cum sub nulla specie qualitatis contineatur. Non enim est habitus, ut probatum est; nec dispositio, cum non sit facile mobilis, immo omnino indelebilis; nec iterum est potentia naturalis, ut probatum est; nec impotentia, quia tunc sacramenta quae characterem imprimunt, magis officerent quam juvarent; nec iterum est passio, ut probatum est; nec passibilis qualitas, cum non sit natus aliquam passionem sensui inferre, nec a passione aliqua innascatur; nec iterum est forma, et circa aliquid constans figura, quia figura est termina-

OBJ. 1: To the first we proceed thus. It seems that the character is not in the soul. For, as the Philosopher says in *Ethics* 2,[15] everything that is in the soul is either a power, or a passion, or a habit. But a character is not a power, for powers are common to all men, but a character is not, since it is a distinctive sign, as its name shows; and besides, powers are from nature, but a character is not. Nor again is it a passion, for passions of the soul are produced with a certain bodily change, as is said in *On the Soul* 1;[16] and they pertain to the sensitive part, as is said in *Physics* 7.[17] Nor again is it a habit, for a habit is ordered to acting, as is evident from Augustine's definition: *a habit is that whereby one acts, when he does a work.*[18] Therefore, the character conferred in baptism is not anything in the soul.

OBJ. 2: Furthermore, all that there is is reducible to some genus of being. But a character does not seem to be reducible to any category of being, except perhaps for quality. But it cannot be a quality, since it is contained under no species of quality.[19] For it is not a habit, as has been proved; nor is it a disposition, since it is not easily moveable, but rather completely indelible. Nor again is it a natural power, as has been proved; nor is it an inability, since then the sacraments that imprint characters would do more to hinder than to help; nor again is it a passion, as has been proved; nor a passible quality, since it is not such as to cause a passion in the senses, nor is it born from any passion. Nor again is it a form, and a figure standing firm around anything, for a fig-

---

14. Parallels: below, a. 4, qa. 1, ad 1; *ST* III, q. 63, a. 1; *De eccles. sacram.*

15. Aristotle, *Nicomachean Ethics*, Bk. 2, ch. 4, 1105b19–20.

16. Moos's edition has Thomas referring to *Nicomachean Ethics*, Bk. 4, ch. 9, at 1128b14–15; but there are pertinent passages in *On the Soul*, e.g., Bk. 1, ch. 1, 403a3ff.

17. Aristotle, *Physics*, Bk. 7, ch. 2, 244b11–12.

18. Augustine, *On the Good of Marriage*, ch. 21, par. 25 (CSEL 41:219). The exact words are: "Ipse est enim habitus, quo aliquid agitur, cum opus est; cum autem non agitur, potest agi, sed non opus est."

19. As given by Aristotle in the *Categories*, ch. 8.

tio quantitatis, anima autem non habet quantitatem. Ergo character nihil est.

PRAETEREA, contraria sunt in eodem genere. Sed ea quae Christo competunt, sunt contraria his quae ad diabolum pertinent. Cum ergo character bestiae, de qua dicitur Apoc. 13, nihil aliud sit quam peccatum mortale, videtur quod supra virtutem et gratiam non oporteat in anima aliquem characterem poni.

PRAETEREA, ea quae sunt in sacramentis novae legis, ordinantur ad causandum gratiam. Sed character non videtur posse gratiam causare, quia multi characterem habere dicuntur qui gratia carent. Ergo non videtur in sacramentis aliquis character imprimi.

PRAETEREA, si dicatur quod est dispositio ad gratiam; contra. Agens infinitum non requirit materiam dispositam. Sed dispositio non est necessaria nisi ad hoc quod materia sit disposita. Cum ergo gratia sit ab agente infinitae virtutis, videtur quod non oporteat characterem dari in sacramentis ad disponendum ad gratiam.

SED CONTRA est quod Damascenus, in definitione baptismi ponit *sigillum*. Sed sigillum impressum in aliquo est character quidam. Ergo in sacramentis character imprimitur.

PRAETEREA, ubicumque est aliqua distinctio competit esse aliquem characterem distinguentem. Sed per sacramenta fit distinctio fidelium ab infidelibus, et fidelium ab invicem. Ergo competit in sacramentis characterem dari.

PRAETEREA, per sacramentum configuramur Christo: quia ab eo sacramenta efficaciam habent, et ipsum significant. Sed configuratio fit per characterem assimilationis. Ergo in sacramentis competit esse characterem.

RESPONDEO dicendum, quod characterem in sacramentis quibusdam imprimi, omnes moderni confitentur; sed in modo ponendi ipsum in anima partim differunt, et partim conveniunt. Conveniunt quidem in hoc quod omnes dicunt per characterem importari relationem triplicem. Est enim character signum distinctivum et configurativum. Inquantum ergo est signum, importat relationem ad signatum; inquantum autem est distinctivum, importat relationem ad ea a quibus distinguit; inquantum autem est configurativum, importat relationem ad ea quibus assimilat.

Differunt autem in hoc, quia quidam ponunt istis relationibus non subesse aliquod accidens absolutum, sed immediate in anima fundari istas relationes. Hoc autem esse non potest: quia signum per formam quam sensibus vel intellectui imprimit, facit aliquid in cognitionem ve-

ure is a termination of quantity, but the soul does not have any quantity. Therefore, a character is nothing.

OBJ. 3: Furthermore, contraries are in the same genus. But the things that belong to Christ are contrary to those things that belong to the devil. Therefore, since the character of the Beast, which is spoken of in Revelation 13, is nothing other than mortal sin, it seems that it is not fitting for any character to be stamped in the soul beyond virtue and grace.

OBJ. 4: Furthermore, the things that are in the sacraments of the New Law are ordered to causing grace. But a character does not seem able to cause grace, for many are said to have a character who lack grace. Therefore, it does not seem that any character is imprinted in the sacraments.

OBJ. 5: Furthermore, if it is said that it is a disposition toward grace, then to the contrary: an infinite agent does not require disposed matter. But a disposition is only necessary in order that matter be disposed. Therefore, since grace is from an agent of infinite power, it seems that it is not necessary for a character to be given in sacraments in order to dispose one for grace.

ON THE CONTRARY, Damascene includes *seal* in the definition of baptism.[20] But a seal impressed on something is a certain character. Therefore, in the sacraments a character is imprinted.

FURTHERMORE, anywhere there is a certain distinction, it is appropriate that there be a certain character distinguishing it. But through the sacraments the faithful are distinguished from unbelievers, and the faithful from each other. Therefore, it is appropriate that a character be given in the sacraments.

FURTHERMORE, by a sacrament we are configured to Christ, for the sacraments have their efficacy from him, and they signify him. But configuration happens by a character of likening. Therefore, it is fitting that there be a character in the sacraments.

I ANSWER THAT, nowadays all confess there to be a character imprinted in certain sacraments; but as to placing it in the soul, they differ on some things and agree on others. All of them agree in saying that the character brings with it a threefold relation. For a character is a distinctive and configuring sign. Therefore, inasmuch as it is a sign, it conveys a relation to the thing signified; but inasmuch as it is distinctive, it conveys a relation to those things from which it is distinguished; while inasmuch as it is configurative, it carries a relation to those things to which it likens.

However, they differ in this: certain ones hold that under these relations there is no absolute accident, but that these relations are founded directly in the soul. But this cannot be. For a sign, through the form it imprints on the senses or the intellect, makes something come into the un-

---

20. *On the Orthodox Faith*, Bk. 4, ch. 9 (PG 94:1122).

nire. Similiter etiam nihil distinguitur ab alio nisi per aliquam formam. Similitudo etiam est relatio super unitate qualitatis fundata, ut dicitur in 5 *Metaphysica*. Unde patet quod quaelibet illarum relationum quam importat character, requirit aliquam formam substratam; et cum non sit forma substantialis, quia forma substantialis in sacramentis non datur, relinquitur quod forma substrata sit qualitas quaedam, cujus unitas consignificationis similitudinem facit.

Et ideo quidam dicunt, quod non est in aliqua quatuor specierum qualitatis, et tamen est in genere qualitatis, innitentes illi verbo Philosophi in *Praedicamentis*: *fortasse*, inquit, *apparebunt alii qualitatis modi*. Sed haec est fuga quaedam: quia quamvis sint alii modi qualitatis, tamen omnes reducuntur ad has species: quod patet ex hoc quod nulla alia species inveniri adhuc potuit.

Et ideo dicunt alii, quod est in quarta specie qualitatis: quia ipsa configuratio quam character suo nomine exprimit, importat unitatem figurae, quae est in specie quarta qualitatis. Et quidam dicunt hanc figuram esse crucem Christi. Sed hoc non potest stare: quia aut figura proprie accipitur, aut metaphorice. Si proprie accipitur, sic importat terminationem quantitatis dimensivae, quam constat in anima non esse. Si autem metaphorice dicatur, tunc oportet quod metaphora reducatur ad proprietatem: quia res non ponitur in genere per id quod de eo metaphorice dicitur; sicut non dicitur quod apostoli sint in genere qualitatis, quia eis dictum est, Matth. 5: *vos estis lux mundi*. Nec poterit aliquid in quarta specie qualitatis inveniri quod sit in anima secundum proprietatem; unde character, de quo loquimur, non potest fundari supra qualitatem quartae speciei.

Et ideo quidam dicunt, quod est in tertia specie qualitatis, eo quod sensui spirituali infert quamdam muliebrem passionem, inquantum animam ornat et decorat. Sed hoc iterum non potest stare: quia, sicut probat Philosophus in 7 *Physic.*; tertia species qualitatis non est nisi in sensibili parte animae: character autem a nullo ponitur in hac parte animae, sed in intellectiva. Et praeterea illae qualitates semper habent ordinem ad aliquam transmutationem corporalem, vel quam inferunt, vel a qua causantur.

Et ideo alii dicunt, quod est in prima specie qualitatis, et est quasi media inter dispositionem et habitum. Inquantum enim est difficile mobilis, convenit cum habitu, inquantum autem non est ultima perfectio, sed ad gratiam disponit, cum dispositione convenit. Sed hoc non potest stare: quia secundum Philosophum in 2 *Ethic.*, habitus est quo habemus nos ad passiones bene vel male; et

derstanding. In the same way too, nothing is distinguished from something else except by a certain form. A likeness is a relation founded upon oneness of quality, as is said in *Metaphysics* 5.[21] Hence it is clear that whichever of these relations a character conveys, it requires a certain underlying form; and since there is no substantial form (for a substantial form is not given in the sacraments), it remains that the underlying form be a certain quality, whose unity of consignification makes the likeness.

And therefore certain people say that it is not in any of the four species of quality, and nevertheless it is in the genus of quality, resting on that word of the Philosopher in the *Categories*: *perhaps*, he says, *other modes of quality will appear*.[22] But this is an evasion: for although there may be other modes of quality, nevertheless, all of them are reducible to these species, which is evident from the fact that no other species has been able to be found to this day.

And so others say that it is in the fourth species of quality: for that configuration, which character expresses in its name, conveys unity of figure, which is in the fourth species of quality. And some people say that this figure is the cross of Christ. But this cannot stand: for figure is taken either properly or metaphorically. If it is taken properly, then it conveys the termination of a dimensive quantity, which clearly does not exist in the soul. But if it is said metaphorically, then the metaphor must be traced back to a proper sense; just as it is not being said that the apostles are in the genus of quality when it is said to them, *you are the light of the world* (Matt 5:14). Nor could anything be found in the fourth species of quality that is in the soul in the proper sense. Hence the character of which we speak cannot be founded on a quality of the fourth species.

And so some people say that it is in the third species of quality, by the fact that it causes a certain feminine passion in one's spiritual perception insofar as it ornaments and beautifies the soul. But this, again, cannot stand; for, as the Philosopher proves in *Physics* 7,[23] the third species of quality exists only in the sensible part of the soul; however, no one considers a character to be in this part of the soul, but in the intellective part. And furthermore, those qualities always have an order to a certain physical change, which either they bring about, or by which they are caused.

And so others say that it is in the first species of quality and is like a middle term between disposition and habit. Inasmuch as it is difficult to move, it resembles habit, while inasmuch as it is not the last perfection but disposes to grace, it resembles disposition. But this cannot stand, for according to the Philosopher in *Ethics* 2,[24] a habit is what orders us well or badly to passions; and to anyone who

---

21. Aristotle, *Metaphysics*, Bk. 5, ch. 15, 1021a10.
22. Aristotle, *Categories*, ch. 8, 10a25.
23. Aristotle, *Physics*, Bk. 7, ch. 2, 244b15–245a5.
24. Aristotle, *Nicomachean Ethics*, Bk. 2, ch. 4, 1105b25–26.

universaliter consideranti haec apparet differentia inter habitum et potentiam, quia potentia est qua possumus aliquid simpliciter, habitus autem quo possumus illud bene vel male; sicut intellectus quo consideramus, scientia qua bene consideramus, concupiscibilis qua concupiscimus, temperantia qua bene concupiscimus, intemperantia qua male; et similiter est de dispositione: quia nihil aliud est dispositio quam quidam habitus incompletus. Cum ergo character ordinetur ad aliquid simpliciter non ad illud bene vel male non potest esse quod qualitas, super quam fundatur relatio characteris sit habitus, sed magis potentia.

Unde relinquitur quod non sit in prima specie qualitatis; sed magis reducitur ad secundam, ut quidam alii dicunt; et hoc sic patet. Sicut enim cujuslibet existentis in aliqua natura, sunt aliquae operationes propriae, ita etiam in spirituali vita regenerati, ut Dionysius dicit. Ubicumque autem sunt operationes propriae, oportet quod sint principia propria illarum operationum. Unde sicut in aliis rebus sunt potentiae naturales ad proprias operationes, ita etiam renati in vitam spiritualem habent quasdam potentias, secundum quas possunt illa opera: quae potentiae sunt similes illis virtutibus quibus sacramenta efficaciam habent sibi inditam: quia sicut sacramenta causant gratiam instrumentaliter, ut supra, dist. 1, qu. 1, art. 4, dictum est, ita recipientes characterem operantur divina per ministerium. Minister autem est sicut instrumentum ejus cui ministrat; unde dicit Philosophus, quod servus est sicut organum animatum; et ideo tam virtus sacramenti quam minister et character est instrumentalis.

Et quod hujusmodi potentia sit character, patet si quis diligenter considerat verba Dionysii, a quo prima traditio characteris nobis advenit. Assignans enim ministerium ritus cujusdam qui in primitiva ecclesia erat, quando adulti baptizabantur, quod accedenti ad baptismum hierarcha, idest pontifex, manum imponebat, et signabat eum signo crucis, et praecipiebat eum describi inter nomina Christianorum, ut de cetero ad divina cum aliis admitteretur, dicit, quod *sic accedentem*, scilicet ad vitam spiritualem, *divina beatitudo in sui participationem recipit, sicut sacerdos baptizandum in proprio lumine quasi quodam signo ipsi tradit*, scilicet sui participationem, *perficiens eum*, scilicet *divinum et communicantem divinorum*, etc. Patet ergo quod ipse per hoc signum nihil aliud intendit quam illud quod facit eum participantem divinarum operationum; unde hoc signum nihil aliud est quam quaedam potentia qua potest in actiones hierarchicas, quae sunt ministrationes et receptiones sacramentorum, et aliorum quae ad fideles pertinent. Et ad

considers, this difference appears between habit and power, that a power is that by which we are able to do something simply, but by a habit we are able to do it well or badly; just as understanding is that by which we consider, but knowledge is that by which we consider well, or the concupiscible is that by which we desire, but temperance is that by which we desire well, and intemperance that by which we desire badly. And it is similar with a disposition, for a disposition is nothing other than a certain incomplete habit. Therefore, since a character is ordered to something simply speaking, not to doing it well or badly, it cannot be that the quality upon which the relation of a character is founded is a habit; it is rather a power.

Hence it remains that it is not in the first species of quality, but rather it is reduced to the second, as others say; and this is evident for the following reason. Just as anything existing in a certain nature has certain proper operations, so too in the spiritual life of one reborn, as Dionysius says.[25] But anywhere that there are proper operations, there need to be proper principles of those operations. Hence, just as in other things there are natural powers for proper operations, so also those reborn in spiritual life have certain powers, by which they can do those works—and these powers are like those virtues by which sacraments are endowed with efficacy, for just as sacraments cause grace instrumentally (as was said above in Distinction 1, Question 1, Article 4), so, too, those receiving the character accomplish divine things through their office. A minister, however, is like an instrument of the one of whom he is minister; hence the Philosopher says that a slave is like an animate tool.[26] And thus, the virtue of the sacrament as well as the minister and the character are instrumental.

And that a character is a power of this kind is evident if someone considers diligently the words of Dionysius, from whom the tradition of a character first came to us. For, when assigning the ministry of a certain rite that existed in the early Church when adults were being baptized—that the hierarch, that is, the pontiff, placed his hand on the one approaching baptism, and made the sign of the Cross over him, and ordered him to be inscribed among the names of Christians, so that he might be admitted to the rest of the divine things with the others—he says that *the divine blessedness thus welcomes the one approaching*, namely to spiritual life, *into a participation in itself, just as the priest in his own light as though by a certain sign imparts to the one to be baptized*, namely, participation in himself, *perfecting him*, namely, *as someone divine and sharing in divine things*, etc. Therefore, it is clear that by this sign, he means nothing other than what makes one a participant in the divine operations. Hence this sign is nothing other than a certain power by which one is capable of hierarchical actions,

---

25. Pseudo-Dionysius, *Ecclesiastical Hierarchy*, ch. 2 (PG 3:391).
26. Aristotle, *Nicomachean Ethics*, Bk. 8, ch. 11, 1161b4.

hoc quod has operationes bene exerceat indiget habitu gratiae, sicut et aliae potentiae habitibus indigent.

Ad primum ergo dicendum, quod non sunt habitus nec passiones, sed sunt potentiae quaedam consequentes animam, secundum quod est in vita spirituali regenerata; et ideo non oportet quod omnibus insint, vel quod a natura sint.

Ad secundum dicendum, quod reducitur ad secundam speciem qualitatis, et est alius modus ab illo quem Philosophus ibi ponit: quia Philosophus non cognoscebat nisi operationes naturales, et ita non nisi potentias naturales. Constat autem quod apud nos oportet ponere potentias spirituales, sicut potentiam conficiendi, et absolvendi, et hujusmodi et quod ad secundam speciem qualitatis reducantur; sicut habitus infusi in eadem specie qualitatis sunt cum habitibus naturalibus, vel acquisitis.

Ad tertium dicendum, quod per hoc quod homo configuratur bestiae, non accipit aliquam spiritualem potestatem, sicut per aliquam potestatem spiritualem homo assimilatur Christo; et ideo non est simile. Tamen ex littera apostoli colligitur quod charactere bestiae configuratur quis ad saeculares operationes; unde dicit: *ut non possit emere vel vendere* etc., et similiter charactere Christi aliquis configuratur ad actiones Christi.

Ad quartum dicendum, quod character est causa sacramentalis gratiae; et quod quidam cum charactere gratiam non recipiunt, est ex eorum indispositione ad gratiam suscipiendam.

Ad quintum dicendum, quod character est dispositio ad gratiam per quamdam congruitatis dignitatem. Ex hoc enim ipso quod homo mancipatus est divinis actionibus, et inter membra Christi connumeratus, fit ei quaedam congruitas ad gratiam suscipiendam: quia Deus perfecte in sacramentis homini providet; unde simul cum charactere, quo datur homini ut possit exercere spirituales actiones fidelium, vel passiones seu receptiones, datur gratia qua haec bene possit.

which are ministrations and receptions of the sacraments, and of other things that pertain to the faithful; and in order to exercise these operations well, one needs the habit of grace, just as other powers also need habits.

Reply Obj. 1: They are neither habits nor passions, but they are certain powers attendant on the soul according as it is regenerated in spiritual life; and thus they do not need to be in all men, nor do they need to be from nature.

Reply Obj. 2: It is reduced to the second species of quality, and it is a different mode from the one that the Philosopher includes there; for the Philosopher did not recognize any operations but natural ones, and thus no powers but natural ones. It is clear that for us, however, it is necessary to posit spiritual powers, like the power of consecrating the Eucharist, and of absolving, and things of that sort, and that these may be reduced to the second species of quality, just as there are infused habits in the same species of quality with natural or acquired habits.

Reply Obj. 3: By being configured to the Beast, a man does not receive any spiritual power, as a man is assimilated to Christ by a certain spiritual power; and therefore, it is not a similar case. Nevertheless, from the text of the Apostle it is inferred that someone is configured by the character of the Beast for worldly operations; hence he says: *so that no one may buy or sell who does not have the mark*, etc. (Rev 13:17). And similarly, by the character of Christ, someone is configured to the actions of Christ.

Reply Obj. 4: A character is a cause of sacramental grace; and the fact that some people with the character do not receive grace is from their own indisposition to receiving grace.

Reply Obj. 5: A character is a disposition to grace by a certain dignity of fittingness. For by the fact that a man is surrendered to divine actions and numbered among the members of Christ, a certain fittingness for receiving grace happens to him: for God provides for man perfectly in the sacraments; hence at the same time as the character, by which it is given to man to be able to exercise the spiritual actions of the faithful, or the passions or receptions, grace is also given by which he can do these things well.

ARTICLE 2

What the baptismal character is

Quaestiuncula 1

AD SECUNDUM SIC PROCEDITUR. Videtur quod definitio quae attribuitur Dionysio de charactere, non bene assignetur, quae talis est: *character est signum sanctum communionis fidei, et sanctae ordinationis, datum divina beatitudine a hierarcha.* Signum enim, ut in 1 dist. dictum est, est quod speciem aliquam sensibus ingerit, et praeter eam aliquid facit in cognitionem venire. Sed character nullam sensibus formam ingerit. Ergo non est signum.

PRAETEREA, potentiis quae sunt principium actionis vel passionis, magis congruit significari quam significare: quia causae per effectus significantur. Sed character, ut dictum est, est potentia spiritualis. Ergo non est signum.

PRAETEREA, quidam habent characterem qui non habent fidem, sicut qui post baptismum in haeresim dilabuntur. Sed qui non habet fidem non communicat in fide. Ergo character non est signum communionis fidei; vel erit signum falsum; quod absurdum est sentire de signo divinitus dato.

PRAETEREA, definitio debet omnibus quae continentur sub definito, communiter convenire. Sed esse signum sacrae ordinationis non convenit omni characteri, sed solum characteri qui imprimitur in ordine. Ergo non est definitio bene assignata.

PRAETEREA, hierarcha, ut dictum est, est pontifex. Sed in aliquibus sacramentis, quae conferuntur a simplicibus sacerdotibus, vel etiam a laicis, imprimitur character. Ergo non debuit dicere: *datum a hierarcha.*

OBJ. 1: To the second we proceed thus. It seems that the definition of character attributed to Dionysius is not well-formulated, which is as follows:[27] *character is a sacred sign of the communion of faith, and of holy ordination, given by a hierarch in divine blessedness.* For a sign, as was said in Distinction 1, is something that impresses a certain species on the senses and makes something beyond it come into the understanding. But a character does not impress anything on the senses. Therefore, it is not a sign.

OBJ. 2: Furthermore, it is more fitting for the powers that are the principle of action or passion to be signified rather than to signify, for causes are signified by their effects. But character, as was said, is a spiritual power. Therefore, it is not a sign.

OBJ. 3: Furthermore, some people bear a character who do not have faith, like those who crumble into heresy after baptism. But anyone who does not have faith does not communicate in faith. Therefore, the character is not a sign of the communion of faith—or else it would be a false sign, which is absurd to think of a sign that was divinely given.

OBJ. 4: Furthermore, the definition should fit equally everything that is contained under the defined. But to be the sign of a sacred ordination does not correspond to every character, but only the character that is imprinted in holy orders. Therefore, it is not a well-formulated definition.

OBJ. 5: Furthermore, the hierarch, as was said, is the pontiff. But in certain sacraments, which are conferred by simple priests, or even by laymen, a character is imprinted. Therefore, the definition should not have said: *given by a hierarch.*

Quaestiuncula 2

ULTERIUS. Videtur quod non bene assignetur quaedam alia definitio magistralis quae talis est: *character est distinctio a charactere aeterno impressa animae rationali secundum imaginem, consignans trinitatem creatam Trinitati creanti et recreanti; et distinguens a non configuratis secundum statum fidei.* Ubi enim est magna differentia, non oportet signa distinctionis dari. Sed infideles a

OBJ. 1: Moreover, it seems that a certain other teacher's definition was not well-formulated, which is as follows:[28] *a character is a distinguishing mark imprinted from the eternal character on a rational soul according to the image, sealing a created trinity to the creating and recreating Trinity, and distinguishing from those not configured according to the state of faith.* For where there is a great difference, it is not nec-

---

27. Parallel: *ST* III, q. 63, a. 2.
28. Parallel: *ST* III, q. 63, a. 3.

fidelibus maxime differunt et in vita et in ritu. Ergo non oportet quod detur aliquod signum distinctivum.

PRAETEREA, aut istud signum distinctionis fit propter hominem, aut propter Deum, aut propter angelos. Non propter hominem, quia nec alii homines possunt cognoscere characterem, nec ipsemet qui habet, percipit se habere; signum autem oportet esse notum: nec quo ad Deum, qui sine hoc signo scit fideles ab infidelibus discernere; et similiter nec quo ad angelos. Ergo illud signum distinctionis character non est.

PRAETEREA, homo non configuratur Trinitati nisi per imaginem et similitudinem. Sed prima configuratio est per naturam, secunda per gratiam. Ergo character nullo modo configurat.

PRAETEREA, caritas est excellentior virtus quam fides. Sed caritati non ponitur aliquod distinguens signum, nec aliis virtutibus. Ergo nec fidei debet poni.

PRAETEREA, contrarium distinguit sufficienter a suo contrario. Sed fides infidelitati contraria est. Ergo sufficienter fideles ab infidelibus distinguit; et ita non oportet quod per characterem distinguantur.

essary for a sign of distinction to be given. But unbelievers differ tremendously from the faithful, both in life and in religious practice. Therefore, it is not necessary that any distinctive sign be given.

OBJ. 2: Furthermore, a sign of distinction like this is either done for the sake of men, for the sake of God, or for the sake of the angels. But this is not for the sake of men, since not only are other men incapable of recognizing this character, but even the one who has it cannot perceive that he has it, whereas a sign needs to be noticeable. Nor is this a sign for God, who knows how to discern believers from unbelievers without this sign; and likewise, neither is it for the angels. Therefore, a character is not that sign of distinction.

OBJ. 3: Furthermore, man is only configured to the Trinity by image and likeness. But the first configuration is by nature, and the second by grace. Therefore, a character does not configure us in any way.

OBJ. 4: Furthermore, charity is a more excellent virtue than faith. But no distinguishing sign is posited for charity, nor for the other virtues. Therefore, it should not be posited for faith.

OBJ. 5: Furthermore, a contrary distinguishes sufficiently from its contrary. But faith and unbelief are contraries. Therefore, believers are sufficiently distinguished from unbelievers; and so it is not necessary that they be distinguished by a character.

Response to Quaestiuncula 1

RESPONDEO dicendum ad primam quaestionem, quod illa definitio nusquam invenitur a Dionysio posita, sed potest accipi ex verbis ejus supra inductis; et acciperetur adhuc convenientius si sic diceretur: *character est signum communionis potestatis*[29] *divinorum, et sacrae ordinationis fidelium, datum a divina beatitudine.* Et tangit quatuor causas. Primo genus characteris inquantum est character, scilicet signum, quod pertinet ad causam formalem. Secundo finem: datur enim hoc signum ad duo, ut scilicet recipiens configuretur quasi ascriptus ad communicandum divinis sacramentis, et actionibus sacris; et quantum ad hoc dicit: *communionis divinorum potestatis;*[30] et ut configuretur coordinandus aliis, quibus eadem potestas data est, quod tangit in hoc quod dicit: *et sacrae ordinationis fidelium*; quae duo excommunicatio suspendit ad tempus: quia privat hominem participatione divinorum et communione fidelium. Tertio ponit mate-

TO THE FIRST QUESTION I answer that definition is nowhere found laid down by Dionysius, but it can be taken from the words of his cited above; and it may be taken more fittingly if it were said as follows: *character is a sign of communion in a share of divine things and of the sacred ordination of the faithful, given by divine blessedness.* And it touches upon the four causes. First, the genus of character as character, namely, sign, which pertains to the formal cause. Second, the final cause, for this sign is given for two things—namely, so that the one receiving it may be configured as inscribed in the sharing of divine sacraments and sacred actions; and with regard to this he says: *of the communion in a share of divine things*; and so that the one to be added to this order may be configured to the others to whom the same power has been given, which he refers to in saying: *and of the sacred ordination of the faithful*; which two things excommunication suspends for a time, for it de-

---

29. *potestatis.—partis* PLE.
30. *potestatis.—partis* PLE.

riam in qua, in hoc quod dicit: *datum a sacerdote*. Quarto efficiens, scilicet *a divina beatitudine*.

Tamen definitio prius posita potest etiam sustineri, ut in idem redeat cum ista; ut hoc quod dicit: *communionis fidei*, referatur ad participationem sacramentorum et actionum fidelium. Quod autem dicit: *et sanctae ordinationis*, ponitur coordinatio ejus ad alios: *accedenti datum a hierarcha* ponitur quantum ad causam efficientem instrumentalem scilicet ministrum, qui configuratione exteriori figurat interiorem.

AD PRIMUM ergo dicendum, quod character accipit rationem signi, secundum quod per sacramentum visibile exterius efficitur et significatur.

AD SECUNDUM dicendum, quod cum qualibet potestate exterius datur aliquod visibile signum illius potestatis, sicut regi in signum regiae potestatis datur corona et sceptrum; et pontifici mitra et baculus et anulus; et similiter cum spirituali potestate, quae in sacramentis confertur, datur signum sacramentale exterius; et per comparationem ad illud exterius signum, ipsa spiritualis potentia dicitur signum, inquantum homo per eam configuratur et determinatur ad actiones spirituales.

AD TERTIUM dicendum, quod communio fidei, ut patet per verba Dionysii, oportet quod recipiatur pro communione in sacramentis fidei, et aliis actionibus quae fidelibus competunt, ad quas nullus admittitur antequam characterem suscipiat spiritualis potestatis respectu illorum. Nec oportet quod omnis qui characterem habet, illas actiones bene exerceat, sicut nec omnis qui habet potentiam, bene operatur actum illius potentiae.

AD QUARTUM dicendum, quod ordinatio non accipitur hic pro ordinis sacramento, sed pro coordinatione ad alios fideles, ut in coetu fidelium aggregetur, quantum ad ea quae fideles facere dicuntur, vel quantum ad ea quae pro fidelibus fiunt.

AD QUINTUM dicendum quod hoc quod dicitur: *datum accedenti a hierarcha*, non potest accipi a verbis Dionysii, sed magis sic: *datum accedenti a divina beatitudine*; et sic cessat objectio. Si autem accipiatur dans ministerio, sic dicitur a hierarcha dari character baptismalis quantum ad maximam solemnitatem baptismi, quae quandoque per pontifices celebratur: sic enim Dionysius ibi ritum baptismi tradit, summum sacerdotem ministrum baptismi ponens, ut patet litteram ejus intuenti.

prives a man of participation in divine things and the communion of the faithful. Third, he includes the matter in which, by saying: *given by a priest*.[31] Fourth, the efficent cause, namely *by divine blessedness*.

Nevertheless, the definition laid down before can also be defended, so that it amounts to the same thing as this one; so that the phrase *of the communion of the faith* may be referred to the participation in the sacraments and the actions of the faithful. But when he says, *and of holy ordination*, he lays down the ordering of one to another; *given to the one approaching by the hierarch* is included as to the efficient instrumental cause, which is the minister, who represents the interior agent cause by external configuration.

REPLY OBJ. 1: Character receives the account of a sign according as it is made outwardly visible and is signified through the sacrament.

REPLY OBJ. 2: With any power, some outward, visible sign of that power is given, as a crown and scepter are given to a king as a sign of royal power, and a miter and crozier and ring are given to a pontiff. And in like manner, together with the spiritual power conferred in the sacraments, an outward sacramental sign is given; and in relation to that outward sign, the spiritual power itself is called a sign, inasmuch as by it a man is configured and determined to spiritual actions.

REPLY OBJ. 3: The communion of faith, as is clear from the words of Dionysius, must be received by communion in the sacraments of the faith, and other actions that befit the faithful, to which no one is admitted before he received this character of spiritual power with respect to these things. Nor is it necessary that every one who has a character exercise these actions well, just as neither does everyone who has a power perform the act of that power well.

REPLY OBJ. 4: Ordination is not taken here for the sacrament of holy orders, but for being integrated into the order of the other believers, so that one is joined to the society of the faithful as regards those things that the faithful are said to do, or as regards those things that are done for the faithful.

REPLY OBJ. 5: This phrasing—*given to the one approaching by the hierarch*—cannot be taken from the words of Dionysius, but rather this one: *given to the one approaching by divine beatitude*, and in this way the objection ceases. But if it is taken as the minister giving it, then in that way the baptismal character is said to be given by the hierarch as to baptism's greatest solemnity, which is sometimes celebrated by pontiffs; for in this way Dionysius hands on the rite of baptism there, placing the high priest as the minister of baptism, as is clear to anyone considering his text.

---

31. This phrase, *datum a sacerdote*, is not present in either the original or the rephrased definition, but it seems to parallel *datum a hierarcha*, discussed below.

Response to Quaestiuncula 2

AD SECUNDAM QUAESTIONEM dicendum, quod in illa etiam definitione tanguntur quatuor causae characteris. Nam causa formalis tangitur in hoc quod ponitur genus, cum dicit, *distinctio*, id est distinctivum signum; et est genus[32] in praecedenti definitione positum. Causa efficiens tangitur in hoc quod dicit: *charactere aeterno*, idest filio, qui est figura substantiae patris; Hebr. 1. Causa autem materialis in qua ponitur cum dicit: *animae rationali impressa secundum imaginem*. Causa vero finalis ponitur duplex, scilicet configuratio, in hoc quod dicit: *consignans trinitatem creatam Trinitati creanti et recreanti*, idest configurans; et distinctio in hoc quod dicit: *et distinguens a non configuratis secundum statum fidei*. Et sicut hic ponitur genus proximum, ita finis proximus, et subjectum proximum, et efficiens appropriatum: in quo excedit praedictam definitionem haec definitio, inquantum per causas magis proximas datur.

AD PRIMUM ergo dicendum quod character non est signum tantum ut distinctionis nota, sed ut distinctionem causans, sicut et alia sacramentalia signa; et ideo eo indigetur ad distinctionem faciendam.

AD SECUNDUM dicendum, quod istud distinctionis signum est et propter ipsum hominem qui suscipit, qui eo accipit distinctum posse ab aliis; et propter alios homines qui eum admittunt ad spirituales actiones, ex consignatione sacramentali exteriori interiorem perpendentes; et quoad Deum, qui ejus actionibus spiritualibus efficaciam praebet.

AD TERTIUM dicendum, quod configuratio ista attenditur ad Deum secundum participationem divinae potestatis, quae non est neque per gratiam virtutum, neque per naturam.

AD QUARTUM dicendum, quod fides hominis nota est, caritas autem incerta. Nihil enim est alicui certius sua fide, ut Augustinus dicit; sed an habeat caritatem non est alicui certum, et ideo distinctio[33] data magis respicit fidem quam caritatem vel alias virtutes. Vel dicendum, quod ista distinctio[34] praecipue attenditur quantum ad operationes, et receptiones, quae sunt in sacramentis, in quibus maxime operatur fides.

AD QUINTUM dicendum, quod fides sufficienter distinguit fideles ab infidelibus quantum ad actus fidei, non tamen quantum ad actus spirituales qui competunt fidelibus, quia ad hoc oportet quod spiritualis potentia addatur.

TO THE SECOND QUESTION it should be said that in that definition as well, the four causes of a character are touched upon. For the formal cause is touched upon in including the genus, when he says, *distinguishing mark*, i.e., distinctive sign; and it is a more proximate genus than that included in the preceding definition. The efficient cause is touched upon in saying, *eternal character*, i.e., the Son, who is the figure of the substance of the Father (Heb 1:3). It puts down the material cause in which, when it says: *imprinted on the rational soul according to the image*. But the final cause is included in two ways—namely, configuration, when it says, *sealing a created trinity to the creating and recreating Trinity*, i.e., configuring; and distinction, when it says, *and distinguishing from those not configured according to the state of faith*. And just as here a proximate genus is laid down, so also a proximate end, and a proximate subject, and an appropriated efficient cause—in which this definition surpasses the definition mentioned, as it is given rather through proximate causes.

REPLY OBJ. 1: A character is a sign not only as a mark of distinction, but as something causing distinction, even as the other sacramental signs are; and thus it needs this for bringing about the distinction.

REPLY OBJ. 2: That sign of distinction is for the sake of the very man who receives it, who takes from it a power distinct from others; for the sake of other men who admit him to spiritual actions, assessing his interior from the external sacramental seal; and toward God, who supplies its efficacy for spiritual actions.

REPLY OBJ. 3: That configuration is related to God according to a participation of divine power, which exists neither through the grace of the virtues nor through nature.

REPLY OBJ. 4: The faith of a man is something one can perceive, but charity is uncertain. For nothing is more certain to someone than his own faith, as Augustine says; but whether one has charity is not certain to anyone, and thus the definition given regards faith more than charity or the other virtues. Or it could be said that this definition chiefly deals with the operations and receiving of things that are in the sacraments, in which faith is most at work.

REPLY OBJ. 5: Faith sufficiently distinguishes the faithful from unbelievers with respect to the act of faith, but not as to the spiritual acts that pertain to the faithful, since for these a spiritual power must be added.

---

32. *genus in.—genus magis proximum quam genus in* PLE.
33. *distinctio.—definitio* PLE.
34. *distinctio.—definitio* PLE.

ARTICLE 3

What the baptismal character is in

Quaestiuncula 1

AD TERTIUM SIC PROCEDITUR. Videtur quod character sit in essentia animae quasi in subjecto. Dispositio enim et habitus sunt in eodem subjecto. Sed character disponit ad habitum gratiae. Cum ergo gratia sit in essentia animae sicut in subjecto, videtur quod etiam character.

PRAETEREA, nihil est subjectum potentiae animae nisi essentia animae. Sed character, ut dictum est, est quaedam spiritualis potentia. Ergo est in essentia animae sicut in subjecto.

SED CONTRA, character configurat trinitatem creatam increatae, ut patet ex definitione supra posita. Sed Trinitas increata consistit in potentiis, unitas autem in essentia, ut in 1 Lib., dist. 3, dictum est. Ergo character non est in essentia animae.

OBJ. 1: It seems that character is in the essence of the soul as a subject.[35] For dispositions and habits are in the same subject. But a character disposes one for the habit of grace. Since, therefore grace is in the essence of the soul as its subject, it seems that the character is as well.

OBJ. 2: Furthermore, the powers of the soul have no subject but the essence of the soul. But a character, as has been said, is a certain spiritual power. Therefore, it is in the essence of the soul as its subject.

ON THE CONTRARY, character configures a created trinity to the uncreated one, as is clear from the definition cited above. But the uncreated Trinity consists in powers, while its unity is in the essence, as was said in Book I, Distinction 3. Therefore, the character is not in the essence of the soul.

Quaestiuncula 2

ULTERIUS. Videtur quod non sit in una potentia, sed in pluribus. Quia, sicut ex praedicta definitione patet, character est in anima rationali secundum imaginem, secundum quam etiam est configuratio hominis ad Deum. Sed imago non consistit in una tantum potentia, sed in pluribus. Ergo nec character.

PRAETEREA, cujus est potentia, ejus est actio, et e converso, ut dicitur in 1 *de Somno et vigilia*. Sed actio spiritualis, ad quam character ordinatur, est per plures potentias, scilicet quia requiritur et affectiva et intellectiva. Ergo character est in pluribus potentiis, sicut spiritualis potentia.

SED CONTRA, unum accidens non est in pluribus subjectis. Sed in uno sacramento imprimitur unus character. Ergo non est in pluribus potentiis.

OBJ. 1: Moreover, it seems that it is not in one power, but in several.[36] For, as is evident from the definition given, a character is in a rational soul as an image, according to which is the configuration of man to God as well. But an image does not consist in one power alone, but in several. Therefore, neither does a character.

OBJ. 2: Furthermore, whatever has a power has an action, and vice versa, as is said in *On Sleep and Waking* 1.[37] But spiritual action, to which a character is directed, is through several powers, since both affective and intellective powers are required for it. Therefore, the character, as a spiritual power, is in several of the powers.

ON THE CONTRARY, one accident is not in several subjects. But in one sacrament, one character is imprinted. Therefore, it is not in several subjects.

---

35. Parallel: *ST* III, q. 63, a. 4.
36. Parallel: *ST* III, q. 63, a. 4.
37. Aristotle, *On Sleep*, ch. 1, 454a8.

Quaestiuncula 3

ULTERIUS. Videtur quod sit magis in affectiva quam cognitiva. Quia character disponit ad gratiam. Sed gratia magis respicit affectivam. Ergo et character.

PRAETEREA, character est ad assimilandum nos Deo. Sed per affectum maxime Deo appropinquamus, et similes ei efficimur. Ergo character est in affectiva.

SED CONTRA, characterem Dionysius lumini comparat. Sed lumen magis intellectivae competit quam affectivae. Ergo et character.

OBJ. 1: Moreover, it seems that it is in the affective power rather than the cognitive power.[38] For a character disposes for grace. But grace regards the affections more. Therefore, so does a character.

OBJ. 2: Furthermore, a character is for the sake of likening us to God. But it is through the affections that we grow most near to God and become most like him. Therefore, a character is in the affective power.

ON THE CONTRARY, Dionysius compares the character to a light. But light applies more to the intellective than to the affective part of the soul. Therefore, so also does the character.

Quaestiuncula 4

ULTERIUS. Videtur quod character non indelebiliter insit potentiae cui inest. Accidens enim diuturnitatem habet ex causa et subjecto. Sed gratia est ab eadem causa et in eodem subjecto cum charactere. Ergo cum gratia amitti possit, et character similiter deleri poterit.

PRAETEREA: *cum venerit quod perfectum est, evacuabitur quod ex parte est*; 1 Corinth. 13, 10. Sed character est ex parte: datur enim ad distinguendum in operibus sacramentalibus, quae competunt secundum statum viae. Ergo in patria character cessabit, et ita est delebilis.

SED CONTRA, si character deleretur, maxime per culpam deleretur. Sed per culpam non deletur, quia sacerdos malus non reordinatur, ut iterum characterem accipiat. Ergo character est indelebilis.

OBJ. 1: Moreover, it seems that the character is not indelibly impressed on the power in which it is.[39] For accidents have endurance from their cause and from their subject. But grace is from the same cause and in the same subject as a character. Therefore, since grace can be lost, a character can likewise also be erased.

OBJ. 2: Furthermore, *when what is perfect has come, what is partial shall be emptied out* (1 Cor 13:10). But character is partial: for it is given to distinguish one in sacramental works, which belong to the state of the wayfarer. Therefore, in the fatherland the character will cease, and thus it is effaceable.

ON THE CONTRARY, if a character could be erased, it would certainly be erased by sin. But it is not erased by sin, for a wicked priest is not reordained so that he may again receive the character. Therefore, the character is indelible.

Quaestiuncula 5

ULTERIUS. Videtur quod Christus habuerit characterem. Ipse enim sacerdos fuit secundum ordinem Melchisedech, Heb. 7, quod est sacerdotium novi testamenti. Sed tale sacerdotium requirit characterem. Ergo Christus habuit characterem.

PRAETEREA, nihil quod est perfectionis quantum ad animam, vel dignitatis, Christo subtrahendum est. Sed character decorat et nobilitat animam in qua est. Ergo character in Christo fuit.

SED CONTRA, character est regeneratorum, et accipientium aliquid a sacramentis. Sed Christus non accepit aliquid a sacramentis, nec renatus est etiam: quia, sicut dicit Augustinus, in *Enchiridion*, ipse solus ita potuit

OBJ. 1: Moreover, it seems that Christ had a character.[40] For he himself was a priest *according to the order of Melchizedek* (Heb 7:17), which is the priesthood of the New Testament. But this priesthood requires a character. Therefore, Christ had a character.

OBJ. 2: Furthermore, nothing of perfection, whether in the soul or in dignity, should be denied to Christ. But a character beautifies and ennobles a soul in which it is. Therefore, in Christ there was a character.

ON THE CONTRARY, a character is for those who have been regenerated, and who receive something from the sacraments. But Christ did not receive anything from the sacraments, nor again was he reborn, since, as Augustine

---

38. Parallel: *ST* III, q. 63, a. 4, ad 3.
39. Parallels: *ST* III, q. 63, a. 5; q. 66, a. 9; *Super Rom.* 7, lec. 1.
40. Parallel: *ST* III, q. 63, a. 3.

nasci, ut non esset ei opus renasci. Ergo non habet characterem.

says in the *Enchiridion*, he alone was able to be born so that it was not necessary for him to be reborn.[41] Therefore, he does not have a character.

Response to Quaestiuncula 1

RESPONDEO dicendum ad primam quaestionem, quod natura proportionaliter spiritualitati substernitur, sicut perfectibile perfectioni. Unde sicut gratia, quae est spiritualis vitae principium, est in essentia animae sicut in subjecto; ita et character, qui est spiritualis potentia, est sicut in subjecto in naturali potentia animae, et non in essentia animae, ut quidam dicunt, nisi mediante potentia animae.

AD PRIMUM ergo dicendum, quod dispositionem esse in eodem cum eo ad quod disponit, non est necesse, nisi quando dispositio postea fit perfectio, sicut scientia quae prius fuit dispositio, postea fit habitus; et ideo scientia dispositio et scientia habitus sunt in eodem subjecto proximo. Non autem hoc oportet quando dispositio et perfectio differunt per essentiam; sed possunt esse in diversis subjectis; et praecipue quando illa diversa habent ordinem ad invicem; sicut operatio sensibilis est dispositio ad intelligibilem operationem, et similiter character est dispositio ad gratiam.

AD SECUNDUM dicendum, quod illa objectio procedit de potentiis naturalibus; sed potentias spirituales oportet fundari in naturalibus.

THE FIRST QUESTION I answer by saying that nature is laid out as a substratum proportionate to spirituality, as the perfectible is related to perfection. Hence, just as grace, which is the principle of spiritual life, is in the essence of the soul as its subject, so also character, which is a spiritual power, has as its subject the natural power of the soul, and not (as some people say) the essence of the soul, except indirectly through the powers of the soul.

REPLY OBJ. 1: It is not necessary for a disposition to be in the same genus as that to which it disposes, except when a disposition becomes a perfection afterward, as science, which was first a disposition, afterward becomes a habit; and thus science the disposition and science the habit are in the same proximate subject. But when the disposition and the perfection differ by essence, this is not necessary; rather, they can be in diverse subjects, especially when they have a different order to each other, as when a sensible operation is a disposition to an intelligible operation. And in a similar way, character is a disposition to grace.

REPLY OBJ. 2: That objection has to do with natural powers; but the spiritual powers must be founded on natural ones.

Response to Quaestiuncula 2

AD SECUNDAM QUAESTIONEM dicendum, quod esse in pluribus potentiis est dupliciter: aut ita quod aequaliter sit in omnibus, sicut essentia animae est in omnibus potentiis; aut ita quod sit in una per prius, et per posterius respiciat alias mediante illa in qua primo est; sicut electio est in intellectu et appetitu, et formaliter in appetitu perficitur, ut patet per Philosophum in 6 *Ethic*. Primo ergo modo nullum accidens potest esse in pluribus potentiis quia accidens numeratur et distinguitur penes materiam et distinctionem subjecti; et ideo cum character sit accidens, non potest esse in pluribus potentiis animae primo modo, sed secundo modo: quia unam respicit per prius, et alias per posterius.

AD PRIMUM ergo dicendum, quod etiam potentiae magis habent ordinem ad invicem, ut in 1 Lib. dictum est; et ideo quod est in una, potest aliquando ad alias redundare.

TO THE SECOND QUESTION, it should be said that something can exist in multiple powers in two ways: either such that it is equally in all of them, as the essence of the soul is in all the powers; or such that it is in one primarily and, as a result, it relates to the others by means of the one in which it first is; as choice is in the intellect and the appetite, and it is formally perfected in the appetite, as is clear from the Philosopher in *Ethics* 6.[42] In the first way, therefore, no accident can exist in several powers, for an accident is numbered and distinguished by virtue of matter and distinction of subject. And thus, since a character is an accident, it cannot be in several powers of the soul in the first way, but only in the second way, for it regards one [power] first, and the others consequently.

REPLY OBJ. 1: Even powers have considerable order to each other, as was said in Book I; and thus, what is in one can sometimes overflow into the others.

---

41. Augustine, *Enchiridion on Faith, Hope, and Charity* (CCSL 46), ch. 14: "qui solus potuit ita nasci ut ei non opus esset renasci."
42. Aristotle, *Nicomachean Ethics*, Bk. 6, ch. 2, 1139b4–5.

Ad secundum dicendum, quod quando ad unam actionem requiruntur plures potentiae, in illa actione est principalis una potentia quasi movens et trahens alias in obsequium sui, et aliae induunt quodammodo formam ipsius; et ideo ex eo quod est in principali potentia, potest actio illa sufficienter perfici.

Reply Obj. 2: When many powers are required for one action, one power is principal in that action as the mover and the one drawing all the others into its service; and the others, in a way, put on its form; and thus, from what is in the principal power, that action can be sufficiently completed.

Response to Quaestiuncula 3

Ad tertiam quaestionem dicendum, quod imago principaliter consistit in potentia cognitiva, quia ex memoria et intelligentia oritur voluntas; unde tota imago est in intellectiva parte sicut in radice; et ideo omne quod attribuitur homini ratione imaginis, principaliter respicit intellectivam, et ex consequenti affectivam: quia etiam ex intellectiva parte habet homo quod sit homo; sed ex affectiva quod sit bonus vel malus; et ideo quia character respicit imaginem, principaliter est in intellectiva parte.

Ad primum ergo dicendum, quod gratia non est neque in intellectiva neque in affectiva, sed in essentia animae; tamen magis de propinquo respicit affectivam, quia gratia datur ad bene operandum; qualiter autem aliquis operetur, praecipue ex voluntate pendet. Sed character datur ad exercendas actiones spirituales aliquas simpliciter: quod autem bene vel male fiant, hoc est per gratiam et per habitum virtutum; et ideo non est similis ratio de charactere et gratia.

Ad secundum dicendum, quod assimilatio in bonitate praecipue est ad Deum per voluntatem; sed assimilatio in esse et posse magis est ex parte intellectus: quia ex hoc ipso quod aliquid esse immateriale habet, intellectivum est, et potentiam habet quodammodo infinitam, secundum quod intellectus universalium est, quae quodammodo infinita sunt virtute; et ideo cum conformitas characteris respiciat spiritualem potestatem, magis competit intellectivae parti quam affectivae.

To the third question, it should be said that the image chiefly consists in the cognitive power. For the will arises from memory and intelligence; hence the whole image is in the intellective part as its root. And thus, everything that is attributed to man by reason of this image chiefly concerns the intellective part, and, in consequence, the affective part. For it is from the intellective part that a man is a man, but it is from the affective part that a man is good or bad. And so, since character regards the image, it is chiefly in the intellective part.

Reply Obj. 1: Grace is neither in the intellective nor in the affective, but in the essence of the soul. Nevertheless, it concerns the affective more closely, since grace is given for acting well. Now, how well someone may act depends especially on the will. But a character is given simply for exercising certain spiritual actions; and whether they are done well or badly is by grace and by the habit of virtues. And thus, the same argument does not apply to grace and to the character.

Reply Obj. 2: Assimilation in goodness toward God is especially through willing, while assimilation in being and ability is rather from the intellectual part—since from the fact that something has immaterial being, it is intellective and has a certain infinite power, since understanding has to do with universals, which are in a certain way infinite in power; and thus, since conformity of character has to do with spiritual power, it applies more to the intellective part than to the affective part.

Response to Quaestiuncula 4

Ad quartam quaestionem dicendum, quod impressio characteris est per quamdam animae rationalis sanctificationem, prout sanctificatio dicitur deputatio alicujus ad aliquid sacrum. Ad hanc autem sanctificationem non magis active comparatur anima sanctificanda, quam aqua sanctificanda, vel oleum vel chrisma, ad sui sanctificationem; nisi quod homo se subjicit tali sanctificationi per consensum, res autem praedictae subjiciuntur, quia libero arbitrio carent; et ideo qualitercumque anima varietur per proprias operationes, nunquam characterem amittit; sicut nec chrisma nec oleum nec panis

To the fourth question, it should be said that the imprinting of a character is through a certain sanctification of the rational soul, just as sanctification is called an appointment of something for something sacred. Now for this sanctification, the soul to be sanctified is not more actively prepared than water, or oil, or chrism to be sanctified, except in that man subjects himself to this sanctification by his own consent, while the things mentioned are subjected to it since they lack free will; and so, no matter how the soul is changed by its proper operations, it will never lose its character, just as neither do chrism, oil, or consecrated

consecratus unquam sanctificationem perdunt, qualiter-cumque transmutentur, dummodo non corrumpantur.

AD PRIMUM ergo dicendum, quod causa indelebi-litatis characteris est ex parte subjecti, quod est incor-ruptibile, et ex parte causae, quae est invariabilis. Gratia autem habet aliquo modo causam non efficientem, sed disponentem ex parte subjecti: quia, secundum Augusti-num: *qui creavit te sine te, non justificabit te sine te*; et ideo per indispositionem subjecti gratia amittitur.

AD SECUNDUM dicendum, quod per characterem homo configuratur ad hoc quod sit de coetu fidelium, et particeps hierarchicarum actionum. ecclesiasticae au-tem hierarchiae succedit caelestis; et ideo ad communio-nem fidelium in ecclesia triumphante, et ad participatio-nem actionum caelestis hierarchiae character in patria perficiet; et sic erit ad alios actus; sicut virtutes et dona in damnatis etiam manent. Sed hoc est per accidens praeter intentionem imprimentis characterem, quod recipiens damnetur; et ideo non est ibi ordinatus ad aliquem fi-nem: quia quae praeter intentionem accidunt, carent or-dine ad finem. Tamen Deus, qui nihil inordinatum relin-quit, elicit ex hoc aliquod bonum, scilicet quod appareat justior eorum damnatio qui tantum munus neglexerunt.

bread ever lose their sanctification, however much they are changed, so long as they are not corrupted.

REPLY OBJ. 1: The cause of the indelibility of a charac-ter is on the part of the subject, which is incorruptible, and on the part of the cause, which is invariable. However, grace has in a certain way a cause that is not efficient but dispos-ing on the part of the subject: for, according to Augustine, *he who created you without you, will not justify you without you*.[43] And thus, by the indisposition of the subject, grace is lost.

REPLY OBJ. 2: By a character, man is configured to what has to do with the society of the faithful, and he becomes partaker of the actions of the hierarchy. But the ecclesias-tical hierarchy gives way to the heavenly one; and thus, in heaven, the character will make more perfect the commu-nion of the faithful in the Church Triumphant, and the par-ticipation in the actions of the heavenly hierarchy. And in this way it will be for other acts, just as the virtues and gifts remain even in the damned. But it is *per accidens* outside the intention of the one imprinting the character that the recipient should be damned; and thus, in that case, it is not ordered to a certain end, for what happens outside the in-tention lacks ordering to an end.[44] Nevertheless God, who leaves nothing disordered, draws some good out of this— namely, that the damnation of those who have neglected such a great gift would appear more just.

Response to Quaestiuncula 5

AD QUINTAM QUAESTIONEM dicendum, quod qui-dam dicunt, quod Christus non habuit characterem bap-tismalem, quia a baptismo nihil accepit: habuit autem characterem ordinis, qui pertinet ad quemdam eminen-tem statum. Sed melius est, si dicatur, quod Christus nullum characterem habuit: quia ipse habuit potestatem plenitudinis in sacramentis, quasi ea instituens, et eis efficaciam praebens. Unde sicut poterat inducere effec-tum sacramenti in aliquo sine sacramento exteriori, ita ex parte ipsius ad hoc non requirebatur aliquod sacra-mentale interius.

AD PRIMUM ergo dicendum, quod ipse fuit sacerdos, quasi sacerdotium instituens; et ideo ejus non est habere characterem, sed illius qui aliunde sacerdotium recipit, ut per characterem principali sacerdoti configuretur.

AD SECUNDUM dicendum, quod aliquid est perfec-tionis in nobis quod non esset Christi, sicut gratia adop-tionis; et similiter est de charactere, qui poneret in eo po-testatem spiritualem coarctatam, et ab alio derivatam.

TO THE FIFTH QUESTION it should be said that some people say that Christ did not have a baptismal character, since he received nothing from baptism, but that he did have the character of holy orders, which pertains to a cer-tain eminent status. But it is better if it were said that Christ had no character; for he had the fullness of power in the sacraments, as the one instituting them and providing them with their efficacy. Hence, just as he could induce the effect of a sacrament in someone without an outward sacrament, in the same way no interior sacramental character was re-quired for this on his part.

REPLY OBJ. 1: He himself was a priest as the one in-stituting the priesthood; thus to have a character does not pertain to him but to that man who receives his priesthood from elsewhere, so that he may be configured to the princi-pal priest by the character.

REPLY OBJ. 2: Some things pertain to perfection in us which would not be so in Christ, like the grace of adoption. And it is similar with the character, which would put in him a spiritual power that was restricted and derived from an-other.

---

43. See Augustine, *Sermon* 169, n. 11 (PL 38:923): "qui ergo fecit te sine te, non te iustificat sine te."
44. That is, the character in a damned soul is no longer serving its essential purpose, as it would be doing in a blessed soul.

ARTICLE 4

Whence comes the baptismal character

Quaestiuncula 1

AD QUARTUM SIC PROCEDITUR. Videtur quod non solum in sacramentis novae legis character imprimatur. Characteris enim effectus est configurare et distinguere. Sed hoc faciunt virtutes: quia in eis boni et a malis distinguuntur, et Deo assimilantur. Ergo per virtutes, et non per sacramenta novae legis tantum, character imprimitur.

PRAETEREA, sicut per sacramenta novae legis distinguitur populus fidelis ab infideli, ita per sacramenta veteris legis distinguebatur. Ergo sacramenta novae legis non magis imprimunt characterem quam sacramenta veteris legis.

SED CONTRA, habens characterem non baptizatur, quia alii characteres baptismum praesupponunt, qui etiam iterari non debet. Sed habentes virtutem, et qui sacramenta veteris legis susceperant, baptizabantur. Ergo neque per virtutes neque per sacramenta veteris legis character imprimitur.

OBJ. 1: To the fourth we proceed thus. It seems that a character is not imprinted only in the sacraments of the New Law.[45] For the effect of a character is to configure and distinguish. But the virtues do this: for in them the good are distinguished from the bad and made like unto God. Therefore, a character is imprinted by the virtues and not only by the sacraments of the New Law.

OBJ. 2: Furthermore, just as by the sacraments of the New Law a faithful people is distinguished from unbelievers, so were they distinguished by the sacraments of the Old Law. Therefore, the sacraments of the New Law do not imprint a character any more than the sacraments of the Old Law.

ON THE CONTRARY, someone having a character is not baptized, for the other characters presuppose baptism, which should also not be given again. But those who have virtue, and those who received the sacraments of the Old Law, were baptized. Therefore, neither by virtues nor by sacraments of the Old Law is a character imprinted.

Quaestiuncula 2

ULTERIUS. Videtur quod per omnia sacramenta legis novae imprimatur character. In quolibet enim sacramento novae legis est aliquid quod est sacramentum tantum, et aliquid quod est res tantum, et aliquid quod est res et sacramentum. Sed character in baptismo est illud quod est res et sacramentum. Ergo in quolibet sacramento novae legis imprimitur character.

PRAETEREA, quolibet sacramento novae legis confertur gratia, et distinguitur recipiens a non recipiente. Cum ergo character sit disponens ad gratiam, et distinguat, videtur quod in quolibet sacramento novae legis character imprimatur.

SED CONTRA, nullum sacramentum, in quo character imprimitur, iteratur: quia character indelebilis est. Sed quaedam sacramenta iterantur. Ergo non omnia sacramenta novae legis characterem imprimunt.

OBJ. 1: Moreover, it seems that a character is imprinted by all the sacraments of the New Law.[46] For in every sacrament of the New Law there is something that is purely a sacrament, and something that is purely a reality, and something that is reality-and-sacrament. But in baptism, that which is reality-and-sacrament is the character. Therefore, in any sacrament of the New Law a character is imprinted.

OBJ. 2: Furthermore, in every sacrament of the New Law grace is conferred, and the one receiving it is distinguished from the one not receiving it. Therefore, since a character disposes for grace and distinguishes, it seems that in any sacrament of the New Law a character is imprinted.

ON THE CONTRARY, no sacrament in which a character is imprinted can be received again, for the character is indelible. But certain sacraments are received over and over. Therefore, not all sacraments of the New Law imprint a character.

---

45. Parallels: *ST* III, q. 63, a. 5; *Super Heb.* 11. lec. 7.
46. Parallels: below, d. 7, q. 2, a. 1, qa. 1; d. 23, q. 1, a. 2, qa. 3; *ST* III, q. 63, a. 6; *De eccles. sacram.*; *Super Heb.* 11, lec. 7.

Quaestiuncula 3

ULTERIUS. Videtur quod in sacramento baptismi character non imprimatur. Baptismus enim sanguinis est dignior quam baptismus fluminis, quia meretur aureolam. Sed in baptismo sanguinis non imprimitur character. Ergo nec in baptismo fluminis.

PRAETEREA, baptismus fluminis non habet supra baptismum flaminis nisi aquam. Sed baptismus ratione aquae non potest imprimere characterem: alias baptismus Joannis impressisset characterem: quod esse non potest, cum baptizati a Joanne iterum baptizarentur, ut supra, dist. 2, art. 4, dictum est. Ergo nec baptismus fluminis characterem imprimit.

SED CONTRA est auctoritas Dionysii, ex qua characteris traditio derivatur: quia ipse inducit verba illa unde definitio characteris accipitur in tractatu de baptismo.

OBJ. 1: Moreover, it seems that in the sacrament of baptism a character is not imprinted. For baptism of blood is more worthy than baptism with water, for it merits a golden crown.[47] But in baptism of blood, no character is imprinted. Therefore, neither in baptism of water.

OBJ. 2: Furthermore, the only thing baptism of water has over and above baptism of spirit is water. But baptism cannot imprint its character by reason of the water, otherwise the baptism of John would have imprinted a character, which cannot be, since those baptized by John were baptized again, as was said above in Distinction 2, Article 4. Therefore, neither does baptism of water imprint a character.

ON THE CONTRARY, is the authority of Dionysius, from whom the tradition of the character is derived, for it was in the treatise on baptism that he himself brought forward those words from which the definition of character is taken.

Quaestiuncula 4

ULTERIUS. Videtur quod character sit sicut a causa efficiente prima a solo Filio. *Character enim est distinctio a charactere aeterno impressa* etc., ut supra, Art. 2, quaestiunc. 2, dictum est. Sed character aeternus est solus Filius, sicut et imago. Ergo a solo Filio character imprimitur.

PRAETEREA, charactere configuratur et assimilatur anima Deo. Sed principium assimilationis ad Deum est Filius; unde Augustinus Filium nominat similitudinem, per quam ad unitatem reformamur, ut patet 1 Lib., dist. 3. Ergo character est tantum a Filio.

SED CONTRA est quod Dionysius dicit, quod signum characteris *datur a divina beatitudine*. Sed divina beatitudo est communis tribus personis. Ergo character non datur a solo Filio.

OBJ. 1: Moreover, it seems that the character is from the Son alone as its first efficient cause.[48] For *character is a distinction imprinted on the rational soul by the eternal character*, etc., as was said above in Article 2, Subquestion 2. But the eternal character is the Son alone, just as he is also the image. Therefore, the character is imprinted by the Son alone.

OBJ. 2: Furthermore, by a character the soul is configured and made to be like God. But the principle of likening to God is the Son; hence Augustine names the Son 'the Likeness', by whom we are reformed unto oneness, as is clear from Book I, Distinction 3. Therefore, the character is only from the Son.

ON THE CONTRARY, Dionysius says that the sign of a character is *given by divine blessedness*. But divine blessedness is common to the three Persons. Therefore, the character is not given by the Son alone.

Response to Quaestiuncula 1

RESPONDEO dicendum ad primam quaestionem, quod, sicut in 2 *Ethic.*, dicit Philosophus: *virtus ex quibus innascitur, ea operatur*, loquens de virtute acquisita; et similiter est in omnibus virtutibus quae ex aliquibus

THE FIRST QUESTION I answer by saying that, as the Philosopher says in *Ethics 2*, *virtue works those things from which it is born*,[49] speaking of acquired virtue; and it is similar in all virtues that are caused in some way from cer-

---

47. Aquinas uses the term *aureola*, "little crown," to express an extra honor or distinction awarded to some of the blessed in addition to the *aurea*, "golden crown" or "halo" that represents the main substantial reward of heavenly beatitude. See the more thorough explanation at Dist. 49, question 5. See also Dist. 8, q. 1, a. 2, qa 1, ad 2.

48. Parallel: *ST* III, q. 63, a. 3.

49. Aristotle, *Nicomachean Ethics*, Bk. 2, ch. 2, 1104a27–29; that is, the kind of actions that give rise to a virtue are the very actions the virtue empowers the agent to perform.

actibus aliquo modo causantur. Unde cum character sit virtus, seu potentia spiritualis ad actiones sacramentales ordinata, si ex aliquo quod per nos fiat, imprimi character debeat, oportet quod per sacramenta novae legis imprimatur, et per ea tantum, quia ad illas actiones tantum directe illa potentia ordinatur.

Ad primum ergo dicendum, quod actiones spirituales ad quas character ordinat, intra ecclesiam tantum exercentur; et ideo pro nihilo potestas ad illas actiones daretur alicui, nisi tali modo quod innotesceret illis qui sunt de ecclesia, ut eum ad tales actiones admittant. Per gratiam autem, et virtutes non posset innotescere quia ignotae sunt; et ideo oportet quod imprimatur character per signa visibilia sacramentorum.

Ad secundum dicendum, quod sacramenta veteris legis ex opere operato nihil conferebant, et ideo illae actiones non requirebant aliquam spiritualem potestatem; et ideo nec ab illis, nec ad illa imprimebatur character.

tain actions. Hence, since a character is a virtue or spiritual power ordered to sacramental actions, if a character should be imprinted from something that is done by us, it has to be imprinted by the sacraments of the New Law, and by them alone, for that power is directly ordered only to those actions.

Reply Obj. 1: The spiritual actions to which a character is ordered are exercised only within the Church; and thus the power for these actions would be given to someone for naught unless it were given in such a way that it might become known to those who are in the Church, so that they admitted him to such actions. But by grace and the virtues he could not become known, since they are unknown; and thus, it was necessary that the character be imprinted by the visible signs of the sacraments.

Reply Obj. 2: Sacraments of the Old Law conferred nothing by the work performed, and thus those actions did not require any spiritual power; and therefore neither from them nor for them was a character imprinted.

Response to Quaestiuncula 2

Ad secundam quaestionem dicendum, quod sacramenta legis novae sunt sanctificationes quaedam. Sanctificatio autem duobus modis accipitur. Uno modo pro emundatione, quia sanctum est mundum. Alio modo pro mancipatione ad aliquod sacrum, sicut dicitur altare sanctificari, vel aliquod hujusmodi. Omnia ergo sacramenta sunt sanctificationes primo modo, quia omnia dantur in remedium contra aliquem defectum, ut dictum est prius, dist. 2, sed quaedam sunt sanctificationes etiam secundo modo, sicut patet praecipue in ordine, quia ordinatus mancipatur ad aliquid sacrum: non autem omnia, sicut patet de poenitentia. Quicumque autem mancipatur ad aliquid sacrum spirituale exercendum, oportet quod habeat spiritualem potestatem, et solum talis; et ideo non omnia sacramenta novae legis characterem imprimunt, sed quaedam, quae etiam secundo modo sanctificationes sunt.

Ad primum ergo dicendum, quod quamvis illud quod est res et sacramentum, in baptismo sit character, non tamen oportet quod sit character in omnibus sacramentis in quibus est res et sacramentum. Quid autem sit res et sacramentum in singulis, postea singillatim ostendetur.

Ad secundum dicendum, quod quamvis quodlibet sacramentum distinguat a non habente, non tamen tali distinctione indelebili, qualis est distinctio in sacramentis sanctificantibus secundo modo; et ideo non est simile de omnibus sacramentis.

To the second question it should be said that sacraments of the New Law are a kind of sanctification. But 'sanctification' is taken in two ways. In one way, as a cleansing, for what is holy is clean. In another way, for a dedication to something sacred, as an altar, or something like it, is said to be sanctified. All the sacraments, therefore, are sanctifications in the first way, for they are all given as a remedy against some defect, as was said before in Distinction 2; but some of them are also sanctifications in the second way, as is particularly evident in holy orders, for the ordained is dedicated to something sacred; but not all the sacraments, as is clear in the case of penance. Now anyone who is dedicated to exercising something sacred and spiritual, and only such a person, needs to have a spiritual power. And therefore not all the sacraments of the New Law imprint a character, but certain ones that are also sanctifications in the second way.

Reply Obj. 1: Although the reality-and-sacrament in baptism happens to be a character, nevertheless it is not necessary that it be a character in all the sacraments in which there is a reality-and-sacrament. But that which is the reality-and-sacrament in each will be shown further on, one sacrament at a time.[50]

Reply Obj. 2: Although any sacrament may distinguish those receiving from those not receiving it, nevertheless it does not do so with such an indelible distinction, of which sort is the distinction in those sacraments that sanctify in the second way; and thus it is not the same with all the sacraments.

---

50. For more about the sacrament alone, reality alone, and sacrament-and-reality, see the footnote at Dist.1, q.1, a.4, qa. 1, main response.

Response to Quaestiuncula 3

AD TERTIAM QUAESTIONEM, dicendum, quod sicut in naturalibus est potentia activa et potentia naturalis passiva; ita etiam in spiritualibus est potentia spiritualis quasi passiva per quam homo efficitur susceptivus spiritualium actionum; et talis spiritualis potentia confertur in baptismo: quia non baptizatus effectum aliorum sacramentorum suscipere non posset, unde et per consequens nec aliis tradere: et haec est prima distinctio, qua communiter totus populus fidelis, cujus est sacramentorum participem esse, ab aliis distinguitur. Alia potentia est activa spiritualis ordinata ad sacramentorum dispensationem, et aliarum sacrarum hierarchicarum actionum exercitium; et haec potestas traditur in confirmatione et ordine, ut suis locis patebit. Et quia in ecclesiastica hierarchia non omnes sunt agentes, ut puta perficientes purgantes, et illuminantes, sicut omnes sunt recipientes puta purgandi, illuminandi, perficiendi, ut dicit Dionysius; ideo isti duo characteres non distinguunt populum Dei universaliter ab aliis, sed quosdam de populo ab aliis.

AD PRIMUM ergo dicendum, quod baptismus sanguinis non habet efficaciam sacramentalem, sed solum meritoriam; et ideo ibi non confertur potestas spiritualis ad actiones hierarchicas, nec character sicut in baptismo fluminis, quod est sacramentum.

AD SECUNDUM dicendum, quod nec baptismus flaminis tantum, nec baptismus aquae tantum sufficit ad sacramentum novae legis; et ideo neuter eorum characterem imprimit.

TO THE THIRD QUESTION it should be said that just as in natural things there is an active power and a natural passive power, so also in spiritual things there is, as it were, a passive spiritual power by which a man is made receptive to spiritual actions. And this kind of spiritual power is conferred in baptism, for the non-baptized are not able to receive the effects of the other sacraments, and hence, accordingly, they are also not able to give them to others. And this is the first distinction, by which all the faithful people, to whom it belongs to take part in the sacraments, are together distinguished from others. There is another active spiritual power that is ordered to the administering of the sacraments, and the exercise of other sacred hierarchical actions; and this power is bestowed in confirmation and holy orders, as will be clear when we treat them in their own places. And since not all are agents in the ecclesiastical hierarchy (as, for instance, perfecting, purifying, and illuminating), as all are recipients of purification, illumination, and perfecting (as Dionysius says),[51] therefore these two characters do not distinguish the people of God universally from others, but certain members of the people from others.

REPLY OBJ. 1: Baptism of blood does not have sacramental efficacy, but only meritorious efficacy; and thus, there is no spiritual power conferred there for hierarchical actions, nor is there a character as in baptism of water, which is a sacrament.

REPLY OBJ. 2: Neither baptism of spirit alone nor baptism of water alone suffices for a sacrament of the New Law; and thus, neither of these imprints a character.

Response to Quaestiuncula 4

AD QUARTAM QUAESTIONEM dicendum, quod omnis effectus in creatura est communiter a tota Trinitate; unde et character non est tantum a Filio, sed a tribus personis. Attribuitur autem Filio tum propter rationem similitudinis ad proprium personae, quia ipse per proprietatem est imago et figura, sive character Patris; tum quia virtus passionis Christi operatur in sacramentis.

ET PER HOC patet solutio ad objecta.

TO THE FOURTH QUESTION it should be said that every effect in creation is commonly from the whole Trinity; hence the character, too, is not only from the Son, but from the three Persons. However, it is attributed to the Son on the one hand because of the account of likeness to what is proper to the Person, since he is image and figure by appropriation, or the character of the Father; on the other hand, because the virtue of Christ's Passion is working in the sacraments.

AND BY THIS the solution to the objections is clear.

---

51. Pseudo-Dionysius, *Ecclesiastical Hierarchy*, ch. 6, PG 3:530.

QUESTION 2

THE EFFECTS OF BAPTISM

Deinde quaeritur de effectu baptismi, qui est res et non sacramentum; et circa hoc quaeruntur tria:

primo, de effectu ipsius quantum ad remotionem mali;

secundo, de effectu ipsius quantum ad collationem boni;

tertio, utrum effectus ejus aequaliter participetur.

Next we will inquire as to the effect of baptism, which is the reality and not the sacrament; and concerning this, three questions arise:

first, its effect as to the removal of evil;

second, its effect as to the conferral of good;

third, whether its effect is equally partaken of by all.

ARTICLE 1

Baptism's effect as to the removal of evil

Quaestiuncula 1

AD PRIMUM SIC PROCEDITUR. Videtur quod baptismus non tollat actualem culpam. Baptismus enim non tollit actualem culpam nisi adsit contritio: quia nullus suae voluntatis arbiter constitutus in quo solum potest esse actualis culpa potest inchoare novam vitam, nisi poeniteat eum veteris vitae, ut in littera dicitur. Contritio autem per se etiam sine baptismo delet culpam actualem. Ergo baptismus nihil facit ad deletionem actualis culpae.

PRAETEREA, diversorum diversae sunt medicinae: quia non sanat oculum quod sanat calcaneum, ut dicit Hieronymus. Sed baptismus directe ordinatur ut medicina contra peccatum originale. Ergo non potest salvare ab actuali.

PRAETEREA, aliquis qui est in proposito peccandi, non potest consequi peccati remissionem. Sed contingit aliquem dum baptizatur, peccare venialiter, vel in proposito peccandi venialiter remanere; nec tamen propter hoc reputatur fictus. Ergo etiam in non fictis baptismus non tollit culpam actualem.

SED CONTRA est quod dicit Augustinus in *Enchiridion*: *baptizati non uni tantum peccato, sed multis magis aut omnibus moriuntur quaecumque jam propria com-*

OBJ. 1: To the first we proceed thus. It seems that baptism does not remove actual fault.[52] For baptism does not take away actual sin unless contrition is present: for no one who is constituted arbiter of his own will, which is the only place actual sin can be, can embark upon a new life unless he repents of his old life, as it says in the text. But contrition in and of itself, even without baptism, blots out actual fault. Therefore, baptism does nothing toward the effacement of actual fault.

OBJ. 2: Furthermore, there are different medicines for different things: since *what heals the heel does not heal the eye*, as Jerome says.[53] But baptism is directly ordained as a medicine against original sin. Therefore, it cannot heal from actual sin.

OBJ. 3: Furthermore, someone who plans to continue sinning cannot obtain the remission of sin. But it does happen that someone sins venially while being baptized, or deliberately remains in venial sin; but he is not considered insincere on that account. Therefore, baptism does not take away actual guilt even among those who are not insincere.

ON THE CONTRARY, Augustine says in the *Enchiridion*: *the baptized die not only to one sin, but to many more, or even to all, whatsoever they have now committed by their*

---

52. Parallels: *In II Sent.*, d. 32, q. 1, a. 1, arg. 1 and a. 2, ad 3; below, d. 12, q. 2, a. 2, qa. 1, ad 3; d. 14, q. 2, a. 1, qa. 2, ad 3; d. 17, q. 2, a. 2, qa. 6, ad 3; *ST* III, q. 69, a. 1; q. 79, a. 5, ad 1; *SCG* IV, chs. 69 & 72.

53. See Pseudo-Jerome, *Expositio Euangelii secundum Marcum*, ch. 9: *medicina cuiusque uulneris adhibenda est ei. Non sanat oculum quod calcaneo adhibetur* (CCSL 82:42).

miserunt vel cogitatione vel locutione vel opere. Sed haec sunt peccata actualia. Ergo baptismus tollit culpam actualem.

PRAETEREA, baptismus est ordinatus ad tollendum culpam originalem. Sed originale non potest tolli sine actuali, etiam ei qui utrumque habet: quia impium est a Deo dimidiam sperare veniam, ut infra dicetur, dist. 15. Ergo baptismus etiam tollit culpam actualem.

own acts, whether in thought or speech or deed.[54] But these things are actual sins. Therefore, baptism takes away actual fault.

FURTHERMORE, baptism is ordered to the removal of original fault. But original sin cannot be removed without actual sin, even for him who has both: for it would be impious to hope for half-forgiveness from God, as will be said below, in Distinction 15. Therefore, baptism takes away actual fault.

Quaestiuncula 2

ULTERIUS. Videtur quod non tollit omnem poenam temporalem debitam actuali peccato. Quia sicut Augustinus dicit, peccatum aut homo punit, aut Deus. Si ergo homo in seipso non puniat peccatum quod commisit a Deo punietur; et ita per baptismum actualis peccati poena non totaliter tollitur.

PRAETEREA, culpa non potest ordinari nisi per poenam. Sed Deus nil inordinatum relinquit. Ergo non dimittit quin pro culpa aliquam poenam infligat; et sic baptismus non absolvit ab omni poena.

PRAETEREA, Eucharistia est perfectius sacramentum quam baptismus, quia est speciale repraesentativum passionis Christi a qua est efficacia in sacramentis. Sed Eucharistia non absolvit etiam non indigne percipientes ab omni poena. Ergo multo minus baptismus.

SED CONTRA est quod dicit Ambrosius Rom. 11 super illud: *sine poenitentia enim sunt dona Dei. Gratia Dei* (inquit) *in baptismo non requirit gemitum vel planctum vel aliquod opus, sed omnia gratis condonat.*

PRAETEREA, Christus sua simplici morte scilicet poenae, duas mortes in nobis consumpsit ut dicitur in Glossa Rom. 6, scilicet culpae et poenae. Sed in baptismo configuratur homo morti Christi, ut ibidem dicit apostolus. Ergo absolvitur et a culpa et a poena.

OBJ. 1: Moreover, it seems that it does not take away all the temporal punishment due to actual sin.[55] For as Augustine says, either man punishes sin, or God does.[56] Therefore, if man did not punish a sin that he himself had committed, it would be punished by God; and in this way, the punishment for actual sin is not completely taken away by baptism.

OBJ. 2: Furthermore, guilt can only be ordered by punishment. But God leaves nothing disordered. Therefore, he does not forgive anything without inflicting a certain penalty for the fault; and thus baptism does not absolve from all punishment.

OBJ. 3: Furthermore, the Eucharist is a more perfect sacrament than baptism, for it is a special re-presentation of the Passion of Christ, from which the efficacy of the sacraments comes. But the Eucharist does not absolve from all punishment even those who are receiving not unworthily. Therefore, much less does baptism.

ON THE CONTRARY, Ambrose says on that verse of Romans: *for the gifts of God are without repentance* (Rom 11:29). He says, *the grace of God in baptism does not require groaning or weeping or any work, but it pardons all things freely.*[57]

FURTHERMORE, as is said in the Gloss on Romans 6:6, by suffering his single death as punishment, Christ consumed two deaths in us, namely, of fault and of punishment. But in baptism, man is configured to the death of Christ, as the Apostle says in the same place. Therefore, he is absolved from both fault and punishment.

---

54. Augustine, *Enchiridion on Faith, Hope, and Charity*, ch. 13, l. 39 (CCSL 46), where the text reads: "sed ideo etiam ipsi mori peccato plerumque dicuntur cum procul dubio non uni sed multis peccatis omnibus que moriantur quaecumque iam propria commiserunt uel cogitatione uel locutione uel opere."

55. Parallels: below, d. 14, q. 2, a. 1, qa. 2, ad 3; d. 18, q. 1, a. 3, qa. 2; *In III Sent.*, d. 19, a. 3, qa. 2 and exposition of the text; *ST* III, q. 49, a. 3, ad 2; q. 68, a. 5; q. 69, a. 2; q. 79, a. 5, ad 1; q. 86, a. 4, ad 3; *SCG* IV, chs. 59 & 72; *Super Rom.* 11, lec. 4.

56. See Augustine, *Exposition of Psalm 58* (CCSL 39), n. 13: "iniquitas omnis, parua magna ue sit, puniatur necesse est, aut ab ipso homine paenitente, aut a deo uindicante."

57. Ambrosiaster, *Commentarius in Pauli epistulam ad Romanos*, on 11:29 (CSEL 81.1:385), which reads: "verum est, quia gratia Dei in baptismate non quaerit gemitum aut planctum aut opus aliquod nisi solam ex corde confessionem." A variant is given in Gratian's *Decretals*, Part 2, On Penance, dist. 1, can. 87: "Gratia Dei in baptismate non requirit gemitum uel planctum, non opus aliquod, sed solam confessionem cordis, et omnia gratis condonat." Cf. *Decretals*, Part 3, On Consecration, dist. 4, can. 99.

Quaestiuncula 3

ULTERIUS. Videtur quod etiam tollat omnem poenam originalis peccati. Efficacius enim est donum Christi quam peccatum Adae, ut dicit apostolus, Rom. 5. Sed omnis poena peccati originalis est inducta per peccatum Adae. Ergo per donum Christi, quod maxime in baptismo operatur omnis poena tollitur.

PRAETEREA, baptismus directius ordinatur contra peccatum originale quam contra peccatum actuale. Sed tollit omnem poenam actualis peccati, ut Ambrosius dicit. Ergo et tollit omnem poenam originalis.

PRAETEREA, cessante causa cessat effectus. Sed causa poenae est culpa. Si ergo tollit culpam originalem, et per consequens aufert poenam.

PRAETEREA, nullus qui est debitor alicujus poenae, evolat statim. Sed baptizatus, si statim moriatur, evolat. Ergo non est debitor alicujus poenae; et sic baptismus absolvit ab omni poena etiam originalis.

SED CONTRA est quia in baptizatis etiam *caro concupiscit adversus spiritum*. Sed haec pugna est ex peccato originali consecuta. Ergo non tollitur omnis poena originalis peccati per baptismum.

PRAETEREA, necessitas moriendi, et incinerationis et poenalitates hujus vitae sunt poenae originalis peccati. Sed istae adhuc manent in baptizatis. Ergo baptismus non tollit omnem poenam originalis peccati.

OBJ. 1: Moreover, it seems that it also removes every punishment of original sin.[58] For the gift of Christ is more efficacious than the sin of Adam, as the Apostle says in Romans 5. But every punishment for original sin was incurred through the sin of Adam. Therefore, every punishment is taken away by the gift of Christ, which is most at work in baptism.

OBJ. 2: Furthermore, baptism is ordered more directly against original sin than against actual sin. But it takes away all the punishment due to actual sin, as Ambrose says.[59] Therefore, it also takes away all the punishment for original sin.

OBJ. 3: Furthermore, once a cause ceases, the effect ceases. But the cause of punishment is fault. If, therefore, it takes away original fault, it also removes the punishment as a result.

OBJ. 4: Furthermore, no one to whom a certain punishment is due flies free right away. But a baptized person who dies flies away at once into heaven. Therefore, to him no punishment is due; and thus, baptism absolves one also from all punishment for original sin.

ON THE CONTRARY, even among the baptized, *the flesh lusts against the spirit* (Gal 5:17). But this fight is the consequence of original sin. Therefore, not all punishment for original sin is removed by baptism.

FURTHERMORE, the necessity of dying, and of being reduced to dust, and the sufferings of this life, are all punishments for original sin. But these things still remain among the baptized. Therefore, baptism does not take away all punishment for original sin.

Response to Quaestiuncula 1

RESPONDEO dicendum ad primam quaestionem, quod in generatione qualibet per introductionem formae omnis contraria forma expellitur, et etiam dispositio ad formam contrariam, nisi quandoque relinquatur ex indispositione recipientis formam. Unde cum baptismus sit regeneratio in vitam spiritualem, omne quod est vitae spirituali contrarium, quod scilicet cum gratia stare non potest, quae est spiritualis vitae principium per baptismum tollitur; et ideo baptismus delet et originalem et actualem culpam mortalem, et quantum est de se etiam venialem, quae disponit ad privationem gratiae; quamvis quandoque culpa venialis remaneat post baptismum mortali remota propter indispositionem recipientis baptismum.

THE FIRST QUESTION I answer by saying that in the generation of anything, the introduction of a form drives out all contrary forms, and even the disposition to the contrary form—except sometimes when it remains from an indisposition of the thing receiving the form. Hence, since baptism is a regeneration unto spiritual life, everything that is contrary to spiritual life, i.e., that cannot coexist with grace which is the principle of spiritual life, is removed by baptism; and thus, baptism wipes away both original sin and actual mortal sin, and considered in itself even wipes away venial sin, which disposes to a privation of grace, although sometimes when mortal sin is removed, venial sin may remain after baptism because of an indisposition of the one receiving baptism.

---

58. Parallels: below, d. 46, q. 2, a. 2, qa. 1, ad 3; *In II Sent.*, d. 32, q. 1, a. 2; d. 44, q. 2, a. 2, ad 2 & 3; *ST* I-II, q. 85, a. 5, ad 2; q. 87, a. 7, ad 1; q. 109, a. 9; *ST* II-II, q. 104, a. 6, ad 1; *ST* III, q. 49, a. 3, ad 3; q. 52, a. 5, ad 2; q. 69, a. 3 and a. 7, ad 3; *SCG* IV, ch. 55; *De malo*, q. 4, a. 6, ad 4; *Quodl.* VI, q. 9, a. 1.
59. In the reference just above.

AD PRIMUM ergo dicendum, quod baptismus non requirit contritionem quasi continuam[60] ad destructionem peccati actualis quasi de se ad hoc non sufficiat, sed solum ad removendam fictionem quae est contraria dispositio impediens effectum baptismi.

AD SECUNDUM dicendum, quod baptismus non ordinatur tantum contra culpam originalem alias circumcisis in primitiva ecclesia non fuisset necessarius baptismus, sed ordinatur ad destruendum omnem culpam quam inveniat, et ad regenerandum in novam vitam destructa omni vetustate; et ideo est sicut totum potentiale habens completam potentiam ad destruendum totaliter peccatum. Sed poenitentia participat aliquid de potentia, quasi pars potentialis ordinata contra alia peccata, scilicet actualia; quia baptismus iterari non potest.

AD TERTIUM dicendum, quod quantum est de se, baptismus, ut dictum est, tollit omnem culpam originalem et actualem non solum mortalem, sed venialem; quae quamvis non contrarietur gratiae simpliciter, contrariatur tamen gratiae baptismali, quae debet esse perfecta ratione novitatis vitae. Sed potest impediri effectus ejus ex parte recipientis, si sit indispositus per fictionem. Sed cum fictio sit peccatum, sicut peccatum mortale est peccatum simpliciter, ita facit fictum simpliciter, et totaliter effectum baptismi impedit quantum ad remissionem culpae. Sed peccatum veniale quod in actu vel in proposito est, facit fictum secundum quid, et est secundum quid peccatum, ut dispositio ad peccatum; et ideo impedit effectum baptismi non simpliciter, sed quantum ad remissionem illius venialis.

REPLY OBJ. 1: For the destruction of actual sin, baptism does not require contrition as a co-cause as though it were not sufficient for this by itself, but it requires contrition only to avoid its being received insincerely, which is a contrary disposition impeding baptism's effect.

REPLY OBJ. 2: Baptism is not ordained against original sin alone, otherwise in the early church it would not have been necessary for those who had already been circumcised. Rather, it is ordered toward destroying all sin that it finds and to regenerating someone into a new life, once all the oldness of sin has been destroyed. And therefore it is like a potential whole, having complete potency for destroying sin entirely. But repentance shares in something of this potency, as a potential part ordered against other sins, namely, actual sin; for baptism cannot be received more than once.

REPLY OBJ. 3: Baptism, of itself, as has been said, removes all sin, original and actual, and not only mortal but also venial. For venial sin, although not opposed to grace simply speaking, is nevertheless opposed to baptismal grace, which should be perfect by reason of the newness of life. But baptism's effect can be impeded on the part of the one receiving it, if he is indisposed because of insincerity. But since pretending is a sin, just as mortal sin is sin simply speaking, it thus makes it false, simply speaking, and completely impedes the effect of baptism for the remission of fault. But a venial sin, whether actual or in the intention, makes it false in a certain respect, and is a sin in a certain respect, as a disposition to sin; and thus, it impedes baptism's effect not simply, but only regarding the remission of that venial sin.

Response to Quaestiuncula 2

AD SECUNDAM QUAESTIONEM dicendum, quod Christus per mortem suam sufficienter satisfecit pro peccatis totius humani generis, etiam si essent multo plura. Et quia homo per baptismum in mortem Christi baptizatur, et ei commoritur et consepelitur, ut dicitur Roman. 6, ideo baptismus, quantum in se est, totam efficaciam passionis in baptizatum influit; et propter hoc absolvit non solum a culpa, sed a poena satisfactoria.

AD PRIMUM ergo dicendum, quod per baptismum homo incorporatur Christo, et efficitur membrum ejus; et ideo poena quam Christus sustinuit, reputatur isti in satisfactionem: quia si patitur unum membrum, omnia alia compatiuntur, ut dicitur 1 Corinth. 12. Et ideo Deus in Christo peccata illa punivit, sicut dicitur Isai. 53: *posuit in eo iniquitatem omnium nostrum.*

TO THE SECOND QUESTION, it should be said that by his own death Christ sufficiently satisfied for the sins of the entire human race—even if there had been many more of them. And since by baptism man is baptized into the death of Christ, and dies and is buried together with him, as it says in Romans 6, for this reason baptism, considered in itself, imparts the whole efficacy of the Passion to the baptized; and because of this it absolves not only from fault, but from the punishment for satisfaction.

REPLY OBJ. 1: By baptism man is incorporated into Christ and made his member; thus, the punishment that Christ underwent is reputed as satisfaction for him, for if one member suffers, all the others suffer with it, as is said in 1 Corinthians 12:26. And thus, God in Christ punished those sins, as is said: *the Lord has laid on him the iniquity of us all* (Isa 53:6).

---

60. *continuam.—concausam* PLE.

Ad secundum dicendum, quod poena ordinat culpam dupliciter. Uno modo ut satisfaciens; et sic culpa remanet ordinata per satisfactionem Christi. Alio modo ut medicina sanans, vel resecans membrum sanabile, et sic culpa in baptizatis ordinatur ut sanata per gratiam oppositam.

Ad tertium dicendum, quod quamvis Eucharistia sit memoriale passionis Christi, non ordinatur tamen ad hoc quod per ipsam homo regeneretur in membrum Christi crucifixi, sed ut jam regeneratus ei adhaereat, et in ipso perficiatur; et ideo non est similis ratio de baptismo et Eucharistia.

Reply Obj. 2: Punishment orders fault in two ways. In one way, as satisfying for it; and in this way the fault remains ordered by Christ's satisfaction. In another way, as a medicine curing or checking the curable member; and in this way, fault in the baptized is ordered as cured by the opposing grace.

Reply Obj. 3: Although the Eucharist is a memorial of the Passion of Christ, nevertheless it is not for the sake of a man being regenerated by it as a member of Christ crucified, but that someone already regenerated may cleave to him and be perfected in him; and thus baptism and the Eucharist do not have the same account.

Response to Quaestiuncula 3

Ad tertiam quaestionem dicendum, quod in peccato originali talis fuit processus quod persona corrupit naturam, et natura personam corrupit; unde aliquid consideratur in hoc peccato quod pertinet ad naturam, aliquid quod pertinet ad personam. Passio autem Christi sufficienter peccatum originale abstulit quantum ad utrumque. Sed quia sacramenta personis adhibentur, ideo baptismus hoc ab homine tollit quod ex corruptione naturae in personam redundabat; et propter hoc ipsam infectionem culpae, prout afficit personam, et poenam illam quae actum personae privabat, scilicet carentiam visionis divinae, baptismus aufert; sed non aufert actu infectionem prout afficit naturam: quod patet ex hoc quod baptizatus per actum naturae originale transmittit in prolem, similiter nec poenas quae consequuntur principia naturae destitutae gratia innocentiae primi status, cujusmodi sunt rebellio carnis ad spiritum, mors, et hujusmodi poenalitates, quae consequuntur ex hoc ipso quod homo ex contrariis compositus est et quantum ad corpus et quantum ad animam quodammodo, scilicet quantum ad appetitum sensus et intellectus. Sed per gratiam baptismalem efficitur ut hae poenae remanentes non dominentur in personam, sed magis ei subjiciantur, et in utilitatem ipsius cedant, inquantum sunt materia virtutis, et occasio humilitatis et exercitii.

Ad primum ergo dicendum, quod passio Christi sufficienter aufert et illud quod est personae, et illud quod est naturae per causam. Sed quia omnes homines in natura communicant, ideo effectus secundum legem communem curationis naturae non erit nisi in fine mundi; quando omnibus electis jam congregatis, simul cum eis etiam alia creatura insensibilis liberabitur a servitute corruptionis, ut dicitur Rom. 8.

Ad secundum dicendum, quod ea quae ad peccatum actuale pertinent, sunt tantum personae, quia ac-

To the third question, it should be said that in original sin the progression was such that a person corrupted the nature, and the nature corrupts the person. Hence, one thing is considered in this sin that pertains to the nature, and another that pertains to the person. Now, Christ's Passion sufficiently took away original sin as to both. But since the sacrament is applied to persons, for this reason baptism takes away from man whatever redounded into the person from the corruption of the nature; and because of this, baptism removes the very infection of fault insofar as it affects the person, and that punishment which the person's act incurred, namely, the loss of the divine vision; but it does not actually remove the infection as it affects the nature, which is clear by the fact that a baptized person transmits original sin to his offspring by the act of nature. Likewise, neither does it remove the punishments that follow upon the principles of nature when stripped of the grace of the first state of innocence, of which sort are the rebellion of the flesh against the spirit, death, and other penalties like that, which follow from the fact that man is composed of contraries both as regards his body and, in a certain way, as regards his soul, namely, in the sensual appetite and the intellect. But by baptismal grace it is brought about that these remaining punishments do not dominate in the person but rather are subjected to him, and they fall to his benefit, inasmuch as they are the matter of virtue, and the occasion of humility and discipline.

Reply Obj. 1: The Passion of Christ, in the manner of a cause, sufficiently removes both that evil which is of the person and that which is of the nature. But since all men share in nature, the effect, according to the shared law of the healing of nature, will not be until the end of the world, when, with all the elect already gathered, together with them the rest of insensible creation will also be freed from its servitude to corruption, as it says in Romans 8:21.

Reply Obj. 2: Those things that pertain to actual sin belong only to the person, since actions are of individuals,

tus individuorum sunt, secundum Philosophum; et ideo non est simile de poena actualis et originalis.

Ad tertium dicendum, quod tollitur culpa originalis per baptismum inquantum est infectiva personae, non autem inquantum est infectiva naturae per actum generationis; et ideo poenae quae ad corruptionem naturae pertinent, etiam non tolluntur.

Ad quartum dicendum, quod baptizatus statim evolat, quia nulla poena debetur sibi ratione personae, sed ratione naturae humanae, quae post mortem non manet secundum hunc statum, in quo sibi poena debetur.

according to the Philosopher;[61] and so it is not the same with the punishment for original sin as for actual sin.

Reply Obj. 3: Original fault is removed by baptism insofar as it infects the person, but not insofar as it infects the nature through the act of generation; and so the punishment that pertains to the corruption of nature is also not taken away.

Reply Obj. 4: A baptized person flies away immediately to heaven because punishment is due to him not by reason of his person but only by reason of human nature, which, after death, does not remain in that state in which punishment is due to it.

---

61. Aristotle, *Metaphysics*, Bk. 1, ch. 1, 981a17.

ARTICLE 2

Baptism's effect as to the conferral of good

Quaestiuncula 1

AD SECUNDUM SIC PROCEDITUR. Videtur quod per baptismum non conferantur pueris gratia et virtutes. Dicit enim Augustinus in libro *de baptismo parvulorum*: *parvulos fideles facit non fides ea quae consistit in credentium voluntate, sed fidei sacramentum.* Sed fides quae est virtus, consistit in credentium voluntate, ut in 3 libro, dist. 23, quaest. 2, art. 3, quaestiunc. 1, dictum est. Ergo parvuli baptizati non habent virtutem fidei, et pari ratione nec alias virtutes, quae etiam in voluntate consistunt.

PRAETEREA, si aliquid de novo recipiatur in aliquo, oportet quod recipiens vel influens alio modo se habeat nunc quam prius. Sed anima pueri baptizati non alio modo se habet dum baptizatur quam prius: quia proprium motum non habet, carens liberi arbitrii usu; nec Deus, qui est influens gratiam et virtutes. Ergo pueri in baptismo gratiam et virtutes non recipiunt.

PRAETEREA, Damascenus dicit, quod substantia nullo modo est sine propria operatione. Sed constat quod in puero non sunt operationes virtutum, quia non habet electionem, ut dicitur in 3 Ethic., quae in opere virtutis requiritur. Ergo non habet virtutes.

PRAETEREA, virtutes, cum sint habitus, habilitant ad actum. Sed pueri non sunt habiles ad agendum quae secundum virtutem sunt. Ergo non recipiunt virtutes in baptismo.

SED CONTRA, Augustinus dicit, quod fides datur et nutritur in baptismo: datur quantum ad parvulos, nutritur quantum ad adultos. Sed fides est virtus. Ergo virtutes dantur parvulis in baptismo, et eadem ratione aliae virtutes.

PRAETEREA, nullus admittitur ad gloriam nisi habeat vestem nuptialem, quae est caritas. Sed pueri baptizati, si moriantur, statim evolant. Ergo habent caritatem, quae est magistra virtutum, et per consequens alias virtutes.

OBJ. 1: To the second we proceed thus. It seems that by baptism, grace and virtues are not conferred on children.[62] For Augustine says in his book *On the Baptism of Infants*: *The faith that exists in the will of believers does not make infants members of the faithful, but rather the sacrament of faith does.*[63] But the faith that is a virtue exists in the will of believers, as was said in Book III, Distinction 23, Question 2, Article 3, Subquestion 1. Therefore, baptized infants do not have the virtue of faith, and by the same argument neither do they have other virtues that also exist in the will.

OBJ. 2: Furthermore, if anything is newly received into something, either the recipient or the one infusing must be different than before. But the soul of a baptized child does not carry itself differently after he is baptized than before, for he has no proper motion, lacking the use of free will; nor does God, who is the one infusing grace and virtues. Therefore, children do not receive grace and virtues in baptism.

OBJ. 3: Furthermore, Damascene says that no substance is without its proper operation.[64] But it is evident that in a child there are no operations of virtue, for it does not have choice, as is clear in *Ethics* 3,[65] and this is required for the work of virtue. Therefore, it does not have virtues.

OBJ. 4: Furthermore, virtues, since they are habits, enable certain acts. But children are not capable of doing the things that are according to virtue. Therefore, they do not receive virtues in baptism.

ON THE CONTRARY, Augustine says that faith is given and nourished in baptism: it is given to infants, and it is nourished in adults.[66] But faith is a virtue. Therefore, virtues are given to infants in baptism, and by the same argument, other virtues as well.

FURTHERMORE, no one is admitted to glory unless he has the nuptial garment, which is charity. But baptized children, if they die, go immediately to heaven. Therefore, they have charity, which is the instructress of virtue, and as a result, the other virtues.

---

62. Parallels: *ST* II-II, q. 47, a. 14, ad 3; *ST* III, q. 69, a. 6.

63. See Augustine, *Epistle 98, to Boniface*, n. 10: "Itaque parvulum etsi nondum fides illa, quae in credentium voluntate consistit, iam tamen ipsius fidei sacramentum fidelem facit" (CSEL 34.2:531).

64. John Damascene, *On the Orthodox Faith*, Bk. 2, ch. 23 (PG 94:950).

65. Aristotle, *Nichomachean Ethics*, Bk. 3, ch. 3, 1111b8.

66. Moos offers no citation, and the text as given here does not appear in Augustine's works. Thomas cites this text only in this one place.

Quaestiuncula 2

ULTERIUS. Videtur quod in adultis virtutes per baptismum non augeantur. Augmentum enim virtutum est per meritum: quia secundum Augustinum, caritas meretur augeri, ut aucta mereatur et perfici. Sed in baptismo non operatur meritum baptizati quantum ad opus operatum. Ergo ex opere operato virtutes in baptismo non augentur.

PRAETEREA, cibus corporalis in eo qui jam pervenit ad quantitatem determinatam, non facit augmentum. Sed potest esse quod aliquis ante baptismum perveniat ad quantitatem gratiae baptismalis quam puer recipit, in quo nullum est impedimentum. Ergo baptismus nihil supra gratiam adjiciet.

SED CONTRA, super illud Psal. 22: *super aquam refectionis educavit me*, dicit Glossa: *per augmentum virtutis et bonae operationis educavit in baptismo*. Ergo baptismus auget virtutes habentibus.

OBJ. 1: Moreover, it seems that in adults, virtues are not increased by baptism.[67] For the increase of virtues happens by merit, since, according to Augustine, charity merits an increase so that once increased, it may merit also to be perfected.[68] But in baptism, no merit of the baptized works for the work being performed. Therefore, by this work being performed, the virtues are not increased in baptism.

OBJ. 2: Furthermore, in the one who has already reached his determinate quantity, physical food does not cause growth. But it can be that someone before baptism reaches the quantity of baptismal grace that a child receives, in whom there is no impediment. Therefore, baptism adds nothing above grace.

ON THE CONTRARY, commenting on the Psalm: *he has led me beside waters of refreshment* (Ps 23 [22]:2), the Gloss says: *he has led me by the increase of virtue and good works in baptism*.[69] Therefore, baptism increases the virtues in those who have them.

Quaestiuncula 3

ULTERIUS. Videtur quod baptismi effectus non sit illuminatio. Quia illuminatio ad doctrinam pertinet. Sed doctrina fidei est per catechismum, qui praecedit baptismum. Ergo non est effectus baptismi.

PRAETEREA, illuminatio contra ignorantiam ordinatur. Sed secundum quosdam baptismus non ordinatur contra ignorantiam, sed magis ordo. Ergo illuminatio non est effectus baptismi, sed magis ordinis.

SED CONTRA est quod Damascenus, ponit inter effectus baptismi illuminationem, ut patet ex ejus definitione in praecedenti dist. inducta.

OBJ. 1: Moreover, it seems that the effect of baptism is not illumination.[70] For illumination relates to teaching. But the teaching of the faith happens through catechising, which precedes baptism. Therefore, it is not the effect of baptism.

OBJ. 2: Furthermore, illumination is ordered against ignorance. But according to some, baptism is not directed against ignorance, but rather holy orders is. Therefore, illumination is not an effect of baptism, but rather of holy orders.

ON THE CONTRARY, Damascene[71] includes illumination among the effects of baptism, as is clear from his definition cited in the previous distinction.

Quaestiuncula 4

ULTERIUS. Videtur quod fecundatio non sit effectus baptismi. Non enim idem est quo aliquis active generat, et passive generatur. Sed baptismus est regeneratio passiva baptizati. Cum ergo fecunditas importet generationem activam, videtur quod non pertineat ad baptismum.

OBJ. 1: Moreover, it seems that making one fruitful is not an effect of baptism.[72] For that by which one actively generates and that by which one is passively generated are not the same. But baptism is the passive regeneration of the baptized. Therefore, since fruitfulness implies active generation, it seems that it does not pertain to baptism.

---

67. Parallels: above, d. 3, q. 1, a. 1, qa. 3; below, d. 9, a. 1, qa. 2; d. 18, q. 1, a. 3, qa. 1; *ST* III, q. 69, a. 4.

68. See Augustine, *Epistle 186*, ch. 3, n. 10: "ipsa gratia meretur augeri, ut aucta mereatur et perfici" (CSEL 57:53).

69. See Lombard, *Commentarium in Psalmos*, Ps. 22:2 (PL 191:242).

70. Parallels: above, d. 3, q. 1, a. 1, qa. 4 and ad 3; a. 3, qa. 1; d. 5, q. 2, a. 1, qa. 2; d. 8, q. 1, a. 1, qa. 1, ad 1; *ST* III, q. 69, a. 5.

71. John Damascene, *On the Orthodox Faith*, Bk. 4, ch. 9 (PG 94:1122).

72. See the preceding qa. 3.

PRAETEREA, fecunditas est proprietas consequens aliquid quantum ad perfectum statum sui: quia, ut dicitur in 4 *Meteor.*, perfectum unumquodque est, quando potest alterum generare. Sed baptismus non ordinatur ad perficiendum, sicut Eucharistia et confirmatio, secundum Dionysium, sed magis ad illuminandum et purgandum. Ergo baptismus non habet fecunditatem pro effectu.

SED CONTRA est quod dicit Glossa super illud Psal. 22: *super aquam refectionis: anima peccatorum ariditate sterilis fecundatur per baptismum.*

OBJ. 2: Furthermore, fruitfulness is a property that results from something attaining its own perfect state, for, as is said in *Meteorology* 4,[73] a thing is perfect when it can generate another. But according to Dionysius,[74] baptism is not ordered toward perfecting, like the Eucharist and confirmation, but rather toward illuminating and purifying. Therefore, baptism does not have fruitfulness as one of its effects.

ON THE CONTRARY, the Gloss says on that phrase of the Psalm: *on the water of refreshment* (Ps 23 [22]:2): *the souls of sinners, barren with drought, are made fruitful through baptism.*[75]

Quaestiuncula 5

ULTERIUS. Videtur quod incorporari Christo non sit effectus baptismi. Aliquis enim incorporatur Christo et membris ejus per fidem formatam, ut in 3 Lib., dist. 23, dixit Magister. Sed aliquis habet fidem formatam etiam ante baptismum. Ergo incorporatio non est effectus baptismi.

PRAETEREA, incorporatio est effectus Eucharistiae. Sed ad eumdem effectum non ordinantur diversa sacramenta. Ergo non est effectus baptismi.

SED CONTRA est quod Augustinus dicit ad Bonifacium quod in baptismo aliquis membrum Christi efficitur. Sed hoc est Christo incorporari. Ergo incorporatio est effectus baptismi.

OBJ. 1: Moreover, it seems that being incorporated into Christ is not an effect of baptism.[76] For someone is incorporated into Christ and his members by formed faith, as the Master said in Book III, Distinction 23. But even before baptism, someone might have formed faith. Therefore, incorporation is not an effect of baptism.

OBJ. 2: Furthermore, incorporation is an effect of the Eucharist. But different sacraments are not ordained to the same effect. Therefore, this is not an effect of baptism.

ON THE CONTRARY, Augustine says to Boniface, that in baptism one is made a member of Christ.[77] But this is to be incorporated into Christ. Therefore, incorporation is an effect of baptism.

Quaestiuncula 6

ULTERIUS. Videtur quod apertio januae non sit effectus baptismi. Quidam enim ante passionem Christi baptizati sunt. Sed tunc eis janua non est aperta: quia si aliquis eorum tunc decessit, regnum non introivit. Ergo baptismus non aperit januam regni caelestis.

PRAETEREA, baptismus repraesentat passionem Christi, non resurrectionem, ut videtur. Sed in resurrectione est aperta janua, ut patet per collectam quae dicitur in die resurrectionis: *Deus qui in hodierna die per unigenitum tuum aeternitatis nobis aditum devicta morte reserasti.* Ergo non debet iste effectus baptismo attribui.

OBJ. 1: Moreover, it seems that the opening of the door of heaven is not an effect of baptism.[78] For before Christ's Passion, some people were baptized. But the door was not open to them at that time, for if some of them then died, they did not enter the kingdom. Therefore, baptism does not open the door of the kingdom of heaven.

OBJ. 2: Furthermore, baptism represents Christ's Passion, not his resurrection, as it seems. But in the resurrection the door is opened, as is clear from the Collect that is said on Easter: *O God, who, on this day, through Thine Only-begotten, hast, by having conquered death, unsealed to us the entrance to eternity.* Therefore, this effect should not be attributed to baptism.

73. Aristotle, *Meteorology*, Bk. 4, ch. 3, 380a14–16; cf. *On the Soul*, Bk. 2, ch. 4, 415a26–30.
74. Pseudo-Dionysius, *Ecclesiastical Hierarchy*, ch. 5, p. 1, n. 3 (PG 3:503).
75. See Lombard, *Commentarium in Psalmos*, Ps. 22:3 (PL 191:242).
76. See the preceding qa. 3.
77. See Augustine, *Epistle 98*, n. 1: "hoc est baptismi salutaris esse uirtutem in sancta compage corporis christi" (CSEL 34.2:520).
78. Parallels: *In III Sent.*, d. 18, a. 6, qa. 3, ad 2; *ST* III, q. 39, a. 5; q. 69, a. 7; *SCG* IV, ch. 69.

SED CONTRA est auctoritas Bedae supra inducta, dist. 1, quod in hoc differebat circumcisio a baptismo quod aditum regni caelestis non aperiebat.

ON THE CONTRARY, is the authority of Bede cited above, Distinction 1, that circumcision differed from baptism in the fact that it did not open the entrance to the heavenly kingdom.

Response to Quaestiuncula 1

RESPONDEO dicendum ad primam quaestionem, quod circa hoc est multiplex opinio. Quidam enim dixerunt, quod pueris in baptismo nullo modo virtutes dantur, sed solum a peccato originali mundantur; sed postea quando decedunt, vel quando ad perfectam aetatem veniunt, eis virtutes conferuntur, si innocentiam servent. Sed haec opinio non potest stare: quia lignum cum praecisum fuerit, ubi ceciderit, ibi stabit, Eccle. 11; et ideo si pueris ante mortem non fuissent collatae virtutes, et gratia operans et cooperans, nec in morte eis conferrentur, et sic non salvarentur; quod falsum est. Videtur autem haec opinio venisse ex hoc quod virtutes actus tantum esse credebant; quod falsum est, ut in 2 libro, dist. 27, quaest. 1, art. 1, dictum est.

Et ideo alii dicunt, quod pueris in baptismo dantur gratia et virtutes non in seipsis, sed in radice sua, scilicet gratia quae est radix virtutum, sicut essentia animae potentiarum; sed postea quando solvuntur potentiae, perfectis organis, effluunt virtutes in ipsa ab ipsa essentia animae. Sed hoc pro tanto esse non potest, quia tunc si puer in furiam verteretur antequam ad perfectam aetatem veniret, nunquam in ipso potentiae solverentur, et ita nunquam virtutes explicite haberet: et praeterea quod potentiae sint ligatae aliquo impedimento, non impedit habitum, sed actum: quia dormientes et vinolenti habitus habent, sed ligatos.

Et ideo alii dicunt, et melius, quod pueris in baptismo dantur gratia et virtutes; sed habitus illi ligati sunt propter pueritiam, sicut in dormiente propter somnum: sed pueritia discedente inclinant ad bene operandum, nisi aliquis Spiritui Sancto resistat.

AD PRIMUM ergo dicendum, quod Augustinus loquitur de fide et voluntate actuali, quae in pueris esse non potest.

AD SECUNDUM dicendum, quod quamvis agens principale sit immobile, tamen agens instrumentale non eodem modo se habet nunc et prius ad puerum: quia nunc adhibetur sibi baptismus, non autem prius. Tamen etiam sine aliqua mutabilitate sui Deus alicui puero posset gratiam conferre, etiam sine adhibitione sacramenti, si ab aeterno disposuisset se ei daturum, sicut patet de sanctificatis in utero.

TO THE FIRST QUESTION, I answer that there are several opinions about this. For certain people have said that no virtues at all are given to infants in baptism, but they are only cleansed from original sin; but afterward, when they die or when they arrive at adulthood, virtues are conferred on them, if they have preserved their innocence. But this opinion cannot stand: for *wood, when it has been cut, will stay where it falls* (Eccl 11:3). And therefore if virtues, as well as operating and cooperating grace, were not conferred on children before they died, neither will they be conferred on them in death, and then they would not be saved, which is false. However, this opinion seems to have come from believing virtues to be only their acts, which is false, as was said in Book II, Distinction 27, Question 1, Article 1.

And thus, others say that grace and virtues are given to children in baptism, not in themselves, but in their root, namely, grace, which is the root of all the virtues, just as the essence of the soul is the root of the powers of the soul. But afterward, when the powers are released, once the organs are completed, the virtues flow out into those powers from the very essence of the soul. But this cannot be so for many reasons, since then if the child should go mad before reaching adulthood, the powers would never be released in him, and then he would never have the virtues explicitly; and furthermore, because if the powers were bound by some impediment, it would impede the act, not the habit, for people who are sleeping and drunk have habits, but those habits are hampered.

And thus, others say, and better, that grace and virtues are given to children in baptism, but those habits are hampered by their childhood, just as they are hampered by sleep in someone sleeping. But once childhood has ended, they incline the person toward acting well, except for someone who resists the Holy Spirit.

REPLY OBJ. 1: Augustine speaks of actual faith and will, which cannot be in infants.

REPLY OBJ. 2: Although the principal agent is unchangeable, nevertheless, the instrumental agent is not ordered to the child in the same way now as before; for now baptism is applied to him, but before it was not. Even without any mutability, however, God could confer grace on any child, even without the administration of a sacrament, if from eternity he had been disposed to give it to him, as is seen among those sanctified in the womb.

AD TERTIUM dicendum, quod duplex est actus virtutum. Unus primus, qui est perficere animam et potentias ejus; et hunc actum etiam pueri habent. Alius est secundus, qui est operari cum electione; et hunc actum non semper habent: quia earum operationes sunt voluntariae, et voluntas non habet necesse semper agere, etiam in adultis.

AD QUARTUM dicendum, quod habitus facit habilem ad actum tollendo inhabilitatem quae est ex imperfectione potentiae, non autem tollit inhabilitatem quae est ex parte corporis, sicut patet in dormientibus.

REPLY OBJ. 3: The actuality of virtues is twofold. One is first actuality, which is to perfect the soul and its powers, and this actuality even children have. The other is second actuality, which is to operate with choice; and they do not always have this actuality, for their operations are voluntary, and the will need not always be acting, even among adults.

REPLY OBJ. 4: A habit makes one capable of acting by taking away the incapacity that comes from the imperfection of the power; but it does not take away any incapacity on the part of the body, as is clear from the case of sleepers.

Response to Quaestiuncula 2

AD SECUNDAM QUAESTIONEM dicendum, quod per easdem causas virtus generatur et augetur, ut dicit Philosophus in 2 *Ethic.*; et ideo, quia baptismi est conferre virtutem et gratiam non habentibus, oportet quod in habentibus augeat.

AD PRIMUM ergo dicendum, quod in baptismo quamvis non operetur meritum baptizati, operatur ibi tamen meritum Christi, quod est efficacius.

AD SECUNDUM dicendum, quod gratia non habet aliquem determinatum terminum ad quem pertingat, vel ultra quem procedere non possit, sicut est de quantitate animalis; et ideo non est simile.

TO THE SECOND QUESTION, I answer that a virtue is generated and increased by the same causes, as the Philosopher says in *Ethics* 2;[79] and thus, since it belongs to baptism to confer virtue and grace on those who do not have them, it must also increase them in those who do have them.

REPLY OBJ. 1: Although in baptism the merit of the baptized is not at work, nevertheless the merit of Christ is at work there, which is more efficacious.

REPLY OBJ. 2: Grace does not have any determinate limit to which it extends, or beyond which it cannot continue, such as constrains the quantity of an animal; therefore, there is no parallel.

Response to Quaestiuncula 3

AD TERTIAM QUAESTIONEM dicendum quod lumen est quo dirigimur in visionem alicujus rei. Baptismus autem dirigit in visionem spiritualem exteriorem et interiorem. Interiorem quidem inquantum baptismus dicitur sacramentum fidei, quae oculum mentis idoneum facit ad visionem divinorum; exteriorem vero, quia baptizatis conceditur inspicere sacram Eucharistiam, et non aliis, ut Dionysius dicit; et ideo tam Damascenus quam Dionysius baptismo vim illuminativam attribuunt.

AD PRIMUM ergo dicendum quod fides principaliter est ex infusione; et quantum ad hoc per baptismum datur; sed quantum ad determinationem suam est ex auditu; et sic homo ad fidem per catechismum instruitur.

AD SECUNDUM dicendum, quod scientia plus dicit quam illuminatio. Importat enim comprehensionem eorum ad quorum visionem illuminatio dirigebat; et ideo scientia ad perfectionem pertinet; unde Dionysius doctos perfectos nominat, et doctores perfectores: et sic contra ignorantiam ordo datur, ut scilicet ordinati sint docti, et etiam doctores aliorum.

TO THE THIRD QUESTION, it must be said that light is that by which we are led to the vision of a certain thing. Now, baptism leads to external and interior spiritual vision: interior, inasmuch as baptism is called the sacrament of faith, which makes the eye of the mind suited to seeing divine things; and external, because it is granted to the baptized and not to others to gaze upon the sacred Eucharist, as Dionysius says;[80] and thus both Damascene and Dionysius attribute illuminative force to baptism.

REPLY OBJ. 1: Faith comes chiefly from infusion, and in this regard is given by baptism; but as to its determination, it comes from hearing; and thus man is prepared for faith by catechism.

REPLY OBJ. 2: 'Science' says more than 'illumination'. For it implies comprehension of those things toward which illumination directed one's vision; and therefore science pertains to perfection. Hence Dionysius calls the learned 'perfected', and teachers 'perfecters': and in this way holy orders is established against ignorance, so that those ordained may be learned, and also the teachers of others.

---

79. Aristotle, *Nicomachean Ethics*, Bk. 2, ch. 1, 1103b7.
80. Pseudo-Dionysius, *Ecclesiastical Hierarchy*, ch. 3, n. 7 (PG 3:436).

Response to Quaestiuncula 4

AD QUARTAM QUAESTIONEM dicendum, quod fecunditas dicitur dupliciter. Uno modo respectu fructus producendi in ipso qui dicitur fecundari, sicut operationes virtutum quidam fructus boni dicuntur; et hoc modo fecundatur anima in baptismo, cum in eo dentur virtutes non habentibus, et augeantur habentibus. Alio modo respectu fructus producendi in altero, sicut cum aliquis per doctrinam et solicitudinem pastoralem in plebe Dei fructum facit; et hoc modo fecundatio non pertinet ad baptismum, sed magis ad sacramentum ordinis.

AD PRIMUM ergo dicendum, quod ex eodem ex quo aliquid habet generationem in natura aliqua, habet quod faciat operationes illius naturae; et ideo cum per baptismum homo regeneretur in vitam spiritualem, per ipsum homo efficitur active fecundus, et quasi genitor spiritualium operum.

AD SECUNDUM dicendum quod ratio illa procedit de secunda fecundatione.

TO THE FOURTH QUESTION, it should be answered that fruitfulness is said in two ways. In one way, with respect to the fruit produced in whatever is said to be made fruitful, as operations of the virtues are called certain fruits of good; and in this way the soul is made fruitful in baptism, since in it the virtues are given to those who do not have them and are increased in those who do have them. In another way, fruitfulness is said with respect to the fruit produced in another, as when someone brings about fruit in the people of God by teaching and pastoral care; and in this way fruitfulness does not pertain to baptism but more to the sacrament of Orders.

REPLY OBJ. 1: That by which something has generation in a certain nature is that by which it performs the operations of that nature. And thus, since by baptism man is regenerated unto spiritual life, by it man is also made actively fruitful, and, as it were, a generator of spiritual works.

REPLY OBJ. 2: That argument deals with the second kind of making fruitful.

Response to Quaestiuncula 5

AD QUINTAM QUAESTIONEM dicendum, quod incorporari Christo contingit dupliciter, scilicet merito et numero. Merito quidem potest aliquis de ecclesia effici (quod est Christo incorporari) etiam ante baptismum actu susceptum, sed non ante baptismi propositum vel ipsum baptismum post tempus gratiae revelatae; sed numero non potest aliquis effici de ecclesia nisi per baptismum; unde aliquis ante baptismum non admittitur ad perceptionem Eucharistiae et aliorum sacramentorum ecclesiae, ut prius dictum est.

AD PRIMUM ergo dicendum, quod objectio illa procedit de prima incorporatione.

AD SECUNDUM dicendum, quod perceptio Eucharistiae praesupponit incorporationem absolute: quia capitis virtus non communicatur membro nisi jam unito. Sed per Eucharistiam est perfecta influentia a capite in membro; et quantum ad hanc perfectionem incorporatio est effectus Eucharistiae.

TO THE FIFTH QUESTION, it should be answered that to be incorporated into Christ happens in two ways, namely, by merit, and in number. For by merit someone can indeed be made part of the Church (which is to be incorporated into Christ) even before actually receiving baptism, although after the time of revealed grace this does not happen before a person plans to be baptized or is baptized. But someone cannot be made a member of the Church in number except by baptism; hence no one is admitted to the reception of the Eucharist and the other sacraments before he has been baptized, as was said before.

REPLY OBJ. 1: That objection deals with the first kind of incorporation.

REPLY OBJ. 2: The reception of the Eucharist absolutely presupposes incorporation into Christ: for the powers of the head are not shared with a member unless it is already united to it. But by the Eucharist the influence of the head over the member is perfected; and with respect to this perfection, incorporation is an effect of the Eucharist.

Response to Quaestiuncula 6

AD SEXTAM QUAESTIONEM dicendum, quod aperiri januam regni caelestis nihil aliud est quam amovere impedimentum quo aditus in regnum caeleste toti naturae humanae prohibebatur. Hoc ergo impedimentum

TO THE SIXTH QUESTION, it should be said that for the gate of the heavenly kingdom to be opened is nothing other than to remove the impediment by which the entrance to the heavenly kingdom was blocked for the whole of hu-

absolute quantum ad omnes remotum fuit sufficienter per passionem Christi; sed illa remotio efficienter fit quo ad istum, secundum quod particeps fit passionis Christi jam factae per baptismum; et sic baptismus quasi causa instrumentalis aperit januam regni caelestis quo ad istum, sed passio ut causa satisfactoria quo ad omnes.

AD PRIMUM ergo dicendum, quod haec ratio erat, quia passio Christi, in cujus virtute baptismus agit, nondum facta erat, nec per eam aditus regni caelestis apertus; unde ratio probat quod baptismus non habeat hanc virtutem quasi causa principalis.

AD SECUNDUM dicendum, quod aditus regni caelestis aperitur tripliciter. Uno modo quantum ad gloriam animae; et sic in passione apertus est; unde dictum est latroni, Luc. 23, 43: *hodie mecum eris in paradiso.* Alio modo quantum ad gloriam corporis; et sic apertus est in resurrectione. Alio modo quantum ad locum gloriae congruentem; et sic apertus est in ascensione. Et his tribus modis baptismus instrumentaliter aperit quo ad istum: agit enim virtute et passionis et resurrectionis et ascensionis, inquantum homo configuratur Christo passo per immersionem, qua quodammodo Christo consepelitur, et ei resurgenti quantum ad nitorem qui resultat ex aqua, et ascendenti quantum ad elevationem baptizati de sacro fonte. Unde baptismus passioni appropriatur: quia etiam gloria animae principalior est, et causa quodammodo aliorum; et in hujus signum baptizato Domino caeli aperti sunt super eum; Matth. 3.

man nature. This impediment, therefore, was absolutely removed for all men sufficiently by the Passion of Christ; but that removal happens effectively in any particular person according as he is now made a participant of Christ's Passion by baptism; and so baptism, in the manner of an instrumental cause, opens the gate of the heavenly kingdom with respect to that particular person, but the Passion does so as a satisfactory cause with respect to all.

REPLY OBJ. 1: The reason for this was that Christ's Passion, by the power of which baptism acts, had not yet happened; nor had the entrance to heaven been opened by it. Hence, this argument proves that baptism would not have this power as a principal cause.

REPLY OBJ. 2: The entrance to heaven is opened in three ways. In one way, as to the glory of the soul; and in this way it was opened by the Passion. Hence it was said to the good thief: *today you will be with me in paradise* (Luke 23:43). In a second way, as to the glory of the body; and in this way it was opened by the resurrection. In a third way, as to the place suited to that glory; and in this way it was opened by the ascension. And in these three ways, baptism instrumentally opens the entrance with respect to an individual, for it acts by the power of the Passion, the resurrection, and the ascension, inasmuch as man is configured to the suffering Christ by immersion, in which he is in a way buried with Christ; and to the risen Christ as to the shimmering that comes from the water; and to the ascending Christ as to the elevation of the baptized from the sacred font. Hence baptism is appropriated to the Passion, for the glory of the soul is more important and, in a way, the cause of the other things; and as a sign of this, when the Lord was baptized the heavens were opened above him (Matt 3:16).

ARTICLE 3

Whether baptism's effect is equally partaken of by all[81]

Quaestiuncula 1

AD TERTIUM SIC PROCEDITUR. Videtur quod baptismus non aequalem effectum habeat in omnes quantum ad remotionem mali. In adultis enim removet peccatum actuale et originale; sed in pueris originale tantum. Ergo plus efficit in adultis quam in pueris quantum ad mali remotionem.

PRAETEREA, mitigatio fomitis est effectus baptismi. Sed post baptismum in quibusdam invenitur fomes magis mitigatus quam in aliis. Ergo in eis efficacius baptismus se habuit in remotione mali.

SED CONTRA, baptismus habet efficaciam ad removendum malum, secundum quod habet quamdam similitudinem mortis. Sed morientium unus non magis moritur quam alius. Ergo et baptismus aequaliter in omnibus mala aufert.

OBJ. 1: To the third we proceed thus. It seems that baptism does not have an equal effect on all as to the removal of evil. For in adults it removes actual and original sin; but in children, only original sin. Therefore, it effects more in adults than in children as to the removal of evil.

OBJ. 2: Furthermore, the mitigation of the kindling for sin is an effect of baptism. But after baptism this kindling is found to be more mitigated in certain people than in others. Therefore, baptism is more efficacious in them for removing evil.

ON THE CONTRARY, baptism has efficacy for removing evil according as it has a certain likeness of death. But among the dying, no one dies more than another. Therefore, baptism takes away evils equally for all.

Quaestiuncula 2

ULTERIUS. Videtur quod etiam aequalis gratia omnibus in baptismo conferatur, qui non ficte accedunt. In baptismo enim operatur passio Christi, quae habet quodammodo efficaciam infinitam. Sed finitum infinito additum nihil majus efficit. Cum ergo devotio accedentis qua unus alium excedit, sit quoddam bonum finitum, videtur quod devotio vel aliquid hujusmodi, efficere non possit quin omnes in baptismo aequalem gratiam consequantur.

PRAETEREA, ad baptismi effectum capiendum non requiritur alia concausa, sed solum ut impedimentum removeatur. Sed nullus recipit gratiam in baptismo nisi ab eo sit impedimentum remotum. Ergo omnes recipiunt gratiam aequalem.

SED CONTRA, Damascenus dicit, quod peccatorum remissio cunctis aequaliter in baptismo datur, gratia autem Spiritus Sancti secundum proportionem fidei, et secundum[83] purgationem. Sed non omnes cum aequali fide nec aequaliter praeparati ad baptismum accedunt. Ergo non omnes aequaliter gratiam consequuntur.

OBJ. 1: Moreover, it seems that in baptism equal grace, too, is conferred on all who do not receive it insincerely. For in baptism Christ's Passion is at work, which has, in a way, infinite efficacy. But something finite added to the infinite does not make anything greater. Therefore, since the devotion of the one approaching baptism, which is greater in one person than in another, is a certain finite good, it seems that neither devotion nor anything else of the sort could make it so that all did not obtain an equal grace in baptism.

OBJ. 2: Furthermore, a cooperating cause is not required for obtaining the effect of baptism, but only for the removal of any impediment. But no one receives grace in baptism unless impediments be removed from him. Therefore, all receive equal grace.

ON THE CONTRARY, Damascene says[82] that the remission of sins is given equally to all in baptism, but the grace of the Holy Spirit is given proportionate to one's faith and through purification. But all do not receive baptism with equal faith, nor equally prepared. Therefore, all do not obtain equal grace.

---

81. Parallel: *ST* III, q. 69, a. 8.
82. John Damascene, *On the Orthodox Faith*, Bk. 4, ch. 9 (PG 94:1122).
83. *secundum.—per* PLE.

Quaestiuncula 3

Ulterius. Videtur quod nec etiam pueri in baptismo consequantur aequalem gratiam. Quia in angelis secundum quantitatem naturalium gratia infundebatur. Sed unus puerorum habet meliora naturalia quam alius. Ergo et majorem gratiam in baptismo recipit.

Praeterea, quidam in baptismo recipiunt gratiam finalem, qui innocentiam baptismalem usque ad finem servant, quidam autem non. Ergo etiam de pueris aliqui aliis majorem gratiam consequuntur.

Sed contra, gratia baptismalis in pueritia non opponitur nisi peccato originali. Sed unus puer non habet plus de peccato originali quam alius. Ergo nec majorem gratiam baptismalem recipit unus alio.

Obj. 1: Moreover, it seems that neither do infants obtain equal grace in baptism. For among the angels, grace was infused according to the quantity of natural endowments. But one child has better natural endowments than another. Therefore, he also receives greater grace in baptism.

Obj. 2: Furthermore, some people, who preserve their baptismal innocence until the end, receive final grace in baptism, but others do not.[84] Therefore among infants, too, some obtain greater grace than others.

On the contrary, baptismal grace in infancy is not opposed to anything but original sin. But one child does not have more original sin than another. Therefore, neither does one receive greater grace than another.

Response to Quaestiuncula 1

Respondeo dicendum, ad primam quaestionem, quod baptismus universaliter aufert in eo qui non ficte accedit, culpam personam inficientem, quam invenit, ut dictum est, et sic accedit ad terminum. Ea autem quae in termino sunt, intensionem non recipiunt; et ideo quantum ad remotionem culpae, aequalem effectum habet in omnibus baptismus; et similiter est de poena personali, quae respondet culpae originali prout est inficiens personam, scilicet carentia divinae visionis. Sed contra aliam poenam ex principiis naturae corruptae consequentem, sicut est concupiscentia vel fomes, remedium adhibetur in baptismo, ut non dominentur per gratiam in baptismo collatam; et ideo simile est de poena illa et de gratia.

Ad primum ergo dicendum, quod hoc non est de efficacia baptismi quod non tot peccata destruit in uno quot in alio:[86] in quolibet enim destruit omnia quae invenit.

Ad secundum dicendum, quod illa objectio procedit de secunda poena, quae habet reprimi per baptismum ex parte gratiae collatae.

To the first question, I answer that baptism, in anyone who does not receive it insincerely, universally removes any guilt infecting the person that it finds, as has been said, and in this way it attains an extreme.[85] Now things that are in the extreme cannot receive extension, and therefore as to the removal of guilt, baptism has an equal effect in all; and it is the same with the personal punishment, which corresponds to original sin as it infects the person, namely, the loss of the divine vision. But against any other punishment following upon the principles of corrupted nature, such as concupiscence or the kindling for sin, a remedy is applied in baptism, so that through the grace conferred in baptism they may not dominate. And so it is the same with that punishment as with grace.

Reply Obj. 1: It is not from baptism's efficacy that it does not destroy as many sins in one person as in another, but it is because it did not find as many in one person as in another; for in anyone it destroys all the sins that it finds.

Reply Obj. 2: That objection concerns the second kind of punishment, which can be curbed by baptism through the grace conferred.

Response to Quaestiuncula 2

Ad secundam quaestionem dicendum, quod actus activorum recipiuntur in passivis secundum suam dispositionem; et ideo quamvis baptismus (ut et passio Christi, quae in eo operatur) quantum est de se, aequalem respectum ad omnes habeat; quia tamen quidam ad

To the second question, it should be said that the acts of active things are received in a passive thing according to its own disposition; and so, although baptism in itself (as also Christ's Passion, which is at work in it) is related equally to all, nevertheless, since some people approach

---

84. "Final grace" is what we would call today the grace of perseverance.

85. Parallels: below, d. 6, q. 1, a. 2, qa. 3, ad 2; d. 23, q. 2, a. 2, qa. 3, ad 2; d. 25, q. 2, a. 1, ad 2; d. 34, a. 4, ad 1; *ST* I-II, q. 113, a. 3, ad 1; *ST* III, q. 68, a. 12; *De veritate*, q. 28, a. 3, ad 2.

86. *alio.—alio, sed quia non tot invenit in uno quot in alio*; PLE.

baptismum cum majori praeparatione fidei et devotionis accedunt quam alii, ideo quidam aliis majorem gratiam consequuntur. Nullus enim gratiam in termino recipit, ut intendi non possit per baptismum.

AD PRIMUM ergo dicendum, quod devotio baptizati non additur quasi concausa, ut efficienter agat ad gratiae receptionem; sed additur quasi dispositio materialis; et ideo secundum diversitatem ipsius participatur baptismi effectus.

AD SECUNDUM dicendum, quod quando adultus baptizatur, non solum requiritur ad percipiendum baptismi effectum removens prohibens, scilicet fictionem, sed etiam requiritur dispositio quasi materialis, scilicet devotio et fides recipientis baptismum; et secundum quod magis vel minus invenitur dispositus, effectum baptismi diversimode consequitur.

baptism with a greater preparation of faith and devotion than others, for this reason some people obtain greater grace. For no one receives a maximum grace such that it could not be extended by baptism.

REPLY OBJ. 1: The devotion of the baptized is not added in the manner of a cooperating cause, such that it would act efficiently for the reception of grace; but it is added in the manner of a material disposition. And therefore the effect of baptism is participated in according to this diversity.

REPLY OBJ. 2: When an adult is baptized, in order to receive baptism's effect not only is it required that whatever prevents it be removed, such as insincerity, but also necessary is a kind of material disposition, which is the devotion and faith of the one receiving baptism. And, according as he is found more or less disposed, he receives the effect of baptism differently.

Response to Quaestiuncula 3

AD TERTIAM QUAESTIONEM dicendum, quod in pueris baptizatis nihil ex parte eorum requiritur, sed habent quasi pro dispositione ad salutem fidem ecclesiae, et pro effectivo salutis virtutem passionis Christi, quae operatur in baptismo; et haec duo aequaliter ad pueros se habent; et ideo non differunt quantum ad effectum baptismi suscipiendum, sed omnes aequalem gratiam suscipiunt.

AD PRIMUM ergo dicendum, quod non est simile de pueris et de angelis: quia angeli differunt specie, secundum multorum opinionem, pueri autem non; unde non est tanta differentia naturalium in pueris sicut in angelis. Vel dicendum, quod in angelis secundum proportionem gradus naturalium erat etiam proportio conatus qui ex parte eorum requirebatur, et ideo accipiebant gratiam secundum proportionem naturalium; in pueris autem non requiritur aliquis actus ex parte eorum; et ideo non est simile.

AD SECUNDUM dicendum, quod gratia accepta in pueris, non facit eis necessitatem ad bonum, sed inclinationem tantum; et ideo postquam ad perfectam aetatem pervenerint, possunt diversimode gratia recepta uti; et inde est quod quidam proficiunt et perseverant, quidam vero deficiunt; non ex diversa quantitate gratiae in baptismo perceptae.

TO THE THIRD QUESTION, it should be said that for the baptism of infants, nothing is required on their part; but for a disposition to salvation, they have, as it were, the faith of the Church, and for the bringing about of salvation, the power of Christ's Passion, which is at work in baptism. And these two things are equally related to infants, and thus they do not differ in receiving the effect of baptism, but all receive equal grace.

REPLY OBJ. 1: It is not the same with infants as with angels, for the angels differ in species, according to the opinion of many, but infants do not; hence there is not such a great difference in natural endowments among infants as among angels. Or it could be said that among the angels the proportion of exertion that was required on their part was also in proportion to the level of their natural endowments, and therefore they received grace according to the proportion of their natural endowments; but among infants no act is required on their part, so it is not the same.

REPLY OBJ. 2: Grace received by infants does not bring about in them a necessary bond to the good, but only an inclination; and thus, after they have attained a mature age, they can use the grace received in many different ways; and this is why some people advance and persevere, but others fall away—not because of receiving different amounts of grace in baptism.

QUESTION 3

Deinde quaeritur de recipientibus baptismum; et circa hoc quaeruntur tria:

primo, de pueris, et aliis usu rationis carentibus, quos constat sacramentum et rem sacramenti percipere;

secundo, de fictis qui recipiunt sacramentum, et non rem sacramenti;

tertio, de baptizatis baptismo flaminis et sanguinis, qui non recipiunt sacramentum, sed rem sacramenti.

Then inquiry is made about those receiving baptism; and about this, three questions arise:

first, about infants and others lacking the use of reason, who everyone agrees do receive the sacrament and the reality of the sacrament;

second, about the insincere, who receive the sacrament and not the reality of the sacrament;

third, about those baptized with the baptism of the spirit and of blood, who do not receive the sacrament but do receive the reality of the sacrament.

ARTICLE 1

About infants and others lacking the use of reason, who everyone agrees do receive the sacrament and the reality of the sacrament

Quaestiuncula 1

AD PRIMUM SIC PROCEDITUR. Videtur quod pueri sacramentum suscipere non possint. Marc. ult., 16: *qui crediderit et baptizatus fuerit, salvus erit*; ex quo patet quod credere praesupponitur ad baptismum. Sed pueri non possunt credere, quia non possunt aliquid cum assertione cogitare. Ergo pueri non possunt suscipere sacramentum baptismi.

PRAETEREA, in baptismo fit quaedam obligatio hominis ad ea quae sunt fidei Christianae servanda. Sed obligatio non potest fieri nisi ab eo qui est suae voluntatis arbiter constitutus. Ergo pueri sacramentum baptismi suscipere non possunt.

PRAETEREA, per baptismum, ut dicit Dionysius, fit aliquis particeps communionis divinorum. Sed pueris non competit sacra communicare. Ergo non competit eis sacramentum baptismi.

SED CONTRA est quod Dionysius dicit, quod *divini nostri duces*, scilicet apostoli, *probaverunt infantes recipi*

OBJ. 1: To the first we proceed thus. It seems that infants cannot receive the sacrament.[87] For it says at the end of Mark (16:16): *whoever believes and is baptized, will be saved*; from which it is evident that believing is presupposed for baptism. But children cannot believe, for they are not able to think about anything with assent. Therefore, infants cannot receive the sacrament of baptism.

OBJ. 2: Furthermore, in baptism there comes to be a certain obligation in a man to those things that are to be kept in the Christian faith. But an obligation cannot arise except in someone who is established as arbiter of his own will. Therefore, infants cannot receive the sacrament of baptism.

OBJ. 3: Furthermore, by baptism, as Dionysius says,[88] one becomes a participant in the sharing of divine things. But it is not fitting to share sacred things with infants. Therefore, the sacrament of baptism is not fitting for them.

ON THE CONTRARY, Dionysius says: *our divine leaders*, that is, the Apostles, *certified that infants were to be*

---

87. Parallels: below, d. 9, a. 5, qa. 4, ad 2; d. 18, q. 1, a. 3, qa. 1; *ST* I-II, q. 113, a. 3, ad 1; *ST* III, q. 68, a. 9; *De malo*, q. 4, a. 1; *Quodl.* IV, q. 7, a. 1 and q. 12, a. 1.

88. Pseudo-Dionysius, *Ecclesiastical Hierarchy*, ch. 2 (PG 3:391).

ad baptismum. Ergo pueri possunt sacramentum baptismi recipere.

PRAETEREA, baptismus circumcisioni successit. Sed circumcisio pueris conferebatur. Ergo et baptismus pueris debet dari.

received unto baptism.[89] Therefore, infants can receive the sacrament of baptism.

FURTHERMORE, baptism replaces circumcision. But circumcision was conferred on infants. Therefore, baptism should also be conferred on infants.

Quaestiuncula 2

ULTERIUS. Videtur quod melius sit baptismum differri quam statim in pueritia dare, nisi necessitas mortis emergat. Quia omnis Christi actio, nostra est instructio. Sed Christus baptismum accipere voluit in tricesimo anno vitae suae, ut dicitur Luc. 3. Ergo et similiter apud nos debet usque ad tempus perfectae aetatis differri.

PRAETEREA, medicina efficax debet sumi quando maxime potest juvare. Sed baptismus maxime juvaret in fine vitae, vel saltem in perfecta aetate; quia per ipsum omnia delicta adolescentiae et juventutis solverentur. Ergo usque tunc deberet differri.

PRAETEREA, magis afficitur homo ad ea quae ex seipso acquirit quam ad ea quae ab alio accipit; unde et illi qui ex propria acquisitione divitias habent, non sunt ita liberales sicut qui ab aliis acceperunt, ut dicit Philosophus in 4 *Ethic*. Sed pueri qui baptizantur, quasi ab aliis baptismum suscipiunt; adulti autem ex seipsis ad baptismum accedunt. Ergo magis afficerentur ad fidem Christianam, quae in baptismo suscipitur, si baptizarentur adulti, quam si baptizarentur infantes.

SED CONTRA, medicina debet quam citius morbo apponi. Sed baptismus est medicina contra originale peccatum, quod etiam in pueris est. Ergo debet eis baptismus dari statim.

PRAETEREA, melius est impedire malum ne fiat, quam jam factum destruere. Sed per baptismum debilitatur fomes, ne dominetur in nobis, et in peccatum actuale ne nos praecipitet; et sic in pueritia susceptus futura peccata impedit. Ergo melius est tunc dari baptismum quam postea ad destruendum peccata praeterita.

OBJ. 1: Moreover, it seems that it would be better if baptism were deferred, rather than being given right away in infancy, unless a necessity of imminent death arose.[90] For every action of Christ is for our instruction. But Christ willed to receive baptism in the thirtieth year of his life, as is said in Luke 3:23. Therefore, among us it should likewise be deferred until adulthood.

OBJ. 2: Furthermore, effective medicine should be taken when it will help most. But baptism would help most at the end of one's life, or at least in adulthood; for then it would wash away all the crimes of adolescence and youth. Therefore, it should be deferred until then.

OBJ. 3: Furthermore, a man is more affected by what he acquires for himself than by what he receives from another; hence, too, those who have wealth of their own acquiring are not as spendthrift as those who have received it from others, as the Philosopher says in *Ethics* 4.[91] But infants who are baptized receive baptism in a certain way from others, whereas adults approach baptism of themselves. Therefore, they are more affected by the Christian faith that they receive in baptism if they were baptized as adults than if they were baptized as infants.

ON THE CONTRARY, medicine should be applied to a disease as quickly as possible. But baptism is a medicine against original sin, which is even in infants. Therefore, it should be given to them right away.

FURTHERMORE, it is better to impede evil lest it occur, than to destroy it when it has already occurred. But by baptism the kindling of sin is weakened, so that it does not dominate in us, and it will not fling us into actual sin; and in this way, being baptized impedes future sins. Therefore, it is better for baptism to be given at that time than afterward to destroy past sins.

Quaestiuncula 3

ULTERIUS. Videtur quod adultis usu rationis carentibus baptisma dari non debet. In adultis enim non solum per baptismum originale, sed etiam actualia peccata solvuntur. Sed contra actuale peccatum quod quis ex seipso commisit, requiritur proprius motus liberi arbi-

OBJ. 1: Moreover, it seems that baptism should not be given to adults lacking the use of reason. For in adults, not only is original sin washed away through baptism, but also actual sins as well. But against actual sin that someone has committed himself, the proper movement of free will is

---

89. Pseudo-Dionysius, *Ecclesiastical Hierarchy*, ch. 7, n. 11 (PG 3:566).
90. Parallels: below, d. 6, q. 2, a. 1, qa. 2, ad 1; d. 17, q. 3, a. 1, qa. 4; *ST* III, q. 39, a. 3, ad 1; q. 68, a. 3.
91. Aristotle, *Nicomachean Ethics*, Bk. 4, ch. 2, 1120b10ff.

trii. Ergo his adultis qui usum liberi arbitrii non habent, baptismus dari non debet.

PRAETEREA, nulli contradicenti sacramentum exhiberi oportet. Sed quandoque amentes et furiosi contradicunt. Ergo eis baptismus dari non debet.

PRAETEREA, dormientes secundum Philosophum, vivunt vita plantae. Sed baptismus non datur nisi viventi vita humana, quae est secundum animam rationalem. Ergo dormienti baptismus dari non oportet.

SED CONTRA est quod Augustinus dicit 4 Confess., de amico suo, qui cum desperaretur, baptizatus est nesciens; et tamen in ipso baptismus efficaciam habuit: quod patet ex hoc quod postea perversae suasioni contradixit. Ergo etiam carentibus usu rationis baptismus dari potest.

PRAETEREA, pueri, qui nunquam habuerunt usum rationis, baptizantur. Ergo multo amplius illi qui aliquando habuerunt, quamvis nunc non habeant.

required [as a condition for baptism]. Therefore, to these adults who do not have the use of free will, baptism should not be given.

OBJ. 2: Furthermore, a sacrament should not be administered to anyone speaking against it. But sometimes the mentally disabled and insane speak against it. Therefore, baptism should not be given to them.

OBJ. 3: Furthermore, according to the Philosopher, sleepers live the life of plants.[92] But baptism is given only to those living a human life, which is according to the rational soul. Therefore, baptism should not be given to someone sleeping.

ON THE CONTRARY, Augustine says in Confessions 4,[93] about his friend, who, since he was despaired of, was baptized without knowing it; and nevertheless the baptism had efficacy in him, which was evident by the fact that afterward he spoke out against Augustine's perverse persuasion. Therefore, baptism can also be given to those lacking the use of reason.

FURTHERMORE, infants who never had the use of reason are baptized. Therefore, much more should those be baptized who had it at one time, although they no longer have it.

Response to Quaestiuncula 1

RESPONDEO dicendum, ad primam quaestionem, quod diversi status mundi comparantur diversis aetatibus unius hominis, sicut Augustinus dicit in Lib. 83 Quaestionum. Unde sicut nullus status mundi fuit in quo esset humano generi praeclusa via salutis, ita nulla aetas hominis unius est in qua sibi via salutis praecludatur. Unde cum in pueris sit peccatum originale, per quod a consecutione aeternae salutis impediuntur, oportet quod eis adhiberi possit aliquod remedium ad removendum praedictum impedimentum. Hoc autem est baptismus. Unde divinae misericordiae contradicit qui negat baptismum parvulis posse exhiberi; et propter hoc haereticum est hoc dicere.

AD PRIMUM ergo dicendum, quod pueri quamvis non habeant actum fidei, habent tamen habitum, quem in baptismo suscipiunt, sicut et habitus aliarum virtutum. Sed si verbum Domini intelligatur de actu fidei, tunc referendum est ad illos tantum qui per doctrinam apostolorum imbuendi erant, de quibus praedixerat: praedicate Evangelium omni creaturae; nulli enim eorum quibus Evangelium praedicandum erat, baptismus dari debebat, nisi crederet.

TO THE FIRST QUESTION, I answer that different states of the world are compared to the different ages of one man, as Augustine says in the Eighty-Three Questions.[94] Hence as there was no state of the world in which the path of salvation was closed off to the human race, so too there is no state of a man in which the path of salvation is closed off to him. Hence, since there is original sin in infants, by which they are prevented from obtaining eternal salvation, it is necessary that some remedy be applied to them to remove this impediment. But this is baptism. Hence, whoever denies that baptism can be administered to infants speaks against divine mercy; and thus to say this is heresy.

REPLY OBJ. 1: Although infants do not have the act of faith, nevertheless, they have the habit that they receive in baptism, just as they also have the habit of other virtues. But if the word of the Lord were understood about the act of faith, then it is to be referred to those only who were to be instructed by the teaching of the Apostles, of whom it is said, preach the Gospel to all creation (Mark 16:15); for none of those to whom the Gospel was preached should have been baptized unless he believed.

---

92. Aristotle, On the Generation of Animals, Bk. 5, ch. 1, 779a1–3.
93. Augustine, Confessions (CCSL 27), Bk. 4, ch. 4.
94. Augustine, de Diuersis quaestionibus octoginta tribus (CCSL 44A), qu. 58: "sunt enim aetates sex etiam in uno homine: infantia, pueritia, adolescentia, iuuentus, grauitas et senectus."

AD SECUNDUM dicendum, quod obligatio in baptismo non fit ad aliquid ad quod non omnis homo teneatur.

AD TERTIUM dicendum, quod sicut ille qui ascribitur ad militiam non oportet quod statim in pugnam vadat, sed quando opportunitas imminet; ita nec ille qui in baptismo ascribitur ad divinas actiones, oportet quod statim ad eas admittatur, sed quando tempus opportunum fuerit.

REPLY OBJ. 2: The obligation in baptism does not arise with regard to anything to which not every man is bound.

REPLY OBJ. 3: Just as it is not fitting to send a man into battle immediately after he has been conscripted into military service, but rather when the time is right; so neither is it fitting that someone who is conscripted to divine actions in baptism should be admitted to them immediately, but rather when the right time has come.

Response to Quaestiuncula 2

AD SECUNDAM QUAESTIONEM dicendum, quod magis laudabile est quod pueri quam citius poterint baptizentur commode, non expectata perfecta aetate, propter tres rationes. Primo, quia propter imbecillitatem naturae de facili mori possunt et damnari; unde ut damnationis periculum evitetur, debent baptismo praeveniri. Secundo propter infestationes daemonum, qui non habent tantam potestatem in pueris baptizatis ab originali mundatis, quantum in illis qui adhuc originale habent, neque quantum ad nocumenta spiritualia, neque quantum ad nocumenta corporalia. Tertio, quia in pueritia facilius homo ad aliqua inducitur, et firmius inhaeret, secundum quod Philosophus dicit in 2 *Ethic.*, cap. 1: *non parum differt ex juvene confestim assuefieri, sed multum; magis autem omne*; et hanc causam assignat Dionysius in fine *Eccles. Hierarc.* dicens: *tradit autem puerum sacris symbolis*, idest sacramentalibus signis, *summus sacerdos, ut cum eis conversetur, et neque formetur in vitam alteram, nisi divina contemplantem semper.*

AD PRIMUM ergo dicendum, quod Christus suscepit baptismum quasi ipsum instituens vel consecrans. Hoc autem ad doctoris vel sacerdotis officium pertinet, nuntiare viam salutis; et ideo ante tempus perfectae aetatis, quod competit esse in doctore vel sacerdote, baptizari non debuit. Nec est simile de aliis qui baptismum suscipiunt, ut ab eo juventur.

AD SECUNDUM dicendum, quod in baptismo confertur gratia ad bene vivendum, et peccata tolluntur praeterita, et impediuntur futura; et ideo quamvis baptismus in fine vitae susceptus plura peccata praeterita tolleret, tamen pauciora impediret, et ad pauciora bona promoveret; et ideo minus esset utilis. Praeterea multis casibus subjacet humana vita, et posset contingere ut qui baptismum in fine accipere expectaret, morte subita praeventus expectatione sua fraudaretur.

TO THE SECOND QUESTION, it should be said that it is more praiseworthy that infants be baptized as soon as conveniently possible, not waiting for a mature age, for three reasons. First, because, on account of the weakness of nature, they can easily die and be damned; hence, in order to avoid the danger of damnation, baptism should come to them beforehand. Second, on account of the attacks of demons, who do not have as much power, whether for spiritual harm or for bodily harm, among baptized children cleansed of original sin as they do among those who still have it. Third, because in infancy a man can be more easily led to something and it will stick with him more firmly, as the Philosopher says in *Ethics* 2, Chapter 1: *to have been accustomed to something immediately from youth makes no small difference, but a great one; or rather, all the difference*;[95] and Dionysius gives this reason at the end of the *Ecclesiastical Hierarchy*, where he says: *however the high priest hands the child to the sacred symbols*, that is, sacramental signs, *so that he may be familiar with them, and may not form any other life than the one that always contemplates divine things.*[96]

REPLY OBJ. 1: Christ received baptism as the one instituting it and consecrating it. To announce the way of salvation, however, pertains to the office of teacher or priest; and thus, he could not be baptized before the age of maturity that befits a teacher or priest. Nor is it the same with others who receive baptism so that they might be helped by it.

REPLY OBJ. 2: In baptism grace is conferred for living well and past sins are taken away, while future ones are impeded; and so, although baptism received at the end of life would take away more past sins, nevertheless it would impede fewer sins and would advance fewer goods; and thus it would be less beneficial. Furthermore, human life is exposed to many chances, and it could happen that someone who looked forward to receiving baptism in the end was thwarted in his expectation by a sudden death.

---

95. Aristotle, *Nicomachean Ethics*, Bk. 2, ch. 1, 1103b23–25.
96. Pseudo-Dionysius, *Ecclesiastical Hierarchy*, ch. 7, n. 11 (PG 3:567).

AD TERTIUM dicendum, quod gratia baptismalis non est per acquisitionem hominis, sed dono Dei. Praeterea status paupertatis ante divitias acquisitas non inclinat affectum ut homo paupertatem sequatur, sed magis ut paupertatem fugiat; status autem peccati ante gratiam vel virtutem relinquit propter assuetudinem inclinationem in anima ut facilius in peccatum labatur; et ideo non est simile de acquisitione pecuniae, et gratiae vel virtutis.

REPLY OBJ. 3: Baptismal grace is not through man's acquisition but by the gift of God. Furthermore, a state of poverty before the acquisition of riches does not incline the affections so that a man pursues poverty, but rather so that he flees it, whereas the state of sin before grace or virtue, because of habituation, leaves behind an inclination in the soul so that it more easily slips into sin; and thus, it is not the same with the acquisition of money as with grace and virtue.

Response to Quaestiuncula 3

AD TERTIAM QUAESTIONEM dicendum, quod de amentibus distinguendum est. Quidam enim sunt qui ex nativitate amentes fuerunt, et nunquam habent aliqua lucida intervalla; et de talibus videtur esse idem judicium quod de pueris. Quidam autem amentiam incurrerunt ex infirmitate vel aliquo hujusmodi, et habent aliqua lucida intervalla; et de istis dicendum est, quod si antequam amentiam incurrerunt, vel dum habent lucida intervalla, fuerunt in proposito baptismum suscipiendi, si necessitas sit, possunt baptizari, et baptismi sacramentum suscipiunt, et rem sacramenti, etiam si tunc actu dissentiant quando baptizantur in amentia existentes. Si autem ante amentiam contradixerint, non recipiunt sacramentum neque rem sacramenti.

AD PRIMUM ergo dicendum, quod sicut in adulto qui habet usum rationis, disponit ad gratiam baptismalem suscipiendam motus liberi arbitrii quem habet dum baptizatur; ita in amente motus liberi arbitrii quem habebat dum sanae mentis erat.

AD SECUNDUM dicendum, quod effectus baptismi in mente suscipitur, nec impeditur nisi ex contradictione mentis. Illi autem qui mentis usum non habent, non contradicunt mente, sed magis phantasia ducti; et ideo talis contradictio effectum baptismi non impedit, quando mentis consensus praecessit.

AD TERTIUM dicendum, quod dormientes baptizandi non sunt, nisi periculum mortis immineat; et tunc similiter distinguendum est de dormientibus sicut de illis qui amentiam incurrunt post statum sanae mentis.

TO THE THIRD QUESTION, it should be said that a distinction must be made about the mentally disabled. For some have been mentally disabled from birth, and never have any lucid intervals; and for these, the same judgment holds as for infants. But some have incurred mental disability from an illness or something of the sort, and they do have certain lucid intervals; and for these people it should be said that if before they incurred mental disability, or during lucid intervals, they had planned to receive baptism, then they can be baptized if there be necessity, and they can receive the sacrament of baptism as well as the reality of the sacrament, even if, at the moment they are baptized, the mental disability has returned and they actually dissent. However, if they spoke against baptism before the mental disability, they do not receive either the sacrament or the reality of the sacrament.

REPLY OBJ. 1: Just as in an adult who has the use of reason, the movement of free will, which he has while he is baptized, disposes him to receive baptismal grace, so also does the movement of free will in a mentally disabled person, which he had when he was of sound mind.

REPLY OBJ. 2: The effect of baptism is received in the mind, nor is it impeded except by the mind's contradiction. However, those who do not have the use of their mind do not mentally contradict, but rather are led by imagination. And thus, a contradiction of this kind does not impede the effect of baptism, when the mind's consent has gone before.

REPLY OBJ. 3: People are not to be baptized while sleeping, unless they are in danger of death; and then the same distinctions would be made about sleepers as about those who became mentally disabled after a state of sound mind.

ARTICLE 2

About the insincere, who receive the sacrament and not the reality of the sacrament

Quaestiuncula 1

AD SECUNDUM SIC PROCEDITUR. Videtur quod nulla indispositio voluntatis humanae possit effectum baptismi impedire. Ea enim quae sunt a natura, sunt magis permanentia quam ea quae sunt a voluntate. Sed originale est peccatum naturae, quod baptismi effectum non impedit. Ergo nec aliqua indispositio voluntatis baptismum in suo effectu impedire potest.

PRAETEREA, in naturalibus indispositio materiae non impedit effectum agentis totaliter, nisi quando contraria dispositio quae est in materia, est fortior quam virtus agentis, sicut patet de aquositate lignorum per comparationem ad calorem ignis. Sed virtus divina, quae in sacramentis secretius operatur salutem, ut Augustinus dicit, est potentior qualibet indispositione nostrae voluntatis. Ergo non potest propter indispositionem voluntatis effectus baptismi totaliter tolli.

PRAETEREA, baptismus, sicut et alia sacramenta, instrumentum est divinae misericordiae operantis salutem. Sed divina misericordia operans salutem etiam voluntatem in bonum mutat per gratiam praevenientem. Ergo et baptismus indispositionem voluntatis magis tollit quam ab ea impediatur.

SED CONTRA, Rom. 2, super illud: *sine poenitentia sunt dona Dei et vocatio*, dicit Ambrosius, quod gratia Dei in baptismo non requirit nisi solam fidem et contritionem. Sed per haec duo tollitur omnis contrarietas voluntatis ad gratiam. Ergo requiritur ad baptismum ut indispositio voluntatis tollatur.

PRAETEREA, secundum Augustinum, *qui creavit te sine te, non justificabit te sine te.* Sed ille qui habet indispositam voluntatem, non cooperatur Deo, immo magis in contrarium operatur. Ergo in baptismo non justificatur.

OBJ. 1: To the second we proceed thus. It seems that no indisposition of the human will could impede the effect of baptism.[97] For things that are by nature are more permanent than things that are by will. But original sin is a sin of the nature, yet it does not impede baptism's effect. Therefore, neither can any indisposition of the will impede baptism in its effect.

OBJ. 2: Furthermore, in natural things an indisposition of matter does not completely impede an agent's effect, except when the contrary disposition in the matter is stronger than the agent's power, as is seen when the wetness of wood is compared to the heat of a fire. But divine power, which is invisibly working our salvation in the sacraments, as Augustine says,[98] is more powerful than any indisposition whatsoever of our will. Therefore, the effect of baptism cannot completely be taken away because of an indisposition of the will.

OBJ. 3: Furthermore, baptism, like all the other sacraments, is an instrument of divine mercy working salvation. But divine mercy working salvation also turns the will to good by prevenient grace. Therefore, baptism removes the indisposition of the will rather than being impeded by it.

ON THE CONTRARY, Ambrose says about this text, *the gifts and the calling of God are without repentance* (Rom 11:29), that the grace of God in baptism requires nothing but faith and contrition.[99] But by these two things, all of the will's contrariety toward grace is removed. Therefore, it is required for baptism that the will's indisposition be removed.

FURTHERMORE, according to Augustine, *he who created you without you will not justify you without you.*[100] But someone who has an indisposed will does not cooperate with God, but rather works against him. Therefore, he is not justified in baptism.

Quaestiuncula 2

ULTERIUS. Videtur quod hujusmodi voluntatis indispositio non debeat dici fictio. Secundum enim unum-

OBJ. 1: Moreover, it seems that an indisposition of the will like this should not be called insincerity. For the will

---

97. Parallels: above, q. 2, a. 1, qa. 1, ad 3; d. 12, q. 2, a. 1, qa. 3, ad 3; *ST* III, q. 69, a. 9; q. 87, a. 3, ad 2.

98. Cf. Isidore, *Etymologiarum* (ed. Lindsay), Bk. 6, ch. 19, par. 40.

99. See Ambrosiaster, *Commentarius in Pauli epistulam ad Romanos*, on 11:29 (CSEL 81.1:385).

100. See Augustine, *Sermon* 169, n. 11 (PL 38:923).

quodque genus peccati contingit voluntatem esse indispositam ad baptismalis gratiae susceptionem. Sed fictio est speciale peccatum, quia opponitur speciali virtuti, scilicet veritati, ut patet per Philosophum in 4 *Ethic.* Ergo non debet dici universale impedimentum baptismalis gratiae.

PRAETEREA, Augustinus dicit, quod fictus est qui non credit. Sed sicut in baptismo datur fides, ita et aliae virtutes, et praecipue caritas, per quam aliquis fit filius Dei. Ergo fictio non magis debet poni impedimentum baptismi, quam opposita aliarum virtutum.

PRAETEREA, secundum Augustinum aliquo modo fictus est qui indevotus accedit. Sed indevotio potest esse sine peccato mortali; talis autem non habet aliquod impedimentum baptismi. Ergo impedimentum baptismi non debet dici fictio.

PRAETEREA, secundum Augustinum, alio modo dicitur fictus qui aliter celebrat. Sed qui non servat formam ecclesiae, non confert sacramentum, neque suscipit. Ergo talis fictio non est sacramenti impedimentum.

PRAETEREA, fictus alio modo ab Augustino dicitur qui contemnit suscipere. Sed talis non suscipit. Ergo talis fictio non impedit sacramenti effectum.

can be indisposed to receive baptismal grace by every genus of sin. But insincerity is a special sin, because it is opposed to a special virtue, namely, truthfulness, as is clear from what the Philosopher says in *Ethics* 4.[101] Therefore, it should not be called the universal impediment to baptismal grace.

OBJ. 2: Furthermore, Augustine says that he is insincere who does not believe.[102] But just as faith is given in baptism, so too are the other virtues, and especially charity, by which one becomes a child of God. Therefore, insincerity should not be considered an impediment to baptism, any more than what is opposed to the other virtues.

OBJ. 3: Furthermore, according to Augustine,[103] it is insincere in a certain way if someone approaches baptism without devotion. But lack of devotion can exist without mortal sin; yet such a person does not have any impediment to baptism. Therefore, the impediment to baptism should not be called insincerity.

OBJ. 4: Furthermore, according to Augustine,[104] in another way, someone is called insincere who celebrates differently. But whoever does not preserve the Church's form does not confer the sacrament, nor does he receive it. Therefore, this kind of insincerity is not an impediment to the sacrament.

OBJ. 5: Furthermore, in another way someone is said to be insincere by Augustine if he scorns to receive the sacrament. But such a person does not receive the sacrament. Therefore, this kind of insincerity does not impede the effect of the sacrament.

Quaestiuncula 3

ULTERIUS. Videtur quod recedente fictione baptismus effectum non consequatur. Opus enim mortuum nunquam vivificatur, ut infra, dist. 14, dicetur. Sed opus mortuum dicitur quod in peccato mortali factum est. Cum ergo ficte accedens ad baptismum, in peccato mortali sit, baptismus ille nunquam vivificari poterit, ut ei gratiam conferat.

PRAETEREA, effectus baptismi est ab omni culpa et poena absolvere. Sed hoc non accidit recedente fictione: quia a poena peccatorum quae post baptismum commisit, non absolvitur alias esset majoris efficaciae in ficte accedentibus quam in aliis, quibus ad deletionem sequentium peccatorum baptismus non operatur. Ergo recedente fictione baptismus non habet suum effectum.

OBJ. 1: Moreover, it seems that baptism would not have its effect once the insincerity has ended.[105] For the work of the dead is never to be brought to life, as will be said later in Distinction 14. But whatever happens in mortal sin is called the work of the dead. Since, then, someone who approaches baptism insincerely is in mortal sin, that baptism will never bring him to life such that it would confer grace on him.

OBJ. 2: Furthermore, the effect of baptism is to absolve from all fault and punishment. But this does not happen when the insincerity has ended, for such a one is not absolved from the punishment of the sins he has committed after baptism, otherwise it would be of greater efficacy to people receiving it insincerely than to others for whom it does not accomplish the wiping out of subsequent sins. Therefore, baptism does not have its effect once the insincerity has stopped.

---

101. Aristotle, *Nicomachean Ethics*, Bk. 4, ch. 7, 1127a20.
102. Augustine, *On Baptism Against the Donatists*, Bk. 1, ch. 12, par. 18 (CSEL 51:162); cf. Bk. 7, ch. 53, par. 101 (CSEL 51:372).
103. Ibid.
104. Ibid.
105. Parallels: above, d. 1, q. 2, a. 4, qa. 1, ad 3; d. 15, q. 1, a. 3, qa. 3, ad 2; *ST* III, q. 69, a. 10.

PRAETEREA, sicut aliquis ficte accedit ad baptismum, ita etiam ad Eucharistiam. Sed recedente fictione Eucharistiae effectum non percipit qui prius fictus accesserat. Ergo nec etiam recedente fictione aliquis baptismi effectum percipit.

SED CONTRA, remota causa removetur effectus. Sed causa impediens effectum baptismi erat fictio. Ergo remota fictione baptismus effectum suum habebit.

PRAETEREA, cuilibet culpae in statu viae potest remedium adhiberi. Sed contra originalem culpam non est aliud remedium quam baptismus. Ergo cum ficte accedentibus originale non remittatur, oporteret baptismum iterari si recedente fictione baptismus effectum suum non haberet quod est inconveniens et haereticum.

OBJ. 3: Furthermore, just as someone may approach baptism insincerely, so also may he approach the Eucharist. But someone who approached it insincerely before does not secure the Eucharist's effect once the insincerity has passed. Therefore, neither would someone receive baptism's effect once the insincerity has passed.

ON THE CONTRARY, when a cause is removed, the effect is removed. But the cause impeding the effect of baptism was insincerity. Therefore, once the insincerity is removed, baptism will have its effect.

FURTHERMORE, a remedy can be applied to any fault in the wayfaring state. But against original sin there is no other remedy than baptism. Therefore, since original sin is not remitted in those who approach insincerely, it would be necessary for baptism to be repeated if, once the insincerity had been removed, baptism did not have its effect—which is unfitting and heretical.

Response to Quaestiuncula 1

RESPONDEO dicendum ad primam quaestionem, quod duplex est effectus baptismi. Primus est res et sacramentum, scilicet character. Et quia character non imprimitur ad praeparandum hominis voluntatem, ut aliquid bene fiat, cum non sit habitus, sed potentia, ut dictum est, ideo hunc effectum voluntatis indispositio non impedit, dummodo aliqualis sit voluntas recipiendi sacramentum. Alius effectus est qui est res et non sacramentum, scilicet gratia, et quae ad ipsam consequuntur, per quae hominis voluntas praeparatur ut bene cooperetur; et ideo ad hunc effectum percipiendum non sufficit quaelibet voluntas sacramentum recipiendi, sed requiritur voluntas talis a qua removeatur omnis indispositio contraria gratiae baptismali quia contraria non se compatiuntur; unde manente contraria dispositione, baptismus ultimum suum effectum habere non posset.

AD PRIMUM ergo dicendum, quod peccatum originale eo ipso quod non est voluntarium voluntate hujus personae, habet quod in voluntate, in qua ultimus effectus baptismi effici debet, indispositionem aliquam non causet; et ideo effectum baptismi impedire non potest.

AD SECUNDUM dicendum, quod de ratione voluntatis est ut cogi non possit; et ideo non est similis ratio de indispositione voluntatis et aliarum rerum naturalium, quae per violentam actionem agentis dispositiones contrarias admittunt.

AD TERTIUM dicendum, quod sicut in his quae ad esse naturae spectant, quaedam Deus operatur mediantibus rebus naturalibus, quaedam autem sibi reservavit, ita etiam in aliis quae ad gratiam pertinent, quaedam operatur mediantibus sacramentis, quaedam autem im-

TO THE FIRST QUESTION, I answer that there are two effects of baptism. The first is the reality-and-sacrament, which is the character. And because the character is not imprinted for preparing man's will so that something might be done well, since it is not a habit, but a power, as has been said, for this reason an indisposition of will does not impede this effect, as long as the will to receive the sacrament exists in some way. The other effect is that which is reality and not sacrament, namely, grace and the things that follow from it, by which man's will is prepared to cooperate well; and thus, to receive *this* effect, not just any will to receive the sacrament suffices, but it requires the kind of will from which all indisposition contrary to baptismal grace is removed, for contrary things cannot coexist; hence, while a contrary disposition remains, baptism could not have its final effect.[106]

REPLY OBJ. 1: By the very fact that original sin is not something voluntary in a person's will, it is not capable of causing a certain disposition in the will, wherein the final effect of baptism should be effected; and thus, it cannot impede the effect of baptism.

REPLY OBJ. 2: It is in the nature of the will that it cannot be forced; and thus, no parallel argument can be made between the indisposition of the will and the indisposition of other natural things that, by the violent action of an agent, admit contrary dispositions.

REPLY OBJ. 3: Just as in what looks to the being of nature, God works certain things by the mediation of natural things, but certain things he has reserved to himself, so too among those matters that pertain to grace, he works certain things by means of the sacraments, but certain others he

---

106. For more about the sacrament alone, reality alone, and sacrament-and-reality, see the footnote at Dist.1, q.1, a.4, qa. 1, main response.

mediate operatur; et quandoque praeter legem naturae, sicut et miracula facit praeter rationes seminales seu naturales; et de hujusmodi est permutatio voluntatis eorum qui gratiae contrariam voluntatem habent non solum habitu (quod quandoque contingit in his qui non ficte accedunt, se ad gratiam disponentibus, quam in ipso momento baptismi consequuntur), sed etiam eorum qui contrariam actu voluntatem habent, sicut de Paulo accidit; Act. 9.

works without intermediaries, and sometimes outside the law of nature, as he also performs miracles beyond seminal or natural reasons. And one of these things is changing the will not only of those who have their wills contrary to grace habitually (which sometimes happens among people who do not approach baptism insincerely, disposing themselves for grace, which they receive in the very moment of baptism), but even of those who actively hold their wills contrary to grace, as happened in the case of Paul (cf. Acts 9).

Response to Quaestiuncula 2

AD SECUNDAM QUAESTIONEM dicendum, quod ad hoc quod aliquis alicujus agentis effectum percipere debeat, oportet quod se habeat in debita dispositione ad causam agentem, et ad effectum percipiendum; et ideo indispositio voluntatis, quae effectum ultimum baptismi impedit est duplex: una secundum ordinem ad ipsum sacramentum; alia secundum ordinem ad effectum sacramenti.

Ad ipsum autem sacramentum contingit voluntatem esse indispositam dupliciter: uno modo per subtractionem necessarii; alio modo per positionem contrarii. Quia autem omnis actio est per contactum; ideo necessarium est quod recipiens sacramentum quodammodo contingat ipsum et per intellectum quem quidem contactum facit fides et per affectum quem contactum facit devotio; et ideo indispositus reputatur et qui non credit, et qui indevotus accedit. Similiter autem duplex est contrarium, quod subtrahi oportet. Unum est ex parte eorum quae exterius aguntur; et sic indispositus est qui aliter celebrat. Aliud est ex parte virtutis intrinsecae, quae secretius operatur salutem; et sic indispositus est qui contemnit.

Similiter autem per comparationem ad effectum baptismi, oportet quod disponatur aliquis adhibendo necessarium, scilicet fidem, quae cor purificat, et quod removeat contrarium, scilicet peccatum, per contritionem; et ideo Ambrosius dicit quod non sunt necessaria ex hac parte nisi fides et contritio, tamen contritio etiam in devotione includitur.

AD PRIMUM ergo dicendum, quod fictio proprie est cum aliquis aliquid ostendit dicto vel facto, quod non est in rei veritate. Hoc autem contingit dupliciter. Uno modo quando ex hac intentione aliquid dicitur vel fit, ut aliud ostendatur quam rei veritas habet; et tunc fictio est speciale peccatum, et sic non accipitur hic. Alio modo quando aliquid ostenditur quod rei veritas non habet dicto vel facto, etiam si non propter hoc dicatur vel fiat; et sic accipitur hic fictio. Quicumque enim ad baptismum accedit, ostendit se veteri vitae abrenuntiare, et novam inchoare; unde si voluntas ejus adhuc in vetusta-

TO THE SECOND QUESTION, it should be said that for someone to receive the effect of a certain agent, it is necessary that he have the due disposition to the acting cause, as well as to the effect to be received. And thus, there are two kinds of indisposition of the will that impede the final effect of baptism: one in its ordering to the sacrament itself, the other in its ordering to the sacrament's effect.

Now toward the sacrament itself, the will can be indisposed in two ways: one way by the removal of what is necessary; another way, by the lodging of something contrary. Since every action is by contact, however, the one receiving the sacrament must somehow make contact with it, both by the intellect, which makes contact through faith, as well as by the affections, which make contact through devotion. And thus, someone is considered indisposed who does not believe, as is he who approaches without devotion. Likewise, there are two contraries that must be taken away. One is on the part of the things that are done outwardly; and indisposed in this way is he who celebrates otherwise than the Church does. The other is on the part of the internal power that secretly works salvation; and this is how someone who scorns the sacrament is indisposed.

Again, in like manner, if we look to the effect of baptism, it is necessary that someone be disposed by bringing to bear what is necessary, that is, faith, which purifies the heart, and what removes what is contrary, that is, sin, through contrition; and thus, Ambrose says that nothing is necessary on our part except faith and contrition, since contrition is also included in devotion.

REPLY OBJ. 1: Insincerity, properly speaking, is when someone shows something in his words or deeds that is not there in the truth of the matter. Now this happens in two ways. In one way, when something is said or done with the intention of showing something other than the truth of the matter; and then insincerity is a special sin, which is not the way it is taken here. The other way is when something is shown that, in word or deed, does not possess the truth of the matter, even if it is not said or done with that aim; and this is the way insincerity is taken here. For whoever approaches baptism shows himself as having renounced his

te vitae remaneat, aliud ostendit quam sit in rei veritate; et ideo est fictio.

AD SECUNDUM dicendum, quod in sacramentis praecipue fides operatur, per quam sacramenta quodammodo continuantur suae causae principaliter agenti, et etiam ipsi recipienti; et ideo defectus fidei specialius pertinet ad fictionem quae est in sacramentis, quam defectus aliarum virtutum.

AD TERTIUM dicendum, quod devotio hic accipitur voluntas consequendi baptismum totaliter, et quantum ad sacramentum et quantum ad rem sacramenti; et hujus devotionis defectus non potest sine peccato mortali esse; quamvis defectus devotionis prout importat fervorem caritatis in reverentia Dei et divinorum, possit esse sine peccato mortali.

AD QUARTUM dicendum, quod aliter celebrans quandoque non variat ea quae sunt de essentia sacramenti, et tunc confertur sacramentum; sed non consequitur aliquis rem sacramenti, nisi suscipiens sacramentum sit immunis a culpa aliter celebrantis.

AD QUINTUM dicendum, quod non loquimur hic de contemptu quo aliquis abjicit sacramentum non recipiens ipsum, sed quo aliquis parvipendit non aestimans in eo esse efficaciam ad salvandum.

old life and begun a new one; hence, if his will still remains in the oldness of life, he shows something different from the truth of the matter; and thus, it is insincerity.

REPLY OBJ. 2: Faith is at work above all in the sacraments, for in a way it connects the sacraments with their principal agent cause as well as with the person receiving them; and thus, a lack of faith pertains more especially than the lack of other virtues to the kind of insincerity that affects the sacraments.

REPLY OBJ. 3: Devotion is here taken as the will to receive baptism completely, both as to the sacrament and as to the reality of the sacrament; and such devotion cannot be lacking without mortal sin—although one could lack devotion insofar as it implies the fervor of charity in reverence for God and divine things without mortal sin.

REPLY OBJ. 4: Sometimes the one who celebrates a sacrament differently does not vary the things that are essential to the sacrament, and in that case the sacrament is conferred; but the recipient does not obtain the reality of the sacrament unless he is immune from the fault of the one celebrating it that way.

REPLY OBJ. 5: We are not speaking here about the contempt of someone who rejects a sacrament by not receiving it, but of someone views it as unimportant, not considering it to be efficacious for salvation.

Response to Quaestiuncula 3

AD TERTIAM QUAESTIONEM dicendum, quod in baptismo imprimitur character, qui est immediata causa disponens ad gratiam; et ideo, cum fictio non auferat characterem, recedente fictione, quae effectum characteris impediebat, character, qui est praesens in anima, incipit habere effectum suum; et ita baptismus recedente fictione, effectum suum consequitur.

AD PRIMUM ergo dicendum, quod baptismus non habet efficaciam solum ex opere operante sed magis ex opere operato, quod est opus Dei et non hominis; et ideo non potest esse mortuum.

AD SECUNDUM dicendum, quod baptismus recedente fictione habet illum effectum quem prius habuisset, si fictio non fuisset; et ideo peccata praecedentia baptismum remittit et quo ad culpam et quo ad poenam; sed peccata sequentia remittuntur virtute contritionis quae fictionem amovet, quantum ad culpam, sed non quantum ad poenam totaliter.

AD TERTIUM dicendum, quod in Eucharistia non imprimitur character cujus virtute possit aliquis virtu-

To THE THIRD QUESTION, I answer that in baptism a character is imprinted, which is the immediate cause disposing one to grace; and thus, since insincerity does not take away the character, once the insincerity that was impeding the effect of the character has ended, the character, which is present in the soul, begins to have its effect; and in this way, baptism obtains its effect once the insincerity has ceased.

REPLY OBJ. 1: Baptism has efficacy not only by the action of the one doing it, but still more from the action itself being accomplished, which is a work of God and not of man; and thus, it cannot be a work of the dead.

REPLY OBJ. 2: Once the insincerity has ceased, baptism has that effect that it would have had before, if there had been no insincerity; and thus, it remits the sins that preceded baptism as to both fault and punishment; but the sins following baptism are remitted as to fault by virtue of the contrition that drove away the insincerity, but not entirely as to punishment.

REPLY OBJ. 3: In the Eucharist, no character is imprinted by virtue of which someone could receive the ef-

tem[107] sacramenti percipere fictione recedente; et ideo non est simile.

fects of the sacrament once his insincerity had ceased; and thus it is not the same.

107. *virtutem.—efficaciam* PLE.

ARTICLE 3

About those baptized with the baptism of the spirit and of blood, who do not receive the sacrament but do receive the reality of the sacrament

Quaestiuncula 1

AD TERTIUM SIC PROCEDITUR. Videtur quod praeter baptismum fluminis non debeant alia baptismata esse. In omnibus enim quae sunt unius speciei, est unus modus generationis. Sed baptismus est regeneratio in vitam spiritualem, quae est unius rationis in omnibus generatis. Ergo non debet esse regeneratio nisi unius modi, et ita tantum baptismus fluminis.

PRAETEREA, baptismus condividitur contra alia sacramenta novae legis. Sed alia sacramenta non multiplicantur: non enim sunt plures confirmationes neque plura sacerdotia, et sic de aliis. Ergo praeter baptismum etiam fluminis non debet esse aliquod baptisma.

PRAETEREA, sacramentum est genus baptismi. Sed alia quae dicuntur baptismata non sunt sacramenta, quia non servatur debita forma et debita materia. Ergo non sunt baptismata.

SED CONTRA est quod Damascenus determinat plura genera baptismatum.

PRAETEREA, Heb. 6, super: *Baptismatum doctrinae*, dicit Glossa: *plura dicit, quia est baptisma aquae, poenitentiae, et sanguinis*. Ergo sunt plura genera baptismatum.

OBJ. 1: To the third, we proceed thus. It seems that, besides baptism of water, there should not be other baptisms.[108] For in all things that are of one species, there is one manner of generation. But baptism is regeneration unto spiritual life, which has the same account in all who are generated. Therefore, there should not be regeneration except in one manner, and so there should be only baptism of water.

OBJ. 2: Furthermore, baptism is condivided against the other sacraments of the New Law. But the other sacraments do not exist in multiple forms, for there are not several confirmations or priesthoods, and the same holds for the others. Therefore, besides the baptism of water, there should not be any other baptism.

OBJ. 3: Furthermore, sacrament is the genus of baptism. But the other things that are called baptisms are not sacraments, because the due form and due matter are not observed. Therefore, they are not baptisms.

ON THE CONTRARY, Damascene defines several kinds of baptism.[109]

FURTHERMORE, commenting on the text *instruction about baptisms* (Heb 6:2), the Gloss states: *it speaks in the plural because there is baptism of water, repentance, and blood*.[110] Therefore, there are several kinds of baptism.

Quaestiuncula 2

ULTERIUS. Videtur quod poenitentiae baptismus non sufficiat ad salutem. Character enim baptismalis videtur esse de pertinentibus ad salutem, eo quod per ipsum distinguitur populus Dei a non populo Dei. Sed per baptismum poenitentiae non imprimitur character. Ergo non sufficit ad salutem.

PRAETEREA, posita causa sufficiente superfluum videtur aliam causam addere. Si ergo baptismus poenitentiae ad salutem sufficeret necessitate imminente, tunc

OBJ. 1: Moreover, it seems that baptism of repentance does not suffice for salvation.[111] For the baptismal character seems to be one of the things pertaining to salvation, in the fact that by it the people of God are distinguished from those not of the people of God. But no character is imprinted by the baptism of repentance. Therefore, it does not suffice for salvation.

OBJ. 2: Furthermore, once a sufficient cause is given, it seems superfluous to add other causes. If therefore baptism of repentance sufficed for salvation in cases of imminent

---

108. Parallels: *ST* III, q. 66, a. 11; *Quodl.* VI, q. 3, a. 1; *Super Ioan.* 3, lec. 1.
109. John Damascene, *On the Orthodox Faith*, Bk. 4, ch. 9 (PG 94:1124).
110. Cf. *Glossa Lombardi* on Hebrews 6:2: "fundamentum etiam *doctrinae baptismatum*, pluraliter dicit, quia est baptismus in aqua, in poenitentia, in sanguine, quia sic mundatur homo a peccatis per poenitentiam vel sanguinis effusionem, sicut per lavacrum baptismi" (PL 192:440).
111. Parallels: *ST* III, q. 66, a. 11; *Quodl.* VI, q. 3, a. 1; *Super Ioan.* 3, lec. 1.

aliquis necessitatis articulum evadens non deberet baptismo aquae baptizari: quod falsum est.

PRAETEREA, aetas puerilis magis est ad misericordiam inclinans quam aetas perfecta, ut patet per Glossam Rom. 5 super illud: *vix pro justo quis moritur*, etc. Sed pueris non remittitur peccatum originale pro sola fide et contritione aliorum, nisi baptismus aquae eis adhibeatur. Ergo videtur quod nec adultis remittatur originale et actuale simul sine baptismo aquae.

SED CONTRA, salus hominis cum sit de maximis bonis, non potest homini invito auferri. Sed in potestate hominis est impedire alium ne baptizetur baptismo aquae. Ergo sine baptismo aquae per solam fidem et contritionem potest esse salus.

PRAETEREA, Rom. 6, 23, dicitur: *gratia Dei vita aeterna*. Sed contritio non est sine gratia. Ergo qui habet, fidem et contritionem, etiam sine baptismo aquae salvatur.

need, then once the emergency was over, the person would not have to be baptized with the baptism of water, which is false.

OBJ. 3: Furthermore, the age of childhood inclines one to mercy more than the age of maturity, as is clear in the Gloss on that text: *one would hardly die for a just man, though perhaps for a good man one will dare even to die* (Rom 5:7).[112] But original sin is not remitted in children by the faith and contrition of others unless the baptism of water is administered to them. Therefore, it seems that original and actual sin are also not remitted in adults without the baptism of water.

ON THE CONTRARY, the salvation of man, since it is one of the greatest goods, cannot be withdrawn from man against his will. But it is within man's power to impede another from being baptized with water. Therefore, there can be salvation by faith and contrition alone, without the baptism of water.

FURTHERMORE, it is said, *the grace of God is eternal life* (Rom 6:23). But contrition is not without grace. Therefore, whoever has faith and contrition may be saved even without baptism of water.

Quaestiuncula 3

ULTERIUS. Videtur quod baptismus sanguinis non suppleat vicem baptismi aquae. Baptismus enim aquae habet efficaciam ex opere operato, baptismus autem sanguinis solum ex opere operante; unde sine caritate non prodest, ut dicitur 1 Corinth. 13. Sed in pueris nihil habet efficaciam ex opere operante, quia usum liberi arbitrii non habent. Ergo in eis baptismus sanguinis non supplet vicem baptismi aquae.

PRAETEREA, in baptismo sanguinis non est nisi poena et causa. Sed poena quandoque non est proportionata ad tollendam totam poenam debitam pro peccatis; nec etiam devotio ad causam passionis, cum quis pro Deo patitur, ad hoc sufficeret. Ergo baptismus sanguinis non semper totam poenam debitam pro peccatis tollit, et ita non supplet in omnibus vicem baptismi aquae.

PRAETEREA, alia multa sunt genera supererogationum, sicut virginitas, cui etiam debetur aureola; et doctrina, et hujusmodi. Sed haec non supplent locum baptismi. Ergo nec martyrium, ut videtur.

OBJ. 1: Moreover, it seems that baptism of blood does not take the place of baptism of water.[113] For baptism of water has its efficacy by the work done, but baptism of blood only by the work of the one doing it; hence, without charity it would be no benefit, as is said in 1 Corinthians 13:1–3. But in children, nothing has efficacy by the work of the one doing it, because they do not have the use of free will. Therefore, in them, baptism of blood cannot take the place of baptism of water.

OBJ. 2: Furthermore, in the baptism of blood, there is nothing but suffering and the reason for it. But sometimes the suffering is not proportionate to taking away the whole punishment due to sins; nor would even devotion to the reason for the suffering, when someone suffers for God, suffice for doing this. Therefore, baptism of blood does not always take away the whole punishment due to sin, and so, it would not take the place of baptism of water in everything.

OBJ. 3: Furthermore, there are many other things in the genus of the supererogatory, like virginity, to which a special reward is also given, and teaching, and other things of that sort.[114] But these do not take the place of baptism. Therefore, neither does martyrdom, as it seems.

---

112. Cf. *Glossa Lombardi* on Romans 5:7: "Justus autem bonum naturae suae exercitio melioravit, et licet justus secundum modum quo hic accipitur melior sit quam bonus, innocentiae tamen causa est miserabilior quam justitiae, quia non est hujusmodi justitia sine severitate."

113. Parallels: *ST* III, q. 66, a. 11; *Quodl.* VI, q. 3, a. 1; *Super Ioan.* 3, lec. 1.

114. See note below, in qa. 4, on the vocabulary of *aurea* and *aureola*.

SED CONTRA est quod Augustinus dicit de Cypriano, quod si quid in eo purgandum erat, passionis falce ablatum est. Ergo baptismus sanguinis purgat universaliter, et etiam supplet locum baptismi aquae.

PRAETEREA, baptismus aquae efficaciam habet ex passione Christi, cui nos conformat. Sed similiter baptismus sanguinis nos passioni Christi conformat. Ergo supplet vicem baptismi.

ON THE CONTRARY, Augustine says of Cyprian, that if anything had to be purified in him, it was taken away by the scythe of his suffering.[115] Therefore, baptism of blood purifies completely, and even takes the place of baptism of water.

FURTHERMORE, baptism of water has efficacy from the Passion of Christ, to which it conforms us. But baptism of blood likewise conforms us to the Passion of Christ. Therefore, it takes the place of baptism.

Quaestiuncula 4

ULTERIUS. Videtur quod baptismus aquae sit potior quam baptismus sanguinis. Baptismus enim sanguinis efficaciam habet ex opere operante illius qui patitur, baptismus autem aquae ex passione Christi. Cum ergo passio Christi sit efficacior quam opus operans alicujus puri hominis, baptismus aquae nobilior erit quam baptismus sanguinis.

PRAETEREA, per baptismum aquae datur homini gratia per quam debetur ei aurea, sed per baptismum sanguinis debetur homini aureola. Ergo cum aurea sit nobilior quam aureola, et baptismus aquae erit nobilior quam baptismus sanguinis.

SED CONTRA est quod dicitur in Glossa, Judic. 6, super illud *Tolle vitulum*, etc.: *Baptismus in sanguine puriores reddit quam baptismus aquae.*

OBJ. 1: Moreover, it seems that baptism of water is more powerful than baptism of blood.[116] For baptism of blood has its effect by the work of the one doing it, who is the one suffering. But baptism of water has its efficacy from the Passion of Christ. Therefore, since the Passion of Christ is more effective than the work of some mere man acting, baptism of water will be nobler than baptism of blood.

OBJ. 2: Furthermore, by baptism of water, grace is given to man through which the golden crown is owed to him, but by baptism of blood a man is owed a special reward.[117] Therefore, since the golden crown is nobler than any special reward, baptism of water will also be nobler than baptism of blood.

ON THE CONTRARY, on this text: *Take the meat and the unleavened cakes, and put them on this rock, and pour the broth over them* (Judg 6:20), a Gloss says, *baptism in blood makes them purer than baptism of water.*

Response to Quaestiuncula 1

RESPONDEO dicendum ad primam quaestionem, quod proprie loquendo, unum est tantum baptisma, quod in aqua celebratur sub determinata forma verborum, de qua Dominus dicit Matth. ult., 19: *docete omnes gentes, baptizantes eos in nomine Patris et Filii et Spiritus Sancti.* Alia autem dicuntur baptismata per ordinem ad illud baptisma; et hoc tripliciter.

Primo dicitur aliquid baptisma quasi signum hujus baptismi; et sic diluvium dicitur baptismus, inquantum significat nostrum baptismum quantum ad salvationem spiritualis vitae ex salvatione humani generis tunc facta in arca, ut patet 1 Petr. 3, et transitus maris rubri, qui significat baptismum nostrum quantum ad liberationem a servitute daemonum, ut dicitur 1 Corinth. 10 et ablutiones quae fiebant in lege, quae significant nostrum bapti-

THE FIRST QUESTION I answer by saying that, properly speaking, there is only one baptism, which is celebrated in water under a determinate form of words, of which the Lord says: *teach all nations, baptizing them in the name of the Father, and of the Son, and of the Holy Spirit* (Matt 28:19). The other kinds are called baptisms by their order to this baptism, and this in three ways.

In the first way, something is called a baptism as being a sign of this baptism; and this is the way the Flood is called a baptism, inasmuch as it signifies our baptism with respect to the salvation of the spiritual life by the salvation of the human race that happened then in the ark, as is clear from 1 Peter 3:20; and the crossing of the Red Sea, which signifies our baptism with respect to liberation from slavery to demons, as is clear from 1 Corinthians 10:1–2; and the

---

115. Augustine, *De unico baptismo*, ch. 13: "Sic et in martyre gloriosissimo Cypriano, . . . si quid habebat purgandum, si nulla re alia, certe passionis falce ultima tolleretur" (CSEL 53:22).

116. Parallels: *ST* III, q. 66, a. 12; *Super Heb.* 6, lec. 1.

117. The "golden crown" or *aurea* refers to the essential reward of heaven, the beatific vision, while the "special reward" or *aureola*, literally the little golden crown, refers to an additional reward given for some outstanding manifestation of Christian virtue.

sma quantum ad purgationem peccatorum quae in ipso fit.

Alio modo dicitur baptisma quasi causa aliqua nostri baptismi; et sic baptismus Joannis dicitur baptisma ut disponens ad nostrum baptisma; et baptisma quo Christus baptizatus est, ut dans efficaciam nostro baptismo.

Alio modo dicitur aliquid baptismus secundum proportionem ad eumdem effectum; et sic dicitur baptismus poenitentiae et baptismus sanguinis de quibus Magister hic loquitur: vel quantum ad effectum secundarium, qui est consummatio in bono; et sic dicitur baptismus spiritus, de quo dicitur Act. 1. Et haec novem genera baptismatum ponit Damascenus; sed Magister hic tangit illa tantum quae habent convenientiam cum sacramento baptismi in principali effectu.

AD PRIMUM ergo dicendum, quod baptismus sanguinis et baptismus poenitentiae habent vim eamdem regenerandi cum baptismo aquae; quia baptismus sanguinis et poenitentiae non valent ad regenerationem nisi ei qui habet baptismum aquae in proposito, scilicet quando articulus necessitatis non contemptus religionis sacramentum excludit, ut in littera dicitur, et sic quodammodo agunt in vi baptismi aquae.

AD SECUNDUM dicendum quod alia sacramenta non sunt tantae necessitatis sicut baptismus; et ideo non oportuit quod haberent aliqua supplentia cum articulus necessitatis sacramentum excludit.

AD TERTIUM dicendum, quod duo baptismata de quibus Magister facit mentionem in littera, non conveniunt cum baptismi sacramento in significando, sed solum in causando; et ideo non proprie possunt dici sacramenta: propter quod in littera dicitur quod tales suscipiunt rem sacramenti sine sacramento.

washings that were done under the law, which signify our baptism in the purification of sins that happened in it.

In another way, something is called baptism as if a certain cause of our baptism; and this is the way the baptism of John is called baptism, as disposing toward our baptism; and the baptism with which Christ was baptized, as giving efficacy to our baptism.

In another way, something is called baptism either according to its proportion to the same effect, which is the way baptism of repentance and baptism of blood (of which the Master is speaking here) are called baptisms; or as regards its secondary effect, namely, consummation in good, which is the way baptism of the spirit, spoken of in Acts 1:5, is called baptism. And Damascene lists these nine kinds of baptism;[118] but the Master is here discussing only those that resemble the sacrament of baptism in its principal effect.

REPLY OBJ. 1: Baptism of blood and baptism of repentance have the same force of regenerating as baptism of water; for baptism of blood and of repentance do not avail for regeneration except in someone who intends to be baptized in water—namely, when necessity and not contempt of religion excludes the sacrament, as is said in the text. And this is how, in a way, they act by force of baptism of water.

REPLY OBJ. 2: Other sacraments are not so necessary as baptism, and thus it is not necessary that they have certain replacements when necessity prevents the sacrament.

REPLY OBJ. 3: The two baptisms that the Master mentions in the text do not resemble the sacrament of baptism in signifying, but only in causing; and thus, they cannot properly be called sacraments. And for this reason it is said in the text that such people receive the reality of the sacrament without the sacrament.

Response to Quaestiuncula 2

AD SECUNDAM QUAESTIONEM dicendum, quod aliquid dicitur ad salutem[119] dupliciter. Uno modo simpliciter et absolute; et sic baptismus poenitentiae sine baptismo aquae non sufficit ad salutem. Alio modo secundum quid et in casu; et sic sufficit, quando articulus necessitatis sacramentum excludit ne actu percipi possit. Tunc enim quamvis sit poenitentia sine baptismo in actu est tamen cum desiderio et proposito baptismi; et voluntas pro facto reputatur ei qui non habet tempus operandi.

TO THE SECOND QUESTION, I answer that something is said to be sufficient for salvation in two ways. In one way, simply and absolutely; and in this way, baptism of repentance without baptism of water is not sufficient for salvation. In another way, in a certain respect and in certain cases; and in this way, it is sufficient, when a moment of dire need prevents the sacrament from being actually received. For at times like that, although there is repentance without actual baptism, it is nevertheless with the desire and intention of baptism; and the will is counted in place of the deed for someone who does not have the time to act.

---

118. John Damascene, *On the Orthodox Faith*, Bk. 4, ch. 9, (PG 94:1123).
119. *salutem dupliciter.—salutem sufficere dupliciter* PLE.

AD PRIMUM ergo dicendum, quod eadem ratio est de charactere baptismali, et de ablutione aquae exteriori: quia utrumque simpliciter est necessarium ad salutem, sed in casu sufficit propositum, quando articulus necessitatis sacramentum excludit.

AD SECUNDUM dicendum, quod ratio illa procederet bene, si baptismus poenitentiae esset simpliciter et absolute ad salutem sufficiens.

AD TERTIUM dicendum, quod quamvis puerorum aetas sit magis miserabilis, tamen oportet si salvari debeant, quod in eis aliqua causa salutis sit. Et quia per proprium motum liberi arbitrii salvari non possunt, oportet quod per sacramentum baptismi salventur. Plus enim valet adulto fides propria, quam parvulo fides aliena. Quod enim aliquando fides aliena puero ad salutem sufficiebat cum aliqua protestatione hoc erat inquantum illa protestatio habebat vim sacramenti quam nunc habet baptismus aquae.

REPLY OBJ. 1: The account of the baptismal character is the same as of the outward washing with water: both are, simply speaking, necessary for salvation, but in certain cases the intention suffices, when a moment of dire need prevents the sacrament.

REPLY OBJ. 2: That argument would proceed well if baptism of repentance were sufficient for salvation, simply speaking and absolutely.

REPLY OBJ. 3: Although the age of children makes them more deserving of mercy, nevertheless if they should be saved, there would have to be some cause of salvation in them. And since they cannot be saved by a proper movement of free will, they have to be saved through the sacrament of baptism. For an adult's own faith avails more for him than someone else's faith avails for a child. For if, at one time, the faith of another person, along with some profession, was sufficient for a child's salvation, it was to the extent that that profession had the power of the sacrament that baptism of water now has.

Response to Quaestiuncula 3

AD TERTIAM QUAESTIONEM dicendum, quod baptismus aquae efficaciam habet a passione Christi, inquantum eam sacramentaliter repraesentat; Baptismus autem sanguinis passioni Christi conformat realiter, non sacramentali repraesentatione; et ideo in his quae sacramentalia sunt baptismus sanguinis non supplet vicem baptismi aquae, sicut est impressio characteris et hujusmodi, sed in eo quod est res tantum, supplet totaliter vicem baptismi aquae quando articulus necessitatis sacramentum excludit. Sicut enim in baptismo aquae liberatur homo ab omni culpa praecedente et poena, ita in baptismo sanguinis.

AD PRIMUM ergo dicendum, quod baptismus sanguinis non habet hoc tantum ex opere operante, neque quantum ad poenam qua aliquis martyrium explet, quam contingit non esse sufficientem ad satisfaciendum pro peccato; neque quantum ad devotionem justae voluntatis: quia contingit quod voluntate majori caritate informata aliquis sine martyrio non potest ab omni poena liberari, sed hoc habet ex imitatione passionis Christi; unde de martyribus dicitur Apocal. 7, 14: *laverunt stolas suas in sanguine agni*; et ideo pueri quamvis usum liberum arbitrium non habeant, si occidantur pro Christo, in suo sanguine baptizati salvantur.

AD SECUNDUM dicendum, quod quamvis illa poena in se considerata, non esset sufficiens ad liberandum ab omni poena peccati, tamen relata ad causam passionis, accipit efficaciam a passione Christi, cui aliquis per ta-

TO THE THIRD QUESTION, I answer that baptism of water has its efficacy from the Passion of Christ, inasmuch as it represents the Passion sacramentally; however, baptism of blood conforms one to the Passion of Christ not by a sacramental representation, but in reality. And therefore, in those things that are sacramental, like the imprinting of the character and things of that sort, baptism of blood does not supply the place of baptism of water; but in the fact that it is the reality alone, it completely supplies the place of baptism of water, when a dire need prevents the sacrament. For just as man is freed from all existing fault and punishment by the baptism of water, so too in the baptism of blood.

REPLY OBJ. 1: Baptism of blood does not have this efficacy only by the work of the one doing it—neither as regards the punishment by which someone completes martyrdom, which sometimes happens to be not sufficient for satisfying for sins, nor as regards the devotion of a just will, for it sometimes happens that someone with a will informed by greater charity cannot be freed from all punishment without martyrdom; but rather, it has this efficacy by its imitation of the Passion of Christ. Hence it is said of the martyrs, *they have washed their robes in the blood of the Lamb* (Rev 7:14); and thus, although children do not have the use of free will, if they are killed for Christ, they are saved, baptized in his blood.

REPLY OBJ. 2: Although that suffering, considered in itself, would not be enough to free one from every punishment for sin, nevertheless, when it is referred to the reason for the suffering, it receives efficacy from the Passion

lem poenam conformatur, et ex hoc ab omni poena absolvere potest.

Ad tertium dicendum, quod in aliis supererogationis vel perfectionis operibus vel statibus, non est ita expressa conformitas ad passionem Christi sicut in baptismo sanguinis, neque etiam in baptismo poenitentiae; et ideo non oportet quod in eis omnis poena dimittatur. Tamen in *Vitis patrum* dicitur, quod quidam patrum vidit eamdem gratiam descendentem super eum qui habitum religionis assumit, et super eum qui baptizatur. Sed hoc non est, quia talis a satisfactione absolvatur, sed quia eo ipso quod suam voluntatem etiam in servitutem redigit propter Deum, plenarie jam pro omni peccato satisfecit, quia eum cariorem habet omnibus rebus mundi, de quibus tantum posset dare quod eleemosynis omnia peccata redimeret, etiam quantum ad poenam.

of Christ, to which someone is conformed by such suffering; and by that fact, he can be absolved from every punishment.

Reply Obj. 3: In other works or states of supererogation or perfection, and even in baptism of repentance, there is not such an explicit conformity to the Passion of Christ as there is in baptism of blood; and therefore it is not fitting that all one's punishment should be dismissed in these things. Nevertheless, in the *Lives of the Fathers* it is said that a certain father saw the same grace descending on the one who assumed a religious habit as upon the one who was baptized. But this is not the case because someone like that is absolved from making satisfaction, but because by the very fact that he rendered his own will in servitude for the sake of God, he has now satisfied fully for every sin, since he holds God dearer than all the things of the world, of which he could give so much that by almsgiving he would redeem all his sins, even as to the punishment.

Response to Quaestiuncula 4

Ad quartam quaestionem dicendum, quod uterque baptismus habet efficaciam a passione Christi, secundum quod ei conformat. Et quia baptismus aquae conformat ei sacramentali significatione, baptismus autem sanguinis realiter; ideo quantum ad sacramentalia excedit baptismus aquae, sicut est impressio characteris, et hujusmodi; sed quantum ad ea quae sunt res sacramenti, excedit baptismus sanguinis, quia et gratia in baptismo sanguinis magis augetur habenti, et amplior datur non habenti, si impedimentum non adsit; et remissio peccatorum quamvis non sit plenior, quia uterque omnem poenam et culpam tollit, tamen est in baptismo sanguinis efficacior et fructuosior, quia secundis maculis non inquinatur, ut Damascenus dicit. Quod enim quidam dicunt, quod in baptismo sanguinis gratia non confertur, apparet falsum esse in pueris qui pro Christo occiduntur, et etiam in adultis, quibus potest in ipso actu passionis gratia dari, sicut et in baptismo aquae, si se ad eam disposuerint, et obicem aliquem non ponant Spiritui Sancto. Et hoc patet per Augustinum, qui loquens de comparatione horum baptismatum, ait: *baptizatus confitetur fidem suam coram sacerdote, martyr coram persecutore; ille post professionem aspergitur aqua, hic sanguine; ille per impositionem manus pontificis recipit Spiritum Sanctum, hic templum efficitur Spiritus Sancti.* Nullus au-

To the fourth question, it is to be said that either of these baptisms has its efficacy from the Passion of Christ, according as each conforms one to it. And since baptism of water conforms someone to the Passion by sacramental signification, but baptism of blood does it in reality, for this reason, in regard to sacramental things, like the imprint of the character and such, baptism of water is superior. But in regard to those things that are the reality of the sacrament, baptism of blood is superior, for in baptism of blood the grace is both increased more in the one who has it, and given more to the one who does not have it, if there is no impediment to it; and although the remission of sins is no greater, since both baptisms take away all fault and punishment, nevertheless, it is more efficacious and fruitful in the baptism of blood, since one is not soiled by second stains, as Damascene says.[120] For what some people say, that in baptism of blood grace is not conferred, appears to be false in the case of the children who are killed for Christ, and also the adults, to whom grace can be given in the very act of suffering, just like in the baptism of water, if they are disposed to it and do not place any obstacle to the Holy Spirit. And this is clear from Augustine, who, comparing these baptisms, says: *the baptized person professes his faith before the priest, the martyr, before his persecutor; the former is sprinkled with water after his profession, the latter, with*

---

120. In the text cited immediately above.

tem efficitur templum Spiritus Sancti nisi gratiam accipiendo.

AD PRIMUM ergo dicendum, quod etiam baptismus sanguinis efficaciam habet a passione Christi, cui expressius conformat quam baptismus aquae.

AD SECUNDUM dicendum, quod in baptismo sanguinis aliquis non solum aureolam meretur, sed etiam auream per gratiam tunc collatam, vel augmentatam.

blood; *the former receives the Holy Spirit by the imposition of the hands of the bishop, the latter is made a temple of the Holy Spirit.*[121] But no one is made a temple of the Holy Spirit except by receiving grace.

REPLY OBJ. 1: Baptism of blood, too, has its efficacy from the Passion of Christ, to which it conforms more expressly than baptism of water.

REPLY OBJ. 2: In baptism of blood one merits not only a special reward, but also the golden crown by the grace conferred or increased at that moment.

---

121. St. Thomas attributed this quotation to Augustine's *Ad Fortunatus*, but it is found in Gennadius Massiliensis, *De ecclesiasticis dogmatibus*, ch. 41 (PL 58:1220).

EXPOSITION OF THE TEXT

Omnes parvuli qui in baptismo ab originali mundantur, sacramentum et rem suscipiunt. Non tamen soli parvuli, sed etiam adulti quandoque. Tamen de parvulis non est dubium quin recipiant; de adultis autem est, quia per fictionem impediri possent; et ideo parvulis potius exemplificat.

Nisi poeniteat, eum veteris vitae. Contra. Ergo baptismus non est primum sacramentum, sed poenitentia. Et dicendum, quod loquitur de poenitentia prout est virtus, non prout est sacramentum.

Non[124] *redire dimissa* etc., hoc qualiter verum sit, infra, dist. 22, quaest. 1, art. 1, in corp., dicetur.

Induunt homines Christum aliquando, etc. Induere Christum nihil aliud est quam Christi similitudinem assumere; quod contingit exterius per sacramentalem repraesentationem, et interius per realem imitationem.

Nec tantum passio vicem baptismi implet, sed etiam fides et contritio, ubi necessitas excludit sacramentum. Contritio non totaliter supplet: quia non semper a tota poena absolvit, quamvis absolvat ab omni culpa.

Neque enim ille latro pro nomine Christi crucifixus est. Contra est quod Hieronymus dicit, quod Christus homicidii poenam in illo latrone fecit esse martyrium. Et dicendum quod habuit aliquid de martyrio, scilicet poenam, et justam voluntatem; et aliquid defecit ad martyrium, scilicet causa; sicut in innocentibus defuit justa voluntas; sed fuit poena et causa.

Quem regeneraturus eram, amisi. Amisisse se eum dicit, quia gaudium et meritum quod de baptizatione ejus habiturus erat, amisit differens baptismum ejus usque ad solemne tempus secundum morem ecclesiae qui tunc erat, vel usque ad perfectam instructionem. Iste autem gratiam baptismi non amisit, quia cum desiderio ejus decessit; et hoc est verum quantum ad remissionem culpae, sed non quantum ad remissionem omnis poenae.

All children who in baptism are cleansed from original sin, receive both the sacrament and thing.[122] However, not only little ones, but also sometimes adults. Nevertheless, with infants there is no doubt that they receive it; there is, however, with adults, for they can impede it by insincerity; and therefore he uses children in his example instead.

"Unless he repent of his old life."[123] To the contrary: then baptism is not the first sacrament, but repentance. And it should be said that he speaks of repentance as a virtue, not as a sacrament.

For . . . sins which have been forgiven return, etc.[125] How this is true will be said below, in Distinction 22, Question 1, Article 1.

"Men put on Christ sometimes", etc.[126] 'To put on Christ' is nothing other than to assume the likeness of Christ, which happens outwardly by sacramental representation, and inwardly by real imitation.

Nor is it suffering alone which fills the role of baptism, but also faith and contrition, where necessity precludes the sacrament.[127] Contrition does not completely substitute, for it does not always absolve from all punishment, although it may absolve from all fault.

"For that thief was not crucified for the name of Christ."[128] Against this is what Jerome says, that Christ made that thief's punishment for homicide into martyrdom.[129] And it should be said that it did have something of martyrdom, namely, suffering, and a just will; and it also lacked something of martyrdom, namely, the reason for the suffering—even as the Holy Innocents were lacking a just will, but they had both the suffering and the reason for it.

"I lost the one whom I was about to bring to new life."[130] He says he 'lost' him, for the joy and merit that he was about to have from his baptizing, he lost by the deferral of his baptism until the time of a solemnity, according to the custom of the Church in those days, or until his instruction was complete. However, that man did not lose the grace of baptism, since he died longing for it; and this is true as to the remission of guilt, but not as to the remission of all punishment.

---

122. Peter Lombard, *Sententiae* IV, 4.1 (26). 2.

123. *Sent.* IV, 4.2 (27), 2, citing Pseudo-Augustine, *Sermo 351* or *Liber de poenitentia*, ch. 2, n. 2.

124. *Non.*—-*Nam* PLE.

125. *Sent.* IV, 4. 2 (27), 4, citing Augustine, *De baptismo contra Donatistas*, bk.1, c. 12, n. 20.

126. *Sent.* IV, 4.3 (28), 1, citing Augustine, *De baptismo contra Donatistas*, Bk. 5, ch. 24, n. 34.

127. *Sent* IV, 4.4 (29). 3.

128. *Sent.* IV, 4.4 (29), 3, citing Augustine, *De baptismo contra Donatistas*, Bk. 4, ch. 22, n. 29.

129. Jerome, *Epistle 58, to Bishop Paulinus*: "At e contrario latro crucem mutat paradiso et facit homicidii poena martyrem" (CSEL 54:528).

130. *Sent.* IV, 4.4 (97), 5 citing Ambrose, *De obitu Valetiniani*, nn. 29–30.

Ubi tota sacramenta baptismi complentur. Verum est quantum ad id quod est tantum res in sacramento.

Aeterno supplicio puniendos, supplicium improprie nominat poenam damni, quam solam pueri sustinebunt, ut in 2 Lib., dist. 33, quaest. 2, art. 2, dictum est.

Quia fidelium consortio non separantur. Orationes tamen illae non sunt pro eis suffragia, sed gratiarum actiones.

"In which all the sacraments of baptism are accomplished."[131] It is true as to what is the reality alone in the sacrament.

Will be punished by an eternal punishment.[132] 'Punishment' is not the proper word for the suffering of loss that is all children will endure, as was said in Book 2, Distinction 33, Question 2, Article 2.

These are not separated from the fellowship of the faithful when the Church prays for the faithful who have died.[133] Nevertheless those prayers are not offerings on their behalf, but thanksgiving.

---

131. *Sent.* IV, 4.4 (29), 9 citing Gennadius, *Liber sive diffinitio ecclesiasticorum dogmatum*, ch. 74.
132. *Sent.* IV, 4. 4 (29), 12, attributed to Augustine but actually Fulgentius, *De fide ad Petrum*, c. 27, n. 70.
133. *Sent.* IV, 4.4 (29), 13.

DISTINCTION 5

THE CAUSE OF BAPTISM

Postquam determinavit Magister de baptismo per comparationem ad recipientes, hic determinat de ipso per comparationem ad dantes; et dividitur in duas partes: in prima ostendit a quibus dari possit baptismus; in secunda a quibus et qualiter dari debeat, 6 dist.: *nunc quibus liceat baptizare, addamus.*

Prima in tres: in prima ostendit a quibus dari possit baptismus, quia a bonis et a malis; in secunda assignat hujus rationem, ibi: *quia ministerium tantum habent, non potestatem baptismi*; in tertia removet quamdam dubitationem, ibi: *hic quaeritur quae sit potestas baptismi quam Christus sibi retinuit.*

Hic est duplex quaestio. Prima de potestate baptizandi. Secunda de ipsis baptizantibus.

After the Master has examined baptism in relation to its recipients, here he examines it in relation to those giving it; and this is divided into two parts. In the first, he shows by whom baptism can be given; in the second, by whom and how it ought to be given, at Distinction 6: *Now let us add something about those for whom it is lawful to baptize.*[1]

The first is in three parts: in the first, he shows by whom baptism can be given, since it may be given by good men and bad; in the second, he assigns the reason, at: *[This is] because they have only the ministry, not the power, of baptism*;[2] in the third, he expels a particular doubt, at: *Here it is asked what is that power of baptism that Christ retained for himself.*[3]

Here, there is a two-fold question: first, about the power of baptizing; second, about those who do the baptizing.

---

1. Peter Lombard, *Sententiae* IV, 6.1 (36), 1.
2. *Sent.* IV, 5.2 (34), 1.
3. *Sent.* IV, 5.3 (35), 1.

QUESTION 1

THE POWER OF BAPTIZING

Circa primum quaeruntur tria:
primo, quam potestatem Christus, secundum quod homo, in baptizando habuit;
secundo, quam ministris contulerit;
tertio, quam conferre potuerit, sed non contulit.

Concerning the first, three questions arise:
first, what power Christ, as man, had in baptizing;

second, what power he conferred on his ministers;
third, what power he could have conferred, but did not confer.

ARTICLE 1

What power Christ, as man, had in baptizing[4]

AD PRIMUM SIC PROCEDITUR. Videtur quod Christus, secundum quod homo, habuit potestatem dimittendi peccata. Matth. 9, 6, dicitur: *ut autem sciatis quia filius hominis habet potestatem in terra dimittendi peccata, dixit paralytico: surge, et ambula.* Sed non oportebat signum ostendere ad probandum quod Deus haberet potestatem dimittendi peccatum: quia hoc Judaei confitebantur. Ergo etiam secundum quod homo habuit hanc potestatem.

PRAETEREA, Christus, secundum quod homo, est redemptor, ut in 3, dist. 19, qu. 1, art. 4, quaestiunc. 1, dictum est. Sed non potest aliquis liberari a servitute peccati nisi sibi peccatum dimissum sit. Ergo Christus, secundum quod homo, habuit potestatem dimittendi peccata.

PRAETEREA, super illud Joan. 5: *sicut pater suscitat mortuos* etc., dicit Augustinus: *judicat, et suscitat corpora, non Pater, sed Filius, secundum humanitatis dispensationem, qua minor est Patre.* Sed suscitatio corporum attestatur suscitationi animarum, quae fit per dimissionem peccati. Ergo Christus, secundum quod homo, potuit peccatum dimittere.

PRAETEREA, majus est imperium ejus quam invocatio nominis ejus. Sed ad invocationem nominis Christi dabatur baptismus et remissio peccatorum in primitiva ecclesia. Ergo et ipse Christus suo imperio poterat peccata dimittere.

PRAETEREA, Christus amplioris gloriae prae Moyse habitus est, quia non sicut servus vel minister, sicut Moyses, est in domo Dei, sed sicut dominus et heres, ut di-

OBJ. 1: To the first we proceed thus. It seems that Christ, as man, had the power of forgiving sins. For it is said: *but so that you may know that the Son of Man has the power on earth to forgive sins, he said to the paralytic, "rise, and walk"* (Matt 9:6). But it was not necessary to show a sign in order to prove that God had the power of forgiving sins, for the Jews professed this. Therefore, he had this power also as man.

OBJ. 2: Furthermore, Christ as man is the Redeemer, as was said in Book 3, Distinction 19, Question 1, Article 4, Subquestion 1. But someone cannot be freed from slavery to sin unless his sins are forgiven him. Therefore, Christ had the power of forgiving sins as man.

OBJ. 3: Furthermore, concerning the passage in John: *Just as the Father raises the dead and gives them life, so also the Son gives life to whomever he wishes* (John 5:21), Augustine says he judges, and he raises bodies—not the Father, but the Son, according to the dispensation of his humanity, in which he is less than the Father.[5] But the raising of bodies attests to the raising of souls, which happens by the forgiving of sins. Therefore, Christ, as man, could forgive sin.

OBJ. 4: Furthermore, his power is greater than the invocation of his name. But in the early Church, baptism and the remission of sins were granted at the invocation of Christ's name. Therefore, Christ himself, too, could forgive sins by his own power.

OBJ. 5: Furthermore, Christ was held to have greater glory than Moses, for he was not in the house of God as a servant or minister, like Moses, but as lord and heir, as is

---

4. Parallels: *ST* III, q. 64, a. 3; *Super Ioan.* 1, lec. 14; *Super I ad Cor.* 1, lec. 2.
5. See Augustine, *In Iohannis euangelium tractatus* (CCSL 36), Tract. 23, n. 13.

citur Hebr. 3. Sed si non haberet potestatem dimittendi peccatum, secundum quod homo, non esset sicut dominus, sed solum sicut minister, sicut et alii. Ergo habet potestatem dimittendi peccata.

SED CONTRA, illud quod est solius Dei, non convenit Christo inquantum est homo. Sed dimittere peccatum est hujusmodi; ut patet Isai. 43: *ego sum qui deleo iniquitates tuas propter me.* Ergo non convenit Christo.

PRAETEREA, nulli dimittitur peccatum, nisi per Spiritum Sanctum. Sed Christus, secundum quod homo, non poterat dare Spiritum Sanctum, ut dist. 15, 1 Lib., quaest. 5, art. 1, quaestiunc. 4, dictum est. Ergo non potest remittere peccata secundum quod homo.

PRAETEREA, Augustinus dicit, quod Christus secundum quod est Filius Dei, est vita quae vivificat animas. Sed quod convenit sibi inquantum est Filius Dei, non competit ei secundum quod est homo. Ergo vivificare animas remittendo peccata, non competit ei secundum quod homo.

RESPONDEO dicendum, quod triplex est potestas absolvendi a peccato in baptismo. Una potestas auctoritatis; et haec solius Dei est, quia propria virtute peccata dimittit, quasi principalis causa remissionis peccati; unde tali potestate Christus, secundum quod homo, peccata remittere non poterat. Alia potestas est ministerii, quae eis competit qui sacramenta dispensant, in quibus divina virtus secretius operatur salutem. Tertia est media inter has duas, quae dicitur potestas excellentiae; et hanc Christus prae aliis habuit.

Attenditur autem haec excellentia quantum ad tria. Primo quantum ad hoc quod ex merito passionis ejus baptismus efficaciam habet, non autem ex merito alicujus alterius baptizantis; unde non est melior baptismus a meliore baptizante datus. Secundo quantum ad hoc quod Christus sine sacramento sacramentorum effectum conferre poterat quasi Dominus et institutor sacramentorum; quod de aliis non est verum. Tertio quantum ad hoc quod ad invocationem nominis ejus dabatur remissio peccatorum in baptismo in primitiva ecclesia. Sed quia secundae rationes videntur procedere de prima potestate, ideo concedendae sunt illae, et respondendum est ad primas.

AD PRIMUM ergo dicendum, quod Filius Hominis habebat potestatem auctoritatis dimittendi peccata, non secundum quod homo, sed secundum quod Deus; et ideo per miraculum ostensum hic probatur quod ille homo esset Deus, cui natura obediebat quasi proprio creatori.

AD SECUNDUM dicendum, quod redemptor dicitur dupliciter. Uno modo propter usum potestatis auctoritativae in absolvendo a peccato, et sic Christus secundum

said in Hebrews 3:3. But if he did not have the power of forgiving sins as man, he would not be as the lord, but only as the minister, just like all the others. Therefore, he has the power of forgiving sins.

ON THE CONTRARY, what belongs to God alone does not belong to Christ as man. But to forgive sin is one of these things, as is clear from Isaiah: *I am he who blots out your transgressions for my own sake* (Isa 43:25). Therefore, it does not belong to Christ as man.

FURTHERMORE, sin is forgiven no one except by the Holy Spirit. But Christ, as man, could not give the Holy Spirit, as was said in Book 1, Distinction 15, Question 5, Article 1, Subquestion 4. Therefore he, as man, cannot remit sins.

FURTHERMORE, Augustine says that Christ, according as he is the Son of God, is the life that gives life to souls. But what belongs to him insofar as he is Son of God does not befit him according as he is man. Therefore, to give life to souls by the remission of sins does not belong to him as man.

I ANSWER THAT, there are three kinds of power for absolving from sin in baptism. One is the power of authority, and this pertains to God alone, who forgives sins by his own power, as the principal cause of the remission of sins; hence Christ as man could not forgive sins with that kind of power. Another power is that of the minister, which belongs to those who dispense the sacraments, in which divine power invisibly works our salvation. The third is a mean between these two, which is called the power of excellence; and this Christ had above everyone else.

Now this excellence has three aspects. First, baptism has its efficacy from the merit of his Passion, but not from the merit of anyone else who baptizes; hence a baptism given by a better baptizer is not a better baptism. Second, Christ, as Lord and institutor of the sacraments, could confer the effect of the sacraments without a sacrament, which is not true of the others. Third, in the early Church, the remission of sins was given at the invocation of his name in baptism. But because the second arguments seem based on the first power, therefore they should be conceded, and the first ones should be answered. [6]

REPLY OBJ. 1: The Son of Man had the power of authority for forgiving sins, not insofar as he was man, but insofar as he was God; and thus, by the miracle displayed here, it is proved that that man was God, whom nature obeyed as its proper creator.

REPLY OBJ. 2: 'Redeemer' is said in two ways. In one way, because of the use of authoritative power in absolving from sins, and in this way, Christ, as God, was the re-

---

6. The first arguments are the objections, the second arguments the *sed contras*.

quod Deus, redemptor est. Alio modo propter effectum humilitatis; et sic competit ei secundum quod homo, inquantum per humilitatem passionis nobis remissionem meruit peccatorum; et hoc pertinet ad potestatem excellentiae, ut dictum est.

AD TERTIUM dicendum, quod potestas quam Christus secundum quod homo habuit suscitandi corpora, non est potestas tantum ministerii, sicut et Petrus mortuos suscitavit; neque est iterum potestas auctoritatis, quia hoc solius Dei est: sed est potestas cujusdam excellentiae, quae ei competit ex unione ad Deum, ut scilicet imperio, non prece, mortuos suscitaret: et similiter habuit potestatem excellentiae in remittendo peccata.

AD QUARTUM dicendum, quod hoc quod ad invocationem nominis ejus conferebatur remissio peccatorum in baptismo, pertinet ad potestatem excellentiae.

AD QUINTUM dicendum, quod non habuit tantum ministerii potestatem, sed altiorem, ut dictum est.

deemer. In another way, because of the effect of humility; and in this way, it applied to him as man, inasmuch as by the humility of his Passion, he merited for us the remission of sins; and this belongs to the power of excellence, as was said.

REPLY OBJ. 3: The power of raising bodies that Christ had, according as he was man, is not the power of a mere minister, even as Peter also raised the dead; nor is it the power of authority, for this belongs to God alone; but it is the power of a certain excellence, which belongs to him by his union with God, so that he could raise the dead by command, not by prayer. And he had this power of excellence likewise in remitting sins.

REPLY OBJ. 4: The fact that the remission of sins in baptism was conferred at the invocation of his name pertains to the power of excellence.

REPLY OBJ. 5: He did not have the power of a mere minister, but a higher power, as was said.

ARTICLE 2

What power Christ conferred on his ministers[7]

AD SECUNDUM SIC PROCEDITUR. Videtur quod ministris contulerit potestatem cooperandi ad interiorem emundationem. Ministris enim data est aliqua spiritualis potestas. Sed ad emundationem corporalem non requiritur aliqua spiritualis potestas, sed sufficit corporalis. Ergo ministri cooperantur ad emundationem interiorem.

PRAETEREA, sicut sanctificatio quaedam adhibetur rebus sacramentalibus, ita etiam ministris sacramentorum. Sed res sacramentales ex sanctificatione invisibilem gratiam continent et conferunt, secundum Hugonem de sancto Victore. Ergo ministri sanctificati, in sua sanctificatione ad interiorem emundationem, quae est per gratiam, operantur.

PRAETEREA, inter creaturas dignior est creatura rationalis quam aliqua forma accidentalis. Sed gratia operatur interius ad peccati remissionem. Ergo et homo multo fortius habet potestatem interius cooperandi.

PRAETEREA, omnis actio alicujus formae attribuitur habenti formam illam, quia calor agit secundum calidum. Sed remissio culpae est actio gratiae. Ergo habenti gratiam competit cooperari ad remissionem culpae.

PRAETEREA, secundum Dionysium, ad ministros ecclesiae pertinet purgare, illuminare, perficere. Sed purgatio in ecclesia fit a sordibus mentis. Ergo ministri ecclesiae cooperantur ad interiorem emundationem.

SED CONTRA, emundatio interior a peccatis fit per Spiritum Sanctum. Sed ministri ecclesiae non dant Spiritum Sanctum. Ergo nec cooperantur ad interiorem emundationem.

PRAETEREA, majus est justificare impium quam creare caelum et terram. Sed in creatione caeli et terrae nihil Deo cooperatur. Ergo nec in justificatione impii.

PRAETEREA, hominis operatio etiam in actibus hierarchicis est sub operatione angeli, ut dicit Dionysius. Sed angeli non possunt imprimere in affectum, ut in 2 Lib., dist. 8, qu. 1, art. 5, dictum est. Ergo cum affectum

OBJ. 1: To the second we proceed thus. It seems that he conferred upon his ministers the power of cooperating in interior cleansing. For a certain spiritual power was given to the ministers. But for bodily cleansing no spiritual power is required; bodily power suffices. Therefore, the ministers cooperate in the interior cleansing.

OBJ. 2: Furthermore, just as a certain sanctification is applied to the things used in the sacraments, so the same is done to the ministers of the sacraments. But things used in the sacraments contain and confer invisible grace by their sanctification, according to Hugh of St. Victor.[8] Therefore, sanctified ministers, in their own sanctification, work interior cleansing, which is by grace.

OBJ. 3: Furthermore, among created things, the rational creature is more noble than any accidental form. But grace works interiorly for the remission of sins. Therefore, much more has a man the power of cooperating interiorly.

OBJ. 4: Furthermore, every action of a certain form is attributed to what has that form, for heat acts through whatever is hot. But the remission of fault is the action of grace. Therefore, it belongs to the one having grace to cooperate in the remission of fault.

OBJ. 5: Furthermore, according to Dionysius,[9] it belongs to the ministers of the Church to purify, illuminate, and perfect. But purification from the filth of the mind happens in the Church. Therefore, the ministers of the Church cooperate in the interior cleansing.

ON THE CONTRARY, interior cleansing from sins is done by the Holy Spirit. But the ministers of the Church do not give the Holy Spirit. Therefore, neither do they cooperate in the interior cleansing.

FURTHERMORE, it is a greater thing to justify the wicked than to create heaven and earth.[10] But in the creation of heaven and earth nothing cooperates with God. Therefore, neither in the justification of the wicked.

FURTHERMORE, even in hierarchical actions, man's operation is under the operation of an angel, as Dionysius says.[11] But the angels cannot make an impression on the affective part, as was said in Book 2, Distinction 8, Question

---

7. Parallel: *ST* III, q. 64, aa. 1 & 4.

8. Hugh of St. Victor, *De sacramentis fidei*, Bk. 1, pt. 9, ch. 2 (PL 176:317).

9. Pseudo-Dionysius, *Ecclesiastical Hierarchy*, ch. 5, n. 3 (PG 3:503).

10. Augustine, *In Iohannis euangelium tractatus* (CCSL 36), Tract. 72, n. 3: "intellegat qui potest, iudicet qui potest, utrum maius sit iustos creare quam impios iustificare."

11. Pseudo-Dionysius, *Celestial Hierarchy*, ch. 9, n. 2 (PG 3:259).

oporteat a peccatis mundari, videtur quod nec cooperentur ad emundationem interiorem.

Respondeo dicendum, quod cooperari alicui agenti dicitur quatuor modis. Uno modo sicut adjuvans ei cui auxilium praebet, cooperatur. Alio modo sicut consilium praebens. Tertio modo sicut quo mediante agens primum suum effectum inducit, sicut cooperantur instrumenta principali agenti. Quarto modo sicut disponens materiam ad effectum agentis principalis suscipiendum.

Primis ergo duobus modis in nulla actione aliquid Deo cooperatur propter perfectam ejus potentiam, quae auxilio non indiget, et propter perfectam sapientiam, quae non indiget consilio, Isai. 40, 13: *quis adjuvit spiritum Domini, aut quis consiliarius ejus fuit?*

Sed tertio modo cooperatur aliqua creatura Deo in aliqua actione, non tamen in omnibus. Cum enim Deus sit primum agens omnium naturalium actionum, quidquid natura agit, hoc efficit quasi instrumentale agens cooperans primo agenti, quod est Deus. Sed quaedam sunt quae sibi Deus retinuit, immediate ea operans; et in his creatura Deo non cooperatur hoc tertio modo, sed quarto modo potest ei cooperari; sicut patet in creatione animae rationalis, quam immediate Deus producit, sed tamen natura disponit materiam ad animae rationalis receptionem.

Et quia recreatio animae rationalis creationi ipsius respondet, ideo in emundatione ipsius immediate operatur; nec aliquis ei quantum ad hoc cooperatur tertio modo, sed quarto; et hoc dupliciter: vel ex opere operante, sive docendo, sive merendo; et sic homines ei cooperantur in peccatorum remissione, de quibus dicitur 1 Corinth. 3, 9: *Dei adjutores sumus*, vel ex opere operato, sicut qui conferunt sacramenta, quae ad gratiam disponunt, per quam fit remissio peccatorum; et haec est cooperatio ministerii, quae ministris ecclesiae competit, de quibus dicitur 1 Corinth. 4, 1: *sic nos existimet homo ut ministros Christi.*

Ad primum ergo dicendum, quod potestas spiritualis quae ministris ecclesiae conceditur, ad aliquid interius se extendit, sicut virtus sacramentalis sed non ad collationem gratiae, per quam est remissio peccatorum, nisi dispensando,[13] sicut et de sacramentis dictum est.

1, Article 5.[12] Therefore, since the affective part has to be cleansed from sin, it seems that neither do they cooperate in interior cleansing.

I answer that, there are four ways that someone may be said to cooperate with any agent. In one way, as someone helping another to whom he offers assistance cooperates with him. In another way, by offering counsel. In a third way, in being the means by which an agent brings about his first effect, as instruments cooperate with the principal agent. In the fourth way, by disposing the matter for receiving the effect of the principal agent.

In the first two ways, therefore, nothing cooperates with God in any action, on account of his perfect power, which needs no assistance, and his perfect wisdom, which needs no counsel: *who helps the spirit of the Lord, or who has been his counselor?* (Isa 40:13)

But in the third way, some creatures cooperates with God in certain actions, but not in all. For since God is the first agent in all natural activities, whatever nature does, it brings about as the instrumental agent cooperating with the first agent, which is God. But there are certain things that God reserves to himself, working them without intermediaries; and in these matters, creation does not cooperate with God in the third way, but it can cooperate with him in the fourth way—as is clear in the creation of the rational soul, which God produces without intermediaries, yet nevertheless nature disposes the matter for the reception of the rational soul.

And since the re-creation of the rational soul corresponds to its creation, thus he works without intermediaries in its cleansing; nor does anyone cooperate with him for this in the third way, but only in the fourth. And this happens in two ways: either by the action of the one doing it, whether by teaching, or by meriting (and men cooperate with him in this way in the remission of sins, of whom it is said, *we are God's helpers*, 1 Cor 3:9); or else by the work itself being done, like those who confer the sacraments, which dispose to grace, by which the remission of sin happens—and the latter is the cooperation of a minister, which is applicable to the ministers of the Church, of whom it is said, *Let a man so consider us as ministers of Christ* (1 Cor 4:1).

Reply Obj. 1: The spiritual power granted to the ministers of the Church, like sacramental power, does extend to something interior, but not to the conferral of grace that causes the remission of sins—except in the manner of administering the means whereby grace is conferred, as was also said of the sacraments.

---

12. Thomas writes here *affectum*, but from the context it has to mean "will." In Bk. 2, d. 8, q. 1, a. 5, ad 7, Thomas writes: "Demons are called instigators insofar as they stir up the blood, and in this way dispose the soul to concupiscence, just as certain foods provoke to sensuality. To make an impression on the will, however, belongs to God alone, which is owing to the freedom of the will, which is lord of its own acts, and is not compelled by its object as the intellect is compelled by a demonstration. Hence it is clear from the foregoing that demons make an impression on the imagination, and angels, in addition, on the intellect; but God alone on the will."

13. *dispensando.—-disponendo* PLE.

Unde patet solutio ad secundum.

Ad tertium dicendum, quod gratia non remittit culpam effective, sed formaliter, sicut albedo aufert nigredinem; et ideo non sequitur quod creaturae rationali competat, quae non est forma.

Ad quartum dicendum, quod est duplex operatio formae alicujus: scilicet prima, quae pertinet ad informationem subjecti sicut scientia et secunda, quae dicitur usus vel actio, sicut considerare. Primam ergo operationem non participat habens formam,[14] sed solum secundam. Remittere autem culpam competit gratiae quantum ad operationem primam; sicut albedo eadem ratione qua facit album, aufert et nigredinem a subjecto in quo est; et ideo non oportet quod habens gratiam, hoc per gratiam participet.

Ad quintum dicendum, quod purgatio, de qua Dionysius loquitur, est a tenebris ignorantiae, sicut ipsemet dicit; unde magis pertinet ad intellectum quam ad affectum.

Hence the solution to the second objection is clear.

Reply Obj. 3: Grace does not remit fault effectively, but formally, as whiteness removes blackness; and thus, it does not follow that it befits the rational creature, which is not a form.

Reply Obj. 4: The operation of a form is twofold: namely, first act, which pertains to the informing of the subject, e.g., knowledge, and second act, which is called use or action, e.g., considering. What has the form, therefore, does not take part by its form in the first operation, but only the second. However, to forgive fault belongs to grace as regards the first operation, just as whiteness, by the same account by which it makes something white, also removes the blackness from the subject in which it is. And thus, it is not necessary that the one having grace take part in this by grace.

Reply Obj. 5: The purification of which Dionysius speaks is purification from the darkness of ignorance, as he himself says. Hence it pertains more to the understanding than to the affection.

---

14. *formam sed.—formam a forma sed* PLE.

ARTICLE 3

What power Christ could have conferred, but did not confer[15]

Quaestiuncula 1

AD TERTIUM SIC PROCEDITUR. Videtur quod ministris conferri potuit a Deo potestas cooperationis. Nam super illud Joan. 1: *hic est qui baptizat*, dicit Augustinus, quod Joannes didicit, quod potestatem mundandi a peccatis Christus dare potuit, sed non dedit: dedit autem potestatem ministerii. Ergo videtur quod potuerit dare, potestatem cooperationis.

PRAETEREA, major est potestas auctoritatis quam cooperationis. Sed super illud 1 Corinth. 1: *divisus est Christus?* Dicit Glossa, quod potuit eis dare auctoritatem baptizandi quibus contulit ministerium. Ergo multo fortius potuit dare cooperationem interius emundandi.

PRAETEREA, plus est expellere daemonem quam seminatum per ipsum, scilicet peccatum. Sed Deus dedit hominibus potestatem daemones expellendi, ut patet Luc. 10. Ergo multo fortius potuit dare potestatem expellendi peccatum.

SED CONTRA, omne agens oportet quod sit simul cum patiente, ut probatur in 7 *Physica*. Sed non potest conferri alicui creaturae quod illabatur in animam rationalem. Ergo non potest conferri quod cooperetur ad interiorem emundationem.

PRAETEREA, gratia est quaedam inchoatio gloriae. Sed non potest alicui creaturae communicari quod ab ipsa sit gloria, sicut neque quod sit summum bonum. Ergo potestas cooperationis ad gratiam habendam, per quam fit peccatorum remissio, homini conferri non potuit.

OBJ. 1: To the third question we proceed thus. It seems that the power of cooperation could have been conferred on the ministers by God. For concerning the text, *he is the one who baptizes with the Holy Spirit* (John 1:33), Augustine says that John said that Christ could give the power of cleansing from sins, but he did not give it: he did, however, give the power of administering it.[16] Therefore, it seems that he could have given the power of cooperating.

OBJ. 2: Furthermore, the power of authority is greater than the power of cooperating. But concerning the text, *Has Christ been divided?* (1 Cor 1:13), the Gloss says that he could have given the authority of baptizing to those on whom he conferred the ministry.[17] Therefore, much more could he have given the power of cooperation in interior cleansing.

OBJ. 3: Furthermore, it is greater to expel a demon than to expel what has been sown by it, namely, sin. But God gave men the power of expelling demons, as is clear from Luke 10. Therefore, much more could he have given them the power of expelling sins.

ON THE CONTRARY, it is necessary that every agent be simultaneous with the patient, as is proved in *Physics* 7.[18] But it cannot be conferred on any created thing that it infiltrate a rational soul. Therefore, cooperation in interior cleansing cannot be conferred.

FURTHERMORE, grace is a certain beginning of glory. But it cannot be shared with any creature that glory be from it, as neither that it be the supreme good. Therefore, the power of cooperation in bestowing grace, by which the remission of sins happens, could not be conferred on any man.

Quaestiuncula 2

ULTERIUS. Videtur quod nec potestas excellentiae. Quia Matth. 25, dicitur, quod dedit unicuique secundum propriam virtutem. Sed non dedit potestatem excellentiae nisi soli Christo. Ergo non potuit aliis conferri.

OBJ. 1: Moreover, it seems that neither could the power of excellence be conferred. For it is said in Matthew 25 that he gave to each according to his own strength (Matt 25:15). But he did not give the power of excellence to any but Christ alone. Therefore, he could not confer it on others.

---

15. Parallels: above, a. 2; *ST* III, q. 64, a. 4; *De veritate*, q. 27, a. 3, ad 17; *Super Ioan.* 1, lec. 14; *Super I ad Cor.* 1, lec. 2.

16. Augustine, *In Iohannis euangelium tractatus* (CCSL 36), Tract. 5, n. 7.

17. See *Glossa Lombardi*, PL 191:1539. Here, "authority" means the ability to institute a sacrament, not merely to confer it.

18. Aristotle, *Physics*, Bk. 7, ch. 2, 244a5ff.; cf. *Physics*, Bk. 2, ch. 3, 195b16–21.

PRAETEREA, potestas excellentiae competit Christo, secundum quod meritum ejus operatur ad remissionem omnium peccatorum, ut dictum est. Sed hoc non competit Christo nisi secundum quod ejus meritum habet quamdam infinitatem, ut in 3 Lib. dictum est, dist. 18, quaest. 2, art. 6, quaestiunc. 1, et dist. 19, quaest. 1, art. 1, quaestiunc. 1. Cum ergo habere efficaciam infinitam in merendo non possit alicui creaturae purae conferri, videtur quod nec potestas excellentiae.

PRAETEREA, potestas excellentiae competit Christo secundum quod est caput ecclesiae de cujus plenitudine omnes accipimus. Sed hoc competit ei quia est unigenitus a Patre, ut dicitur Joan. 1. Ergo nulli purae creaturae communicari potuit.

SED CONTRA, quidquid competit Christo secundum quod homo, potest et alii homini communicari. Sed potestas excellentiae, ut dictum est, competit Christo secundum quod homo est. Ergo potest aliis hominibus communicari.

PRAETEREA, ad potestatem excellentiae pertinet quod ad invocationem nominis Christi remissio peccatorum in ipso[19] detur. Sed potuit etiam hoc Deus conferre Petro vel Paulo, ut ad invocationem nominis ejus baptisma conferretur, ut dicit *Glossa* 1 Corinth., 1. Ergo potestas excellentiae potuit aliis conferri.

OBJ. 2: Furthermore, the power of excellence belongs to Christ according as his merit works unto the remission of all sins, as was said. But this belongs to Christ only according as his merit has a certain infinity, as was said in Book 3, Distinction 18, Question 2, Article 6, Subquestion 1, and Distinction 19, Question 1, Article 1, Subquestion 1. Therefore, since having infinite efficacy in meriting could not be conferred on any mere creature, it seems that neither could the power of excellence.

OBJ. 3: Furthermore, the power of excellence belongs to Christ according as he is the Church's head, of whose fullness we all receive. But this belongs to him because he is the Only-begotten Son of the Father, as is said in John 1:14. Therefore, it could not be shared with any mere creature.

ON THE CONTRARY, whatever belongs to Christ as man can also be shared with other men. But the power of excellence, as was said, belongs to Christ as man. Therefore, it can also be shared with other men.

FURTHERMORE, it belongs to the power of excellence that the remission of sins be given at the invocation of Christ's name in baptism. But God could also have conferred this on Peter or Paul, such that at the invocation of his name baptism would be conferred, as the Gloss on 1 Corinthians 1 says.[20] Therefore, the power of excellence could have been conferred on others.

Quaestiuncula 3

ULTERIUS. Videtur quod potentia creandi potuerit creaturae communicari. Plus enim Deus potest facere quam homo possit intelligere; *quia non est impossibile apud Deum omne verbum*, ut dicitur Luc. 1, 37. Sed quidam philosophi posuerunt in aliquibus creaturis potentiam creandi, sicut Avicenna, qui dicit, quod intelligentia prima producit secundam, et sic deinceps. Ergo Deus posset hoc creaturae communicare.

PRAETEREA, nihil potentiae divinae absolute acceptae subtrahendum est quod in se contradictionem non implicat vel defectum. Sed quod aliqua creatura habeat potentiam creandi hoc nullam contradictionem implicat, ut videtur; neque in aliquem defectum sonat, immo magis in perfectionem divinam: quia perfectum est quod potest alterum facere quale ipsum est, ut dicitur in 4 *Meteor.*; et sic non ponit imperfectionem in Deo, quod ipse Creator alios creatores constituat. Ergo hoc potentiae ejus subtrahendum non est.

OBJ. 1: Moreover, it seems that the power of creating could have been communicated to a creature. For God can do more than man can understand; *since no word is impossible with God* (Luke 1:37). But some philosophers posited a power of creating in certain creatures, like Avicenna, who says that the first intelligence produces the second intelligence, and so on in succession.[21] Therefore, God could communicate this to a creature.

OBJ. 2: Furthermore, nothing should be withdrawn from the scope of divine power, understood absolutely, unless it implies self-contradiction or defect. But that some creature should have the power of creating implies no contradiction, as it seems; nor does it convey any defect, but rather, more the divine perfection, for the perfect is what can make another like itself, as is said in *Meteorology* 4;[22] and in this way, that the Creator himself should establish other creators posits no imperfection in God. Therefore, this should not be withdrawn from his power.

---

19. *ipso.—baptismo* PLE.
20. See *Glossa Lombardi*, PL 191:1538.
21. Here Thomas refers to Avicenna's theory of the emanation of spiritual creatures or pure intellects from the highest to the least, each coming from the one before.
22. Aristotle, *Meteorology*, Bk. 4, ch. 3, 380a14–15.

PRAETEREA, forma est nobilior quam materia. Sed aliquibus creaturis collatum est ut possint producere formas. Ergo et potuit creaturae conferri ut possit producere materiam; et hoc est creare: ergo potentia creandi creaturae communicari potuit.

PRAETEREA, quanto est major resistentia tanto est major difficultas in actione. Sed contrarium magis resistit actioni quam non ens, quod non potest agere. Si ergo creaturae collatum est ut possit aliquid ex contrario facere, multo fortius potuit ei conferri ut possit aliquid ex non ente facere, quod est creare.

SED CONTRA, creaturae non potest conferri quod habeat potentiam infinitam, cum sit essentiae finitae. Sed creatio est opus potentiae infinitae, quod patet per distantiam infinitam quae est inter ens et non ens. Ergo potentia creandi creaturae communicari non potuit.

PRAETEREA, Creatori debetur latria. Sed hoc non potest creaturae communicari ut ei latria debeatur, sicut nec quod sit Deus. Ergo creaturae non potest communicari potentia creandi.

PRAETEREA, nihil agit nisi secundum quod est actu. Sed creaturae non potest communicari quod sit actus purus. Ergo non potest sibi communicari quod agat se tota; ergo neque quod agat totum quod est in re, quod est creare.

OBJ. 3: Furthermore, form is more noble than matter. But it was conferred on other creatures that they be able to produce forms. Therefore, it could also have been conferred that they produce matter, and this is to create. Therefore, the power of creating could have been shared with a creature.

OBJ. 4: Furthermore, the greater the resistance, the more difficult the act. But a contrary resists action more than non-being, which cannot act. Therefore, if it was conferred on a creature to be able to make something out of its contrary, much more could there be conferred the ability to make something out of non-being, which is to create.

ON THE CONTRARY, it cannot be conferred on a creature that it have infinite power, since it is of finite essence. But creation is a work of infinite power, which is clear from the infinite distance that there is between being and non-being. Therefore, the power of creating could not be communicated to a creature.

FURTHERMORE, adoration is owed to the Creator. But it cannot be shared with a creature that adoration be owed to it, just as neither can it be communicated to it that it be God. Therefore, the power of creating cannot be communicated to a creature.

FURTHERMORE, nothing acts except to the extent that it is in act. But it cannot be communicated to a creature that it be pure act. Therefore, it cannot be shared with it that it act wholly from itself; therefore, neither can it be that it enact everything that is in a thing, which is to create.

Response to Quaestiuncula 1

RESPONDEO dicendum ad primam quaestionem, quod dupliciter dicitur aliquid non posse communicari alicui creaturae: aut quia nulli creaturae communicari potest aut quia alicui potest communicari sed non isti. Quidquid enim communicatum alicui traheret ipsum extra terminos suae speciei, non potest sibi communicari sicut equo non potest communicari quod habeat rationem, quamvis hoc communicatum sit homini. Quod autem communicatum alicui trahit ipsum extra terminos creaturae non potest alicui creaturae communicari. Potestas ergo auctoritatis communicata alicui traheret ipsum extra terminos creaturae: quia non potest esse quod creatura sit agens principale respectu nobilissimi effectus, quo ultimo fini conjungimur, cujusmodi est gratia per quam fit remissio peccatorum. Et ideo omnes dicunt, quod potestas auctoritatis nulli creaturae communicari potuit.

Sed de potentia cooperationis est duplex opinio. Magister enim in littera videtur dicere, quod potentia cooperationis ad emundationem interiorem possit alicui creaturae conferri, quamvis non sit collata: quod non

TO THE FIRST QUESTION, I answer that there are two ways of saying that something cannot be shared with any created thing: either because it can be communicated to no creature, or because it can be communicated to some creature, but not this one. For anything that, once communicated to another, would draw it outside the bounds of its own species, cannot be communicated to it, as it cannot be communicated to a horse that he have reason, although this could be shared with a man. But that which, communicated to something, draws it outside the bounds of creation cannot be shared with any created thing. Therefore, the power of authority communicated to another would draw him beyond the bounds of creation—for it cannot be that a creature be the principal agent with respect to the noblest effect, by which we are joined to the last end, and that is the kind of thing grace is, through which the remission of sins happens. And thus, all say that the power of authority could not be shared with any creature.

But there are two opinions about the power of cooperation. For the Master seems to say in the text that the power of cooperation in interior cleansing could be conferred on some creature, although it was not conferred—which can-

potest intelligi de cooperatione quae fit per modum dispositionis quia haec collata est ministris ecclesiae, ut dictum est. Alii autem dicunt contrarium, quod conferri non potuit. Utraque autem opinio aliquo modo sustineri potest. Cooperatur enim aliquid Deo instrumentaliter duobus modis. Uno modo ita quod per virtutem aliquam habentem esse absolutum et completum in natura operetur ad effectum aliquem producendum non solum secundarium, sed principalem, sicut ignis cooperatur Deo in generatione ignis alterius; et hoc modo accipiendo cooperationem, non poterat conferri homini ut Deo cooperetur in interiori mundatione quae fit per gratiam: quia gratia elevat hominem ad vitam quandam quae est supra conditionem omnis naturae creatae; est enim esse gratiae supra esse naturale et hominis et angeli, quae sunt supremae creaturae; et ideo agens quod propria virtute sibi animam assimilat per gratiam, oportet quod sit supra omnem virtutem creatam, et sic talis cooperatio excedet terminos creaturae. Alio modo aliquid cooperatur Deo non per virtutem quae habeat esse perfectum in natura, neque ad ultimum principalem effectum directe pertingendo, sicut de sacramentis in 1 dist., qu. 1, art. 4, dictum est, et hoc modo cooperari Deo in interiori emundatione, ut quidam dicunt, disponendo, potuit homini conferri sine sacramentis, sicut sacramenta praebendo facit; et hoc modo cooperari pertinet ad potestatem excellentiae in Christo, ut dictum est.

Ad primum ergo dicendum, quod hoc intelligitur de potestate excellentiae quam Christus habuit etiam secundum quod homo; quae includit potestatem cooperationis secundo modo dictae; non autem de potestate cooperationis primo modo dictae.

Ad secundum dicendum, quod auctoritas ibi accipitur non respectu emundationis, sed respectu institutionis sacramentorum, eis efficaciam praebendo per meritum baptizantis, quod ad potestatem excellentiae pertinet; et hoc potuit eis conferri. Vel dicendum, quod non loquitur de auctoritate prima sed de subauctoritate: quod patet ex eo quod sequitur in Glossa: *ita scilicet quod ipse principalis auctor existeret.*

Ad tertium dicendum, quod hominibus datur potestas expellendi daemones quantum ad effectum nocumenti corporalis, quem in vexatis faciunt, non autem quantum ad effectum spiritualis nocumenti, quod est peccatum[23] expellere, et a servitute daemonis liberare. Joan. 8, 36: *si Filius vos liberaverit, vere liberi eritis.*

not be understood of the cooperation that happens in the manner of disposition, since this was conferred on the ministers of the Church, as was said. However, others say the opposite, that it could not have been conferred. Now both opinions can be supported in a certain way. For something cooperates with God instrumentally in two ways. In one way, so that by a certain power having absolute and complete being in nature, it may work to produce not only a secondary effect but a principal one, as fire cooperates with God in the generation of another fire. And in this way of taking cooperation, it could not be conferred on man that he cooperate with God in the interior cleansing that happens by grace, for grace elevates man to a certain life that is above the condition of all created nature; indeed, the being of grace is above the natural being of both men and angels, who are the highest creatures. And thus, the agent, who by his own power likens the soul to himself by grace, must be above all created power, and so this kind of cooperation surpasses the creature's limits. In another way, something cooperates with God not by a power that has being perfect in nature, nor by extending directly to the final principal effect, as was said of the sacraments in Distinction 1, Question 1, Article 4; and in this way, to cooperate with God in interior cleansing by (as some say) disposing, could have been conferred on man without the sacraments, just as he does it by offering the sacraments; and to cooperate in this way belongs to the power of excellence in Christ, as was said.

Reply Obj. 1: This is understood concerning the power of excellence, which Christ had also as man, which includes the second kind of power of cooperation mentioned, but not the first kind of power of cooperation mentioned.

Reply Obj. 2: Authority is taken here not with respect to cleansing, but with respect to the institution of the sacraments, furnishing efficacy to them by the merit of the one baptizing, which belongs to the power of excellence; and this he could have conferred upon them. Or it could be said that it is not speaking of primary authority, but of subauthority, which is clear from what follows in the Gloss: *namely, such that he himself would exist as principal author.*

Reply Obj. 3: To men is given the power of expelling demons as to the effect of the physical harm they cause in those they trouble, but not as to the effect of spiritual harm, which is the power to expel sin and to free someone from slavery to the demon: *if the Son makes you free, you will be free indeed* (John 8:36).

---

23. *peccatum expellere.—peccatum quia hoc solius dei est peccatum* PLE.

Response to Quaestiuncula 2

AD SECUNDAM QUAESTIONEM dicendum, quod potestatem excellentiae Deus homini puro conferre potuit, sed tamen non fuit decens, ne spes in homine poneretur, et ut ecclesiae unum caput esse ostenderet, a quo omnia membra spiritualem sensum et motum reciperent.

AD PRIMUM ergo dicendum, quod hoc intelligitur de illis quae sunt necessaria ad perfectionem hominis vel quantum ad esse naturae vel quantum ad esse gratiae. Non enim oportet quod Deus homini dederit omnem gratiam gratis datam quam dare potest: quia divisiones gratiarum sunt, et dat unicuique sicut vult; 1 Corinth., 12.

AD SECUNDUM dicendum, quod ad hoc quod homo purus cooperaretur Deo in interiori emundatione modo praedicto non oportet quod haberet efficaciam infinitam in merendo, quamvis Christus quodammodo habuerit infinitatem in merendo: quia non cooperaretur respectu omnium, nec ita plene sicut Christus.

AD TERTIUM dicendum, quod gratia capitis in Christo distinguitur a gratia unionis: quamvis ex ipsa unione per quamdam condecentiam plenitudo omnis gratiae, et capitis et singularis personae in illa anima fuerit. Nec tamen sequitur quod si alicui quantum ad aliquid potestas excellentiae conferretur, puta quod in nomine ejus baptismus daretur vel quod meritum ejus aliquo modo operaretur ad effectum baptismi in illo baptizato, quod esset simpliciter caput.

TO THE SECOND QUESTION, it should be said that God could have conferred the power of excellence on a mere man, but nevertheless it was not fitting, lest hope should be placed in a man, and so that he might show that there was one head of the Church, from whom all the members would receive spiritual sensation and movement.

REPLY OBJ. 1: This is understood concerning those things that are necessary for man's perfection, whether as to the being of nature or as to the being of grace. For it was not necessary that God give man every gratuitous grace that he can give: for there are divisions of graces, and he gives to each as he wills (1 Cor 12).

REPLY OBJ. 2: In order for a mere man to cooperate with God in the interior cleansing in the way just mentioned, it is not necessary that he have infinite efficacy in meriting, although Christ had, in a certain way, infinity in meriting; for a mere man would not be cooperating with respect to all things, nor so fully as Christ.

REPLY OBJ. 3: The grace of headship in Christ is distinguished from the grace of union, although from that very union, by a certain congruence, came the fullness of all grace, both of headship and of the singular person in that soul. Nevertheless, it does not follow that, if the power of excellence were conferred on someone for some purpose—for example, baptism were given in his name, or his merit somehow worked toward the effect of baptism in a particular baptized person—then he would be the head simply speaking.

Response to Quaestiuncula 3

AD TERTIAM QUAESTIONEM dicendum, quod communis opinio habet, quod creatio non potest alicui creaturae communicari: quia est opus infinitae potentiae, propter distantiam infinitam quae est inter simpliciter ens et simpliciter non ens, inter quae est mutatio creationis; potentia autem infinita non potest esse in essentia finita. Unde ex hoc ipso quod ponitur potentia infinita alicui communicari, ponitur consequenter quod illud habeat essentiam infinitam, et per hoc habeat esse non receptum, sed purum et simplex; et sic ponitur extra terminos creaturae; et ideo nulli creaturae secundum communem opinionem communicari potest talis potentia.

AD PRIMUM ergo dicendum, quod illi philosophi qui hoc posuerunt, non intellexerunt plene rationem creationis, et quomodo requirit potentiam infinitam agentem; et ideo non intellexerunt incompossibilitatem suae positionis.

TO THE THIRD QUESTION, it should be said that the common opinion holds that creation cannot be communicated to any creature: for it is a work of infinite power, because of the infinite distance there is between simply being and simply non-being, which the change of creation must cross. However, infinite power cannot be in a finite essence. Hence, by the very fact that infinite power is claimed to be communicated to something, it means consequently that that thing would have an infinite essence, and by this fact it would have being that was not received, but pure and simple. This is how it is placed outside the bounds of creation, and so, according to the common opinion, such power can be communicated to no creature.

REPLY OBJ. 1: Those philosophers who posited this did not understand fully the notion of creation, and how it requires an infinite power of acting; and thus, they did not understand the inconsistency of their position.

AD SECUNDUM dicendum, quod hoc etiam implicat contradictionem, inquantum ponitur creaturam habere essentiam infinitam; et per consequens non esse creaturam; et sonat in defectum divinae majestatis, cui ponitur aliquid in essentiae infinitate posse aequari. Non enim oportet ut quod est perfectionis apud nos, scilicet posse aliquid facere aequale sibi sit perfectionis apud Deum ut scilicet possit facere aliquid aequale sibi.

AD TERTIUM dicendum, quod nullum agens creatum facit formam, quia formae non fiunt ut probatur in 7 *Metaphysica*, sed educuntur de potentia materiae. Sed materia non potest educi de potentia alterius; et ideo non est simile de forma et materia.

AD QUARTUM dicendum, quod contrarium ex quo fit generatio, non impedit actionem agentis nisi dupliciter. Uno modo, debilitando virtutem agentis, quod etiam non est universaliter verum, sed in his tantum in quibus est mutua actio et passio, unde hoc accidit. Alio modo, per se loquendo, elongando potentiam passivam patientis per indispositionem a receptione effectus agentis; et hoc est in omnibus. Constat autem quod nulla indispositio potest potentiam passivam tantum elongare ab effectu agentis percipiendo, quantum subtractio ipsius potentiae totaliter; et ideo multo majoris virtutis est facere aliquid ex nihilo quam ex contrario, simpliciter loquendo; quamvis secundum quid hoc habeat aliquam difficultatem quae non est in illo.

Quia tamen Magister in littera dicit, quod potest creaturae communicari ministerium creationis et non auctoritatis: si quis vellet eum in hoc sustinere, posset dicere, quod tunc proprie aliquid creatur quando fit ex nullo praeexistente. Unde patet quod creatio de sui ratione excludit praesuppositionem alicujus praeexistentis.

Hoc autem contingit dupliciter. Uno modo ita quod excludat omne praeexistens et ex parte agentis et ex parte facti, ut scilicet creatio dicatur quando nec agens agit virtute alicujus agentis prioris, nec factum sit ex aliqua praeexistente materia: et haec est potentia auctoritatis in creando, et est infinita; et ideo nulli creaturae communicari potest.

Alio modo ita quod excludat praeexistens ex parte facti, sed non ex parte agentis, ut scilicet dicatur creatio, sed minus proprie, quando aliquod agens virtute alicujus prioris agentis ex non praesupposita materia aliquem effectum producit, et sic erit creationis ministerium; et ita aliqui philosophi posuerunt aliquas creaturas creare;

REPLY OBJ. 2: This also implies contradiction, inasmuch as a creature is posited to have infinite essence, and consequently not to be a creature; and it conveys a defect in divine majesty to claim that something can equal it in infinity of essence. For it is not necessary that what belongs to perfection in us, namely, to be able to make something equal to oneself, be a perfection in God, such that he could make something equaling himself.

REPLY OBJ. 3: No created agent makes a form, for forms are not made, as is proved in *Metaphysics* 7,[24] but rather they are drawn out of the potency of matter. But matter cannot be drawn out of any other potency; and thus, it is not the same with form as with matter.

REPLY OBJ. 4: The contrary from which generation occurs only impedes the action of the agent in two ways. In one way, by weakening the agent's power—and that is not even universally the case, but only in those things in which there is mutual action and suffering, from which this occurs.[25] In another way, speaking *per se*, by diminishing the passive power of the one suffering, through an indisposition to receive the agent's effect. And this is found in all cases of receptivity. It is clear, however, that no indisposition can so remove the passive potency from receiving the agent's effect as to take this potency away completely; and thus, it takes much more power to make something out of nothing than out of a contrary, simply speaking; although in some respect, the latter has a certain difficulty that is not in the former.

Since, however, the Master says in the text that the ministry of creation *can* be communicated to a creature, but not the ministry of authority, if anyone wanted to support him in this, he could say that something is created, properly speaking, at the moment that it comes to be out of no pre-existing thing. Hence, it is clear that creation in its very notion excludes the presupposition of anything pre-existing.

Now this happens in two ways. In one way, such that it excludes everything pre-existing, both on the part of the agent and on the part of the thing made, such that it is called 'creation' when neither the agent acts by virtue of some prior agent nor the thing made comes from any pre-existing matter: and this is the power of authority in creating, and it is infinite, and so can be communicated to no creature.

In another way, such that it excludes anything pre-existing on the part of the thing made, but not on the part of the agent, such that it is called 'creation' (but less properly) when something acting by the power of a prior agent produces an effect from non-presupposed matter; and in this way, it will be the ministry of creation. And thus, some

---

24. Aristotle, *Metaphysics*, Bk. 7, ch. 8, 1033b5–6.

25. In those things that are acted upon when they act, namely material things, to act upon another is, at the same time and *per accidens*, to suffer something; for example, a stove's electric heating element is slightly cooled when a pot of cold water is placed on it, even though in itself, it is the heating agent and the water is the heatable patient.

et sic Magister dicit quod potuit communicari potentia creandi, non est autem alicui communicata.

Secundum hoc ergo ad quintum dicendum esset secundum Magistrum, quod distantia inter ens et non ens requirit absolute infinitatem potentiae in eo qui facit aliquid ex simpliciter non ente. Quod enim in motibus virtus moventis proportionetur distantiae quae est inter terminos, ideo contingit, quia ab illa distantia motus accipit quantitatem. *Quanta enim est via, tantus est motus,* ut dicitur in 4 *Physic.* Motus autem est proprius effectus virtutis moventis, inquantum hujusmodi, ei proportionatus.

Sed in creatione non sic est: quia non ens purum non est per se terminus creationis, sed per accidens se habet ad ipsam: dicitur enim aliquid fieri ex non ente, idest post non ens. Unde creatio non habet quantitatem ex distantia non entis ad ens, sed ab ente quod creatur; et ideo non oportet quod potentia creantis proportionetur distantiae quae est inter ens et non ens, sed solum ei quod creatur, quod non est infinitum; et ideo non requiritur potentia infinita simpliciter, sed infinita secundum quid, scilicet non commensurata alicui materiae determinatae, sicut sunt omnia agentia naturalia et materialia: ignis enim non habet effectum nisi in aliqua materia determinata, quia virtus ejus materialis est. Et ideo etiam philosophi non posuerunt creationem secundo modo, nisi in substantiis incorporeis et immaterialibus.

Vel dicendum, quod non est distantia infinita inter ens et non ens ex parte ipsius entis, nisi ens sit infinitum: quia tantum distat aliquid ab uno oppositorum, quantum participat de altero; unde non distat in infinitum a non esse nisi quod esse infinitum habet, scilicet Deus, cui quanto reliqua entia sunt proximiora, tanto magis a non esse distant, sicut Augustinus dicit in Lib. 12 *Confession.*, quod angelus factus est prope Deum, materia prope nihil.

Sed verum est quod dicta distantia est quodammodo infinita ex parte non entis simpliciter, eo quod neque[28] determinatam distantiam ab aliquo ente signato transcendit, quia nihil potest magis distare ab ente quam non ens. Contingit enim aliquam distantiam esse infinitam ex una parte et finitam ex altera, sicut quandocumque fit comparatio finiti ad infinitum. Nisi enim esset aliquo modo talis distantia finita, non distaret minus una creatura a Deo quam altera; et nisi esset aliquo modo infinita, posset intelligi aliquid magis distans a creatu-

philosophers posited that certain creatures create; and in this manner, the Master says that the power of creating could have been shared, but it was not shared with anyone.

Reply Obj. 5: In keeping with this, therefore, it would be said to the fifth, according to the Master, that the distance between being and non-being absolutely requires infinity of power in him who makes something out of non-being simply. For the reason that, in motions, the power of the mover is proportionate to the distance between the two terminuses is because motion takes its quantity from that very distance. *For as great as the path is, so great is the movement,* as is said in *Physics* 4.[26] Now motion is more properly the effect of the power of the mover, as such, proportioned to it.

But in creation it is not thus, for pure non-being is not a *per se* terminus of creation, but stands to it only *per accidens*—for something is said to be 'made from non-being,' that is, after non-being. Hence, creation does not have quantity from a distance of non-being to being, but by the being that is created. And thus, it is not necessary that the power of the one creating be proportionate to the distance that is between being and non-being, but only to what is created, which is not infinite. And thus, a power that is simply infinite is not required, but one that is infinite in a certain respect, namely, not commensurate with any determinate matter, as all natural and material agents are; for fire does not have an effect except in a certain determinate matter, since its power is material. And thus, even the philosophers did not posit creation in the second way except among incorporeal and immaterial substances.

Or it could be said that there is not an infinite distance between a being and non-being on the part of the being itself, unless the being is infinite; for, to the extent that something is distant from one of two opposites, it is closer to the other; hence the only thing infinitely distant from not being is what has infinite being, namely, God, and to the degree that the remaining beings are closer to him, so much more are they distant from non-being, just as Augustine says in Book 12 of the *Confessions* that an angel is made close to God, matter close to nothing.[27]

But it is true that the distance mentioned is in a way infinite on the part of non-being simply, by the fact that it transcends every determinate distance from any being represented, since nothing can be more distant from being than non-being. For it happens that a certain distance is infinite from one side and finite from the other, as whenever a comparison is made between the finite and the infinite. For unless there were such a finite distance in some way, one creature would not be less distant from God than another; and unless there were in some way an infinite distance, some-

---

26. Aristotle, *Physics*, Bk. 4, ch. 11, 219a9ff.

27. See Augustine, *Confessions* (CCSL 27), Bk. 12, ch. 7: "tu eras et aliud nihil, unde fecisti caelum et terram, duo quaedam, unum prope te, alterum prope nihil, unum, quo superior tu esses, alterum, quo inferius nihil esset."

28. neque.—omnem PLE.

ra quacumque quam Deus. Creatio autem non respicit hanc distantiam ex parte non entis, sed magis ex parte entis, quod est creationis terminus.

AD SEXTUM dicendum, quod latria debetur Creatori inquantum ipse est primum agens, cujus virtute omnia alia agunt, et ipse non agit virtute alterius; et hoc non potest alicui creaturae communicari.

AD SEPTIMUM dicendum, quod quamvis nulla creatura sit in qua non sit aliquid de potentia, ad minus secundum quod ejus natura se habet ad esse quod recipit a Deo sicut potentia ad actum; tamen aliqua creatura est in qua nihil de potentia remanet quae non sit completa per actum, sicut est angelus; et ideo talis creatura se tota potest agere, quamvis primum principium suae actionis sit aliquid aliud ab ipsa, scilicet Deus, qui est primum agens.

thing might be understood more distant from any creature than from God. Creation, however, does not regard this distance from the side of non-being, but rather from the side of being, which is the terminus of creating.

REPLY OBJ. 6: Adoration is due to the Creator inasmuch as he is the first agent, with whose power all others act, while he himself does not act by virtue of another; and this cannot be shared with any creature.

REPLY OBJ. 7: Although there is no creature in which there is not something of potency, at least as far as its nature is ordered to the being that it receives from God as potency is ordered to act, nevertheless, there is a certain creature in which no potency remains that is not completed by act, as an angel. And so, such a creature can wholly act from itself, although the first beginning of its action is something other than it, namely, God, who is the first agent.

QUESTION 2

WHO CAN BAPTIZE

Deinde quaeritur, qui possint baptizare; et circa hoc quaeruntur tria:

primo, utrum possint baptizare tam ordinati quam non ordinati;

secundo, utrum possint baptizare tam boni, quam mali;

tertio, utrum possint baptizare tam homines quam angeli.

Next is asked who can baptize; and concerning this, three questions arise:

first, whether the non-ordained can baptize, as well as the ordained;

second, whether the bad can baptize, as well as the good;

third, whether angels can baptize, as well as men.

ARTICLE 1

Whether the non-ordained can baptize, as well as the ordained

Quaestiuncula 1

AD PRIMUM SIC PROCEDITUR. Videtur quod nullus possit baptizare nisi habeat ordinem. Actum enim hierarchicum nullus potest exercere nisi sit hierarchiae particeps. Sed illi qui non habent ordinem, non sunt participes hierarchiae, quia non habent aliquem sacrum principatum. Ergo cum baptizare sit actus hierarchicus, quia baptismus est purgatio et illuminatio, ut dicit Dionysius in *Eccl. Hierarc.*, videtur quod nullus possit baptizare nisi habeat ordinem.

PRAETEREA, sicut baptismus est sacramentum necessitatis, ita et poenitentia. Sed nullus potest absolvere sacramentaliter in poenitentia nisi habeat ordinem. Ergo et similiter nullus non ordinatus potest baptizare.

SED CONTRA est quod Isidorus dicit, quod cum ultima necessitas cogit, etiam laicis fidelibus permittitur baptizare. Sed laici non habent ordinem. Ergo, etc.

OBJ. 1: To the first question, we proceed thus. It seems that no one could baptize unless he has holy orders.[29] For no one can exercise a hierarchical act unless he takes part in the hierarchy. But those who do not have holy orders are not partakers of the hierarchy, for they do not have any sacred rulership. Therefore, since baptizing is a hierarchical act (because baptism is a purification and illumination, as Dionysius says in the *Ecclesiastical Hierarchy*[30]), it seems that no one could baptize except unless he had holy orders.

OBJ. 2: Furthermore, just as baptism is a necessary sacrament, so also is penance. But no one can absolve someone sacramentally in penance except someone with holy orders. In like manner, therefore, no one who is not ordained can baptize.

ON THE CONTRARY, Isidore says that when extreme necessity compels, even lay members of the faithful are permitted to baptize.[31] But laymen do not have holy orders. Therefore, etc.

---

29. Parallels: below, d. 17, q. 3, a. 3, qa. 2, ad 3; d. 20, a. 1, qa. 2, ad 3; d. 23, q. 2, a. 1, qa. 1; *ST* I-II, q. 100, a. 2, ad 1; *ST* III, q. 67, a. 3.

30. Pseudo-Dionysius, *Ecclesiastical Hierarchy*, ch. 5, n. 3 (PG 3:503).

31. Isidore, *De ecclesiasticis officiis* (CCSL 113), Bk. 2, ch. 25, n. 9: "Cuiusque ministerium nec ipsis diaconibus explere est licitum absque episcopo uel presbitero, nisi his procul absentibus ultima langoris cogat necessitudo, quod etiam et laicis fidelibus plerumque permittitur, ne quisquam sine remedio salutari de saeculo euocetur."

Quaestiuncula 2

Ulterius. Videtur quod baptizare sit proprium ordinis diaconi. Quia, secundum Dionysium, diaconi habent vim purgativam. Sed baptismus principaliter ad purgandum est institutus. Ergo diaconis competit baptizare ex proprio officio.

Praeterea, Marc. ult., simul injungitur officium baptizandi cum praedicatione Evangelii. Sed praedicatio Evangelii pertinet ad diaconos ex proprio officio. Ergo et baptizare.

Sed contra, est quod Isidorus dicit, quod baptismi ministerium nec ipsis diaconibus implere est licitum.

Obj. 1: Moreover, it seems that baptizing is proper to the order of deacon.[32] For, according to Dionysius, deacons have purifying power. But baptism was instituted chiefly for purifying. Therefore, baptizing belongs to the deacon as proper to his office.

Obj. 2: Furthermore, the duty of baptizing is enjoined at the same time as the preaching of the Gospel, as given at the end of Mark (cf. Mark 16:15–16). But the preaching of the Gospel pertains to deacons as proper to their office. Therefore, so does baptism.

On the contrary, Isidore says that deacons are not permitted to fulfill the ministry of baptism.[33]

Quaestiuncula 3

Ulterius. Videtur quod non baptizati baptizare non possint. Minus enim est sacramentum recipere quam sacramentum conferre. Sed non baptizati non possunt sacramentum aliquod recipere: quia, secundum Dionysium, non sunt ad spirituales et hierarchicas actiones idonei. Ergo nec sacramentum baptismi conferre possunt.

Praeterea, si non baptizatus posset baptizare, et ipse baptismo indigeret, posset seipsum baptizare. Sed hoc est impossibile: tum quia nulla res, secundum Augustinum, seipsam gignit ut sit; Baptismus autem regeneratio quaedam est: tum quia non posset servari forma ecclesiae. Ergo non baptizatus baptizare non potest.

Sed contra est quod in littera dicitur, quod Romanus pontifex non hominem judicat qui baptizat, sed Spiritum Dei, quamvis paganus sit qui baptizat. Sed paganus non est baptizatus. Ergo non baptizatus potest baptizare.

Obj. 1: Moreover, it seems that the unbaptized may not baptize.[34] For it is a smaller thing to receive a sacrament than to confer one. But the unbaptized cannot receive any sacrament: for, according to Dionysius, they are not suited to spiritual and hierarchical acts.[35] Therefore, neither can they confer the sacrament of baptism.

Obj. 2: Furthermore, if an unbaptized person could baptize, and he himself needed baptism, then he could baptize himself. But this is impossible, both because, according to Augustine, nothing gives birth to itself so that it may be,[36] while baptism is a certain regeneration; and because the form of the Church could not be preserved in that case. Therefore, an unbaptized person cannot baptize.

On the contrary, is what is said in the text, that the Roman pontiff judges that it is not man who baptizes, but the spirit of God, even if it is a pagan who baptizes. But a pagan is not baptized. Therefore, a non-baptized person can baptize.

Response to Quaestiuncula 1

Respondeo dicendum ad primam quaestionem, quod baptisma inter alia sacramenta est maximae necessitatis: tum quia pueris non potest aliter subveniri; tum quia etiam nec adultis quantum ad remissionem totius poenae; et ideo ea quae ad necessitatem sacramenti requiruntur, debuerunt esse communissima et ex parte materiae, scilicet aquae, quae ubique haberi potest, et ex parte ministri, ut quilibet homo baptizare possit; et

To the first question, I answer that baptism is the most necessary of all the sacraments: both because children cannot be rescued any other way, and because neither can even adults as to the remission of all guilt; and thus, those things that are required as necessary for the sacrament must be the most common both on the part of the matter, namely, water, which can be had anywhere, and on the part of the minister, such that any man may baptize.

---

32. Parallel: *ST* III, q. 67, a. 1.
33. See the text given just above.
34. Parallel: *ST* III, q. 67, a. 5.
35. Pseudo-Dionysius, *Ecclesiastical Hierarchy*, ch. 2, p. 1 (PG 3:391).
36. Cf. Augustine, *De Trinitate* (CCSL 50), Bk. 1, ch. 1: "nulla enim omnino res est quae se ipsam gignat ut sit."

sic sanctificatio materiae et benedictio praecedens baptismum non est de necessitate sacramenti, sed de solemnitate, quam non licet praetermittere propter ecclesiae institutionem. Ita etiam ordinatio ministri non est de necessitate sacramenti, sed de solemnitate; et peccat si aliquis non ordinatus baptizet, nisi necessitate imminente, tamen sacramentum confert.

AD PRIMUM ergo dicendum, quod homini non competit actus hierarchicus ex natura sua, sed ex divina institutione et sanctificatione; et quamvis simpliciter gradum hierarchicum non contulit omni homini, tamen actum istum hierarchicum omnibus hominibus contulit propter necessitatem, sicut omnibus aquis vim regenerativam dedit.

AD SECUNDUM dicendum, quod non est simile de poenitentiae sacramento, et baptismo: quia aliquis sine absolutione sacramenti poenitentiae potest salvari in necessitate nec iterum absolutio sacerdotalis a tota poena absolvit; sed in pueris non est aliquid aliud per quod possint salvari, nec quo adulti possint a tota poena liberari; et ideo est majoris necessitatis quam poenitentia.

And in this way, the sanctification of the matter and the blessing preceding baptism are not necessary for the sacrament, but only for its solemnity, which, on account of the Church's institution of it, one is not permitted to omit. Thus, even the ordination of the minister is not necessary for the sacrament, but only for its solemnity; and if, apart from a case of imminent need, someone not ordained baptized, he would sin, yet nevertheless would confer the sacrament.

REPLY OBJ. 1: A hierarchical act does not belong to a man by his own nature, but by divine institution and sanctification; and although, simply speaking, he did not confer the hierarchical degree on every man, nevertheless he conferred this particular hierarchical act on all men on account of necessity, just as he gave regenerative power to all waters.

REPLY OBJ. 2: It is not the same with the sacrament of penance as with the sacrament of baptism: for in a case of necessity someone can be saved without the absolution of the sacrament of penance, nor again does priestly absolution absolve from all punishment. But there is nothing else among children by which they may be saved, nor among adults by which they may be freed from all punishment; and thus, it is of greater necessity than penance.

Response to Quaestiuncula 2

AD SECUNDAM QUAESTIONEM dicendum, quod in potentiis ordinatis ita est quod quidquid potest potentia inferior, potest superior; sed non convertitur. Unde cum potestas sacerdotalis ordinis sit supra potestatem diaconi, sacerdos habet vim purgativam cum illuminativa; sed diaconus habet purgativam tantum sine illuminativa. Et quia in omnibus sacramentis novae legis est illuminatio gratiae cum purgatione, ideo non est diaconus proprius minister baptismi nec alicujus sacramenti sed aliquorum sacramentalium, sicut exorcismi, et expulsionis immundorum a divinis, ut cum dicit: *si quis Judaeus est, abscedat*; et eruditionis eorum qui ignorant qualiter se habere debeant ad divina, ut cum dicit: *flectamus genua*, et *humiliate vos, ad benedictionem*, vel aliud hujusmodi.

AD PRIMUM ergo dicendum, quod baptismus non habet tantum purgare, sed illuminare, ut dicit Dionysius; et ideo non competit diacono, sed sacerdoti.

AD SECUNDUM dicendum, quod ad diaconum pertinet praedicare Evangelium, et in ecclesia recitare, quod

TO THE SECOND QUESTION, it should be said that among ordered powers it is such that whatever a lower power can do, the higher power can as well, but not vice versa. Hence, since the power of an ordained priest is above the power of a deacon, the priest has purifying power together with illuminative, but a deacon has only purifying power, without the illuminative. And because in all the sacraments of the New Law there is the illumination of grace together with purification, for this reason, the deacon is not the proper minister of baptism or of any sacrament, but rather, of certain sacramentals, like exorcism and the banishment of those unclean from divine things, as when he says: *If anyone is a Jew, let him depart*,[37] and the instruction of those who do not know how they should behave toward divine things, as when he says: *Let us kneel*, and *Humble yourselves for the blessing*, or anything like this.

REPLY OBJ. 1: Baptism is not only for purifying, but for illuminating, as Dionysius says,[38] and thus it belongs not to the deacon but to the priest.

REPLY OBJ. 2: It pertains to the deacon to preach the Gospel, and to read aloud in the church, which is like

---

37. In some of the ancient liturgies is found a proclamation by the deacon at the end of the Mass of Catechumens, to the effect of "Let all the unbaptized depart." One celebrated formula from a Missal of the 11th-12th century read: "If anyone is a catechumen, let him depart; if anyone is a heretic, let him depart; if anyone is a Jew, let him depart; if anyone is a pagan, let him depart; if anyone is an Arian, let him depart; anyone for whom this is not his concern, let him depart."

38. Pseudo-Dionysius, *Ecclesiastical Hierarchy*, ch. 5, p. 1, n. 3 (PG 3:502).

est quasi loqui linguis; sed ad presbyterum pertinet interpretari et exhortari, quod est quasi prophetare.

speaking in tongues; but it pertains to the priest to interpret and to exhort, which is like prophesying.

Response to Quaestiuncula 3

Ad tertiam quaestionem dicendum, quod sicut aqua absque omni sanctificatione est materia baptismi, ita etiam homo absque omni sacramentali sanctificatione est baptismi minister quantum ad necessitatem sacramenti; unde non baptizatus potest baptizare, dummodo servet formam ecclesiae, et habeat intentionem baptizandi.

Ad primum ergo dicendum, quod receptio aliorum sacramentorum non est tantae necessitatis quantae collatio istius; et ideo potest aliquis conferre hoc sacramentum qui alia non posset percipere.

Ad secundum dicendum, quod quamvis posset aliquis non baptizatus baptizare alium, non tamen potest seipsum baptizare rationibus praedictis in objectione. Sed quod Innocentius tertius in decretali quadam dicit: *Judaeus qui se ipsum in aquam immersit, dicens: ego baptizo me in nomine patris* etc. *si decessisset, ad patriam evolasset,* intelligendum est propter vim contritionis et devotionis, ex cujus magnitudine hoc procedere videbatur, ut inter Judaeos existens, quasi periculo mortis se offerret.

To the third question, it should be said that just as water without any sanctification is the matter of baptism, so also a man without any sacramental sanctification is the minister of baptism, regarding what is necessary for the sacrament; hence, the non-baptized person can baptize, as long as he preserves the form of the Church and has the intention of baptizing.

Reply Obj. 1: The reception of other sacraments is not of such great necessity as the conferral of this one; and thus, someone who cannot receive the other sacraments can still confer this one.

Reply Obj. 2: Although someone unbaptized could baptize someone else, he is nevertheless not able to baptize himself, for the reasons cited in the objection. But what Innocent III says in a certain decretal—*A Jew who immerses himself in water, saying, "I baptize myself in the name of the Father, etc.,"* if he should pass away, will go straight to heaven—should be understood on account of the force of his contrition and devotion, from the greatness of which this seems to proceed, namely, that living among Jews he would so to speak expose himself to danger of death.

Article 2

Whether the bad can baptize, as well as the good

Quaestiuncula 1

Ad secundum sic proceditur. Videtur quod mali sacramentum baptismi conferre non possint. Sicut enim ad baptismum requiritur forma et materia, ita et minister. Sed si sit materia indebita vel forma, non erit baptismus. Ergo et similiter si sit minister indebitus. Sed mali non sunt debiti ministri: quia, sicut dicit Augustinus, *justos oportet esse per quos baptizatur*. Ergo mali sacramentum conferre non possunt.

Praeterea, membrum aridum non participat aliquam actionem corporis. Sed baptizare est aliqua actio corporis mystici. Cum ergo mali sint quasi membrum aridum, carentes pinguedine caritatis et gratiae, videtur quod baptismum conferre non possint.

Sed contra sunt plures rationes in littera.

Obj. 1: To the second we proceed thus. It seems that bad men cannot confer the sacrament of baptism.[39] For just as form and matter are required for baptism, so also is a minister. But if there is undue matter or form, there will not be baptism. Therefore, it is the same if there is an undue minister. But the wicked are not the due ministers: for as Augustine says, *it must be just men who baptize*.[40] Therefore the wicked cannot confer this sacrament.

Obj. 2: Furthermore, a withered member does not partake in any action of the body. But to baptize is an action of the Mystical Body. Therefore, since the wicked are like withered members, lacking the oil of charity and grace, it seems they cannot confer baptism.

On the contrary, are the multiple reasons in the text.

Quaestiuncula 2

Ulterius. Videtur quod per eos non conferatur res sacramenti. Eccli. 34, 4: *ab immundo quis mundabitur?* Sed peccator omnis est immundus. Ergo ab eo nullus potest mundari. Cum ergo mundatio sit res sacramenti baptismi, videtur quod per malos res sacramenti non conferatur.

Praeterea, sacerdotes sunt medii inter Deum et plebem, divina in sacris praebentes populo et doctrinam, et ea quae sunt populi repraesentantes Deo per orationem. Sed orationes malorum sacerdotum non prosunt plebi: quia, secundum Gregorium in pastorali, *cum is qui displicet, ad intercedendum mittitur, irati animus ad deteriora provocatur*. Ergo nec sacramenta per malos ministros data prosunt ad effectum salutis.

Sed contra est quod in littera dicitur: *cum baptizat malus, illud quod datum est, unum est, nec impar propter impares ministros*. Sed boni baptizando conferunt sacramentum et rem sacramenti. Ergo et mali.

Obj. 1: Moreover, it seems that the reality of the sacrament is not conferred by them: *What can be made clean by the unclean?* (Sir 34:4) But every sinner is unclean. Therefore, no one can be made clean by one. Therefore, since cleansing is the reality of the sacrament of baptism, it seems that the reality of the sacrament is not conferred.

Obj. 2: Furthermore, priests are mediators between God and the people, presenting divine things to the people in sacred rites and teaching, and representing to God the needs of the people by prayer. But the prayers of wicked priests do not benefit the people, for, according to Gregory in his pastoral letter, *when someone displeasing is sent to intercede, the spirit of the angry one is provoked to worse things*.[41] Therefore, neither are sacraments given by wicked ministers beneficial for the effect of salvation.

On the contrary, is what is said in the text: *when a wicked man baptizes, what is given is one, nor is it inferior because of the inferior ministers*. But when good men baptize, they confer the sacrament and the reality of the sacrament. Therefore, so do wicked men.

---

39. Parallels: below, d. 7, q. 3, a. 1, qa. 1, ad 2; *ST* III, q. 64, aa. 5 and 9; *SCG* IV, ch. 77; *Super Heb.* 7, lec. 2.
40. Augustine, *In Iohannis euangelium tractatus* (CCSL 36), Tract. 15, n. 5.
41. Gregory, *Regula pastoralis* (CCSL 141), p. 1, ch. 10.

Quaestiuncula 3

ULTERIUS. Videtur quod per meliorem ministrum baptismus datus majorem effectum habeat. Multiplicata enim causa multiplicatur effectus. Sed baptismus ex opere operato gratiam confert: similiter etiam patet quod sancti homines ex opere operante gratiam alicui merentur. Ergo si opus operans baptizantis adjungatur cum efficacia baptismi, major gratia dabitur.

PRAETEREA, baptismus magis est ordinatus ad spiritualem salutem quam ad corporalem. Sed aliquis baptizatus a sancto homine, meritis et intercessione baptizantis quandoque salutem corporalem consequitur; quod non est ex opere operato; quia baptismus ad hoc efficaciam non habet; sicut patet de Constantino, quem Silvester baptizavit. Ergo etiam quantum ad spiritualem salutem baptismus a bono ministratus potest ampliorem effectum spiritualis salutis habere.

SED CONTRA est quod in littera dicitur: *non est melior baptismus qui per meliorem ministrum datur; sed per ministros dispares Dei munus est aequale.*

OBJ. 1: Moreover, it seems that baptism given by a better minister has a greater effect. For when the cause is multiplied, the effect is multiplied. But baptism confers grace by the very work being accomplished: similarly also it is clear that holy men merit grace for others by their own work. Therefore, if the work of the one baptizing is added to the efficacy of baptism, a greater grace will be given.

OBJ. 2: Furthermore, baptism is more ordered to spiritual health than to bodily health. But someone baptized by a holy man sometimes obtains bodily health by the merits and intercession of the one baptizing, which is not from the work itself being performed, since baptism does not have efficacy for this. This is how it happened with Constantine, whom Silvester baptized. Therefore also, for spiritual health baptism by good ministers can have a greater effect.

ON THE CONTRARY, is what is said in the text: *The baptism that is given by a better minister is not better, but the gift of God given through unequal ministers is equal.*

Quaestiuncula 4

ULTERIUS. Videtur quod malus minister peccet baptizans. Quia, sicut Augustinus in *Littera* dicit, *justos oportet esse per quos baptizatur.* Si ergo non sint justi cum baptizent, faciunt quod non oportet. Ergo peccant.

PRAETEREA, Eucharistiae sacramentum non est majoris efficaciae quam baptismi. Sed peccat sacerdos indigne accedens ad illud sacramentum, ut patet 1 Corinth., 11. Ergo et peccat, si sit malus, baptizando.

SED CONTRA, ex officio habet quod baptizet. Ergo exequendo suum ministerium non peccat.

PRAETEREA, ipse tenetur baptizare. Ergo si baptizando peccat, esset perplexus; quod non potest esse.

OBJ. 1: Moreover, it seems that when a wicked minister baptizes, he sins.[42] For, as Augustine says in the text, *it must be just men who baptize.*[43] Therefore, if they are not just when they baptize, they do what is not fitting. Therefore, they sin.

OBJ. 2: Furthermore, the sacrament of the Eucharist is not of greater efficacy than baptism. But a priest who unworthily approaches that sacrament, sins, as is clear from 1 Corinthians 11:27. Therefore, he also sins by baptizing if he is bad.

ON THE CONTRARY, he is able to baptize by his office. Therefore, he does not sin in executing his office.

FURTHERMORE, he is bound to baptize. Therefore, if he sinned by baptizing, he would be trapped; which cannot be the case.

Quaestiuncula 5

ULTERIUS. Videtur quod recipiens in se vel in alio sacramentum a malo sacerdote, peccat. Quia consentiens peccanti ipse peccat. Sed sacerdos in aliquo casu peccat indigne baptizans. Ergo et ab eo baptismum accipiens vel exigens.

PRAETEREA, esto quod sacerdos non velit baptizare sine pretio, constat quod si datur ei pretium, simonia

OBJ. 1: Moreover, it seems that someone who receives a sacrament for himself or another from a bad priest, sins. For anyone consenting to sin sins. But in a certain case the priest baptizing unworthily sins. Therefore, also the person receiving or requesting baptism from him sins.

OBJ. 2: Furthermore, when a priest refuses to baptize without payment, it is clear that if payment is given him,

---

42. Parallels: below, d. 24, q. 1, a. 4, qa. 5; *ST* III, q. 64, a. 6.
43. See citation just above.

committitur; quod sine peccato fieri non potest. Ergo in alio casu peccat accipiens sacramentum baptismi a malo ministro.

SED CONTRA est quod Augustinus in littera dicit: *nec timeo adulterum nec homicidam.* Esset autem timendus, si ab eo accipiens sacramentum peccaret. Ergo nec peccat ab eo accipiens sacramentum.

simony is committed; which cannot happen without sin. Therefore, in some cases the one receiving the sacrament of baptism from a bad minister sins.

ON THE CONTRARY, Augustine says in the text: *I fear neither the adulterer nor the murderer.*[44] But if he would sin by receiving the sacrament from them, that would be something to be feared. Therefore, the one receiving the sacrament from them does not sin.

Response to Quaestiuncula 1

RESPONDEO dicendum, ad primam quaestionem quod in sacramentis est aliquid quod est de substantia sacramenti, et aliquid quod est de convenientia sacramenti et solemnitate. Si ergo subtraheretur aliquid quod est de substantia sacramenti, non erit verum sacramentum; si autem subtraheretur aliquid eorum quae requiruntur ad solemnitatem vel convenientiam sacramenti, propter hoc non desinit esse sacramentum. Unde cum bonitas ministri non sit de substantia sacramenti, quia non omnino certa est, sed quandoque ignorata, ea autem quae sunt de substantia sacramenti oportet esse certa; patet quod subtracta bonitate ministri adhuc est sacramentum, dummodo alia quae sunt de sacramenti substantia, observentur.

AD PRIMUM ergo dicendum, quod debitum dicitur dupliciter. Uno modo, debito necessitatis; et sic est debitus minister baptismi quilibet homo. Alio modo, debito convenientiae et congruitatis; et sic oportet ministrum esse bonum, sicut oportet aquam in qua fit baptismus, esse mundam ob reverentiam sacramenti; tamen si sit immunda, nihilominus fit in ea baptismus; et similiter si sit minister malus, nihilominus confertur baptismus.

AD SECUNDUM dicendum, quod duplex est actio corporis. Una est intranea, sicut sentire, vivere, et hujusmodi; et tali actione non participat membrum aridum; et similiter nec homo malus actione virtutum, quae huic proportionatur. Alia est actio ad extra; et talis actio bene potest fieri per membrum aridum, sicut percutere, quod etiam omnino re inanimata fit, ut baculo; et huic proportionaliter respondet ministratio sacramentorum.

TO THE FIRST QUESTION, I answer that in the sacraments there is something that belongs to the substance of the sacrament, and something that belongs to its fittingness and solemnity. Therefore, if something were taken away that belonged to the sacrament's substance, it would not be a valid sacrament; but if something were taken away that was required for the sacrament's solemnity or fittingness, it would not cease to be a sacrament because of this. Hence since the goodness of the minister does not belong to the sacrament's substance, for it is not at all certain, but sometimes it is unknown; yet those things that belong to the sacrament's substance need to be certain; it is clear that if the goodness of the minister is taken away, there is still a sacrament, as long as the other things that belong to the sacrament's substance are observed.

REPLY OBJ. 1: 'Due' is said in two ways. In one way, what is necessarily due; and in this way the due minister of baptism is any man. In the other way, what is due for fittingness and harmony: and in this way the minister should be a good man, just as it is fitting that the water in which the baptism happens should be clean out of reverence for the sacrament; but if it were dirty, the baptism would happen in it nevertheless. And it is the same way if the minister is wicked; the baptism is conferred nevertheless.

REPLY OBJ. 2: There are two kinds of bodily action. One is internal, like sensing, living, and things like that; and a withered member does not partake in actions like these. And similarly neither does a bad man partake in the action of the virtues, which is proportionate to this. The other kind of action is outwardly directed; and this kind of action can be done well by withered members, like striking, which can even be done by an entirely inanimate thing, like a stick; and this corresponds proportionally to the administering of the sacraments.

Response to Quaestiuncula 2

AD SECUNDAM QUAESTIONEM dicendum, quod duplex est agens; unum principale, et aliud instrumenta-

TO THE SECOND QUESTION, it should be said that there are two kinds of agents: one is the principal agent, and the

---

44. Augustine, *In Iohannis euangelium tractatus* (CCSL 36), Tract 5, n. 18.

le. Agens autem principale, cum agat sibi simile, oportet quod habeat formam, quam inducit per suam actionem in agentibus univocis, vel aliquam nobiliorem in agentibus non univocis. Sed agens instrumentale non oportet quod habeat formam quam inducit ut disponentem ipsum, sed solum per modum intentionis, sicut de forma scamni in serra patet, ut in 1 dist., quaest. 1, art. 4, quaestiunc. 1 et 2, dictum est. Agens autem principale in baptizando est ipse Deus per auctoritatem, et ipse Christus secundum quod homo, cujus meritum operatur in baptismo; et ex plenitudine divinae bonitatis et gratiae Christi pervenit gratia ad baptizatum. Sed baptizans est tantum agens instrumentale; unde non refert ad rem sacramenti percipiendam, utrum ipse gratiam habeat, vel non.

AD PRIMUM ergo dicendum, quod actio non attribuitur instrumento secundum Philosophum, proprie, sed principali agenti. Unde proprie et per se loquendo iste malus minister non est qui mundat, sed Christus, de quo dictum est, Joan. 1, 33: *hic est qui baptizat.*

AD SECUNDUM dicendum, quod in oratione orans est sicut principale agens, non solum sicut instrumentale; et ideo requiritur ad efficaciam orationis quod ex opere operante effectum sortiatur, non solum ex opere operato, sicut est in sacramentis; et ideo malorum orationes infructuosae sunt, quantum ex eis est; sed possunt esse fructuosae aliis pro quibus oratur, propter eorum devotionem, vel inquantum orant in persona ecclesiae.

other is instrumental. But a principal agent, since it makes something like itself, must have the form which it imposes by its own action, among univocal agents, or some nobler form, among non-univocal agents. But an instrumental agent does not need to have the form that it imposes as something disposing itself, but only by the mode of intention, as we see regarding the form of a stool in a saw, as was said in Distinction 1, Question 1, Article 4, Subquestions 1 and 2. However, the principal agent in baptizing is God himself by authority, and Christ himself as man, whose merit is at work in baptism; and from the fullness of divine goodness and the grace of Christ grace reaches the baptized. But the person baptizing is only an instrumental agent; hence it makes no difference to receiving the reality of the sacrament whether he has grace himself or not.

REPLY OBJ. 1: According to the Philosopher, an action is not attributed properly to an instrument, but to the principal agent.[45] Hence, speaking properly and *per se*, that wicked minister is not the one who cleanses, but Christ is, of whom it is said, *He is the one who baptizes* (John 1:33).

REPLY OBJ. 2: In prayer, the one praying is like the principal agent, not only like an instrumental one; and hence it is required for the effectiveness of the prayer that it bring about its effect by the work of the one doing it, not only by the work itself having been done, as it is in the sacraments. And for this reason the prayers of the wicked are unfruitful, inasmuch it is from them; but they can be fruitful for the others for whom they pray, because of the others' devotion, or inasmuch as they pray in the person of the Church.

Response to Quaestiuncula 3

AD TERTIAM QUAESTIONEM dicendum, quod aliquid dicitur effectus alicujus per se et per accidens. Per se quidem effectus alicujus est quod per ipsum ad hoc ordinatum producitur, sicut domus aedificatoris. Per accidens quod conjungitur ei quod est effectus per se, sicut si inhabitatio domus dicatur effectus aedificatoris. Sic ergo dico, quod effectus per se baptismi aequalis est a quocumque detur, vel a malo vel a bono, ceteris paribus ex parte baptizati.

Sed cum effectu baptismi potest aliquid aliud baptizato conferri, sive pertineat ad salutem corporis, sive animae, ex merito baptizantis; et hoc non est proprie effectus baptismi: quia baptismus non est causa nisi instrumentalis, et non est instrumentum agens in virtute

TO THE THIRD QUESTION, it should be said that something can be called the effect of something else directly or incidentally. A direct effect of something is what is produced by it as ordered to this, as a house is of a housebuilder. An incidental effect is what is joined to the direct effect, as when living in the house is called the effect of the builder. Therefore, this is how I say that the direct effect of baptism is equal, no matter whom it is given by, whether a bad man or a good man, all other things being equal on the part of the one baptized.

But along with baptism's effect, something else, other than the effect of baptism, whether pertaining to the health of the body or of the soul, can be conferred on the baptized, by the merit of the one baptizing—and this is not, properly speaking, baptism's effect: for baptism is only an in-

---

45. See Aristotle, *Generation of Animals*, Bk. 2, ch. 1, 734b28–30: "And just as we should not say that an axe or other instrument or organ was made by the fire alone, so neither shall we say that foot or hand were made by heat alone."

ministri, qui et ipse instrumentum est, agens in virtute Christi et Dei.

Et per hoc patet solutio ad objecta.

strumental cause, and it is not an instrument acting by the power of the minister, who is himself also an instrument, acting by the power of Christ and of God.

And by this the solutions to the objections are clear.

Response to Quaestiuncula 4

Ad quartam quaestionem dicendum, quod quicumque in peccato mortali existens, exhibet se ministrum ecclesiae in quocumque spirituali, peccat, secundum quorumdam opinionem satis probabilem, et quae per auctoritatem Dionysii, confirmatur, ut infra dist. 24, quaest. 1, art. 3, quaestiunc. 1, melius ostendetur; et ideo sacerdos baptizans cum solemnitate, ministrum ecclesiae se exhibens, peccat mortaliter; si autem simpliciter baptizet in articulo necessitatis, non quasi minister ecclesiae, sed sicut vetula baptizare posset, non peccat.

Ad primum ergo dicendum, quod auctoritas Augustini non multum cogit, quia loquitur de opportunitate congruentiae; et praeterea loquitur de illis qui baptizant ut ministri ecclesiae; unde subdit: *justos oportet esse tanti judicis ministros.*

Ad secundum dicendum, quod secus est de Eucharistia: quia illud sacramentum nunquam nisi a ministris ecclesiae perfici potest; et ideo semper aliquis celebrans illud sacramentum, ministrum ecclesiae se exhibet.

Ad tertium dicendum, quod quamvis ex officio competat sibi quod baptizet, tamen officium suum debet juste exercere, sicut dicitur Deut. 16, 20: *juste quod justum est exequeris.*

Ad quartum dicendum, quod ipse non est perplexus: quia potest conteri de peccato, et tunc baptizare et conficere.

To the fourth question, it should be said that according to the more probable opinion of certain people, anyone in mortal sin who presents himself as minister of the Church in anything spiritual, sins, and this is confirmed by the authority of Dionysius, as will be shown better later on in Distinction 24, Question 1, Article 3, Subquestion 1. And thus a priest, baptizing with solemnity, presenting himself as the minister of the Church, does sin mortally. But if he baptizes simply in a moment of dire need, not as the minister of the Church, but just as any old woman could baptize, he does not sin.

Reply Obj. 1: The text from Augustine does not have much force, since he is speaking about the situation of greatest congruity; and furthermore he speaks of those who baptize as ministers of the Church; hence he adds: *it is fitting for the ministers of such a judge to be just.*

Reply Obj. 2: It is different with the Eucharist, for that sacrament can never be accomplished without ministers of the Church; and thus anyone celebrating that sacrament presents himself as minister of the Church.

Reply Obj. 3: Although it applies to the one baptizing by his office, nevertheless, his office must be justly exercised, as is said in Deuteronomy 16:20: *Justly shall you carry out what is just.*

Reply Obj. 4: This is not a trap, for someone can be contrite for his sin, and then baptize and consecrate.

Response to Quaestiuncula 5

Ad quintam quaestionem dicendum, quod malus minister aut est praecisus ab ecclesia aut non. Si sit praecisus ab ecclesia, tunc peccat ab eo accipiens sacramentum, nisi in necessitate in qua posset etiam a Pagano vel a Judaeo suscipere. Si autem non sit praecisus ab ecclesia, non peccat ab eo accipiens sacramentum, nisi per accidens scilicet si ejus peccato communicet.

Ad primum ergo dicendum, quod dato quod malus sacerdos peccet baptizando, non tamen oportet quod ille qui ab eo baptismum recipit vel exigit, etiam excepto casu necessitatis, peccet propter duas rationes. Primo quia isti non potest esse certum quod ille sit in peccato mortali, cum in uno instanti Spiritus operetur justificationem impii. Secundo, quia iste petit quod justum est quia a suo

To the fifth question, it should be said that either a wicked minister is cut off from the Church, or he is not. If he is cut off from the Church, then whoever takes the sacrament from him sins, except in the kind of dire need in which one could even receive it from a Jew or pagan. But if he is not cut off from the Church, then one does not sin by receiving the sacrament from him, unless incidentally, when one shares in his sin.

Reply Obj. 1: Granted that a wicked priest sins by baptizing, it is, however, not necessary that the one who receives or requests baptism from him should sin, even apart from the case of dire need; and this is for two reasons. First, because he cannot be certain that the priest is in mortal sin, since the Holy Spirit may work the justification of the wicked in an instant. Second, because he asks what is

sacerdote debet sacramenta percipere. Nec propter hoc cogit vel inducit eum ad peccandum: quia ille potest reddere quod debet non peccando.

AD SECUNDUM dicendum, quod aut ille qui est baptizandus, est adultus, aut non. Si est adultus, sufficit ei petere baptismum ad salutem, quia baptizatur baptismo flaminis; nec debet propter hoc simoniam committere. Si autem sit puer qui est baptizandus, tunc potius debet ipsemet puerum baptizare, quam pretium sacerdoti pro baptismo simoniace dare. Et tamen licitum est ei aquam emere, si alias habere non posset, quia aqua non est sacrum quid: et si sit sanctificata non operatur ad baptismum de necessitate ejus existens quasi sanctificata, sed quasi aqua; et ideo non emit aquam sanctificatam, sed aquam. Quidam vero dicunt, quod potest pretium dare: quia hoc non est simoniam committere, sed redimere vexationem suam. Sed primum melius videtur.

right, for one should receive the sacraments from one's own priest. Nor does this force or induce the priest to sin, since he could render what he should without sinning.

REPLY OBJ. 2: The person who is baptized is either an adult or not. If he is an adult, it is enough for his salvation for him to seek baptism, since he is baptized by baptism of the spirit; nor does he have to commit simony because of this. But if it is a child who is baptized, then it is better for the one requesting baptism to baptize the child himself than to give money to a simonist priest to baptize. But it is nevertheless permitted for him to buy the water, if it could not be had any other way, for water is not sacred in itself: and if it is holy water it does not work in baptism by the fact of having been blessed, but only as water; and therefore one does not buy holy water, but water. But some people say that one can give money to the priest, since this is not committing simony but compensating him for his disturbance. But the first argument seems better.

ARTICLE 3

Whether angels can baptize, as well as men[46]

Quaestiuncula 1

AD TERTIUM SIC PROCEDITUR. Videtur quod daemon in figura hominis apparens possit baptizare. Dicit enim Augustinus super *Joan.*, quod *talis est baptismus, qualis ille in cujus potestate datur.* Si ergo diabolus baptizet invocando potestatem Trinitatis, bonus est baptismus.

PRAETEREA, in baptizante non requiritur assimilatio ad Deum per gratiam, quia etiam mali possunt baptizare; nec etiam assimilatio per characterem, quia etiam Pagani baptizare possunt. Ergo sufficit assimilatio per naturam. Sed hoc est in daemonibus. Ergo possunt baptizare.

SED CONTRA, ministri baptismi ad Christum est aliqua conventio. Sed nulla est conventio Christi ad diabolum, ut patet 2 Corinth., 6. Ergo diabolus non potest conferre sacramentum baptismi.

OBJ. 3: To the third we proceed thus. It seems that a demon appearing in the figure of a man could baptize. For Augustine says in his *Tractates on John*, that *baptism is as good as the one in whose power it is given.*[47] If therefore the devil should baptize by invoking the power of the Trinity, then the baptism is good.

OBJ. 2: Furthermore, in the person baptizing, no assimilation to God by grace is required, for even the wicked can baptize; nor is even any assimilation by the character needed, for even pagans can baptize. Therefore, the assimilation that we have by nature suffices. But this is also in the demons. Therefore, they can baptize.

ON THE CONTRARY, there is a certain conformity to Christ in the minister of baptism. But there is no conformity to Christ in the devil, as is clear from 2 Corinthians 6:15. Therefore, the devil cannot confer the sacrament of baptism.

Quaestiuncula 2

ULTERIUS. Videtur quod bonus angelus in figura hominis apparens, baptizare possit. Baptismus enim est actio hierarchica: quia est *illuminatio et purgatio*, secundum Dionysium. Sed angeli exercent in nos hierarchicas actiones: quia purgant nos perficiunt, et illuminant. Ergo possunt baptizare.

PRAETEREA, in actionibus hierarchicis ita est quod quamcumque actionem potest facere inferior, potest facere superior: sicut quidquid potest diaconus, potest sacerdos. Sed, secundum Dionysium, quilibet angelus est major summo sacerdote apud nos, qui ex eorum potestatis participatione angelus dicitur, Malach. 2. Si ergo sacerdos homo potest baptizare multo fortius angelus.

SED CONTRA, baptismus est actio militantis ecclesiae. Sed angeli non sunt neque actu neque potentia de ecclesia militante. Ergo baptizare non possunt.

OBJ. 1: Moreover, it seems that a good angel appearing in the figure of a man could baptize. For baptism is a hierarchical act, for it is *illumination and purification*, according to Dionysius.[48] But angels exercise hierarchical acts for us, for they purify, perfect, and illuminate us. Therefore, they can baptize.

OBJ. 2: Furthermore, among hierarchical acts it is such that anything that an inferior can do, a superior can do, so that whatever a deacon can do, a priest can do. But according to Dionysius,[49] any angel is greater than the highest priest among us, who is called an angel by a partaking in their power (cf. Malachi 2:7). If therefore a human priest can baptize, much more can an angel.

ON THE CONTRARY, baptism is an act of the Church Militant. But angels are not members of the Church Militant, whether in act or in potency. Therefore, they cannot baptize.

---

46. Parallel: *ST* III, q. 64, a. 7.

47. Augustine, *In Iohannis euangelium tractatus* (CCSL 36), Tract. 5, par. 6: "baptisma enim tale est, qualis est ille, in cuius potestate datur; non qualis est ille per cuius ministerium datur."

48. Pseudo-Dionysius, *Ecclesiastical Hierarchy*, ch. 5, p. 1, n. 3 (PG 3:503).

49. Pseudo-Dionysius, *Celestial Hierarchy*, ch. 12, n. 1 (PG 3:292).

Response to Quaestiuncula 1

RESPONDEO dicendum ad primam quaestionem, quod diabolus in figura sacerdotis apparens potest immergere, sed non sacramentum conferre, propter duas rationes. Primo, quia dispensatio sacramentorum non est concessa nisi hominibus, qui conveniunt cum Verbo incarnato, a quo sacramenta fluxerunt in natura assumpta; et etiam cum sacramentis, in quibus est spiritualis virtus in corporeis elementis, sicut et homines ex natura spirituali et corporali compositi sunt. Secundo si baptizare se fingeret, semper esset timendum quod non faceret intentione baptizandi, quae ad sacramentum exigitur, sed intentione decipiendi: quia non esset probabile quod tantum bonum homini procuraret, sicut est spiritualis regeneratio.

AD PRIMUM ergo dicendum, quod ubi datur baptismus, talis est qualis ille in cujus potestate datur. Sed diabolus nullo modo dare potest.

AD SECUNDUM dicendum, quod homo peccator habet similitudinem cum Deo non solum quantum ad naturam divinam per imaginem, sed etiam quantum ad naturam assumptam; et iterum in malis hominibus possibile est esse similitudinem per gratiam, non autem in daemonibus. Et praeterea quod omnibus hominibus concessa est baptizandi potestas, hoc est propter necessitatem sacramenti, ut omnibus possit de facili adesse baptizans. Sed diaboli conversatio non est cum hominibus; unde non juvaret ad necessitatem sacramenti, si sibi potestas illa concederetur.

TO THE FIRST QUESTION, I answer that the devil appearing in the figure of a priest can immerse someone in water, but he cannot confer the sacrament for two reasons. First, because administering the sacraments is only granted to men, who share with the Incarnate Word, from whom the sacraments flowed, in the nature he assumed; and also with the sacraments, in which there is a spiritual power in physical elements, just as men are also composed of a spiritual and physical nature. Second, if he pretended to baptize, it would always be feared that he did not act with the intention of baptizing, which is required for the sacrament, but with the intention of deceiving: for it would not be probable that he would procure so great a good for man as spiritual rebirth.

REPLY OBJ. 1: Where baptism is given, it is as great as the One in whose power it is given. But the devil cannot give it in any way.

REPLY OBJ. 2: A human sinner has a resemblance not only to God's divine nature by his image, but also to his assumed nature; and again it is possible for there to be a likeness by grace in wicked men, but not among the demons. And furthermore the fact that the power of baptizing is granted to all men derives from the necessity of this sacrament, so that a person who can baptize may be easily found by everyone. But the devil does not have fellowship with men; hence it would not be helpful for the necessity of this sacrament if its power were granted to him.

Response to Quaestiuncula 2

AD SECUNDAM QUAESTIONEM dicendum quod angelis bonis non est collata potestas baptizandi, propter duas rationes. Primo, quia non habent praedictam convenientiam cum sacramento, et cum Christo, qui est auctor sacramenti. Secundo, quia ad necessitatem baptismi non valeret potestas eis concessa, cum non sint in promptu hominibus, ut per eos baptizentur. Sed sicut Deus potentiam suam sacramentis non alligavit, ita nec potestatem consecrandi sacramenta alligavit aliquibus ministris; unde qui dedit hanc potestatem hominibus, posset dare et angelis. Nec angelus bonus baptizaret nisi divinitus potestate sibi concessa; unde si baptizaret, non esset rebaptizandus, dummodo constaret quod bonus angelus esset; sicut et judicatum est, templum quod per angelos consecratum est, non oportere per hominem consecrari, ut legitur in historia dedicationis sancti Michaelis.

TO THE SECOND QUESTION, it should be said that the power of baptizing is not conferred on the good angels for two reasons. First, because they do not have the conformity mentioned above with the sacrament, and with Christ, who is the author of the sacrament. Second, because if this power were granted to them it would be of no avail for the necessity of the sacrament, since they are not seen by men, so that men could be baptized by them. But just as God did not bind his own power in the sacraments, so neither did he restrict the power of consecrating sacraments to certain ministers; hence he, who gave this power to men, could give it to angels as well. Nor would a good angel baptize anyone except by power divinely granted to him; hence if he did baptize, one would not need to be rebaptized, as long as it was certain that he was a good angel; just as it was also judged that a temple that was consecrated by angels did not need to be consecrated by man, as is read in the story of the dedication of St. Michael's.[50]

---

50. The legend of St. Michael the Archangel's apparition at Mount Gargano is related in the *Breviarium Romanum* for May 8 as well as in the *Legenda*

AD PRIMUM ergo dicendum, quod angeli actiones hierarchicas eis proportionaliter exequuntur, scilicet invisibiliter: non autem eis est proportionale ut per corporalia hierarchicas actiones perficiant.

AD SECUNDUM dicendum, quod non oportet quod superior potestas eodem modo operetur quo inferior, sed modo altiori; et ideo non oportet si homines sacerdotes per sacramentalia symbola actiones hierarchicas exequuntur, quod hoc angeli possint facere, sed modo altiori.

REPLY OBJ. 1: Angels can perform the hierarchical acts proportionate to them, namely, the invisible ones; but it is not proportionate to them that they perform hierarchical acts through physical things.

REPLY OBJ. 2: It is not necessary that a greater power work in the same way as a lower power, but in a higher way; and thus it is not necessary if human priests perform hierarchical acts through sacramental symbols, that angels be able to do this, but rather in a higher way.

Aurea of Jacobus de Voragine. Around the year 490 St. Michael appeared several times to the Bishop of Sipontum near a cave, asking that the cave be dedicated to Christian worship and promising protection of the nearby town of Sipontum from invaders. Pope Gelasius I (492–96) directed that a basilica be erected enclosing the space.

EXPOSITION OF THE TEXT

Quid noverat Joannes Baptista? Dominum. Sciendum est, quod Joannes antequam intraret eremum, Christum cognovit personaliter ex conversatione, cum fuerit ejus cognatus per carnem et scivit etiam dignitatem ejus ex prophetica revelatione sed propter longam moram amiserat vultus ejus imaginationem; unde personaliter eum non cognoscebat. Et ideo Christo veniente ad baptismum, tria didicit, secundum diversos sanctos: quia, secundum Chrysostomum, didicit quod iste in persona erat ille quem praedicaverat venturum: secundum Augustinum, didicit quod haberet potestatem excellentiae quam sibi retineret, tamen posset eam servis largiri quod tamen in generali prius sciverat, sed tunc in speciali de hac persona cognovit; sed secundum Hieronymum didicit, quod per baptismum Christi non solum gratia conferretur mundans a culpa, sed etiam ab omni poena absolvens, quod habet ab ejus passione.

Tot essent baptismi quot servi. Hoc non videtur esse inconveniens; quia per hoc non differrent baptismi secundum speciem, cum haberent unam formam et unum effectum, sed differrent tantum secundum materiam, sicut et nunc differunt. Et dicendum, quod differrent secundum virtutem, et secundum invocationem; et sic esset occasio schismatis in ecclesia, ut unus diceret: *ego sum Pauli,* alius, *ego sum Petri.*

"What did John the Baptist know? The Lord."[51] It should be known that before John entered the wilderness, he knew Christ personally by spending time with him, since he was his relative in the flesh, and he also knew his dignity from the prophetic revelation, but because of the long delay he had lost the memory of his face; hence he did not recognize him in person. And thus when Christ came for baptism, John learned three things, according to several saints: for according to John Chrysostom,[52] he learned that this man in person was the one he had been preaching would come; according to Augustine,[53] he learned that Christ had the power of excellence which he reserved to himself, although he could endow his servants from it, which John had known before in a general way, but now he understood it about this specific person; but according to Jerome,[54] he learned that by Christ's baptism not only would there be conferred a grace that cleansed from sin, but also a grace that absolved from all punishment, which came from his Passion.

"There would be as many baptisms as there are servants."[55] This does not seem to be unfitting, since these baptisms would not differ according to species, since they would have the same form and the same effect, but they would differ only according to matter, just as they differ now. And it should be said that should they differ according to power, and according to invocation, then in that way there would be the chance of schism in the church, so that one person would say, "I am of Paul," and another would say, "I am of Peter."

---

51. *Sent.* IV, 5.2 (34), 1, citing Augustine, *In Iohannis euangelium tractatus* (CCSL 36), Tract. 5, ch. 11.
52. John Chrysostom, *Homilies on John*, Homily 17, n. 3 (PG 59:378).
53. Augustine, *In Iohannis euangelium tractatus* (CCSL 36), Tract. 5, n. 6.
54. Jerome on Ezekiel 47:3, in *Commentary on Ezekiel*, Bk. 4 (PL 25:469).
55. *Sent.* IV, 5.2 (34), 2, citing Augustine, *In Iohannis euangelium tractatus* (CCSL 36), Tract. 5, n. 7.

DISTINCTION 6
CONDITIONS FOR BAPTISM

Superius determinavit Magister, qui possunt baptizare; hic intendit, determinare qui et qualiter congrue baptizent; et dividitur in partes tres: in prima ostendit qualiter congrue fiat baptismus ex parte baptizantis; in secunda qualiter congrue fiat ex parte baptizandi; utrum scilicet aliquis sit rebaptizandus, vel non, ibi: *de illis vero qui ab haereticis baptizantur, utrum rebaptizandi sint quaeri solet*; in tertia qualiter congrue fiat quantum ad ritum baptismi, ibi: *cognoscendum est etiam, in baptizandis electis duo tempora esse servanda*; secunda pars dividitur in tres: in prima ostendit utrum aliquis sit rebaptizandus propter defectum baptizantis; in secunda, utrum sit rebaptizandus propter defectum baptizati, ibi: *illud etiam ignorandum non est, quod in materno utero nullus baptizari potest*; in tertia, utrum sit rebaptizandus propter defectum eorum quae pertinent ab baptismum, ibi: *quaeri autem solet, si corrupte proferantur verba illa, an baptismus sit.*

Prima dividitur in tres: in prima ostendit quod baptizati ab haereticis non sunt rebaptizandi; in secunda excludit opinionem contrariam, ibi: *sunt tamen nonnulli doctorum . . . qui dicere videntur, ab haereticis non posse tradi baptismum*; in tertia removet quamdam objectionem, quae rebaptizantibus patrocinari videtur, ibi: *hoc etiam sciendum est*, etc.

Illud autem ignorandum non est, etc. Hic inquirit, utrum sit aliquis rebaptizandus propter defectum nativitatis ex utero; et circa hoc duo facit: primo ostendit quod illi qui nondum nati sunt, in maternis uteris existentes, non susceperunt baptismum baptizatis matribus; unde baptizandi sunt; secundo objicit in contrarium, et solvit, ibi: *si vero opponitur de Hieremia, et Joanne . . . dicimus*, etc.

Quaeri autem solet, si corrupte proferantur verba illa, an baptismus sit. Hic inquirit, utrum sint aliqui rebaptizandi propter defectum eorum quae ad baptismum requiruntur: et primo utrum propter corruptionem formae; secundo utrum propter incertitudinem baptismalis

Above the Master delineated who could baptize; here he means to determine who baptizes fittingly, and how; and this is divided into three parts: in the first, he shows how baptism is fittingly done on the part of the one baptizing; in the second, how it is fittingly done on the part of the one baptized; namely, whether anyone should be rebaptized or not, at: *But it is usual to ask concerning those who were baptized by heretics whether they ought to be re-baptized;*[1] in the third part, how it is fittingly done as to the rite of baptism, at: *it is also to be known that "in baptizing those who have been chosen, two times are to be observed."*[2] The second part is divided into three parts: in the first, he shows whether someone should be rebaptized because of a defect in the baptizer; in the second, whether someone should be rebaptized because of a defect in the one baptized, at: *Nor is it to be overlooked that no one can be baptized in his mother's womb;*[3] in the third, whether someone should be rebaptized because of a defect in the things that pertain to baptism, at: *It is also usual to ask whether there is a baptism, if the aforementioned words are uttered in a corrupt form.*[4]

The first is divided into three parts: in the first part, he shows that people baptized by heretics are not to be rebaptized; in the second, he excludes the contrary opinion, at: *but there are some among the doctors . . . who seem to say that baptism cannot be given by heretics;*[5] in the third, he removes a certain objection, which seems to defend rebaptizing, at: *It is also to be known that "although there is a triple immersion,"* etc.[6]

Nor is it to be overlooked that no one can be baptized in his mother's womb, etc. Here he inquires whether someone should be rebaptized because of not having been born from the womb; and concerning this he does two things: first, he shows that those who are not yet born, existing in their mothers' wombs, have not received baptism by their mothers' baptism; hence they must be baptized. Second, he objects to the contrary, and resolves it, at: *But if it is objected that we read of Jeremias and John the Baptist that they were sanctified in the womb*, etc.[7]

It is also usual to ask whether there is a baptism, if the aforementioned words are uttered in a corrupt form. Here he inquires whether there may be some people who have to be rebaptized because of the lack of what is required for baptism. And first, whether because of a corruption of

---

1. Peter Lombard, *Sententiae* IV, 6.2 (37), 1.
2. *Sent.* IV, 6.4 (39), 3 Leo I, *Epistola 16 (ad universos episcopos Siciliae)*, chs. 5–6.
3. *Sent.* IV, 6.3 (38), 1.
4. *Sent.* IV, 6.4 (39), 1.
5. *Sent.* IV, 6.2 (37), 4.
6. *Sent.* IV, 6.2 (37), 6 citing Jerome, *In quatuor epistolas Paulinas*, Eph. 4:5.
7. *Sent.* IV, 6.3 (38), 2 citing Jer 1:5; Lk 1:15.

ablutionis, ibi: *praeterea sciendum est, quod illi de quibus nulla extant indicia inter propinquos vel domesticos vel vicinos, a quibus baptizati fuisse doceantur, agendum est ut renascantur, ne pereant;* tertio utrum propter defectum intentionis, ibi: *solet etiam quaeri de illo qui jocans, sicut mimus, commemoratione tamen Trinitatis immergitur.*

Cognoscendum est etiam, in baptizandis electis duo tempora esse servanda. Hic ostendit qualiter baptismus congrue fiat ex parte ritus, et circa hoc tria facit: primo ostendit quod tempus sit deputatum ad solemnem baptismi celebrationem; secundo determinat de professione quae praecedit baptismum, ibi: *porro cuncti ad baptismum venientes fidem suam profiteri debent;* tertio determinat de catechismo et exorcismo, in quibus hujusmodi professio fit, ibi: *illa autem interrogatio et responsio fidei fit in catechismo.* Circa secundum duo facit: primo ostendit propositum; secundo movet duas quaestiones; primam ibi: *si vero quaeritur ex quo sensu pro parvulo dicatur, credo, vel fidem peto; dicimus de sacramento fidei id esse intelligendum;* secundum ibi: *sed adhuc quaeritur, ex quo sensu pro parvulo respondeatur, credo in Deum patrem,* etc.

Hic est duplex quaestio. Prima de his quae requiruntur ad baptismum ex parte baptizantis et baptizati. Secunda de ritu baptismi.

the form; second, whether because of uncertainty about the baptismal pouring, at: *it is also to be known that those concerning whom "no proofs exist among their relatives nor among the clergy or neighbors, whereby they may be shown to have been baptized, action must be taken for their regeneration, lest they perish;"* [8] third, whether because of a defect of intention, at: *it is also usual to ask concerning one who, in jest, like an actor, is immersed with the commemoration of the Trinity.* [9]

It is also to be known that "*in baptizing those who have been chosen, two times are to be observed.*" Here he shows how baptism is fittingly done on the part of the rite, and concerning this he does three things: first, he shows what time is deputed for the solemn celebration of baptism; second, he examines the profession that precedes baptism, at: *next all who come to baptism are to profess their faith;* [10] third, he considers the catechism and exorcism, in which a profession like this is made, at: *however that interrogation and response as to faith is done with the catechumen.* [11] Concerning the second he does two things: first, he shows the argument; second, he raises two questions, the first one at: *But if it is asked in what sense I believe or I seek faith, is said on behalf of the child, we say that it is to be understood of the sacrament of faith;* [12] the second, at: *But it is also asked in what sense is the response: I believe in God the Father,* etc. [13]

Here there are two questions. First, concerning what is required for baptism on the part of the one baptizing and the one being baptized. Second, concerning the rite of baptism.

---

8. *Sent.* IV, 6.4 (39), 2 citing Pope Leo I, *Epistola 167 (ad Rusticum Narbonensem)*, inq. 16–17.
9. *Sent.* IV, 6.5 (40), 1.
10. *Sent.* IV, 6.2 (41), 1.
11. *Sent.* IV, 6.7 (42), 1.
12. *Sent.* IV, 6.6 (41), 2.
13. *Sent.* IV, 6.6 (41), 3.

QUESTION 1

Circa primum quaeruntur tria:

primo, utrum requiratur in baptizando nativitas ex utero;

secundo, utrum requiratur in utroque intentio et voluntas;

tertio, utrum requiratur fides.

About the first, three questions arise:

first, whether birth out of the womb is required for baptizing;

second, whether both will and intention are required;

third, whether faith is required.

ARTICLE 1

Whether birth out of the womb is required for baptizing[14]

Quaestiuncula 1

AD PRIMUM SIC PROCEDITUR. Videtur quod nativitas ex utero non sit expectanda. Nulli enim statui hominis praecluditur via salutis ab eo *qui vult omnes homines salvos fieri*. Sed existentes in maternis uteris homines sunt, cum sint jam animam rationalem sortiti, et sunt in periculo damnationis propter peccatum originale contractum, et facilitatem corruptionis. Ergo cum eis non possit remedium adhiberi perveniendi ad vitam nisi per baptismum, videtur quod debeant baptizari.

PRAETEREA, puer in materno utero existens est quasi quaedam pars matris, sicut fructus pendens in arbore, pars arboris. Ergo baptizata matre, baptizatur puer in ventre ejus existens.

PRAETEREA, contingit quandoque quod aliqua pars prius egreditur, sicut legitur, Gen. 25, de Esau, quod exivit primo manus; et tamen timetur de periculo mortis. Ergo videtur quod saltem in tali casu non sit expectanda nativitas ex utero sed pars egressa aspergenda baptismali aqua.

PRAETEREA, mors aeterna pejor est quam mors corporalis in infinitum. Sed de duobus malis eligendum est minus malum. Ergo debet mater scindi, et extrahi puer, ut baptizatus a morte aeterna liberetur et non expectari nativitas ex utero.

SED CONTRA, 1 Corinth. 15, 46: *non prius quod spirituale est, sed quod animale, deinde quod spirituale.*

OBJ. 1: To the first we proceed thus. It seems that one should not wait for birth out of the womb. For in no state of man is the way of salvation closed off by him *who wills all men to be saved* (1 Tim 2:4). But existing in their mothers' wombs they are humans, since they are already endowed with a rational soul, and they are in danger of damnation because of the original sin they have contracted, and the ease of corruption. Therefore, since for them no remedy can be applied for attaining life except through baptism, it seems they must be baptized.

OBJ. 2: Furthermore, the child existing in his mother's womb is almost like a part of the mother, as a fruit hanging from a tree is a part of the tree. Therefore, when the mother is baptized, the child in her womb is baptized.

OBJ. 3: Furthermore, sometimes it happens that a certain part comes out first, as is read of Esau, that his hand came out first; and nevertheless danger of death is feared (cf. Gen 25:25). Therefore, it seems that at least in this case one should not wait for birth from the womb, but the part emerging should be sprinkled with baptismal water.

OBJ. 4: Furthermore, eternal death is infinitely worse than bodily death. But the lesser of two evils is always to be chosen. Therefore, the mother should be cut open and the child taken out, so that, baptized, he may be freed from eternal death, and his birth from the womb should not be waited for.

ON THE CONTRARY, *What is spiritual does not come first, but what is animal, and then the spiritual* (1 Cor 15:46).

---

14. Parallel: *ST* III, q. 68, a. 11.

Sed baptismus est quaedam regeneratio spiritualis. Ergo prius homo animali, et carnali nativitate nasci debet quam baptizetur.

Praeterea, sacramentum est actio militantis ecclesiae. Sed quamdiu puer est in ventre matris, nondum connumeratur aliis membris ecclesiae. Ergo non potest sibi baptismus exhiberi.

But baptism is a certain spiritual regeneration. Therefore, man must be born by his animal and fleshly birth before being baptized.

Furthermore, a sacrament is an act of the Church Militant. But while a child is in his mother's womb, he is not yet numbered with the other members of the Church. Therefore, baptism cannot be administered to him.

Quaestiuncula 2

Ulterius. Videtur quod nullus etiam in materno utero possit sanctificari per gratiae gratum facientis donum. Quia, ut Isidorus dicit, *regeneratio in eo dici non potest in quem generatio non praecessit*. Sed per gratiam gratum facientem fit homo filius Dei, et ita regeneratur. Ergo non potest homo sanctificari antequam nascatur ex utero.

Praeterea, sicut peccatum actuale contrahitur ex actu, ita originale contrahitur ex origine. Sed peccatum actuale non potest remitti quamdiu homo est in actu peccandi. Ergo nec peccatum originale potest remitti puero in materno utero existenti, qui adhuc est actualiter in origine existens.

Praeterea, ubi est majus periculum, ibi magis divina misericordia subvenit. Sed illi qui morituri sunt antequam ex utero nascantur, sunt in majori periculo quam Joannes Baptista et Hieremias, qui ex utero postmodum nati sunt. Si ergo non dicimus pueros dictos sanctificari in utero, ne praeveniantur morte, videtur quod multo fortius nec Joannes nec Hieremias sanctificati fuerunt.

Sed contra est quod dicitur Hierem. 1, 5: *antequam exires de vulva sanctificavi te*; et Luc. 1, 16, dicitur de Joanne: *et Spiritu Sancto replebitur adhuc ex utero matris suae*. Ergo aliqui in utero sanctificantur.

Praeterea, de nullo celebrat ecclesia festum, nisi de sancto aliquo. Sed celebrat nativitatem Joannis. Ergo tunc nascens sanctus erat; ergo in utero sanctificatus fuit.

Obj. 1: Moreover, it seems that also no one can be sanctified in his mother's womb by the gift of sanctifying grace.[15] For as Isidore says, *regeneration cannot be asserted in one for whom generation has not gone before*.[16] But by sanctifying grace man becomes a son of God, and in this way he is regenerated. Therefore, a human cannot be sanctified before being born from the womb.

Obj. 2: Furthermore, just as actual sin is contracted by our acts, so also original sin is contracted through our origin. But actual sin cannot be remitted as long as a man is actually sinning. Therefore, neither can original sin be forgiven in a child existing in this mother's womb, who is still actually existing in his origin.

Obj. 3: Furthermore, where danger is greater, there divine mercy comes to the rescue. But those who are about to die before they are born from the womb are in greater danger than John the Baptist and Jeremiah, who were born after their sanctification. If, therefore, we do not say those children mentioned are sanctified in the womb lest they be prevented by death, it seems that much less were John the Baptist and Jeremiah sanctified in the womb.

On the contrary, is what is said: *before you came forth out of the womb, I sanctified you* (Jer 1:5); and what is said of John, *and he will be filled with the Holy Spirit even from his mother's womb* (Luke 1:15). Therefore, certain people have been sanctified *in utero*.

Furthermore, the Church only celebrates a feast day for someone who is a saint. But it celebrates the birth of John. Therefore, he was holy at his birth; therefore, he was sanctified *in utero*.

Quaestiuncula 3

Ulterius. Videtur quod in utero sanctificati non sunt baptizandi. In sanctificatione enim in utero datur major gratia quam in baptismo: quia sanctificationis gratia dicitur esse confirmans saltem[17] contra mortale peccatum. Sed injuriam faceret baptismo qui baptizatum iterum baptizaret. Ergo injuriam facit sanctificatio-

Obj. 1: Moreover, it seems that those sanctified in the womb do not need to be baptized. For in sanctification *in utero*, greater grace is given than in baptism; for the grace of sanctification is said to be a grace that strengthens salvation against mortal sin. But whoever baptized a baptized person would do injury to baptism. Therefore, whoever sanctified

---

15. Literally, "grace that makes pleasing."
16. Isidore, *Sententiae* (CCSL 111), ch. 22, n. 5.
17. *saltem.—salutem* PLE.

ni in utero qui sanctificatum iterum baptizando sanctificaret.

Praeterea, natura non facit per plura quod per unum potest facere. Sed operatio gratiae est ordinatior quam natura. Cum ergo ad salutem sufficiat gratia sanctificationis, videtur quod frustra baptismus addatur.

Praeterea, divina operatio non est minus efficax in sanatione spirituali quam corporali. Sed in illis quos curavit corporaliter, non oportebat aliquem medicum ab homine superaddi. Ergo et in illis quos curat per gratiam sanctificationis interius non sunt adhibenda sacramentorum medicamenta.

Sed contra, baptismus circumcisioni successit. Sed Joannes sanctificatus in utero, octavo die legitur circumcisus, Luc. 1. Ergo et sanctificatus in utero esset baptizandus.

Praeterea, sanctificatio in utero est baptismus flaminis. Sed adulti baptizati per contritionem baptismo flaminis, sunt baptizandi baptismo fluminis. Ergo et similiter sanctificati in utero.

a sanctified person by baptizing him again, would do injury to sanctification *in utero*.

Obj. 2: Furthermore, nature does not work through many things what it can work through one. But the operation of grace is more ordered than that of nature. Since, therefore, the grace of sanctification suffices for salvation, it seems that baptism would be added in vain.

Obj. 3: Furthermore, divine operation is not less effective in spiritual healing than in physical healing. But among those whom it has cured physically, no curative needed to be added by man. Therefore, also among those whom it has healed by the grace of interior sanctification the medicine of the sacraments need not be applied.

On the contrary, baptism took the place of circumcision. But John, who was sanctified in the womb, is read to have been circumcised on the eighth day after birth (Luke 1:59). Therefore, those sanctified in the womb would also have needed to be baptized.

Furthermore, sanctification in the womb is a baptism of spirit. But adults baptized with the baptism of the spirit through their contrition do need to be baptized with the baptism of water. Therefore, it is also the same with those sanctified in the womb.

Response to Quaestiuncula 1

Respondeo dicendum ad primam quaestionem, quod baptismus est actio hierarchica secundum Dionysium; unde per ministros ecclesiae conferendus est, vel per eos qui in necessitate vicem ministrorum obtinent. Puer autem quamdiu est in utero matris existens, non potest subjici operationi ministrorum ecclesiae nec est hominibus notus; et ideo tunc baptizari non potest.

Quidam autem assignant alias causas, quae non sunt magni ponderis: quarum una est quod divina justitia exigit quod peccatum quodlibet non dimittatur sine poena aliqua, quam puer in baptismo sentit, quod esse non posset, dum adhuc est in utero matris. Sed hoc nihil est quia baptismus, secundum Ambrosium, non requirit poenam exteriorem. Et praeterea peccato originali non debetur poena sensibilis inflicta. Alia est quod gratia dat esse ordinatum; et ideo regeneratio gratiae praesupponit generationem naturae. Alia est quod puer quamdiu est in materno utero, adhuc conjungitur causae originalis peccati; et ideo non potest ab eo mundari. Sed hae duae causae repugnant sanctificationi in utero, sicut et baptismo. Alia est quod in baptismo debet esse aqua et spiritus contra infectionem carnis, et animae per originale; et ideo oportet praeexistere ad baptismum nativi-

To the first question, I answer that baptism is a hierarchical act according to Dionysius;[18] hence it must be conferred by the ministers of the Church, or by those who occupy the place of ministers in necessity. However, while a baby exists in the womb of his mother, he cannot be subjected to the operation of the ministers of the Church, nor is he known to people; and thus he cannot be baptized at that time.

However, some people assign other reasons, which are not of great weight: one of which is that divine justice requires that no sin be forgiven without some penalty suffered, which the baby experiences in baptism, which could not happen while he is still in his mother's womb. But this is nothing, because baptism, according to Ambrose,[19] does not require external penalty to be suffered. And furthermore for original sin no sensible penalty is required to be inflicted. Another argument is that grace gives ordered being; and therefore the regeneration of grace presupposes the generation of nature. Another is that while a baby is in the mother's womb, he is still joined to the cause of original sin; and so he cannot be cleansed of it. But these two reasons are opposed to sanctification in the womb, as well as baptism. Another argument is that in baptism there should be water and spirit against the infection of the flesh and soul

---

18. Pseudo-Dionysius, *Ecclesiastical Hierarchy*, ch. 2, (PG 3:391).
19. Actually Ambrosiaster, *On the Epistle to the Romans* 11:29 (CSEL 81.1:385).

tatem in utero, qua infunditur anima, et nativitatem ex utero, qua nascitur corpus. Sed hoc nihil est: quia nativitas neque est animae neque corporis, sed conjuncti; unde in nativitate in utero nascitur et corpus et anima. Unde primae rationi standum est.

AD PRIMUM ergo dicendum, quod non est ex defectu divinae misericordiae quod pueris in maternis uteris existentibus remedium non exhibetur, sed quia non sunt capaces illius remedii, per quod secundum legem communem participes passionis Christi efficiantur, a qua est remissio peccatorum: quia non possunt subjici operationi ministrorum ecclesiae, per quos talia remedia ministrantur.

AD SECUNDUM dicendum, quod puer in materno utero existens, quamvis sit conjunctus matri secundum corpus, quod ab ipsa traxit tamen est omnino distinctus secundum animam rationalem quam ab extrinseco habet; et ideo secundum immutationem corporalem matris, immutatur corporaliter, sed non oportet quod sanctificata matre per baptismum, spiritualiter sanctificetur.

AD TERTIUM dicendum, quod expectanda est totalis egressio ex utero, nisi periculum mortis timeatur; tunc autem egressa parte principali scilicet capite, in quo operationes animae magis manifestantur, ut quidam dicunt, baptizari debet: secus autem est de aliis partibus, ut de manu et pede, quamvis non noceat etiam si tunc aspergerentur illae partes baptismali aqua, quia divina misericordia non est arctanda. Si tamen postea plenarie nascatur non est rebaptizandus, secundum quosdam. Sed nihil periculi accidit, si ad majorem cautelam baptizetur sub hac forma: *si non es baptizatus, ego te baptizo*, etc.

AD QUARTUM dicendum, quod *non sunt facienda mala, ut veniant bona*, sicut dicitur Rom. 3; et ideo homo potius debet dimittere perire infantem quam ipse pereat, homicidii crimen in matre committens.

by original sin; and thus before baptism can happen, conception in the womb must happen, by which the soul is infused, as well as birth from the womb, by which the body is born. But this is nothing: for birth is neither of the soul nor of the body, but of the two joined; hence at conception in the womb the soul and the body are both brought to life. Hence the first argument should be upheld.

REPLY OBJ. 1: It is not from a lack of divine mercy that children in their mothers' wombs are not given the remedy, but because they are not capable of this remedy, by which, according to the common rule, they would be made partakers in the Passion of Christ, from which comes the remission of sins. For they cannot be subject to the operation of the ministers of the Church by which this kind of remedy is administered.

REPLY OBJ. 2: A baby in his mother's womb, although he is joined to his mother in his body, which he drew from her, nevertheless is entirely distinct in his rational soul, which he has from outside. And thus according to any physical change in the mother, he is changed bodily, but it is not necessary that when the mother is sanctified through baptism, he should be spiritually sanctified.

REPLY OBJ. 3: Complete delivery from the uterus should be waited for, unless a danger of death is feared; but then once the principal part is delivered, namely the head, where the operations of the soul are most evident, as some people say, he should be baptized. However, it is different with the other parts, like the hand and the foot, although there is no harm if then those parts were also to be sprinkled with baptismal water, for divine mercy is not to be constricted. However, if afterward he should be completely born, he is not to be rebaptized, according to some people. But no danger would befall if, for safety's sake, he were baptized under this form: *if you are not baptized, I baptize you*, etc.

REPLY OBJ. 4: *Bad things should not be done so that good things will come*, as is said in Romans 3:8. And thus someone should rather allow the infant to perish than perish himself by committing murder against the mother.

Response to Quaestiuncula 2

AD SECUNDAM QUAESTIONEM dicendum, quod sicut Deus non alligavit virtutem suam rebus naturalibus, ut non possit praeter eas operari cum voluerit quod in miraculosis actibus facit, ita non alligavit virtutem suam sacramentis, ut non possit sine sacramentorum ministris aliquem sanctificare; et ideo aliquos praeter legem communem quasi miraculose in maternis uteris sanctificasse legitur, illos praecipue qui immediatius ordinabantur ad ejus sanctissimam conceptionem; et ideo mater sanctificata creditur, et Joannes Baptista, qui ei in utero existenti testimonium perhibuit, et Hieremias, qui ip-

TO THE SECOND QUESTION, it should be said that just as God did not bind his own power to natural things so that he would not be able to work without them when he willed what he does in miraculous acts; so also he did not bind his power to the sacraments so that he would not be able to sanctify someone without the ministry of the sacraments; and thus it is read that certain people, outside the common rule, have been sanctified almost miraculously in their mothers' wombs, particularly those who were more immediately ordered to his most holy conception; and thus his mother is believed to have been sanctified, and John

sius conceptionem vaticinio expresso praedixit: *novum*, inquit, *faciet Dominus super terram. Mulier circumdabit virum*: Hierem. 31, 22; et ideo etiam in Beata Virgine fuit amplior sanctificatio, in qua fomes adeo debilitatus est vel extinctus, ut ad peccatum actuale nunquam inclinaretur; in aliis autem inclinavit ad veniale, non autem ad mortale; et in Joanne Baptista etiam fuit expressior quam in Hieremia cujus interior sanctificatio exultatione quadam in notitiam hominum prodiit, quia dictum est: *exultavit infans in utero ejus*, Luc. 1, 41, ut secundum gradum propinquitatis ad Christum sit gradus sanctificationis.

AD PRIMUM ergo dicendum, quod generatio spiritualis praesupponit naturalem sibi correspondentem; et ideo generatio spiritualis quae fit per ministerium hominum in baptismo praesupponit nativitatem ex utero, qua homo in notitiam et societatem hominum prodit. Sed regeneratio quae fit divinitus, non praesupponit de necessitate nisi nativitatem in utero, qua homo a Deo creatus, formatus est.

AD SECUNDUM dicendum, quod jam formato puerperio anima rationali infusa, puer non accipit a matre nisi nutrimentum. Peccatum autem originale non contrahitur per actum nutritivae, sed generativae; et ideo non est actu in contrahendo originale, nisi in ipsa infusione animae; et propter hoc nihil prohibet puerum in statu illo post infusionem a peccato originali mundari.

AD TERTIUM dicendum, quod ea quae fiunt praeter legem communem, non fiunt principaliter ad subveniendum uni personae, sed ad insinuationem et commendationem gratiae; et ideo quamvis non fuerit tantum periculum in sanctificatis in utero, qui prodituri erant, tamen quia eligebantur divinitus ut gratiae speciales praecones et ministri, ideo tali privilegiata sanctificatione dotati sunt.

the Baptist, who bore witness to him while he was in his mother's womb, and Jeremiah, who foretold his conception in the prophecy he announced: *The Lord will do something new upon the earth. A woman shall encompass a man* (Jer 31:22). And thus in the Blessed Virgin there was also a fuller sanctification, in which the kindling for sin was weakened or quenched to the extent that she would never be inclined to actual sin. In others, though, it inclined to venial sin, but not to mortal sin; and in John the Baptist, whose internal sanctification welled up in a certain exultation observable by others, it was also more explicit than in Jeremiah, since it is said: *the infant leapt in her womb* (Luke 1:41), so that the degree of sanctification follows the degree of closeness to Christ.

REPLY OBJ. 1: Spiritual generation presupposes the natural one corresponding to it; and thus the spiritual generation that occurs through the ministry of men in baptism presupposes birth from the womb, by which a man comes forth into the awareness and society of men. But the regeneration that happens divinely does not necessarily presuppose anything but conception in the womb, by which a man created by God is formed.

REPLY OBJ. 2: Once the rational soul is infused in the now-formed unborn child, he does not receive anything from his mother but nourishment. However, original sin is not contracted by the nutritive act, but by the generative act; and thus the child is only in the act of contracting original sin in the moment of the soul's infusion; and consequently nothing prohibits a child in this state from being cleansed of original sin after the soul's infusion.

REPLY OBJ. 3: Those things that happen outside the common rule do not happen chiefly for the benefit of one person, but for the instilling and committal of grace; and thus even if there was not such great danger among those sanctified in the womb, who were about to come forth, nevertheless since they were divinely chosen as special heralds of grace and ministry, thus they were endowed with such a privileged sanctification.

Response to Quaestiuncula 3

AD TERTIAM QUAESTIONEM dicendum, quod sanctificatus in utero debet baptizari, propter tres rationes. Primo propter acquirendum characterem, quo annumeretur in populo Dei, et quasi deputetur ad percipienda divina sacramenta. Secundo, ut per baptismi perceptionem passioni Christi etiam corporaliter conformetur. Tertio propter bonum obedientiae: quia praeceptum de baptismo omnibus datum est, et ab omnibus impleri debet, nisi articulus necessitatis sacramentum excludat.

AD PRIMUM ergo dicendum, quod baptismus quantum ad aliquid extensive excedit sanctificationem: quia

TO THE THIRD QUESTION, it should be said that those sanctified in the womb should be baptized for three reasons. First, in order to acquire the character, by which they will be numbered among the people of God and entitled in a certain way to receive the divine sacraments. Second, so that by receiving baptism they may be conformed to the Passion of Christ bodily as well. Third, on account of the good of obedience, for the command about baptism was given to all and should be fulfilled by all, unless an emergency should exclude the sacrament.

REPLY OBJ. 1: Baptism surpasses sanctification in its extension; for in baptism a character is imprinted, and man

in baptismo imprimitur character, et corporaliter homo morti Christi configuratur: quamvis intensive in sanctificatione amplior gratia fortassis praebeatur; et ideo non fit injuria sanctificationi, si sanctificatis baptismus conferatur.

AD SECUNDUM dicendum, quod non totum quod facit baptismus, factum est per sanctificationem, quia non imprimit characterem; et ideo non frustra baptismus additur, in quo etiam sanctificatis gratia augetur.

AD TERTIUM dicendum, quod per medicinam corporalem nihil addi posset ad salutem eorum quos Christus curaverat; et ideo non est similis ratio.

is bodily configured to Christ's death; although in intensity a fuller grace may perhaps be supplied in sanctification; and thus it causes no injury to sanctification if baptism is conferred on someone already sanctified.

REPLY OBJ. 2: Not all that baptism does is done by sanctification, for it does not imprint a character; and thus baptism is not added to it in vain. Moreover, in baptism grace is increased even in the sanctified.

REPLY OBJ. 3: Nothing could be added to the health of those Christ cured by bodily medicine; and so the situation is not the same.

ARTICLE 2

Whether both will and intention are required for baptism

Quaestiuncula 1

AD SECUNDUM SIC PROCEDITUR. Videtur quod intentio baptizantis non requiratur ad baptismum. Intentio enim non requiritur ad opus nisi in principali agente, qui praestituit finem, et per imperium suum alios movet ad finem intentum a se. Sed sacerdos baptizans non est principale agens, sed instrumentale, ut dictum est supra. Ergo non requiritur ejus intentio ad baptismum.

PRAETEREA, intentio hominis non est alicui certa nisi sibi. Si ergo requiratur intentio ad baptismum, non erit certum de aliquo quod sit baptizatus, nisi apud eum qui baptizavit; et hoc est inconveniens quod homo sit in tanto dubio salutis.

PRAETEREA, sicut Augustinus dicit, *ebriosus et furiosus baptizare possunt.* Sed isti, ut videtur, non possunt habere intentionem, quia privantur usu rationis. Ergo intentio non requiritur ad baptismum.

PRAETEREA, intentio cogitationem requirit. Sed frequenter et de facili cogitatio ad alia rapitur. Ergo frequenter baptismus impediretur.

SED CONTRA, ea quae fiunt praeter intentionem, sunt casualia. Sed hoc sacramentis non competit, cum habeant determinatos effectus, et determinatas causas. Ergo requiritur intentio in baptismo, et in aliis sacramentis.

PRAETEREA, opera quae fiunt a voluntate, determinantur et specificantur intentione. Unde Ambrosius dicit quod *affectus tuus operi tuo imponit nomen*; et in *Glossa,* Matth. 12, dicitur: *quantum intendis, tantum facis.* Sed baptizare est actus voluntarius. Ergo requiritur in ipso intentio ex parte baptizantis.

OBJ. 1: To the second we proceed thus. It seems that the intention of the one baptizing would not be required for baptism.[20] For intention is not required for any work except in the principal agent, who has predetermined the end, and by his command moves others to the end intended by himself. But the priest baptizing is not the principal agent, but an instrumental one, as was said above. Therefore, his intention is not required for baptism.

OBJ. 2: Furthermore, a man's intention is not certainly known by anyone but himself. Therefore, if his intention were required for baptism, it would not be certainly known whether anyone had been baptized, except to the one who baptized him; and it is unfitting that a man should be in so much doubt of his salvation.

OBJ. 3: Furthermore, just as Augustine says, *madmen and drunks can baptize.*[21] But it would seem that they cannot have the intention, since they are lacking the use of reason. Therefore, an intention is not required for baptism.

OBJ. 4: Furthermore, an intention requires thought. But thoughts are often easily swept away to other things. Therefore, baptism would often be prevented.

ON THE CONTRARY, those things that happen outside of intention are by chance. But this does not apply to the sacraments, since they have determinate effects and determinate causes. Therefore, intention is required in baptism and the other sacraments.

FURTHERMORE, works that flow from the will are determined and specified by the intention. Hence, Ambrose says *your desire imposes a name on your work*;[22] and in the Gloss on Matthew 12 it is said, *however much you intend, that much you do.*[23] But to baptize is a willed act. Therefore, intention is required in it on the part of the one baptizing.

Quaestiuncula 2

ULTERIUS. Videtur quod requiratur intentio recta. Requiritur enim intentio faciendi quod facit ecclesia. Sed hoc intendere est rectae intentionis. Ergo ad baptismum requiritur recta intentio.

OBJ. 1: Moreover, it seems that right intention is required.[24] For the intention of doing what the Church does is required. But to intend this belongs to the right intention. Therefore, the right intention is required for baptism.

---

20. Parallels: below, d. 7, q. 3, a. 1, qa. 1, ad 3; d. 8, q. 2, a. 4, qa. 3, ad 1; d. 30, q. 1, a. 3, ad 3; *ST* III, q. 60, a. 8; q. 64, a. 8.
21. Augustine, *In Iohannis euangelium tractatus* (CCSL 36), Tract. 5, n. 17.
22. Ambrose, *De Officiis,* Bk. 1, ch. 30 (CCSL 15:53): "Affectus tuus nomen imponit operi tuo: quomodo a te proficiscitur sic aestimatur."
23. *Glossa interlinearis* on Matthew 12:35.
24. Parallels: below, exposition of the text; d. 11, q. 2, a. 1, qa. 3, ad 1; d. 30, q. 1, a. 3, ad 3; *ST* III, q. 64, a. 10; q. 74, a. 2, ad 2.

Praeterea, in omnibus ad quae requiritur intentio, ita est quod per pravam intentionem vitiantur. Sed baptismus, dummodo detur, non potest esse pravus, ut in praecedenti distinctione dictum est. Ergo videtur quod prava intentio non possit conferre baptismum.

Sed contra, baptismus non impeditur ex malitia baptizantis. Sed perversa intentio pertinet ad malitiam baptizantis. Ergo perversa intentio in aliis non impedit baptismi effectum.

Obj. 2: Furthermore, in anything requiring an intention, a corrupt intention would ruin it. But baptism, when it is truly given, cannot be corrupt, as was said in the preceding distinction. Therefore, it seems that a wicked intention could not confer baptism.

On the contrary, baptism is not impeded by the wickedness of the one baptizing. But a wrong intention pertains to the wickedness of the one baptizing. Therefore, a wrong intention in others does not impede the effect of baptism.

Quaestiuncula 3

Ulterius. Videtur quod intentio vel voluntas non requiratur in baptizato. Baptismus enim contra peccatum originale datur. Sed peccatum originale praeter voluntatem et intentionem contrahitur. Ergo intentio et voluntas non requiruntur ad baptismum in baptizando.

Praeterea, pueri, dormientes et amentes possunt baptizari, ut supra, dist. 4, quaest. 3, art. 1, quaestiunc. 2 et 3, dictum est. Sed illi carent intentione baptismi. Ergo ad baptismum non requiritur intentio ex parte baptizandi.

Praeterea, *unaquaeque res per eadem corrumpitur et fit, contrarie tamen facta*, ut dicitur in 2 *Ethic*. Si ergo intentione baptizandi fieret baptismus, tunc intentione ipsius character baptismalis deleri posset; quod falsum est.

Sed contra, in baptismo fit quoddam spirituale connubium animae ad Deum. Sed in conjugio requiritur consensus. Ergo et in baptismo.

Praeterea, baptismi effectus magis impeditur ex parte baptizati quam ex parte baptizantis: quia malitia baptizantis non impedit receptionem gratiae in baptismo, quae impediri potest per malitiam recipientis sacramentum. Sed defectus intentionis ex parte baptizantis impedit sacramentum. Ergo multo fortius defectus intentionis ex parte baptizati.

Obj. 1: Moreover, it seems that the intention or the will is not required in the one baptized.[25] For baptism is given against original sin. But original sin is contracted without will or intention. Therefore, intention and will in the one to be baptized are not required for baptism.

Obj. 2: Furthermore, children, sleeping persons, and the mentally disabled can be baptized, as was said above in Distinction 4, Question 3, Article 1, Subquestions 2 and 3. But they all lack the intention of baptism. Therefore, for baptism intention is not required on the part of the one being baptized.

Obj. 3: Furthermore, *any thing may be corrupted by the same things that made it, just acting in the opposite way*, as is said in *Ethics* 2.[26] Therefore, if by the intention of the one being baptized baptism was done, then the baptismal character could be erased by his intention as well, which is false.

On the contrary, in baptism a certain spiritual wedding takes place of the soul to God. But in marriage, consent is required. Therefore, also in baptism.

Furthermore, baptism's effect is impeded more on the part of the one being baptized than on the part of the one baptizing, for the wickedness of the one baptizing does not impede the reception of grace in baptism, but it can be impeded by the wickedness of the one receiving the sacrament. But a defect of intention on the part of the one baptizing impedes the sacrament. Therefore, much more would a defect of intention on the part of the baptized.

Response to Quaestiuncula 1

Respondeo dicendum, ad primam quaestionem, quod cum unius effectus una sit causa, si ex aliquibus pluribus causis unus effectus procedat, oportet quod illae causae sint aliquo modo factae unum ad invicem. Ad effectum autem sacramenti videmus multa concurrere; scilicet ministrum, formam verborum, et materiam.

To the first question, I answer that since a single effect has a single cause, if a single effect proceeds from several causes, it is necessary that those causes be in some way made one with each other. Now for a sacrament's effect we see that many things must concur; namely, the minister, the form of the words, and the matter. However, these things

---

25. Parallels: below, d. 27, q. 1, a. 2, qa. 4; *ST* III, q. 68, a. 7; q. 69, a. 9.
26. Aristotle, *Nicomachean Ethics*, Bk. 2, ch. 1, 1103b7.

Haec autem non possunt colligari ad invicem ut sint una causa, nisi per intentionem baptizantis, qui scilicet formam ad materiam applicat, suum vero ministerium ad utrumque, et totum hoc ad sacramenti collationem;[27] et ideo requiritur intentio baptizantis. Et similiter etiam in omnibus aliis sacramentis requiritur intentio ministri cum debita materia et forma, non solum ad effectum sacramenti consequendum, sed ad sacramenti perceptionem.

AD PRIMUM ergo dicendum, quod duplex est instrumentum, scilicet animatum, ut servus, et inanimatum ut securis, ut dicitur in 8 *Ethic.* In instrumento igitur inanimato non requiritur intentio propria, quia ipsa inclinatio instrumenti ad effectum per motum principalis agentis, locum intentionis supplet; sed in instrumento animato, quod non tantum agitur, sed aliquo modo agit, utpote per imperium agens, et non per impulsum motus, requiritur intentio exequendi ministerium ad quod applicatum est.

AD SECUNDUM dicendum, quod ad hoc dupliciter secundum diversas opiniones respondetur. Quidam enim dicunt, quod si desit mentalis intentio in baptizante, non confert sacramentum baptismi; tamen in adulto supplet fides et devotio effectum baptismi, ut periculum ex hoc baptizato, qui ignorat intentionem baptizantis, nullum proveniat. Si autem sit puer, creditur pie, quod summus sacerdos, scilicet Deus, defectum suppleat, et salutem ei conferat. Si tamen non facit, non injuste facit, sicut nec in illo qui sacramento non subjicitur. Alii dicunt, quod in baptismo et in aliis sacramentis quae habent in forma actum exercitum, non requiritur mentalis intentio, sed sufficit expressio intentionis per verba ab ecclesia instituta; et ideo si forma servatur, nec aliquid exterius dicitur quod intentionem contrariam exprimat, baptizatus est. Non enim sine causa in sacramentis necessitatis, scilicet baptismo, et quibusdam aliis, actus baptizantis tam solicite expressus est ad intentionis expressionem.

AD TERTIUM dicendum, quod quamvis actu ebrius intentionem habere non possit, tamen ebriosus potest esse non actu ebrius, et intentionem baptizandi habens, baptizare.

AD QUARTUM dicendum, quod quamvis minister sacramenti debeat niti ad custodiendum cor suum quantum potest, ut maxime in verbis sacramentalis formae intentionem habeat actualem; quia tamen cogitatio est valde labilis, etiam si tunc non adsit actualis intentio quando verba profert, dummodo prius intenderit, et contraria intentio non intervenerit, sacramentum non

cannot be united into one cause except by the intention of the one baptizing, who actually applies the form to the matter, and indeed his own ministry to both, and all this pertains to the conferral of the sacrament. And thus the intention of the one baptizing is required. And likewise, in all the other sacraments also the intention of the minister is required with the due matter and form, not only for bringing about the sacrament's effect, but for receiving the sacrament.

REPLY OBJ. 1: As it says in *Ethics* 8, there are two kinds of instruments, namely, animate, like a slave, and inanimate, like an axe.[28] Therefore, a proper intention is not required in an inanimate instrument, for the instrument's very inclination to the effect by the motion of the principal agent takes the place of an intention. But in an animate instrument, which is not only used but acts in some way, namely acting by a command, and not moved by a force, intention is required to exercise the ministry to which it is applied.

REPLY OBJ. 2: There are two ways of answering this according to different opinions. For some people say that if mental intention is lacking in the one baptizing, he does not confer the sacrament of baptism; however, in an adult, faith and devotion can supply the effect of baptism, so that danger from this would not affect the one baptized who did not know the intention of the one baptizing. But if it were a child, it is piously believed that the highest priest, namely, God, would supply the defect, and confer on him salvation. Nevertheless, if he does not do this, he does not act unjustly, just as neither does he act unjustly in someone who is not subjected to the sacrament. Other people say that in baptism and in the other sacraments that have in their form the act exercised, a mental intention is not required but the expression of the intention by the words instituted by the Church suffices. And thus if the form is preserved, and nothing is said outwardly that expresses a contrary intention, the person is baptized. For not without reason in the sacraments of necessity, namely, baptism, and certain others, is the act of the one baptizing expressed so carefully for the expression of the intention.

REPLY OBJ. 3: Although someone who is drunk cannot have an actual intention, nevertheless a drunk can be sober at a certain moment, and baptize having the intention of baptizing.

REPLY OBJ. 4: Although the minister of the sacrament may have to struggle to guard his own heart as much as he can, so that he actually has the intention of the form as much as possible in the sacramental words, nevertheless, since thought is so distractible, even if the actual intention is not present at the moment when he utters the words, as long as he intended it before, and no contrary intention has

---

27. *collationem.—collationem pertinet* PLE.
28. Aristotle, *Nicomachean Ethics*, Bk. 8, ch. 13, 1161b4.

impeditur: quia operatur tunc in vi principalis intentionis. Non enim oportet quod in opere semper intentio conjungatur in actu, sed sufficit quod opus ab intentione procedat.

occurred in the meantime, the sacrament is not impeded; for it works at that moment by the force of the principal intention. For it is not necessary that in a work the intention is always actually joined to it, but it suffices that the work proceeds from the intention.

Response to Quaestiuncula 2

Ad secundam quaestionem dicendum, quod rectum est cujus medium non exit ab extremis. Sacramentum autem baptismi est quo mediante acquiritur effectus baptismi in anima baptizati; unde tunc est recta intentio quando baptizans seu baptizatus sacramentum ordinat ad effectum sacramenti, qui est salus.

To the second question, it should be said that something is "right" or "straight" when its middle does not depart from the end points. Now the sacrament of baptism stands in the middle between the effect of baptism and the baptized soul aquiring the effect; hence the intention is "right" or "straight" when the one baptizing or the one baptized orders the sacrament to the effect of baptism, which is salvation.

Si ergo intentio adsit in baptizante, quia intendit sacramentum conferre; sed desit rectitudo, quia ordinat sacramentum ad finem indebitum; non propter hoc in recipiente impeditur perceptio sacramenti, quia ad hoc fertur intentio baptizantis; neque effectus sacramenti, quia mundatio interior a ministro non est, unde ejus intentio ad hoc nihil facit. Si autem in baptizato sit intentio percipiendi sacramentum, sed desit rectitudo intentionis, recipit quidem quod intendit sacramentum, sed non rem sacramenti: quia obicem per pravam intentionem Spiritui Sancto ponit.

Therefore, if the intention is present in the one baptizing, for he does intend to confer the sacrament, but rectitude is lacking, because he orders the sacrament to an undue end, this does not impede the sacrament's reception in the one receiving it, for the one baptizing intends the sacrament's reception. Nor does it impede the sacrament's effect, for interior cleansing does not come from the minister, and thus his intention does nothing toward this. But if in the baptized there were the intention of receiving the sacrament, but rectitude of intention were lacking, he would indeed receive the sacrament he intends, but not the reality of the sacrament: for he places an obstacle to the Holy Spirit by his wicked intention.

Ad primum ergo dicendum, quod quamvis ad sacramentum requiratur intentio faciendi quod facit ecclesia, non tamen requiritur quasi de necessitate sacramenti existens, facere quod facit ecclesia propter hoc quod ecclesia facit: et in hoc consistit rectitudo intentionis.

Reply Obj. 1: Although the intention of doing what the Church does is required for the sacrament, nevertheless it is not required as being necessary for the sacrament that one does what the Church does for the reason that the Church does it: and this is what rectitude of intention consists in.

Ad secundum dicendum, quod baptismus non habet bonitatem ex ministro, sicut alia operatio voluntaria habet bonitatem ex operante; et ideo non est simile.

Reply Obj. 2: Baptism does not have goodness from its minister in the way that other operations of the will have goodness from the one doing them; and thus it is not the same.

Response to Quaestiuncula 3

Ad tertiam quaestionem dicendum, quod in baptismo baptizatus duo recipit, scilicet sacramentum, et rem sacramenti; sed ad haec duo recipienda non requiritur aliquid causans ex parte recipientis, sed solum impedimentum removens: quod quidem impedimentum nihil aliud est quam voluntas contraria alteri praedictorum; et ideo in adultis et in habentibus usum rationis, in quibus potest esse contraria voluntas actu vel habitu, requiritur et contritio; sive devotio, ad percipiendam rem sacramenti, et intentio, vel voluntas ad recipiendum sacramentum; in pueris autem absque utroque

To the third question, it should be said that in baptism a baptized person receives two things, namely, the sacrament and the reality behind the sacrament. But to receive these two things, nothing is required on the part of the one receiving baptism that would cause them, but only the removal of the impediment, which is nothing other than a will contrary to one of the things mentioned. And thus, among adults and those having the use of reason, in whom a contrary will can exist either actually or habitually, baptism requires contrition or devotion, to receive the reality behind the sacrament; as well as intention or will, to receive

percipitur et sacramentum et res sacramenti; et similiter est in carentibus usu rationis, nisi contraria voluntas habitu insit, etsi non actu.

Tamen sciendum, quod non requiritur in adulto voluntas absoluta suscipiendi quod ecclesia confert, sed sufficit voluntas conditionata, sicut est in voluntariis mixtis, ut dicitur in 3 *Ethic.*; et ideo si sit coactio sufficiens, ita quod principium sit ex toto extra, nil conferente vim passo, ut cum aliquis reclamans immergitur violenter, tunc talis nec sacramentum suscipit, nec rem sacramenti. Si autem sit coactio inducens, sicut minis vel flagellis, ita quod baptizatus potius eligat baptismum suscipere quam talia pati; tunc suscipit sacramentum, sed non rem sacramenti.

Ad primum ergo dicendum, quod intentio vel voluntas in baptizato, ut dictum est, non requiritur quasi causans deletionem culpae originalis, sed solum quasi removens prohibens, scilicet contrariam voluntatem.

Ad secundum dicendum, quod in pueris non potest esse contraria voluntas neque actu neque habitu; et ideo non requiritur voluntas vel intentio in eis, qua prohibens removeatur. In amentibus autem et dormientibus potest esse voluntas contraria habitualis, quamvis non sit actualis; et ideo si ante somnum vel furiam fuerunt contrariae voluntatis, non recipiunt sacramentum, quia adhuc illa voluntas habitualiter manet. Si autem habuerunt propositum recipiendi baptismum, et hoc per aliqua signa innotuit, tunc in articulo necessitatis debet eis conferri baptismus; et suscipiunt sacramentum et rem sacramenti, etiam si furiosus tunc contradicat: quia illa contradictio non procedit a voluntate rationis, secundum quam est capax baptismalis gratiae. Si autem necessitas non sit, debet in furiosis expectari lucidum intervallum, vel in dormientibus vigilia. Si tamen baptizetur in statu illo, sacramentum suscipit, quamvis peccet baptizans.

Ad tertium dicendum, quod voluntas vel intentio baptismum suscipiendi non requiritur ad baptismum quasi causa vel dispositio characteris, sed solum sicut removens prohibens: ideo ratio non valet.

the sacrament. But among children lacking in either one, both the sacrament and the reality are received; and likewise among those lacking the use of reason, unless there is a will to the contrary in them habitually, even if not actually.[29]

Nevertheless, it should be known that an absolute will to receive what the Church confers is not required in an adult, but it is enough to will it conditionally, as happens in matters of mixed willing, which is discussed in *Ethics* 3;[30] and thus if it is completely forced, such that its principle is completely external, with the one undergoing it contributing nothing, as when someone is violently dunked while crying out in protest, that person receives neither the sacrament nor the reality behind it. But if it is compelling inducement, as with threats or beating, such that the baptized chooses to receive baptism rather than suffer such things, then he does receive the sacrament, but not the reality behind it.

Reply Obj. 1: Intention or willing in the baptized, as was said, is not required as something causing the effacement of original sin, but only as something removing what prevents it, namely, a contrary will.

Reply Obj. 2: Among children there cannot be a contrary will either actually or habitually; and thus in them neither willing nor intention is required for any impediment to be removed. But among those mentally disabled or asleep there can be a habitual contrary will, although it may not be actual; and thus if before they fell asleep or lost their wits they were of contrary will, they do not receive the sacrament, for that will remains habitually afterward. But if they had planned to receive baptism, and made this known through some kind of sign, then emergency baptism should be conferred on them, and they receive both the sacrament and the reality behind it, even if they should speak against it in their mental illness: for that contradiction does not proceed from their rational will, by which they are capable of baptismal grace. But if there is no necessity, a lucid interval should be waited for in the mentally ill, and waking in the ones sleeping. But if someone should be baptized in that state, he does receive the sacrament, although the one baptizing him sins.

Reply Obj. 3: The will or intention to receive baptism is not required for baptism as a cause or disposition to the character, but only as removing what prevents it; therefore the argument does not hold.

---

29. For more about the sacrament alone, reality alone, and sacrament-and-reality, see the footnote at Dist.1, q.1, a.4, qa. 1, main response.
30. Aristotle, *Nicomachean Ethics*, Bk. 3, ch. 1, 1110a11.

ARTICLE 3

Whether faith is required for baptism

Quaestiuncula 1

AD TERTIUM SIC PROCEDITUR. Videtur quod in baptizato fides requiratur ad hoc quod sacramentum suscipiat. Baptismus enim sacramentum fidei dicitur. Sed nonnisi propter fidem recipientis ipsum. Ergo requiritur fides baptizandi.

PRAETEREA, Marc. ult. 16, dicitur: *qui crediderit et baptizatus fuerit.* Ergo videtur quod requiritur in adulto quod credat ad hoc quod baptizetur.

PRAETEREA, fides essentialior est sacramento quam voluntas. Sed voluntas requiritur, ut dictum est. Ergo multo amplius fides.

SED CONTRA, adulti non sunt pejoris conditionis quam pueri. Sed in pueris sufficit fides ecclesiae ad baptismum, et non requiritur fides personae illius. Ergo nec in adultis.

PRAETEREA, caritas propinquior est ad gratiam quam fides: quia caritas non potest esse sine gratia sicut fides. Sed non requiritur caritas in recipiente baptismum, quia sic nullus adultus de novo acciperet ibi gratiam. Ergo non requiritur fides.

OBJ. 1: To the third question we proceed thus. It seems that in baptism faith is required for one to receive the sacrament.[31] For baptism is called the sacrament of faith. But this would only be on account of the faith of the person receiving it. Therefore, faith is required in the person to be baptized.

OBJ. 2: Furthermore, it is said, *whoever believes and is baptized* (Mark 16:16). Therefore, it seems that it is required in an adult that he believe in order to be baptized.

OBJ. 3: Furthermore, faith is more essential to the sacrament than will. But will is required, as has been said. Therefore, faith is required much more.

ON THE CONTRARY, adults are not in a worse condition than children. Yet among children the faith of the Church suffices for baptism, and the faith of the person himself is not required. Therefore, neither is it required in adults.

FURTHERMORE, charity is closer to grace than faith is, since charity cannot exist without grace, as faith can. But charity is not required in the one receiving baptism, since then no adult would receive grace again then. Therefore, faith is not required there.

Quaestiuncula 2

ULTERIUS. Videtur quod requiratur fides in baptizante. Requiritur enim in baptizante intentio conferendi sacramentum. Sed infidelis quantum ad articulum baptismi non credit sacramentum baptismi. Ergo non potest intendere conferre illud, et ita non potest baptizare.

PRAETEREA, baptismus est sacramentum ecclesiae. Sed fides est per quam membra ecclesiae primo ad invicem uniuntur. Ergo qui non habet fidem, nec potest baptizare, cum non sit de ecclesia.

PRAETEREA, propinquius se habet ad baptismum baptizans quam offerens puerum ad baptizandum. Sed in offerente requiritur fides, quia respondet, *credo*. Ergo multo fortius requiritur in baptizante.

SED CONTRA est quod in littera determinatur quod haeretici verum baptismum conferunt. Haeretici autem infideles sunt. Ergo, etc.

OBJ. 1: Moreover, it seems that faith is required in the one baptizing.[32] For the intention of conferring the sacrament is required in the one baptizing. But an unbeliever does not believe in the sacrament of baptism as far as the article of the Creed goes. Therefore, he cannot intend to confer it, and thus he cannot baptize.

OBJ. 2: Furthermore, baptism is a sacrament of the Church. But faith is how members of the Church are first united with each other. Therefore, anyone who has no faith cannot baptize, since he is not of the Church.

OBJ. 3: Furthermore, the person baptizing is more closely related to baptism than the one offering the child to be baptized. But faith is required in the one offering, for he is the one who answers, *I believe.* Therefore, much more is it required in the one baptizing.

ON THE CONTRARY, it is determined in the text that heretics confer valid baptism. But heretics are unbelievers. Therefore, etc.

---

31. Parallels: above, d. 2, q. 2, a. 4; d. 6, q. 1, a. 3, qa. 1, and q. 2, a. 2, qa. 3; d. 9, a. 2, qa. 2, ad 2; *ST* III, q. 68, a. 8.
32. Parallel: *ST* III, q. 64, a. 9.

Quaestiuncula 3

Ulterius. Videtur quod recipientes baptismum ab haereticis non consequantur rem sacramenti. Quia Augustinus dicit, quod *qui foris ecclesiam baptizantur, non sumunt baptismum ad salutem, sed ad perniciem.* Sed baptizati ab haereticis sumunt baptismum extra ecclesiam. Ergo non sumunt ad salutem; et ita rem sacramenti non consequuntur.

Praeterea, quicumque accipit aliquid ab aliquo qui non habet jus dandi illud, injuste accipit. Sed haereticus non habet jus dandi baptismum, ut dicit Augustinus: *si*, inquit, *haereticus jus baptizandi non habuit, tamen Christi est quod dedit.* Ergo accipiens ab haeretico, injuste accipit, et ita peccat.

Sed contra, peccatum baptizantis non polluit baptismum, ut dictum est supra. Sed infidelitas est quoddam peccatum. Ergo non impedit effectum baptismi in baptizato.

Obj. 1: Moreover, it seems that those receiving baptism from heretics do not obtain the reality behind the sacrament.[33] For Augustine says that *those who are baptized outside the Church do not receive baptism to salvation, but to their ruin.*[34] But those baptized by heretics receive baptism outside the Church. Therefore, they do not receive it to their salvation, and so they do not receive the reality behind the sacrament.

Obj. 2: Furthermore, whoever receives something from someone who does not have the right to give it receives unjustly. But a heretic does not have the right to give baptism, as Augustine says: *if a heretic did not have the right to baptize, nevertheless, it is Christ's that he gave.*[35] Therefore, anyone receiving from a heretic receives unjustly, and so he sins.

On the contrary, the sin of one baptizing does not soil baptism, as was said above. But unbelief is a certain sin. Therefore, it does not impede baptism's effect in the baptized.

Response to Quaestiuncula 1

Respondeo dicendum ad primam quaestionem, quod cum quaeritur utrum fides requiratur, velut necessaria ad baptismum, non intelligitur quaestio de necessitate absoluta, sed de necessitate quae est ex conditione finis. Est autem duplex finis in baptizatis. Primus est perceptio sacramenti; secundus est perceptio rei sacramenti. Dico ergo, quod in adultis requiritur fides etiam personalis necessitate quae est ex suppositione finis secundi: quia nisi credat, reputatur fictus, ut supra, dist. 4, quaest. 3, art. 2, quaestiunc. 1, 2, et 3, dictum est, et ita non consequitur rem sacramenti. Non autem requiritur ad primum finem consequendum: quia sacramentum percipit aliquis etiam si non credat. Unde Augustinus dicit quod *prorsus fieri potest ut aliqui verum baptisma habeant, et non habeant veram fidem.* In parvulis autem sufficit fides ecclesiae ad utrumque.

Ad primum ergo dicendum, quod baptismus dicitur fidei sacramentum, quia per eum homo coetibus fidelium aggregatur; et ideo qui accipit baptismum, osten-

To the first question, I answer that when it is asked whether faith is required as something necessary for baptism, the question is not understood as dealing with absolute necessity, but the necessity that comes from the condition of the end. But there are two ends in baptism. The first is the reception of the sacrament; the second is the reception of the reality behind the sacrament. Therefore, I say that in adults a personal faith is also required by the necessity arising from the second end: for unless someone believes, he is considered a fake, as was said above in Distinction 4, Question 3, Article 2, Subquestions 1, 2, and 3; and accordingly he does not obtain the reality behind the sacrament. But it is not required for obtaining the first end: for someone can receive the sacrament even if he does not believe. Hence Augustine says that *it can absolutely happen that some people have valid baptism who do not have true faith.*[36] However, for children the faith of the Church suffices for both ends.

Reply Obj. 1: Baptism is called the sacrament of faith because by it a man is brought together into the assemblies of the faithful. And thus whoever receives baptism shows

---

33. Parallel: *ST* III, q. 68, a. 9.

34. In fact, Pseudo-Augustine, *Dialogus quaestionum 65 Orosii percontantis et Augustini respondentis*, qu. 59; but there are many similar passages in Augustine, e.g.: "Sed propterea dolemus errantes et eos per caritatem Christi lucrari Deo cupimus, ut sanctum sacramentum, quod foris ab ecclesia habent ad perniciem, in pace ecclesiae habeant ad salutem" (*Epistle* 61, CSEL 34.2:223).

35. Augustine, *On Baptism, Against the Donatists*, Bk. 5, ch. 15 (CSEL 51:278).

36. Augustine, *On the One Baptism*, ch. 11 (CSEL 53:18).

dit se fidem habere; et si non habet, reputatur fictus, et rem sacramenti cum sacramento percepto non percipit.

AD SECUNDUM dicendum, quod Dominus in verbis illis ostendit quid requiritur in baptizando ad salutem consequendam, quae est res sacramenti; unde subdit: *qui crediderit et baptizatus fuerit, salvus erit.*

AD TERTIUM dicendum, quod sacramentum baptismi in anima recipitur quantum ad characterem. Anima autem non potest alicui subjici invita; et ideo voluntas seu intentio facit ad hoc quod homo se sacramento subjiciat; sed fides facit ad hoc quod debito modo se subjiciat. Unde fides requiritur tantum ad perceptionem rei sacramenti, sed intentio ad perceptionem rei[37] simpliciter.

ET QUIA ALIAE RATIONES PROBANT, quod nec quantum ad ultimum effectum fides requiratur, ideo ad quartum dicendum, quod in pueris non potest esse contrarium gratiae baptismalis ex personali voluntate; et ideo non requiritur personalis fides, sicut requiritur in adultis ad consequendam rem sacramenti, in quibus potest esse personalis infidelitas.

AD QUINTUM dicendum, quod recta intentio requiritur ad consequendam rem sacramenti. Fides autem intentionem dirigit, et sine ea non potest esse, praecipue in talibus, intentio recta; sed caritas ulterius facit intentionem meritoriam; et ideo ad hoc quod homo praeparet se ad gratiam in baptismo percipiendam, praeexigitur fides, sed non caritas: quia sufficit attritio praecedens, etsi non sit contritio.

that he has faith; and if he does not have it, he is considered a fake, and he does not receive the reality behind the sacrament he has received.

REPLY OBJ. 2: The Lord shows in those words what is required in the one to be baptized to obtain salvation, which is the reality behind the sacrament; hence he adds afterwards, *whoever believes and is baptized will be saved* (Mark 16:16).

REPLY OBJ. 3: The sacrament of baptism is received in the soul as a character. But a soul cannot be subject to something unwillingly; and thus by will or intention a man makes himself subject to the sacrament. But by faith a man makes himself subject in the right way. Hence faith is required only for the reception of the reality behind the sacrament, but intention for the reception of the sacrament simply speaking.

REPLY OBJ. 4: And since the other arguments prove that faith is not required for the final effect either, for this reason it should be said to the fourth objection that in children there cannot be anything contrary to baptismal grace from their personal will; and thus personal faith is not required for obtaining the reality behind the sacrament, as it is required in adults in whom there can be personal unbelief.

REPLY OBJ. 5: Right intention is required to obtain the reality behind the sacrament. But faith directs intention, and without it there can be no right intention, especially in matters like these; but charity makes the intention meritorious as well. And thus for a man to prepare himself to receive grace in baptism, faith is prerequisite, but not charity: for beforehand attrition is enough, even if it is not contrition.

Response to Quaestiuncula 2

AD SECUNDAM QUAESTIONEM dicendum, quod dum haereticus vel quicumque infidelis debitam formam servet, et intentionem baptizandi habeat, verum sacramentum confert: quia baptismus non habet efficaciam ex merito baptizantis, sed ex merito Christi, qui operatur in baptizato per fidem propriam in adultis, vel per fidem ecclesiae in pueris.

AD PRIMUM ergo dicendum, quod quamvis ille qui non credit baptismum esse sacramentum, aut habere aliquam spiritualem virtutem, non intendat dum baptizat conferre sacramentum; tamen intendit facere quandoque quod facit ecclesia, etsi illud reputet nihil esse; et quia ecclesia, aliquid facit, ideo ex consequenti et implicite intendit aliquid facere, quamvis non explicite.

TO THE SECOND QUESTION, it should be said that when heretics or any kind of unbelievers keep the due form and have the intention of baptizing, they confer a valid sacrament: for baptism does not have efficacy from the merit of the one baptizing, but from the merit of Christ, who works in the baptized person through his own faith, for an adult, or through the faith of the Church for a child.

REPLY OBJ. 1: Although the person who does not believe baptism to be a sacrament or to have any spiritual power, does not intend when he baptizes to confer a sacrament, nevertheless, he does at that time intend to do what the Church does, even if he considers that to be nothing; and since the Church does do something, therefore consequently and implicitly he does intend to do something, although not explicitly.

---

37. *rei.—sacramenti* PLE.

Ad secundum dicendum, quod quamvis haereticus per fidem rectam non sit membrum ecclesiae, tamen inquantum servat morem ecclesiae in baptizando, baptismum ecclesiae tradit; unde regenerat filios Christi et ecclesiae, non sibi vel haeresi suae. Sicut enim Jacob genuit filios per liberas et ancillas, ita Christus per Catholicos et haereticos, bonos et malos, ut Augustinus dicit contra Donatum.

Ad tertium dicendum, quod non requiritur fides personalis offerentium puerum ad baptismum, nec alicujus personae determinatae, sed solum fides ecclesiae militantis; quam non est possibile deficere totaliter, Deo sic ordinante, qui dixit, Matth. ult., 20: *ecce ego vobiscum sum usque ad consummationem saeculi.* Si tamen deficeret, illud suppleret quod de fide remansit in ecclesia triumphante, scilicet visio: nec offerens puerum ad baptismum in persona sua dicit, *credo*, sed in persona pueri, ut sit sensus: *credo*, idest, *sacramentum fidei praesto sum recipere.*

Reply Obj. 2: Although a heretic is not a member of the Church by true faith, nevertheless as far as he preserves the custom of the Church in baptizing, he hands on the baptism of the Church; hence he regenerates sons of Christ and of the Church, not for himself or his heresy. For just as Jacob begot sons by free women and slave girls (Gen 40), so does Christ by Catholics and heretics, good men and bad, as Augustine says against Donatus.[38]

Reply Obj. 3: Personal faith is not required of those offering a child for baptism, nor of any particular person, but only the faith of the Church Militant, which is not possible to fail completely, with God so ordering it, as he said: *behold I am with you even to the end of the age* (Matt 28:20). But nevertheless if it were to fail, what faith remained in the Church Triumphant, namely, the vision, would supply. Nor does the one offering a child for baptism say in his own person, *I believe*, but in the person of the child, so that the sense is, *I believe*, i.e., *I am ready to receive the sacrament of faith.*

Response to Quaestiuncula 3

Ad tertiam quaestionem dicendum, quod ille qui ab haeretico baptizatur, propter peccatum haeretici non privatur gratia baptismali, sed quandoque propter peccatum proprium. Unde si sit puer, in quem culpa actualis non cadit, si baptizatur in forma ecclesiae, recipit sacramentum et rem sacramenti: similiter si sit adultus, et baptizans non sit haereticus manifestus et ab ecclesia praecisus, vel si baptizatus sit in articulo necessitatis. Si autem sciat ipsum esse haereticum, et baptismum ab ipso suscipiat, hoc contingit vel quia favet haeresi suae, vel in contemptum ecclesiae, vel propter aliquod temporale commodum; et sic ipsemet peccat; unde proprio peccato obicem ponit Spiritui Sancto, ne consequatur rem sacramenti.

Ad primum ergo dicendum, quod Augustinus loquitur in casu illo quando aliquis in favorem haeresis vel aliquo alio malo fine ab haeretico baptismum suscipit.

Ad secundum dicendum, quod jus dandi baptisma est ex duobus; scilicet ex ordine sacerdotali, et ex jurisdictione. In haeretico ergo ab ecclesia praeciso manet jus dandi baptisma quantum ad ordinem sacerdotalem, si primo in ecclesia sacerdos fuerit; non tamen manet quantum ad jurisdictionem, quam amittit. Nec tamen sequitur quod baptismum ab haeretico suscipiens, semper injuste accipiat, cum credit eum habere jus dandi, et

To the third question, I say that no one who is baptized by a heretic is deprived of baptismal grace because of the sin of the heretic, but sometimes because of his own sin. Hence if it is a child, in whom actual fault does not happen, if he is baptized in the form of the Church, he receives the sacrament and the reality behind the sacrament.[39] Likewise, if it is an adult, and the one baptizing is not an obvious heretic, cut off from the Church, or if the baptized is in a state of emergency. But if he knows that the other is a heretic, and he receives baptism from him, then it happens because he either supports his heresy, or acts in contempt of the Church, or for the sake of some temporal convenience; and in this way the baptized person sins. Hence by his own sin he places an obstacle to the Holy Spirit, so that he does not obtain the reality behind the sacrament.

Reply Obj. 1: In this case Augustine speaks of when someone receives baptism from a heretic in support of the heresy or for some other bad end.

Reply Obj. 2: The right to give baptism comes from two sources, namely, from the priestly order, and from legal authority. Therefore, in a heretic who has been cut off from the Church, the right of giving baptism remains as to the priestly order, if he was a priest in the Church before. However, it does not remain as to legal authority, which he has lost. Nevertheless, it does not follow that someone receiving baptism from a heretic always receives it illicitly, since

---

38. Augustine, *On Baptism, Against the Donatists* (CSEL 51), Bk. 5, ch. 15.
39. For more about the sacrament alone, reality alone, and sacrament-and-reality, see the footnote at Dist.1, q.1, a.4, qa. 1, main response.

non esse haereticum, vel in casu necessitatis, in quo quilibet habet potestatem baptizandi.

he believes that the other has the right to give it and is not a heretic, or it is an emergency situation, in which anyone has the power to baptize.

QUESTION 2

THE RITE OF BAPTISM

Deinde quaeritur de ritu baptismi; et circa hoc quaeruntur tria:

primo, de ritu ipsius baptismi;
secundo, de ritu catechismi;
tertio, de ritu exorcismi.

Next, inquiry is made about the rite of baptism; and concerning this, three questions arise:

first, about the rite of baptism itself;
second, about the rite of catechism;
third, about the rite of exorcism.

ARTICLE 1

About the rite of baptism itself

Quaestiuncula 1

AD PRIMUM SIC PROCEDITUR. Videtur quod baptismus iterari possit. Quia Eucharistia est sacramentum excellentius quam baptismus: quia est perfectio, secundum Dionysium. Sed Eucharistia iteratur. Ergo et baptismus iterari potest.

PRAETEREA, gratia est principalior effectus baptismi quam character. Sed gratia amittitur, quamvis character non deleatur. Ergo videtur quod ratione gratiae recuperandae baptismus iterari debeat.

PRAETEREA, sicut ad unitatem actionis requiritur unitas temporis, ita et unitas agentis. Sed plures possunt aliquem simul baptizare, quia unus alium non impedit; et praecipue hoc necessarium est, si unus sit mutus, qui verba proferre non possit, et alius mancus, qui non possit immergere. Ergo et similiter potest aliquis pluries diversis temporibus baptizari.

SED CONTRA est quod dicitur Ephes. 4, 5: *una fides, unum baptisma*. Ergo iterari non debet.

PRAETEREA, baptismus contra originale datur. Sed originale peccatum non iteratur. Ergo nec baptismus iterari debet.

OBJ. 1: To the first question we proceed thus. It seems that baptism can be received again.[40] For the Eucharist is a more excellent sacrament than baptism, since it is perfection, according to Dionysius.[41] But the Eucharist can be received again. Therefore, baptism can also be received again.

OBJ. 2: Furthermore, grace is a more important effect of baptism than the character. But grace may be lost, although the character is not erased. Therefore, it seems that baptism may be received again for the sake of regaining grace.

OBJ. 3: Furthermore, a single action requires not just singularity of time, but also a single agent. But many people can baptize someone at the same time, for one person does not impede another; and this is particularly necessary if one person is mute and cannot utter the words, and the other one is disabled and cannot immerse the baptized. Therefore, in the same way someone can be baptized by several people at different times.

ON THE CONTRARY, is what is said: *there is one faith, one baptism* (Eph 4:5). Therefore, it should not be received again.

FURTHERMORE, baptism is given against original sin. But original sin is not contracted again. Therefore, neither should baptism be received again.

---

40. Parallels: above, d. 2, q. 1, a. 2, ad 2; d. 12, q. 3, a. 1, qa. 1, ad 2; d. 14, q. 1, a. 4, qa. 3; *ST* III, q. 66, a. 9; q. 80, a. 10, ad 1; q. 84, a. 10, ad 1 & 5; *SCG* IV, chs. 69 & 71; *Super Ioan*. 3, lec. 1; *Super Eph*. 4, lec. 2; *Super Heb*. 6, lec. 1.

41. Pseudo-Dionysius, *Ecclesiastical Hierarchy*, ch. 3 (PG 3:423).

Quaestiuncula 2

Ulterius. Videtur quod non debeant esse illa duo tempora determinata ad baptismum, scilicet sabbatum Paschae, et Pentecostes. Quia periculo quantocius succurrendum est. Sed homo propter fragilitatem naturae semper est in periculo vitae suae. Ergo non debet expectari tempus aliquod determinatum ad baptismum, sed statim baptizari.

Praeterea, per baptismum homo regeneratur in filium Dei ad imaginem Christi. Ergo praecipue in festo nativitatis baptismus celebrari deberet.

Praeterea, baptismus Christi contulit aquis vim regenerativam. Sed Christus in die Epiphaniae baptizatus fuit. Ergo tunc praecipue homo deberet baptizari.

Praeterea, baptismus habet efficaciam a passione Christi. Ergo in die passionis Dominicae magis deberet celebrari baptismus, quam in sabbato Paschae.

Obj. 1: Moreover, it seems that there should not be those two times designated for baptism, namely, Holy Saturday and the eve of Pentecost.[42] For when someone is in danger, help should be brought him, the sooner the better. But man, because of the frailty of his nature, is always in danger of his life. Therefore, he should not have to wait for any designated time for baptism, but should be baptized immediately.

Obj. 2: Furthermore, by baptism a man is reborn as a son of God in the image of Christ. Therefore, baptism should especially be celebrated in the feast of the Nativity.

Obj. 3: Furthermore, Christ's baptism conferred on the waters the regenerative power. But Christ was baptized on the day of the Epiphany. Therefore, a man should especially be baptized on that day.

Obj. 4: Furthermore, baptism has its efficacy from the Passion of Christ. Therefore, baptism should be celebrated on the day of the Lord's Passion rather than on Holy Saturday.

Quaestiuncula 3

Ulterius. Videtur quod sacramentalia baptismi male ponantur a Dionysio. Ponit enim primo receptionem baptizandi ab episcopo quem summum sacerdotem dicit praesente omni ecclesiae plenitudine. Debet enim baptizandus recipi ab eo qui est proprius baptismi minister. Talis autem est sacerdos, et non episcopus. Ergo non oportet ponere receptionem ab episcopo.

Praeterea, per manus impositionem datur Spiritus Sanctus ad robur; quod ad confirmationem pertinet, quae baptismum sequitur. Ergo inconvenienter ponit quod episcopus baptizando recepto manus ei ante baptismum imponit.

Praeterea, baptizandis sal in os mittitur, et aures et nares sputo liniuntur. Cum ergo de his Dionysius mentionem non faciat, videtur quod sacramentalia baptismi ponat insufficienter.

Praeterea, ipse ponit olei inunctionem ante baptismum, quo inungatur Christianus quasi ad pugnam, ut ipse dicit. Sed ad pugnam spiritualem praecipue ordinatur sacramentum confirmationis. Ergo videtur quod talis inunctio non debeat fieri in baptismo.

Obj. 1: Moreover, it seems that the sacramentals of baptism are wrongly listed by Dionysius.[43] For he lists first the reception of the person to be baptized by the bishop, whom he calls the highest priest, with all the existing fullness of the Church.[44] For the one to be baptized must be received by the one who is most properly the minister of baptism. But that is the priest, and not the bishop. Therefore, it should not include reception by the bishop.

Obj. 2: Furthermore, the Holy Spirit is given by the imposition of the hands for strengthening, which pertains to confirmation, which follows baptism. Therefore, it is unfitting that he includes the bishop imposing his hands on the one to be baptized before baptism.

Obj. 3: Furthermore, salt is placed in the mouth of the one to be baptized, and his ears and nostrils are anointed with saliva. Therefore, since Dionysius makes no mention of these, it seems that he lists baptism's sacramentals incompletely.

Obj. 4: Furthermore, he includes the anointing with oil before baptism, by which the Christian would be anointed as before a fight, as he himself says. But the sacrament of confirmation is particularly ordained to the spiritual battle. Therefore, it seems that this anointing should not take place in baptism.

---

42. Parallel: *ST* III, q. 66, a. 10, ad 1.
43. Pseudo-Dionysius, *Ecclesiastical Hierarchy*, ch. 2, n. 2 (PG 3:394ff.).
44. Parallel: *ST* III, q. 66, a. 10.

PRAETEREA, sacramenta sunt distincta. Ergo videtur quod non debeat simul cum baptismo connumerare Eucharistiae perceptionem, et sacri chrismatis linitionem.

OBJ. 5: Furthermore, the sacraments are distinct. Therefore, it seems that he should not count the reception of the Eucharist and anointing with sacred chrism together with baptism.

Response to Quaestiuncula 1

RESPONDEO dicendum, ad primam quaestionem, quod baptismus nullo modo iterari debet propter quatuor rationes. Prima sumitur ex morbo contra quem datur, scilicet originale peccatum, quod non iteratur; unde nec medicina iterari debet. Secunda sumitur ex re sacramenti: quia in baptismo deletur culpa et poena totaliter. Unde si frequenter liceret homini baptismum suscipere, esset quaedam provocatio ad peccandum: quia facilitas veniae incentivum praebet delinquendi, ut dicit Gregorius. Tertia sumitur ex sua significatione: quia configurat morti Christi, qui semel tantum mortuus est. Quarta sumitur ex ipso sacramento, scilicet charactere, qui indelebiliter manet; unde fieret injuria sacramento si baptismus iteraretur, quasi prima sanctificatio non suffecisset; et iterum, quia ipsum sacramentum regeneratio quaedam est: cujuslibet autem generatio est tantum semel. Quod autem nescitur esse factum, non iteratur. Unde si inveniatur pro certo aliquis defectus fuisse in baptismo eorum quae sunt de essentia sacramenti, debet absolute iterum baptizari sub hac forma: *baptizo te, si non es baptizatus, in nomine patris*, etc.

TO THE FIRST QUESTION, I answer that baptism should not be repeated at all, for four reasons. The first is taken from the disease against which baptism is given, namely, original sin, which is not contracted again; hence neither should its medicine be given again. The second is taken from the reality behind the sacrament: for in baptism guilt and punishment are completely wiped away. Hence if it were permitted for someone to receive baptism frequently, it would be a provocation to sin, for the ease of forgiveness would present an incentive for wrongdoing, as Gregory says.[45] The third is taken from its signification: for it configures one to the death of Christ, who only died once. The fourth is taken from the sacrament itself, namely, the character, which remains indelibly; hence injury would be done to the sacrament if baptism were received over and over, as though the first sanctification was not enough; and again, because this sacrament is a certain regeneration, while any given thing is generated only once. But when it is unknown whether something has been done, it is not done again. Hence if it were found for certain that someone had been lacking one of the things that belong to the essence of the sacrament, he must absolutely be baptized again, with the following form: *If you are not baptized, I baptize you in the name of the Father*, etc.

AD PRIMUM ergo dicendum, quod sicut in Eucharistiae sacramento sanctificatur materia, ita in baptismo sanctificatur recipiens[46] characteris impressionem. Unde sicut fieret injuria Eucharistiae, si hostia consecrata consecraretur iterum; ita fit injuria baptismo, si aliquis semel baptizatus iterum baptizaretur: quia sicut ibi sanctificatio refertur ad materiam, ita hic ad suscipientem sacramentum.

REPLY OBJ. 1: Just as in the sacrament of the Eucharist matter is sanctified, so in baptism the person receiving is sanctified by the imprint of the character. Hence just as injury would be done to the Eucharist if a consecrated host were consecrated again, in the same way injury would be done to baptism if someone already baptized were baptized again. For just as in the first case the sanctification is directed to the matter, so in the second case it is directed to the one receiving the sacrament.

AD SECUNDUM dicendum, quod quamvis gratia sit dignior effectus baptismi quam character, et sit quodammodo principalior; non tamen est ita proprius effectus ejus, et in hoc non ita principalis: quia gratia amissa, per alia sacramenta recuperari potest; et ideo non oportet quod ad ipsam recuperandam iteretur baptismus.

REPLY OBJ. 2: Although grace is a nobler effect of baptism than the character, and in a certain way it is more important, nevertheless it is not for this reason more properly its effect and in this it is not so important: for grace lost can be recovered through the other sacraments; and thus it is not necessary that baptism be received again for its recovery.

AD TERTIUM dicendum, quod si plures simul immergerent, ita quod uterque diceret, *ego te baptizo* etc., baptizatum esset; quamvis peccarent non servantes ri-

REPLY OBJ. 3: If several people immersed someone at the same time, such that each one said, *I baptize you* etc., there would be a baptism, although they would sin in not

---

45. In fact, Ambrose, *On Psalm 118*, ch. 26 (CSEL 62:165): "facilitas enim ueniae incentiuum tribuit delinquendi."

46. *recipiens characteris.—recipiens per characteris* PLE.

tum ecclesiae: nec tamen essent puniendi tamquam iterantes baptisma, nisi hoc intenderent: quia contingit eamdem actionem et ab uno et a pluribus exerceri; non autem contingit eamdem actionem esse quae in diversis temporibus fit. Si autem dicant: *nos baptizamus te,* non erit baptismus: quia non servatur debita forma, ut supra, dist. 3, qu. 1, art. 2, quaestiunc. 2, dictum est. Similiter non erit baptismus, si unus sit mancus et alius mutus, uno proferente verba, et alio immergente: quia ipsa verba formae ostendunt quod ab eodem debet fieri immersio et verborum pronuntiatio.

observing the rite of the Church: nevertheless they would not be punished for baptizing again unless they had intended that: for it happens that the same action may be executed by one person and by several, but it cannot happen that it is the same action that is done at several different times. But if they said, *We baptize you,* there would be no baptism: for the due form was not preserved, as was said above in Distinction 3, Question 1, Article 2, Subquestion 2. In the same way there will be no baptism if one person is crippled and the other one mute, and one utters the words while the other does the immersion: for the words of the form themselves show that the immersion and pronouncement of words must be done by the same person.

Response to Quaestiuncula 2

AD SECUNDAM QUAESTIONEM dicendum, quod in baptismo duo considerantur; scilicet substantia sacramenti, et solemnitas; et quantum ad substantiam sacramenti non est aliquod tempus determinatum ad baptismum; immo quolibet die et qualibet hora baptismus celebrari potest. Sed solemnis celebratio baptismi in ecclesia habet tempus deputatum, scilicet duplex sabbatum, de quo in littera dicitur; cujus ratio est, quia baptismus habet efficaciam ex duobus; scilicet ex virtute Spiritus Sancti; et ideo in vigilia Pentecostes celebratur solemniter baptismus: item ex passione Christi, cujus morti aliquis configuratur per baptismum quasi *consepultus Christo in mortem,* ut dicitur, Rom. 6; et ideo celebratur solemniter in die sepulturae Christi, idest in vigilia Paschae.

AD PRIMUM ergo dicendum, quod in necessitate non oportet expectare ista duo tempora. Unde dicitur, *de Consecr.,* dist. 3: *de catechumenis baptizandis id decretum est ut in paschali festivitate vel Pentecostes veniant ad baptismum; in ceteris autem solemnitatibus infirmi tantum debent baptizari.* Et quia pueri infirmi computantur propter naturae imbecillitatem, et propter periculum damnationis, a qua non possunt aliter liberari; ideo nunc ipsi pueri baptizantur ut in pluribus, et non expectantur haec duo tempora, sicut in adultis expectari solebant.

AD SECUNDUM dicendum, quod in festo nativitatis recolitur nativitas Domini secundum carnem. Nos autem non efficimur fratres ejus nativitate carnis, sed spiritus; et ideo non oportet quod tunc baptismus celebretur.

AD TERTIUM dicendum, quod per baptismum Christi est tantum materia praeparata ad actum baptismi; sed virtus agens in baptismo est meritum passionis Christi, et virtus Spiritus Sancti. Et quia agens in omnibus est principalius quam materia, ideo potius in duobus de-

TO THE SECOND QUESTION, it should be said that two things must be considered in baptism, namely, the sacrament's substance and its solemnity. And as to its substance there is no predetermined time for baptism; on the contrary, baptism can be celebrated on any day at any hour. But the solemn celebration of baptism in the Church has a designated time, namely, the two Saturdays that were mentioned in the text. And the reason for this is that baptism has efficacy from two things, namely, the power of the Holy Spirit, and therefore baptism is solemnly celebrated on the vigil of Pentecost; and also from the Passion of Christ, to whose death someone is configured through baptism as *buried with Christ into death* (Rom 6:3–4); and thus it is solemnly celebrated on the day Christ lay in the grave, which is Holy Saturday.

REPLY OBJ. 1: In emergencies, it is not necessary to wait for these two times. Hence it is said in the *Decretals: Concerning the catechumens to be baptized, this is decreed, that they should come for baptism on the feast of Easter or Pentecost; however, the sick or frail alone should be baptized in the remaining solemnities.*[47] And since infants are considered frail because of the feebleness of nature, and because of the danger of damnation from which they cannot otherwise be freed, for this reason nowadays those infants are baptized right away in most cases, and those two times are not awaited, as it was customary to wait for adults.

REPLY OBJ. 2: In the feast of Christmas, the Lord's birth is commemorated according to the flesh. But we are not made his brothers by birth in the flesh, but in the spirit; and thus it is not fitting that baptism be celebrated then.

REPLY OBJ. 3: By Christ's baptism, all that happened was that the matter was prepared for the act of baptism; but the acting power in baptism is the merit of Christ's Passion and the power of the Holy Spirit. And since what acts in something is more important than its matter, for this

---

47. See Gratian's *Decretals,* Part 3, *De consecratione,* d. 4, ch. 15 (PL 187:1798).

terminatis temporibus baptismus celebrari debet quam in Epiphania. Tamen ideo non est specialiter institutum baptismum celebrari in die illa, ut excluderetur error quorumdam, qui dicebant, nunquam baptismum, posse conferri nisi illa die qua Dominus baptizatus est.

Ad quartum dicendum, quod homo in baptismo configuratur passioni Christi per modum cujusdam consepelitionis, ut apostolus, Rom. 6, dicit; et ideo in die sepulturae congruentius fit quam in die passionis.

reason baptism is celebrated at the two designated times rather than at Epiphany. Nevertheless, the reason it was not specifically established that baptism be celebrated on that day was to exclude the error of certain people, who said that baptism can never be conferred except on that day on which the Lord was baptized.

Reply Obj. 4: Man is conformed to Christ's Passion in baptism by a certain manner of being buried with him, as the Apostle says in Romans 6:4; and thus it is done more becomingly on the day of his entombment than on the day of his Passion.

Response to Quaestiuncula 3

Ad tertiam quaestionem dicendum, quod Dionysius prosequitur ritum baptismi qui in primitiva ecclesia servabatur in solemni celebratione baptismi, quando adulti ad baptismum veniebant; et ideo quatuor per ordinem ponit; quorum primum pertinet ad catechismum, secundum ad exorcismum, tertium ad baptismum, quartum ad baptismi complementum.

Quantum ad catechismum pertinent haec quae hic per ordinem tanguntur. Primo instructio de fide per praedicationem episcopi. Secundo conversio infidelis ad fidem, et accessus ad episcopum mediante patrino, quem anadochum dicit. Tertio gratiarum actio et oratio ab episcopo et clericis facta. Quarto petitio baptismi et professio observantiae Christianae religionis. Quinto manus impositio, et signatio ejus signo crucis. Sexto conscriptio baptizandi et anadochi.

Sed quantum ad exorcismum ponuntur quatuor. Primo exsufflatio versus occidentalem partem, et abrenuntiatio. Secundo manuum ad caelum erectio cum sacra confessione fidei, et professione Christianae religionis. Tertio oratio, benedictio, et manus impositio. Quarto denudatio, et unctio oleo sancto, quod dicitur ad catechumenos.

Sed quantum ad baptismum ponit trinam immersionem cum aliis quae requiruntur ad baptismum; quantum vero ad perfectionem baptismi, quae consequitur, ponit tria scilicet vestis traditionem, linitionem chrismatis in vertice, et Eucharistiae perceptionem.

Ad primum ergo dicendum, quod Dionysius tradit ritum baptismi quantum ad maximam sui solemnitatem; et ideo non ponit solum ministrum sufficientem, sed excellentem.

Ad secundum dicendum quod circa baptismum ut ex praedictis patet, triplex manus impositio datur. Una in catechismo, ut homo in fide roboretur in seipso; alia in exorcismo, ut roboretur in pugna adversus diabolum;

To the third question, it should be said that Dionysius describes the rite of baptism that was observed in the early Church in the solemn celebration of baptism, when adults were coming for baptism; and for this reason he sets down four things in order, of which the first pertains to catechizing, the second to exorcising, the third to baptizing, and the fourth to baptism's completion.

To catechesis pertain these things, which he touches on in order. First, instruction in the faith by the preaching of the bishop. Second, conversion of the unbeliever to the faith, and approach to the bishop by means of the godparent, whom he calls the anadochus. Third, thanksgiving and prayer made by the bishop and clerics. Fourth, the requesting of baptism and profession of observing the Christian religion. Fifth, the imposition of hands, and signing the catechumen with the sign of the cross. Sixth, the conscription of the person to be baptized and the anadochus.

But as regards exorcism, he lists four things. First, blowing toward the west and renunciation of the devil. Second, raising the hands to heaven with the sacred confession of the faith and profession of the Christian religion. Third, prayer, benediction, and imposition of hands. Fourth, disrobing and anointing with holy oil, which is called the oil of catechumens.

But as to baptism, he sets down a threefold immersion with the other things that are required for baptism; and as to the completion of baptism, which follows, he lists three things, namely the handing over of the garment, the anointing with chrism on the crown of the head, and the reception of the Eucharist.

Reply Obj. 1: Dionysius is handing on the rite of baptism in its greatest solemnity; and for this reason he sets down not just the sufficient minister, but the most excellent one.

Reply Obj. 2: As is clear from above, three impositions of hands are given in the course of baptism. One during the catechesis, so that a man may be strengthened in himself in faith; another in the exorcism, so that he may be strength-

tertia in confirmatione, ut roboretur in confessione fidei contra pressuras mundi.

Ad tertium dicendum, quod de illis sacramentalibus quae pertinent ad solemnitatem baptismi, quaedam fuerunt in primitiva ecclesia quae nunc non sunt; et quaedam postea superaddita sunt. Unde exorcismo aliquid subtractum est, ut patet per ritum quem docet Rabanus, scilicet conversio ad Occidentalem partem et Orientalem; et aliquid additum, scilicet salis cibatio, et aurium et naris sputo linitio, ad designandum remotionem illorum quae praecipue possunt impedire fidei doctrinam, cujus sacramentum percipiendum est. Potest enim impediri ne recipiatur, et contra hoc adaperiuntur aures sputo ad recipiendam fidem ex auditu per verbum Dei, et nares ad quaerendum doctrinam fidei per odorem bonum notitiae suae sparsum in conversatione et doctrina sanctorum; ad similitudinem ejus quod Dominus luto ex sputo facto linivit oculos caeci nati. Ideo autem oculi non liniuntur, quia visus inventioni servit, fides autem non est per inventionem humanam. Potest etiam impediri divulgatio fidei in confitentibus et docentibus ipsam; et ideo apponitur in ore sal discretionis, ut omnis sermo fidelium sit sale conditus.

Ad quartum dicendum, quod circa baptismum est triplex inunctio. Una ante baptismum, quae fit oleo sancto, quod dicitur ad catechumenos et hoc secundum Dionysium et Ambrosium, fit in signum pugnae contra inimicum, sicut athletae inunguntur; vel secundum Rabanum, ut nullae reliquiae latentis inimici resideant: quia quod emollitum est, facilius ablui ab intrinsecis sordibus potest. Secunda fit post baptismum chrismate in vertice, ut sicut per ablutionem aquae significatur emundatio a peccatis. Ita per chrismatis linitionem in vertice significetur gratia collata in mente ad bene operandum, ut odor boni exempli ad alios diffundatur. Tertia fit in confirmatione, de qua post dicetur.

Ad quintum dicendum, quod illa linitio chrismatis non est sacramentum confirmationis, sed datur tantum in signum, sicut et vestis candida, et candela accensa; ut per vestem candidam significetur novitas vitae et puritas, per chrisma odor bonae famae, per candelam accensam veritas doctrinae. Eucharistiae autem perceptio non ponitur a Dionysio quasi sacramentale baptismi, sed quia jam baptizatus est configuratus admittitur ad sacra-

ened in the fight against the devil; the third in confirmation, so that he may be strengthened to confess the faith against the pressures of the world.

Reply Obj. 3: Concerning those sacramentals that belong to the solemnity of baptism, certain ones existed in the early Church that are no longer, and certain ones were added later. Hence something has been taken away from the exorcism, as is evident from the rite that Rabanus teaches,[48] namely, turning toward the west and the east; and something has been added, namely, feeding the salt and anointing the ears and nostrils with saliva, to designate the removal of anything that could especially impede the teaching of the faith, whose sacrament is about to be received. For it can be prevented from being received, and against this the ears are opened with saliva, to receive the faith by hearing the word of God, and the nostrils to seek the teaching of the faith by the good odor its news spread in the fellowship and teaching of holy men; in imitation of the Lord who made mud out of saliva and anointed the eyes of the man born blind. The reason the eyes are not anointed is that sight is in service of discovery, while faith does not come from human discovery. The sharing of the faith can also be prevented among those confessing and teaching it; and thus the salt of discretion is placed in the mouth, so that every utterance of the faithful may be kept with salt.

Reply Obj. 4: There are three anointings surrounding baptism. The first is done before the baptism with holy oil, which is called the oil of catechumens, and according to Dionysius[49] and Ambrose,[50] this is done as a sign of the fight against the enemy, just as athletes are anointed; or, according to Rabanus,[51] so that no trace of the hidden enemy may remain: for what has been softened can more easily be washed away from internal filth. The second anointing is done after the baptism with chrism on the head, so that cleansing from sins is signified, just as by washing with water. In this way, the grace to act well in the mind may be signified by the anointing with chrism on the head, as the odor of good example is diffused to others. The third is done in confirmation, about which we will speak below, in Distinction 7, Question 3, Article 3, Subquestion 2.

Reply Obj. 5: That anointing with chrism is not the sacrament of confirmation, but it is given only as a sign, just like the white garment and the lit candle; so that by the white garment may be signified the newness and purity of life, by the chrism, the odor of good reputation, by the lit candle, truth of teaching. However, the reception of the Eucharist is not listed by Dionysius as a sacramental of baptism, but because the now-baptized person is config-

---

48. Rabanus Maurus, *De institutione clericorum*, Bk. 1, ch. 25 (PL 107:311).
49. In the text cited above.
50. Ambrose, *On the Sacraments*, Bk. 1, ch. 2 (CSEL 73:17).
51. In the text just cited.

mentalem mensam; et iterum quia omne sacramentum per Eucharistiam consummatur, ut Dionysius dicit.

ured, he is admitted to the sacramental table; and again because every sacrament is consummated by the Eucharist, as Dionysius says.[52]

---

52. Pseudo-Dionysius, *Ecclesiastical Hierarchy*, ch. 3, p. 1 (PG 3:423).

Article 2

About the rite of catechism

Quaestiuncula 1

Ad secundum sic proceditur. Videtur quod catechismum baptismum praecedere non debeat. Quia, sicut dicit Augustinus in Lib. *de Catechizandis rudibus*: *narratio plena est cum quisque primo catechizatur, ab eo quod scriptum est, in principio creavit Deus caelum et terram, usque ad praesentia tempora ecclesiae*. Sed hoc non potest fieri nisi longissimo tempore. Cum ergo periculosum sit tantum differri baptismum, videtur quod non debeat baptismum catechismus praecedere.

Praeterea, Matth. 7, 6, dicitur: *nolite sanctum dare canibus*. Sed *sanctum* ibi dicitur doctrina sacra, quae non est committenda immundis, ut Dionysius dicit. Cum ergo non baptizati sint immundi, videtur quod non debeant catechizari non baptizati.

Praeterea, baptismus est spiritualis regeneratio, per quam datur esse spirituale, ut Dionysius dicit. Sed prius est accipere esse quam doctrinam. Ergo baptismus debet praecedere catechismum.

Sed contra est quod dicitur Matth. ult., 19: *docete omnes gentes, baptizantes eos*, etc. Ergo doctrina fidei quae ad catechismum pertinet, debet praecedere baptismum.

Praeterea, nullus digne accedit ad baptismum qui fictus accedit. Sed non credens reputatur fictus secundum Augustinum. Cum ergo *fides sit ex auditu, auditus autem per verbum Christi*, ut dicitur Rom. 10, videtur quod oporteat prius instrui aliquem per verbum Christi quam ad baptismum accedat.

Obj. 1: To the second question we proceed thus. It seems that catechism should not precede baptism.[53] For as Augustine says in *On Catechizing the Uninstructed*: *The narration is full when each person is catechized in the first instance from what is written in the text, "In the beginning God created the heaven and the earth," all the way to the present time of the Church*.[54] But this cannot be done without taking a long time. Therefore, since it is dangerous to defer baptism so much, it seems that catechism should not precede baptism.

Obj. 2: Furthermore, it is said in Matthew 7:6: *do not give what is holy to dogs*. But *holy* there is said of sacred doctrine, which is not to be entrusted to the unclean, as Dionysius says.[55] Since, therefore, the unbaptized are unclean, it seems that the unbaptized should not be catechized.

Obj. 3: Furthermore, baptism is a spiritual regeneration by which something spiritual is given, as Dionysius says.[56] But receiving being comes before receiving teaching. Therefore, baptism should precede catechism.

On the contrary, is what is said: *teach all nations, baptizing them*, etc. (Matt 28:19). Therefore, the teaching of the faith that pertains to catechism must precede baptism.

Furthermore, no one approaches baptism worthily who approaches falsely. But someone who does not believe is considered false according to Augustine. Since therefore, *faith is from hearing, but hearing is through the word of Christ* (Rom 10:17), it seems that someone would have to be instructed through the word of Christ before approaching baptism.

Quaestiuncula 2

Ulterius. Videtur quod catechizare non sit officium sacerdotis. Quia, secundum Dionysium in Eccl. Hierarch., diaconi habent officium super omnes immundos, quia ipsi habent purgativam virtutem. Sed primus gradus immundorum sunt cathecumeni, ut ipse dicit. Ergo ad diaconos pertinet eorum instructio.

Obj. 1: Moreover, it seems that to catechize is not the duty of a priest.[57] For, according to Dionysius in *Ecclesiastical Hierarchy*,[58] deacons are responsible for all the unclean, for they have the purifying power. But to be a catechumen is the first step of one unclean, as he himself says. Therefore, their instruction belongs to the deacons.

---

53. Parallel: *ST* III, q. 71, a. 1.
54. Augustine, *On Catechizing the Uninstructed* (CCSL 46), ch. 3.
55. Pseudo-Dionysius, *Ecclesiastical Hierarchy*, ch. 1 (PG 3:370).
56. Ibid., ch. 2 (PG 3:391).
57. Parallel: *ST* III, q. 71, a. 4.
58. Ibid., ch. 5, p. 1, n. 6 (PG 3:507).

Praeterea, illius videtur esse instruere baptizandum cujus est ad baptismum eum adducere. Hoc autem est anadochi, idest patrini, secundum Dionysium, et non sacerdotis. Ergo et catechizare non erit sacerdotis officium.

Sed contra est quod dicit Nicolaus Papa: *catechismi baptizandorum a sacerdotibus uniuscujusque ecclesiae fieri possunt*. Ergo videtur esse officium sacerdotum.

Obj. 2: Furthermore, instructing those to be baptized and leading them to baptism seem to belong to the same person. But this is the *anadochus*, i.e., the godparent, according to Dionysius, and not the priest. Therefore, neither will catechizing be the duty of the priest.

On the contrary, Pope Nicholas says: *the catechizing of those to be baptized can be done by the priests of each church*.[59] Therefore, it seems to be the duty of priests.

Quaestiuncula 3

Ulterius. Videtur quod pueri non debeant catechizari. Frustra enim adhibetur instructio ei qui non est perceptibilis disciplinae. Sed puer non est perceptibilis disciplinae, quia non habet usum liberi arbitrii. Ergo non debet ei instructio adhiberi.

Praeterea, in catechismo requiritur confessio fidei, et professio Christianae religionis, ut per Dionysium patet. Sed hoc per se puer facere non potest, nec aliquis pro puero: quia nullus potest ex voto alterius obligari. Ergo videtur quod non debeant pueri catechizari.

Praeterea, si ipse pro puero confitetur ergo videtur quod ipse patrinus obligetur ad instruendum puerum de his quae pertinent ad fidem Christianam; et ita videtur quod sit valde periculosum puerum de sacro fonte levare, cum raro aliquis de pueri instructione curam gerat.

Sed contra est quod ritus baptismi debet in omnibus similiter observari, ut ostendatur unitas baptismi. Si ergo adulti catechizantur, et similiter pueri catechizari debent.

Praeterea, ad hoc est generalis ecclesiae consuetudo.

Obj. 1: Moreover, it seems that children should not be catechized.[60] For instruction is given in vain to anyone who is not able to learn. But a child is not able to learn, for he does not have the use of his free will. Therefore, instruction should not be applied to him.

Obj. 2: Furthermore, the confession of the faith and the profession of the Christian religion are required in catechism, as is clear from Dionysius.[61] But this is something a child cannot do by himself, nor can anyone do it for him: for no one can be obliged by the vow of another. Therefore, it seems that children should not be catechized.

Obj. 3: Furthermore, if a godparent professes the faith on behalf of a child, it seems therefore that that godparent is obliged to instruct the child in those things that belong to the Christian faith; and so it seems that it would be extremely dangerous to lift a child from the baptismal font, since rarely does anyone take care of the instruction of a child.

On the contrary, the rite of baptism must be observed in all matters the same, so that the unity of baptism may be shown. If therefore, adults are catechized, then children should be catechized likewise.

Furthermore, this is the general custom of the Church.

Response to Quaestiuncula 1

Respondeo dicendum ad primam quaestionem, quod sicut in aliis scientiis et doctrinis quaedam sunt communia, quibus ignoratis necesse est artem ignorare; quaedam autem propria, quae sine ignorantia illius doctrinae ignorari possunt; ita etiam in doctrina fidei quaedam dicuntur quae sunt fidei communia rudimenta, ad quae credenda explicite omnes tenentur, sicut est fides Trinitatis, et incarnationis, et passionis, et divini judicii, et providentiae Dei de factis hominum; et talis instruc-

To the first question, I answer that just as in other sciences and teachings, certain things are common, so that not knowing them means not knowing this art. But others are proper, which can be unknown without ignorance of that teaching. So also in the teaching of the faith certain things are said that are the common rudiments of the faith, which all men are bound to believe explicitly, such as the faith in the Trinity, the Incarnation, the Passion, divine judgment, and the providence of God about the deeds of

---

59. See Gratian's *Decretals*, Part 3, *De consecratione*, d. 4, ch. 57 (PL 187:1818).
60. Parallel: *ST* III, q. 71, a. 1, ad 2.
61. Pseudo-Dionysius, *Ecclesiastical Hierarchy*, ch. 2, p. 2, nn. 5–6 (PG 3:394–95).

tio catechismus dicitur: de aliis autem debet instrui post baptismum temporis processu.

AD PRIMUM ergo dicendum quod non est necessarium quod omnia in particulari addiscat quae in tota Biblia continentur sed in quadam summa, ut scilicet videat quomodo in quolibet statu mundi Deo fuit cura de hominibus.

AD SECUNDUM dicendum quod Dominus loquitur de illis immundis qui fidei contrariantur non de illis qui ad fidem accedere volunt; unde sequitur: *ne ipsi conversi dirumpant vos.*

AD TERTIUM dicendum quod generatio naturalis non praesupponit aliquam cognitionem; et ideo non potest praeexistere aliqua instructio; sed spiritualis regeneratio praesupponit vitam naturae; et ideo potest praeexistere aliqua instructio.

men; and this kind of instruction is called catechism: but about the other things one should be instructed after baptism over time.

REPLY OBJ. 1: It is not necessary that every thing that is contained in the whole Bible be taught individually, but just a certain summary, so that one sees just how in every state of the world God had care of men.

REPLY OBJ. 2: The Lord speaks of those uncleansed who oppose the faith, not of those who want to embrace the faith; hence he continues, *lest they turn and maul you* (Matt 7:6).

REPLY OBJ. 3: Natural generation does not presuppose any understanding, and so no instruction can precede it; but spiritual regeneration presupposes the life of nature, and thus some instruction can precede it.

Response to Quaestiuncula 2

AD SECUNDAM QUAESTIONEM dicendum, quod triplex est instructio fidei. Una admonitoria, qua quis ad fidem convertitur, et haec proprie est sacerdotum, quorum est praedicare et docere; unde et Dionysius, hanc instructionem episcopo attribuit. Alia est instructio disciplinalis, qua quis instruitur qualiter ad baptismum accedere debet, et quid credere debeat; haec pertinet ad officium diaconi, et per consequens sacerdotis: quia quidquid est diaconi, est etiam sacerdotis. Tertia, quae sequitur baptismum, et haec pertinet ad anadochum, et ad praelatos ecclesiae. Praelati enim ecclesiae habent quasi doctrinam generalem, quae per officium anadochi specialiter ad hunc vel illum adaptatur secundum quod ei competit.

AD PRIMUM ergo dicendum, quod in primitiva ecclesia, quando adulti ad baptismum veniebant, qui magna instructione indigebant, hoc per diaconos exercebatur, sacerdotibus circa majora occupatis; et ideo Dionysius diaconibus attribuit.

AD SECUNDUM dicendum, quod anadochus non instruit ante baptismum de fide, sed conversum jam recipit, ad instructionem praesentans.

AD TERTIUM dicendum, quod quidquid est diaconi, licet etiam sacerdotibus facere; unde per hoc non removetur quin catechizare sit officium diaconi.

TO THE SECOND QUESTION, I answer that there are three kinds of instruction in the faith. First, admonitory instruction, by which someone is converted to the faith, and this is properly for priests, to whom it belongs to preach and teach; hence Dionysius also attributes this instruction to the bishop.[62] Another is disciplinal instruction, by which someone is instructed how he should approach baptism and what he should believe; this belongs to the office of deacon, and consequently to the priest, for whatever belongs to a deacon also belongs to a priest. Third, the instruction that follows baptism, and this pertains to the *anadochus*, and to the prelates of the Church. For the prelates of the Church have a sort of general teaching which is adapted by the office of *anadochus* to this or that in particular according as it suits him.

REPLY OBJ. 1: In the early Church, when adults came to baptism who needed a lot of instruction, this was accomplished by the deacons, since priests were occupied by bigger things; and hence Dionysius attributes it to deacons.

REPLY OBJ. 2: An *anadochus* does not instruct someone in the faith before baptism, but he receives him once he has converted and provides him with instruction.

REPLY OBJ. 3: Whatever a deacon can do, priests can also do; hence the fact that a priest can catechize does not do away with the fact that to catechize is the office of a deacon.

---

62. Pseudo-Dionysius, *Ecclesiastical Hierarchy*, ch. 5, p. 1, nn. 6–7 (PG 3:506).

Response to Quaestiuncula 3

AD TERTIAM QUAESTIONEM dicendum, quod catechismus est quasi quaedam dispositio ad baptismum. Dispositiones autem debent proportionari illis ad quae disponunt; unde in adultis, in quibus in baptismo requiritur propria fides et propria voluntas, requiritur etiam quod ipse per se catechizetur, et per se confiteatur, et Christianam religionem profiteatur. In puero autem cujus baptismus operatur tantum ex fide ecclesiae et merito Christi, fit instructio mediante alio; unde eadem quibus instruendus est, proponuntur praesente anadocho, cui committitur in his instruendus; et ipse loco ejus confessionem et professionem facit.

AD PRIMUM ergo dicendum, quod quamvis non sit tunc actu perceptibilis disciplinae, tamen habet hujusmodi perceptibilitatem in radice quantum ad potentiam rationis quam habet ex natura, et quantum ad habitum fidei, quem recipit in baptismo.

AD SECUNDUM dicendum, quod quamvis puer confiteri non possit per se, vel profiteri, tamen alius vicem ejus supplet, non quidem suam propriam fidem confitens sed fidem pueri, et quantum ad id quod nunc est, ut sit sensus: *credo*, idest, *sacramentum fidei praesto sum accipere*, in persona pueri loquens, ut Augustinus exponit, et quantum ad id quod futurum est, ut fit sensus, *credo*, idest, *quando ad perfectam aetatem veniam, fidei consentiam*, ut Dionysius exponit; et hoc quidem confiteri potest ex proposito solicitudinis circa ipsum adhibendae, ut alio modo possit esse sensus, *credo*, idest, *operam dabo ad hoc quod credat*; et in hoc ipse puer obligatur, et anadochus: quia de illis ad quae omnes tenentur, non est inconveniens si unus alium obliget; secus autem est de consiliis, ad quae non omnes tenentur.

AD TERTIUM dicendum, quod non est ibi magnum periculum quantum ad modernum tempus: quia parentes pueri sunt Christiani, et satis probabiliter potest aestimari quod eum in fide nutrient, et etiam ex aliis quibus convivet, fidem addiscet. Secus autem erat in primitiva ecclesia, ubi pueri cum infidelibus conversabantur; et ideo diligentior cura adhibenda erat ab anadocho vel patrino. Et similiter etiam nunc, si pueri parentes de infidelitate suspecti essent, vel si inter infideles conversaturus forte puer esset.

TO THE THIRD QUESTION, I answer that catechism is like a certain disposition to baptism. Now, dispositions should be proportioned to whatever they dispose toward; hence in adults, in whom personal faith and willing are required for baptism, it is also required that each one be catechized himself, and confess for himself, and profess the Christian religion. However, in a child whose baptism works only by the faith of the Church and the merit of Christ, instruction happens by means of someone else; hence the same things in which he is to be instructed are proposed to the *anadochus* standing by, to whom he is entrusted to be instructed in these things; and he makes the confession and profession in place of the child.

REPLY OBJ. 1: Although the child is not actually able to learn at that time, nevertheless, he has the root ability in his power of reason, which he has by nature, and in the habit of faith which he receives in baptism.

REPLY OBJ. 2: Although a child may not be able to confess by himself, or to profess, nevertheless another may supply it in his stead, not indeed confessing his own personal faith but the faith of the child, both according to what currently exists, so that the sense of it is: *I believe*, that is, *I am ready to receive the sacrament of faith*, speaking in the person of the child, as Augustine explains;[63] and according to what will be, so that the sense becomes, *I believe*, that is, *when I reach maturity, I will consent to the faith*, as Dionysius explains;[64] and this indeed can be confessed from the intention of having concern for him, so that in another way the sense could be, *I believe*, that is, *I will work toward his believing*; and in this the child himself is obligated, as well as the *anadochus*: for concerning those things that all are bound to, it is not unfitting if one person obliges another; however, it is different with the counsels, to which not all are bound.

REPLY OBJ. 3: Here there is no great danger in modern times, for the child's parents are Christians, and it can be expected with enough probability that they will nourish him in the faith, and also that he will learn more of the faith from the others with whom he lives. However, it was different in the early Church where a child would be living with unbelievers; and thus more care had to be taken by the *anadochus* or godparent. And it would be likewise even now if the child's parents were suspected of unbelief, or if the child were perhaps going to be living among unbelievers.

---

63. In the text of Lombard for this distinction; cf. *Epistola 98 ad Bonifacium*, n. 9 (CSEL 34.2:531).
64. Pseudo-Dionysius, *Ecclesiastical Hierarchy*, ch. 7, n. 11 (PG 3:566).

Article 3

About the rite of exorcism

Quaestiuncula 1

Ad tertium sic proceditur. Videtur quod exorcismus in eodem non debet praecedere baptismum. Exorcismi enim contra energumenos instituti sunt. Sed non omnes qui accedunt ad baptismum, sunt energumeni. Ergo non omnes sunt exorcizandi.

Praeterea, prius debet curari causa quam curetur effectus. Sed peccatum est causa quare in quibusdam diabolus potestatem habeat. Si ergo exorcismi sunt ad potestatem diaboli pellendam, videtur quod prius deberet aliquis per baptismum a peccato mundari quam per exorcismum a potestate diaboli.

Praeterea, ad idem superfluum est diversa remedia ordinari. Sed ad potestates daemonis arcendas sufficit aqua benedicta. Ergo non oportet ad hoc alios exorcismos esse.

Sed contra est quod Caelestinus Papa dicit: *sive parvuli sive juvenes ad regenerationis veniant sacramentum, non fontem vitae prius adeant quam exorcismis et exsufflationibus clericorum immundus spiritus ab eis abjiciatur.*

Praeterea, alia quae sanctificantur, prius exorcizantur, sicut patet in aqua benedicta, et in sale quod apponitur. Cum ergo in baptismo homo consecretur, videtur quod prius debeat exorcizari.

Obj. 1: To the third question we proceed thus. It seems that exorcism should not precede baptism in the same person.[65] For exorcisms were established against possession. But not everyone who approaches baptism is possessed. Therefore, not everyone should be exorcised.

Obj. 2: Furthermore, a cause should be cured before an effect may be cured. But sin is the cause of the devil having power in certain people. Therefore, if exorcisms are to expel the power of the devil, it seems that someone should first be cleansed from sin by baptism before being cleansed from the power of the devil by exorcism.

Obj. 3: Furthermore, it is superfluous to apply different remedies to the same thing. But holy water suffices for protecting from the power of the Devil. Therefore, there do not need to be other exorcisms for this.

On the contrary, Pope Celestine says: *whether little ones or the youth come to the sacrament of regeneration, they may not go to the font of life before the unclean spirit is driven out of them by the priests' exorcism and blowing upon them.*[66]

Furthermore, other things that are sanctified are first exorcised, as is seen in the case of holy water and in the salt that is inserted. Therefore, since in baptism a man is consecrated, it seems that first he should be exorcised.

Quaestiuncula 2

Ulterius. Videtur quod exorcismus non habeat aliquem effectum, sed sit ad significandum tantum. Nihil enim plus exigitur ad sacramentum novae legis nisi quod significet, et efficiat quod significat. Si ergo ea quae sunt in exorcismo, non solum significant, sed etiam efficiunt, tunc per se sacramenta sunt, et non sacramentalia.

Praeterea, sicut exorcismus praecedit baptismum, ita et quaedam alia sacramentalia consequuntur ipsum, sicut prius dictum est. Sed illa consequentia sunt tantum ad significandum. Ergo et exorcismus.

Praeterea, si aliquis exorcizatus puer ante baptismum moriatur, constat quod hoc eum a daemone non

Obj. 1: Moreover, it seems that the exorcism does not have any effect, but it is only for the sake of signifying.[67] For nothing more is required for a sacrament of the New Law but that it signifies and effects what it signifies. If therefore those things that are in the exorcism do not just signify but also effect, then they are themselves sacraments, and not sacramentals.

Obj. 2: Furthermore, just as exorcism precedes baptism, so also certain other sacramentals follow it, as was said before. But those things that follow are only for the sake of signifying. Therefore, so also is exorcism.

Obj. 3: Furthermore, if some child should die after the exorcism but before baptism, it is clear that this would not

---

65. Parallels: below, qa. 2, ad 4; *ST* III, q. 71, a. 2.
66. See Gratian's *Decretals*, Part 3, *De consecratione*, d. 4, ch. 53 (PL 187:1818).
67. Parallel: *ST* III, q. 71, a. 3.

liberet. Ergo ad minus in anima ejus exorcismus nullum effectum habuit.

Praeterea, sicut dicit Cyprianus: *scias nequitiam diaboli permanere usque ad aquam salutarem posse; in baptismo autem nequitiam amittere.* Sed aliquando etiam post baptismum exorcismus fit in illis quibus in articulo necessitatis exorcismus omissus fuerit, si periculum evadant. Ergo non liberat a potestate daemonis, et nullum effectum habere videtur.

Sed contra, Gregorius super Ezech.: *sacerdos dum per exorcismi gratiam manus imponit credentibus, et habitare malignos spiritus in eorum mente contradicit, quid aliud facit, nisi quia daemones ejicit?* Ergo habet aliquem effectum.

Praeterea, exorcismi Salomonis habebant aliquem effectum ad pellendos daemones. Ergo multo fortius exorcismi ecclesiae.

free him from the demon. Therefore, at least in his soul, exorcism would have had no effect.

Obj. 4: Furthermore, as Cyprian said: *you should know that the wickedness of the devil can remain until the saving water; but in baptism the wickedness drops away.*[68] But when an exorcism is omitted because of an emergency, sometimes if the danger has passed, it is done also after baptism. Therefore, it does not free from the power of the demon, and it seems to have no other effect.

On the contrary, Gregory says on Ezekiel: *when the priest by the grace of exorcism places his hands on the believers, and speaks against the malignant spirits living in their minds, what else does he do but cast out demons?*[69] Therefore, it does have some effect.

Furthermore, the exorcisms of Solomon had a certain effect in driving back demons.[70] Therefore, much stronger are the exorcisms of the Church.

Quaestiuncula 3

Ulterius. Videtur quod exorcizare sit officium eorum qui in sacris ordinibus constituuntur. Quia operari in immundis, secundum Dionysium, ad diaconum pertinet. Sed inter immundos, secundum Dionysium, locum tenent energumeni. Cum ergo exorcizatio sit ad eos sicut catechizatio ad catechumenos, videtur quod sit eorum qui sunt in sacris ordinibus.

Praeterea, catechismus praecedit exorcismum. Sed in artibus operativis ita est, quod operatio principalioris artis semper sequitur, sicut patet de arte quae secat ligna, et quae compaginat navem. Cum ergo catechismus per diaconos vel sacerdotes fiat, videtur quod exorcismus non possit fieri per illos qui sunt in minoribus ordinibus.

Praeterea, ad hoc est consuetudo ecclesiae: quia exorcizatio solum per sacerdotes fit; quod etiam ex auctoritate Gregorii inducta patet.

Sed contra est quod infra, dist. 24, dicit Magister quod ad exorcistas pertinet exorcismos memoriter tenere, manus super energumenos imponere. Ergo cum exorcista non sit sacer ordo, videtur quod ille qui est in minoribus ordinibus constitutus possit exorcizare ex officio.

Obj. 1: Moreover, it seems that to exorcise is the office of those who are established in sacred orders.[71] For to work among the unclean, according to Dionysius, pertains to the deacon.[72] But the possessed hold a place among the unclean, according to Dionysius. Since therefore exorcising is to them as catechizing is to catechumens, it seems that it belongs to those who are in sacred orders.

Obj. 2: Furthermore, catechism precedes exorcism. But among operative arts it is such that the more important operation of an art comes later, as is clear from the art of cutting wood and the art of ship-building. Since therefore catechism is done by deacons or priests, it seems that exorcism could not be done by those who are in minor orders.

Obj. 3: Furthermore, this is the custom of the Church, since exorcising is done by priests alone, which is also clear from the authority of Gregory cited.

On the contrary, the Master says below, Distinction 24, that it pertains to exorcists to hold exorcisms by memory, and to place their hands on the possessed. Therefore, since "exorcist" is not a sacred order, it seems that someone who is established in minor orders could exorcise by his office.

---

68. Cf. Cyprian, *Epistle 69* (CCSL 3), ch. 15: "Quod si aliquis in illo mouetur quod quidam de his qui aegri baptizantur spiritibus adhuc inmundis temptabantur, sciat diaboli nequitiam pertinacem usque ad aquam salutarem ualere, in baptismo uero omne nequitiae suae uirus amittere."

69. Gregory, *Homilies on the Gospels*, Bk. 2, Homily 29, n. 4 (CCSL 141:248).

70. Thomas refers to King Solomon as an exorcist in one other place, namely, *De Potentia*, q. 6, a. 10, obj. 3 and ad 3. Given that Aquinas apparently knew Josephus (see, e.g., *ST* I-II, q. 102, a. 4), the probable source of his information on Solomon is Josephus's *Antiquities of the Jews*, Bk. 8, ch. 2, n. 5.

71. Parallel: *ST* III, q. 71, a. 4.

72. Pseudo-Dionysius, *Ecclesiastical Hierarchy*, ch. 5, n. 6 (PG 3:507).

Response to Quaestiuncula 1

Respondeo dicendum ad primam quaestionem, quod propter peccatum hominis diabolus potestatem accipit in hominem, et in omnia quae in usum hominis veniunt, in ipsius nocumentum. Et quia nulla conventio est Christi ad Belial, ideo quandocumque aliquid sanctificandum est ad cultum divinum, prius exorcizatur, ut liberatum a potestate diaboli, qua illud in nocumentum hominis assumere poterat, Deo consecretur; et hoc patet in benedictione aquae, in consecratione templi, et in omnibus hujusmodi. Unde cum propria[73] sanctificatio qua homo Deo consecratur, sit in baptismo, oportet quod etiam homo prius exorcizetur quam baptizetur, multo fortiori ratione quam alia res: quia in ipso homine est causa quare diabolus potestatem accepit in hominem, et in alia quae sunt propter hominem, scilicet peccatum originale vel actuale; et hoc significant ea quae in exorcismo dicuntur, ut cum dicitur: *recede ab eo Satana*, et hujusmodi; et similiter ea quae ibi fiunt: quia ipsa exsufflatio significat daemonis expulsionem; benedictio autem cum manus impositione praecludit expulso viam, ne redire possit; sal autem in os missum, et narium et aurium sputo linitio significat remotionem impedimenti ipsius daemonis respectu fidei docendae vel addiscendae, ut dictum est; sed olei inunctio significat expeditionem hominis in pugna quam adversus diabolum suscipit, a cujus potestate exemptus est.

Ad primum ergo dicendum, quod energumeni dicuntur interius laborantes, ab *en*, quod est in, et *ergon*, quod est labor. Et quamvis non omnes baptizandi sint energumeni, nec interius laborantes a diabolo vexati corporaliter, tamen interius laborant vel infirmantur propter infectionem fomitis diabolo in eis potestatem habente.

Ad secundum dicendum quod quando effectus confirmat causam, tunc prius laborandum est ad curandum effectum, ut sic expeditius procedatur ad curationem causae. Potestas autem daemonis, quae ex peccato consequitur, et tenet et conservat hominem in malitia et in peccato; et ideo prius evacuanda est potestas daemonis, vel debilitanda, quod in exorcismo fit, ne curationem causae, idest peccati, in baptismo factam impedire possit.

Ad tertium dicendum, quod diabolus impugnat nos et ab exteriori et ab interiori. Aqua ergo benedicta ordinatur contra impugnationem diaboli quae est ab exteriori, sed exorcismus contra impugnationem quae est ab interiori. Unde et illi contra quos datur, dicuntur *energumeni*, idest interius laborantes.

To the first question, I answer that because of man's sin the devil received power over man, and over all things that come under man's use, for harming him. And since there is no agreement between Christ and Belial (cf. 2 Cor 6:15), for this reason whenever something is to be sanctified for divine worship, it is first exorcised, so that freed from the devil's power, by which he could use it to harm man, it may be consecrated to God; and this is evident in the blessing of water, in the consecration of a temple, and in everything like this. Hence since the first sanctification by which man is consecrated to God is in baptism, it is fitting that a man is also exorcised before he is baptized, for a much greater reason than with other things: because in a man himself is the cause by which the devil received power over man and the other things that are for man's sake (namely, original and actual sin). And this is what the things said in an exorcism signify, as when it is said: *depart from him, Satan*, and other things like that. And similarly, what is done then: because the blowing symbolizes the expulsion of the demon; moreover, the blessing with the imposition of hands blocks the way for the one who has been cast out, so that he cannot return; while the salt placed in the mouth and the anointing of the nostrils and ears with saliva represents the removal of impediments from that demon with respect to teaching or learning the faith, as was said; but the anointing with oil represents man's charging into the fight that he has undertaken against the devil, from whose power he has been released.

Reply Obj. 1: Possessed people are said to be laboring inwardly, from the Greek word, *energumens*, which means labor inside. And although not all those to be baptized are possessed, nor are they laboring inwardly in the sense of being physically plagued by the devil, nevertheless they labor or suffer inwardly from the infection of sin's tinderwood because of the devil having power over them.

Reply Obj. 2: When the effect strengthens the cause, then one should first work to cure the effect, so that in that way one may proceed more expeditiously to the cure of the cause. But the power of a demon, which results from sin, both holds and keeps man in malice and sin, and thus, first the power of the demon must be eradicated or diminished, which is done in an exorcism, lest it should impede the curing of the cause, i.e., sin, accomplished in baptism.

Reply Obj. 3: The devil attacks us both from inside and from without. Therefore, holy water is ordered against the devil's attacks that come from outside, but exorcism against the attacks that come from inside. Hence those to whom exorcism is applied are called *energumens*, that is, laboring inwardly.

73. *propria.—prima* PLE.

Response to Quaestiuncula 2

Ad secundam quaestionem dicendum, quod circa hoc est duplex opinio. Quidam enim dicunt quod ea quae in exorcismo aguntur, sunt tantum signa eorum quae postea in baptismo complentur, in quo potestas daemonis totaliter evacuatur, ut Cyprianus dicit in auctoritate inducta. Sed hoc est contra auctoritatem Gregorii inductam, et contra ea quae in exorcizando dicuntur, quae frustra dicerentur, nisi aliquem effectum haberent, praecipue cum per modum imperii, et non solum per modum orationis dicantur in hoc quod dicitur: *ergo, maledicte diabole, exi ab eo*, etc. Et ideo dicendum secundum alios, quod non tantum significant, sed etiam efficiunt aliquid, non tantum in corpore, sed etiam in anima, quia in utroque est infectio fomitis. Effectus autem iste est debilitatio potestatis daemonis, ne tantum possit in homine sicut ante, ne baptismum et alia bona in ipso impediat; sed potestas praedicta totaliter in baptismo aufertur: sicut etiam Pharao prius flagellatus est populo nondum de Aegypto egresso, et postea totaliter in mari rubro, quod est figura baptismi, submersus.

Ad primum ergo dicendum, quod sacramenta novae legis habent effectum in conferendo gratiam qua perfecte morbo subvenitur, contra quem sacramentum ordinatur; sed sacramentalia habent effectum in removendo contrarias dispositiones, vel impedimenta gratiae; et ideo secundum diversa impedimenta multiplicantur, nec in eis gratia confertur.

Ad secundum dicendum quod non est simile de sacramentalibus quae sequuntur et quae praecedunt: quia ex quo baptismus plene effectum suum habet, non oportet quod impedientia baptismum tollantur, quia jam impediri non potest; tamen non est remotum quin unctio chrismatis post baptismum in vertice facta aliquem effectum ad gratiam conferendam vel conservandam habeat.

Ad tertium dicendum quod Praepositinus dixit, quod exorcizatus ante baptismum decedens, minores tenebras patietur. Sed hoc nihil est: quia tenebrae illae in sola carentia divinae visionis consistunt, cum non habeant aliam poenam sensibilem; et hoc in omnibus aequaliter erit. Et ideo dicendum aliter, quod non habet effectum in collatione gratiae, sed solum in debilitatione potestatis daemonis; et ideo hoc valet ei tantum in vita.

Ad quartum dicendum, quod ad hoc quod uniformitas baptismi observetur, oportet quod exorcismus si praetermissus fuit, post baptismum suppleatur; et tunc tantum significat; vel forte additur etiam aliqua cohibitio ab impugnatione diaboli. Nec hoc est inconveniens,

To the second question, it should be said that concerning this there are two opinions. For some people say that the things that are done in an exorcism are only signs of those things that are fulfilled afterward in baptism, in which the power of the demon is completely driven out, as Cyprian says in the text cited. But this is contrary the text of Gregory cited, and contrary to the things that are said in exorcising, which would be said in vain unless they had a certain effect, particularly since they are said in the mode of command and not only in the mode of prayer, by the fact that it is said: *therefore, cursed devil, go out from him*, etc. And thus it should be said, following others, that these words do not only represent but also effect something, not only in the body but also in the soul, since the infection of the *fomes* is in both. However, that effect is a weakening of the power of the devil, only so that he cannot be in a man as before, lest he impede the baptism and other goods in him. But the power mentioned is completely removed in baptism, just as also Pharaoh was first afflicted with scourges when the Jewish people had not yet left Egypt, and afterward he was completely drowned in the Red Sea, which is a figure of baptism.

Reply Obj. 1: Sacraments of the New Law have an effect by conferring the grace by which one is perfectly rescued from the disease that the sacrament is ordered against, but sacramentals have their effect by removing contrary dispositions, or impediments to grace; and thus they are multiplied according to the different impediments, nor is grace conferred in them.

Reply Obj. 2: The sacramentals that follow a sacrament are not the same as the ones that precede it: for once baptism has its full effect, the things impeding baptism do not need to be taken away, since it can no longer be impeded; nevertheless, this does not take away the fact that chrism oil on the crown of the head after baptism has some effect in conferring or preserving grace.

Reply Obj. 3: Praepositinus said that someone who dies after being exorcised but before baptism will suffer less darkness. But this amounts to nothing: for that darkness consists only of the absence of the divine vision, since they do not have any sensory punishment; and this darkness will exist equally for all. And thus it should be said rather that it will not have an effect in conferring grace, but only in weakening the power of the demon; and so this benefits someone only in life.

Reply Obj. 4: So that uniformity may be observed in baptism, if the exorcism has been left out, it may be supplied after the baptism; and then it only signifies, or perhaps it adds a certain inhibition against attacks from the devil. Nor is this unfitting, since some power of the devil is

cum etiam per aquam benedictam, qua post baptismum aspergimur, aliqua potestas daemonis reprimatur.

also repressed by the holy water that is sprinkled after baptism.

Response to Quaestiuncula 3

AD TERTIAM QUAESTIONEM dicendum, quod exorcizare ad exorcistas pertinet ex proprio officio ordinis; nihilominus tamen est et superiorum ordinum. Tamen propter ostendendam unitatem baptismi, consuetum est in ecclesia ut totum quod ad baptismum pertinet, expleatur ab uno, scilicet a sacerdote; et praecipue nunc, quando non venit magna multitudo simul ad baptismum, et sunt multi sacerdotes. In primitiva autem ecclesia quandoque magna turba simul ad baptismum accedebat, et erant pauci sacerdotes; unde hujusmodi sacramentalia relinquebantur in minoribus ordinibus.

AD PRIMUM ergo dicendum, quod Dionysius sub ministris comprehendit omnes ordines inferiores; et ideo ministris qui diaconi dicuntur, attribuit omnia quae sunt inferiorum ordinum: quia forte in primitiva ecclesia nondum erant illi ordines ita distincti propter paucitatem ministrorum.

AD SECUNDUM dicendum, quod sicut exorcismus primo pertinet ad exorcistam, ita etiam primus ordo, qui habet actum in catechizando, est ordo lectorum, quamvis hoc postea per superiores ordines compleatur; et ideo sicut catechismus praecedit exorcismum, ita ordo lectoris praecedit ordinem exorcistae.

AD TERTIUM dicendum, quod completa potestas in exorcizando competit sacerdoti; et ideo quando non est magna necessitas, ipse secundum consuetudinem ecclesiae exorcismi actum exequitur; et secundum hanc consuetudinem loquitur auctoritas Gregorii.

TO THE THIRD QUESTION, it should be said that exorcising pertains to exorcists by their proper office of order; but nevertheless it is also of superior orders. But for the sake of showing the unity of baptism, it is customary in the Church that all that pertains to baptism be fulfilled by one person, namely, by the priest; and particularly now, when a great number of people are not coming to be baptized at the same time, and there are many priests. But in the early Church sometimes a great crowd came to be baptized at once, and there were few priests; hence sacramentals like this were left to those in minor orders.

REPLY OBJ. 1: Under the term 'ministers', Dionysius includes all the lower orders; and thus to the ministers who are called deacons, he attributed everything that belongs to the lower orders: for perhaps in the early Church those orders did not yet exist as distinct, because of the scarcity of ministers.

REPLY OBJ. 2: Just as the exorcism pertains to the exorcist in the first place, so also the first order, which whose act is catechizing, is the order of lectors, although afterward this may be completed by higher orders; and thus just as catechism precedes exorcism, so does the order of lector precede the order of exorcist.

REPLY OBJ. 3: Complete power in exorcising belongs to the priest; and thus when there is no great necessity, he performs the act of exorcism according to the custom of the Church; and this custom is what the authority of Gregory speaks about.

EXPOSITION OF THE TEXT

Hoc etiam sciendum est, quod licet ter immergatur propter mysterium Trinitatis, tamen unum baptisma reputatur. De trina immersione supra, dist. 3, dictum est.

Acceleratus est usus rationis. Quia Augustinus super hoc ambigue loquitur, ideo diversimode quidam de hoc senserunt. Dixerunt enim quidam, quod Joannis exultatio non fuit aliquis motus corporalis, sed miraculosus quasi gaudentis, ut matri innotesceret matris salvatoris adventus. Alii autem dicunt aliter et melius, quod ad illud momentum datus est ei usus rationis; nec est inconveniens si postea sit subtractus, sicut et gratia raptus ad momentum datur: secus autem est de gratia gratum faciente, quae non subtrahitur sine culpa.

Non errorem inducens, etc. Quia si errorem vellet inducere, intendens mutare formam ecclesiae, hoc ipso non intenderet facere quod ecclesia facit; et ideo non baptizaret. De corruptione autem formae supra, dist. 3, dictum est.

Divinum judicium per alicujus revelationis miraculum oratione implorandum esse censerem. Videtur quod male dicat: quia divinum judicium non est hoc modo requirendum nisi in dubiis. Certum autem videtur, quod si ludo fecit, intentio defuit, et verus baptismus non fuit. Et dicendum, quod ludus aliquando excludit intentionem, et aliquando non. Cum enim ludo fieri dicantur quae praeter intentionem alicujus utilitatis fiunt ad solam delectationem, ludus baptizantium potest excludere intentionem respectu utriusque effectus ablutionis, scilicet sacramenti collationis, et rei sacramenti; et tunc non intendit facere quod facit ecclesia in collatione sacramenti; et ita talis ludus evacuat intentionem quae requiritur in sacramento: vel potest excludere tantum secundam utilitatem, ut scilicet velit de hoc ludum suum facere ex eo quod baptismi sacramentum conferat, non propter sanctificationem baptizandi hoc faciens; et tunc manet intentio quae sufficit ad baptismum. Et ideo propter hoc dubium dixit Augustinus: *implorandum est divinum judicium*; et ideo dicitur quod puer Athanasius ludendo simulans se episcopum baptizavit quosdam, et judicatum est ab Alexandro episcopo ut non rebaptizarentur: quia inventum est quod ipse intentionem baptizandi ha-

It is also to be known, that "although there is a triple immersion for the mystery of the Trinity, yet it is held to be one baptism."[74] The threefold immersion was discussed above, in Distinction 3.

"If in the child the use of reason is accelerated."[75] Since Augustine speaks about this ambiguously, people have understood it in various ways. For some people have said that John's exultation was not any bodily movement, but a miraculous kind of rejoicing, so that the arrival of the mother of the Savior would be made known to his mother. But others say differently, and better, that he was given the use of reason at that moment; nor is it unfitting if afterward it was taken away, just as also someone is taken up to heaven by a grace given for a moment; but it is different with sanctifying grace, which is not taken away without blame.

"If the one who baptized did not introduce any error,"[76] etc. Since if someone wanted to lead into error, intending to change the Church's form, he would by this very fact not intend to do what the Church does; and thus he would not baptize. But corruption of the form has been discussed above, at Distinction 3.

"I would think that we ought to pray imploringly for the declaration of God's judgment through the miracle of some revelation."[77] It seems that Augustine speaks poorly: for divine judgment is not required in this way, except in matters of doubt. But it seems certain that if someone did this in jest, the intention was lacking, and there was no valid baptism. And it should be said that joking sometimes excludes the intention, and sometimes does not. For when things are said to be done in jest that are done only for pleasure, without the intention of a certain benefit, the joke of the ones baptizing in jest can exclude the intention with respect to both effects of the pouring, namely, the conferral of the sacrament and of the reality behind the sacrament; and then a person does not intend to do what the Church does in conferring a sacrament; and so this kind of joke removes the intention that is required for the sacrament. Or it can exclude only the second benefit, namely, so that someone wants to make his joke out of conferring the sacrament of baptism, not doing it for the sake of the sanctification of the one to be baptized, and then an intention remains that suffices for baptism. And thus, on account of this doubt Augustine said to *pray imploringly for the declaration of divine judgment*;[78] and thus it is said that as a child, Athanasius

---

74. *Sent* IV, 6.2 (37). 6 citing Jerome, *In quatuor epistolas Paulinas*, Eph. 4,5.
75. *Sent.* IV, 6.2 (38), 2, citing Augustine, *Epistola 187*, ch. 7, n. 24.
76. *Sent* IV, 6.4 (39). 1 citing Pope Zacharias, *Epistola 7*.
77. *Sent.* IV, 6.5 (40), 1, Augustine, *De baptismo contra Donatistas*, Bk. 7, ch. 53, n. 102.
78. See Augustine, *On Baptism, Against the Donatists*, Bk. 7, ch. 53 (CSEL 51:374).

buit; quod etiam patet ex hoc quod non baptizabat nisi catechumenos.

Cui additur exorcismus, etc. Videtur quod exorcismus debeat praecedere catechismum: quia prius removendum est malum quam perficiatur aliquis in bono. Et dicendum, quod verum est, si utrumque in eodem genere accipiatur. Sed catechismus ordinat ad bonum non efficiendo aliquid, sed solum instruendo; exorcismus autem removet malum in operando; et instructio in talibus debet operationem praecedere, ut sciat homo quid in eo fieri debeat.

while playing pretended to be a bishop and baptized certain people, and it was judged by Bishop Alexander that they were not to be rebaptized: for it was found that he had the intention of baptizing; which is also clear from the fact that he only baptized catechumens.[79]

Exorcism follows catechism, etc.[80] It seems that an exorcism should precede catechism, since evil must be removed before someone can be perfected in good. And it should be said that this is true if both things are in the same genus. But catechism is ordered to the good not by effecting anything but only by instructing, while exorcism removes evil in its working; and instruction in such things should precede operation so that a man might know what should be done in it.

---

79. The story is recounted thus by the Orthodox Church of America: "A group of children, which included Athanasius, were playing at the seashore. The Christian children decided to baptize their pagan playmates. The young Athanasius, whom the children designated as 'bishop,' performed the Baptism, precisely repeating the words he heard in church during this sacrament. Patriarch Alexander observed all this from a window. He then commanded that the children and their parents be brought to him. He conversed with them for a long while, and determined that the Baptism performed by the children was done according to the Church order. He acknowledged the Baptism as real and sealed it with the sacrament of Chrismation. From this moment, the Patriarch looked after the spiritual upbringing of Athanasius and in time brought him into the clergy, at first as a reader, and then he ordained him as a deacon." From http://oca.org/saints/lives/2014/05/02/101269-st-athanasius-the-great-the-patriarch-of-alexandria, accessed January 9, 2015.

80. *Sent.* IV, 6.7 (42), 1.

DISTINCTION 7

CONFIRMATION

Postquam Magister determinavit de sacramento intrantium, scilicet de baptismo, hic intendit determinare de sacramentis quae pertinent ad progredientes in via Dei; et dividitur in partes duas: in prima determinat de sacramentis quibus progredientes in bono perficiuntur; in secunda de sacramento quo a malo sublevantur quos cadere accidit, scilicet de poenitentia, dist. 14, ibi: *post hoc de poenitentia agendum est.*

Prima in duas: in prima determinat de sacramento confirmationis qua aliquis in seipso perficitur ad modum quo forma perficit; in secunda de Eucharistia, qua aliquis perficitur per conjunctionem ad finem, 8 dist., ibi: *post sacramentum baptismi et confirmationis sequitur Eucharistiae sacramentum.*

Prima in duas: in prima tangit ea quae sunt intra essentiam sacramenti, scilicet materiam et formam; in secunda ea quae sunt extra essentiam ipsius, ibi: *hoc sacramentum ab aliis perfici non potest, nisi a summis pontificibus.*

Et circa hoc tria facit: primo determinat ministrum hujus sacramenti; secundo effectum, ibi: *virtus autem hujus sacramenti est donatio Spiritus Sancti*; tertio ritum, ibi: *hoc sacramentum tantum a jejunis accipi, et jejunis tradi debet.*

Circa primum duo facit: primo determinat veritatem; secundo removet quamdam objectionem, ibi: *Melchiades,*[6] etc. Hic est triplex quaestio. Prima de ipso sacramento confirmationis. Secunda de effectu ejus. Tertia de celebratione ejus.

After the Master has examined the sacrament of those entering, namely baptism, here he intends to examine those sacraments that pertain to those progressing on the path of God; and this is divided into two parts: in the first, he examines the sacraments in which those who are progressing are perfected in the good; in the second, the sacrament in which those who fall are helped up again, namely, penance, at Distinction 14: *After these matters, we must treat of penance.*[1]

The first is in two parts: in the first he examines the sacrament of confirmation in which someone is perfected in himself in the way that a form perfects a thing; in the second, the Eucharist, in which someone is perfected by being joined to the end, at Distinction 8: *After the sacrament of baptism and the one of confirmation, follows the sacrament of the Eucharist.*[2]

The first is in two parts: in the first, he touches on those things that are within the essence of the sacrament, namely, matter and form; in the second, those things that are outside its essence, at: *that "sacrament cannot be performed by anyone other than the highest priests."*[3]

And concerning the latter he does three things: first, he determines the minister of this sacrament; second, its effect, at: *but the power of this sacrament is the giving of the Holy Spirit;*[4] third, its rite, at: *this sacrament ought to be conferred and received by people who are fasting.*[5]

About the first he does two things: first, he determines the truth; second, he removes a certain objection, at: *And yet Gregory writes,* etc.[7] Here there are three questions: First, concerning the sacrament of confirmation itself. Second, its effect. Third, its celebration.

---

1. Peter Lombard, *Sententiae* IV, 14.2 (74), 1.
2. *Sent.* IV, 8.1 (48), 1.
3. *Sent.* IV, 7.2 (44), 1 citing Pseudo-Eusebius, *Epistola 3 (ad episcopos Tusciae et Campaniae).*
4. *Sent.* IV, 7.3 (45), 1.
5. *Sent.* IV, 7.4 (46), 2.
6. *Melchiades.—Gregorius tamen* PLE.
7. *Sent.* IV, 7.2 (44), 2.

QUESTION 1

THE ESSENCE OF CONFIRMATION

Circa primum quaeruntur tria:
primo, utrum confirmatio sit sacramentum per se;
secundo, de materia ejus;
tertio, de forma.

Concerning the first, three questions arise:
first, whether confirmation is a sacrament in itself;
second, its matter;
third, its form.

ARTICLE 1

Whether confirmation is a sacrament in itself[8]

Quaestiuncula 1

AD PRIMUM SIC PROCEDITUR. Videtur quod confirmatio non sit sacramentum. Omne enim sacramentum efficaciam habet ab institutione divina. Sed confirmatio non legitur a Domino instituta. Ergo non est sacramentum.

PRAETEREA, illud cujus est usus in omnibus vel pluribus sacramentis, non videtur esse sacramentum per se. Sed, sicut dicit Dionysius, usus sacri unguenti, scilicet chrismatis, est in aliis sacramentis pluribus, sicut patet in baptismo, in quo infunditur chrisma in aqua baptismi, et baptizatus in vertice chrismate inungitur, et similiter pontifices chrismatis inunctione consecrantur, et altare etiam in quo Eucharistia consecranda est, chrismate linitur, et calix similiter. Ergo confirmatio, quae dicitur chrismatio, non est aliquod sacramentale.[10]

PRAETEREA, sacramenta novae legis in veteri praefigurata fuerunt. Sed nulla figura confirmationis in lege veteri legitur praecessisse. Ergo confirmatio non est sacramentum.

SED CONTRA est quod Melchiades in littera dicit: *scitote utrumque magnum esse sacramentum,* scilicet confirmationem et baptismum.

PRAETEREA, hoc patet per definitionem sacramenti, quae competit confirmationi, quae habet significationem gratiae in linitione olei, et habet efficaciam, ut

OBJ. 1: It seems that confirmation is not a sacrament. For every sacrament has its efficacy from divine institution. But nowhere do we read that confirmation was instituted by the Lord. Therefore, it is not a sacrament.

OBJ. 2: Furthermore, what is used in all or most sacraments does not seem to be a sacrament itself. But as Dionysius says,[9] the use of holy ointment, namely, chrism, is in several other sacraments, as evident in baptism, in which chrism is poured into the baptismal water and the baptized is anointed on the crown of the head with chrism, and similarly, pontiffs are consecrated by an anointing with chrism, and also the altar on which the Eucharist is consecrated is anointed with chrism, and the chalice in the same way. Therefore, confirmation, which is called chrismation, is not any specific sacrament, but rather a sacramental.

OBJ. 3: Furthermore, sacraments of the New Law were prefigured in the Old Law. But no figure of confirmation is read to have been the forerunner of confirmation in the Old Law. Therefore, confirmation is not a sacrament.

ON THE CONTRARY, Melchiades says in the text: *Know that each of these is a great sacrament,* namely, confirmation and baptism.[11]

FURTHERMORE, it is clear from the definition of a sacrament that it applies to confirmation, because it has the signification of grace in the anointing with oil, and has effi-

---

8. Parallels: above, d. 2, q. 1, a. 2; *ST* III, q. 65, a. 1; q. 72, a. 1; *SCG* IV, ch. 58.
9. Pseudo-Dionysius, *Ecclesiastical Hierarchy,* ch. 4, p. 3, n. 10 (PG 3:483).
10. *aliquod sacramentale.—aliquod speciale sacramentum sed magis sacramentale* PLE.
11. Pseudo-Pope Melchiades, *Epistola ad omnes Hispaniae episcopos,* Bk. 2, cited in Gratian's *Decretals,* Part 3, *De consecratione,* d. 5, canon 3 (*Corpus iuris canonici,* pars prior, ed. E. Friedberg, p. 1413).

in littera dicitur, in collatione gratiae ad plenitudinem sanctitatis. Ergo est sacramentum.

cacy, as it says in the text, in the conferral of grace for fullness of sanctity. Therefore, it is a sacrament.

Quaestiuncula 2

ULTERIUS. Videtur quod sit sacramentum necessitatis. Quia, ut Rabanus in littera dicit, *omnes fideles debent post baptismum per episcopos accipere Spiritum Sanctum, ut pleni Christiani inveniantur*. Sed hoc est de necessitate salutis, ut aliquis sit plenus Christianus. Ergo sacramentum confirmationis est sacramentum necessitatis.

PRAETEREA, sacramentum confirmationis contra morbum peccati ordinatur. Sed hoc est de necessitate salutis, ut quis a morbo peccati liberetur. Ergo confirmatio est sacramentum necessitatis.

PRAETEREA, sicut ad justitiam exigitur recessus a malo, ita et accessus ad bonum. Sed baptismus operatur ad recessum a malo, quod ipsum ablutionis nomen ostendit; confirmatio autem ad accessum ad bonum, quod etiam ex nomine patet. Ergo sicut baptismus est de necessitate sanctificationis, ita et confirmatio.

SED CONTRA, sine eo quod est de necessitate salutis, non est salus. Sed pueri baptizati salvantur si ante confirmationem moriantur. Ergo non est sacramentum necessitatis.

PRAETEREA gratia et virtus sufficiunt ad salutem. Sed in baptismo confertur gratia et plenitudo virtutum. Ergo baptismus sufficit ad salutem; et ita confirmatio non est sacramentum necessitatis.

OBJ. 1: Moreover, it seems that it is a sacrament of necessity. For, as Rabanus says in the text, *after baptism all the faithful must receive the Holy Spirit through the bishops, so that they may be found to be full Christians*.[12] But it is necessary to salvation that someone be a full Christian. Therefore, the sacrament of confirmation is a sacrament of necessity.

OBJ. 2: Furthermore, the sacrament of confirmation is directed against the disease of sin. But it is necessary to salvation that a person be freed from the disease of sin. Therefore, confirmation is a sacrament of necessity.

OBJ. 3: Furthermore, just as justice requires withdrawing from evil, so it also requires advancing toward good. But baptism works toward the withdrawal from evil, which is shown by the word 'cleansing', while confirmation works for the advancement toward good, as is also clear from its name. Therefore, just as baptism is necessary to sanctification, so is confirmation.

ON THE CONTRARY, without what is necessary to salvation, there is no salvation. But baptized children are saved if they die before confirmation. Therefore, it is not a sacrament of necessity.

FURTHERMORE, grace and virtue suffice for salvation. But in baptism, grace, along with the fullness of virtues, is conferred. Therefore, baptism is enough for salvation; and so confirmation is not a sacrament of necessity.

Quaestiuncula 3

ULTERIUS. Videtur quod baptismus sit nobilius sacramentum quam confirmatio: quia essentialia rei accidentalibus digniora sunt, sicut substantia accidente. Sed baptismus essentialiter se habet ad salutem, cum sit sacramentum necessitatis; confirmatio autem[13] accidentaliter, cum non sit necessitatis sacramentum. Ergo baptismus est nobilius sacramentum confirmatione.

PRAETEREA, effectus proportionatur suae causae. Sed baptismus habet majorem efficaciam in efficiendo: quia delet omnem culpam et poenam, quod non facit confirmatio. Ergo est nobilius sacramentum.

SED CONTRA, ad nobiliorem actionem ordinatur nobilius ministerium. Sed confirmatio datur a nobiliori mi-

OBJ. 1: Moreover, it seems that baptism is a more noble sacrament than confirmation: for the essentials of a thing are more worthy than the accidentals, just as a substance is more worthy than an accident. But baptism is related to salvation essentially, since it is a sacrament of necessity; but confirmation is somewhat incidentally related to salvation, since it is not a sacrament of necessity. Therefore, baptism is more noble than confirmation.

OBJ. 2: Furthermore, an effect is proportionate to its cause. But baptism has greater efficacy in effecting, for it erases all fault and punishment, which confirmation does not do. Therefore, it is a more noble sacrament.

ON THE CONTRARY, to a nobler action, a nobler office is ordered. But confirmation is given by a nobler minis-

---

12. Pseudo-Pope Urban, *Epistola ad omnes christianos*, Bk. 7, cited in Gratian's *Decretals*, Part 3, *De consecratione*, d. 5, canon 1 (*Corpus iuris canonici*, pars prior, ed. E. Friedberg, p. 1413).

13. *autem.—quasi* PLE.

nistro quam baptismus. Ergo confirmatio est nobilius sacramentum baptismo.

Response to Quaestiuncula 1

RESPONDEO dicendum ad primam quaestionem, quod actiones quae sunt ordinatae ad aliquos effectus proprios et determinatos, recipiunt distinctionem secundum proportionem ad suos effectus; unde si ad duos effectus distinctos ordinentur, erunt duae diversae[14] actiones. Si autem ordinentur ad unum effectum, ita quod una disponat vel impedimentum removeat, et alia perficiat, et alia ornet perfectum; totum computatur pro una integra actione, sicut patet in operibus artificum. Unde cum sacramenta sint quaedam actiones hierarchicae secundum Dionysium, ordinatae ad aliquos effectus salutis, quando plures actiones sacramentales ordinantur ad unum effectum, una ut perficiens, alia ut disponens, vel impedimentum removens, vel aliquo modo ornans, tunc in illa quae efficit effectum principalem consistit essentialiter ratio sacramenti. Aliae autem non dicuntur per se sacramenta, sed sacramentalia quaedam, quasi sacramentis adjuncta, sicut patet ex his quae dicta sunt circa baptismum in exorcismo et catechismo et aliis hujusmodi concurrere. Quando autem sunt plures actiones ordinatae ad effectus omnino distinctos, tunc sunt diversa sacramenta. Et ideo cum confirmatio habeat per se effectum distinctum ab effectu baptismi, ut patebit, non est sacramentale baptismi, sed potius per se est principale sacramentum.

AD PRIMUM ergo dicendum, quod circa institutionem hujus sacramenti est triplex opinio. Una enim dicit, quod hoc sacramentum non fuit institutum nec a Christo nec ab apostolis, sed postea processu temporis in quodam Concilio; et dicunt quod Dominus rem sacramenti hujus sine sacramento conferebat manus imponendo, similiter et apostoli, eo quod ipsi confirmati fuerunt immediate a Spiritu Sancto. Sed hoc videtur valde absonum: quia secundum hoc ecclesia tota die posset nova sacramenta instituere, quod falsum est, cum ipsi non sint latores legis, sed ministri, et fundamentum cujuslibet legis in sacramentis consistit; et praeterea in littera dicitur quod *tempore apostolorum . . . non ab aliis quam ab apostolis fuit peractum.*

Ideo alii dicunt, quod non fuit a Christo sed ab apostolis institutum hoc sacramentum. Sed hoc etiam non competit: quia et ipsi apostoli quamvis erant bases ecclesiae, tamen non fuerunt legislatores; unde ad eos non pertinebat sacramenta instituere.

ter than baptism. Therefore, confirmation is a nobler sacrament than baptism.

TO THE FIRST QUESTION, I answer that actions that are ordered to certain proper and determinate effects gain distinction according to their proportion to those effects. Thus if they are ordered to two distinct effects, they will be two distinctly different actions. But if they are ordered to one effect, such that one disposes or removes impediments, and the other perfects, while another adorns what has been perfected, then the whole is counted as one complete action, as is seen in the works of craftsmen. Therefore since the sacraments, according to Dionysius,[15] are certain hierarchical actions ordered to certain effects of salvation, when several sacramental actions are ordered to one effect, one as perfecting, another as disposing or removing impediments, or in some way adorning, then the notion of sacrament essentially subsists in the one that brings about the main effect. But the others are not called sacraments *per se*, but are a kind of sacramental, like something connected with the sacraments, as is evident from what was said about baptism in regard to exorcism and catechism, and it corresponds to other things like them. But when there are several actions ordered to completely different effects, then there are different sacraments. And therefore since confirmation has an essentially different effect from baptism's effect, as will be made clear, it is not a sacramental of baptism, but rather it is a main sacrament in itself.

REPLY OBJ. 1: There are three opinions about the institution of this sacrament. For one says that this sacrament was not instituted by Christ or the apostles, but afterward, over the passing of time at a certain council; and they say that the Lord conferred the reality behind this sacrament without conferring the sacrament by the imposition of his hands, and the apostles did the same, by the fact that they had been confirmed directly by the Holy Spirit. But this seems extremely discordant: for according to this the Church could institute new sacraments any day, which is false, since they are not proposers of the law, but ministers, and the foundation of any law whatsoever consists in its sacraments. And furthermore it says in the text that *in the time of the apostles . . . it had not been carried out by others than the apostles.*

Therefore, others say that this sacrament was not instituted by Christ but by the apostles. But this also does not apply: for although those apostles were also the foundations of the Church, nevertheless they were not the lawmakers; hence it did not pertain to them to institute sacraments.

---

14. *diversae.—diversae distincte* PLE.
15. Pseudo-Dionysius, *Ecclesiastical Hierarchy*, ch. 5, n. 1 (PG 3:499).

Et ideo probabilior videtur aliorum opinio, qui dicunt, hoc sacramentum, sicut et omnia alia, a Christo fuisse institutum: quod patet ex hoc quod ipse etiam Dominus manus pueris imponebat, ut patet Matth. 19. Nec obstat quod in Evangelio vel in actibus apostolorum non fit mentio de materia vel forma hujus sacramenti: quia formae sacramentales et alia quae in sacramentis exiguntur occultanda erant in primitiva ecclesia propter irrisiones gentilium, ut Dionysius dicit; unde etiam in fine *Eccl. Hier.* excusat se a determinatione formarum sacramentalium. Secus autem de baptismo quod erat sacramentum necessitatis, et statim cuilibet offerebatur in principio.

AD SECUNDUM dicendum, quod quamvis materia confirmationis, scilicet chrismate, utantur ecclesiae ministri in diversis sacramentis; tamen hoc sacramentum non consistit tantum in materia, sed in forma verborum, et actu, sicut et sacramentum baptismi; et hoc non utuntur in aliis sacramentis; et ideo est per se sacramentum.

AD TERTIUM dicendum, quod hoc sacramentum est ad perfectionem gratiae. Et quia status legis erat status imperfectionis, eo quod *nihil ad perfectum adduxit lex*, Hebr. 7, 19, ideo hoc sacramentum non habuit aliquid sibi respondens in veteri lege: quamvis aliquo modo sit figuratum in unctione pontificum, qua significabatur unctio Christi, a quo haec unctio derivatur.

And so the opinion of others seems to be more probable, who say that this sacrament, like all the others, was instituted by Christ; which is clear from the fact that the Lord himself placed his hands on the heads of children, as is evident from Matthew 19:15. Nor is it problematic that no mention of the matter and form of this sacrament is made in the Gospel or the Acts of the Apostles: for sacramental forms and other things that are required in the sacraments had to be concealed in the early Church because of the derision of the pagans, as Dionysius says. This is why also at the end of the *Ecclesiastical Hierarchy* he excuses himself from detailing the forms of sacramentals.[16] However, it is different with baptism which was a sacrament of necessity, and was offered immediately to anyone in the beginning.

REPLY OBJ. 2: Although the matter of confirmation, namely, chrism, may be used by the ministers of the Church in different sacraments, nevertheless this sacrament does not consist only in its matter, but in the form of words, and in the action, just as the sacrament of baptism does; and these things are not used in any other sacrament; and so it is a sacrament in itself.

REPLY OBJ. 3: This sacrament is for the perfection of grace. And since the state of the Law was the state of imperfection, by the fact that *the law brought nothing to perfection* (Heb 7:19), for this reason this sacrament did not have anything that corresponded to it in the Old Law, although in another way it was prefigured in the anointing of priests, by which Christ's anointing was symbolized, from which this anointing is derived.

Response to Quaestiuncula 2

AD SECUNDAM QUAESTIONEM dicendum, quod est triplex necessitas. Una est necessitas absoluta, sicut necessarium est Deum esse, vel triangulum habere tres angulos. Alia est necessitas ex causa efficiente, quae dicitur necessitas coactionis. Tertia est necessitas ex suppositione finis; et est duplex. Quia uno modo dicitur necessarium sine quo aliquis non potest conservari in esse, sicut nutrimentum animali. Alio modo sine quo non potest haberi quod pertinet ad bene esse, sicut equus dicitur necessarius ambulare volenti, et medicina ad hoc quod homo sane vivat. Primis ergo duobus modis non dicitur aliquod sacramentum esse necessitatis, sed tertia necessitate; quaedam quidem quantum ad primum modum, illa scilicet sine quibus non potest homo in spirituali vita vivere, sicut est baptismus et poenitentia; quaedam autem sine quibus non potest consequi aliquem effectum qui est ad bene esse spiritualis vitae; et hoc modo confirmatio et omnia alia sunt necessaria. Verumtamen con-

TO THE SECOND QUESTION, it should be said that there are three kinds of necessity. One is absolute necessity, as it is necessary that God exist, or that a triangle have three angles. Another is the necessity of an efficient cause, which is called the necessity of compulsion. The third is the necessity that arises from the supposition of the end; and this happens in two ways. For in one way something is called necessary when someone cannot be preserved in being without it, like nourishment for an animal. In another way when what pertains to well-being cannot be had without it, as a horse is said to be necessary to someone who wants to travel, and medicine for a man to live healthily. Now no sacrament is said to be necessary with the first two kinds of necessity, but only with the third kind of necessity; and then some of them indeed are necessary in the first way, namely those that a human being cannot live without in the spiritual life, like baptism and penance. But without certain others he cannot accomplish any effect that is for the well-

---

16. Pseudo-Dionysius, *Ecclesiastical Hierarchy*, ch. 7, p. 3, n. 10 (PG 3:566).

temptus cujuslibet sacramenti est periculosus. Objectiones autem procedunt de primo modo tertiae necessitatis.

ET IDEO DICENDUM AD PRIMUM, quod est plenitudo Christianae gratiae sufficiens ad salutem, et haec datur in baptismo; et est plenitudo copiae gratiae ad fortiter resistendum contra pressuras mundi, et haec datur in confirmatione, et sine hac potest esse salus.

AD SECUNDUM dicendum quod morbus peccati dupliciter expellitur. Uno modo quo ad culpam originalem in baptismo, et actualem in poenitentia; et haec expulsio sufficit ad salutem. Alio modo quo ad poenam inclinantem ad culpam; et sic expellitur in confirmatione, et in aliis sacramentis; et haec non est de necessitate salutis.

AD TERTIUM dicendum, quod in baptismo datur gratia quae a peccato mundat, et ad bene operandum perficit quantum ad sufficientiam salutis; sed in confirmatione additur amplius munus gratiae, quod non est de necessitate salutis.

being of the spiritual life, and confirmation and all the others are necessary in this way. Still, it is dangerous to treat any sacrament lightly. But the objections proceed from the first kind of the third necessity.

REPLY OBJ. 1: There is a fullness of Christian grace sufficient for salvation, and this is given in baptism. And there is a fullness of abundant grace for bravely resisting the pressures of the world, and this is given in confirmation, and without this there can be salvation.

REPLY OBJ. 2: The disease of sin is expelled in two ways. There is the way that original sin is expelled in baptism, and actual sin in penance; and this expulsion suffices for salvation. But there is also the penalty inclining us to sin; and this is driven out by confirmation and the other sacraments; and this is not necessary to salvation.

REPLY OBJ. 3: In baptism, grace is given that cleanses us from sin and perfects us for acting sufficiently well for salvation; but in confirmation a fuller gift of grace is added, which is not necessary for salvation.

Response to Quaestiuncula 3

AD TERTIAM QUAESTIONEM dicendum, quod quinque modis unum sacramentum dicitur esse dignius alio. Uno modo quo ad rem sacramenti, sive effectum ejus; et sic baptismus, qui delet omnem culpam et aufert omnem poenam, est maximum sacramentorum. Alio modo quantum ad id quod continetur in sacramento; et sic Eucharistia est nobilissimum, in qua continetur ipse Christus. Tertio quantum ad gradum dignitatis in quo constituit; et sic ordo est dignissimum sacramentum. Quarto quantum ad ministrum; et sic confirmatio, et etiam ordo, sunt dignissima, quia non nisi per episcopum ministrantur. Quinto quantum ad significatum et non contentum; et sic matrimonium est dignissimum, quia significat conjunctionem duarum naturarum in persona Christi.

Si tamen has dignitates ad invicem comparemus, invenitur illa dignitas potissima quam sacramentum habet ex contento, quia est essentialior; et ideo sacramentum Eucharistiae est simpliciter dignissimum, et ad ipsum quodammodo alia sacramenta ordinantur. Dignitas autem quae est in efficiendo, praevalet ei quae est in significando; et illa quae est in efficiendo respectu boni, simpliciter loquendo, praevalet ei quae est in amotione mali; et ideo, simpliciter loquendo, post Eucharistiam nobilius sacramentum est ordo, per quod homo et in gratia et in gradu dignitatis ponitur; et post hoc confirmatio, per quam perfectio gratiae confertur; et post baptismus, per quem fit plena remissio culpae et poenae; et post matrimonium, quod habet maximam significationem. Poenitentia autem et extrema unctio ponuntur

TO THE THIRD QUESTION, it should be said that there are five ways of saying that one sacrament is nobler than another. In one way, as to the reality of the sacrament, or its effect; and in this way, baptism, which takes away every fault and removes all punishment, is the greatest of the sacraments. In another way, as to what the sacrament contains; and in this way the Eucharist is the noblest, for Christ himself is contained in it. The third, as to the level of dignity in which it establishes someone; and in this way holy orders is the most worthy sacrament. The fourth, as to the minister; and in this way confirmation, and also orders, are the noblest, since they are only administered by a bishop. The fifth way, as to what is signified and not contained; and in this way marriage is the most noble, for it signifies the union of the two natures in the person of Christ.

But nevertheless if we compare these dignities with each other, we find the greatest dignity is the one that the sacrament has from its content, because that is the most essential; and this is why the sacrament of the Eucharist is the most noble, simply speaking, and the other sacraments are ordered to it in some fashion. However, the dignity that is in effecting is greater than that which is in signifying; and the dignity of effecting with respect to the good, simply speaking, is greater than that which removes evil; and so simply speaking, after the Eucharist the most noble sacrament is holy orders, by which a man is placed both in grace and in a level of dignity; and after this confirmation, by which the perfection of grace is conferred, and after this baptism, by which the full remission of guilt and punishment happens; and after this, marriage, which has the greatest signi-

inter baptismum et matrimonium: quia ordinantur directe ad remotionem mali: quamvis in hoc poenitentia habeat minorem efficaciam quam baptismus; quia ordinatur contra culpam actualem tantum, et non delet totaliter poenam; et adhuc minorem extrema unctio, quae contra reliquias peccati ordinatur.

AD PRIMUM ergo dicendum, quod quamvis confirmatio se habeat quasi accidentaliter ad vitam spiritualem simpliciter acceptam, tamen ad vitam spiritualem secundum sui perfectam differentiam non habet se accidentaliter, sed essentialiter; et ideo non oportet quod sit minoris dignitatis quam baptismus. Sicut etiam rationale est differentia nobilior quam sensibile: quamvis animali inquantum animal accidat esse rationale, cui inquantum hujusmodi per se convenit esse sensibile. Vel dicendum, ut quidam dicunt, quod confirmatio praesupponit baptismum; unde dupliciter possunt comparari. Uno modo ut accipiatur confirmatio cum praesuppositione baptismi; et sic confirmatio simpliciter est nobilior: sicut etiam esse substantiale perfectum per accidentalia simpliciter, nobilius est quam esse substantiale simpliciter. Alio modo cum praecisione baptismi; et sic quodammodo baptismus est nobilior quantum ad majorem efficaciam in removendo malum.

AD SECUNDUM dicendum, quod baptismus non habet majorem efficaciam simpliciter, sed solum in remotione mali, ut dictum est.

fication. However, penance and extreme unction are placed between baptism and marriage, because penance and extreme unction are ordered directly to the removal of evil; although in this penance has less efficacy than baptism, for it is ordered against actual guilt alone, and does not blot out punishment entirely; and extreme unction has still less efficacy, for it is ordered against the remnants of sin.

REPLY OBJ. 1: Although confirmation is related almost accidentally to the spiritual life taken simply, nevertheless for the spiritual life according to its own perfect difference it is not related accidentally but essentially; and so it is not necessary that it have less dignity than baptism. In the same way rational is a nobler difference than sensible; although for an animal as animal it is accidental to be rational, insofar as it is 'something of this kind' it belongs to it *per se* to be sensible. Or it could be said, as some people say, that confirmation presupposes baptism; hence they can be compared in two ways. In one way, so that confirmation is taken with the presupposition of baptism, and in this way, confirmation is simply more noble, just as also substantial being perfected by accidental being is simply nobler than substantial being simply. In another way, prescinding from baptism, and then in a certain way baptism is the nobler sacrament in having a greater efficacy for removing evil.

REPLY OBJ. 2: Baptism does not have a greater efficacy simply speaking, but only in the removal of evil, as was said.

ARTICLE 2

The matter of confirmation

Quaestiuncula 1

AD SECUNDUM SIC PROCEDITUR. Videtur quod sacramentum istud materiam non habeat. Sacramenta enim habent efficaciam ex divina institutione. Sed materia hujus sacramenti non legitur a Domino instituta. Ergo non habet determinatam materiam.

PRAETEREA, confirmatio datur ad plenitudinem sancti spiritus percipiendam. Sed super apostolos in die Pentecostes descendit Spiritus Sancti plenitudo absque omni materia. Ergo hoc sacramentum materia non indiget.

PRAETEREA, apostoli formam nobis ecclesiastici ritus tradiderunt. Sed ipsi confirmabant manus imponendo sine aliqua materia, ut legitur in Act. apostolorum. Ergo hoc sacramentum materiam non habet.

SED CONTRA est, quia, secundum Hugonem de s. Victore, *sacramentum est materiale elementum*. Ergo debet omne sacramentum habere materiam.

PRAETEREA, si omittitur aliquid quod non sit de substantia sacramenti, non impeditur perceptio sacramenti. Sed si omitteret episcopus chrismatis linitionem, non conferret sacramentum. Ergo materia est de essentia hujus sacramenti.

OBJ. 1: To the second question we proceed thus. It seems that this sacrament does not have matter.[17] For sacraments have efficacy from divine institution. But nowhere do we read that the matter of this sacrament was instituted by the Lord. Therefore, it does not have determinate matter.

OBJ. 2: Furthermore, confirmation is given for receiving the fullness of the Holy Spirit. But the fullness of the Holy Spirit descended on the apostles on the day of Pentecost without any matter. Therefore, this sacrament does not need any matter.

OBJ. 3: Furthermore, the apostles handed down the form of ecclesiastical rites to us. But they confirmed by the imposition of hands, without any matter, as we read in the Acts of the Apostles 8:17. Therefore, this sacrament does not have matter.

ON THE CONTRARY, according to Hugh of St. Victor, *a sacrament is a material element*.[18] Therefore, every sacrament ought to have matter.

FURTHERMORE, if something were omitted that did not belong to the substance of a sacrament, it does not prevent the reception of the sacrament. But if the bishop omitted the anointing with chrism, he would not confer the sacrament. Therefore, the matter is of the essence of this sacrament.

Quaestiuncula 2

ULTERIUS. Videtur quod chrisma non sit materia competens. In sacramentis enim uniformitas observari debet. Sed in baptismo est materia simplex elementum, scilicet aqua. Ergo etiam in confirmatione aliquod elementum debet esse materia.

PRAETEREA, virtus agentis proportionatur agenti. Sed virtus agens in sacramentis est simplex. Ergo et materia debet esse simplex; et ita materia confirmationis non debet esse commixta ex duobus liquoribus, scilicet oleo et balsamo.

PRAETEREA, materia sacramenti debet esse omnibus communis: quia omnibus sacramenta proponuntur

OBJ. 1: Moreover, it seems that chrism is not the appropriate matter.[19] For uniformity should be observed in the sacraments. But in baptism the matter is a simple element, namely, water. Therefore, also in confirmation some element should be the matter.

OBJ. 2: Furthermore, the power of an agent is proportionate to that agent. But the acting power in the sacraments is simple. Therefore, the matter should also be simple; and so the matter of confirmation should not be mixed from two liquids, oil and balsam.

OBJ. 3: Furthermore, the matter of a sacrament should be common to all: for the sacraments are proposed to all for

---

17. Parallels: *ST* III, q. 72, a. 2; q. 84, a. 1, ad 1; *SCG* IV, ch. 60.
18. Hugh of St. Victor, *De sacramentis fidei*, Bk. 1, pt. 9, ch. 2 (PL 176:317).
19. Parallels: *ST* III, q. 72, a. 2; q. 84, a. 1, ad 1; *SCG* IV, ch. 60.

in salutem. Sed oleum olivae et balsamum non est apud omnes. Ergo non sunt conveniens materia alicujus sacramenti.

PRAETEREA, ex aliis etiam rebus fit oleum quam ex oliva, sicut ex nucibus et papavere. Ergo videtur quod etiam ex tali oleo posset fieri chrisma.

PRAETEREA, sacramentum confirmationis est ad roborandum hominem in pugna spirituali. Sed vinum facit homines bonae spei, secundum Philosophum, quod ad fortitudinem pugnae exigitur; et similiter *panis cor hominis confirmat*, ut dicitur in Psal. 103. Ergo panis et vinum esset hujus sacramenti convenientior materia quam oleum et balsamum.

PRAETEREA, materia sacramenti debet habere significationem et respectu effectus, et respectu alicujus quod in Christo praecessit, a quo sacramenta profluxerunt. Sed per hujusmodi liquores nihil significatur in Christo praecedens. Ergo hujusmodi liquores non sunt conveniens materia hujus sacramenti.

salvation. But not everyone has olive oil and balsam. Therefore, they are not fitting matter for any sacrament.

OBJ. 4: Furthermore, oil can be made from other things besides olives, like nuts and poppies. Therefore, it seems that also those oils could be made into chrism.

OBJ. 5: Furthermore, the sacrament of confirmation is for fortifying a person in his spiritual fight. But according to the Philosopher,[20] wine makes men of good hope, which is necessary for courage in the fight; and likewise *bread strengthens a man's heart*, as it says in Psalm 103:15. Therefore, bread and wine would be more fitting matter for this sacrament than oil and balsam.

OBJ. 6: Furthermore, the matter of a sacrament should have signification both with respect to the effect and with respect to something that preceded in Christ from whom the sacrament flowed forth. But nothing pre-existing in Christ is symbolized by liquids like these. Therefore, these liquids are not fitting matter for this sacrament.

Quaestiuncula 3

ULTERIUS. Videtur quod non exigatur materia prius sanctificata. Confirmatio enim, ut in littera dicitur, non est majoris virtutis quam baptismus. Sed in baptismo non requiritur materia prius sanctificata. Ergo nec in confirmatione.

PRAETEREA, secundum Augustinum, *accedit verbum ad elementum, et fit sacramentum*. Si ergo oporteret quod materia aliquibus verbis prius sanctificaretur, tunc etiam ipsum chrisma per se est quoddam sacramentum, et non sacramenti materia.

PRAETEREA, sanctificatio non est iteranda circa idem. Sed per formam sacramenti sanctificatur materia, ut patet in baptismo, cujus materia est aqua verbo vitae sanctificata; quod verbum supra, dist. 3, dixit Magister esse formam baptismi. Ergo non debet ante prolationem formae sacramentalis aliqua sanctificatio circa materiam confirmationis adhiberi.

SED CONTRA est communis usus ecclesiae, et etiam determinatio Dionysii, qui ponit ritum consecrationis chrismatis.

OBJ. 1: Moreover, it seems that it does not require matter previously sanctified.[21] For confirmation, as it says in the text, is not more powerful than baptism. But in baptism no previously sanctified matter is required. Therefore, neither in confirmation.

OBJ. 2: Furthermore, according to Augustine, *the word is combined with the element and the sacrament occurs*.[22] If therefore it were necessary that the matter be sanctified by certain words beforehand, then the chrism itself would also be a certain sacrament, and not the matter of a sacrament.

OBJ. 3: Furthermore, sanctification is not to be repeated for the same thing. But the matter is sanctified by the form of a sacrament, as is clear in baptism, whose matter is the water sanctified by the word of life, and above, in Distinction 3, the Master called this word the form of baptism. Therefore, no sanctification of the matter should be applied to the matter of confirmation before the uttering of the sacramental form.

ON THE CONTRARY is the common use of the Church, and also the determination of Dionysius,[23] who includes the rite of consecrating the chrism.

Response to Quaestiuncula 1

RESPONDEO dicendum ad primam quaestionem, quod materia sacramenti dicitur illa res visibilis sub cu-

TO THE FIRST QUESTION, I answer that a sacrament's matter is called the visible reality under cover of which di-

---

20. Aristotle, *Nichomachean Ethics*, Bk. 3, ch. 11, 1117a14–15.

21. Parallels: above, d. 2, q. 1, a. 1, qa. 2, ad 2; below, d. 23, q. 1, a. 3, qa. 2 & 3; *ST* III, q. 72, a. 3; *De veritate*, q. 27, a. 4, ad 10.

22. Augustine, *In Iohannis euangelium tractatus* (CCSL 36), Tract. 80, par. 3.

23. Pseudo-Dionysius, *Ecclesiastical Hierarchy*, ch. 4, p. 2 (PG 3:474).

jus tegumento divina virtus secretius operatur salutem; et ideo ad hoc necessaria est materia sacramentis, ut ad effectum, ad quem virtus humana nullatenus attingit neque operando neque cooperando, divina virtus in re visibili operans perducat. Et ideo in poenitentia et in matrimonio cujus effectus aliquo modo dependet ex operatione humana, scilicet dolore de peccatis, et consensu etiam in copulam conjugalem, non requiritur talis materia. In baptismo autem, cujus effectus totaliter est ab extrinseco, nil cooperante interius baptizante neque eo qui baptizatur, nisi ad removendum impedimentum, requiritur materia sensibilis. Cum ergo effectus confirmationis, qui est plenitudo Spiritus Sancti, sit omnino ab extrinseco, non per aliquam operationem humanam, non est dubium quod in sacramento confirmationis materia exigatur.

AD PRIMUM ergo dicendum, quod plenitudo Spiritus Sancti non erat danda ante Christi resurrectionem et ascensionem, sicut dicitur Joan. 7, 39: *nondum erat spiritus datus, quia nondum erat Jesus glorificatus*; et ideo secundum unam opinionem, ea quae ad hoc sacramentum pertinent non fuerunt ante Christi ascensionem instituenda. Sed aliquo modo praefiguratum fuit hoc sacramentum in manus impositione Christi super pueros; quamvis etiam illa manus impositio possit referri magis ad manus impositionem quae fit super catechumenos, ut dictum est. Nec hoc differt, sive Dominus ipsemet instituit, sive apostoli ejus speciali praecepto. Secundum vero aliam opinionem dicendum, quod Dominus materiam hujus sacramenti per seipsum instituit, sicut et adventum Spiritus Sancti promisit; sed denuntiandam apostolis dereliquit, quando usus sacramenti competebat, scilicet post plenam Spiritus Sancti missionem.

AD SECUNDUM dicendum quod sicut sacramentum baptismi incepit in baptismo Christi; ita sacramentum confirmationis incepit in adventu Spiritus Sancti in apostolos. Et quia principia rerum debent esse notissima, ideo utrobique Spiritus Sanctus apparuit visibiliter; in baptismo quidem in columbae specie, et in confirmatione apostolorum in linguis igneis; et propter hoc non oportuit esse materiam, in qua Spiritus Sanctus secretius operaretur salutem, ut Augustinus dicit.

AD TERTIUM dicendum, quod apostoli non confirmabant sine materia, nisi forte quando praeter legem communem visibilibus signis Spiritus Sanctus in eos descendebat quibus per apostolos manus impositio facta fuerat: tunc enim illa visibilis apparitio supplebat locum elementi visibilis. Quod autem aliquando materia uterentur, patet per Dionysium in 4 cap. *Eccl. Hier.* in principio, ubi dicitur, quod *est quaedam perfectiva operatio quam duces nostri*, quos apostolos nominat, *chrismatis*

vine power works our salvation in a hidden way; and for this reason matter is necessary to the sacraments, so that for an effect that human power does not bring about at all, whether by working or by cooperating, divine power carries it out by working in a visible thing. And this is why in penance and marriage, whose effects depend in a certain way on human acting, namely, in sorrow for sins and consent to conjugal union, matter such as this is not required. But in baptism, whose effect is completely from outside, with no interior working on the part of the one baptizing nor the one baptized, except in removing impediments, a sensible matter is required. Since therefore the effect of confirmation, which is the fullness of the Holy Spirit, is entirely from outside, not by any human operation, there is no doubt that matter is needed in the sacrament of confirmation.

REPLY OBJ. 1: The fullness of the Holy Spirit was not to be given before Christ's Resurrection and ascension, as it says: *for as yet the Spirit had not been given, because Jesus was not yet glorified* (John 7:39). And so according to one opinion, those things that pertain to this sacrament had not been instituted before Christ's ascension. But in some way this sacrament was prefigured in the imposition of Christ's hands on the children; although that imposition of hands could be referred more to the imposition of hands that is done upon catechumens, as was said. Nor does it make any difference whether the Lord himself instituted it or his apostles did by special command. But according to another opinion it should be said that the Lord instituted the matter of this sacrament by himself, just as he also promised the coming of the Holy Spirit; but he left its announcement to the apostles when the use of the sacrament was available, namely, after the full sending of the Holy Spirit.

REPLY OBJ. 2: Just as the sacrament of baptism began at the baptism of Christ, so also the sacrament of confirmation began in the coming of the Holy Spirit upon the apostles. And because the principles of a thing should be the most known, for this reason the Holy Spirit appeared visibly on both occasions: at the baptism in the form of a dove, and at the confirmation of the apostles in tongues of fire; and because of this it was not necessary for there to be matter in which the Holy Spirit would work our salvation in a hidden way, as Augustine says.[24]

REPLY OBJ. 3: The apostles did not confirm without matter, except perhaps when, outside of the usual course of things, the Holy Spirit descended by visible signs upon those on whom the apostles had imposed their hands; for then that visible appearance would supply the place of the visible element. But the fact that they ever used matter is clear from Dionysius in the beginning of Chapter 4 of the *Ecclesiastical Hierarchy*, where it says that *there is a certain perfective operation, which our leaders*, as he calls the apos-

---

24. Rather, Isidore, *Etymologiarum* (ed. Lindsay), Bk. 6, ch. 19, par. 40.

hostiam nominant, hostiam dicens communiter omnem ritum sacramenti.

tles, *name the sacrifice of chrism*, calling every sacrament's rite commonly a sacrifice.[25]

Response to Quaestiuncula 2

AD SECUNDAM QUAESTIONEM dicendum, quod, sicut dictum est, hoc sacramentum initium sumpsit ab adventu Spiritus Sancti in discipulos, qui quamvis prius Spiritum Sanctum habuissent in munere gratiae, quo perficiebantur ad ea quae ad singulares personas eorum pertinebant, tamen in die etiam Pentecostes acceperunt Spiritum Sanctum, sed in munere gratiae quo perficiebantur ad promulgationem fidei in salutem aliorum; et ideo facta est apparitio Spiritus Sancti linguis igneis, *ut verbis essent proflui* ad divulgandam fidem Christi; *et caritate fervidi*, aliorum salutem quaerentes; et propter hoc dicitur Act. 2, 4: *repleti sunt Spiritu Sancto, et coeperunt loqui.* Igni autem nihil convenientius accipi potuit loco ejus in materia confirmationis quam oleum, tum quia lucet, tum quia maxime est nutritivum ignis. Figurae autem linguae nihil convenientius esse potuit quam balsamum propter odorem, quia propter confessionem linguae odor bonae notitiae Dei diffunditur in omni loco. Et ideo sicut visibilis apparitio Spiritus Sancti fuit in igne figurato figura linguae, ita materia confirmationis est oleum balsamatum, ut oleum pertineat ad conscientiam quam oportet nitidam habere eos qui confessores divinae fidei constituuntur; et balsamum ad famam, quam oportet diffundere et verbis et factis fidei confessores.

AD PRIMUM ergo dicendum, quod non debet in omnibus sacramentis observari uniformitas identitatis, sed proportionalitatis; ut sicut materia unius sacramenti competit illi sacramento, ita materia alterius sacramenti etiam competat alii. Et quia baptismus est janua sacramentorum, quasi principium et elementum omnium aliorum, ideo sibi competit materia quae sit simplex elementum, non autem ita aliis sacramentis, in quibus additur aliquid speciale; sicut corpora mixta habent aliquas virtutes superadditas speciem consequentes.

AD SECUNDUM dicendum, quod virtus hujus sacramenti quamvis sit simplex in essentia, tamen est multiplex in effectu: quia et hominem facit ferventem in conscientia, et famosum per confessionem; et ideo materia hujus sacramenti est et una et multiplex: una in actu, sed multiplex in virtute, sicut et alia mixta.

AD TERTIUM dicendum, quod illa ratio procedit in sacramentis necessitatis, cujusmodi non est hoc sacra-

TO THE SECOND QUESTION, it should be said that, as was said, this sacrament took its beginning from the coming of the Holy Spirit among the disciples, who, although they had had the Holy Spirit before in the gift of grace by which they were perfected for the things that pertain to individual persons, nevertheless on the day of Pentecost received the Holy Spirit, but in a gift of grace by which they were perfected for the promulgation of faith in Christ for the salvation of others. And thus the apparition of the Holy Spirit in tongues of fire happened *so that they might be fluent in words* to share the faith of Christ; *and fervid in charity*, seeking the salvation of others;[26] and because of this it says: *they were filled with the Holy Spirit, and they began to speak* (Acts 2:4). Now, nothing could be taken more fittingly in place of fire than oil, both because it shines, and because it is the greatest fuel for fire. Now, nothing could be more fittingly taken for the figure of tongues than balsam, on account of the odor, since because of the confession of the tongue the odor of the good tidings of God is diffused in every place. And thus as the visible apparition of the Holy Spirit was figured in fire with the shape of a tongue, so the matter of confirmation is oil with balsam, so that the oil pertains to the conscience which must shine in those who are constituted confessors of the divine faith; and balsam to the good news which confessors of the faith must spread both in words and in deeds.

REPLY OBJ. 1: The uniformity of sameness should not be observed in all the sacraments, but uniformity of proportionality; so that just as the matter for one sacrament befits that sacrament, so the matter of another sacrament is suited to it. And since baptism is the door of the sacraments, like a principle and element of all the others, for this reason it befits it to have matter that is a simple element, but not so with the other sacraments in which something specific is added on; just as compound bodies have certain superadded properties resulting from their species.

REPLY OBJ. 2: It is the virtue of this sacrament that, although it is simple in essence, it nevertheless has a compound effect: for it makes man both fervent in conscience and renowned for his confession; and for this reason the matter of this sacrament is both one and compound: one in acting, but compound in power, just like other mixed things.

REPLY OBJ. 3: This argument works with sacraments of necessity, but this sacrament is not one of those. However,

---

25. Pseudo-Dionysius, *Ecclesiastical Hierarchy*, ch. 4, n. 1 (PG 3:471).
26. These two phrases are from the Lauds hymn *Beata nobis gaudia* of the Feast and Octave of Pentecost.

mentum. Tamen oleum et balsamum quamvis non ubique terrarum crescant, tamen ubique de facili transportari possunt.

AD QUARTUM dicendum quod proprietates olei perfectius in oleo olivae inveniuntur, unde antonomastice oleum dicitur; et praeterea ipsa oliva propter virorem perpetuum quem servat, aliquid adjuvat ad significationem mysterii.

AD QUINTUM dicendum quod vinum et panis roborant hominem per modum nutrimenti confortando hominem in seipso; ideo magis competunt Eucharistiae; sed oleum facit expeditum et ferventem ad ea quae exterius sunt; et ideo etiam pugiles oleo unguntur; et ideo competit magis oleum huic sacramento.

AD SEXTUM dicendum quod hac unctione, ut dicit Hugo de sancto Victore, significatur illa unctio qua Christus unctus est ut rex et sacerdos oleo laetitiae prae consortibus suis. Unde etiam a chrismate Christus dicitur, et a Christo Christianus; et propter hoc etiam Dionysius per chrisma Christum significari dicit.

although oil and balsam do not grow in every land, nevertheless they can be easily transported anywhere.

REPLY OBJ. 4: The properties of oil are found more perfectly in olive oil, hence it is called oil antonomastically; and furthermore, the olive itself, because of the long-lasting freshness that it keeps, adds something to the representation of the mystery.

REPLY OBJ. 5: Wine and bread fortify a person by the mode of nourishment, strengthening the person in himself, and this is why they are better suited to the Eucharist. But oil makes a person slick and warmed up for what is external, and for this reason boxers are also rubbed with oil; and so oil is better suited to this sacrament.

REPLY OBJ. 6: By this anointing, as Hugh of St. Victor says, that anointing is represented in which Christ was anointed as king and priest with the oil of gladness above his brethren.[27] This is the reason Christ is also said from chrism, and from Christ, Christian is said; and because of this Dionysius says that Christ is also represented by the chrism.[28]

Response to Quaestiuncula 3

AD TERTIAM QUAESTIONEM dicendum, quod materia sacramenti est quasi instrumentum sanctificationis; est autem instrumentum et principalis agentis et ministri qui materia sacramenti utitur ad significandum. Quodlibet autem sacramentum determinat sibi principale agens quantum ad necessitatem sacramenti, quia non habet efficaciam aliquam nisi ex auctoritate Domini et merito Christi; sed non quodlibet sacramentum determinat sibi ministrum quantum ad necessitatem sacramenti, sed quandoque solum quantum ad solemnitatem, sicut patet in baptismo. Et ideo ut materia sacramenti etiam principali agenti respondeat proportionaliter et ministro, illa sacramenta quae ministrum sibi determinant, materiam sanctificatam exigunt, ut dispositio sacramenti a ministris ecclesiae descendere ostendatur. Sacramentum autem quod non determinat sibi ministrum nisi quantum ad solemnitatem, non habet materiam sanctificatam quantum ad necessitatem sacramenti, sed solum quantum ad solemnitatem, in cujus materia etiam chrisma in modum crucis effunditur. Et quia sacramentum confirmationis determinat sibi ministrum, ut dicetur, ideo materiam sanctificatam requirit ab eo qui est minister sacramenti, scilicet ab episcopo.

AD PRIMUM ergo dicendum quod ad hoc nihil facit virtus sacramenti, sed determinatio ministri, ut dictum

TO THE THIRD QUESTION, it should be said that the sacrament's matter is like an instrument of sanctification, but it is an instrument of both the principal agent and the minister who uses the sacrament's matter for signifying. Now every sacrament has its principal agent determined for it regarding what is necessary for the sacrament, for it does not have any efficacy except from the authority of the Lord and the merit of Christ. But not every sacrament has its minister determined for it as something necessary for the sacrament, but sometimes only for the sake of its solemnity, as is seen in baptism. And therefore, so that the sacrament's matter might correspond proportionally to the principal agent and to the minister, those sacraments that have their minister determined for them require sanctified matter so that the sacrament's disposition might be shown to come from the ministers of the Church. But a sacrament that does not have its minister determined except for the sake of solemnity does not require sanctified matter as something necessary to it, but only for its solemnity, and it is in this matter that chrism is applied in the shape of the Cross. And since minister of the sacrament of confirmation is determined for it, as will be said, for this reason it requires matter sanctified by the one who is the minister of the sacrament, namely, the bishop.

REPLY OBJ. 1: The power of the sacrament has nothing to do with this, but the determination of the minister, as

---

27. Hugh of St. Victor, *De sacramentis fidei*, Bk. 2, pt. 2, ch. 2 (PL 176:416).
28. Pseudo-Dionysius, *Ecclesiastical Hierarchy*, ch. 4, p. 3, n. 10 (PG 3:483).

est. Vel dicendum, quod baptismus est sacramentum necessitatis; et ideo materiam communissimam habet; et propter hoc sanctificatione non indiget.

AD SECUNDUM dicendum, quod quidam dicunt ipsum chrisma esse sacramentum. Sed hoc falsum apparet in hoc quod usus chrismatis in pluribus est quam sacramentum confirmationis; sicut patet in baptizato, qui chrismate in fronte linitur, et de pontifice, cujus caput chrismate tangitur. Et ideo dicendum, quod sacramentum confirmationis non est ipsum chrisma, sed linitio chrismatis sub forma praescripta verborum. Illa autem benedictio vocalis chrismatis non est forma sacramenti, sed magis est quaedam benedictio sacramentalis, sicut benedictio aquae vel altaris.

AD TERTIUM dicendum, quod sicut instrumentum virtutem instrumentalem acquirit dupliciter, scilicet quando accipit formam instrumenti, et quando movetur a principali agente ad effectum; ita etiam materia sacramenti duplici sanctificatione indiget: una qua instituitur materia propria sacramenti, et ad hoc est sanctificatio materiae; alia est quando applicatur ad effectum, quae fit per formam sacramenti. Et ideo non fit injuria sanctificationi, si duplex sanctificatio in talibus adhibeatur.

was said. Or it could be said that baptism is a sacrament of necessity, and for this reason it has the most common matter; and because of this it does not need sanctification.

REPLY OBJ. 2: Certain people say that the chrism itself is the sacrament. But this appears false in the fact that chrism is used in more things than the sacrament of confirmation; as is seen in a baptized person, who is anointed with chrism on the forehead, and with a pontiff, whose head is touched with chrism. And so it should be said that the sacrament of confirmation is not chrism itself, but the anointing with chrism under the prescribed form of words. But that blessing pronounced over the chrism is not the form of the sacrament, but rather a certain sacramental blessing, like the blessing of water or an altar.

REPLY OBJ. 3: Just as an instrument acquires instrumental power in two ways, namely, when it receives the form of the instrument, and when it is moved by a principal agent to its effect, so also the matter of a sacrament needs two sanctifications: one in which it is established as the proper matter of the sacrament, and this is the sanctification of the matter; the other is when it is applied to its effect, which happens through the sacrament's form. And in this way no injury is done to sanctification, if two sanctifications are applied in this kind of thing.

ARTICLE 3

The form of confirmation[29]

Quaestiuncula 1

AD TERTIUM SIC PROCEDITUR. Videtur quod sacramentum confirmationis non habeat formam. Sacramenta enim a Christo descenderunt. Sed Christus non legitur aliqua forma usus, manus imponens. Ergo cum illa manus impositio confirmationem designet, videtur quod confirmationis sacramentum non habeat aliquam formam.

PRAETEREA, apostoli etiam leguntur per manus impositionem Spiritum Sanctum dedisse. Sed illa manus impositio, ut sancti dicunt, fuit confirmatio illorum quibus manus imponebant. Ergo cum non legatur eos sub aliqua forma verborum manus imposuisse, sicut leguntur in nomine Christi baptizasse, videtur quod hoc sacramentum non habeat formam.

PRAETEREA, sacramenta quae habent formam, sub eisdem verbis apud omnes perficiuntur. Sed sacramentum confirmationis non perficitur eisdem verbis apud omnes. Dicunt enim quidam: *consigno te signo crucis, et confirmo te chrismate salutis in nomine patris et filii et Spiritus Sancti*. Quidam autem dicunt: *chrismate sanctificationis*. Ergo hoc sacramentum non habet aliquam formam.

SED CONTRA est quod Magister dixit in 1 dist., quod duo sunt in quibus sacramenta consistunt, verbum, et res. Verba autem ad formam pertinent.

PRAETEREA, Augustinus dicit: *accedit verbum ad elementum, et fit sacramentum*.

OBJ. 1: To the third question we proceed thus. It seems that the sacrament of confirmation does not have a form. For sacraments came down from Christ. But we do not read that Christ used any form when he imposed his hands on anyone. Therefore, since that imposition of hands designates confirmation, it seems that the sacrament of confirmation does not have any form.

OBJ. 2: Furthermore, we also read that the apostles gave the Holy Spirit through the imposition of hands (Acts 8:17). But that imposition of hands, as holy men say, was the confirmation of those people on whom they placed their hands. Therefore, since we do not read that they imposed their hands under any form of words, as we do read that they baptized in the name of Christ (Acts 2, 8, and 10), it seems that this sacrament does not have any form.

OBJ. 3: Furthermore, sacraments that have form are administered by anyone under the same words. But the sacrament of confirmation is not administered by everyone with the same words. For some people say: *I sign you with the sign of the Cross and I confirm you with the chrism of salvation in the name of the Father and of the Son and of the Holy Spirit*. But others say: *with the chrism of sanctification*. Therefore, this sacrament does not have a certain form.

ON THE CONTRARY, the Master said in Distinction 1 that there are two things in which the sacraments consist: a word and a thing. But the words pertain to the form.

FURTHERMORE, Augustine says: *the word is combined with the element, and the sacrament happens.*[30]

Quaestiuncula 2

ULTERIUS. Videtur quod illa forma verborum non sit competens. In quolibet enim sacramento exigitur intentio. Sed ad designandum intentionem in forma baptismi exprimitur persona baptizans hoc pronomine *ego*. Ergo et in forma confirmationis hoc pronomen *ego* apponi debet.

PRAETEREA, consignatio videtur ad characteris impressionem pertinere. Sed characterem non imprimit minister magis hic quam in baptismo. Cum ergo in baptismo nulla fiat mentio de consignatione in forma, nec hic fieri deberet de ipsa mentio.

OBJ. 1: Moreover, it seems that this form of words is not appropriate. For in every sacrament an intention is required. But in the form of baptism the person baptizing expresses his intention in the pronoun *I*. Therefore, also in the form of confirmation, the pronoun *I* should be added.

OBJ. 2: Furthermore, sealing seems to pertain to the impression of a character. But the minister does not imprint a character here more than in baptism. Since therefore in baptism no mention is made of a seal in the form, neither should mention be made of it here.

---

29. Parallels: *ST* III, q. 72, a. 4; q. 84, a. 3; *De forma absol.*, ch. 1.
30. Augustine, *In Iohannis euangelium tractatus* (CCSL 36), Tract. 80, par. 3.

PRAETEREA, per baptismum homo maxime configuratur passioni Christi. Sed in forma baptismi non fit mentio aliqua de Christi passione. Ergo nec in forma ista deberet fieri mentio de cruce.

PRAETEREA, sicut confirmatio habet formam determinatam, ita et baptismus. Sed in baptismi forma non fit mentio de materia ipsius: non enim dicitur: *baptizo te aqua*. Ergo nec hic deberet fieri mentio de chrismate.

PRAETEREA, forma est de essentia sacramenti:[31] quia multi accipiunt sacramentum qui non accipiunt rem sacramenti. Ergo non debet res sacramenti poni in forma, sicut hic ponitur, *chrismate salutis*.

OBJ. 3: Furthermore, by baptism most of all a person is configured to the Passion of Christ. But in the form of baptism no mention is made at all of Christ's Passion. Therefore, neither should mention be made of the Cross in this form.

OBJ. 4: Furthermore, just as confirmation has a determinate form, so also does baptism. But in baptism's form no mention is made of the matter itself; for it is not said, *I baptize you with water*. Therefore, neither should mention be made here of chrism.

OBJ. 5: Furthermore, form is essential to the sacrament, but the reality behind the sacrament is not essential to the sacrament: for many receive the sacrament who do not receive the reality behind the sacrament. Therefore, the reality behind the sacrament should not be included in the form, as it is included here: *with the chrism of salvation*.

Quaestiuncula 3

ULTERIUS. Videtur quod forma ista non habeat in hoc sacramento aliquam efficaciam. Quia, secundum Hugonem de sancto Victore, *sacramentum ex sanctificatione invisibilem gratiam continet*. Sed materia hujus sacramenti est sanctificata etiam ante formae prolationem. Ergo formae prolatio nullam efficaciam praebet sacramento.

PRAETEREA, sicut in Eucharistia est sanctificatio hostiae et usus ipsius, ita et hic. Sed ibi tota virtus sacramenti est in hostia sanctificata, ut patet in forma verborum quae proferuntur, cum quis hostiam sumit, cum dicitur: *corpus Domini nostri*, etc. Ergo et similiter hic virtus sacramenti non consistit in verbis praemissis, quae in usu materiae hujus sacramenti dicuntur.

SED CONTRA est, quod forma est principalior in re quam in materia. Si ergo materia aliquid efficit, multo fortius forma.

OBJ. 1: Moreover, it seems that this form does not have any efficacy in this sacrament. For according to Hugh of St. Victor, *a sacrament contains invisible grace from its sanctification*.[32] But the matter of this sacrament is sanctified before the form is even uttered. Therefore, the uttering of the form furnishes no efficacy to the sacrament.

OBJ. 2: Furthermore, just as in the Eucharist there is the consecration of the host and its use, so also here. But in the former, the sacrament's whole power is in the consecrated host, as is clear in the form of words that are uttered when someone consumes the host, since it is said: *May the Body of Our Lord*, etc.[33] Therefore also, in the same way here the power of the sacrament does not consist in the words uttered in the use of the sacrament.

ON THE CONTRARY, form is more important in a thing than matter. If therefore the matter effects something, much more will the form.

Response to Quaestiuncula 1

RESPONDEO dicendum ad primam quaestionem, quod ministri sacramentorum operantur in sacramentis benedicendo et sanctificando; et ideo secundum quod ad aliquod sacramentum requiritur minister, ita requiritur forma qua minister sacramentum dispensat.

AD PRIMUM ergo dicendum, quod, sicut dictum est, illa manus impositio quam Dominus pueris exhibebat, non erat proprie sacramentum confirmationis,

TO THE FIRST QUESTION, I answer that the ministers of the sacraments work in the sacraments by blessing and sanctifying; and thus according as a minister is required for any sacrament, a form is also required by which the minister may administer the sacrament.

REPLY OBJ. 1: As was said, the Lord's imposition of hands upon the children was not properly a sacrament of confirmation, which it was not appropriate to display be-

31. *sacramenti.—sacramenti, sed res sacramenti non est de essentia sacramenti* PLE.
32. Hugh of St. Victor, *De sacramentis fidei*, Bk. 1, pt. 9, ch. 2 (PL 176:317).
33. Thomas is referring to the traditional formula with which the minister of holy communion says to the recipient as he places the host on his or her tongue: *Corpus Domini nostris Jesu Christi custodiat animam tuam in vitam aeternam, Amen.*

quod non conveniebat exhiberi ante ipsius glorificationem; sed vel erat signum quoddam futurae confirmationis, vel erat talis manus impositio, qualis fit in catechismo et exorcismo. Si tamen Dominus confirmasset sine forma vel materia, non esset inconveniens; quia ipse habebat excellentiae potestatem in sacramentis, qui poterat effectum sacramenti sine sacramentalibus praebere; quod non est de aliis.

AD SECUNDUM dicendum, quod quidam dicunt quod apostoli propter dignitatem et auctoritatem ipsorum confirmabant sine materia et forma per solam manus impositionem. Sed hoc non videtur bene dictum: quia quantumcumque ipsi essent magnae auctoritatis, tamen potestatem excellentiae in sacramentis dispensandis non habebant. Et ideo dicendum, quod apostoli aliqua forma utebantur, quamvis non sit scripta. Multa enim apostoli servabant in sacramentorum dispensatione quae nolebant divulgari propter irrisionem gentilium evitandam, sicut patet per apostolum, qui dicit 1 Corinth. 11, 34: *cetera, cum venero, disponam*; et loquitur de celebratione sacramenti Eucharistiae; et hoc est etiam quod Dionysius dicit in fine *Eccl. Hier.*: *consummativas autem invocationes*, idest verba quibus perficiuntur sacramenta, *non est justum Scripturas interpretantibus, neque mysticum earum [sensum], aut in ipsis operatas ex Deo virtutes, ex occulto ad commune adducere; sed, ut nostra sacra traditio habet, sine pompa*, idest occulte, *eas edocere*, etc. Ex quibus verbis tria possumus accipere. Primo, quia apostoli in sacramentis utebantur forma verborum certa, quia ipse alibi in eodem Lib. dicit, quod tradit ritum sacramentorum sicut apostoli docebant. Secundo, quod in occulto tradebantur hujusmodi sacramentalia in primitiva ecclesia. Tertio, quod in ipsis verbis est aliqua virtus, quod quidam negant.

AD TERTIUM dicendum, quod variatio formae in his quae non sunt de essentia formae, potest tolerari secundum diversas ecclesiarum consuetudines, dummodo substantia formae apud omnes servetur. Hoc autem quod a quibusdam dicitur, *chrismate salutis*, vel *sanctificationis*, quasi in unum redit; et ideo per hoc non removetur quin hoc sacramentum habeat determinatam formam.

fore his glorification; but it was either a sign of future confirmation or an imposition of hands of the kind that is done in catechism and exorcism. But even so, if the Lord had confirmed without form or matter, it would not have been unfitting; for he himself had the power of excellence in the sacraments, which could furnish the effect of a sacrament without sacramentals; and this is not the case with others.

REPLY OBJ. 2: Certain people say that the apostles confirmed without matter and form, by the imposition of hands alone, because of their own dignity and authority. But this does not seem to be well said: for notwithstanding their great authority, they still did not have the power of excellence in administering the sacraments. And so it should be said that the apostles used some form, although it was not written down. For the apostles preserved many things in the administering of the sacraments that they did not wish to publish in order to avoid the derision of the pagans, as is clear from the Apostle, who says, *the rest I will dispose when I come* (1 Cor 11:34); and he speaks of the celebration of the sacrament of the Eucharist; and this is also what Dionysius says in the end of the *Ecclesiastical Hierarchy*: *However, as to the consummative invocations*, that is, the words by which the sacraments are performed, *it is not right for those interpreting the Scriptures nor their mystery, or the powers worked in them by God, to draw out their hidden sense in public; but as our sacred tradition has it, without pomp*, that is, secretly, *to teach them*, etc.[34] From these words we can gather three things. First, that the apostles were using a certain form of words in the sacraments, since he says elsewhere in the same book[35] that he hands on the rite of the sacraments just as the apostles taught it. Second, that they were handing on sacramentals like this in secret in the early Church. Third, that there is a certain power in those words, which some people deny.

REPLY OBJ. 3: A variation of form among those things that are not essential to the form can be tolerated according to the different customs of the churches, as long as the substance of the form is preserved among all. But whether some people say *chrism of salvation* or *chrism of sanctification*, it amounts to the same thing; and so this does not prevent this sacrament from having a determinate form.

Response to Quaestiuncula 2

AD SECUNDAM QUAESTIONEM dicendum, quod sicut definitio debet indicare totum esse rei, si sit perfecta; ita per formam sacramenti debet innotescere totum quod ad sacramentum pertinet. Sacramentum autem et

TO THE SECOND QUESTION, it should be said that just as a definition should indicate the entire being of a thing, if it is complete, so also by a sacrament's form everything the sacrament pertains to should be made known. How-

---

34. Pseudo-Dionysius, *Ecclesiastical Hierarchy*, ch. 7, n. 10 (PG 3:566).
35. Pseudo-Dionysius, *Ecclesiastical Hierarchy*, ch. 1, n. 5 (PG 3:375).

est ad aliquem finem ordinatum, et ab aliqua causa principali efficaciam habet. Et ideo tria ponuntur in forma hujus sacramenti; quorum primum pertinet ad finem ad quem institutum est hoc sacramentum, qui est confessio fidei Christianae, cujus tota summa consistit in passione Christi; unde apostolus 1 Corinth. 2, 2: *non enim judicavi me aliquid scire inter vos, nisi Jesum Christum et hunc crucifixum*; iterum et hujus articuli confessio majorem habet difficultatem: quia, sicut dicitur in eadem epistola, 1 Corinth. 1, 23, *nos autem praedicamus Christum crucifixum, Judaeis quidem scandalum, gentibus autem stultitiam*; et ad hoc pertinet cum dicitur: *consigno te signo sanctae crucis*, ut crucis verbum non erubescat, sed publice confiteatur. Secundo ponitur ipse sacramentalis actus cum sua materia et effectu, ut sic tangatur et id quod est sacramentum tantum, in hoc quod dicitur, *chrismate*; et id quod est res et sacramentum, in hoc quod dicit, *confirmo*, idest sacramentum confirmationis praebeo; et id quod est res et non sacramentum, in hoc quod dicit, *salutis*. Sed causa agens principalis, unde sacramentum effectum habet, tangitur in hoc quod dicit: *in nomine patris et filii et Spiritus Sancti.*

AD PRIMUM ergo dicendum, quod baptismus est sacramentum necessitatis; et ideo intentio baptizantis magis est arctanda ad actum sacramenti. Vel dicendum quod baptizare potest quilibet, confirmare autem solus ille qui est in summo gradu ecclesiae, de quo praesumitur quod minus possit in dispensatione sacramenti deficere; et ideo non requiritur tanta arctatio intentionis per verba in forma apposita.

AD SECUNDUM dicendum, quod consignatio quae ponitur in forma, non pertinet ad consignationem characteris, sed ad consignationem crucis, quae fit in fronte linitione chrismatis propter confessionem fidei crucis; et talis signatio non fit in baptismo, quia baptizatus non consecratur ad aliquid speciale, sed universaliter ad spiritualem vitam; consignatio autem importat quamdam ascriptionem, vel aliquid speciale, quod est in sacramento confirmationis.

AD TERTIUM dicendum, quod ille qui baptizatur, configuratur passioni Christi per fidem ejus, quam habere in corde debet; et ideo non exigitur aliqua consignatio crucis exterius, sed sufficit consignatio interior quae est per characterem et[37] conformatio ad passionem Christi in consepelitione aquae. Sed confirmatio est sacramentum confessionis passionis Christi, sicut baptismus sacramentum fidei; et ideo exterius in manifesto imprimitur crucis signaculum, et in forma exprimitur.

ever, a sacrament is also ordered to a certain end, and has its efficacy from a certain principal cause. And so these three things are included in the form of this sacrament; the first of them pertains to the end for which this sacrament was instituted, which is the confession of the Christian faith, whose complete summary consists in Christ's Passion; hence the Apostle says: *for I have not considered myself to know anything among you, except Jesus Christ, and him crucified* (1 Cor 2:2); and, moreover, the confession of this article has greater difficulty, for, as he says in the same letter (1 Cor 1:23), *but we preach Christ crucified, a scandal to Jews and a foolishness to gentiles*; and this is why it is said, *I seal you with the sign of the holy Cross*, so that one may not be embarrassed by the name of the Cross, but confess it publicly. Second is included the sacramental act itself, with its own matter and effect, so that in this way may be touched upon both what the sacrament is alone, in saying, *with chrism*, and what the reality-and-sacrament[36] is, in saying, *I confirm you*, that is, 'I present you with a sacrament of strengthening'; as well as the reality that is not symbolized, by saying, *of salvation*. But the principal agent cause, from which the sacrament has its effect, is touched upon in saying: *in the name of the Father and of the Son and of the Holy Spirit.*

REPLY OBJ. 1: Baptism is a sacrament of necessity; and so the intention of the one baptizing needs to be more protected for the sake of the sacrament's act. Or it could be said that anyone can baptize, but only someone in the highest level of the Church can confirm, and it is presumed of him that he may fail less in the administering of the sacrament; and thus not so much protection of the intention is required in the words applied in the form.

REPLY OBJ. 2: The seal that is included in the form does not pertain to the sealing of a character, but to the seal of the Cross, which is made on the forehead with an anointing of chrism because of the confession of faith in the Cross. And no stamp is done like this in baptism, because the one baptized is not consecrated to anything specific, but to the spiritual life generally. However, a seal conveys a certain conscription, or something specific, which is there in the sacrament of confirmation.

REPLY OBJ. 3: Someone who is baptized is configured to the Passion of Christ by his faith, which he should have in his heart; and therefore no external seal of the cross is required, but the interior seal that exists through the character, that is, the conformity to the Passion of Christ by being buried with him in water are enough. But confirmation is the sacrament of confessing the Passion of Christ, just as baptism is the sacrament of faith; and therefore the sign of the Cross is imprinted in the sight of all and expressed in the form.

---

36. For more about the sacrament alone, reality alone, and sacrament-and-reality, see the footnote at Dist.1, q.1, a.4, qa. 1, main response.
37. *et.—scilicet* PLE.

AD QUARTUM dicendum quod in ipso actu baptizationis intelligitur determinata materia baptismi: non autem materia confirmationis intelligitur in ipso actu confirmandi; et ideo oportet quod materia addatur.

AD QUINTUM dicendum, quod in actu ablutionis magis expresse significatur res sacramenti in baptismo quam in linitione chrismatis; et ideo non[38] oportet quod addatur effectus salutis ad majorem expressionem.

REPLY OBJ. 4: In the very act of baptizing, the determinate matter of baptism is understood; but the matter of confirmation is not understood in the very act of confirming, and hence the matter must be added in the form.

REPLY OBJ. 5: The reality behind the sacrament is more expressly represented in the act of washing in baptism than in the anointing with chrism, and this is why the effect of salvation needs to be added for greater expression.

Response to Quaestiuncula 3

AD TERTIAM QUAESTIONEM dicendum, quod formae sacramentorum sunt ad perficiendum sacramenta; unde Dionysius vocat eas *consummativas invocationes*, ut dictum est; et ideo in illo sacramento quod totum consistit in illa re sensibili sanctificata, et non in usu illius rei, forma sacramenti dicitur illud quo materia sanctificatur, non autem illa verba quae in materiae usu proferuntur, sicut patet in Eucharistia. In illis autem sacramentis quae perficiuntur in usu materiae, sicut baptismus in ipsa tinctione vel ablutione, forma sacramenti est quae dicitur in usu materiae, non quae dicitur in sanctificatione materiae, quia illa sacramentale quoddam est. Et ideo cum sacramentum confirmationis, ut dictum est, perficiatur in usu materiae, constat quod illa verba quae dicit episcopus confirmans, sunt forma sacramenti, et habent efficaciam sicut et aliae formae sacramentorum.

AD PRIMUM ergo dicendum, quod duplex est sanctificatio sacramenti, ut dictum est. Ex prima ergo sanctificatione quae fit in benedictione materiae, non habet ut actu conferat gratiam, sed ex secunda.

AD SECUNDUM dicendum quod aliter est in sacramento Eucharistiae quam in aliis sacramentis: quia ibi totum sacramentum consistit in ipsa hostia consecrata, eo quod ibi Christus realiter continetur, et non virtute tantum, sicut in aliis sacramentis; et ideo forma sacramenti illius est verba prolata in sanctificatione hostiae.

TO THE THIRD QUESTION, I answer that the forms of the sacraments are for completing the sacraments, which is why Dionysius calls them *consummative invocations*, as was said. And therefore in the sacrament that entirely consists in a sanctified sensible thing, and not in the use of the thing, the sacrament's form is said to be the words by which the matter is sanctified, but not those words that are uttered at the use of the matter, as is seen in the Eucharist. But in those sacraments that are completed in the matter's use, like baptism is in the very immersion or washing, the sacrament's form is what is said at the matter's use, not what is said in the matter's sanctification, because that is just a sacramental. And so since the sacrament of confirmation, as was said, is completed in the use of the matter, it is clear that those words that the bishop says when he confirms are the form of the sacrament, and they have efficacy just like the other forms of sacraments.

REPLY OBJ. 1: There are two kinds of sanctification in a sacrament, as has been said. Therefore, it does not have the capacity to confer actual grace from the first kind of sanctification, which happens in blessing the matter, but only from the second kind.

REPLY OBJ. 2: It is different in the sacrament of the Eucharist than in the other sacraments, for there the whole sacrament consists in the consecrated host itself, by the fact that Christ is contained there in reality, and not only in power as in all the other sacraments; and thus the form of that sacrament is the words uttered in the sanctification of the host.

---

38. *ideo non oportet.—ideo oportet* PLE.

QUESTION 2

THE EFFECTS OF CONFIRMATION

Deinde quaeritur de effectu confirmationis; et circa hoc quaeruntur duo:

primo, de effectu qui est res et sacramentum, scilicet character;

secundo, de effectu qui est res tantum, scilicet gratia.

Next, inquiry is made about the effect of confirmation; and concerning this, two questions arise:

first, about the effect that is reality-and-sacrament, namely, the character;

second, about the effect that is reality alone, namely, grace.

ARTICLE 1

About the effect that is reality-and-sacrament, namely, the character

Quaestiuncula 1

AD PRIMUM SIC PROCEDITUR. Videtur quod in confirmatione character non imprimatur. Character enim, ut supra, dist. 4, quaest. 1 art. 1 in corp., dictum est, est signum distinctivum. Sed pugna spiritualis omnibus indicitur. Cum ergo confirmationis sacramentum detur ad roborandum in pugna spirituali, videtur quod in ipsa non fiat aliqua distinctio alicujus ab altero per impressionem characteris.

PRAETEREA, in veteri lege erat necessaria pugna spiritualis, sicut et in nova. Sed in lege veteri non erat aliquod sacramentum characterem imprimens, ut supra dictum est. Ergo nec confirmatio characterem imprimit.

PRAETEREA, supra dictum est, quod character est spiritualis potestas. Sed potestas spiritualis passiva, scilicet participandi sacramenta alia, sufficienter traditur in baptismo; potestas autem activa, scilicet dispensandi sacramenta, ad ordinem pertinet. Cum ergo confirmatus non constituatur in gradu alicujus ordinis vel dignitatis, videtur quod in confirmatione character non imprimatur.

SED CONTRA, character est signum conformans nos Trinitati. Sed sicut oportet nos conformari in sapientia et potentia, ita et in bonitate. Cum ergo in baptismo imprimatur character fidei, conformans nos divinae sapientiae, et in ordine character potestatis, conformans nos divinae potentiae; videtur quod in confirmatione im-

OBJ. 1: To the first we proceed thus. It seems that in confirmation a character is not imprinted.[39] For a character is a distinctive sign, as was said above in Distinction 4, Question 1, Article 1. But spiritual battle is appointed for everyone. Therefore, since the sacrament of confirmation is given to fortify for the spiritual battle, it seems that no distinction of one person from another should be made in it by the impression of the character.

OBJ. 2: Furthermore, in the Old Law, spiritual battle was necessary, just as in the New Law. But in the Old Law there was no sacrament imprinting a character, as was said above. Therefore, neither does confirmation imprint a character.

OBJ. 3: Furthermore, it was said above that a character is a spiritual power. But a passive spiritual power, namely, for partaking of the other sacraments, is sufficiently granted in baptism; however, active power, namely, for dispensing sacraments, pertains to holy orders. Since therefore someone who has been confirmed is not constituted in any degree of holy orders or dignity, it seems that in confirmation a character is not imprinted.

ON THE CONTRARY, a character is a sign conforming us to the Trinity. But just as we must be conformed in wisdom and power, so also in goodness. Since therefore in baptism a character of faith is imprinted conforming us to divine wisdom, and in holy orders a character of power, conforming us to divine power, it seems that in confirmation a charac-

---

39. Parallels: below, d. 3, a. 3, qa. 3; *ST* III, q. 63, a. 6; q. 72, a. 5.

primatur character plenitudinis Spiritus Sancti, conformans nos divinae bonitati.

PRAETEREA, per characterem quasi ascribimur ad familiam Jesu Christi. Sed Christus sicut est pater noster et sacerdos, ita est et rex noster. Cum ergo per characterem baptismalem ascribamur ei quasi patri filii regenerati per baptismum, et per characterem ordinis quasi ministri sacerdoti summo, videtur quod simili ratione in confirmatione debeat imprimi character, quo conformemur ei quasi minister[40] regi.

ter of the fullness of the Holy Spirit is imprinted, conforming us to divine goodness.

FURTHERMORE, by the character it is as if we were enrolled in the family of Jesus Christ. But just as Christ is our father and priest, so also he is our king. Since therefore by the baptismal character we are ascribed to him like regenerated sons to a father in baptism, and by the character of holy orders like ministers to the high priest, it seems that by the same argument in confirmation a character should be imprinted by which we may be conformed to him like soldiers to a king.

Quaestiuncula 2

ULTERIUS. Videtur quod idem sit character confirmationis per essentiam, et baptismi. Quia ad eamdem formam seu speciem non potest esse nisi una assimilatio. Sed in Trinitate, ut Hilarius dicit, est species indifferens. Ergo cum character sit signum assimilans Trinitati, videtur quod character confirmationis non possit esse alius a charactere baptismi.

PRAETEREA, in corporibus[42] ita est quod duo characteres non possunt esse in eadem parte. Sed characteris subjectum est universaliter una pars animae, ut supra dictum est. Ergo post primum characterem non potest alius character superaddi.

PRAETEREA, ad ea quae se necessario consequuntur, aliquis eodem charactere ascribitur; sicut idem character est in sacerdote ad conficiendum et ad absolvendum. Sed confessio fidei, cujus sacramentum est confirmatio, consequitur de necessitate ad fidem, cujus sacramentum est baptismus; quia *corde creditur ad justitiam, ore confessio fit ad salutem*; Rom. 10, 10. Ergo idem character est in baptismo et in confirmatione.

SED CONTRA, character est proprius effectus sacramenti et immediatus. Sed diversarum causarum proprii effectus sunt diversi. Cum ergo baptismus et confirmatio sint diversa sacramenta, et characteres impressi erunt diversi.

PRAETEREA, ideo baptismus iterari non potest, quia character est indelebilis. Si ergo idem esset character baptismi et confirmationis, post baptismum confirmatio non adderetur.

OBJ. 1: Moreover, it seems that confirmation's character is the same in essence as baptism's. For things cannot be assimilated to the same form or species without being one. But in the Trinity, as Hilary says, there is an undiffering species.[41] Therefore, since a character is a sign assimilating us to the Trinity, it seems that the character of confirmation cannot be different from the character of baptism.

OBJ. 2: Furthermore, among physical things it is the case that two characters cannot exist in the same part. But the subject of a character is always the same part of the soul, as was said. Therefore, after the first character another character cannot be superadded.

OBJ. 3: Furthermore, for those things that necessarily follow, someone is ascribed with the same character, just as the same character exists in a priest for confessing and absolving. But the confession of faith, whose sacrament is confirmation, necessarily follows from faith, whose sacrament is baptism; because *one believes with the heart unto justice, and with the mouth confession is made unto salvation* (Rom 10:10). Therefore, it is the same character in baptism and confirmation.

ON THE CONTRARY, a character is the proper and direct effect of a sacrament. But the proper effects of different causes are different. Since therefore baptism and confirmation are different sacraments, the characters they impress are also different.

FURTHERMORE, baptism cannot be received again for this reason, that the character is indelible. If therefore the character were the same for baptism and confirmation, then confirmation would not be added after baptism.

---

40. *minister.—milites* PLE.
41. Hilary, *De Synodis*, n. 13 (PL 10:490).
42. *corporibus.—corporalibus* PLE.

Quaestiuncula 3

ULTERIUS. Videtur quod character confirmationis non praesupponat characterem baptismalem. Character enim confirmationis ad hoc datur quod homo fortiter Christum confiteatur. Sed aliqui ante baptismum fortiter Christum confessi sunt, ad martyrii palmam pervenientes. Ergo ante baptismum potest aliquis accipere characterem confirmationis.

PRAETEREA, character confirmationis est sacramentum et res. Sed homo etiam non baptizatus potest percipere id quod est sacramentum et res in Eucharistia, scilicet Corpus Domini verum; quamvis rem sacramenti non consequatur, inordinate accipiens; nisi forte credat se baptizatum. Ergo et similiter characterem confirmationis consequi potest non baptizatus.

PRAETEREA, sicut baptismus naturaliter praecedit confirmationem, ita unus ordo naturaliter praecedit alium. Si autem aliquis accipit ordinis consequentis characterem qui non accepit characterem praecedentis, tamen non reordinatur, sed quod defuerat suppletur. Ergo et characterem confirmationis potest homo accipere sine charactere baptismali.

SED CONTRA est quod Dionysius dicit, quod nihil divinitus traditarum operari potest qui non est regeneratus per baptismum. Sed character confirmationis est hujusmodi; ergo non potest aliquis characterem confirmationis percipere qui non est baptizatus.

Praeterea, baptismus dicitur esse principium spiritualis vitae, secundum Dionysium, et Damascenum. Sed remoto principio aufertur quod est post principium. Ergo qui non est baptizatus, non potest characterem confirmationis accipere.

OBJ. 1: Moreover, it seems that the character of confirmation does not presuppose the baptismal character.[43] For the character of confirmation is given so that a person may bravely confess Christ. But some people bravely confessed Christ before baptism, attaining the palm of martyrdom. Therefore, before baptism someone can receive the character of confirmation.

OBJ. 2: Furthermore, the character is the sacrament-and-reality of confirmation. But even a non-baptized person can receive what is the sacrament-and-reality in the Eucharist, namely, the true Body of the Lord; although receiving it out of order, he would not obtain the reality behind the sacrament, unless perhaps he believed he had been baptized. Therefore, in the same way a non-baptized person can obtain the character of confirmation.[44]

OBJ. 3: Furthermore, just as baptism naturally precedes confirmation, so also one degree of holy orders naturally precedes another. But if someone receives the character attendant on holy orders who has not received the character of the previous degree of holy orders, he still is not re-ordained, but what was lacking is supplied. Therefore, a person can also receive the character of confirmation without the baptismal character.

ON THE CONTRARY, Dionysius says[45] that someone who is not regenerated by baptism can work nothing of those things divinely handed down. But the character of confirmation is this kind of thing; therefore no one can receive the character of confirmation who is not baptized.

FURTHERMORE, baptism is said to be the principle of the spiritual life, according to Dionysius[46] and Damascene.[47] But when the principle is removed, whatever is after the principle is removed. Therefore, whoever is not baptized cannot receive the character of confirmation.

Response to Quaestiuncula 1

RESPONDEO dicendum ad primam quaestionem, quod character est distinctivum signum, quo quis ab aliis distinguitur ad aliquid spirituale deputatus. Sed ad spirituale potest aliquis tripliciter deputari. Uno modo ut aliquis in se spiritualia participet; et ad hoc quis deputatur in baptismo, quia jam baptizatus potest esse particeps omnis spiritualis receptionis; unde character baptismalis, ut supra dictum est, est quasi quaedam spiritualis potentia passiva. Alio modo ut spiritualia quis

TO THE FIRST QUESTION, I answer that a character is a distinctive sign by which someone is distinguished from others and deputed for something spiritual. But someone can be deputed for something spiritual in three ways. In one way, so that the person in himself takes part in spiritual things; and for this a person is deputed in baptism, for once baptized he can be partaker of every spiritual thing that can be received; hence the baptismal character, as was said above, is something like a passive spiritual power. In

---

43. Parallel: *ST* III, q. 72, a. 6.
44. For more about the sacrament alone, reality alone, and sacrament-and-reality, see the footnote at Dist.1, q.1, a.4, qa. 1, main response.
45. Pseudo-Dionysius, *Ecclesiastical Hierarchy*, ch. 2, p. 1 (PG 3:391).
46. Ibid.
47. John Damascene, *On the Orthodox Faith*, Bk. 4, ch. 9 (PG 94:1122).

in notitiam ducat per eorum[48] fortem confessionem; et ad hoc quis deputatur in confirmatione; unde etiam tempore persecutionis eligebantur aliqui qui deberent in loco persecutionis remanere ad publice nomen Christi confitendum, aliis occulte credentibus, sicut patet in legenda beati Sebastiani. Tertio modo ut etiam spiritualia credentibus tradat; et ad hoc deputatur aliquis per sacramentum ordinis. Et ideo sicut in baptismo confertur character et in ordine, ita et in confirmatione.

Ad primum ergo dicendum, quod pugna spiritualis qua quis pugnat contra impedientes salutem sui ipsius, omnibus indicitur; sed ad hoc non datur sacramentum confirmationis, sed ad persistendum fortiter in pugna qua quis nomen Christi impugnat, et ut invictus confessor Christi permaneat; et huic pugnae non omnes exponuntur, sed solum confirmati.

Ad secundum dicendum quod in veteri lege non erat tempus *per stultitiam praedicationis* propagandi cultum Dei, sed magis per generationem carnalem; et ideo tunc talis pugna de confessione fidei non multum erat necessaria. Nihilominus tamen erat distinctio hujus characteris in veteri lege figurata, sicut et aliorum. In distinctione enim filiorum Israel ab Aegyptiis, significabatur character baptismalis; in distinctione timidorum a fortibus in bellis, character confirmationis; in distinctione Levitarum a fratribus suis, character ordinis.

Ad tertium dicendum, quod potestas characteris hujus est potestas activa, non ad conferendum spiritualia, quod est ordinis, sed magis ad confitendum publice; et ideo confirmatus non constituitur in gradu alicujus ordinis, quia nullus ei subjicitur in receptione divinorum ab ipso.

another way, so that the person brings spiritual things into notice by his brave confession of Christ; and this is what a person is commissioned for in confirmation. This is also why certain people were chosen in the time of persecution who had to remain in the place of persecution to confess Christ's name publicly, while others were secret believers, as is seen in the legend of Saint Sebastian.[49] In the third way, so that a person may also hand on spiritual things to believers; and someone is deputed for this by the sacrament of holy orders. And thus just as a character is conferred in baptism and holy orders, so also in confirmation.

Reply Obj. 1: The spiritual battle in which someone fights against those hindering his own salvation is appointed for everyone; but the sacrament of confirmation is not given for this, but for persisting bravely in the battle in which someone attacks the name of Christ, and so that he may remain an unconquered confessor of Christ; and not everyone is exposed to this battle, but only the confirmed.

Reply Obj. 2: Under the Old Law it was not the time for spreading the worship of God by *foolishness of preaching*, but rather by physical generation; and therefore at that time such a battle concerning the confession of the faith was not much necessary. Nevertheless, there was still a distinguishing of this kind of character figured in the Old Law, along with the others. For in the distinguishing of the sons of Israel from the Egyptians, the baptismal character was signified; in the distinguishing of the timid from the brave in war, the character of confirmation; and in the distinguishing of the Levites from their brethren, the character of holy orders.

Reply Obj. 3: The power of this character is an active power, not for conferring spiritual things, which belongs to holy orders, but rather for confessing in public; and therefore, one who has been confirmed is not constituted in any degree of holy orders, because no one is subject to him in receiving divine things from him.

Response to Quaestiuncula 2

Ad secundam quaestionem dicendum, quod quaelibet potentia de sui ratione importat ordinem ad aliquid; et ideo oportet potentiam proportionatam esse actui ad quem est: quia proprius actus non fit nisi in propria materia, secundum Philosophum in 2 *de Anima*; et ideo oportet quod potentiae distinguantur per distinctionem actuum ad quos ordinantur, sive sint potentiae activae, sive passivae; et quia character, ut supra dictum est, dist. 4, quaest. 1, art. 1, in corp., est potentia spiritualis, ideo cum character baptismalis non ad idem ordine-

To the second question, it should be said that any power, by its very nature, carries an ordering to something; and therefore all power must be proportionate to the act it produces, since its proper act will not happen except in the proper matter, according to the Philosopher in Book 2 of *On the Soul*.[50] Therefore powers must be distinguished by the distinction of the acts they are ordered to, whether they are active powers or passive powers; and as was said above in Distinction 4, Question 1, Article 1, since a character is a spiritual power, and since the baptismal character is not

---

48. *eorum.—Christi* PLE.
49. See the account of St. Sebastian in Jacobus de Voragine, *The Golden Legend*, trans. William Granger Ryan (Princeton, NJ: Princeton University Press, 1993), 97–101.
50. Aristotle, *On the Soul*, Bk. 2, ch. 2, 414a11.

tur cum charactere confirmationis, ut ex dictis patet, planum est quod non est idem uterque character.

AD PRIMUM ergo dicendum, quod ad unam speciem seu formam, quam aliquid perfecte repraesentat, non potest esse nisi una assimilatio; et ideo patris non est nisi una perfecta imago, scilicet filius. Sed si non sit perfecta repraesentatio, tunc possunt esse diversae assimilationes ad unum simplex; et ideo diversae creaturae diversimode secundum suum modum divinam similitudinem habent; et propter hoc non est inconveniens, si sint diversi characteres in anima, Trinitati secundum diversa conformantes.

AD SECUNDUM dicendum, quod character corporalis attenditur secundum figuram, quae consistit in terminatione figurati. Et quia impossibile est esse diversas terminationes unius rei, ideo impossibile est ut idem corpus secundum eamdem partem diversimode figuretur aut characterizetur. Sed character spiritualis attenditur secundum aliquam spiritualem proprietatem. Non est autem inconveniens diversas proprietates non oppositas eisdem inesse secundum eamdem partem; et ideo in eadem parte animae plures characteres esse possunt.

AD TERTIUM dicendum, quod quamvis cujuslibet baptizati et credentis sit confiteri, quando confessio ab eo expectatur; non tamen est cujuslibet se libere exponere, sed tantum confirmati. Et hoc etiam patet in apostolis, in quibus hoc sacramentum initium sumpsit: quia ante adventum Spiritus Sancti confirmantis eos erant clausae fores coenaculi propter metum Judaeorum; postea repleti Spiritu Sancto coeperunt loqui cum fiducia et publice verbum Dei, ut patet in actibus.

ordered to the same thing as the character of confirmation, as is clear from what has been said, it is plain that the two characters are not the same.

REPLY OBJ. 1: There can only be one assimilation to one species or form that something perfectly represents; which is why there is only one perfect image of the Father, namely the Son. But if it is not a perfect representation, then there can be various assimilations to one single thing; and for this reason different creatures have divine likeness in different ways, each according to its own mode. And because of this it is not unfitting if there are different characters in the soul, conforming to the Trinity in various ways.

REPLY OBJ. 2: Bodily character is found according to figure, which consists in the boundaries of the figure. And since it is impossible for there to be different boundaries to one thing, it is therefore impossible for the same body to have different figures or characters in the same part. But a spiritual character is found according to a certain spiritual property. Nor is it unfitting if there are different properties that are not opposed to each other in the same part of the same thing; and for this reason several characters can exist in the same part of the soul.

REPLY OBJ. 3: Although it belongs to anyone baptized and believing to confess when confession of the faith is required, nevertheless, it is not for just anyone to expose himself freely, but only for those who have been confirmed. And this is also evident in the apostles, among whom this sacrament took its beginning: for before the coming of the Holy Spirit to confirm them, they were locked in the Cenacle out of fear of the Jews; but afterward, filled with the Holy Spirit, they began to speak the word of God publicly and with confidence, as is seen in the Acts of the Apostles.[51]

Response to Quaestiuncula 3

AD TERTIAM QUAESTIONEM dicendum, quod nihil potest participare actionem aut proprietatem alicujus naturae nisi prius habeat subsistentiam in natura illa; unde cum per baptismum, qui est spiritualis regeneratio, homo acquirat subsistentiam in vita spirituali Christianae religionis, non potest non baptizatus aliquid eorum quae ad hanc spiritualem vitam pertinent, participare; et ideo non potest percipere confirmationis characterem; et hanc rationem Dionysius assignat in 2 cap. *Eccl. Hier.*

AD PRIMUM ergo dicendum, quod ad ea quae sunt necessitatis, homo admittitur, etiam si illud hoc non competat ei ex officio; sicut patet quod etiam non habens ordinem in casu necessitatis baptizare potest licite, quamvis hoc non competat sibi ex officio. Similiter

TO THE THIRD QUESTION, I answer that nothing can take part in an action or property of a certain nature unless it first has subsistence in that nature; hence, since a person acquires subsistence in the spiritual life of the Christian religion through baptism, which is a spiritual regeneration, a non-baptized person cannot partake in anything that pertains to this spiritual life; and for this reason he cannot receive the character of confirmation, and Dionysius assigns this reason in Chapter 2 of the *Ecclesiastical Hierarchy.*[52]

REPLY OBJ. 1: For those things that are necessary, a man is admitted even if it does not pertain to him by office, as is evident from the fact that someone without holy orders can licitly baptize in case of emergency, although this does not belong to him by office. Similarly since confessing the

---

51. Namely, in Chapters 1 and 2.
52. Pseudo-Dionysius, *Ecclesiastical Hierarchy*, ch. 2, p. 1 (PG 3:391).

etiam quia confiteri nomen Christi, ubi confessio exquiritur, est necessitatis, ideo etiam non baptizatis hoc competit, quamvis hoc non habeant ex officio characteris in sacramento confirmationis suscepti.

AD SECUNDUM dicendum, quod in sacramento Eucharistiae illud quod est res et sacramentum, est extra suscipientem; et ideo indispositio illius non impedit quin sit illud quod est res et sacramentum, scilicet corpus Christi verum. Sed hoc quod est res et sacramentum in confirmatione est aliqua forma in suscipiente recepta; et ideo indispositio recipientis impedit impressionem characteris.

AD TERTIUM dicendum, quod ordo potentiae passivae ad activam est ordo necessitatis: quia qui non habet potentiam passivam ad aliquid recipiendum, nihil recipit nisi miraculose: sed ordo potentiae inferioris activae ad superiorem est tantum ordo congruitatis; et ideo carens baptismali charactere, qui est potentia passiva recipiendi spiritualia, nihil potest recipere de aliis spiritualibus; carens autem charactere inferioris ordinis, qui est potentia activa, potest recipere characterem superioris ordinis.

name of Christ, when confession is expected, is also necessary, for this reason it also belongs to the non-baptized, although they do not have this from the office bestowed by the character in the sacrament of confirmation.

REPLY OBJ. 2: In the sacrament of the Eucharist, what is reality-and-sacrament is outside the one receiving it; and thus that person's indisposition does not impede it from being reality-and-sacrament, in this case, the true Body of Christ. But what is reality-and-sacrament in confirmation is a certain form taken in by the person receiving it; and for this reason an indisposition of the recipient does impede the imprint of a character.[53]

REPLY OBJ. 3: The order of a passive power to an active one is an order of necessity: for whoever does not have the passive power to receive something will receive nothing, except miraculously. But the order of an inferior active power to a superior one is only the order of congruity, and for this reason anyone lacking a baptismal character, which is the passive power of receiving spiritual things, can receive nothing of anything spiritual; but someone lacking the character of lower holy orders, which is an active power, can receive the character of higher orders.

---

53. For more about the sacrament alone, reality alone, and sacrament-and-reality, see the footnote at Dist.1, q.1, a.4, qa. 1, main response.

ARTICLE 2

About the effect that is reality alone, namely, grace[54]

Quaestiuncula 1

AD SECUNDUM SIC PROCEDITUR. Videtur quod gratia gratum faciens, in confirmatione non conferatur. Gratia enim gratum faciens ordinatur contra culpam, et non contra poenam. Sed confirmatio ordinatur contra poenam, et non contra culpam; quia ille qui confirmatur jam non est impius, per baptismum justificatus. Ergo non recipit gratiam gratum facientem.

PRAETEREA, baptismus non habet minus ordinem ad gratiam gratum facientem quam confirmatio. Sed ille qui prius habuit gratiam, per baptismum non accipit gratiam gratum facientem. Ergo cum confirmatus jam habeat gratiam quam in baptismo suscepit, sicut patet in pueris, videtur quod in confirmatione gratia gratum faciens non conferatur.

PRAETEREA, ad id quod potest fieri in mortali peccato non requiritur gratia gratum faciens. Sed aliqui in peccato mortali existentes possunt fortiter nomen Christi confiteri. Ergo cum confirmatio sit sacramentum confessionis Christi, videtur quod non detur ibi gratia gratum faciens.

SED CONTRA, sacramentum novae legis efficit quod figurat. Sed per unctionem chrismatis significatur unctio gratiae. Ergo in confirmatione gratia gratum faciens confertur.

PRAETEREA, in littera dicitur, quod ibi datur Spiritus Sanctus. Sed in primo libro, dist. 16, qu. 1, art. 2, dictum est, quod missio Spiritus Sancti non est sine gratia gratum faciente. Ergo in confirmatione datur gratia gratum faciens.

OBJ. 1: To the second question we proceed thus. It seems that sanctifying grace[55] is not conferred in confirmation. For sanctifying grace is directed against guilt, and not against punishment. But confirmation is directed against punishment, and not against guilt, for someone who is confirmed is no longer wicked, since he was justified by baptism. Therefore, he does not receive sanctifying grace.

OBJ. 2: Furthermore, baptism does not have less order to sanctifying grace than confirmation. But someone who had grace before does not receive sanctifying grace through baptism. Therefore, since the confirmed person already has the grace that he received in baptism, as we see among children, it seems that in confirmation sanctifying grace is not conferred.

OBJ. 3: Furthermore, anything that can be done while in mortal sin does not require sanctifying grace. But someone sunk in mortal sin is able to bravely confess the name of Christ. Therefore, since confirmation is the sacrament of confessing Christ, it seems that sanctifying grace is not given in it.

ON THE CONTRARY, a sacrament of the New Law brings about what it represents. But by the anointing with chrism the unction of grace is represented. Therefore, sanctifying grace is conferred in confirmation.

FURTHERMORE, the text says that the Holy Spirit is given in confirmation. But in Book I, Distinction 16, Question 1, Article 2, it was said that the sending of the Holy Spirit is not without sanctifying grace. Therefore, in confirmation sanctifying grace is given.

Quaestiuncula 2

ULTERIUS. Videtur, quod sit eadem cum gratia baptismali. Duo enim accidentia ejusdem speciei non possunt esse in eodem simplici et indivisibili. Sed subjectum gratiae gratum facientis est essentia animae, quae est una et simplex. Ergo in ea non possunt esse diversae gratiae; et ideo cum gratia baptismalis sit ibi, gratia in confirmatione data erit penitus idem.

PRAETEREA, eadem est gratia quae est in virtutibus et donis. Sed per baptismum confertur gratia cum om-

OBJ. 1: Moreover, it seems that it is the same as baptismal grace. For two accidents of the same species cannot be in the same simple and indivisible thing. But the subject of sanctifying grace is the essence of the soul, which is one and simple. Therefore, in those things there cannot be different graces; and so since baptismal grace is there, the grace given in confirmation will be fundamentally the same.

OBJ. 2: Furthermore, it is the same grace that is in the virtues and gifts. But in baptism grace is conferred with all

---

54. Parallel: *ST* III, q. 72, a. 7.
55. Literally, "grace that makes pleasing."

nibus virtutibus, ut supra dictum est, dist. 1, qu. 1, art. 4, quaestiunc. 5; in confirmatione autem datur gratia cum septiformi plenitudine Spiritus Sancti, ut in littera dicitur, quod ad septem dona pertinet. Ergo eadem est gratia quae datur in confirmatione et in baptismo.

PRAETEREA, major est distinctio virtutum quam gratiae. Sed ad eamdem virtutem pertinet credere et confiteri, scilicet ad fidem. Ergo multo fortius pertinet ad eamdem gratiam; ergo gratia baptismalis quae perficit ad credendum et gratia confirmationis quae perficit ad confitendum, est eadem gratia.

SED CONTRA, causae diversae inducunt diversos effectus. Sed aliud est sacramentum exterius in baptismo quam in confirmatione, et alius character interior, ut dictum est, quae sunt causa gratiae. Ergo et alia est gratia utrobique.

PRAETEREA, contra diversos morbos datur diversa medicina. Sed contra alium morbum ordinatur confirmatio et baptismus, ut supra, dist. 2, qu. 1, art. 1 in corp., dictum est. Ergo alia est gratia quae in medicinam morbi in sacramento utroque datur.

virtues, as was said above, Distinction 1, Question 1, Article 4, Subquestion 5. But in confirmation grace is given with the sevenfold fullness of the Holy Spirit, as it says in the text that it pertains to the seven gifts. Therefore, the grace that is given in confirmation is the same as that given in baptism.

OBJ. 3: Furthermore, there is greater distinction among the virtues than among graces. But it pertains to the same virtue to believe and to confess, namely, to faith. Therefore, much more does it pertain to the same grace; therefore the baptismal grace that perfects for believing and the grace of confirmation that perfects for confessing are the same grace.

ON THE CONTRARY, diverse causes bring about diverse effects. But the external sacrament is different in baptism than in confirmation, and the interior character is different, as has been said, and these are the causes of grace. Therefore, the grace in each is also different.

FURTHERMORE, against different ailments different medicines are given. But confirmation is directed against another ailment than baptism, as was said above in Distinction 2, Question 1, Article 1. Therefore, the grace that is given in each sacrament as medicine for its ailment is also different.

Quaestiuncula 3

ULTERIUS. Videtur quod gratia confirmationis non perficiat gratiam baptismalem. Omnis enim perfectio quae confirmationi ascribitur, ad dona vel virtutes pertinet; sicut fortiter confiteri, et persistere, quod est fortitudinis virtutis vel doni. Sed in baptismo, ubi confertur gratia, conferuntur et virtutes et dona, quae in gratia connexionem habent, ut dictum est supra. Ergo gratia confirmationis non perficit gratiam baptismalem.

PRAETEREA, ex eodem habitus operatur[57] et perficitur, ut dicitur in 2 Ethic. Sed gratia baptismalis per baptismum acquiritur. Ergo non perficitur per confirmationem.

PRAETEREA, in augmento fit idem ex eo quod auget et quod augetur. Sed gratia baptismalis differt a gratia confirmationis. Ergo gratia confirmationis non perficit gratiam baptismalem.

SED CONTRA, secundum Dionysium, baptismus est illuminatio, chrisma autem perfectio. Sed perfectio consummat illuminationem sicut illuminatio purgationem. Ergo confirmatio chrismatis consummat gratiam baptismalem.

OBJ. 1: Moreover, it seems that the grace of confirmation does not complete baptismal grace. For every perfection that is ascribed to confirmation pertains to the gifts or virtues, as bravely confessing and persevering belong to the virtue or gift of fortitude. But in baptism, where grace is conferred, both the virtues and the gifts are conferred, which are bound together with grace, as was said above.[56] Therefore, the grace of confirmation does not perfect baptismal grace.

OBJ. 2: Furthermore, a habit is generated and is completed by the same thing, as is said in Ethics 2.[58] But baptismal grace is acquired by baptism. Therefore, it is not completed by confirmation.

OBJ. 3: Furthermore, when a thing is increased, what is increased and what increases it become the same. But baptismal grace differs from the grace of confirmation. Therefore, the grace of confirmation does not complete baptismal grace.

ON THE CONTRARY, according to Dionysius, baptism is an illuminating, but chrism is a perfecting.[59] But perfection brings illumination to its fullness just as illumination does for purification. Therefore, confirmation with chrism brings baptismal grace to its fullness.

---

56. Different editions give different references. The two most pertinent texts are Bk. 3, d. 36, a. 3, and Bk. 4, d. 1, q. 1, a. 4, qa. 5.
57. *operatur.—generatur* PLE.
58. Aristotle, *Nicomachean Ethics*, Bk. 2, ch. 1, 1103b7.
59. Pseudo-Dionysius, *Ecclesiastical Hierarchy*, ch. 5, p. 1, n. 3 (PG 3:503).

Praeterea, in omnibus perfectionibus ordinatis ad invicem ita est quod secunda perficit primam. Sed confirmationis gratia superadditur ad gratiam baptismalem. Ergo gratia confirmationis perficit gratiam baptismalem.

Furthermore, in all perfectings ordered to each other it is such that the second one perfects the first. But the grace of confirmation is superadded to baptismal grace. Therefore, the grace of confirmation perfects baptismal grace.

Response to Quaestiuncula 1

Respondeo dicendum ad primam quaestionem, quod in quolibet sacramento est aliqua sanctificatio. Sed quaedam est sanctificatio in sacramento quae est communis omnibus sacramentis, scilicet emundatio a peccato vel a reliquiis peccati; et quaedam sanctificatio quae est specialis quibusdam sacramentis imprimentibus characterem, scilicet deputatio ad aliquid sacrum. Utraque autem sanctificatio gratiam gratum facientem requirit: quia illud quod directe contrariatur peccato, est gratia; contraria autem contrariis curantur. Unde idem remedium adhiberi non potest contra peccatum et sequelas ejus, nisi per gratiam gratum facientem. Et ideo in omni sacramento novae legis gratia gratum faciens confertur, ut dictum est supra, dist. 2, qu. 1, art. 1, quaestiunc. 1 et 2. Similiter autem accessus ad sacra non est licitus immundis, nec aliquis ab immunditia liberari potest nisi per gratiam, nec effici idoneus ad sacra administranda vel percipienda; et ideo oportet quod in sacramentis quae characterem imprimunt, gratia gratum faciens imprimatur. Cum ergo confirmatio sit sacramentum novae legis characterem imprimens, ex duplici parte necessarium est quod gratiam gratum facientem conferat.

Ad primum ergo dicendum, quod confirmatio ordinatur contra poenam quae est ex culpa causata, et ad culpam inclinans; et ideo ex consequenti habet repugnantiam ad gratiam; et propter hoc contra ipsam oportet quod gratia gratum faciens detur; et ideo si invenit aliquam culpam quae fictum non faciat, delet illam, sicut patet de culpa veniali; quamvis non principaliter contra culpam ordinetur.

Ad secundum dicendum quod baptismus est sacramentum necessitatis; et ideo gratia quae confertur in baptismo, ordinatur in communem statum salutis, et non in aliquem specialem effectum; et propter hoc per baptismum ei qui habuit gratiam gratum facientem, non additur alia gratia nova, sed illa quae prius inerat, augetur. Secus autem est de confirmatione, quae non est sacramentum necessitatis; unde ejus gratia ad aliquem specialem effectum ordinatur; et propter hoc gratia confirmationis potest addi ad gratiam quae perficit in communi statu vitae.

Ad tertium dicendum, quod quamvis aliquis possit constanter, etiam si sit in mortali peccato, fidem Christi confiteri, non tamen est idonea illa confessio, quia *non est speciosa laus in ore peccatoris*, Eccli. 15, 9, nec iterum

To the first question, I answer that in any sacrament there is a certain sanctification. But there is one sanctification in a sacrament that is common to all sacraments, namely cleansing from sin or the remnants of sin; and there is another sanctification that is specific to those sacraments that imprint a character, namely a delegating to something sacred. But either sanctification requires 'the grace that makes one pleasing', because what is directly opposed to sin is grace, while contrary things cure their opposites. Hence the same remedy cannot be applied against sin and its secondary infections, except by sanctifying grace. And thus in every sacrament of the New Law, sanctifying grace is conferred, as was said above, in Distinction 2, Question 1, Article 1, Subquestions 1 and 2. But in the same way, approaching sacred things is not permitted to the unclean, nor can anyone be freed from uncleanness, nor be made worthy of administering or receiving the sacred things, except by grace. Therefore, it is necessary that in the sacraments that imprint a character sanctifying grace be imprinted. Since, therefore, confirmation is a sacrament of the New Law that imprints a character, it is necessary that it confer sanctifying grace for both reasons.

Reply Obj. 1: Confirmation is ordered against the punishment that is caused by our sin and that inclines us to sin, and that is consequently opposed to grace; and for this reason sanctifying grace must be given against it. And this is why if it finds any sin that does not constitute a deception, it wipes it away, as we see in the case of venial sin, although it is not chiefly directed against sin.

Reply Obj. 2: Baptism is a sacrament of necessity, and the grace that is conferred in baptism is ordered to the common state of salvation and not to any special effect; and because of this by baptism no other new grace is added to someone who had sanctifying grace, but the grace that was in him before is increased. However, it is different with confirmation, which is not a sacrament of necessity; hence its grace is ordered to a specific effect, and because of this the grace of confirmation can be added to the grace that perfects one in the common state of life.

Reply Obj. 3: Although someone could resolutely confess faith in Christ even if he were in mortal sin, it would nevertheless not be a worthy confession, for *praise is not seemly in the mouth of a sinner* (Sirach 15:9), nor again is it

est meritoria ad salutem. Sacramentum autem ordinatur non solum ad hoc quod aliquid fiat qualitercumque, sed ad hoc quod aliquid idonee fiat, nisi sit defectus ex parte recipientis sacramentum.

meritorious for his salvation. But the sacrament is ordered not only to doing this in any manner whatsoever, but to doing it in a worthy manner, unless there is a defect on the part of the one receiving the sacrament.

Response to Quaestiuncula 2

AD SECUNDAM QUAESTIONEM dicendum, quod, sicut supra dictum est, sacramentales gratiae ab invicem distinctae sunt secundum distinctionem eorum ad quae ordinantur, sicut et virtutes; quamvis earum distinctio non ita appareat sicut distinctio virtutum, quia earum effectus non sunt ita manifesti sicut effectus virtutum. Ita autem videmus in virtutibus moralibus; quia ubi est specialis difficultas, requiritur specialis virtus; unde alia est virtus quae dirigit in magnis sumptibus secundum magnificentiam, ab ea quae in communibus donis et sumptibus perficit, scilicet liberalitate. Et quia gratia baptismalis datur ad perficiendum in his quae pertinent ad communem statum vitae Christianae, gratia autem confirmationis ad perficiendum in his quae sunt difficillima in isto statu, scilicet confiteri nomen Christi contra persecutores; ideo speciali gratia ad hoc indigetur; et propter hoc alia est gratia confirmationis a gratia baptismi, et contra alium defectum datur. Gratia enim baptismi datur contra defectum qui impedit communem statum justitiae in vita Christiana, scilicet contra peccatum originale et actuale; gratia autem confirmationis contra defectum oppositum robori quod exigitur in confessoribus nominis Christi, scilicet infirmitati.

AD PRIMUM ergo dicendum, quod gratia confirmationis et baptismi non sunt ejusdem speciei, ut dictum est, et ideo nihil prohibet quod in eodem indivisibili sint. Vel dicendum, quod gratia baptismalis ex essentia animae derivatur in intellectum, quod est ad recte et perfecte credendum; sed gratia confirmationis respicit magis irascibilem, ad quam pertinet fortitudo et robur.

AD SECUNDUM dicendum, quod gratia sacramentalis, quae est principalis effectus sacramenti, quamvis habeat connexionem cum gratia quae est in virtutibus et donis, tamen est alia ab ea: quia gratia sacramentalis perficit removendo primo et principaliter defectum ex peccato consequentem; sed gratia virtutum et donorum perficit inclinando ad bonum virtutis et doni; sicut gratia confirmationis removendo infirmitatis morbum; fortitudinis autem donum vel virtus inclinando ad bonum quod est proprium virtuti vel dono. Et ideo quamvis in baptismo dentur virtutes et dona, et similiter in confirmatione, non oportet quod sit eadem gratia sacramentalis utrobique.

AD TERTIUM dicendum quod confiteri ubi ex confessione imminet mortis periculum, non est tantum fi-

TO THE SECOND QUESTION, it should be said that, just as was said above, sacramental graces are distinguished from each other according to what they are ordered toward, just like virtues, although their distinction is not as apparent as the distinction of virtues, for their effects are not so manifest as the effects of virtues. We see this in the moral virtues, for where there is a special difficulty, a special virtue is required; hence the virtue that directs a person in large expenses, that is, magnificence, is different from the one that perfects one in ordinary gifts and expenses, namely, liberality. And since baptismal grace is given for perfecting someone in those things that pertain to the common state of Christian life, but the grace of confirmation for perfecting in those things that are the most difficult in that state, namely, confessing the name of Christ against persecutors, a special grace is needed for this; and this is why the grace of confirmation is different from the grace of baptism, and is given against another defect. For the grace of baptism is given against the defect that impedes the common state of justice in Christian life, which is original and actual sin; but the grace of confirmation is given against the defect opposed to the firmness that is demanded in confessing the name of Christ, that is, against weakness.

REPLY OBJ. 1: The graces of confirmation and baptism are not of the same species, as was said, and that is why nothing prevents them from being in the same indivisible thing. Or it could be said that baptismal grace is drawn from the essence of the soul into the intellect, since it is for believing rightly and perfectly, but the grace of confirmation regards more the irascible appetite, to which belong fortitude and firm resolve.

REPLY OBJ. 2: Sacramental grace, which is the chief effect of the sacrament, although it may be bound together with the grace that is in the virtues and gifts, is nevertheless something different from it: for sacramental grace perfects first and chiefly by removing the defect resulting from sin; but the grace of the virtues and gifts perfects by inclining one toward the good of the virtue or gift, just as the grace of confirmation does by removing the ailment of weakness, but the gift or virtue of fortitude by inclining one to the good that is proper to the gift or virtue. And so although in baptism virtues and gifts are given, and likewise in confirmation, it is not necessary that the same sacramental grace be given in both.

REPLY OBJ. 3: To confess when there is an imminent danger of death from that confession is not only from faith

dei, sed indiget auxilio alterius virtutis, scilicet fortitudinis; et similiter etiam indiget alia gratia sacramentali, quae removeat effectum oppositum fortitudini.

but also requires the help of another virtue, which is fortitude; and likewise it also requires another sacramental grace, which takes away the effect of sin opposed to fortitude.

Response to Quaestiuncula 3

Ad tertiam quaestionem dicendum, quod, ut supra dictum est, dist. 1, quaest. 1, art. 4, quaestiunc. 5, sicut gratia gratum faciens, quae essentiam animae perficit, differt a virtutibus et donis quae ab ipsa fluunt, ita etiam differt a gratia quae est proprius effectus sacramentorum; tamen est ei connexa, sicut et connexionem habet ad virtutes et dona; unde in sacramentis principaliter datur gratia sacramentalis, quae differt in diversis sacramentis; et per consequens gratia virtutum et donorum, quae est communis in omnibus sacramentis. Secundum hoc ergo dico quod gratia baptismalis potest dici dupliciter. Uno modo illa quae est principalis et proprius effectus baptismi, operans contra morbum: alio modo gratia quae est effectus baptismi ex consequenti, et per quamdam connexionem: et similiter distinguendum est de gratia confirmationis. Accipiendo ergo gratiam baptismalem et confirmationis primo modo, sic sunt diversae gratiae; et ideo non perficit eam directe, quasi cedens in eamdem essentiam cum ipsa, sed directe perficit ipsum baptizatum ad aliquid altius; et per consequens etiam ipsa baptismalis gratia perfectius et nobilius esse habet, sicut anima sensibilis est perfectior adjuncta rationali, et virtus adjuncta dono, et liberalitas adjuncta magnificentiae. Accipiendo autem gratiam baptismalem et confirmationis secundo modo, sic directe auget eam, cadens in eamdem essentiam cum ipsa, sicut baptismus directe auget gratiam quam prius invenit.

To the third question, it should be said that, as was said above in Distinction 1, Question 1, Article 4, Subquestion 5, just as sanctifying grace, which perfects the essence of the soul, differs from the virtues and gifts that flow from it, so also it differs from the grace that is the proper effect of each of the sacraments. Nevertheless, it is connected with it, just as it is also connected with the virtues and gifts; hence in the sacraments sacramental grace, which is different in different sacraments, is given chiefly, and the grace of the virtues and gifts, which is common to all the sacraments, as a consequence. Accordingly, therefore, I say that baptismal grace can be said two ways. In one way, for the grace that is the chief and proper effect of baptism, working against an ailment; in another way the grace that is baptism's effect as a consequence, and by a certain connection; and the same distinction can be made about the grace of confirmation. Therefore, if we take baptismal grace and the grace of confirmation in the first way, they are different graces; and so the latter does not perfect the former directly, as though reducible to the same essence as it, but it directly perfects the person baptized for something higher; and accordingly baptismal grace has a more perfect and nobler being in itself, just as the sensible soul is more perfect when joined to the rational, and a virtue is more perfect when combined with a gift, and liberality is more perfect when attached to magnificence. But if we take baptismal grace and the grace of confirmation in the second way, then the grace of confirmation directly increases it, and is reducible to the same essence with it, just as baptism directly increases any grace that it finds before it.

Et per hoc patet responsio ad utramque partem.

And by this the answer to each objection is clear.

QUESTION 3

CONFERRAL OF CONFIRMATION

Deinde quaeritur de celebratione hujus sacramenti; et circa hoc quaeruntur tria:

primo, quis possit conferre hoc sacramentum;

secundo, quis debeat recipere;

tertio, de ritu et modo recipiendi.

Next, inquiry is to be made about the celebration of this sacrament, and concerning this, three questions arise:

first, who can confer this sacrament;

second, who should receive it;

third, the rite and mode of receiving it.

ARTICLE 1

Who can confer confirmation[60]

Quaestiuncula 1

AD PRIMUM SIC PROCEDITUR. Videtur quod quilibet non ordinatus possit alium confirmare. Efficacia enim sacramentorum est a virtute verborum. Sed quilibet, etiam non ordinatus, potest verba proferre quae sunt forma hujus sacramenti. Ergo non ordinatus potest confirmare.

PRAETEREA, unumquodque potest agere secundum formam quam habet: quia unumquodque agit secundum quod est actu. Sed aliquis non ordinatus habet characterem confirmationis. Ergo potest confirmare.

PRAETEREA, quanto aliquod sacramentum est majoris necessitatis, tanto indiget majori discretione et attentione in ministrando. Sed baptismus est sacramentum necessitatis. Ergo cum illud quod requirit majorem discretionem debeat majoribus committi, videtur quod ex quo non ordinatus potest baptizare, etiam possit confirmare.

SED CONTRA est quod Hugo de s. Victore dicit, quod administratio ecclesiae consistit in ordinibus ministrorum, et sacramentis. Ergo sicut sine sacramento non potest quis confirmari, ita nec sine ordine confirmantis.

PRAETEREA, unctio confirmationis est dignior quam extremae unctionis. Sed illa non potest fieri nisi ab ordinatis, ut patet Jacob. ult. Ergo nec ista.

OBJ. 1: To the first we proceed thus. It seems that any non-ordained person can confirm another. For the efficacy of the sacraments is from the power of the words. But even someone who is not ordained can utter the words that are the form of this sacrament. Therefore, someone who has not been ordained can confirm.

OBJ. 2: Furthermore, everything is able to act according to the form that it has: for anything acts according as it is in act. But someone who has not been ordained can have the character of confirmation. Therefore, he can confirm.

OBJ. 3: Furthermore, the greater the necessity of a certain sacrament, the more discernment and attention are needed to administer it. But baptism is the sacrament of necessity. Therefore, since what requires greater discernment should be entrusted to greater persons, it seems that since a non-baptized person can baptize, he can also confirm.

ON THE CONTRARY, Hugh of St. Victor says, that the administration of the Church consists in the orders of its ministers and in the sacraments.[61] Therefore, just as someone cannot be confirmed without the sacrament, so neither without holy orders in the one confirming.

FURTHERMORE, the anointing of confirmation is nobler than that of extreme unction. But that anointing cannot be done except by an ordained minister, as is evident from James 5:14. Therefore, neither can confirmation.

---

60. Parallels: above, d. 2, q. 2, a. 4, ad 1; below, d. 13, q. 1, a. 1, qa. 2, ad 2; d. 25, q. 1, a. 1; *ST* III, q. 65, a. 3, ad 3; q. 72, a. 11; *SCG* IV, ch. 60; *De eccles. sacr.*; *Quodl.* XI, q. 7.

61. Hugh of St. Victor, *De sacramentis fidei*, Bk. 2, pt. 2, ch. 5 (PL 176:418).

Quaestiuncula 2

ULTERIUS. Videtur quod sacerdos simplex, etiam si non sit episcopus, possit confirmare. Baptismus enim quantum ad aliquid est majoris efficaciae quam confirmatio. Sed sacerdos ex suo officio potest baptizare. Ergo et confirmare.

PRAETEREA, sicut confirmationis sacramentum ad perfectionem pertinet, ita et Eucharistiae, secundum Dionysium. Sed sacerdos est proprius minister sacramenti Eucharistiae. Ergo ipse potest confirmare.

PRAETEREA, in sacramentis ex parte conferentis requiritur ordo et intentio. Sed episcopus non habet aliquem ordinem vel characterem quem non habeat simplex sacerdos. Ergo sicut episcopus, ita et sacerdos potest confirmare, si intentionem confirmandi habeat.

SED CONTRA, soli episcopi in loco apostolorum succedunt. Sed soli apostoli in primitiva ecclesia manus imponebant, quod erat confirmare. Ergo soli episcopi nunc possunt confirmare.

PRAETEREA, in ordine ecclesiasticae hierarchiae, secundum Dionysium, soli episcopi sunt perfectores. Sed, secundum eumdem, sicut aliquis per exorcismum purgatur, et per baptismum illuminatur, ita per confirmationem chrismatis perficitur. Ergo soli episcopi possunt confirmare.

OBJ. 1: Moreover, it seems that a simple priest, even if he is not a bishop, can confirm. For baptism in a certain respect has greater efficacy than confirmation. But a priest can baptize by his office. Therefore, he can also confirm.

OBJ. 2: Furthermore, just as the sacrament of confirmation pertains to perfection, so does the Eucharist, according to Dionysius.[62] But the priest is the proper minister of the sacrament of the Eucharist. Therefore, he can confirm.

OBJ. 3: Furthermore, holy orders and intention are required on the part of the someone conferring the sacraments. But a bishop does not have any order or character that a simple priest does not have. Therefore, since a bishop can confirm, a priest can also, if he has the intention of confirming.

ON THE CONTRARY, only bishops are the successors of the apostles. But in the early Church only the apostles imposed their hands on the faithful, which was to confirm. Therefore, only the bishops can confirm nowadays.

FURTHERMORE, in the order of the ecclesiastical hierarchy, according to Dionysius, only bishops are perfecters.[63] But according to him, as someone is purified by exorcism and illuminated by baptism, so he is perfected by confirmation. Therefore, only bishops can confirm.

Quaestiuncula 3

ULTERIUS. Videtur quod sacerdos simplex ex commissione Papae non possit confirmare. Sicut enim se habet hoc quod est sacerdotis ad sacerdotem, ita quod est episcopi ad episcopum. Sed nullus non sacerdos potest propter Papae commissionem Eucharistiam conficere, quod est sacerdotum. Ergo similiter ex commissione Papae nullus potest non episcopus confirmare, quod est episcopi.

PRAETEREA, sicut conferre sacerdotalem ordinem est episcopi, ita et confirmare. Sed nullus non episcopus ex mandato Papae posset aliquem in sacerdotem promovere. Ergo nullus ex Papae mandato, qui non sit episcopus, potest praebere confirmationis sacramentum.

PRAETEREA, quicumque potest ex mandato vel ex commissione alicujus baptizare, si sine commissione baptizat eum qui non est sibi subditus, extra casum necessitatis, baptizatus est, quamvis peccet. Sed si sacerdos

OBJ. 1: Moreover, it seems that a simple priest cannot confirm by the commission of the Pope. For what pertains to priests is related to priests in just the same way that what pertains to bishops is related to a bishop. But even by the Pope's commission, someone who is not a priest cannot consecrate the Eucharist, because that belongs to priests. Therefore in the same way, no one who is not a bishop can confirm by the Pope's commission, because that belongs to bishops.

OBJ. 2: Furthermore, to confer priestly ordination belongs to a bishop, just like confirmation. But no one who is not a bishop could ordain anyone a priest by the Pope's command. Therefore, neither by the Pope's command could anyone who is not a bishop provide the sacrament of confirmation.

OBJ. 3: Furthermore, if someone who can baptize by another's command or commission, should baptize without commission someone who is not subject to him outside of the case of necessity, then the person would be bap-

---

62. Pseudo-Dionysius, *Ecclesiastical Hierarchy*, ch. 5, p. 1, n. 2 (PG 3:503).
63. Ibid., n. 5 (PG 3:506).

sine commissione alicujus confirmet, non est confirmatum. Ergo non potest ex commissione Papae confirmare.

SED CONTRA est quod in littera dicitur, quod Gregorius in casu permisit quod simplices sacerdotes possent confirmare.

PRAETEREA, majus est ordinem conferre quam confirmare. Sed ex mandato Papae aliqui non episcopi conferunt quosdam ordines; sicut sunt presbyteri cardinales, qui conferunt minores ordines. Ergo multo fortius ex mandato Papae potest aliquis simplex sacerdos confirmare.

tized, although he would have sinned. But if a priest without anyone's commission confirmed someone, that person would not be confirmed. Therefore, he cannot confirm by the commission of the Pope.

ON THE CONTRARY, in the text it says that Pope Gregory allowed that in certain cases simple priests could confirm.

FURTHERMORE, it is a greater thing to confer holy orders than confirmation. But by the Pope's mandate, certain people who are not bishops confer certain orders; for example, cardinal presbyters, who confer minor orders. Therefore much more can some simple priest confirm by the Pope's mandate.

Response to Quaestiuncula 1

RESPONDEO dicendum ad primam quaestionem, quod proprii dispensatores sacramentorum sunt ministri ecclesiae per sacramentum ordinis consecrati, ut sint medii inter Deum et plebem, divina populo tradentes; et ideo solis eis competit ex officio sacramenta ministrare, nec per alium conferri possunt, excepto baptismo propter necessitatem. Unde cum confirmatio non sit sacramentum necessitatis, non poterit nisi ab ordinatis conferri.

AD PRIMUM ergo dicendum, quod efficacia sacramenti non tantum est ex verbis prolatis, sed etiam ex materia debita, et persona conveniente; et ideo, si sit defectus in persona ministri, verba prolata ab alio non possunt efficaciam sacramento praebere.

AD SECUNDUM dicendum, quod perfectio personalis hujus vel illius nihil facit ad collationem sacramentorum: quod patet ex hoc quod sacramenta conferuntur a bonis ministris et a malis; sed exigitur quod sit perfectio hujus inquantum est minister ecclesiae, sicut in naturalibus ad hoc quod forma se in alteram materiam transfundat per sui similitudinem, requiritur qualitas activa. Et ideo quia per confirmationis sacramentum non efficitur aliquis minister ecclesiae, quamvis quamdam naturalem perfectionem consequatur, ideo non oportet quod quilibet confirmatus confirmare possit.

AD TERTIUM dicendum quod omnia sacramenta indigent aequaliter intentione; sed illa quae omnibus sunt conferenda, non indigent discretione, qua unus repellatur, et alius admittatur: quia a sacramentis necessitatis nullus debet excludi; et ideo cuilibet etiam sacerdoti committitur illa sacramenta conferre, non autem illa quibus aliquis ad statum perfectionis promovetur.

TO THE FIRST QUESTION, I answer that the proper ministers of the sacraments are the ministers of the Church consecrated by the sacrament of holy orders, as they are intermediaries between God and the people, handing over divine things to the people; and so it belongs to them alone to administer the sacraments by their office, nor can they be conferred by anyone else, except baptism in an emergency. Hence since confirmation is not a sacrament of necessity, it can only be conferred by ordained ministers.

REPLY OBJ. 1: The sacrament's efficacy comes not only from the words pronounced, but also from the due matter and the appropriate person. And so if there is a lack in the person of the minister, words uttered by someone else cannot supply the sacrament with efficacy.

REPLY OBJ. 2: The personal perfection of any given person has nothing to do with the conferral of the sacraments, which is evident from the fact that the sacraments are conferred by good ministers and by bad ones. But it is required that he have a perfection insofar as he is a minister of the Church, just as in natural things an active quality is required for a form to transfer itself into another matter by its own likeness. And thus, since by the sacrament of confirmation no one is made a minister of the Church, although he attains a certain natural perfection, for this reason it is not necessary that someone confirmed should be able to confirm.

REPLY OBJ. 3: All the sacraments need equal intention. But the ones that are conferred on everyone do not need discernment, by which one person would be rejected and another admitted: for no one should be excluded from the sacraments of necessity; and for this reason it is committed to any priest whatsoever to confer these sacraments, but not those in which someone is advanced to a state of perfection.

Response to Quaestiuncula 2

AD SECUNDAM QUAESTIONEM dicendum, quod in omnibus artibus et potentiis ordinatis, vel habitibus, ita est quod ultima perfectio reservatur inducenda per supremam artem in genere illo; sicut artes quae operantur circa materiam navis, reservant inductionem formae arti superiori, quae navim compaginat; et illa reservat ulterius finem, scilicet usum navis, arti superiori, scilicet gubernatoriae. Unde cum episcopi in ecclesiastica hierarchia teneant supremum locum, illud quod est ultimum in actionibus hierarchicis, eis reservandum fuit. Et quia perficere aliquem hoc modo quod sit supra communem statum aliorum, est supremum in actionibus hierarchicis, ideo sacramentum confirmationis et ordinis, quibus hoc efficitur, solis episcopis dispensanda reservantur.

AD PRIMUM ergo dicendum, quod baptismus, cum sit sacramentum necessitatis, communiter omnibus competit; et ideo per ipsum non ponitur aliquis supra communem statum, sicut fit per confirmationem, ut prius etiam dictum est.

AD SECUNDUM dicendum, quod Eucharistia, sicut confirmatio et ordo, est sacramentum perficiens; sed in hoc differt ab aliis, quia in ordine et confirmatione illud quod est ibi res et sacramentum, est aliquid in suscipiente acquisitum; et ideo suscipientem haec sacramenta promovent ad perfectionem quamdam ultra communem statum fidelium; sed Eucharistia habet illud quod est res et sacramentum, in se, non in suscipiente; et ideo per sumptionem Eucharistiae non acquirit aliquis perfectionem ultra communem statum, cum non imprimatur character; sed perficit unumquemque in suo statu; et ideo etiam secundum Dionysium cuilibet sacramento Eucharistiae perceptio adjungitur; et ideo non est simile de Eucharistia et de aliis.

AD TERTIUM dicendum, quod quamvis episcopus non habeat aliquem ordinem supra sacerdotem, secundum quod ordines distinguuntur per actus relatos ad Corpus Domini, verumtamen habet aliquem ordinem supra sacerdotem, secundum quod ordines distinguuntur per actus supra corpus mysticum. Unde Dionysius in *Eccles. Hier.*, ponit episcopatum ordinem; unde et cum quadam consecratione dignitas episcopalis confertur; et ideo in promotione membrorum corporis mystici aliquid potest competere episcopo quod non competit simplici sacerdoti.

TO THE SECOND QUESTION, I answer that in all arts and ordered powers, or habits, it is the case that the last perfection is reserved to be instilled by the highest art in that genus; for example, those skills that work with the material of ships defer induction of the form to the higher art, which builds the ship; and that art defers the further end, which is the use of the ship, to an even higher skill, navigation. Therefore, since the bishops in the ecclesiastical hierarchy hold the highest place, whatever is last in hierarchical actions is reserved to them. And since perfecting someone in such a way that he is above the common state of others is supreme among hierarchical actions, for this reason the sacraments of confirmation and holy orders, in which this is done, are reserved to be dispensed by bishops alone.

REPLY OBJ. 1: Baptism, since it is a sacrament of necessity, applies commonly to all; and therefore no one is set above the common state by it, as happens by confirmation, as has already been said.

REPLY OBJ. 2: The Eucharist, like confirmation and holy orders, is a perfecting sacrament; but it differs from the others in this, that in holy orders and confirmation the reality-and-sacrament is something acquired in the recipient, and so these sacraments advance the recipient to a certain perfection beyond the common state of the faithful. But the Eucharist contains its reality-and-sacrament in itself, not in the recipient; and so by the consumption of the Eucharist a person does not acquire a perfection beyond the common state, since no character is imprinted.[64] But it does perfect each person in his own state, and therefore also according to Dionysius the reception of the Eucharist is joined with every sacrament,[65] and so it is not the same with the Eucharist as with others.

REPLY OBJ. 3: Although the bishop does not have an order above a priest according to the distinction of acts related to the body of the Lord, nevertheless, he does have a certain order above a priest according to the distinction of acts concerning the Mystical Body. This is why Dionysius, in the *Ecclesiastical Hierarchy*, includes the order of bishops;[66] this is also why the episcopal dignity is conferred with a certain consecration; and so in the advancement of members of the Mystical Body something can apply to a bishop that does not apply to a simple priest.

---

64. For more about the sacrament alone, reality alone, and sacrament-and-reality, see the footnote at Dist.1, q.1, a.4, qa. 1, main response.
65. Pseudo-Dionysius, *Ecclesiastical Hierarchy*, ch. 3, p. 1 (PG 3:424).
66. Pseudo-Dionysius, *Ecclesiastical Hierarchy*, ch. 5, p. 1, n. 5 (PG 3:506).

Response to Quaestiuncula 3

AD TERTIAM QUAESTIONEM dicendum, quod circa hoc est multiplex opinio. Quidam enim dicunt, quod presbyter simplex non possit ex mandato Papae confirmare; et quod dicitur de Gregorio ad Januarium scribente, exponunt quod illi presbyteri ex mandato Papae non conferebant sacramentum confirmationis, sed aliquid sacramentale simile illi sacramento, sicut alicui porrigitur panis benedictus loco Eucharistiae. Sed non videtur conveniens, ut talem simulationem in dispensatione sacramentorum induxisset Gregorius, vel sustinuisset: quia dispensatio sacramentorum pertinet ad veritatem doctrinae, quae non est propter scandalum dimittenda.

Et ideo alii dicunt, quod auctoritas Papae tanta est quod ejus mandato quilibet potest conferre quod habet, ut confirmatus confirmare, sacerdos sacerdotium conferre, diaconus diaconatum; non autem mandato ipsius potest aliquis conferre quod non habet, ut diaconus ordinem sacerdotalem.

Sed haec opinio videtur nimis ampla; et ideo media via secundum alios tenenda est. Et ideo sciendum est, quod cum episcopatus non addat aliquid supra sacerdotium per relationem ad corpus Domini verum, sed solum per relationem ad corpus mysticum, Papa per hoc quod est episcoporum summus, non dicitur habere plenitudinem potestatis per relationem ad corpus Domini verum, sed per relationem ad corpus mysticum. Et quia gratia sacramentalis descendit in corpus mysticum a capite, ideo omnis operatio in corpus mysticum sacramentalis, per quam gratia datur, dependet ab operatione sacramentali super corpus Domini verum; et ideo solus sacerdos potest absolvere in foro poenitentiali, et baptizare ex officio.

Et ideo dicendum, quod promovere ad illas perfectiones quae non respiciunt corpus Domini verum, sed solum corpus mysticum, potest a Papa, qui habet plenitudinem pontificalis potestatis, committi sacerdoti, qui habet actum summum super corpus Domini verum; non autem diacono, vel alicui inferiori, qui non habet perficere corpus verum, sicut nec absolvere in foro poenitentiali. Non autem potest simplici sacerdoti committere promovere ad perfectionem quae respicit aliquo modo corpus Domini verum; et ideo simplex sacerdos ex mandato Papae non potest conferre ordinem sacerdotii: quia ordines sacri habent actum supra corpus Domini verum, vel supra materiam ejus. Potest autem concedere simplici sacerdoti quod conferat minores ordines, quia isti nullum actum habent supra corpus Domini verum, vel materiam ejus, nec etiam supra corpus mysticum habent actum per quem gratia conferatur; sed habent ex offi-

TO THE THIRD QUESTION, it should be said that concerning this there are many opinions. For certain people say that a simple priest cannot confirm by the command of the Pope, and concerning what is said about Gregory writing to Januarius, they explain that those priests were not conferring the sacrament of confirmation by the command of the Pope, but some sacramental resembling that sacrament, just as blessed bread is offered to someone in place of the Eucharist. But it does not seem appropriate that Gregory would have introduced such a pretense in the administering of the sacraments, or that he would have allowed it, for administering the sacraments pertains to the truth of doctrine, which is not to be omitted because of scandal.

And therefore others say that the Pope's authority is such that by his command anyone can confer anything he himself has, so that someone confirmed could confirm, a priest could confer the priesthood, and a deacon the diaconate; however, no one could confer by his command something that he himself did not have, so a deacon could not confer priestly orders.

But this opinion seems too broad; and for this reason a middle way is to be held, according to some others. And therefore it should be known that since the episcopate does not add anything above the priesthood in relation to the true Body of the Lord, but only in relation to the mystical body, the Pope, by the fact that he is the highest of bishops, is not said to have fullness of power by relation to the true Body of the Lord, but in relation to the Mystical Body. And since sacramental grace comes down to the Mystical Body from the head, for this reason any sacramental operation in the Mystical Body by which grace is given depends on the sacramental operation upon the true Body of the Lord. And therefore only a priest can absolve in the penitential forum, and baptize by his office.

And so it should be said that to advance people to those perfections that do not regard the true Body of the Lord, but only the Mystical Body, can be granted by the Pope, who has the fullness of pontifical power, to a priest, who has the highest act upon the true Body of the Lord; however, it cannot be given to a deacon or to anyone below him, who does not have the ability to consecrate the true Body, nor to absolve in the penitential forum. But it cannot be granted to a simple priest to bring someone to the perfection that has anything to do with the true Body of the Lord, and therefore a simple priest cannot confer the order of priesthood by the Pope's command: for the sacred orders have act upon the true Body of the Lord, or upon its matter. However, he can grant to a simple priest that he confer minor orders, since those have no act upon the true Body of the Lord, or its matter, nor even upon the Mystical Body do they have the act by which grace is conferred; but by their office they

cio quosdam actus secundarios et praeparatorios; et similiter potest concedere alicui sacerdoti quod confirmet: quia confirmatio perficit eum in actu corporis mystici, non autem habet aliquam relationem ad corpus Domini verum.

ET PER HOC de facili patet solutio ad objecta.

have certain secondary and preparatory acts. And in the same way he can grant to a certain priest that he may confirm: for confirmation perfects one in the act of the Mystical Body, but it does not have any relation to the true Body of the Lord.

AND BY THIS the answers to the objections can be easily seen.

ARTICLE 2

Who should receive confirmation

Quaestiuncula 1

AD SECUNDUM SIC PROCEDITUR. Videtur quod Christus debuerit sacramentum confirmationis accipere. Sacramentum enim confirmationis confert majorem plenitudinem gratiae quam baptismus. Sed Christus baptizari voluit, ut tactu mundissimae suae carnis efficaciam baptismo praeberet. Ergo similiter debuit confirmationem accipere.

PRAETEREA, confirmatio ad hoc datur ut homo in confessione veritatis usque ad mortem firmiter stet. Sed Christus dedit omnibus exemplum pro veritate moriendi. Ergo hoc sacramentum maxime debuit accipere.

SED CONTRA, confirmatur quod infirmum est. Sed infirmitas spiritualis in Christo non fuit. Ergo nec confirmari debuit.

OBJ. 1: To the second we proceed thus. It seems that Christ should have received the sacrament of confirmation.[67] For the sacrament of confirmation confers greater fullness of grace than baptism. But Christ desired to be baptized, so that by the touch of his most pure flesh he might supply efficacy to baptism. Therefore, in the same way he should have received confirmation.

OBJ. 2: Furthermore, confirmation is given to allow a man to stand firmly in the confession of the truth even unto death. But Christ gave the example to all of dying for the truth. Therefore, he should especially have received this sacrament.

ON THE CONTRARY, what is weak needs to be strengthened. But there was no spiritual weakness in Christ. Therefore, neither should he have been confirmed.

Quaestiuncula 2

ULTERIUS. Videtur quod hoc sacramentum pueris non sit conferendum. Quia hoc sacramentum supra communem statum promovet, sicut et sacramentum ordinis. Sed illud sacramentum non confertur pueris. Ergo nec istud.

PRAETEREA, hoc sacramentum datur ad confitendum fidem, et ad pugnandum pro ipsa. Sed hoc non competit pueris. Ergo non debent hoc sacramentum suscipere.

SED CONTRA, gratia baptismalis est immediata dispositio ad gratiam confirmationis. Sed baptismus confertur pueris. Ergo confirmatio debet pueris dari.

OBJ. 1: Moreover, it seems that this sacrament should not be conferred on children.[68] For this sacrament advances one above the common state, just like the sacrament of holy orders. But that sacrament is not conferred on children. Therefore, neither should this one be.

OBJ. 2: Furthermore, this sacrament is given for confessing the faith and for fighting for it. But this does not apply to children. Therefore, they should not receive this sacrament.

ON THE CONTRARY, baptismal grace is an immediate disposition to the grace of confirmation. But baptism is conferred on children. Therefore, confirmation should be given to children.

Quaestiuncula 3

ULTERIUS. Videtur quod non debeat dari omnibus adultis. Illud enim quod omnibus datur, non excedit communem statum. Sed confirmatio ponit supra communem statum, ut dictum est. Ergo non debet omnibus dari.

OBJ. 1: Moreover, it seems that it should not be given to all adults.[69] For whatever is given to all does not exceed the common state. But confirmation places one above the common state, as was said. Therefore, it should not be given to all.

---

67. Parallel: *ST* III, q. 39, a. 1.
68. Parallel: *ST* III, q. 72, a. 8, corp. and ad 2.
69. Parallel: *ST* III, q. 72, a. 8.

PRAETEREA, hoc sacramentum est ad robur in pugna spirituali. Sed pugnare non est mulierum propter imbecillitatem sexus. Ergo nec hoc sacramentum eis competit.

PRAETEREA, confirmatio est sacramentum confessionis. Sed muti non possunt confiteri. Ergo non debet eis dari hoc sacramentum.

PRAETEREA, morientes a pugna hujus vitae subtrahuntur. Sed ad robur in pugna hujus vitae datur confirmatio. Ergo non debet morientibus dari.

SED CONTRA est quod dicit Hugo de s. Victore, quod omnino periculosum esset, si ab hac vita sine confirmatione migrare contingeret. Ergo omnibus dandum est hoc sacramentum.

PRAETEREA, ad robur in hoc sacramento datur septiformis gratia Spiritus Sancti. Sed haec omnibus est necessaria. Ergo et sacramentum confirmationis omnibus dari competit.

OBJ. 2: Furthermore, this sacrament is for fortifying in the spiritual fight. But to fight is not for women because of the weakness of their sex. Therefore, this sacrament does not apply to them.

OBJ. 3: Furthermore, confirmation is the sacrament of confessing. But those who are mute cannot confess. Therefore, this sacrament should not be given to them.

OBJ. 4: Furthermore, those who are dying are taken away from the fight of this life. But confirmation is given to fortify one in the fight of this life. Therefore, it should not be given to the dying.

ON THE CONTRARY, Hugh of St. Victor says, that it would be extremely dangerous if someone happened to depart this life without confirmation.[70] Therefore, this sacrament is to be given to all.

FURTHERMORE, the sevenfold grace of the Holy Spirit is given in this sacrament to fortify one. But this is necessary for everyone. Therefore, it is also appropriate to give the sacrament of confirmation to everyone.

Response to Quaestiuncula 1

RESPONDEO dicendum ad primam quaestionem, quod suscipere baptismum est in praecepto, cum sit sacramentum necessitatis; et ideo Dominus voluit baptizari, quamvis in baptismo nihil susciperet, sed magis contulerit ut forma obediendi mandatis omnibus praeberetur per ipsum; et propter hoc dixit ad baptismum veniens: *sic decet nos implere omnem justitiam*; Matth. 3, 15. Justitia enim consistit in obedientia legis, ut Philosophus dicit in 5 *Ethic.* Sed sacramentum confirmationis non est necessitatis, sed utilitatis alicujus consequendae causa accipitur; et ideo cum Dominus non acceperit aliquid a sacramentis, non debuit sacramentum confirmationis accipere, sicut nec sacramentum ordinis: quia potestas excellentiae in sacramentis, et plenitudo Spiritus Sancti in ipso a sui conceptione fuit, et sic non oportebat nisi quod in ipso erat innotescere; quod factum est per adventum columbae super ipsum.

ET PER HOC patet solutio ad objecta.

TO THE FIRST QUESTION, I answer that to receive baptism is commanded since it is the sacrament of necessity, and that is why the Lord wanted to be baptized, even though he received nothing in baptism, but rather he established that the form of obedience to all commands would be provided by him; and for this reason he said when he came to baptism: *it is proper for us in this way to fulfill all righteousness* (Matt 3:15). For righteousness consists in obedience to the law, as the Philosopher says in *Ethics* 5.[71] But the sacrament of confirmation is not of necessity, but it is received for the sake of a certain benefit that follows from it. And so since the Lord did not gain anything from the sacraments, he did not have to receive the sacrament of confirmation, just as neither the sacrament of holy orders: for the power of excellence in the sacraments and the fullness of the Holy Spirit were in him from his conception, and this is why it was not necessary except to make known what there was in him; which happened by the coming of the dove upon him.

AND BY THIS the answers to the objections are evident.

Response to Quaestiuncula 2

AD SECUNDAM QUAESTIONEM dicendum, quod perfectio quae confertur in ordine et confirmatione, in hoc differunt, quod perfectio ordinis est ad aliquid dispensandum, perfectio autem confirmationis est ad

TO THE SECOND QUESTION, it should be said that the perfection that is conferred in holy orders differs from that of confirmation in this: the perfection of holy orders is for administering something, but the perfection of confirma-

---

70. Hugh of St. Victor, *De sacramentis fidei*, Bk. 2, pt. 7, ch. 3 (PL 176:460).
71. Aristotle, *Nicomachean Ethics*, Bk. 5, ch. 2, 1129a33.

standum fortiter in seipso. Ad hoc autem quod dispensatio alicujus rei detur alicui, requiritur idoneitas aliqua praeexistens in eo qui dispensationem recipit propter periculum quod potest imminere ex prava dispensatione; et ideo perfectio ordinis non confertur pueris. Sed perfectio qua quis in seipso perficitur, non praeexigit aliam perfectionem, sed ipsa perfectione quis idoneus redditur; nec ex hoc aliquod periculum imminere potest; et ideo confirmatio potest puero tradi, et convenienter traditur: quia infantilis aetas non patitur fictionem, qua effectus sacramenti impediatur; et ideo quamvis tunc non competat ei confiteri vel pugnare, certum tamen est quod effectum sacramenti plene recipit, per quem erit idoneus ad pugnam et confessionem ad perfectam aetatem veniens, nisi gratiam acceptam per peccatum amittat.

ET PER HOC patet solutio ad objecta.

tion is for standing bravely in oneself. But for the ministry of a thing to be given to someone, a certain worthiness is required pre-existing in the one who gets to distribute it, because of the risk of danger if it is badly administered; and for this reason the perfection of holy orders is not conferred on children. But a perfection by which a person is perfected in himself does not require any other pre-existing perfection, but he is rendered worthy by this very perfection itself. Nor can there be any risk of danger from this, and so confirmation can be given to a child and it is fitting that it be given: for someone in infancy cannot pretend falsely, which would impede the effect of this sacrament. And so although at that time confessing and fighting do not apply to the child, nevertheless it is certain that he receives the effect of the sacrament fully, by which he will be made worthy of fighting and confessing once he is mature, unless by sin he loses the grace he received.

AND BY THIS the answers to the objections are evident.

Response to Quaestiuncula 3

AD TERTIAM QUAESTIONEM dicendum, quod sicut dictum est, perfectio in confirmatione collata non praeexigit aliam perfectionem, sed per eam quis in seipso perficitur, ut sit idoneus ad pugnam spiritualem. Et quia cuilibet est conveniens et bonum, ut in pugna spirituali fortitudinem habeat; ideo ab hoc sacramento nullus excludi debet qui sit baptizatus.

AD PRIMUM ergo dicendum quod non ponit supra communem statum quantum ad dispensationem alicujus sacramenti, sed quantum ad confessionem sacramentorum; et haec perfectio vel excellentia omnibus membris ecclesiae competit per hoc sacramentum collata.

AD SECUNDUM dicendum, quod etiam quaedam mulieres in pugna spirituali gloriosum reportaverunt de hoste triumphum, sicut patet de beata Agnete, et beata Caecilia et aliis; unde ab hoc sacramento mulieres non sunt excludendae.

AD TERTIUM dicendum, quod quamvis muti non possint confiteri ore, possunt confiteri nutibus, et possunt habere voluntatem et propositum confitendi; et ideo eis non debet denegari hoc sacramentum.

AD QUARTUM dicendum, quod quamvis morientes abstrahantur a pugna, tamen vadunt ad locum praemii, in quo secundum mensuram gratiae datur mensura gloriae; et ideo indigent plenitudine gratiae, quae in pugna perficit, propter finem pugnae consequendum.

TO THE THIRD QUESTION, it should be said that just as was said, in the conferral of confirmation, no prerequisite perfecting is required, but a person is perfected in himself by it, so that he is worthy of the spiritual fight. And since it is good and fitting for anyone to have fortitude in the spiritual battle, for this reason no one should be excluded from this sacrament who is baptized.

REPLY OBJ. 1: It does not place someone above the common state in the administering of any sacrament, but in the confessing of the sacraments; and this perfection or excellence befits all members of the Church through the conferral of this sacrament.

REPLY OBJ. 2: Even some women have won a glorious triumph from the enemy in the spiritual battle, as is seen in the case of blessed Agnes and blessed Cecilia and others. Therefore, women are not to be excluded from this sacrament.

REPLY OBJ. 3: Although those who are mute cannot confess with their mouths, they can confess with nods, and they can have the will and the aim of confessing; and so this sacrament should not be denied them.

REPLY OBJ. 4: Although the dying are being withdrawn from the fight, nevertheless they are going to the place of the reward, in which the measure of glory will be given according to the measure of grace; and therefore they need the fullness of grace, which perfects in a fight, for the sake of the end resulting from the fight.

ARTICLE 3

The rite and mode of receiving confirmation

Quaestiuncula 1

AD TERTIUM SIC PROCEDITUR. Videtur quod non exigatur quod aliquis tangat[72] aliquem ad confirmationem. Ille enim qui habet immediatam relationem ad principem, sicut liberi, non oportet quod mediantibus aliquibus coram principe compareat, sicut servi comparent mediantibus dominis et filiifamilias mediantibus patribus. Sed confirmandus jam habet immediatam relationem ad principem ecclesiae, cum sit membrum ecclesiae per baptismum. Ergo quamvis baptizatus per alium debeat praesentari, tamen confirmandus nullo modo debet per alium ad confirmationem teneri, praecipue si sit adultus.

PRAETEREA, fortitudo minus competit mulieribus quam viris. Prov. ultim. 10: *mulierem fortem quis inveniet?* Sed confirmatio est sacramentum fortitudinis, quia in eo datur Spiritus Sanctus ad robur. Ergo ad minus mulier non debet tenere virum ad confirmationem.

SED CONTRA, videtur etiam quod non confirmatus possit tenere ad confirmationem. Quia majus est sacramentum conferre quam ad sacramentum suscipiendum aliquem tenere. Sed non confirmatus potest sacramentum baptismi conferre. Ergo multo fortius potest ad confirmationem tenere.

OBJ. 1: To the third we proceed thus. It seems that it is not required that someone hold a person for confirmation.[73] For anyone who has an immediate relation to the prince, like free men, it is not fitting that he appear in the sight of the prince by intermediaries, the way that servants act as emissaries to their lords and sons of the family act as emissaries to their fathers. But a confirmand already has an immediate relation to the Prince of the Church, since he is a member of the Church by baptism. Therefore, although a person to be baptized should be presented by another, nevertheless the confirmand should in no way be held by another for his confirmation, especially if he is an adult.

OBJ. 2: Furthermore, fortitude applies less to women than to men: *who will find a strong woman?* (Prov 31:10) But confirmation is a sacrament of fortitude, for the Holy Spirit is given in it to fortify us. Therefore, at least a woman should not hold a man for confirmation.

ON THE CONTRARY, it seems also that someone not confirmed could hold someone for confirmation. For it is a greater thing to confer a sacrament than to hold someone receiving a sacrament. But a someone unconfirmed can confer baptism. Therefore, much more can he hold someone in his confirmation.

Quaestiuncula 2

ULTERIUS. Videtur quod non debeat fieri linitio chrismatis tantum in fronte. Quia vertex est nobilior pars corporis quam frons, quia ibi est organum cogitativae, hic autem organum phantasiae. Sed sacerdos, qui est inferior quam episcopus, ungit baptizatos chrismate in vertice. Ergo episcopus non debet ungere chrismate confirmando in fronte.

PRAETEREA, confirmatio est sacramentum confessionis. Sed confessio fit ore. Ergo unctio confirmationis magis deberet in ore fieri.

PRAETEREA, frons est locus nudus et patens. Sed hic de facili sordes contrahit. Cum ergo chrisma sit servandum ab omni inquinamento, videtur quod non congrue fiat unctio in fronte.

OBJ. 1: Moreover, it seems that the anointing with chrism should not only be done on the forehead. For the crown of the head is a nobler part of the body than the forehead, because the organ of thought is there, while at the forehead is the organ of imagination. But a priest, who is lower than a bishop, anoints the baptized with chrism on the crown. Therefore, the bishop should not anoint the confirmand with chrism on the forehead.

OBJ. 2: Furthermore, confirmation is the sacrament of confessing the faith. But confession is made with the mouth. Therefore, the anointing of confirmation should rather be done on the mouth.

OBJ. 3: Furthermore, the forehead is a place that is bare and exposed. But this collects dirt easily. Therefore, since chrism should be preserved from all impurity, it seems that it is not fitting to make the anointing on the forehead.

---

72. *tangat.—teneat* PLE.
73. Parallels: *ST* III, q. 72, a. 9; a. 11, ad 3; *SCG* IV, ch. 60; *Quodl.* VI, q. 7; *Super Rom.*, ch. 1, lec. 5 and ch. 10, lec. 2.

SED CONTRA, in confirmatione datur Spiritus Sanctus ad robur. Sed robur in fronte significatur, ut patet Ezech. 3, 8: *ecce dedit . . . frontem tuam duriorem frontibus eorum.* Ergo in fronte debet fieri unctio confirmationis.

PRAETEREA, Apocal. 7, 3, angelus dicit: *quoadusque signemus servos Dei vivi in frontibus eorum.* Sed episcopi dicuntur angeli, ut patet Apoc. 3. Ergo eorum est in fronte signare.

ON THE CONTRARY, the Holy Spirit is given to fortify in confirmation. But fortification is symbolized by the forehead: *behold he has made . . . your forehead harder than their foreheads* (Ezek 3:8). Therefore, the anointing of confirmation should be done on the forehead.

FURTHERMORE, the angel says: *until we have marked the servants of the living God with a sign on their foreheads* (Rev 7:3). But the bishops are said to be angels, as is clear from Revelation 3. Therefore, it belongs to them to mark the sign on the forehead.

Quaestiuncula 3

ULTERIUS. Videtur quod confirmatio possit iterari. Sicut enim confirmatio datur ad robur fidei, ita Eucharistia ad robur caritatis. Sed Eucharistia iteratur. Ergo et confirmatio.

PRAETEREA, si morbus iteratur, et medicina iterari debet. Sed morbus contra quem datur hoc sacramentum, potest iterari, scilicet spiritualis infirmitas. Ergo et sacramentum debet iterari.

SED CONTRA, sicut in baptismo imprimitur character, ita et in confirmatione. Sed baptismus non iteratur. Ergo nec confirmatio.

OBJ. 1: Moreover, it seems that confirmation can be received again.[74] For just as confirmation is given to fortify one in the faith, so the Eucharist is given to fortify one in charity. But the Eucharist is received over and over. Therefore, so can confirmation be.

OBJ. 2: Furthermore, if someone gets sick over and over, the medicine should be given over and over. But the sickness that this sacrament is against, spiritual weakness, can happen over and over. Therefore, this sacrament should also be given over and over.

ON THE CONTRARY, just as a character is imprinted in baptism, so it is also imprinted in confirmation. But baptism is not received again. Therefore, neither should confirmation be.

Response to Quaestiuncula 1

RESPONDEO dicendum ad primam quaestionem, quod in sacramento confirmationis datur Spiritus Sanctus ad robur. Unde propter hoc aliquis ad confirmationem accedit, quia se habere robur standi non praesumit; et ideo institutum fuit ut ab altero teneatur, ad significandum quod per se stare non posset.

AD PRIMUM ergo dicendum, quod ille qui est mediator in hoc sacramento, non habet officium repraesentandi quasi extraneum, sicut est in baptismo, neque suscipiendi quasi instruendum: sed solum tenendi quasi infirmum.

AD SECUNDUM dicendum, quod fortitudo spiritualis est per Christum, in quo *non est masculus et femina*, ut dicitur ad Galat. 3; et ita non differt utrum vir mulierem, vel mulier virum teneat; quamvis quidam contrarium dicant, scilicet quod mulier virum tenere non potest.

TO THE FIRST QUESTION, I answer that in the sacrament of confirmation the Holy Spirit is given to fortify. Therefore, someone approaches confirmation because of the fact that he presumes he does not have the strength of standing, and so it was established that he would be held by another, to symbolize that he cannot stand on his own.

REPLY OBJ. 1: The person who is the mediator in this sacrament does not have the office of representing him as though he were an outsider, as is the case in baptism, nor of receiving him as though to instruct him, but only of holding him as though he were weak.

REPLY OBJ. 2: Spiritual fortitude is through Christ, in whom *there is no male or female* (Gal 3:28); and so it makes no difference whether a man holds a woman or a woman holds a man; although certain people say the opposite, namely that a woman cannot hold a man.

---

74. Parallel: *ST* III, q. 72, a. 5.

Response to Quaestiuncula 2

AD SECUNDAM QUAESTIONEM dicendum, quod homo potest impediri a libera et aperta confessione nominis Christi propter duo; scilicet propter timorem mortis, et propter confusionem, quae est timor ignominiae. Utriusque autem signum praecipue in facie manifestatur: quia *pallescunt timentes, et rubent verecundati,* ut dicitur in 4 *Ethic.,* et praecipue in fronte quae est pars magis aperta, et imaginationi, ex qua procedunt passiones praedictae, vicina; et ideo cum confirmatio detur ad liberam confessionem nominis Christi, convenienter unguntur confirmati in fronte.

AD PRIMUM ergo dicendum, quod unctio quae datur in vertice a sacerdote, significat dignitatem regalem et sacerdotalem in baptizato, quia incipit esse de numero illorum quibus dicitur: *vos estis gens sancta, regale sacerdotium,* 1 Petr. 2, 9; et ideo in vertice fit ad significandum eminentiam dignitatis collatae. Sed unctio confirmationis datur ad fortiter defendendam dignitatem acceptam, quod amplius est; et ideo in loco publico dari debet.

AD SECUNDUM dicendum quod non datur hoc sacramentum ad confessionem simpliciter, sed ad libertatem confessionis; et ideo debet dari ubi apparent illae passiones quae liberam confessionem impedire possunt.

AD TERTIUM dicendum, quod ex hoc non est periculum: quia ligatur frons confirmati quousque desiccetur locus; et postmodum etiam secundum Hugonem, debet esse sub quadam disciplina custodiendi chrisma, ne scilicet caput lavet usque ad septem dies propter septem dona Spiritus Sancti, sicut etiam ecclesia septem diebus adventum Spiritus Sancti in discipulos celebrat.

TO THE SECOND QUESTION, it should be said that a man can be prevented from a free and open confession of Christ's name by two things: namely, the fear of death, and shame, which is the fear of disgrace. But the sign of either one is particularly manifest in the face, for *people turn pale when they are afraid, and red when they are ashamed,* as it says in *Ethics* 4;[75] and particularly in the forehead, which is the most open part and closest to the imagination, from which the passions mentioned come forth; and therefore since confirmation is given for the free confession of Christ's name, it is fitting that those confirmed are anointed on the forehead.

REPLY OBJ. 1: The anointing that is given on the crown of the head by the priest represents the dignity of king and priest in the newly baptized, for he begins to be of the number of those to whom it is said: *you are a holy people, a royal priesthood* (1 Pet 2:9); and therefore it is done on the crown to represent the eminence of the dignity conferred. But the anointing of confirmation is given for bravely defending the dignity received, which is greater; and so it should be given on a more public place.

REPLY OBJ. 2: This sacrament is not given for confessing simply, but for freedom of confession, and so it should be given where those passions appear that can impede free confession.

REPLY OBJ. 3: There is no danger of collecting dirt; for the forehead of the confirmed person is tied until the place is dry;[76] and afterward also, according to Hugh, there should be a certain instruction in protecting the chrism, so that one does not wash his head for seven days, on account of the seven gifts of the Holy Spirit, just as also the Church celebrates for seven days the coming of the Holy Spirit upon the apostles.

Response to Quaestiuncula 3

AD TERTIAM QUAESTIONEM dicendum, quod sacramentum quod habet effectum semper permanentem, non potest iterari sine injuria sacramenti: et quia in confirmatione imprimitur character, qui est indelebilis, ideo non debet iterari.

AD PRIMUM ergo dicendum, quod Eucharistia non imprimit characterem; nec illud quod est res et sacra-

TO THE THIRD QUESTION, it should be said that a sacrament that has an effect that endures forever cannot be received again without injury to the sacrament; and because a character is imprinted in confirmation that is indelible, for that reason it should not be received again.

REPLY OBJ. 1: The Eucharist does not imprint a character; nor is its reality-and-sacrament any form received in

---

75. Aristotle, *Nicomachean Ethics,* Bk. 4, ch. 15, 1128b13–14.

76. According to a long-standing custom, a white cloth or ribbon was tied around the forehead immediately after the anointing, out of reverence for the sanctity of the chrism, which is a holy object consecrated by the bishop. Although instructions to this effect remained in liturgical books well into the twentieth century, it became common by the nineteenth century for an assistant to wipe the chrism off with a cloth immediately after the anointing and to dispose of the cloth as any holy object would be disposed of.

mentum, est aliqua forma recepta in recipiente sacramentum, sicut est in confirmatione; et ideo non est similis ratio.

Ad secundum dicendum, quod confirmatio datur contra infirmitatem, prout est contracta per originale peccatum; et sic non redit, quamvis infirmitas actualis peccati redeat.

the one receiving the sacrament, as it is in confirmation; and so the account is not the same.[77]

Reply Obj. 2: Confirmation is given against the weakness that is specifically contracted by original sin; and that is why it does not return, although the weakness that comes from actual sin may return.

---

77. For more about the sacrament alone, reality alone, and sacrament-and-reality, see the footnote at Dist.1, q.1, a.4, qa. 1, main response.

EXPOSITION OF THE TEXT

Donatio Spiritus Sancti ad robur. Contra. *Panis cor hominis confirmat*; Psalm. 103. Ergo magis pertinet ad Eucharistiam quam ad confirmationem. Et dicendum, quod per Eucharistiam roboratur caritas, per hoc autem sacramentum fides: in his enim duabus virtutibus tota virtus spiritualis aedificii consistit. Vel dicendum quod caritas perficit et roborat ad standum in seipso per modum cibi, sed confirmatio ad pugnam quam quis ab aliis patitur in confessione nominis Christi contra adversarios audaciam praebens.

Hoc sacramentum tantum a jejunis accipi et jejunis tradi debet. Propter eminentiam Spiritus Sancti, qui cum sua plenitudine in hoc sacramento datur ad robur.

The giving of the Holy Spirit for strengthening.[78] Against this: *Bread strengthens the heart of men* (Ps 103:15). Therefore, this pertains more to the Eucharist than to confirmation. And it should be said that by the Eucharist charity is strengthened, but by this sacrament, faith is: for in these two virtues all the strength of the spiritual edifice consists. Or it could be said that charity perfects and strengthens for standing on one's own in the manner of food, but confirmation by supplying boldness for the fight that someone must undergo against others in the confession of Christ's name against adversaries.

This sacrament ought to be conferred and received by people who are fasting.[79] Because of the eminence of the Holy Spirit, who, with his fullness, is given in this sacrament for strengthening.

78. *Sent.* IV, 7.3 (45), 1.
79. *Sent.* IV, 7.4 (46), 2.

DISTINCTION 8

THE SACRAMENT OF THE EUCHARIST

Postquam Magister determinavit de baptismo et confirmatione, hic tertio determinat de Eucharistiae sacramento; et dividitur in partes duas: in prima determinat ea quae pertinent ad ipsum sacramentum; in secunda determinat de dispensantibus sacramentum, 13 dist., ibi: *solet etiam quaeri, utrum pravi sacerdotes hoc sacramentum conficere queant.*

Prima in duas: in prima determinat ea quae requiruntur ad hoc sacramentum in generali; in secunda prosequitur de eis in speciali, dist. 10, ibi: *sunt item alii praecedentium insaniam transcendentes.*

Prima iterum in duas: in prima determinat ea quae requiruntur ad hoc sacramentum; in secunda determinat usum sacramenti, 9 dist., ibi: *et sicut duae sunt res illius sacramenti, ita et duo modi manducandi.*

Prima autem in tres: in prima determinat praecedentia Eucharistiam quibus hoc sacramentum figuratur; in secunda determinat concomitantia, quibus hoc sacramentum integratur, scilicet formam et institutionem, ibi: *hic etiam ante alia consideranda occurrunt quatuor*; in tertia determinat consequentia, quae in hoc sacramento efficiuntur vel significantur, ibi: *nunc quid ibi sacramentum sit et quid res, videamus.*

Secunda pars dividitur in tres: in prima determinat institutionem; in secunda formam, ibi: *forma vero est quam ipse ibidem edidit*; in tertia movet quamdam quaestionem, et solvit, ibi: *ubi consideratione dignum est quare illud sacramentum post coenam dedit discipulis.*

Nunc quid ibi sit sacramentum et quid res, videamus. Hic determinat de sacramento Eucharistiae per comparationem ad significatum vel causatum ejus: et circa hoc duo facit. Primo ostendit quid sit ibi res, et quid sacramentum. Secundo concludit eorum numerum et ordinem, ibi: *sunt igitur, hic tria distinguenda*, etc.

Hic est duplex quaestio. Prima de ipso Eucharistiae sacramento. Secunda de forma ipsius.

After the Master has examined baptism and confirmation, here he examines the sacrament of the Eucharist. And this is divided into two parts: in the first part, he defines those things that pertain to this sacrament; in the second, he considers those who administer this sacrament, in Distinction 13, at: *It is usual to ask whether bad priests are able to confect this sacrament.*[1]

The first part is in two parts: in the first part he determines what things are required for this sacrament in general; in the second, he describes these specifically, at Distinction 10: *There are also others who go beyond the insanity of those already mentioned.*[2]

The first again is in two parts: in the first, he determines those things required for this sacrament; in the second, he determines the use of the sacrament, at Distinction 9: *And just as there are two things of that sacrament, so also there are "two ways of eating."*

Now the first section is in three parts: in the first, he examines those things that preceded the Eucharist by which this sacrament was prefigured; in the second, he examines the concomitant things with which this sacrament is renewed, namely, its form and institution, at: *Here too before anything else, four things are to be considered*;[3] in the third, he examines the results that are brought about or symbolized in this sacrament, at: *Now let us see what in it is the sacrament and what the thing.*[4]

The second part is divided into three: in the first he examines its institution; in the second, its form, at: *As for the form, it is what he himself made known*;[5] in the third, he raises a certain question and resolves it, at: *Here it is worth considering why he gave that sacrament to the disciples after supper.*[6]

Now let us see what in it is the sacrament and what the thing. Here he examines the sacrament of the Eucharist in reference to what it signifies or causes: and concerning this he does two things. First, he shows what is the reality in it, and what is the sacrament. Second, he draws a conclusion about their number and order, at: *And so there are three things to distinguish here*, etc.[7]

Here there are two questions. The first concerns the sacrament of the Eucharist itself; the second concerns its form.

1. Peter Lombard, *Sententiae* IV, 13.1 (72), 1.
2. *Sent.* IV, 10.1 (58), 1.
3. *Sent.* IV, 8.3 (50), 1.
4. *Sent.* IV, 8.6 (53), 1.
5. *Sent.* IV, 8.4 (51), 1.
6. *Sent.* IV, 8.5 (52), 1.
7. *Sent.* IV, 8.7 (54), 2.

QUESTION 1

THE EUCHARIST IN GENERAL

Circa primum quaeruntur quatuor:
primo, utrum Eucharistia sit sacramentum;
secundo, de significatione ejus;
tertio, de institutione;
quarto, de ordine sumendi hunc cibum respectu
    aliorum ciborum.

About the first, four questions arise:
first, whether the Eucharist is a sacrament;
second, its signification;
third, its institution;
fourth, the order of consuming this food in relation to
    other foods.

ARTICLE 1

Whether the Eucharist is a sacrament

Quaestiuncula 1

AD PRIMUM SIC PROCEDITUR. Videtur quod Eucharistia non sit sacramentum. Ad idem enim non debent diversa ordinari. Sed confirmatio est ad perficiendum, secundum Dionysium. Cum ergo secundum ipsum Eucharistia etiam sit perfectio, videtur quod superfluat hoc sacramentum.

PRAETEREA, in omni sacramento novae legis idem quod figuratur, efficitur per signum figurans. Sed species panis et vini, quae figurant corpus Christi verum et mysticum, non efficiunt illud. Ergo Eucharistia non est sacramentum novae legis.

PRAETEREA, *sacramentum est elementum materiale*, secundum Hugonem, *exterius oculis suppositum*. Sed corpus Christi verum quod dicitur hic sacramentum et res similiter, non est oculis videntium suppositum. Ergo non est sacramentum.

PRAETEREA, omne sacramentum in ipsa sui susceptione consecratur et perficitur, sicut patet de baptismo, quod perficitur in ipsa ablutione. Sed Eucharistia consecratur ante sumptionem. Ergo non est sacramentum.

PRAETEREA, in omni alio sacramento illud quod est res et sacramentum, est aliquid effectum in suscipiente, sicut character in baptismo. Sed corpus Christi verum, quod ponitur hic res et sacramentum, non est aliquid in

OBJ. 1: To the first question we proceed thus. It seems that the Eucharist is not a sacrament.[8] For different things should not be ordered to the same end. But confirmation is for perfecting, according to Dionysius.[9] Since therefore according to him the Eucharist is also a perfection, it seems that this sacrament is superfluous.

OBJ. 2: Furthermore, in every sacrament of the New Law, what is represented is brought about by the sign representing it. But the species of bread and wine, which represent the Body of Christ really and mystically, do not bring it about. Therefore, the Eucharist is not a sacrament of the New Law.

OBJ. 3: Furthermore, *a sacrament is a material element externally placed before our eyes*, according to Hugh.[10] But the true Body of Christ, which both this sacrament and its reality are called, is not set before our eyes. Therefore, this is not a sacrament.

OBJ. 4: Furthermore, every sacrament is consecrated and completed by its very reception, as is evident in the case of baptism, which is completed by the very act of washing. But the Eucharist is consecrated before its consumption. Therefore, it is not a sacrament.

OBJ. 5: Furthermore, in every other sacrament the reality-and-sacrament is a certain effect in the receiver, like the character in baptism. But the true Body of Christ which is here considered as reality-and-sacrament, is not anything

---

8. Parallels: *ST* III, q. 65, a. 1; q. 73, a. 1; q. 79, aa. 5 & 7; *SCG* IV, ch. 61; *Super I ad Cor.* 11, lec. 5.
9. Pseudo-Dionysius, *Ecclesiastical Hierarchy*, ch. 5, p. 1, n. 3 (PG 3:503).
10. Hugh of St. Victor, *De sacramentis fidei*, Bk. 1, pt. 9, ch. 2 (PL 176:317).

recipiente effectum. Ergo non est sacramentum ejusdem rationis cum aliis.

SED CONTRA est quod in Collecta dicitur: *praesta ut hoc tuum sacramentum non sit nobis reatus ad poenam.*

PRAETEREA, omnis actio per ministros ecclesiae dispensata, in qua ex ipso opere operato gratia confertur, est sacramentum. Sed Eucharistia est hujusmodi. Ergo est sacramentum.

effected in the receiver. Therefore, it is not a sacrament with the same nature as the others.

ON THE CONTRARY, is what is said in the Collect: *Grant that this Thy sacrament may not be unto us a condemnation.*[11]

FURTHERMORE, every action administered by the ministers of the Church in which grace is conferred by the very action performed, is a sacrament. But the Eucharist is one of these. Therefore, it is a sacrament.

Quaestiuncula 2

ULTERIUS. Videtur quod non sit unum sacramentum, sed multa. Primo per hoc quod in Collecta dicitur: *purificent nos, quaesumus Domine, sacramenta quae sumpsimus.*

PRAETEREA, sacramentum est in genere signi. Sed ea quae sunt in genere signi, sicut nomina, plurificantur ad pluralitatem signantium, quamvis sit idem signatum; sicut Marcus et Tullius sunt duo nomina, quamvis sit eadem res significata. Ergo cum in Eucharistia sint plura signantia, sicut species panis et vini, videtur quod sint plura sacramenta.

PRAETEREA, unitas rei est ex forma sua. Sed in Eucharistia sunt duae formae, una ad consecrationem panis, alia ad consecrationem sanguinis. Ergo sunt duo sacramenta.

PRAETEREA, ea quae nec in genere nec in specie conveniunt, sunt plura simpliciter. Sed corpus Christi verum cum speciebus panis et vini sunt differentia et specie et genere. Ergo sunt plura simpliciter. Cum ergo utrumque dicatur sacramentum in Eucharistia, videtur quod non sit unum sacramentum.

PRAETEREA, ex duobus perfectis non fit aliquid unum. Sed Christus perfecte est sub utraque specie, scilicet panis et vini. Ergo ex his duobus non fit unum sacramentum.

SED CONTRA est, quia si essent duo, tunc sacramenta novae legis non essent tantum septem.

PRAETEREA, quaecumque ordinantur ad idem efficiendum et significandum, pertinent ad unum sacramentum. Sed omnia quae in Eucharistia sunt, pertinent ad idem repraesentandum, scilicet mortem Domini, et idem efficiendum, scilicet gratiam, per quam homo incorporatur corpori mystico. Ergo est unum tantum sacramentum.

OBJ. 1: Moreover, it seems that it is not one sacrament, but many.[12] First, because it says in the Collect: *May the sacraments that we have received purify us, we beseech Thee, O Lord.*[13]

OBJ. 2: Furthermore, a sacrament is in the genus of signs. But those things that are in the genus of signs, like names, are multiplied when the signifiers are multiplied, even when they signify only one thing; for example, Marcus and Tullius are two names, although the thing signified is the same. Therefore, since in the Eucharist there are several signifying things, like the species of bread and wine, it seems that there are several sacraments.

OBJ. 3: Furthermore, the singularity of a thing comes from its form. But in the Eucharist there are two forms, one at the consecration of the bread, another at the consecration of the Blood. Therefore, there are two sacraments.

OBJ. 4: Furthermore, things that do not share either in genus or in species are simply different things. But the true Body of Christ is different from the appearance of bread and wine in both genus and species. Therefore, they are simply different things. Since, then, either may be called the sacrament of the Eucharist, it seems that it is not one sacrament.

OBJ. 5: Furthermore, some single thing is not made out of two complete things. But Christ is completely under both species, that is, bread and wine. Therefore, one sacrament is not made out of these two things.

ON THE CONTRARY, if these were two things, then there would not be only seven sacraments of the New Law.

FURTHERMORE, any things that are ordered to effecting and signifying the same thing pertain to the same sacrament. But all the things that are in the Eucharist pertain to representing the same thing, namely, the death of the Lord; and bringing about the same thing, namely, the grace by which man is incorporated into the Mystical Body. Therefore, this is only one sacrament.

---

11. This phrase is found in the third Lenten postcommunion, "for the Living and the Dead," found in missals printed prior to the reduction of orations to one set only.

12. Parallels: *ST* III, q. 73, a. 2; q. 78, a. 6, ad 2.

13. In the same postcommunion as above.

Quaestiuncula 3

ULTERIUS. Videtur quod non convenientibus nominibus nominetur. Nomen enim proprium alicui debet imponi ex eo quod sit sibi proprium. Sed bonitas gratiae est communis omnibus sacramentis. Ergo ex hoc non debet imponi nomen proprium uni sacramento, ut dicatur Eucharistia.

PRAETEREA, sicut in littera dicitur, hoc sacramentum ideo *viaticum appellatur, quia in via nos reficiens, usque ad patriam deducit.* Sed hoc est commune omnibus sacramentis, quae non nisi viatoribus dantur ad perveniendum ad gloriam patriae, quae est res non contenta, et significata in omnibus sacramentis. Ergo non convenienter 'viaticum' appellatur.

PRAETEREA, causae per effectus denominari solent. Sed adducere ad communionem fidelium est effectus baptismi, secundum Dionysium, ut ex praedictis patet. Ergo baptismus magis debet dici communio vel synaxis, quam hoc sacramentum.

PRAETEREA, in quolibet sacramento fit aliquid sacrum. Sed hoc importat sacrificii nomen. Ergo sacrificium etiam non est nomen proprium hujus sacramenti.

PRAETEREA, hostia videtur idem quod sacrificium. Sed Dionysius confirmationem nominat chrismatis hostiam. Ergo neque hostia neque sacrificium est nomen proprium huic sacramento.

OBJ. 1: Moreover, it seems that it is not named with fitting names.[14] For a name proper to a certain thing should be imposed from what is proper to it. But the goodness of grace is common to all the sacraments. Therefore, it should not be imposed as a name proper to one sacrament, so that we call it 'Eucharist.'

OBJ. 2: Furthermore, as it says in the text, this sacrament *is called viaticum, "way-bread," because it renews us on the journey until it leads us to the heavenly fatherland.* But this is common to all the sacraments, that they are only given to those on the journey in order to arrive at the glory of the homeland, which is the reality not contained but signified in all the sacraments. Therefore, it is not fittingly called 'viaticum.'

OBJ. 3: Furthermore, causes are usually named from their effects. But to lead one into communion with the faithful is the effect of baptism, according to Dionysius,[15] as is clear from what was said above. Therefore, baptism, rather than this sacrament, should be called Communion or 'synaxis.'

OBJ. 4: Furthermore, in any sacrament something sacred is done. But this is what the name 'sacrifice' conveys. Therefore, 'sacrifice' is also not a name proper to this sacrament.

OBJ. 5: Furthermore, 'host,' sacrificial offering, seems to be the same thing as 'sacrifice.' But Dionysius calls confirmation *the host of chrism.*[16] Therefore, neither 'host' nor 'sacrifice' is a name proper to this sacrament.

Response to Quaestiuncula 1

RESPONDEO dicendum ad primam quaestionem, quod Eucharistia sacramentum quoddam est, alio tamen modo ab omnibus aliis sacramentis. Sacramentum enim secundum sui nominis proprietatem sanctitatem active importat; unde secundum hoc aliquid habet sacramenti rationem secundum quod habet rationem sanctificationis, qua sanctum aliquid fit.

Dicitur autem aliquid sanctum dupliciter. Uno modo simpliciter et per se, sicut quod est subjectum sanctitatis, sicut dicitur homo sanctus. Alio modo secundario et secundum quid, ex eo quod habet ordinem ad hanc sanctitatem, vel sicut habens virtutem sanctificandi, sicut chrisma dicitur sanctum; vel quocumque alio modo ad aliquid sanctum deputetur, sicut altare sanctum.

TO THE FIRST QUESTION, I answer that the Eucharist is a certain sacrament, but in a different way from all the other sacraments. For a sacrament, according to the property of its own name, conveys holiness in an active way; and so accordingly something has the nature of a sacrament to the extent that it has the nature of a sanctification, by which something is made holy.

But something is said to be holy in two ways. In one way, simply speaking and in itself, like something that is the subject of holiness, as a man is said to be holy. The other way is secondary and only in a certain respect, by the fact that it has an order to the first holiness, either as something having the power of sanctifying, as chrism is called holy; or in some other way it may be set aside for something holy, like a holy altar.

---

14. Parallels: *ST* III, q. 73, a. 4; q. 79, a. 2, ad 1.

15. Pseudo-Dionysius, *Ecclesiastical Hierarchy*, ch. 3, p. 1 (PG 3:391).

16. Pseudo-Dionysius, *Ecclesiastical Hierarchy*, ch. 4, p. 1 (PG 3:471).

Et ideo ea quibus aliquid fit sanctum primo modo, dicuntur sacramenta simpliciter; illa autem quibus fit aliquid sanctum secundo modo, non dicuntur sacramenta, sed sacramentalia magis. In aliis ergo sacramentis fit aliquid sanctum primo modo, sicut homo suscipiens sacramentum; non autem elementum corporale sanctificans hominem, quia hoc est sanctum secundo modo; et ideo hoc quod pertinet ad sanctificationem materiae in omnibus sacramentis non est sacramentum, sed sacramentale; sed hoc quod pertinet ad usum materiae qua homo sanctificatur, est sacramentum.

In hoc autem sacramento illud quod est sanctificans hominem, est sanctum primo modo, quasi subjectum sanctitatis, quia est ipse Christus; et ideo ipsa sanctificatio materiae est hic sacramentum; sed sanctificatio hominis est effectus sacramenti. Et ideo hoc sacramentum in se consideratum, est dignius omnibus sacramentis, quia habet absolutam sanctitatem etiam praeter suscipientem; alia autem non habent nisi in ordine ad aliud; et ideo hoc sacramentum est perfectio aliorum sacramentorum; quia omne quod est per aliud, reducitur ad id quod est per se, sicut patet de accidente et substantia.

AD PRIMUM ergo dicendum quod *perfectum unumquodque est, cum attingit propriam virtutem,* ut dicitur in 7 *Phys. Virtus autem est ultimum in re,* ut dicitur in 1 *de Caelo et Mundo;* et ideo perfectio rei consistit in hoc quod res ad sui ultimum perducatur. Est autem dupliciter ultimum rei; unum quod est in re, et aliud quod est extra rem; sicut in corporibus ultimum in corpore est superficies corporis contenti; ultimum extra, locus qui est superficies corporis continentis. Ultimum autem cujuslibet rei in re ipsa est ipsa rei operatio, propter quam res est: *forma enim est finis generationis, non ipsius generati,* ut dicit Commentator in 2 *Physica.* Unde res quae habet formam substantialem per quam est, esse non dicitur perfecta simpliciter, sed perfecta in esse, vel perfecta perfectione prima; et talem perfectionem quantum ad esse spirituale acquirit homo in baptismo, quo est regeneratio spiritualis; et ideo Dionysius non ponit baptismum habentem vim perfectivam simpliciter, sed magis purgativam et illuminativam. Sed simpliciter perfectum dicitur quod habet operationem convenientem suae formae. In hoc enim consistit virtus rei, secundum Philosophum in 2 *Ethic.,* per cujus consecutionem aliquid dicitur perfectum, ut dictum est.

And therefore those things by which something becomes holy in the first way are called sacraments simply speaking. But those things by which something is made holy in the second way are not called sacraments, but rather sacramentals. Therefore, in the other sacraments, something is made holy in the first way, like the man receiving the sacrament, but not the physical element sanctifying the man, because that is holy in the second way; and so what pertains to the sanctification of the matter in all the sacraments is not a sacrament, but a sacramental; but what pertains to the use of the matter by which the man is sanctified is the sacrament.

However, in the sacrament of the Eucharist, what is sanctifying the man is holy in the first way, as the subject of holiness, because it is Christ himself; and thus the sanctification of the matter is this sacrament, but the sanctification of the man is the effect of the sacrament. And thus this sacrament considered in itself is more worthy than all the other sacraments, because it has absolute holiness even apart from anyone receiving it, but the others only have this as ordered to something else. And so this sacrament is the perfection of the other sacraments, for everything that is through another can be reduced to what is through itself, as is evident with accidents and substance.

REPLY OBJ. 1: *Anything is perfect when it has attained its proper power,* as is said in *Physics* 7.[17] However, *power is what comes last in a thing,* as it says in *On the Heavens and the Earth* 1.[18] And so the perfection of a thing consists in its being brought to what is last for it. However, what is last for a thing is twofold: one is in the thing, the other is outside it; just as in bodies what is last in a body is the surface of the body contained; while what comes last outside the body is its place, which is the surface of the containing body. However, what comes last for any thing in the thing itself is the thing's very operation, for the sake of which the thing exists; *for a form is the end of generation, but not of the thing generated,* as the Commentator says about *Physics* 2.[19] Hence a thing that has the substantial form by which it exists is not said to be perfect simply speaking, but perfect in being, or perfect with the first kind of perfection; and man acquires this kind of perfection as to spiritual being in baptism, by which there is a spiritual regeneration. And this is why Dionysius does not consider baptism to have simply perfective force, but rather purifying and illuminative force.[20] But what is perfect simply speaking has the operation befitting its own form. For according to the Philosopher in *Ethics* 2,[21] the power of a thing consists in the execution of whatever enables something to be called perfect, as was said.

---

17. Aristotle, *Physics*, Bk. 7, ch. 3, 246a13–14.
18. Aristotle, *On the Heavens and the Earth*, Bk. 1, ch. 11, 281a5 ff.
19. Comment 75 on the text of the *Physics*.
20. See Pseudo-Dionysius, *Ecclesiastical Hierarchy*, throughout ch. 2.
21. Aristotle, *Nicomachean Ethics*, Bk. 2, ch. 1, 1109a25.

Hominis autem operatio spiritualis est duplex. Una ipsius inquantum est persona privata; et quantum ad hoc perficit confirmatio, quae facit hominem non impeditum aliquo mundano timore in confessione fidei, et aliis quae ad Christianam religionem spectant. Alia, inquantum est persona publica, quasi membrum principale, et influens aliis membris; et quantum ad hoc perficit sacramentum ordinis.

Ultimum autem cujuslibet rei extra seipsam, est principium a quo res habet esse: quia per conjunctionem ad ipsum res complentur et firmantur, et propter distantiam ab ipso deficiunt, sicut corruptibilia propter longe distare a primo, ut dicitur in 2 *de Generat.*; et ideo primum agens habet etiam rationem ultimi finis perficientis. Fons autem Christianae vitae est Christus; et ideo hoc modo Eucharistia perficit, Christo conjungens; et ideo hoc sacramentum est perfectio omnium perfectionum, ut Dionysius dicit; unde et omnes qui sacramenta alia accipiunt, hoc sacramento in fine confirmantur, ut ipse dicit.

AD SECUNDUM dicendum quod sicut ad species sensibiles aliorum sacramentorum se habet virtus quae interius inest, quae sanctificationem acquirit, ex qua sacramentum efficit, secundum Hugonem, ita in hoc sacramento se habet ipsum corpus Christi, quod per consecrationem sub speciebus illis fit. Unde sicut in aliis sacramentis materiale elementum non est causa virtutis quae in ipso est, neque alicujus spiritualis effectus in homine, nisi mediante virtute, secundum quod ex elemento et virtute quasi unum efficitur; ita in hoc sacramento species non sunt causa corporis Christi, neque alicujus effectus in anima spiritualis, nisi mediante corpore Christi vero, secundum quod ex speciebus et corpore Christi fit unum sacramentum. Utrum autem species illae secundum se habeant aliquem effectum corporalem, sicut aqua corporaliter abluit in baptismo, etiam non mediante spirituali virtute, infra dicetur.

AD TERTIUM dicendum, quod omne sacramentum est visibile; non tamen oportet quod quidquid est in sacramento, sit visibile. Videtur enim species visibilis aquae in baptismo, sed non videtur virtus spiritualis, quae secretius operatur salutem; et similiter hic videntur species, sed non videtur verum corpus Christi. Vel dicendum, quod est visibile non in se, sed in speciebus quae ipsum tegunt; sicut et substantia aliorum corporum videtur mediante colore.

AD QUARTUM dicendum, quod sanctitas quae est in materiis aliorum sacramentorum, non est forma sanctitatis absolute, sed secundum ordinem ad aliud, ut in 1

Now a man's spiritual operation is twofold. One is as a private person, and confirmation perfects him in this, for it makes a man unhindered by any earthly fear in confessing the faith or other things that regard the Christian religion. The other is as a public person, like a principal member who influences the other members, and the sacrament of holy orders perfects him in this.

But what comes last for any thing outside of itself is the beginning from which the thing has its being: for by joining with it, things are completed and strengthened, and they fail because of the distance from it, as corruptible things do because of their great distance from what is first, as it says in *On the Generation of Animals* 2.[22] And so the first agent also has the nature of a perfecting last end. However, the font of Christian life is Christ, and thus the Eucharist perfects in this way, by uniting us to Christ. And so this sacrament is the perfection of all perfections, as Dionysius says; hence all who receive the other sacraments are confirmed in their end by this sacrament, as he himself says.[23]

REPLY OBJ. 2: According to Hugh,[24] as the interior power, which acquires sanctification, from which the sacrament works, stands in relation to the sensible species of the other sacraments, so in this sacrament stands the very Body of Christ, which comes to be under these species by the consecration. Hence just as in other sacraments the material element is not a cause of the power that is in it, nor of any spiritual effect in man (except by means of the power, according as an element and a power could be made to be like one thing); so also in this sacrament the species are not the cause of the Body of Christ, nor of any spiritual effect in the soul, except by means of the true Body of Christ, according as one sacrament is made out of the species and the Body of Christ. But whether those species have any physical effect in themselves, the way that water physically cleanses in baptism, even without spiritual power mediating, will be addressed below.[25]

REPLY OBJ. 3: Every sacrament is visible, but nevertheless it is not necessary that whatever is in the sacrament be visible. For the visible appearance of water is seen in baptism, but its spiritual power, which works our salvation in a hidden way, is not seen. And similarly here the appearances are seen, but the true Body of Christ is not seen. Or it could be said that it is not visible in itself, but under the appearances that cover it; just as also the substance of other bodies is seen by means of color.

REPLY OBJ. 4: The holiness that is in the matters of the other sacraments is not the form of holiness absolutely, but a holiness that is ordered to something else, as was said in

22. Aristotle, *On the Generation of Animals*, Bk. 2, ch. 10, 336b30.
23. Pseudo-Dionysius, *Ecclesiastical Hierarchy*, ch. 3 (PG 3:423).
24. Hugh of St. Victor, *De sacramentis fidei*, Bk. 1, pt. 9, ch. 2 (PL 176:317).
25. See d. 12, q. 1, a. 2, qa. 5.

dist. dictum est; et ideo non est simile de aliis sacramentis et de hoc, ut ex dictis patet.

AD QUINTUM dicendum, quod ex hoc ipso quod alia sacramenta perficiuntur in acceptione vel collatione, contingit quod illud quod est in eis sacramentum et res, est aliquid acquisitum in suscipiente; in hoc autem sacramento aliter est, ut ex dictis patet.

Distinction 1; and therefore it is not the same with the other sacraments as with this one, as is clear from what has been said.

REPLY OBJ. 5: The fact that the other sacraments are perfected in their reception or conferral means that their sacrament-and-reality is something acquired in the recipient; but in this sacrament it is different, as is clear from what has been said.[26]

Response to Quaestiuncula 2

AD SECUNDAM QUAESTIONEM dicendum, quod per se unum simpliciter, et quod est numero unum, tribus modis dicitur. Uno modo sicut indivisibile est unum, ut punctum et unitas, quod neque est multa actu neque potentia. Alio modo quod est unum ex continuitate, quod tamen est multa potentia, sicut linea. Tertio modo quod est unum perfectione, sicut dicitur calceamentum unum, quia habet omnes partes quae requiruntur ad calceamentum; et haec unitas dicitur in omnibus illis ad quorum integritatem aliqua exiguntur, sicut unus homo, una domus. Et quia ad esse sacramenti multa concurrunt, sicut forma et materia, et hujusmodi; ideo ab hac unitate perfectionis[27] dicitur sacramentum unum esse. Illa enim sunt de integritate alicujus instrumenti quae requiruntur ad operationem illam ad quam instrumentum deputatum est. Hoc autem sacramentum deputatum est ex divina institutione ad cibationem spiritualem, quae per cibationem corporalem significatur. Et quia cibatio corporalis duo requirit, scilicet aliquid per modum cibi, et aliquid per modum potus; ideo ad integritatem hujus sacramenti ex divina institutione est aliquid per modum cibi, scilicet corpus Christi; et aliquid per modum potus, scilicet sanguis.

AD PRIMUM ergo dicendum, quod dicitur pluraliter sacramenta propter materialem diversitatem signorum.

AD SECUNDUM dicendum, quod ratio illa procedit quando utrumque signum habet integram significationem; sic autem non est hic: quia cibatio spiritualis non significatur perfecte neque per panis tantum neque per vini tantum sumptionem, sed per utrumque simul, sicut est in significatione nominum compositorum.

AD TERTIUM dicendum, quod ratio illa procederet, si utraque forma responderet toti sacramento; sed hoc falsum est: quia una forma respondet uni, et alia alii eorum quae ad sacramentum exiguntur.

AD QUARTUM dicendum, quod quamvis non sint unum in genere vel specie naturae, possunt tamen esse unum per relationem ad unam operationem, ex qua unitate sumitur unitas sacramenti.

TO THE SECOND QUESTION, it should be said that what is one thing in itself simply, and what is one in number, can be said in three ways. In one way, as the indivisible is one thing, like a point and oneness, which is not many things either in act or in potency. In another way, what is one thing by continuity, which is, however, many things in potency, like a line. In the third way, what is one in perfection, as a shoe is said to be one thing because it has all the parts that are required for a shoe; and this oneness is said about anything that requires several things for its integrity, like one man or one house. And because many things converge for the being of a sacrament, like form and matter and things like that, for this reason a sacrament is said to be one thing by this oneness. For those things are integral to a certain instrument which are required for whatever operation the instrument is designed for. But this sacrament is designed by its divine institution as a spiritual meal, which is signified by the physical meal. And since two things are required for a physical meal, namely, something in the mode of food and something in the mode of drink, therefore for this sacrament's integrity by divine institution there is something in the mode of food, namely the Body of Christ, and something in the mode of drink, namely, his Blood.

REPLY OBJ. 1: 'Sacraments' is said in the plural because of the material diversity of the signs.

REPLY OBJ. 2: That argument works when either sign has the full signification, but that is not the case here: for a spiritual meal is not perfectly represented by the consumption of either bread or wine alone, but of both of them together, as it happens in the case of composite names.

REPLY OBJ. 3: That argument would work if either form corresponded to the whole sacrament; but this is false: for one form corresponds to one and the other to the other of those things that are required for the sacrament.

REPLY OBJ. 4: Although they are not one thing in natural genus or species, nevertheless they can be one thing by their relation to one operation, and the oneness of the sacrament is taken from this unity.

---

26. For more about the sacrament alone, reality alone, and sacrament-and-reality, see the footnote at Dist.1, q.1, a.4, qa. 1, main response.
27. *unitate perfectionis dicitur.—unitate dicitur* PLE.

AD QUINTUM dicendum, quod quamvis Christus perfectus sit sub utraque specie, non tamen quantum ad integrum usum sacramenti est sub utroque, sed quantum ad diversos usus.

REPLY OBJ. 4: Although Christ is perfect under either species, he is not under each as to the integral use of the sacrament, but as to different uses.

Response to Quaestiuncula 3

AD TERTIAM QUAESTIONEM dicendum, quod in quolibet sacramento est tria considerare; scilicet originem, perfectionem, et finem ad quem est. Origo autem omnium sacramentorum est passio Christi, de cujus latere in cruce pendentis sacramenta profluxerunt, ut sancti dicunt; perfectio autem sacramenti est in hoc quod continet gratiam; finis autem sacramenti est duplex; proximus, scilicet sanctificatio recipientis, et ultimus, scilicet vita aeterna. Haec autem per quamdam excellentiam in Eucharistia inveniuntur. Quia hoc sacramentum est specialiter in memoriam Dominicae Passionis; unde Matthaei 26: *quotiescumque feceritis, in mei memoriam facietis*; et ideo quantum ad originem vocatur sacrificium vel hostia. Similiter etiam gratiam non per modum intentionis continet sicut alia sacramenta, sed plenitudinem gratiae in suo fonte; et ideo antonomastice Eucharistia dicitur. Similiter etiam quia ipsa est consummatio omnium sanctificationum, ut Dionysius dicit, id quod est omnium, scilicet congregari ad unum, huic sacramento attribuitur; et dicitur communio vel synaxis, quod idem est, inquantum scilicet homo congregatur ad unum et ad seipsum et ad alios, ei quod est maxime unum conjunctus. Similiter etiam quantum ad ultimum finem consequendum maximam efficaciam habet, inquantum realiter continet hoc quo janua caeli nobis aperta est, scilicet sanguinem Christi; et ideo specialiter viaticum appellatur.

ET PER HAEC patet solutio ad objecta: quia ab eo quod est commune, aliquid antonomastice denominari potest.

TO THE THIRD QUESTION, it should be said that in any sacrament there are three things to consider: namely, its origin, its perfection, and the end it is directed to. Now the origin of all the sacraments is the Passion of Christ, from whose side the sacraments poured forth while he was hanging on the Cross, as the saints say. And a sacrament's perfection resides in the fact that it contains grace. However, a sacrament's end is twofold: the proximate end, namely, the sanctification of the recipient, and the ultimate end, namely, eternal life. But these things are found with a certain excellence in the Eucharist. For this sacrament is especially a memorial of the Lord's Passion; hence Matthew 26: *whenever you do this, you will do it in memory of me*; [28] and so in regard to its origin it is called 'sacrifice' or 'host,' which means 'victim.' Likewise it also does not contain grace in the mode of intention, like the other sacraments, but the fullness of grace in its source; and so it is called 'Eucharist' antonomastically. Likewise also because it is the consummation of all sanctifications, as Dionysius says, whatever belongs to all of them, namely, to bring together into one, is particularly attributed to this sacrament; and so it is called 'Communion' or 'synaxis,' which is the same thing, because a man is brought together in one both in himself and with others, since he is united to that which is most one. Likewise, as to attaining the ultimate end, it has the greatest efficacy, inasmuch as it really contains what opened the gates of heaven for us, namely, the Blood of Christ; and so it is especially called 'viaticum,' food for the journey.

AND FROM THIS the answers to the objections are clear: for something can be named antonomastically from what is common to all.

---

28. In fact, Luke 22:18; cf. 1 Corinthians 11:25.

ARTICLE 2

The signification of the Eucharist

Quaestiuncula 1

AD SECUNDUM SIC PROCEDITUR. Videtur quod huic sacramento figurae assignari non debeant. Nihil enim disponitur per aliquid sui generis; albedinis enim non est albedo, nec motus est motus. Sed sacramentum est signum. Ergo sacramento non debet aptari aliqua figura, quia in infinitum iretur.

PRAETEREA, sacramenta veteris legis dicuntur sacramentis novae legis respondere, in quantum signant ipsa. Sacramentis autem novae legis quae sunt maximae perfectionis non respondebant aliqua sacramenta in veteri lege, ut quidam dicunt. Cum ergo hoc sacramentum sit maximae perfectionis, videtur quod non debeant ei aliquae figurae assignari.

PRAETEREA, sicut praefigurata Eucharistia est in agno paschali, ita et baptismus in transitu maris rubri, ut dicitur 1 Corinth., 10. Cum ergo Magister non assignaverit aliquas figuras baptismi, videtur quod nec Eucharistiae figuras assignare debeat.

SED CONTRA, hoc sacramentum memoriale passionis Christi est specialiter. Sed passionem Christi praecipue oportebat praefigurari, per quam nos redemit, ut fides antiquorum ad redemptorem ferretur. Ergo praecipue competebat hoc sacramentum figurari.

PRAETEREA, hoc sacramentum est dignissimum, et difficillimum ad credendum. Sed talia maxime consueverunt praefigurari. Ergo, etc.

OBJ. 1: To the second question we proceed thus.[29] It seems that figures should not be assigned to this sacrament. For nothing is disposed by anything of its own kind; for there is not a whiteness of white, nor a motion of motion. But a sacrament is a sign. Therefore, no figure should be applied to a sacrament, for it will result in an infinite regress.

OBJ. 2: Furthermore, sacraments of the Old Law are said to correspond to sacraments of the New Law, inasmuch as they represent them. But the sacraments of the New Law that are of the greatest perfection have no correspondents in the Old Law, as some people say. Since therefore this sacrament is of the greatest perfection, it seems that there should not be any figures assigned to it.

OBJ. 3: Furthermore, just as the Eucharist is prefigured in the Paschal lamb, so also baptism is prefigured in the crossing of the Red Sea, as it says in 1 Corinthians 10:1–2. Therefore, since the Master did not assign any figures to baptism, it seems that neither should he assign any figures to the Eucharist.

ON THE CONTRARY, this sacrament is especially the memorial of the Passion of Christ. But it was particularly fitting that the Passion of Christ, by which he redeemed us, be prefigured, so that the faith of the ancients might be raised toward their redeemer. Therefore it was most of all fitting that this sacrament be prefigured.

FURTHERMORE, this sacrament is the most noble and the most difficult to believe in. But that kind of thing is the most likely to be prefigured. Therefore, etc.

Quaestiuncula 2

ULTERIUS. Videtur quod Magister inconvenienter assignet figuras hujus sacramenti. Hoc enim sacramentum post baptismum datur. Sed agnus paschalis praecessit transitum maris rubri, in quo baptismus est praefiguratus. Ergo non est congrua figura hujus sacramenti.

PRAETEREA, in hoc sacramento aliquid offertur Deo. Sed Melchisedech non legitur Deo obtulisse, sed homini, scilicet Abrahae, cui obtulit panem et vinum, ut dicitur Gen. 14. Ergo illa oblatio non est conveniens figura hujus sacramenti.

OBJ. 1: Moreover, it seems that the Master inappropriately assigns figures to this sacrament.[30] For this sacrament is given after baptism. But the Paschal lamb preceded the crossing of the Red Sea, in which baptism is prefigured. Therefore, it is not a fitting figure for this sacrament.

OBJ. 2: Furthermore, in this sacrament something is offered to God. But Melchizedek is not read to have offered to God but to a man, namely, Abraham, to whom he offered bread and wine, as it says in Genesis 14:18. Therefore, that offering is not an appropriate figure for this sacrament.

---

29. Parallels: *ST* III, q. 61, a. 3, ad 3; q. 73, a. 6; q. 80, a. 10, ad 2.
30. Parallel: *ST* III, q. 73, a. 6.

PRAETEREA, idem non est signum sui ipsius. Sed sanguis qui consecratur in altari, est illemet quem Christus in cruce fudit pro nobis. Ergo ille non est signum vel figura istius.

PRAETEREA, manna habebat in se omnem saporis suavitatem, ut dicitur Sap. 16. Sed hoc sacramentum non habet in se omnem saporem spiritualem: quia sic haberet effectus omnium sacramentorum, et alia sacramenta superfluerent. Ergo manna non est figura hujus sacramenti.

PRAETEREA, nobilioris rei nobilior debet esse figura. Sed Eucharistia est nobilius sacramentum quam baptismus. Cum ergo baptismus habuerit figuram quae praebebat remedium ex ipso opere operato contra originale, scilicet circumcisionem; supradictae autem figurae non fuerunt tales; videtur quod fuerunt incompetentes.

PRAETEREA, in canone Missae fit mentio de sacrificio Abrahae et Abel; et similiter omnia sacrificia legalia hujus veri sacrificii figura fuerunt. Ergo insufficienter posuit Magister figuras hujus sacramenti.

OBJ. 3: Furthermore, the same thing is not a sign of itself. But the Blood that is consecrated on the altar is the very same that Christ shed for us on the Cross. Therefore, it is not a sign or figure of itself.

OBJ. 4: Furthermore, manna had in itself all sweetness of flavor, as it says in Wisdom 16:20. But this sacrament does not have in itself all spiritual flavor, for then it would have the effect of all the sacraments, and the other sacraments would be superfluous. Therefore, manna is not a figure of this sacrament.

OBJ. 5: Furthermore, something nobler should be the figure of a nobler thing. But the Eucharist is a nobler sacrament than baptism. Therefore, since there was a figure of baptism which furnished a remedy against original sin by its very act being performed, namely, circumcision, while the figures mentioned above had nothing like that, it seems that those figures were inadequate.

OBJ. 6: Furthermore, in the canon of the Mass mention is made of the sacrifice of Abraham and Abel; [31] and likewise all the sacrifices of the law were figures of this true sacrifice. Therefore, the Master has not sufficiently listed the figures of this sacrament.

Quaestiuncula 3

ULTERIUS. Videtur quod in lege Moysi expressius fuit figuratum hoc sacrificium quam in lege naturae. Quia, secundum Hugonem, quanto magis appropinquavit passio salvatoris, tanto signa fuerunt evidentiora. Sed ea quae fuerunt in lege Moysis, fuerunt propinquiora. Ergo expressiora.

PRAETEREA, in sacrificiis legis Moysi fiebat sanguinis effusio. Sed oblatio Melchisedech fuit sanguinis sine effusione. Ergo legalia sacrificia expressius figurabant sacramentum passionis Christi quam oblatio Melchisedech.

SED CONTRA, Christus dicitur sacerdos secundum ordinem Melchisedech, non autem secundum sacerdotium legis Moysi, quod est sacerdotium leviticum, ut patet Hebr. 7. Ergo oblatio Melchisedech magis convenit cum sacrificio Christi quam sacrificium legis Moysi.

OBJ. 1: Moreover, it seems that this sacrament was more explicitly prefigured under the law of Moses than under the law of nature. For, according to Hugh, as the Passion of the Savior grew closer, the signs became more evident. [32] But the ones under the law of Moses were closer. Therefore, they were more explicit.

OBJ. 2: Furthermore, in the sacrifices of the law of Moses, blood was spilled. But the offering of Melchizedek was of blood without spilling it. Therefore, the sacrifices of the law prefigured the sacrament of the Passion of Christ more explicitly than the offering of Melchizedek.

ON THE CONTRARY, Christ is said to be a priest according to the order of Melchizedek, but not according to the priesthood of the law of Moses, which is the levitical priesthood, as is clear from Hebrews 7. [33] Therefore, the offering of Melchizedek fits more with Christ's sacrifice than any sacrifice of the law of Moses.

Response to Quaestiuncula 1

RESPONDEO dicendum ad primam quaestionem, quod sacramenta novae legis tripliciter se habent ad

TO THE FIRST QUESTION, I answer that the sacraments of the New Law are related in three ways to the Old Law. For

---

31. St. Thomas is referring to the Roman Canon or Eucharistic Prayer I, which includes the following petition: "Upon which vouchsafe to look with a propitious and serene countenance, and to accept them, as Thou wert graciously pleased to accept the gifts of Thy just servant Abel, and the sacrifice of our patriarch Abraham, and that which Thy high priest Melchisedek offered to Thee, a holy Sacrifice, a stainless Victim."

32. Hugh of St. Victor, *De sacramentis fidei*, Bk. 2, pt. 6, ch. 3 (PL 176:447).

33. See verses 11 and 17.

veterem legem. Quaedam enim essentialiter fuerunt in veteri lege, quamvis non ut sunt sacramenta novae legis, sed magis secundum quod sunt in officium vel actum virtutis; sicut poenitentia, ordo, et matrimonium. Quaedam fuerunt secundum aliquid eis respondens non essentialiter, sicut baptismus et Eucharistia. Quaedam autem nihil respondens habuerunt in veteri lege, sicut confirmatio et extrema unctio. Cujus ratio est, quia prima tria sacramenta non solum sunt sacramenta; sed poenitentia est actus virtutis; ordo autem pertinet ad officium dispensationis sacramentorum; matrimonium autem ad officium naturae; et ideo in qualibet lege requiruntur.

Baptismus autem et Eucharistia sunt sacramenta tantum gratiam continentia; et ideo ante tempus gratiae esse non debuerunt. Sed quia sunt sacramenta necessitatis, baptismus quidem quantum ad effectum, Eucharistia autem quantum ad fidem ejus quod repraesentatur per ipsam; ideo oportuit quod in lege Moysi haberent aliquid respondens: sed confirmatio et extrema unctio sunt sacramenta gratiam continentia; et ideo in veteri lege esse non debuerunt. Et quia non sunt sacramenta necessitatis, sed cujusdam superabundantis perfectionis; ideo non oportet quod haberent aliquid respondens, cum non esset tempus plenitudinis gratiae; et ideo haec duo non fuerunt praefiguranda aliquibus expressis figuris, similiter neque prima tria, sed tantum duo media, scilicet Eucharistia et baptismus.

Ad primum ergo dicendum, quod oppositae relationes possunt inesse eisdem respectu diversorum, eo quod esse relativi est ad aliud se habere, non autem proprietates absolutae; et ideo in relativis contingit aliquid disponi per aliquid sui generis per accidens, et non per se; sicut filii est filius, non inquantum filius, sed inquantum pater; et similiter signi potest esse signatum. In absolutis autem non contingit hoc; unde qualitatis non est qualitas nec per se nec per accidens.

Ad secundum dicendum, quod una perfectio dicitur alia major dupliciter: aut simpliciter, aut secundum statum; sicut praemium essentiale quod aurea dicitur, est simpliciter majus quam praemium accidentale, quod dicitur aureola; sed aureola est major quantum ad statum habentis, quia non cuilibet datur, sed tantummodo illis qui sunt in statu perfectionis. Et similiter dico, quod perfectio Eucharistiae est simpliciter major quam perfectio confirmationis et extremae unctionis, sed illae sunt majores secundum statum: quia perfectio Eucharistiae, quae est per conjunctionem ad principium sanctitatis est omnibus de necessitate salutis; sed perfectio Spiritus Sancti ad robur quae est in confirmatione, vel perfectio purgationis a reliquiis peccati, quae est in extrema unctione, non sunt omnibus necessaria; et ideo perfectioni

certain of them essentially existed in the Old Law, although not as they exist as sacraments of the New Law, but rather as an office or an act of virtue, like penance, holy orders, and marriage. Some of them existed in something corresponding to them non-essentially, like baptism and the Eucharist. But some had nothing corresponding to them under the Old Law, like confirmation and extreme unction. The reason for this is that the first three sacraments mentioned are not only sacraments, but penance is an act of virtue, holy orders pertains to the office of administering sacraments, and marriage is an office of nature; and so these are required under any law.

Baptism and the Eucharist, however, only exist as sacraments containing grace, and therefore before the time of grace they could not exist. But because they are necessary sacraments, baptism as regards its effect and the Eucharist as regards faith in him who is represented by it, for this reason it was fitting that they have something corresponding to them under the law of Moses. But confirmation and extreme unction are sacraments containing grace, and so they could not exist under the Old Law. And since these sacraments are not necessary but exist for the sake of a superabundant perfection, for this reason it is not necessary for them to have anything corresponding to them when it was not the time of the fullness of grace; and therefore these two did not need to be prefigured by any explicit figures, nor did the first three mentioned, but only the middle two, the Eucharist and baptism.

Reply Obj. 1: Opposite relations can be in the same things with respect to different things by the fact that to be related is to be related to another; however, absolute properties cannot. And this is why in relative things it happens that something may be disposed by something of its own genus accidentally, and not essentially, as a son may have a son, not as a son, but as a father; and in the same way a thing signified can also be a sign. However, this does not happen among absolutes; hence no quality is of a quality, whether essentially or accidentally.

Reply Obj. 2: One perfection is said to be greater than another in two ways: either simply, or according to one's status; just as the essential reward, which is called the golden crown of heaven, is simply speaking greater than the accidental reward, which is called a special distinction; but the special distinction is greater with respect to the status of the one having it, for it is not given to just anyone, but only to those who are in the state of perfection. And in the same way I say that the perfection of the Eucharist is simply speaking greater than the perfection of confirmation and extreme unction, but those are greater according to their state: for the perfection of the Eucharist, which is by the union to the principle of holiness, is necessary for the salvation of all; but the perfection of the Holy Spirit for strengthening, which is in confirmation, or the perfection

Eucharistiae debet aliquid respondere in qualibet lege, non autem perfectioni confirmationis et extremae unctionis nisi in lege in qua est status perfectionis, quae est lex gratiae.

Ad tertium dicendum quod praefiguratio Eucharistiae erat magis necessaria quam baptismi, tum ratione dignitatis, tum ratione difficultatis, tum propter necessitatem fidei ejus quod figuratur in Eucharistia. Tamen Magister supra aliquas figuras baptismi posuit, scilicet circumcisionem et baptismum Joannis.

of purification from the last traces of sin, which is in extreme unction, are not necessary for all; and so something must correspond to the perfection of the Eucharist in every law, but not to the perfection of confirmation and extreme unction, except in a law in which there is a state of perfection, which is the law of grace.

Reply Obj. 3: The prefiguring of the Eucharist was more necessary than baptism, both by reason of its dignity and by reason of its difficulty, as well as because of the necessity of faith in the one who is figured in the Eucharist. Nevertheless, the Master listed above[34] certain figures of baptism, namely, circumcision and the baptism of John.

Response to Quaestiuncula 2

Ad secundam quaestionem dicendum, quod aliquid potest figurari dupliciter. Uno modo per id quod est signum et causa: et hoc modo effusio sanguinis et aquae ex latere Christi fuerunt figura hujus sacramenti. Alio modo per id quod est signum tantum; et sic quantum ad id quod est sacramentum tantum in Eucharistia, fuit figura ejus oblatio Melchisedech; quantum autem ad id quod est res et sacramentum, scilicet ipsum Christum passum, fuit figura agnus paschalis; quantum autem ad id quod est res tantum, scilicet gratiam, fuit signum manna, quod reficiebat, omnem saporem suavitatis habens.

Ad primum ergo dicendum, quod ratio illa valeret, si baptismi et Eucharistiae tantum esset una figura: sunt autem plures; et ideo non est inconveniens quod aliquam figuram baptismi praecedat aliqua figura Eucharistiae, et ab aliqua praecedatur; sicut praecedit agnus paschalis transitum maris rubri, et sequitur circumcisionem.

Ad secundum dicendum, quod Eucharistia offertur Deo in sanctificatione hostiae, et offertur populo in ipsius sumptione; et hoc significatum fuit in oblatione Melchisedech, qui obtulit Abrahae panem et vinum, et benedixit Deo excelso.

Ad tertium dicendum, quod nihil sub eadem specie manens est signum sui ipsius; sed aliquid secundum quod est in una specie, potest esse signum sui secundum quod est sub alia specie; et similiter est in proposito dicendum, quod aqua fluens de latere Christi figurabat populum, qui ejus sanguine redimendus et reficiendus erat; et ideo significabat aqua sanguini admixta hujus sacramenti usum.

Ad quartum dicendum, quod hoc sacramentum habet omnem suavitatem, inquantum continet fontem omnis gratiae, quamvis non ordinetur ejus usus ad om-

To the second question, it should be said that anything can be prefigured in two ways. In one way, by that which is sign and cause, and in this way, the shedding of blood and of water from Christ's side were a figure of this sacrament. In another way, by what is only a sign, and in this way, regarding what is sacrament alone in the Eucharist, the offering of Melchizedek was a figure of it; but regarding what is reality-and-sacrament, namely, Christ himself crucified, the figure was the Paschal lamb; but regarding what is reality alone, namely, grace, the sign was manna, which refreshed, having all flavor of sweetness.[35]

Reply Obj. 1: That argument would hold if there were only one figure of baptism and Eucharist; however, there are several, and so it is not unfitting that a certain figure of the Eucharist should precede a certain figure of baptism, and be preceded by a certain other, as the Paschal lamb came before the crossing of the Red Sea, and followed circumcision.

Reply Obj. 2: The Eucharist is offered to God in the sanctification of the host, and it is offered to the people in its consumption; and this was represented in the offering of Melchizedek, who offered bread and wine to Abraham and blessed the Most High God.

Reply Obj. 3: Nothing remaining under the same species is a sign of itself, but something according as it is in one species can be a sign of itself as it is under another species; and it is the same way in the example given: the water flowing from Christ's side symbolized the people who were to be redeemed and remade by his blood; and so the water mixed with blood represented the use of this sacrament.

Reply Obj. 4: This sacrament has all sweetness inasmuch as it contains the fount of all grace, although its use is not ordered to all effects of sacramental grace. Or it could

---

34. See Distinctions 1 and 2.
35. For more about the sacrament alone, reality alone, and sacrament-and-reality, see the footnote at Dist.1, q.1, a.4, qa. 1, main response.

nes effectus sacramentalis gratiae. Vel dicendum, quod etiam quantum ad effectum habet omnem suavitatis effectum in reficiendo, quia hoc solum sacramentum per modum refectionis operatur. Vel dicendum, secundum Dionysium, quod omnium sacramentorum effectus huic sacramento possunt ascribi, inquantum perfectio est omnis sacramenti, habens quasi in capitulo et summa omnia quae alia sacramenta continent singillatim.

AD QUINTUM dicendum, quod baptismus est sacramentum necessitatis quantum ad effectum, quia delet peccatum originale, quo manente non est salus; et ideo oportebat quod in veteri lege responderet sibi aliqua figura, quae contra originale remedium praeberet, scilicet circumcisio. Sed Eucharistia est sacramentum necessitatis quantum ad fidem ejus quod repraesentat, scilicet opus nostrae redemptionis; et ideo non oportuit quod haberet figuras remedium praebentes, sed significantes tantum.

AD SEXTUM DICENDUM, quod quamvis in veteri lege fuerint figurae plures materialiter, tamen omnes ad has reducuntur: quia in omnibus sacrificiis et oblationibus antiquorum significabatur illud quod est res et sacramentum in Eucharistia, quod etiam significatur per agnum paschalem, scilicet ipse Christus qui obtulit se Deo patri pro nobis oblationem et hostiam. Vel dicendum, quod istae figurae repraesentant corpus Christi secundum quod est in usu fidelium per esum, quod patet de oblatione Melchisedech, qui panem et vinum edendum obtulit Abrahae; et similiter agnus paschalis edendus a populo occidebatur; et etiam manna ad esum populi a Deo providebatur: aqua etiam sanguini admixta in passione Christi populum significat Christi sanguine communicantem. Non autem ita est in aliis sacrificiis; et ideo quamvis sint figurae Christi passi, non tamen sunt propriae figurae hujus sacramenti. Fit autem in canone Missae mentio de oblatione Abrahae et Abel magis propter devotionem offerentium quam propter figuram rei oblatae.

be said that even in its effect it has every effect of sweetness in refreshing, for this sacrament alone works by the mode of refreshing. Or it could be said that, according to Dionysius,[36] the effect of all the sacraments can be ascribed to this sacrament, inasmuch as it is the perfection of every sacrament, having in capsule and sum, as it were, all that the other sacraments contain piecemeal.

REPLY OBJ. 5: Baptism is a necessary sacrament in its effect of blotting out original sin, for there is no salvation where original sin remains. And so Baptism had to have some corresponding figure in the Old Law, which would furnish a remedy against original sin, namely, circumcision. But the Eucharist is a necessary sacrament as regards faith in what it represents, namely, the work of our redemption; and so it was not necessary that it have figures presenting a remedy, but only representing.

REPLY OBJ. 6: Although in the Old Law there had been several material figures, nevertheless all are reducible to these: for in all the sacrifices and offerings of the ancients was signified what is reality-and-sacrament in the Eucharist, which is also signified by the Paschal lamb, namely, Christ himself, who offered himself to God the Father as offering and victim on our behalf. Or it could be said that those figures represent the Body of Christ according as it is for the use of the faithful by eating, which is clear from the offering of Melchizedek, who offered bread and wine to Abraham to eat. And likewise, the Paschal lamb was killed to be eaten by the people, and also manna was provided by God for the people to eat; also, water mixed with blood in Christ's Passion symbolized the people partaking of the blood of Christ. However, it is not this way in other sacrifices; and so although they may be figures of the suffering Christ, they are nevertheless not proper figures of this sacrament. However, mention is made in the canon of the Mass of the offerings of Abraham and Abel because of the devotion of the ones making the sacrifice rather than because of any figure in the thing offered.

Response to Quaestiuncula 3

AD TERTIAM QUAESTIONEM dicendum, quod quantum ad id quod est signum tantum in hoc sacramento, expressior figura hujus sacramenti fuit oblatio Melchisedech quam figurae legis Moysi; sed quantum ad id quod est res et sacramentum; expressior fuit figura legis Mosaicae, qua expressius Christus passus significabatur. Et quia ritus sacramenti consistit in signis exterioribus; ideo sacerdotium Christi quantum ad ritum magis con-

TO THE THIRD QUESTION, it should be said that as for what is sign alone in this sacrament, the oblation of Melchizedek was a more explicit figure of this sacrament than the figures in the law of Moses; but as for what is reality-and-sacrament, the Mosaic law's figure was more explicit, for the suffering Christ was more expressly symbolized in it. And because a sacrament's rite consists in outward signs, for this reason Christ's priesthood as to the rite

---

36. Pseudo-Dionysius, *Ecclesiastical Hierarchy*, ch. 3 (PG 3:423).

venit cum sacerdotio Melchisedech quam cum sacerdotio levitico; et etiam quantum ad alias conditiones Melchisedech, quas apostolus plenius prosequitur.

Et per hoc patet solutio ad objecta.

shares more with the priesthood of Melchizedek than with the levitical priesthood; and also as to the other conditions of Melchizedek, which the Apostle describes more fully.

And from this the solutions to the objections are evident.

ARTICLE 3

The institution of the Eucharist[37]

Quaestiuncula 1

AD TERTIUM SIC PROCEDITUR. Videtur quod nulla fuerit necessitas instituendi hoc sacramentum. Veniente enim veritate debet cessare figura. Sed hoc sacramentum agitur in figuram Dominicae Passionis, quae jam realiter venit. Ergo non debuit hoc sacramentum institui.

PRAETEREA, eadem in actione aliquid instituitur et a contraria dispositione removetur. Sed ad eamdem actionem non debet institui nisi unum sacramentum, sicut unum instrumentum est unius actionis. Cum ergo per baptismum mundemur a malo, videtur quod non oportuit institui aliquod sacramentum per quod *in bono confirmemur,* scilicet Eucharistiam, ut in littera dicitur.

PRAETEREA, *ex eisdem ex quibus sumus, et nutrimur,* ut in 2 *de Generat.* dicitur. Sed per baptismum, qui est spiritualis regeneratio, acquirimus esse spirituale, ut Dionysius dicit. Ergo per gratiam reficimur baptismalem; et ita non oportet hoc sacramentum institui ad spiritualiter reficiendum, ut in littera dicitur.

SED CONTRA, quia ad perfectionem corporis exigitur quod membra capiti conjungantur. Sed per hoc sacramentum membra ecclesiae suo capiti conjunguntur; unde Joan. 6, 57, dicitur: *qui manducat carnem meam, et bibit sanguinem meum, in me manet, et ego in eo.* Ergo necessaria fuit hujus sacramenti institutio.

PRAETEREA, caritas non est minus necessaria quam fides. Sed habemus unum sacramentum fidei, scilicet baptismum. Cum ergo caritatis sacramentum sit Eucharistia, unde et communio dicitur; videtur quod ejus institutio fuerit necessaria.

OBJ. 1: To the third we proceed thus. It seems that it was not necessary to institute this sacrament. For when the truth comes, the figure must cease. But this sacrament is performed as a figure of the Lord's Passion, which has now come in reality. Therefore, this sacrament did not need to be instituted.

OBJ. 2: Furthermore, by the same action, something is instituted and removed from contrary dispositions. But for the same action only one sacrament needs to be instituted, since a single action only needs a single instrument. Therefore, since one is cleansed from evil by baptism, it seems that it was not necessary to institute another sacrament by which *one is strengthened in good,* namely the Eucharist, as it says in the text.

OBJ. 3: Furthermore, *we are nourished from the same things of which we are made,* as it says in *On Generation and Corruption* 2.[38] But by baptism, which is a spiritual regeneration, we acquire spiritual being, as Dionysius says.[39] Therefore, we are re-made by baptismal grace; and so it is not necessary to institute this sacrament for spiritual renewal, as it says in the text.

ON THE CONTRARY, for the perfection of the body, it is required that members be united with the head. But by this sacrament the members of the Church are united with their head; for this reason it is said, *whoever eats my flesh and drinks my blood remains in me and I in him* (John 6:56). Therefore, the institution of this sacrament was necessary.

FURTHERMORE, charity is not less necessary than faith. But we have one sacrament of faith, namely, baptism. Therefore, since the sacrament of charity is the Eucharist, which is why it is also called 'Communion,' it seems that its institution was necessary.

Quaestiuncula 2

ULTERIUS. Videtur quod ante adventum Christi debuerit institui. Christus enim est caput hominum justorum qui fuerunt a principio mundi, ut in 3 Lib., dist. 13, qu. 2, art. 2, quaest. 2 ad 4, dictum est. Si ergo per hoc sacramentum membra corporis mystico suo capiti con-

OBJ. 1: Moreover, it seems that it should have been instituted before Christ's coming. For Christ is the head of the just men who were from the beginning of the world, as was said in Book III, Distinction 13, Question 2, Article 2, Subquestion 2, reply to the fourth objection. If therefore the

---

37. Parallels: *ST* III, q. 73, a. 5; q. 83, a. 2, ad 3; *De ven. sacram. altar.,* ch. 1; *Super Matt.* 26; *Super I ad Cor.* 11, lec. 4.
38. Aristotle, *On Generation and Corruption,* Bk. 2, ch. 8, 335a10.
39. Pseudo-Dionysius, *Ecclesiastical Hierarchy,* ch. 2, p. 1 (PG 3:391).

jungantur, videtur quod debuerit a principio mundi institui.

PRAETEREA, populus Israel fuit populus a Deo dilectissimus; unde dicitur Exod. 4, 22: *filius meus primogenitus Israel.* Sed hoc sacramentum est sacramentum caritatis, ut dictum est. Ergo debuit institui adhuc priore populo habente statum.

PRAETEREA, hoc sacramentum dicitur viaticum, quia tendentes ad patriam in via confortat, et quotidianos etiam lapsus reparat. Sed patres qui erant ante adventum Christi, ad patriam tendebant, hospites et peregrinos se vocantes super terram, ut dicitur Hebr. 11, et etiam quotidianis peccatis impediebantur. Ergo ante adventum Christi debuit hoc sacramentum institui.

SED CONTRA, hoc sacramentum continet verbum incarnatum realiter. Ergo institui non potuit ante incarnationem verbi.

PRAETEREA, hoc sacramentum continet gratiae plenitudinem; unde et Eucharistia dicitur. Sed tempus plenitudinis incepit ab incarnatione Christi. Ergo ante incarnationem hoc sacramentum institui non potuit.

members of the body are united to their mystical head by this sacrament, it seems that it should have been instituted at the beginning of the world.

OBJ. 2: Furthermore, the people of Israel was a people most beloved by God; hence it says, *Israel is my firstborn son* (Exod 4:22). But this sacrament is the sacrament of charity, as was said. Therefore, it should have been instituted before, for the nation first having that status.

OBJ. 3: Furthermore, this sacrament is called 'viaticum,' for it strengthens those striving on their way to the fatherland, and it revives as well those who tend to fall. But the patriarchs who were before Christ's coming were striving for the fatherland, calling themselves strangers and pilgrims on earth, as it says in Hebrews 11:13; and they too were hindered by habitual sins. Therefore, this sacrament should have been instituted before Christ's coming.

ON THE CONTRARY, this sacrament really contains the Incarnate Word. Therefore, it could not have been instituted before the Incarnation of the Word.

FURTHERMORE, this sacrament contains the fullness of grace; hence it is also called 'Eucharist.' But the time of fullness began at Christ's Incarnation. Therefore, before the Incarnation this sacrament could not have been instituted.

Quaestiuncula 3

ULTERIUS. Videtur quod post passionem institui debuit. Quia hoc sacramentum est in memoriam Dominicae Passionis, ut patet 1 Corinth., 11. Sed memoria praeteritorum est. Ergo et praeterita passione Christi institui debuit.

PRAETEREA, Eucharistia non nisi baptizatis debet dari. Sed baptismus fuit institutus post Christi passionem, quando Dominus discipulis formam baptizandi dedit, Matth. ult. Ergo et post passionem institui debuit Eucharistia.

PRAETEREA, in his quae sibi invicem continue succedunt, ultimum primi debet conjungi primo secundi. Sed Dominus voluit in coena ostendere terminationem veteris legis, et continuationem novae legis ad ipsam, ut ex littera habetur. Ergo debuit post coenam paschalem statim instituere primum sacramentum novae legis, et alia per ordinem; et sic post passionem Eucharistiam, quae est ultimum.

SED CONTRA, videtur quod debuerit institui a principio praedicationis Christi. Quia quae primo capiuntur, arctius memoriae imprimuntur, ut patet de his quae homo a pueritia capit. Sed Dominus voluit ut hoc sacramentum arctissime memoriae commendaretur. Ergo debuit a principio hoc instituere.

OBJ. 1: Moreover, it seems that it should have been instituted after the Passion. For this sacrament is in memory of the Lord's Passion, as is clear from 1 Corinthians 11:24–26. But a memorial has to do with the past. Therefore, it should have been instituted once Christ's Passion was past.

OBJ. 2: Furthermore, the Eucharist should not be given to anyone but the baptized. But baptism was instituted after Christ's Passion, when the Lord gave the form of baptizing to his disciples (Matt 28:19). Therefore, the Eucharist should also have been instituted after the Passion.

OBJ. 3: Furthermore, among those things that succeed each other in a continuous way, the end of the first should be joined to the beginning of the second. But in the Last Supper the Lord wanted to display the end of the Old Law, and the continuation of the New Law with it, as is maintained in the text. Therefore, he should have instituted the first sacrament of the New Law immediately after the Passover supper, and the others in order; and so after the Passion, the Eucharist, which is last.

ON THE CONTRARY, it seems that it should have been instituted at the beginning of Christ's preaching. For the things that are grasped first are imprinted more firmly on the memory, as is evident from those things that a man holds from his childhood. But the Lord wanted this sacrament to be committed most firmly to memory. Therefore, he should have instituted it from the beginning.

Response to Quaestiuncula 1

RESPONDEO dicendum ad primam quaestionem, quod in quolibet genere actionum in quo inveniuntur plures actiones ordinatae diversis agentibus ordinatis distributae, oportet quod principalis illarum actionum attribuatur principali agenti, cujus virtute secundarii agentes operantur secundarias actiones; sicut patet in artibus quae sub invicem continentur, ut militaris, equestris, et frenorum factrix. Et quia invenimus diversas actiones sacramentales diversis sacramentis distributas, quae in virtute verbi incarnati agunt, oportet ad perfectam actionem hujus generis esse aliquam sacramentalem actionem quae ipsimet principali agenti attribuatur, quod est verbum incarnatum. Et ideo oportuit esse sacramentum Eucharistiae, quod ipsum verbum incarnatum contineret, ceteris sacramentis tantum in virtute ipsius agentibus.

Et ideo convenienter in figura cibi hoc sacramentum institutum est: quia inter alios sensus solus tactus est cui suum sensibile realiter conjungitur, similitudinibus tantum sensibilium ad alios sensus per medium pervenientibus: gustus autem tactus quidam est: et inter alia quae ad tactum pertinent, solus cibus est qui agit per conjunctionem sui ad cibatum, quia nutriens et nutritum fit unum; alia vero tangibilia agunt efficiendo aliquas impressiones in eo quod tangitur, sicut patet de calido et frigido, et hujusmodi. Et ideo cum omne sacramentum in figura alicujus rei sensibilis proponi debeat, convenienter sacramentum in quo ipsum verbum incarnatum nobis conjungendum continetur, proponitur nobis in figura cibi, non quidem convertendi in nos per suam conjunctionem ad nos, sed potius sua conjunctione nos in se ipsum convertens, secundum quod Augustinus ex persona verbi incarnati dicit: *non tu me mutabis in te, sicut cibum carnis tuae; sed tu mutaberis in me.*

AD PRIMUM ergo dicendum, quod secundum Dionysium nostra hierarchia est media inter caelestem et eam quae in veteri lege erat. Tempore enim legis erat veritas promissa tantum; sed in statu novae legis est veritas inchoata per Jesum Christum; in patria autem erit veritas consummata. Et ideo in veteri lege figurae sine rebus proponebantur; in nova autem proponuntur figurae cum rebus; in patria autem res sine figuris. Et ideo orat ecclesia *ut quod nunc spe gerimus in via, rerum veritate capiamus in patria.*

AD SECUNDUM dicendum, quod objectio illa procedit de perfectione illa qua aliquid ad formam receptam

TO THE FIRST QUESTION, I answer that in any category of actions where many ordered actions are found distributed to diverse ordered agents, the chief of these actions must be attributed to the principal agent, by whose power the secondary agents work secondary actions; and this is clear in the case of arts that are subsumed under each other, as the art of harness-making is under the art of horsemanship, which is under the art of warfare. And since we find diverse sacramental actions distributed to diverse sacraments, which act in virtue of the Incarnate Word, it is necessary that for a complete action of this kind there must be some sacramental action that is attributed to the principal agent, which is the Incarnate Word. And so it was necessary that there be the sacrament of the Eucharist, which would contain the Incarnate Word himself, while the other sacraments work only in virtue of him.

And therefore this sacrament was fittingly instituted in the figure of food: for among the other senses, only touch is united to its sensible object in a real way, for the sensible object only reaches the other senses in a likeness through a medium. However, taste is a kind of touch, and among the other things that pertain to touch, food is the only one that acts by joining itself to the one fed, for nourishment and the one nourished become one thing; but other tangible things act by bringing about certain impressions on whatever is touched, as is seen in the case of hot and cold, and things like that. And so since every sacrament should be set forth in the figure of a certain sensible thing, the sacrament in which the Incarnate Word himself is contained for the purpose of being joined to us, is fittingly set before us in the figure of food, not of course changing into us by his union with us, but rather changing us into himself by his union, as Augustine says in the person of the Incarnate Word: *you will not change me into you, like food of your flesh; but you will be changed into me.*[40]

REPLY OBJ. 1: According to Dionysius, our hierarchy is a middle one between the heavenly one and the one that was in the Old Law.[41] For at the time of the law, the truth was only promised; but in the state of the New Law, truth has been initiated by Jesus Christ; however, in the fatherland the truth will be consummated. And so under the Old Law, figures were set forth without realities, while in the New Law, figures are set forth with realities; but in the fatherland there will be realities without figures. And this is why the Church prays *that what we now bear in hope on the way, we may possess in the truth of reality in the fatherland.*[42]

REPLY OBJ. 2: That objection proceeds from the perfection with which something is perfected when it receives a

---

40. Augustine, *Confessions* (CCSL 27), Bk. 7, ch. 10.

41. See Pseudo-Dionysius, *Ecclesiastical Hierarchy*, ch. 5, p. 1.

42. From the Postcommunion of the Mass of Ember Saturday in September. The full text as it appears in the *Missale Romanum* 1962: "Perficiant in nobis, Domine, quaesumus, tua sacramenta quod continent; ut quae nunc spe gerimus, rerum veritate capiamus."

perficitur, qualis perfectio fit per baptismum; non autem de illa quae est per conjunctionem ad principium perfectionis, quae fit per Eucharistiam, ut supra dictum est.

AD TERTIUM dicendum, quod de nutrimento corporali verum est nos eisdem nutriri ex quibus sumus, quia debet cibum carnis nostrae in nos transmutari, et ideo oportet quod nobiscum in materia conveniat; secus autem de cibo spirituali, qui nos in seipsum transmutat.

form, which is the kind of perfection that happens through baptism; however, it is not the kind that occurs in being joined to the principle of perfection, which happens through the Eucharist, as was said above.

REPLY OBJ. 3: Concerning physical nourishment it is true that we are nourished by the same things from which we exist, for the food of our flesh ought to be transformed into us, and that is why it must be appropriate to us in its matter. However, it is different with spiritual food, which transforms us into it.

Response to Quaestiuncula 2

AD SECUNDAM QUAESTIONEM dicendum, quod sicut dictum est, in hoc sacramento ipse Christus, qui est sanctificationis principale agens, realiter nobis proponitur. In veteri autem lege non exhibebatur, sed promittebatur, incarnatione nondum facta; et ideo in veteri lege hujus sacramenti institutio esse non potuit. Unde sacramenta veteris legis habebant se ad modum sensibilium quae per medium cognoscuntur, quae quidem realiter sentienti non conjunguntur, sed suas similitudines ad sensus a longinquo transmittunt. Sacramenta vero alia novae legis, in quibus virtus Christi operatur, cum ipsum realiter non contineant, assimilantur sensibilibus jam dictis, quae quidem non incorporantur sentienti, sed secundum aliquam qualitatem immutant. Hoc autem sacramentum, ut dictum est, quasi majoris perfectionis, similatur illi sensibili quod incorporatur sentienti, scilicet cibo; unde magis distat a modo sacramentorum veteris legis quam sacramenta novae legis.

AD PRIMUM ergo dicendum, quod Christus ab initio mundi erat caput sanctorum, non quasi habens actu conformitatem in natura cum membris ecclesiae, incarnatione nondum facta, sed solum secundum fidem incarnationem expectantium; et ideo conjunctio corporis mystici ad suum caput pro tempore illo non poterat fieri per aliquod sacramentum realiter continens ipsum caput membris conforme, sed poterat per aliqua sacramenta figurari.

AD SECUNDUM dicendum, quod populus Israel erat dilectissimus pro tempore illo comparatione aliorum populorum, qui idolis serviebant, non autem comparatione populi novi testamenti, de quo dicitur 1 Petr. 2, 9: *vos estis gens sancta, populus acquisitionis.* Vel dicendum, secundum apostolum Rom. 9: *non qui sunt secundum carnem, sed qui ex promissione, hi computantur in semine.* Unde populus novi testamenti non excluditur ab illo privilegio amoris ratione cujus Israel primogenitus Dei dicebatur.

AD TERTIUM dicendum, quod quamvis antiqui patres in via essent, tendentes ad patriam, non tamen erant

TO THE SECOND QUESTION, it should be said that, as has been said, in this sacrament Christ himself, who is the principal agent of sanctification, is really set before us. Now in the Old Law he was not presented, but he was promised, for the Incarnation had not yet happened; and so in the Old Law this sacrament could not have been instituted. Hence sacraments of the Old Law were like the mode of sensible things that are known through a medium, which are not joined to the one sensing them in a real way, but transmit their likenesses to the senses from afar. But the sacraments of the New Law in which the power of Christ is working, although they do not contain him in reality, are like the sensed objects just mentioned, which indeed are not incorporated into the one sensing, but alter him according to a certain quality. This sacrament, however, as was said, as belongs to greater perfection, is like that sensible object that is incorporated into the one sensing it, namely, food; hence it is more distant from the mode of sacraments of the Old Law than the other sacraments of the New Law.

REPLY OBJ. 1: From the beginning of the world Christ was head of holy men, not as though having actual conformity of nature with the members of the Church, since the Incarnation had not yet happened, but only according to the faith of the ones awaiting the Incarnation; and this is why the union of the Mystical Body with its head could not have happened for that time through any sacrament really containing the head himself similar to his members, but it could be prefigured by certain other sacraments.

REPLY OBJ. 2: The people of Israel was most beloved for that time by comparison with the other peoples, who served idols, but not by comparison with the people of the New Testament, of whom it says, *you are a holy nation, a purchased people* (1 Pet 2:9). Or it could be said, according to the Apostle in Romans 9:8: *not those who are according to the flesh, but who are from the promise, these are counted as descendents.* Therefore, the people of the New Testament are not excluded from that privilege of love by reason of which Israel was called God's firstborn.

REPLY OBJ. 3: Although the ancient patriarchs were journeying and striving for the fatherland, nevertheless

in statu perveniendi ante Christi incarnationem; et ideo non competebat pro tempore illo viaticum esse, quo statim ad patriam perducimur.

they were not in the state of arriving there before the Incarnation of Christ. And so it was not appropriate at that time for there to be that viaticum by which we are led immediately to heaven.

Response to Quaestiuncula 3

AD TERTIAM QUAESTIONEM dicendum, quod propter quatuor rationes hoc sacramentum in coena institui debuit, et non ante. Prima apparet ex ipsa necessitate sacramenti assignata: quia ad perfectionem nostram exigebatur ut caput nostrum etiam nobis realiter conjungeretur; et ideo quamdiu sub propria specie cum hominibus conversatus est, non oportebat hoc sacramentum institui, sed quando ejus corporali praesentia destituenda erat ecclesia; et haec ratio tangitur in littera ab Eusebio: *quia*, inquit, *corpus assumptum ablaturus erat*, etc.

Secunda sumitur ex ejus figura. Christus enim quamdiu in mundo conversatus est, figuras legis observare voluit, *factus sub lege, ut eos qui sub lege erant redimeret*. Et quia veniente veritate cessat figura, ideo non debuit hoc sacramentum institui nisi Christo abscedente per mortem, quando figurae veteris legis terminandae erant.

Tertia ratio sumitur ab ipsa repraesentatione hujus sacramenti. Est enim repraesentativum Dominicae Passionis; et ideo congrue jam passione imminente instituitur.

Quarta ratio sumitur ex ritu quo frequentandum est hoc sacramentum, ut ultimo traditum magis memoriae teneretur.

AD PRIMUM ergo dicendum, quod imminente passione corda discipulorum magis erant affecta ad passionem, quam passione jam peracta, quando jam erant immemores pressurae passionis propter gaudium resurrectionis; et ideo memoriale passionis magis erat eis proponendum ante quam post. Nec tunc erat memoriale, sed instituebatur ut in memoriam in posterum celebrandum.

AD SECUNDUM dicendum, quod baptismus etiam ante passionem institutus est quantum ad aliquid, ut supra dictum est; et praeterea non oportet quod sit idem ordo institutionis sacramentorum et perceptionis: quia ad finem qui nobis praestituitur, ultimo pervenimus. Sed Eucharistia est quodammodo finis baptismi: quia per baptismum aliquis consecratur ad Eucharistiae percep-

TO THE THIRD QUESTION, it should be said that for four reasons this sacrament had to be instituted at the Last Supper and not before. The first appears from the very necessity ascribed to the sacrament: for it was necessary for our perfection that our head be joined also to us in a real way. And so as long as he was keeping company with men under his proper appearance,[43] it was not necessary to institute this sacrament, but only when the Church was to be deprived of his physical presence. And this reason is touched upon in the letter from Eusebius: *since he was going to withdraw his assumed body from their eyes*, etc.[44]

The second reason is taken from its figure. For as long as Christ was spending time in the world, he wished to observe the figures of the law, he who was *made under the law, that he might redeem those who were under the law* (Gal 4:4–5). And since figures cease when the truth comes, for this reason this sacrament should not have been instituted unless Christ had withdrawn through death, when the figures of the Old Law were to be ended.

The third reason is taken from the representation itself of this sacrament. For it represents the Lord's Passion; and so it is fittingly instituted at the moment the Passion was imminent.

The fourth reason is taken from the rite by which this sacrament is to be repeated, so that, handed down last, it might be held better in the memory.

REPLY OBJ. 1: Since the Passion was imminent, the hearts of the disciples were more affected toward the Passion than if the Passion had already been accomplished, when the pressures of the Passion had been forgotten because of the joy of the resurrection. And this is why the memorial of the Passion had to be set forth for them before rather than after. Nor was it a memorial then, but it was instituted as something to be celebrated in memorial afterwards.

REPLY OBJ. 2: Baptism was instituted even before the Passion in a certain respect, as was said above; and furthermore it is not necessary that the sacraments have the same order of institution and of receiving, since we attain to that end last which was predetermined for us. But the Eucharist is in a way the end of baptism: for by baptism someone is consecrated for the reception of the Eucharist, just as some-

---

43. *Species* has many meanings. Here it refers to Christ's appearance in his humanity as contrasted with his existence under the appearance of bread and wine in the Eucharist.

44. Eusebius of Gaul, *Homilia XVII seu VI de Pascha*, n.1; elsewhere as Pseudo-Jerome, *Epistle 38*.

tionem, sicut per ordinem ad ejus consecrationem. Et ideo ratio non procedit.

Ad tertium dicendum, quod quamvis hoc sacramentum sit quasi ultimum in perceptione, est tamen primum in intentione. Institutio autem ordini intentionis respondet; et ideo terminatis sacramentis legalibus hoc primo instituendum fuit.

Ad quartum dicendum, quod ratio illa procedit de illis quae a principio quis capere potest. Apostoli autem a principio non tanti capaces erant mysterii; et ideo in fine hoc eis proponendum fuit. Et praeterea ratio illa procedit de illis quae memoriae imprimuntur propter seipsa; in illis autem quae memoriae imprimit affectio ad dicentem, secus est: quia tunc firmius imprimuntur quando affectionis motus ad dicentem major sentitur. Quanto autem aliquis ad amicum diutius conversatur, fit major dilectio; et quando ab amicis separamur, sentitur motus dilectionis ferventior propter dolorem separationis; et ideo verba amicorum a nobis recedentium finaliter dicta magis memoriae imprimuntur.

one is set aside for its consecration by holy orders. And so the argument does not proceed.

Reply Obj. 3: Although this sacrament is like the last one in reception, it is nevertheless the first one in intention. However, the institution corresponds to the order of intention; and so when the sacraments of the law were ended, this one was the first to be instituted.

Reply Obj. 4: That argument proceeds from those things that someone can understand from the beginning. However, the apostles were not ready for so great a mystery in the beginning; and so this had to be set down for them at the end. And furthermore, that argument deals with things that are imprinted on the memory for their own sake; but in these things that affection for the speaker impressed upon their memories, it is different: for when the emotion of affection for the speaker is more strongly felt, then the impressions are fixed more strongly. However, the more someone spends time with a friend, the greater his love becomes, and when he is separated from his friends, he feels the emotion of love more fervently because of the sorrow of separation; and this is why the last words spoken by friends as they leave us are more impressed upon our memory.

ARTICLE 4

The order of consuming this food in relation to other foods[45]

Quaestiuncula 1

AD QUARTUM SIC PROCEDITUR. Videtur quod hoc sacramentum a non jejunis licite sumi possit. Hoc enim sacramentum a Domino in coena institutum est. Sed ecclesia observat ea quae Dominus servavit in sacramentorum traditione, sicut formam et materiam. Ergo et ritum deberet servare, ut jam pransis hoc sacramentum traderetur.

PRAETEREA, 1 Corinth. 11, 33, dicitur: *dum convenitis ad manducandum, invicem expectate. Si quis autem esurit, domi manducet.* Loquitur autem de manducatione corporis Christi. Ergo postquam aliquis domi manducaverit, potest in ecclesia corpus Christi manducare licite.

PRAETEREA, *de Consecratione*, dist. 1 dicitur: *sacramenta altaris non nisi a jejunis hominibus celebrantur, excepto uno die anniversario, quo coena Domini celebratur.* Ergo ad minus illo die potest aliquis post alios cibos corpus Christi sumere.

SED CONTRA est quod dicitur *de Consecr.*, dist. 2: *placuit Spiritui Sancto in honorem tanti sacramenti prius in os Christiani Dominicum Corpus intrare.*

PRAETEREA, hoc sacramentum cum magna reverentia sumendum est. Sed post cibum non est aliquis ita sobrius et modestus sicut ante. Ergo non debet post cibum sumi.

OBJ. 1: To the fourth we proceed thus. It seems that this sacrament can be licitly received by those who have not fasted. For this sacrament was instituted by the Lord at supper. But in handing down the sacraments, the Church observes what the Lord kept, like form and matter. Therefore, it should have also kept the rite, so that this sacrament would be given out to those who have just eaten.

OBJ. 2: Furthermore, it is said, *when you come together to eat, wait for each other. But if anyone is hungry, let him eat at home* (1 Cor 11:33–34). However, he is speaking about eating the body of Christ. Therefore, after someone has eaten at home, he can licitly eat the body of Christ in the Church.

OBJ. 3: Furthermore, Distinction 1 of *On Consecration* says, *the sacraments of the altar are not to be celebrated by any but fasting men, except for on the one day in the year when the Lord's Supper is celebrated.*[46] Therefore, at least on that day someone can receive the body of Christ after other foods.

ON THE CONTRARY, in *On Consecration*, Distinction 2, it says: *it pleased the Holy Spirit in honor of so great a sacrament for the Lord's body to enter first into the mouths of Christians.*[47]

FURTHERMORE, this sacrament is to be consumed with the greatest reverence. But after a meal one is not as sober and reserved as before. Therefore, it should not be consumed after a meal.

Quaestiuncula 2

ULTERIUS. Videtur quod non quaelibet cibi sumptio perceptionem hujus sacramenti impediat. Quia sumptio cibi et potus in parva quantitate in nullo sobrietatem diminuit, immo magis auget naturam confortando. Sed ideo oportet a jejunis sumi, ut cum reverentia sumatur et sobrietate. Ergo non quaelibet sumptio cibi impedit perceptionem hujus sacramenti.

PRAETEREA, ad perceptionem hujus sacramenti exigitur quod homo sit jejunus. Sed quaedam sunt quae non frangunt jejunium, sicut aqua, et medicinae quaedam.

OBJ. 1: Moreover, it seems that not every consumption of food would prevent the reception of this sacrament. For the consumption of food and drink in small quantities diminishes sobriety in no one, but on the contrary, rather increases nature by strengthening. But the reason it must be consumed by those who have fasted is so that it is received with reverence and sobriety. Therefore, not every consumption of food hampers the reception of this sacrament.

OBJ. 2: Furthermore, it is required for the reception of this sacrament that a person be fasting. But there are certain things that do not break one's fast, like water and cer-

---

45. Parallels: *ST* II-II, q. 147, a. 6, ad 2; *ST* III, q. 80, a. 8; *Super I ad Cor.* 11, lec. 4.
46. Gratian's *Decretals*, Part 3, *De consecratione*, d. 1 (PL 187:1721); cf. Third Council of Carthage, can. 29.
47. Gratian's *Decretals*, Part 3, *De consecratione*, d. 2 (PL 187:1757).

Ergo videtur quod post earum susceptionem homo possit hoc sacramentum percipere.

Praeterea, corpus Christi sicut in os intrat, ita in ventrem trajicitur. Sed si aliquae cibi reliquiae in ore remaneant, et postmodum de mane in ventrem trajiciantur, non impeditur quis a sumptione corporis Christi: quia hoc posset sacerdoti accidere etiam dum est in ipsa celebratione sacramenti, quando non deberet a sumptione corporis Christi desistere. Ergo nec cibus in os missus debet perceptionem hujus sacramenti impedire, in parva quantitate sumptus.

Sed contra est quod ex hoc ipso sacramento reverentia exhibetur quod prius in os Corpus Domini sumitur a Christianis. Sed quicumque cibus praeponeretur, et in quacumque quantitate, non esset Corpus Domini prius acceptum. Ergo quaelibet sumptio cibi impedit a perceptione hujus sacramenti.

tain medicines. Therefore, it seems that after taking them a man could receive this sacrament.

Obj. 3: Furthermore, just as the body of Christ enters into the mouth, so it is also passed into the stomach. But if certain traces of food remain in the mouth, and afterward in the morning they are passed into the stomach, one is not prevented from receiving the body of Christ, for this could happen to a priest even while he is in the middle of celebrating the sacrament, when he could not abstain from receiving the body of Christ. Therefore, neither should food left behind in the mouth, if consumed in small amount, prevent the reception of this sacrament.

On the contrary, reverence is shown to this sacrament by this very fact, that the body of the Lord is consumed in the mouth of Christians first. But if any food were taken beforehand, in any amount whatsoever, then the body of the Lord would not be received first. Therefore, any consumption of food impedes one from receiving this sacrament.

Quaestiuncula 3

Ulterius. Videtur quod homo non statim debet comedere post corporis Christi sumptionem, per hoc quod dicitur *de Consecr.*, dist. 2: *si mane Dominica portio editur, usque ad sextam ministri jejunent qui eam consumpserunt, et si in tertia vel quarta hora acceperint, jejunent usque ad vesperam.*

Praeterea, non minor reverentia exhibenda est sacramento jam sumpto quam sumendo. Sed ante perceptionem non est aliquis cibus sumendus. Ergo nec post, quousque in ventre remaneat.

Sed contra est contraria consuetudo totius ecclesiae.

Obj. 1: It seems that a person should not immediately eat after receiving the body of Christ, by the fact that it says in *On Consecration*, Distinction 2: *if Sunday morning a portion is eaten, let the ministers who have consumed it fast until the sixth hour, and if they have received it in the third or fourth hour, let them fast until evening.*[48]

Obj. 2: Furthermore, no less reverence is to be shown to this sacrament once it has been received than when it is about to be received. But before its reception no food is to be taken. Therefore, neither should it be taken afterward, as long as it remains in the stomach.

On the contrary stands the contrary custom of the entire Church.

Response to Quaestiuncula 1

Respondeo dicendum ad primam quaestionem, quod hoc sacramentum a jejunis tantum percipi debet, nisi propter necessitatem imminentis mortis, ne contingat sine viatico ex hac vita transire: quod oportet in reverentiam tanti sacramenti, praecipue propter tria institutum esse. Primo propter ipsam sanctitatem sacramenti; ut os Christiani, quo sumendum est, non sit alio cibo prius imbutum, sed quasi novum et purum ad perceptionem ejus reservetur. Secundo propter devotionem quae exigitur ex parte recipientis, et attentionem quae ex cibis acceptis impediri posset, fumis a stomacho ad

To the first question, I answer that this sacrament should only be received by those who are fasting, unless out of necessity because of imminent death, lest it happen that someone should have to exit this life without viaticum. Fasting must be established in reverence for such a sacrament, for three reasons in particular. First, because of the very sanctity of the sacrament; so that the mouth of a Christian, by which it is to be consumed, would not be first drenched with other food, but would be reserved for its reception as something new and pure. Second, because of the devotion that is required on the part of the one re-

---

48. Gratian's *Decretals*, Part 3, *De consecratione*, d. 2 (PL 187:740).

caput ascendentibus. Tertio propter periculum vomitus, vel alicujus hujusmodi.

AD PRIMUM ergo dicendum, quod forma et materia sunt servata a Domino instituente hoc sacramentum quasi essentialia sacramento; et ideo oportuit quod ecclesia haec retineret. Sed ordinem sumendi servavit Dominus quasi convenientem institutioni sacramenti; unde non oportet quod ecclesia servet: quia non oportet quod illud quod convenit principio vel generationi alicujus rei quod competat ei quando jam est in esse perfecto; et similiter quod competit sacramento quantum ad sui institutionem, non oportet quod competat ei quantum ad suum usum.

AD SECUNDUM dicendum, quod apostolus non intendit quod fideles post cibos sumptos domi in ecclesia corpus Christi sumant; sed illos redarguit qui hunc cibum volebant aliis cibis commiscere, quos in ecclesia sumebant.

AD TERTIUM dicendum, quod forte ecclesia aliquo tempore sustinuit in die coenae sumi corpus Christi post alios cibos in repraesentationem Dominicae coenae; sed nunc abrogatum est decretum illud per communem consuetudinem: vel loquitur quantum ad astantes qui non sumunt.

ceiving, and the attention that could be distracted by having taken food, with gases rising from the stomach to the head. Third, because of the danger of vomiting, and other things like that.

REPLY OBJ. 1: Form and matter are preserved from the Lord's instituting of this sacrament as essentials for the sacrament, and so the Church had to retain these. But the Lord observed the order of consuming as befitting the sacrament's institution; and so it is not necessary that the Church preserve this: for something that befits the beginning or the generation of a certain thing does not necessarily apply to it when it has reached its perfect being; and likewise, what applies to the sacrament at its institution does not necessarily apply to it in its use.

REPLY OBJ. 2: The Apostle does not intend that the faithful consume Christ's body in the Church after having eaten at home; but he refuted those who wanted to commingle this food with other foods, which they would consume in the Church.

REPLY OBJ. 3: Perhaps at one time the Church permitted the body of Christ to be consumed on the day of the Lord's Supper after other foods representing the Last Supper, but now that decree has been repealed by common custom; or it speaks about those in attendance who do not consume.

Response to Quaestiuncula 2

AD SECUNDAM QUAESTIONEM dicendum, quod, sicut dictum est, in reverentiam sanctitatis hujus sacramenti institutum est quod os Christiani suscipientis corpus Christi quasi novum ad ipsum sumendum accedat. Quantalibet autem cibi assumptio hanc auferret novitatem; et ideo quaelibet cibi sumptio impedimentum praebet Eucharistiae sumptioni.

AD PRIMUM ergo dicendum, quod legis praecepta se habent ad ea quae agenda sunt sicut universalia ad singularia, ut dicitur in 5 *Ethic*. Quia enim legislator non potest ad omnes eventus attendere, oportet quod ad ea quae in pluribus accidunt attendens, universalem legem constituat, ut lex universalis sit. Et quia ut frequenter per cibum turbatur hominis discretio et sobrietas, quae praecipue in hoc sacramento exigitur, ideo universaliter prohibitum est post cibum corpus Christi sumi, quamvis aliqua cibi sumptio non impediat rationem; praecipue cum nihil periculi accidat, si post cibum sumptum abstineatur a perceptione hujus sacramenti, quia in articulo necessitatis licet accipere post alios cibos.

TO THE SECOND QUESTION, it should be said that, just as has been said, in reverence for the holiness of this sacrament it was established that the mouth of a Christian receiving the body of Christ should be presented to receive it as though new. However, even the slightest consumption of food would strip away this newness; and so any consumption of food presents an impediment to the consumption of the Eucharist.

REPLY OBJ. 1: The precepts of the law are ordered to those things that must be done as universals to singulars, as it says in *Ethics* 5.[49] For since a lawmaker cannot foresee all events, he must establish a universal law in attending to those things that happen most of the time, so that the law may be universal. And since as frequently happens, a person's discretion and sobriety, which is particularly required in this sacrament, is disturbed by food, this is the reason that it is universally prohibited to receive the body of Christ after food, even though some consumption of food may not impede reason; particularly since no danger occurs, if after taking food one abstains from receiving this sacrament, since in an emergency it is permitted to take it after other foods.

49. Aristotle, *Nicomachean Ethics*, Bk. 5, ch. 14, 1137b13–14.

Ad secundum dicendum, quod duplex est jejunium; scilicet naturae et ecclesiae. Jejunium naturae est quo quis jejunus dicitur ante cibum sumptum illa die, etiam si pluries postea comesturus sit: et quia hoc jejunium dicitur ex privatione cibi praeassumpti, ideo quaelibet cibi sumptio hoc jejunium tollit. Jejunium autem ecclesiae est quo quis dicitur jejunans secundum modum ab ecclesia institutum ad carnis afflictionem; et hoc jejunium manet etiam post unicam comestionem, nec solvitur nisi per secundam sumptionem illorum quae in cibum et refectionem de se consueverunt assumi; et ideo ea quae propter alios cibos accipi consueverunt, vel digerendos, sicut electuaria, vel deducendos per membra, sicut potus vini aut aquae, hujusmodi jejunium non solvunt quamvis etiam aliquo modo nutriant. Ad debitam ergo sumptionem Dominici corporis non exigitur jejunium ecclesiae, quia etiam praeter dies jejunii hoc sacramentum celebratur; sed requiritur jejunium naturae propter reverentiam sacramenti; et ideo secundum communem sententiam electuaria et vinum praeassumpta impediunt a perceptione Eucharistiae. Sed de aqua, diversa est opinio. Quidam enim dicunt, quod quia nullo modo nutrit, non solvit neque jejunium naturae neque jejunium ecclesiae. Sed quamvis aqua in se non nutriat, tamen commixta nutrit. In stomacho autem oportet quod aliis humoribus admisceatur; et ideo in nutrimentum cedere potest; et propter hoc alii probabilius et securius dicunt quod etiam post aquae potum corpus Christi non sumendum est.

Ad tertium dicendum, quod jejunium naturae dicitur per privationem actus comestionis, secundum quod comestio etiam potationem includit. Comestio autem principaliter dicitur a sumptione exterioris cibi, quamvis terminetur ad trajectionem cibi in ventrem, et ulterius ad nutritionem; et ideo quae interius geruntur sine exterioris cibi sumptione, non videntur solvere jejunium naturae, nec impedire Eucharistiae perceptionem, sicut deglutitio salivae; et similiter videtur de his quae infra dentes remanent, et etiam de eructationibus: tamen propter reverentiam, nisi necessitas incumbat, potest sine periculo abstineri.

Reply Obj. 2: There are two kinds of fasts: namely, natural fasts and ecclesial fasts. A natural fast is when someone is said to have fasted before the first food taken that day, even if he will eat several times afterward: and since this is called a fast because of the lack of food taken beforehand, any consumption of food whatsoever breaks this fast. However, the Church's fast is when someone is said to be fasting according to the mode established by the Church for the affliction of the flesh; and this fast remains even after eating one thing, nor is it broken except by a second consumption of those things that were customarily taken in the meal and for the sake of replenishment; and so those things that were customarily taken for the sake of other foods, either for digesting them, like electuaries, or for drawing them out to the members, like a drink of wine or water, do not break this kind of fast although they do also nourish in some way. Therefore, for the right consumption of the Lord's body, a Church fast is not required, since even outside fasting days this sacrament is celebrated. Rather it requires a natural fast out of reverence for the sacrament; and so according to the common opinion, electuaries and wine taken beforehand impede the reception of the Eucharist. But concerning water, there are different opinions. For some people say that since it does not nourish in any way, it neither breaks the natural fast nor the Church's fast. But although water in itself does not nourish, nevertheless, it does nourish when mixed with other things. Now in the stomach it must mix with other fluids, and so it can result in nourishment; and because of this, others say more probably and securely that also after drinking water the body of the Lord is not to be received.

Reply Obj. 3: A fast is called natural by the absence of the act of eating, where eating also includes drinking. However, 'eating' mainly refers to the consumption of external food, although it ends in the passing of food into the stomach, and finally in nourishment; and so the foods that are borne internally without the consumption of external food do not seem to break a natural fast, nor prevent the reception of the Eucharist, just like the swallowing of saliva. And it seems to be the same with those things that remain stuck in the teeth, and also those that are burped up. Nevertheless, for the sake of reverence, if necessary one can abstain from receiving without danger.

Response to Quaestiuncula 3

Ad tertiam quaestionem dicendum, quod secundum consuetudinem ecclesiae propter reverentiam tanti sacramenti, post ejus sumptionem homo debet in gratiarum actione persistere; unde etiam in Missa oratio gratiarum actionis post communionem dicitur, et sacerdotes post celebrationem suas speciales orationes habent ad gratiarum actionem; et ideo oportet esse aliquod in-

To the third question, it should be said that according to the custom of the Church, out of reverence for so great a sacrament, after having received it, a man should remain in thanksgiving; and the prayer of thanksgiving after Communion in the Mass is also said, and the priests after celebrating Mass have special prayers for thanksgiving. And so it is fitting that there should be a certain interval be-

tervallum inter sumptionem Eucharistiae et aliorum ciborum. Sed quia non requiritur magnum intervallum, et quod parum deest, nihil deesse videtur, ut dicitur in 2 *Physic.*, ideo possemus sub hoc sensu concedere quod statim potest aliquis cibos alios sumere post Eucharistiae sumptionem.

AD PRIMUM ergo dicendum quod illud decretum loquitur secundum consuetudinem primitivae ecclesiae, quando propter paucitatem ministrorum rarius Missarum solemnia celebrabantur, et cum majori praeparatione. Unde Dionysius narrat de Carpo in suis epistolis quod nunquam Missam celebrabat nisi aliqua divina revelatione prius percepta; et ideo nunc per contrariam consuetudinem abrogatum est.

AD SECUNDUM dicendum, quod sacramentum post sui sumptionem, effectum proprium causat; et ideo oportet actualiter in ipsa sumptione cor hominis in devotione persistere: sed post perceptionem sufficit quod habitu devotio teneatur, quia non potest semper in actu esse; et ideo ea quae possunt actum impedire, prohibentur magis ante sumptionem sacramenti quam post.

tween consuming the Eucharist and other foods. But since a great interval is not required, and what lacks something small seems to lack nothing, as it says in *Physics* 2,[50] for this reason we might concede that in this sense a person can take other food immediately after receiving the Eucharist.

REPLY OBJ. 1: That decree speaks according to the custom of the early Church, when because of the scarcity of ministers, the solemn rites of Masses were rarely celebrated, and then, with greater preparation. Hence Dionysius tells of Carpus in his letters that he never celebrated Mass unless he had first received a divine revelation;[51] and so nowadays this has been repealed by the contrary custom.

REPLY OBJ. 2: After a sacrament's reception, it causes its proper effect, and so a man's heart must actually persist in devotion during the reception itself; but after the reception of it, it is enough that devotion be held habitually, for it cannot always be in act; and so those things that can impede the act are prohibited before the sacrament's reception, rather than after.

---

50. Aristotle, *Physics*, Bk. 2, ch. 5, 197a29–30.
51. Pseudo-Dionysius, *Epistle* 8, n. 6 (PG 3:1098).

QUESTION 2

THE FORM OF THE SACRAMENT

Deinde quaeritur de forma hujus sacramenti; et circa hoc quaeruntur quatuor:

primo, de forma qua corpus Christi consecratur;

secundo, de forma qua consecratur ipsius sanguis;
tertio, de virtute utriusque;
quarto, de comparatione unius ad aliam.

Next inquiry is made about the form of this sacrament; and concerning this, four questions arise:

first, the form with which the body of Christ is consecrated;

second, the form with which his blood is consecrated;
third, the power of each;
fourth, a comparison of the two.

ARTICLE 1

The form with which the body of Christ is consecrated

Quaestiuncula 1

AD PRIMUM SIC PROCEDITUR. Videtur quod haec non sit forma consecrationis panis: *hoc est corpus meum.* Sacramenta enim habent efficaciam ex institutione divina. Sed Dominus instituens hoc sacramentum non consecravit his verbis, sed post consecrationem et fractionem haec verba protulit; unde dicitur Matth. 26, 26: *coenantibus illis accepit Jesus panem, et benedixit, et fregit, deditque discipulis suis, et ait: accipite et comedite; hoc est corpus meum.* Ergo in praedictis verbis non consistit forma consecrationis panis.

PRAETEREA, forma baptismi consistit in verbis quae dicuntur in ipso usu baptismi. Sed haec verba non dicuntur in usu Eucharistiae, sed magis in sanctificatione materiae. Ergo in his verbis non consistit forma hujus sacramenti.

OBJ. 1: To the first we proceed thus. It seems that this is not the form of consecrating the bread: *this is my body.*[52] For sacraments have their efficacy from divine institution. But when the Lord was instituting this sacrament, he did not consecrate with these words, but uttered them after the consecration and breaking of the bread; hence it says, *while they were eating, Jesus took the bread and blessed it and broke it, and gave it to his disciples and said: take and eat; this is my body* (Matt 26:26). Therefore, the form of the consecration of the bread does not consist in the words mentioned.

OBJ. 2: Furthermore, the form of baptism consists in the words that are said in the use itself of baptism. But these words are not said in the use of the Eucharist, but rather in the sanctification of its matter. Therefore, the form of this sacrament does not consist in these words.

Quaestiuncula 2

ULTERIUS. Videtur quod non tantum in his verbis consistat forma: *hoc est corpus meum.* Sicut enim dicit Eusebius Emissenus, *invisibilis sacerdos visibiles creaturas in suum corpus convertit dicens: accipite et comedite,* etc. Ergo haec etiam est forma: *accipite et comedite.*

PRAETEREA, illud quod non est de substantia formae, non debet interponi inter substantialia formae, in

OBJ. 1: Moreover, it seems that the form does not only consist in these words: *this is my body.*[53] For as Eusebius of Emesa says, *the invisible priest changes visible creatures into his own body when he says, 'Take and eat', etc.*[54] Therefore, the form is also this: *Take and eat.*

OBJ. 2: Furthermore, whatever is not of the form's substance must not be interposed between the substantial ele-

---

52. Parallels: below, a. 2, qa. 1; a. 4, qa. 3; *ST* III, q. 78, a. 1; *Super Matt.* 26; *Super I ad Cor.* 11, lec. 5.
53. Parallel: *ST* III, q. 78, a. 1, ad 2.
54. See Gratian's *Decretals*, Part 3, *De consecratione*, d. 2, ch. 35 (PL 187:1745).

hoc sacramento, sicut nec in aliis. Sed inter haec verba, in libris Romanis interposita invenitur haec conjunctio *enim*. Ergo hoc etiam est de forma, et non tantum verba praedicta.

ments of the form in this sacrament, just as neither in the others. But in the Roman canon is found interposed between these words the conjunction *for*. Therefore, this is also part of the form, and not only the words mentioned.

Quaestiuncula 3

ULTERIUS. Videtur quod forma haec non sit conveniens. In forma enim sacramenti debet exprimi hoc quod in sacramento geritur per actum convenientem materiae, sicut in forma baptismi dicitur: *ego te baptizo*; et in forma confirmationis: *confirmo te chrismate salutis*. Sed non ponitur in verbis praemissis aliquid pertinens ad transubstantiationem, quae fit in hoc sacramento, panis scilicet in corpus Christi. Ergo non est conveniens forma.

PRAETEREA, dispensatur hoc sacramentum per ministros ecclesiae, sicut et alia sacramenta. Sed in formis aliorum sacramentorum ponitur aliquid pertinens ad ministrum. Ergo cum in hac forma non ponatur actus ministri, videtur quod sit incompetens.

OBJ. 1: Moreover, it seems that this form is not fitting.[55] For in the form of a sacrament should be expressed what is carried out in the sacrament by the act suited to its matter, as in the form of baptism it is said, *I baptize you*, and in the form of confirmation, *I confirm you with the chrism of salvation*. But in the words mentioned nothing is included that pertains to transubstantiation, which is the turning of the bread into the body of Christ that happens in this sacrament. Therefore, the form is not fitting.

OBJ. 2: Furthermore, this sacrament is administered by the ministers of the Church, just like the other sacraments. But in the form of the other sacraments, something is included that pertains to the minister. Therefore, since the act of the minister is not included in this form, it seems that it is inadequate.

Quaestiuncula 4

ULTERIUS. Videtur quod singulae partes inconvenienter ponantur. Hoc enim pronomen hoc demonstrativum est. Aut ergo importat demonstrationem ut conceptam, aut ut exercitam. Si ut conceptam, sic sumitur ut res quaedam, et non ut habens ordinem ad rem aliam, ut si dicerem: *hoc pronomen hoc*. Sed sanctificatio sacramenti non fit nisi per hoc quod verba formae ordinantur ad materiam ex intentione proferentis. Ergo secundum hoc non posset verbis praedictis fieri consecratio aliqua corporis Christi. Si autem importat demonstrationem ut exercitam; aut facit demonstrationem ad intellectum, aut ad sensum. Si ad intellectum, ut sit sensus: *hoc*, idest significatum per hoc, *est corpus meum*, tunc iterum significatio verborum non refertur ad hanc materiam panis. Sed sacramenta significando efficiunt; et de formis sacramentorum Augustinus dicit: *accedit verbum ad elementum, et fit sacramentum*. Ergo adhuc per verba praedicta non fit transubstantiatio. Si autem faciat demonstrationem ad sensum, ergo demonstrabit substantiam contentam sub illis speciebus sensibilibus. Sed illa substantia est panis, de quo non potest dici quod sit cor-

OBJ. 1: Moreover, it seems that the individual parts are unfittingly laid down.[56] For the pronoun 'this' is demonstrative. Therefore, it conveys demonstration as conceived or as carried out in practice. If as conceived, then it is taken as a certain thing, and not as something having an order to another thing, as it would be if I were to say, *This pronoun this*. But the sanctification of the sacrament only happens by the fact that the words of the form are directed to the matter by the intention of the one uttering them. Therefore, according to this no consecration of the body of Christ could be done by the words mentioned. But if it conveys demonstration as carried out in practice, either it makes a demonstration for the intellect or for the senses. If for the intellect, so that the sense would be, *this*, i.e., what is represented by this, *is my body*, then again the meaning of the words does not refer to this matter of bread. But sacraments bring about by signifying, and concerning the forms of the sacraments Augustine says, *the word is combined with the element and the sacrament occurs*.[57] Therefore no transubstantiation has happened up to the point of the words mentioned. But if it makes a demonstration for the senses, then

---

55. Parallels: *ST* III, q. 75, a. 2; q. 78, a. 2; *Super Matt.* 26; *Super I ad Cor.* 11, lec. 5.

56. Parallels: *ST* III, q. 78, a. 2; *Super Matt.* 26; *Super I ad Cor.* 11, lec. 5.

57. Augustine, *In Iohannis euangelium tractatus* (CCSL 36), Tract. 80, par. 3.

pus Christi. Ergo non erit vera haec locutio: *hoc est corpus meum.*

PRAETEREA, quod transit in aliquid, non est illud: quia omnis motus et factio est ex incontingenti, ut dicit Philosophus in 1 *Physica*. Sed verum est dicere quod haec substantia demonstrata fit corpus Christi vel transit in corpus Christi. Ergo non vere dicitur: *hoc est corpus meum.*

PRAETEREA, significatum debet respondere signo. Sed panis est corpus homogeneum. Ergo significatio ejus est respectu alicujus partis homogeneae corporis Christi. Non nisi carnis: quia de ipsa dicit Dominus, Joan. 6, 56: *caro mea vere est cibus*. Ergo potius dici debuit: *haec est caro mea*, quam *hoc est corpus meum.*

PRAETEREA, sicut dictum est, oportet quod hoc pronomen hoc faciat demonstrationem exercitam, ad hoc quod fiat consecratio corporis Christi ex hac materia. Sed non potest hoc esse, nisi quando demonstratio profertur ex persona loquentis: quia si proferretur a recitante verba alterius, non faceret demonstrationem ad istam materiam, sed quasi materialiter sumerentur. Ergo oportet quod verba praedicta proferantur quasi ex persona sacerdotis ea enuntiantis. Sed panis non convertitur in corpus sacerdotis, sed in corpus Christi. Ergo deberet dicere: hoc est corpus Christi; et non: *hoc est corpus meum*: quia hoc posset esse erroris materia.

it will demonstrate the substance contained under those sensible appearances. But that substance is bread, about which it cannot be said that it is the body of Christ. Therefore this sentence will not be true: *this is my body.*

OBJ. 2: Furthermore, what is transformed into something is not it in the first place: for every motion and doing is from not-happening, as the Philosopher says in *Physics* 1.[58] But it is true to say that this substance indicated becomes the body of Christ or turns into the body of Christ. Therefore, one cannot say truly, *this is my body.*

OBJ. 3: Furthermore, what is signified by a sign must correspond to the sign. But bread is a homogeneous body. Therefore, its signification regards some homogeneous part of the body of Christ. But this could only be his flesh, for the Lord says about this, *my flesh is true food* (John 6:56). Therefore it should have been said, *this is my flesh*, rather than, *this is my body.*

OBJ. 4: Furthermore, as was said, this pronoun 'this' must make a demonstration in practice for the consecration of the body of Christ to happen from this matter. But this can only happen when the demonstration is uttered in the person of the one speaking; for if it were uttered by reciting the words of another, it would not be a demonstration to this matter, but it would be taken quasi-materially. Therefore, the words mentioned must be uttered as though in the person of the priest pronouncing them. But bread is not changed into the body of the priest, but into the body of Christ. Therefore he should have said: *this is the body of Christ*, and not, *this is my body*: for this could be matter for error.

Quaestiuncula 5

ULTERIUS. Videtur quod verba quae circa formam dicuntur, non convenienter ponantur. Sicut enim Dionysius dicit in principio *de Divin. Nom.*, *non est audendum dicere aliquid de divinis praeter ea quae nobis ex sacris eloquiis sunt expressa*. Sed in Evangeliis non legitur quod Dominus instituens hoc sacramentum in coena, oculos ad caelum levaverit. Ergo inconvenienter praemittitur: *sublevatis oculis in caelum.*

PRAETEREA, in baptismo non licet fieri mutationem verborum etiam per verba ejusdem significationis, ut pro loco *Patris*, Genitoris poneretur. Sed in nullo Evangelio sunt haec verba: *accipite et manducate*; sed *accipite et comedite*. Ergo inconvenienter dicitur: *manducate.*

OBJ. 1: It seems that the words that are spoken surrounding the form are not fittingly set down.[59] For as Dionysius says in the beginning of the *Divine Names, we must not dare to say anything about divine things apart from those things that are expressed for us in the sacred words.*[60] But in the Gospels it is not read that when the Lord was instituting this sacrament at Supper, he lifted his eyes to heaven.[61] Therefore, it is unfittingly said beforehand, *with eyes raised to heaven.*

OBJ. 2: Furthermore, in baptism no changing of the words is permitted, even by words of the same meaning, as if in place of *Father*, 'Creator' were said. But in no Gospel are these words: *take and eat* [manducate], but *take and eat* [comedite]. Therefore, 'manducate' is unfittingly said.

---

58. Aristotle, *Physics*, Bk. 1, ch. 4, 188a31ff.
59. Parallel: *ST* III, q. 78, a. 1.
60. Pseudo-Dionysius, *Divine Names*, ch. 1 (PG 3:587).
61. Yet this phrase is found in the Roman Canon: "Who, the day before He suffered, took bread into His holy and venerable hands, and with His eyes lifted up towards heaven, unto Thee, God, His almighty Father . . ."

PRAETEREA, in nullo Evangeliorum ponitur *omnes*. Ergo videtur quod praesumptuosum fuit addere.

OBJ. 3: Furthermore, in none of the Gospels is *all of you* set down. Therefore, it seems that it was a presumptuous thing to add.

Response to Quaestiuncula 1

RESPONDEO dicendum ad primam quaestionem, quod per formam cujuslibet sacramenti oportet quod exprimatur hoc in quo substantia sacramenti consistit; sicut in forma baptismi ablutio exprimitur, qua baptismi perficitur sacramentum. Tota autem perfectio hujus sacramenti in ipsa materiae consecratione consistit, quae est per transubstantiationem panis in corpus Christi: et hanc transubstantiationem exprimunt verba haec: *hoc est corpus meum*; et ideo haec verba sunt forma hujus sacramenti.

AD PRIMUM ergo dicendum, quod circa hoc est quadruplex opinio.

Quidam enim dixerunt, quod Christus, qui habebat potestatem excellentiae in sacramentis, absque omni forma virtute divina confecit, et postea verba protulit, sub quibus alii deinceps consecrabant; et hanc opinionem tangit Innocentius, dicens: *sane dici potest, quod Christus virtute divina confecit, et postea formam expressit sub qua posteri benedicerent*. Sed hoc non videtur conveniens: quia in textu Evangelii dicitur: *benedixit*, quod aliquibus verbis factum est. Innocentius autem loquitur opinionem narrando, vel tangendo ordinem quo virtus consecrationis a Christo, in quo primo erat, ad verba derivata est.

Et ideo alii dicunt, quod confecit quidem sub aliqua forma verborum, non autem sub his, sed sub aliis verbis ignotis. Sed hoc etiam videtur inconveniens: quia sacerdos his verbis conficiens ea profert ut tunc a Christo prolata; unde si tunc eis non fiebat confectio, nec modo fieret.

Et ideo alii dicunt, quod confecit sub eisdem verbis, sed ea bis protulit: primo tacite, cum benedixit; secundo aperte, cum distribuit, ut formam consecrandi aliis traderet. Sed hoc etiam videtur inconveniens: quia non proferuntur a sacerdote consecrante in persona Christi, ut in occulto prolata: non enim benedixit dicens: *hoc est corpus meum*, sed dedit dicens: *accipite*, etc.

Et ideo alii dicunt, et melius, quod Christus ea semel tantum protulit, et eis semel prolatis consecravit, et formam consecrandi dedit. Hoc enim participium *dicens* non importat concomitantiam solum ad hoc verbum *de-*

TO THE FIRST QUESTION, I answer that the form of any sacrament must express what the substance of the sacrament consists in; as in the form of baptism cleansing is expressed, in which the sacrament of baptism is completed. But the whole perfection of this sacrament consists in the very consecration of its matter, which is by the transubstantiation of bread into the body of Christ. And these words express this transubstantiation: *this is my body*; and so these words are the form of this sacrament.

REPLY OBJ. 1: There are four opinions about this.

For some people have said that Christ, who had the power of excellence in the sacraments, consecrated without any form, by divine power, and afterward pronounced the words by which others consecrated thereafter; and Innocent touches on this opinion, saying: *it can be soundly said that Christ consecrated by divine power, and afterward expressed the form under which future generations would bless it.*[62] But this does not seem fitting: for in the text of the Gospel it says, *he blessed it*, which was done by certain words. However, Innocent states this opinion by way of giving his own view, or by referring to the order by which the power of consecrating was imparted to the words from Christ, in whom this power first existed.

And so others say that he did consecrate under a certain form of words, though not these, but other words we do not know. But this also seems unfitting: for a priest consecrating by these words utters them as uttered by Christ at that moment. For this reason if at that moment the consecration was not happening through them, then it would not happen now either.

And so others say that he consecrated under these same words, but he pronounced them twice: the first time, silently, when he blessed the bread, and the second time, openly, when he distributed it, so that he might impart to the others the form of consecrating. But even this seems unfitting: for they are not uttered by the consecrating priest in the person of Christ as uttered in secret: for he did not bless it saying, *this is my body*, but he gave it saying, *take and eat*, etc.

And so others say, and this is better, that Christ uttered these words only once, and by uttering them once, he both consecrated the bread and gave the form of consecrating. For this participle, *saying*, does not convey simultaneity

62. Pope Innocent, *De Myster. Missae*, Bk. 4, ch. 6 (PL 217:859).

dit, sed ad hoc cum aliis praedictis, ut sit sensus: dum benedixit et fregit, et dedit discipulis, haec verba protulit: *accipite*, etc. Vel, secundum quosdam, Evangelista non observat ordinem verborum quo a Domino fuerunt prolata; ordo enim fuit talis: accepit panem, et benedixit, dicens: *accipite*, etc. Sed primum melius est.

Ad secundum dicendum, quod perfectio aliorum sacramentorum consistit in usu materiae, istius autem in materiae consecratione; et ideo forma etiam in aliis sacramentis est in verbis quae dicuntur in usu sacramenti; in hoc autem forma sacramenti est in verbis quae dicuntur in consecratione materiae.

only with the word *gave*, but with all the other things mentioned, so that the sense would be: while he blessed it and broke it, and gave it to his disciples, he uttered these words: *take and eat*, etc. Or, according to certain others, the Gospel writer does not observe the order in which the words were uttered by the Lord; for the order went like this: he took the bread, and blessed it, saying, *take and eat*, etc. But the former explanation is better.

Reply Obj. 2: The completion of the other sacraments consists in the use of the matter, but this one in the consecration of the matter. And this is why in the other sacraments the form too is in the words that are said in the use of the sacrament, while in this one, the form of the sacrament is in the words that are said in the consecration of the matter.

Response to Quaestiuncula 2

Ad secundam quaestionem dicendum, quod in hoc sacramento, sicut in aliis, duo sunt; scilicet consecratio materiae, et usus materiae consecratae; et haec duo per verba Domini exprimuntur. In hoc enim quod dicitur, *Accipite et manducate ex hoc omnes*, praecipitur usus sacramenti; in hoc autem quod dicitur, *hoc est corpus meum*, traditur materiae consecratio. Et quia consecratio materiae est ad usum fidelium, ideo usus praemittitur in demonstratione sacramenti, quamvis sequatur in executione: quia finis est prior in intentione et cognitione, et ultimus in operatione. Sed quia, ut dictum est, usus materiae in hoc sacramento non est de essentia sacramenti, sicut in aliis; ideo illa verba quae ad usum pertinent, non sunt de forma, sed tantum illa quae ad consecrationem materiae pertinent, scilicet, *hoc est corpus meum*.

Ad primum ergo dicendum, quod quamvis sacramenti usus non sit de essentia sacramenti, est tamen ad completum esse ipsius, inquantum pertingit ad hoc quod institutum est; et ideo quandoque dicuntur esse de forma non solum illa quae pertinent ad consecrationem, sed etiam illa quae pertinent ad usum; et sic loquitur Ambrosius et Eusebius et Magister in littera.

Ad secundum dicendum, quod haec conjunctio *enim* importat ordinem consecrationis ad usum materiae consecratae; et ideo sicut verba quae pertinent ad usum, non sunt de forma, ita nec praedicta conjunctio. Apponi autem debet secundum usum Romanae ecclesiae, quae a beato Petro initium sumpsit. Nec est simile de hoc sacramento et de aliis. Verba enim formae hujus sacramenti proferuntur a ministro in persona Christi quasi recitative; et ideo oportet apponere continuationem ad recitationem praemissam, quam facit conjunctio

To the second question, it should be said that in this sacrament, as in the others, there are two things: namely, the consecration of matter and the use of the consecrated matter; and these two things are expressed by the words of the Lord. For in saying, *take and eat of it all of you*, the use of the sacrament is commanded; but in saying, *this is my body*, the consecration of the matter is given. And since the consecration of the matter is for the use of the faithful, for this reason the use is stated first in the sacrament's demonstration, although it follows in execution: since the end is prior in intention and understanding, and last in operation. But since, as was said, the use of the matter in this sacrament is not of the essence of the sacrament, as it is in the others, for that reason those words that pertain to the use do not belong to the form, but only the words that pertain to the consecration of the matter, namely, *this is my body*.

Reply Obj. 1: Although the sacrament's use is not of the essence of the sacrament, nevertheless it does contribute to the sacrament's fullness, inasmuch as it attains what it was instituted for; and so sometimes not only those words are said to be of the form that pertain to the consecration, but also those that pertain to the use; and this is how Ambrose and Eusebius are speaking, as well as the Master in the text.

Reply Obj. 2: This conjunction *for* conveys the order of the consecration to the use of the matter once consecrated; and thus just as words that pertain to the use are not of the form, likewise neither is the conjunction mentioned. However, it must be included according to the use of the Roman Church, which took its beginning from blessed Peter. Nor is it the same with this sacrament as with others. For the words of this sacrament's form are uttered by the minister in the person of Christ, as though quoting. And this is why the link must be made with the previous quota-

enim. Aliorum autem sacramentorum formae ex persona ministri proferuntur; et ideo non oportet interponere aliquid quod non sit de forma ratione continuationis, cum absolute proferantur.

tion, which the conjunction *for* does. The forms of the other sacraments, on the other hand, are uttered in the person of the minister; and so nothing that is not of the form need be interposed to link it to something else, since it is uttered absolutely.

Response to Quaestiuncula 3

AD TERTIAM QUAESTIONEM dicendum, quod minister in sacramentis dupliciter operatur. Uno modo, verba pronuntians; alio modo actum aliquem exteriorem exercens, ut in baptismo patet; et utrumque istorum est sacramentalis causa ejus quod divina virtute, quae in sacramentis latet, perficitur. Causa autem sacramentalis significando efficit; unde in illis sacramentis in quibus utroque modo minister operatur, oportet quod verba prolata significent actum exercitum, et actus exterior significet interiorem effectum, ut in baptismo patet: quia ablutio exterior, quam verba formae exprimunt, significat interiorem ablutionem, quam divina virtus perficit in sacramento latens. Ubi ergo minister non operatur nisi verba pronuntians, oportet quod verborum significatio immediate ad hoc quod efficitur, referatur. In hoc autem sacramento, cujus perfectio in ipsa materiae consecratione consistit, non habet minister actum nisi pronuntiationem verborum, sicut nec in aliqua alia materiae sanctificatione. Unde oportet quod verba formae significent hoc quod virtus divina in secreto facit; hoc autem est esse corpus Christi sub speciebus illis; et ideo haec est conveniens forma huic sacramento: *hoc est corpus meum,* quae hoc quod dictum est, significat.

AD PRIMUM ergo dicendum, quod in hoc sacramento non geritur aliquid a ministro quod sit de essentia sacramenti, sicut erat in baptismo; unde oportet quod verba significent illud tantum quod divina virtute geritur. Omne autem faciens causat ipsam factionem in hoc quod factum est; nec oportet esse assimilationem factionis ad facientem, sed facti ad facientem, quia ad hoc est intentio facientis. Sicut autem in operibus artis et naturae requiritur inter faciens et factum similitudo secundum formam naturalem et artificialem; ita in causis sacramentalibus requiritur assimilatio vel repraesentatio per modum significationis; unde verba prolata in hoc sacramento non deberent significare ipsam factionem vel transubstantiationem ut in fieri, sed ut in factum esse; unde haec non esset conveniens forma hujus sacramenti: *hoc fit corpus meum*: quia per hoc non significatur aliquid esse vel non esse; et similiter nec haec: *hoc mutetur, vel transubstantietur in corpus meum*: quia non significatur esse vel non esse *hoc*, quod est principaliter intentum in hoc sacramento. Vel dicendum, quod alia verba significant agere et pati, et ita motum aliquem, et quia in

TO THE THIRD QUESTION, it should be said that in the sacraments the minister can work two ways. In one way, pronouncing the words; in another way, as the one performing a certain outward act, as is evident in baptism; and both of these are the sacramental cause of what is accomplished by the divine power that is hidden in the sacraments. Now a sacramental cause effects by signifying; hence in those sacraments in which the minister works in both of these ways, the words uttered must signify the act performed, and the outward act must signify the interior effect, as is seen in baptism: for the external cleansing, which the words of the form express, signifies an interior cleansing, which divine power, hidden in the sacrament, accomplishes. Therefore, where the minister works only by pronouncing the words, it is necessary that the signification of the words refer directly to what is accomplished; however, in this sacrament, whose completion consists in the actual consecration of the matter, the minister has no act but the pronouncing of the words, nor any other sanctification of the matter. Hence the words of the form must signify what divine power is doing imperceptibly; but this is for the body of Christ to exist under those appearances, and therefore this is the fitting form for this sacrament: *this is my body*, which signifies what has been said.

REPLY OBJ. 1: In this sacrament nothing is carried out by the minister that is of the essence of the sacrament, as it was in baptism; for this reason the words must signify only what is brought about by divine power. However, everything that does something causes the very doing in the fact that it was done; nor must there be a resemblance between the doing and the one doing it, but between the deed and the one doing it, since this is the intention of the one acting. However, just as works of art and nature require a resemblance between the one doing and the deed done according to the natural and artificial form, so also sacramental causes require a likening or representation by the mode of signifying; which is why words uttered in this sacrament did not have to signify this doing or transubstantiation itself as something happening, but as something that has happened; therefore this would not be a fitting form for this sacrament: *this is becoming my body*, for by this no being or non-being is signified; and likewise, nor would these words: *may this be changed or transubstantiated into my body*, for *this* is not signified as being or non-being, which is chiefly intended in this sacrament. Or it could be said that other words sig-

transubstantiatione non est motus aliquis, cum non sit subjectum commune, nec mutatio, quia terminus transubstantiationis est praeexistens actu; ideo per nullum verbum congrue potuit tradi forma sacramenti hujus, nisi per verbum substantivum.

Ad secundum dicendum, quod minister non habet actum exteriorem in consecratione, in qua consistit essentia hujus sacramenti; quamvis habeat actum exteriorem in dispensatione, quae consequitur ad sacramentum; et ideo actus ministri in forma quae est de essentia sacramenti, poni non debuit.

nify acting or being passive, and thus a certain motion, and since there is no motion in transubstantiation, since there is no common subject, nor a change, since the terminus of transubstantiation is pre-existing in act; for this reason no adequate word could have been handed down as this sacrament's form, except a substantive.

Reply Obj. 2: A minister does not have an outward act in the consecration, in which the essence of this sacrament consists; although he has an outward act in the distribution to the faithful, which comes after this sacrament; and so the minister's act need not be included in the form that is of the essence of the sacrament.

Response to Quaestiuncula 4

Ad quartam quaestionem dicendum, quod, sicut dictum est, verba formae transubstantiationem in suo termino significare debent, non secundum quod consideratur ut in fieri. Esse autem est terminus transubstantiationis, cujus extrema vel termini sunt duae substantiae; et ideo in verbis formae significantur duo termini transubstantiationis, et ipsa transubstantiatio prout est in suo termino per verbum *essendi*. In termino autem transubstantiationis substantia quae erat terminus a quo, non manet quantum ad naturam speciei, sed solum quantum ad accidentia, quibus ejus individuatio cognoscebatur; sed substantia quae est terminus ad quem, in termino transubstantiationis continetur in sacramento integre, et quo ad naturam speciei, et quo ad accidentia propria. Et ideo ex parte termini a quo, non ponitur illud quod significaret naturam speciei, sed pronomen demonstrativum, quod notificat individuationem per accidentia, prout cadunt sub sensu: ex parte autem termini ad quem, ponitur nomen designans naturam speciei, et pronomen non demonstrativum hujus substantiae prout est sub sacramento, sed prout est Christi in propria specie visibilis, quia sic verba formae pronuntiavit. Unde patet quod congrue in his verbis quatuor forma consistit: *hoc est corpus meum.*

Ad primum ergo dicendum, quod circa hoc est multiplex opinio.

Quidam enim dicunt, quod hoc pronomen *hoc* nullam demonstrationem facit, quia sumitur materialiter, cum verba illa recitative a sacerdote proferantur. Sed hoc non potest stare: quia secundum hoc verba illa nullum ordinem haberent ad materiam praesentem, et sic non fieret sacramentum. Augustinus enim dicit: *accedit verbum ad elementum, et fit sacramentum.* Et praeterea eadem difficultas remanet de verbis istis secundum quod fuerunt ab ipso Christo prolata.

To the fourth question, it should be said that as has been said, the words of the form should signify transubstantiation in its terminus, but not considered as happening. However, being is the terminus of transubstantiation, for its extremes or terminuses are the two substances; and so in the form's words the two terminuses of transubstantiation are signified, and transubstantiation itself as it exists in its terminus by the word *is.* However, in the terminus of transubstantiation that was the starting terminus, the nature of the species does not remain but only the accidents, by which its individuation was recognized; but the substance that is the ending terminus is wholly contained in the sacrament, both as to the nature of the species and as to its proper accidents. And so on the part of the starting terminus, what signifies the nature of the species is not stated, but a demonstrative pronoun, which indicates its individuation by the accidents, just as it is perceived by the senses. On the part of the ending terminus, however, a noun is used designating the nature of the species, and a pronoun not demonstrative of this substance as it is under the sacrament, but as it is Christ's in his proper visible species, for that is how he pronounced the words of the form. Hence it is evident that the form consists adequately in these four words: *this is my body.*

Reply Obj. 1: Concerning this there are several opinions.

For certain people say that this pronoun, *this*, makes no demonstration, for it is taken materially, since those words are uttered by the priest as though quoting. But this cannot stand: for then those words would have no order to the matter present, and so there would be no sacrament. For Augustine says: *the word is combined with the element, and a sacrament occurs.*[63] And furthermore, the same difficulty remains about those words as uttered by Christ himself.

---

63. Augustine, *In Iohannis euangelium tractatus* (CCSL 36), Tract. 80, par. 3.

Et ideo alii dicunt, quod facit demonstrationem ad intellectum, et est sensus: *hoc est corpus meum*; idest, *per hunc panem vel per has species significatur corpus meum*: vel, *significatum per hoc, est corpus meum*. Sed illud iterum stare non potest: quia cum in sacramentis non efficiatur nisi quod significatur virtute dictorum verborum, non fieret corpus Christi in altari secundum rei veritatem, sed secundum significationem tantum, quod est haereticum; vel verba praemissa non essent forma hujus sacramenti. Nec potest dici quod intentio proferentis verba facit ut his verbis consecretur virtute divinitus collata: quia virtus data sacramentis consequitur significationem; et intentio ministri non potest ad alium effectum sacramenta perducere, nisi qui eis significatur.

Et ideo alii dicunt, quod ly *hoc* facit demonstrationem ad sensum, et demonstrat panem non simpliciter, sed secundum quod est transubstantiatus in corpus Christi. Sed contra hoc est, quia panis transubstantiatus jam non est panis. Sed dum profertur hoc pronomen *hoc*, nondum facta est transubstantiatio, quia jam alia verba non essent de essentia formae. Cum igitur non possit ad sensum demonstrari quod actu non subest sensui, non poterit praedicto modo demonstratio sumi; nisi dicatur, sicut alii dicunt, quod totus sensus locutionis et omnium partium ejus referendus est ad ultimum instans pronuntiationis verborum, quia pro illo instanti pro quo res est, habet locutio veritatem; et est simile cum dicitur, nunc taceo vel nunc bibo, si statim tacere vel bibere incipiat. Sed hoc iterum non potest stare: quia secundum hoc significatio horum verborum praesupponeret transubstantiationem jam factam: ergo virtute verborum non fieret. Et praeterea secundum hoc sensus hujus locutionis erit: corpus meum est corpus meum: quod quidem virtute horum verborum non fit.

Et ideo aliter dicendum, quod ea quae sunt in voce, proportionantur his quae sunt in anima. Conceptio autem animae duobus modis se habet. Uno modo ut repraesentatio rei tantum, sicut est in omnibus cognitionibus acceptis a rebus; et tunc veritas conceptionis praesupponit entitatem rei sicut propriam mensuram, ut dicitur in 10 *Metaphysica*; et per modum hujusmodi conceptionum se habent locutiones, quae causa significationis tantum proferuntur. Alio modo conceptio animae non est repraesentativa rei, sed magis praesignativa, sicut exemplar factivum, sicut patet in scientia practica, quae est causa rei; et veritas hujus conceptionis non praesupponit entitatem rei, sed praecedit ipsam naturaliter quasi causa, etsi simul sint tempore: et ad hunc modum se habent verba praemissa, quia sunt significativa et

And so others say that he makes a demonstration for the intellect, and the sense is: *this is my body*; that is, *by this bread or by these appearances, my body is represented*, or *the thing symbolized by this, is my body*. But this too, cannot stand: for since in the sacrament nothing is effected except what is signified by the power of the words spoken, the body of Christ would not come to be on the altar as to the truth of the thing, but only in symbol, which is heretical; or else the words mentioned would not be the form of this sacrament. Nor can it be said that the intention of the one uttering the words makes it so that with these words it is consecrated by power divinely conferred; for the power given to the sacraments follows on their signification, and the intention of the minister cannot direct the sacraments to an effect other than the one signified by the words.

And so others say that the *this* makes a demonstration for the senses, and indicates the bread not simply, but according as it is transubstantiated into the body of Christ. But against this is that the bread once transubstantiated is not bread. But when this pronoun *this* is uttered, the transubstantiation has not happened, for the other words to that point were not of the essence of the form. Therefore, since what is actually not sensible could not be demonstrated to the senses, it could not be taken as a demonstration in the mode mentioned; unless it were said, as others say, that the whole sense of the sentence and all parts of it is to be referred to the last instant of pronouncing the words, since in that instant where the reality is, the speech has truth. And it is the same when someone says, "Now I am silent" or "now I drink," if he immediately begins to be silent or to drink. But this again cannot stand: for then the meaning of those words presupposes the transubstantiation to have already happened; therefore it would not happen by the power of the words. And furthermore according to this the sense of the expression would be, *My body is my body*, which indeed is not being done by the power of these words.

And so it is to be said rather that those things expressed by the voice are proportionate to those that are in the soul. But the soul's concept can work in two ways. In one way as the representation of a thing alone, as is the case in all understanding taken from things; and so the truth of a concept presupposes the thing's existence as its proper measure, as is said in *Metaphysics* 10.[64] And speech that is uttered for the sake of signifying alone is characterized by this mode of concepts. In the other way, the concept in the soul is not representative of the thing, but rather presignative, like the exemplar of something to be made, as is seen in practical knowledge, which is the cause of a thing; and the truth of this concept does not presuppose the existence of the thing, but precedes it naturally as its cause, even if they are simultaneous in time; and this is the mode belonging to

---

64. See Aristotle, *Metaphysics*, Bk. 10, ch. 1, 1053a31.

factiva ejus quod significatur. Unde veritas et significatio hujus locutionis praecedit naturaliter entitatem rei quam significat, et non praesupponit ipsam, quamvis sit simul cum ipsa tempore, sicut causa propria cum proprio effectu.

Sed quia significatio et veritas locutionis, quae est simul tempore cum transubstantiatione, consurgit ex consignificationibus partium successive prolatarum; ideo oportet quod dictio ultimo prolata compleat significationem locutionis, sicut differentia specifica; et simul cum significatione fiat entitas rei; et per consequens significationes primarum partium praecedant transubstantiationem, quae quidem non successive fit, sed in instanti ultimo per significationem locutionis jam perfectam. Sic ergo hoc pronomen *hoc* neque demonstrat terminum ad quem transubstantiationis determinate, quia jam significatio locutionis praesupponeret entitatem rei significatae, et non esset causa ejus; neque iterum demonstrat terminum a quo determinate, quia ejus significatio impediret veritatem significationis totius locutionis, cum terminus a quo non remaneat in ultimo instanti locutionis. Relinquitur ergo quod demonstret hoc quod est commune utrique termino indeterminate. Sicut autem in formalibus mutationibus commune utrique termino est subjectum vel materia; distinguuntur autem termini per formas accidentales vel substantiales; ita in transubstantiatione commune est accidentia sensibilia, quae remanent; diversitas autem est substantiarum. Unde sensus est: hoc contentum sub his speciebus est corpus meum. Et haec est causa quare cum pronomine non ponitur aliquod nomen, ne demonstratio ad aliquam speciem substantiae determinetur. Sicut enim in locutione quae significat tantum alterationem, per se subjectum est subjectum commune alterationis, ut cum dicitur, hoc fit album; ita oportet quod in locutione quae facit transubstantiationem, subjectum sit hoc quod est commune in transubstantiatione.

Ad secundum dicendum, quod ratio illa procederet, si demonstratio pronominis ferretur ad contentum sub speciebus, secundum quod est determinatum ad speciem panis: quia corpus Christi non potest praedicari de pane, nisi cum verbo importante transitum. Sed sic non intelligitur demonstratio pronominis, sed sicut dictum est.

Ad tertium dicendum, quod Dominus, Joan. 6, loquebatur de hoc sacramento tantum secundum quod est activum refectionis; et quia refectioni magis convenit caro quam corpus secundum similitudinem ad refectionem corporalem; ideo ibi potius dixit carnem quam corpus. Sed in forma sacramenti debet exprimi et essentia sacramenti et significatio ipsius; et ideo potius debet dici corpus quam caro: tum quia essentialiter in hoc sa-

the words mentioned, for they are significative and effective of what they signify. This is why the truth and signification of this expression naturally precedes the existence of the thing that it signifies, and does not presuppose it, although it may be simultaneous with it in time, like a proper cause with its proper effect.

But since the signification and the truth of the speech, which is simultaneous with transubstantiation, arises from the consignifications of the parts uttered one after another, for this reason it is necessary that the last statement uttered complete the signification of the speech, like a specific difference; and the existence of the thing happens at the same time as the signification, and as a result the significations of the first parts may precede transubstantiation, which indeed does not happen successively, but in the last instant through the speech's signification then completed. In this way, therefore, the pronoun *this* neither demonstrates transubstantiation's ending terminus determinately, for now the speech's signification would presuppose the being of the signified thing, and would not be its cause; nor again does it demonstrate the starting terminus definitely, since the signification of that would impede the whole phrase's truth of signification, since the starting terminus does not remain in the last instant of the speech. Therefore, it is left that it demonstrate indeterminately what is shared by both terminuses. However, just as in formal changes the subject or the matter is common to both terminuses, but the terminuses are distinguished by accidental or substantial forms, so also in transubstantiation the sensible accidents that remain are shared, while the substances differ. And so this is the sense: *This thing contained under these appearances is my body*. And this is the reason why there is no noun set down with the pronoun, lest the demonstration be determined to a certain species of substance. For just as in the speech that signifies only change the subject *per se* is the shared subject of the change, as when someone says, "This is becoming white," so also in the speech that causes transubstantiation, the subject must be what is shared in transubstantiation.

Reply Obj. 2: That argument would proceed if the demonstration of the pronoun were directed to what was contained under those appearances, according as it is determined to the appearance of bread: for the body of Christ cannot be predicated of bread, except with a word that conveys a change. But this is not how the demonstration of the pronoun is understood, but rather as was said above.

Reply Obj. 3: The Lord, in John 6, was speaking of this sacrament only as it is effectual of restoration, and since flesh is more suited for restoration than body, according to the resemblance to bodily restoration, for that reason he said 'flesh' at that point rather than 'body'. But in the form of the sacrament the essence of the sacrament and its signification should be expressed; and therefore 'body' should be said rather than 'flesh', both because in this sacrament

cramento continetur ex vi sacramenti non solum caro, sed totum corpus Christi: tum quia hoc sacramentum significat repraesentando Christi passionem, quae erat per totum corpus. Significat etiam, quasi rem ultimam, corpus mysticum, scilicet ecclesiam, quae propter distinctionem officiorum habet similitudinem cum toto corpore ratione distinctionis membrorum. Panis autem non est figura rei contentae in sacramento secundum quod est corpus homogeneum, sed secundum quod ex diversis conficitur granis; unde sua significatio magis aptatur ad totum corpus quam ad carnem.

Ad quartum dicendum, quod hoc sacramentum directe repraesentativum est Dominicae Passionis, qua Christus ut sacerdos et hostia Deo se obtulit in ara crucis. Hostia autem quam sacerdos offert, est una cum illa quam Christus obtulit secundum rem, quia Christum realiter continet; minister autem offerens non est idem realiter; unde oportet quod sit idem repraesentatione; et ideo sacerdos consecrans prout gerit personam Christi, profert verba consecrationis recitative ex persona Christi, ne hostia alia videatur. Et quia per ea quae gerit respectu exterioris materiae, Christi personam repraesentat; ideo verba illa simul et recitative et significative tenentur respectu praesentis materiae, quae est figura illius quam Christus praesentem habuit; et propter hoc dicitur convenientius: *hoc est corpus meum*, quam: hoc est corpus Christi. Vel etiam propter hoc quod sacerdos non habet actum exteriorem, qui sit sacramentaliter causa consecrationis; sed in solis verbis prolatis consistit virtus consecrationis; et ideo ex persona illius proferuntur cujus virtute fit transubstantiatio.

not only the flesh but the whole body of Christ is essentially contained by the sacrament's power, and because this sacrament signifies by representing Christ's Passion, which took place throughout his whole body. In addition it signifies, as a final reality, the mystical body, namely, the Church, which because of the distinction of offices has a resemblance to a whole body by reason of the distinction of its members. However, bread is not a figure of the reality contained in the sacrament as a homogeneous body, but as something confected from many different grains; hence its signification is more suited to a whole body than to flesh.

Reply Obj. 4: This sacrament is directly representative of the Lord's Passion, in which Christ as priest and victim offered himself to God on the altar of the Cross. Now, the victim that the priest offers is one with the one that Christ offered according to reality, for it really contains Christ; however, the minister offering it is not really the same. Therefore, it is necessary that he be the same in representation, and so the consecrating priest, as bearing the person of Christ, utters the words of consecration as though speaking in the person of Christ, lest it seem to be a different victim. And since by those things that he enacts with regard to the external matter, he represents the person of Christ, this is how those words, at once in recitation and in signification, are bound to the matter present, which is the figure of what Christ had present. And because of this it is fittingly said, *this is my body*, rather than *this is the body of Christ*. Or also because of the fact that the priest does not have an outward act that would be the cause of the consecration sacramentally, but the power of consecration consists in the spoken words alone; and so the words are uttered in the person of him by whose power the transubstantiation happens.

Response to Quaestiuncula 5

Ad quintam quaestionem dicendum, quod multa sunt a Domino facta vel dicta quae Evangelistae non scripserunt, ut patet Joan. 21, quae tamen ecclesia postea ab apostolis accepta fideliter conservavit.

Et secundum hoc dicendum ad primum quod, sicut Innocentius Papa dicit, quod quamvis nusquam in sacra Scriptura legatur quod Dominus ad caelum oculos sublevaverit in coena; tamen hoc ecclesia ex traditione apostolorum recitat, et satis rationabiliter potest ex aliis locis Scripturae colligi. Legitur enim Joan. 11, quod in suscitatione Lazari oculos ad patrem elevaverit; et similiter Joan. 17, orationem ad patrem fundens. Hoc autem in arduis faciebat, gratias agens, et exemplum nobis ad Deum recurrendi praebens, secundum illud Psal. 122,

To the fifth question, it should be said that there are many things said and done by the Lord that the Gospel writers did not write down, as is evident from John 21, which things the Church nevertheless faithfully kept afterwards as received from the apostles.

Reply Obj. 1: And accordingly, as Pope Innocent says, although nowhere in Sacred Scripture is it read that the Lord raised his eyes to heaven at the Last Supper, nevertheless the Church recites this as something handed down from the apostles, and it can be gathered reasonably enough from other places in Scripture.[65] For it is read in John 11:41 that in the raising of Lazarus he lifted his eyes to his Father, and likewise in John 17:1, when pouring out a prayer to his Father. Moreover, he often did this in difficult times, giving thanks, and presenting an exam-

---

65. Innocent, *De Sacro Altaris Mysterio*, Bk. 4, ch. 5 (PL 217:858).

1: *Ad te levavi oculos meos qui habitas in caelis.* Et quia hoc sacramentum arduissimum est, ideo instituens hoc sacramentum probabiliter colligitur quod oculos ad patrem levaverit, gratias agens patri de reparatione humani generis, quae hoc sacramento figuratur, et nobis ostendens virtute divina hoc confici sacramentum.

AD SECUNDUM dicendum, quod, sicut dictum est, haec verba: *accipite et manducate ex hoc omnes,* non sunt de substantia formae; et ideo non est tanta vis facienda, ut penitus eadem observentur. Et praeterea comedere et manducare, in nullo differentem habent significationem; et quamvis circa ista verba non ponatur in Evangeliis verbum manducandi, ponitur tamen parum ante, Luc. 22, 15: *desiderio desideravi hoc Pascha manducare vobiscum antequam patiar.*

AD TERTIUM dicendum, quod quamvis non exprimatur in Evangelio haec determinatio omnes, tamen intelligitur: quia sacramentalis manducatio est omnium, quamvis non spiritualis; ideo autem exprimitur circa sumptionem sanguinis in Evangeliis praedicta dictio, quia sanguis in redemptionem effusus est; redemptio autem est omnium quantum ad sufficientiam, quamvis non quantum ad efficaciam. Vel quia ultimo traditur sumptio sanguinis, quod circa eam dicitur, circa sumptionem corporis similiter intelligendum est.

ple to us of turning to God, according to the Psalm, *but to you I have lifted my eyes, O you who dwell in the heavens!* (Ps 123[122]:1). And since this sacrament is the most difficult, for this reason when he was instituting this sacrament he probably lifted his eyes to his Father, giving thanks to his Father for the restoration of the human race, which is figured by this sacrament, and showing us that this sacrament was confected by divine power.

REPLY OBJ. 2: Just as has been said, these words, *take and eat of it all of you,* do not belong to the form's substance. And so there is not so much effort having to be made that the same things be so carefully observed. And furthermore, 'comedere' and 'manducare' have no difference in meaning 'eat'; and although a word from 'manducare' is not included among these words in the Gospels, nevertheless a little before it is written, *with longing I have desired to eat* [manducare] *this Passover with you before I suffer* (Luke 22:15).

REPLY OBJ. 3: Although this determination 'all of you' is not expressed in the Gospel, nevertheless, it is understood, for sacramental eating is for all, although not spiritual eating. Thus, the phrase mentioned is expressed concerning the consumption of the blood in the Gospels, for the blood was poured out in the redemption, and while redemption is for all as to sufficiency, it is not so as to efficacy. Or since the consumption of the blood is handed on last, what is said about it can be understood in the same way about the consumption of the body.

ARTICLE 2

The form with which his blood is consecrated[66]

Quaestiuncula 1

AD SECUNDUM SIC PROCEDITUR. Videtur quod forma consecrationis sanguinis consistat in his tantum verbis: *hic est calix sanguinis mei*; et hoc quod additur: *novi et aeterni testamenti, mysterium fidei, qui pro vobis et pro multis effundetur in remissionem peccatorum* non sit de forma. Evangelistae enim convenire debent in his quae sunt de substantia formae hujus sacramenti: quia verba formae hujus sacramenti recitative dicuntur ex persona Christi. Sed non conveniunt in verbis illis appositis, quia in nullo Evangelistarum leguntur, nec ab apostolo, 1 Corinth. 11, haberi possunt. Ergo non sunt de forma hujus sacramenti.

PRAETEREA, sicut panis transubstantiatur in corpus Christi per consecrationem, ita vinum in Christi sanguinem. Sed consecratio quae fit his verbis, *hoc est corpus meum*, sufficit ad transubstantiationem panis in corpus Christi. Ergo et haec verba: *hic est calix sanguinis mei*, sufficiunt ad transubstantiationem vini in sanguinem Christi; ergo verba quae sequuntur non sunt de forma.

Praeterea, proprietates naturaliter consequuntur substantiam rei. Sed illud quod sequitur substantiam, non potest esse factivum transubstantiationis. Ergo cum illa verba quae sequuntur designent aliquas proprietates sanguinis in quem fit transubstantiatio, videtur quod non sint de forma.

SED CONTRA est quia Luc. 22, 20, interponuntur praedicta verba verbis formae; ita enim dicitur: *hic est calix novi testamenti in meo sanguine.*

PRAETEREA hoc videtur ex ritu consecrationis: quia sacerdos non deponit calicem usque ad verba illa: *haec quotiescumque feceritis*, quae non sunt de forma, quamvis sint Domini verba.

OBJ. 1: To the second we proceed thus. It seems that the form of the consecration of the blood consists in these words alone: *this is the chalice of my blood*, and what is added, *the blood of the new and eternal covenant, the mystery of faith, which is poured out for you and for many in remission of sins*, is not of the form. For the Gospel writers should agree on those things that are of the form of this sacrament: for words of this sacrament's form are said quoting, as though in the person of Christ. But they do not agree in adding those words, for they are not read in any Gospel, nor can they be found in the text of the Apostle (1 Cor 11). Therefore, they are not of the form of this sacrament.

OBJ. 2: Furthermore, just as bread is transubstantiated into the body of Christ by the consecration, wine is transubstantiated into Christ's blood. But the consecration that happens by these words, *this is my body*, suffices for transubstantiation of the bread into the body of Christ. Therefore also these words, *this is the chalice of my blood*, are sufficient for transubstantiation of the wine into the blood of Christ. Therefore the words that follow are not of the form.

OBJ. 3. Furthermore, natural properties follow upon the substance of a thing. But what follows upon substance cannot be effective of transubstantiation. Therefore, since these words that follow designate certain properties of the blood into which transubstantiation happens, it seems that they are not of the form.

ON THE CONTRARY, the words in question are interposed in the words of the form in Luke 22:20: *this is the chalice of the new covenant in my blood.*

FURTHERMORE, this appears from the rite of consecration: since the priest does not set down the chalice until these words: *however often you do this*, which are not of the form, although they are the Lord's words.

Quaestiuncula 2

ULTERIUS. Videtur quod haec verba inconvenienter ponantur: *hic est calix sanguinis mei.* Unius enim modi est transubstantiatio panis in corpus Christi, et vini in sanguinem. Sed in transubstantiatione panis in corpus Christi ponitur corpus Christi in recto. Ergo in consecratione vini poni debet sanguis Christi in recto, ut di-

OBJ. 1: Moreover, it seems that these words are unfittingly set down: *this is the chalice of my blood*. For transubstantiation of the bread into the body of Christ and of the wine into the blood of Christ happen in the same way. But in the transubstantiation of the bread into the body of Christ, the body of Christ is named directly. Therefore, in

66. Parallels: *ST* III, q. 78, a. 3; *Super Matt.* 26; *Super I ad Cor.* 11, lec. 6.

catur, sicut Magister dicit in littera: *hic est sanguis meus*; sicut etiam habetur Matth. 26.

Praeterea, in forma transubstantiante ex parte praedicati poni debet terminus in quem fit transubstantiatio, ut ex dictis patet. Sed transubstantiatio non fit in calicem alicujus. Ergo non debet praedicari in forma transubstantiante.

Praeterea, in forma sacramenti non debet poni aliquid quod non sit de substantia sacramenti. Sed calix non est de substantia sacramenti cum sit vas quoddam. Ergo non debet poni in forma sacramenti.

Sed contra est quod dicitur Luc. 22, 20: *hic calix novi testamenti in meo sanguine*. Ad idem est etiam usus ecclesiae.

the consecration of the wine, the blood of Christ should be named directly, so that it would be said, as the Master says in the text: *this is my blood*, as Matthew 26:28 also has it.

Obj. 2: Furthermore, in the part mentioned of the transubstantiating form, the terminus to which transubstantiation happens should be included, as is clear from what has been said. But nothing is transubstantiated into a chalice. Therefore, it should not be named in the transubstantiating form.

Obj. 3: Furthermore, in the sacrament's form nothing should be included that is not of the substance of the sacrament. But a chalice is not of the substance of the sacrament, since it is a kind of vessel. Therefore, it should not be included in the sacrament's form.

On the contrary, it says, *this is the chalice of the new covenant in my blood* (Luke 22:20). And the Church's use amounts to the same thing.

Quaestiuncula 3

Ulterius. Videtur quod etiam verba quae sequuntur, inconvenienter ponantur. Testamentum enim videtur pertinere ad traditionem mandatorum; unde et tabulae continentes decem praecepta, dicuntur tabulae testamenti. Sed traditio sacramentorum est alia a traditione mandatorum. Ergo in sacramentis non debet fieri mentio de testamento.

Praeterea, Ambrosius dicit, nostra sacramenta antiquiora esse sacramentis Judaeorum. Sed sacramenta Judaeorum non pertinent ad novum testamentum, sed ad vetus. Ergo nec in sacramento isto, de quo Ambrosius loquitur, debet apponi: *novi testamenti*.

Praeterea, novum et aeternum videntur ad invicem contrarietatem habere: quia aeternum est quod caret principio, novum autem est quod quantum ad sui principium est propinquum. Ergo est oppositio in adjecto.

Praeterea, illud quod potest esse juvamentum erroris, non debet apponi in forma sacramenti. Sed, sicut dicit Innocentius III, quod dicitur hoc, *mysterium*, quibusdam est adjuvamentum erroris, qui dicunt corpus Christi verum in altari non contineri, sed per significationem tantum. Ergo inconvenienter ponitur in forma.

Praeterea, hoc sacramentum, ut prius dictum est, praecipue videtur esse sacramentum caritatis, sicut et baptismus sacramentum fidei. Ergo inconvenienter dicitur: *mysterium fidei*; sed magis dicendum esset: *mysterium caritatis*.

Obj. 1: Moreover, it seems that also the words that follow are unfittingly included. For 'covenant' seems to pertain to the handing down of commands; hence also the tables containing the Ten Commandments are called tables of the covenant. But the handing down of sacraments is different from the handing down of commands. Therefore, in the sacraments no mention should be made of a covenant.

Obj. 2: Furthermore, Ambrose says that our sacraments are older than the sacraments of the Jews.[67] But the sacraments of the Jews do not pertain to the new covenant, but to the old. Therefore, nor should *new covenant* be included in the sacrament, of which Ambrose speaks.

Obj. 3: Furthermore, new and eternal seem to be contrary to each other, for the eternal is what has no beginning, but the new is what is closest to its beginning. Therefore, the adjectives are opposites.

Obj. 4: Furthermore, whatever is grounds for error should not be included in a sacrament's form. But as Innocent III says, that which is said—*mystery*—offers grounds for error to some people, who say that the true body of Christ is not contained on the altar but is only there by signification.[68] Therefore, it is unfittingly included in the form.

Obj. 5: Furthermore, this sacrament, as was said before, seems especially to be the sacrament of charity, as also baptism is the sacrament of faith. Therefore, it is unfittingly said, *mystery of faith*, but rather it should be said, *mystery of charity*.

---

67. See Ambrose, *On the Sacraments*, Bk. 4, ch. 3: "Accipe, quae dico: et anteriora esse mysteria Christianorum quam Iudaeorum et diviniora esse sacramenta Christianorum quam Iudaeorum" (CSEL 73:49).

68. Innocent III, *De Sacro Altaris Mysterio*, Bk. 4, ch. 35 (PL 217:878).

PRAETEREA, sicut sanguis Christi pro nobis est effusus, ita corpus Christi pro nobis est traditum, ut ex verbis etiam Domini habetur, Luc. 22, 19: *hoc est corpus meum, quod pro vobis tradetur*. Cum ergo hoc non apponatur in forma corporis consecrandi, nec in consecratione sanguinis de effusione fieri mentio deberet.

PRAETEREA, quod dicitur: *pro vobis et pro multis effundetur*, aut accipitur de effusione quantum ad sufficientiam, aut quantum ad efficaciam. Si quantum ad sufficientiam, sic pro omnibus effusus est, non solum pro multis; si autem quantum ad efficaciam, quam habet solum in electis, non videtur distinguendum fuisse inter apostolos et alios.

PRAETEREA, baptismus magis ordinatur contra amotionem mali quam Eucharistia, quae maxime ordinatur ad perfectionem in bono. Sed in forma baptismi non fit mentio de remissione peccatorum. Ergo nec hic deberet dici: *in remissionem peccatorum*.

OBJ. 6: Furthermore, just as the blood of Christ was poured out for us, so also the body of Christ was handed over for us, so that from the Lord's words we also have, *this is my body, which will be given up for you* (Luke 22:19). Since therefore this is not added to the form of consecrating the body, neither should mention be made of this outpouring in the consecration of the blood.

OBJ. 7: Furthermore what is said, *which will be poured out for you and for many*, is to be understood concerning the effusion either to sufficiency or to efficacy. If as to sufficiency, then it was poured out for all, not only for many; but if as to efficacy, which it has only among the elect, then it seems that it did not have to distinguish between the apostles and others.

OBJ. 8: Furthermore, baptism is more directed against the removal of evil than the Eucharist, which is most of all directed toward perfecting in good. But in the form of baptism no mention is made of the remission of sins. Therefore, neither should it be said, *in remission of sins*.

Response to Quaestiuncula 1

RESPONDEO dicendum ad primam quaestionem, quod circa hoc aliqui diversimode dixerunt. Quidam enim dicunt, quod hoc est tantum de forma: *hic est calix sanguinis mei*, ut forma utriusque consecrationis sit consimilis. Sed quia conditiones appositae ad subjectum vel praedicatum sunt de integritate locutionis alicujus; ideo alii probabilius dicunt, quod totum quod sequitur, est de forma, cum totum hoc quod additur non sit locutio per se, sed sit determinatio praedicati.

AD PRIMUM ergo dicendum, quod verba supradicta ex magna parte possunt ex diversis locis sacrae Scripturae colligi, quamvis non inveniantur alicubi simul scripta. Quod enim dicitur: *hic est calix*, habetur Luc. 22, et 1 Corinth. 2. Quod autem dicitur: *novi testamenti*, ex tribus habetur, Matth. 26, et Marc. 14, et Luc. 22. Quod autem dicitur, *aeterni*, et iterum, *mysterium fidei*, ex traditione Domini habetur, quae per apostolos ad ecclesiam pervenit, secundum illud 1 Corinth. 11, 23: *ego accepi a Domino quod et tradidi vobis*. Evangelistae enim non intendebant formas et ritus sacramentorum tradere, sed dicta et facta Domini enarrare.

AD SECUNDUM dicendum, quod cum Eucharistiae sacramentum sit memoriale Dominicae Passionis, in consecratione corporis Christi non repraesentatur nisi passionis subjectum; sed in consecratione sanguinis repraesentatur passionis mysterium: non enim a corpore Christi sanguis ejus seorsum fuit nisi per passionem; et ideo conditiones Dominicae Passionis exprimuntur per verba sequentia magis in consecratione sanguinis quam in consecratione corporis.

TO THE FIRST QUESTION, I answer that concerning this people have spoken in different ways. For certain people say that this alone belongs to the form: *this is the chalice of my blood*, so that the form of both consecrations may be alike. But since conditions in apposition to a subject or a predicate are integral to any sentence, for this reason others say more probably that all that follows belongs to the form, since everything that is added is not a sentence on its own, but the determination of a predicate.

REPLY OBJ. 1: For the most part, the words above can be gathered from different places in the Sacred Scriptures, although they are not found anywhere written all together. For the phrase, *this is the chalice*, is found in Luke 22:20 and 1 Corinthians 11:25; the phrase, *of the new covenant*, is had from three places, Matthew 26:28, Mark 14:24, and Luke 22:20; the phrases, *eternal*, and, *the mystery of faith*, are had from the Lord by the tradition that came to the Church from the apostles, as it says, *I received from the Lord what I have handed on to you* (1 Cor 11:23). For the Gospel writers did not intend to give the forms and rites of the sacraments, but to tell the deeds and sayings of the Lord.

REPLY OBJ. 2: Since the sacrament of the Eucharist is the memorial of the Lord's Passion, the body of Christ is only represented in the consecration as the subject of the Passion; but in the consecration of the blood, the mystery of the Passion is represented, for Christ's blood was not parted from his body except by the Passion. And so the conditions of the Lord's Passion are expressed by the words that follow more in the consecration of the blood than in the consecration of the body.

AD TERTIUM dicendum, quod quamvis illa quae sequuntur sint ut proprietates consequentes Christi sanguinem inquantum hujusmodi, sunt tamen essentiales sanguini Christi inquantum est per passionem effusus. Non autem seorsum a corpore consecraretur sanguis Christi, sicut nec aliae partes ejus, nisi pro eo quod est in passione effusus; et ideo illa quae sequuntur, sunt essentialia sanguini, prout in hoc sacramento consecratur; et ideo oportet quod sint de substantia formae.

REPLY OBJ. 3: Although those things said afterward are like properties of the blood of Christ consequent to it as the kind of thing it is, they are nevertheless essential to the blood of Christ as poured out through his Passion. However, the blood of Christ would not be consecrated apart from the body, just as neither would any other parts, except for the fact that it was shed in the Passion; and so the things said after are essential to the blood as it is consecrated in this sacrament; and so it is necessary that they belong to the form's substance.

Response to Quaestiuncula 2

AD SECUNDAM QUAESTIONEM dicendum, quod haec locutio: *hic est calix sanguinis mei*, figurativa est, et potest intelligi dupliciter. Uno modo ut sit metonymica locutio, ut ponatur continens pro contento, secundum quod dicere consuevimus, bibe calicem vini, idest vinum contentum in calice. Ideo autem talis modus locutionis congruus est formae huic, quia sanguis de sui ratione non dicit aliquid potabile, immo magis aliquid quod natura abhorret in potum. Et quia in hoc sacramento sanguis Christi consecratur ut potus, ideo oportuit aliquid addi quod ad potum pertineret, scilicet *calicem*. Alio modo potest intelligi, ut sit metaphorica locutio, ut per calicem passio Christi designetur. Sicut enim calix vini inebriat, ita et passio sui amaritudine quasi hominem extra se ponit: Thren. 3, 15: *replevit me amaritudinibus, inebriavit me absynthio*; et hoc modo loquendi usus est Dominus de sua passione loquens, ut patet Matth. 26, 39: *transeat a me calix iste*; et hic modus loquendi etiam est conveniens in hac forma: quia, ut dictum est, in consecratione sanguinis exprimitur directe mysterium passionis. Nec obstat quod solet objici, quod locutiones figurativae faciunt distrahere intellectum, et ita sunt causa evagationis: quia mens sacerdotis debet esse adeo fixa ad ea quae dicit, quod non qualibet levi actione evagetur.

TO THE SECOND QUESTION, it should be said that this speech, *this is the chalice of my blood*, is figurative, and can be understood in two ways. In one way as an expression of metonomy, so that the container is said in place of the contents, just as we often say, "Drink a cup of wine," i.e., the wine contained in the cup. But this is why such a mode of speaking fits with this form, that blood by its own nature does not mean something to drink, but rather something that nature abhors drinking. And because in this sacrament the blood of Christ is consecrated as a drink, it is necessary for something to be added that relates it to drinking, namely, *chalice*. It can be understood another way, as metaphorical speech, so that by the chalice the Passion of Christ is designated. For just as a chalice of wine inebriates, so also the Passion by its bitterness rendered him a man beside himself, as it were: *he has filled me with bitterness, he has inebriated me with wormwood* (Lam 3:15). And this manner of speaking is used by the Lord, speaking of his Passion (as is clear from Matthew 26:39: *let this cup pass from me*); and this manner of speaking is also suited to this form, for as was said, in the consecration of the wine the mystery of the Passion is directly expressed. Nor is what people often object a problem, namely that figurative speech distracts the understanding, and so is a cause of the mind wandering: for the mind of the priest must be so fixed on what he is saying that it does not wander by any light action.

AD PRIMUM ergo dicendum, quod corpus de sui ratione non dicit aliquid repugnans cibo ex ipsa sui nominatione, sicut sanguis repugnat potui; et ideo non est similis ratio. Magister autem non posuit formam quantum ad verba, sed quantum ad sensum.

REPLY OBJ. 1: The body of its own nature does not convey anything repugnant to food by its very naming, as blood is repugnant to drinking; and so the reasoning is not the same. Moreover, the Master did not set down the form as to the words, but as to the sense.

AD SECUNDUM dicendum, quod transubstantiatio vini in ipsum calicem non fit, sed in contentum, scilicet sanguinem Christi, prout potus est, et prout est per passionem fusus; et ideo objectio cessat.

REPLY OBJ. 2: Transubstantiation of wine does not happen to the chalice itself, but to the contents, namely, the blood of Christ, as it is a drink and as it is poured out through the Passion; and so the objection ceases.

AD TERTIUM dicendum, quod quamvis vas illud non sit de substantia sacramenti, tamen contentum et significatum est de substantia sacramenti; et secundum hoc intelligitur locutio.

REPLY OBJ. 3: Although this vessel does not belong to the sacrament's substance, nevertheless what it contains and what it signifies do belong to the sacrament's substance; and this is how the speech is understood.

Response to Quaestiuncula 3

AD TERTIAM QUAESTIONEM dicendum, quod, sicut dictum est, verba illa quae adduntur in consecratione sanguinis, exprimunt conditiones passionis, et praecipue secundum quod operantur in sacramentis. Sunt autem tria in passione consideranda, secundum quod in sacramentis operatur. Primo effectus quem inducit, qui est remissio peccatorum; et hoc tangitur in hoc quod dicit: *qui pro vobis et pro multis effundetur in remissionem peccatorum.* Secundo medium quo iste effectus in alios traducitur, quod est fides, qua mediante habet effectum et in his qui praecesserunt et in his qui sequuntur; et quantum ad hoc dicit, *mysterium fidei;* quod quidem potest referri et ad ipsam passionem, quae est mysterium fidei, ut occultum quoddam latens in fide omnium Christi fidelium, et praecipue antiquorum, apud quos erat in mysterio abscondita diversimode figurata; et ad ipsum sanguinem, prout in sacramento continetur, quod quidem latet sub speciebus, et maximam habet difficultatem ad credendum; unde antonomastice dicitur, *mysterium fidei.* Tertio finis ad quem perducit, qui est aeternorum perceptio, ad quem introducit Christus per sanguinem propriae passionis: in quo novum testamentum confirmatur, non quidem promittens temporalia, ut prius, sed aeterna; et quantum ad hoc dicit: *novi et aeterni testamenti.* Et quia finis prius est in intentione, ideo, fine praemisso, per medium ad effectum passionis ostendendum verba formae perducunt.

AD PRIMUM ergo dicendum, quod testamentum proprie est hereditatis percipiendae institutio filiis a patre; et ideo testamentum proprie pertinet ad promissionem bonorum, quae nobis a patre caelesti disponuntur; ad quod quidem testamentum praecepta se habent sicut via ad consequendum hereditatem promissam; et ita per posterius testamentum ad mandata pertinet.

AD SECUNDUM dicendum, quod antiquitas illa intelligitur quantum ad similitudinem ritus. Dicitur autem hoc testamentum *novum* et ratione hujus sacramenti, quod in renovatione mundi institutum est tempore gratiae, et iterum ratione promissionis per sanguinem Christi confirmatae, quae vetus impedimentum consequendae hereditatis amovit; et sic quasi quaedam innovatio promissionis per mortem Christi facta est.

AD TERTIUM dicendum, quod dicitur *novum et aeternum* diversis rationibus: *novum* quidem ratione jam dicta; *aeternum*, vel ratione bonorum aeternorum, de quibus est testamentum; vel ratione hujus sacramenti continentis Christum, qui est persona aeterna; vel ratione praedestinationis aeternae hanc gratiam praeparantis.

TO THE THIRD QUESTION, it should be said that, as has been said, those words that are added to the consecration of the blood express the conditions of the Passion especially as they are at work in the sacraments. However, there are three things to be considered in the Passion as it is at work in the sacraments. First, the effect that it brings about, which is the remission of sins; and this is touched upon by saying: *which is poured out for you and for many for the remission of sins.* Second, the medium by which this effect is transferred to others, which is faith, by means of which it has an effect on both those who went before and those who come after; and as to this it says, *the mystery of faith;* which indeed can be referred both to the Passion itself, which is the mystery of faith (as a certain secret thing hidden in the faith of all the Christian faithful, and particularly of the ancients, among whom it was figured in different ways in a hidden mystery) and to the blood itself as it is contained in the sacrament, which indeed hides under the appearances and holds the greatest difficulty for believing; hence it is said antonomastically, *the mystery of faith.* Third, the end to which it draws us, which is the reception of eternal things, which Christ led us into by the blood of his own Passion, in which the new covenant is confirmed, not indeed promising temporal things as before but eternal things; and as to this it says: *of the new and eternal covenant.* And since the end is first in intention, for this reason once the end is stated the words of the form lead to showing the effect of the Passion through the means.

REPLY OBJ. 1: Covenant is properly the establishment of an inheritance to be received by children from their father, and so covenant properly belongs to the promising of goods, which are allotted to us by our heavenly Father. To this covenant the commandments are indeed related as a path to obtaining the promised inheritance; and so the covenant pertains to the commandments *per posterius.*

REPLY OBJ. 2: That antiquity should be understood as to likeness of rite. However, this covenant is called *new* both by reason of this sacrament, which was established for the renewal of the world in the time of grace, and again by reason of the promise confirmed through the blood of Christ, which took away the old impediment to obtaining the inheritance; and so a certain renewal of the promise was made through the death of Christ.

REPLY OBJ. 3: *New and eternal* is said with many different notions: for *new,* indeed with the notion already given; *eternal* either with the notion of eternal goods, which the covenant is concerned with; or with the notion of this sacrament containing Christ, who is an eternal person; or with the notion of eternal predestination preparing this grace.

Ad quartum dicendum, quod nihil prohibet id quod est in aliquo occultatum et figuratum, secundum veritatem ibidem esse; et ideo frivolum juvamentum sui erroris accipiunt qui negant Christi sanguinem secundum veritatem in altari esse, propter hoc quod est ibi etiam secundum mysterium.

Ad quintum dicendum, quod Eucharistia dicitur sacramentum caritatis Christi expressivum, et nostrae factivum; sed fides supponitur ad effectum hujusmodi sacramenti, quo mediante aliquis effectum participet; et ideo potius ponit ut medium perducens ad effectum fidem quam caritatem.

Ad sextum dicendum, quod hujus solutio ex dictis patet: quia hoc accidit propter hoc quod in consecratione corporis non signatur passio, sicut in consecratione sanguinis.

Ad septimum dicendum, quod sanguis Christi effusus est pro omnibus quo ad sufficientiam, sed pro electis tantum quo ad efficaciam; et ne putaretur effusus pro Judaeis tantum electis, quibus promissio facta fuerat, ideo dicit, *vobis*, qui ex Judaeis, et *multis*, scilicet multitudine gentium. Vel per apostolos sacerdotes significat, quibus mediantibus ad alios effectus passionis per dispensationem sacramentorum pervenit, qui etiam pro seipsis et pro aliis orant.

Ad octavum dicendum, quod remissio peccatorum non ponitur hic ut proprius effectus hujus sacramenti, sed ut effectus passionis, quae per consecrationem sanguinis exprimitur. De mutatione autem, additione et subtractione, idem dicendum est hic quod supra dictum est de forma baptismi, distinct. 3.

Reply Obj. 4: Nothing prohibits what is hidden and symbolized in a certain thing from being there according to the truth; and so those who deny that the blood of Christ is on the altar according to the truth, because of the fact that it is also there according to mystery, take foolish grounds for their error.

Reply Obj. 5: The Eucharist is called the sacrament of charity because it expresses Christ's charity and causes ours; but faith is presupposed for the effect of this kind of sacrament, since someone may partake of the effect by means of it; and so he includes faith as a means leading to the effect rather than charity.

Reply Obj. 6: The answer to this is evident from what has been said: for this happens because of the fact that in the consecration of the body the Passion is not represented as in the consecration of the blood.

Reply Obj. 7: The blood of Christ was poured out for all as to sufficiency, but only for the elect as to efficacy; and lest it be considered poured out only for the Jewish elect to whom the promise had been made, for this reason he says, *for you*, who are of the Jews, *and for many*, namely, the multitude of gentiles. Or, in the persons of the apostles, it signifies priests, by means of whom the effect of the Passion reaches others through the administering of the sacraments, and who also pray for themselves and others.

Reply Obj. 8: The remission of sins is not included here as the proper effect of this sacrament, but as the effect of the Passion, which is expressed by the consecration of the blood. However, concerning changes, whether additions or subtractions, the same thing should be said here that was said above concerning the form of baptism, Distinction 3.[69]

---

69. See q. 1, a. 2, qa. 2, 3, and 4.

Article 3

The power of each consecration[70]

Ad tertium sic proceditur. Videtur quod verbis praedictis non insit aliqua vis creata ad transubstantiationem faciendam. Damascenus enim dicit, quod *sola virtute Spiritus Sancti fit conversio panis in corpus Christi.* Sed virtus Spiritus Sancti non est virtus creata. Ergo nulla virtus creata inest his verbis, per quam fiat transubstantiatio.

Praeterea, opus transubstantiationis videtur esse difficilius quam opus creationis; quia citius ratio consentit creationi quam huic conversioni; cum quidam etiam philosophi ratione naturali ducti creationem posuerint. Sed nulla virtus creata, secundum communem opinionem, potest Deo cooperari in opere creationis. Ergo multo minus in opere hujus conversionis.

Praeterea, difficilius est convertere panem in substantiam corporis Christi, quam purissimos sanguines Virginis: quia corpus Christi et sanguines Virginis habent materiam communem, quae est subjectum conversionis; quod non potest esse in conversione panis in corpus Christi. Sed in formatione corporis Christi ex Virgine non fuit aliqua virtus creata active operans transformationem, ut in 3 Lib., distinct. 3, dictum est. Ergo nec verbis praedictis inest aliqua virtus creata ad transubstantiandum.

Praeterea, nulla virtus creata potest operari aliquid supra naturam. Sed conversio panis in corpus Christi est maxime supra naturam, cum non servetur modus mutationis naturalis: quia neque est subjectum commune, et terminus ad quem est praeexistens actu. Ergo non potest per virtutem creatam verbis formae collatam hujusmodi conversio fieri.

Praeterea, virtus activa directe proportionatur ei ad quod actio terminatur: quia hoc est intentum ab agente, et ex eo denominatur actio. Sed corpus Christi ad quod terminatur conversio, est multo dignius qualibet pura creatura. Ergo cum agens debet esse nobilius facto, non potest aliqua virtute creata aliquid in corpus Christi converti.

Praeterea, faciens et factum, causa et causatum, debent esse simul: quia quod non est, non potest aliquid facere, vel alicujus causa existere. Sed cum conversio praedicta fiat in instanti, et verba formae successive proferantur; quando fit conversio, verba illa non possunt simul esse, nisi secundum aliquid minimum sui. Ergo in

Obj. 1: To the third we proceed thus. It seems that in the words mentioned there is no created power for bringing about transubstantiation. For Damascene says that *the conversion of the bread into the body of Christ happens by the power of the Holy Spirit alone.*[71] But the power of the Holy Spirit is not a created power. Therefore, no created power is in these words by which transubstantiation happens.

Obj. 2: Furthermore, the work of transubstantiation seems to be more difficult than the work of creation, for reason more quickly consents to creation than to this conversion, since even certain philosophers led by natural reason deduced creation. But no created power, according to common opinion, can cooperate with God in the work of creation. Therefore, much less in this work of conversion.

Obj. 3: Furthermore, it is more difficult to convert bread into the substance of the body of Christ than to convert the most pure blood of the Virgin into the body of Christ; for the body of Christ and the Virgin's blood have shared matter, which is the subject of conversion; which there cannot be in the conversion of bread into the body of Christ. But in the formation of the body of Christ from the Virgin there was no created power actively working the transformation, as was said in Book III, Distinction 3.[72] Therefore, neither is there any created power for transubstantiating in the words mentioned.

Obj. 4: Furthermore, no created power can work something above nature. But the conversion of bread into the body of Christ is extremely beyond nature, since the mode of natural change is not preserved, for neither is there a common subject, and the ending terminus is actually preexisting. Therefore, a conversion like this cannot happen by the created power conferred on the words of the form.

Obj. 5: An active power is directly proportionate to what its action terminates in, for this is intended by the agent, and 'action' is named from the agent. But the body of Christ in which the conversion ends is much more worthy than any pure creature. Therefore, since an agent should be more noble than what it makes, nothing can be converted into the body of Christ by any created power.

Obj. 6: Furthermore, the one doing and the thing done, the cause and the caused, should exist simultaneously, for what is not cannot make anything, or exist as cause of anything. But since the conversion mentioned happens in an instant, and the words of the form are uttered in succession, when the conversion happens those words cannot be simul-

---

70. Parallels: *ST* III, q. 78, a. 4; *Super Matt.* 26.
71. Damascene, *On the Orthodox Faith*, Bk. 4, ch. 13 (PG 194:1139).
72. See q. 2, a. 2.

virtute aliqua quae insit verbis, non potest fieri hujusmodi conversio.

Praeterea, verba ista non habent virtutem ex seipsis: hoc planum est. Si ergo habent aliquam hujusmodi virtutem, oportet quod eis sit divinitus data. Oportet autem hanc virtutem esse simplicem, cum ejus effectus sit in instanti. Simplex autem virtus non potest successive dari, et ejus subjectum oportet esse simplex. Cum ergo verba praedicta compositionem habeant et successionem, non potest ipsis talis virtus esse collata.

Praeterea, inconveniens videtur facere aliquid nobilissimum, quod statim desinat esse. Sed virtus transubstantians est nobilissima, quod patet ex nobilitate effectus. Ergo cum verba formae statim esse desinant, inconveniens videtur, si ei virtus transubstantiandi data est a Deo.

Praeterea, verba ista non faciunt conversionem praedictam, nisi a sacerdote dicta. Sed anima sacerdotis magis est capax virtutis alicujus divinae quam verba prolata ab ipso. Ergo magis dicendum est quod haec virtus in sacerdote sit quam in verbis; si tamen aliqua virtus creata ad transubstantiationem operetur.

Sed contra est quod Dionysius dicit in fine *Eccl. Hier.*, *in ipsis*, scilicet *consummativis invocationibus*, idest formis sacramentorum, *esse virtutes operativas ex Deo*. Sed verba praedicta sunt forma dignissimi sacramenti. Ergo est in ipsis aliqua virtus ad transubstantiandum.

Praeterea, Ambrosius dicit, quod sermo Christi creaturas mutat, et sic ex pane fit corpus Christi consecratione caelestis verbi. Verbum autem Christi est forma praedicta a Christo instituta, et ex ejus persona recitata. Ergo virtute horum verborum fit transubstantiatio.

Praeterea, sacerdos non operatur ad transubstantiationem nisi proferendo verba. Si ergo verbis non inesset virtus ad transubstantiandum, tunc sacerdos non haberet aliquam potestatem spiritualem conficiendi; et sic non haberet ordinem, qui est quaedam potestas ad hoc principaliter.

Respondeo dicendum, quod circa hoc est duplex opinio. Quidam enim dicunt, quod nulla virtus creata inest his verbis, qua fiat transubstantiatio; sed quod dicitur aliquando virtute horum verborum transubstantiationem fieri, intelligendum est, quod divina institutione firmatum est ut ad prolationem horum verborum conversio praedicta fiat virtute divina tantum; et sic etiam

taneous with it, except for a tiny part of them. Therefore, a conversion like this cannot happen by any power that is in the words.

Obj. 7: Furthermore, those words do not have power on their own; that is plain. Therefore, if they have any power like this, it would have had to be divinely given to them. Moreover, it is necessary for this power to be simple, since its effect is in an instant. However, a simple power cannot be given successively, and its subject must be simple. Therefore since the words mentioned are composite and successive, this power cannot be conferred on them.

Obj. 8: Furthermore, it seems unfitting to make something that is of the greatest nobility that immediately stops existing. But transubstantiating power is the most noble, which is evident from the nobility of its effect. Therefore, since the words of the form cease to exist immediately, it seems unfitting if the power of transubstantiating is given to them by God.

Obj. 9: Furthermore, those words do not bring about the conversion mentioned unless spoken by a priest. But the soul of a priest is more receptive of a divine power than words uttered by him. Therefore, it should be said that this power is in the priest rather than the words, if some created power is working transubstantiation.

On the contrary, Dionysius says at the end of the *Ecclesiastical Hierarchy*: *in those very invocations, once completed*, i.e., the forms of the sacraments, *there is power working from God*.[73] But the words mentioned are the form of this most worthy of sacraments. Therefore, the power of transubstantiating is in them.

Furthermore, Ambrose says that the words of Christ change creatures, and so the body of Christ is made out of bread with these heavenly words in the consecration.[74] However, Christ's word is the form instituted by Christ and spoken in the person of Christ. Therefore, the transubstantiation happens by the power of these words.

Furthermore, the priest does not work the transubstantiation except by uttering words. If therefore the power of transubstantiating was not in the words, then the priest would not have any spiritual power of consecrating, and thus he would not have holy orders, which is a kind of power directed chiefly to this.

I answer that, there are two opinions about this. For some people say that no created power by which transubstantiation happens is in these words; but the fact that transubstantiation is sometimes said to happen by the power of those words is to be understood as that it has been established by divine institution that the conversion happen by divine power alone at the utterance of those words; and

---

73. Pseudo-Dionysius, *Ecclesiastical Hierarchy*, ch. 7, p. 3, n. 10 (PG 3:566).
74. See Ambrose, *On the Sacraments*, Bk. 4, ch. 4.

dicunt in omnibus aliis sacramentis, ut supra, distinct. 1, dictum est.

Sed haec opinio dignitati sacramentorum novae legis derogat, et dictis sanctorum obviare videtur. Et ideo dicendum est, quod in verbis praedictis, sicut et in aliis formis sacramentorum, inest aliqua virtus ex Deo; sed haec virtus non est qualitas habens esse completum in natura, qualiter est virtus alicujus principalis agentis secundum formam suam, sed habet esse incompletum, sicut virtus quae est in instrumento ex intentione principalis agentis, et sicut similitudines colorum in aere, ut supra, dist. 1 dictum est.

Ad primum ergo dicendum, quod dictio exclusiva adjuncta principali agenti non excludit agens instrumentale: non enim sequitur: solus hic faber facit cultellum; ergo martellus nihil ad hoc operatus est. Virtus enim instrumenti non est nisi quaedam redundantia virtutis agentis principalis; unde in toto actio non attribuitur instrumento, sed principali agenti, secundum Philosophum; et propter hoc ex hoc quod dicitur, quod sola virtute Spiritus Sancti fit hujusmodi conversio, non excluditur virtus instrumentalis, quae est in verbis praemissis.

Ad secundum dicendum, quod virtus creata praesupponit materiam in qua operetur; quod quidem contingit esse dupliciter. Uno modo ita quod sit mutationis subjectum, sicut accidit in conversionibus naturalibus. Alio modo ita quod subsit termino a quo, non autem mutationi, sicut accidit in dicta conversione. Sed creatio neutro modo materiam praesupponit; et ideo magis potest aliquid Deo instrumentaliter cooperari in hac conversione quam in opere creationis. Utrum autem majoris virtutis sit ista conversio, vel creatio, dicetur infra, distinct. 11.

Ad tertium dicendum, quod si in conceptione unio includatur, quae simul cum ipsa facta est, major difficultas fuit in conceptione quam in transubstantiatione: quia illa unio est terminata ad esse divinae personae: haec autem transubstantiatio ad corpus Christi, quia panis non convertitur nisi in corpus Christi. Si autem conceptionis opus includat tantum conversionem sanguinum purissimorum Virginis in corpus Christi, sic major difficultas est in hac conversione quam in illa; unde potuit etiam alicui creaturae conferre quod in illa conceptione sibi cooperaretur; quamvis non fuisset conveniens propter dignitatem Christi servandam, quod tunc fiebat simpliciter, prius non existens: quod hic non accidit; et ideo nihil deperit dignitati corporis Christi, si aliqua creatura

they say the same thing about all the other sacraments, as was said in Distinction 1. [75]

But this opinion disparages the dignity of the sacraments of the New Law, and it seems to go against the things the saints have said. And so it should be said that in the words mentioned, as also in the forms of the other sacraments, there is a certain power from God, but this power is not a quality having complete being in nature, like the power of any principal agent according to its own form, but it has incomplete being, like the power that is in an instrument from the intention of the principal agent, and like the similitudes of color in the air, as was said above in Distinction 1.

Reply Obj. 1: An excluding term (e.g., 'alone'), when attributed to a principal agent does not exclude there being an instrumental agent, for it does not follow: this craftsman makes a knife alone; therefore the hammer did no work toward this. For the power of the instrument is only a certain overflow of the power of the principal agent; hence the action in whole is not attributed to the instrument, but to the principal agent, according to the Philosopher; [76]and because of this, when it is said that this conversion happens by the power of the Holy Spirit alone, the instrumental power that is in these words is not excluded.

Reply Obj. 2: A created power presupposes matter on which it works, which indeed happens in two different ways. In one way such that it is a subject of the change, as happens in natural conversions. In another way, such that it underlies the starting terminus but not the change, as happens in the conversion stated. But creation presupposes matter in neither way; and so something can cooperate with God instrumentally more in this conversion than in the work of creation. However, whether there is greater power in this conversion or in creation, will be said further on in Distinction 11. [77]

Reply Obj. 3: If the union is included in the conception, which happened at the same time with it, then there was a greater difficulty in the conception than in transubstantiation: for that union has its terminus in a divine person's being, while transubstantiation has its terminus in the body of Christ, for bread is not converted into anything but the body of Christ. However, if the work of conception includes only the conversion of the most pure blood of the Virgin into the body of Christ, then the greater difficulty is in this conversion rather than in that one; hence he could have also conferred on a certain creature that it cooperate with him in that conception, although for the sake of preserving the dignity of Christ it would not have been fitting, since [the body of Christ] was being made simply at

---

75. See q. 2, a. 2, qa. 2.
76. Aristotle, *Generation of Animals*, Bk. 2, ch. 1, 734b28–30; cf. ch. 6, 742a25.
77. See q. 1, a. 3, qa. 4.

accipiat instrumentalem virtutem operandi in id quod in corpus Christi transubstantiatur.

AD QUARTUM dicendum, quod nulla creatura potest agere ea quae sunt supra naturam quasi principale agens; potest tamen agere quasi agens instrumentale a virtute increata motum: quia sicut creaturae inest obedientiae potentia, ut in ea fiat quidquid Creator disposuerit, ita ut ea mediante fiat, quod est ratio instrumenti.

AD QUINTUM dicendum, quod virtus agentis principalis respicit principaliter terminum ad quem; sed virtus causae instrumentalis non attingit ad terminum ad quem, sed habet operationem suam in his quae sunt circa terminum; sicut qualitates activae elementares non attingunt ad animae rationalis introductionem. Et similiter hic contingit: quia virtus illa instrumentalis quae inest verbis, habet operationem supra substantiam panis, quia *verbum ad elementum accedit*, secundum Augustinum, non est autem aliquo modo causa eorum quae in termino ad quem sunt, sicut quod sint accidentia sine subjecto, vel alicujus hujusmodi; et ideo objectio cessat.

AD SEXTUM dicendum, quod virtus haec conversiva quae est in his verbis, cum sit sacramentalis, sequitur significationem, ut dictum est; significatio autem existentis conversionis, cum importet ordinem unius ad alterum, non potest fieri per dictionem, sed oportet quod per orationem fiat; cujus partes quamvis successive proferantur, tamen significatio est tota simul, quod tunc complet ultima orationis particula ad modum differentiae ultimae in definitionibus; et hac significatione existente, in ultimo prolationis instanti fit transubstantiatio.

AD SEPTIMUM dicendum, quod significatio orationis, quamvis relata ad partes quibus fit significatio, videatur composita, tamen relata ad rem significatam simplex est, inquantum significat unum quid, scilicet compositionem hujus cum hoc; sicut etiam Philosophus dicit in 5 *Metaphysica*, quod substantia senaria non est bis tria, sed semel sex quam ibi qualitatem nominat. Unde sicut ad hanc qualitatem senarii se habent partes ejus ut dispositiones materiales, non ut qualitates partium, sicut partes unius qualitatis totius; ita significationes partium sunt dispositiones ad significationem totius orationis, quae consurgit ex significatione ultimae partis in ordine ad omnes praecedentes: quia virtus conversiva sequitur significationem, ut dictum est; et ideo in ipso complemento significationis datur illa virtus ora-

that time, not existing before, which does not happen here; and therefore nothing is taken away from Christ's dignity, if some creature should receive instrumental power of working upon what is transubstantiated into the body of Christ.

REPLY OBJ. 4: No creature can do those things that are above nature as principal agent; however, it can cause a motion by uncreated power as instrumental agent: for as there is an obediential potency in creation, so that whatever the Creator has disposed happens in it, thus also so that it happens by means of it, which is the definition of an instrument.

REPLY OBJ. 5: The power of the principal agent regards principally the ending terminus, but the power of an instrumental cause does not reach to the ending terminus, but has its own operation in those things that surround the terminus, just as active elementary qualities do not attain to introducing the rational soul. And this happens similarly, because that instrumental power that is in the words has its operation upon the substance of the bread, for *the word is combined with the element* according to Augustine.[78] However, it is not in any way a cause of those things that are in the ending terminus, as that accidents exist without a subject, or something like that; and so the objection ceases.

REPLY OBJ. 6: Since this power of converting which is in these words is sacramental, it follows the signification, as was said. However, the signification of a conversion of something existing, since it conveys an order of one thing to another, cannot be brought about through a word or phrase but must be brought about through a complete statement, whose signification is whole and simultaneous even if its parts are uttered successively, because the last particle of the statement completes the signification at that moment, in the manner of the final difference in definitions. And once this signification exists, the transubstantiation happens in the last instant of the utterance.

REPLY OBJ. 7: Although in relation to the parts that bring about its signification the signification of the statement seems composite, yet relative to the reality signified it is simple, inasmuch as it signifies one thing, namely the composition of this with that; just as the Philosopher also says in *Metaphysics* 5, that the substance of six is not three twice, but six once, which names the quality there.[79] Hence just as for this quality of six its parts are related to it as material dispositions, not as qualities of parts, like the parts of one entire quality, so also the significations of the parts are dispositions to the signification of the whole utterance, which arises from the signification of the last part, taken in an order to all those preceding it: for the power to convert follows the signification, as was said; and so in what completes the signification that power is given to the whole ut-

78. Augustine, *In Iohannis euangelium tractatus* (CCSL 36), Tract. 80, par. 3.
79. Aristotle, *Metaphysics*, Bk. 5, ch. 14, 1020b7–8.

tioni toti, ita quod partes singulae se habent materialiter tantum ad illam virtutem.

AD OCTAVUM dicendum, quod valde conveniens est quod omne quod est propter aliquid, esse desinat perfecto hoc propter quod erat; et quia virtus illa non erat ad perfectionem ejus cui dabatur, sed magis ad faciendum conversionem de qua loquimur, cum sit tantum instrumentalis virtus, ut dictum est; ideo non est inconveniens, si statim conversione facta, et verba et virtus verborum esse desinant.

AD NONUM dicendum, quod quando aliquod opus perficitur pluribus instrumentis, virtus instrumentalis non est complete in uno, sed incomplete in utroque, sicut manu et penna scribitur; et similiter contingit in proposito: quia virtus instrumentalis ad faciendam praedictam conversionem non tantum est in verbo sed in sacerdote, sed in utroque incomplete: quia nec sacerdos sine verbo, nec verbum sine sacerdote conficere potest. Et quia sacerdos est similior principali agenti quam verbum, quia gerit ejus figuram; ideo, simpliciter loquendo, sua virtus instrumentalis est major et dignior (unde etiam permanet, et ad multos hujusmodi effectus se habet): virtus autem verbi transit, et ad semel tantum est: sed secundum quid est potentior virtus verbi, inquantum effectui propinquior, quasi signum ipsius; sicut etiam penna est scripturae propinquior, sed manus scribenti.

terance, so that the individual parts are related only materially to that power.

REPLY OBJ. 8: It is extremely fitting that everything that is for the sake of something stop existing once this thing is complete that it was for the sake of; and since that power was not for the perfection of what it was given to, but rather for making the conversion of which we speak, since it is only an instrumental power, as was said, for this reason it is not unfitting if, once the conversion is done, both the words and the power of the words immediately cease to be.

REPLY OBJ. 9: When some work is completed by several instruments, the instrumental power is not completely in one but incompletely in each, as one writes with a pen and the hand; and it happens the same way in this case: for an instrumental power for making the conversion mentioned is not only in the word but also in the priest, yet in each incompletely: for neither the priest without the word nor the word without the priest can consecrate. And since a priest is more like the principal agent than a word, since he bears his figure, for this reason, simply speaking, his instrumental power is greater and more worthy (for which reason also it remains, and is related to many effects like this). However, the power of the word is transient, and only exists for one time; but in a certain respect, the power of the word is greater, as closer to the effect, like a sign of it; just as also a pen is closer to the writing, but a hand is closer to the writer.

ARTICLE 4

A comparison of the two consecrations

Quaestiuncula 1

AD QUARTUM SIC PROCEDITUR. Videtur quod formae expectent se in operando. Sicut enim se habet res ad rem, ita se habet forma ad formam. Sed res corporis non est sine re sanguinis: quia non consecratur corpus Christi sine sanguine. Ergo nec forma corporis operatur sine forma sanguinis.

PRAETEREA, hoc sacramentum est unum. Sed propter unitatem sacramenti species duae, scilicet panis et vini, se habent in ratione unius signi, ut dictum est. Ergo similiter duae formae se habent in ratione unius formae. Sed in una forma partes se expectant invicem ad agendum, ut dictum est. Ergo et forma corporis expectat formam sanguinis.

PRAETEREA, in baptismo tres immersiones se expectant in agendo. Ergo et similiter hae duae prolationes verborum.

SED CONTRA, si statim verbis prolatis, quando est orationis significatio, non esset ibi verum corpus Christi, haec esset falsa: *hoc est corpus meum*. Sed in sacramento veritatis non contingit aliquid esse falsum. Ergo forma prima non expectat secundam in operando.

PRAETEREA, hostia non est adoranda ante consecrationem. Sed secundum communem morem ecclesiae, statim dictis primis verbis formae super panem, ante formam sanguinis elevatur hostia a populo adoranda. Ergo ante formam sanguinis hostia est consecrata.

OBJ. 1: To the fourth we proceed thus. It seems that the forms depend on each other in working.[80] For just as one reality is related to another reality, so also is a form related to a form. But the reality of the body does not exist without the reality of the blood: for the body of Christ is not consecrated without the blood. Therefore, neither does the form of consecrating the body work without the form of consecrating the blood.

OBJ. 2: Furthermore, this sacrament is one. But because of the unity of the sacrament the two species, namely, bread and wine, are interrelated in the notion of one sign, as has been said. Therefore, in the same way, the two forms are interrelated in the notion of one form. But in one form the parts are dependent on each other in order to act, as has been said. Therefore, the form of consecrating the body also depends on the form of the blood.

OBJ. 3: Furthermore, in baptism three immersions depend on each other in acting. Therefore, also these two utterances of words do in the same way.

ON THE CONTRARY, if once the words are uttered, when there is the signification of the prayer, the true body of Christ were not there immediately, then this would be false: *this is my body*. But in the sacrament of truth nothing can happen that is false. Therefore, the first form does not depend on the second one to work.

FURTHERMORE, the host should not be adored before its consecration. But according to the common custom of the Church, immediately once these first words of the form are said over the bread, before the form of the blood, the host is raised for the people to adore. Therefore, before the form of the blood the host is consecrated.

Quaestiuncula 2

ULTERIUS. Videtur quod deficiente sacerdote post corporis Christi consecrationem non debet alius procedere ad consecrationem sanguinis. Quia unius sacramenti unus debet esset minister. Sed consecratio utraque ad unum sacerdotem pertinet. Ergo ab uno ministro fieri debet.

OBJ. 1: Moreover, it seems that if the priest fails[81] after the consecration of the body of Christ, another should not proceed to the consecration of the blood.[82] For one person should be the minister for one sacrament. But both consecrations belong to one priest. Therefore, they should be done by one minister.

---

80. Parallels: below, d. 11, q. 2, a. 1, qa. 1, ad 4; *ST* III, q. 78, a. 6; *Super Matt.* 26; *Super I ad Cor.* 11, lec. 6.

81. "Fails" is meant to cover any scenario in which the priest who consecrated the bread becomes suddenly unable to consecrate the wine, e.g., if he passes out and cannot be revived, or has a heart attack on the spot and dies.

82. Parallel: *ST* III, q. 83, a. 6, ad 1.

PRAETEREA, sacerdos consecrans gerit figuram Christi, ex cujus persona verba proferuntur. Sed Christus non est divisus, ut dicitur 1 Corinth. 1. Ergo nec verba dividi debent ut a diversis proferantur.

SED CONTRA, ad perfectionem hujus sacramenti utraque consecratio requiritur. Si ergo consecrato corpore non consecratur sanguis, sacramentum remanet imperfectum, quod est inconveniens.

OBJ. 2: Furthermore, the consecrating priest bears the figure of Christ, in whose person the words are uttered. But Christ is not divided, as it says in 1 Corinthians 1:13. Therefore, neither should the words be divided by being uttered by different people.

ON THE CONTRARY, for the completion of this sacrament both consecrations are required. If, therefore, when the body is consecrated, the blood is not consecrated, the sacrament remains incomplete, which is unfitting.

Quaestiuncula 3

ULTERIUS. Videtur quod haec verba sine aliis quae in canone Missae dicuntur, non habeant vim conficiendi. Quia in hoc sacramento requiritur intentio faciendi quod facit ecclesia; et sic intentio debet esse secundum statuta ecclesiae regulata. Sed proferens haec verba tantum, non servat ecclesiae statuta. Ergo non conficit.

PRAETEREA, verba quibus fit consecratio, per se prolata, ad personam dicentis referuntur. Sed conversio panis et vini non fit in corpus et sanguinem dicentis, sed in corpus et sanguinem Christi. Ergo sine verbis praemissis, quibus verba formae determinantur ad personam Christi, scilicet: *qui pridie quam pateretur*, etc., non potest fieri conversio.

PRAETEREA, si verbis praedictis tantum posset fieri consecratio, tunc aliquis in periculo mortis existens, posset licite sine verbis praecedentibus conficere, sicut aliquis in necessitate potest baptizare omissis illis quae sunt ad decorem sacramenti. Sed hoc nunquam licet. Ergo sine verbis aliis ista non habent vim convertendi.

SED CONTRA est quod Ambrosius dicit: *sacramentum istud quod accipis, sermone Domini conficitur*; et loquitur de verbis praedictis. Ergo sine aliis ista prolata habent vim conficiendi.

PRAETEREA, virtus conversiva sequitur significationem verborum, ut dictum est. Sed verba formae absque praecedentibus sufficienter significant hoc quod in sacramento hoc faciendum est. Ergo sine aliis habent vim conversivam.

OBJ. 1: Moreover, it seems that these words, without the others that are said in the canon of the Mass, would not have the power of consecrating. For in this sacrament the intention of doing what the Church does is required, and so the intention should be according to the statutes of the Church. But uttering these words alone does not preserve the statutes of the Church. Therefore, it does not consecrate.

OBJ. 2: Furthermore, the words by which the consecration happens, uttered by themselves, are referred to the person of the speaker. But the conversion of bread and wine does not happen into the body and blood of the speaker, but into the body and blood of Christ. Therefore, without the foregoing words, namely, *who the day before he suffered*, etc., by which the form's words are determined to the person of Christ, this conversion cannot happen.

OBJ. 3: Furthermore, if the consecration could happen by the words in question alone, then someone in danger of death could licitly consecrate without the prefatory words, just as someone can baptize in necessity while omitting those things that are for the embellishment of the sacrament. But this is never permitted. Therefore, without the other words, these words do not have the force of conversion.

ON THE CONTRARY, Ambrose says: *this sacrament which you receive is confected by the word of the Lord*; [83] and he is speaking of the words discussed. Therefore, without any others, those have the force of consecrating once uttered.

FURTHERMORE, the conversive power follows the signification of the words, as was said. But the words of the form without any preface sufficiently signify what is being done in this sacrament. Therefore, without any others they have the force to convert.

Response to Quaestiuncula 1

RESPONDEO dicendum ad primam quaestionem, quod quidam dixerunt, quod prima forma non habet ef-

TO THE FIRST QUESTION, I answer that certain people say that the first form does not have its effect unless the sec-

---

83. The idea is discussed in Ambrose, *On the Sacraments*, Bk. 4, ch. 4 (CSEL 73).

fectum suum nisi prolata forma secunda; nec secunda haberet effectum, nisi prima prius prolata: nec tamen periculose adoratur hostia ante consecrationem sanguinis, quia non adoratur quod est, sed quod erit. Sed illud non potest stare: quia forma materiae proportionari debet; unde sicut materiae distinctae sunt nec ad invicem commixtae, ita formae divisim operantur; quod patet ex hoc quod utraque per se completam significationem habet. Et ideo dicendum cum aliis, quod formae praedictae non expectant se mutuo in operando.

AD PRIMUM ergo dicendum, quod in hoc sacramento dupliciter aliquid continetur; scilicet ex vi sacramenti, et ex naturali concomitantia; et quia sacramentum est institutum in usum fidelium, ideo ex vi sacramenti continetur in hoc sacramento quod in usum fidelium venit. Et quia in pane consecrato non continetur sanguis Christi secundum quod est in usum potus fidelium, ideo non continetur ibi ex vi sacramenti, sed ex naturali concomitantia, qua convenit ut corpus Christi non sit sine sanguine; et e contrario est de vino consecrato. Unde panis non convertitur per vim primorum verborum in corpus exsangue, sed in corpus sine sanguine veniente in usum potus fidelium. Causa autem quare divisim sanguis a corpore consecratur, cum nunc non sit divisus, potest sumi ex usu ad quem est sacramentum, quia manducatio in cibo et potu consistit; et ex eo quod per sacramentum repraesentatur, quia in passione sanguis Christi a corpore divisus fuit.

AD SECUNDUM dicendum, quod duae formae in hoc sacramento non pertinent ad unum sacramentum quasi unam formam constituant, sicut ex diversis dictionibus constituitur una forma; sed pertinent ad unum sacramentum mediantibus diversis partibus hujus sacramenti; et ideo utraque habet seorsum effectum suum supra partem ad quam ordinatur.

AD TERTIUM dicendum, quod tres immersiones referuntur ad unum characterem, qui est res et sacramentum in baptismo; sed diversae formae referuntur ad diversa, quae sunt res et sacramentum hic; et ideo non est simile.

ond form is uttered; nor would the second have effect unless the first had been uttered before; nor is it dangerous to adore the host before the consecration of the blood, for it is not adored as what it is, but as what it will be. But this cannot stand: for the form must be proportionate to the matter, and therefore just as there are distinct matters which are not mixed with each other, so the forms work separately, which is evident from the fact that both have complete signification in themselves. And so it should be said, with other people, that the forms in question do not mutually depend upon each other to work.

REPLY OBJ. 1: In this sacrament something is contained in two ways: namely, by the force of the sacrament, and by a natural concomitance. And since the sacrament is instituted for the use of the faithful, for this reason what is contained in this sacrament by the force of the sacrament is there for the use of the faithful. And since in the consecrated bread the blood of Christ is not contained as a drink available to the faithful, it is therefore not contained there by the force of the sacrament, but by natural concomitance, by which it is fitting that the body of Christ not be without its blood; and the same is true of the consecrated wine. Hence by the force of the first words the bread is not converted into bloodless body, but into the body without the blood coming into use as a drink for the faithful. However, the reason why the blood is consecrated separately from the body (although now it is not divided) can be taken from the use to which the sacrament is directed, because eating consists in food and drink, and from that which is represented by the sacrament, since the blood of Christ was divided from the body in the Passion.

REPLY OBJ. 2: The two forms in this sacrament do not pertain to the one sacrament as though constituting one form, as one form is instituted from many different words. Rather they pertain to the one sacrament via the different parts of this sacrament, and so each has its own separate effect upon the part that it is ordered to.

REPLY OBJ. 3: The three immersions are referred to one character, which is the reality-and-sacrament in baptism, but the diverse forms are referred to diverse things, which are the reality-and-sacrament here; and so it is not the same.[84]

Response to Quaestiuncula 2

AD SECUNDAM QUAESTIONEM dicendum, quod secundum statutum Concilii Toletani, si sacerdos impeditur ut coeptum Missarum officium explere non possit, alius sacerdos debet explere quod ille inchoavit, ita quod

TO THE SECOND QUESTION, it should be said that according to the Council of Toledo,[85] if a priest is prevented so that having begun the office of the Mass he cannot complete it, another priest must complete what he has begun, so

---

84. For more about the sacrament alone, reality alone, and sacrament-and-reality, see the footnote at Dist.1, q.1, a.4, qa. 1, main response.
85. See Gratian's *Decretals*, c. 7, q. 1, "Nihil contra" (PL 187:572).

incipiat sequens sacerdos ubi primus dimisit, si sciatur: si autem nesciatur, debet a capite incipere: non enim dicitur iteratum quod nescitur esse factum. Nec aliquid per hoc derogatur unitati sacramenti: quia omnes unum sumus in Christo propter fidei unitatem. Secundum tamen Innocentium tertium consultius est ut illa hostia jam consecrata seorsum posita, super aliam deinceps totum officium iteretur.

ET PER HOC patet solutio ad objecta.

that the following priest begins where the first left off, if it is known. If it is not known, however, he should begin from the top: for what is not known to have been done is not said to have been repeated. Nor is anything detracted from the unity of the sacrament by this, for we all are one in Christ because of the unity of faith. Nevertheless, according to Innocent III,[86] it is more advised that that host that was already consecrated be set apart, and the entire office be repeated with another one afterward.

AND BY THIS the answers to the objections are evident.

Response to Quaestiuncula 3

AD TERTIAM QUAESTIONEM dicendum, quod quidam dixerunt quod verba ista, in quibus forma consistit, ut dictum est, si per se dicantur sine aliis, non faciunt conversionem, ad minus sine illis quae sunt in canone Missae. Sed hoc non videtur probabile: quia secundum Augustinum, *accedit verbum ad elementum, et fit sacramentum.* Verbum autem quo accedente ad elementum fit sacramentum, a sanctis dicitur esse verbum salvatoris; unde alia sunt de solemnitate sacramenti, non de necessitate. Et ideo cum aliis dicendum est quod in his verbis sine aliis potest confici corpus Christi, quamvis graviter peccaret qui hoc faceret. Et quod haec opinio sit verior, patet ex hoc quod non sit idem canon Missae apud omnes, et secundum diversa tempora, diversa sunt in canone Missae superaddita.

AD PRIMUM ergo dicendum, quod ad sacramentum requiritur intentio faciendi quod facit ecclesia in essentialibus sacramento, non autem in his quae pertinent ad decorem vel solemnitatem sacramenti, sicut in baptismo patet.

AD SECUNDUM dicendum, quod ex ipsa intentione proferentis possunt verba formae ad personam Christi referri, etiam verbis aliis non praemissis, si sacerdos verba praedicta in persona Christi dicere intenderet.

AD TERTIUM dicendum, quod baptismus est sacramentum necessitatis; et ideo concessum est ut imminente necessitatis articulo possit aliquis baptizare sine solemnitate ab ecclesia instituta. Secus autem est de hoc sacramento: quia alicui in necessitate constituto sufficeret spiritualiter manducare, si sacramentaliter manducare non posset; et ideo in nullo casu a peccato excusaretur.

TO THE THIRD QUESTION, it should be said that certain people have said, as has been said, that if those words that the form consists in are said by themselves without the others, at least without those that are in the canon of the Mass, then they do not cause the conversion. But this does not seem probable, for according to Augustine, *the word is combined with the element and the sacrament occurs.*[87] However, the word that combined with the element makes the sacrament is said by the saints to be the word of the Savior. This is why the other things are of the solemnity of the sacrament, not necessary to it. And so it should be said with other people that in these words without any others the body of Christ can be confected, although one would gravely sin who did this. And that this opinion is truer is clear from the fact that the canon of the Mass is not the same for everyone, and in different ages different things are added to the canon of the Mass.

REPLY OBJ. 1: The intention of doing what the Church does is required for a sacrament in those things essential to it, but not in those things that pertain to the sacrament's beauty or solemnity, as is evident in baptism.

REPLY OBJ. 2: By the very intention of the one uttering the words, the words of the form can be referred to the person of Christ, even without saying the prefatory words, if the priest intended to say the words mentioned in the person of Christ.

REPLY OBJ. 3: Baptism is a sacrament of necessity, and so it was granted that in an imminent emergency someone could baptize without the solemnity instituted by the Church. But it is different with this sacrament: because for anyone in an emergency it would be enough to spiritually eat, if he could not eat sacramentally, and therefore in no case would it be excused from sin.

---

86. Innocent III, *De sacro altaris mysterio*, Bk. 4, ch. 22 (PL 217:872).
87. Augustine, *In Iohannis euangelium tractatus* (CCSL 36), Tract. 80, par. 3.

Exposition of the Text

Post sacramentum baptismi et confirmationis sequitur Eucharistiae sacramentum. Videtur quod male ordinet. Quia quod est per essentiam, prius est quam id quod est per participationem. In hoc autem sacramento continetur Christus per essentiam, in aliis vero per participationem suae virtutis. Ergo hoc sacramentum ante omnia alia determinare debuit. Praeterea, Dionysius aliter ordinat. Prius enim de baptismo, et postea de Eucharistia, et postea de chrismate determinat. Ergo videtur quod Magister hic ordinem pervertat. Et dicendum ad primum, quod sacramenta sunt ordinata ad usum fidelium; unde ordo sacramentorum non attenditur secundum contentorum ordinem sed secundum quod veniunt in usum fidelium; et ideo baptismus ante Eucharistiam ab omnibus ponitur. Ad secundum dicendum, quod Dionysius determinat de sacramentis secundum quod sunt actiones hierarchicae, ut supra, dist. 2, qu. 1, art. 2 in corp., dictum est; et ideo ordinem sacramentorum attendit, secundum quod per ea distinguuntur personae, ut in hierarchia et ordine. Et quia Eucharistia non importat aliquam distinctionem supra baptismum, cum ex hoc ipso quod baptizatur aliquis, ad Eucharistiae perceptionem deputetur; confirmatio autem addit; ideo praemittit Eucharistiam confirmationi, sicut commune ad proprium. Magister autem determinat de sacramentis secundum quod sacramenta sunt medicinae quaedam sanctificantes; et ideo secundum ordinem sanctificationum ordinat sacramenta; et quia amplioris sanctificationis est Eucharistia quam confirmatio; ideo postremo de ea determinat.

Intelligi datur antiquiora esse sacramenta Christianorum quam Judaeorum. Videtur hoc esse falsum: quia hoc sacramentum quo ad rem non fuit ante adventum Christi; quo ad speciem autem et ritum fuerunt sacrificia, quae erant sacramenta Judaeorum, etiam ante Melchisedech. Et dicendum, quod loquitur quantum ad figuram hujus sacramenti per similitudinem speciei et ritus. Sacramenta autem quae in lege naturae fiebant, non erant figurae sacramentorum veteris legis, sed magis passionis Christi.

Consecratio quibus fit verbis? etc. Videtur falsum esse quod dicit: quia non dicitur: accipite et edite, sed manducate; et praeterea hoc non est de forma, ut dictum est supra, qu. 2, art. 2. Item non dicitur: hic est sanguis meus, sed: hic est calix sanguinis mei. Et dicendum, quod Ma-

After the sacrament of baptism and the one of confirmation, follows the sacrament of the Eucharist.[88] It seems that this is badly ordered. For what is by essence is before what is by participation. However, in this sacrament Christ is contained in his essence, but in the others by participation in his power. Therefore, this sacrament should be examined before all the others. Furthermore, Dionysius puts them in a different order.[89] For he examines baptism first, and then the Eucharist, and then chrismation. Therefore, it seems that the Master has disturbed this order. And it should be said to the first that the sacraments are in an order according to their use by the faithful; hence the order of the sacraments does not depend on the order of what they contain but on how they are available to the faithful. And so baptism is placed before the Eucharist by all. And to the second it should be said that Dionysius examines the sacraments according as they are hierarchical actions, as was said above in Distinction 2, Question 1, Article 2. And so he puts them in an order following how persons are distinguished by them as in the hierarchy and in orders. And because the Eucharist does not convey any distinction above baptism, since by the very fact that someone is baptized, he is authorized for reception of the Eucharist, but confirmation does add something, for this reason he places the Eucharist before confirmation, as the common before the proper. However, the Master considers the sacraments according as sacraments are a kind of sanctifying medicine. And so he ranks the sacraments according to the order of sanctifications. And because the Eucharist is of a fuller sanctification than confirmation, he considers it afterward.

It is given to be understood that "the sacraments of the Christians are earlier than those of the Jews."[90] This seems to be false, for this sacrament did not exist in its reality before the coming of Christ; and as to its appearance and rite, there were sacrifices, which were the sacraments of the Jews, even before Melchizedek. And it should be said that he speaks of the figure of this sacrament by the resemblance of its appearance and rite. But the sacraments which were done under the law of nature were not figures of the sacraments of the Old Law, but rather of the Passion of Christ.

"By which words is the consecration done? etc."[91] What he says seems to be false: for it is not said: Take and "eat" [edite], but, Take and eat [manducate]; and furthermore, this does not belong to the form, as was said above in Question 2, Article 2. Besides, it is not said, This is my blood, but

---

88. *Sent.* IV, 8.1 (48), 1.

89. In the *Ecclesiastical Hierarchy*, Pseudo-Dionysius first treats of illumination (baptism) in ch. 2, then the synaxis (communion) in ch. 3, and finally the ointment (chrismation, confirmation) in ch. 4.

90. *Sent.* IV, 8.2 (49), 4, citing Ambrose, *De sacramentis*, Bk. 4, ch. 3, n. 10.

91. *Sent.* IV, 8.4 (51), 1, citing Ambrose, *De sacramentis*, Bk. 4, chs. 4–5, nn. 14, 19, 21, 22.

gister non intendit hic definite ponere verba quibus fit consecratio, sed explanare quod verbis Domini fit; non tamen in omnibus verbis quae ipse ponit, nec eisdem numero, sed eisdem quo ad sensum.

Per reliqua autem omnia quae dicuntur, laus Deo defertur. Sciendum, quod eorum quae in officio Missae dicuntur, quaedam dicuntur per sacerdotem, quaedam per ministros, quaedam a toto choro. Ea quidem quibus populus immediate ordinatur ad Deum, per sacerdotes tantum dicuntur, qui sunt mediatores inter populum et Deum; quorum quaedam dicuntur publice, spectantia ad totum populum, in cujus persona ipse solus ea Deo proponit, sicut orationes et gratiarum actiones; quaedam privatim, quae ad officium ipsius tantum spectant, ut consecrationes et hujusmodi orationes quas ipse pro populo facit, non tamen in persona populi orans; et in omnibus praemittit: *Dominus vobiscum*, ut mens populi Deo conjungatur ad ipsum per intentionem erecti. Et quia populus in his quae ad Deum sunt, sacerdotem ducem habet, ideo in fine cujuslibet orationis populus consentit respondens: *amen*; unde et omnis sacerdotis oratio alte terminatur, etiam si privatim fiat. Ad ea vero quae per ministerium aliorum divinitus sunt tradita, per ministros altaris populus ordinatur. Ea vero quae ad dispositionem populi pertinent, chorus prosequitur: quorum quaedam a sacerdote inchoantur, quae ad ea pertinent quae rationem humanam excedunt, quasi divinitus accepta: quaedam chorus per seipsum, quibus illa declarantur quae rationi sunt consona. Item quaedam pertinent ad populum ut praeparatoria ad divina percipienda; et haec a choro praemittuntur his quae a ministris et sacerdote dicuntur; quaedam vero ex perceptione divinorum in populo causata; et haec sequuntur.

His ergo visis, sciendum est, quod quia omnis nostra operatio a Deo inchoata, circulariter in ipsum terminari debet; ideo Missae officium incipit ab oratione, et terminatur in gratiarum actione. Unde tres habet partes principales; scilicet principium orationis quod durat usque ad epistolam; medium celebrationem ipsam quae durat usque ad postcommunionem; et finem gratiarum actionis exinde usque in finem.

Prima pars duo continet; scilicet populi praeparationem ad orationem, et ipsam orationem. Praeparatur autem populus ad orationem tripliciter. Primo per devotionem, quae excitatur in introitu; unde et sumitur ex aliquo pertinente ad solemnitatem, in cujus devotionem populus congregatur, et etiam adjungitur Psalmus. Secundo humilitatem, quae fit per *kyrie eleison*, quia mi-

This is the chalice of my blood. And it should be said that the Master does not intend here to set down precisely the words by which the consecration happens, but to explain what is done by the Lord's words; not of course in all the words that he said, nor the same in number, but the same in sense.

As for all the other things that are said, by them praise is given to God.[92] It should be known that of those things that are said in the office of the Mass, some are said by the priest, some by the ministers, and some by the whole choir. Those indeed by which the people are directly ordered to God are said only by the priests, who are the mediators between the people and God. And some of the priest's words are said publicly, on behalf of the whole people, in the person of whom he alone speaks them to God, like prayers and thanksgiving. But some are said privately, which regard only his own office, like consecrations and prayers of the sort that he does for the people, but not praying in the person of the people; and in all of these he prefaces his words with, *May the Lord be with you*, so that the minds of the people may be united with him by a right intention. And since in what is directed to God the people have the priest as their leader, for this reason at the end of every prayer the people consent by answering *amen*; and this is also why every prayer of the priest ends aloud, even if it is done privately. But for those things that are divinely handed down through the ministry of others, the people are directed by the ministers of the altar. But those things that pertain to disposing the people, the choir accomplishes: of these, the ones that pertain to those things that surpass human reason are started by the priest, as though divinely received; the ones that are consonant with reason are declared by the choir by itself. Likewise, some pertain to the people as preparatory to receiving divine things; and these are said by the choir before those that are said by the ministers and priest. But some things are caused by the reception of divine things in the people, and these follow what the priest says.

Therefore, having seen these things, it should be known that since all our work is begun by God, it should end in him, coming full circle. And this is why the office of the Mass begins from a prayer and ends in thanksgiving. Hence it has three principal parts: namely, the beginning of the prayer that lasts until the epistle; the middle celebration itself that lasts until the postcommunion; and the end of thanksgiving from there until the end.

The first part contains two things, namely, the preparation of the people for prayer, and the prayer itself. Now the people are prepared for prayer in three ways. The first is by devotion, which is aroused in the Introit; hence it is taken from something pertaining to the solemnity, in the devotion of which the people are brought together, and the psalm is also added. Second, by humility, which is done

---

92. *Sent.* IV, 8.4 (51), 1, citing Ambrose, *De sacramentis*, Bk. 4, chs. 4–5, nn. 14, 19, 21. 22.

sericordiam petens miseriam profitetur; et dicitur novies propter novem choros angelorum, vel propter fidem Trinitatis, secundum quod quaelibet persona in se consideratur et in ordine ad alias duas. Tertio per rectam intentionem, quae ad caelestem patriam et gloriam dirigenda est, quae omnem rationem humanam excedit; et hoc fit per *gloria in excelsis*, quam chorus prosequitur sacerdote inchoante; et ideo non dicitur nisi in solemnitatibus quae nobis caelestem solemnitatem repraesentant; in officiis vero luctus omnino intermittitur. Deinde sequitur oratio ad Deum pro populo fusa, quam sacerdos publice proponit praemisso *Dominus vobiscum*, quod sumitur de Ruth 2. Pontifex autem dicit: *pax vobis*, gerens typum Christi qui his verbis discipulos post resurrectionem allocutus est, Joan. 20.

Secunda autem pars principalis tres partes continet. Prima est populi instructio usque ad offertorium; secunda, materiae oblatio usque ad praefationem; tertia, sacramenti consummatio usque ad post communionem. Instructio autem populi fit per verbum Dei, quod quidem a Deo per ministros suos ad populum pervenit; et ideo ea quae ad instructionem plebis pertinent, non dicuntur a sacerdote, sed a ministris.

Ministerium autem verbi Dei est triplex. Primum auctoritatis, quod competit Christo qui dicitur *minister*, Rom. 15, de quo dicitur Matth. 7, 29: *erat autem in potestate docens*. Secundum manifestae veritatis quae competit praedicatoribus novi testamenti, de quo dicitur 2 Corinth. 3, 6: *qui et idoneos nos fecit ministros*, etc. Tertium figurationis, quod competit praedicatoribus veteris testamenti; et ideo doctrinam Christi proponit diaconus. Et quia Christus non solum est homo, sed Deus; ideo diaconus praemittit: *Dominus vobiscum*, ut ad Christum quasi ad Deum homines attentos faciat. Doctrina vero praedicatorum novi testamenti proponitur per subdiaconos. Nec obstat quod aliquando ab eis legitur loco epistolae aliquid de veteri testamento, quia praedicatores novi testamenti etiam vetus praedicant. Doctrina vero praedicatorum veteris testamenti per inferiores ministros legitur non semper, sed illis diebus quibus praecipue configuratio novi et veteris testamenti designatur, ut in jejuniis quatuor temporum, et quando aliqua celebrantur quae in veteri lege figurata sunt, sicut passio, nativitas, baptismus, et aliquod hujusmodi. Et quia utraque doctrina ordinat ad Christum, et eorum qui praeibant, et eorum qui sequebantur; ideo doctrina Christi postponitur quasi finis.

Ex doctrina autem ordinante ad Christum duplex effectus populo provenit, quibus etiam homo praeparatur ad doctrinam Christi: scilicet profectus virtutum, qui

by the *Kyrie eleison*, for the one seeking mercy declares his wretchedness; and it is said nine times because of the nine choirs of angels, or because of faith in the Trinity, according as any Person is considered in himself and in relation to the other two. Third, by right intention, which is directed to the heavenly fatherland and glory, which exceeds all human reason; and this is done by the *glory to God in the highest*, which the choir completes once the priest has started it. And so it is only said on solemnities which represent to us heavenly solemnity; but in the offices of mourning it is completely omitted. Next comes the prayer poured out to God for the people, which the priest publicly pronounces after *the Lord be with you*; which is taken from Ruth 2:4. However, the high priest says: *Peace be with you*, bearing the type of Christ who addressed his disciples with these words after the Resurrection, in John 20:19 and 21.

Now the second main part contains three parts. The first is the instruction of the people until the offertory; the second, the offering of the matter until the Preface; the third, the consummation of the sacrament until the postcommunion. Now the instruction of the people is done through the word of God, which indeed reaches the people from God through his ministers; and so those things that pertain to the instruction of the people are not said by the priest, but by the ministers.

Now there are three kinds of ministry of the word of God. The first is from authority, which belongs to Christ who is called 'minister' in Romans 15:8, of whom it is said, *but he was teaching as one having power* (Matt 7:29). The second is from the truth made plain which applies to the preachers of the New Testament, of whom it says, *he has made us also worthy ministers*, etc. (2 Cor 3:6). The third is from prefiguration, which applies to the preachers of the Old Testament. And thus a deacon sets forth Christ's teaching; and because Christ is not only man, but God, the deacon says first, *the Lord be with you*, so that he might make men attentive to Christ as God. But the teaching of the preachers of the New Testament is announced by subdeacons. Nor is it inconsistent that sometimes in place of an epistle something is read by them from the Old Testament, since the preachers of the New Testament also preached the Old. But the teaching of the preachers of the Old Testament by lower ministers is not always read, but specifically on those days on which the configuration of the New and Old Testaments is indicated, as in the fasts of the four seasons, and when certain things are celebrated that were prefigured in the Old Law, like the Passion, the Nativity of Christ, his Baptism, and things like that. And since both teachings direct to Christ, both of those who went before and of those who came after, this is why the teaching of Christ is reserved for the end.

However, from the teaching that directs to Christ, two effects arise for the people, by which effects a man is also prepared for Christ's teaching: namely, progress in the

per graduale insinuatur: dicitur enim a gradu quo ascenditur de virtute in virtutem, vel a gradibus altaris ante quos dicitur; et exultatio habita de aeternorum spe, quod insinuat *alleluja;* unde et replicatur propter stolam animae et corporis. In diebus vero et officiis luctus intermittitur, et loco ejus, tractus ponitur, qui asperitate vocum et prolixitate verborum praesentis miseriae incolatum insinuat. Tempore autem resurrectionis duplex *alleluja* dicitur propter gaudium resurrectionis capitis, et membrorum. Effectus autem evangelicae doctrinae est fidei confessio; quae quia supra rationem est, a sacerdote inchoatur symbolum fidei et chorus prosequitur, nec dicitur nisi in illis solemnitatibus de quibus fit mentio in symbolo, sicut de nativitate, resurrectione, de apostolis, qui fidei fundatores extiterunt, ut dicitur 1 Corinth. 3, 10: *ut sapiens architectus fundamentum posui.*

Deinde sequitur secunda pars partis secundae principalis quae pertinet ad materiae consecrandae oblationem; et hic tria continentur. Praemittitur enim offerentium exultatio, quasi praeparatoria, in offertorio, quia *hilarem datorem diligit Deus,* 2 Corinth. 9, 7: exprimitur ipsa oblatio dum dicitur: *suscipe sancta Trinitas:* petitur oblationis acceptatio per orationes secreto dictas, quia hoc sacerdotis tantum est Deum oblationibus placare: ad quam orationem sacerdos per humiliationem se praeparat dicens: *in spiritu humilitatis et in animo contrito suscipiamur a te Domine.* Et quia haec tria praedicta exigunt mentis erectionem ad Deum, ideo omnibus tribus praemittitur: *Dominus vobiscum,* loco cujus quando oratio secreta facienda est, dicitur: *orate fratres.*

Tertia pars secundae principalis partis, quae ad sacramenti perceptionem pertinet, tria continet. Primo praeparationem; secundo sacramenti perfectionem, ibi: *te igitur* etc., tertio sacramenti sumptionem, ibi: *oremus. Praeceptis salutaribus moniti, et divina institutione formati audemus dicere.* Praeparatio autem populi et ministrorum et sacerdotis ad tantum sacramentum fit per devotam Dei laudem; unde in praefatione, in qua fit dicta praeparatio, tria continentur. Primo populi excitatio ad laudem, ubi sacerdos praemisso *Dominus vobiscum,* quod ad totam hanc tertiam partem referendum est, inducit ad mentis erectionem, dicens: *sursum corda,* et ad gratiarum actionem, dicens: *gratias agamus Domino Deo nostro.* Secundo Deum implorat ad

laudem suscipiendum, ostendens laudis debitum, dicens: *vere dignum,* ratione Dominii (unde subdit: *Domine sancte); justum* ratione paternitatis (unde subdit: *pater omnipotens); aequum,* ratione deitatis (unde subdit: *aeterne Deus); salutare,* ratione redemptionis (unde subdit: *per Christum Dominum nostrum*). Quando-

virtues, which is suggested by the Gradual, for it is named from the step by which one ascends from one virtue to another, or from the steps of the altar before which it is said; and the exultation possessed from the hope of eternal things, which the *Alleluia* suggests; this is also why it is repeated, because of the stole of the soul and body. But on days and in offices of mourning it is omitted, and a Tract is put in its place, which by the harshness of voices and the long duration of the words suggests our residence in this present misery. However, during Eastertide, two alleluias are said because of the joy of the Resurrection of the head and of the members. But the effect of Gospel teaching is the confession of faith, and since this is above reason, the Creed is begun by the priest and completed by the choir, nor is it said except on those solemnities that are mentioned in the Creed, like the Nativity, the Resurrection, and the feasts of the Apostles, who stood out as founders of the faith, as it says: *like a skilled architect I have laid the foundation* (1 Cor 3:10).

Next comes the second part of the second main part, which pertains to the offering of the matter to be consecrated; and this contains three things. For the exultation of the ones offering is stated first as preparatory, in the Offertory, for *God loves a cheerful giver* (2 Cor 9:7). The offering itself is expressed when it is said, *Receive, O Holy Trinity;* the acceptance of the offering is sought by prayers silently spoken, for it belongs to the priest alone to appease God by these offerings. The priest prepares himself for this prayer through humiliation, saying: *humbled in spirit and contrite of heart may we find favor with you, O Lord.* And since these three things named require that the mind be raised to God, this is why before all three is said, *The Lord be with you* (but in place of this he says *Pray brethren* when the prayer is to be said silently).

The third part of the second main part, which pertains to the sacrament's reception, contains three things. First, preparation; second, the sacrament's completion, at: *Therefore, we humbly pray and beseech you, most merciful Father,* etc.; third, the consuming of the sacrament, at: *Let us pray. At the Savior's command and formed by divine institution, we dare to say.* Now, the preparation of the people, ministers, and priest for such a great sacrament is done by devout praise of God; therefore in the Preface, in which the preparation mentioned happens, three things are contained. First, the people's arousal to praise, where the priest, having said *the Lord be with you,* which is to be referred to this entire third part, invites them to raise their minds, saying, *Lift up your hearts,* and to thanksgiving, saying, *Let us give thanks to the Lord our God.* Second, he implores God to receive our praise, showing that praise is due, saying: *Truly it is worthy,* by reason of his dominion (hence he adds, *Holy Lord*), *and just,* because of his fatherhood (hence he adds: *all-powerful Father*); *right,* because of his deity (hence he adds, eternal God); *and for our salvation,* because of our

que vero adjungitur aliqua alia laudis materia secundum congruentiam solemnitatis, sicut: *et te in assumptione Beatae Mariae semper Virginis collaudare*; etiam proponens laudis exemplum: *per quem majestatem tuam laudant angeli*. Tertio populus laudes exsolvit divinitatis, assumens angelorum verba: *sanctus, sanctus, sanctus Dominus Deus exercituum*, Isa. 6, 3, et humanitatis Christi, assumens verba puerorum, Matth. 21, 10: *benedictus qui venit in nomine Domini*.

Illa autem pars quae perfectionem sacramenti continet, in tres dividitur, secundum tria quae sunt de integritate hujus sacramenti: scilicet aliquid quod est sacramentum tantum; aliquid quod est res et sacramentum; aliquid quod est res tantum. In prima ergo parte continetur benedictio oblatae materiae, quae est tantum sacramentum; in secunda corporis et sanguinis Christi consecratio, quod est res et sacramentum, ibi: *quam oblationem*; in tertia, effectus sacramenti postulatio quod est res tantum, ibi: *supra quae propitio ac sereno vultu respicere digneris*. Circa primum duo facit sacerdos: primo petit oblationis benedictionem, quae dicitur *donum* a Deo nobis datum, *munus* Deo a nobis oblatum, *sacrificium* ad nostram salutem a Deo sanctificatum; secundo petit *offerentibus*, sive pro quibus offertur, salutem, ibi: *in primis quae tibi offerimus*, etc.

Ubi tria facit: primo commemorat eos pro quorum utilitate offertur hostia tam quantum ad generalem statum ecclesiae, quam quantum ad personas speciales, ibi: *memento*; secundo commemorat eos in quorum offertur reverentia, ibi: *communicantes*; et ponitur Virgo quae Christum in templo obtulit, apostoli qui ritum offerendi nobis tradiderunt, et martyres qui seipsos Deo obtulerunt, non autem confessores, quia de eis antiquitus non solemnizabat ecclesia, vel quia non sunt passi sicut Christus, cujus passionis memoriale est hoc sacramentum: tertio concluditur expresse quid per oblationem hostiae impetrandum petatur, ibi: *hanc igitur oblationem*, etc.

Quam oblationem, etc. Haec pars ad consecrationem pertinet, quae tria continet: primo imploratur consecrantis virtus; secundo perficitur consecratio, ibi: *qui pridie quam pateretur, accepit panem*; tertio exponitur rei consecratae commemoratio, ibi: *unde et memores*, etc. Verba autem illa quae ibi dicuntur: *benedictam, adscriptam, ratam, rationabilem, acceptabilemque*, possunt referri uno modo ad hoc quod est res contenta in hoc sacramento, scilicet Christum, qui est hostia benedicta ab omni macula peccati immunis; adscripta, idest praefigurata figuris veteris testamenti, et praedestinatione divina praeordinata; rata, quia non transitoria; rationabilis,

redemption (hence he adds: *through Christ our Lord*). But sometimes there is added some other matter of praise appropriate to the solemnity, such as, *and to praise you in the assumption of Blessed Mary, ever Virgin*; also setting forth an example of praise, *through whom the angels praise your majesty*. Third, the people offer up praises of the divinity, taking up the words of the angels: *Holy, Holy, Holy, Lord God of hosts* (Isa 6:3); and of Christ's humanity, taking up the words of the children: *blessed is he who comes in the name of the Lord* (Matt 21:9).

Now the part that contains the sacrament's completion is divided in three, according to the three things that are integral to this sacrament: namely, what is the sacrament alone, what is the reality-and-sacrament, and what is the reality alone. In the first part, therefore, is contained the blessing of the matter offered, which is the sacrament alone; in the second part, the consecration of the body and blood of Christ, which is the reality-and-sacrament, at: *bless and approve this our offering*; in the third, the request of the sacrament's effect, which is the reality alone, at: *vouchsafe to look upon them with a gracious and tranquil countenance*. Concerning the first, the priest does two things: first, he asks a blessing on the offering, which is called a *gift* as given to us by God, a *present* as something offered to God by us, and a *sacrifice* as something sanctified by God for our salvation. Second, he asks salvation for the ones offering it, or for whom it is offered, at: *which we offer up to you in the first place*, etc.

There he does three things. First, he commemorates those for whose benefit the victim is offered: for the general state of the Church, as well as for particular persons, at: *Remember your servants*. Second, he commemorates those in whose reverence it is offered, at: *in union with the whole church*, and there is included the Virgin who offered Christ in the temple, the Apostles who handed down this rite of offering to us, and the martyrs who offered themselves to God, but not confessors, because in ancient times the Church did not invoke them in solemnizing, or because they did not suffer like Christ, whose Passion this sacrament is the memorial of. Third, what is sought to be obtained by the offering of this victim is expressly concluded, at: *accept this offering*, etc.

Bless and approve this our offering, etc. This part belongs to the consecration, which contains three things: first, the power of consecrating is implored; second, the consecration is completed, at: *who the day before he suffered, took the bread*; third, the commemoration of the thing consecrated is explained, at: *wherefore, calling to mind* etc. However, the words that are said here: *bless, consecrate, and approve this our offering, making it reasonable and acceptable*, can be referred in one way to what is the reality contained in this sacrament, namely, Christ, who is the *blessed* victim free from any stain of sin; *written down*, i.e., prefigured by the figures of the Old Testament, and by divine predesti-

propter congruitatem ad placandum; acceptabilis, propter efficaciam. Alio modo possunt referri ad ipsam hostiam, quae est sacramentum tantum; quam petit fieri *benedictam*, ut Deus eam consecret; sed ut confirmet quantum ad memoriam: *adscriptam*; quantum ad propositum immobile: *ratam*; ut eam acceptet: *rationabilem*, quantum ad judicium rationis; *acceptabilem*, quantum ad beneplacitum voluntatis. Tertio modo possunt referri ad effectum; unde dicit, *benedictam*, per quam benedicimur; *adscriptam*, per quam in caelis ascribamur; *ratam*, per quam in membris Christi censeamur; *rationabilem*, per quam a bestiali sensu eruamur; *acceptabilem*, per quam Deo accepti simus.

Supra quae propitio ac sereno vultu respicere digneris. Hic petit sacerdos sacramenti effectum; et primo effectum gratiae; secundo effectum gloriae, ibi: *memento etiam Domine famulorum famularumque tuarum.* Circa primum duo facit: primo petit acceptari sacramentum, quod est gratiae causa; secundo petit dari gratiae donum, ibi: *supplices te rogamus*; cujus expositio infra, dist. 13, ponetur. Effectum autem gloriae primo petit jam mortuis, ibi, *memento*, secundo adhuc vivis, ibi: *nobis quoque peccatoribus.* Completur autem canon Missae more aliarum orationum in Christo, ibi: *per Christum Dominum nostrum*, per quem hoc sacramentum originem habet et quantum ad substantiam; unde dicit, *creas* propter esse naturae; *sanctificas*, propter esse sacramenti: et quantum ad virtutem; unde dicit, *vivificas*, propter effectum gratiae, quae est vita animae; *benedicis*, propter gratiae augmentum; et quantum ad operationem, sive usum; unde dicit: *et praestas nobis.*

Oremus. Praeceptis salutaribus moniti, et divina institutione formati audemus dicere. Hic ponitur sacramenti perceptio, ad quam praemittitur praeparatio communis et specialis. Communis triplex: primo enim ponitur sacramenti petitio in oratione Dominica, in qua dicitur: *panem nostrum quotidianum da nobis hodie*; secundo percipientium expiatio per orationem sacerdotis: *libera nos*; tertio pacis adimpletio, ibi: *pax Domini.* Hoc enim sacramentum est sanctitatis et pacis; et quia pax Christi exsuperat omnem sensum, ideo pacis petitio a sacerdote inchoatur, cum dicit *pax Domini*, et a choro completur, cum dicitur, *agnus Dei*; et sic tria a sacerdote incepta prosequitur, scilicet, *gloria in excelsis*, quod pertinet ad spem; *credo in unum Deum*, quod pertinet ad fidem; *pax Domini*, quod pertinet ad caritatem. Petit autem populus misericordiam quantum ad amotionem mali contra miseriam culpae et poenae, et pacem quantum ad consecutionem omnis boni; unde ter *agnus Dei*, dicitur. Praeparatio autem specialis sacerdotis sumentis fit per ora-

nation foreordained; *approved*, because not transitory; *reasonable*, because of its suitability for appeasing; *acceptable*, because of its efficacy. In another way it can be referred to the host itself, which is the sacrament only; which he asks to be *blessed*, that God consecrate it; but that he confirm it as regards memory, *approved*, and as regards a fixed purpose, *ratified*; that he may accept it, *reasonable*, as regards the judgment of reason; *acceptable*, as regards something pleasing to the will. In a third way, it can be referred to the effect, hence he says, *blessed*, by which we are blessed; *approved*, by which we may be enrolled in heaven; *ratified*, by which we may be counted among Christ's members; *reasonable*, by which we may be torn from all beastly sensuality; *acceptable*, by which we may be accepted by God.

Vouchsafe to look upon them with a gracious and tranquil countenance. Here the priest asks for the effect of the sacrament; and first the effect of grace; second, the effect of glory, at: *remember also your servants, Lord.* Concerning the first he does two things: first, he asks that the sacrament be received, which is the cause of grace; second, he asks that the gift of grace be given, at: *we humbly pray and beseech you*, the exposition of which will be given further on, at Distinction 13. However, he first asks the effect of glory for those already dead, at: *remember*; second, for those still living, at: *for us, though sinners.* However, the canon of the Mass is completed by the custom of other prayers in Christ, at: *through Christ our Lord*, through whom this sacrament has its origin, both as to its substance, hence he says, *you create*, because of the natural being; *you sanctify*, because of the sacrament's being; and as to its power, hence he says, *you give life*, because of the effect of grace, which is the life of the soul; *you bless*, because of the increase of grace; and as to its operation, or use, hence he says: *and bestow on us.*

Let us pray. At the Savior's command and formed by divine institution, we dare to say. Here the reception of the sacrament is set down, before which is the general and specific preparation. The general preparation has three parts: for first the sacrament's petition is set down in the Lord's Prayer, in which is said, *give us this day our daily bread*; second, the expiation of those receiving through the prayer of the priest: *deliver us, Lord, from all evil*; third, the fulfillment of peace, at, *the peace of the Lord be with you.* For this is the sacrament of holiness and peace; and since the peace of Christ exceeds all the senses, for this reason the petition of peace is begun by the priest, when he says, *the peace of the Lord be with you*, and it is completed by the choir, when it says, *Lamb of God.* And in this way it finishes three things begun by the priest, namely, *Glory to God in the highest*, which pertains to hope; *I believe in one God*, which pertains to faith; and *the peace of the Lord be with you*, which pertains to charity. Now the people ask mercy in the removal of evil against the wretchedness of fault and punish-

tiones quas privatim dicit, *Domine Jesu Christe*, et si quae aliae sunt.

Tertia pars principalis est gratiarum actionis; et continet duo: rememorationem accepti beneficii in cantu antiphonae post communionem, et gratiarum actionem in oratione, quam sacerdos prosequitur, ut conformiter finis Missae principio respondeat.

Sciendum autem, quod in officio Missae, ubi passio repraesentatur, quaedam continentur verba Graeca, sicut, *kyrie eleison*, idest Domine miserere: quaedam Hebraica, sicut *alleluja*, idest laudate Deum; *Sabaoth*, idest exercituum; *hosanna*, salva obsecro; *amen*, idest vere, vel fiat: quaedam Latina, quae patent: quia his tribus linguis scriptus est titulus crucis Christi, Joan. 19.

ment, and peace, in the accomplishment of all good; and for this the *Lamb of God* is said three times. However, the special preparation of the priest before consuming happens through the prayers he says privately, *Lord, Jesus Christ*, and whatever others there are.

The third main part is the thanksgiving, and it contains two things: the calling to mind of the benefit received, in singing the antiphon after Communion, and thanksgiving in prayer, which the priest carries out, so that the end of the Mass might correspond in likeness to the beginning.

Now it should be known that in the office of the Mass, where the Passion is represented, certain Greek words are contained, like *kyrie eleison*, i.e., Lord have mercy; and certain Hebrew words, like *alleluia*, i.e., praise God; *Sabaoth*, i.e., of hosts; *hosanna*, save I beg; *amen*, i.e., truly, or so be it; and certain Latin ones, which are evident. For the placard over the Cross of Christ was written in these three languages (Jn 19:20).

DISTINCTION 9
RECEPTION OF THE EUCHARIST

Postquam determinavit Magister de sacramento Eucharistiae secundum se, hic determinat de usu ipsius; et dividitur in partes tres: in prima distinguit duos modos manducandi corpus Christi; in secunda excludit ex determinatis quemdam errorem, ibi: *haec verba et alia hujusmodi . . . quidam obtuso corde legentes, erroris caligine involuti sunt*; in tertia manifestat quaedam dubia ex praedeterminatis, ibi: *secundum hos duos modos sumendi intelligentia quorumdam verborum ambigue dictorum distinguenda est.* Secunda dividitur in duas: in prima ponit errorem; in secunda excludit ipsum, ibi: *sed indubitanter tenendum est, a bonis sumi non modo sacramentaliter, sed et spiritualiter.*

After the Master has considered the sacrament of the Eucharist in itself, here he considers its use; and this is divided into three parts: in the first, he distinguishes two modes of eating the body of Christ; in the second, he excludes a certain error from the considerations, at: *These words and others like them . . . have enveloped in the darkness of error some people who read them with an obtuse heart;*[1] in the third, he shows clarifies doubts from what had already been considered, at: *In accordance with these two modes of receiving, we need to distinguish the meaning of some words which have been used ambiguously.*[2] The second is divided into two parts: in the first, he sets down the error; in the second, he excludes it, at: *But without a doubt it is to be held that they are received by the good not only sacramentally, but also spiritually.*[3]

---

1. Peter Lombard, *Sententiae* IV, 9.2 (56), 1.
2. *Sent.* IV, 9.3 (57), 1.
3. *Sent.* IV, 9.3 (56), 1.

QUESTION 1

HOLY COMMUNION

Hic quaeruntur quinque:	Here five questions arise:
primo, de manducatione corporis Christi;	first, about eating the body of Christ;
secundo, qui possint manducare;	second, who may eat of it;
tertio, utrum peccatoribus liceat corpus Christi manducare;	third, whether sinners are permitted to eat the body of Christ;
quarto, utrum corporaliter pollutis;	fourth, whether those who are bodily impure may eat of it;
quinto, utrum cuilibet sit dandum ad manducandum.	fifth, whether it may be given to anyone to eat.

ARTICLE 1

About eating the body of Christ

Quaestiuncula 1

AD PRIMUM SIC PROCEDITUR. Videtur quod corpus Christi non debeat sumi per modum manducationis. Quia quod manducatur, per os intrat. Omne autem quod *per os intrat, in ventrem vadit, et per secessum emittitur,* ut dicitur Matth. 15; quod dignitati corporis Christi non competit. Ergo non debet per modum manducationis sumi.

PRAETEREA, quod manducatur, ad manducantem trahitur. Sed, sicut dicit Dionysius, nos non trahimus Deum ad nos, sed magis nos in Deum. Ergo non debemus Deo conjungi per modum manducationis.

PRAETEREA, hoc sacramentum ordinatur ad refectionem mentis. Sed refectio mentis, quae erit in patria, erit per visionem. Ergo corpus Christi deberet dari videndum, non manducandum.

SED CONTRA, est quod dicitur Joan. 6, 56: *caro mea vere est cibus.* Sed usus cibi non est ut videatur, sed ut manducetur. Ergo non debet videri tantum corpus Christi, sed manducari.

PRAETEREA, oportet membra capiti realiter conjungi, ad hoc quod vivificentur. Sed per visum non conjungitur nobis aliquid realiter, sed secundum similitudinem tantum. Ergo non per visum, sed per manducationem corpus Christi sumi debet.

OBJ. 1: To the first we proceed thus. It seems that the body of Christ should not be received by way of eating. For whatever is eaten enters through the mouth. But everything that *enters through the mouth goes into the stomach and is expelled into the sewer* (Matt 15:17), which is unbecoming to the dignity of the body of Christ. Therefore, it should not be received by way of eating.

OBJ. 2: Futhermore, whatever is eaten is drawn into the eater. But as Dionysius says, we do not draw God into us, but rather we are drawn into God.[4] Therefore, we should not be united to God by way of eating.

OBJ. 3: Furthermore, this sacrament is ordered to the renewal of the mind. But the renewal of the mind that will be in the fatherland will be through vision. Therefore, the body of Christ should be given for seeing, not for eating.

ON THE CONTRARY, it is said, *my flesh is true food* (Jn 6:56). But the use of food is not that it be seen, but that it be eaten. Therefore, the body of Christ should not only be seen, but eaten.

FURTHERMORE, it is necessary for the members to be united with the head in reality, for them to be kept alive. But by vision nothing is joined to us in reality, but only according to a likeness. Therefore, the body of Christ should be consumed not by vision but by eating.

---

4. Pseudo-Dionysius, *On the Divine Names*, ch. 4 (PG 3:693).

Quaestiuncula 2

ULTERIUS. Videtur quod manducatio corporis Christi sit de necessitate salutis. Sicut enim dicitur de baptismo, Joan. 3, 5: *nisi quis renatus fuerit ex aqua et Spiritu Sancto, non potest intrare in regnum caelorum*; ita dictum est Joan. 6, 54: *nisi manducaveritis carnem filii hominis, et biberitis ejus sanguinem, non habebitis vitam in vobis*. Sed propter verba praedicta dicitur baptismus sacramentum necessitatis. Ergo eadem ratione manducatio corporis Christi est de necessitate salutis.

PRAETEREA, Innocentius III dicit, quod *manducandus est agnus, ut a vastante angelo protegamur*. Sed protegi a vastante angelo est de necessitate salutis. Ergo et praedicta manducatio.

PRAETEREA, per istam manducationem Christo incorporamur. Sed hoc est de necessitate salutis, sicut et a peccato mundari. Ergo praedicta manducatio est de necessitate salutis, sicut et poenitentia et baptismus, quibus a peccatis mundamur.

SED CONTRA, pueri baptizati salutem consequuntur, cum gratia in baptismo detur. Sed eis non datur corpus Christi manducandum. Ergo manducatio praedicta non est de necessitate salutis.

PRAETEREA, baptismi ministerium propter hoc quod est de necessitate salutis, omnibus est concessum in casu necessitatis. Sed hoc sacramentum per solos sacerdotes perfici potest. Ergo non est sacramentum necessitatis.

OBJ. 1: Moreover, it seems that eating the body of Christ is necessary to salvation. For as it is said of baptism, *unless you are born again of water and the Holy Spirit, you cannot enter the kingdom of heaven* (John 3:5); so also it is said, *unless you eat the flesh of the Son of Man, and drink his blood, you will not have life in you* (John 6:54). But because of the words mentioned baptism is called a sacrament of necessity. Therefore, by the same reasoning eating the body of Christ is necessary to salvation.

OBJ. 2: Furthermore, Innocent III says that *the lamb must be eaten, so that we may be protected from the destroying angel*.[5] But to be protected from a ravaging angel is necessary to salvation. Therefore, so is this eating.

OBJ. 3: Furthermore, we are incorporated into Christ by this eating. But this is necessary to salvation, as is also being cleansed from sin. Therefore, eating this is necessary to salvation, just as also penance and baptism, by which we are cleansed from sin.

ON THE CONTRARY, baptized infants obtain salvation, since grace is given in baptism. But they are not given the body of Christ to eat. Therefore, this eating is not necessary to salvation.

FURTHERMORE, it is granted to anyone to administer baptism in case of necessity, because of the fact that it is necessary for salvation. But this sacrament can be accomplished by priests alone. Therefore, it is not a sacrament of necessity.

Quaestiuncula 3

ULTERIUS. Videtur quod male distinguantur duo modi manducationis in littera. Corpus enim Christi est cibus spiritualis. Sed cibi corporalis manducatio semper est corporalis. Ergo et hujus cibi manducatio semper est spiritualis; et ita non sunt duo modi manducationis.

PRAETEREA, in aliis sacramentis non attenditur aliqua distinctio nisi ex parte recipientis tantum, sicut quod quidam accedunt ficti, quidam non. Sed haec distinctio videtur esse ex parte ipsius sacramenti. Ergo inconvenienter ponitur.

PRAETEREA, ubi unum propter alterum, ibi unum tantum. Sed manducatio sacramentalis est propter spiritualem. Ergo una non debet contra alteram distingui.

SED CONTRA, videtur quod sint plures modi. Quia usus hujus sacramenti dicitur manducatio. Sed in hoc sacramento sunt tria; scilicet id quod est sacramentum

OBJ. 1: Moreover, it seems that the two modes of eating are poorly distinguished in the text.[6] For the body of Christ is spiritual food. But eating bodily food is always bodily. Therefore, eating this food is also always spiritual, and so there are not two modes of eating it.

OBJ. 2: Furthermore, in the other sacraments no distinction is found except on the part of the receiver alone, like the fact that some people receive them under false pretenses, while others do not. But this distinction seems to be on the part of the sacrament itself. Therefore, it is unfittingly set down.

OBJ. 3: Furthermore, where one thing exists for the sake of another, there is only one thing. But sacramental eating is for the sake of the spiritual. Therefore, one kind of eating should not be distinguished from the other.

ON THE CONTRARY, it seems that there are more modes. For the use of this sacrament is said to be eating. But in this sacrament there are three things, namely, what

---

5. Innocent III, *De sacro altaris mysterio*, Bk. 4, ch. 42 (PL 217:883).
6. Parallels: *ST* III, q. 80, a. 1; *De ven. sacram. altar.*, serm. 17; *Super Ioan.* 6, lec. 6 & 7; *Super I ad Cor.* 11, lec. 7.

tantum, et id quod est res et sacramentum, et id quod est res tantum. Ergo debent esse tres modi manducationis.

PRAETEREA, in baptismo etiam fit trimembris divisio suscipientium: quidam enim suscipiunt rem et sacramentum; quidam sacramentum et non rem; quidam rem, et non sacramentum. Sed susceptio hujus sacramenti dicitur manducatio. Ergo hic etiam debet distingui triplex modus manducandi.

is sacrament alone, and what is reality-and-sacrament, and what is reality alone. Therefore, there should be three kinds of eating.

FURTHERMORE, those who receive baptism also fall into three categories of recipients: for some receive the reality-and-sacrament; some receive the sacrament and not the ality; and some receive the reality, but not the sacrament. But the reception of this sacrament is called eating. Therefore, this too should be distinguished into three kinds of eating.

Response to Quaestiuncula 1

RESPONDEO dicendum ad primam quaestionem, quod, sicut supra dictum est, ad perfectionem sacramentorum novae legis exigitur quod sit sacramentum aliquod in quo Christus nobis realiter conjungatur et uniatur, non solum per participationem virtutis ejus, sicut est in aliis sacramentis; et quia sacramentum est sensibile signum, ideo oportet quod alicui sensui usus sacramenti approprietur. In sensibilibus autem est triplex differentia. Quaedam enim sentientibus neque conjunguntur neque uniuntur, sicut ea quae sentiuntur per medium extrinsecum, ut in visu praecipue accidit et auditu et olfactu, sed solum similitudines sensibilium ad sensum referuntur. Quaedam autem sensibilia conjunguntur quidem, sed non uniuntur realiter, sed secundum assimilationem qualitatis tantum, sicut accidit in tactu: quia qualitates tangibilium immutant tactum; nec tamen ex tangente et tacto fit unum nisi secundum quid. Quaedam autem et conjunguntur et uniuntur, sicut accidit in cibis et potibus. Et ideo sumptio hujus sacramenti congrue per modum manducationis fit. Alia vero sacramenta novae legis, quibus per virtutem eis inditam Christo similamur, fiunt in tangendo tantum, ut baptismus. Figurae autem veteris testamenti quae solam similitudinem Christi venturi habebant, significabant per modum visionis. Competit etiam manducatio passioni Christi in hoc sacramento repraesentatae, per quam corpus Christi vulneratum fuit; convenit etiam effectui, qui est robur animae.

AD PRIMUM ergo dicendum, quod ratio illa procedit de cibo qui ordinatur ad refectionem corporis quem oportet digeri, et sic impuro separato in membra converti; sed cibus iste ordinatur ad refectionem mentis: et propter hoc ratio non sequitur.

AD SECUNDUM dicendum, quod de ratione manducationis est quod aliquid per os introrsum sumatur; sed esse in aliter in spiritualibus, et aliter in corporalibus su-

TO THE FIRST QUESTION, I answer that, as was said above,[7] for the completion of sacraments of the New Law it is required that there be a certain sacrament in which Christ is really joined and united to us, not only by participation in his power, as it is in the other sacraments; and since a sacrament is a sensible sign, therefore the use of the sacrament must be adapted to a certain sense. However, there are three differences among sensible things. For some things are neither joined nor united to the senses, like those that are sensed through an external medium, as happens in sight especially, as well as hearing and smell, where only likenesses of the sensible objects are brought to the senses. However, certain sensible objects are indeed joined, but not united in reality, but only according to the likeness of a certain quality, as happens in touch: for the qualities of tangible things change what is touched; nor, however, are the toucher and the touched made one except under a certain aspect. But some things are both joined and united, as happens in food and drink. And so the reception of this sacrament happens fittingly by way of eating. But the other sacraments of the New Law, by which we are likened to Christ through the power he bestowed on them, happen only by touching, like baptism. However, the figures of the Old Testament that had only a resemblance to the Christ who was to come were represented by the mode of vision. Eating also befits this sacrament in its representation of Christ's Passion, by which the body of Christ was wounded; and it also suits the effect, which is the fortification of the soul.

REPLY OBJ. 1: That argument proceeds from the food that is ordered to the renewal of the body, which must be digested so it may be converted into the members once the impure has been separated from it; but this food is ordered to the renewal of the mind, and because of this the argument does not follow.

REPLY OBJ. 2: The nature of eating is that something is consumed internally through the mouth, but 'being in' is taken one way in spiritual things, and another way in bod-

---

7. See d. 8, q. 1, a. 1, qa. 1.

mitur: quia in corporalibus quod est in, continetur sicut locatum in loco; in spiritualibus autem quod est in continet sicut anima corpus. Et ideo convenienter cibus corporis trahitur ad corpus, ut contentum ad continens: cibus autem mentis trahit ad se mentem, ut continens contentum: propter quod Augustinus dicit sibi dictum: *non tu me mutabis in te, sicut cibum carnis tuae; sed tu mutaberis in me.*

AD TERTIUM dicendum, quod res visa beatificans per essentiam suam videnti conjungetur in patria; quod quidem non accidit in visione corporali. Et quia oportebat hanc conjunctionem significari per aliquod sensibile signum, oportuit illud sensibile ad hoc assumi quod realiter conjungatur et uniatur. In patria autem signis sacramentalibus opus non erit; nihilominus propter similitudinem ad ea quae nunc geruntur, frequenter illa beata visio nobis per figuram manducationis in Scriptura exprimitur.

ily things: for in bodily things, what is 'in' is contained, like something in a place; but in spiritual things what is 'in' contains, as the soul contains the body. And so food is properly drawn into a body, as something contained into the container: but the food of the mind draws the mind into itself, as a container draws its contents: because of which Augustine speaks this as said to himself: *you will not change me into you, like the food of your flesh, but you will be changed into me.*[8]

REPLY OBJ. 3: The reality that, once seen, beatifies by its very essence is joined to the one seeing in the fatherland; which certainly does not happen in physical vision. And since this union had to be signified by some sensible sign, that sensible object had to be assumed in such a way that it is joined and united in reality. In the fatherland, however, sacramental signs will not be needed; nevertheless, because of a resemblance to those the activities we carry on in this life, that beatific vision is often expressed to us in Scripture by the figure of eating.

Response to Quaestiuncula 2

AD SECUNDAM QUAESTIONEM dicendum, quod gratia est sufficiens causa gloriae; unde omne illud sine quo potest haberi gratia, non est de necessitate salutis. Hoc autem sacramentum gratiam praesupponit, quia praesupponit baptismum, in quo gratia datur: nec debet peccato praeveniri, quod gratiam privet; et ideo quantum est de se, non est de necessitate salutis. Sed de ordinatione ecclesiae homines obligantur secundum ecclesiae statutum corpus Christi semel in anno sumere.

AD PRIMUM ergo dicendum, quod Dominus loquitur de manducatione spirituali sine qua non potest esse salus.

AD SECUNDUM dicendum, quod Innocentius loquitur quantum ad instructionem ecclesiae, vel etiam quantum ad manducationem spiritualem.

AD TERTIUM dicendum, quod incorporatio spiritualis ad Christum potest esse sine manducatione sacramentali; et ideo non oportet quod sit sacramenti susceptio de necessitate salutis.

TO THE SECOND QUESTION, it should be said that grace is a sufficient cause of glory; hence anything that grace can be had without is not necessary to salvation. But this sacrament presupposes grace, for it presupposes baptism, in which grace is given, nor should it be preceded by sin, which deprives us of grace; and so in itself it is not necessary to salvation. But by the Church's ordination, people are obliged to receive the body of Christ once per year by Church law.

REPLY OBJ. 1: The Lord speaks of spiritual eating, without which there can be no salvation.

REPLY OBJ. 2: Innocent speaks as to the Church's instruction, or as to spiritual eating.

REPLY OBJ. 3: Spiritual incorporation in Christ can take place without sacramental eating; and so the reception of this sacrament need not be necessary to salvation.

Response to Quaestiuncula 3

AD TERTIAM QUAESTIONEM dicendum, quod divisio formalis alicujus sumitur penes id quod competit ei per se, et non per accidens. Usus autem alicujus rei per se et non per accidens, est quando utitur quis re aliqua ad hoc ad quod instituta est. Unde cum manducatio dicat usum hujus sacramenti, quod quidem ad hoc institutum

TO THE THIRD QUESTION, it should be said that the formal division of a thing is taken according to what applies to it *per se*, and not *per accidens*. But the use of any thing *per se* and not *per accidens* is when someone uses the thing for that for which it was instituted. Since eating is called the use of this sacrament, which was certainly instituted so that

---

8. Augustine, *Confessions* (CCSL 27), Bk. 7, ch. 10.

est ut quis re sacramenti potiatur; distinguetur manducatio secundum duas res hujus sacramenti: ut manducatio sacramentalis respondeat ei quod est res et sacramentum; manducatio vero spiritualis ei quod est res tantum.

Ad primum ergo dicendum, quod manducatio cibi corporalis non praesupponit aliam manducationem quae sit ejus causa sicut manducatio spiritualis praesupponit sacramentalem quasi causam. Unde in his qui sacramentaliter manducant, potest ex defectu manducantium impediri effectus sacramenti, qui est spiritualis manducatio; et ideo possunt haec manducationes ab invicem separari, et propter hoc oportet eas distinguere.

Ad secundum dicendum, quod perfectio aliorum sacramentorum in ipso usu consistit; et ideo eorum distinctio non potest nisi ex parte recipientium sumi: sed perfectio hujus sacramenti in ipsa materiae consecratione consistit; et ideo potest esse hic distinctio ex parte ipsius sacramenti.

Ad tertium dicendum, quod verbum illud intelligitur in his quae hoc modo ad se invicem ordinantur quod ab invicem separari non possunt; sicut quando talis effectus nunquam potest esse sine tali causa, nec e converso; et tunc etiam non excluditur diversitas rerum inter causam et causatum, sed ponitur necessitas ordinis.

Ad quartum dicendum, quod id quod est hic res et sacramentum, nunquam separatur ab eo quod est sacramentum tantum; et si separaretur usus ejus quod est sacramentum tantum, esset accidentalis usus; et ideo penes hoc non debet sumi aliquis modus manducationis specialis.

Ad quintum dicendum, quod hic etiam posset fieri talis distinctio. Quibusdam enim conjunguntur duae manducationes, et hi suscipiunt rem et sacramentum; et in quibusdam separantur, et hi suscipiunt vel rem tantum, vel sacramentum tantum. Sed quia haec divisio magis se tenet ex parte suscipientium quam ex parte sacramenti; ideo non est propria huic sacramento sicut baptismo.

a person might possess the reality behind the sacrament, therefore eating may be distinguished according to the two realities of this sacrament. And so sacramental eating corresponds to what is the reality-and-sacrament, but spiritual eating to what is the reality alone.[9]

Reply Obj. 1: Eating physical food does not presuppose any other eating that is its cause, as spiritual eating presupposes sacramental eating as its cause. For this reason, among those who eat sacramentally, the effect of the sacrament, which is spiritual eating, can be impeded by a defect in the ones eating. And so these two kinds of eating can be separated from each other, and because of this it is necessary to distinguish them.

Reply Obj. 2: The completion of the other sacraments consists in their very use, and so no distinction between them can be made except on the part of the recipients, but the completion of this sacrament consists in the matter's consecration itself, and so there can be a distinction here on the part of the sacrament itself.

Reply Obj. 3: That word is understood in those things that are ordered toward each other in such a way that they cannot be separated from each other, like when a certain effect can never exist without a certain cause, nor vice versa; and even in that case the real difference between cause and caused is not excluded, but it is placed in a necessary order.

Reply Obj. 4: What is reality-and-sacrament here is never separated from what is sacrament alone; and if the use of what is sacrament alone were separated, it would be an accidental use. And so no special mode of eating pertaining to such use need be established.

Reply Obj. 5: Here, too, a distinction like that could be made. For some people, the two kinds of eating are joined, and these people receive the reality and the sacrament; and in some people, they are separated, and these receive either the reality alone or the sacrament alone. But because this division has more to do with the ones receiving than with the sacrament, for this reason it is not proper to this sacrament as it is for baptism.

---

9. For more about the sacrament alone, reality alone, and sacrament-and-reality, see the footnote at Dist.1, q.1, a.4, qa. 1, main response.

ARTICLE 2

Who may eat of the body of Christ

Quaestiuncula 1

AD SECUNDUM SIC PROCEDITUR. Videtur quod peccator non manducet corpus Christi sacramentaliter. Quia, ut dicitur Sap. 1, 4, *in malevolam animam non introibit sapientia, nec habitabit in corpore subdito peccatis.* Sed Christus, qui est res contenta in hoc sacramento, est Dei sapientia, ut habetur 1 Corinth. 1. Ergo a peccatore sumi non potest.

PRAETEREA, cibus iste non vadit in ventrem, sed in mentem. Non autem vadit in mentem peccatoris. Ergo nullo modo corpus Christi sumit.

PRAETEREA, nihil indecens debet fieri a sapiente. Sed hoc est valde indecens quod corpus tam pretiosum in immundo corpore ponatur. Ergo cum corpus peccatoris sit immundum, non recipiet verum corpus Christi.

SED CONTRA, majus videtur consecrare corpus Christi quam sumere. Sed peccator potest consecrare. Ergo et sumere.

PRAETEREA, Christi corpus non est magis nobile sub sacramento quam in specie propria. Sed in specie propria permisit se a peccatoribus tractari. Ergo et sub specie sacramenti a peccatoribus manducari potest.

OBJ. 1: To the second we proceed thus. It seems that a sinner may not eat the body of Christ sacramentally.[10] For, as it says, *wisdom will not enter a deceitful soul, nor dwell in a body enslaved to sin* (Wis 1:4). But Christ, who is the reality contained in this sacrament, is the wisdom of God, as is maintained by 1 Corinthians 1:24. Therefore he cannot be received by a sinner.

OBJ. 2: Furthermore, this food does not enter the stomach but the mind. However, it does not enter the mind of a sinner. Therefore, in no way does he receive the body of Christ.

OBJ. 3: Furthermore, nothing indecent should be done by a wise man. But it is extremely indecent that a body so precious should be placed in a body so unclean. Therefore, since the body of a sinner is unclean, he will not receive the true body of Christ.

ON THE CONTRARY, it is a greater thing to consecrate the body of Christ than to consume it. But a sinner can consecrate. Therefore, he also can receive it.

FURTHERMORE, the body of Christ is not more noble under this sacrament than in its proper species. But in his proper species, he permitted himself to be handled by sinners. Therefore, also under the species of the sacrament he can be eaten by sinners.

Quaestiuncula 2

ULTERIUS. Videtur quod infideles sacramentaliter comedunt. Quia, sicut dicit Hugo de s. Victore, quamdiu sensus corporalis afficitur, praesentia carnis non tollitur. Sed sensus corporalis infidelis afficitur. Ergo praesentiam corporalem carnis Christi non amittit.

PRAETEREA, infidelis potest recipere characterem, qui est res et sacramentum, in baptismo. Sed fides operatur in baptismo sicut in Eucharistia. Ergo et corpus Christi sacramentaliter potest manducare.

PRAETEREA, plus est conficere corpus Christi quam sumere. Sed haereticus habens ordinem potest confice-

OBJ. 1: Moreover, it seems that unbelievers eat sacramentally.[11] For as Hugh of St. Victor says,[12] as long as bodily sense is affected, the presence of the flesh is not taken away. But the physical sense of an unbeliever is affected. Therefore, he does not lose the physical presence of the flesh.

OBJ. 2: Furthermore, an unbeliever can receive a character, which is the reality-and-sacrament in baptism. But faith works in baptism just as in the Eucharist. Therefore, he can also eat the body of Christ sacramentally.

OBJ. 3: Furthermore, it is a greater thing to consecrate the body of Christ than to consume it. But a heretic who

---

10. Parallels: *ST* III, q. 80, a. 3; *Super I ad Cor.* 11, lec. 7.
11. Parallels: *ST* III, q. 80, a. 3; *Super I ad Cor.* 11, lec. 7.
12. Hugh of St. Victor, *De sacramentis fidei*, Bk. 2, pt. 8, ch. 13 (PL 176:471).

re, ut infra dicetur. Ergo et potest sacramentaliter manducare.

SED CONTRA, in forma hujus sacramenti ponitur *mysterium fidei*. Ergo hi qui fide carent, sacramentaliter manducare non possunt.

PRAETEREA, de ratione sacramenti est quod significet et efficiat. Sed in eo qui non habet fidem non efficit aliquid, nec aliquid, ei signat. Ergo sacramentaliter non manducat.

has holy orders can consecrate, as will be said further on.[13] Therefore, he can also eat sacramentally.

ON THE CONTRARY, in the form of this sacrament is included *the mystery of faith*. Therefore, those who lack faith cannot eat sacramentally.

FURTHERMORE, it is in the definition of a sacrament that it signifies and effects. But in someone who does not have faith, it does not effect anything, nor does it represent anything to him. Therefore, he cannot eat it sacramentally.

Quaestiuncula 3

ULTERIUS. Videtur quod creatura irrationalis non sumat aliqualiter corpus Christi. Primo per hoc quod Magister infra dicit, quod hoc quod a brutis sumitur, non est corpus Christi.

PRAETEREA, hoc sacramentum est majoris perfectionis quam baptismus. Sed quantumcumque animal brutum aqua abluatur, non dicitur baptismi sacramentum percipere aliquo modo. Ergo neque sacramentum corporis Christi poterit aliquo modo percipere.

PRAETEREA, constat quod non percipit spiritualiter, quia non credit; neque sacramentaliter, quia sacramenta creaturae rationali sunt tradita. Si ergo aliquo modo sumat, erit tertius modus manducandi praeter duos in littera assignatos.

SED CONTRA, Deus magis abominatur peccatorem quam creaturam irrationalem, in qua non est nisi quod Deus in ea fecit, qui solum culpam non fecit. Sed, sicut in littera determinatur, corpus Christi verum a peccatoribus sumitur. Ergo et a brutis.

PRAETEREA, si corpus Christi per negligentiam vel quocumque modo in aliquem locum immundum projiciatur, non dicitur quod desinat esse sub speciebus corpus Christi. Ergo non oportet dici, quod sub speciebus a brutis comestis desinat esse corpus Christi. Sed species possunt a brutis manducari. Ergo et corpus Christi.

OBJ. 1: Moreover, it seems that an irrational creature may not receive the body of Christ in any way.[14] First, because of what the Master says below, namely that what is consumed by animals is not the body of Christ.

OBJ. 2: Furthermore, this sacrament is of greater perfection than baptism. But no matter how much a brute animal is washed with water, it is not said to receive the sacrament of baptism in any way. Therefore, neither could it receive the sacrament of the body of Christ in any way.

OBJ. 3: Furthermore, it is clear that it does not receive it spiritually, for it does not believe; nor sacramentally, since the sacraments are given to rational creation. If therefore it received in any way, it would be in a third way of eating besides those two that were assigned in the text.

ON THE CONTRARY, God abominates a sinner more than an irrational creature, in whom there is nothing but what God made, who alone does no wrong. But as is determined in the text, the body of Christ is consumed by sinners. Therefore, also by animals.

FURTHERMORE, if through negligence or carelessness the body of Christ were thrown out into some unclean place, it is not said that the body of Christ would cease to exist under these species. Therefore, it must not be said that if it were eaten by animals under these species, it would cease to be the body of Christ. But these species can be eaten by animals. Therefore, so can the body of Christ.

Quaestiuncula 4

ULTERIUS. Videtur quod qui non manducat sacramentaliter, non manducet spiritualiter. Sacramentalis enim manducatio est propter spiritualem. Si ergo spiritualis sine corporali haberi possit, frustra aliquis sacramentali uteretur.

PRAETEREA, spiritualis manducatio est per fidem et caritatem, per quae aliquis Christo incorporatur. Sed antiqui patres fidem et caritatem habuerunt. Ergo si spiri-

OBJ. 1: Moreover, it seems that whoever does not eat sacramentally does not eat spiritually.[15] For sacramental eating is for the sake of spiritual eating. If therefore spiritual eating can be had without physical, sacramental eating would serve no purpose.

OBJ. 2: Furthermore, spiritual eating takes place through faith and charity, by which one is incorporated into Christ. But the ancient fathers had faith and charity. There-

---

13. See d. 13, q. 1, a. 1, qa. 3.
14. Parallel: *ST* III, q. 80, a. 3.
15. Parallel: *ST* III, q. 80, a. 2.

tualis manducatio esse posset sine sacramentali, ipsi spiritualiter manducassent; quod non potest esse, quia usus sacramenti non potest esse ante ejus institutionem.

SED CONTRA, aliquis potest percipere rem baptismi sine sacramento, ut supra, dist. 4, dictum est. Sed baptismi sacramentum est majoris necessitatis quam hoc. Ergo potest etiam spiritualiter manducare quis sine sacramenti manducatione.

fore if spiritual eating could exist without sacramental eating, they would have eaten spiritually; which cannot be, since the sacrament's use cannot exist before its institution.

ON THE CONTRARY, someone can receive the reality of baptism without the sacrament, as was said above, in Distinction 4.[16] But the sacrament of baptism is of greater necessity than this one. Therefore, someone can also eat spiritually without eating of the sacrament.

Quaestiuncula 5

ULTERIUS. Videtur quod etiam angelus corpus Christi possit manducare spiritualiter: quia super illud, Psalm. 72, *panem angelorum manducavit homo*, dicit Glossa: *idest corpus Christi, qui est vere cibus angelorum.*

PRAETEREA, quicumque potest manducare sacramentaliter, potest etiam manducare spiritualiter. Sed angelus in carne assumpta potest manducare sacramentaliter. Ergo etiam sine corpore assumpto potest manducare spiritualiter.

SED CONTRA, manducare est usus sacramenti. Sed sacramenta non sunt data angelis ad usum, sed hominibus. Ergo angeli non possunt spiritualiter manducare.

OBJ. 1: Moreover, it seems that even an angel can eat the body of Christ spiritually.[17] For commenting on the psalm, *man ate the bread of angels* (Ps 78 [72]:25), the Gloss says, *that is, the body of Christ, which is the true food of angels.*[18]

OBJ. 2: Furthermore, whoever can eat sacramentally can also eat spiritually. But an angel who has assumed flesh can eat sacramentally. Therefore also, without assuming flesh, it can eat spiritually.

ON THE CONTRARY, eating is the use of the sacrament. But sacraments are not given to angels to use, but to men. Therefore, the angels cannot eat spiritually.

Response to Quaestiuncula 1

RESPONDEO dicendum ad primam quaestionem, quod quidam dixerunt corpus Christi secundum rei veritatem a peccatoribus non sumi: quia quam cito labiis peccatoris tangebatur, desinebat sub speciebus esse corpus Christi: intantum dignitati sacramenti deferentes quod derogabant veritati. Si enim vere corpus Christi sub speciebus erat per conversionem panis et vini in substantiam corporis Christi, speciebus remanentibus, non poterit esse quod desinat ibi esse corpus Christi, nisi per aliquam contrariam mutationem ejus quod prius convertebatur in corpus Christi. Et quia de illo non manent nisi species solae, quae ad utramque substantiam communiter se habent, sicut subjectum in naturalibus mutationibus duabus formis; ideo quamdiu species non mutantur, nullo modo desinit ibi esse corpus Christi; sicut nec in mutationibus formalibus forma introducta desinit esse in subjecto, donec subjectum ad formam aliam transmutetur. Speciebus autem in aliquid transmutari non competit nisi secundum quod habent aliquam proprietatem substantiae in hoc quod sunt sine subjecto; unde nihil potest eas transmutare ad aliam substantiam, nisi quod transmutaret substantiam panis et vini, si ibi

TO THE FIRST QUESTION, I answer that some people said the body of Christ was not received by sinners according to the truth of reality, for as soon as it was touched by the lips of sinners, it would cease to be the body of Christ under those appearances: deferring so much to the dignity of the sacrament that they detracted from its truth. For if indeed the body of Christ under the appearances was by the conversion of bread and wine into the substance of the body of Christ, with the appearances remaining, it could not cease to be the body of Christ except by a certain contrary change of what before was converted into the body of Christ. And because nothing of that remains except the appearances alone, which are related in common to both substances, as a subject in natural changes is related to both forms, therefore as long as the appearances do not change, in no way does the body of Christ cease to be there, just as neither in formal changes does the form introduced cease to be in the subject, until the subject is transformed into another form. However, it does not belong to the appearances to be changed into something except according as they have a certain property of substance in the fact that they are without a subject; hence nothing can change them

---

16. See d. 4, q. 3, a. 3.
17. Parallel: *ST* III, q. 80, a. 2.
18. See the *Glossa ordinaria*, PL 113:969.

esset; quod solus tactus labiorum, vel divisio quae est per dentes, vel trajectio in ventrem non faceret, sed sola digestio, quae est a calore naturali convertente cibum. Unde patet quod veritati sacramenti derogat qui dicit, quod ad solum tactum labiorum desinit esse corpus Christi a peccatore sumptum. Et ideo hac opinione tamquam haeretica de medio sublata, ejus contrarium ab omnibus tenetur.

AD PRIMUM ergo dicendum, quod auctoritas illa loquitur de spirituali inhabitatione, et non de sacramentali vel corporali: quia Christus etiam peccatoribus corpus suum tractandum exhibuit.

AD SECUNDUM dicendum, quod cum dicitur, *cibus iste non transit in ventrem, sed in mentem*, haec praepositio *in* non denotat terminum motus localis, sed finem sumptionis: vadit enim quasi localiter quocumque species vadunt; sed non sumitur propter ventris repletionem, sicut corporales cibi, sed propter mentis refectionem, in qua ejus effectus recipitur, non ipsa materia corporis, quia mentem inhabitare per essentiam sola divinitas potest.

AD TERTIUM dicendum, quod ex hoc quod corpus Christi sumitur a peccatoribus, nullo modo corpus Christi aliquam immunditiam contrahit: quia labia peccatoris non tangunt nisi species, sub quibus secundum veritatem est corpus Christi; et praeterea in hoc dat exemplum mansuetudinis et humilitatis.

into another substance, except what would have changed the substance of bread and wine, if it were there; which a mere touch of the lips or biting of the teeth or transferal to the stomach would not do, but only digestion, which comes from natural heat converting the food. Hence it is clear that anyone who says that the body of Christ received by a sinner stops existing at the mere touch of his lips, detracts from the truth of the sacrament. And so such a heretical opinion having been put out of the way, its opposite is held by all.

REPLY OBJ. 1: That authority speaks of spiritual indwelling, and not sacramental or physical: for Christ also presented his own body to sinners to handle.

REPLY OBJ. 2: When it is said, *this food does not go into the stomach, but into the mind*, this preposition *into* denotes not the terminus of local motion, but the end of consumption: for in terms of place it goes wherever the species go, but it is not consumed for the sake of filling the stomach, like physical food, but for the sake of renewing the mind, in which its effect is received, not the very matter of the body, for only divinity can inhabit the mind by its essence.

REPLY OBJ. 3: The body of Christ in no way contracts any impurity from the fact that it is received by sinners: for the lips of sinners touch nothing but the appearances under which the body of Christ exists according to truth; and furthermore, in this he gives an example of meekness and humility.

Response to Quaestiuncula 2

AD SECUNDAM QUAESTIONEM dicendum, quod manducatio est actus transiens a manducante in manducatum. Unde sacramentaliter manducare potest intelligi dupliciter. Uno modo ut adverbium determinet manducationem ex parte manducati; et sic quicumque sumit species, sacramentaliter manducat; idest, sumit hoc quod est sacramentum in Eucharistia, idest verum corpus Christi. Alio modo ut determinet manducationem ex parte manducantis; et sic solus ille sacramentaliter manducat qui utitur illo cibo visibili ut sacramento. Infidelis autem circa id quod est significatum in hoc sacramento, errans, non utitur speciebus illis ut sacramento, sive non credit in Christum secundum quod sub hoc sacramento continetur; unde talis non sacramentaliter manducat. Et quia actio est magis propinqua agenti quam patienti, ideo sensus secundus est magis proprius; et ideo secundum hunc sensum dicendum, quod infidelis non credens rem hujus sacramenti, non manducat sacramentaliter.

TO THE SECOND QUESTION, it should be said that eating is an act passing from the eater into what is eaten. Hence to eat something sacramentally can be understood in two ways. In one way so that the adverb describes the eating on the part of what is eaten; and in this way whoever consumes the outward appearances eats sacramentally, i.e., he consumes what is sacrament in the Eucharist, i.e., the true body of Christ. In another way, so that the adverb describes the eating on the part of the eater; and in this way only the person who uses this visible food as a sacrament eats it sacramentally. However, an unbeliever, who is in error about what is represented in this sacrament, does not use those appearances as a sacrament, or he does not believe in Christ as contained under this sacrament. And so someone like this does not eat sacramentally. And since action is closer to the agent than what is acted upon, for this reason the second meaning is more proper; and so according to this meaning it should be said that an unbeliever who does not believe in the reality behind this sacrament does not eat sacramentally.

AD PRIMUM ergo dicendum, quod illa objectio procedit secundum primum sensum.

AD SECUNDUM dicendum, quod percipiens baptismum se habet tantum ut patiens. Unde ad hoc quod aliquis recipiat sacramentaliter baptismum, non exigitur nisi quod subjiciat se actioni ecclesiae, ut scilicet intendat recipere quidquid illa facit, quamvis quandoque credat illam nihil facere; sed percipiens Eucharistiam non solum se habet ut recipiens, seu patiens, sed etiam ut agens, inquantum manducat; ideo ad hoc quod sacramentaliter manducet, oportet quod ipsemet utatur sacramento ut sacramento.

AD TERTIUM dicendum, quod consecrare Eucharistiam non est uti sacramento, sed quodammodo efficere ipsum; sed manducare est uti sacramento; actio autem utentis recipit modum ab eo quo quis utitur, sed actio efficientis non recipit modum ab eo quod quis efficit, sed a virtute activa: unde aliquis dicitur conficere sacramentum, et non conficere sacramentaliter; dicitur autem manducare et sacramentum, et sacramentaliter. Et ideo non est mirum, si aliquid requiritur ad hoc quod aliquis manducet sacramentaliter quod non requiritur ad hoc quod efficiat sacramentum.

REPLY OBJ. 1: That objection proceeds according to the first meaning.

REPLY OBJ. 2: The person receiving baptism is only having something done to him. For this reason, to receive baptism sacramentally requires only that one subject himself to the action of the Church, namely that he intend to receive whatever the Church does, although sometimes he may believe that she does nothing. But someone receiving the Eucharist is not only related to it as recipient, or having something done to him, but also as agent, inasmuch as he eats. And so in order to eat this sacramentally, it is necessary that he himself use the sacrament as a sacrament.

REPLY OBJ. 3: To consecrate the Eucharist is not to use the sacrament, but in a certain way to effect it. But to eat is to use the sacrament; however, the action of the one using receives its mode from what someone uses, but the action of the one effecting does not receive its mode from what someone effects, but from an active power. Hence someone is said to confect the sacrament and not to confect sacramentally, but he is said both to eat the sacrament and to eat sacramentally. And so it is not surprising if something is required for someone to eat sacramentally that is not required for someone to effect the sacrament.

Response to Quaestiuncula 3

AD TERTIAM QUAESTIONEM dicendum, quod circa hoc est duplex opinio. Quidam enim dicunt, quod corpus Christi non manducatur a brutis ita quod in ventrem trajiciatur, eo quod corpus Christi non est sub speciebus illis nisi prout est ordinabile ad usum humanum. Ex quo autem in ventrem muris descendunt species, non possunt ordinari ad usum humanum; et ideo desinit esse corpus Christi. Sed haec ratio non valet propter duo. Primo, quia supponit falsum. Cum enim non statim species in ventrem trajectae esse desinant, vel in aliud convertantur, possent adhuc de ventre animalis extrahi, et in usum venire. Secundo, quia quamvis aliquid ordinetur ad usum aliquem, non tamen oportet quod esse desinat, quando quis eo uti non potest. Et ideo secundum alios dicendum, quod verum corpus Christi manet adhuc sub speciebus a brutis ore acceptis, et in ventrem trajectis.

AD PRIMUM ergo dicendum, quod nulla ordinatio bruti est ad corpus Christi, secundum quam possit Christo incorporari; et ideo non sumunt corpus Christi nisi per accidens, inquantum sumunt illud sub quo est corpus Christi; et sic Magister intellexit quod non sumitur corpus Christi a brutis; vel loquitur secundum aliam opinionem.

TO THE THIRD QUESTION, it should be said that concerning this there are two opinions. For some people say that the body of Christ is not eaten by animals such that it is transferred into their stomach, because the body of Christ is only under those appearances as available to human use. However, by the fact that the species descend into the stomach of a mouse, they cannot be put to human use; and so it ceases to be the body of Christ. But this reasoning is not strong enough, for two reasons. First, because it supposes something false. For when the species are swallowed into the stomach they do not cease to exist or become converted into something else immediately, so for a while they can be taken out of the stomach of the animal, and come into use. Second, because although something is ordered to a certain use, nevertheless it is not necessary that it cease to exist when someone cannot use it. And so according to others it should be said that the true body of Christ still remains, under its appearances, when taken into the mouth of an animal and swallowed into its stomach.

REPLY OBJ. 1: Animals have no ordering to the body of Christ according to which they could be incorporated into Christ, and so they do not receive the body of Christ except incidentally, inasmuch as they consume something under which the body of Christ exists; and this is how the Master understood that the body of Christ is not received by animals; or else he speaks according to the other opinion.

Ad secundum dicendum quod illud quod est sacramentum in baptismo, est aliquis effectus inductus in recipiente, cujus creatura irrationalis capax esse non potest; et ideo sacramentum baptismi creatura irrationalis neque per se neque per accidens recipit: sed sacramentum Eucharistiae consistit in ipsa materiae consecratione; et ideo potest creatura irrationalis ipsum accipere non per se, sed per accidens.

Ad tertium dicendum, quod creatura irrationalis nullo modo spiritualiter manducat, neque sacramentaliter: quia neque utitur manducato ut sacramento, neque manducat sacramentum secundum rationem sacramenti, sicut neque sacramentaliter dicitur manducare infidelis qui intendit recipere hoc quod recipit ecclesia, quamvis hoc credat nihil esse. Et similiter etiam ille qui manducaret hostiam consecratam, nesciens eam consecratam esse, non manducaret sacramentaliter aliquo modo, quia non manducaret sacramentum nisi per accidens: nisi quod plus accederet ad sacramentalem manducationem, inquantum est aptus natus sacramentum ut sacramentum manducare, quod bruto non competit. Nec tamen oportet quod sit alius modus manducationis tertius a duobus praedictis; quia hoc quod est per accidens, in divisionem non cadit.

Reply Obj. 2: What is sacrament in baptism is a certain effect brought about in the recipient, which an irrational creature is not capable of receiving. And that is why an irrational creature receives the sacrament of baptism neither *per se* nor incidentally. But the sacrament of the Eucharist consists in the very matter of consecration; and so an irrational creature can receive it not *per se*, but incidentally.

Reply Obj. 3: An irrational creature cannot at all eat spiritually, nor sacramentally, for it neither uses what is eaten as a sacrament, nor eats the sacrament according to the notion of sacrament, as neither is an unbeliever said to eat sacramentally when he intends to receive what the Church receives, although he believes that to be nothing. And likewise also a person who ate the consecrated host without knowing that it was consecrated would not be eating sacramentally in any way, since he would only be eating the sacrament incidentally; except that he would come closer to sacramental eating, inasmuch as he is fit by nature to eat this sacrament as a sacrament, which does not apply to an animal. Nor, however, need there be another, third, mode of eating besides the two mentioned, for what is incidental is not the basis for division.

Response to Quaestiuncula 4

Ad quartam quaestionem dicendum, quod Christus est spiritualis electorum cibus, non quidem in alios conversus, sed ad se convertens eos quos reficit; unde spiritualiter Christum manducare est Christo incorporari, quod per fidem et caritatem contingit. Et quia Christus in seipso est spiritualis cibus, ideo in sacramentali cibo significatur et continetur. Prius ergo naturaliter est Christum esse cibum spiritualem quam esse cibum spiritualem sub sacramento contentum: quia prius est aliquid naturaliter proprietatem aliquam habens, quam similitudinem proprietatis illius ei significatio aliqua adhibeat. Unde non quicumque manducat Christum spiritualiter, manducat hoc sacramentum spiritualiter; utroque tamen modo convenit[19] spiritualiter manducare non manducantem sacramentaliter. Manducat enim spiritualiter Christum qui fidem et caritatem ad ipsum habet sine ordine ad hoc sacramentum; non tamen manducat talis spiritualiter hoc sacramentum, sed solum ille qui habet fidem et caritatem ad Christum cum devotione et proposito sumendi hoc sacramentum, etiam si sacramentaliter non manducet.

Ad primum ergo dicendum, quod baptizatus baptismo flaminis emundationem consecutus est propter propositum baptismi sacramentalis, et accipiens sacra-

To the fourth question, it is to be said that Christ is the spiritual food of the elect, not indeed changing into them, but changing into himself those whom he refreshes; and so to eat Christ spiritually is to be incorporated into Christ, which happens by faith and charity. And since Christ in himself is spiritual food, he is signified and contained in sacramental food. Therefore, it is naturally prior for Christ to be spiritual food than to be spiritual food contained under a sacrament; for it is prior for something to have a certain property naturally than for a certain signification to apply a likeness of that property to it. Hence not everyone who spiritually eats Christ eats this sacrament spiritually; nevertheless in both ways it happens that someone not eating sacramentally eats spiritually. For someone spiritually eats Christ who has faith and charity for him without relation to this sacrament; however, someone like that does not eat this sacrament spiritually, but only the person who has faith and charity for Christ with devotion and the purpose of receiving this sacrament, even if he does not eat it sacramentally.

Reply Obj. 1: One baptized with the baptism of the Spirit has obtained cleansing because of his aim of sacramental baptism, and when he receives the sacrament he

---

19. *convenit.—contingit* PLE.

mentum ampliorem gratiam consequitur; ita etiam qui spiritualiter manducavit, in proposito et devotione habuit manducationem sacramentalem, ad quam accedens ex ipsa vi sacramenti majorem gratiam consequitur; unde non sequitur quod sacramentalis manducatio superfluat.

AD SECUNDUM dicendum, quod antiqui patres non manducaverunt spiritualiter hoc sacramentum quia nondum erat institutum, nec consecratio praecesserat; manducaverunt tamen spiritualiter Christum; et secundum hoc dicitur 1 Corinth. 10, quod *omnes eamdem escam manducaverunt spiritualem.*

acquires even more abundant grace; so also whoever has eaten spiritually in his purpose and devotion has had sacramental eating, and when he does approach the sacrament he obtains greater grace by the very force of the sacrament. Hence it does not follow that sacramental eating is superfluous.

REPLY OBJ. 2: The ancient fathers did not eat this sacrament spiritually because it had not been instituted, nor had its consecration ever happened before. Nevertheless they did eat Christ spiritually, and according to this it is said that *all have eaten the same spiritual food* (1 Cor 10:3).

Response to Quaestiuncula 5

AD QUINTAM QUAESTIONEM dicendum, quod manducare hoc sacramentum spiritualiter non competit angelis: quia eis Christus sub sacramento non proponitur, sed in nuda veritate. Christum tamen quodammodo spiritualiter manducant, et quodammodo non. Cum enim spiritualiter manducare sit Christo incorporari, secundum hoc aliquis Christum manducare potest secundum quod ejus membrum effici potest et Christus esse caput ejus. Est autem Christus caput angelorum quodammodo, quia secundum rationem influentiae, et secundum conformitatem naturae in genere; et quodammodo non, quia non secundum conformitatem in specie, ut in 3 Lib., dist. 13, qu. 1, art. 2, quaestiunc. 1, in corp., dictum est; et ideo uno modo spiritualiter manducant Christum, et alio modo non.

AD PRIMUM ergo dicendum, quod Christus dicitur esca angelorum et secundum divinitatem, inquantum angelos reficit; et secundum humanitatem, secundum quod in ipsum *desiderant angeli prospicere*, 1 Petr. 1; non tamen secundum conformitatem naturae in specie.

AD SECUNDUM dicendum, quod si angelus assumpto corpore species masticaret, non tamen manducaret sacramentaliter: quia non manducaret sacramentum secundum rationem sacramenti, cum non habeat fidem, sed manifestam visionem; neque habet conformitatem naturae; et ideo non manducaret sacramentum nisi per accidens.

TO THE FIFTH QUESTION, it should be said that to eat this sacrament spiritually does not apply to angels, for Christ is not presented to them under a sacrament, but in naked truth. However, they eat Christ spiritually in a certain way and in a certain way not. For since to eat spiritually is to be incorporated into Christ, someone can eat Christ to the extent that he can be made his member and Christ can be his head. Now Christ is head of the angels in a certain way, namely according to the notion of influence and according to a conformity of nature in genus; and in a certain way he is not, namely according to a conformity in species, as was said in Book III, Distinction 13, Question 1, Article 2, Subquestion 1, main response. And so in one way they eat Christ spiritually, and in another way they do not.

REPLY OBJ. 1: Christ is called the food of angels both according to his divinity, inasmuch as he refreshes the angels, and according to his humanity, according to which *the angels long to gaze* on him (1 Pet 1:12); not, however, according to a conformity of nature in species.

REPLY OBJ. 2: If an angel, having assumed a body, chewed, he would still not eat sacramentally, for he would not eat the sacrament according to the nature of a sacrament, since he would not have faith, but manifest vision; nor does he have the likeness of nature, and so he would not eat the sacrament except accidentally.

ARTICLE 3

Whether sinners are permitted to eat the body of Christ

Quaestiuncula 1

AD TERTIUM SIC PROCEDITUR. Videtur quod non peccet quis cum conscientia peccati mortalis corpus Christi manducans. Quia secundum Augustinum, maximis bonis nullus male utitur. Sed corpus Christi de maximis bonis est. Ergo nullus potest ipso utendo peccare.

PRAETEREA, infirmi non minus egent medicina quam medico. Sed Christus in propria specie veniens ut medicus, non refugit peccatorum consortium: quia, sicut ipse dicit, Luc. 5, 31, *non egent qui sani sunt medico, sed qui male habent.* Ergo cum Christus sub sacramento proponatur ut medicina, non debet peccatoribus subtrahi.

PRAETEREA, nullus peccat faciendo id quod tenetur. Sed iste peccator tenetur ex praecepto ecclesiae semel in anno corpus Christi sumere. Ergo quamvis sit in proposito peccandi, non peccat corpus Christi sumendo.

SED CONTRA, 1 Corinth. 11, 29: *qui manducat indigne, judicium sibi manducat.* Sed qui cum conscientia peccati mortalis manducat, indigne manducat. Ergo, etc.

PRAETEREA, Deus magis horret sordes spirituales, quae sunt peccata, quam sordes corporales. Sed peccaret qui corpus Christi in lutum projiceret. Ergo peccat qui Christum in corpus suum peccato infectum intromittit.

OBJ. 1: To the third we proceed thus. It seems that someone who ate the body of Christ with the consciousness of mortal sin would not sin.[20] For according to Augustine, no one uses the greatest goods badly.[21] But the body of Christ is one of the greatest goods. Therefore, no one can use it to sin.

OBJ. 2: Furthermore, the sick do not need less medicine than a doctor. But Christ coming in his own appearance as doctor did not recoil from fellowship with sinners, for as he himself says, *those who are well do not need a doctor, but those who are ill* (Luke 5:31). Therefore, since Christ is presented under the sacrament as a medicine, he should not be taken away from sinners.

OBJ. 3: Furthermore, no one sins by doing what he is bound to do. But any sinner is bound by the precept of the Church to receive the body of Christ once a year. Therefore, even if he intends to sin, he does not sin by receiving the body of Christ.

ON THE CONTRARY, *Whoever eats unworthily, eats to his own judgment* (1 Cor 11:29). But whoever eats while conscious of mortal sin eats unworthily. Therefore, etc.

FURTHERMORE, God abhors spiritual filth, which is sin, more than physical filth. But one would sin if he threw the body of Christ into the mud. Therefore, he sins who takes Christ into his own body infected with sin.

Quaestiuncula 2

ULTERIUS. Videtur quod etiam ille qui non habet conscientiam peccati mortalis, in peccato mortali existens peccet corpus Christi sumendo. Peccatum enim facit hominem indigne accedere ad corpus Christi. Sed ignorantia peccati cui homo subjacet, non tollit peccatum, immo gravissime peccat qui ignorat, secundum Ambrosium. Ergo cum indigne accedens peccet mortaliter, videtur quod habens peccatum cujus non est conscius, accedens peccet.

PRAETEREA, in meliori statu est justus habens conscientiam peccati mortalis, cui non subjacet, quam peccator subjacens peccato cujus non est conscius: quia hoc

OBJ. 1: Moreover, it seems that even someone existing in mortal sin who is not conscious of it would sin by receiving the body of Christ.[22] For sin makes a man unworthy of approaching the body of Christ. But ignorance of a sin to which a man is subject does not take away the sin; rather, he sins most gravely who is unaware, according to Ambrose. Therefore, since someone approaching unworthily sins mortally, it seems that someone having a sin of which he is not conscious would sin by approaching the body of Christ.

OBJ. 2: Furthermore, the just man who thinks he has a mortal sin which he has not committed is in a better state than a sinner guilty of sin that he is not conscious of. For

---

20. Parallels: *ST* III, q. 80, a. 4; q. 79, a. 3; *Super I ad Cor.* 11, lec. 7.
21. Augustine, *On Free Choice of the Will* (CCSL 29), Bk. 2, ch. 19.
22. Parallels: *ST* III, q. 79, a. 3; q. 80, a. 4; *Super I ad Cor.* 11, lec. 7.

videtur esse praesumptionis, primum autem humilitatis: quia secundum Gregorium, *bonarum mentium est ibi culpam agnoscere ubi culpa non est.* Sed justus carens peccato peccat, si cum conscientia peccati mortalis accedat. Ergo multo fortius peccator, qui peccati sui sibi non est conscius.

PRAETEREA, ubicumque requiritur examinatio, ibi est necessaria rei veritas, et non opinio tantum. Sed ad hoc quod aliquis digne accedat ad corpus Christi, requiritur diligens examinatio sui ipsius, ut patet 1 Corinth. 11, 28: *probet seipsum homo, et sic de pane illo edat.* Ergo necessarium est quod sit puritas a peccato secundum veritatem, et non solum secundum aestimationem.

SED CONTRA, Eccl. 9, 1, dicitur: *nemo scit utrum odio vel amore dignus sit.* Si ergo habens peccatum cujus non est conscius, peccaret corpus Christi sumendo; quicumque sumit, exponeret se periculo peccati mortalis; et ita nullus sumere deberet.

PRAETEREA, ignorantia facti excusat. Sed ignorantia peccati est hujusmodi. Ergo excusat.

the latter seems to have presumption, while the former has humility, for according to Gregory, *it belongs to good minds to admit to guilt where there is no guilt.*[23] But the just man without sin sins if he approaches the sacrament believing he is in mortal sin. Therefore, much more would the sinner who is not conscious of his own sin.

OBJ. 3: Furthermore, wherever examination is required, there the truth of the matter is necessary, and not just opinion. But for someone to worthily approach the body of Christ, a diligent examination of himself is required, as is clear: *let every man examine himself, and then he may eat of the bread* (1 Cor 11:28). Therefore, it is necessary that there be purity from sin according to the truth, and not just according to one's estimation.

ON THE CONTRARY, it is said, *no one knows whether he is worthy of love or of hatred* (Eccl 9:1). Therefore, if someone having a sin of which he is not conscious should sin by receiving the body of Christ, whoever consumes it would expose himself to the danger of mortal sin, and then no one should consume it.

FURTHERMORE, ignorance of a deed excuses it. But ignorance of sin is of this kind. Therefore, it excuses it.

Quaestiuncula 3

ULTERIUS. Videtur quod manducans indigne corpus Christi, magis peccat quam quodcumque aliud peccatum committat. Super illud Marc. 14: *vae homini illi* etc., dicit Glossa: *vae homini illi qui ad mensam Domini accedit indigne: iste enim in exemplum Judae filium hominis tradit*; et in 1 Corinth. 11 dicitur, quod est *reus sanguinis Domini.* Sed Judas et illi qui sanguinem Domini fuderunt, gravissime peccaverunt. Ergo et hoc peccatum est ceteris gravius.

PRAETEREA, plus peccaret qui corpus Christi in lutum projiceret quam qui aliquod aliud peccatum committeret, puta fornicationem, vel aliquid hujusmodi. Sed Deus plus horret sordes peccati quam sordes luti. Ergo peccator sumens corpus Christi gravius peccat quam quodlibet aliud peccatum committens.

SED CONTRA, quod est per se malum, est majus malum quam quod est per accidens malum. Sed alia peccata sunt per se mala, ut fornicatio. Manducare autem corpus Christi est per se bonum, et per accidens malum. Ergo est minus malum.

OBJ. 1: Moreover, it seems that the one eating the body of Christ unworthily sins more than someone who commits any other sin.[24] For commenting on the text, *woe to that man by whom the Son of Man is betrayed*, etc. (Mark 14:21), the Gloss says, *woe to that man who approaches the table of the Lord unworthily: for he follows the example of Judas in handing over the Son of Man.*[25] And it is said that *he is answerable for the blood of the Lord* (1 Cor 11:27). But Judas and those who shed the blood of the Lord, sinned most gravely. Therefore, this sin is also more grave than the rest.

OBJ. 2: Furthermore, a person who threw Christ's body into the mud would sin more than someone who committed any other sin, for instance, fornication, or something like that. But God abhors the filth of sin more than the filth of mud. Therefore, a sinner receiving the body of Christ sins more gravely than someone committing any other sin.

ON THE CONTRARY, what is evil in itself is a greater evil than what is evil incidentally. But other sins, like fornication, are evil in themselves, whereas eating the body of the Lord is good in itself, and evil incidentally. Therefore, it is a lesser evil.

---

23. Gregory the Great, *Epistles*, Bk. 11, Epistle 64 (PL 77:1195).
24. Parallels: *ST* III, q. 80, a. 5; *Super I ad Cor.* 11, lec. 7.
25. *Glossa ordinaria*, PL 114:231.

Quaestiuncula 4

ULTERIUS. Videtur quod minus peccat haereticus manducans corpus Christi quam fidelis peccator. Quia pejus est contemnere Christum quam contemnere sacramentum Christi. Sed fidelis peccator manducans contemnit Christum, quem sub sacramento vere esse credit; infidelis autem contemnit sacramentum in hoc quod sub eo Christum esse non credit. Ergo infidelis minus peccat.

PRAETEREA, quanto aliquod peccatum est magis dissonum a ratione, tanto est gravius. Sed peccatum fidelis indigne sumentis est contra rationem naturalem manifeste: non autem illius qui non credit sub hoc sacramento Christum secundum veritatem esse: quia hoc supra rationem est, et supra sensum. Ergo infidelis minus peccat.

SED CONTRA, quanto aliquis magis elongatur a Christo realiter, tanto magis debet elongari sacramentaliter. Sed infidelis magis elongatur realiter: quia prima unio ad Christum est per fidem, qua ille caret. Ergo magis peccat accedendo ad Christum sacramentaliter.

OBJ. 1: Moreover, it seems that a heretic eating the body of Christ sins less than a sinful believer. For it is worse to despise Christ than to despise the sacrament of Christ. But a sinful believer who eats, despises Christ, whom he believes to be truly present under the sacrament; but an unbeliever despises the sacrament in the fact that he does not believe Christ to be in it. Therefore, the unbeliever sins less.

OBJ. 2: Furthermore, the more a certain sin is at odds with reason, the more grave it is. But the sin of a believer unworthily receiving is manifestly against natural reason, but not the sin of someone who does not believe Christ to exist according to the truth under this sacrament: for this is above reason, and above sense. Therefore, an unbeliever sins less.

ON THE CONTRARY, the more removed someone is from Christ in reality, the more removed he should be from him sacramentally. But an unbeliever is more distant in reality, since he lacks the first union to Christ, which is by faith. Therefore, he sins more by approaching Christ sacramentally.

Quaestiuncula 5

ULTERIUS. Videtur quod subjacens peccato carnis, magis peccat accedens ad hoc sacramentum quam subjacens peccato spirituali. Quia peccatum manducantium corpus Christi in peccato carnis existentium comparatur peccato Judae; unde Hieronymus: *quid tibi cum feminis qui ad altare cum Deo fabularis? . . . Dic sacerdos, dic clerice, qualiter eisdem labiis filium Dei oscularis, quibus osculatus es filiam meretricis? O Juda, osculo filium hominis tradis.* Sed peccatum Judae fuit gravissimum. Ergo talis gravius peccat.

PRAETEREA, in peccato carnis est immunditia mentis et corporis. Ergo magis facit contumeliam sacramento qui cum peccato carnis corpus Christi manducat, quam qui manducat cum peccato spirituali, ubi est immunditia mentis tantum.

SED CONTRA, Gregorius dicit, quod *peccata spiritualia sunt majoris culpae*; cujus ratio est quia peccata carnis magis ex infirmitate accidunt. Sed ex hoc est aliquis indignus corporis et sanguinis Domini quod culpae subjacet. Ergo minus peccat accedens cum peccato carnis quam cum peccato spirituali.

OBJ. 1: Moreover, it seems that someone subject to sin of the flesh sins more by approaching this sacrament than someone subject to spiritual sin. For the sin of those eating the body of Christ while existing in sins of the flesh is compared to the sin of Judas; hence Jerome says, *what do you mean by conversing with women, you who do the same with God at the altar? . . . Tell, priest, tell, cleric, how you kiss the Son of God with those same lips, with which you have kissed the daughter of a prostitute? O Judas, you hand over the Son of man with a kiss.*[26] But the sin of Judas was the most grave. Therefore, such a person sins more gravely.

OBJ. 2: Furthermore, in a sin of flesh there is an uncleanness of the mind and of the body. Therefore, someone who eats the body of Christ while guilty of a sin of the flesh does a greater disgrace to the sacrament than someone who eats it with spiritual sin, where there is only uncleanness of mind.

ON THE CONTRARY, Gregory says that *spiritual sins have greater guilt,*[27] and the reason for this is that sins of the flesh happen more from weakness. But someone is unworthy of the Lord's body and blood who is subject to guilt. Therefore, he sins less by approaching the sacrament with sin of the flesh than with spiritual sin.

---

26. Jerome, *Epistle 69, to Oceanum*, n. 2 (CSEL 54:680).
27. Gregory the Great, *Moralia in Iob* (CCSL 143B), Bk. 31, ch. 45.

Quaestiuncula 6

ULTERIUS. Videtur quod peccator peccat videndo corpus Christi. Quia corpus Christi est dignius quam arca testamenti. Sed Bethsamitae videntes arcam Domini, quia peccatores erant, percussi sunt, ut dicitur 1 Reg. 6. Ergo multo fortius peccator videns corpus Christi peccat.

PRAETEREA, publicanus laudatur, Luc. 18, de hoc quod oculos non levabat ad caelum. Sed corpus Christi est dignius caelo. Ergo debent peccatores ab aspectu corporis Christi abstinere.

SED CONTRA est consuetudo ecclesiae, secundum quam elevatur corpus Christi ab omnibus aspiciendum sine aliqua discretione videntium. Ergo non peccat peccator videns.

OBJ. 1: Moreover, it seems that a sinner sins by seeing the body of Christ. For the body of Christ is more noble than the ark of the covenant. But the Bethshemites who saw the ark of the Lord, since they were sinners, were struck down, as it says in 1 Sam 6:19. Therefore, much more would any sinner who saw the body of the Lord sin.

OBJ. 2: Furthermore, the tax collector is praised for not raising his eyes to heaven (Luke 18:13). But the body of Christ is more noble than heaven. Therefore, sinners should abstain from looking on the body of Christ.

ON THE CONTRARY, is the custom of the Church, according to which the body of Christ is elevated for all to look upon without any distinction of those looking. Therefore, a sinner does not sin by looking.

Response to Quaestiuncula 1

RESPONDEO dicendum ad primam quaestionem, quod quilibet cum conscientia peccati mortalis manducans corpus Christi, peccat mortaliter, quia abutitur sacramento: et quanto sacramentum est dignius, tanto abusus est periculosior. Ratio autem hujus ex tribus potest sumi. Primo ex eo quod est sacramentum tantum, ex quo apparet, quod hoc sacramentum in modum cibi proponitur; cibus autem non competit nisi viventi: unde si carens vita spirituali per peccatum mortale accipiat hoc sacramentum, abutitur ipso. Secundo ex eo quod est ibi res et sacramentum, quod est ipse Christus, qui est sanctus sanctorum; unde receptaculum ejus debet esse sanctum; et ideo si aliquis cum contrario sanctitatis corpus Christi sumat, sacramento abutitur. Tertio ex eo quod est res tantum, quod est corpus Christi mysticum; quia ex hoc ipso quod aliquis ad hoc sacramentum accedit, significat se ad unitatem corporis mystici tendere; unde si peccatum in conscientia teneat, per quod a corpore mystico separatur, fictionis culpam incurrit, et ita abutitur sacramento.

AD PRIMUM ergo dicendum, quod verbum Augustini intelligendum est de eo quo utitur quis sicut eliciente actum usus: sic enim virtutibus, quas maxima bona dicit, nullus male utitur. Sed non est intelligendum de eo quo quis utitur quasi objecto usus: sic enim etiam virtutibus aliquis male utitur, qui de virtutibus gloriatur et superbit; et ita etiam aliquis potest corpore Christi male uti sicut objecto.

AD SECUNDUM dicendum, quod duplex est medicina. Una est removens morbum; et talis infirmis debetur; et huic comparatur baptismus et poenitentia. Alia est promovens in perfectam sanitatem; et talis non de-

TO THE FIRST QUESTION, I answer that anyone conscious of mortal sin who eats the body of the Lord sins mortally, for he abuses the sacrament, and the greater the dignity of the sacrament, the more dangerous is the abuse. Now the reason for this can be taken from three things. First, from that which is sacrament alone, from which it is apparent that this sacrament is set forth in the mode of food; but food belongs only to the living: hence if someone who lacks spiritual life through mortal sin receives this sacrament, he abuses it. Second, from that which is reality-and-sacrament here,[28] which is Christ himself, who is the holy of holies; hence his receptacle should be holy, and so if anyone receives the body of Christ with the opposite of sanctity, he abuses the sacrament. Third, from that which is reality alone, which is the mystical body of Christ; since by the fact that someone approaches this sacrament, he signifies that he longs for unity with the mystical body; hence if he holds any sin in his conscience by which he is separated from the mystical body, he incurs the guilt of false pretenses, and so he abuses the sacrament.

REPLY OBJ. 1: The word of Augustine is to be understood as having to do with what someone uses as the thing eliciting the act of use: for this is how no one uses the virtues badly, which he calls the greatest goods. But this is not to be understood of the object of use: for this is how someone does use the virtues badly, when he glories in the virtues and grows proud; and likewise someone can use the body of Christ badly, as an object.

REPLY OBJ. 2: There are two kinds of medicine. One is what removes disease, and this kind is owed to the sick; and baptism and penance are compared to this. The other is what advances someone to perfect health, and this kind

---

28. For more about the sacrament alone, reality alone, and sacrament-and-reality, see the footnote at Dist.1, q.1, a.4, qa. 1, main response.

betur infirmis, sed jam sanis; et huic comparatur haec medicina. Utraque autem medicina per medicum datur. Unde non sequitur, si medicus non fugit infirmi consortium, quod quaelibet ejus medicina infirmis dari debeat.

AD TERTIUM dicendum, quod habens conscientiam mortalis quod dimittere non proponit, peccat accedens ad sumendum corpus Christi, quia indigne accedit. Peccat etiam non accedendo tempore ab ecclesia constituto, quia inobediens est. Non tamen est perplexus, quia potest se ab hoc dubio eripere, peccati propositum dimittendo. Nihilominus tamen manente tali proposito minus peccat non sumendo quam sumendo; quia illud quod est malum secundum se, est majus malum quam illud quod est malum quia prohibitum; unde potius se debet dimittere excommunicari, quam cum proposito peccati corpus Christi sumat.

is not owed to the sick, but to those already healthy; and this medicine is compared to this. However, both medicines are given by the doctor. Hence it does not follow, if the doctor does not refuse the fellowship of the sick, that he should give every medicine he has to them.

REPLY OBJ. 3: Someone having on his conscience a mortal sin that he does not plan to give up, sins if he approaches to receive the body of Christ, for he approaches unworthily. He also sins if he does not receive at the time established by the Church, since he is disobedient. However, he is not stuck in a predicament, for he can tear himself from this doubt by giving up the fixed purpose of sin. Nevertheless, if he still remains intent on such a purpose, he sins less by not receiving than by receiving, for what is evil in itself is more evil than what is evil because it is prohibited; hence he should rather give himself up to be excommunicated than receive the body of Christ with the fixed purpose of sinning.

Response to Quaestiuncula 2

AD SECUNDAM QUAESTIONEM dicendum, quod ignorantia circumstantiae a peccato excusat, adhibita debita diligentia, praecipue quando est talis circumstantia, cujus certitudo plene haberi non potest. Quod autem homo sit omnino a peccato immunis, per certitudinem sciri non potest; 1 Corinth., 4, 4: *nihil mihi conscius sum, sed non in hoc justificatus sum*. Potest tamen de hoc haberi aliqua conjectura, praecipue per quatuor signa, sicut Bernardus dicit. Primo, cum quis devote verba Dei audit: quia *qui est ex Deo, verba Dei audit*; Joan. 8, 47. Secundo, cum quis se promptum ad bene operandum invenit: quia *probatio dilectionis exhibitio est operis*, ut dicit Gregorius. Tertio, cum quis a peccatis abstinendi in futurum propositum habet. Quarto, cum de praeteritis dolet: quia in his vera poenitentia, secundum Gregorium, consistit. Unde si aliquis per hujusmodi signa facta diligenti discussione suae conscientiae, quamvis forte non sufficienti, ad corpus Christi devote accedat, aliquo peccato mortali in ipso manente, quod ejus cognitionem praeterfugiat, non peccat, immo magis ex vi sacramenti peccati remissionem consequitur. Unde Augustinus dicit in quodam sermone, quod *quando corpus Christi manducatur, vivificat mortuos*.

AD PRIMUM ergo dicendum, quod duplex est ignorantia peccati. Una qua ignoratur an aliquid peccatum sit; et haec quidem ignorantia si sit in sola cognitione consistens, quandoque excusat peccatum, sicut cum ignoratur circumstantia quae peccatum facit, sicut cum

TO THE SECOND QUESTION, it should be said that ignorance of the circumstances excuses from sin, if due diligence has been applied, particularly when the circumstances are the kind of which certitude cannot be had fully. However, that man is completely free from sin cannot be known with certainty: *I am not conscious of anything in me, but I am not thereby justified* (1 Cor 4:4). However, some conjecture can be had about this, particularly by four signs, as Bernard says.[29] First, when someone listens devoutly to the word of God: for anyone who is of God, hears the word of God (John 8:47). Second, when someone finds himself prompt in doing good works: for *the display of a work is the proof of love*, as Gregory says.[30] Third, when someone has the purpose of abstaining from sin in the future. Fourth, when he grieves over past sins: for in these true repentance consists, according to Gregory.[31] Hence if someone having made a diligent search of his conscience by signs like this, although perhaps not sufficiently, approaches the body of Christ devoutly, with some mortal sin remaining in him, which has escaped his awareness, he does not sin, but rather he obtains the remission of the sin by the force of the sacrament. Hence Augustine says in a certain sermon that *when the body of Christ is eaten, it gives life to the dead.*[32]

REPLY OBJ. 1: There are two kinds of ignorance of sin. One in which one does not know whether something is a sin, and this kind of ignorance, if it consists in the understanding alone, sometimes excuses the sin, as when someone is ignorant of the circumstances that make a sin, like

29. Bernard of Clairvaux, *Sermones in Septuagesima*, Sermon 1 (*Bernardi opera*, ed. Leclercq and Rochais, 4:344ff.).
30. Gregory the Great, *Homilies on the Gospels*, Homily 30, n. 1 (CCSL 141:256).
31. Gregory the Great, *Epistles*, Bk. 11, Epistle 45 (PL 77:1163).
32. See Gratian's *Decretals*, Part 3, *De consecratione*, d. 2, ch. "Invitat" (PL 187:1766).

quis commiscetur alienae quam credit suam; et hic non habet locum auctoritas Ambrosii.

Quandoque autem non excusat, sicut cum est ignorantia universalis juris; immo ipsa ignorantia grave peccatum est; et videtur in his quae per se mala sunt, ad infidelitatem pertinere; in his autem quae sunt mala quia prohibita, ad negligentiam; et hic habet aliquo modo locum verbum Ambrosii propter ignorantiae periculum; quia medicina non quaeritur cum morbus ignoratur; et etiam propter infidelitatem, quae est gravissimum peccatum. Si autem sit talis ignorantia in cognitione simul et affectione consistens, sicut ignorantia electionis, quando quis in illicitum improhibite fertur ac si esset licitum, sicut dicit Philosophus de his qui ex habitu alicujus vitii operantur, ut intemperati, tunc gravissime peccat qui ignorat, quia haec ignorantia provenit ex contemptu.

Alia ignorantia peccati est, qua id quod scitur esse peccatum, jam non creditur esse, sed sibi dimissum esse; et talis ignorantia non excusat nec aggravat illud peccatum, cujus ignorantia dicitur; sed potest excusare respectu sequentis peccati, respectu cujus peccatum praecedens, quod ignoratum est, se habet ut circumstantia, quae peccatum in actu sequenti induceret, si sciretur; et ita est in proposito. Unde quamvis sit indignus ratione praecedentis peccati, non tamen indigne accedit, quia ignorantia excusat a peccato illum accessum, ut dictum est.

AD SECUNDUM dicendum, quod sicut ignorantia circumstantiae quae excusat[34] peccatum, excusat a peccato, ita error circumstantiae talis causat peccatum, ut patet in eo qui accedit ad suam, quam credit non esse suam. Et similiter est in proposito: quia justus credens se peccatorem, errat in hac circumstantia. Unde si tali opinione manente corpus Christi manducaret; constat quod eligeret se peccatorem corpus Christi manducare; et ita electio esset prava, et peccaret. Sed electio non est prava in eo qui peccatum habet quod nescit; et ideo quamvis justus sit simpliciter melius dispositus, tamen est pejus dispositus quantum ad hoc.

AD TERTIUM dicendum, quod examinatio requiritur, ne ignorantia ex negligentia procedat; quia talis ignorantia non excusaret.

if someone lay with someone else's wife, whom he believed his own; and here the text of Ambrose is irrelevant.

Sometimes, though, it does not excuse the sin, as when it is ignorance of universal law; rather, that kind of ignorance is itself a grave sin; and among those things that are evil in themselves it seems to pertain to infidelity; but among those things that are evil because they are prohibited, it pertains to negligence. And the word of Ambrose is relevant here in a certain way because of the danger of ignorance, for medicine is not sought for a disease that is unknown; and also because of infidelity, which is the gravest sin. But if it is the kind of ignorance that consists both in the understanding and the emotions, like ignorance of choice, when someone is carried away unrestrained into something illicit as if it were licit, like the Philosopher says about those who operate from the habit of a certain vice, like the intemperate, then he sins most gravely who does not know, for this ignorance arises from scorn.[33]

There is another kind of ignorance of sin, in which what is known to be a sin, is not believed to be present, but is dismissed by oneself; and this kind of ignorance neither excuses nor worsens that sin of which the ignorance is said; but it can excuse with respect to what follows after the sin, with respect to which the preceding sin, which was unknown, is related as circumstances, which would have made the following act a sin, if it had been known, and this is how it is in this case. Hence although he is unworthy by reason of the preceding sin, nevertheless he does not approach unworthily, since ignorance excuses his reception from sin, as was said.

REPLY OBJ. 2: Just as the ignorance of a circumstance that causes sin also excuses from sin, so does the error of such a circumstance cause sin, as is clear in the case of someone who approaches his wife, believing her not to be his wife. And it is the same in this case: for the just man who believes himself a sinner errs in this circumstance. Hence if he, remaining in this opinion, were to eat the body of Christ, it is clear that he would be choosing to eat the body of Christ as a sinner and so his choice would be wrong, and he would sin. But the choice is not wrong in someone who has a sin that he does not know; and so although the just man is simply-speaking better disposed, nevertheless, he is worse disposed in this respect.

REPLY OBJ. 3: An examination of conscience is required lest ignorance come from negligence, for that kind of ignorance would not excuse.

---

33. Aristotle, *Nicomachean Ethics*, Bk. 7, ch. 8 (1151a10–20).
34. *excusat.—causat* PLE.

Response to Quaestiuncula 3

AD TERTIAM QUAESTIONEM dicendum, quod sicut meritum praecipue consistit penes caritatem, ita demeritum praecipue consistit penes contemptum Dei; unde secundum quod aliquis Deum per actum peccati magis contemnit, secundum hoc majorem reatum incurrit; et ideo illa peccata quae in actuali contemptu consistunt, sunt graviora illis in quibus non est contemptus nisi ex consequenti, et quasi interpretatus; sicut accidit in fruitione creaturae, per quam aliquis delectationi intendit, ex cujus intentione a praeceptis Dei discedit, et sic per consequens percipientem[35] contemnit. Peccatum autem blasphemiae in contemptu principaliter consistit; et similiter peccatum accedentis indigne ad corpus Christi, irreverentia quaedam et contemptus essentialiter est.

Sciendum autem, quod contemptus ex duplici parte mensurari potest. Uno modo ex parte contemnentis; et sic non potest fieri comparatio unius generis peccati ad aliud genus, sed unius particularis peccati ad aliud: quia contingit in uno veniali peccato ex genere esse majorem contemptum actualem quam in uno gravissimo peccato mortali ex genere. Alio modo ex parte ejus quod contemnitur; et sic est talis ordo peccatorum, quod illud in quo ipse Deus in seipso etiam contemnitur, est peccatum gravissimum, sicut peccatum infidelitatis et blasphemiae; et post hoc illud peccatum in quo contemnitur Deus in sacramento, et inter alia praecipue in isto, in quo essentialiter Christus Deus et homo continetur (non tamen contemptus iste est circa Christum, ut est Deus et homo, sed prout est in sacramento); et post, peccatum illud in quo contemnitur Deus in membris suis; et post, peccatum in quo contemnitur Deus in praeceptis suis, quod commune est omni peccato mortali; et secundum hoc patet quod peccatum de quo nunc agitur, neque est omnium gravissimum, neque est omnium minimum; sed est medium inter peccata quae committuntur in Deum, et alia peccata quae committuntur in proximum, vel in seipsum; unde ad utraque argumenta oportet respondere.

AD PRIMUM ergo dicendum, quod peccatum indigne corpus Christi manducantium comparatur peccato Christum occidentium, inquantum utrumque peccatum in ipsum Christum committitur; sed tamen peccatum Christum occidentium majus est: quia illud peccatum commissum est in ipsam Christi personam; hoc autem peccatum committitur in ipsum, secundum quod est sub sacramento.

AD SECUNDUM dicendum, quod ille qui corpus Christi in lutum projiceret, magis peccaret quam manducans peccator: quia magis abutitur sacramento, se-

TO THE THIRD QUESTION, it should be said that just as merit especially consists in charity, likewise demerit especially consists in contempt of God; hence according as someone shows more contempt for God by an act of sin, he incurs greater culpability; and so those sins that consist in actual contempt are more grave than those in which contempt is shown only as a consequence, and interpreted in a certain way; as happens in the enjoyment of creatures, by which someone intends pleasure, and by intending it he departs from God's commands, and, in this way, he holds in contempt the one who gave the commands. But the sin of blasphemy consists in contempt principally; and likewise the sin of approaching the body of Christ unworthily is essentially a certain irreverence and contempt.

However, it should be known that contempt can be measured by two things. In one way, on the part of the one showing contempt, and in this way a sin from one genus cannot be compared with a sin from another, only one particular sin with another particular sin, for one sin that is venial in kind may turn out to show greater actual contempt than a sin that is mortal in kind. In another way, it may be measured on the part of what is condemned, and in this way the order of sins is such that the sin that shows contempt of God in himself is the gravest sin, like a sin of unbelief and blasphemy; and after that the sin that shows contempt for God in a sacrament, and among those, especially in this sacrament, in which Christ is contained essentially as God and man (not that this contempt is directed at Christ as he is God and man, but only as he is in the sacrament); and after that a sin that shows contempt for God in his members; and after that a sin that shows contempt for God in his commands, which is common to every mortal sin; and according to this it is clear that the sin now under discussion is neither the most grave of all, nor is it the least of all, but it is in the middle between sins that are committed against God and other sins that are committed against one's neighbor or oneself; hence it is necessary to respond to both arguments.

REPLY OBJ. 1: The sin of those who eat the body of Christ unworthily is compared to the sin of those who killed Christ inasmuch as both sins were committed against Christ, but even so the sin of those killing Christ is greater; for that sin was committed against Christ in his very person, but this sin is committed against Christ according as he is under the sacrament.

REPLY OBJ. 2: Anyone who threw the body of Christ in the mud would sin more than a sinner eating it, for there is greater abuse of the sacrament according as it departs far-

---

35. *percipientem—precipientem* PLE.

cundum quod longius a debito usu sacramenti recedit quo ab homine justo sumendum est.

AD TERTIUM dicendum, quod quamvis corpus Christi manducare non sit malum nisi per accidens, tamen manducare corpus Christi indigne est malum per se. Nullum enim peccatum dicitur malum per se nisi propter corruptionem alicujus circumstantiae.

ther from the right use of the sacrament, by which it is to be received by a just man.

REPLY OBJ. 3: Although eating the body of Christ is not evil except incidentally, nevertheless to eat the body of Christ unworthily is evil in itself. For no sin is called evil in itself except because of a corruption in some circumstance.

Response to Quaestiuncula 4

AD QUARTAM QUAESTIONEM dicendum, quod in indigne manducante est duo peccata considerare; scilicet peccatum quo indignus redditur ad manducandum, et peccatum quo indigne manducat. Quia ergo peccatum infidelitatis est gravius ceteris aliis peccatis, ideo infidelis manducans indignior est ad manducandum. Sed quia non credit illud quod sumitur esse tantae dignitatis quantae est, ideo non tantum peccat in abusu: quia ignorantia infidelitatis quamvis non excuset sequens peccatum a toto, excusat tamen a tanto, ut patet de peccato occidentium Christum: quia, *si cognovissent, nunquam Dominum gloriae crucifixissent*, 1 Corinth. 2, 8; et per hanc ignorantiam eorum peccatum alleviatum est, ut dicit Anselmus; et similiter Paulus de seipso dicit, 1 Timoth. 1, 14: *misericordiam consecutus sum, quia ignorans feci in incredulitate mea*. Et ideo infidelis indignior manducat, sed peccator fidelis magis indigne.

AD PRIMUM ergo dicendum, quod infidelis quantum ad peccatum infidelitatis contemnit Christum in sua persona, quia ejus doctrinae repugnat; quantum autem ad manducationem contemnit quidem non expresse sed interpretative, inquantum illa ignorantia qua Christum sub sacramento esse non credit, non est invincibilis; unde quia potest facere ut credat, perinde reputatur ac si credat, in genere peccati; quamvis actualis et expressus contemptus aggravet quantitatem istius peccati; et sic quantum ad ipsam manducationem magis fidelis peccator peccat.

AD SECUNDUM dicendum, quod quamvis ea quae sunt fidei, et praecipue circa hoc sacramentum, non sint ita rationi humanae consona secundum se considerata, tamen ut dicta a Deo, et prodigiis approbata, sunt maxime rationi consona. Nihil enim est adeo rationi consonum, sicut quod Deo sit credendum in omnibus quae dicit et contestatur. Doctrina autem fidei *cum accepisset principium enarrandi a Domino, contestante Deo signis et prodigiis, et variis Spiritus Sancti distributionibus, per eos qui audierunt, in nos confirmata est*, Hebr. 2, 3; et ideo peccatum infidelitatis est gravius etiam quam peccatum indigne manducantis.

TO THE FOURTH QUESTION, it should be said that there are two sins to consider in someone who eats unworthily, namely, the sin by which he was rendered unworthy for eating, and the sin of eating unworthily. Therefore, since the sin of unbelief is graver than all other sins, the unbeliever eating is more unworthy to eat. But since he does not believe that what is received is of such great dignity as it is, he does not only sin in abuse, for the ignorance of unbelief, although it does not excuse what follows from sin completely, nevertheless it excuses it somewhat, as is seen in the sin of those killing Christ: for *if they had known, they never would have crucified the Lord of glory* (1 Cor 2:8). And by this ignorance of theirs their sin was lightened, as Anselm says;[36] and likewise Paul says about himself, *I received mercy because I acted ignorantly in my unbelief* (1 Tim 1:13). And so an unbeliever is more unworthy to eat, but a believing sinner eats more unworthily.

REPLY OBJ. 1: An unbeliever shows contempt for Christ in his own person in the sin of unbelief, for he rejects his teaching; but in eating the body of Christ he shows contempt not expressly but implicitly, inasmuch as that ignorance by which he does not believe Christ to be present under the sacrament is not invincible ignorance; hence because he can act as if he believed, likewise he is judged as if he believed, in that genus of sin; although actual and explicit contempt would worsen the quantity of this sin, and so as to the eating itself a sinful believer sins more.

REPLY OBJ. 2: Although those things that belong to faith, and particularly those surrounding this sacrament, are not so consonant with human reason considered in themselves, nevertheless as spoken by God and proved by portents they are extremely consonant with reason. For nothing is as consonant with reason as that God is to be believed in everything that he says and attests. However, the teaching of the faith, *since it had taken its beginning in being told by the Lord, with signs and portents attesting, and various distributions of the Holy Spirit, was confirmed in us by those who heard him* (Heb 2:3); and so the sin of unbelief is more grave even than the sin of eating unworthily.

---

36. See Anselm, *Cur Deus Homo*, Bk. 2, ch. 15 (*Opera Omnia*, ed. Schmitt, 2:115).

TERTIUM AUTEM argumentum concludit, quod infidelis indignior sit; et hoc concedendum est.

REPLY OBJ. 3: However, the third objection concludes that an unbeliever is more unworthy, and this should be granted.

Response to Quaestiuncula 5

AD QUINTAM QUAESTIONEM dicendum, quod ad hoc quod aliquis digne corpus Christi manducet, duo requiruntur: scilicet ut sit in statu gratiae, per quam capiti Christo unitur; et quod in actu mens ejus feratur ad divina; unde et sacerdos monet populum sursum corda ad Deum habere. Peccatum autem quanto est gravius, tanto magis a gratia elongat; unde cum peccata spiritualia secundum genus sint graviora carnalibus, ut per Gregorium patet, quamvis aliquod carnale aliquo spirituali sit gravius loquendo in genere; per peccatum spirituale aliquis efficitur magis indignus manducationis corporis Christi quam per peccatum carnale quantum ad primum quod requirebatur ad digne manducandum. Sed quia per peccatum carnale, per luxuriam praecipue, mens humana deprimitur ut ad superna ferri non possit, quia etiam *in actu matrimoniali Spiritus Sanctus corda prophetarum non tangit*, ut Hieronymus dicit, et secundum Philosophum in 7 *Ethic.*, impossibile est hominem aliquid intelligere in ipsa delectatione venereorum; ideo per peccatum carnale homo magis indignus redditur quantum ad secundum quod exigebatur ad digne manducandum. Sed quia multo gravius est habitum gratiae tollere quam actum virtutis impedire, cum illud pertineat ad peccatum mortale semper, hoc autem interdum ad veniale; major indignitas relinquitur, ex defectu primi quam ex defectu secundi; et ideo, simpliciter loquendo, plus peccat qui peccato majori irretitus accedit, nisi per ignorantiam excusetur. Certius autem cognosci potest peccatum mortale in peccatis carnis, praecipue luxuria, quam in peccatis spiritualibus; et ideo quantum ad hoc per accidens peccat plus accedens cum carnali peccato; quamvis simpliciter et per se loquendo peccet plus accedens cum spirituali, si spirituale carnali sit gravius.

AD PRIMUM ergo dicendum, quod hoc idem quod de peccato luxuriae dicit Hieronymus, de quolibet peccato mortali dici potest: quia qui manducat indigne, reus est corporis et sanguinis Domini aliquo modo, ut dictum est.

AD SECUNDUM dicendum, quod illa immunditia corporis procedit ex immunditia mentis: quia non inqui-

TO THE FIFTH QUESTION, it should be said that for someone to eat the body of Christ worthily, two things are required: namely, that he be in the state of grace, by which he is united to Christ the head; and that his mind be actually directed toward divine things; hence also the priest advises the people to have their hearts lifted to God. However, the more grave the sin, the more it removes one from grace; hence since spiritual sins are more grave according to their kind than fleshly sins, as Gregory shows,[37] although some carnal sin may be more grave than a spiritual one when speaking in kind, by spiritual sin someone is made more unworthy of eating the body of Christ than by carnal sin as to the first thing that was required for eating worthily. But since by carnal sin, particularly lust, the human mind is pressed down so that it cannot be directed to higher things—for even *in the matrimonial act the Holy Spirit does not touch the hearts of the prophets*, as Jerome says,[38] and according to the Philosopher in the *Ethics* 7,[39] it is impossible for a man to understand anything in the moment of sexual pleasure—thus by carnal sin a man is rendered more unworthy as to the second thing that is required for eating worthily. But since it is much graver to take away a habit of grace than to prevent an act of virtue, since the former always pertains to mortal sin, while the latter is sometimes venial, a greater unworthiness remains from the defect of the first kind than from a defect of the second kind. And so, simply speaking, someone sins more who approaches entangled in a greater sin, unless he is excused by ignorance. However, mortal sin can more certainly be recognized in sins of the flesh, particularly lust, than in spiritual sins. And so in that respect someone sins more incidentally by approaching the sacrament with carnal sin, although simply and essentially speaking he sins more who approaches with spiritual sin, if the spiritual is more grave than the carnal.

REPLY OBJ. 1: The same thing that Jerome says about the sin of lust can be said about any mortal sin: for whoever eats unworthily is answerable for the body and blood of the Lord in some way, as has been said.

REPLY OBJ. 2: That uncleanliness of body proceeds from an uncleanliness of mind, for the body is not polluted

---

37. Gregory the Great, *Moralia in Iob* (CCSL 143B), Bk. 31, ch. 45.
38. Jerome, *Adversus Jovinianum*, Bk. 1, n. 36 (PL 23:255).
39. Aristotle, *Nicomachean Ethics*, Bk. 7, ch. 5 (1147a15).

natur corpus nisi de consensu mentis, ut dicit Lucia. Unde magis pensatur indignitas ex mente quam ex carne.

without the consent of the mind, as Lucy says.[40] Hence it is considered a greater indignity from the mind than from the body.

Response to Quaestiuncula 6

AD SEXTAM QUAESTIONEM dicendum, quod ea quae in sacramentis geruntur exterius, debent respondere his quae interius geruntur; unde secundum quod homo ad Christum accedit interius mente, ita ad ejus sacramentum debet accedere corpore. Quidam autem non accedunt neque fide neque caritate; unde tales arcendi sunt ab inspectione sacramenti et assumptione. Quidam autem accedunt fide sine caritate; et tales possunt videre, sed non sumere: quia per caritatem aliquis Christo incorporatur; sed per fidem accedens, adhuc longius stat.

AD PRIMUM ergo dicendum, quod hoc non erat propter dignitatem arcae, quod prohibita erat videri, sed propter figuram: *omnia enim in figura contingebant illis*, 1 Corinth. 10, 11: quia non licet nisi majoribus et perfectis secreta fidei, quae per arcam significantur, curiose scrutari: quia *qui perscrutator est majestatis, opprimetur a gloria*; Prov. 25, 27.

AD SECUNDUM dicendum, quod humilitas alicujus commendatur in hoc etiam quod a licitis abstinet; et ideo non sequitur, si aliquis peccator abstinens ab hoc ad tempus laudatur, quod propter hoc non abstinens peccet.

TO THE SIXTH QUESTION, it should be said that the things that are done outwardly in the sacraments should correspond to those things that are accomplished inwardly; hence according as a man comes close to Christ inwardly, in his mind, so he should approach the sacrament of him bodily. However, some people approach with neither faith nor charity; hence they are to be kept away from looking at or receiving the sacrament. But some people approach with faith but without charity; and they can see, but not receive, because by charity someone is incorporated into Christ, but someone who approaches with faith is still standing a long way off.

REPLY OBJ. 1: It was not because of the dignity of the Ark that it was forbidden to be seen, but because of the figure: *for everything happened to them in figure* (1 Cor 10:11). For the secrets of the faith, which were symbolized by the Ark, were only permitted to be gazed upon intently by the greater and more perfect, since *whoever is a searcher of majesty, shall be overwhelmed by glory* (Prov 25:27).

REPLY OBJ. 2: Someone's humility is revealed in the fact that he even abstains from what is permitted; and so it does not follow, if some sinner abstaining from this for a time is praised, that because of this he would sin if he did not abstain.

---

40. See *The Golden Legend*, ch. 4, in Ryan, 1:28.

ARTICLE 4

Whether those who are bodily impure may eat of the body of Christ[41]

Quaestiuncula 1

AD QUARTUM SIC PROCEDITUR. Videtur quod nocturna pollutio quae in somnis accidit, sit peccatum. Meritum enim et demeritum, cum sint contraria, nata sunt fieri circa idem. Sed homo in somnis mereri potest, sicut patet de Salomone, qui dormiens a Domino sapientiae donum impetravit: 2 Paralip. 1. Ergo et potest aliquis demereri: ergo si in somnis in aliquod peccatum consentiat, peccatum est, quod in nocturna pollutione frequenter accidit.

PRAETEREA, quicumque non habet mentem ligatam, non excusatur a peccato, si aliquod turpe committere consentiat. Sed mens dormientis non videtur esse ligata, cum non sit actus corporis ex cujus passione somnus accidit; immo videtur quod debeat esse magis libera, quia immobilitatis exterioribus sensibus, interiores, a quibus immediate mens accipit, confortantur; et quaedam quandoque de futuris mente dormiens percipit quae vigilans percipere non potest. Ergo non excusatur a peccato, si in aliquod turpe consentiat; et sic idem quod prius.

PRAETEREA, quicumque potest deliberare et ratiocinari, videtur usum liberi arbitrii habere, quod inquirendo eligit. Sed dormiens, ut experimento scitur, interdum argumentatur, et argumenta solvit. Ergo habet usum liberi arbitrii et sic idem quod prius.

PRAETEREA, quicumque potest consentire et dissentire alicui turpi, reus esse videtur, si consentiat: quia talis videtur esse dominus sui actus. Sed dormiens aliquando dissentit turpitudini praesentatae, aliquando autem consentit. Ergo quando consentit, videtur esse reus peccati.

PRAETEREA, actiones et motus ex terminis judicantur. Sed nocturna pollutio frequenter vigilia finitur quamvis in somno inchoetur. Ergo est judicanda ac si in vigilia fieret; et ita est peccatum.

SED CONTRA, est quod Augustinus dicit, 12 super Genes. ad litteram: *ipsa phantasia quae fit in cogitatione sermocinantis, cum expressa fuerit in visione somniantis, ut inter illam et veram conjunctionem corporum non*

OBJ. 1: To the fourth we proceed thus. It seems that nightime ejaculations that happen during sleep are a sin. For merit and demerit, since they are opposites, come to be regarding the same thing. But a man can merit while asleep, as is clear from the case of Solomon, who begged the gift of wisdom from the Lord while sleeping (2 Chr 1:10). Therefore, someone can also demerit, for if he consents to any sin during sleep, it is a sin, and this frequently happens during nocturnal emissions.

OBJ. 2: Furthermore, anyone whose mind is not bound is not excused from sin, if he consents to commit anything base. But the mind of someone sleeping does not seem to be bound, since it is not the act of the body by whose passion sleep happens, but rather it seems to be more free, since when the external senses are immobilized, the interior senses, from which the mind receives directly, are strengthened; and some people sometimes perceive future things in their minds while sleeping, which the waking mind cannot perceive. Therefore, it is not excused from sin, if it consents to anything base, and so, the same as in the first objection.

OBJ. 3: Furthermore, anyone who is able to deliberate and reason seems to have the use of his free will, which chooses by inquiring. But when we are sleeping, as is known by experience, sometimes we debate and resolve a debate. Therefore, we have the use of free will, and so the same as above.

OBJ. 4: Furthermore, anyone who can consent to and dissent from something base seems to be culpable if he consents, for a person like this seems to be master of his own acts. But someone who is sleeping sometimes dissents from the baseness that is presented to him, and sometimes consents. Therefore, when he consents, he seems to be culpable for sin.

OBJ. 5: Furthermore, actions and motions are judged by their ends. But nocturnal emission frequently ends in waking, although it starts during sleep. Therefore, it is to be judged as though it happened while awake, and then it is a sin.

ON THE CONTRARY, as Augustine says in his literal commentary on Genesis: *when those imaginations that happen in someone's thought while talking, have been made explicit in the mind's eye of someone sleeping, so that the distinc-*

---

41. Parallel: *ST* III, q. 80, a. 7.

discernatur, continue movetur caro, et sequitur quod eum motum sequi solet; cum hoc tam sine peccato fiat, quam sine peccato a vigilantibus dicitur, quod ut diceretur sine dubio cogitatum est.

PRAETEREA, Philosophus dicit in 1 *Ethic.*, quod secundum dimidium vitae, scilicet somnum, non differt felix a misero neque vitiosus a studioso. Sed secundum peccatum differunt. Ergo peccatum non potest in somnis accidere.

tion between that union and the true union of bodies cannot be discerned, the flesh is moved persistently, and what follows is what usually follows this movement; since this happens as much without sin as it is spoken of without sin by those who are awake, which was thought so that it might be said without doubt.[42]

FURTHERMORE, the Philosopher says in *Ethics* 1 that in the half of life, namely sleep, there is no difference between a happy man and a miserable one, or between a vicious one and a diligent one.[43] But these do differ in sin. Therefore, sin cannot happen in sleep.

Quaestiuncula 2

ULTERIUS. Videtur quod non impediat a sumptione corporis Christi. Veniale enim peccatum magis displicet Deo quam quaelibet immunditia corporalis quae fit sine peccato. Sed nocturna pollutio non est peccatum, ut ex auctoritate Augustini inducta patet. Ergo cum veniale peccatum non impediret a sumptione corporis Christi, multo minus nocturna pollutio impedit.

PRAETEREA, non est dubium quin peccatum mortale plus impedit quam nocturna pollutio. Sed aliquis post peccatum mortale confessum, potest corpus Christi manducare. Ergo multo fortius qui pollutionem nocturnam confessus est, potest eadem die manducare corpus Christi.

PRAETEREA, homo debet impedire peccatum alterius mortale, quantumcumque potest. Sed si aliquis in peccato mortali existens celebret Missam, constat quod peccat mortaliter. Ergo si aliquis non habens conscientiam peccati mortalis possit hoc impedire celebrando loco ejus, videtur quod debeat celebrare, etiam si sit nocturna pollutione pollutus.

PRAETEREA, turpis cogitatio aliquando sine peccato accidit, ut ex verbis Augustini inductis patet: crapulatio autem sine peccato accidere non potest. Sed secundum Gregorium, pollutio quae ex crapula accidit, a communione non impedit, si necessitas incumbat. Ergo nec illa quae ex turpi cogitatione praecedente in vigilia procedit, nec illa quae ex infirmitate naturae, ut Gregorius dicit. Ergo nulla pollutio impedit.

SED CONTRA est quod dicitur Levit. 15, 16: *vir a quo egreditur semen coitus . . . immundus erit usque ad vesperam.* Sed immundis non licet sancta tangere. Ergo multo minus corpus Christi manducare.

PRAETEREA, Isidorus dicit, et habetur in Decr. dist. 6: *qui nocturna illusione polluitur, quamvis extra memo-*

OBJ. 1: Moreover, it seems that it would not prevent the reception of the body of Christ. For venial sin displeases God more than any bodily uncleanness that happens without sin. But nocturnal emission is not a sin, as can be concluded from the authority of Augustine. Therefore, since venial sin would not prevent someone from receiving the body of Christ, much less should nocturnal emission.

OBJ. 2: Furthermore, there is no doubt whether mortal sin prevents more than nocturnal emission. But someone after confessing a mortal sin can eat the body of Christ. Therefore, much more can someone who has confessed nighttime emission eat the body of Christ on the same day.

OBJ. 3: Furthermore, a man should prevent the mortal sin of another as much as he can. But if someone should celebrate Mass in mortal sin, it is clear that he sins mortally. Therefore, if someone who is not conscious of mortal sin could prevent this by celebrating Mass in his place, it seems he should celebrate, even if he had been soiled by nighttime emission.

OBJ. 4: Furthermore, base thoughts sometimes happen to one, without sin, as is evident from the words of Augustine cited. However, intoxication cannot happen without sin. But according to Gregory,[44] the soiling that happens by intoxication does not prevent someone from Holy Communion, if necessity presses him. Therefore, neither do those things that proceed from base thoughts one had while awake, nor those things that proceed from the weakness of nature, as Gregory says. Therefore, no pollution prevents it.

ON THE CONTRARY, it is said: *a man from whom seed of copulation goes out . . . will be unclean until evening* (Lev 15:16). But it is not permitted to the unclean to touch holy things. Therefore, much less to eat the body of Christ.

FURTHERMORE, Isidore says, and it is had in the Decretal, Distinction 6: *whoever is polluted by nocturnal illusion,*

---

42. Augustine, *On the Literal Meaning of Genesis*, Bk. 12, par. 15 (CSEL 28.1:400).
43. Aristotle, *Nicomachean Ethics*, Bk. 1, ch. 13 (1102b5).
44. Gregory the Great, *Epistles*, Bk. 9, Epistle 64 (PL 77:1198).

riam turpium cogitationum se sentiat inquinatum, tamen hoc ut tentaretur suae culpae tribuat, et suam immunditiam statim fletibus tergat. Sed ille qui purgatione indiget, debet a perceptione hujus sacramenti abstinere. Ergo pollutus nocturna pollutione impeditur a perceptione corporis Christi.

although he feels himself stained without the memory of base thoughts, nevertheless, so that he may be tried, let him attribute this to his own guilt, and immediately wash away his uncleanness with tears.[45] But a person who needs purification should abstain from receiving this sacrament. Therefore, someone polluted by nocturnal emission is impeded from receiving the body of Christ.

Quaestiuncula 3

ULTERIUS. Videtur quod propter immunditiam pure corporalem aliquis a perceptione hujus sacramenti impediatur. Deut. 23, 12: *habebitis locum extra castra*, dicit Glossa: *corporalem munditiam diligit Deus*. Ergo corporalem immunditiam odit; et ita propter corporalem immunditiam debet homo ab hoc sacramento abstinere.

PRAETEREA, major est dignitas hujus sacramenti quam omnium sacramentorum veteris testamenti. Sed in veteri lege et mulieres post partum, et patientes fluxum menstrui, et seminiflui immundi reputabantur respectu sacramentorum veteris testamenti. Ergo multo fortius debent abstinere a perceptione hujus sacramenti.

PRAETEREA, sacerdoti leproso interdicitur facultas celebrandi, ut patet Extra. de clerico aegrotante vel debilitato: *tua nos*. Ergo eadem ratione propter lepram debet laicus a perceptione hujus sacramenti abstinere.

SED CONTRA, poena non debetur poenae, sed culpae: alioquin consurgeret duplex tribulatio, quod est contra id quod dicitur Nahum 1. Sed omnes praedictae immunditiae corporales poenae quaedam sunt. Ergo propter eas non debet aliquis a sacramento altaris impediri, quod est maxima poena.

PRAETEREA, naturalibus non meremur neque demeremur. Sed omnes praedictae immunditiae ex causis naturalibus accidunt. Ergo propter eas non meretur aliquis a participatione hujus sacramenti impediri.

OBJ. 1: Moreover, it seems that because of purely bodily uncleanness someone is impeded from receiving this sacrament. For the Gloss on this text, *you will have a place outside the camp* (Deut 23:12), says, *God loves bodily cleanliness.*[46] Therefore, he hates bodily uncleanness, and so because of bodily uncleanness a man should abstain from this sacrament.

OBJ. 2: Furthermore, the dignity of this sacrament is greater than all of the sacraments of the Old Testament. But in the Old Law, women after childbirth, and those suffering their monthly period, and men suffering a flow of semen were all considered unclean with regards to the sacraments of the Old Testament. Therefore, much more should they abstain from the reception of this sacrament.

OBJ. 3: Furthermore, the faculty of celebrating Mass is forbidden to a leprous priest, as is evident from the *Decretals* concerning sick or debilitated clergy. Therefore, by the same reasoning a lay person should abstain from this sacrament on account of leprosy.

ON THE CONTRARY, no punishment is due to a punishment, but only to a fault; otherwise two troubles would arise, which is against what is said in Nahum 1:9. But all the bodily uncleannesses that have been mentioned are some kind of punishment. Therefore, no one should be prevented from the sacrament of the altar because of them, for this is the greatest punishment.

FURTHERMORE, we neither merit nor demerit by natural things. But all the mentioned uncleannesses happen from natural causes. Therefore, someone does not deserve to be impeded from partaking of this sacrament by them.

Response to Quaestiuncula 1

RESPONDEO dicendum ad primam quaestionem, quod omne peccatum, secundum Augustinum, est in voluntate: motus autem voluntatis praesupponit judicium rationis, eo quod est apparentis boni vel vere vel false; unde ubi non potest esse judicium rationis, non

TO THE FIRST QUESTION, I answer that every sin, according to Augustine, is in the will;[47] but the movement of the will presupposes the judgment of reason, by the fact that it moves toward an apparent good either truly or falsely. For this reason, where there is no judgment of reason there can-

---

45. Isidore, *Sententiae*, Bk. 3, ch. 6, sent. 14 (CCSL 111:220); Gratian's *Decretals*, p. 1, d. 6, can. 3 (PL 187:42).
46. *Glossa ordinaria*, PL 113:478.
47. Augustine, *De libero arbitrio* (CCSL 29), Bk. III, ch. 17; *De duabus animabus* (CSEL 25), ch. 10.

potest esse voluntatis motus. In somnis autem judicium rationis impeditur. Judicium enim perfectum haberi non potest de aliqua cognitione, nisi per resolutionem ad principium unde cognitio ortum habet; sicut patet quod cognitio conclusionum ortum habet a principiis; unde judicium rectum de conclusione haberi non potest nisi resolvendo ad principia indemonstrabilia. Cum ergo omnis cognitio intellectus nostri a sensu oriatur, non potest esse judicium rectum nisi reducatur ad sensum. Et ideo Philosophus dicit in 6 *Ethic.*, quod sicut principia indemonstrabilia, quorum est intellectus, sunt extrema, scilicet resolutionis, ita et singularia, quorum est sensus. In somno autem sensus ligati sunt; et ideo nullum judicium animae est liberum, neque rationis neque sensus communis; et ideo neque motus appetitivae partis est liber; et propter hoc non potest aliquis peccare in somno, neque mereri. Sed tamen potest in somno accidere signum peccati vel meriti, inquantum somnia habent causas imaginationis vigilantium; unde dicit Philosophus in 1 *Ethic.*, quod *inquantum paulatim pertranseunt quidam motus*, scilicet a vigilantibus ad dormientes, *meliora sunt phantasmata studiosorum quam quorumlibet*; et Augustinus, 12 *super Genes.*, quod *propter affectionem animae bonam etiam in somnis quaedam ejus merita clarent.*

AD PRIMUM ergo dicendum, quod secundum quod Augustinus ibidem dicit, Salomonis petitio in somnis facta placuisse Deo et remunerationem invenisse dicitur pro bono desiderio prius habito, quod in somno per signum sanctae petitionis claruit; non quod tunc in somno intellexit.

AD SECUNDUM dicendum, quod mens humana habet duos respectus: unum a superiora, quibus illustratur: alium ad corpus a quo recipit, et quod regit. Ex parte illa qua anima a supernis accipit, per somnum non ligatur, immo magis libera redditur quanto fit a corporalibus curis magis absoluta; et ideo etiam ex influentia superni luminis aliqua de futuris percipere potest dormiens quae vigilans scire non posset. Ex parte autem illa qua a corpore recipit, oportet quod ligetur quantum ad ultimum judicium et completum, ligatis sensibus a quibus ejus cognitio initium sumit; quamvis etiam imaginatio ejus non ligetur, quae immediate ei species rerum subministrat.

AD TERTIUM dicendum, quod liberi arbitrii est eligere, secundum quod patet ex Augustini definitione in 2 Lib., dist. 24, quaest. 1, art. 1, posita: electio autem est quasi conclusio consilii, ut dicitur in 3 *Ethic.* unde ad judicium pertinet, vel judicium praesupponit; et ideo

not be a movement of the will. Now in sleep the judgment of reason is impeded. For a perfect judgment cannot be had about any thought, except through retracing back to the beginning whence the thought arose; just as it is clear that the knowledge of conclusions has its source in the principles. And so a right judgment of a conclusion cannot be had without retracing it to indemonstrable principles. Since, therefore, every thought of our intellect arises from the senses, there cannot be a right judgment that is not traceable to sensation. And so the Philosopher says, in *Ethics* 6,[48] that just as indemonstrable principles, which pertain to the understanding, are at the ends, namely of logical reasoning, so also are the singulars, which pertain to the senses. However, in sleep the senses are bound; and so no judgment of the soul is free, whether of reason or of the common sense; and so neither is any movement of the appetitive part free, and because of this a person can neither sin during sleep, nor merit. But nevertheless there can be a sign of sin or merit in sleep, inasmuch as the causes of images in dreams come from waking images; hence the Philosopher says, in *Ethics* 1,[49] that *inasmuch as certain movements only pass little by little*, namely from waking to sleeping, *the imaginations of the diligent are better than anyone else's*; and Augustine says in his *Commentary on Genesis* that *because of a soul's good affections, certain of its merits may shine even in sleep.*[50]

REPLY OBJ. 1: According to what Augustine says in the same place, Solomon's request made in sleep is said to have pleased God and found reward because of the good desire he already had, which shone forth in his dream by the sign of this holy request, not because he had understanding of anything in his sleep.

REPLY OBJ. 2: The human mind has two considerations: one is from higher things, by which it is illuminated; the other is for the body from which it receives and which it rules. On the side of the soul's reception of things from above, it is not bound by sleep, but on the contrary, it is rendered more free to the extent that it is more released from bodily cares. And so also by the inflowing of higher light someone can perceive things about the future while sleeping, which, awake, he could not know. However, on the side of its reception from the body, it must be bound as to the last and complete judgment, since the senses are bound from which its thinking takes its beginning; although its imagination is not also bound, which directly supplies to it the species of things.

REPLY OBJ. 3: It pertains to free will to choose, as is clear from the definition of Augustine in Book II, Distinction 24, Question 1, Article 1. But choice is like the conclusion of counsel, as it says in *Ethics* 3.[51] And so it pertains to judgment, or presupposes judgment. And so although

48. Aristotle, *Nicomachean Ethics*, Bk. 6, ch. 12 (1143a36 et seq.).
49. Aristotle, *Nicomachean Ethics*, Bk. 1, ch. 13 (1102b10).
50. Augustine, *De Genesi ad litteram*, Bk. 12, ch. 15 (CSEL, 28,1:400).
51. Aristotle, *Nicomachean Ethics*, Bk. 3, ch. 5 (1113a4).

quamvis aliquem usum alicujus rationis homo dormiens habere possit, secundum quod sensus minus ligantur, tamen usum liberi arbitrii in eligendo habere non potest.

Ad quartum dicendum, quod secundum quod sensus magis vel minus ligatur a passione somni, hoc etiam judicium rationis magis vel minus impeditur. Unde quandoque homo dormiens considerat, haec quae apparent somnia esse. Sed quia in dormiendo nunquam sunt sensus soluti ex toto, ideo etiam rationis judicium non est ex toto liberum; unde semper cum aliqua falsitate judicium rationis est, etiam si quantum ad aliquid sit verum; et inde contingit quod aliquis in somno aliquando consentit turpitudini, aliquando non. Quia tamen judicium rationis non est omnino liberum, et per consequens nec liberi arbitrii usus; ideo nec talis consensus vel dissensus potest esse meritorius vel demeritorius in se.

Ad quintum dicendum, quod corporales motus non pertinent ad meritum vel demeritum, nisi secundum quod a voluntate quasi a principio causantur; et ideo nocturna pollutio magis judicatur quantum ad rationem meriti vel demeriti, secundum principium quod est in dormiendo, quam secundum terminum qui est in vigilando: quia ex quo in dormiendo excitatus est motus carnis, non subjacet voluntati vigilantis ulterius motus ille, nec reputatur evigilasse, quousque perfectum usum liberi arbitrii recuperavit. Potest tamen contingere quod in ipsa evigilatione peccatum oriatur, si quidem pollutio propter delectationem placeat: quod quidem erit veniale peccatum, si sit ex surreptione talis placentia; mortale autem, si sit cum deliberante consensu, et praecipue cum appetitu futuri. Ista autem placentia non facit praeteritam pollutionem peccatum, quia ipsius causa non est, sed ipsa in se peccatum est. Si autem placeat ut naturae exoneratio, vel alleviatio, peccatum non creditur.

a man asleep may have a certain use of some reason, according as his senses are less bound, nevertheless, he cannot have the use of free will in choosing.

Reply Obj. 4: To the degree that the senses are more or less bound by the passion of sleep, this judgment of reason is also more or less impeded. And this is why whenever a man asleep considers something, those things that appear are dreams. But since while sleeping the senses are never completely shut off, for this reason also the judgment of reason is not completely free; hence the judgment of reason is always with a certain falsity, even if it is true in a certain respect; and so it happens that someone asleep sometimes consents to something base, but sometimes does not. For nevertheless the judgment of reason is not entirely free, and as a result neither is the free will; and so this kind of consent or dissent cannot be meritorious or demeritorious in itself.

Reply Obj. 5: Bodily movements do not pertain to merit or demerit, except to the extent that they are caused by the will as their principle. And so nighttime emission is judged as to merit or demerit more according to the beginning that is in sleeping, rather than the end terminus that is in waking, because from the fact that the movement of the flesh was excited while asleep, that final movement is not subject to the will once awake, nor is it considered to have been awake until the point that it recovered the perfect use of the free will. Nevertheless it can happen that at the moment of waking a sin will arise, if someone should enjoy the emission because of pleasure, which indeed would be a venial sin, if this pleasure should be on the sly; but it would be mortal if it were with the consent of someone deliberating, and particularly with a future desire. However, this pleasure does not make the foregoing emission a sin, for it did not cause it, but is a sin on its own. However, if someone were pleased at the natural unburdening or relief, that is not believed to be a sin.

Response to Quaestiuncula 2

Ad secundam quaestionem dicendum, quod ad hoc quod homo digne ad sacramentum Eucharistiae accedat, tria requiruntur. Primo munditia conscientiae; quae non nisi per peccatum tollitur. Secundo erectio mentis ad Deum per actualem devotionem; et haec per mentis hebetudinem vel occupationem aut evagationem interdum sine peccato amittitur. Tertio etiam munditia corporalis; unde et celebrantes, vel tractaturi aliquod sacramentum, propter reverentiam manus lavant. Unde primo et principaliter peccatum impedit; secundo indevotio sive hebetudo mentis; tertio corporalis immunditia; et haec tria quandoque concurrunt in aliqua pollutione nocturna, quandoque duo ex his, quandoque unum tantum; et secundum hoc homo magis vel minus

To the second question, it should be said that for a man to be worthy to approach the sacrament, three things are required. First, cleanness of conscience, which can only be taken away by sin. Second, raising the mind to God by active devotion, and this is lost sometimes without sin by the mind's being sluggish, or distracted, or wandering. Third, also cleanness of body, which is why those celebrating or about to handle some sacrament also wash their hands out of reverence. And this is why sin impedes, first and principally; second, lack of devotion or sluggishness of mind; third, bodily uncleanness. And sometimes in nighttime emission, these three things come together, or sometimes two of them, sometimes just one; and according to this, a man is more or less impeded. And so the different

impeditur; et ideo distinguendae sunt pollutionum differentiae. Distinguitur autem dupliciter pollutio nocturna.

Primo quantum ad causam. Eorum enim quae in somnis apparent, triplex est causa. Una extrinseca spiritualis, sicut in his quae per spirituales substantias nobis revelantur. Alia intrinseca spiritualis, sicut quando phantasmata quae apparent dormientibus, sunt reliquiae praecedentium cogitationum. Tertia est corporalis intrinseca, sicut quando phlegma dulce ad linguam decurrit, somniat homo comedere dulcia; unde medici ex somnis, corporis dispositionem conjiciunt. Pollutio ergo quandoque ex illusione accidit, quando phantasmata per causam extrinsecam spiritualem, scilicet daemones, commoventur; quandoque ex reliquiis praeteritarum cogitationum, quod est causa spiritualis intrinseca; quandoque ex causa intrinseca naturali: quae quidem causa vel fuit voluntati subjecta, sicut est quando ex superfluitate cibi aut potus praecedente pollutio accidit; vel non fuit voluntati subjecta, sicut sive accidat ex debilitate naturae impotentis retinere semen, sive ex ejus virtute superflua expellentis, sive quocumque alio modo, quod in idem redit.

Secundo distinguitur pollutio quantum ad modum: quia quandoque accidit sine imaginatione, quandoque cum imaginatione; et hoc dupliciter: quia quandoque in ipsa somni imaginatione homo turpitudini consentit, quandoque dissentit, et tamen pollutio accidit. Quando igitur sine imaginatione pollutio accidit, signum est quod pollutio ex causa sit corporali intrinseca. Sed quando cum imagine, potest sic vel sic esse. In omnibus igitur praedictis pollutionibus corporalis immunditia est communis; sed quaedam mentis hebetatio non est nisi in illis pollutionibus quae cum imaginatione accidunt: quia in illis quae sine imaginatione accidunt, anima nihil participare videtur. Nulla autem dictarum est peccatum, ut ex dictis patet, sed potest esse effectus peccati significans praecedens peccatum veniale vel mortale. Peccatum autem mortale ex necessitate praecepti a perceptione Eucharistiae impedit, quia mortaliter peccat qui cum conscientia peccati mortalis accedit. Hebetudo autem mentis et immunditia corporalis est quaedam indecentia honestatis: quia indevotio quaedam videtur sic accedere, nisi necessitas urgeat.

Et ideo considerandum est, utrum in causa pollutionis possit inveniri peccatum praecedens: quia cogitatio turpium quandoque est sine peccato, sicut cum in cogitatione tantum manet, ut cum quis disputans de talibus, oportet quod loquens cogitet; aliquando etiam cum peccato veniali, quando ad affectionem cogitatio pertingens in sola delectatione finitur; quandoque autem etiam mortali, quando consensus adjungitur. Et quia cogitationi tali de propinquo est delectatio, et delectationi consensus, unde in dubium potest verti, utrum sequens

kinds of pollution are to be distinguished, and this in two ways.

First, as to cause. For there can be three causes for things that appear in dreams. One is external and spiritual, like in those things that are revealed to us by spiritual substances. Another is internal and spiritual, as when the images that appear to us asleep are left behind by the thoughts we had before. Third is internal and physical, as when sweet mucus runs onto the tongue, a man dreams that he is eating sweets; and this is how doctors infer the disposition of the body from dreams. Therefore, pollution sometimes happens from an illusion, when images are provoked by extrinsic spiritual causes, namely, demons; sometimes from the remains of past thoughts, which is the intrinsic spiritual cause; sometimes from an intrinsic natural cause, which cause was either subject to the will, as it is when pollution happens from an excess of food or drink beforehand; or else it was not subject to the will, as if it happens from the natural weakness of someone unable to retain semen, or from an excessive power of expelling it, or in any other way that ends up the same.

Second, pollution is distinguished as to its mode, for sometimes it happens without imagination, sometimes with imagination, and this in two ways: for sometimes in the dreaming itself a man consents to something base, and sometimes he dissents, and still the pollution occurs. Therefore, when the pollution occurs without imagination, it is a sign that the pollution is from an internal physical cause. But when it happens with images, it can be this way or that way. Therefore all the pollutions brought up have bodily uncleanness in common. But a certain stupor of the mind only exists in those pollutions that happen with imagination, since in those that happen without imagining, the soul seems to take no part. However, none of the examples given is a sin, as is clear from what has been said, but it can be an effect of sin, signifying a foregoing sin that was venial or mortal. Now a mortal sin impedes the reception of the Eucharist by the necessity of a precept, for anyone conscious of mortal sin who approaches this sacrament sins mortally. But mental stupor and bodily uncleannness are a kind of unbecomingness of honor; for it seems to be a certain lack of devotion to approach in this condition, unless necessity should urge one.

And so it should be considered whether in the cause of the pollution a foregoing sin was to be found, for thinking about base things is sometimes without sin, as when it remains only in the thoughts, like when someone discussing these things has to think about them to speak about them. Sometimes it is also with venial sin, when the thought reaching into the emotions ends in pleasure alone; but sometimes it is mortal, when consent is given to it. And since pleasure is very close to this kind of thinking, and consent is right beside pleasure, for this reason it is open

pollutio ex peccato acciderit, vel non, et aut veniali, aut mortali; satis tamen probabiliter potest conjici non praecessisse consensus, quando in ipsa somni imaginatione anima dissentit; non tamen oportet quod, si consentiat, quod consensus in vigilando praecessit: quia hoc potest accidere propter ligamen judicii rationis, quod quandoque magis quandoque minus est liberum in somno. Unde in tali pollutione si ad causam recurrens dubitet de consensu, omnino abstinere debet. Si autem expresse inveniat consensum non praecessisse, et necessitas urgeat, aut aliqua causa potior reformet pactum, potest accedere, aut etiam celebrare non obstante corporis immunditia, aut hebetatione mentis: alias si necessitas non incumbat, videtur non exhibere debitam reverentiam sacramento. Non tamen si celebrat, mortaliter peccat, sed venialiter, sicut cum quis quandoque mentis evagationem patitur. Quando autem ex illusione accidit, si illusionis causa in nobis praecessit, puta cum quis indevotus ad dormiendum accesserit; idem est judicium et de pollutione quae ex cogitatione praecedenti causatur.

Si autem in nobis causa non praecesserit, immo magis causa contraria, et hoc frequenter accidat, et praecipue in diebus quibus quis communicare debet; signum est quod diabolus homini fructum Eucharistiae percipiendae auferre conatur. Unde in tali casu consultum fuit cuidam monacho, ut in collationibus patrum legitur, quod, communicaret; et sic diabolus videns se non posse consequi intentum, ab illusione cessavit. Si autem ex cibo praecedenti aut potu acciderit, idem est judicium et de pollutione quae ex turpi cogitatione processit; nisi intantum quod non ita de facili accidit peccare mortaliter in sumptione cibi sicut in cogitatione turpi. Et quia aliquando haec pollutio sine imaginatione accidit, illa vero nunquam; illa autem quae ex naturae dispositione accidit, non est signum alicujus peccati, sed potest hebetationem mentis inducere, si cum imaginatione contingat, immunditiam autem corporalem habet; et ideo si necessitas immineat, vel devotio exposcat, talis non impeditur, et praecipue quando non cum imaginatione accidit. Tamen si propter reverentiam abstineat, laudandus est, quando infirmitas non est perpetua. Et quia non ita de facili potest percipi ex qua causa contingat, ideo tutius est abstinere, nisi necessitas incumbat. Debet autem abstinere, ut dicunt, usque ad vigintiquatuor horas: quia in tali spatio natura deordinata per corporalem immunditiam et mentis hebetationem, reordinatur.

AD PRIMUM ergo dicendum, quod quamvis peccatum quodlibet veniale magis ad impuritatem pertineat

to question whether the pollution following happened from sin, or not, and whether it was venial or mortal. Nevertheless it can be deduced probably enough that consent did not happen first, when in the dream itself the soul dissented. Still, if he consented, it does not necessarily mean that consent would have preceded if he had been awake, for this can happen because of the binding of the judgment of reason, which is sometimes more and sometimes less free in sleep. For this reason, in this kind of pollution, if going back to the cause one should be unsure of whether he consented, he should abstain entirely. But if he finds explicitly that consent did not happen first, and necessity urges, or some stronger reason shapes his intention, he can approach, or even celebrate despite his uncleanness of body or stupor of mind; otherwise if necessity does not compel him, he would seem not to show due reverence to the sacrament. Still, if he celebrates, he does not sin mortally, but venially, like when someone sometimes allows his mind to wander. However, when it happens by an illusion, if the cause of the illusion was in us before, for example when someone falls asleep out of a lack of devotion, the judgment is the same as when the pollution is caused by the preceding thoughts.

However, if the cause was not in us before, but rather the opposite cause, and this happens often, and particularly on those days when someone should receive Communion, then it is a sign that the devil is trying to take away the fruit of receiving the Eucharist from a man. And so in this case a certain monk was advised, as is read in the *Conferences of the Fathers*,[52] that he receive Communion; and so the devil, seeing that he could not accomplish his aim, stopped the illusion. However, if it had happened from food or drink taken before, the judgment is the same as of pollution that proceeded from base thoughts, except inasmuch as it is not quite as easy to fall into mortal sin in the consumption of food as in thinking base things. And since the pollution from food sometimes happens without any imagination, but the pollution from base thoughts never does, while that which happens from the disposition of nature is not a sign of any sin, but it can introduce a mental stupor if it happens with imagination, although it has bodily uncleanness; thus if there is risk of an emergency, or devotion demands it, someone in this state is not impeded, and especially when it happens without imagination. Nevertheless, if he should abstain out of reverence, he is to be praised, when the infirmity is not perpetual. And since what caused it cannot so easily be perceived, for this reason it is safer to abstain unless necessity compels. Moreover, he should abstain, as they say, for twenty-four hours: for in such an interval nature, which was disordered by bodily uncleanness and mental stupor, is reordered.

REPLY OBJ. 1: Although any venial sin pertains more to impurity of the mind in itself than nighttime pollution

---

52. See John Cassian, *Collationes*, collection 23, ch. 6 (CSEL 13:621).

mentis secundum se quam pollutio nocturna, et secundum hoc magis Deo displiceat; tamen peccatum veniale non ita hebetat animam et corpus inquinat, nec ita de facili est signum peccati mortalis, sicut pollutio; et ideo ratio non sequitur.

AD SECUNDUM dicendum, quod non esset consulendum alicui quod statim post peccatum mortale etiam contritus et confessus, ad Eucharistiam accederet; sed deberet, nisi magna necessitas urgeret, per aliquod tempus propter reverentiam abstinere; et praeterea confessio purgat maculam mentis, non autem immunditiam corporalem et hebetudinem, quae contingit in mente ex depressione ipsius ad carnem.

AD TERTIUM dicendum, quod quidam dicunt quod homo debet peccare venialiter, ut alium a peccato mortali impediat. Sed hoc dictum contradictionem implicat: quia ex hoc ipso quod dicitur peccatum, ponitur indebitum fieri. Unde si aliquid fit quod nullo modo possit non esse peccatum, non debet fieri, nec etiam bonum est fieri, nec licitum, ut alius a peccato mortali liberetur; quamvis ad hoc ex quadam pietate animi etiam multi boni inclinarentur. Sed potest hoc contingere ut aliquid quod alias esset peccatum veniale, ex tali causa factum desineret esse peccatum; sicut dicere aliquod verbum jocosum quod non esset otiosum si diceretur causa piae utilitatis; unde si talis pollutio sit, quae in casu necessitatis non impediat, deberet pollutus in casu proposito celebrare; alias non.

AD QUARTUM dicendum, quod turpis cogitatio dicitur non solum quae de turpibus est (quia de eis non potest esse honesta cogitatio); sed quae turpitudinem habet propter delectationem vel consensum adjunctum; et haec quidem turpitudo magis horrenda est quam illa quae in cibo accidit: tum quia magis vitari potest, cum difficillimum sit in cibo modum tenere: tum quia est magis propinqua ad mortale peccatum.

does, and accordingly, it displeases God more, nevertheless, venial sin does not dull the soul and soil the body so much, nor is it so easily a sign of mortal sin, as pollution; and so the argument does not follow.

REPLY OBJ. 2: No one would be counseled to approach the Eucharist immediately after a mortal sin, even if it were repented and confessed, but he should abstain for some time out of reverence, unless a great necessity urged him. And furthermore, confession purifies the mind's stain, but not the bodily uncleanness and stupor that happens to the mind from its sinking down to the flesh.

REPLY OBJ. 3: Some people say that a man should sin venially to prevent another from sinning mortally. But this saying implies a contradiction: for by the very fact that it is called sin, it is set down as the wrong thing to be done. For this reason if something is done that in no way could not be a sin, it should not be done, nor is it a good thing to do, nor is it permitted so that someone might be freed from sinning mortally; although many good men may be inclined to it out of a certain piety of soul. But it can happen that something that would otherwise be a venial sin may cease to be a sin when done for a reason like this, like saying a certain joking word that would not be idle if it were said for the sake of a pious benefit. Therefore, if there were that kind of pollution, which would not impede in a case of necessity, the one suffering it should celebrate in the case proposed, but otherwise not.

REPLY OBJ. 4: Thoughts are called base not only when they are about base things (since there cannot be decent thoughts about these things) but when they dwell on base things for the sake of the pleasure or consent joined to them; and this baseness is indeed more abhorrent than the kind that happens from food: both because it is more able to be avoided, since it is most difficult to keep moderate in food, and because it is closer to mortal sin.

Response to Quaestiuncula 3

AD TERTIAM QUAESTIONEM dicendum, quod cum iste cibus non sit corporis sed mentis cibus, magis in ejus sumptione consideranda est dispositio mentis quam corporis; et ideo distinguendum est in immunditia corporali tantum: quia aut est perpetua, sicut lepra, aut diuturna; vel est temporalis et cito purgabilis. Si quidem sit perpetua vel diuturna, tunc nullo modo propter hoc quis abstinere debet, ne propter immunditiam corporis perdatur fructus mentis, sicut accidit in leprosis patientibus fluxum sanguinis vel seminis. Si autem sit temporalis et facile expurgabilis, tunc si aliquis in mente sit bene dispositus, sumere non prohibetur; quamvis etiam possit ad

TO THE THIRD QUESTION, it should be said that since that food is not for the body but for the mind, the disposition of the mind is more to be considered in its consumption than that of the body. And so the kinds of bodily uncleanness should be distinguished: for either it is perpetual or long-lasting, like leprosy, or it is temporary and quickly purified. If indeed it is perpetual or chronic, then in no way should someone abstain because of it, lest because of the uncleanness of the body the fruit of the mind should be lost, as happens among lepers suffering a hemorrhage of blood or flow of semen. However, if it is temporary and easily purified, then if someone is well disposed in mind, it is not for-

tempus laudabiliter abstinere propter reverentiam tanti sacramenti.

AD PRIMUM ergo dicendum, quod Deus diligit corporalem munditiam, et immunditiam odit, secundum quod pertinet ad reverentiam vel irreverentiam sacramenti; et ideo si ex devotione mentis, non propter irreverentiam, aliquis cum immunditia corporali accedat, Deus acceptat.

AD SECUNDUM dicendum, quod prohibitio immundorum in lege a sanctis magis erat propter significationem quam propter ipsas res; et ideo non oportet quod similiter fiat in novo testamento, ubi veniente veritate figurae cessaverunt.

AD TERTIUM dicendum, quod interdicitur sacerdoti leproso ne celebret publice coram populo propter horrorem; tamen secrete bene potest ex devotione celebrare, nisi sit adeo corruptus quod ministerium sine periculo explere non possit. Leprosus tamen ad sacerdotium promoveri non debet.

bidden for him to receive; although he could also abstain for a time laudably out of respect for so great a sacrament.

REPLY OBJ. 1: God loves bodily cleanness, and hates uncleanness, according as it is related to reverence or irreverence for the sacrament. And so if out of mental devotion, not because of irreverence, someone should approach with bodily uncleanness, God would accept him.

REPLY OBJ. 2: The prohibition of the unclean from holy things under the law was more for the sake of the signification than because of the things themselves; and so it is not necessary that it be done the same way in the New Testament, where, since the truth has come, the figures have ceased.

REPLY OBJ. 3: It is forbidden to a leprous priest to celebrate publicly before the people, on account of the shock; nevertheless, he can celebrate well privately out of devotion, unless he is so debilitated that he cannot fulfill his ministry without danger. And someone with leprosy already should not be advanced to the priesthood.

ARTICLE 5

Whether the body of Christ may be given to anyone to eat

Quaestiuncula 1

AD QUINTUM SIC PROCEDITUR. Videtur quod sacerdos dare non debet corpus Christi petenti, si sciat ipsum esse peccatorem. Medicus enim non debet dare infirmo medicinam quam scit ei esse mortiferam. Sed sacerdos scit peccatori corpus Christi esse mortis causam. Ergo non debet ei dare.

PRAETEREA, contra veritatem vitae non est faciendum aliquid propter vitandum scandalum. Sed dare corpus Christi peccatori est contra veritatem vitae, cum sit contra praeceptum Domini, Matth. 7, 6: *nolite sanctum dare canibus.* Ergo quantumcumque possit sequi scandalum, nullo modo est ei dandum: sicut nec pro aliquo scandalo vitando deberet dari cani, aut in lutum projici.

PRAETEREA, de duobus malis minus malum eligendum est. Sed peccatori minus est malum si infametur, quam si corpus Christi manducet indigne. Ergo magis sacerdos debet ei negare in publico, etiamsi crimen ipsius in notitiam venire debeat, quam ei dare.

PRAETEREA, si dat ei hostiam non consecratam, nullum scandalum erit. Ergo videtur quod hoc debet magis facere.

SED CONTRA, omnis Christi actio nostra est instructio. Sed Christus dedit corpus suum in coena Judae, ut habetur Joan. 13, et Dionysius dicit, *quamvis sciret eum peccatorem.* Ergo et sacerdos peccatori petenti denegare non debet.

PRAETEREA, Augustinus dicit: *non prohibeat dispensator pingues terrae,* idest peccatores, *mensam Domini manducare.*

OBJ. 1: To the fifth we proceed thus. It seems that the priest should not give the body of Christ to someone who asks, if he knows that person to be a sinner.[53] For a doctor should not give to a sick person a medicine that he knows to be lethal. But the priest knows that the body of Christ is lethal to someone in sin. Therefore, he should not give it to him.

OBJ. 2: Furthermore, nothing should be done to avoid scandal that is against the truth of life. But to give the body of Christ to a sinner is against the truth of life, since it is against the command of the Lord, *do not give what is holy to dogs* (Matt 7:6). Therefore, no matter how much scandal might follow, it should in no way be given to him; just as neither should it be given to a dog or thrown in the mud to avoid scandal.

OBJ. 3: Furthermore, the lesser of two evils should be chosen. But for a sinner it is less of an evil if he is defamed than if he eats the body of Christ unworthily. Therefore, a priest should refuse him in public, and should even make his crime publicly known, rather than give him Communion.

OBJ. 4: Furthermore, if he gives him an unconsecrated host, there will be no scandal. Therefore, it seems he should rather do this.

ON THE CONTRARY, every action of Christ is our instruction. But Christ gave his own body to Judas at the Last Supper, as it is had in John 13:26, and as Dionysius says, *although he knew him to be a sinner.*[54] Therefore, the priest should also not refuse a sinner who asks.

FURTHERMORE, Augustine says, *may the steward not prohibit the fat of the land,* i.e., sinners, *to eat at the Lord's table.*[55]

Quaestiuncula 2

ULTERIUS. Videtur quod suspectis de crimine etiam dari debeat. Suspicio enim dubitationem importat. Sed dubia in meliorem partem interpretanda sunt. Ergo videtur quod debeat ei dari ac si esset justus.

OBJ. 1: Moreover, it seems that those suspected of a crime should also be given the sacrament. For suspicion implies doubt. But doubt should be interpreted toward the better part. Therefore, it seems that it should be given to him as though he were a just man.

---

53. Parallels: below, d. 11, q. 3, a. 2, qa. 2, ad 1; *ST* III, q. 80, a. 6; q. 81, a. 2; *Quodl.* V, q. 6, a. 2.
54. Pseudo-Dionysius, *Ecclesiastical Hierarchy,* ch. 3, p. 3, n.1 (PG 3:427).
55. See the *Glossa ordinaria,* PL 113:875.

PRAETEREA, experimentum non sumitur de aliquo crimine, nisi de quo suspicio praecessit. Sed corpus Christi dandum est aliquando alicui ad experimentum de peccato sumendum sub his verbis: *corpus Domini sit tibi ad probationem hodie*; ut dicitur in Decret. Caus. 2, qu. 4, cap. saepe contingit. Ergo dari debet suspectis.

SED CONTRA, si suspectis de crimine daretur corpus Christi, esset scandalum populo videnti et scienti. Sed scandalum vitandum est. Ergo non oportet eis dari corpus Christi.

OBJ. 2: Furthermore, no crime is tried unless there was first a suspicion of it. But the body of Christ is sometimes to be given to someone as a test of sin to be taken under these words: *the body of the Lord is a test for you today*, as it says in the *Decretals*.[56] Therefore, it should be given to those suspected.

ON THE CONTRARY, if those suspected of a crime were given the body of the Lord, it would be a scandal for the people who saw and knew. But scandal is to be avoided. Therefore, the body of Christ must not be given to them.

Quaestiuncula 3

ULTERIUS. Videtur quod amentibus corpus Christi dari non debeat. Quia ad hoc quod aliquis corpus Christi sumat, requiritur diligens examinatio, ut patet 1 Corinth. 11, 28: *probet autem seipsum homo, et sic de pane illo edat et de calice bibat*. Sed hoc non potest in amente procedere. Ergo non debet ei Eucharistia dari.

PRAETEREA, inter amentes etiam energumeni computantur, secundum Dionysium in *Eccl. Hier.*: *energumeni etiam ab inspectione divinorum arcentur*; unde statim post Evangelium in primitiva ecclesia per vocem diaconi cum catechumenis excludebantur. Ergo non debet eis dari Eucharistia.

SED CONTRA Cassianus dicit: *eis qui ab incommodis vexantur spiritibus, communionem sacrosanctam a senioribus nostris nunquam meminimus interdictum*. Ergo cum tales sint amentes, amentibus debet dari.

PRAETEREA, in Decret. Caus. 26, qu. 1, cap.: qui recedunt, dicitur: *amentibus etiam quaecumque pietatis sunt, conferenda sunt*; et loquitur de reconciliatione et sacra communione.

OBJ. 1: Moreover, it seems that the body of Christ should not be given to the mentally disabled.[57] For to receive the body of Christ, a diligent examination of conscience is required, as is clear from 1 Corinthians 11:28: *but let a man examine himself, and then he may eat of that bread and drink of that chalice*. But this cannot happen in someone mentally disabled. Therefore, he ought not to be given the Eucharist.

OBJ. 2: Those possessed are also counted among the mentally disabled, according to Dionysius in the *Ecclesiastical Hierarchy*: *the possessed are also to be kept away from gazing upon divine things*;[58] hence immediately after the Gospel in the early Church they were sent away with the catechumens by the voice of the deacon. Therefore, the Eucharist should not be given to them.

ON THE CONTRARY, Cassian says, *we recall that the most holy Communion was never forbidden by our elders to those who are harassed by troublesome spirits*.[59] Therefore, since such people are mentally disabled, it should be given to the mentally disabled.

FURTHERMORE, in the *Decretals* it is said, *whatever things belong to piety are to be conferred on the mentally disabled*;[60] and it is speaking of reconciliation and sacred Communion.

Quaestiuncula 4

ULTERIUS. Videtur quod etiam pueris dandum sit corpus Christi. Quia per baptismum aliquis ascribitur ad corporis Christi sumptionem; unde et baptizato conferendum est, ut Dionysius dicit. Sed pueri baptizati sunt. Ergo et eis corpus Christi debet dari.

OBJ. 1: Moreover, it seems that the body of Christ should also be given to children.[61] For by baptism someone is enrolled for the consumption of the body of Christ; hence it should be conferred on one who is baptized, as Dionysius says.[62] But children have been baptized. Therefore, the body of Christ should also be given to them.

---

56. See Gratian's *Decretals*, d. 2, q. 5, ch. 23 (PL 187:615).
57. Parallels: below, d. 23, q. 2, a. 2, qa. 3 & 4; *ST* III, q. 80, a. 8; *Super Ioan.* 6, lec. 7.
58. Pseudo-Dionysius, *Ecclesiastical Hierarchy*, ch. 3, p. 1 (PG 3:423).
59. John Cassian, *Collationes*, collection 7, ch. 30 (CSEL 13:207).
60. See Gratian's *Decretals*, cause 26, q. 6, ch. 7 (PL 187:1359).
61. Parallels: below, d. 23, q. 2, a. 2, qa. 3 & 4; *ST* III, q. 80, a. 8; *Super Ioan.* 6, lec. 7.
62. Pseudo-Dionysius, *Ecclesiastical Hierarchy*, ch. 2, p. 2, n. 7 (PG 3:395).

PRAETEREA, vita spiritualis sicut est per baptismum, ita est per Eucharistiam: quia dicitur Joan. 6, 58: *qui manducat me, vivit propter me.* Sed pueris datur baptismus ut habeant spiritualem vitam. Ergo et similiter debet dari eis Eucharistia.

SED CONTRA est quod iste *cibus est grandium*, ut patet per Augustinum. Sed pueri nondum sunt grandes in fide. Ergo non debet eis dari.

OBJ. 2: Furthermore, just as by baptism there is spiritual life, so also by the Eucharist: for it says, *whoever eats me, lives because of me* (John 6:57). But baptism is given to children so that they may have spiritual life. Therefore, in the same way the Eucharist should also be given to them.

ON THE CONTRARY, *This food is for the full-grown*, as is clear from Augustine.[63] But children are not yet full-grown in faith. Therefore, it should not be given to them.

Response to Quaestiuncula 1

RESPONDEO DICENDUM ad primam quaestionem, quod si sacerdos sciat peccatum alicujus qui Eucharistiam petit, per confessionem vel alio quolibet modo, distinguendum est: quia aut peccatum est occultum, aut manifestum. Si est occultum, aut exigit in occulto, aut in manifesto. Si in occulto, debet ei denegare, et monere ne in publico petat. Si autem in manifesto petit, debet ei dare. Primo, quia pro peccato occulto poenam inferens publicam, revelator est confessionis, aut proditor criminis. Secundo, quia quilibet Christianus habet jus in perceptione Eucharistiae, nisi illud per peccatum mortale amittat. Unde cum in facie ecclesiae non constet istum amisisse jus suum, non debet ei in facie ecclesiae denegari: alias daretur facultas malis sacerdotibus pro suo libito punire maxima poena quos vellent. Tertio propter incertitudinem status sumentis: quia *spiritus ubi vult, spirat*, Joan. 3, 8, unde subito potest esse compunctus, et divinitus a peccato purgatus, et divina inspiratione ad sacramentum accedere. Quarto, quia esset scandalum, si denegaretur. Si vero peccatum est manifestum, debet ei denegari sive in occulto sive in manifesto petat.

AD PRIMUM ergo dicendum, quod potius deberet eligere medicus medicinam esse mortiferam infirmo quam sibi, si alterum oporteret. Et similiter sacerdos potius deberet eligere quod peccator assumat ad perditionem suam, quam ipse deneget in perditionem propriam, scandalizando et peccatum occultum revelando. Et praeterea non est certum utrum sit ei mortifera, quia subito homo spiritu Dei mutatur. Et iterum in ipsa petitione peccavit mortaliter in mortale peccatum consentiens.

AD SECUNDUM dicendum, quod non dimittitur tantum propter scandalum, sed propter alias causas quae faciunt; nec esset contra veritatem vitae, si negaret. Dominus ergo non prohibuit simpliciter dare, sed voluntatem dandi, dicens: *nolite sanctum dare canibus.* Sacerdos autem in casu proposito non dat propria sponte, sed magis coactus. Nec est similis ratio de animalibus brutis, et

TO THE FIRST QUESTION, I answer that if a priest knew the sin of someone who seeks the Eucharist, by confession or by some other way, a distinction must be made: for either the sin is hidden, or it is manifest. If it is hidden, either he demands Communion privately or publicly. But if privately, he should deny him, and warn him against asking in public. But if he asks for holy Communion in public, the priest should give it to him. First, because imposing a public penalty for a secret sin is to reveal what is heard in confession, or to betray a crime. Second, because any Christian has the right to receive the Eucharist, unless he loses it by mortal sin. Hence since it is not established in the sight of the Church that this person has lost his right, one ought not to deny it him in the sight of the Church: otherwise faculty would be given to bad priests to punish at will whomever they want with the greatest punishment. Third, because of uncertainty of the status of the recipient: for *the Spirit blows where it will* (John 3:8). And from that he can be suddenly contrite and divinely purified of his sin, and have come to the sacrament by divine inspiration. Fourth, because there would be scandal if he were refused. But if the sin is well known, the priest should refuse him whether he asks in secret or in public.

REPLY OBJ. 1: A doctor should rather choose lethal medicine for the sick person than for himself, if he must choose one or the other. And likewise, the priest should rather choose that a sinner be taken to his perdition than that he should refuse him to his own perdition, by scandalizing and revealing his secret sins. And furthermore, it is not certain whether it would be deadly to him, for by the Spirit of God a man might change in an instant. And again in his very asking the person consenting to a mortal sin has sinned mortally.

REPLY OBJ. 2: He is not to be sent away only because of scandal, but because of other reasons that make it advisable; nor would it be against the truth of life, if he refused. Therefore, the Lord did not simply prohibit giving it, but the will of giving it, by using the verb *nolle* to say, *do not give what is holy to dogs.* But a priest in the case proposed does not give of his own accord, but rather compelled. Nor

---

63. Augustine, *Confessions* (CCSL 27), Bk. 7, ch. 10.

de projectione in lutum: quia causae praedictae non sunt ibi.

AD TERTIUM dicendum, quod secundum Innocentium tertium, *cum nemo debeat unum mortale committere ut proximus aliud non committat, eligendum est potius sacerdoti non prodere peccatorem, quam ut ille non peccet; sed peccator debet potius eligere ut abstinendo reddatur suspectus quam communicando manducet indignus.*

AD QUARTUM dicendum, quod nullo modo debet dari hostia non consecrata pro consecrata: tum quia in sacramento veritatis non debet esse aliqua fictio: tum quia cum manducans adoret quod manducat, ut dicit Augustinus, daret sacerdos ei occasionem idolatrandi. Unde decretalis dicit in casu consimili, quod *falsa sunt abjicienda remedia quae sunt veris periculis graviora.*

RATIONES QUAE SUNT ad oppositum, procedunt solum quando peccator occultus publice petit.

is there any similarity to the argument about brute animals or throwing in the mud: because none of aforementioned reasons are present there.

REPLY OBJ. 3: According to Innocent III,[64] *since no one should commit one mortal sin so that his neighbor does not commit another, it should be chosen rather that the priest not expose the sinner, than that he not sin himself; but the sinner should choose to make himself suspect by abstaining, rather than eat unworthily by receiving Communion.*

REPLY OBJ. 4: In no way should an unconsecrated host be given in place of a consecrated one: both because in the sacrament of truth there should be no pretense, and because when someone who eats it adores what he eats, as Augustine says, the priest would have given him the occasion of idolatry.[65] Hence the Decretal says that in a case like this, *one should reject false remedies, which are more dangerous than true dangers.*[66]

THE ARGUMENTS that are made to the contrary proceed only when a secret sinner requests Communion publicly.

Response to Quaestiuncula 2

AD SECUNDAM QUAESTIONEM dicendum, quod triplex est suspicio. Quaedam violenta, ad cujus contrarium non admittitur probatio; sicut si inveniatur solus cum sola nudus in lecto, loco secreto, et tempore apto ad commixtionem. Alia est probabilis, sicut si inveniatur solus cum sola colloquens in locis suspectis, et frequenter. Tertia est praesumptuosa, quae ex levi conjectura ortum habet. Haec autem ultima deponenda est; in secunda non debet denegari, quia poena non infligitur ubi culpa ignoratur; sed de prima est idem judicium quod de peccato. Unde si sit suspicio procedens ex fama publica, non debet ei dari neque in occulto neque in manifesto; si autem sit singularis ipsius sacerdotis, sic debet dari in publico, sed non in occulto.

AD PRIMUM ergo dicendum, quod quamvis non habeatur in prima suspicione certitudo sensibilis, vel per demonstrationem, tamen habetur talis certitudo quae sufficit ad probationem juris. Non enim in omnibus est similiter certitudo requirenda, ut dicitur 1 *Ethic.*

AD SECUNDUM dicendum, quod decretum illud abrogatum est: quia facere tales probationes est tentare Deum. Vel dicendum, quod intentio illius decreti non est

TO THE SECOND QUESTION, it should be said that there are three kinds of suspicion. One kind is violent, and admits of no evidence to the contrary, as when a man and a woman are found alone, naked in bed, in a hidden place and at a time suited to intercourse. Another is probable, as when a man and woman are found alone often, talking in a suspicious place. The third kind is presumption, which has its origin in a light conjecture. However, this last kind should be laid aside. In the second kind, a person should not be denied, because a penalty is not imposed where guilt is not known; but the first kind is judged the same as the sin. Hence if there is suspicion proceeding from public reputation, the Eucharist should not be given to him in private or in public; but if the suspicion is only in this individual priest, then it should be given to him in public, but not in private.

REPLY OBJ. 1: Although in the first kind of suspicion there is no sensible certitude, or certainty by demonstration, nevertheless, there is the kind of certitude that suffices for proof in the law. For the same kind of certitude is not required for everything, as it says in *Ethics* 1.[67]

REPLY OBJ. 2: That decree has been repealed, because tests like that tempt God. Or it could be said that the intention of that decree is not that a purification like that be

---

64. Innocent III, *De sacro altaris mysterio*, Bk. 4, ch. 13 (PL 217:865).

65. Moos gives as the citation Augustine, *Ennarationes in Psalmos*, Psalm 18, n. 9 (PL 36:1264), which does not seem to be correct. The original passage has remained elusive.

66. From the *Decretalium Gregorii papae IX compilationis*, Bk. 3, title 41, ch. 7, "De homine," retrieved from http://www.hs-augsburg.de/~harsch/Chronologia/Lspost13/GregoriusIX/gre_3t41.html on January 30, 2015.

67. Aristotle, *Nicomachean Ethics*, Bk. 1, ch. 1 (1094b13).

ut talis purgatio fiat, sed ut propter timorem talis purgationis a futuris abstineat.

made, but that out of fear of such a purification, one would abstain in the future.

Response to Quaestiuncula 3

AD TERTIAM QUAESTIONEM dicendum, quod de amentibus distinguendum est. Quidam enim dicuntur large amentes, quia debilem mentem habent, sicut dicitur invisibile quod male videtur; et tamen sunt aliquo modo docibiles eorum quae ad fidem et devotionem sacramenti pertineant: et talibus non oportet corpus Christi denegari. Quidam vero sunt omnino carentes judicio rationis; et isti vel fuerunt tales a nativitate, et tunc eis non debet dari, quia non possunt ad devotionem induci quae requiritur ad hoc sacramentum (quamvis quidam contrarium dicant): vel inciderunt in amentiam post fidem et devotionem sacramenti, et tunc debet eis dari, nisi timeatur periculum vel de vomitu vel de exspuitione, aut aliquo hujusmodi. Et hoc patet per hoc quod habetur in *Decretis*, 26, qu. 6: *si is qui infirmitate poenitentiam petit et dum sacerdos invitatus ad eum venit, vertatur in phrenesim, accepto testimonio ab astantibus qui petitionem audierunt, et reconcilietur, et Eucharistia ejus ori infundatur.*

AD PRIMUM ergo dicendum, quod in isto casu praecedens devotio computatur ei ad dignam manducationem.

AD SECUNDUM dicendum quod daemoniacis non est deneganda communio, nisi forte certum sit quod pro aliquo crimine a diabolo torqueantur; et de talibus loquitur Dionysius. Vel dicendum, et melius, quod ipse vocat *energumenos* illos in quibus adhuc viget virtus daemonis propter peccatum originale nondum extirpatum, eo quod nondum baptismi gratiam consecuti sunt, quibus adhibetur exorcismus post catechismum ante baptismum; unde ipse ponit eos secundo loco post catechumenos.

TO THE THIRD QUESTION, it should be said that a distinction must be made about the mentally disabled. For some of them are called mentally disabled broadly, because they have a weak mind, as something hard to see is called invisible. And nevertheless they can be taught in some way about what would pertain to faith and devotion to the sacrament, and it is not necessary to refuse the body of Christ to such as these. But some are completely lacking in any judgment of reason, and either they were this way from birth, and then it should not be given to them, for they cannot be led to the devotion that is required for this sacrament (although some people say the opposite); or else they fell into mental illness after faith and devotion to the sacrament; and then it should be given to them unless there is a danger of vomiting or spitting out or anything like this. And this is clear from what it says in the *Decretals*, Cause 26, Question 6: *if someone who in his illness seeks penance and while the priest invited to him comes, he reverts to madness, once the testimony is taken from those standing by that they heard his request, let him be both reconciled, and let the Eucharist be placed into his mouth.*[68]

REPLY OBJ. 1: In this case, the devotion he had before is reckoned to him for a worthy reception.

REPLY OBJ. 2: Communion is not to be refused to demoniacs, unless perhaps it is sure that they are being tormented by the devil for some crime; and that is what Dionysius is speaking about. Or it could be said, and better, that he calls *possessed* those in whom the power of the devil still thrives because original sin has not yet been uprooted, by the fact that the grace of baptism has not yet been obtained, for which the exorcism is employed after the catechesis before baptism. And this is why he includes these in second place after the catechumens.

Response to Quaestiuncula 4

AD QUARTAM QUAESTIONEM dicendum, quod pueris carentibus usu rationis, qui non possunt distinguere inter cibum spiritualem et corporalem, non debet Eucharistia dari; quamvis quidam Graeci contrarium teneant, irrationabiliter autem: quia ad Eucharistiae sumptionem exigitur actualis devotio, quam tales pueri habere non possunt. Pueris autem jam incipientibus habere discretionem, etiam ante perfectam aetatem, pu-

TO THE FOURTH QUESTION, it should be said that to children lacking the use of reason, who cannot distinguish between spiritual and bodily food, the Eucharist should not be given, although some of the Byzantines maintain the opposite, though irrationally: because actual devotion is required for the consumption of the Eucharist, which children of that age cannot have. However, once children have begun to have discretion, even before the age of ma-

---

68. Gratian's *Decretals*, cause 26, q. 6, ch. 8 (PL 187:1359).

ta cum sint decem vel undecim annorum, aut circa hoc, potest dari, si in eis signa discretionis appareant et devotionis.

AD PRIMUM ergo dicendum, quod pueri baptizati acquirunt jus percipiendi corpus Christi, non tamen statim, sed tempore competenti; sicut et jus percipiendae hereditatis habent, quamvis eam statim non possideant. Dionysius autem assignat ritum baptismi quoad adultos, ut patet inspicienti verba ejus.

AD SECUNDUM dicendum, quod per baptismum datur primus actus vitae spiritualis, unde est de necessitate salutis; et ideo pueris baptismus dandus est: sed per Eucharistiam datur complementum spiritualis vitae; et ideo illis qui perfectionis secundae, quae est per actualem devotionem, possunt esse capaces, debet dari, prout habetur *de Consecr.*, distinct. 4, cap. in ecclesia, ubi dicitur: *non cogitent vitam habere posse qui sunt expertes corporis et sanguinis Domini*; et loquitur de pueris. Intelligendum est autem quantum ad rem sacramenti, quae est unitas ecclesiae, extra quam non est salus nec vita, et non quantum ad sacramentalem manducationem.

turity, for example when they are ten or eleven years old, or around then, it can be given to them, if signs of discretion and devotion appear in them.

REPLY OBJ. 1: Baptized infants acquire the right to receive the body of Christ, not right away though, but at the fitting time; just as they have the right of receiving their inheritance, although they do not possess it immediately. However, Dionysius describes the rite of baptism for adults, as is clear to anyone who studies his words.

REPLY OBJ. 2: By baptism the first act of the spiritual life is given, which is why it is necessary for salvation; and so baptism must be given to children. But by the Eucharist is given the completion of the spiritual life, and so it should be given to those who can be capable of the second perfection, which is by actual devotion, as it says in the *Decretals*: *let them not think that those who have no share in the Lord's body and blood can have life*; and it is speaking of children. [69] This is to be understood, however, not as to receiving the sacrament, but as to the reality behind the sacrament, which is the unity of the Church, outside of which there is no salvation, nor life.

---

69. Gratian's *Decretals*, Part 3, *De consecratione*, d. 4, ch. 130 (PL 187:1845).

EXPOSITION OF THE TEXT

Crede, et manducasti. Intelligendum est de manducatione spirituali, et fide formata. Ideo autem potius fidem commemorat, quia ipsa est quae maxime in sacramentis operatur.

Nos corpus Christi facti sumus. Ergo spiritualiter manducamus nosipsos. Et dicendum, quod nos non sumus corpus ipsius nisi ratione unionis, quam manducando spiritualiter acquirimus.

Ecce factum est malum. Contrarium dicit supra eodem capite: *indigne quis sumens corpus Christi, non efficit ut malum sit quod accipit.* Et dicendum, quod non sit malum in se, sed sit malum, idest nocivum, isti.

Ita spiritualiter sumamus. Contra: quia in patria nullus usus sacramenti erit; ergo nec spiritualis sumptio. Et dicendum, quod dicitur sumptio consecutio rei sacramenti, quam sacramentum statim non efficit, sed tantum significat, scilicet fruitio divinitatis, quam etiam significat sacramentalis manducatio.

"Believe, and you will have eaten."[70] This is to be understood of spiritual eating and formed faith. However, he commemorates faith rather because it is what is most at work in the sacraments.

"We too have been made the body [of Christ]."[71] Thus, we eat ourselves spiritually. And it should be said that we are not his body except by reason of the union, which we acquire by eating spiritually.

"For you see, wickedness is done."[72] He says the opposite below in the same chapter: *"One who receives the body of the Lord unworthily, does not thereby make that which he receives evil."*[73] And it should be said that it is not evil in itself, but it is evil, that is, harmful, to him.

So we may receive it spiritually.[74] To the contrary: for in heaven there will be no use of the sacrament; therefore neither will there be spiritual reception. And it should be said that what is called reception is obtaining the reality behind the sacrament, which the sacrament does not cause immediately, but only signifies, namely, the enjoyment of the divinity, which sacramental eating also signifies.

---

70. Peter Lombard, *Sententiae* IV, 9.1 (55). 2 citing Augustine, *In Ioannem*, tr. 25 n12.
71. *Sent.* IV, 9.1 (55), 3, citing Augustine, *Sermo 229: De sacramentis fidelium.*
72. *Sent.* IV, 9.2 (56), 2, citing Augustine, *In Iohannis euangelium tractatus* (CCSL 36), Tract. 62, n. 1.
73. *Sent.* IV, 9.2 (56), 3, citing Augustine, *De baptismo contra Donatistas*, Bk. 5, ch. 8, n. 9.
74. *Sent.* IV, 9.3 (57), 3.

DISTINCTION 10
THE BODY OF CHRIST IN THE EUCHARIST

Postquam Magister determinavit quod in hoc sacramento tria inveniuntur, aliquid quod est sacramentum tantum, et aliquid quod est res et sacramentum, et aliquid quod est res tantum; et secundum hoc diversimode diversi manducant: in parte ista incipit prosequi de singulis dictorum trium in speciali; unde dividitur in partes tres: in prima determinat de ipso vero corpore Christi, quod est sacramentum, et res contenta in sacramento; in secunda de speciebus panis et vini, quae sunt in sacramentum tantum;[1] 12 dist., ibi: *si autem quaeritur de accidentibus quae remanent . . . in quo subjecto fundentur, potius mihi videtur fatendum existere sine subjecto quam esse in subjecto*; in tertia determinat de effectu sacramenti, qui est res tantum, in fine dist., ibi: *institutum est hoc sacramentum duabus de causis.*

Prima in duas: in prima ostendit verum corpus Christi in altari contineri sub sacramento; in secunda determinat de transubstantiatione, per quam fit ut ibi sit verum corpus Christi, dist. 11: *si autem quaeritur, qualis sit illa conversio . . . definire non sufficio.*

Prima in tres: in prima ponit errorem quorumdam negantium veritatem quam asserere intendit, et probationes eorum; in secunda solvit probationes ipsorum, ibi: *quae ex eadem ratione omnia accipienda sunt*; in tertia inducit auctoritates ad veritatem probandam, ibi: *haec et his similia objiciunt*, etc.

Secunda pars dividitur in partes tres: in prima exponit auctoritates quas illi errantes pro se inducunt, et expositionem sanctorum praedictam confirmat; in secunda ostendit dubitationem esse de quadam auctoritate Augustini inducta pro se, ibi: *deinde addit quod magis movet*; in tertia exponit eam, ibi: *attende his diligenter.*

After the Master has determined that three things are found in this sacrament, something that is sacrament alone, something that is reality-and-sacrament, and something that is reality alone, and according to this difference people eat of it in different ways, in this part he begins to describe individually these three things in particular. For this reason it is divided into three parts: in the first, he considers the true body of Christ itself, which is the sacrament, and the reality contained in the sacrament; in the second, the species of bread and wine, which are the sacrament alone, at Distinction 12: *But if it is asked about the accidents which remain . . . in what subject they inhere, it seems to me to be better to profess that they exist without a subject than that they are in a subject*;[2] in the third, he considers the effect of the sacrament, which is the reality alone, at the end of the distinction: *And this sacrament was instituted for two causes.*[3]

The first is in two parts: in the first, he shows that the true body of Christ is contained under the sacrament on the altar; in the second, he considers transubstantiation, by which it comes about that the true body of Christ is there, Distinction 11: *But if it is asked what is the nature of that change . . . I am not up to the task of defining it.*[4]

The first is in three: in the first, he sets down the error of some people who deny the truth that he intends to assert, and their evidence; in the second, he unravels their arguments, at: *All of these statements are to be taken according to the same line of reasoning*;[5] in the third, he cites authorities for the truth to be proved, at: *They make objection by these and similar texts*, etc.[6]

The second part is divided into three parts: in the first, he explains the authorities that those men cite for their error, and confirms the exposition mentioned of the saints; in the second, he shows that there is a doubt about a certain text of Augustine cited for it, at: *He then adds what troubles the reader more*;[7] in the third, he explains it, at: *Attend to these words with diligence.*[8]

---

1. *in sacramentum tantum—-sacramentum tantum* PLE.
2. Peter Lombard, *Sententiae* IV, 12.1 (66), 1.
3. *Sent* IV, 12.6 (71). 1.
4. *Sent.* IV, 11.3 (60), 1.
5. *Sent.* IV, 10.1 (58), 4.
6. *Sent.* IV, 10.2 (59), 1.
7. *Sent.* IV, 10.2 (58), 7.
8. *Sent.* IV, 10.1 (58), 8.

QUESTION 1

THE BODY OF CHRIST IN THE EUCHARIST

Hic quatuor quaeruntur:

primo, utrum verum corpus Christi contineatur in hoc sacramento;

secundo, utrum totus Christus contineatur in sacramento sub speciebus quae manent;

tertio, qualiter sit ibi;

quarto, quomodo possit agnosci corpus Christi secundum quod est sub sacramento.

Here four questions arise:

first, whether the true body of Christ is contained in this sacrament;

second, whether the whole Christ is contained in this sacrament;

third, how it is there;

fourth, how the body of Christ can be recognized as it exists under this sacrament.

ARTICLE 1

Whether the true body of Christ is contained in this sacrament[9]

AD PRIMUM SIC PROCEDITUR. Videtur quod in sacramento altaris non contineatur verum corpus Christi. In his enim quae ad pietatem et reverentiam pertinent divinam, nihil debet esse quod in crudelitatem vel irreverentiam sonet. Sed manducare carnes hominis sonat in quamdam bestialem crudelitatem et irreverentiam manducati. Ergo et in sacramento pietatis, quod ad manducationis usum ordinatur, non debet esse verum corpus Christi quod manducatur.

PRAETEREA, sacramenta ordinantur ad utilitatem nostram. Sed Joan. 6, 64, dicitur: *caro non prodest quidquam.* Ergo corpus Christi, sive ejus caro, non debet esse in hoc sacramento, sed solum ejus spiritualis virtus.

PRAETEREA, Gregorius dicit in Homil. de regulo: *corporalem praesentiam Domini quaerebat, qui per spiritum nunquam deerat. Minus itaque in illum credidit, quem non putabat posse salutem dare, nisi praesens esset in corpore.* Sed non ponimus quod corpus Christi sit in altari, nisi ut nobis sit causa salutis. Ergo videtur quod ex infirmitate fidei procedat.

PRAETEREA, nihil potest esse nunc ubi prius non fuit, loco praeexistente, nisi ipsum mutetur. Sed corpus Christi ante consecrationem non erat in altari. Si ergo post consecrationem sit ibi secundum veritatem, oportet quod aliquo modo sit mutatum; quod non potest dici. Ergo non est verum ibi corpus Christi.

OBJ. 1: To the first we proceed thus. It seems that the true body of Christ is not contained in the sacrament of the altar. For in those things that pertain to piety and divine reverence, there should be nothing that implies cruelty or irreverence. But to eat the flesh of a man suggests a certain bestial cruelty and an irreverence for what is eaten. Therefore, in the sacrament of piety which is ordered toward eating as its use, it should not be the true body of Christ that is eaten.

OBJ. 2: Furthermore, sacraments are ordained to our benefit. But it is said: *the flesh does not profit anything* (John 6:63). Therefore, the body of Christ, or his flesh, should not be in this sacrament but only his spiritual power.

OBJ. 3: Furthermore, Gregory says on his Homily on Regulus: *he was seeking the bodily presence of the Lord, who was never lacking through the Spirit. And so he believed less in him, whom he did not believe could give salvation unless he were bodily present.*[10] But we do not hold that the body of Christ is on the altar unless as it is a cause of salvation for us. Therefore, it seems that it proceeds from weakness of faith.

OBJ. 4: Furthermore, nothing can be now in a place where it was not before unless it is changed, assuming the place already existed. But the body of Christ before the consecration was not on the altar. If therefore after the consecration it is there according to the truth, it is necessary that it has changed in some way, which cannot be said. Therefore, the true body of Christ is not there.

---

9. Parallels: *ST* III, q. 75, a. 1; *SCG* IV, chs. 61ff.; *De ven. sacr. altar.*, serm. 11; *Super Matt.* 26; *Super Ioan.* 6, lec. 6; *Super I ad Cor.* 11, lec. 5.

10. Gregory the Great, *Homilies on the Gospels*, Bk. 2, homily 28, par. 1 (CCSL 141:240).

PRAETEREA, nullum corpus potest esse simul in diversis locis. Sed corpus Christi est in caelo vere, quo ascendit. Ergo impossibile est quod sit in altari. Probatio primae. Nihil continetur extra suos terminos, si termini cujuslibet corporis locati sunt simul cum terminis corporis locantis. Ergo nullum corpus locatum in uno loco, potest esse extra terminos illius loci; et ita non potest esse in duobus locis simul.

PRAETEREA, eadem ratione potest poni corpus Christi esse in diversis locis et esse ubique, sicut ponentes angelum esse in diversis locis, dicunt quod est etiam ubique si velit. Sed ponere quod corpus Christi ubique possit esse, est haereticum: quia hoc solius divinitatis est. Ergo non potest esse in diversis locis simul.

PRAETEREA, angelus est simplicior quam corpus Christi. Sed angelus non potest esse simul in pluribus locis. Ergo neque corpus Christi: et sic idem quod prius.

PRAETEREA, corpus Christi, inquantum corpus, non habet quod sit in pluribus locis, quia sic cuilibet corpori conveniret; neque inquantum gloriosum, quia multo fortius spiritui glorificato conveniret; neque inquantum divinitati unitum, quia unio non ponit ipsum extra limites corporis. Ergo nullo modo sibi competit.

SED CONTRA, 1 Corinth. 11, 19: *qui manducat et bibit indigne, judicium sibi manducat et bibit, non dijudicans corpus Domini.* Sed si esset corpus Christi ibi secundum solam significationem, non oporteret dijudicare hunc cibum ab aliis: quia quilibet panis eadem ratione significat corpus Christi. Ergo oportet ponere quod sit ibi verum corpus Christi.

PRAETEREA, veritas in novo testamento debet respondere figuris veteris testamenti. Sed in veteri testamento ipse agnus, qui figurabat Christum, sumebatur in cibum, ut patet Exod. 12: ergo in nova lege ipsum verum corpus Christi quod per agnum significatur, debet manducari.

PRAETEREA, Deuter. 32, 4 dicitur: *Dei perfecta sunt opera.* Sed non perfecte conjungeremur Deo per sacramenta quae nobis tradit, nisi sub aliquo eorum ipse vere contineretur. Ergo in hoc sacramento verum corpus Christi continetur: quia non est aliud assignare sacramentum in quo Christus realiter contineatur.

AD HOC etiam sunt multae auctoritates in littera positae.

RESPONDEO dicendum, quod sub sacramento altaris continetur verum corpus Christi, quod de Virgine traxit: et contrarium dicere est haeresis, quia derogatur veritati Scripturae, qua Dominus dicit, Mat. xxvi et alibi: *hoc est corpus meum.* Ratio autem quare oportet quod in hoc sacramento ipse Christus contineatur, in principio hu-

OBJ. 5: Furthermore, no body can be in different places at the same time. But the body of Christ is truly in heaven, where he ascended. Therefore, it is impossible for it to be on the altar. Proof of the first: nothing is contained outside its limits, if the limits of any contained body are simultaneous with the limits of the containing body. Therefore, no body located in one place can be outside the limits of that place, and so it cannot be in two places at once.

OBJ. 6: Furthermore, by the same reasoning it can be stated that the body of Christ is in different places and that it is everywhere, as those who say an angel can be in different places say that it is also everywhere if it wills. But to state that the body of Christ can be everywhere is heretical: for that only belongs to divinity. Therefore, it cannot be in different places at once.

OBJ. 7: Furthermore, an angel is simpler than the body of Christ. But an angel cannot be in many places at one time. Therefore, neither can the body of Christ: and so the same as before.

OBJ. 8: Furthermore, the body of Christ is not able to be in several places just insofar as it is a body, for then this ability would belong to any body; nor is it able to be in several places at once insofar as it is glorified, for this ability would belong with even more reason to a glorified spirit; nor as united to the divinity, for the union does not place it outside the limits of a body. Therefore, it does not apply to it in any way.

ON THE CONTRARY, *Whoever eats and drinks unworthily, eats and drinks to his own judgment, not discerning the body of the Lord* (1 Cor 11:27, 29). But if the body of Christ were there only according to signification, it would not be necessary to discern this food from others: for any bread signifies the body of Christ by that reasoning. Therefore, it is necessary to state that it is the true body of Christ.

FURTHERMORE, the truth in the New Testament should correspond to the figures of the Old Testament. But in the Old Testament the very lamb that prefigured Christ was taken as food, as is clear from Exodus 12. Therefore, in the New Law the true body of Christ itself, which was symbolized by the lamb, must be eaten.

FURTHERMORE, it is said, *the works of God are perfect* (Deut 32:4). But we would not be perfectly united to God by the sacraments that he gives us, unless he himself were contained in one of them. Therefore, in this sacrament the true body of Christ is contained, since there is no other sacrament one could designate as really containing Christ.

FOR THIS many authorities are also cited in the text.

I ANSWER THAT, the true body of Christ, which he drew from the Virgin, is contained under the sacrament of the altar: and to say the opposite is heresy, for it detracts from the truth of Scripture, where the Lord says, in Matthew 26:26 and elsewhere: *this is my body.* Now the reason why it is necessary that Christ be contained in this sacrament was

jus tractatus, dist. 8, dicta est: quia scilicet non ita perfecte nobis Christus conjungeretur, si sola sacramenta illa haberemus in quibus conjungitur nobis Christus per virtutem suam in sacramentis illis participatam; et ideo oportet esse aliquod sacramentum in quo Christus non participative, sed per suam essentiam contineatur, ut sit perfecta conjunctio capitis ad membra. Consequuntur autem et aliae utilitates, sicut ostensio maximae caritatis in hoc quod seipsum dat nobis in cibum, sublevatio spei ex tam familiari conjunctione ad ipsum, et maximum meritum fidei in hoc quod creduntur multa in hoc sacramento quae non solum praeter rationem sunt, sed etiam contra sensum, ut videtur; et multae aliae utilitates, quae explicari sufficienter non possunt.

Ad primum ergo dicendum, quod in crudelitatem saperet, et maximam irreverentiam, si corpus Christi ad modum cibi corporalis manducaretur, ut scilicet ipsum verum corpus Christi dilaniaretur et dentibus attereretur. Hoc autem non contingit in sacramentali manducatione: quia ipsum per manducationem non laceratur, sed manducantes integros facit, speciebus, sub quibus latet, divisis, ut infra dicetur, dist. 12.

Ad secundum dicendum, quod nihil prodesset caro Christi corporaliter manducata, ut dictum est; multum autem prodest sacramentaliter manducata. Unde Augustinus dicit: *caro non prodest quidquam; sed quomodo illi intellexerunt: sic enim intellexerunt carnem quomodo in cadaver venditur, aut in macello dilaniatur.*

Ad tertium dicendum, quod non dicimus verum corpus Christi esse in altari, eo quod aliter non posset salutem conferre, sicut Regulus credebat; sed quia iste est convenientissimus modus salvandi, sicut et convenientissimus modus reparationis humanae fuit per hoc quod *verbum caro factum est, et habitavit in nobis*: quamvis etiam alius modus reparationis fuit possibilis.

Ad quartum dicendum, quod non oportet semper illud quod est nunc ubi prius non fuit localiter, mutatum esse: quia potest aliquid esse conversum in ipsum, sicut cum aer in ignem convertitur. Sed tamen ignis mutatur mutatione generationis; et hoc accidit, quia ignis in illa conversione non est terminus generationis, sed compositum ex subjecto generationis, scilicet materia, et termino, scilicet forma; unde forma ipsa quae est terminus, per se non generatur, ut in 7 *Metaphysica* probatur: generatur autem per accidens, quia non est per se subsistens, sed in alio, quo mutato mutari dicitur. Corpus ergo Christi est in altari cum prius non fuerit, quia panis conversus est in ipsum, ita quod ipsum totum corpus est terminus per se conversionis, sicut ibi erat forma: non tamen est ens in alio sicut forma, sed per se subsistens; et ita

said at the beginning of this treatise, Distinction 8: namely, because Christ would not be so perfectly united with us if we only had those sacraments in which Christ is joined to us by his power participated by those sacraments. And so there has to be a certain sacrament in which Christ is contained not by participation but by his own essence, so that there is a complete union of head with members. There also follow other benefits, however, like showing the greatest charity in the fact that he gives himself to us as food; the increase of hope from such an intimate union with him; and the greatest merit of faith in that many things are believed in this sacrament that are not only beyond reason, but even against our senses, as it seems; and many other benefits that cannot sufficiently be explained.

Reply Obj. 1: It would savor of cruelty and the greatest irreverence if the body of Christ were eaten in the mode of physical food, namely so that the true body of Christ itself were torn to pieces and ground up by our teeth. However, this does not happen in sacramental eating, for it is not mangled by this eating, but it makes the ones eating it whole, when they divide the appearances under which it is hidden, as will be said below at Distinction 12.

Reply Obj. 2: The flesh of Christ would have profited nothing if it were eaten physically, as was said; however, it profits much when eaten sacramentally. Hence Augustine says, *flesh profits nothing, but how did they understand, for they understood flesh as what is sold as a carcass, or is torn to pieces at the butcher's.*[11]

Reply Obj. 3: We do not say the true body of Christ is on the altar as though it could not confer salvation in any other way, as Regulus believed; but because this is the most fitting mode of being saved, just as also the most fitting mode of human reparation was by the fact that *the Word became flesh, and dwelt among us* (John 1:14), although another mode of reparation was also possible.

Reply Obj. 4: It is not always necessary that something that is now where it was not before be changed, for something can be converted into it, just as when air is converted into fire. Nevertheless, fire is changed by the change of the generation, and this happens because fire is not in that conversion as the terminus of generation but as a composite of the subject of generation, namely, the matter, and the terminus, namely, the form. And this is why the form that is the terminus is not generated *per se*, as is proved in *Metaphysics* 7.[12] However, it is generated *per accidens*, since it does not subsist on its own, but in something else, and it is said to have changed when that changes. Therefore, the body of Christ is on the altar when it was not before, since the bread has converted into it, so that the whole body itself is the terminus of the conversion *per se*, just as the form

---

11. See Augustine, *In Iohannis euangelium tractatus* (CCSL 36), Tract. 27, n. 5: "quid est ergo: non prodest quidquam caro? non prodest quidquam, sed quomodo illi intellexerunt: carnem quippe sic intellexerunt, quomodo in cadauere dilaniatur, aut in macello uenditur, non quomodo spiritu uegetatur."

12. Aristotle, *Metaphysics*, Bk. 7, ch. 6 (1033b5–6).

non oportet quod sit localiter motum, neque generatum per se, neque per accidens.

AD QUINTUM dicendum, quod nullum corpus comparatur ad locum nisi mediantibus dimensionibus quantitatis; et ideo ibi corpus est aliquod ut in loco, ubi commensurantur dimensiones ejus dimensionibus loci; et secundum hoc corpus Christi non est nisi in uno loco tantum, scilicet in caelo. Sed quia conversa est in corpus Christi substantia panis, qui prius erat in hoc loco determinate mediantibus dimensionibus suis, quae manent transubstantiatione facta; ideo manet locus, non quidem immediate habens ordinem ad corpus Christi secundum proprias dimensiones, sed secundum dimensiones panis remanentes, sub quibus succedit corpus Christi substantiae panis. Et ideo non est hic ut in loco, per se loquendo, sed ut in sacramento, non solum significante, sed continente ipsum ex vi conversionis factae. Et sic patet quod corpus Christi non est extra terminos loci sui per quem modum competit ei esse alicubi vel esse extra aliquid ex dimensionibus propriis. Esse autem alicubi per commensurationem propriarum dimensionum est per se alicubi esse. Et similiter esse extra aliquid secundum situm propriarum dimensionum est per se extra aliquid esse. Sed corpus Christi est extra terminos loci sui qui competit ei secundum proprias dimensiones, quasi per accidens, et hoc modo est sub sacramento quo competit ei esse alicubi ratione illarum dimensionum quae remanserunt ex illo corpore quod conversum est in corpus Christi.

AD SEXTUM dicendum, quod sicut ex dictis patet, corpus Christi non dicitur esse alicubi nisi ratione dimensionum propriarum, et illius corporis quod in ipsum conversum est. Non est autem possibile quod dimensiones ejus propriae sint ubique, neque quod corpus in ipsum convertendum ubique sit; et ideo quamvis corpus Christi sit in pluribus locis aliquo modo, non tamen potest esse ubique.

AD SEPTIMUM dicendum, quod ratio illa bene sequeretur, si ratione propriorum terminorum esset in pluribus locis, quod multo fortius angelo conveniret; sed convenit ei inquantum aliquod corpus convertitur in corpus Christi, non autem in angelum.

AD OCTAVUM dicendum, quod hoc non competit corpori Christi neque inquantum est corpus, neque inquantum est glorificatum, neque inquantum divinitati unitum, sed inquantum est terminus conversionis; unde similiter accideret de corpore lapidis, si Deus simili modo panis substantiam in lapidem converteret, quod non est dubium eum posse.

was in the other case. Yet the body of Christ is not a being in another as form is, but subsists in itself; and so there is no need that it be moved in place, or generated, whether *per se* or *per accidens*.

REPLY OBJ. 5: No body is compared to a place unless by means of the dimensions of quantity, and so the body is there as something in a place where its dimensions are commensurate with the dimensions of the place; and in this regard the body of Christ is in only one place, namely, in heaven. But since the substance of the bread is converted into the body of Christ, which bread before was in this place determinately by means of its dimensions, which remain once transubstantiation has happened; therefore the place remains not indeed immediately, having an order to the body of Christ according to that body's own dimensions, but according to the remaining dimensions of bread, under which the body of Christ takes the place of the substance of bread. And therefore it is not here as in a place, speaking *per se*, but as in a sacrament, not only signifying, but containing it by the power of the conversion made. And so it is clear that the body of Christ is not outside the boundaries of its own place according as it belongs to it to be somewhere or to be outside something by its proper dimensions. Now, to be somewhere by the measure of proper dimensions is to be somewhere *per se*, and likewise to be outside something according to the situation of proper dimensions is to be outside something *per se*. But the body of Christ is outside the boundaries of its place, which belongs to it according to its proper dimensions, as if *per accidens*, and this is how it is under the sacrament, by which it belongs to it to be somewhere by reason of those dimensions which remain from that body which was converted into the body of Christ.

REPLY OBJ. 6: As is clear from what has been said, the body of Christ is only said to be somewhere by reason of its proper dimensions, and those of the body that was converted into it. However, it is not possible that its proper dimensions be everywhere, nor that the body converted into it be everywhere; and so although the body of Christ is in many places in a certain way, nevertheless, it cannot be everywhere.

REPLY OBJ. 7: That argument would work well if the body of Christ were in many places by reason of its own boundaries, which applies even more to an angel; but to be in several places at once applies to it inasmuch as a certain body is converted into the body of Christ, but not into an angel.

REPLY OBJ. 8: This does not apply to the body of Christ as a body, nor as glorified, nor as united with the divinity, but as a terminus of a conversion. And that is why it would happen the same way with the body of a stone, if God in a similar way changed the substance of bread into a stone, and there is no doubt that he could do so.

ARTICLE 2

Whether the whole Christ is contained in this sacrament

Quaestiuncula 1

AD SECUNDUM SIC PROCEDITUR. Videtur quod Christus non contineatur sub sacramento quantum ad animam. Quia Christo non competit esse in altari, ut dictum est, nisi secundum quod panis in ipsum convertitur. Sed constat quod panis non convertitur in animam Christi. Ergo anima Christi non est ibi.

PRAETEREA, Christus est in sacramento altaris, ut cibus fidelium. Sed non est cibus secundum animam, sed secundum corpus: quia dicit Joan. 6, 55: *caro mea vere est cibus.* Ergo non est ibi secundum animam.

PRAETEREA, forma sacramenti debet respondere sacramento. Sed in forma non fit mentio de anima, sed solum de corpore: quia dicitur: *hoc est corpus meum.* Ergo non est ibi secundum animam.

SED CONTRA, quaecumque non separantur secundum esse, ubicumque est unum, et aliud. Sed unum est esse animae Christi et corporis, sicut materiae et formae. Ergo cum corpus Christi sit in altari, erit ibi anima.

PRAETEREA, corpus Christi non est in sacramento inanimatum. Sed corpus sine anima est inanimatum. Ergo Christus non est ibi secundum corpus tantum, sed etiam secundum animam.

OBJ. 1: To the second we proceed thus. It seems that Christ is not contained under the sacrament as to his soul.[13] For it does not belong to Christ to be on the altar, as was said, except insofar as the bread is converted into him. But the bread is obviously not converted into the soul of Christ. Therefore, the soul of Christ is not there.

OBJ. 2: Furthermore, Christ is in the sacrament of the altar as the food of the faithful. But he is not food in his soul, but only in his body: for he says, *my flesh is true food* (John 6:55). Therefore, he is not there according to his soul.

OBJ. 3: Furthermore, a sacrament's form should correspond to the sacrament. But in the form no mention is made of the soul, but only of the body, for it is said, *this is my body.* Therefore, he is not there according to his soul.

ON THE CONTRARY, whenever there are two things that are not separated according to being, where one is, the other is too. But Christ's body and soul are one being, like matter and form. Therefore, since the body of Christ is on the altar, his soul will be there too.

FURTHERMORE, the body of Christ is not an inanimate thing in the sacrament. But a body without a soul is an inanimate thing. Therefore, Christ is not there according to his body alone, but also according to his soul.

Quaestiuncula 2

ULTERIUS. Videtur quod sub specie panis Christus non contineatur inquantum[15] ad carnem animatam. Quia, ut dictum est, corpus Christi est ibi secundum quod cibus. Sed esse cibum non convenit nisi carni; unde Joan. 6, 55: *caro mea vere est cibus.* Ergo non est ibi aliqua pars corporis, nisi caro.

PRAETEREA, quod jam est, non oportet fieri. Si ergo in pane consecrato sunt omnes partes corporis Christi, erit ibi sanguis; ergo non oporteret quod per consecrationem vini iterum ibi fieret.

PRAETEREA, Deus in revelationibus veritatem ostendit: alias revelatio esset causa erroris, quod est inconveniens. Sed species panis ostensa est aliquando ut

OBJ. 1: Moreover, it seems that under the appearance[14] of bread Christ is only contained as living flesh.[16] For, as has been said, the body of Christ is there as food. But being food only applies to the flesh; hence, *my flesh is true food* (John 6:55). Therefore, no part of the body is there except the flesh.

OBJ. 2: Furthermore, what is already does not need to come to be. Therefore, if all the parts of the body of Christ are in the consecrated bread, the blood will be there; therefore it will not be necessary that it come to be there again by the consecration of the wine.

OBJ. 3: Furthermore, God shows truth in his revelations: otherwise the revelation would be the cause of error, which is unfitting. But sometimes the appearance of bread

---

13. Parallels: *ST* III, q. 76, aa. 1 & 2; *SCG* IV, ch. 64; *Quodl.* VII, q. 4, a. 1; *Super Matt.* 26; *Super Ioan.* 6, lec. 6; *Super I ad Cor.* 11, lec. 6.

14. The word *species* has many meanings, including appearance, kind, form, beauty, and the species that is opposed to genus. When Aquinas uses *species* to refer to the Eucharist, he means the substance of the body and blood of Christ under the *appearance* (or accidents) of bread and wine.

15. *contineatur inquantum.—contineatur nisi quantum* PLE.

16. Parallels: *ST* III, q. 76, a. 2; *SCG* IV, ch. 64; *Super Ioan.* 6, lec. 6; *Super I ad Cor.* 11, lec. 6.

caro tantum, sicut legitur in vita beati Gregorii. Ergo non est sub specie panis aliquid de corpore Christi nisi caro, et non sanguis vel os, vel aliquid hujusmodi.

SED CONTRA, sicut corpus Christi significatur in sacramento, ita continetur ibi. Sed significatur secundum quod est; alias significatio esset falsa. Ergo est ibi secundum quod est. Sed caro non est sine sanguine et aliis partibus corporis. Ergo est ibi non solum caro, sed etiam aliae partes corporis.

PRAETEREA, in specie panis significatur totum id quod est res tantum sine sacramento, scilicet unitas corporis mystici, et similiter in vino, ut ex dictis, 8 dist., patet. Sed sicut significatur id quod est res tantum, ita significatur et continetur id quod est res et sacramentum. Ergo et totus Christus, qui est res et sacramentum, continetur sub utraque specie.

is shown as though only flesh were there, as is read in the life of blessed Gregory.[17] Therefore, under the appearance of bread there is not anything of the body of Christ but the flesh, and not blood or bone, or anything else like that.

ON THE CONTRARY, just as the body of Christ is represented in the sacrament, so it is also contained there. But it is represented according as it is, otherwise the signification would be false. Therefore, it is there according as it is. But the flesh is not without blood and other parts of the body. Therefore there is not only flesh there, but also the other parts of the body.

FURTHERMORE, in the species of bread, and likewise in the wine, is represented all that is reality alone without the sacrament, namely, the unity of the mystical body, as is clear from what was said in Distinction 8. But just as what is reality alone is represented, so also what is reality-and-sacrament is represented and contained. Therefore, the whole Christ, who is reality-and-sacrament, is contained under both species.

Quaestiuncula 3

ULTERIUS. Videtur quod non sit ibi corpus Christi secundum propriam qualitatem.[18] Nihil enim quod manet convertitur in alterum. Sed quantitas panis manet. Ergo non convertitur in quantitatem corporis Christi. Sed corpus Christi non est in altari, ut dictum est, nisi ut est terminus conversionis. Ergo non est ibi secundum propriam quantitatem.

PRAETEREA, secundum Philosophum in 4 *Physica*, corpus naturale non potest esse simul cum dimensionibus separatis: quia tunc duae dimensiones essent simul. Sed dimensiones panis manent. Ergo sub eisdem dimensionibus non potest esse corpus Christi cum dimensionibus propriae quantitatis.

PRAETEREA, accidens plus dependet a substantia quam substantia ab accidente. Sed ex parte ejus quod est sacramentum tantum, invenitur accidens sine substantia. Ergo multo magis potest poni ex parte ejus quod est res et sacramentum, quod sit substantia sine accidente; et ita corpus Christi sine quantitate.

PRAETEREA, sicut dictum est supra, ubicumque est corpus aliquod secundum proprias dimensiones, est ibi ut in loco. Sed corpus Christi non est sub sacramento ut in loco, quia jam esset extra terminos loci proprii. Ergo

OBJ. 1: Moreover, it seems that the body of Christ is not there according to its proper quantity.[19] For nothing that remains has been converted into something else. But the quantity of bread remains. Therefore, it is not converted into the quantity of the body of Christ. But the body of Christ is only on the altar, as was said, as the terminus of conversion. Therefore it is not there according to its own quantity.

OBJ. 2: Furthermore, according to the Philosopher in the *Physics* 4,[20] a natural body cannot exist at the same time with separated dimensions, for then two dimensions would exist at the same time. But the dimensions of the bread remain. Therefore, the body of Christ cannot exist under the same dimensions with the dimensions of its own proper quantity.

OBJ. 3: Furthermore, an accident depends more on a substance than a substance on an accident. But on the side of what is sacrament alone, an accident is found without substance. All the more therefore can can one posit on the side of what is reality-and-sacrament that it be a substance without an accident; and so the body of Christ is without quantity.

OBJ. 4: Furthermore, just as was said above, wherever there is a body according to its own dimensions, it is there as in a place. But the body of Christ is not under the sacrament as in a place, since it would then be outside the

---

17. See John the Deacon, *The Life of Saint Gregory the Great*, Bk. 2, n. 41 (PL 75:103).
18. *qualitatem.—quantitatem* PLE.
19. Parallels: *ST* III, q. 76, a. 3; *SCG* IV, ch. 67; *Quodl.* VII, q. 4, a. 1; *Super Matt.* 26; *Super I ad Cor.* 11, lec. 5.
20. Aristotle, *Physics*, Bk. 4, ch. 1 (209a4–6).

impossibile est quod sit ibi secundum dimensiones propria.

SED CONTRA, subjectum nunquam separatur a propria passione. Sed substantiae corporalis propria passio est quantitas dimensiva. Ergo cum substantia corporis Christi sit sub sacramento et quantitas ejus dimensiva erit.

PRAETEREA, de ratione corporis vivi est organizatio, ut patet in 2 *de Anima*. Sed organizatio requirit diversum situm partium; situs autem praesupponit quantitatem. Ergo oportet, cum corpus Christi sit vivum sub sacramento, quod sit ibi sub propria quantitate.

boundaries of its own proper place. Therefore, it is impossible that it be there under its proper dimensions.

ON THE CONTRARY, a subject is never separated from its proper passion. But the proper passion of a bodily substance is dimensive quantity. Therefore, since the substance of the body of Christ is under the sacrament, so will his dimensive quantity also be.

FURTHERMORE, organization is of the nature of a living body, as is clear from *On the Soul* 2.[21] But organization requires a diverse positioning of parts, while a positioning presupposes quantity. Therefore, it is necessary, since the living body of Christ is under the sacrament, that it have its proper quantity there.

Quaestiuncula 4

ULTERIUS. Videtur quod non sit ibi secundum totam quantitatem suam. Constat enim quod quantitas corporis Christi non invenitur extra corpus Christi, ut corpus Christi sit sine propria quantitate. Sed constat quod corpus Christi non est ultra dimensiones panis, neque aliqua pars dimensionis est sub qua non sit corpus Christi. Ergo si est ibi quantitas tota corporis Christi, neque excedit dimensiones panis, neque exceditur. Sed communis animi conceptio est quod duae quantitates, quarum una alteri superposita neque excedit neque exceditur, sunt aequales, ut patet in principio Euclidis. Ergo quantitas corporis Christi tota aequatur quantitati panis: quod est falsum; quia contingit esse etiam majorem et minorem.

PRAETEREA, nullum corpus secundum totam suam quantitatem potest contineri indifferenter a magna et parva quantitate extrinseca. Sed corpus Christi continetur indifferenter sub parva parte vel magna panis consecrati. Ergo non est ibi secundum totam suam quantitatem.

PRAETEREA, quandocumque sub aliqua quantitate extrinseca continetur corpus aliquod habens partes distinctas secundum suam intrinsecam quantitatem totam; contingit assignare sub qua parte illius quantitatis singulae partes contineantur. Sed corpus Christi, cum sit organicum, habet partes distinctas. Si ergo secundum totam suam quantitatem continetur sub dimensionibus, erit assignare ubi sit caput ejus et manus et pes; quod est impossibile: quia parvitas quantitatis non sufficit ad talem distantiam; et praecipue cum partes habeant distantias determinatas.[23]

OBJ. 1: Moreover, it seems that it is not there according to its whole quantity.[22] For it is obvious that the quantity of the body of Christ is not found outside the body of Christ, so that the body is without its proper quantity. But it is evident that the body of Christ is not beyond the dimensions of the bread, nor is there any part of its dimension under which the body of Christ is not. Therefore, if the entire quantity of the body of Christ is there, it neither exceeds the dimensions of the bread, nor is it exceeded. But it is a common conception of the soul that two quantities, of which one superimposed on the other neither exceeds nor is exceeded, are equal, as is clear in the beginning of Euclid. Therefore the whole quantity of the body of Christ is equal to the quantity of bread, which is false, because it happens to be also greater and less.

OBJ. 2: Furthermore, no body according to its whole quantity can be contained equally by a great and small external quantity. But the body of Christ is contained equally in small and large pieces of consecrated bread. Therefore, it is not there according to its own entire quantity.

OBJ. 3: Furthermore, whenever a body having distinct parts according to its own entire intrinsic quantity is contained under a certain extrinsic quantity, it is possible to assign under which part of that quantity individual parts are contained. But the body of Christ, since it is organic, has distinct parts. If, therefore, it is contained under these dimensions according to its whole quantity, one will be able to assign where its head and hands and feet are; which is impossible. For the smallness of quantity is not enough for such a distance, and particularly for parts having determinate distances, because of the many intermediate things having determinate quantities.

---

21. Aristotle, *On the Soul*, Bk. 2, ch. 1 (412a27–412b6).
22. Parallels: *ST* III, q. 76, a. 4; *SCG* IV, chs. 63–64 and 67; *Quodl.* VII, q. 4, a. 1.
23. *determinatas.—determinatas propter multa intermedia quae habent quantitates determinatas* PLE.

SED CONTRA, totalitas corporis attenditur secundum totalitatem quantitatis ejus; quia secundum quantitatem dividitur et partes habet. Sed secundum Augustinum, *Christus totus manducatur in sacramento*. Ergo est ibi secundum totam suam quantitatem.

PRAETEREA, impossibile est aliquid esse alicubi secundum partem quantitatis et non secundum totam, nisi divisa quantitate ipsius. Sed quantitas corporis Christi non dividitur actu, quia corpus illud est impassibile. Ergo cum in sacramento contineatur aliquid quantitatis corporis ejus, impossibile est dicere quod non contineatur in toto.

ON THE CONTRARY, the totality of a body depends on the totality of its quantity, for according to quantity it is divided and has parts. But according to Augustine, *the whole Christ is eaten in this sacrament*.[24] Therefore, he is there according to his whole quantity.

FURTHERMORE, it is impossible for something to be somewhere according to a part of its quantity and not according to the whole, unless its quantity has been divided. But the quantity of the body of Christ is not actually divided, because that body is impassible. Therefore, since a certain quantity of his body is contained in the sacrament, it is impossible to say that it is not contained in its entirety.

Response to Quaestiuncula 1

RESPONDEO dicendum ad primam quaestionem, quod in sacramento altaris continetur aliquid dupliciter: uno modo ex vi sacramenti, alio modo ex naturali concomitantia.

Ex vi quidem sacramenti continetur ibi illud ad quod conversio terminatur. Ad quid autem terminatur conversio, sciri potest ex tribus. Primo ex eo quod convertebatur: non enim convertitur materia sacramenti nisi in id ad quod habet similitudinem secundum proprietatem naturae suae, sicut vinum in sanguinem. Secundo ex significatione formae, cujus virtute fit conversio; unde in illud conversio terminatur quod est significatum per formam. Tertio ex usu sacramenti: quia quod pertinet ad cibum, continetur sub specie panis ex vi sacramenti; quod pertinet ad potum, sub specie vini.

Ex naturali autem concomitantia, et quasi per accidens, continetur sub sacramento illud quod per se non est terminus conversionis, sed sine quo terminus conversionis esse non potest. Secundum hoc ergo patet quod cum anima Christi non habeat similitudinem cum substantia panis, nec in forma sacramenti de anima fiat mentio, nec anima conveniat ad usum sacramenti, qui est manducare et bibere; ad animam non terminatur conversio panis nec vini, sed ad corpus et sanguinem Christi, quae ab anima separata non sunt; et ideo anima non continetur ibi ex vi sacramenti, sed tamen continetur ibi ex naturali concomitantia ad corpus quod vivificat. Unde si fuisset facta conversio panis in corpus Christi quando erat mortuum, anima non fuisset sub sacramento. Et quod dictum est de anima, debet intelligi

TO THE FIRST QUESTION, I answer that there are two ways something can be contained in the sacrament of the altar: in one way, by the power of the sacrament, in another, by natural concomitance.

By the power of the sacrament is contained what the conversion terminates in. Now, what it is that the conversion terminates in can be known by three things. First, from what was converted: for the matter of the sacrament is only converted into something that it bears a resemblance to according to the properties of its own nature, like wine into blood. Second, from the signification of the form, by whose power the conversion happens; and this is why whatever the conversion terminates in is signified by the form. Third, by the use of the sacrament: for what pertains to food is contained under the appearance[25] of bread by the power of the sacrament; what pertains to drink, under the appearance of wine.

Now by natural concomitance, and almost incidentally, there is contained under the sacrament something that is not *per se* a terminus of the conversion, but without which the terminus of conversion cannot exist. According to this, therefore, it is is evident that since the soul of Christ does not have any resemblance to the substance of bread, nor is any mention made of it in the sacrament's form, nor is his soul suited to the use of the sacrament, which is to eat and drink, neither the conversion of the bread nor that of the wine terminates in the soul, but in the body and blood of Christ, which are not now separated from the soul. And this is why the soul is not contained there by the power of the sacrament, but nevertheless it is contained there by natural concomitance with the body that it animates. Hence if the conversion of the bread into the body of Christ had hap-

---

24. See Gratian's *Decretals*, Part 3, *de Consecratione*, d. 2, ch. 75 (PL 187:1772).

25. *Species* has many meanings, including appearance, form, kind, beauty, and the species that is contrasted with a genus. In reference to the Eucharist, Aquinas uses *species* to mean the substance of the body and blood of Christ under the *appearance* (or accidents) of bread and wine.

de divinitate; nisi quod divinitas ejus, etiam praeter sacramentum, est ubique.

ET PER HOC patet responsio ad objecta.

pened when he was dead, the soul would not have been under the sacrament. And what was said about his soul must be understood about his divinity; except that his divinity is everywhere, even apart from the sacrament.

AND BY THIS the answers to the objections are evident.

Response to Quaestiuncula 2

AD SECUNDAM QUAESTIONEM dicendum, quod duplex est usus sacramenti; scilicet manducare et bibere. Manducare autem est usus cibi sicci; sed bibere est usus cibi humidi, qui 'potus' dicitur; et ideo sub specie panis, qui ad usum manducationis ordinatur, continetur ex vi sacramenti non solum caro Christi, sed os, et omnes hujusmodi partes; non autem sanguis, quia continetur ex vi sacramenti sub specie vini, qui ad usum potus ordinatur; quamvis ex naturali concomitantia et sanguis sit sub specie panis, et caro sub specie vini.

AD PRIMUM ergo dicendum, quod ponitur ibi pars pro toto, scilicet caro pro toto corpore: et hanc partem specialiter posuit, ut per similitudinem manducationis corporalis, cui praecipue caro apta est, manuduceret ad sacramentalem, quamvis etiam ossa et aliae hujusmodi partes manducationi aliquo modo competant, cum secundum Avicennam quaedam animalia ipsis nutriantur.

AD SECUNDUM dicendum, quod illud quod jam est, non fit eo modo quo est, sed alio modo potest fieri; quia quod est potentia, fit actu; et ideo sanguis Christi, qui est sub sacramento hostia consecrata non ex vi sacramenti, fit ibi per consecrationem vini ex vi sacramenti existens; sicut etiam quod est in uno loco per accidens, fit ibi per se quandoque.

AD TERTIUM dicendum, quod visus corporalis, ut dicetur, non potest videre corpus Christi secundum quod est sub sacramento. Quid autem illud sit quod quandoque in hoc sacramento in specie carnis aut sanguinis apparet, infra dicetur, art. 4, quaestiunc. 2.

TO THE SECOND QUESTION, it should be said that there are two uses of the sacrament, namely, eating and drinking. But eating is the use of dry food, while drinking is the use of wet food, which is called 'drink.' And so under the species of bread, which is ordered to the use of eating, there is contained by the power of the sacrament not only the flesh of Christ but his bones, and every such part; but not his blood, which is contained by the power of the sacrament under the appearance of wine, which is ordered to the use of drinking; although by natural concomitance the blood is also under the appearance of bread, and the flesh is under the appearance of wine.

REPLY OBJ. 1: The part is included there for the whole, namely, flesh for the whole body: and this part was specifically named, so that by its likeness to physical eating, which flesh is particularly suited for, it would pave the way for the sacrament, although also bones and other parts like this are in some way suited to eating, since according to Avicenna some animals are nourished by these things.[26]

REPLY OBJ. 2: What already exists does not come to be in the way in which it exists, but it can come to be in another way, since what is in potency can come into act; and so the blood of Christ, which, once the host is consecrated, exists under the sacrament not by the power of the sacrament, is made to exist there by the power of the sacrament through the consecration of the wine. Likewise also, what is in one place incidentally can at some time be made to be there essentially.

REPLY OBJ. 3: Physical sight, as will be said, cannot see the body of Christ as it is under the sacrament. However, what it is that sometimes appears in this sacrament in the appearance of flesh or blood will be said later in Article 4, Subquestion 2.

Response to Quaestiuncula 3

AD TERTIAM QUAESTIONEM dicendum, quod substantia panis, quae convertitur in corpus Christi, non habet aliquam proportionem similitudinis ad quantitatem

TO THE THIRD QUESTION, it should be said that the substance of bread, which is converted into the body of Christ, does not have any relation of similarity to the quan-

---

26. At their Early Science Lab website, Paula Findlen and Rebecca Bence, explaining early views of the skeleton, cite the following text from Avicenna: "The bone . . . is, however, moister than hair, because bone is derived from the blood, and its fume is dry, so that it dries up the humors naturally located in the bones. This accounts for the fact that many animals thrive on bones, whereas no animal thrives on hair—or at least it would be a very exceptional thing if hair ever did provide nourishment" (see https://web.stanford.edu/class/history13/earlysciencelab/body/skeletonpages/skeleton.html, accessed January 22, 2015).

vel alia accidentia Christi, sed tantummodo ad substantiam ejus corporis: et ideo, cum nihil convertatur in corpus Christi de pane nisi substantia panis, quia accidentia manent, constat quod conversio illa terminatur directe ad substantiam, non autem ad accidentia, quia accidentia panis remanent; et ideo quantitas et alia accidentia propria corporis non sunt ibi ex vi sacramenti; sunt tamen ibi secundum rei veritatem ex naturali concomitantia accidentis ad subjectum, ut de anima dictum est.

AD PRIMUM ergo dicendum, quod ratio illa probat quod non sit ibi ex vi sacramenti; et hoc concedo.

AD SECUNDUM dicendum, quod quia dimensiones corporis Christi non sunt ibi ex vi sacramenti, sed solum ex eo quod concomitantur inseparabiliter substantiam, constat quod contrario ordine sunt ibi dimensiones propriae corporis Christi, et dimensiones locati corporis in loco. Corporis enim locati substantia non habet ordinem ad locum nisi mediantibus dimensionibus; et ideo, quia dimensiones corporis locati non possunt esse simul cum aliis dimensionibus, sequitur ex consequenti quod substantia corporis locati non possit esse simul cum aliis dimensionibus, neque separatis, neque in alio corpore existentibus. Sed hic e contrario substantia corporis Christi per se immediate ordinatur ad hoc quod sit sub sacramento; et dimensiones ejus propriae ex consequenti et per accidens. Substantia autem ex hoc quod est substantia non prohibetur esse simul cum dimensionibus quibuscumque, sive conjunctis sibi, sive separatis, aut existentibus in alio subjecto; sicut substantia angeli potest esse simul ubi est aliud corpus; et ideo etiam corpus Christi sub propria quantitate potest esse sub dimensionibus panis.

AD TERTIUM dicendum, quod non potest fieri sine mutatione panis, quod ejus accidentia sine substantia remaneant: et similiter non posset fieri quod substantia corporis Christi esset sine accidentibus sine sua mutatione. Posset autem Deus hoc facere ut sine accidentibus propriis esset, ad minus aliquibus, sine mutatione intrinseca; et quia non est inconveniens panem mutari, esset autem inconveniens Christum mutari;[27] ideo non est simile quod inducit ratio.

AD QUARTUM dicendum, quod quamvis corpus Christi cum quantitate propria sit sub sacramento, non est tamen ibi mediante sua quantitate; et ideo non est ibi ut in loco.

tity or other accidents of Christ, but only to the substance of his body; and so, since nothing of the bread is converted into the body of Christ except its substance, since the accidents remain, it is clear that this conversion terminates directly in substance, but not in accidents, for the accidents of the bread remain. And so the quantity and other proper accidents of his body are not there by the power of the sacrament, but they are there according to the truth of reality by the natural concomitance of an accident in a subject, as was said about the soul.

REPLY OBJ. 1: That argument proves that it is not there by the power of the sacrament, and this I grant.

REPLY OBJ. 2: Because the dimensions of the body of Christ are not there by the power of the sacrament, but only by the fact that they are inseparably concomitant with the substance, it is evident that the proper dimensions of Christ's body are there in an order contrary to the dimensions of a body located in a place. For the substance of a body in place only has a relation to the place by means of the dimensions; and so, because the dimensions of a body in place cannot be together with other dimensions, it follows as a result that the substance of a body in place cannot exist together with other dimensions, whether separated or existing in another body. But here, to the contrary, the substance of the body of Christ is related immediately and *per se* to existing under the sacrament, and its proper dimensions as a result and incidentally. Substance, however, by the fact that it is substance, is not prevented from being together with any dimensions, whether united with it or separated, or existing in another subject, as the substance of an angel can exist simultaneously where there is another body; and so the body of Christ, too, under its proper quantity can exist under the dimensions of bread.

REPLY OBJ. 3: It cannot happen that the accidents of the bread remain without its substance, unless by some change of the bread, and likewise it cannot happen that the substance of the body of Christ exist without accidents unless by some change in itself. However, God could bring it about that it exist without its proper accidents, at least certain ones, without an intrinsic change. And since it is not unfitting for bread to be changed, but it would be unfitting for Christ to be changed by an intrinsic change, therefore what the argument concludes is not the same.

REPLY OBJ. 4: Although the body of Christ with its proper quantity exists under the sacrament, it is still not there by means of its own quantity, and so it is not there as in a place.

---

27. *mutari; ideo.—mutari intrinseca mutatione; ideo* PLE.

Response to Quaestiuncula 4

AD QUARTAM QUAESTIONEM dicendum, quod qua ratione ponitur ibi pars quantitatis, eadem ratione ibi poni debet etiam tota quantitas: quia sicut corpus Christi non separatur a propria quantitate, ita una pars quantitatis non separatur ab alia: utrumque enim sine mutatione intrinseca corporis Christi non posset evenire.

AD PRIMUM ergo dicendum, quod in superpositione directe quantitas applicatur quantitati. Et quia quantitas Christi non directe applicatur quantitati panis, quia non mediante ipsa corpus Christi sub dimensione panis est; ideo non est ibi aliqua superpositio quantitatis ad quantitatem, nec aliqua commensuratio quantitatum; et ideo non sequitur quod sint aequales.

AD SECUNDUM dicendum, quod sicut illa quae non habent quantitatem, possunt esse indifferenter sub parva et magna quantitate, sicut patet de anima, quae est indifferenter in magno et parvo corpore; ita illud quod non ratione suae quantitatis continetur sub aliqua quantitate, potest esse indifferenter in magna et parva quantitate, sicut est in proposito.

AD TERTIUM dicendum, quod situs, sicut objectio tangit, quantitatem praesupponit; et quia quantitas Christi nullam habitudinem habet ad dimensiones panis, ideo etiam nec situs partium corporis Christi; et ideo quamvis corpus Christi, prout est sub sacramento, habeat partes distinctas, et situatas situ naturali, non est tamen assignare in partibus dimensionum panis, ubi singulae partes corporis Christi jaceant. Nec tamen sequitur quod dicamus corpus Christi confusum, quia ordinem habent partes in se; sed secundum ordinem illum non comparantur ad dimensiones exteriores.

TO THE FOURTH QUESTION, it should be said that by the same account by which part of the quantity is said to be there, the whole quantity must also be said to be there: for just as the body of Christ is not separated from its proper quantity, so one part of the quantity is not separated from another; for without an intrinsic change in the body of Christ neither one can come about.

REPLY OBJ. 1: In superimposing, a quantity is directly applied to a quantity. And since the quantity of Christ is not directly applied to the quantity of bread, because the body of Christ does not exist under the dimensions of the bread by means of that quantity, there is not any superimposing of quantity on quantity, nor any alignment of quantities, and so it does not follow that they are equal.

REPLY OBJ. 2: Just as those things that do not have quantity can exist equally under small and large quantity, as is seen in the case of the soul, which is equally in large and small bodies, so also that which is contained under a certain quantity not by reason of its own quantity can be equally in large and small quantity, as is the case in the question at hand.

REPLY OBJ. 3: As the objection mentions, position presupposes quantity, and since the quantity of Christ has no relationship to the dimensions of the bread, neither has the position of the parts of Christ's body. And so although the body of Christ, as it exists under the sacrament, has distinct parts situated in natural position, nevertheless one cannot assign in the parts of the dimensions of the bread where individual parts of the body of Christ lie. Nor, however, does it follow that we may call the body of Christ confused, since the parts do have order in themselves; but they are not related to external dimensions according to that order.

ARTICLE 3

How the body of Christ is there

Quaestiuncula 1

Ad tertium sic proceditur. Videtur quod corpus Christi contineatur sub sacramento circumscriptive. Omne enim corpus quod est in loco, circumscribitur. Sed corpus Christi est sub sacramento sicut in loco: quod patet, quia non est alium modum assignare de modis essendi in quos assignat Philosophus in 4 *Physica*. Ergo corpus Christi est in loco circumscriptive.

PRAETEREA, in *Sex principiis* dicitur, quod *proprium est positionis primo loco substantiae inhaerere*. Sed corporis Christi substantia non denudatur aliis proprietatibus, prout est sub sacramento. Ergo neque positione: ergo secundum quod est sub sacramento, est in loco: quia positio ordinem partium in loco dicit.

PRAETEREA, omne corpus quod continetur superficie alterius corporis, ita quod non excedit neque exceditur, circumscribitur illa superficie sicut loco. Sed corpus Christi totum, ut dictum est, continetur sub ultima superficie dimensionum panis quae manent, et nec excedit nec exceditur. Ergo est sicut in loco circumscriptive.

PRAETEREA, omne quod replet locum, circumscribitur loco. Sed corpus Christi replet locum dimensivum, alias esset vacuum. Ergo corpus Christi circumscribitur speciebus illis.

SED CONTRA, omne corpus quod circumscribitur loco, commensuratur loco circumscribenti: quia locus et locatum sunt aequalia, ut dicitur in 4 *Physica*. Sed corpus Christi non commensuratur quantitati dimensionum, ut dictum est, art. praec. Ergo non est ibi sicut in loco circumscriptive.

PRAETEREA, omne corpus quod circumscribitur loco aliquo, partes ejus habent situm determinatum in loco illo. Sed hoc, ut dictum est, non convenit corpori Christi ratione dimensionum illarum. Ergo non continetur eis circumscriptive.

OBJ. 1: To the third we proceed thus. It seems that the body of Christ is contained under the sacrament circumscriptively.[28] For every body that is in a place is circumscribed. But the body of Christ is under the sacrament as in a place, which is evident because there is no other mode of 'being in' that the Philosopher assigns in the *Physics* 4 that one can assign to it.[29] Therefore, the body of Christ is in the place circumscriptively.

OBJ. 2: Furthermore, in *Six Principles*[30] it is said that *it is proper first of all to position to inhere in a substance*. But the substance of the body of Christ, as it exists under the sacrament, is not stripped of its other properties. Therefore, neither is it stripped of position, and so according as it is under the sacrament, it is in a place. For position describes the order of parts in place.

OBJ. 3: Furthermore, every body that is contained by the surface of another body, such that it neither exceeds nor is exceeded, is circumscribed by that surface as its place. But the whole body of Christ, as was said, is contained under the outer surface of the bread's dimensions which remain, and it does not exceed nor is it exceeded. Therefore, it is as in a place circumscriptively.

OBJ. 4: Furthermore, everything that fills its place is circumscribed by the place. But the body of Christ fills the dimensions of the place, for otherwise there would be a vacuum. Therefore, the body of Christ is circumscribed by these appearances.

ON THE CONTRARY, every body that is circumscribed by a place is commensurate with the place that circumscribes it: for place and the thing located there are equals, as it says in the *Physics* 4.[31] But the body of Christ is not commensurate with the quantity of the dimensions [of the species], as was said in the preceding article. Therefore, it is not there as in a place circumscriptively.

FURTHERMORE, every body that is circumscribed by some place has its parts determinately situated in that place. But as was said, this does not apply to the body of Christ by reason of those dimensions. Therefore, it is not contained circumscriptively by them.

---

28. Parallels: above, at the end of a. 1; *ST* III, q. 75, a. 1, ad 3; q. 76, a. 5; *SCG* IV, chs. 62, 64, and 67; *De 36 art.*, a. 33.
29. Aristotle, *Physics*, Bk. 4, ch. 3 (210a14ff.).
30. Gilbert de la Porrée (Gilbertus Porretanus), *Sex principiis* (ed. Heysse), n. 25, p. 27.
31. Aristotle, *Physics*, Bk. 4, ch. 4 (211a1–2).

Quaestiuncula 2

ULTERIUS. Videtur quod contineatur sub eis saltem definitive. Quia plus distat a natura loci angelus quam corpus Christi. Sed angelus non potest esse in loco quin loco definiatur, ut communiter dicitur. Ergo multo fortius corpus Christi est definitive sub speciebus illis.

PRAETEREA, omne corporale individuum est determinatum ad hic et nunc. Sed corpus Christi est hujusmodi. Ergo determinatur ad hic. Ergo est definitive sub speciebus.

PRAETEREA, omne finitum existens alicubi, definitive est ibi. Sed corpus Christi est hujusmodi. Ergo, etc.

SED CONTRA, omne quod est definitive alicubi, ita est ibi quod non alibi. Sed corpus Christi non ita est sub speciebus quod non alibi. Ergo non est definitive sub eis.

PRAETEREA, omne quod potest sine sua mutatione alibi esse quam hic, non est hic definitive: propter hoc enim ponimus angelos moveri, quia loco definiuntur. Sed corpus Christi potest alicubi esse quam sub speciebus istis sine omni mutatione vel sua vel specierum; puta, si alibi corpus Christi consecratur. Ergo non erat hic definitive.

OBJ. 1: Moreover, it seems that it is contained under the species' dimensions at least as limited by their boundaries.[32] For there is more difference between an angel's nature and place than between the body of Christ and place, but an angel cannot be in a place unless it is limited by that place, as it is commonly said. Therefore, much more is the body of Christ limited under these species.

OBJ. 2: Furthermore, every individual physical thing is determined to 'here' and 'now'. But the body of Christ is one of these things. Therefore, it is determined to the 'here'. Therefore, it is limited by the boundaries of the species.

OBJ. 3: Furthermore, every finite thing existing somewhere is limited by the boundaries of that place. But the body of Christ is one of these things. Therefore, etc.

ON THE CONTRARY, everything that exists somewhere limited by its boundaries exists so that it is there and not elsewhere. But the body of Christ does not exist under the species such that it is there and not elsewhere. Therefore, it does not exist limited by the boundaries of the species.

FURTHERMORE, everything that can exist somewhere other than here without a change in itself does not exist here as limited by its boundaries: for we say that angels are moved because of this, that they are limited by the boundaries of a place. But the body of Christ can be somewhere else than under those species without any change either of itself or of the species; for example, if the body of Christ is consecrated elsewhere. Therefore, it was not here as limited by those boundaries.

Quaestiuncula 3

ULTERIUS. Videtur quod corpus Christi non possit esse totum sub qualibet parte specierum. Dimensiones enim panis remanentes possunt in infinitum dividi. Si ergo in qualibet parte dimensionum illarum esset corpus Christi totum, esset infinities sub eisdem dimensionibus; quod est impossibile.

PRAETEREA, quaecumque uni et eidem sunt simul, sibi invicem sunt simul. Sed si in qualibet parte dimensionum est totum corpus Christi, ubicumque est pars corporis Christi, esset totum corpus Christi. Ergo ubi esset una pars, esset alia, et hoc repugnat distinctioni partium, quae requiritur in corpore organico. Ergo non est possibile quod totum corpus Christi sub qualibet parte specierum sit.

PRAETEREA, Augustinus dicit, quod *proprium est spiritus quod possit simul in diversis partibus totus esse.*

OBJ. 1: Moreover, it seems that the body of Christ cannot exist in its entirety under each part of the species.[33] For the dimensions of the bread remaining can be divided infinitely. If, then, the whole body of Christ were in each part of those dimensions, it would be infinitely repeated under the same dimensions, which is impossible.

OBJ. 2: Furthermore, whatever things exist together with one and the same thing exist together with each other. But if in every part of the dimensions is the whole body of Christ, then wherever there is a part of the body of Christ there would be the whole of the body of Christ. Therefore, wherever one part was, another would be, and this conflicts with the distinction of parts, which is required in an organic body. Therefore it is not possible that the whole body of Christ exist under every part of the species.

OBJ. 3: Furthermore, Augustine says that *it is proper to spirit that it can exist wholly in different parts at the same*

---

32. See also the preceding qa.
33. Parallels: *ST* III, q. 76, a. 3; *SCG* IV, ch. 67; *Quodl.* VII, q. 4, a. 1; *Super Matt.* 26; *Super I ad Cor.* 11, lec. 5.

Sed corpus Christi non ponitur neque per unionem neque per gloriam extra limites corporis, ut possit percipere proprietatem spiritus. Ergo corpus Christi non est totum in qualibet parte specierum.

SED CONTRA est quod Hilarius dicit de Cons., dist. 2, cap. ubi: *ubi pars est corporis, et totum*; et loquitur de corpore Domini in sacramento. Sed in qualibet parte dimensionum est aliqua pars corporis Domini. Ergo in qualibet parte dimensionum est totum.

PRAETEREA, panis consecratus est quoddam totum homogeneum, idest unius rationis in toto et in partibus. Sed sub toto est totum corpus. Ergo sub qualibet parte corporis est totum.

time.[34] But the body of Christ is not placed, whether by union or by glory, outside the limits of "body" such that it could receive the property of a spirit. Therefore, the body of Christ does not exist whole in each part of the species.

ON THE CONTRARY, Hilary says: *where there is part of the body, there is also the whole*; [35] and he is speaking of the body of the Lord in the sacrament. But in any part of the dimensions there is a certain part of the Lord's body. Therefore, in any part of the dimensions there is the whole.

FURTHERMORE, consecrated bread is a certain homogeneous whole thing, i.e., of one single notion in the whole and in the parts. But under the whole is the whole body. Therefore, under any of the body's parts is the whole.

Quaestiuncula 4

ULTERIUS. Videtur quod corpus Christi movetur ad motum hostiae. Omne enim quod desinit esse ubi prius erat, et incipit esse ubi prius non erat, movetur vel per se vel per accidens. Sed corpus Christi translata hostia desinit esse ubi prius erat, scilicet in altari; et incipit esse ubi prius non erat, scilicet in pixide, vel in ore. Ergo corpus Christi movetur ad motum hostiae, vel per se vel per accidens.

PRAETEREA, secundum Philosophum in 2 *Topicor.*, *moventibus nobis, moventur ea quae in nobis sunt*. Sed corpus Christi vere continetur sub speciebus illis. Ergo speciebus translatis, et ipsum transfertur.

PRAETEREA, anima vel angelus magis recedit a natura loci quam corpus Christi. Sed anima vel angelus movetur per accidens, moto corpore unito vel assumpto. Ergo multo fortius corpus Christi.

SED CONTRA, nullum quietum manens in eodem loco movetur per se vel per accidens. Sed corpus Christi est hujusmodi. Ergo, etc.

PRAETEREA, quod movetur per accidens ad motum alterius, definitive est in illo; unde Deus non movetur ad motum alicujus, nec anima ad motum manus. Sed corpus Christi non est definitive sub speciebus illis. Ergo non movetur ad motum illarum.

OBJ. 1: Moreover, it seems that the body of Christ is moved when the host is moved.[36] For everything that stops being where it formerly was and begins to be where it formerly was not, is moved either *per se* or incidentally. But when the host is transferred, the body of Christ stops being where it was before, namely, on the altar, and begins to be where it was not before, namely, in the pyx, or in the mouth. Therefore, the body of Christ is moved when the host is moved, either *per se* or incidentally.

OBJ. 2: Furthermore according to the Philosopher in *Topics* 2,[37] *when we are moving, those things that are in us are moved*. But the body of Christ is truly contained under those species. Therefore, when the species are transferred, it too is transferred.

OBJ. 3: Furthermore, the soul or an angel differs more from the nature of place than the body of Christ. But a soul or an angel is moved incidentally, when the body united to it or assumed by it is moved. Therefore, much more is the body of Christ.

ON THE CONTRARY, no resting thing remaining in the same place is moved *per se* or incidentally. But the body of Christ is one of these things. Therefore, etc.

FURTHERMORE, what is moved incidentally at the motion of another is in it as limited by its boundaries; hence God is not moved at the movement of anything, nor is the soul at the movement of the hand. But the body of Christ is not under those species as limited by the boundaries. Therefore, it is not moved at the movement of those species.

---

34. Augustine, *Epistle 166*, n. 4 (PL 33:721).
35. Gratian's *Decretals*, Part 3, *De consecratione*, d. 2, ch. 78 (PL 187:1773).
36. Parallels: *ST* III, q. 76, a. 6; *De 36 art.*, a. 34.
37. Aristotle, *Topics*, Bk. 2, ch. 7 (113a29–30).

Response to Quaestiuncula 1

RESPONDEO dicendum ad primam quaestionem, quod locus dicitur circumscribere locatum ex eo quod in circuitu describit figuram locati: quia loci proprii et locati oportet esse unam figuram; figura autem est qualitas circa quantitatem. Et quia corpus Christi non habet ordinem ad species sub quibus continetur mediante quantitate, sed e converso, ut dictum est; ideo neque figura corporis Christi respondet figurae specierum, sicut patet ad sensum. Et ideo patet quod non est sub speciebus circumscriptive, et per consequens nec est in eis sicut in loco: quia nihil per se, proprie loquendo, est in loco ut in loco, nisi quod loco circumscribitur.

AD PRIMUM ergo dicendum, quod comparatio corporis Christi ad species sub quibus est, non est similis alicui comparationi naturali; et ideo non potest reduci, proprie loquendo, ad aliquem modorum a Philosopho assignatorum; tamen habet aliquam similitudinem cum illo modo quo aliquid dicitur esse in loco secundum quod esse in loco est esse in aliquo separato extra substantiam suam, quod non est ejus causa: et secundum hoc etiam Innocentius dicit corpus Christi esse in pluribus locis, quod continetur sub pluribus speciebus.

AD SECUNDUM dicendum, quod quamvis corpus Christi non denudetur positione, neque aliqua suarum proprietatum, ex hoc quod est sub sacramento, non tamen sequitur quod secundum quod habet figuram et quantitatem et positionem, comparetur ad species sacramenti; sicut homo non comparatur ad locum ex hoc quod habet animam, vel mediante anima; quamvis hoc quod in loco est, anima non privetur.

AD TERTIUM dicendum, quod ad circumscriptionem plus exigitur, scilicet quod locatum configuretur loco, aut e converso: et hoc non est in proposito, ratione jam dicta.

AD QUARTUM dicendum, quod corpus naturale non habet quod repleat locum ex parte materiae, neque ex parte[39] dimensionum; unde secundum Philosophum in 4 *Physica*, et in 3 *Metaphysica*, dimensiones separatae si ponantur esse (vel corpus mathematicum, quod idem est), replent locum, et non possunt esse simul cum alio corpore. Nec obstat quod ipse in 4 *Physica*, cap. 6, de vacuo videtur uti dimensionibus separatis quasi vacuo: quia procedit ex suppositione illorum qui ponebant dimensiones separatas existentes inter terminos corporis continentis, esse locum. Unde sequitur quod quando illae dimensiones fuerunt sine corpore sensibili quod di-

TO THE FIRST QUESTION, I answer that place is said to circumscribe what is in a place by the fact that it encompasses the figure of the thing in the place, for proper place and the thing in that place must have one shape; however, shape is the quality of quantity. And because the body of Christ does not have a relation to the species under which it is contained by means of quantity but vice versa, as was said, therefore neither does the shape of the body of Christ correspond to the shape of the species as it appears to the senses. And therefore it is evident that it is not under the species as though limited by their boundaries, and consequently neither is it in them as in a place, for nothing *per se*, properly speaking, is in a place as in a place, except what is limited by the boundaries in the place.

REPLY OBJ. 1: The relation of the body of Christ to the species under which it exists is not like any natural comparison; and so it cannot be reduced, properly speaking, to any of the modes assigned by the Philosopher. Nevertheless, it has a certain likeness to that mode of saying that something is in a place according as being in a place is being in something separate outside of one's own substance, which is not the cause of it. And this is also how Innocent says that the body of Christ is in many places, because it is contained under many species.[38]

REPLY OBJ. 2: Although the body of Christ is not stripped of position, nor any of its own properties, by the fact that it is under the sacrament, nevertheless it does not follow that it is related to the sacrament's species according as it has figure and quantity and position; just as a man is not related to a place by the fact that he has a soul, or by means of his soul; although by the fact that he exists in a place, he is not deprived of his soul.

REPLY OBJ. 3: For something to be circumscribed more is required, namely, that what is in a place be configured to the place, or vice versa; and this is not the case in question, for the reason already given.

REPLY OBJ. 4: A natural body is not capable of filling its place on account of its matter, nor on account of its form, but on account of its dimensions; hence according to the Philosopher in *Physics* 4 and in *Metaphysics* 3,[40] if one posits dimensions existing on their own (or a mathematical body, which is the same thing), they fill their place, and they cannot be there at the same time as another body. Nor is it a problem that he himself in *Physics* 4,[41] on the nature of a vacuum, seems to use the separated dimensions like a vacuum: for it proceeds from the supposition of those who stated that separated dimensions existing between the boundaries of a containing body were place. Hence it fol-

---

38. Cf. Innocent III, *De sacro altaris mysterio*, Bk. 4, ch. 27 and ch. 44 (PL 217:875, 886).

39. *parte dimensionum.—parte formae, sed ex parte* PLE.

40. Aristotle, *Physics*, Bk. 4, ch. 1 (290a4–6); *Metaphysics*, Bk. 3, ch. 2 (998a13).

41. Aristotle, *Physics*, Bk. 4, ch. 6 (213a11ff.).

catur vacuum; sic enim vacuum ponebant. Et ideo dicendum est in proposito, quod cum corpus Christi non comparetur ad locum istum in quo est sub sacramento, mediantibus propriis dimensionibus, non replet locum; neque tamen locus ille est vacuus, quia repletur dimensionibus separatis sacramenti corporis Christi.

lows that when those dimensions were without sensible body, which is called a vacuum, they would thus posit a vacuum. And so it should be said in this case that since the body of Christ is not related by means of its proper dimensions to that place in which it exists under the sacrament, it does not fill the place. Nor, however, is that place empty, for it is filled by the separated dimensions of the sacrament of the body of Christ.

Response to Quaestiuncula 2

AD SECUNDAM QUAESTIONEM dicendum, quod ad hoc quod aliquid sit in loco definitive, duo requiruntur. Primum est ut competat ibi esse ei, quia quod non est in aliquo loco, non potest loco illo definiri. Secundum est quod sit ibi sicut in loco commensurato aliquo modo suae quantitati vel virtuti. Corpus enim bicubitale non definitur loco unius cubiti, quamvis aliquo modo sit ibi; neque anima est definitive in manu, quia est in aliis partibus, eo quod non est in manu secundum totam virtutem suam. Et ideo omne quod habet quantitatem finitam, vel virtutem, oportet quod sit definitive in loco in quo est; et ideo angeli definitive sunt in loco, non tamen Deus. Corpus autem Christi quamvis secundum veritatem sit sub speciebus, non tamen competit ei esse ibi ratione sui: quia neque ratione suae quantitatis, ut dictum est, neque ratione suae virtutis, sed ratione illius quod in ipsum conversum est ibi praeexistens, cujus dimensiones adhuc manent, quibus ad locum illum determinabatur; et ideo non definitur loco illo, sed simili modo potest esse alibi, ubicumque fuerint panis dimensiones conversi in ipsum.

AD PRIMUM ergo dicendum, quod angelus est in loco quo definitur, non quia aliquid convertatur in ipsum, sed ratione suae operationis, virtutis, et essentiae; et ideo non potest esse nisi in uno loco, quia substantia rei non est nisi semel.

AD SECUNDUM dicendum, quod corpus Christi, sicut et alia corpora, determinatur ad unum locum qui competit ei ratione suae quantitatis, quia ibi est ut in loco; sed non hoc modo sub speciebus est; et ideo ratio non sequitur.

AD TERTIUM dicendum, quod finitum et infinitum sunt passiones quantitatis, secundum Philosophum in 1 *Physica*; unde cum corpus Christi non habeat ex ratione suae quantitatis quod sit ubi consecratur, sed magis ex conversione alterius in ipsum corpus Christi; sic esse in pluribus, et non definitive in uno, non pertinet ad ejus

TO THE SECOND QUESTION, it should be said that for something to be in a place as limited by its boundaries, two things are required. The first is that it belongs to it to be there, for what is not in a certain place cannot be in that place as limited by its borders. The second is that it is there as in a place commensurate in some way with its quantity or power. For a bicubital body is not bound by a space of one cubit, although it might be there in some sense; nor is the soul bound by existing in the hand, for it is in the other parts, by the fact that it is not in the hand according to its whole power. And so everything that has finite quantity, or power, must be in the place where it is, as bound by it. And that is why angels are in a place as bound, but God is not. However, although the body of Christ in truth exists under the species, it nevertheless does not belong to it to be 'there' by reason of itself, because it exists there neither by reason of its own quantity, as was said, nor by reason of its own power, but by reason of that thing pre-existing there that was converted into it, and the dimensions of that thing remain afterward, by which it is determined to that place; and so it is not bound by the limits of that place, but it can be elsewhere in the same way, wherever were the dimensions of the bread that was converted into it.

REPLY OBJ. 1: An angel is in the place by which it is bound not because something is converted into it, but by reason of its own operation, power, and essence; and so it cannot be anywhere but one place, because the substance of a thing is only once.

REPLY OBJ. 2: The body of Christ, just like other bodies, is determined to one place which belongs to it by reason of its quantity, for it is there as in a place; but it is not under the species in this way; and so the argument does not follow.

REPLY OBJ. 3: Finite and infinite are characteristics of quantity, according to the Philosopher in *Physics* 1.[42] Hence, since it is not by the nature of its quantity that the body of Christ is able to exist where it is consecrated, but rather by the conversion of something else into the body of Christ itself, in the same way, to be in many things and not

---

42. Aristotle, *Physics*, Bk. 1, ch. 2 (185a33–34).

finitatem vel infinitatem, sed magis ad numerum eorum quae convertuntur in ipsum.

in one as bound by its limits, does not pertain to its finiteness or infiniteness but rather to the number of those things that are converted into it.

Response to Quaestiuncula 3

AD TERTIAM QUAESTIONEM dicendum, quod circa hoc est duplex opinio: quidam enim dicunt, quod hostia remanente integra, Christus totus est sub tota hostia, non tamen sub qualibet hostiae parte; sed hostia divisa, Christus totus remanet sub qualibet parte. Et ponunt exemplum de speculo; quia Augustinus dicit, quod sicut fracto speculo multiplicantur species vel imagines; sic post fractionem quot sunt partes, toties est ibi Christus: constat autem quod ante fractionem speculi non erat ibi nisi una imago. Istud autem non potest stare; quia hostia integra manente, aliquo modo est corpus Christi sub partibus hostiae. Si ergo non sit ibi secundum totum, erit secundum partem: sed omne quod est totum in toto, et pars ejus in parte, est ibi situaliter; et ita corpus Christi esset situaliter sub sacramento, et circumscriptive; quod est impossibile. Exemplum autem non est conveniens: quia imago speculi non est ibi ut forma absolute quiescens in subjecto, sed aggeneratur ex reverberatione; et ideo quamdiu est una superficies speculi, fit una reverberatio, et per consequens una imago resultat; fracto autem speculo sunt multae superficies, et per consequens multae reflexiones, et imagines multae resultantes. Si autem esset forma absolute quiescens in subjecto; aut esset consequens quantitatem, sicut albedo quae fundatur in superficie; aut praecedens quantitatem, sicut forma substantialis. Si primo modo, de necessitate esset tota in toto et pars in parte ante fractionem speculi et post; si autem esset praecedens quantitatem, esset ante et post, et tota in toto, et tota in partibus, sicut tota forma substantialis ligni est in qualibet parte ejus, quia totalitas formae substantialis non recipit quantitatis totalitatem, sicut est de totalitate formarum accidentalium, quae fundantur in quantitate, et praesupponunt ipsam.

Corpus autem Christi continetur absolute sub speciebus; et hoc non convenit substantiae mediante quantitate, ut dictum est, sed ratione substantiae, inquantum substantia panis est conversa; et ideo etiam ante fractionem est totum in tota, et totum in partibus: quia ubicumque erat tota natura panis, est tota natura corporis Christi, et per consequens etiam totum corpus, et tota

TO THE THIRD QUESTION, it should be said that there are two opinions about this. For some people say that while the host remains complete, Christ is whole under the whole host, not, however, under any little part of the host; but once the host is divided, the whole Christ remains under any part. And they give the example of a mirror, for Augustine says that just as appearances or images are multiplied by a broken mirror, in the same way after the bread is broken, Christ is there in every part.[43] However, it is evident that before the mirror was broken there was only one image there. But that cannot stand; for while the host remains whole, in some way the body of Christ exists under the parts of the host. Therefore, if it is not there as a whole, it will be there as a part, but everything that is whole in a whole, and its part in a part, is there as in a place, and so the body of Christ would be present as in a place under the sacrament, and circumscriptively; which is impossible. Moreover, the example is not fitting: for the image in a mirror is not there as a form resting absolutely in a subject, but produced by reflection, and so as long as there is a surface of mirror, a reflection will be made, and an image results; however, once the mirror is broken there are many surfaces, and consequently many reflections, and many resulting images. But if there were a form reposing absolutely in a subject, either it would follow quantity, as whiteness is founded in a surface; or it would precede quantity, like substantial form. If in the first way, it would necessarily be whole in the whole and a part in the part before the breaking of the mirror as well as after. But if it preceeded quantity, it would be whole in the whole and whole in the parts both before and after, as the whole substantial form of wood is in each part of it; for the totality of substantial form does not receive the totality of quantity, as it is with the totality of accidental forms, which are founded in quantity and presuppose it.

However, the body of Christ is contained absolutely under the species; and this does not happen to the substance by means of quantity, as was said, but by reason of the substance, inasmuch as the substance of the bread has been converted. And so also before the breaking, the whole is in all and the whole is in the parts, for wherever there was the whole nature of bread, there is the whole nature of the body

---

43. By the time he wrote the *Summa theologiae*, Thomas knew that this had not been said by Augustine; instead he merely says "quidam dicunt" (*ST* III, q. 76, a. 3). The editors of the Editiones Paulinae *ST* note that this opinion was recounted by, among others, Innocent III (*De sacro altaris mysterio*, Bk. 4, ch. 8 [PL 217:861]) and Bonaventure (*In IV Sent*. d. 10, p. 1, a. 1, q. 5 [Quarrachi ed., IV:224]).

quantitas ejus. Et haec est alia opinio quae magis vera videtur.

Ad primum ergo dicendum, quod unitas rei consequitur esse ipsius: partes autem alicujus homogenei continui ante divisionem non habent esse actu, sed potentia tantum; et ideo nulla illarum habet unitatem propriam in actu; unde actu non est accipere ipsarum numerum, sed potentia tantum. Et propter hoc forma quae est tota in toto tali, et tota in partibus ejus, non dicitur ante divisionem continui esse ibi pluries actu, sed solum potentia: sed post divisionem multiplicatur secundum actum, sicut patet de anima in animalibus anulosis. Et similiter corpus Christi ante divisionem hostiae, quamvis sit totum sub qualibet parte hostiae, non est tamen pluries actu sub partibus illis, sed tantum potentia. Nec est inconveniens quod sit ibi infinities in potentia.

Ad secundum dicendum, quod confusio opponitur ordini partium qui pertinet ad rationem situs: et quia corpus Christi non est situaliter sub sacramento, ideo non sequitur ibi aliqua confusio partium ex hoc quod in quolibet signato hostiae est totum corpus, et quaelibet pars ejus. Quamvis enim non sit accipere ordinem partium corporis Christi secundum comparationem ad partes hostiae, tamen est accipere ordinem ipsarum partium ad invicem in corpore Christi secundum propriam quantitatem.

Ad tertium dicendum, quod spiritui competit esse totum in toto, et in qualibet parte: quia non habet quantitatem, nec a quantitate substantia ejus dependet. Corpus autem Christi quamvis in se consideratum non absolvatur a propria quantitate, tamen non comparatur ad hostiam sub qua est, secundum propriam quantitatem; et ideo non est spiritus, sed participat quantum ad aliquid proprietatem spiritus secundum comparationem ad species sub quibus continetur.

of Christ, and consequently also the whole body, and all its quantity. And this is the other opinion, which seems more true.

Reply Obj. 1: The unity of a thing is consequent on its being. However, if something is continuous and homogeneous, its parts do not have actual being before it is divided, but only potential being; and thus none of them have proper unity actually. Hence their number cannot be taken in act but only in potency. And because of this, the form that is whole in a whole like this, and whole in its parts, is not said to be there actually many times before the division of its continuum, but only potentially. But after the division it is multiplied actually, as is evident with the soul in anulose animals. And similarly, although before the division of the host, the body of Christ is whole under any tiny piece of the host, nevertheless, it does not exist many times under those pieces actually, but only potentially. Nor is it unfitting that it exists there an infinite number of times potentially.

Reply Obj. 2: Confusion is the opposite of the ordering of parts that is the nature of position. And since the body of Christ does not exist as localized under the sacrament, therefore the fact that in any tiny thing representing the host there is the whole body, and any part of it, does not result in a confusion of parts. For although one cannot take the order of the parts of Christ's body according to their relation to the pieces of the host, nevertheless one can take the order of those very parts to each other in the body of Christ according to proper quantity.

Reply Obj. 3: It belongs to spirit to be completely in the whole, as well as in any part, for it does not have quantity, nor does its substance depend on quantity. However, although the body of Christ considered in itself is not cut off from its proper quantity, nevertheless, it is not related according to its proper quantity to the host under which it exists. And therefore it is not spirit, but it partakes of a certain property of spirit in its relation to the species under which it is contained.

Response to Quaestiuncula 4

Ad quartam quaestionem dicendum, quod moveri in loco includit esse in loco; unde ad hoc quod aliquid per se moveatur in loco, oportet quod per se sit in loco, et quod per se moveatur, non ad motum alterius. Sed per accidens aliquid movetur in loco dupliciter: uno modo quia per accidens est in loco, sicut formae moventur per accidens; alio modo quia per se est in loco, sed per accidens movetur in loco, sicut patet in his quae vehuntur; quia locus quem mutant, est per se eorum proprius locus, vel communis. Corpus autem Christi in loco quem species transmutant, non est per se neque sicut in loco proprio, neque sicut in loco communi, sicut ex dictis patere potest; et ideo per se in illo moveri non po-

To the fourth question, it should be said that to be moved in a place includes being in a place; hence for something to be moved *per se* in a place it is necessary that it be *per se* in a place, and that it be moved *per se*, not at the movement of another. But something is moved incidentally in a place in two ways: in one way, when it is incidentally in a place, as forms are moved incidentally; in another way when it is *per se* in a place, but it is moved in the place incidentally, as is seen in things that are carried, for the place that they change is *per se* their proper or common place. But the body of Christ is not *per se* in the place which the species change, neither as in a proper place nor as in a common place, as can be seen from what has been said. And

test, neque per accidens, sicut corpora per accidens moventur; sed hoc modo quo aliquid et per accidens est in loco, et per accidens movetur. Nec differt, ut quidam dicunt differre, utrum species moveantur in eodem loco, aut transferantur de loco ad locum: quia quod in eodem loco secundum substantiam manens movetur, mutat locum non solum secundum partes, sed secundum totum, ut in 6 Physic. probatur.

ET SECUNDUM HOC patet solutio ad utramque partem, praeter ultimum.

AD SECUNDUM dicendum, quod quamvis non definiatur hoc loco, tamen perfecte est ibi et quantum ad substantiam et quantum ad virtutem, tamen per accidens: non autem in manu perfecte est anima; unde non est simile.

so in that place it cannot be moved *per se*, nor incidentally, like bodies are moved incidentally, but in that way in which something is both incidentally in a place and is moved incidentally. Nor does it make any difference, as some people say it does, whether the species are moved in the same place or transferred from one place to another: for what, remaining in the same place according to its substance, is moved, changes place not only according to parts but according to the whole, as is proved in *Physics* 6.[44]

AND ACCORDING TO THIS the answers to both parts are evident, except the last.

REPLY OBJ. 2: Although it is not limited by this place, nevertheless it is completely there both as to its substance and as to its power, though incidentally. However, the soul is not perfectly present in the hand, and so it is not the same.

---

44. Aristotle, *Physics*, Bk. 6, ch. 9 (240a29ff.).

ARTICLE 4

How the body of Christ can be recognized as it exists under this sacrament

Quaestiuncula 1

AD QUARTUM SIC PROCEDITUR. Videtur quod oculus glorificatus possit videre ipsum verum corpus Christi sub speciebus existens. Ipse enim Christus sub speciebus existens, videt seipsum ibi corporali oculo. Sed corpora glorificata conformantur corpori ejus, ut dicitur Philipp. 3. Ergo et alius oculus glorificatus, puta Virginis, potest hoc idem.

PRAETEREA, ideo, ut infra dicetur, corpus Christi sub alia specie proponitur, ut fides habeat meritum. Sed illi qui sunt in gloria, non habent fidem. Ergo ipsi ad ipsam substantiam corporis ejus videndam pertingunt corporali oculo, etiam secundum quod est sub sacramento.

PRAETEREA, propter velamen specierum quibus verum corpus Christi velatur, decipitur sensus viatoris. Sed status gloriae non patitur deceptionem neque velamen. Ergo ipsam substantiam corporis Christi sub sacramento vident.

SED CONTRA, major magnitudo in aequali distantia visa, sub majori angulo videtur, ut perspectivi probant. Sed major est quantitas corporis Christi quam hostiae hujus, et distantia ad oculum est eadem. Ergo oculus videns corpus Christi et hostiam, videt corpus Christi sub majori angulo. Sed corpus Christi videtur sub specie hostiae. Ergo minor angulus continet majorem, quod est impossibile.

PRAETEREA, corpus non est natum movere visum nisi moto medio. Sed medium non movetur a colore corporis Christi, quia nos etiam videremus. Ergo impossibile est quod ab aliquo oculo videatur; nullus enim oculus videt, nisi motus a colore.

OBJ. 1: To the fourth we proceed thus. It seems that the eyes of the glorified can see the very body of Christ existing under these appearances.[45] For Christ himself existing under these appearances sees himself there with his bodily eyes. But a glorified body is conformed to his body, as it says in Philippians 3:21. Therefore also, the eyes of someone else glorified, for example the Virgin, can do the same.

OBJ. 2: Furthermore, as will be said later, the body of Christ is set forth under a different appearance, so that faith may have merit. But those who are in glory do not have faith. Therefore, they attain to seeing the very substance of his body with their bodily eyes, even as he exists under the sacrament.

OBJ. 3: Furthermore, because of the veil of the species under which the true body of Christ is veiled, the senses of those wayfaring in this life are deceived. But the state of glory does not admit of deception nor of veils. Therefore, they see the very substance of the body of Christ under the sacrament.

ON THE CONTRARY, the greater magnitude seen from an equal distance seems to be under a greater angle, as perspectives proves. But the quantity of the body of Christ is greater than that of the host, and the distance to the eye is the same. Therefore, the eye seeing the body of Christ and the host sees the body of Christ under a greater angle. But the body of Christ is seen under the appearance of the host. Therefore the smaller angle contains the larger, which is impossible.

FURTHERMORE, it is not the nature of a body to move the sight except by moving the medium. But the medium is not moved by the color of the body of Christ, for then we too would see it. Therefore, it is impossible that it be seen by any eyes; for no eyes see unless moved by color.

Quaestiuncula 2

ULTERIUS. Videtur quod quando apparet in specie carnis vel pueri in altari, quod videatur in specie propria. Corpus enim Christi non est nisi sub specie propria, vel sub specie panis. Sed tunc desinunt ibi esse species panis.

OBJ. 1: Moreover, it seems that when it appears in the appearance of flesh or of a child on the altar that it is seen in its proper appearance.[46] For the body of Christ does not exist except under its proper species or the species of bread.

---

45. Parallel: *ST* III, q. 76, aa. 7–8.
46. Parallels: *ST* III, q. 76, a. 8; *De ven. sacr. altar.*, serm. 11.

Ergo si non est species propria illa in qua videtur, nullo modo erit ibi.

Praeterea, illa ostensio est ad aedificationem fidei. Sed non confirmaretur fides, si Christus in specie alterius carnis appareret. Ergo in specie propria ibi apparet.

Praeterea, nihil potest apparere in aliquo quod non est in eo. Sed in sacramento altaris non est nisi species panis quae est tantum sacramentum; et corpus Christi, quod est res contenta; illud autem quod ibi apparet, non est species panis. Ergo est species corporis Christi.

Sed contra, cum in hoc sacramento non sit aliqua deceptio, ergo oportet secundum veritatem ibi esse illud quod sensus percipit. Sed sensus percipit ibi quasdam parvas dimensiones quarum judicium ad ipsum pertinet. Ergo sunt ibi illae dimensiones. Sed illae non sunt dimensiones corporis Christi, cum sint multo minores. Ergo sunt ibi aliae dimensiones quam dimensiones corporis Christi, et super illas fundantur species quae ibi apparent. Cum ergo species corporis Christi non fundentur nisi super dimensiones proprias, non videtur ibi corpus Christi in propria specie.

Praeterea, superficies illius speciei quae ibi apparet, tangit aerem circumstantem. Ergo illud cujus est illa superficies, est ibi sicut in loco. Sed corpus Christi non est ibi sicut in loco, ut dictum est. Ergo illa species quae ibi apparet, non est species corporis Christi.

But in this case the species of bread cease to be there. Therefore, if that is not the proper species in which it is seen, it will be there in no way at all.

Obj. 2: Furthermore, an apparition like that is for building up the faith. But faith would not be confirmed if Christ appeared under the appearance of some other flesh. Therefore, he appears there in his own appearance.

Obj. 3: Furthermore, nothing that is not in a thing can appear in it. But in the sacrament of the altar there is nothing but the appearance of the bread that is sacrament alone, and the body of Christ, which is the reality contained; however, what appears there is not the species of bread. Therefore, it is the species of the body of Christ.

On the contrary, since in this sacrament there is no deception, therefore what the senses perceive there must be there according to the truth. But the senses perceive there certain small dimensions, and the judgment of them belongs to the senses. Therefore, those dimensions are there. But they are not the dimensions of the body of Christ, since they are much smaller. Therefore other dimensions are there than the dimensions of the body of Christ, and the species which appear there are grounded in those dimensions. Therefore, since the species of the body of Christ are not grounded in anything but their own proper dimensions, it does not seem that the body of Christ is there in its own species.

Furthermore, the surface of that species that appears there touches the air surrounding it. Therefore, what possesses that surface is there as in a place. But the body of Christ is not there as in a place, as was said. Therefore that species that appears there is not the species of the body of Christ.

Quaestiuncula 3

Ulterius. Videtur quod in hoc casu debeat sumi. Quia in sumente exigitur devotio. Sed talis ostensio fit ad augmentandam devotionem. Ergo tunc magis debet sumi.

Praeterea, ille qui consecrat, secundum canones debet sumere: quod non posset nisi illud quod sub specie carnis apparet, sumeret. Ergo debet sumere.

Sed contra, nihil horrendum est committendum in hoc sacramento. Sed horrendum est comedere carnem crudam. Ergo illud quod in substantia carnis crudae apparet, non est sumendum.

Obj. 1: Moreover, it seems that in this case it should be consumed. For devotion is required in the one receiving. But such an apparition happens to increase devotion. Therefore, when this happens, all the more should it be consumed.

Obj. 2: Furthermore, whoever consecrates must consume, according to the canons; and this could not happen unless what appears under the species of flesh were consumed. Therefore, he must consume it.

On the contrary, nothing abhorrent is to be committed in this sacrament. But it is abhorrent to eat raw flesh. Therefore, what appears in the substance of raw flesh is not to be consumed.

Quaestiuncula 4

Ulterius. Videtur quod nec angelus possit videre corpus Christi sub sacramento. Quia quidam sancti sunt majores quibusdam angelis, ut habetur per Glossam 1 Corinth., 6, super illud: *angelos judicabimus*. Sed oculus glorificatus hominis sancti non potest ipsum videre. Ergo nec angelus.

Praeterea, quod est visibile, si ab aliquo non videatur, hoc est propter defectum videntis. Sed oculus glorificatus, qui non videt corpus Christi sub sacramento, ab omni defectu est immunis. Ergo corpus Christi non est de se visibile sub sacramento existens. Sed quod de se non est visibile, a nullo potest videri. Ergo nec angelus corpus Christi videre potest sub sacramento.

Sed contra, Gregorius: *quia est quod non videant qui videntem omnia vident?* Sed angeli vident Deum videntem omnia, ut patet Matth. 18, 10: *angeli eorum semper vident faciem patris*. Ergo vident corpus Christi sub sacramento.

Obj. 1: Moreover, it seems that neither can an angel see the body of Christ under the sacrament. For certain saints are greater than some of the angels, as is held in the Gloss on this text: *we will judge angels* (1 Cor 6:3).[47] But the eyes of a glorified human saint cannot see it. Therefore, neither can an angel.

Obj. 2: Moreover, if something that is visible is not seen by anyone, this is because of a defect in the one seeing. But the eyes of the glorified, who do not see the body of Christ under the sacrament, are immune from all defect. Therefore, the body of Christ is not visible in itself when existing under the sacrament. But what is not visible in itself can be seen by no one. Therefore neither can an angel see the body of Christ under the sacrament.

On the contrary, Gregory says: *for what is there they may not see who see the one who sees all?*[48] But angels see God, who sees all things, as is clear from that text, *their angels are always looking upon the face of the Father* (Matt 18:10). Therefore, they see the body of Christ under the sacrament.

Quaestiuncula 5

Ulterius. Videtur quod comprehendi possit intellectu viatoris. Quod enim est supra intellectum, est supra sermonem, ut patet in Lib. *de Causis*. Sed nos loquimur de corpore Christi sub sacramento contento. Ergo non est omnino supra intellectum nostrum.

Praeterea, nullus tenetur ad impossibile. Sed quilibet tenetur concedere, et mente tenere, corpus Christi verum esse sub sacramento. Ergo mente capi potest.

Sed contra, intellectus noster ortum habet a sensu. Sed corpus Christi sub sacramento non cadit in sensum, ut probatum est. Ergo non cadit in intellectum nostrum.

Obj. 1: Moreover, it seems that it can be comprehended by the understanding of someone wayfaring in this life. For what is above the understanding is above speech, as is clear in the *Book of Causes*.[49] But we speak of the body of Christ contained under the sacrament. Therefore, it is not entirely above our understanding.

Obj. 2: Furthermore, no one is bound to what is impossible. But anyone is bound to concede and to hold in his mind, that the true body of Christ is under the sacrament. Therefore, it can be grasped by the mind.

On the contrary, our understanding has its origin in our senses. But the body of Christ under the sacrament is not perceptible to the senses, as was proved. Therefore, it is not available to our understanding.

Response to Quaestiuncula 1

Respondeo dicendum, ad primam quaestionem, quod nihil videtur corporali visu, nisi per hoc quod oculus ejus movetur ab objecto secundum similitudinem coloris in ipso existentis: quae quidem similitudo primo fit in medio, et deinde in sensu. Corpus autem Christi non habet ordinem ad species, sub quibus est, ratione

To the first question, I answer that nothing is seen by physical sight unless its eye is moved by the object according to the likeness of color existing in it, which likeness indeed first happens in the medium, and then in the senses. But the body of Christ does not stand in a relationship to the species under which it exists by reason of its quantity;

---

47. See the *Glossa Lombardi*, PL 191:1576.

48. Cf. Gregory the Great, *Moralia in Iob* (CCSL 143), Bk. 2, ch. 3: "Quid enim de his quae scienda sunt nesciunt qui scientem omnia sciunt?"

49. Proposition 6. For the text of this proposition as well as discussion of it, see Thomas's *Commentary on the Book of Causes*, trans. Vincent Guagliardo, Charles Hess, and Richard Taylor (Washington, DC: The Catholic University of America Press, 1996), 45–52.

quantitatis suae; et ideo non potest aggenerari similitudo coloris ejus in aere contingente species, duplici ratione. Primo, quia omnis actio corporalis requirit contactum; tactus autem corporalis consequitur quantitatem, quia nihil aliud est quam conjunctio terminorum duarum quantitatum; et ideo corpus Christi non tangit aerem circumstantem; et propter hoc non potest in ipso aggenerare similitudinem coloris sui. Secundo, quia color consequitur quantitatem, cum immediatum subjectum ejus sit superficies: et quia corpus Christi non habet ordinem ad hunc locum ratione suae quantitatis, ideo nec ratione sui coloris; et ideo sicut non conjungitur aeri circumstanti secundum quantitatem, ita non assimilat sibi ipsum, aggenerando similitudinem coloris sui in eo.

AD PRIMUM ergo dicendum, quod si oculus Christi esset extra species sacramenti, non videret substantiam suam intra species contentam ex natura gloriae nisi miraculose; et ideo non oportet quod oculus glorificatus videat, nisi forte per miraculum.

AD SECUNDUM dicendum, quod comprehensores, quamvis non videant forte corporali visione corpus Christi sub sacramento, vident tamen visione intellectuali plena; et ideo non oportet quod habeant de eo fidem, sed perfectam cognitionem.

AD TERTIUM dicendum, quod sensus in hoc sacramento non decipitur: quia sensus non habet judicare de substantia, sed de formis sensibilibus; et ideo cum formae sensibiles sint ibi vere, in judicio sensus non est deceptio. Sed potest esse deceptio in judicio intellectus, nisi adsit fides, vel plena cognitio: et quamvis lateat visum corporalem beatorum, non tamen latet ipsos, quia intellectu conspiciunt; sicut etiam essentiam Dei non videt oculus corporis, sed oculus mentis ipsorum, ut Augustinus dicit in Lib. *de Videndo Deum*.

and so a likeness of its color cannot be replicated in the air touching the species, for two reasons. First, because every physical action requires contact, but bodily touch follows quantity, for it is nothing else than the union of the boundaries of two quantities; and so the body of Christ does not touch the surrounding air; and because of this it cannot generate in it a likeness of its color. Second, because color follows quantity, since its immediate subject is the surface; and because the body of Christ does not stand in a relationship to this place by reason of its quantity, neither does it by reason of its color; and so just as it is not joined to the air surrounding it according to quantity, so also it does not assimilate it to itself by generating the likeness of its own color in it.

REPLY OBJ. 1: If the eyes of Christ were outside the species of the sacrament, they would not see its substance contained within the species by the nature of glory, except miraculously; and so it would not be necessary that the eyes of the glorified see it, except perhaps by a miracle.

REPLY OBJ. 2: Those who possess the beatific vision, although they do not perhaps see the body of Christ by physical sight under the sacrament, do see by full intellectual sight; and so it is not necessary that they have faith about it, but perfect knowledge.

REPLY OBJ. 3: The senses are not deceived in this sacrament, for the senses are not able to judge about substance, but about sensible forms; and so since the sensible forms are true there, there is no deception in the judgment of the senses. But there can be deception in the judgment of the understanding, unless faith is present, or full knowledge. And although it may be hidden from the physical sight of the blessed, nevertheless it is not hidden from the blessed themselves, who look with understanding; just as also their physical eyes do not see the essence of God, but the eyes of their minds do, as Augustine says in his book *On Seeing God*.[50]

Response to Quaestiuncula 2

AD SECUNDAM QUAESTIONEM dicendum, quod absque omni dubio dicendum est, illud quod ibi apparet, esse verum corpus Christi (alias non adoraretur), sicut et prius erat quando in specie panis videbatur. Sed utrum species illa quae ibi apparet, sit species corporis Christi, difficile est determinare.

Quidam enim dicunt, quod species illa carnis vel pueri est tantum in oculo videntis: et hoc forte aliquando verum est, cum ab uno videatur in specie panis, et ab alio in specie carnis vel pueri; et ab eodem etiam quandoque post modicum iterum in specie panis videtur, quod prius in specie carnis videbatur: et secundum hoc potest fie-

TO THE SECOND QUESTION, it should be said that without any doubt what appears there is the true body of Christ (otherwise it may not be adored), just as it also was before when it was seen in the species of bread. But whether that species which appears there is the species of the body of Christ is difficult to determine.

For some people say that that appearance of flesh, or of the Christ-child, is only in the eye of the one seeing: and so perhaps it is true sometimes, when it is seen by one person in the species of bread, and by another in the species of flesh or of a child; and even sometimes after a little while it is seen again by the same person in the species of bread,

---

50. See Augustine, *Epistle 148*, n. 5 (CSEL 44:347).

ri divino miraculo ut similitudo corporis Christi fiat in oculo, sicut naturaliter fieret, si corpus Christi praesens esset. Nec est deceptio; quia non fit nisi ad instructionem fidei, et devotionem excitandam.

Sed quia aliquando ab omnibus ita videtur, et quandoque ita diu servatur in tali specie; ideo alii dicunt, quod vera species corporis Christi extra[51] visum immutat. Nec obstat quod videtur in minori quantitate, et non in specie gloriosa: quia in potestate corporis gloriosi est, ut se ostendat in toto vel in parte, et in specie gloriosa vel non gloriosa. Sed quia mutatio visus ab aliquo corpore per medium, fit per contactum ejus quod sentitur, ad medium quo sentitur, oportebit secundum hoc dicere quod corpus Christi secundum hoc tangat medium visionis, et per consequens quod sit ibi sicut in loco; et ita quod vel sit simul in pluribus locis, vel quod localiter motum sit de caelo descendens; quod tamen ei non est impossibile.

Sed huic obviat quod Guitmundus dicit, quod *de multorum episcoporum consilio sigillatum fuit hoc quod apparebat in specie corporis Christi, et positum in altari.* Corpus autem Christi, si ibi esset localiter, dispareret postquam apparuisset, sicut accidit discipulis euntibus in Emaus; nullo autem modo reservaretur inclusum.

Et ideo securius videtur dicere, quod sicut quando videbatur corpus Christi in specie panis, erant quaedam dimensiones subsistentes, et in illis alia sensibilia accidentia sensibilia fundabantur; ita illae eaedem dimensiones manent, et eis alia accidentia superducuntur divina virtute, quae speciem carnis praetendunt, sicut et accidentia quae prius erant, praetendebant speciem panis: et potest esse quod postea eadem virtute, illis accidentibus recedentibus, iterum accidentia panis reducantur, cum etiam naturali actione aliquod illorum accidentium quandoque immutari posset, dimensionibus manentibus, sicut odor vini vel sapor, si diu conservaretur.

AD PRIMUM ergo dicendum, quod adhuc species panis manent quantum ad dimensiones quae prius subsistebant, et principales erant in sacramento, quamvis color et alia hujusmodi non maneant, divina virtute hoc faciente; et ideo sub illis dimensionibus adhuc manet corpus Christi.

AD SECUNDUM dicendum, quod aedificatur fides, et excitatur devotio: quia illa accidentia sunt similia omnino accidentibus carnis Christi verae, quod non erat de

which before was seen in the species of flesh; and according to this it can happen by a divine miracle that a likeness of the body of Christ comes about in the eye, just as would have happened naturally, if the body of Christ were present. Nor is it a deception, because it only happens for instruction in the faith, and for exciting devotion.

But since sometimes it is seen this way by everyone, and sometimes it is kept this way for a long time under such appearances, therefore others say that the true species of the body of Christ changes the outward appearance. Nor does it matter that it is seen in a smaller quantity, and not in its glorified appearance, for it is in the power of the glorified body to show itself in whole or in part, as glorified or not glorified. But since a change in appearance by a body through the medium happens by the contact of what is sensed with the medium by which it is sensed, it would be necessary according to this to say that the body of Christ would touch the medium of sight, and as a result, that it would be there as in a place, and so either it would be in many places at the same time, or it would be locally moved, by coming down from heaven, which is nevertheless not impossible for it.

This contradicts what Guitmund says,[52] that *it was confirmed by the agreement of many bishops that what appeared in the species of the body of Christ was sealed and placed upon the altar.* But the body of Christ, if it was there as in a place, would disappear after it had appeared, as happened to the disciples going to Emmaus; and in no way would it be reserved enclosed.

And so it seems safer to say that just as when the body of Christ was seen under the appearance of bread there were certain subsistent dimensions, and in them other sensible accidents were based, so also those same dimensions remain, and other accidents are brought in to replace them by divine power, which display the appearance of flesh, just as also the accidents which existed before displayed the appearance of bread. And it can be that afterwards, by the same power, once those accidents are removed, the accidents of bread may again return, since even by natural action something of those accidents might be changed sometime while the dimensions remain, like the odor of the wine or its flavor, if it is kept a long time.

REPLY OBJ. 1: The appearance of the bread still remains in the dimensions that were subsisting before, and they were principal in the sacrament, although color and other things like that do not remain, when divine power does this; and so under those dimensions the body of Christ still remains.

REPLY OBJ. 2: Faith is built up and devotion is excited because those accidents are entirely like the accidents of the true body of Christ, which was not the case with the acci-

---

51. *extra visum.—extra existens visum* PLE.
52. Guitmundus, *De veritate Eucharistiae*, Bk. 2 (PL 149:1449–50).

accidentibus panis; quamvis non sint ipsamet accidentia corporis Christi.

AD TERTIUM dicendum, quod quamvis illa accidentia carnis ibi prius non essent, tamen sunt superinducta ad fidei instructionem divina virtute.

dents of bread, although they are not the very accidents of the body of Christ.

REPLY OBJ. 3: Although those accidents of flesh were not there before, nevertheless they are brought in by divine power for the instruction of the faith.

Response to Quaestiuncula 3

AD TERTIAM QUAESTIONEM dicendum, quod usus sacramenti debet materiae sacramenti competere, sicut ablutio aquae in baptismo. Et quia corpus Christi in hoc sacramento sub specie panis nobis proponitur, ideo usus sacramenti est per manducationem, ut supra dictum est. Cum ergo in specie propria, vel in specie carnis cruentatae apparens, vel in simili specie, non habeat rationem cibi, non debet assumi ab eo cui sic apparet, sed ab alio cui sub specie panis apparet. Si autem omnibus sub specie carnis appareret, tunc deberet cum reliquiis poni.

AD PRIMUM ergo dicendum, quod devotio non excitatur hic ad manducandum, quia non in specie cibi proponitur, sed ad venerandum.

AD SECUNDUM dicendum, quod in tali casu sacerdos debet iterum celebrare, ut quidam dicunt, et corpus Christi sumere; et si secundo hoc accideret, iterum tertio. Quidam autem dicunt, quod in tali casu sufficit spiritualis manducatio, nec propter hoc efficitur transgressor constitutionis ecclesiae: quia ad ea quae frequentius accidunt, leges aptantur.

TO THE THIRD QUESTION, it should be said that the use of this sacrament should be suited to the sacrament's matter, as washing is suited to water in baptism. And since in this sacrament the body of Christ is presented to us under the appearance of bread, therefore the use of the sacrament is by eating, as was said above. Therefore, when appearing in its proper species, or in the species of raw flesh, or in a similar species, it does not have the account of food, and so it should not be received by anyone to whom it appears in these ways, but by another to whom it appears under the species of bread. However, if it appears to everyone under the species of flesh, then it should be set aside with the relics.

REPLY OBJ. 1: In this case, devotion is not excited by eating, but by venerating, since it is not presented under the appearance of food.

REPLY OBJ. 2: In such a case the priest must celebrate again, as some people say, and consume the body of Christ. And if this should happen again the second time, he should celebrate again a third time. However, certain people say that in such a case spiritual eating suffices, nor is a priest made a transgressor of the regulations of the Church on account of this, because the laws are tailored to the things that usually happen.

Response to Quaestiuncula 4

AD QUARTAM QUAESTIONEM dicendum, quod angelus nihil videt corporali visione; quia etsi corpus assumat, non tamen conceditur quod videat per corpus assumptum; unde relinquitur quod in ipso non est nisi intellectualis visus, qui quidem non est recipiendo a sensibilibus, ut in 2 Lib. dictum est, dist. 3, qu. 2, art. 1 ad 2, sed vel per species innatas, quantum ad ea quae naturali cognitione intelligunt, vel per Verbum quod vident, quantum ad ea quae supra naturalem cognitionem ipsorum sunt. Et quia angeli sunt beati, oportet quod habeant plenam visionem eorum omnium de quibus est fides quantum ad visionem gloriosam, quae fidei succedit; et ideo sicut fides credit corpus Christi esse sub sacramento, ita in visione beata angeli vident. Credo autem quod omnia quae sunt fidei, sunt supra naturalem cognitionem angelorum, sicut supra rationem naturalem hominum; et ideo mysteria fidei dicuntur esse *abscondita a*

TO THE FOURTH QUESTION, it should be said that an angel sees nothing with bodily vision, for even if he assumed a body, it is still not granted that he see by means of his assumed body; hence it remains that in him there is only intellectual vision, which indeed is not through receiving from sensible objects, as is said in Book II, Distinction 3, Question 2, Article 1, reply to the second objection, but either by inborn species, for things that they understand by natural knowledge, or else, what they see through the Word, for those things that are above their natural understanding. And since angels are blessed, they must have full vision of all those things that faith deals with in the glorified vision, which replaces faith; and so just as faith believes the body of Christ to exist under the sacrament, in the same way the angels see it in the beatific vision. However, I believe that all those things that are of the faith are above the natural knowledge of the angels, just as they are above the

saeculis in Deo, ut dicitur Eph. 3; unde naturali cognitione non vident angeli corpus Christi sub sacramento, sed solum beata. Daemones vero nullo modo vident plenarie, sed *credunt, et contremiscunt.*

AD PRIMUM ergo dicendum, quod beati visione intellectuali gloriae vident corpus Christi sub sacramento, quamvis non corporali, in qua cum angelis non communicant.

AD SECUNDUM dicendum, quod de se secundum quod est sub sacramento, non est visibile corpus Christi visu corporali; est tamen visibile visu intellectuali.

natural reason of men. And this is why the mysteries of the faith are said to be *hidden in God from the ages*, as it says in Ephesians 3:9; hence the angels do not see the body of Christ under the sacrament by their natural knowledge, but only by beatified vision. But the demons do not see it fully in any way, but *they believe and tremble* (Jas 2:19).

REPLY OBJ. 1: The blessed see the body of Christ under the sacrament with the intellectual vision of glory, although not with bodily vision, in which they do not share with the angels.

REPLY OBJ. 2: According as it is under the sacrament the body of Christ in itself is not visible by bodily vision; however, it is visible by intellectual vision.

Response to Quaestiuncula 5

AD QUINTAM QUAESTIONEM dicendum, quod sicut in 3 Lib. dictum est, dist. 34, qu. 1, art. 2, quaestiunc. 1, illa tantum intellectus noster videre dicitur, proprie loquendo, quorum essentiae ei repraesentantur sive lumine naturali, sive lumine gratiae aut gloriae; et ideo per consequens videre dicitur illa a principio quae statim cognitis terminis, quasi visis essentiis terminorum, cognoscuntur, et per consequens tantum illa quae reducuntur in illa principia, sicut conclusiones scientiarum; quae vero nullo modo ordinem habent ad principia naturaliter cognita, nec ad sensus perceptionem, non potest in statu viae videre. Et quia corpus Christi esse sub sacramento nullum ordinem habet ad principia naturaliter cognita, quae sunt principia scientiarum, nec etiam sensu a nobis apprehendi potest; ideo intellectus viatoris nullo modo hoc videre potest, et multo minus comprehendere: quia aliquid videtur quod non comprehenditur, sicut essentia divina in patria: nisi videre largo modo dicto, secundum quod dicimur ea quae sunt fidei, videre *in speculo et aenigmate*, 1 Corinth. 13.

AD PRIMUM ergo dicendum, quod sicut imperfecte videmus, ita etiam et deficienter loquimur.

AD SECUNDUM dicendum, quod nullus tenetur videre in praesenti, sed tenetur credere. Fides autem de non visis est, credere autem est possibile.

TO THE FIFTH QUESTION, it should be answered that as was said in Book III, Distinction 34, Question 1, Article 2, Subquestion 1, our intellect is only said to see those things, properly speaking, whose essences are represented to it whether by natural light or by the light of grace or of glory. And so consequently it is said to see first those things that are known immediately when their terms are known, when as it were the essences of terms are seen, and only subsequently to see those things that are reduced to those principles, like the conclusions of the sciences; but things that in no way have an order to naturally known principles, nor to the perception of the senses, cannot be seen in the wayfaring state. And since the body of Christ under the sacrament has no order to naturally known principles, which are the principles of the sciences, nor can it even be apprehended by us through our senses, for this reason the intellect of a wayfarer cannot see it in any way, and much less understand it. For something is seen that is not comprehended, like the divine essence in the heavenly fatherland; unless 'to see' is said broadly, as we say we see those things that are of faith *in a mirror dimly* (1 Corinthians 13:12).

REPLY OBJ. 1: Just as we see imperfectly, so also we speak deficiently.

REPLY OBJ. 2: No one is bound to see in the present, but one is bound to believe. Now while faith is about things that are not seen, believing, on the other hand, is possible.

EXPOSITION OF THE TEXT

Non hoc corpus quod videtis, manducaturi estis. Intelligendum est per se, idest secundum quod videtur in forma sua.

Ipsum quidem et non ipsum corpus. Videtur esse contradictio. Et dicendum, quod non est: quia ipsum corpus Christi in propria specie non manducatur; et hoc dicit *visibiliter* Augustinus, quia in propria specie corpus Christi videri potest; sed sub specie panis manducatur; et hoc dicit *invisibiliter*, quia in propria specie videri non potest.

Sacrificium ecclesiae duobus confici. Non quod ex eis fiat unum in essentia, sed quia ex eis fit unum sacramentum. Qualiter autem persona Christi dicatur composita ex duabus naturis, dictum est, in 3 Lib., dist. 6.

Caro carnis, et sanguis sacramentum est sanguinis. Videtur hoc esse falsum: quia nihil est signum sui ipsius. Et dicendum, quod carnem quae significat, nominat ipsas species, quae sunt signum carnis; et hoc tropice, ut Magister dicit: et ipsae species cum carne contenta dicuntur caro invisibilis, quia sub specie illa caro Christi non videtur. Carnem autem significatam nominat ipsam carnem Christi, secundum quod sub propria forma videtur; unde et visibiliter dicitur.

Quis audeat manducare Dominum suum? Ad primam harum rationum responsum est in primo articulo hujus distinctionis. Ad secundam patebit solutio ex his quae dicentur in 2 art. dist. sequentis.

Si tantum valuit sermo Eliae ut ignem de caelo deponeret, non valebit tantum sermo Christi ut substantias mutet? Locus est a minori; unde intelligendum est quod plus valeat sermo Christi, et in persona Christi prolatus: quia sermo Eliae in seipso non habebat virtutem aliquam, sed operabatur per modum intercessionis; sermo autem Christi, scilicet forma hujus sacramenti habet virtutem intraneam, de qua supra, dist. 8, dictum est.

Quid ergo hic quaeris naturae ordinem? Ergo videtur quod non licet disputare per rationes de hoc sacramento. Et dicendum, quod loquitur contra illos qui nihil in hoc sacramento, et in aliis quae sunt fidei, volunt credere, nisi quod per naturalem rationem probari potest;

"It is not this body, which you can see, which you will eat."[53] This is to be understood per se, i.e., according as it is seen in its own form.

"The body that is eaten is the same and not the same as the one which was seen."[54] It seems to be a contradiction. And it should be said that it is not: for this very body of Christ in its proper species is not eaten; and Augustine says this, *visibly*, because in its proper species the body of Christ can be seen, but under the species of bread it is eaten. And he says *invisibly*, because in its proper species it cannot be seen.[55]

"The sacrifice of the Church is confected in two things."[56] Not that from those one thing is made in essence, but because from those one sacrament is made. But the way that the person of Christ may be said to be composed from two natures was said in Book III, Distinction 6.

"The flesh is the sacrament of flesh, and the blood of blood."[57] This seems to be false: for nothing is a sign of itself. And it should be said that he calls these species the flesh that signifies, which species are the sign of the flesh, and this figuratively, as the Master says; and those species with flesh contained are called the invisible flesh, for under that species the flesh of Christ is not seen. However, he calls the very flesh of Christ the flesh signified, according as it is seen under its proper form; hence it is also said 'visibly'.

"Who would dare to eat his Lord?"[58] To the first of these arguments the answer is in the first article of this distinction. To the second, the solution will be clear from what will be said in Article 2 of the next distinction.

"If the word of Elias had such power as to bring down fire from heaven, shall the word of Christ not have such power to change substances?"[59] This text argues from the lesser, and so it is to be understood that the word of Christ, and the word uttered in the person of Christ, has greater strength; for the word of Elijah had no power in itself, but it worked by way of intercession. However, the word of Christ, namely, this sacrament's form, has intrinsic power, as was said above in Distinction 8.

"Why then do you seek the order of nature?"[60] Therefore, it seems that it is not permitted to discuss this sacrament with rational arguments. And to this it should be said that he is speaking against those who wish to believe nothing in this sacrament or in the other sacraments of the faith except

---

53. *Sent.* IV, 10.1 (58), 2, citing Augustine, *Enarrationes in Psalmos*, on Ps. 54, n. 23.
54. *Sent* IV, 10.1 (58). 4 citing Lanfranc, *Liber de corpore et sanguine Domini*, c18.
55. For the text atttributed to Augustine, see Lanfranc, *Liber de corpore et sanguine Domini*, ch. 18 (PL 150:430).
56. *Sent* IV, 10.1 (58). 6 citing Lanfranc, *Liber de corpore et sanguine Domini*, c10.
57. *Sent* IV, 10.1 (58). 7 citing Lanfranc, *Liber de corpore et sanguine Domini*, c14.
58. *Sent* IV, 10.1 (58). 10 citing Augustine, *Sermo Mai 129*, n1.
59. *Sent* IV, 10.2 (59). 3 citing Ambrose, *De mysteriis*, c9 n52.
60. *Sent* IV, 10.2 (59). 4 citing Ambrose, *De mysteriis*, c9 n53.

non autem contra illos qui ex principiis fidei disputant, et qui ex principiis naturalibus non volunt probare quae sunt fidei, sed sustinere: quia quae sunt fidei, quamvis sint supra rationem, non tamen sunt contra rationem: alias Deus esset sibi contrarius, si alia posuisset in ratione quam rei veritas habet.

Si tanta vis est in sermone Domini ut incipiant esse quae non erant, quanto magis operatorius est, ut sint quae erant, et in aliud commutentur? Videtur quod haec probatio non valeat: quia sermo quo omnia facta sunt ex nihilo, est Verbum increatum; nunc autem loqui debuit de verbo creato, scilicet forma sacramenti. Et dicendum, quod auctoritas hujus virtutis residet in Verbo increato, sed in verbo creato est instrumentaliter, ut dictum est.

Sicut per Spiritum Sanctum vera Christi caro sine coitu creatur, ita per eumdem ex substantia panis et vini idem corpus Christi et sanguis consecratur. Videtur quod ista transubstantiatio non debeatur[62] Spiritui Sancto, sed magis filio. Et dicendum est, quod appropriatur filio sicut operanti, quia ipse est sacerdos et hostia; spiritui autem sancto sicut quo operatur: quia ipse est virtus de illo exiens ad sanandum, Luc. 6.

what can be proved by natural reason; but not against those who discuss from the principles of the faith and who do not wish to prove matters of faith from natural principles, but to defend them. For although matters of faith are above reason, nevertheless they are not against reason; otherwise God would be contrary to himself, if he had placed other things in our reason than the truth of the matter holds.

"If such power is in the Lord's word of the Lord that things that were not began to be, how much more effective it is in keeping in being things that already were, even as it changes them into something else."[61] It seems that this proof does not work: for the Word by which all things were made out of nothing is the uncreated Word; but now he must be speaking of the created word, namely, the sacrament's form. And it should be said that the authority of this power resides in the uncreated Word, but it exists in the created word instrumentally, as was said.

"Just as through the Spirit true flesh is created without coition, so through the same Spirit, the same body of Christ and his blood is consecrated from the substance of bread and wine."[63] It seems that this transubstantiation should not be appropriated to the Holy Spirit, but rather to the Son. And it should be said that this is appropriated to the Son as the one working, for he is the priest and victim; but it is appropriated to the Holy Spirit as that by which he works: for he is the power by which healing goes out of Christ (cf. Luke 6:19).

61. *Sent* IV, 10.2 (59). 6 citing Ambrose, *De sacramentis*, Bk. 4 ch. 4 nn15–17 and 19.
62. *debeatur spiritui.—debeat appropriari spiritui* PLE.
63. *Sent* IV, 10.2 (59). 7 citing Paschasius Radbertus, *De corpore et sanguine Domini*, c4 n1.

DISTINCTION 11
SACRAMENT-AND-REALITY IN THE EUCHARIST

Postquam determinavit Magister de re contenta in hoc sacramento, ostendens quod verum corpus ibi continetur, hic intendit determinare de conversione panis in corpus Christi, ex qua contingit ut sub sacramento corpus Christi contineatur; et dividitur in partes duas: in prima determinat de praedicta conversione panis in corpus Christi; in secunda ostendit qualiter species remaneant substantiali conversione facta, ibi: *sub alia autem specie tribus de causis carnem et sanguinem tradidit Christus.*

Circa primum tria facit: primo inquirit qualis sit praedicta conversio; secundo determinat hanc quaestionem quantum ad id in quo omnes conveniunt, ibi: *formalem tamen non esse cognosco*; tertio determinat eam quantum ad id in quo diversi diversa opinantur, ibi: *quibusdam videtur esse substantialis*. Et haec dividitur in partes tres secundum tres opiniones quas ponit; secunda pars incipit ibi: *quidam vero sic dicunt* etc.; tertia ibi: *alii vero putaverunt*, etc.

Circa primum tria facit: primo ponit opinionem; secundo objicit in contrarium, et solvit, ibi: *sed huic sententiae sic opponitur ab aliis*; tertio ostendit quae locutiones sint concedendae vel negandae secundum hanc opinionem, ibi: *nec tamen concedunt quidam quod substantia panis aliquando sit caro Christi.*

Sub alia autem specie tribus de causis carnem et sanguinem tradidit Christus. Hic ostendit qualiter species remaneant substantiali conversione facta; et dividitur in partes duas: in prima ostendit quare sub alia specie corpus Christi verum in sacramento exhibeatur; in secunda determinat de usu sive distributione dictarum specierum, ibi: *colligitur etiam ex praedictis, quod Christus vinum aqua mixtum dedit discipulis, corpus vero tale dedit quale tunc habuit.*

Circa primum tria facit: primo ostendit quare sub alia specie corpus Christi proponatur in sacramento; secundo quare sub duplici, ibi: *sed quare sub duplici spe-*

After the Master has considered the reality contained in this sacrament, showing that the true body is contained there, here he intends to examine the conversion of bread into the body of Christ, by which it happens that the body of Christ is contained under the sacrament. And this is divided into two parts: in the first, he examines this conversion of bread into the body of Christ; in the second, he shows how the species remain when the substantial conversion has happened, at: *Christ gave his body and blood under another species for three reasons.*[1]

Concerning the first he does three things: first, he inquires what the aforementioned conversion is like; second, he considers this question according to what all agree on, at: *And yet I know it is not formal*;[2] third, he considers what different people have different opinions about, at: *To some it seems to be substantial.*[3] And this is divided into three parts according to the three opinions that he cites. The second part begins at: *But some say that*, etc.;[4] the third at: *But others held*, etc.[5]

Concerning the first he does three things: first, he sets forth the opinion; second, he objects to the contrary, and resolves it at: *But the following objection to this position is made by others*;[6] third, he shows which statements are to be conceded or negated according to this opionion, at: *And yet some do not grant that the bread's substance is ever the flesh of Christ.*[7]

Christ gave his body and blood under another species for three reasons.[8] Here he shows how the species remain when the substantial conversion has happened; and this is divided into two parts. In the first he shows why the true body of Christ is displayed in this sacrament under a different appearance; in the second he determines its use, or the distribution of the species mentioned, at: *It is gathered from the foregoing that Christ gave to the disciples wine mixed with water. As for the body, he gave such a one as he then had.*[9]

Concerning the first he does three things: first, he shows why the body of Christ is presented in the sacrament under a different appearance; second, why under two different ap-

---

1. Peter Lombard, *Sententiae* IV, 11.3 (62). 1.
2. *Sent* IV, 11.1 (60). 1.
3. *Sent* IV, 11.1 (60). 1.
4. *Sent* IV, 11.2 (61). 5.
5. *Sent* IV, 11.2 (61). 6.
6. *Sent* IV, 11.1 (60). 2.
7. *Sent* IV, 11.2 (61). 3.
8. *Sent* IV, 11.3 (62). 1.
9. *Sent* IV, 11.6 (65). 1.

cie sumitur? Tertio de admixtione tertii elementi, scilicet aquae, ibi: *aqua vero admiscenda est vino.*

Colligitur etiam ex praedictis, quod Christus vinum aqua mixtum dedit discipulis, etc. Hic determinat de distributione specierum; et primo quomodo Christus distribuerit; secundo quomodo nunc distribuendum sit, ibi: *Eucharistia quoque intincta non debet dari populo pro supplemento communionis.*

Hic est triplex quaestio. Prima de conversione panis in corpus Christi, et vini in sanguinem. Secunda de materia hujus sacramenti, cujus species post conversionem remanent. Tertia de usu sacramenti istius in prima sui institutione, qua Christus ipsum discipulis dedit.

pearances, at: *But why is it taken under a double species?*[10] Third, about the mixing in of a third element, namely, water, at: *But water is to be mixed with the wine.*[11]

It is gathered from the foregoing that Christ gave to the disciples wine mixed with water. As for the body, he gave such a one as he then had, etc. Here he considers the distribution of the species, and first, how Christ distributed it; second, how it should be distributed now, at: *And the Eucharist is not to be given by intinction to the people "as a supplement of communion."*[12]

Here there are three questions. First, concerning the conversion of the bread into the body of Christ, and the wine into his blood. Second, the matter of this sacrament, whose appearances remain after the conversion. Third, the use of this sacrament at its first institution, when Christ gave it to his disciples.

10. *Sent* IV, 11.4 (63). 1.
11. *Sent* IV, 11.5 (64). 1.
12. *Sent* IV, 11.6 (65). 2 citing from the Council of Braga (spurious), c1.

QUESTION 1

TRANSUBSTANTIATION

Circa primum quaeruntur quatuor:

primo, utrum post consecrationem remaneat ibi panis;

secundo, utrum annihiletur;

tertio, utrum convertatur in corpus Christi;

quarto, de locutionibus quae in hac materia concedendae sunt.

Concerning the first, there are four things to be asked:

first, whether the bread remains there after the consecration;

second, whether it is annihilated;

third, whether it is converted into the body of Christ;

fourth, the statements that should be granted in this matter.

ARTICLE 1

Whether the bread remains there after the consecration

Quaestiuncula 1

AD PRIMUM SIC PROCEDITUR. Videtur quod substantia panis remaneat post consecrationem, ut dicit tertia opinio. Damascenus enim dicit: *quia consuetudo est hominibus comedere panem et vinum, conjugavit eis divinitatem, et fecit ea corpus et sanguinem suum.* Sed conjunctio requirit utrumque conjunctorum existere actu. Ergo panis remanet cum corpore Christi.

PRAETEREA, illud quod de pane remanet in hoc sacramento post consecrationem, cum sit sacramentum tantum, debet verum corpus Christi, et etiam mysticum, significare. Sed significatio talis non competit pani nisi ratione substantiae suae secundum quam ex diversis granis conficitur, secundum quam etiam reficere et nutrire habet. Ergo oportet quod remaneat in substantia panis.

PRAETEREA, illud ad quod pauciora difficilia sequuntur, est magis eligendum. Sed ad hanc positionem sequuntur pauciora difficilia, cum nihil aliud sequatur, nisi quod duo corpora sint in eodem loco; quod non est inconveniens de corpore glorioso ratione suae subtilitatis. Ergo haec opinio est alii praeeligenda.

SED CONTRA, hoc pronomen *hoc*, cum sit demonstrativum ad sensum, demonstrat substantiam sub speciebus immediate latentem. Sed si substantia panis ibi remaneret, ipsa sola immediate accidentibus subesset, quia eis afficeretur. Ergo ad ipsam ferretur demonstratio hujus pronominis hoc, cum dicitur: *hoc est corpus meum;*

OBJ. 1: To the first we proceed thus. It seems that the bread's substance remains after the consecration, as the third opinion says.[13] For Damascene says, *since it is the custom for men to eat bread and wine, he has joined them to divinity, and made those things his own body and blood.*[14] But a joining requires that both of the things joined actually exist. Therefore, the bread remains with the body of Christ.

OBJ. 2: Furthermore, what remains of the bread in this sacrament after the consecration, since it is sacrament alone, must signify the true body of Christ, and also the mystical body. But this signification does not belong to bread except by reason of its substance, according to which it is made out of many grains, and according as it is able to restore and nourish. Therefore, it must remain in the substance of bread.

OBJ. 3: Furthermore, what leads to fewer difficulties is rather to be chosen. But this position leads to fewer difficulties, since nothing follows other than that two bodies are together in the same place, which is not unfitting to the glorified body by reason of its subtlety. Therefore, this opinion is to be preferred to the other.

ON THE CONTRARY, this pronoun, *this*, since it is demonstrative in its sense, indicates the substance hidden directly under the appearances. But if the bread's substance remained there, it alone would directly underlie the accidents, for it would be affected by them. Therefore, the demonstration of this pronoun *this*, when it is said, *this is*

---

13. Parallels: *ST* III, q. 75, a. 2; *SCG* IV, ch. 63; *Super Matt.* 26; *Super I ad Cor.* 11, lec. 4.

14. John Damascene, *On the Orthodox Faith*, Bk. 4, ch. 13 (PG 94:1144).

et sic locutio esset falsa; quod est inconveniens et haereticum, quia est in doctrina religionis proposita. Ergo et praedicta positio est haeretica.

PRAETEREA, si substantia panis ibi remaneret, tunc sumens hoc sacramentum non solum sumeret spiritualem cibum, sed etiam corporalem. Sed corporalis cibi sumptio impedit a sacramento ulterius eadem die percipiendo, ut supra, dist. 8, dictum est. Ergo qui semel sumpsisset corpus Christi, non posset iterato sumere; quod est contra ritum hujus sacramenti.

my body, would be directed to it, and then it would be a false statement, which is unfitting and heretical, for it is in the teaching proposed by our religion. Therefore, the position described is heretical.

FURTHERMORE, if the bread's substance remained there, then the one receiving this sacrament would not only receive spiritual food, but also physical food. But the consumption of physical food impedes one from receiving the sacrament for the rest of the day, as was said above in Distinction 8.[15] Therefore, anyone who had consumed the body of Christ once would not be able to receive again, which is against the rite of this sacrament.

Quaestiuncula 2

ULTERIUS. Videtur quod non debeant species panis remanere. Quia in sacramento veritatis non debet esse aliqua deceptio. Sed cum accidentia ducant in cognitionem ejus quod quid est, secundum Philosophum in 1 *de Anima*, deceptio videtur, ostendere illius accidentia cujus substantia non manet. Ergo ex quo substantia panis non manet, non deberent accidentia ejus remanere.

PRAETEREA, causae in littera assignatae non videntur convenientes. Fides enim quamvis experimentum rationis effugiat, tamen rationis contradictionem non requirit: quia ea quae sunt fidei non sunt contra rationem, sed supra. Sed quod sub alia specie videatur, hoc non solum contra rationem, sed etiam contra sensum apparet. Ergo non deberet sub alia specie apparere propter meritum fidei.

PRAETEREA, supposita fide hujus sacramenti, per quam corpus Christi sine sui detrimento manducari creditur, non esset horridum illud sumere in quacumque specie appareret. Sed fides necessaria est ad sumendum. Ergo secunda causa quam assignat, nulla est.

PRAETEREA, illud quod aliquando fit ad confirmationem fidei, si semper fieret, non esset irrisio, sed major confirmatio. Sed aliquando ad confirmationem fidei alicujus dubitantis de hoc sacramento, ostenditur corpus Christi sub specie carnis, sicut legitur in vita beati Gregorii et in *Vitis patrum*. Ergo non esset ad irrisionem, si semper in specie propria ostenderetur.

SED CONTRA, sacramentum est sensibile signum, ut 1 distinct. dictum est. Sed panis est corporis Christi veri

OBJ. 1: Moreover, it seems that the appearance of the bread must not remain.[16] For in the sacrament of truth there should be no deception. But since accidents lead to the recognition of what something is, according to the Philosopher in *On the Soul* 1,[17] it seems to be a deception to display the accidents of something whose substance no longer remains. Therefore, since the bread's substance does not remain, its accidents should not remain.

OBJ. 2: Furthermore, the reasons assigned in the text do not seem fitting. For although faith slips away from the testing of reason, nevertheless it does not require contradicting reason: for those things that are of faith are not against reason, but above it. But what is seen under another appearance is not only against reason, but even appears against the senses. Therefore, it should not have appeared under a different species for the sake of the merit of faith.

OBJ. 3: Furthermore, once we assume faith in this sacrament, by which the body of Christ is believed to be eaten without detriment to him, it would not be horrible to consume it in whatever species it should appear. But faith is necessary for receiving it. Therefore, the second reason that he assigns is null.

OBJ. 4: Furthermore, what happens sometimes for the strengthening of faith, if it always happened, would not be mockery, but greater strengthening. But sometimes to strengthen the faith of someone who is doubting about this sacrament, the body of Christ appears under the species of flesh, as is read in the life of blessed Gregory[18] and in the lives of the fathers. Therefore, it would not be derisive if it always appeared in its proper species.

ON THE CONTRARY, a sacrament is a sensible sign, as was said in Distinction 1.[19] But bread is the sacrament of

---

15. See d. 8, q. 1, a. 4, qa. 2.
16. Parallels: below, d. 12, q. 1, a. 1, qa. 2; *ST* III, q. 75, a. 5; *SCG* IV, chs. 62, 63, and 65; *De rationibus fidei*, ch. 8; *Super I ad Cor.* 11, lec. 5.
17. Aristotle, *On the Soul*, Bk. 1, ch. 1 (402b21).
18. See John the Deacon, *The Life of Saint Gregory the Great*, Bk. 2, n. 41 (PL 75:103).
19. See d. 1, q. 1, a. 1, qa. 1.

sacramentum. Ergo debet remanere quantum ad sensibilia accidentia.

PRAETEREA, usus hujus sacramenti est manducatio, ut supra, dist. 9, dictum est. Sed manducatio requirit divisionem cibi, quae fit per masticationem. Ergo cum divisio non possit fieri in vero corpore Christi, quod est gloriosum, oportuit quod essent ibi species saltem aliae, quarum fractio esset.

the true body of Christ. Therefore, it should remain in its sensible accidents.

FURTHERMORE, the use of this sacrament is eating, as was said above in Distinction 9.[20] But eating requires a sundering of food, which happens by chewing. But since this sundering cannot happen to the true body of Christ, which is glorified, there had to be at least other appearances there, which could be broken up.

Quaestiuncula 3

ULTERIUS. Videtur quod etiam forma substantialis panis debeat remanere. Operatio enim substantialis non potest fieri sine forma substantiali. Sed nutrire est operatio formae substantialis: quia *nutrit inquantum quid cibus*, ut dicitur in 2 *de Anima*. Ergo cum species quae in sacramento remanent, etiam corporaliter nutriant, ut a quibusdam dicitur, videtur quod forma substantialis panis remaneat.

PRAETEREA, illud quod non mutatur in aliquid corporis Christi, oportet quod post consecrationem maneat. Sed forma substantialis panis non convertitur in aliquid corporis Christi: quia si converteretur, oporteret quod converteretur in animam, quae est forma substantialis corporis Christi, in quam non convertitur aliquid, ut ex praecedenti dist. patet. Ergo forma substantialis panis manet sicut et accidentia.

PRAETEREA, panis est quoddam artificiale. Sed formae artificialium sunt accidentia, ut patet in 2 *Physic*. Cum ergo accidentia maneant, videtur quod forma panis secundum quam est panis, maneat.

PRAETEREA, secundum Averroem in Lib. *de Substantia orbis*, et in 1 *Physic*., oportet in materia praeintelligere dimensiones ante formas substantiales aliquo modo in generabilibus et corruptibilibus, alias non possent esse diversae formae in diversis partibus materiae, cum divisio non fiat nisi secundum quantitatem. Sed dimensiones manent. Ergo et forma substantialis manet.

SED CONTRA, remotis accidentibus et forma substantiali, nihil manet nisi subjectum commune. Sed illud quod est commune, non potest converti in aliquid. Ergo non posset intelligi aliqua conversio fieri si forma substantialis remaneret.

OBJ. 1: Moreover, it seems that also the substantial form of bread should remain.[21] For substantial operation cannot happen without substantial form. But to nourish is the operation of a substantial form, for *something nourishes to the extent that it is food*, as it says in *On the Soul* 2.[22] Therefore, since the appearances that remain in the sacrament also nourish physically, as certain people say, it seems that the substantial form of bread remains.

OBJ. 2: Furthermore, what is not changed into something of the body of Christ must remain after the consecration. But the bread's substantial form is not converted into anything of the body of Christ: for if it were converted, it would have had to be converted into the soul, which is the substantial form of the body of Christ, into which nothing is converted, as is evident from the previous distinction.[23] Therefore, the substantial form of bread remains, like the accidents.

OBJ. 3: Furthermore, bread is something man-made. But the forms of man-made things are accidents, as is evident in *Physics* 2.[24] Therefore, since the accidents remain, it seems that the bread's form, according to which it is bread, remains.

OBJ. 4: Furthermore, according to Averroes in his book *On the Substance of the World*,[25] and in his commentary on *Physics* 1,[26] it is necessary in matter to understand dimensions before substantial forms in some way among generable and corruptible things, otherwise there could not be different forms in different parts of the matter, since division only happens according to quantity. But the dimensions remain. Therefore, the substantial form also remains.

ON THE CONTRARY, once accidents and substantial form are removed, nothing remains except the shared subject. But what is shared cannot be converted into something. Therefore, no conversion can be understood to happen if substantial form remains.

---

20. See d. 9, a. 2, qa. 5.
21. Parallels: *ST* III, q. 75, a. 6; *Super I ad Cor.* 11, lec. 4.
22. Aristotle, *On the Soul*, Bk. 2, ch. 4 (416b13).
23. See d. 10, a. 2, qa. 4.
24. Aristotle, *Physics*, Bk. 2, ch. 1 (192b27–32).
25. Averroes, *de Substantia orbis*, ch. 1.
26. Text 63.

PRAETEREA, species panis et vini sensibiles sunt sacramentum tantum in Eucharistia. Ergo debent ducere in illud cujus sunt sacramentum, scilicet in corpus Christi. Sed si remaneret ibi forma substantialis panis, ducerent in ipsam magis quam in corpus Christi, quia sunt ei propinquiora secundum naturam. Ergo videtur quod non remaneat forma substantialis panis.

FURTHERMORE, the sensible appearances of bread and wine are sacrament alone in the Eucharist. Therefore, they must lead to that of which they are the sacrament, namely, the body of Christ. But if the bread's substantial form remained there, the appearances would lead to it rather than to the body of Christ, for they are closer to it according to nature. Therefore it seems that the bread's substantial form does not remain.

Response to Quaestiuncula 1

RESPONDEO dicendum ad primam quaestionem, quod haec positio, quae ponit substantiam panis ibi remanere post consecrationem simul cum vero corpore, incompetens est huic sacramento, et impossibilis, et haeretica.

Incompetens quidem, quia impediret venerationem debitam huic sacramento: esset enim idolatriae occasio, si hostiae veneratio latriae exhiberetur, substantia panis ibi remanente. Esset etiam contra significationem sacramenti: quia species non ducerent in verum corpus Christi per modum signi, sed magis in substantiam panis. Esset etiam contra usum sacramenti: quia jam cibus iste non esset pure spiritualis sed etiam corporalis.

Sed quod sit impossibilis, patet ex hoc quod impossibile est aliquid esse nunc cum prius non fuerit, nihil ipso mutato vel aliquo in ipsum: nec posset etiam per miraculum fieri, sicut quod esset animal rationale mortale, et non esset homo: aliter enim se habere nunc et prius est idem quod moveri vel transmutari. Si ergo corpus Christi verum esset sub sacramento nunc et non prius, oporteret aliquem motum vel mutationem intervenisse. Sed nulla mutatio est ex parte panis facta secundum hanc positionem. Ergo oportet quod corpus Christi sit mutatum saltem localiter, ut dicatur quod corpus Christi est hic, quia per motum localiter huc venit; quod omnino esse non potest: quia cum simul et semel in diversis locis corpus Christi consecretur, oporteret quod simul et semel ad diversa loca unum numero moveretur corpus, quod est impossibile: quia contingeret simul contrarios motus inesse eidem, vel saltem diversos ejusdem speciei.

Quod autem sit haeretica, patet ex hoc quod contradicit veritati Scripturae; non enim esset verum dicere: *hoc est corpus meum*, sed: *hic est corpus meum*.

AD PRIMUM ergo dicendum, quod verbum Damasceni intelligendum est quantum ad species quibus corpus Christi divinitati unitum modo ineffabili conjungitur.

TO THE FIRST QUESTION, I answer that this position, which holds that the bread's substance remains after the consecration together with the true body, is unbecoming to this sacrament, and impossible, and heretical.

It is unbecoming because it would impede the veneration due to this sacrament, for it would be an occasion of idolatry if the veneration of latria were given to the host while the substance of bread remained there. It would also be against the sacrament's signification, for the species would not lead to the true body of Christ by the mode of a sign, but rather they would signify the substance of bread. It would also be against the use of the sacrament, for then this food would not be purely spiritual but also physical.

But that it is impossible is evident from the fact that it is impossible for something to exist now when it did not exist before, when it has not changed and nothing has changed into it. Nor can it even happen by a miracle, like if something were a mortal rational animal and were not a human: for to be related otherwise now and before is the same thing as to be moved or to be transformed. Therefore, if the true body of Christ were under the sacrament now and not before, it would be necessary for some motion or change to happen in between. But no change happens on the part of the bread according to this position. Therefore it is necessary that the body of Christ be changed at least in place, so that it may be said that the body of Christ is here, because it comes here by local motion; which cannot happen in any way: for since the body of Christ is consecrated at one and the same time in different places, it would be necessary that at one and the same time a body one in number would be moved to different places, which is impossible. For at the same time contrary movements would happen in the same thing, or at least different movements of the same species.

But the fact that this is heretical is seen from the fact that it contradicts the truth of Scripture, for it would not be true to say, *this is my body*, but rather, *here is my body*.

REPLY OBJ. 1: The word of Damascene is to be understood as to the appearances to which the body of Christ united to the divinity is joined in an ineffable way.

AD SECUNDUM dicendum, quod species sic remanentes repraesentant aliquo modo substantiam quam prius afficiebant, et per consequens proprietates ejus; et ita habent rationem significandi per quamdam similitudinem corpus Christi verum et mysticum.

AD TERTIUM dicendum, quod hanc positionem sequitur gravius inconveniens quam quod contradictoria sint simul vera: quia ponit definitionem (scilicet aliter nunc quam prius), et non potest ponere definitum (scilicet motum), neque in corpore Domini, neque in substantia panis.

REPLY OBJ. 2: The appearances so remaining represent in a certain way the substance that they previously affected, and as a result, its properties. And in this way they have the account of signifying the true and mystical body of Christ by a certain resemblance.

REPLY OBJ. 3: Something more unfitting results from this position than that contradictory things are simultaneously true. For it posits a definition (namely, different now than before), and cannot posit the thing defined (namely, motion), whether in the body of the Lord or in the bread's substance.

Response to Quaestiuncula 2

AD SECUNDAM QUAESTIONEM dicendum, quod accidentia panis eadem numero remanent ibi. Quomodo autem ibi sint, utrum sine subjecto vel alio modo, in sequenti distinct., qu. 1, art. 1, dicetur. Sed ratio quare remaneant, assignatur in littera ex parte usus sacramenti, et quantum ad manducationem spiritualem, quae est per fidem, ut scilicet fides esset majoris meriti quantum ad manducationem sacramentalem, ne scilicet esset nobis horrori, si in propria specie sumeretur, et infidelibus irrisioni. Potest assignari et alia causa ex parte ipsius sacramenti: quia spiritualia in sacramentis per signa corporalia consueverunt ostendi: et quia corpus Christi verum non est cibus corporalis, sed spiritualis; ideo oportuit quod per similitudines sensibiles cibus corporalis significaretur, et eis contineretur.

AD PRIMUM ergo dicendum, quod in hoc sacramento non est aliqua deceptio neque fictio. Non enim sensus decipitur, quia non habet judicare nisi de sensibilibus speciebus, quae quidem vere ibi sunt sicut et sensui ostenduntur; neque etiam intellectus, qui habet judicium de substantiis rerum per fidem juvatus.

AD SECUNDUM dicendum quod jam patet ex dictis quod non est contra sensum, sed supra; quia sensus non potest pertingere ad illius substantiae cognitionem.

AD TERTIUM dicendum, quod supposita fide, in sumptione corporis Christi in specie propria apparentis non esset horror ex abominatione proveniens, esset tamen horror ex devotione procedens; quia homo non solum refugit immunda tangere ex abominatione, sed etiam sancta ex devotione.

AD QUARTUM dicendum, quod quantum ad ostensionem talis speciei fides potest aedificari; sed si in hac specie sumeretur, magis esset in fidei destructionem: quia corpus Christi quod est gloriosum, passibile ostenderetur, si masticationi subesset.

TO THE SECOND QUESTION, it should be said that the accidents of the bread remain there the same in number. However, how they exist there, whether without their subject or in some other way, will be said in the following distinction, Question 1, Article 1. But the reason why they remain is assigned in the text on account of the sacrament's use, and as to spiritual eating, which is by faith, namely so that faith would be of greater merit in sacramental Communion, and so that it would not be dreadful to us, if it were consumed in his proper appearance, and open to the derision of unbelievers. Another reason can be assigned on the part of the sacrament itself: for spiritual things in sacraments are customarily shown by physical signs. And since the true body of Christ is not physical food, but spiritual food, for this reason it was necessary that through sensible likenesses physical food would be signified, and that it would be contained by those likenesses.

REPLY OBJ. 1: In this sacrament there is neither deception nor pretense. For the senses are not deceived, since they only need to judge sensible species, which indeed are truly there just as they are presented to the senses. Nor is the intellect deceived, which must judge the substance of things aided by faith.

REPLY OBJ. 2: It is already evident from the things said that it is not against the senses, but above them, for the senses cannot attain to understanding of that substance.

REPLY OBJ. 3: If faith is assumed, in the consumption of the body of Christ appearing in its proper species there would not be any horror arising from abomination, but there would be horror proceeding from devotion, for man does not only recoil from touching unclean things out of abomination, but also from touching holy things out of devotion.

REPLY OBJ. 4: In exhibiting this kind of species, faith can be built up, but if it were consumed in this species, it would rather be for the destruction of faith, for the body of Christ, which is glorified, would be presented as vulnerable, if it were subject to chewing.

Response to Quaestiuncula 3

AD TERTIAM QUAESTIONEM dicendum, quod forma panis substantialis non remanet post consecrationem; et hoc propter tres rationes. Primo, quia in qualibet transmutatione vel conversione terminus a quo est ejusdem generis cum termino ad quem. Illud autem ad quod terminatur conversio, non est forma tantum neque materia tantum, sed substantia existens in actu; et hoc declarant verba substantiva[27], quae hoc faciunt quod significant. Unde cum in eis exprimatur per hoc pronomen hoc substantia in actu composita, oportet quod illud quod convertitur in corpus Christi, sit etiam substantia composita, non materia panis tantum; et ita forma panis non manet. Secundo, quia frustra remaneret. Accidentia enim manent ut sint signa, quia ad hoc sunt ut per ea de substantia subjacente cognitionem accipiamus, cum sint sensibilia, et ita ad cognitionem intelligibilium via. Sed forma substantialis non est quid sensibile, sed est ordinata ad esse substantiale. Unde cum substantia panis non remaneat, frustra forma substantialis ibi esset. Tertio, quia accidentia non immediate ducerent in corpus Christi, sed in formam substantialem panis remanentem; et ideo deperiret aliquid significationi sacramenti.

AD PRIMUM ergo dicendum, quod haec ratio movit quosdam ad ponendum formam substantialem ibi remanere; sed patet quod ratione ista magis ponendum esset quod materia panis remaneat quam quod forma. Panis enim non nutrit, nec aliquis cibus, nisi secundum quod convertitur in illud quod nutritur: quod autem naturali conversione convertitur in alterum, non manet quantum ad formam, sed quantum ad materiam, unde forma substantialis panis, si remaneret, nutrire non posset magis quam accidentia. Utrum autem species illae possint nutrire, in sequenti distinctione dicetur.

AD SECUNDUM dicendum, quod anima non est forma quae perficiat uniformiter suum perfectibile in toto et in omnibus partibus; unde singulae partes ex anima consequuntur perfectionem eis proportionalem; unde quamvis in animam Christi secundum quod est perfectio totius, non convertatur aliquid, tamen transubstantiatur substantia panis tota, et quantum ad formam et quantum ad materiam in ipsum corpus Christi totum, secundum quod intelligitur accepisse congruentes perfectiones in singulis partibus, quia sic est organicum, et propria animae materia.

AD TERTIUM dicendum, quod quamvis ars non possit introducere formam substantialem per seipsam, po-

TO THE THIRD QUESTION, it should be said that the bread's substantial form does not remain after the consecration, and this is for three reasons. First, because in any change or conversion, the starting terminus is of the same kind as the ending terminus. Now what the conversion terminates in is not form alone nor is it matter alone, but a substance existing actually; and this is what the transubstantiating words declare that bring about what they signify. Hence since in them the pronoun *this* expresses a composite substance in act, it is necessary that what is converted into the body of Christ is also a composite substance, not the bread's matter alone, and this is why the form of the bread does not remain. Second, because it would remain in vain. For accidents remain so that they can be signs, because this is what they exist for, so that we might receive the understanding of the underlying substance through them, since they are sensible, and in that way they are a path to the understanding of intelligible things. But substantial form is not sensible, but ordered to substantial being. Hence since the substance of the bread does not remain, the substantial form would be there to no purpose. Third, because the accidents would not directly lead to the body of Christ, but to the bread's substantial form remaining, and so something of the sacrament's signification would be destroyed.

REPLY OBJ. 1: This argument moves certain people to claim that substantial form remains there, but it is evident that this argument would lead rather to the conclusion that the bread's matter remains than that its form does. For bread does not nourish, nor does any food, except as it is converted into something that is nourished; but of what is converted into something else by natural conversion, the form does not remain, but the matter does. Hence the bread's substantial form, if it remained, would not be able to nourish more than its accidents do. But whether those appearances can nourish will be said in the next distinction.[28]

REPLY OBJ. 2: The soul is not a form that uniformly perfects its perfectible in the whole and in all the parts; hence individual parts obtain from the soul a perfection proportional to them; hence although nothing is converted into Christ's soul according as it is the perfection of the whole, nevertheless the whole substance of the bread is transubstantiated, both in its form and in its matter, into the whole body of Christ, according to which it is understood to have received congruent perfection in the individual parts, since this is the way with organic things, and the proper matter of the soul.

REPLY OBJ. 3: Although art cannot introduce substantial form by itself, it can, however, introduce it by the power

---

27. *substantiva.—transsubstantiantia* PLE.
28. See d. 12, q. 1, a. 2, qa. 5.

test tamen introducere virtute naturae qua utitur in sua operatione sicut instrumento; sicut patet in hoc quod aquam in vaporem convertit, et aerem in ignem igne mediante. Et similiter cum occiditur animal, recedente anima, alia forma substantialis succedit, sicut generatio unius est corruptio alterius. Ita etiam per commixtionem farinae et aquae et ustionem ignis potest consequi forma aliqua substantialis quae sit forma substantialis per quam panis est panis. Si autem non esset forma substantialis quae est per artem inducta per quam panis est panis, substernitur forma substantialis accidentali, scilicet forma farinae; triticum enim jam a sua specie est corruptum; quia non manet ejus operatio ut possit sibi simile generare.

AD QUARTUM dicendum, quod dimensio quae praeintelligitur ante formam substantialem in materia, non habet esse completum, quia non est dimensio terminata; terminatio enim dimensionis est per formam. Sed dimensiones quae manent post consecrationem, sunt dimensiones terminatae, quia habent certam mensuram et figuram.

of nature which it uses in its operation like an instrument, as is clear in the conversion of water into a vapor, and air into fire by means of fire. And likewise when an animal is killed, once the soul leaves, another substantial form replaces it, as the generation of one thing is the corruption of another. So also by the mixing of flour and water and the burning of fire a certain substantial form can result that is the substantial form by which bread is bread. But if there were not a substantial form that is instilled by art, by which bread is bread, a substantial form underpins the accident, namely, the form of flour; for the wheat has already broken down from its own species, because its operation does not remain so that it can generate something like itself.

REPLY OBJ. 4: The dimension which is understood before substantial form in matter does not have complete being, since it is not a terminated dimension, for the termination of dimension is by form. But the dimensions that remain after the consecration are terminated dimensions, because they have a certain measure and figure.

ARTICLE 2

Whether the bread is annihilated[29]

AD SECUNDUM SIC PROCEDITUR. Videtur quod panis facta conversione annihiletur. In qualibet enim mutatione quae est secundum aliquid intraneum rei, terminus a quo non manet nisi in potentia praejacenti; sicut quando nigrum fit album, nigredo non remanet nisi in potentia subjecti; et quando ex aere fit ignis, forma aeris, quae est terminus a quo, non manet nisi in potentia materiae communis, quae subjicitur mutationi. Sed in conversione de qua loquimur, est terminus a quo, tota substantia panis. Ergo cum non sit accipere aliquid praejacens ad totam substantiam panis, quia non est in subjecto sicut accidens, neque in materia sicut forma, videtur quod omnino annihiletur.

PRAETEREA, respectu ejusdem est aliquid natum esse terminus a quo et terminus ad quem; sicut ex albo fit nigrum, et ex nigro album. Sed mutationis, cujus terminus ad quem est tota substantia rei, terminus a quo est simpliciter nihil, sicut patet in creatione. Ergo similiter cum in conversione de qua loquimur, terminus a quo sit tota substantia panis, terminus ad quem erit simpliciter nihil. Ergo substantia panis annihilatur.

PRAETEREA, si unum contradictorium est falsum, reliquum de necessitate erit verum. Sed facta conversione, haec est falsa: panis est aliquid, vel: de pane est aliquid. Ergo haec est vera: nihil de pane est. Ergo panis est annihilatus.

PRAETEREA, illud annihilari dicitur quod neque in se neque in alio manet. Sed panis substantia non manet in se, facta conversione, ut dictum est, neque manet in corpore Christi, quia sic corpus Christi augeretur. Ergo penitus annihilatur.

PRAETEREA, sicut se habet conversio formalis ad formam, ita substantialis ad substantiam. Sed in conversione formali annihilatur forma, sicut patet cum ex aere fit ignis. Ergo in conversione substantiali, qualis haec esse dicitur, annihilatur substantia panis.

SED CONTRA, Augustinus dicit in Lib. 83 qq., quaest. 21: *ille ad quem non esse non pertinet, non est causa tendendi ad non esse.* Sed Deus est hujusmodi. Ergo ipse ni-

OBJ. 1: To the second we proceed thus. It seems that the bread is annihilated once the conversion has been done. For in any change that is according to something internal to a thing, the starting terminus does not remain except in potency to the thing lying before it, as when something black becomes white, blackness does not remain except in the potency of the subject; and when fire is made from the air, the form of the air, which is the starting terminus, does not remain except in the potency of the shared matter, which is subject to the change. But in the conversion that we are discussing, the starting terminus is the whole substance of the bread. Therefore, since there is not anything to take as underlying the whole substance of the bread, since it is not in a subject as an accident, nor in matter as a form, it seems that it is entirely annihilated.

OBJ. 2: Furthermore, regarding the same thing something is bound to be starting terminus and ending terminus, just as from something white, something black is made, and from something black something white is made. But of a change, of which the ending terminus is the whole substance of a thing, the starting terminus is simply nothing, as is evident in creation. Therefore likewise, since in the conversion that we are discussing the starting terminus is the whole substance of the bread, the ending terminus will simply be nothing. Therefore the substance of the bread is annihilated.

OBJ. 3: Furthermore, if one of two contradictories is false, the other will necessarily be true. But once the conversion has happened this is false: *the bread is something*, or *something of the bread exists.* Therefore, this is true: *nothing of the bread exists.* Therefore the bread is annihilated.

OBJ. 4: Furthermore, something is said to be annihilated which remains neither in itself nor in another. But the bread's substance does not remain in itself, once the conversion happens, as was said; nor does it remain in the body of Christ, for then the body of Christ would be increased. Therefore, it is thoroughly annihilated.

OBJ. 5: Furthermore, formal conversion is related to form just as substantial conversion is related to substance. But in a formal conversion the form is annihilated, as is seen when fire is made out of air. Therefore, in a substantial conversion, as this is said to be, the bread's substance is annihilated.

ON THE CONTRARY, Augustine says in the *83 Questions*, Question 21: *someone to whom non-being does not pertain is not a cause of tending to non-being.*[30] But God is

---

29. Parallels: *ST* III, q. 75, a. 3; *SCG* IV, ch. 63; *Quodl.* V, q. 6, a. 1; *Super Matt.* 26; *Super I ad Cor.* 11, lec. 5.

30. Augustine, *De diuersis quaestionibus octoginta tribus* (CCSL 44A), q. 21: "At ille ad quem non esse non pertinet non est causa deficiendi, id est tendendi ad non esse, quia, ut ita dicam, essendi causa est."

hil in nihilum reducit. Sed conversio praedicta fit divina virtute. Ergo non reducitur substantia panis in nihil.

PRAETEREA, illud quod in aliud convertitur, non annihilatur. Sed panis in corpus Christi convertitur, ut per auctoritates in littera positas ostendi potest. Ergo non annihilatur.

PRAETEREA, defectus perfectioni repugnat. Sed hoc sacramentum est maximae perfectionis, ut supra dictum est, dist. 8, qu. 1, art. 3, quaestiunc. 1. Ergo cum annihilatio sit via ad defectum, non competit huic sacramento.

RESPONDEO dicendum, quod haec opinio duo ponit sub disjunctione; scilicet quod substantia panis resolvitur in praejacentem materiam, vel quod annihilatur; et quantum ad utrumque est falsa.

Si enim in praejacentem materiam resolveretur, hoc non potest intelligi nisi dupliciter. Uno modo quod esset in materia sine forma omni, quod quidem nec per miraculum esse potest, quia haec positio implicat in se contradictionem. Materia enim per essentiam suam est ens in potentia, et forma est actus ejus. Si ergo ponatur materia sine forma esse actu, ponetur actu materia esse et non esse. Alio modo potest intelligi ita quod resolvatur in materialia elementa; et hoc iterum non potest esse; quia illa materialia elementa aut remanerent in eodem loco, et oporteret quod sub illis speciebus esset aliud corpus quam corpus Christi, et quod illud materiale corpus esset simul cum dimensionibus panis, et multa hujusmodi inconvenientia sequerentur: vel non essent in eodem loco, et sic esset motus localis illius elementi materialis; quod non potest esse, quia sentiretur talis mutatio, si esset.

Praeterea, cum motus localis necessario sit successivus, oporteret quod illud materiale elementum prius relinqueret unam partem hostiae quam aliam. Transubstantiatio autem fit in instanti, ut dicetur art. seq., quaestiunc. 2. Unde sequeretur alterum duorum: vel quod aliquando sub aliqua parte specierum non esset neque corpus Christi, neque substantia panis, neque materiale elementum, quod jam abscessit ab illa parte; vel quod aliquando sub eadem parte hostiae esset corpus Christi et materiale elementum, quod est impossibile; et ideo non potest dici quod resolvatur in praejacentem materiam.

Similiter non potest dici quod annihiletur, eo quod omnis motus denominatur a termino ad quem, sicut motus qui est ad albedinem, dicitur dealbatio; unde illa transmutatio tantum posset dici annihilatio, cujus terminus ad quem esset nihil. Hoc autem non potest esse in ista conversione, quia oportet hanc conversionem terminari ad corpus Christi: quia nihil potest incipere hic

such a one. Therefore, he reduces nothing to nothingness. But the conversion mentioned is done by divine power. Therefore the substance of the bread is not reduced to nothing.

FURTHERMORE, what is converted into something is not annihilated. But bread is converted into the body of Christ, as can be shown by the authorities cited in the text. Therefore, it is not annihilated.

FURTHERMORE, a defect is opposed to perfection. But this sacrament is of the greatest perfection, as was said above, in Distinction 8, Question 1, Article 3, Subquestion 1. Therefore, since annihilation is a way to defect, it does not belong to this sacrament.

I ANSWER THAT, this opinion places two things under disjunction: namely, that the bread's substance is resolved into the underlying matter, or that it is annihilated; and both are false.

For if it were resolved into the underlying matter, this can only be understood in two ways. In one way, that it would be in the matter without any form at all, which indeed cannot happen even by a miracle, for this position implies self-contradiction. For matter by its own essence is being in potency, and form is its act. Therefore, if matter were posited to exist in act without form, the matter would be posited actually to be and not to be. The other way it can be understood is such that the bread is resolved into its material elements. And this also cannot be, for those material elements either would remain in the same place, and under those species there would have to be another body other than the body of Christ, and that material body would exist together with the dimensions of the bread, and many other unfitting things like this would result. Or else they would not exist in the same place, and then it would be local motion of that material element, which cannot be, because a change like that would be noticed if it happened.

Furthermore, since local motion is necessarily successive, that material element would have had to leave behind one part of the host before another. But transubstantiation happens in an instant, as will be said in the following article, Subquestion 2. Hence one of two things would follow: either sometimes under a certain part of the species there would be neither the body of Christ nor the substance of bread, nor the material element, which has already passed away from that part; or sometimes under the same part of the host there would be the body of Christ and the material element, which is impossible. And so it cannot be said that it is resolved into the underlying matter.

Likewise it cannot be said that it is annihilated, by the fact that every motion is denominated from the ending terminus, like the motion that is to whiteness is called whitening; hence only that transformation could be called annihilation whose ending terminus was nothing. However, this cannot be the case in that conversion, since this conversion must terminate in the body of Christ: for nothing can be-

esse cum prius hic non fuerit, nisi per motum aut mutationem propriam vel alterius terminatam aliquo modo ad ipsum. Unde si conversio praedicta ad corpus Christi non terminaretur, oporteret quod corpus Christi esset hic in altari facta consecratione, ubi prius non erat, per motum proprium; quod supra est improbatum. Unde patet quod opinio illa falsa est, quae ponebat substantiam panis annihilari.

AD PRIMUM ergo dicendum, quod in mutationibus naturalibus terminus a quo est forma aliqua, quae quidem non convertitur in terminum ad quem; et ideo non annihilatur, nisi quatenus manet in potentia in suo subjecto: sed illud quod convertitur ad terminum ad quem, est subjectum mutationis, non quidem ut sit illud, sed ut sit sub illo; unde subjectum annihilari non dicitur inquantum in aliud convertitur. Unde cum in hac conversione id quod est terminus a quo, scilicet substantia panis, convertatur secundum se totum in terminum ad quem, scilicet corpus Christi, non quidem ut sit sub ipso, sed ut sit ipsummet, patet quod non est annihilatio substantiae panis.

AD SECUNDUM dicendum, quod ratio illa procedit in mutationibus oppositis, quia illud quod est terminus a quo in una, est terminus ad quem in alia; non autem in mutationibus quarum una ordinatur ad aliam sicut perfectum ad imperfectum, sicut mutatio qua acquiritur perfectio[31] secunda. Conversio autem panis in corpus Christi non est mutatio opposita creationi, sed quodam modo perficiens ipsam, inquantum substantia panis nobilius esse per hanc conversionem consequitur; et ideo non oportet quod sit in hac conversione terminus ad quem, quod in creatione erat terminus a quo.

AD TERTIUM dicendum, quod quamvis panis non sit aliquid, tamen illud in quod conversus est panis, est aliquid, conversione facta; et ideo non sequitur quod panis sit annihilatus.

AD QUARTUM dicendum, quod quamvis non maneat panis neque in se neque in alio; manet tamen corpus Christi, in quod conversus est panis; et ideo non sequitur quod sit annihilatus.

AD QUINTUM dicendum sicut ad primum.

gin to be here that was not here before, except by a motion or change of itself or of something else terminating in it in some way. Hence if the conversion mentioned did not terminate in the body of Christ, then the body of Christ by its own motion would have had to be here on the altar after the consecration, where it was not before; which notion was rejected above. Hence it is clear that that opinion is false which holds that the bread's substance is annihilated.

REPLY OBJ. 1: In natural changes the starting terminus is a certain form, which indeed is not converted into the ending terminus, and so it is not annihilated, unless to the extent that it remains in potency in its own subject. But what is converted into the ending terminus is the subject of the change, not indeed so that it is it, but so that it is under it; hence the subject is not said to be annihilated to the extent that it is converted into something else. Hence, since in this conversion what is the starting terminus, namely, the substance of the bread, is completely converted in itself into the ending terminus, namely, the body of Christ, not indeed so that it exists under it, but so that it is it, it is clear that there is no annihilation of the bread's substance.

REPLY OBJ. 2: That argument works in opposed changes, because what is starting terminus in one is ending terminus in the other. But it does not work in changes of which one is ordered to the other as the perfect to the imperfect, as the change by which the first perfection is aquired is ordered to the one by which the second perfection is acquired. Now the conversion of bread into the body of Christ is not a change opposed to creation, but in some way perfecting it, inasmuch as the substance of bread attains a more noble being by this conversion. And so it is not necessary that there be an ending terminus in this conversion that was a starting terminus in creation.

REPLY OBJ. 3: Although the bread is not something, nevertheless what the bread is converted into is something once the conversion is done; and so it does not follow that the bread is annihilated.

REPLY OBJ. 4: Although the bread does not remain in itself or in something else, nevertheless the body of Christ into which the bread is converted remains, and so it does not follow that it is annihilated.

THE FIFTH OBJECTION should be answered like the first.

---

31. *perfectio secunda.—perfectio prima, ordinatur ad illam qua acquiritur perfectio secunda* PLE.

ARTICLE 3

Whether the bread is converted into the body of Christ

Quaestiuncula 1

AD TERTIUM SIC PROCEDITUR. Videtur quod panis non possit converti in corpus Christi. Conversio enim mutatio quaedam est. Sed nulla specie transmutationis in corpus Christi panis convertitur; non enim est ibi generatio et corruptio, quia materia panis non manet; nec est alteratio, quia non manet aliqua substantia ejus actu; nec est augmentum, quia non additur aliquid ad corpus Christi, neque motus localis, non enim ipsum corpus Christi de coelo descendit, ut Damascenus dicit. Ergo videtur quod nullo modo panis in corpus Christi convertatur.

PRAETEREA, in omni conversione oportet esse aliquid quod mutetur. Mutatur autem quod dissimiliter se habet nunc et prius. Si ergo panis in corpus Christi convertatur, oportet aliquid esse idem numero quod prius fuerit de substantia[34] corporis Christi; quod non ponitur. Ergo panis in corpus Christi non convertitur.

PRAETEREA, conversio accidens quodam est; omne enim accidens est in subjecto. Non autem potest dici quod subjectum ejus sit panis neque corpus Christi; quia non est idem subjectum mutationis et terminus a quo vel ad quem. Ergo panis nullo modo convertitur in corpus Christi.

PRAETEREA, omne quod fit aliquid, acquirit hoc quod fieri dicitur. Sed omne singulare est incommutabile. Ergo impossibile est quod aliquod singulare fiat aliud singulare, quamvis possit ei adjungi, et sic esse ejus percipere sicut pars. Sed corpus Christi est quoddam singulare demonstratum. Ergo non potest esse quod aliquid convertatur in ipsum, ita quod fiat ipsummet; sed solum quod adjungatur ei.

SED CONTRA est quod Damascenus dicit, ubi supra: *fecit Christus panem et vinum corpus et sanguinem suum, non quoniam ipsum corpus Christi de caelo descendit, sed quoniam panis et vinum transit in corpus et sanguinem Christi.*

PRAETEREA, illud quod nec in se manet nec annihilatur, oportet quod in aliud convertatur. Sed panis non manet in se, sicut in primo articulo dictum est, nec etiam

OBJ. 1: To the third we proceed thus. It seems that the bread cannot be converted into the body of Christ.[32] For a conversion is a kind of change. But in no kind of change is bread converted into the body of Christ; for that is not generation and corruption, because the matter of the bread does not remain; nor is there an alteration, because none of its substance remains in act; nor is there an increase, because nothing is added to the body of Christ, nor is there local motion, for the body of Christ itself did not descend from heaven, as Damascene says.[33] Therefore, it seems that the bread is in no way converted into the body of Christ.

OBJ. 2: Furthermore, in every conversion there must be something that is changed. Now, what is changed is what is related differently now than before. Therefore, if the bread is converted into the body of Christ, there must be something the same in number that was formerly of the substance of bread and is now of the substance of the body of Christ, which no one holds. Therefore the bread is not converted into the body of Christ.

OBJ. 3: Furthermore, conversion is a kind of accident; for every accident is in a subject. However, it cannot be said that its subject is the bread, nor is it the body of Christ; for the same thing is not the subject of change and the starting or ending terminus. Therefore, the bread is in no way converted into the body of Christ.

OBJ. 4: Furthermore, everything that becomes something acquires what it is said to become. But every singular thing is incommutable. Therefore, it is impossible that some singular thing become another singular thing, although it can be joined to it, and in that way it can partake of its being as a part. But the body of Christ is a certain designated singular. Therefore it cannot be that something is converted into something else so that it becomes it, but only that it is joined to it.

ON THE CONTRARY, Damascene says above: *Christ made bread and wine his body and blood, not because the body of Christ itself descended from heaven, but because bread and wine turn into the body and blood of Christ.*

FURTHERMORE, what neither remains as itself nor is annihilated, must be converted into something else. But bread does not remain in itself, as was said in the first ar-

---

32. Parallels: *ST* III, q. 75, a. 4; *SCG* IV, ch. 63; *Quodl.* V, q. 6, a. 1; *De rationibus fidei*, ch. 8; *Super I ad Cor.* 11, lec. 4 & 5.
33. John Damascene, *On the Orthodox Faith*, Bk. 4, ch. 13 (PG 94:1143).
34. *substantia corporis.—substantia panis et nunc sit de substantia* PLE.

annihilatur, ut ex secundo articulo patuit. Ergo oportet quod in aliud convertatur.

ticle, nor is it annihilated, as was evident from the second article. Therefore, it must be converted into something else.

Quaestiuncula 2

ULTERIUS. Videtur quod ista conversio fiat successive. Fit enim haec conversio virtute verborum. Sed verba non possunt aliquid facere nisi dum sunt. Ergo cum habeant esse in successione, videtur quod successive conversio praedicta fiat.

PRAETEREA, impossibile est in eodem instanti esse aliquid corpus Christi et panem. Ergo non est idem instans in quo est primo corpus Christi, et in quo ultimo est panis. Sed inter quaelibet duo instantia est tempus medium, ut probatur in 6 *Phys*. Ergo conversio panis in corpus Christi est successiva.

PRAETEREA, in omni conversione requiritur ut sit aliquid aliter nunc et prius, cum conversio mutatio quaedam sit. Sed ubicumque est nunc et prius, successio est. Ergo in omni conversione et mutatione oportet esse successionem; et sic idem quod prius.

PRAETEREA, in omni factione est fieri et factum esse. Sed fieri et factum esse non sunt simul: quia quod fit, non est; quod autem factum est, jam est. Ergo est ibi prius et posterius; et sic idem quod prius.

SED CONTRA est, quia virtus infinita operatur subito. Sed haec conversio fit virtute divina, quae est infinita. Ergo fit subito.

PRAETEREA, in omni successiva mutatione prius aliquid est in medio quam in termino. Sed in hac conversione non est invenire aliquid medium inter substantiam panis et corpus Christi. Ergo non est ibi successiva conversio.

OBJ. 1: Moreover, it seems that this conversion happens successively.[35] For this conversion is done by the power of words. But words cannot do something except while they exist. Therefore, since they have being in succession, it seems that the mentioned conversion happens successively.

OBJ. 2: Furthermore, it is impossible for something to be bread and the body of Christ in the same instant. Therefore, there is no single instant in which the body of Christ first exists and the bread last exists. But between two certain instants there is a middle time, as is proved in *Physics* 6.[36] Therefore the conversion of bread into the body of Christ is successive.

OBJ. 3: In every conversion it is required that something be different now than before, since a conversion is a kind of change. But wherever there is now and before, there is succession. Therefore, in every conversion and change there must be succession; and so the same as before.

OBJ. 4: Furthermore, in every making there is becoming and having-been-done. But becoming and having-been-done are not at the same time: for what is becoming does not exist, but what has been done already exists. Therefore, in this there is before and after, and so the same as before.

ON THE CONTRARY, infinite power operates instantly. But this conversion is done by divine power, which is infinite. Therefore, it happens instantly.

FURTHERMORE, in every successive change there is something in the middle before it is in the end. But in this conversion there is not found any middle between the substance of the bread and the body of Christ. Therefore, this is not a successive conversion.

Quaestiuncula 3

ULTERIUS. Videtur quod haec conversio sit miraculosior omni alia mutatione. Quia quanto alicui magis de facili consentit ratio nostra, minus habet de miraculo. Sed non est aliqua miraculosa conversio cui ratio magis non consentiat quam huic; quia creationem etiam quidam philosophi posuerunt ratione naturali ducti, et etiam quod materia obedit substantiis separatis, et maxime Deo, ad omnem formationem. Ergo ista conversio est miraculosior omnibus mutationibus.

PRAETEREA, ubi est plus de resistentia, ibi est major difficultas in convertendo, et per consequens majus mi-

OBJ. 1: Moreover, it seems that this conversion is more miraculous than any other change. For the more easily our reason consents to something, the less miraculous it is. But there is no miraculous conversion that our reason consents to less than this one; for certain philosophers led by natural reason even arrived at creation, and also that matter obeys separated substances, and God most of all, for all its formation. Therefore, this conversion is more miraculous than all those changes.

OBJ. 2: Furthermore, where there is more resistance, there is greater difficulty in making the conversion, and

35. Parallels: *ST* III, q. 75, a. 7; *Quodl*. VII, q. 4, a. 2.
36. Aristotle, *Physics*, Bk. 6, ch. 3 (234a5–10).

raculum. Sed in hac conversione est maxima resistentia, cum oporteat totum converti in totum. Ergo ista conversio est maximae difficultatis; ergo est maxime miraculosa.

PRAETEREA, quanto minus est de potentia ex parte creaturae in qua fit miraculum, tanto est majus miraculum quod fit per potentiam divinam. Sed in hac conversione minimum est de potentia in creatura: quia in quibusdam conversionibus miraculosis est potentia naturalis, sicut quod aqua conversa fuit in vinum, in quibusdam autem potentia obedientiae tantum: sicut quando costa formata est in mulierem; in creatione autem etsi non praecedat aliqua potentia, tamen non est aliqua repugnantia. Ergo cum in hac conversione sit repugnantia, et nulla potentia ex parte creaturae, quia non potest esse aliquid in potentia respectu totius compositi; videtur quod haec conversio sit miraculosior omni alia mutatione.

SED CONTRA, quanto aliqua sunt magis distantia, tanto difficilius in invicem mutantur. Sed magis distat non ens simpliciter ab ente, quam hoc ens ab hoc ente. Ergo difficilius est ex non ente simpliciter facere ens aliquod, quam ex ente hoc facere illud; et ita creatio est majoris virtutis indicativa quam transubstantiatio.

PRAETEREA, quanto terminus mutationis est altior, tanto mutatio est majoris virtutis; sicut majoris virtutis est facere hominem quam animal. Sed assumptio humanae naturae, quae est mutatio quaedam, terminatur ad personam filii Dei, quae est dignius quid quam corpus Christi, ad quod terminatur transubstantiatio. Ergo magis est miraculosa illa mutatio quam ista conversio.

consequently a greater miracle. But in this conversion there is the greatest resistance, since a whole must be converted into a whole. Therefore, this conversion is of the greatest difficulty; therefore it is the most miraculous.

OBJ. 3: Furthermore, the less power there is on the part of the creature in which the miracle is done, the greater the miracle that is done by divine power. But in this conversion the power in the creature is the smallest, for in certain miraculous conversions there is natural power, like when water was converted into wine, while in others there is only potency of obedience, as when the rib was formed into the woman; and in creation, even if no potency precedes, nevertheless there is no opposition. Therefore, since in this conversion there is opposition, and no potency on the part of the creature, because something cannot be in potency with regard to a composite whole, it seems that this conversion is more miraculous than any other change.

ON THE CONTRARY, the greater the distance between things, the more difficult it is to change them into each other. But non-being is more distant simply from being than this being from that being. Therefore, it is simply speaking more difficult to make any being from non-being than to make this being from that being; and thus creation is indicative of greater power than transubstantiation.

FURTHERMORE, the higher the terminus of the change, the greater the power the change takes, just as it takes greater power to make a man than an animal. But the assumption of human nature, which is a certain change, has its end terminus in the person of the Son of God, which is something more worthy than the body of Christ, in which transubstantiation terminates. Therefore, that change is more miraculous than this one.

Response to Quaestiuncula 1

RESPONDEO DICENDUM ad primam quaestionem, quod in mutationibus naturalibus invenitur aliqua mutatio secundum quam nihil variatur de eo quod est intraneum rei, sed solum hoc quod est extra, sicut patet in motu locali; aliqua vero mutatio in qua variatur illud quod inest rei accidentaliter, scilicet quantitas vel qualitas, sicut patet in motu augmenti et alterationis; aliqua vero mutatio est quae pertingit usque ad formam substantialem, sicut generatio et corruptio. Sed naturalis mutatio non potest pertingere usque ad variationem materiae: quia operatur ex supposita materia, sicut quodlibet secundum agens operatur suppositis his quae data sunt sibi a primo agente; et haec principia oportet manere in operatione naturae, ut 1 *Physica* dicitur. Sicut autem esse compositi, quod ex suppositione materiae natura

TO THE FIRST QUESTION, I answer that among natural changes there are some changes in which nothing intrinsic to the thing varies, but only what is outside it, as is clear in the case of local motion. But in some changes what is in a thing incidentally varies, namely, quantity or quality, as is clear in the motion of increase or alteration; other changes extend even to the substantial form, like generation and corruption. But natural change cannot extend to variations of matter: for it works from the underlying matter, just like every second agent works with those underlying things that are given to him by the first agent. And these principles must remain in the operation of nature, as is said in *Physics* 1.[37] But just as the being of a composite, which nature produces from the underlying matter, is subject to nature's operation, so also that matter which nature presup-

---

37. Aristotle, *Physics*, Bk. 1, ch. 7 (190a17ff.).

producit, operationi naturae subjicitur; ita ipsa materia quam praesupponit natura, subjicitur actioni primi agentis, scilicet Dei, a quo hoc ipsum imperfectum esse (scilicet in potentia), quod habet, accepit; unde divina operatio pertingere potest ad variationem materiae, ut scilicet sicut natura facit hoc totum esse hoc totum, ut ex toto aere totam aquam; ita Deus faciat ex hac materia signata illam. Et quia materia signata est individuationis principium, ideo solius Dei operatione hoc fieri potest, ut hoc individuum demonstratum fiat illud individuum demonstratum; et talis modus conversionis est in hoc sacramento, quia ex hoc pane fit hoc corpus Christi.

Ex quo patet quod ista conversio differt ab omnibus naturalibus conversionibus in quatuor. Primo in hoc quod usque ad materiam pertingit, quod in illis non invenitur. Et quia materia est primum subjectum, et ipsum non est aliud subjectum; ideo secundo differt in hoc quod haec conversio non habet subjectum sicut illae habent. Tertio, quod in naturalibus conversionibus convertitur totum in totum, non autem partes essentiales in partes; totus enim aer convertitur in aquam; sed materia aeris non convertitur in aliquid, quia est eadem: forma etiam non convertitur, quia abscedit alia et alia introducitur. Sed hic et totum convertitur in totum, quia panis fit corpus Christi; et partes etiam convertuntur; quia materia panis fit materia corporis Christi, et forma substantialis similiter fit illa forma quae est corpus Christi. Quarto, quia in naturalibus conversionibus transmutatur et id quod convertitur et illud in quod convertitur. Illud quidem quod in alterum convertitur, semper transmutatur corruptione; sed illud in quod aliquid naturaliter convertitur (si quidem sit simplex conversio) transmutatur per generationem, sicut cum aqua generatur ex aere; si autem sit conversio cum additione ad alterum praeexistens, illud cui additur transmutatur secundum augmentum, vel saltem per restaurationem deperditi, sicut accidit in nutrimento. Sed hic, illud in quod fit conversio erat praeexistens, et non ei additur, quia, ut dictum est, illud quod convertitur, convertitur in ipsum, et secundum totum et secundum omnes partes ejus; unde hoc in quod terminatur conversio, nullo modo transmutatur, scilicet corpus Christi, sed solum panis qui convertitur.

Ad primum ergo dicendum, quod haec conversio sub nulla naturalium mutationum continetur, sed ab omnibus differt, ut ex praedictis patet: habet tamen aliquam convenientiam cum transmutatione nutrimenti, inquantum utraque conversio fit in aliquid praeexistens; differt tamen ab ea, inquantum hic non fit aliqua additio sicut ibi.

Ad secundum dicendum, quod in hac transmutatione, seu conversione, est aliquid quod transmutatur, scilicet panis, non quidem ad modum aliarum mutatio-

poses is subject to the action of the first agent, namely, God, from whom this thing receives the imperfect being (namely, being in potency) that it has. Hence divine operation can extend to the variation of matter, namely so that just as nature makes this whole to be this whole, so that it makes the whole water from the whole air, so also God may make that thing from this designated matter. And since designated matter is the principle of individuation, for this reason only by God's operation can it happen that this particular individual thing become that particular individual thing; and that is the kind of conversion that is in this sacrament, since from this bread is made this body of Christ.

From which it is clear that this conversion differs from all natural conversions in four things. First, in the fact that it extends to the level of matter, which is not found in those conversions. And because matter is the first subject, and there is no other subject, for this reason it differs second in the fact that this conversion does not have a subject like the others have. Third, because in natural conversions a whole is converted into a whole but the essential parts are not converted into parts; for the whole air is converted into water, but the matter of the air is not converted into anything, because it is the same; form is also not converted, because one leaves and another is introduced. But here both the whole is converted into a whole, because bread becomes the body of Christ, and even the parts are converted, because the matter of the bread becomes the matter of the body of Christ, and the substantial form likewise becomes that form which is the body of Christ. Fourth, because in natural conversions what is converted and what it is converted into are both transformed. Indeed, what is converted into something else is always transformed by corruption; but what something is naturally converted into (if indeed it is a simple conversion) is transformed by generation, just as when water is generated from air. But if there is a conversion with an addition to something pre-existing, what is added is transformed according to increase, or at least by restoration of what it has lost, as happens in nourishment. But here what is converted into was pre-existing, and it is not added to, because as was said, what is converted is converted into it, both according to the whole and according to all its parts. Hence the thing that the conversion terminates in, namely, the body of Christ, is not transformed in any way, but only the bread that is converted.

Reply Obj. 1: This conversion is contained under none of the natural changes, but rather it differs from all of them, as is clear from what has already been said; however, it has a certain agreement with the transformation of nourishment, inasmuch as both are conversions into something pre-existing. Nevertheless it differs from it in the fact that here no addition is made, as it is there.

Reply Obj. 2: In this transformation or conversion there is something that is transformed, namely, bread; not indeed in the mode of other natural changes, so that some-

num naturalium, ut aliquid ipsius maneat, sed secundum totum et omnes partes ejus, ut dictum est.

AD TERTIUM dicendum, quod transmutatio naturalis panis ponit actum imperfectum, ut patet in 3 *Physica*; et quia idem est subjectum actus perfecti, et imperfecti; ideo oportet quod subjectum transmutationis naturalis sit id quod est subjectum postmodum actus perfecti, scilicet formae, ad quem tendit motus, et non ipsum jam perfectum. Sed transmutatio hujus conversionis non ponit aliquem actum imperfectum, sed solum successionem quamdam perfectorum non solum actuum, sed rerum subsistentium. Successio autem est in succedentibus sibi, sicut et ordo in ordinatis. Sed secundum regulam in 1 Lib., dist. 26, qu. 2, art. 3, ad 1 et 2, de relativis datam, erit ista relatio ordinis hujus successionis secundum rem quidem in ipso pane qui mutatur, non autem in corpore Christi vero, nisi secundum rationem, quia ipsum immutatum permanet.

AD QUARTUM dicendum, quod communicatio importat quamdam collationem; et ideo exigit aliquid recipiens id quod confertur seu datur; unde non habet locum nisi in formalibus conversionibus in quibus mutatio non attingit nisi usque ad formam; et ideo cum in hac conversione nihil maneat cui possit aliquid conferri, non habet locum commutatio.[39]

Response to Quaestiuncula 2

AD SECUNDAM QUAESTIONEM dicendum, quod causa quare aliqua mutatio non est in instanti, est distantia ejus quod movetur a termino motus. Distantiam autem dico non solum secundum dimensionem loci aut quantitatis, sed secundum repugnantiam formae vel naturae; et ideo ubi nihil est repugnans formae introducendae, forma ibi recipitur in instanti, praesente agente; sicut patet de illuminatione diaphani, cum in eo non sit aliquid contrarium vel repugnans luci; et similiter in forma subito introducenda quando materia est necessitans, contrariis dispositionibus ab ea exclusis.

Sicut autem aer subjacet soli ad recipiendum ab eo formam luminis non existente aliquo interposito; ita tota natura creata subditur divino nutui, ut statim fiat omne quod Deus vult; quia quidquid est in creatura est materiale, et non contrarium dispositioni divinae; et ideo ea quae per seipsum facit, potest, cum voluerit, facere in instanti. Quandoque autem successive facit, ut in nobis secundum modum nostrum operetur. Hoc tamen contingit quando hoc quod transmutatur, potest magis vel

thing remains of it, but according to its whole and all its parts, as was said.

REPLY OBJ. 3: The natural transformation of bread includes imperfect act, as is clear in *Physics* 3; [38] and since the same thing is the subject of perfect and imperfect act, for this reason the subject of natural transformation must be that which is the subject afterward of perfect act, namely, of form, to which the motion tends, and not what is already perfected. But the transformation in this conversion does not include any imperfect act, but only a certain succession of not only perfected acts, but also perfected subsistent things. However, succession is in things coming one after the other, as also order is in things that are ordered. But according to the rule given about relations in Book I, Distinction 26, Question 2, Article 3, response to the first and second objections, the relation of this order of succession will exist in reality indeed in the very bread that is changed, but not in the true body of Christ, except according to reason, for it remains unchanged.

REPLY OBJ. 4: Communication conveys a certain conferral, and so it requires something to receive what is conferred or given; hence it does not take place except in formal conversions where the change only extends to the form. And so since in this conversion nothing remains to which anything could be conferred, no communication takes place.

Response to Quaestiuncula 2

TO THE SECOND QUESTION, it should be said that the reason why a given change is not instantaneous is the distance between what is moved and the terminus of motion. However, I say 'distance' not only according to the dimension of place or quantity, but according to the contrariety of form or nature. And thus where nothing is opposed to the form to be introduced, the form is received in an instant as soon as the agent presents it, as is seen in the illumination of something transparent, since in it there is nothing contrary or opposed to light; and it is the same in a form instantaneously introduced when the matter makes it necessary, once contrary dispostions have been expelled from it.

However, just as air lies under the sun to receive from it the form of light with no existing thing interposed in between, so also all created nature is subject to the divine nod, so that everything that God wills is done immediately, because whatever there is in a creature is material and not contrary to divine disposing; and so those things that he does by himself he can, when he wants, do in an instant. However, he sometimes does them successively, so that he works in us according to our own mode. Nevertheless this

---

38. Aristotle, *Physics*, Bk. 3, ch. 1 (201a10ff.).
39. *commutatio—-communicatio* PLE.

minus distare a termino transmutationis, quia secundum hoc fit successio in motu.

Cum autem conversio de qua loquimur, ad ipsam materiae essentiam pertingat, ut dictum est, secundum quam separatis per intellectum formis et dispositionibus, una res non magis convenit cum una quam cum alia, non potest accipi major et minor distantia a termino: quia hoc singulare demonstratum, quantum ad hoc quod convertitur in corpus Christi, tantum distat ab alio singulari suae speciei quantum a singulari alterius speciei; et ideo conversio praedicta fit in instanti.

Ad primum ergo dicendum, quod verba formae habent sacramentalem virtutem; unde non efficiunt nisi quod significant; et ideo, cum significatio illius formae non sit perfecta nisi in ultimo instanti, tunc habet efficaciam suam.

Ad secundum dicendum, quod ad hoc argumentum multipliciter respondetur a diversis.

Quidam concedunt quod est signare ultimum instans in quo est panis sicut et primum in quo est corpus Christi, propter hoc quod in toto quodam tempore fuit panis, et ita in quolibet instanti illius temporis. Unde quidam istorum dicunt quod unum est instans secundum rem in quo est panis et corpus Christi, sed differt secundum rationem: quia inquantum illud instans est finis praeteriti temporis, est in eo panis; inquantum autem est principium futuri, est in eo corpus Christi. Sed hoc non potest stare: quia contradictoria simul esse secundum rem est impossibile; simul autem secundum rem maxime sunt quae sunt in eodem instanti secundum rem. Unde impossibile est duo contradictoria esse in instanti quod est unum secundum rem, quantumcumque sit differens ratione: quia ex illa ratione non habet ordinem ad mensuratum et tempus, cujus est terminus; sed ad animam. Et quia si ponamus simul esse corpus Christi et panem, sequitur duo contradictoria simul esse; quia dum est panis non est corpus Christi; ideo impossibile est quod sit unum instans secundum rem in quo nunc ultimo est panis, et nunc primo corpus Christi.

Ideo alii dicunt, quod istud nunc est quodammodo unum realiter, et quodammodo diversum; et ponunt exemplum de duabus lineis se tangentibus, de quibus constat quod habent duo puncta, et tamen illa puncta conjunguntur in uno puncto lineae continentis; contigua enim sunt quorum termini sunt simul. Et similiter dicunt quod esse panem et esse corpus Christi in altari, contiguantur; unde est unum instans extra mensurans, in quo primo est corpus Christi et ultimo panis; sed tamen sunt duo instantia si accipiamus ut duorum

happens when what is transformed can be more or less distant from the terminus of transformation, because the succession in motion happens according to this.

However, since the conversion of which we speak extends to the very essence of matter, as was said, according to which, forms and dispositions having been separated by the intellect, one thing does not share more with one thing than with another, a greater and lesser distance from the terminus cannot be taken, because this singular designated thing, in respect of its being converted into the body of Christ, is as distant from another singular of its own species as it is from a singular of another species; and so the conversion mentioned happens in an instant.

Reply Obj. 1: The words of the form have sacramental power; hence they bring about nothing but what they signify, and so, since the signification of that form is only complete in the last instant, at that moment it has its efficacy.

Reply Obj. 2: This argument has been answered many ways by different people.

Some grant that one can designate the last instant in which bread exists as the first in which the body of Christ exists, because of the fact that in a certain whole time the bread existed, and so also in any instant of that time. Hence some of these people say that according to reality there is one instant in which there is bread and the body of Christ, but it differs according to reason; for inasmuch as that instant is the end of past time, the bread exists in it; but inasmuch as it is the beginning of the future, the body of Christ exists in it. But this cannot stand, because it is impossible that contradictories exist at the same time according to reality; but things that exist at the same instant according to reality exist most of all at the same time according to reality. Hence it is impossible that two contradictories exist in an instant that is one according to reality, no matter how much it differs according to reason: because by that reasoning it would have no order to what is measured and the time of which it is the terminus, but only to the soul. And since if we hold that the body of Christ and the bread exist at the same moment, it follows that two contradictories exist at the same time, since when there is bread there is not the body of Christ, for this reason it is impossible that there be one instant according to reality in which now the bread last exists and now the body of Christ first exists.

Therefore, others say that this 'now' is in one way one in reality, and in another way different; and they cite the example of the two lines touching each other, in which it is clear that they have two points, and nevertheless those points are joined in one point of the containing line; for things whose terminuses are together, are contiguous. And similarly they say that the being of the bread and the being of the body of Christ on the altar are contiguous; hence there is one outside measuring instant, in which the body of Christ first exists, and the bread last exists. But neverthe-

temporum quibus mensuratur esse panis in altari et esse corporis Christi: et sic inter duo instantia quasi contiguata non est necesse esse tempus medium, sicut nec inter duo puncta contiguata lineam. Sed illud non potest stare: quia cum punctum sit terminus lineae, quae potest esse mensura et intranea et extranea, possibile est puncta assignare et intrinseca et extrinseca; sed instans est terminus temporis quod nunquam est nisi mensura extrinseca; unde non est accipere instans nisi quod se habet per modum extra jacentis puncti. Et ideo haec positio redit in idem impossibile cum prima.

Et propter hoc alii dicunt, quod sicut probatur 4 *Physica*, in toto tempore non est accipere nisi unum nunc secundum substantiam; et quod numerentur duo instantia, hoc est secundum ordinem temporis ad motum, et actionem quam mensurant; prout scilicet tempus excedens mensurat aliquam actionem; et ita principium et finis illius actionis est in tempore; et secundum hoc in tempore numerantur duo instantia; et ideo ordo et habitudo duorum instantium ad invicem est consideranda secundum actiones et motus qui mensurantur. Unde si accipiantur duo instantia respectu ejusdem motus, prout tempus mensurat principium et finem illius motus, sic oportet quod inter duo instantia sit tempus medium, sicut inter principium motus et finem est motus medius. Si autem accipiantur duo instantia per comparationem ad diversos motus secundum quod mensurant principium unius et finem alterius, sic inter duo instantia non est tempus medium, sicut nec motus est medius inter principium unius motus et finem alterius; et ideo cum quies mensuretur tempore, sicut et motus, duo instantia sunt se invicem consequentia, quorum unum mensurat finem quietis in quo erat panis, et alterum principium quietis in quo est corpus Christi. Sed hoc iterum non potest stare; quia instantia temporis distinguuntur per comparationem ad illum motum a quo tempus potest habere unitatem vel multitudinem, ad quam comparatur non solum sicut mensura ad mensuratum, sed sicut accidens ad subjectum; scilicet motum caeli, quia est continuus, et interruptionem non patitur secundum naturam; unde qualitercumque signes duo instantia in tempore, semper est accipere tempus medium, quia est accipere inter quaelibet momenta motus caeli motum medium; et ideo in aliis motibus non ferret, sive comparentur diversa instantia ad eumdem motum, sive ad diversos. Patet etiam quod haec positio contradicit dicto Philosophi in 8 *Physica*, ubi probat quod inter quoslibet motus contra-

less there are two instants if we take it as of the two times by which are measured the being of the bread on the altar and the being of the body of Christ. And so between the two instants that are contiguous, as it were, there does not need to be a middle time, just as neither is a line necessary between two contiguous points. But that cannot stand, because since a point is a terminus of a line, which can be both an intrinsic and an extrinsic measure, it is possible to assign both an intrinsic and an extrinsic point. But an instant is a terminus of time, which is only ever an extrinsic measure. Hence an instant can only be taken as what is ordered by the mode of an outlying point. And so this position results in the same impossibility as the first.

And on account of this, others say that just as is proved in *Physics* 4,[40] in the whole time only one now can be taken according to substance, and when two instants would be counted, this is according to the order of time to motion, and the action that they measure, namely as passing time measures some action. And in this way the beginning and end of that action is in time, and according to this two instants are numbered in time; and so the order and relation of the two instants to each other is to be considered according to the actions and motions that are measured. Hence if two instants are taken with regard to the same motion, as time measures the beginning and end of that motion, then it is necessary that there be a middle time between the two instants, as between the beginning of motion and the end there is a middle motion. But if the two instants are taken by comparison with different movements according as they measure the beginning of one and the end of the other, in that way between the two instants there is no middle time, just as neither is there a middle motion between the beginning of one motion and the end of another. And therefore when a rest is measured by time, just like with motion, the two instants are subsequent, one of them measuring the end of the period in which the bread existed, and the other measuring the beginning of the period in which the body of Christ exists. But this also cannot stand, for instants of time are distinguished by comparison with the motion that gives time unity or multitude, to which it is compared not only as a measure to what is measured, but as accident to subject; namely, the motion of the sky, because it is continuous, and does not admit of any interruption according to nature. Hence however you may designate two instants in time, a middle time can always be taken, because between any moments of the sky's movement there is a middle movement. And so it would not bring in other motions, whether different instants are compared to the same motion or to different motions. It is also evident that this position contradicts

---

40. Aristotle, *Physics*, Bk. 4, ch. 11 (219b10ff.).

rios est quies media; quod non oporteret, si duo instantia modo praedicto possent se invicem consequi.

Et ideo alii dicunt, quod ista conversio, cum sit supra naturam, non habet ordinem ad motum caeli; unde non mensuratur tempore, sed instanti, quod est mensura motus caeli; et propter hoc non est inconveniens, si duo instantia succedunt sibi sine tempore medio, sicut in 1 Lib., dist. 37, qu. 4, art. 3, dictum est de motu angeli. Sed hoc iterum stare non potest; quia ista conversio sequitur motum prolationis verborum, qui habet reduci ad mensuram motus caeli, sicut illuminatio sequitur ad motum localem, quo defertur illuminans; et ideo oportet quod instantia accipiantur in hac conversione secundum mensuram motus caeli.

Et propter hoc alii dicunt, quod non est simul signare duo instantia in quorum uno primo sit corpus Christi, et in alio ultimo sit panis, quia sic de necessitate esset inter ea tempus medium; sed tamen utrumlibet eorum potest per se signari. Sed hoc iterum nihil est; quia designatio nostra nihil facit ad hoc quod tempus intersit vel non intersit; unde si sint duo instantia secundum rem, in quorum uno est panis ultimo, et in alio corpus Christi primo, sive signentur a nobis sive non, oportet esse tempus medium. Praeterea, ex quo instans illud est signabile, non videtur quod possit designatio ejus impediri per designationem alterius instantis, cum istae duae designationes non sint contrariae.

Et ideo aliter dicendum, quod non est designare ultimum instans, sed ultimum tempus in quo est panis. Inter tempus autem et instans non cadit necessario tempus medium, sicut cadit medium inter duo instantia. Et veritas hujus quaestionis apparet ex hoc quod Philosophus dicit in 8 *Physica*, quod quando ex albo fit nigrum, in toto tempore mensurante motum alterationis erat album, sed in ultimo instanti illius temporis est nigrum; unde, secundum ipsum, non est dandum quod in toto illo tempore sit album, sed in toto praeter ultimum nunc. Et quia ante ultimum nunc alicujus temporis non est accipere penultimum, sicut nec ante ultimum punctum lineae penultimum, ideo non est accipere ultimum instans in quo erat album, sed ultimum tempus; et similiter est de illis mutationibus quae sunt termini motus, sicut generatio est terminus alterationis; quia cum ex aere fit ignis, in toto tempore alterationis praecedentis erat aer, praeter ultimum instans, in quo est ignis; et similiter est in illuminatione respectu motus localis. Et ideo cum conversio sit terminus cujusdam motus, scilicet prolationis

the Philosopher's statement in *Physics* 8,[41] where he proves that between any contrary motions there is a middle rest, which would not be necessary if two instants could follow one another in the way mentioned.

And so others say that this conversion, since it is above nature, does not have order to the motion of the sky; hence it is not measured by time, but by the instant, which is the measure of the sky's movement. And because of this it is not unfitting if two instants succeed each other without a middle period, as was said about the angels' movement in Book I, Distinction 37, Question 4, Article 3. But this again cannot stand; for this conversion follows the motion of uttering the words, which can be reduced to the measure of the sky's movement, just as illumination is attendant on local motion, by which the illuminating thing is borne. And so it is necessary that instants be taken in this conversion according to the measure of the sky's movement.

And because of this others say that one cannot designate two instants at the same time in one of which the body of Christ first exists, and in the other the bread last exists, for then there would necessarily be a middle time between them. But either of them can still be marked by themselves. But this is also nothing, because our marking does nothing to the fact that there is time in between or not; hence if there are two instants according to reality, in which one is the bread's last instant and the other is the body of Christ's first, whether it is marked by us or not, there must be a middle time. Furthermore, in the fact that that instant can be marked, it does not seem that its designation can be impeded by the designation of another instant, since those two designations are not contraries.

And so it should be said otherwise that one cannot mark a last instant, but a last time when there is bread. But between a time and an instant no middle time necessarily falls, as a middle falls between two instants. And the truth of this question appears from what the Philosopher says in *Physics* 8,[42] that when something black is made from something white, in the whole time measuring the motion of the change it was white, but in the last instant of that time it is black. Hence, according to him, one should not think that in that whole time it is white, but in the whole time until the last 'now'. And since before the last 'now' of a certain time a penultimate cannot be taken, just as neither before the last point of a line is there a penultimate point, for this reason there is not a last instant in which the thing was white, but only a last time; and it is similar with those changes that are the terminuses of motion, as generation is the terminus of alteration. For when fire is made from the air, in the whole time of the preceding alteration, it was air, up until the last instant, in which it is fire; and it is the same in illumination with regard to local motion. And so since the conversion is

41. Aristotle, *Physics*, Bk. 8, ch. 8 (264b28ff.).
42. Aristotle, *Physics*, Bk. 8, ch. 8 (263b9–26).

verborum, in toto tempore praecedenti erat panis, praeter ultimum instans, in quo est corpus Christi.

Ad tertium dicendum, quod in qualibet mutatione oportet designari nunc et prius secundum duos terminos mutationis, qui sunt incontingentes, ut dicitur in 1*Physica*; idest, qui non possunt simul esse. Unde secundum diversitatem terminorum in diversis mutationibus, secundum hoc diversimode signatur ibi nunc et prius. Aliqua enim mutatio est inter cujus terminos potest accipi medium quod minus distat ab uno extremorum quam aliud; unde antequam perveniatur ad ultimum mutationis terminum, fiunt recessus ab uno termino et accessus ad alterum, in quo consistit mutationis ratio; et ideo utrumque ad illam mutationem pertinet; et nunc scilicet in quo terminatur accessus et recessus, et prius illud in quo incepit: et ideo talis mutatio non est in instanti, sed in tempore.

Aliqua vero mutatio est, inter cujus terminos non potest accipi medium in eodem subjecto, nisi forte per accidens, sicut inter affirmationem et negationem: quia contradictio est oppositio, cujus non est medium secundum se, ut dicitur in 1 *Poster.* Per accidens autem potest accipi ibi medium ex parte negationis cui aliquid adjungatur, quod magis vel minus distat ab affirmatione, sive illud sit contrarium in eodem genere directe, sive dispositio contraria; sicut inter non album et album accipitur per accidens medium ex parte coloris cui conjungitur negatio albedinis, secundum quod magis vel minus distat ab albedine; et inter non ignem et ignem accipitur medium, secundum quod aliquid est magis vel minus frigidum aut humidum. Unde in omnibus mutationibus, in quibus sunt affirmatio et negatio tantum, seu privatio et forma tantum, per se loquendo, non potest esse recessus a termino vel accessus ad terminum ante perventionem ad ultimum terminum: et ideo illud principium non pertinet, per se loquendo, ad hanc mutationem, sed solum per accidens ratione illius adjuncti ad negationem, secundum quod per accidens negatio recipiebat magis et minus, et per consequens medium; unde, per se loquendo, pertinet ad motum praecedentem, sicut ad alterationem quae praecedit generationem, et ad motum localem qui praecedit illuminationem; et propter hoc istae mutationes dicuntur esse in instanti.

Et quia, ut dictum est, inter substantiam panis et substantiam corporis Christi non est accipere medium quod magis sit propinquum corpori Christi quam substantia panis quantum ad hoc quod convertatur in ipsum divina virtute; ideo simile est judicium de ista conversione et de praedictis mutationibus; unde ad hanc conversionem non pertinet nisi illud nunc in quo desinit esse

the terminus of a certain movement, namely, the uttering of the words, it was bread in the entire preceding time, up until the last instant, in which it is the body of Christ.

Reply Obj. 3: In any change it is necessary to designate 'now' and 'before' according to the two terminuses of change, which do not touch one another, as it says in *Physics* 1;[43] that is, they cannot exist at the same time. Hence according to the different terminuses in different changes, now and before are marked differently. For one kind of change exists when the middle of two terminuses is less distant from one of the extremes than the other; hence before it reaches the last terminus of the change, a withdrawal from one terminus and an approach to the other happen, in which the nature of this change consists; and so both belong to this change: both 'now', namely, when this approach and withdrawal is terminated, and 'before' when it began. And so a change like this is not in an instant, but in a time.

But there is another kind of change, in which a middle cannot be taken between its terminuses in the same subject, except perhaps incidentally, like between affirmation and negation: for contradiction is opposition, for which there is no middle in itself, as is said in *Posterior Analytics* 1.[44] But a middle can be found there incidentally on the part of the negation to which something is added, which is more or less distant from affirmation, whether it is directly contrary in the same genus, or a contrary disposition; just as between one white thing and another a middle can be taken incidentally on the part of a color to which the negation of white is joined, according as it is more or less distant from whiteness; and between fire and not fire a middle is taken, according as something is more or less cold or wet. Hence in all changes in which there is only affirmation and negation, or only privation and form, speaking *per se*, there cannot be receding from a terminus or approaching a terminus before reaching the last terminus: and so that principle does not belong to this change, speaking *per se*, but only incidentally by reason of what is attached to the negation, according as incidentally the negation is received more and less, and consequently, middle. Hence, speaking *per se*, it belongs to the preceding motion, like the alteration that precedes generation, and to the local motion that precedes illumination, and because of this those changes are said to exist in an instant.

And since, as was said, between the bread's substance and the body of Christ's substance a middle cannot be taken that is closer to the body of Christ than to the bread's substance in that it is converted into it by divine power, for this reason the judgment is the same of that conversion and the changes mentioned above. Hence the only 'now' that pertains to this conversion is the one in which the bread ceases

---

43. Aristotle, *Physics*, Bk. 1, ch. 5 (188a31ff.).
44. Aristotle, *Posterior Analytics*, Bk. 1, ch. 2 (71a12).

panis, et incipit esse corpus Christi; sed illud primum pertinet ad totum tempus praecedens quod mensurabat prolationem verborum, quae quodammodo efficit conversionem.

AD QUARTUM dicendum, quod mutatio, ut dictum est, in instanti est; sed motus praecedens est in tempore. Si ergo includatur in factione tam motus praecedens quam mutatio quae est terminus ejus, sicut generatio alterationis; tunc fieri pertinebit ad motum praecedentem, et factum esse ad terminum motus qui est ipsa generatio: et sic non simul fit et factum est. Si autem factio non extendat se ad mutationem illam, tunc utrumque est simul, et fieri et factum esse; et sic quod fit est (si dicatur fieri ratione ipsius mutationis quae tunc est); sed factum est ratione termini mutationis; sicut dicimus quod simul terminatur motus et terminatus est, simul illuminatur aer et illuminatus est: et similiter etiam est in conversione de qua loquimur.

to exist and the body of Christ begins to exist; but that 'first' pertains to the whole preceding time that measured the uttering of the words, which somehow bring about the conversion.

REPLY OBJ. 4: The change, as was said, is in an instant, but the preceding motion is in time. Therefore, if the preceding motion is included in the becoming as much as the change that is its terminus, as generation is of alteration, then 'becoming' will pertain to the preceding motion, and 'being done' to the terminus of motion that is the generation itself, and so becoming and being-done do not happen at the same time. But if the becoming does not extend to that change, then both are at once, both becoming and being-done; and so what 'is becoming' exists (if it may be called 'becoming' by reason of that change which is at that moment); but it 'has become' by reason of the term of the change; just as we say that a motion terminates and has been terminated at the same time, and that at the same time that the air is illuminated, it has been illuminated; and similarly also in the conversion of which we speak.

Response to Quaestiuncula 3

AD TERTIAM QUAESTIONEM dicendum, quod quanto aliquid est permanentius, tanto difficilius transmutatur. Et quia subjectum in qualibet mutatione manet, ideo in omnibus mutationibus materia est maxime manens, cum sit subjectum omnium mutationum; unde illa mutatio quae ad ipsam materiam attingit, est difficilior et majoris virtutis ostensiva quam quaecumque alia transmutatio ex parte ejus quod transmutatur. Et quia creatio et haec conversio pertingunt usque ad essentiam materiae, ut ex praedictis patet, constat has mutationes esse majoris virtutis ostensivas quibuscumque aliis, in quibus mutatur vel forma substantialis vel accidentalis, aut locus exterior. Sed inter has duas videtur creatio, simpliciter loquendo, praecellere, quia per ipsam materiae essentia producitur; ex quo consequitur ut a producente per hanc conversionem possit in alterum transmutari. Sed ex parte ejus ad quod est mutatio, mutatio quae est in unione humanae naturae ad divinam personam, praecellit has et omnes alias mutationes in difficultate; unde ipsa est miraculum miraculorum omnium.

AD PRIMUM ergo dicendum, quod mutatio ista fit ex existenti in existens praeter modum aliarum mutationum, quae fiunt etiam ex existentibus in existentia, ex quarum inspectione intellectus noster sibi suas conceptiones formavit: et ideo haec conversio videtur esse contra conceptiones intellectus; et propter hoc difficilius ei assentitur quam creationi, quae est ex omnino non existenti, cujusmodi mutationem non vidit.

TO THE THIRD QUESTION, it should be said that the more permanent something is, the more difficult it is to change over. And because the subject remains in any change, for this reason matter remains the most in all changes, since it is subject of all changes. And so that change that extends to matter itself is more difficult and displays greater power than any other transmutation, with regard to what is changed. And since creation and this conversion extend all the way to the essence of matter, as is clear from what has been said, it is clear that these changes show greater power than any others, in which substantial or accidental form is changed, or an external place. But between these two, it seems that creation, simply speaking, surpasses the other, because by it matter's essence is produced, from which it results that it can be transformed into something else by the one who produced it through this conversion. But on the part of what it is changed into, the change that is in the union of human nature to a divine person surpasses these and all other changes in difficulty; and therefore it is the miracle of all miracles.

REPLY OBJ. 1: That change happens from an existing thing into an existing thing in a way beyond other changes, which also happen from existing things into existing things, and from whose examination our intellect formed its own conceptions; and that is why this conversion seems to be against the conceptions of the intellect. And because of this it is more difficult to assent to it than to creation, which is from what does not exist in any way, which sort of change our intellect does not see.

AD SECUNDUM dicendum, quod in aliqua actione potest esse resistentia dupliciter. Uno modo ex parte agentis, quando scilicet ex contrario agente virtus ipsius debilitatur; alio modo ex parte ipsius effectus, quando ex contraria dispositione impeditur effectus. In omni autem actione ubi agens non patitur, prima resistentia non habet locum, sed secunda solum; unde in operationibus divinis non attenditur difficultas secundum resistentiam ad agentem, sed secundum impedimentum effectus. Magis autem impeditur effectus per subtractionem potentiae recipientis quam per rationem[45] contrariae dispositionis: quia contraria dispositio non impedit effectum nisi inquantum facit potentiam indispositam. Et ideo major difficultas est in creatione, ubi omnino materia non praeexistit, quam ubi in praeexistente materia est aliquid quod effectui, contrariando, repugnat.

AD TERTIUM dicendum, quod sicut se habet potentia naturalis ad mutationes naturales, ita se habet potentia obedientiae ad conversiones miraculosas; unde secundum modum miraculosae conversionis est etiam modus obedientialis potentiae in creatura in aliud convertendo. Sicut ergo in conversionibus formalibus inest potentia obedientiae ad recipiendum talem formam, ita in hac substantiali conversione inest potentia obedientiae ut haec substantia convertatur in illam; unde majoris virtutis ostensiva est creatio, in qua nulla potentia obedientiae praeexistit, quam haec conversio.

REPLY OBJ. 2: In any action there can be resistance in two ways. In one way on the part of the agent, when, namely, its power is weakened by a contrary agent; in another way on the part of the effect itself, when the effect is impeded by a contrary disposition. Now in every action where the agent is not acted upon, the first resistance does not take place, but only the second. Hence in divine operations no difficulty is found in resistance to the agent, but only in impediments to the effect. However, an effect is more impeded by taking away the potency of the receiver than by the opposition of a contrary disposition, because a contrary disposition does not impede an effect except insofar as it makes the potency indisposed. And so there is a greater difficulty in creation, where no matter pre-exists at all, than where there is something in the pre-existing matter that resists the effect by opposing it.

REPLY OBJ. 3: Natural potency is related to natural changes just as the potency of obedience is related to miraculous conversions. Hence the mode of obediential potency in the creature to be converted into something else is also according to the mode of miraculous conversion. Therefore, just as in formal conversions there is a potency of obedience to receiving this sort of form, so also in this substantial conversion there is a potency of obedience in this substance so that it may be converted into that one. Hence creation displays a greater power than this conversion, for there no potency of obedience pre-exists.

---

45. *rationem.—oppositionem* PLE.

ARTICLE 4

The statements that should be granted in this matter[46]

Quaestiuncula 1

Ad quartum sic proceditur. Videtur quod praedicta conversio possit exprimi per verbum substantivum alterius temporis quam praesentis, ut dicatur: quod *est panis, erit corpus Christi*, vel: *quod est corpus Christi, fuit panis*. Ambrosius enim dicit in Lib. *de Sacramentis*, quod erat panis ante consecrationem.[47]

Praeterea, major est convenientia, quanto perfectior est conversio. Sed haec conversio est perfectior omnibus aliis: quia in hac convertitur totum in totum et partes in partes, sicut ex praedictis patet. Cum ergo in aliis conversionibus utamur tali modo loquendi, scilicet, quod erat aqua est vinum: vel, quod erat aer est ignis: videtur multo fortius hic quod possit dici: *quod est corpus Christi, erat panis*.

Sed contra, 'quod' est relativum suppositi ejusdem. Sed non est accipere aliquod suppositum quod sit quandoque panis, quandoque corpus Christi, ut ex praedictis patet. Ergo non est dicendum: *quod est corpus Christi, fuit panis*.

Obj. 1: To the fourth we proceed thus. It seems that the conversion mentioned can be expressed by a substantive verb of another tense than the present, so that it might be said, "What is bread, will be the body of Christ," or "What is the body of Christ was bread." For Ambrose says in his book *On the Sacraments* that what was bread before the consecration is now after the consecration the body of Christ.[48]

Obj. 2: Furthermore, there is more fittingness when the conversion is more perfect. But this conversion is more perfect than all others, for in it a whole is converted into a whole and parts into parts, as is clear from what has been said. Therefore, since in other conversions we use this way of speaking, namely, that what was water is wine, or that what was air is fire, it seems much more that this can be said: "What was bread, is the body of Christ."

On the contrary, 'What' [*quod*] is a relative of the same supposit. But one cannot take any supposit that is at one time bread, at another time the body of Christ, as is clear from what was said. Therefore, it should not be said, "What has been bread, is the body of Christ."

Quaestiuncula 2

Ulterius. Videtur quod haec sit vera: *panis fit corpus Christi*. Ad omne enim facere sequitur fieri. Sed Christus fecit ea, scilicet panem et vinum, corpus suum et sanguinem suum, ut Damascenus dicit. Ergo panis fit corpus Christi.

Praeterea, omne quod convertitur in alterum, fit illud. Sed panis convertitur in corpus Christi. Ergo fit corpus Christi.

Sed contra, omne fieri terminatur ad factum esse. Sed haec nunquam erit vera: *panis est factus corpus Christi*: quia quod factum est, est; panis autem nunquam est corpus Christi. Ergo et haec est falsa: *panis fit corpus Christi*.

Obj. 1: Moreover, it seems that this is true: "bread becomes the body of Christ." For in everything making follows becoming. But Christ made them, namely, bread and wine, his body and blood, as Damascene says.[49] Therefore, the bread becomes the body of Christ.

Obj. 2: Furthermore, everything that is converted into something else becomes it. But bread is converted into the body of Christ. Therefore, it becomes the body of Christ.

On the contrary, every becoming terminates in a being-done. But this will never be true: "the bread has been made the body of Christ." For what has been made, is; however, the bread is never the body of Christ. Therefore, this is also false: "the bread becomes the body of Christ."

---

46. Parallel: *ST* III, q. 75, a. 8.

47. *consecrationem.—consecrationem iam est corpus Christi post consecrationem* PLE.

48. See Ambrose, *On the Sacraments*, Bk. 4, ch. 4, par. 15 (CSEL 73:53): "Ergo tibi ut respondeam, non erat corpus Christi ante consecrationem, sed post consecrationem dico tibi, quia iam corpus est Christi."

49. John Damascene, *On the Orthodox Faith*, Bk. 4, ch. 13 (PG 94:1146).

Quaestiuncula 3

ULTERIUS. Videtur quod haec sit falsa: *de pane fit corpus Christi*. Ex eodem enim fit aliquid et factum est. Sed haec est falsa: *corpus Christi factum est de pane, vel ex pane*. Ergo et haec, corpus Christi fit de pane.

PRAETEREA, *de* notat consubstantialitatem, ut Magister dicit in 1, dist. 36. Sed nulla consubstantialitas est panis ad corpus Christi. Ergo non potest dici quod corpus Christi fit de pane vel ex pane.

SED CONTRA, Ambrosius dicit: *ubi accessit consecratio, de pane fit corpus Christi*.

OBJ. 1: Moreover, it seems that this is false: "The body of Christ comes to be from this bread." For something comes to be and is made out of the same thing. But this is false: "the body of Christ is made from bread, or out of bread." Therefore also this, "the body of Christ comes to be from this bread."

OBJ. 2: Furthermore, 'from' denotes consubstantiality, as the Master says in Book I, Distinction 36. But there is no consubstantiality of the bread with the body of Christ. Therefore, it cannot be said that the body of Christ comes to be from bread or out of bread.

ON THE CONTRARY, Ambrose says, *where the consecration approaches, the body of Christ comes to be from bread.*[50]

Quaestiuncula 4

ULTERIUS. Videtur quod haec sit vera: 'panis potest esse corpus Christi.' Motus enim est actus existentis in potentia. Sed panis mutatur in corpus Christi. Ergo panis est potentia corpus Christi: ergo potest esse corpus Christi.

PRAETEREA, Ambrosius dicit, quod panis potest esse corpus Christi consecratione, quae fit Christi sermone.

SED CONTRA, quod potest esse aliquid nihil prohibet si ponatur illud: quia possibili posito, secundum Philosophum, non sequitur inconveniens. Sed inconveniens sequitur, si dicatur: 'panis est corpus Christi.'[53] Ergo haec est falsa: 'panis potest esse corpus Christi.'

OBJ. 1: Moreover, it seems that this is true: "bread can be the body of Christ." For motion is the act of what exists in potency. But bread is changed into the body of Christ. Therefore, bread is the body of Christ in potency: therefore it can be the body of Christ.

OBJ. 2: Furthermore, Ambrose says that bread can be the body of Christ by consecration, which is done by the words of Christ.[51]

ON THE CONTRARY, if something can be something else, nothing prevents us from calling it that: for when what is possible is posited, according to the Philosopher,[52] nothing unfitting follows. But something unfitting follows if it were said, "bread is the body of Christ," or "what is or was bread, is the body of Christ." Therefore, this is false: "bread can be the body of Christ."

Response to Quaestiuncula 1

RESPONDEO dicendum ad primam quaestionem, quod haec conversio in hoc differt ab omnibus aliis mutationibus, quod in omnibus aliis mutationibus est aliquod subjectum commune: in hac autem non, sed solum est accipere duos terminos conversionis; et ideo omnes locutiones exprimentes mutationem per quam importatur ordo termini ad terminum, sunt concedendae in hac materia, sicut haec: *panis convertitur in corpus Christi*; locutiones vero quae exprimunt identitatem subjecti, non sunt concedendae, proprie loquendo. Sed quia in hac conversione est aliquid simile identitati subjec-

TO THE FIRST QUESTION, I answer that this conversion differs from all other changes in this, that in all other changes there is a certain shared subject. But in this one there is not, but only two terminuses of conversion. And so all statements expressing a change in which the order of a terminus to a terminus is implied, are granted in this matter, like this one: "Bread is converted into the body of Christ." But statements that express an identity of subject are not granted, properly speaking. But because in this conversion there is something like identity of subject, namely, shared appearances, which remain here from there, al-

---

50. See Ambrose, *On the Sacraments*, Bk. 4, ch. 4, par. 14 (CSEL 73:51): "Sed panis iste panis est ante verba sacramentorum; ubi accesserit consecratio, de pane fit caro Christi."

51. This claim is pieced together from various things said by Ambrose in the preceding *loci*.

52. Aristotle, *Metaphysics*, Bk. 9, ch. 4 (1047b11).

53. *Christi.'—Christi' vel 'id quod est aut fuit panis, est corpus Christi.'* PLE.

ti, scilicet communitas specierum, quae manent hinc inde, quamvis illae species non sint mutationis subjectum; ideo etiam tales locutiones aliquando a sanctis positae inveniuntur, ut identitas importata non referatur ad subjectum sed ad species easdem. Unde tales locutiones non sunt extendendae, quia sunt impropriae; et haec locutio quae est: *hoc fuit illud*, vel: *quod est hoc erit illud*, expresse important identitatem subjecti mutationis propter naturam relationis; ideo non est simpliciter concedenda.

AD PRIMUM ergo dicendum, quod verbum Ambrosii est exponendum: *quod erat panis est corpus Christi*; idest, quod est sub speciebus panis, primo fuit panis, et postea corpus Christi.

AD SECUNDUM dicendum, quod secundum Philosophum in 2 *de Anima*, passum in principio est dissimile, sed in fine est simile; unde perfecta conversio requirit perfectam distantiam in principio, et perfectam unitatem in fine. Sed hoc nomen panis importat quod erat in principio, quia importat terminum a quo; ideo quanto perfectior est conversio, tanto minus potest corpus Christi de pane praedicari.

though those appearances are not the subject of the change, for this reason also statements like those quoted from the saints are sometimes found, so that the identity implied is not referred to the subject but to the same appearances. Hence such statements are not to be extended, because they are improper; and the statements, "this was that," or "what is this will be that," expressly convey an identity of the subject of the change because of the nature of relation; and so they should not be granted simply speaking.

REPLY OBJ. 1: The words of Ambrose are to be explained: *what was bread is the body of Christ*; i.e., what is under the appearances of bread, was first bread, and afterward is the body of Christ.

REPLY OBJ. 2: According to the Philosopher in *On the Soul* 2, in the beginning what suffers is dissimilar, but in the end it is the same.[54] Hence perfect conversion requires perfect distance in the beginning, and perfect unity in the end. But this noun 'bread' conveys what was there in the beginning, because it conveys the starting terminus; therefore the more perfect the conversion, the less the body of Christ can be predicated of the bread.

Response to Quaestiuncula 2

AD SECUNDAM QUAESTIONEM dicendum, quod cum dicitur: *hoc fit illud*, ex vi locutionis in ly hoc importatur subjectum factionis; unde haec est per se: homo fit albus; sed haec est per accidens: nigrum fit album. Subjectum autem factionis commune est utrique termino; unde patet quod praedicta locutio importat communitatem subjecti, et proprie non est concedenda.

AD PRIMUM ergo dicendum, quod exponendum est verbum Damasceni sicut expositum est verbum Ambrosii, ut relatio importata in ly ea designet unitatem specierum, et non subjecti unitatem.

AD SECUNDUM dicendum, quod in hac locutione: *panis convertitur in corpus Christi*, importatur tantum ordo unius termini ad alterum; in hac autem: *panis fit corpus Christi*, importatur unitas subjecti; et ideo non est similis ratio de utraque.

TO THE SECOND QUESTION, it should be said that when it is said, "This becomes that," by the force of the speech the subject of the doing is conveyed in the 'this'; hence this is *per se*: "a man becomes white"; and this is incidental: "black becomes white." However, the subject of the doing is common to both terminuses; therefore it is clear that the statement mentioned conveys a shared subject, and that should not properly be granted.

REPLY OBJ. 1: The words of Damascene should be explained like the words of Ambrose, so that the relation conveyed by the 'them' designates oneness of appearances and not oneness of subject.

REPLY OBJ. 2: This statement, "The bread is converted into the body of Christ," conveys only the order of one terminus to another. But this statement, "The bread becomes the body of Christ," conveys unity of subject, and so the account is not the same for both.

Response to Quaestiuncula 3

AD TERTIAM QUAESTIONEM dicendum, quod, sicut patet in 1 *Physic.*, *hoc fit hoc*, dicimus in permanentibus per se, sed in non permanentibus per accidens; sed *ex hoc fit hoc* dicitur proprie in non permanentibus. Dicimus enim: *ex non albo fit album*. Et si aliquando dicatur

TO THE THIRD QUESTION, it should be said that as is clear in *Physics* 1,[55] we say, "This becomes this," in things enduring in themselves, but not for things enduring incidentally; but "This comes to be out of this," is said properly of non-enduring things. For we say, *a white thing comes to*

---

54. Aristotle, *On the Soul*, Bk. 2, ch. 4 (416b3).
55. Aristotle, *Physics*, Bk. 1, ch. 7 (190a21ff.).

aliquid fieri ex permanente, hoc est inquantum intelligitur cum permanente aliquid non permanens; sicut cum dicitur: *ex aere fit statua*, intelligitur *ex aere infigurato*.

Et sic patet quod haec locutio: *hoc fit hoc*, exprimit identitatem subjecti; haec autem locutio: *ex hoc fit hoc*, principaliter exprimit ordinem terminorum ad invicem, et per consequens quandoque unitatem subjecti; unde quandoque importat tantum ordinem sine hoc quod importet subjectum, ut cum dicitur: *ex mane fit meridies*, idest post, ut dicitur in 2 *Metaphysica*; et secundum hoc erit incongrua: *panis fit corpus Christi*; sed haec erit concedenda: *ex pane fit corpus Christi*, si ly ex non denotet subjectum, et quasi causam materialem, sed tantum ordinem terminorum conversionis ad invicem. Sed haec: *de pane fit corpus Christi*, est minus propria: quia haec propositio de notat consubstantialitatem, ut Ambrosius tangit; tamen quandoque de ponitur pro ex, et sic potest concedi quod de pane fit corpus Christi sicut *ex pane*.

Ad primum ergo dicendum, quod cum dicitur: *de pane factum est corpus Christi*, ly de potest importare ordinem in essendo: quia quod significatur in *factum esse*, significatur jam esse; et sic non conceditur quod de pane sit factum corpus Christi: quia significaretur quod panis haberet ordinem ad corpus Christi in essendo, quod falsum est, quia non est materia ejus. Potest etiam importare ordinem in fieri, quod praecessit factum esse; et sic sicut conceditur haec: *de pane fit corpus Christi*; ita potest concedi ista: *ex pane factum est corpus Christi*.

Ad secundum patet solutio ex dictis.

be from a non-white thing. And if ever something is said to come to be from something permanent, this is inasmuch as something non-permanent is understood with the permanent thing, as when it is said, *a statue comes to be out of bronze*, it is understood, *out of unshaped bronze*.

And in this way it is clear that this statement, *this becomes this*, expresses identity of subject; but this statement, *this comes to be out of this*, principally expresses the order of terminuses to each other, and consequently, sometimes oneness of subject; hence sometimes it conveys only order without conveying subject, as when it is said, *out of the morning the noon comes to be*, that is, after, as it says in *Metaphysics* 2;[56] and accordingly, this will be incongruous: *bread becomes the body of Christ*; but this will be granted: *out of bread the body of Christ comes to be*, if the *out of* does not denote a subject, and something like a material cause, but only the order of the terminuses of conversion to each other. But this: *from bread the body of Christ comes to be* is less proper, because the preposition 'from' denotes consubstantiality, as Ambrose mentions; nevertheless, 'from' is sometimes used for 'out of' and so it can be granted that from bread the body of Christ is made as meaning *out of bread*.

Reply Obj. 1: When it is said, *the body of Christ has come to be from bread*, the 'from' can convey order in being, because *to have become* signifies what exists right now. And so it is not granted that the body of Christ has come to be from bread, because this would signify that bread had an order to the body of Christ in being, which is false, because bread is not its matter. It can also convey an order in becoming, which precedes being done; and then as this is granted: *the body of Christ comes to be from bread*, so this can also be granted: *the body of Christ has come to be out of bread*.

The solution to the second objection is clear from what has been said.

Response to Quaestiuncula 4

Ad quartam quaestionem dicendum, quod cum potentia pertineat ad subjectum, non est dubium quod cum dicitur: *panis potest esse corpus Christi*, importatur unitas subjecti; et ideo non est concedenda, quia nihil panis unquam erit aliquid corporis Christi: sed sicut conceditur ista: *panis convertitur in corpus Christi*, ita potest concedi ista: panis potest converti: quia cujus est potentia, ejus est actus, ut dicitur in Lib. *de Somno et vigilia*.

Ad primum ergo dicendum, quod ista definitio non habet locum in ista conversione, ut ex praedictis patet.

To the fourth question, it should be said that since potency pertains to the subject, there should be no doubt that when it is said, *bread can be the body of Christ*, it conveys oneness of subject. And this is why it is not to be granted, because nothing of bread will ever be anything of the body of Christ. But just as this is granted: *bread is converted into the body of Christ*, so this can also be granted: *bread can be converted*; because whatever has a potency has an act, as is said in the book *On Sleep and Waking*.[57]

Reply Obj. 1: That definition does not apply to this conversion, as is clear from what has been said.

56. Aristotle, *Metaphysics*, Bk. 2, ch. 2 (994b1).
57. Aristotle, *On Sleep and Waking*, ch. 1 (454a8).

AD SECUNDUM dicendum, quod illud verbum Ambrosii exponendum est, sicut prius dictum est.

REPLY OBJ. 2: Those words of Ambrose are to be explained as was said before.

QUESTION 2

THE MATTER OF THE EUCHARIST

Deinde quaeritur de materia hujus sacramenti; et circa hoc quaeruntur quatuor:

primo, utrum panis et vinum sint materia hujus sacramenti;

secundo, qualis panis;

tertio, quale vinum hujus sacramenti materia esse possit;

quarto, de aquae admixtione.

Next we ask about the matter of this sacrament; and concerning this, four questions arise:

first, whether bread and wine are the matter of this sacrament;

second, what kind of bread;

third, what kind of wine can be the matter of this sacrament;

fourth, about the mixing in of water.

ARTICLE 1

Whether bread and wine are the matter of this sacrament

Quaestiuncula 1

AD PRIMUM SIC PROCEDITUR. Videtur quod non debeat esse duplex materia hujus sacramenti. Quanto enim aliquid est simplicius, tanto nobilius; unde et simplicissima sunt nobilissima. Sed hoc sacramentum est nobilius aliis. Ergo debet esse simplicius. Cum ergo alia sacramenta unam tantum materiam habeant, sicut baptismus aquam, confirmatio chrisma; videtur quod non debeat esse duplex materia hujus sacramenti.

PRAETEREA, materia sacramenti debet respondere ei quod est sacramentum et res in sacramento, quia est signum ejus. Sed totum illud quod est res et sacramentum, continetur sub specie panis, scilicet totus Christus. Ergo panis est tota materia hujus sacramenti; et sic idem quod prius.

PRAETEREA, hoc sacramentum ordinatur ad usum fidelium. Sed tantum sub una specie populo hoc sacramentum ministratur, scilicet sub specie panis. Ergo tantum una ejus debet esse materia.

PRAETEREA, posset contingere quod in aliqua terra triticum haberetur et non vinum, vel e converso. Ergo in tali casu liceret et in una specie tantum conficere.

SED CONTRA, sacramentum Eucharistiae a Christo initium sumpsit. Sed Christus discipulis duo in coena

OBJ. 1: To the first we proceed thus. It seems that there should not be a twofold matter for this sacrament.[58] For the simpler something is, the more noble it is; and so the simplest things are also the most noble. But this sacrament is more noble than any others. Therefore, it should be more simple. Therefore since the other sacraments have only one matter, like water for baptism and chrism for confirmation, it seems that there should not be a twofold matter for this sacrament.

OBJ. 2: Furthermore, a sacrament's matter should correspond to what is sacrament-and-reality in the sacrament, for it is a sign of that. But everything that is reality-and-sacrament, namely, the whole Christ, is contained under the appearance of bread. Therefore, bread is the whole matter of this sacrament, and so the same as before.[59]

OBJ. 3: Furthermore, this sacrament is ordered to the use of the faithful. But this sacrament is only administered to the people under one species, namely the species of bread. Therefore, there should only be one matter of it.

OBJ. 4: Furthermore, it could happen that in some land, wheat was available but not wine, or vice versa. Therefore, it seems that in such a case it would be permitted to consecrate also in only one species.

ON THE CONTRARY, the sacrament of the Eucharist took its origin from Christ. But Christ gave his disciples two

---

58. Parallels: *ST* III, q. 74, a. 1; *SCG* IV, ch. 61; *De sacram. altar.*, chs. 9 & 29; *Super I ad Cor.* 11, lec. 5.
59. For more about the sacrament alone, reality alone, and sacrament-and-reality, see the footnote at Dist.1, q.1, a.4, qa. 1, main response.

dedit, scilicet panem et vinum. Ergo debent esse materia hujus sacramenti.

PRAETEREA, materia sacramenti debet respondere usui sacramenti. Sed manducatio, quae est usus hujus sacramenti, ut supra, dist. 9, qu. 1, art. 1, dictum est, requirit cibum et potum. Ergo hujus sacramenti materia debet esse duplex, una quae competat in cibum, et alia quae competat in potum.

things at the Last Supper, namely, bread and wine. Therefore, they should be the matter for this sacrament.

FURTHERMORE, the matter of the sacrament should correspond to the use of the sacrament. But eating, which is the use of this sacrament, as was said above in Distinction 9, Question 1, Article 1, requires food and drink. Therefore, the matter for this sacrament should be twofold, one that applies to food, and another that applies to drink.

Quaestiuncula 2

ULTERIUS. Videtur quod non debeat esse materia hujus sacramenti panis et vinum. Sacramenta enim legis Mosaicae propinquiora fuerunt sacramentis legis novae quam sacramenta legis naturae. Sed in lege Mosaica secundum modum sacramenti manducabantur carnes animalium. Ergo hoc magis debet esse materia hujus sacramenti quam panis et vinum, quae sumebantur in lege naturae per modum sacramenti.

PRAETEREA, materia sacramenti debet competere usui sacramenti et significationi. Sed expressius significaret caro animalis alicujus carnem Christi quam panis: quia majorem habet convenientiam ad ipsam, et iterum magis reficit. Ergo magis debet caro esse materia hujus sacramenti quam panis.

PRAETEREA, sacramenta infirmis ministrari debent, quia medicinae sunt. Sed vinum non datur infirmis. Ergo non debet esse materia hujus sacramenti.

PRAETEREA, illud sacramentum non solum praefiguratum fuit in oblatione Melchisedech, qui obtulit panem et vinum, ut dicitur Genes. 14, sed etiam in favo mellis, quem sumpsit Jonathas, ut dicitur 1 Reg. 14. Ergo etiam mel deberet esse materia hujus sacramenti, et praecipue propter suavitatem.

PRAETEREA, in hoc sacramento continetur Christus ut cibus parvulorum. Sed parvulis datur in cibum lac. Ergo lac deberet esse materia hujus sacramenti.

OBJ. 1: Moreover, it seems that the matter for this sacrament should not be bread and wine. For the sacraments of the Mosaic law were closer to the sacraments of the New Law than the sacraments of the law of nature. But in the Mosaic law the flesh of animals was eaten as a sacrament. Therefore, this should be the matter of this sacrament rather than bread and wine, which were consumed as a sacrament in the law of nature.

OBJ. 2: Furthermore, the sacrament's matter should apply to the sacrament's use and signification. But the flesh of some animal represents the flesh of Christ more explicitly than bread: for it has greater resemblance to it, and again, it restores one more. Therefore, flesh should be this sacrament's matter rather than bread.

OBJ. 3: Furthermore, sacraments should be administered to the sick, for they are medicine. But wine is not given to the sick. Therefore, it should not be this sacrament's matter.

OBJ. 4: Furthermore, this sacrament was not only prefigured in the offering of Melkizedech, who offered bread and wine, as it says in Genesis 14:18, but also in the honeycomb that Jonathan consumed, as it says in 1 Samuel 14:27. Therefore, honey should also have been this sacrament's matter, especially because of its sweetness.

OBJ. 5: Furthermore, in this sacrament Christ is contained as food for little ones. But little ones are given milk for food. Therefore, milk should have been this sacrament's matter.

Quaestiuncula 3

ULTERIUS. Videtur quod panis et vinum non possint esse materia hujus sacramenti nisi sub determinata quantitate. In sacramentis enim intentio requiritur conformis intentioni ecclesiae. Sed si aliquis vellet consecrare totum panem qui est in foro, et totum vinum quod est in cellario, intentio ejus non esset concors intentioni ecclesiae, quae intendit consecrare ad usum fidelium: quod etiam verba instituentis ostendunt: *accipite*, inquit,

OBJ. 1: Moreover, it seems that bread and wine cannot be the matter of this sacrament except under a determinate quantity.[60] For in the sacraments is required an intention conformed to the intention of the Church. But if someone wished to consecrate all the bread that is in the market and all the wine that is in the cellar, his intention would not agree with the intention of the Church, which intends to consecrate for the faithful's use. And the words of institu-

---

60. Parallel: *ST* III, q. 74, a. 2.

et manducate. Ergo requiritur determinata quantitas panis.

PRAETEREA, virtus data verbis et ministro, datur ad venerationem sacramenti, non ad irrisionem. Sed si immoderata quantitas panis et vini consecraretur, verteretur in irrisionem. Ergo non potest consecrari nisi sub determinata quantitate.

PRAETEREA, si aliquis in mari hominem baptizet, illa tantum aqua verbo vitae sanctificatur quae ad usum ablutionis cedit, et non totum mare. Ergo a simili et hic, tantum de pane et vino consecrari potest, quantum potest venire in usum fidelium.

SED CONTRA, secundum Philosophum, omne determinatum est medium duorum extremorum determinatorum. Sed quantitas panis qui consecrari potest, non est medium duorum extremorum determinatorum: quia nunquam est ita parva quantitas panis quin possit consecrari. Ergo non est determinata quantitas etiam secundum magnitudinem.

PRAETEREA, constat quod sacerdos habens paucos parochianos potest tantum de pane consecrare, quantum habens multos, quamvis non debeat. Sed non potest accipi tanta quantitas panis quae non possit venire in usum multorum parochianorum, et praecipue cum unus homo possit et multum et parum in quantitate sumere. Ergo non potest esse tanta materia panis quin possit consecrari etiam a quocumque sacerdote.

tion also show this: for he said, *take and eat*. Therefore, a determinate quantity of bread is required.

OBJ. 2: Furthermore the power given to the words and the minister is given for the sacrament's veneration, not its mockery. But if an immoderate quantity of bread and wine were consecrated, it would be changed to mockery. Therefore, it cannot be consecrated except in a determinate quantity.

OBJ. 3: Furthermore, if anyone baptized a man in the sea, only that water is sanctified by the word of life that is used for the cleansing, and not the whole sea. Therefore, in the same way here, only as much bread and wine can be consecrated as can come into the use of the faithful.

ON THE CONTRARY, according to the Philosopher, every determinate thing is a middle between two determinate extremes.[61] But the quantity of bread which can be consecrated is not a middle between two determined extremes, for there is never such a small quantity of bread that it cannot be consecrated. Therefore, there is no determinate quantity on the side of greatness, either.

FURTHERMORE, it is clear that a priest having few parishioners can consecrate as much bread as one who has many parishioners, although he should not. But there cannot be taken so great a quantity of bread that it cannot come into the use of many parishioners, and particularly since one man can consume either a lot or a little in quantity. Therefore, there cannot be so much matter of bread that it cannot be consecrated also by any priest at all.

Response to Quaestiuncula 1

RESPONDEO dicendum ad primam quaestionem, quod materia sacramenti debet competere et significationi sacramenti et usui; et utroque modo exigitur duplex materia in hoc sacramento. Usus enim hujus sacramenti est manducatio, quae ad sui integritatem et cibum et potum exigit; et ideo hujus sacramenti etiam debet esse duplex materia; una quae in cibum sumitur, et alia quae in potum. Significatio autem sacramenti est duplex. Una secundum quod repraesentat praeteritum; et sic in hoc sacramento significatur passio Christi, in qua separatus fuit ejus sanguis a corpore; et ideo separatim in hoc sacramento offerri debet signum corporis et signum sanguinis, duplici materia existente. Alia significatio sacramenti est de effectu per sacramentum inducendo, quia sacramenta efficiunt quod figurant; et sic, cum hoc sacramentum ad salutem corporis et animae sumatur, oportet quod sub specie panis ad significandam salutem corporis, et sub specie vini ad significandam sa-

TO THE FIRST QUESTION, I answer that the matter of the sacrament should be suited to both the sacrament's signification and its use, and in both ways a twofold matter is required for this sacrament. For this sacrament's use is eating, which requires both food and drink for its completeness; and so there should also be a twofold matter for this sacrament, one that is consumed as food, and the other as drink. However, a sacrament has two significations. One, according to which it represents the past; and so in this sacrament the Passion of Christ is signified, in which his blood was separated from his body; and therefore the sign of his body and the sign of his blood should be offered separately in this sacrament, by existing in a twofold matter. The sacrament's other signification concerns the effect brought about by the sacrament, for sacraments effect what they represent. And in this way, since this sacrament is consumed for the health of soul and body, it is necessary that it be accomplished under the appearance of bread to signify

---

61. Aristotle, *Nicomachean Ethics*, Bk. 2, ch. 8 (1108b9–12).

lutem animae hoc sacramentum perficiatur, ut in littera Magister dicit.

AD PRIMUM ergo dicendum, quod simplicitas per se non est causa nobilitatis; sed perfectio; unde ubi perfecta bonitas in uno simplici invenitur, simplex est nobilius quam compositum; quando autem e converso simplex est imperfectum, compositum vero perfectum, tunc compositum est nobilius quam simplex, sicut homo est nobilior terra; et ideo hoc sacramentum quamvis sit magis compositum ratione materiae, est tamen nobilius, quia est magis perfectum. Quod autem ad perfectionem ejus haec compositio exigatur, patet ex dictis.

AD SECUNDUM dicendum, quod quamvis totus Christus sit sub specie panis secundum rei veritatem, non tamen est ibi ex vi sacramenti nisi corpus ejus, ut ex dictis patet, et secundum quod venit in usum fidelium.

AD TERTIUM dicendum, quod populo non datur sanguis propter periculum: quia facilius una gutta sanguinis citius laberetur quam aliqua particula corporis; unde ministris altaris secundum consuetudinem aliquorum datur participatio sanguinis, de quibus praesumitur quod in talibus magis sint cauti. In lege etiam veteri de libaminibus nihil habebant offerentes, sed soli sacerdotes; per quae significabatur potus hujus sacramenti: de sacrificiis autem habebant, quibus significabatur cibus hujus sacramenti.

AD QUARTUM dicendum, quod quamvis consecratio panis non dependeat a consecratione vini, quod quidam posuerunt, ut supra, dist. 8, qu. 2, art. 4, quaestiunc. 1, dictum est, tamen potius deberet desistere qui non haberet utrumque quam conficere praeter morem ecclesiae in una tantum specie; quamvis etiam si in una tantum specie consecraret, consecratum esset. Peccaret autem graviter: nisi post consecrationem corporis ante consecrationem sanguinis occideretur, vel alias praeter culpam suam impediretur.

the health of the body, and under the appearance of wine to signify the health of the soul, as the Master says in the text.

REPLY OBJ. 1: Simplicity *per se* is not a cause of nobility, but perfection is. Hence where perfect goodness is found in one simple thing, the simple is nobler than the composite; but when on the other hand the simple is imperfect, but the composite is perfect, then the composite is nobler than the simple, just as man is nobler than earth. And so although this sacrament is more composite by reason of its matter, it is nevertheless more noble, for it is more perfect. And the fact that this composition is required for its perfection is clear from what has been said.

REPLY OBJ. 2: Although the whole Christ exists under the appearance of bread according to the truth of reality, nevertheless only his body is there by the power of the sacrament, as is clear from what has been said,[62] and according to that it comes into the faithful's use.

REPLY OBJ. 3: The blood is not given to the people because of the danger, since one drop of blood could fall more easily than any particle of the body; hence according to the custom of some, partaking of the blood is granted to the ministers of the altar, of whom greater caution is presumed in these matters. In the Old Law, too, the ones making the offering had nothing of the libations, but only the priests, by which this sacrament's drink was signified; however, they did receive of the sacrifices, by which this sacrament's food was signified.

REPLY OBJ. 4: As it says above in Distinction 8, Question 2, Article 4, Subquestion 1, although the consecration of the bread does not depend upon the consecration of the wine, which some people claimed, nevertheless someone who did not have both should abstain from consecrating rather than consecrating in one species alone against the Church's practice. Although even if he did consecrate in only one species, it would be consecrated. But he would sin gravely, unless he were killed after the consecration of the body and before the consecration of the blood, or he was impeded in some other way not his fault.

Response to Quaestiuncula 2

AD SECUNDAM QUAESTIONEM dicendum, quod causa quare panis et vinum sunt materia hujus sacramenti inter alios cibos et potus, est institutio divina. Causa autem institutionis multipliciter potest assignari. Prima ex parte usus sacramenti: quia haec duo communius in cibum et potum veniunt; unde convenientius per haec in cibum et potum spiritualem manuducimur. Secunda ex effectu sacramenti: quia, ut dicitur in Glossa 1 Corinth. 11, panis prae ceteris cibis sustentat cor-

TO THE SECOND QUESTION, it should be said that the reason why bread and wine among all foods and drinks are this sacrament's matter is the divine institution. However, many reasons can be assigned for this institution. The first is on the part of the sacrament's use: for these two things are most commonly taken as food and drink, and so we are more fittingly led by them to the spiritual food and drink. Second, from the sacrament's effect, because as it says in the Gloss on 1 Corinthians 11, bread sustains the body be-

---

62. See d. 8, q. 2, a. 4, qa. 1, ad 1.

pus, et vinum laetificat cor: et similiter hoc sacramentum sustentat magis et laetificat caritate inebriatos quam alia sacramenta. Tertia ex ritu celebrationis: quia mundius tractantur quam alia quae in cibum et potum veniunt. Quarta ex significatione duplicis rei hujus sacramenti: quia panis ex multis granis conficitur, et vinum ex multis acinis confluit; quod competit ad significandum corpus Christi verum et mysticum, ut supra, dist. 8, dictum est. Quinta ex repraesentatione ejus quod praecessit: nam grana in area conculcantur, et panis in fornace decoquitur, et vinum in torculari exprimitur; quae omnia competunt ad repraesentandum passionem Christi.

AD PRIMUM ergo dicendum, quod hoc sacramentum non debuit in specie alicujus sacramenti legis Mosaicae institui, ut ostenderetur cessatio legalium, quorum sacerdotium est imperfectius sacerdotio Christi; et ideo convenienter ad illas species in novo testamento reditur, quibus ostenditur sacerdotium novi testamenti praeeminere sacerdotio levitico, scilicet oblationi Melchisedech, ut apostolus probat Hebr. 7.

AD SECUNDUM dicendum, quod caro de ratione sui non dicit aliquid ordinatum in cibum, sed quamdam rem naturae; et ideo non ita competenter significaret caro animalis carnem Christi, ut est cibus fidelium, secundum quod in hoc sacramento continetur sicut panis; quia ad hoc confectus est ut cibus sit.

AD TERTIUM dicendum, quod vinum quamvis non detur infirmis qui morbo febrili subjacent, datur tamen debilibus ut confortentur; et similiter hoc sacramentum non est dandum his qui sunt in febre peccati, sed ad confortationem debilium qui a peccato liberati sunt.

AD QUARTUM dicendum, quod mel quamvis habeat suavitatem, est tamen inflativum; et ideo magis congrue significat suavitatem temporalem quae inflat, quam caritatis quae aedificat; unde et in sacrificiis veteris legis apponi prohibebatur; et ideo etiam non competit huic sacramento.

AD QUINTUM dicendum, quod quamvis cibus iste sit parvulorum per humilitatem, est tamen grandium in fide. Unde Augustinus: *cibus sum grandium*; et ideo non convenit ut sub specie lactis sumatur.

yond all the other foods, and wine delights the heart;[63] and likewise this sacrament sustains and delights those who are drunk with it by charity more than the other sacraments. Third, from the rite of its celebration: for these two things are more cleanly handled than other things that are taken as food and drink. Fourth, from the signification of this sacrament's twofold reality: for bread is composed of many grains, and wine is collected from many grapes, which belongs to the signification of the true and mystical body of Christ, as was said above in Distinction 8. Fifth, from the representation of what preceded it: for grains are crushed on the threshing floor, and bread is baked in an oven, and wine is expressed in a wine-press, which is all fitting to represent the Passion of Christ.

REPLY OBJ. 1: This sacrament should not have been instituted in the species of any sacrament of the Mosaic law, so that it might display the cessation of the prescripts of the law, whose priesthood was more imperfect than the priesthood of Christ. And this is why the return to these species in the New Testament, namely, to the offering of Melchizedek, is fitting, for it shows that the priesthood of the New Testament surpasses the levitical priesthood, as the Apostle proves in Hebrews 7.

REPLY OBJ. 2: The nature of flesh does not mean anything particularly ordered to food, but a certain reality of nature. And so flesh would not signify the body of Christ as it is the food of the faithful, according to which it is contained in this sacrament, so fittingly as bread does, because bread is made to be food.

REPLY OBJ. 3: Although wine is not given to the sick who suffer from a feverish illness, it is nevertheless given to the weak in order to strengthen them. And likewise this sacrament is not to be given to those who are in the fever of sin, but for the strengthening of the weak who have been freed from sin.

REPLY OBJ. 4: Although honey has sweetness, it is nevertheless something that puffs one up, and so it signifies more the temporal sweetness that puffs up than the charity that builds up; hence in the sacrifices of the Old Law it was forbidden to be used, and so neither does it belong in this sacrament.

REPLY OBJ. 5: Although that food is for little ones by humility, it is nevertheless for the fully grown in faith. Hence Augustine: *I am the food of the fully grown*;[64] and so it is not fitting that it be received under the species of milk.

Response to Quaestiuncula 3

AD TERTIAM QUAESTIONEM dicendum, quod quidam dicunt, quod virtus non est data ministro et ver-

TO THE THIRD QUESTION, it should be said that some people say that power is not given to the minister and the

---

63. See the text of Lombard at d. 8, ch. 7, n. 2.
64. Augustine, *Confessions* (CCSL 27), Bk. 7, ch. 10.

bis ad consecrandum panem et vinum sub quacumque quantitate, sed sub tanta quantitate, quanta potest competere ad usum fidelium; sic enim conformabitur intentio consecrantis intentioni ecclesiae. Sed hoc non videtur verum. Non enim potest dici, quod quantitas materiae sit determinata secundum usum qui in praesenti occurrit; quia sic sacerdos in deserto existens non posset conficere tot hostias, quot sacerdos alicujus civitatis habentis multos parochianos, quod falsum est; sed secundum usum qui nunquam occurrere potest. Tantum ergo de pane et vino potest consecrari, quantum est sumibile ab hominibus. Ad hoc autem non est quantitas determinata, praecipue cum unus homo possit sumere in magna et parva quantitate; unde quantitas parva vel magna ad hoc nihil facit.

AD PRIMUM ergo dicendum, quod sacramenta ad aliquid ordinantur; unde in sacramentis est duplex intentio. Una quae ordinatur ad perfectionem sacramenti; et haec est essentialis sacramento; unde ea praetermissa non est sacramentum. Alia quae ordinatur ad finem sacramenti; et haec consequitur sacramentum. Unde ea posita vel remota, nihilominus perficitur sacramentum; sicut si aliquis intendat baptizare aliquem ut lucrum temporale consequatur, sacramentum baptismi verum est, quia secundum primam intentionem conformatur intentioni ecclesiae, quamvis non quantum ad secundam. Et similiter in hoc sacramento si sacerdos intenderet consecrare non ad sumendum, sed ut in veneficiis uteretur, verum corpus Christi esset. Unde etsi aliquis sacerdos intenderet consecrare magnam quantitatem panis et vini non ad usum fidelium, sed in irrisionem, esset consecratum. Non tamen dico quod posset consecrare totum panem qui est in civitate simul, vel qui est in foro; quia ipsa forma pronomine demonstrativo utens, ostendit quod materia consecranda debet esse coram sacerdote. Unde sacerdos existens in domo sua non posset consecrare panem qui est in altari: quod non potest de toto pane qui est in foro, neque de toto vino quod est in cellario. Sed quantacumque sit quantitas panis et vini quae coram sacerdote proponitur, credo quod possit consecrari ab ipso.

AD SECUNDUM dicendum, quod potestas omnis a Deo est, ut dicitur Rom. 13, et quantum est de intentione dantis potestatem, ad bonum est ordinata; nihil tamen prohibet quin potestate accepta abutatur. Unde sicut praelati ecclesiae habent potestatem in aedificationem, et non in destructionem, tamen multa possunt facere quae sunt in destructionem; ita virtus consecrandi data est verbo et ministris ad Dei honorem; tamen potest aliquis abuti, ut ad irrisionem, vel ad lucrum, vel ad aliquid hujusmodi faciat.

AD TERTIUM dicendum, quod perfectio sacramenti in baptismo consistit in ipso usu materiae; et ideo il-

words to consecrate bread and wine under just any quantity, but under as large a quantity as can be suited to the use of the faithful, for in this way the intention of the one consecrating will be conformed to the Church's intention. But this does not seem to be true. For it cannot be said that the quantity of the matter is determined according to the use that happens in the present moment; for then a priest living in the desert could not consecrate so many hosts as a priest of some city having many parishioners, which is false, but he can consecrate according to a use that can never happen. Therefore, as much of the bread and wine can be consecrated as can be consumed by men. However, this is not a determinate quantity, particularly since one man can consume a large or a small quantity; hence a large or small quantity does not matter.

REPLY OBJ. 1: Sacraments are ordered to something; hence in the sacraments there is a twofold intention. One is directed to the completion of the sacrament, and this is essential to the sacrament; hence if it is omitted the sacrament does not exist. The other is directed to the sacrament's end; and this intention is subsequent to the sacrament. Hence, whether it is present or absent, nevertheless the sacrament is completed; just as if someone intends to baptize someone so that he may obtain temporal payment, the sacrament of baptism is valid, for according to the first intention it is conformed to the Church's intention, although not in the second intention. And likewise in this sacrament, if the priest intended to consecrate not for the sake of consuming, but so that it might be used in sorcery, it would be the true body of Christ. Hence even if some priest intended to consecrate a large quantity of bread and wine not for the use of the faithful, but in mockery, it would be consecrated. Now I do not say that he could consecrate all the bread that is in the city at one moment, or all the bread that is in the market; because the form itself, by using a demonstrative pronoun, shows that the matter to be consecrated must be before the priest. Hence a priest while in his own home could not consecrate the bread that is on the altar, which he cannot do for all the bread that is in the market or all the wine that is in the cellar. But however great is the quantity of bread and wine that is set before the priest, I believe that it can be consecrated by him.

REPLY OBJ. 2: All power is from God, as is said in Romans 13:1, and insofar as it is from the intention of the one giving the power, it is ordered to good. Nevertheless nothing prevents the power received from being abused. Hence just as the bishops of the Church have power for building and not for destruction, and yet they can do many things that are destructive, so the power of consecrating is given in the word and ministers for the honor of God; nevertheless, someone can abuse it, so that he does it for mockery, or for money, or something like that.

REPLY OBJ. 3: The completion of the sacrament in baptism consists in the very use of the matter; and so only that

lud tantum aquae consecratur verbo vitae quod in usum venit. Sed perfectio hujus sacramenti consistit in ipsa materiae consecratione, et usus est consequens ad hoc sacramentum; unde perfectio hujus sacramenti non dependet ab usu, sicut est in baptismo.

water is consecrated by the word of life that comes into use. But the completion of this sacrament consists in the very consecration of the matter, and the use comes after the sacrament; hence the completion of this sacrament does not depend on use, as it does in baptism.

ARTICLE 2

What kind of bread

Quaestiuncula 1

AD SECUNDUM SIC PROCEDITUR. Videtur quod non oportet quod sit panis triticeus. Hoc enim sacramentum est memoriale Dominicae Passionis. Sed magis competeret ad significandum passionem, panis hordei, quod est durum et hispidum, quam granum tritici, quod est delicatum. Ergo ex alio frumento panis confectus potest esse materia hujus sacramenti.

PRAETEREA, in omni aqua potest perfici sacramentum baptismi, ut nullus propter defectum materiae a sacramenti perceptione fraudetur. Ergo et similiter omnis panis debet esse materia hujus sacramenti, ut nullum inopia excuset.

PRAETEREA, figura in naturalibus est signum speciei. Sed quaedam frumenta sunt quae habent similem figuram grano tritici, sicut de farre et spelta. Ergo sunt ejusdem speciei cum grano tritici; et ita panis ex illis frumentis confectus poterit esse materia hujus sacramenti.

PRAETEREA, panis, materia hujus sacramenti est, quia ex multis granis confectus unitatem corporis mystici designat, ut supra, dist. 8, dictum est. Sed hoc etiam invenitur in pane de aliis frumentis confecto. Ergo ille panis potest esse materia hujus sacramenti.

SED CONTRA est usus ecclesiae, et hoc quod Dominus se grano frumenti comparavit Joan. 12, et non aliis leguminibus.

OBJ. 1: To the second we proceed thus. It seems that it is not necessary that the bread be from wheat.[65] For this sacrament is a memorial of the Lord's Passion. But more suited to signifying the Passion would be barley bread, because it is hard and rough, rather than the wheat grain, which is delicate. Therefore, bread made from a different grain can be the matter for this sacrament.

OBJ. 2: Furthermore, in any water the sacrament of baptism can be completed, so that no one is cheated of receiving this sacrament because of a lack of the matter. Therefore, in the same way all bread should be the matter for this sacrament, so that poverty would excuse no one.

OBJ. 3: Furthermore, in natural things shape is a sign of species. But there are certain grains that have a similar shape to the grain of wheat, like spelt and grits. Therefore, they are of the same species as the wheat grain, and so bread confected from these grains could be the matter for this sacrament.

OBJ. 4: Furthermore, bread is the matter of this sacrament, because it represents the oneness of the mystical body composed of many grains, as was said above in Distinction 8. But this is also found in bread made from other grains. Therefore, those breads can be the matter for this sacrament.

ON THE CONTRARY, is the practice of the Church, and the fact that the Lord compared himself to the grain of wheat in John 12:24, and not to other seeds.

Quaestiuncula 2

ULTERIUS. Videtur quod, si grano tritici admisceatur aliud frumentum quod possit panis exinde confectus esse materia hujus sacramenti. Quia in siccis commixtio non tollit speciem. Sed granum tritici et alia hujusmodi sunt sicca. Ergo si commisceantur, adhuc manet species tritici, et ita potest inde confici corpus Christi.

PRAETEREA, vix invenitur farina ex solis granis tritici, nisi studiose fiat. Si ergo ex farina commixta ex diversis granis non posset confici panis qui sit materia hujus sacramenti, rarissime hoc sacramentum perficeretur; quod est absurdum.

OBJ. 1: Moreover, it seems that if other grains are mixed in with the grains of wheat, the bread made from this can be the matter of this sacrament. For a mixture of dry things does not destroy the species. But a grain of wheat and other grains are dry. Therefore, if they are mixed together, the species of wheat still remains, and so the body of Christ can be consecrated from this.

OBJ. 2: Furthermore, flour of wheaten grains alone is seldom found unless one tries hard. Therefore, if the bread that is this sacrament's matter could not be made from a mixed flour of assorted grains, this sacrament would very rarely be performed, which is absurd.

---

65. Parallels: below, d. 19, q. 1, a. 2, qa. 3, ad 1; *ST* III, q. 74, a. 3; *SCG* IV, ch. 69; *De sacram. altar.*, ch. 10.

PRAETEREA, per corruptionem magis receditur a specie quam per commixtionem. Sed de pane corrupto potest fieri hoc sacramentum, cum videamus hostias diutissime a quibusdam conservari. Ergo multo magis de pane ex granis commixtis confecto potest perfici hoc sacramentum.

SED CONTRA, medium, neutrum extremorum est. Sed panis commixtus ex diversis granis, est medius inter panem tritici et aliorum granorum. Ergo non est panis triticeus; ergo de eo non potest perfici hoc sacramentum.

PRAETEREA, de amido, ut quidam dicunt, non potest perfici hoc sacramentum. Sed amidum est farina triticea pura. Ergo multo minus potest perfici hoc sacramentum de pane alterius farinae.

OBJ. 3: Furthermore, more is removed from a species by corruption than by admixture. But this sacrament can be done with corrupt bread, since we see hosts kept for an extremely long time by some people. Therefore, much more can this sacrament be performed with bread made from mixed grains.

ON THE CONTRARY, a middle is neither of its extremes. But bread mixed from assorted grains is a middle between bread from wheat and from other grains. Therefore, it is not wheaten bread; therefore this sacrament cannot be completed with it.

FURTHERMORE, this sacrament cannot be completed with wheatmeal, as some people say. But wheatmeal is pure wheaten flour. Therefore, much less can this sacrament be completed with a bread of another flour.

Quaestiuncula 3

ULTERIUS. Videtur quod non debeamus conficere in azymo, sed in fermentato. Nos enim debemus conficere secundum quod Christus confecit. Sed Christus confecit in fermentato, non in azymo. Ergo nec nos debemus in azymo conficere. Probatio mediae. Ante Pascha Judaei azymis non utebantur. Sed coena Domini, in qua hoc sacramentum inchoavit, fuit ante Pascha celebratum, ut patet Joan. 13, 1: *ante diem festum Paschae*, etc. Ergo ipse in fermentato, non in azymis confecit.

PRAETEREA, veritas debet respondere figurae. Sed agnus typicus immolabatur luna decimaquarta, ut habetur Exod. 12. Ergo Christus immolatus fuit luna decimaquarta. Sed in die praecedenti corpus suum dedit discipulis manducandum. Ergo hoc fuit luna decimatertia. Sed Pascha incipiebat luna decimaquarta. Ergo ante Pascha fuit coena Domini, et sic idem quod prius.

PRAETEREA, Joan. 18, dicitur, quod in die passionis Domini Judaei non intraverunt praetorium Pilati, ut non contaminarentur, sed ut manducarent Pascha. Ergo illa die a Judaeis manducabatur Pascha, et sic coena Domini fuit ante Pascha; et sic idem quod prius.

PRAETEREA, Luc. 23, dicitur, quod mulieres viso monumento iverunt, et paraverunt aromata. Sed hoc non licuisset prima die de septem quibus azyma comedebant, quia dies illa erat eis celeberrima, quae quidem dies erat luna decimaquinta. Ergo Christus passus est luna decimaquarta; et sic idem quod prius.

OBJ. 1: Moreover, it seems that we should not consecrate unleavened bread, but bread with leavening.[66] For we should consecrate according to how Christ consecrated. But Christ consecrated leavened bread, not unleavened. Therefore, neither should we consecrate unleavened bread. Proof of the middle: before Passover the Jews did not use unleavened bread. But the Lord's Supper, at which he established this sacrament, was celebrated before Passover, as is clear from John 13:1: *before the day of the Passover feast*, etc. Therefore, he used leavened bread, not unleavened.

OBJ. 2: Furthermore, the truth should correspond to the figure. But the figurative lamb was sacrificed on the fourteenth of the month, as Exodus 12:18 has it. Therefore, Christ was sacrificed on the fourteenth day of the month. But on the day before that he gave his body to his disciples to eat. Therefore it was on the thirteenth day of the month. But the Passover began on the fourteenth. Therefore, the Lord's Supper was before the Passover, and so, the same as above.

OBJ. 3: Furthermore, John 18:28 says that on the day of the Lord's Passion the Jews would not enter Pilate's praetorium, so that they would not be contaminated and so that they might eat the Passover. Therefore, on that day the Passover meal was eaten by the Jews, and so the Lord's Supper was before Passover; and so the same as above.

OBJ. 4: Furthermore, Luke 23:55–56 says that the women went out to visit the grave and prepared spices. But this would not have been permitted on the first day of the seven when they were eating unleavened bread, because that day was the greatest feast for them, which indeed was the fifteenth day. Therefore, Christ suffered on the fourteenth day, and so the same as before.

---

66. Parallels: *ST* III, q. 74, a. 4; *SCG* IV, ch. 69; *Contra errores Graec.*, pt. 2, ch. 39; *Super Ioan.* 13, lec. 1.

PRAETEREA, Joan. 19, dicitur, quod dies sepulturae Dominicae erat *magnus dies sabbati*. Sed in solemnitate azymorum sola prima dies erat celeberrima, et vocabatur magna. Ergo dies sabbati fuit prima dies solemnitatis, quod est luna decimaquinta; et sic dies Veneris fuit luna decimaquarta; et sic idem quod prius.

PRAETEREA, *artos* secundum Graecos significat panem fermentatum. Sed hoc nomen invenitur apud Graecos, ubi nos habemus, *accepit Jesus panes*. Ergo de fermentato confecit; et sic idem quod prius.

PRAETEREA, sacramenta veteris legis tempore revelatae gratiae observata ad litteram, sunt mortifera: quia *littera occidit*, 2 Cor. 3, 6. Sed hoc erat unum de legalibus, comedere in azymis. Ergo videtur esse mortiferum in azymis conficere.

PRAETEREA, hoc sacramentum est specialiter sacramentum caritatis. Sed fermentum caritatem significat, ut patet in Glossa Matth. 13, super illud: *simile est regnum caelorum fermento*, etc. Ergo maxime debet confici de fermentato.

PRAETEREA, sicut album et rubeum sunt accidentia vini; ita azymum et fermentatum sunt accidentia panis. Sed indifferenter conficitur de vino albo et rubeo. Ergo non magis debet attendi de pane an sit azymus vel fermentatus, quam de vino an sit album vel rubeum.

SED CONTRA, prima die azymorum nihil fermentatum esse debebat in domibus Judaeorum, ut patet Exod. 12. Sed Dominus confecit prima die azymorum, ut patet Matth. 26, Marc. 14, Luc. 22. Ergo ipse confecit de azymo; ergo et nos debemus de azymo conficere.

PRAETEREA, Christus non venit legem solvere, sed implere, ut dicitur Matth. 5. Sed secundum legem agnus paschalis comedebatur cum azymis, ut patet Exod. 12. Ergo Christus agnum paschalem cum azymis comedit. Ergo de azymo confecit.

PRAETEREA, materia debet convenire sacramento. Sed panis azymus magis competit huic sacramento quam fermentatus propter puritatem. 1 Cor. 5, 8: *epulemur non in fermento veteri, neque in fermento malitiae et nequitiae, sed in azymis sinceritatis et veritatis*. Ergo debet de pane azymo fieri sacramentum.

OBJ. 5: Furthermore, John 19:31 says that the day of the Lord's burial was *a great day of sabbath*. But in the solemnity of unleavened bread only the first day was the most festive, and it was called 'great'. Therefore, the day of the sabbath was the first day of the solemnity, which is the fifteenth of the month, and so the Friday was the fourteenth, and so the same as above.

OBJ. 6: Furthermore, according to the Byzantines, *artos* means leavened bread. But among the Byzantines, this word *artos* is found where we have, *Jesus took the bread*. Therefore, he consecrated leavened bread, and so the same as before.

OBJ. 7: Furthermore, the sacraments of the Old Law, if observed to the letter in the time of revealed grace, are deadly: for *the letter kills* (2 Cor 3:6). But this was one of the legal statutes, to eat unleavened bread. Therefore, it seems to be deadly to consecrate unleavened bread.

OBJ. 8: This sacrament is especially the sacrament of charity. But yeast represents charity, as is clear from the Gloss on that text: *the kingdom of heaven is like yeast*, etc. (Matt 13).[67] Therefore, it should most certainly be consecrated out of yeast bread.

OBJ. 9: Furthermore, just as white and red are accidents of wine, so unleavened and leavened are accidents of bread. But white wine and red wine can be equally consecrated. Therefore, we should pay no more attention to whether the bread is unleavened or leavened, than to whether the wine is white or red.

ON THE CONTRARY, on the first day of unleavened bread nothing with yeast should have been found in the homes of the Jews, as is evident from Exodus 12:15. But the Lord consecrated on the first day of unleavened bread, as is evident from Matthew 26:17, Mark 14:12, and Luke 22:7. Therefore, he consecrated unleavened bread; therefore, we also must consecrate unleavened bread.

FURTHERMORE, Christ did not come to destroy the law but to fulfill it, as it says in Matthew 5:17. But according to the law the Paschal lamb was eaten with unleavened bread, as is evident from Exodus 12:8. Therefore, Christ ate the Paschal lamb with unleavened bread. Therefore, he consecrated unleavened bread.

FURTHERMORE, the matter should be fitting to the sacrament. But bread without yeast is more suited to the sacrament than bread with yeast, because of its purity: *Let us not feast on the old yeast, the yeast of malice and wickedness, but with the unleavened bread of sincerity and truth* (1 Cor 5:8). Therefore the sacrament should be performed with unleavened bread.

---

67. See the *Glossa ordinaria*, PL 114:133.

Response to Quaestiuncula 1

RESPONDEO dicendum ad primam quaestionem, quod non potest confici nisi de pane triticeo; cujus causa est divina institutio, quia ipse hoc pane confecit. Ratio autem institutionis potest triplex assignari. Prima ex effectu; quia talis panis melius nutrimentum praestat; unde competit ad significandum excellentiam gratiae quae in hoc sacramento confertur. Secunda ex usu sacramenti: quia panis triticeus est qui communius in usum cibi venit, alii autem panes non fiunt nisi propter defectum tritici; unde et panis simpliciter dictus intelligitur de tritico, sicut et oleum de olivis; unde competit huic sacramento, cujus usus est in manducando, ut supra, dist. 9, dictum est. Tertia ex re contenta, quae est Christus, qui se grano frumenti comparavit dicens, Joan. 12, 24: *nisi granum frumenti cadens in terram mortuum fuerit, ipsum solum manet.*

AD PRIMUM ergo dicendum, quod in passione Christi non fuit aliqua duritia ex parte Christi qui patiebatur, sed summa benignitas; et quia hostia panis significat et continet ipsum Christum, ideo non ita competit huic sacramento panis hordeaceus, vel alterius modi, sicut panis triticeus, qui est delicatior et suavior.

AD SECUNDUM dicendum, quod omnis aqua omni aquae est eadem specie, secundum Philosophum; et ideo non differt in quacumque aqua baptismus fiat. Sed non omnia grana ex quibus panis consuevit confici, sunt ejusdem speciei; et ideo non est similis ratio utrobique. Et praeterea sacramentum istud non est tantae necessitatis sicut sacramentum baptismi, ut prius dictum est, dist. 9, qu. 1, art. 1, quaestiunc. 2.

AD TERTIUM dicendum, quod quidam dicunt, quod de spelta potest confici corpus Christi propter similitudinem quam habet ad triticum. Sed, sicut patet intuenti, quantum ad figuram plus appropinquat hordeum ad similitudinem tritici quam spelta, amoto cortice ab utroque, quamvis in colore plus spelta conveniat; sed inter alia omnia hujusmodi plus convenit, maxime in figura, far cum tritico, et similiter in colore. Unde ex identitate figurae non potest haberi quod aliquod istorum sit ejusdem speciei cum grano tritici; sed identitatis speciei potest ex alio experimentum accipi. Generans enim et genitum conveniunt de necessitate in specie, sed non de necessitate in accidentibus, quinimmo accidentia variantur ex causis extrinsecis; unde cum ex grano tritici, ubicumque seminetur, nunquam nascatur spelta vel far aut hordeum, vel aliquid hujusmodi, constat quod omnino ista differunt specie a tritico.

AD QUARTUM dicendum, quod illud quod objectio tangit, est causa quare ex pane fit hoc sacramentum, non

TO THE FIRST QUESTION, I answer that only wheaten bread can be consecrated, and the reason for this is divine institution, for Christ consecrated this bread. But three reasons can be assigned for this institution. The first is from the effect, because this kind of bread provides better nourishment, and so it pertains to signifying the excellence of grace that is conferred in this sacrament. The second is from the use of the sacrament: for wheaten bread is what is more commonly available for use as food, while other breads are only made when there is a lack of wheat. And so 'bread', simply speaking, is understood to be from wheat, as oil from olives, and so it is suited to this sacrament, whose use is in eating, as was said above. The third comes from the reality contained, which is Christ, who compared himself to a grain of wheat, saying, *unless a grain of wheat falls to the earth and dies, it remains just a single grain* (John 12:24).

REPLY OBJ. 1: In Christ's Passion there was not any hardness on the part of Christ who was suffering, but the greatest kindness. And so the host of bread signifies and contains Christ himself, which is why barley bread, or another kind, is not so suited to this sacrament as wheaten bread, which is sweeter and more delicate.

REPLY OBJ. 2: All water is the same species as all other water, according to the Philosopher;[68] and so it does not matter in which water a baptism happens. But not all grains out of which bread is usually made are of the same species, and so the reasoning is not the same for both. And furthermore, this sacrament is not of such great necessity as the sacrament of baptism, as was said above, in Distinction 9, Question 1, Article 1, Subquestion 2.

REPLY OBJ. 3: Some people say that the body of Christ can be consecrated out of spelt bread, because of the resemblance it has to wheat. But, as is clear upon closer inspection, in its shape barley is closer to the likeness of wheat than spelt is, when the husk is removed from either, although in color spelt is more like. But among all the other things like this wheatmeal shares the most in shape with wheat, and likewise in color. And this is why from an identical shape it cannot be held that any of these is the same species as the grain of wheat; but it can be taken for an identical species by another test. For what generates and what is generated necessarily share in species, but not necessarily in accidents, for indeed accidents are varied by extrinsic causes. And this is why since when a grain of wheat is sown anywhere, neither spelt nor barley nor wheatmeal nor anything like them ever grows, it is clear that they are entirely different in species from wheat.

REPLY OBJ. 4: What that objection refers to is the reason why this sacrament is done from bread, but not why it

---

68. Aristotle, *Metaphysics*, Bk. 5, ch. 6 (1016a20).

autem quare ex tali pane; sed hanc oportet superaddere sicut proprium ad commune.

uses this bread; and this must be added as the proper to the common.

Response to Quaestiuncula 2

AD SECUNDAM QUAESTIONEM dicendum, quod admixtio extranei dupliciter potest esse: uno modo ita quod extraneum adjunctum solvat speciem ejus cui adjungitur, vel trahendo ad speciem suam, sicut si amphorae aquae adderetur phiala vini; vel faciendo mediam speciem, sicut quando utrumque aequaliter ponitur, ut aequalitas non accipiatur[69] secundum quantitatem, sed secundum proportionem virtutis. Alio modo ita quod additum non solvat speciem, sed ipsum assumatur ad speciem ejus cui additur; sicut si gutta aquae amphorae vini apponatur. Si ergo fiat tanta admixtio extranei quod solvatur species panis triticei, non poterit confici ex pane illo; si autem adeo sit parva admixtio quod species panis triticei maneat, et illud quod additur, ad naturam tritici convertatur, potest exinde confici sacramentum. Hujus autem signum potest accipi ex accidentibus, scilicet colore, sapore, et hujusmodi; quia accidentia maximam partem conferunt ad cognoscendum quod quid est, secundum Philosophum in 1 *de Anima.*

AD PRIMUM ergo dicendum, quod quamvis sicca, quando integra manent, non amittant speciem ex permixtione, tamen quando dividuntur et conficiuntur, sicut in pane accidit, possunt speciem amittere.

AD SECUNDUM patet solutio ex distinctione praedicta.

AD TERTIUM dicendum, quod si sit tanta corruptio quod species panis non maneat, tunc non potest ex eo confici; si autem specie manente sit aliqua dispositio ad corruptionem, potest exinde confici; quamvis graviter peccet conficiens ex tali scienter propter irreverentiam sacramenti. Et quod species maneat, potest ex hoc cognosci, quod continuitas non est soluta, nec alia accidentia omnino ablata. Et quia amidum fit de farina triticea, quae quidem per attritionem et excolationem et vaporis admixtionem videtur speciem farinae amisisse, vel ad corruptionem omnino esse disposita; ideo ex ea non debet confici, nec potest, secundum quosdam. Quidam autem dicunt, quod amidum cum sit crudum, non potest esse materia hujus sacramenti, sicut nec pasta. Sed si coquatur, poterit exinde confici, quia amidum fit ex farina maxime depurata.

TO THE SECOND QUESTION, it should be said that there are two ways of mixing something extraneous into something: in one way so that the extraneous additive dissolves the species of what it was added to, either by drawing it into its own species, as when a cup of wine is added to a pitcher of water; or by making a middle species, as when both are added equally, so that the equality is not taken only according to quantity, but according to the proportion of strength. In another way such that what is added does not dissolve the species, but it is assumed into the species of what it was added to; as when a drop of water is added to a pitcher of wine. Therefore, if such an admixture of something foreign was made that the species of wheaten bread is dissolved, it could not be consecrated from that bread; but if it were just such a small admixture that the species of wheaten bread remained, and what is added is converted to the nature of wheat, then the sacrament can be consecrated from this. Now the sign of this can be taken from the accidents, namely, color, flavor, and things like that; for the accidents contribute the greatest part to knowing what something is, according to the Philosopher in *On the Soul* 1.[70]

REPLY OBJ. 1: Although dry things, while they remain whole, do not lose their species by combining, nevertheless, when they are ground up and stirred together, as happens in bread, they can lose their species.

REPLY OBJ. 2: The solution is clear from what has been said.

REPLY OBJ. 3: If there is so much corruption that the species of bread does not remain, then the sacrament cannot be consecrated from this; but if there were a certain disposition to corruption while the species remained, it can be consecrated from this bread, although he would sin gravely who knowingly consecrated bread like that, because of irreverence for the sacrament. And that the species remained can be recognized by this, that continuity has not dissolved, nor are the other accidents entirely taken away. And since wheatmeal is made from wheat flour, which indeed by grinding and sifting and mixing in steam seems to have lost the appearance of flour, or to be entirely disposed to corruption, this is why it should not be made out of it, nor can it, according to certain people. However, some people say that when wheatmeal is raw, it cannot be the matter for this sacrament, just as neither can dough. But if it is cooked, it could be made from this, because wheatmeal is made from the most purified flour.

---

69. *accipiatur secundum.—accipiatur tantum secundum* PLE.
70. Aristotle, *On the Soul*, Bk. 1, ch. 1 (402b21).

Response to Quaestiuncula 3

AD TERTIAM QUAESTIONEM dicendum, quod in hoc videtur esse diversitas inter Graecos et Latinos: Graeci enim de fermentato, Latini de azymo conficiunt. Causa autem hujus diversitatis est, quia Dominus in azymo confecit, ut ex tribus Evangelistis habetur manifeste, et ita in primitiva ecclesia apostoli celebrabant; quem morem Romana ecclesia ab apostolis, qui ipsam fundaverunt, accepit, ut Innocentius 3 dicit. Sed postea, ut dicit Leo Papa imminente haeresi Ebionitarum, qui dicebant simul cum Evangelio legalia observanda, sancti patres ne eis consentire viderentur, voluerunt ad tempus instinctu Spiritus Sancti ex fermentato confici sacramentum: postea cessante illa haeresi, ecclesia Romana ad pristinum morem rediit.

Graeci autem servare voluerunt morem ad tempus a patribus introductum, ulterius addentes non posse confici nisi de fermentato: et ad hoc probandum asserere voluerunt Dominum in fermentato confecisse. Et quia tres Evangelistae concorditer dicunt, prima die azymorum Dominum instituisse hoc sacramentum, in tantam infamiam quidam ex eis proruperunt, ut dicerent, Evangelistas illos falsum scripsisse, et a Joanne fuisse correctos qui ante diem Paschae dicit Dominum coenasse cum discipulis.

Sed quod hoc non contradicat, ostendetur. Supposito autem quod Dominus decimatertia luna, ut dicunt, coenam celebrasset, adhuc evidenter ostenditur quod azymo confecit; quia, sicut dicit Chrysostomus super Matth., *apertissime Dominus demonstravit, quia a principio circumcisionis suae usque ad diem Paschae extremum, non erat contrarius divinarum legum, in quibus praecipiebatur ut cum azymis paschalis agnus comederetur.* Et ideo dicendum est, quod Dominus in azymo confecit, et in azymo conficiendum est, quamvis etiam in fermentato confici possit; quamvis peccaret conficiens, ecclesiae morem non servans.

AD PRIMUM ergo dicendum, quod verbum illud Joannis, Graeci hoc modo intelligunt, sicut in objectio procedit. Sed hic intellectus stare non potest, quia est contrarius aliis Evangelistis, quod non est fas in sacra Scriptura dicere. Praeterea non invenitur in lege quod aliquo casu liceret anticipare lunam decimam quartam, sicut dicunt Dominum fecisse praevidens passionem. Unde quidam dixerunt, quod coena qua Dominus la-

TO THE THIRD QUESTION, it should be said that in this there seems to be a difference between Latins and Byzantines: for the Byzantines consecrate bread with yeast, while the Latins consecrate unleavened bread. Now the reason for this difference is that the Lord consecrated unleavened bread, as is manifestly known from the three Gospel writers, and this is how the apostles celebrated it in the early Church, which practice the Roman church received from the apostles, who founded it, as Innocent III says.[71] But afterward, as Pope Leo says,[72] at the threat of the heresy of the Ebionites, who said that the prescripts of the law had to be observed together with the Gospel, the holy fathers, lest they seem to agree with the Ebionites, at the prompting of the Holy Spirit wanted the sacrament to be consecrated from yeast bread for a time. After that heresy had ceased, the Roman church returned to the original practice.

The Byzantines wished to preserve the practice introduced by the fathers for a time, and they added further that only yeast bread can be consecrated, and to prove this they wished to assert that the Lord had consecrated yeast bread. And because three Gospel writers say in agreement that the Lord instituted this sacrament on the first day of the feast of unleavened bread, some of them have charged into such disgrace as to say that those Gospel writers wrote something false, and they were corrected by John who says that the Lord supped with his disciples on the day before Passover.

But it will be shown how this does not contradict. For once it is supposed that the Lord celebrated the Last Supper on the thirteenth of the month, as they say, it is obviously shown that he still consecrated unleavened bread, for as Chrysostom comments on Matthew, *the Lord demonstrated most openly that from the beginning of his own circumcision until the last day of the Passover he was not the opponent of divine laws, among which it was commanded that the paschal lamb be eaten with unleavened bread.*[73] And so it should be said that the Lord consecrated unleavened bread, and unleavened bread is to be consecrated, although yeast bread can also be consecrated; however, whoever did consecrate it would sin by not observing the practice of the Church.

REPLY OBJ. 1: The Byzantines understand those words of John in the way that the objection proceeds. But this understanding cannot stand, for it is contrary to the other Gospel writers, which is not right to say about sacred Scripture. Furthermore, it is not found in the Law that it was permitted in any case to anticipate the fourteenth day of the month, as they say the Lord did in foreseeing his Passion. And this is why certain people say that the Supper at which

---

71. Innocent III, *De sacro altaris mysterio*, Bk. 4, ch. 4 (PL 217:857–58).
72. Leo IX, *Epistle to Michael, Emperor of Constantinople.*
73. John Chrysostom, *Homilies on Matthew*, ch. 26 (PG 56:730).

vit discipulorum pedes, et qua corpus suum consecravit, non fuit eadem, sed una aliam praecessit; et de prima loquitur Joannes, de secunda alii Evangelistae. Sed hoc est contra usum ecclesiae, quae die Jovis ablutionem pedum celebrat, et etiam contra textum Evangelii: quia sicut ex serie Evangelii Joannis apparet, eodem sero quo pedes lavit, a Juda post bucellam recedente traditus est. Et ideo dicendum est, quod dies festus Paschae vocabatur prima dies de septem quae erat celeberrima, et haec erat decimaquinta luna, et in vespere praecedenti immolabatur et comedebatur agnus, luna decimaquarta, cum azymis; et tunc Dominus coenam fecit cum discipulis suis; et hanc diem dicunt alii Evangelistae primam diem azymorum, et Joannes *ante diem festum Paschae.*

AD SECUNDUM dicendum, quod non oportet quod veritas responderet figurae quantum ad omnia; alioquin oportebit nos dicere, quod Dominus ad vesperam passus sit, quia tunc immolabatur agnus, quod est contra omnes Evangelistas; sed quantum ad aliquid veritas figurae respondet; quia quamvis ante Christi resurrectionem dies a mane in mane computaretur, sicut in 2 Lib., dist. 13, dictum est, tamen hoc erat speciale in solemnitatibus legis quod computatur dies a vespera in vesperam. Unde vespera quartaedecimae diei computabatur quantum ad solemnitatem in numero dierum cum quintadecima, in qua Dominus passus est; et etiam immolatio ejus vespere quartaedecimae diei quodammodo inchoavit; quia tunc traditus fuit, et tunc factus est sudor ejus sanguineus, ut dicitur Luc. 22.

AD TERTIUM dicendum, quod Pascha accipitur ibi pro cibis paschalibus, scilicet azymis, qui per omnes septem dies comedebantur. Chrysostomus tamen dicit super Joan., quod intelligitur de agno paschali, quem in alia die ab ea quam lex instituit, comederunt, et legem solverunt, ut animi sui adimplerent desiderium in morte Christi. Christus autem non praeteriit tempus Paschae, diem scilicet Jovis, sed in ipso Pascha comedit.

AD QUARTUM dicendum, quod nulla dies erat adeo celebris quantum ad vacationem ab operibus, sicut dies sabbati; unde in prima die solemnitatis licebat coquere cibos et alia hujusmodi facere quod non licebat facere sabbatis; et ideo mulieres feria sexta paraverunt aromata, videntes quod non sufficerent quae per Nicodemum parata erant; et sabbato secundum legem quieverunt; et transeunte sabbato emerunt aromata, idest empta paraverunt, vel etiam alia superemerunt, videntes non sufficere quae prius feria sexta paraverant, et venerunt ad

the Lord washed his disciples' feet and at which he consecrated his body, were not the same, but one preceded the other, and John speaks of the first, while the other Gospel writers speak of the second. But this is against the practice of the Church, which celebrates the washing of the feet on Holy Thursday; and it is also against the text of the Gospel, for just as appears from the sequence of John's Gospel,[74] at the same late hour that he washed the feet, he was betrayed by Judas after he took the morsel of food. And so it should be said that the feast day of Passover was called the first day of the seven that were the high feast, and this was the fifteenth of the month, and on the previous evening the lamb had been sacrificed and eaten, the fourteenth of the month, with unleavened bread. And that was when the Lord had a supper with his disciples, and the other Gospel writers call this day the first day of unleavened bread, and John calls it *the day before the Passover feast.*

REPLY OBJ. 2: It is not necessary that truth correspond to a figure in all things, otherwise it would be necessary for us to say that the Lord suffered in the evening, because that was when the lamb was sacrificed, which is against all the Gospel writers. But truth corresponds to the figure in something, for although before Christ's resurrection the days were calculated from one morning to another, as was said in Book II, Distinction 13, yet this was specific to solemnities of the law that a day is calculated from one evening to the next. Hence the evening of the fourteenth day was counted for the solemnity in the number of days with the fifteenth, on which the Lord suffered. And also his sacrifice began in a certain way on the evening of the fourteenth day, for he was handed over then, and that was when his sweat became like blood, as it says in Luke 22:44.

REPLY OBJ. 3: Passover is taken there for the paschal foods, like unleavened bread, which were eaten for all seven days. Nevertheless Chrysostom comments on John[75] that it is understood of the paschal lamb which they ate on a different day from the one that the law instituted, and they observed the law, so that their souls would be filled with longing for the death of Christ. However, Christ did not go beyond the time of Passover, namely, the Thursday, but on that day ate the Passover.

REPLY OBJ. 4: No day was so solemn in the exemption from work as the day of the sabbath. And this is why on the first day of the solemnity it was permitted to cook food and do other things like that, which would not be permitted on the sabbath. And so the women prepared spices on the sixth day, seeing that those prepared by Nicodemus were not enough, and they rested on the sabbath according to the law, and once the sabbath was over they bought spices, i.e., they prepared the spices they had bought or even bought more, seeing that those they had prepared before on

---

74. Chapter 13.
75. John Chrysostom, *Commentary on John*, homily 83, n. 3 (PG 69:367).

monumentum. Vel secundum quosdam, opera misericordiae non reputantur inter opera servilia; unde in die solemni licebat aromata ad sepulturam praeparare, quia hoc erat opus misericordiae.

AD QUINTUM dicendum, quod quocumque die de septem diebus azymorum sabbatum veniret, dicebatur magnus dies sabbati propter geminatam solemnitatem, scilicet sabbati et Paschae.

AD SEXTUM dicendum, quod *artos* apud Graecos quandoque etiam pro azymo pane ponitur; et ideo Exod. 12, dicitur in Graecos *artos* ubi nos habemus *panes azymos.*

AD SEPTIMUM dicendum, quod facere aliquid quod in lege fiebat, ut dicit Anselmus, non est judaizare; alioquin et ipsi judaizant conficientes ex fermentato, quia in lege praeceptum erat ut panes primitiarum fermentatos offerent. Sed facere aliquid hac intentione ut legalia observentur, est judaizare. Nos autem non ob hoc ex azymo conficimus ut legem servemus, sed ut Christo conformemur, servantes hoc quod huic competit sacramento ab eo instituto. Significatur enim in azymo puritas vitae, quae semper servanda est, sicut et in thurificatione devotio orationis; unde utrumque in lege nova retinetur.

AD OCTAVUM dicendum, quod in hoc sacramento continetur Christus ut hostia: et quia puritas praecipue in hostia, etiam secundum legem, exigebatur; ideo magis competit huic sacramento ut significetur Christi puritas per panem azymum, quam quod significetur fervor caritatis per fermentum.

AD NONUM dicendum, quod album et rubeum non ita faciunt differentiam in significatione sacramenti circa vinum, sicut azymum et fermentatum circa panem; et ideo non est similis ratio de utroque.

the sixth day were not enough, and they came to the tomb. Or, according to some people, works of mercy are not considered servile work, and so they were allowed to prepare spices for a tomb on a solemn day, because this was a work of mercy.

REPLY OBJ. 5: On whatever day of the seven days of unleavened bread the sabbath should come, it was called a great day of sabbath because of the twin solemnities, namely, the sabbath and Passover.

REPLY OBJ. 6: *Artos* among the Greeks is sometimes also defined as unleavened bread; and thus in Exodus 12 in Greek it says *artos* where we have *unleavened bread.*

REPLY OBJ. 7: To do something that was done under the law, as Anselm says,[76] is not to live like a Jew; otherwise those who consecrated yeast bread, too, are living like Jews, because in the law it was commanded that they offer the breads of first leavening. But to do something with this intention, that the prescripts of the law should be observed, is to live like a Jew. However, we do not consecrate unleavened bread so that we may keep the law, but so that we might be conformed to Christ, observing what befits this sacrament instituted by him. For unleavened bread signifies purity of life, which must always be observed, just as also incensing signifies devotion of prayer; and so both of these are retained in the New Law.

REPLY OBJ. 8: In this sacrament Christ is contained as victim: and since purity was particularly required in the victim, even according to the law, for that reason it was more fitting to this sacrament that Christ's purity be signified by unleavened bread than that the fervor of charity be signified by yeast bread.

REPLY OBJ. 9: White and red do not make such a difference in the signification of the sacrament concerning the wine as unleavened and yeast concerning the bread; and so the argument is not the same for both.

---

76. Anselm, *De fermentato et azymo*, ch. 4 (PL 158:544).

Article 3

What kind of wine can be the matter of this sacrament[77]

Quaestiuncula 1

Ad tertium sic proceditur. Videtur quod non solum de vino vitis debeat sanguis Christi consecrari. Baptismus enim in qualibet aqua fieri potest. Sed vinum est materia hujus sacramenti, sicut aqua baptismi. Ergo et de quolibet vino potest hoc sacramentum fieri, sicut de vino malorum granatorum vel mororum vel hujusmodi.

Praeterea, in aliquibus terris non sunt vites, nec ad eas de facili vinum portari potest. Ergo debuit a divina sapientia provideri ut alius aliquis liquor in loco vini de vite possit in sacramento assumi.

Sed contra, sicut Dominus se comparavit grano frumenti, Joan. 12, ita comparavit se viti, Joan. 15. Ergo sicut non debet in hoc sacramento assumi nisi panis de tritico, ita nec vinum nisi de vite.

Obj. 1: To the third we proceed thus. It seems that Christ's blood does not have to be consecrated only from wine from grapes. For baptism can happen in any water. But wine is this sacrament's matter just as water is baptism's. Therefore, this sacrament can also be done with any wine, like the wine of pomegranates, or mulberries, or the like.

Obj. 2: Furthermore, in some lands there are no grapevines, nor can wine be easily carried to them. Therefore, it must have been provided by divine wisdom that some other liquor can be taken in this sacrament in place of grape wine.

On the contrary, just as the Lord compared himself to a grain of wheat, in John 12:24, so he also compared himself to a vine, in John 15:1. Therefore, just as nothing but wheat bread should be taken in this sacrament, so also no wine but grape wine.

Quaestiuncula 2

Ulterius. Videtur quod possit etiam confici de aceto. Quia, secundum Isidorum, acetum est species vini. Sed de vino vitis potest confici hoc sacramentum. Ergo et de aceto.

Praeterea, si vinum consecratum in acetum converteretur, non desineret ibi esse Christi sanguis. Ergo eadem ratione si ante consecrationem sit acetum, potest exinde sanguis Christi consecrari.

Sed contra, Innocentius dicit, quod *vinum huic sacramento competit: quia cor bibentis et dilatat et exhilarat.* Sed hoc non facit acetum. Ergo ex aceto non potest consecrari sanguis Christi.

Obj. 1: Moreover, it seems that it can also be consecrated from vinegar. For according to Isidore, vinegar is a species of wine.[78] But this sacrament can be consecrated from wine of the vine. Therefore also with vinegar.

Obj. 2: Furthermore, if consecrated wine turned into vinegar, it would not cease to be Christ's blood. Therefore, by the same reasoning if it be vinegar before the consecration, Christ's blood can be consecrated from it.

On the contrary, Innocent says that *wine befits this sacrament: for the heart of the one drinking is enlarged and exhilarated.*[79] But vinegar does not do this. Therefore, the blood of Christ cannot be consecrated from vinegar.

Quaestiuncula 3

Ulterius. Videtur quod de agresta possit sanguis Christi consecrari. Sicut enim agresta non habet speciem perfectam vini, ita nec mustum. Sed de musto dulci

Obj. 1: Moreover, it seems that the blood of Christ may be consecrated from verjuice.[80] For just as verjuice does not have the complete species of wine, so neither does must.

---

77. Parallels: *ST* III, q. 74, a. 5; *SCG* IV, ch. 69.

78. Isidore, *Etymologiarum siue Originum* (ed. Lindsay), Bk. 20, ch. 3, n. 9.

79. Innocent III, *De sacro altaris mysterio*, Bk. 4, ch. 3 (PL 217:854).

80. *Agresta* or verjuice is the juice of unripe grapes. Thus verjuice has not attained the maturity of grape juice, which is needed for the first step in the wine-making process.

potest confici sanguis Christi; dicitur enim *de Consecr.*, dist. 2: *si necesse fuerit, botrus in calice prematur.* Ergo et eadem ratione de agresta.

PRAETEREA, agresta non differt a vino nisi quia immatura est. Sed maturitas et immaturitas sunt accidentia. Ergo non differunt secundum speciem; et ita videtur quod ex agresta sicut ex vino indifferenter sanguis Christi consecrari possit.

SED CONTRA, quod fit, non est, secundum Philosophum. Sed agresta est in via generationis respectu vini. Ergo nondum est vinum; ergo ex ea non potest sanguis Christi consecrari.

But the blood of Christ can be consecrated from sweet must, for it is said in the *Decretals, On Consecration,* Distinction 2, *if it were necessary, a bunch of grapes may be pressed in the chalice.*[81] Therefore, by the same reasoning, also verjuice.

OBJ. 2: Furthermore, verjuice only differs from wine in that it is immature. But maturity and immaturity are accidents. Therefore, it does not differ according to species, and so it seems that the blood of Christ can be equally consecrated from verjuice as from wine.

ON THE CONTRARY, what is still becoming, is not yet, according to the Philosopher.[82] But verjuice is in the process of generation toward wine. Therefore, it is not yet wine, and therefore the blood of Christ cannot be consecrated from it.

Response to Quaestiuncula 1

RESPONDEO dicendum ad primam quaestionem, quod non potest confici sanguis Christi nisi de vino vitis, quia hoc proprie vinum est. Alia vero dicuntur vina per similitudinem hujus vini. Hoc etiam vinum communius sumitur in potum, sicut et panis tritici in cibum; et habet proprietates magis convenientes ad effectum sacramenti, inquantum calefacit et laetificat; et ideo Dominus de vino vitis confecit, ut patet per hoc quod dicitur Matth. 26, 29: *amodo non bibam de hoc genimine vitis.*

AD PRIMUM ergo dicendum, quod omnis aqua est ejusdem speciei; sed non sic est de vino.

AD SECUNDUM dicendum, quod non est aliqua terra ad quam non possit tantum de vino portari quantum sufficeret ad celebrandum; unde illa ratio non cogit.

TO THE FIRST QUESTION, I answer that the blood of Christ can be consecrated only from wine of the grapevine, for that is properly wine. But other things are called wine by their likeness to this wine. This wine is also taken more commonly as a drink, just as wheat bread as food. And it has properties more fitting to the sacrament's effect inasmuch as it warms and delights; and this is why the Lord consecrated wine of the grapevine, as is clear from what is said, *from now on I shall not drink of the fruit of the vine* (Matt 26:29).

REPLY OBJ. 1: All water is of the same species, but that is not how it is with wine.

REPLY OBJ. 2: There is no land to which enough wine cannot be carried for celebrating Mass, and so that argument is not compelling.

Response to Quaestiuncula 2

AD SECUNDAM QUAESTIONEM dicendum, quod secundum Philosophum, in 8 *Metaphysica*, hoc modo fit ex vino acetum, quo ex vivo fit mortuum; unde sicut animal vivum et mortuum non sunt ejusdem speciei, ita nec vinum et acetum; et hoc ostendunt contrariae proprietates: quia vinum est calidum, acetum autem frigidum; et non fit reditus de aceto in vinum, sicut nec de mortuo ad vivum. Et ideo dicendum, quod si vinum sit omnino factum sit acetum, de eo non potest confici; sed si sit acidum quasi in via acescendi, est idem judicium quod de pane qui in via est ad corruptionem; unde sicut de pane

TO THE SECOND QUESTION, it should be said that according to the Philosopher in *Metaphysics* 8,[83] vinegar comes to be from wine in the same way that something dead comes to be from something living. Hence, just as a living animal and a dead one are not of the same species, so neither are wine and vinegar. And the contrary properties show this: for wine is warm, but vinegar is cold; and there is no return from vinegar to wine, just as there is no returning to life from death. And so it should be said that if the wine has become entirely vinegar, it cannot be consecrated. But if it is acid as though in the process of turning sour, the

---

81. Gratian's *Decretals*, Part 3, *De consecratione*, d. 2, ch. 7 (PL 187:1733).
82. Aristotle, *Physics*, Bk. 5, ch. 1 (225a27).
83. Aristotle, *Metaphysics*, Bk. 8, ch. 5 (1044b34–1045a6).

illo potest confici, peccat tamen conficiens propter irreverentiam, ita et hic.

AD PRIMUM ergo dicendum, quod ipse largo modo accipit vinum pro omni liquore qui ex uvis ortum habet.

AD SECUNDUM dicendum, quod si vinum consecratum reservatum omnino acetum fieret, esset idem judicium quod de pane omnino corrupto; unde sicut non remanet ibi corpus Christi, ita nec hic sanguis. Secus autem est de pane qui est in via ad corruptionem, et de vino quod est in via ad acescendum.

judgment is the same as of bread that is in the process of corrupting. And so just as that bread can be consecrated, but the one consecrating sins because of irreverence, so also here.

REPLY OBJ. 1: He takes wine in a broad way for any liquid that arises from grapes.

REPLY OBJ. 2: If consecrated wine that has been reserved becomes vinegar entirely, the judgment would be the same of it as of bread that is completely corrupted; hence just as the body of Christ does not remain in that case, so neither does the blood remain in this one. But it is otherwise with bread that is in the process of corrupting, and wine that is in the process of going sour.

Response to Quaestiuncula 3

AD TERTIAM QUAESTIONEM dicendum, quod nihil recipit speciem nisi in termino generationis: agresta autem adhuc est in via generationis ad vinum, sicut sanguis quando coagulari incipit, est in via generationis ad animal; unde sicut ille sanguis non est animal, ita agresta non est vinum; et propter hoc de ipsa non potest confici sanguis Christi.

AD PRIMUM ergo dicendum, quod mustum jam ad completam speciem vini venit: dulcedo enim ipsius attestatur maturationem quae est digestionis species; digestio autem est completio a naturali calore, ut patet in 4 Meteor.; et ideo ex musto confici potest, sed non decet, propter impuritatem ipsius, ut ex ipso conficiatur, nisi necessitas emergat.

AD SECUNDUM dicendum, quod maturatio est naturalis digestio, per quam digestum ad ultimam perfectionem naturalem perducitur, ut etiam possit alterum generare sibi simile, ut dicitur in 4 *Meteor.*; unde maturum et acerbum differunt sicut completum et incompletum: quae quidem differentia non est tantum accidentalis.

TO THE THIRD QUESTION, it should be said that nothing receives its species except at the terminus of generation: but verjuice is still on the way to generating wine, just as blood when it begins to come together is on the way to generating an animal. And so just as that blood is not an animal, so verjuice is not wine; and because of this the blood of Christ cannot be consecrated from it.

REPLY OBJ. 1: Must has already arrived at the complete species of wine: for its sweetness attests to a maturation that is a species of digestion. Now digestion is the completion of natural heat, as is clear from *Meteorology* 4,[84] and so one can consecrate with must, but it is not as seemly, because of its impurity, that it be consecrated, unless the necessity arises.

REPLY OBJ. 2: Maturation is natural digestion, by which what is digested is brought to its final natural perfection, so that it also is able to generate something else like itself, as is said in *Meteorology* 4.[85] And so mature and sour differ as complete and incomplete: which in fact is not merely an accidental difference.

---

84. Aristotle, *Meteorology*, Bk. 4, ch. 2 (379b18).
85. Ibid., ch. 3 (380a14–15).

ARTICLE 4

About the mixing in of water

Quaestiuncula 1

AD QUARTUM SIC PROCEDITUR. Videtur quod aqua vino admiscenda non sit. De latere enim Domini in cruce pendentis effluxit sanguis et aqua, ut dicitur Joan. 19; per quae duo, sacramenta praecipue intelliguntur, ut dicit Innocentius. Sed aqua competit sacramento regenerationis, scilicet baptismo. Ergo sanguis tantum competit sacramento redemptionis Eucharistiae; et ita vinum sine aqua.

PRAETEREA, vinum et aqua sunt alterius speciei. Si ergo aqua admiscetur vino, erit triplex materia hujus sacramenti, et non solum duplex, ut dictum est.

PRAETEREA, hoc sacramentum sub specie panis et vini celebratur, ut in littera dicitur. Sed ad speciem panis nihil additur. Ergo nec vino aliquid addi debet.

SED CONTRA est quod dicit Alexander Papa: *in sacramentorum oblationibus panis tantum et vinum aqua permixtum offerantur.* Ergo debet admisceri aqua.

PRAETEREA, materia sacramenti debet competere rei significatae. Sed populus significatur per aquam, qui ad corpus mysticum pertinet, quod est res ultima hujus sacramenti. Ergo aqua debet apponi.

OBJ. 1: To the fourth we proceed thus. It seems that water should not be mixed into the wine.[86] For from the Lord's side when hanging on the Cross, blood and water flowed out, as is said in John 19:34, by which two things the sacraments are especially understood, as Innocent says.[87] But water pertains to the sacrament of regeneration, namely, baptism. Therefore, blood alone pertains to the sacrament of redemption, the Eucharist. And so it should be wine without water.

OBJ. 2: Furthermore, wine and water are different species. Therefore, if water is mixed into the wine, there will be a threefold matter for this sacrament, not only a twofold one, as was said.

OBJ. 3: Furthermore, this sacrament is celebrated under the species of bread and wine, as it says in the text. But nothing is added to the species of bread. Therefore, neither should anything be added to the wine.

ON THE CONTRARY, Pope Alexander says: *in the offerings of the sacraments let bread alone and wine mixed with water be offered.*[88] Therefore, it should be mixed with water.

FURTHERMORE, the matter of the sacrament should be suited to the reality signified. But the water signifies the people, who belong to the mystical body, which is the ultimate reality of this sacrament. Therefore, the water should be added.

Quaestiuncula 2

ULTERIUS. Videtur quod absque ea non possit sanguis consecrari. Cyprianus enim dicit: *calix Domini non potest esse aqua sola et vinum solum nisi utrumque misceatur, quoniam nec corpus Domini farina esse potest, nisi utrumque, scilicet farina et aqua, adunatum fuerit.* Sed constat quod ex farina sine aqua nullo modo potest corpus Christi consecrari. Ergo nec ex vino sine aqua.

PRAETEREA, significatio est de essentia sacramenti. Sed aqua significat aliquid quod est principale in sacra-

OBJ. 1: Moreover, it seems that without water the blood of Christ cannot be consecrated.[89] For Cyprian says: *the Lord's chalice cannot be water alone and wine alone unless the two are mixed, since neither can the body of the Lord exist from flour, unless both, that is, flour and water, have been united into one thing.*[90] But it is clear that from flour without water the body of Christ can in no way be consecrated. Therefore, neither from wine without water.

OBJ. 2: Furthermore, signification is of the essence of the sacrament. But water signifies something that is central

---

86. Parallels: *ST* III, q. 74, a. 6; *Super Matt.* 26; *Super I ad Cor.* 11, lec. 6.

87. In his letter *Cum Marthae* to John, Archbishop of Lyons, November 29, 1202: "For it seems to some that, since from the side of Christ two special sacraments flowed—of the redemption in the blood and of regeneration in the water—into those two the wine and water, which are mixed in the chalice, are changed by divine power" (http://www.geocities.ws/caleb1x/documents/cummarthae.html, accessed January 23, 2015).

88. Gratian's *Decretals*, Part 3, *De consecratione*, d. 2, ch. 1 (PL 187:1731).

89. Parallels: *ST* III, q. 74, a. 7; *Super I ad Cor.* 11, lec. 6.

90. Quoted by the Lombard; from Cyprian, *Epistle 63, ad Caecilium* (CCSL 3), ch. 13, par. 4.

mento, scilicet unionem corporis mystici ad caput. Ergo aqua est de necessitate hujus sacramenti, ut sine ea confici non possit.

PRAETEREA, hoc sacramentum est memoriale Dominicae passionis. Sed ex latere Domini patientis non solum fluxit sanguis sed aqua. Ergo ex vino sine aqua sacramentum hoc confici non potest.

SED CONTRA, Graeci non apponunt aquam, ut Magister dicit; sed tamen conficiunt. Ergo sine aquae admixtione confici potest hoc sacramentum.

PRAETEREA, nihil est de substantia sacramenti quod non manet in sacramento. Sed aqua non manet in propria specie in sacramento. Ergo non est de substantia sacramenti.

in the sacrament, namely, the union of the mystical body to its head. Therefore, water is necessary to this sacrament, so that without it it cannot be consecrated.

OBJ. 3: Furthermore, this sacrament is the memorial of the Lord's Passion. But from the Lord's side during his Passion not only blood flowed out but also water. Therefore, from wine without water the sacrament cannot be consecrated.

ON THE CONTRARY, the Byzantines do not add water, as the Master says, but they still consecrate. Therefore, without mixing in water this sacrament can be consecrated.

FURTHERMORE, nothing is of the sacrament's substance that does not remain in the sacrament. But water does not remain in its proper species in the sacrament. Therefore, it is not of the sacrament's substance.

Quaestiuncula 3

ULTERIUS. Videtur quod debeat aqua artificialis apponi. Quia sacramentum dicitur esse uniforme. Sed ex parte corporis est aliquid artificiale, scilicet panis. Ergo ex parte sanguinis debet esse aqua artificialis.

PRAETEREA, si panis ex aqua artificiali, ut rosacea, conficeretur, posset ex eo corpus Christi consecrari. Ergo similiter potest apponi in vino aqua artificialis.

SED CONTRA, baptismus est sacramentum majoris necessitatis quam Eucharistia. Sed in baptismo non potest accipi nisi aqua naturalis, ut supra dictum est. Ergo nec in Eucharistia.

OBJ. 1: Moreover, it seems that manmade water should be added.[91] For the sacrament is said to be uniform. But on the part of the body there is something manmade, namely, bread. Therefore, on the part of the blood there should be manmade water.

OBJ. 2: Furthermore, if bread were made from manmade water, like rose-water, the body of Christ could be consecrated from this. Therefore, likewise artificial water can be added to the wine.

ON THE CONTRARY, baptism is a sacrament of greater necessity than the Eucharist. But in baptism nothing but natural water can be used, as was said above.[92] Therefore, neither in the Eucharist.

Quaestiuncula 4

ULTERIUS. Videtur quod debeat in magna quantitate apponi. Quia quod non est, non potest aliquid significare. Sed quod corruptum est, non est. Cum ergo aqua ponatur ad significandum, videtur quod debeat tantum apponi quod non corrumpatur; et ita tantum quantum de vino vel plus, quia vinum est magis activum.

PRAETEREA, de latere Christi sicut sanguis, ita et aqua sensibiliter fluxit. Sed si parum de aqua poneretur, non posset sentiri. Ergo debet in majori quantitate apponi.

PRAETEREA, si sufficit in parva quantitate aquam apponi, eadem ratione sufficeret ad sacramentum, si gutta aquae in totum dolium projiceretur. Sed hoc videtur ridiculum. Ergo non sufficit quod parva quantitas ponatur.

OBJ. 1: Moreover, it seems that it should be added in great quantity.[93] For what does not exist cannot signify anything. But what is corrupted does not exist. Since therefore water is included to signify, it seems that there should be added so much that it is not corrupted, and that means as much as the wine, or more, because wine is more active.

OBJ. 2: Furthermore, just as blood flowed perceptibly from Christ's side, so also did water. But if only a little water is included, it cannot be perceived. Therefore, it should be added in greater quantity.

OBJ. 3: Furthermore, if it suffices for water to be added in a small quantity, by the same argument it would suffice for the sacrament if a drop of water were put into a whole cask. But this seems ridiculous. Therefore, it is not enough that a small quantity be added.

91. Parallels: *ST* III, q. 74, a. 7; *Super I ad Cor.* 11, lec. 6.
92. See d. 3, a. 3, qa. 2.
93. Parallels: *ST* III, q. 74, a. 8; *Super I ad Cor.* 11, lec. 6.

PRAETEREA, quorumdam consuetudo esse dicitur in terris ubi non crescit vinum, quod pannum vino rubeo intinctum et siccatum aqua lavent; de qua cum ruborem vini acceperit, sanguinem Christi conficiunt. Ergo videtur quod aqua in magna quantitate possit apponi.

SED CONTRA, *illud quod est ex duobus, neutrum illorum est*, ut Damascenus dicit. Sed si magna quantitas aquae apponeretur, esset quaedam mixtio. Ergo non esset vinum; et ita non posset inde sanguis Christi confici.

PRAETEREA, oportet quod aqua consumatur a vino ad hoc quod ex parte sanguinis sit tantum una species, sicut ex parte corporis. Sed non posset consumi, si aqua in magna quantitate poneretur. Ergo non debet in magna quantitate poni.

OBJ. 4: Furthermore, it is said to be the custom of some people in lands where wine does not grow, that they take a cloth dipped in red wine and dried, and wash it with water, which, since it has taken the redness of the wine, they consecrate as Christ's blood. Therefore, it seems that water can be added in great quantity.

ON THE CONTRARY, *What comes from two things is neither of them*, as Damascene says.[94] But if a large amount of water were added, it would be a kind of mixture. Therefore, it would not be wine, and so the blood of Christ could not be consecrated from it.

FURTHERMORE, it is necessary that the water be consumed by the wine so that there will be only one species on the part of the blood, just as on the part of the body. But it cannot be consumed if water is added in a large amount. Therefore, it should not be added in great quantity.

Response to Quaestiuncula 1

RESPONDEO dicendum ad primam quaestionem, quod aqua debet apponi vino propter institutionem: quia Dominus apposuisse probabiliter creditur ex more illius patriae: quia vinum ibi sine aqua nunquam bibitur propter vini fortitudinem: quamvis de aqua in Evangelio mentio non fiat, quia non est principalis materia in hoc sacramento; sed ejus appositio competit huic sacramento et quantum ad[95] significationem rei hujus sacramenti, quae est corpus mysticum per aquam significatum, quia *aquae multae populi multi*, Apocal. 17, 15; et sic appositio aquae ad vinum significat unionem membrorum ad caput ratione ipsius conjunctionis; et amorem capitis patientis pro membris, ad ipsa, ex hoc quod ex duobus conjunctis unum efficitur; et processum redemptionis a capite ad membra, ex ipsa transformatione aquae in vinum. Unde dicit Glossa Marc. 14 super illud: *accepit Jesus panem* etc.: *neque aqua solum neque vinum solum cuilibet licet offerre, ne videatur caput a membris secernere, vel Christum sine nostrae redemptionis amore pati potuisse, vel nos sine illius passione salvari.*

AD PRIMUM ergo dicendum, quod, sicut dicit Gregorius in *Moral.*, *quia natura uniuscujusque ex diversitate componitur, in sacro eloquio per rem quamlibet recte diversa significantur.* Aqua ergo secundum quod habet vim abluendi, significatio ejus competit baptismo; secundum autem quod continue in terram decurrit, habet significare populum: 2 Reg., 14, 14: *omnes morimur, et quasi*

TO THE FIRST QUESTION, I answer that water should be added to wine because of the sacrament's institution: for the Lord is believed to have probably added some by the practice of that country: for wine there without water is never drunk because of the strength of the wine, although no mention is made of water in the Gospel, because it is not the chief matter in this sacrament. But its addition pertains to this sacrament for both the representation of the Passion of Christ and the signification of the reality behind this sacrament, which is the mystical body signified by the water, because *the many waters are many peoples* (Rev 17:15). And so the addition of water to wine signifies the union of the members to the head by reason of its mingling; and the love of the suffering head for his members, by the fact that from two things joined, one is made; and the progress of redemption from the head to his members, by the very transformation of water into wine. Hence on this text, *Jesus took the bread* (Mark 14:22), the Gloss says, *no one is permitted to offer either water alone or wine alone, lest it seem that the head is separated from the members, or that Christ could suffer for our redemption without love, or that we could be saved without his Passion.*[96]

REPLY OBJ. 1: As Gregory says in his *Commentary on Job*, because the nature of any one thing is composed of a diversity, in sacred speech a given thing rightly signifies different things.[97] Therefore, according as water has the power of cleansing, its signification is suited to baptism; but according as it runs uninterrupted over the earth, it can signify people: *we all die and like water will we be spilled on the*

94. John Damascene, *On the Orthodox Faith*, Bk. 3, ch. 3 (PG 94:987).

95. *ad significationem.—ad representationem passionis Christi et quantum ad* PLE.

96. See *Glossa ordinaria*, PL 114:231.

97. Gregory the Great, *Moralia in Iob* (CCSL 143), Bk. 5, par. 21.

aqua dilabimur; et sic ejus significatio competit huic sacramento.

AD SECUNDUM dicendum, quod de aqua apposita est duplex opinio. Quidam enim dicunt, quod aqua manet in sua natura, et solum vinum transubstantiatur; unde aqua non apponitur ibi nisi ad significationem. Alii vero dicunt, quod aqua apposita in vinum convertitur, et sic totum in sanguinem Christi transubstantiatur. Quaecumque autem harum opinionum sit vera, aqua non erit materia hujus sacramenti: quia secundum primam non convertitur in corpus vel sanguinem Christi; secundum secundam non manet in propria specie sed vini. Secunda tamen opinio verior apparet, et secundum rationem naturalem; quia modica aqua vino admixta, quod est magis activum, a vino corrumpitur et in speciem vini transit: et quantum ad ritum sacramenti: quia si aqua in propria natura remaneret, sic calix consecratus non esset tantum potus spiritualis sed etiam corporalis; et ita non liceret post primam sumptionem sanguinis iterum sumere.

AD TERTIUM dicendum, quod aqua apponitur pani in ipsa sua confectione; et ideo non est necesse ut postea apponatur. Vel dicendum, quod effectus redemptionis a capite pervenit ad membra per sanguinis effusionem; et ideo magis apponitur aliquid ad significandum populi unionem ad sanguinem quam ad corpus.

ground (2 Sam 14:14). And in this way its signification is suited to this sacrament.

REPLY OBJ. 2: There are two opinions about the water added. For some people say that the water remains in its own nature, and only the wine is transubstantiated; hence water is not added for anything but the signification. But others say that the water added is converted into wine, and so the whole is transubstantiated into Christ's blood. Whichever of these opinions is true, water will not be this sacrament's matter, for according to the first, it is not converted into the body or blood of Christ; while according to the second it does not remain in its proper species but in the species of wine. Nevertheless, the second opinion appears more true, both according to natural reason, because a small amount of water mixed into wine, which is more active, is corrupted by the wine and passes over into the species of the wine; and as to the rite of the sacrament, because if the water remained in its proper nature, then the consecrated chalice would not be only a spiritual drink, but also a physical one; and so it would not be permitted after the first consumption of the blood to receive it again.

REPLY OBJ. 3: Water is added to bread in its very making; and so it is not necessary that it be added afterward. Or it should be said that the effect of the redemption reaches the members from the head by the shedding of blood; and so it is added to the blood to signify the union of the people rather than to the body.

Response to Quaestiuncula 2

AD SECUNDAM QUAESTIONEM dicendum, quod materia proportionatur sacramento; unde secundum aliquid est de essentia sacramenti.[98] Dictum est autem supra, quod perfectio hujus sacramenti consistit in ipsa consecratione corporis et sanguinis Christi, et non in usu materiae consecratae, sicut est in baptismo et confirmatione; et ideo ex parte materiae illud tantum est de necessitate sacramenti, quod significat corpus et sanguinem Christi, scilicet panis et vinum; illud autem quod significat usum et effectum hujus sacramenti, scilicet aqua, non est de necessitate hujus sacramenti; unde vinum sine aqua potest consecrari, sed consecrans peccat.

AD PRIMUM ergo dicendum, quod exponendum est verbum Cypriani: *non potest*, idest *non debet*; quia illud possumus quod de jure possumus: et ideo quantum ad id quod debet fieri, est simile ex parte corporis et sanguinis; non autem quantum ad id quod fieri potest: quia aqua est de substantia panis, non autem de substantia vini.

TO THE SECOND QUESTION, it should be said that the matter is proportionate to the sacrament; hence it belongs to the essence of the sacrament according as the matter signifies what is of the sacrament's essence. However, it was said above[99] that the completion of this sacrament consists in the very consecration of the body and blood of Christ, and not in the use of the consecrated matter, as is the case in baptism and confirmation. And so on the part of the matter, that alone is necessary to the sacrament which signifies the body and blood of Christ, namely, bread and wine. However, what signifies the use and effect of this sacrament, namely, water, is not necessary to this sacrament; hence wine without water can be consecrated, but the one doing this sins.

REPLY OBJ. 1: The words of Cyprian are to be explained thus: *it cannot*, that is, *it must not*; for we can do what we can do by right, and so as to what should be done, it is the same on the part of the body and blood; but not as to what can be done: for water is of the substance of the bread, but not of the substance of the wine.

---

98. *sacramenti.—sacramenti secundum hoc materia significans illud est de essentia sacramenti.* PLE.
99. See d. 8, q. 1, a. 1, qa. 1.

Ad secundum dicendum, quod non significat aqua aliquid quod sit de substantia hujus sacramenti, ut dictum est, sed effectum vel usum consequentem.

Ad tertium dicendum, quod effusio sanguinis in passione Christi directe pertinebat ad[100] effectum ablutionis a peccatis.

Reply Obj. 2: Water does not signify anything that is of the substance of this sacrament, as was said, but the effect or the resulting use.

Reply Obj. 3: The shedding of blood in Christ's Passion directly pertains to the Passion itself but the emanation pertains even more to the effect of washing from sins.

Response to Quaestiuncula 3

Ad tertiam quaestionem dicendum, quod cum sine aqua possit sanguis consecrari, quantum ad id quod fieri potest non refert quaecumque aqua apponatur, dummodo sit talis aqua quae in vinum converti possit; sed quantum ad id quod fieri debet, non debet apponi nisi aqua naturalis: quia illae aquae non sunt ejusdem speciei, et dicuntur aquae aequivoce, sicut etiam de vino et de pane dictum est.

Ad primum ergo dicendum quod panis artificialiter factus est ejusdem speciei cum illo pane de quo confecit Christus; non autem aqua artificialis cum aqua. Et ideo non est similis ratio.

Ad secundum dicendum, quod quidam dicunt, quod similiter est ex parte panis, quod de pane confecto ex aqua rosacea potest confici corpus Christi, quamvis peccaret scienter ex tali pane conficiens. Sed probabilius videtur quod non possit confici: quia panis est principalis materia hujus sacramenti, de cujus substantia et compositione est aqua; et ideo diversificatio aquae secundum speciem, facit diversitatem speciei in materia sacramenti. Sed aqua non est de substantia vini, quae est principalis materia in hoc sacramento.

Patet etiam responsio ad id quod in oppositum objicitur: quia aqua in baptismo est principalis materia; et ideo si aqua alterius speciei apponatur, non servatur debita materia, et propter hoc non est sacramentum; sed hic est aliter, ut dictum est.

To the third question, it should be said that without water the blood can be consecrated, and as to what can be done it does not matter what kind of water is added, so long as it is a kind that can be converted into wine; but as to what should be done, only natural water should be added; for those waters are not of the same species, and they are only called water equivocally, just as also was said about the wine and bread.

Reply Obj. 1: Manmade bread is of the same species as that bread that Christ consecrated; whereas artificial water is not of the same species as the water. And so the reasoning is not the same.

Reply Obj. 2: Certain people say that it is similar on the part of the bread, which can be consecrated as the body of Christ from bread made with rosewater, although whoever did consecrate it knowingly from such bread would have sinned. But it seems more probable that he would not be able to consecrate it: for this sacrament's chief matter is bread, whose substance and composition includes water. And so a different species of water makes a different species in the matter of the sacrament. But the water is not part of the substance of wine, which is the chief matter in this sacrament.

The response is also clear to what is objected in opposition: for water is the chief matter in baptism, and so if a different species of water is added, it does not preserve the due matter, and because of this the sacrament does not exist; but here it is different, as was said.

Response to Quaestiuncula 4

Ad quartam quaestionem dicendum, quod, sicut dictum est, aqua apposita vino in vinum convertitur, et sic totum convertitur in sanguinem; unde non tantum de aqua debet apponi quod vinum in aquam convertatur, vel in aliquod medium per mixtionem; et ideo semper tutius est apponere parum: quia quantumcumque apponatur parum, significatio servatur.

Ad primum ergo dicendum, quod ex hoc ipso quod in vinum convertitur aqua, habet suam significationem: quia nos in Christum mutamur, non ipse in nos.

To the fourth question, it should be said that as was said, the water added to the wine is converted into wine, and this is how the whole is converted into blood. And this is why not so much water should be added that the wine is converted into water, or into some third thing by mixture. And so it is always safer to add a small amount, because however little is added, the signification is preserved.

Reply Obj. 1: By the very fact that water is converted into wine, it has its own signification: for we are changed into Christ, not he into us.

---

100. *ad effectum.—ad ipsam passionem sed emanatio atque magis pertinebat ad* PLE.

AD SECUNDUM dicendum, quod hoc sacramentum repraesentat Christi passionem quantum ad redemptionem, quae facta est per effusionem sanguinis; sed baptismus quantum ad ablutionem; et ideo in baptismo oportet quod sensibiliter aqua maneat, sicut et vinum hoc quod sanguini respondet; aqua autem haec apposita a vino absorbetur, sicut nostra mortalitas per virtutem passionis Christi.

AD TERTIUM dicendum, quod si apponeretur aqua in dolio, non significaret aliquid; et ideo hoc non sufficeret; sed oportet ut imminente oblatione apponatur ad sacramentum perficiendum.

AD QUARTUM dicendum, quod cum illud sit magis aqua rubea quam vinum, non potest exinde sanguis Christi consecrari; unde illa consuetudo damnatur in canone *de Consec.*, dist. 2, cap. cum omne.

REPLY OBJ. 2: This sacrament represents Christ's Passion as to our redemption, which was accomplished by the shedding of his blood. But baptism represents Christ's passion as to cleansing, and so in baptism it is necessary that water remain sensibly, just as also the wine that corresponds to the blood here; but the water added to the wine here is absorbed, like our mortality by the power of Christ's Passion.

REPLY OBJ. 3: If water were added to a cask, it would not signify anything, and so this would not suffice. But to complete the sacrament it would have to be added when the offering was about to be made.

REPLY OBJ. 4: Since that is more red water than wine, the blood of Christ cannot be consecrated from it; and so this custom is condemned in one of the canons of *On Consecration*, Distinction 2.[101]

---

101. Gratian's *Decretals*, Part 3, *De consecratione*, d. 2, ch. 7 (PL 187:1733).

QUESTION 3

THE EUCHARIST AT THE LAST SUPPER

Deinde quaeritur quomodo Christus hoc sacramento usus sit in ipsa prima sui institutione; et circa hoc quaeruntur quatuor:

primo, utrum ipse corpus suum manducaverit;

secundo, utrum Judae dederit;

tertio, utrum dederit corpus suum passibile, vel impassibile;

quarto, utrum si in pixide reservatum fuisset corpus Christi, ibi moreretur;

sub qua autem forma consecravit, supra, dist. 8, dictum est.

Next it is asked how Christ used this sacrament at its first institution: and concerning this, four questions arise:

first, whether he ate his own body;

second, whether he gave it to Judas;

third, whether he gave his own body as suffering, or impassible;

fourth, if the body of Christ had been reserved in a pyx, whether it would have died there.

However, under what form he consecrated it was discussed above, in Distinction 8.

ARTICLE 1

Whether Christ ate his own body[102]

AD PRIMUM SIC PROCEDITUR. Videtur quod ipse Christus non manducaverit. Quia de his quae Dominus fecit, non sunt alia asserenda, nisi quae nobis in Evangelio narrantur. Sed in Evangelio continetur quod Christus accepit panem in manibus, et dedit discipulis suis manducandum. Ergo non debemus asserere quod ipse manducaverit.

PRAETEREA, omne quod manducatur, in cibum assumitur. Sed *assumens non est assumptum*, ut in 3 Lib., dist. 5, dictum est. Ergo Christus corpus suum manducare non potuit.

PRAETEREA, hoc sacramentum ordinatur ad spiritualem refectionem. Sed ipse spirituali refectione non indigebat. Ergo hoc sacramentum non sumpsit, quia in vacuum accepisset.

PRAETEREA, ut supra, dist. 9, dictum est, duplex est modus manducandi; scilicet spiritualis, et sacramentalis. Sed Christo non competebat sacramentaliter manducare, cum esset verus comprehensor, et sine velamine figurarum ad rem sacramenti pertingeret; nec iterum spiritualiter, quia in ipso gratia non augebatur. Ergo ipse non manducavit.

SED CONTRA, Hieronymus dicit et habetur de Consec., dist. 2: *Dominus Jesus ipse cum apostolis conviva*

OBJ. 1: To the first we proceed thus. It seems that Christ himself did not eat. For with regard to the Lord's deeds, no others are to be asserted beyond those which are recounted for us in the Gospel. But in the Gospel is contained that Christ took the bread in his hands, and gave it to his disciples to eat. Therefore, we should not assert that he himself ate.

OBJ. 2: Furthermore, everything that is eaten is taken as food. But *the one taking is not what is taken*, as it says in Book III, Distinction 5.[103] Therefore, Christ could not eat his own body.

OBJ. 3: Furthermore, this sacrament is ordered to spiritual restoration. But he did not need spiritual restoration. Therefore, he did not take this sacrament, for he would have received it to no purpose.

OBJ. 4: As was said above in Distinction 9,[104] there are two modes of eating, namely, spiritual and sacramental. But it did not pertain to Christ to eat sacramentally, since he was a true comprehensor, and could reach to the reality behind the sacrament without the veil of figures. Nor again did it pertain to him to eat spiritually, for grace did not increase in him. Therefore, he did not eat.

ON THE CONTRARY, Jerome says, and it is quoted in *On Consecration*, Distinction 2: *The Lord Jesus himself was*

---

102. Parallels: *ST* III, q. 81, a. 1; q. 84, a. 7, ad 4.
103. See Bk. 3, d. 5, q. 1, a. 1, qa. 3.
104. See d. 9, a. 1, qa. 3.

507

et convivium; ipse comedens, et qui comeditur. Ergo ipse corpus suum manducavit.

PRAETEREA, sicut Christus instituit baptismum, ita et hoc sacramentum. Sed ipse baptizatus fuit. Ergo similiter debuit hoc sacramentum assumere.

RESPONDEO dicendum, quod circa hoc est duplex opinio. Quidam enim dicunt, quod Christus corpus suum in coena non manducavit, sed tantum manibus accepit; et nituntur solvere auctoritates sanctorum qui contrarium dicunt, quod ipse manducavit et bibit in coena ante consecrationem, sed non corpus suum consecratum. Sed expresse habetur Ruth 3, in Glossa super illud: *cumque comedisset et bibisset,* etc., quod Christus comedit et bibit in coena, cum corporis et sanguinis sui sacramentum discipulis tradidit. Unde quia *pueri communicaverunt carni et sanguini, et ipse participavit eisdem,* Heb. 2. et propter hoc communius tenetur quod manducaverit, secundum quod sancti expresse dicere videntur; unde et ab antiquis versus est factus: *rex sedet in caena, turba cinctus duodena: se tenet in manibus, se cibat ipse cibus.* Non autem manducavit ut aliquem effectum consequeretur a sacramento, sed ut aliis manducandi exemplum daret.

AD PRIMUM ergo dicendum, quod in acceptione panis potest utrumque intelligi, scilicet et acceptio in manibus et manducatio.

AD SECUNDUM dicendum, quod Christus sub specie propria quodammodo distat a seipso sub specie sacramenti; unde nunc in specie propria est in caelo, sed sub specie sacramenti est in altari; et secundum hunc modum non est inconveniens quod seipsum assumat.

AD TERTIUM dicendum, quod illa manducatio non efficiebat in ipso spiritualem refectionem, sed significabat: nullus enim adeo perfecte in ipso reficitur, sicut ipsemet.

AD QUARTUM dicendum, quod Christus manducavit, ut videtur, et sacramentaliter et spiritualiter. Sacramentaliter quidem, quia verum corpus suum sub sacramento sumpsit. Poterat enim in sacramento rem sacramenti inspicere non ex sacramento, ut etiam Deus videt in effectibus causas, sed non ex effectibus. Spiritualiter autem, inquantum in re sacramenti spiritualiter delectaretur. Non tamen haec spiritualis refectio ex sacramento causabatur, nec augmentabatur; unde nec spiritualis manducatio erat in eo sicut in aliis, nec sacramentalis. Et ideo quidam dixerunt, quod neque sacramentaliter neque spiritualiter manducavit. Quidam quod sacramentaliter, sed non spiritualiter.

a banqueter with his apostles, and the banquet; he was eating and the one who was eaten.[105] Therefore, he ate his own body.

FURTHERMORE, just as Christ instituted baptism, so also this sacrament. But he himself was baptized. And likewise he had to receive this sacrament.

I ANSWER THAT, there are two opinions about this. For some people say that Christ did not eat his own body at the Last Supper, but only took it in his hands; and to resolve the authoritative texts of the saints who say the contrary, they say that he ate and drank at the Last Supper before the consecration, but not his own consecrated body. But it expressly says in the Gloss on this text, *and when he had eaten, and drunk, and was merry* (Ruth 3:7), that Christ ate and drank at the supper, when he handed down the sacrament of his body and blood to his disciples. Hence, because *children have shared in the flesh and blood, and he himself partook of the same* (Heb 2:14). And on this account it is more commonly held that he ate, in accordance with what the saints seem to say explicitly; hence the ancient verse: *the king sits at supper, encircled by the crowd of twelve: he holds himself in his hands, he eats himself for food.* But he did not eat so as to obtain any effect from the sacrament, but so that he might give an example of eating to others.

REPLY OBJ. 1: In taking the bread, both can be understood, namely, both taking it in his hands and eating it.

REPLY OBJ. 2: Christ under his proper species stands apart in a certain manner from himself under the species of the sacrament; so for example now in his proper species he is in heaven, but under the species of the sacrament he is on the altar. And in keeping with this manner it is not unfitting that he take himself.

REPLY OBJ. 3: That eating did not bring about a spiritual restoration in him, but it signified one: for no one is so perfectly restored in him as he himself.

REPLY OBJ. 4: Christ ate, it would seem, both sacramentally and spiritually. Sacramentally, indeed, for he received his true body under the sacrament. For he could have looked at the reality behind the sacrament in the sacrament but not from it, as God also sees causes in their effects, but not from their effects. He ate spiritually, however, inasmuch as he delighted spiritually in the reality of the sacrament. Nevertheless this spiritual restoration was not caused or increased by the sacrament, which is why neither spiritual eating nor sacramental eating was in him as it is in others. And so some people said that he ate neither sacramentally nor spiritually. And others say sacramentally but not spiritually.

---

105. Jerome, *Epistle 120* (CSEL 55:480); Gratian's *Decretals,* Part 3, *De consecratione,* d. 2, ch. 87 (PL 187:177).

ARTICLE 2

Whether Christ gave his body to Judas[106]

Quaestiuncula 1

AD SECUNDUM SIC PROCEDITUR. Videtur quod Christus corpus suum Judae non dederit. Ipse enim implevit quod mandavit. Sed mandaverat sanctum non esse canibus dandum, Matth. 7. Ergo ipse non dedit Judae corpus suum sanctissimum.

PRAETEREA, secundum Augustinum, Deus non est causa alicui quod deterior fiat. Sed si Judas corpus Christi sumpsisset, ex hoc factus fuisset deterior, quia sumendo peccasset. Ergo Christus corpus suum ei manducandum non dedit.

PRAETEREA, sicut supra, dist. 9 quaest. 1, art. 1, quaestiunc. 1, dictum est, ideo sacerdos debet peccatori dare, quia non est Dominus, sed dispensator, et reddit quod suum est exigenti. Sed Christus erat Dominus sacramenti, nec Judas ibi jus habere poterat, nisi quod Christus sibi daret. Ergo non debuit Judae corpus tradere.

PRAETEREA, Dominus dixit, quod discipuli bibentes bibituri essent secum illud novum in regno patris sui, et quod erat eis in remissionem peccatorum. Sed neutrum Judae competit. Ergo ipse non sumpsit; et haec est ratio Hilarii.

SED CONTRA est quod Dionysius dicit: *symbolorum conditor partitur sanctissima non unimode ei sacre concoenanti*, scilicet Judae. Sanctissima autem dicit corpus et sanguinem suum, ut ibidem patet. Ergo Judae dedit corpus suum.

PRAETEREA, sine exceptione dicitur Matth. 26, 26: *accipite omnes, et comedite*. Ergo etiam Judae dedit.

OBJ. 1: To the second we proceed thus. It seems that Christ did not give his body to Judas. For he fulfilled what he commanded. But he had commanded that holy things not be given to dogs (Matt 7:6). Therefore, he did not give his most holy body to Judas.

OBJ. 2: Furthermore, according to Augustine, God is not the cause of anyone becoming worse.[107] But if Judas took the body of Christ, it caused him to become worse, for he sinned in taking it. Therefore, Christ did not give his body to him to eat.

OBJ. 3: Furthermore, just as was said above in Distinction 9, Question 1, Article 1, Subquestion 1, for this reason the priest should give to a sinner, because he is not the Lord, but the steward, and renders what is required of him. But Christ was the Lord of the sacrament, nor could Judas have had any right there, unless Christ gave it to him. Therefore, he should not have handed over his body to Judas.

OBJ. 4: Furthermore, the Lord said that the disciples drinking were to drink it anew with him in the kingdom of his Father, and that it was for them for the remission of sins (Matt 26:28–29). But neither applied to Judas. Therefore, he did not receive it; and this is Hilary's argument.[108]

ON THE CONTRARY, Dionysius says, *the creator of symbols shares not only sacred things with him, but the holiest things with the one dining with him*, namely, Judas.[109] However, by "the holiest things" Dionysius means his body and blood, as is clear in the same place. Therefore, he gave Judas his body.

FURTHERMORE, without exception it is said, *take and eat, all of you* (Matt 26:26). Therefore, he also gave it to Judas.

Quaestiuncula 2

ULTERIUS. Videtur quod sub bucella corpus suum ei dedit. Dicit enim Augustinus de Consec.: *non mala erat bucella quae data est Judae a Domino. Salutem medicus dedit; sed ille, quia indignus erat, accepit ad perniciem.*

OBJ. 1: Moreover, it seems that he gave his body to him in the morsel of bread. For Augustine says, *the morsel that was given to Judas by the Lord was not bad. The doctor gave health, but he, who was unworthy, took it to his ruin.*[110]

---

106. Parallels: *ST* III, q. 81, a. 2; *Super Matt.* 26; *Super Ioan.* 13, lec. 3 & 4.
107. See Augustine, *de Diuersis quaestionibus octoginta tribus* (CCSL 44A), q. 3.
108. Hilary, *Commentarius in Matthaeum*, ch. 30, par. 2 (SChr 258:222).
109. Pseudo-Dionysius, *Ecclesiastical Hierarchy*, ch. 3, p. 3, n. 1 (PG 3:427).
110. See Augustine, *In Iohannis euangelium tractatus* (CCSL 36), Tract. 6, par. 15: "Num enim mala erat buccella quae tradita est Iudae a Domino? Absit. Medicus non daret uenenum: salutem medicus dedit; sed indigne accipiendo, ad perniciem accepit, qui non pacatus accepit" (cf. Tract. 26, par. 11); Gratian, *Decretals*, Part 3, *De consecratione*, d. 2, ch. 66 (PL 187:1763).

Non autem fuisset indignus, si bucella illa tantum panis fuisset. Ergo illa bucella erat corpus Christi.

PRAETEREA, diabolum intrare in hominem est effectus peccati. Sed Joan. 13, dicitur, *quod post bucellam introivit in eum Satanas*. Ergo accipiendo bucellam, peccavit: ergo bucella erat corpus Christi.

SED CONTRA est quod habetur in Glossa Joan. 13, super illud: *cui intinctum panem porrexero*, etc.

However, he would not have been unworthy, if that morsel were only bread. Therefore, that morsel was the body of Christ.

OBJ. 2: Furthermore, for the devil to enter into a man is an effect of sin. But it says that *after the morsel, Satan entered into him* (John 13:27). Therefore, by taking the morsel, he sinned: therefore the morsel was the body of Christ.

ON THE CONTRARY is what the Gloss says about John 13:26: *he it is to whom I shall extend the bread I have dipped*, etc.[111]

Response to Quaestiuncula 1

RESPONDEO dicendum ad primam quaestionem, quod secundum Augustinum, Christus corpus suum in coena cum aliis discipulis Judae dedit, ut nobis exemplum daret quod peccatoribus occultis non essent sacramenta deneganda, et ut omnem occasionem ei auferret male faciendi, quam assumere potuisset, si in aliquo ab aliis discipulis ante apertam malitiam fuisset discretus. Hilarius tamen contrarium dicere videtur. Sed primum communius tenetur.

AD PRIMUM ergo dicendum, quod quamvis Judas in rei veritate canis esset, tamen non in manifesto; et ideo noluit eum detegere coram aliis discipulis, ne desperationem incurreret, et sic liberius peccaret.

AD SECUNDUM dicendum, quod Christus non dedit causam nec occasionem Judae peccandi, sed peccatum evitandi ex mansuetudinis suae ostensione ad ipsum; sed ipse ex vitali medicina sumpsit periculum mortis.

AD TERTIUM dicendum, quod illa non est sola causa, sed etiam ne peccatorem occultum prodat.

AD QUARTUM dicendum, quod Judas bibit cum aliis sacramentaliter, sed non spiritualiter; unde nec remissionem peccatorum consecutus est, nec in regno patris secum bibit: quia potus ille tantum spiritualiter bibentibus debetur.

TO THE FIRST QUESTION, I answer that according to Augustine[112] Christ gave his body to Judas at the Last Supper with the other disciples, so that he might give an example to us that the sacraments should not be denied to hidden sinners, and that he might remove from him every occasion for doing evil, which he could have taken if he had been singled out from the other disciples in anything before his malice was made known. However, Hilary seems to say the contrary.[113] But the first is more commonly held.

REPLY OBJ. 1: Although Judas was a dog in the truth of reality, nevertheless, it was not publicly known; and so he did not wish to expose him before the other disciples, lest he be driven to despair and so sin more freely.

REPLY OBJ. 2: Christ did not give Judas cause or occasion for sinning but rather for avoiding sin by displaying his meekness to him; but he took the danger of death from life-giving medicine.

REPLY OBJ. 3: That is not the only reason, but also so that he would not expose a hidden sinner.

REPLY OBJ. 4: Judas drank sacramentally with the others, but not spiritually; hence neither did he obtain remission of sins, nor does he drink with him in the kingdom of the Father; for that drink is only due to those drinking spiritually.

Response to Quaestiuncula 2

AD SECUNDAM QUAESTIONEM dicendum, quod Christus primo Judae dedit corpus suum cum aliis discipulis; sed postea bucella intincta in ostensionem proditionis ejus ei porrecta, purus panis fuit, sicut patet ex Glossa inducta.

AD PRIMUM ergo dicendum, quod Augustinus loquitur non de bucella intincta, sed de eo quod prius cum aliis discipulis acceperat. Vel dicendum, quod dicitur ad

TO THE SECOND QUESTION, it should be said that Christ first gave Judas his body with the other disciples, but afterward when he dipped the morsel and offered it to him in recognition of his betrayal, it was simply bread, as is clear from the Gloss cited.

REPLY OBJ. 1: Augustine is not speaking of the dipped morsel, but of what he had taken before with the other disciples. Or it could be said that he is said to have received

---

111. See *Glossa ordinaria*, PL 114:406.

112. The points may be gathered from *Epistle 44* (CSEL 34.2), n. 5 and *In Iohannis euangelium tractatus* (CCSL 36), Tract. 62, par. 3.

113. In the passage cited just above.

perniciem assumpsisse, quia quod Christus ad salutem suam fecerat porrigendo bucellam, ut videns se deprehensum, ab iniquo proposito desisteret, ille ex hoc magis exasperatus fuit.

Ad secundum dicendum, quod in comestione bucellae intinctae, peccatum Judae augmentatum fuit vel ex hoc quod exasperatus est magis, vel propter praesumptionem qua cum magistro in catinum manum mittebat, ut audacia bonam conscientiam mentiretur, ut dicitur Matth. 26, super illud: *qui intingit manum mecum* etc., et ratione hujus augmenti dicitur diabolus post bucellam in eum intrasse; jam praemissum erat enim in Evangelio, quod diabolus immiserat in cor Simonis Scarioth, ut traderet eum.

it to his ruin, because while Christ had offered the morsel for his salvation, so that seeing that he was caught he might cease from his wicked plan, he was more irritated by it.

Reply Obj. 2: In eating the dipped morsel, Judas's sin was increased either by the fact that he was more aggravated, or because of the presumption with which he put his hand into the bowl with his master, so that by his boldness he might feign a good conscience, as Matthew 26:23 says about that: *whoever dips his hand with me*, etc., and by reason of this increase, it is said that the devil entered into him after the morsel; for it was already mentioned in the Gospel that the devil had gone into the heart of Simon Iscariot, so that he would betray him.

ARTICLE 3

Whether Christ gave his own body as suffering, or impassible[114]

AD TERTIUM SIC PROCEDITUR. Videtur quod Christus in coena discipulis suis corpus impassibile dedit. Quia super illud Matth. 17: *transfiguratus est ante eos*, dicit Glossa: *illud corpus quod habuit per naturam, dedit discipulis in coena, non mortale et corruptibile*.

PRAETEREA, Lev. 2, super illud: *si oblatio tua fuerit de sartagine* etc., dicit Glossa: *crux super omnia fortis carnem Christi, quae ante passionem non videbatur esui apta, post aptam fecit*. Sed Christus in coena dedit carnem suam ut aptam ad manducandum. Ergo dedit eam talem qualis fuit post passionem. Sed post passionem suam fuit impassibilis. Ergo dedit corpus suum impassibile.

PRAETEREA, passibile trahitur ad naturam agentis. Sed Christus in coena dedit corpus suum in cibum, non qui in alios mutaretur, sed qui alios in se mutaret. Ergo non dedit corpus suum passibile.

PRAETEREA, omne corpus passibile ex contactu patitur. Sed corpus Christi a discipulis manducatum non laedebatur. Ergo non erat passibile.

SED CONTRA, Innocentius dicit: *tale corpus tunc dedit quale habuit*, scilicet passibile.

PRAETEREA, constat quod Christus discipulis verum corpus suum tradidit. Sed corpus suum verum erat passibile. Si ergo corpus datum erat impassibile, idem erat passibile et impassibile; quod non est possibile.

RESPONDEO dicendum, quod circa hoc duplex fuit opinio. Hugo enim de s. Victore dicere voluit, quod Christus adhuc existens in carne mortali quandoque unam dotem, quandoque aliam legitur accepisse; sicut claritatem in transfiguratione, subtilitatem in nativitate, agilitatem quando super mare ambulavit; et similiter impassibilitatem quando corpus suum in coena dedit. Non quidem nec tunc simpliciter erat impassibile; sed erat impassibile secundum quod in sacramento dabatur, quia masticatione non laedebatur; sicut etiam in se erat visibile; sed secundum quod in sacramento dabatur, erat invisibile. Sed istud non potest stare; quia substantia corporis Christi eadem est in sacramento et in specie propria; sed comparatione ejus ad exteriora non est eadem; quia in specie propria comparatur ad exteriora secundum situm propriarum dimensionum; sed in sacramento secundum situm dimensionum panis; unde illae proprietates quae insunt absolute corpori Christi, oportet

OBJ. 1: It seems that Christ gave his disciples an impassible body at the Last Supper. For about that text, *he was transfigured before them* (Matt 17:2), the Gloss says, *that body that he had by nature, he gave his disciples at the Last Supper, not the mortal and corruptible one.*[115]

OBJ. 2: Furthermore, about that text, *if your offering is grain prepared in a pan* (Lev 2:7), the Gloss says: *the flesh of Christ which before the Passion did not seem suited to eating, the Cross, strong above all things, made suitable afterward.* But Christ gave his flesh at the Last Supper as suitable for eating. Therefore, he gave it such as it was after the Passion. But after the Passion it was impassible. Therefore, he gave his body as impassible.

OBJ. 3: Furthermore, what is passible is drawn into the nature of what is active. But at the Last Supper, Christ gave his body as food, not such as would be changed into others, but such as would change others into himself. Therefore, he did not give his body as passible.

OBJ. 4: Furthermore, every passible body suffers from contact. But the body of Christ was not injured by the disciples eating it. Therefore, it was not passible.

ON THE CONTRARY, Innocent says, *the body that he gave was such as he had at that time*,[116] namely, passible.

FURTHERMORE, it is clear that Christ gave his true body to his disciples. But his true body was passible. If therefore the body he gave was impassible, the same thing was passible and impassible, which is not possible.

I ANSWER THAT, concerning this there are two opinions. For Hugh of St. Victor[117] wanted to say that Christ while still existing in mortal flesh is read to have taken up sometimes one quality [of a glorified body], sometimes another, like clarity in the Transfiguration, subtlety in the Nativity, agility when he walked on water; and likewise impassibility when he gave his body at the Last Supper. Nor indeed was it simply speaking impassible at that moment, but it was impassible as it was given in the sacrament, for chewing did not hurt it; just as he was also visible in himself, but as he was given in the sacrament he was invisible. But that cannot stand: for the substance of the body of Christ is the same in the sacrament and in its proper species; but by relation to the outside it is not the same; for in its proper species it is related to the exterior according to the location of its proper dimensions, but in the sacrament, according to the location of the dimensions of bread. Hence it is necessary that those properties that are absolutely in the body

---

114. Parallel: *ST* III, q. 81, a. 3.
115. See *Glossa ordinaria*, PL 114:143.
116. Innocent III, *De sacro altaris mysterio*, Bk. 4, ch. 12 (PL 217:866).
117. Hugh of St. Victor, *De sacramentis fidei*, Bk. 2, pt. 8, ch. 3 (PL 176:462).

quod eodem modo insint sibi secundum quod est in sacramento, et secundum quod est in specie propria; sed illae quae conveniunt ei ex comparatione ad aliud corpus extra, non eodem modo, sicut patet de visione. Sed passibilitas est proprietas absolute ipsius corporis; unde cum in propria specie esset passibile, et in sacramento passibile erat, ut alii dicunt, quamvis ibi non pateretur.

Ad primum ergo dicendum, quod dicitur corpus Christi in sacramento non mortale, non passibile, quia per sacramentalem sumptionem non patiebatur neque moriebatur.

Ad secundum dicendum, quod caro Christi non est apta esui nisi prout est sub sacramento; et quia sacramentum hoc est repraesentativum passionis Christi, ideo dicitur quod crux fecit eam esui aptam.

Ad tertium dicendum, quod non ratione passibilitatis, sed virtute divinitatis unitae, habebat corpus Christi quod alios in se converteret.

Ad quartum dicendum, quod masticatio importat respectum corporis Christi ad aliud extra; et ideo quantum ad hoc non comparatur ad manducantem secundum dimensiones proprias, sed secundum dimensiones panis; et inde est quod nunc non laeditur per masticationem, nisi ratione impassibilitatis, quae in ipso corpore nunc est.

of Christ be in it in the same way as it is in the sacrament, and according as it is in its proper species; but those that apply to it by its relation to another body outside it, not in the same way, as is evident from the example of sight. But passibility is an absolute property of this body; hence since it was possible in its proper species, it was also possible in the sacrament, as others say, although it did not suffer there.

Reply Obj. 1: The body of Christ is not said to be mortal in the sacrament, nor passible, because by sacramental consumption it did not suffer, nor did it die.

Reply Obj. 2: The flesh of Christ is only suited to eating as it exists under the sacrament; and since this sacrament is representative of the Passion of Christ, for this reason it is said that the Cross made it ready for eating.

Reply Obj. 3: The body of Christ is able to convert others into itself, not by reason of passibility, but by virtue of being united to the divinity.

Reply Obj. 4: Chewing conveys a relation of the body of Christ to something outside it; and so as to this it is not related to the one chewing according to its proper dimensions, but according to the dimensions of bread; and this is how it is not hurt by chewing, if not by reason of the impassibility that is now in the body itself.

ARTICLE 4

If the body of Christ had been reserved in a pyx, whether it would have died there

Quaestiuncula 1

AD QUARTUM SIC PROCEDITUR. Videtur quod corpus Christi, si fuisset in pixide servatum, non ibi moreretur. Corpus enim Christi non est mortuum nisi crucifixione. Sed ibi non crucifigebatur. Ergo et ibi non moriebatur.

PRAETEREA, actio Judaeorum erat causa mortis Christi, et sanguinis effusio. Sed ibi non effudisset sanguinem, nec actio Judaeorum ibi fuisset. Ergo non fuisset ibi mortuum.

SED CONTRA, unum et idem corpus fuisset tunc in pixide et in cruce. Sed in cruce moriebatur. Ergo et in pixide.

OBJ. 1: To the fourth we proceed thus. It seems that if the body of Christ had been kept in a pyx, it would not have died there.[118] For the body of Christ only died by crucifixion. But it was not crucified there. Therefore, it would not have died there.

OBJ. 2: The Jews' actions were the cause of Christ's death and the shedding of his blood. But he would not have shed his blood there, nor would the actions of the Jews have taken place there. Therefore, he would not have died there.

ON THE CONTRARY, one and the same body would have been in the pyx and on the Cross at that moment. But he died on the Cross. Therefore, he would also have died in the pyx.

Quaestiuncula 2

ULTERIUS. Videtur quod si post mortem Christi aliquis apostolorum confecisset hoc sacramentum, quod fuisset ibi anima Christi; fuisset enim aliter imperfectum sacramentum. Sed de perfectione sacramenti est non solum corpus, sed etiam anima; quia totus Christus in sacramento continetur. Ergo ibi fuisset anima.

PRAETEREA, verba formae non fuissent tunc minoris virtutis quam modo. Sed modo ex vi formae conficitur corpus cum anima. Ergo, etc.

SED CONTRA, corpus Christi non est perfectius sub specie sacramenti quam sub specie propria. Sed tunc corpus Christi erat exanime. Ergo et sub sacramento.

OBJ. 1: Moreover, it seems that if after Christ's death one of the apostles had consecrated this sacrament, the soul of Christ would have been there;[119] for otherwise it would have been an incomplete sacrament. But the sacrament's completion requires not only the body, but also the soul; for the whole Christ is contained in the sacrament. Therefore, the soul would have been there.

OBJ. 2: Furthermore, the words of the form would not have had less power at that time than they do now. But now the body is consecrated with the soul by the force of the form. Therefore, etc.

ON THE CONTRARY, the body of Christ is not more perfect under the sacrament's species than under his proper species. But at that time the body of Christ was lifeless. Therefore, it would also have been so under the sacrament.

Quaestiuncula 3

ULTERIUS. Videtur quod Deus facere potuerit quod tunc anima esset corpori Christi in sacramento existenti unita. Anima enim Christi majorem convenientiam habebat ad corpus proprium quam ad infernum. Sed anima separata a corpore Christi jacente in sepulcro fuit in inferno. Ergo similiter potuisset esse in loco illo ubi corpus Christi sub sacramento conservabatur.

OBJ. 1: Moreover, it seems that God could have caused at that moment the soul to be united to the body of Christ existing in the sacrament. For the soul of Christ belonged more with his proper body than in hell. But when Christ's body lay in the tomb, his separated soul was in hell. Therefore likewise it could have been in that place where the body of Christ was preserved under the sacrament.

---

118. Parallels: above, d. 10, a. 2, qa. 1; *ST* III, q. 81, a. 4; *SCG* IV, ch. 64; *Quodl.* V, q. 6, a. 1, ad 1; *Super Ioan.* 6, lec. 7; *Super ad I Cor.* 11, lec. 6.
119. Parallel: above, d. 10, a. 2, qa. 1.

Praeterea, corpus Christi, quia est divinitati adjunctum, potest esse in sacramento, et in specie propria. Ergo et anima, cum sit divinitati unita, poterat esse simul in inferno, et in corpore Christi sub sacramento.

Sed contra, ex hoc sequeretur quod contradictoria essent simul vera, si corpus Christi esset simul animatum et inanimatum. Sed hoc Deus facere non potest, ut Augustinus dicit contra Faustum. Ergo nec primum.

Obj. 2: Furthermore, the body of Christ, because it is united to divinity, can exist in the sacrament and in its proper species. Therefore, the soul, too, since it is united to the divinity, could be at the same time in hell and in the body of Christ under the sacrament.

On the contrary, this would result in contradictories being true at the same time, if the body of Christ were at the same time animate and inanimate. But God cannot do this, as Augustine says against Faustus.[120] Therefore, neither can he do the first thing.

Response to Quaestiuncula 1

Respondeo dicendum ad primam quaestionem, quod omnia verba quae significant passionem ab extrinseco illatam, non possunt attribui corpori Christi prout est sub sacramento; cujus ratio ex dictis apparet; unde non potest dici, quod in pixide crucifigeretur vel verberaretur, vel aliquid hujusmodi. Nec ex hoc sequitur quod duo contradictoria sint simul vera; quia non secundum idem comparatur ad extra corpus Christi hic et ibi. Omnia enim verba quae significant passionem innatam, conveniunt ei, ut dolet, patitur, et cetera hujusmodi; et similiter potest dici, quod in altari moritur; unde versus: *pixide servato poteris copulare dolorem innatum; sed non illatus convenit illi.*

Ad primum ergo dicendum, quod passiones extrinsecae pertingunt ad substantiam corporis Christi mediantibus dimensionibus propriis, non autem mediantibus dimensionibus panis. Et ideo propter impressiones extrinsecas quae ad species panis pertinent, nulla passio intrinseca corpori Christi attribuitur; sed propter impressiones extrinsecas ad dimensiones proprias pertinentes attribuuntur passiones corpori Christi, et extrinsecae sub specie propria tantum, et intrinsecae etiam sub specie aliena. Et ideo propter crucifixionem in Calvariae loco factam, corpus Christi verum servatum moriebatur sub specie propria, et sub sacramento.

Et per hoc patet solutio ad secundum; quia actio Judaeorum extrinseca erat; fluxus etiam sanguinis ad motum localem pertinet, et sic importat ordinem ad aliquid extra.

To the first question, I answer that no words that signify suffering inflicted from without can be attributed to the body of Christ as it exists under the sacrament; and the reason for this is apparent from what has been said. And this is why it cannot be said that in the pyx he would have been crucified or flogged, or anything like that. Nor does it follow from this that two contradictory things are true at the same time; for the body of Christ is not related to what is outside it in the same way in both cases. For all the words that signify suffering from within do apply to it, such as, he sorrows, he suffers, and others like this; and likewise it can be said that he dies on the altar; hence the verse: *You could collect inward suffering while held in the pyx; but inflicted pain does not apply to this.*

Reply Obj. 1: Outward sufferings pertain to the substance of the body of Christ by means of his proper dimensions, but not by means of the dimensions of the bread. And so because of outward impressions that belong to the species of bread, no inward suffering is attributed to the body of Christ, but because of external impressions belonging to its proper dimensions, suffering is attributed to the body of Christ, both externally under its proper species alone, and inwardly also under its foreign species. And so because of the crucifixion that happened on Calvary, the true body of Christ preserved died under its proper species and under the sacrament.

And by this the answer to the second objection is clear; for the Jews' actions were external, and the flow of blood also belongs to local motion, and so it conveys a relation to something outside.

Response to Quaestiuncula 2

Ad secundam quaestionem dicendum, quod cum animatio sit proprietas intrinseca, constat quod sicut corpus Christi in specie propria erat exanime, ita sub sacramento. Unde si corpus Christi fuisset ab ullo disci-

To the second question, it should be said that since being animate is an intrinsic property, it is clear that just as the body of Christ was lifeless in its proper species, so also under the sacrament. Hence if the body of Christ had been

---

120. Augustine, *Contra Faustum*, Bk. 26, par. 5 (CSEL 25:733).

pulorum consecratum, non fuisset ibi anima. Quidam autem dicunt, quod forma fuit suspensa in illo triduo; et quod si primo consecratum, fuisset reservatum, desineret ibi esse Christo mortuo. Sed haec frivola sunt; quia nec ratione nec auctoritate confirmantur.

Ad primum ergo dicendum, quod, sicut supra dictum est, dist. 10, anima non est ibi ex vi sacramenti, sed propter concomitantiam ad corpus; et ideo corpore sine anima existente, nihil deperit perfectioni sacramenti, si anima ibi non contineatur.

Ad secundum dicendum, quod hoc non est propter defectum virtutis verborum, sed propter diversam dispositionem corporis Christi.

consecrated by any one of the disciples, his soul would not have been there. However, some people say that the form was suspended during that Triduum; and if what had been consecrated before had been reserved, it would have ceased to be there when Christ died. But these are silly things to say, for they are confirmed neither by reason nor by authority.

Reply Obj. 1: Just as was said above in Distinction 10,[121] the soul is not there by the force of the sacrament, but because of its concomitance with the body; and so when the body exists without its soul, there is no injury to the perfection of the sacrament if the soul is not contained there.

Reply Obj. 2: This is not because of a defect of the words' power, but because of the different dispositions of the body of Christ.

Response to Quaestiuncula 3

Ad tertiam quaestionem dicendum, quod Deus bene poterat facere quod anima Christi a corpore separata jacente in sepulcro, esset in loco ubi erat corpus sub sacramento, quia hoc importat respectum ad extra; sed non quod esset ei unita sub sacramento sicut forma, quia hoc pertinet ad dispositionem interiorem; unde inevitabiliter sequeretur duo contradictoria esse simul.

Ad primum ergo dicendum, quod ratio illa non concludit, nisi quod esset ibi sicut in loco; et hoc Deus bene potuit facere.

Et similiter etiam dicendum ad secundum. Tamen non est haec causa quare corpus Christi potest esse aliquo modo in diversis locis, quia est divinitati unitum; sed ratione conversionis alterius corporis in ipsum, fecit[122] quae non fit in animam.

To the third question, it should be said that while Christ's body was lying in the tomb, God could have easily caused Christ's separated soul to be in a place where his body was under the sacrament, for this conveys a relation to without; but under the sacrament it would not have been united to Christ's body as its form, because this pertains to the interior disposition; hence it would inevitably result that two contradictories exist at the same time.

Reply Obj. 1: That argument concludes only that it would be there as in a place, and this God could easily do.

Reply Obj. 2: And the second objection should be answered in a similar way. Nevertheless, the fact that it is united to divinity is not the reason why the body of Christ can exist in a certain way in different places, but by reason of the conversion of another body into it, which is not a conversion into his soul.

---

121. See d. 10, a. 2, qa. 1.
122. *fecit—-factae* PLE.

EXPOSITION OF THE TEXT

De materia de qua in conceptione non fuit factum. Patet quod ex aequivocatione hujus praepositionis de procedunt: quia cum dicitur: *de pane fit corpus Christi,* ly de non denotat habitudinem causae materialis, sed solum ordinem mutationis terminorum.

Investigari salubriter non potest, scilicet ut aliquis comprehendere nitatur: quia praesumptuosum est et periculosum, dum aliquis non vult plus ibi credere quam ratione videre potest; sed investigare pro defensione fidei, utile est.

Quis fidelium habere dubium possit in ipsa immolationis hora ad sacerdotis vocem caelos aperiri? etc. Dicuntur caeli aperiri in ipsa immolationis hora propter efficaciam divinae virtutis, quae operatur in sacramento; summa imis sociari, quia ex speciebus et corpore Christi fit unum sacramentum; et iterum membra capiti uniuntur; et iterum in caelum rapitur corpus Christi, inquantum fidelium devotio non sistit in specie sacramenti, sed fertur usque ad Christum, secundum quod est in caelo sub specie propria, per desiderium.

Vinum operatur sanguinem, in quo est sedes animae. Hoc potest intelligi tripliciter. Uno modo ut sedes animae dicatur conservatio vitae, quae est per sanguinem. Alio modo quia sanguis est potentia totum, quia per actum virtutis nutritivae in membra convertitur. Tertio modo quia per sanguinem in corde generatum vitalis operatio in omnia membra diffunditur, ut Philosophus in Lib. *de Animalibus* dicit.

Caro pro corpore nostro offertur, hoc intelligendum est per quamdam adaptationem de salute corporis, quae erit per gloriam resurrectionis, ad quam hoc sacramentum operatur.

Nec iterari sacramentum, quantum ad id quod est principale in hoc sacramento, scilicet consecratio materiae, quamvis iteretur quantum ad usum.

Ut mixtio illa non possit separari. Sed contra. Alchimistae dicunt, quod per immissionem junci decorticati potest separari. Et dicendum, quod a vino aufertur substantia aquae quae ibi est, propter similitudinem junci,

It is formed of some matter of which it was not made at conception.[123] It is evident that these proceed from equivocation on the preposition 'from': for when it is said, 'The body of Christ is made from bread,' the 'from' does not denote the condition of material cause, but only the order between the terminuses of the change.

"It cannot be healthfully investigated,"[124] namely so that someone strives to comprehend it: for presumption is also dangerous, when someone does not wish to believe more there than he can see with his reason; but to investigate for the defense of the faith is useful.

"Which of the faithful can have any doubt that at the very moment of immolation, the heavens open at the priest's voice?" etc.[125] The heavens are said to be opened at the very moment of immolation because of the efficacy of divine power, which works in the sacrament; the highest is said to be joined with the lowliest, because out of the species and the body of Christ one sacrament is made; and again the members are united with the head; and again the body of Christ is taken up into heaven, inasmuch as the devotion of the faithful does not stop at the species of the sacrament, but it is drawn on through longing to Christ, according as he is in heaven under his proper species.

The wine becomes blood, in which the seat of the soul is said to be.[126] This can be understood in three ways. In one way as the conservation of life, which is by the blood, may be called the seat of the soul. In another way, because the blood is potentially everything, because it is converted into the members by the act of nutritive power. In the third way because by the blood generated in the heart the vital operation is diffused among all the members, as the Philosopher says in the *History of Animals.*[127]

The flesh is offered for our body.[128] This is to be understood as by a certain adaptation for the salvation of the body, which will take place through the glory of resurrection, toward which this sacrament works.

Nor is the sacrament to be repeated,[129] as to what is principal in this sacrament, namely, the consecration of the matter, although it may be received again as to its use.

"This joining . . . is to be so mixed . . . that the commixture cannot be separated."[130] But to the contrary. Alchemists say that it can be separated by filtering it through a peeled rush. And it should be said that the substance of the water that is

---

123. Peter Lombard, *Sententiae* IV, 11.1 (60). 2.
124. *Sent* IV, 11.2 (61). 2 citing Lanfranc, *Liber de corpore et sanguine Domini,* c10.
125. *Sent* IV, 11.2 (61). 8 citing Gregory, *Dialogi,* bk 4 c58.
126. *Sent* IV, 11.4 (63). 1.
127. Aristotle, *History of Animals,* Bk. 3, ch. 19 (521a9–10).
128. *Sent* IV, 11.4 (63). 1 citing Lev. 17, 11; Deut. 12, 23.
129. *Sent* IV, 11.4 (63). 3.
130. *Sent* IV, 11.5 (64). 1 citing Cyprian, *Epistola 63 (ad Caecilium),* c13.

quod etiam porosum est; non tamen illa aqua quae fuit apposita, separatur, quia jam facta est vinum.

Nobis vero non potest ignosci, idest, peccatum nostrum non haberet in se causam veniae, cum non ex ignorantia procederet.

Aqua vero nullatenus sine vino potest offerri in sacrificium. Si autem per errorem contingat ut aqua loco vini ponatur, si ante consecrationem vini percipiat, debet aquam effundere, et vinum imponere. Si autem post, debet incipere consecrationem vini, alio vino super infuso, contritione de negligentia praehabita; vel etiam a capite canonem inchoare super aliam hostiam, hostia prius consecrata posita seorsum, ut Innocentius dicit.

there is taken away from the wine, because of the likeness of the rush, which is also porous; nevertheless, that water that had been added may not be separated, because it has already become wine.

"But we cannot be pardoned,"[131] i.e., our sin would not have in itself any cause for forgiveness, since it would not proceed from ignorance.

But water without the wine can never be offered in sacrifice.[132] However, if by mistake it should happen that water was used in place of wine, if this is perceived before the consecration of the wine, the water should be poured out and wine poured in. If it is perceived after, however, the consecration of the wine should be repeated with other wine poured in, with contrition for the previous negligence; or also one could begin the canon of the Mass from the start, using new hosts, while the host previously consecrated is set apart, as Innocent says.[133]

---

131. *Sent* IV, 11.5 (64). 2 citing Cyprian, *Epistola 63 (ad Caecilium)*, c17.
132. *Sent* IV, 11.5 (64). 3.
133. Innocent III, *De sacro altaris mysterio*, Bk. 4, ch. 22 (PL 217:872).

DISTINCTION 12
APPEARANCE AND EFFECTS OF THE EUCHARIST

Postquam determinavit Magister de uno trium, in quibus consistit integritas hujus sacramenti, scilicet de eo quod est res et sacramentum; in parte ista intendit determinare de aliis duobus, scilicet de eo quod est sacramentum tantum, et de eo quod est res tantum; unde dividitur in partes duas: in prima determinat de eo quod est[1] res tantum, ibi: *institutum est hoc sacramentum duabus de causis.*

Prima in duas: in prima determinat de accidentibus, quae sunt sacramenta, idest signa utriusque corporis Christi, scilicet veri et mystici; in secunda determinat de actu sacerdotis, qui est sacramentum sive signum passionis Christi, ibi: *post haec quaeritur, si quod gerit sacerdos, proprie dicatur sacrificium.*

Circa primum duo facit: primo determinat de ipsis accidentibus; secundo de fractione, quae in eis fundatur, ibi: *solet etiam quaeri de fractione et partitione.* Circa hoc duo facit: primo determinat de ipsa fractione; secundo de partium significatione, ibi: *quid autem partes illae significent, Sergius Papa tradit.*

Circa primum duo facit: primo movet quaestionem; secundo determinat eam, ibi: *ideo quibusdam placet, quod non sit ibi fractio, sicut videtur.* Circa quod quatuor opiniones ponit; secunda incipit ibi: *alii vero dicunt* etc.; tertia ibi: *alii tradunt corpus Christi essentialiter frangi;* quarta, ibi: *sed quia corpus Christi incorruptibile est, sane dici potest fractio illa et partitio non in substantia corporis, sed in ipsa forma panis sacramentaliter fieri.* Et circa hoc duo facit: primo ponit opinionem quartam; secundo confirmat eam, quia prae ceteris vera est, ibi: *ne autem mireris vel insultes, si accidentia videantur frangi.*

Institutum est hoc sacramentum duabus de causis. Hic ponit effectum hujus sacramenti; et quia ex effectu rei accipitur usus ejus, ideo circa hoc duo facit: primo ponit effectum; secundo determinat utendi modum, ibi: *si au-*

After the Master has examined one of the three things in which the integrity of this sacrament consists, namely, what is reality-and-sacrament, in this part he intends to consider the other two things, namely, what is sacrament alone, and what is reality alone. Hence it is divided into two parts: in the first, he considers what is sacrament alone; in the second, the effect of the sacrament which is the reality alone, at: *And this sacrament was instituted for two causes.*[2]

The first is in two parts; in the first, he considers the accidents, which are sacraments, i.e., signs of both the true body of Christ and the mystical body of Christ; in the second, he considers the act of the priest, which is a sacrament or sign of Christ's Passion, at: *After these matters it is asked whether what the priest does is properly called a sacrifice.*[3]

Concerning the first he does two things: first, he considers the accidents themselves; second, the breaking that is founded on them, at: *it is also usual to ask about the breaking and division into parts.*[4] Concerning this he does two things: first, he examines the breaking itself; second, the meaning of the parts, at: *As to what those parts may signify, Pope Sergius teaches.*[5]

Concerning the first he does two things: first, he raises the question; second, he considers it, at: *And so some are pleased to hold that there is no breaking there, as there seems to be.*[6] Concerning this he cites four opinions, the second beginning at: *But others say,* etc.;[7] the third at: *others teach that the body of Christ is broken and divided according to essence;*[8] the fourth at: *but because the body of Christ is incorruptible, it may be truly said that the breaking and division into parts is done not in the substance of the body, but in the sacramental form itself of the bread.*[9] And concerning this he does two things: first, he sets down the fourth opinion; second, he confirms it, for it is true above all the rest, at: *nor should you wonder or scoff if the accidents appear to be broken.*[10]

And this sacrament was instituted for two causes. Here he gives the effect of this sacrament. And because from the effect of a thing, its use is taken, for this reason he does two things about this: first, he sets down the effect; sec-

---

1. *est res.—est sacramentum tantum; in secunda, de effectu sacramenti qui est res* PLE.
2. Peter Lombard, *Sententiae* IV, 12.6 (71). 1.
3. *Sent* IV, 12.5 (70). 1.
4. *Sent* IV, 12.2 (67). 1.
5. *Sent* IV, 12.4 (69). 1.
6. *Sent* IV, 12.2 (67). 2.
7. *Sent* IV, 12.2 (67). 3.
8. *Sent* IV, 12.3 (68). 1.
9. *Sent* IV, 12.3 (68). 2.
10. *Sent* IV, 12.3 (68). 2.

tem quaeritur, utrum quotidie communicandum sit; audi quid inde tradit Augustinus.

Hic est triplex quaestio: prima de accidentibus. Secunda de effectibus hujus sacramenti. Tertia de frequentatione ipsius.

ond, he determines the mode of using it, at: *but if it is asked whether Communion is to be received daily, hear what Augustine teaches about this.*

Here there are three questions: first, about the accidents; second, about this sacrament's effects; third, about its frequency.

QUESTION 1

ACCIDENTS AND THE EUCHARIST

Circa primum quaeruntur tria:
primo, utrum accidentia sint hic sine substantia;

secundo, de operatione illorum accidentium;
tertio, de fractione quae in eis fundatur.

Concerning the first, three questions arise:
first, whether the accidents are here without a substance;

second, about the operation of those accidents;
third, about the breaking which is founded on them.

ARTICLE 1

Whether the accidents are here without a substance

Quaestiuncula 1

AD PRIMUM SIC PROCEDITUR. Videtur quod accidentia sine substantia esse, Deus facere non possit. Si enim esse rei separaretur ab ente, ens esset non ens. Sed hoc Deus non potest facere: quia non potest facere quod duo contradictoria sint simul vera. Ergo non potest separare esse rei ab ente. Sed accidentis esse est inesse, secundum Philosophum. Ergo Deus non potest facere quin accidens insit.

PRAETEREA, quicumque separat definitionem a definito, ponit duo contradictoria esse simul vera: quia hoc ipsum quod est homo, est animal rationale mortale; et ita si ponatur esse homo et non esse animal rationale mortale, ponitur esse homo et non esse. Sed definitio accidentis est quod inest substantiae; unde etiam in definitione singulorum accidentium oportet quod ponatur substantia. Ergo cum Deus non possit facere contradictoria simul esse vera, neque facere poterit quod accidens sit sine substantia.

PRAETEREA, Deus non potest facere quod definitio insit alicui, et definitum non insit eidem, nec quod inter affirmationem et negationem sit medium. Sed si ponamus accidentia esse sine substantia, oportet alterum dictorum sequi. Ergo Deus non potest hoc facere. Probatio mediae. Non esse enim in subjecto, sed per se existere, est definitio substantiae, et opponitur contradictorie ei quod est esse in subjecto. Sed si ponamus aliquod accidens non esse in subjecto; vel ponemus quod aliquid sit

OBJ. 1: To the first we proceed thus. It seems that God cannot make accidents exist without a substance.[11] For if a being were separated from its existence, the being would be a non-being. But God cannot do this, for he cannot make two contradictories to be true at the same time. Therefore, he cannot separate a being from being. But accidental being is to be present-in, according to the Philosopher.[12] Therefore God cannot make it so that an accident is not present in something.

OBJ. 2: Furthermore, whoever separates a definition from the thing defined, holds two contradictories to be true at the same time. For this very thing that is man, is a mortal rational animal; and so if it is held to be a man and not a mortal rational animal, it is held to be a man and not to be one. But the definition of an accident is what is present in a substance; hence also in the definition of individual accidents, substance must be included. Therefore, since God cannot make contradictories true at the same time, neither could he make accidents exist without substance.

OBJ. 3: Furthermore, God cannot make it that a definition is present in something, and the defined thing is not present in the same thing; nor that there be a mean between affirmation and negation. But if we posited that accidents exist without substance, one of these statements would necessarily follow. Therefore, God cannot do this. Proof of the middle: for the definition of substance is not being in a subject, but existing through itself, and it is opposed like a contradictory to what is being in a subject. But if we posited

---

11. Parallels: *I Sent.* d. 47, a. 4; *ST* III, q. 77, a. 1; *SCG* IV, chs. 62–63, 65; *Quodl.* III, a. 1; *Quodl.* IX, q. 3; *De rationibus fidei*, ch. 8; *Super Matt.* 26; *Super I ad Cor.* 11, lec. 5.
12. Aristotle, *Metaphysics*, Bk. 5, ch. 30 (1025a14).

medium inter esse in subjecto et non esse, vel ponemus quod aliquid sit non ens in subjecto, et non sit substantia: quia si est substantia, non est accidens. Ergo si ponamus accidens esse simul[13] subjecto, sequitur alterum duorum: vel quod inter contradictoria sit medium; vel quod definitio separetur a definito, quod iterum implicat contradictoria esse simul vera.

SED CONTRA est quod dicitur Lucae 1, 37: *non erit impossibile apud Deum omne verbum.*

PRAETEREA, potest Deus plura facere quam homo possit intelligere vel imaginari. Sed aliqui philosophi posuerunt dimensiones esse sine subjecto, sicut qui posuerunt mathematica separata. Ergo Deus potest hoc facere.

that a certain accident did not exist in a subject, either we will posit that something is a mean between being in a subject and not being in a subject, or we will posit that something is not a being in a subject, and it is not substance; for if it is substance it is not accident. Therefore if we posit that an accident exists without a subject, one of the two statements follows: either that there is a middle between two contradictories, or that a definition may be separated from what it defines, which again implies contradictories to be true at the same time.

ON THE CONTRARY, it is said: *for no word shall be impossible with God* (Luke 1:37).

FURTHERMORE, God can do more things than a man can understand or imagine. But certain philosophers posited that dimensions can exist without a subject, like those who posited separated mathematicals.[14] Therefore, God can do this.

Quaestiuncula 2

ULTERIUS. Videtur quod non sit congruum huic sacramento quod accidentia sint sine substantia. In sacramento enim perfectissimo non congruit esse aliquid quod divinae ordinationi repugnet. Sed divina ordinatio est quod accidens sit in subjecto. Ergo in hoc sacramento non competit quod sit sine subjecto.

PRAETEREA, sacramentum veritatis non decet aliqua fallacia. Sed hoc sacramentum est maximae veritatis, quia continet illum qui dixit, Joan. 14, 6: *ego sum veritas.* Cum ergo existentibus accidentibus sine subjecto sequatur fallacia; quia accidentia, quantum est in se, significant substantiam propriam subesse: videtur quod non competat huic sacramento accidentia esse sine subjecto.

PRAETEREA, materia debet esse formae proportionata. Sed ex parte formae sacramenti non competeret quod esset accidens verbi sine essentia verbi. Ergo nec ex parte materiae competit quod sit accidens elementi sine elemento.

SED CONTRA, accidens subjecto respondet. Sed substantia panis, qui prius erat subjectum priorum accidentium, mutata est in alterum statum per hoc quod conversa est in corpus Christi. Ergo et accidentia congruit in alterum statum mutari, ut scilicet sint sine subjecto.

PRAETEREA, hoc sacramentum dicitur mysterium fidei. Sed fides non solum est supra intellectum, sed etiam supra sensum. Ergo in hoc sacramento non solum debet aliquid esse supra intellectum, sicut quod corpus

OBJ. 1: Moreover, it seems that it is not fitting to this sacrament that accidents exist without substance.[15] For in the most perfect sacrament it is not suitable that there be anything opposed to divine ordination. But the divine ordination is that accidents be in a subject. Therefore, in this sacrament it is not fitting that it be without a subject.

OBJ. 2: Furthermore, no fallacy is appropriate to the sacrament of truth. But this sacrament is of the greatest truth, because it contains the one who said, *I am the truth* (John 14:6). Therefore, since a fallacy results when accidents exist without a subject, for accidents, in themselves, signify that their proper substance is underlying, therefore it seems that it does not befit this sacrament for accidents to be without a subject.

OBJ. 3: Furthermore, matter should be proportioned to form. But in the sacrament's form it would not be fitting for there to be the accidents of the words without the essence of the words. Therefore, neither in the matter is it fitting that the accidents of the element exist without the element.

ON THE CONTRARY, accidents correspond to their subject. But the substance of bread, which was formerly the subject of the former accidents, is changed into another state by the fact that it is converted into the body of Christ. Therefore, it was fitting that the accidents also be changed into another state, namely, so that they are there without a subject.

FURTHERMORE, this sacrament is called the mystery of faith. But faith is not only above the intellect, but also above the senses. Therefore, in this sacrament there should not only be something above the understanding, like the fact

---

13. *simul*—-*sine* PLE.
14. Thomas would have in mind here either Plato or some of the Platonists, who spoke of the circle as such or the form of the circle, the dyad, etc.
15. Parallels: above, d. 11, q. 1, a. 1, qa. 2; *ST* III, q. 75, a. 5; *SCG* IV, chs. 62–63, 65; *De rationibus fidei*, ch. 8; *Super I ad Cor.* 11, lec. 5.

Christi sub tam parvis panis dimensionibus contineatur; sed etiam supra sensum, scilicet quod accidentibus quae sensui subjacent, substantia propria non subsit.

that the body of Christ is contained under such small dimensions of bread; but also something above the senses, namely, that the accidents that the senses perceive do not exist in their proper substance.

Quaestiuncula 3

Ulterius. Videtur quod accidentia non sint in hoc sacramento sine substantia. Esse enim in substantia aequaliter convenit omnibus accidentibus. Sed albedo non est hic sine subjecto: quod patet ex hoc quod dividitur per accidens, quod non competit nisi existenti in subjecto. Ergo nec quantitas aut aliquod accidens est hic sine subjecto.

Praeterea, illud quod sensus percipit in hoc sacramento, est ibi secundum veritatem; alias esset fictio in hoc sacramento. Sed sensus non tantum percipit ibi quantitatem aut albedinem, sed etiam quantum et album. Ergo non est ibi accidens sine subjecto.

Praeterea, accidens non individuatur nisi ex subjecto, sicut nec forma nisi ex materia. Sed accidentia sunt ibi individuata; alias non essent sensibilia. Ergo non sunt sine subjecto.

Praeterea, omnis forma separata a materia est intellectus in actu, ut a philosophis probatur. Sed si accidentia sunt hic sine subjecto, erunt quaedam formae sine materia: non enim habent materiam partem sui. Ergo erunt intellectus in actu, quod falsum apparet.

Praeterea, quanto aliquid appropinquat ad divinam simplicitatem, tanto est simplicius. Sed si sunt hic accidentia sine substantia, magis appropinquant ad divinam simplicitatem quam angeli: quia in angelis est compositio, ad minus ex quo est et quod est; quae in his accidentibus inveniri non potest. Ergo erunt nobiliora angelis; quod falsum est.

Praeterea, impossibile est densitatem esse sine materia, neque raritatem: quia haec est definitio densi, quod multum de materia contineatur sub parvis dimensionibus; et contraria est definitio rari. Sed tactus percipit in hoc sacramento densitatem. Ergo est ibi materia sub dimensionibus; ergo dimensiones non per se existunt, et ita nec alia accidentia.

Sed contra: sicut, in praecedenti dist., dictum est, ibi non est alia substantia quam corporis Christi. Sed non sunt accidentia quae apparent in corpore Christi sicut in subjecto, quia non denominant ipsum. Ergo non sunt in subjecto aliquo.

Obj. 1: Moreover, it seems that accidents are not in this sacrament without substance.[16] For to be in a substance applies equally to all accidents. But whiteness is not here without a subject, which is clear from the fact that it is divided per accidens, which only belongs to something existing in a subject. Therefore, neither quantity nor any accident is here without a subject.

Obj. 2: Furthermore, what the senses perceive in this sacrament is there according to truth; otherwise there would be false pretenses in this sacrament. But the senses do not only perceive there quantity or whiteness, but also a certain quantity and something white. Therefore, there are no accidents there without a subject.

Obj. 3: Furthermore, an accident is only individuated by its subject, just as form is by matter. But accidents are individuated there, or else they would not be sensible. Therefore, they do not exist without a subject.

Obj. 4: Furthermore, every form separated from matter is understanding in act, as is proved by philosophers. But if accidents are here without a subject, they will be certain forms without matter: for they do not have their own material part. Therefore, they will be understanding in act, which seems false.

Obj. 5: Furthermore, the more something approaches divine simplicity, the more simple it is. But if there are accidents here without substance, they approach divine simplicity more than the angels: for in the angels there is composition, at least of what it is and that it is, which cannot be found in these accidents. Therefore, they will be more noble than the angels, which is false.

Obj. 6: Furthermore, it is impossible for density to exist without matter, nor rarity: for this is the definition of the dense, that a lot of matter is contained under small dimensions; and the definition of the rare is the opposite. But the sense of touch perceives density in this sacrament. Therefore, there is matter here under the dimensions; therefore the dimensions do not exist by themselves, and so neither do the other accidents.

On the contrary, just as was said in the previous distinction, no substance exists there other than that of the body of Christ. But the accidents that appear are not in the body of Christ as in a subject, for they do not denominate it. Therefore, they are not in any subject.

---

16. Parallels: *In I Sent.*, d. 47, a. 4; *ST* III, q. 75, a. 5; q. 77, aa. 1–2; *SCG* IV, chs. 62–63, 65; *Quodl.* III, a. 1; *Quodl.* IX, q. 3; *De rationibus fidei*, ch. 8; *Super I ad Cor.* 11, lec. 5.

PRAETEREA, species ad hoc remanent in sacramento, ut ducant per significationem in corpus Christi. Sed si essent in aliquo sicut in subjecto, non ducerent in corpus Christi, sed magis in cognitionem sui subjecti. Ergo sunt hic accidentia sine subjecto.

FURTHERMORE, the species remain in the sacrament so that they may lead us by their signification to the body of Christ. But if they were in anything as in a subject, they would not lead us to the body of Christ, but more to the knowledge of their own subject. Therefore, there are accidents here without a subject.

Response to Quaestiuncula 1

RESPONDEO dicendum ad primam quaestionem, quod, sicut dicitur prima propositione lib. *de Causis, causa prima est vehementioris impressionis supra causatum causae secundae quam ipsa causa secunda.* Unde quando causa secunda removet influentiam suam a causato, adhuc potest remanere influentia causae primae in causatum illud; sicut remoto rationali, remanet vivum, quo remoto remanet esse. Cum ergo causa prima accidentium et omnium existentium Deus sit; causa autem secunda accidentium sit substantia, quia accidentia ex principiis substantiae causantur; poterit Deus accidentia in esse conservare, remota etiam causa secunda, scilicet substantia. Et ideo absque omni dubitatione dicendum est, quod Deus potest facere accidens sine subjecto.

AD PRIMUM ergo dicendum, quod inesse non dicit esse accidentis absolute, sed magis modum essendi qui sibi competit ex ordine ad causam proximam sui esse. Et quia remoto ordine accidentis ad causam proximam, adhuc potest remanere ordo ipsius ad causam primam, secundum quem modus ipsius essendi non est inesse, sed ab alio esse; ideo potest Deus facere quod sit accidens, et non insit: nec tamen esse accidentis ab accidente removebitur, sed modus essendi.

AD SECUNDUM dicendum, quod sicut probat Avicenna in sua *Metaphysica*, per se existere non est definitio substantiae: quia per hoc non demonstratur quidditas ejus, sed ejus esse; et sua quidditas non est suum esse; alias non posset esse genus: quia esse non potest esse commune per modum generis, cum singula contenta in genere differant secundum esse; sed definitio, vel quasi definitio, substantiae est res habens quidditatem, cui acquiritur esse, vel debetur, non in alio; et similiter esse in subjecto non est definitio accidentis, sed e contrario res cui debetur esse in alio; et hoc nunquam separatur ab aliquo accidente, nec separari potest: quia illi rei quae est accidens, secundum rationem suae quidditatis semper debetur esse in alio. Sed potest esse quod illud quod debetur alicui secundum rationem suae quidditatis, ei virtute divina agente non conveniat; et sic patet quod facere accidens esse sine substantia, non est separare definitionem a definito; et si aliquando hoc dicatur

TO THE FIRST QUESTION, I answer that as is said in the first proposition of the *Book of Causes: the first cause makes a more vehement impression on what is caused by a second cause than the second cause itself.*[17] Hence when the second cause removes its own influence from what is caused, the first cause's influence can still remain in what it caused; just as when rational is removed, living remains, and when that is removed, being remains. Since therefore the first cause of accidents, and of everything existing, is God, but the second cause of accidents is substance, for accidents are caused by the principles of substance, God could keep accidents in being while removing their second cause, namely, substance. And thus without any doubt it must be said that God can make accidents without a subject.

REPLY OBJ. 1: 'To be present-in' does not name the being of an accident absolutely, but rather the mode of being that belongs to an accident by its order to the proximate cause of its being. And since once an accident's order to its proximate cause is removed, its order to its first clause can remain, according to which its mode of being is not being present-in, but being from another, in this way God can make something an accident and not present-in anything; however, he still will not remove an accident's being from the accident, but its mode of being.

REPLY OBJ. 2: As Avicenna proves in his *Metaphysics*, existing through itself is not the definition of a substance: for by this what it is is not demonstrated, but only its being; and what it is is not its being, otherwise it could not be a genus, for being cannot be shared in the manner of a genus, since the individual things contained in a genus differ from each other according to being. But the definition, or quasi-definition, of substance is a thing having whatness, for which being is acquired or due, not in another. And likewise to be in a subject is not the definition of an accident, but on the contrary, it is a thing to which it is due to exist in another. And this is never separated from any accident, nor can it be separated: for to that thing that is an accident it is always due that it exist in another, according to the notion of what it is. But it can be that what is due to something according to the notion of what it is does not apply to it by the power of a divine agent. And so it is clear that to make an accident exist without substance is not to separate a defini-

---

17. For the text of this proposition as well as discussion of it, see Thomas's *Commentary on the Book of Causes*, 5–11.

definitio accidentis, praedicto modo intelligenda est definitio dicta: quia aliquando ab auctoribus definitiones ponuntur causa brevitatis non secundum debitum ordinem, sed tanguntur illa ex quibus potest accipi definitio.

AD TERTIUM dicendum, quod sicut ab accidentibus in hoc sacramento removetur esse in subjecto, ita convenit eis non esse in subjecto; unde non ponitur aliquid medium inter affirmationem et negationem. Nec tamen sequitur quod definitio alicui conveniat cui non convenit definitum; quia non esse in substantia[18] non est definitio substantiae, ut dictum est, sed habere quidditatem cui tale esse competat; et hoc non convenit[19] eis ex ratione suae quidditatis, sed divina virtute.

tion from what it defines; and if this is sometimes called the definition of an accident, the definition mentioned should be understood in the foregoing way: for sometimes definitions are set down by authors for the sake of brevity, not according to due order, but they touch on those things from which a definition can be taken.

REPLY OBJ. 3: Just as being in a subject is removed from the accidents in this sacrament, so it belongs to them not to be in a subject; hence no middle between affirmation and negation is maintained. Nor does it follow, however, that the definition applies to something to which the thing defined does not apply; for not being in a subject is not the definition of substance, as was said, but to have the whatness to which such being belongs; and this does not apply to the accidents in this sacrament because "not being in a subject" does not apply to them by reason of their whatness, but by divine power.

Response to Quaestiuncula 2

AD SECUNDAM QUAESTIONEM dicendum, quod accidentia remanere in hoc sacramento quare congruat, supra dictum est, dist. praec. Sed accidentia esse sine subjecto congruit huic sacramento multipliciter. Primo quantum ad significationem; quia species sine substantia existentes expressius ducunt in corpus Christi, quod sub eis continetur, et immediatius; si enim subjectum haberent, ducerent immediate in subjectum illud. Secundo propter effectum, qui est unio membrorum ad caput, in quo fit per fidem; et ideo in hoc sacramento oportet aliquid esse supra naturam, per quod intellectus noster assuescat ad ea quae sunt fidei credenda. Tertio quantum ad usum, quia est cibus spiritualis; et ideo competit quod nullum accidentibus subjectum subsit, quod cibus corporalis esse possit. Quarto quantum ad perfectionem; quia enim hoc sacramentum est perfectissimum, ideo omnia quae sunt in hoc sacramento, altissimum statum accipiunt, sicut quod substantia panis in corpus gloriosum divinitati unitum convertitur; et propter hoc etiam accidentibus datur in hoc sacramento sine subjecto esse.

AD PRIMUM ergo dicendum, quod divina dispositio quae aliquid ordinat secundum legem communem, etiam sibi aliqua reservat praeter legem communem facienda ad aliquod privilegium gratiae communicandum; nec ex hoc sequitur aliqua inordinatio, quia divina dispositio unicuique rei ordinem imponit.

AD SECUNDUM dicendum, quod de substantia rei judicare non pertinet ad sensum, sed ad intellectum, cu-

TO THE SECOND QUESTION, it should be said that it was said above in the preceding distinction how it is appropriate to this sacrament that the accidents remain. But for the accidents to exist without a subject is fitting to this sacrament in many ways. First, in signification; for species existing without substance more expressly and directly lead us to the body of Christ, which is contained under them; for if they had a subject, they would lead directly to that subject. Second, because of the effect, which is the union of the members to the head, which happens by faith; and so in this sacrament it is necessary for something to be above nature, by which our understanding grows accustomed to the things of faith that are to be believed. Third, as to its use, which is a spiritual food; and so it is fitting that no subject that could be bodily food underlies the accidents. Fourth, as to perfection, for because this sacrament is the most perfect, all the things that are in this sacrament take on their highest state, like the fact that the bread's substance is converted into the glorified body united to the divinity; and because of this it is given to the accidents to exist without subject in this sacrament.

REPLY OBJ. 1: The divine disposing that orders something according to the general law also reserves to itself certain things to be done outside the general law for some privilege of grace to be communicated. Nor does any disordering follow from this, for divine disposing imposes order on every single thing.

REPLY OBJ. 2: Judging about the substance of a thing does not pertain to the senses, but to the understanding,

---

18. *substantia.—subjecto* PLE.
19. *convenit eis.—convenit accidentibus in hoc sacramento quia non esse in subjecto non convenit eis* PLE.

jus objectum est quod quid est, ut dicitur in 3 *de Anima*; et ideo non accidit ibi aliqua deceptio; quia accidentia sunt ibi de quibus sensus judicat; sed de substantia verum judicium habet intellectus fide juvatus. Nec est inconveniens quod intellectus absque fide erret in hoc sacramento, sicut et in aliis quae sunt fidei.

AD TERTIUM dicendum, quod verbo inest virtus transubstantiandi; et ideo ad hoc quod sit vera transubstantiatio, oportet quod sit verum verbum; sed materia est ibi ad significandum; et ideo sufficit quod accidentia remaneant, quibus mediantibus significatio completur.

whose object is what is, as is said in *On the Soul* 3;[20] and so there is no deception there, for accidents are what the senses judge about in this case; but the understanding has true judgment about the substance when helped by faith. Nor is it unfitting that without faith the understanding would err in this sacrament, for it is the same in other matters that are of faith.

REPLY OBJ. 3: The power of transubstantiation is in the words; and so for there to be a true transubstantiation, it is necessary that there be true words; but matter is there for signifying; and so it suffices that the accidents remain by means of which the signification is completed.

Response to Quaestiuncula 3

AD TERTIAM QUAESTIONEM dicendum, quod quidam dixerunt, quod vera substantia panis simul remaneat sub sacramento cum corpore Christi; et secundum hoc accidentia non essent in hoc sacramento sine subjecto. Sed haec opinio in praecedenti dist. improbata est.

Alia opinio est quod remanet ibi forma substantialis, et in ea fundantur omnia accidentia quae apparent. Sed non minus difficile est materialem formam substantialem a materia separare quam accidentia a substantiis. Et praeterea quantitas non respicit formam nisi ratione materiae; unde formae immateriales dimensionibus carent; et ideo, cum alia accidentia mediante quantitate referantur ad substantiam, non poterit forma existens sine materia, accidentium sensibilium subjectum esse. Boethius etiam dicit in Lib. *de Trin.* quod forma simplex subjectum esse non potest.

Et ideo alii dixerunt, quod accidentia illa fundantur in aere sicut in subjecto. Sed haec opinio stare non potest. Constat enim quod ante transubstantiationem sub dimensionibus panis non erat aer. Ergo si conversione facta sit ibi aer, oportet quod aer subintraverit per motum localem dimensiones illas; et iste motus non percipitur. Et praeterea inconveniens est quod subjectum moveatur motu locali ad accidens, et quod accidens transeat de subjecto in subjectum. Probatum est etiam a philosophis, quod corpus naturale et corpus mathematicum non possunt esse simul; unde cum illae dimensiones quae fuerunt, sint quoddam corpus non naturale, sed mathematicum, non poterit aer cum illis dimensionibus simul esse, nec poterit esse subjectum eorum, quia habet dimensiones proprias aer. Cum ergo omnes dimensiones sint ejusdem speciei, in quacumque materia sint, quia materia non intrat in definitionem earum; si

To THE THIRD QUESTION, it should be said that some people said that the bread's true substance remained under the sacrament together with the body of Christ; and according to this the accidents did not exist in this sacrament without a subject. But this opinion was disproved in the previous distinction.

The other opinion is that the substantial form remains there and in it are founded all the accidents that appear. But it is no less difficult to separate the material substantial form from the matter than to separate accidents from substances. And furthermore, quantities do not relate to form except by reason of matter, which is why immaterial forms lack dimensions. And so, since other accidents are referred to substance by means of quantity, no form existing without matter could be the subject of sensible accidents. Boethius also says in his book *On the Trinity* that a simple form cannot be a subject.[21]

And so others have said that those accidents are founded in the air as in their subject. But this opinion cannot stand. For it is clear that before transubstantiation, air was not existing under the dimensions of the bread. Therefore, if there is air there once the conversion has happened, air would have to have entered under those dimensions by local motion; and this motion is not perceived. And furthermore, it is unfitting that the subject be moved to the accidents by local motion, and that the accidents transfer from one subject to another. It has also been proven by philosophers that a natural body and a mathematical body cannot exist together.[22] And so, since those dimensions that did exist are not a natural body, but a mathematical one, air could not have existed together with those dimensions, nor could it be their subject, because air has its own proper dimensions. Therefore since all dimensions are of the same species in whatever matter they exist, because

---

20. Aristotle, *On the Soul*, Bk. 3, ch. 6 (430b27–28).
21. Boethius, *Quomodo trinitas unus Deus ac non tres dii* [*De Trinitate*], ch. 2 (PL 64:1250; Loeb, "Opuscula Sacra," pp. 8–12).
22. See Aristotle, *Physics*, Bk. 4, ch. 8 (216a26ff.).

dimensiones panis iterum sint sicut in subjecto in aere, sequitur quod duo accidentia speciei ejusdem sint in eodem subjecto; quod est contradictoria esse simul; quia accidentium ejusdem speciei numeratio non est nisi ex subjecto; unde si subjectum sit unum, sequitur illa accidentia esse plura et non plura. Constat etiam quod aer non est susceptivus talium accidentium, scilicet duritiei, figurae determinatae, et aliarum hujusmodi quae ibi apparent.

Et ideo dicendum est, quod accidentia sunt ibi sine subjecto; non enim potest dici, quod sint in corpore Christi sicut in subjecto. Sciendum autem, quod substantia corporalis habet quod sit subjectum accidentium ex materia sua, cui primo inest subjici alteri. Prima autem dispositio materiae est quantitas; quia secundum ipsam attenditur divisio ejus et indivisio, et ita unitas et multitudo, quae sunt prima consequentia ens; et propter hoc sunt dispositiones totius materiae, non hujus aut illius tantum. Unde omnia alia accidentia mediante quantitate in substantia fundantur, et quantitas est prior eis naturaliter; et ideo non claudit materiam sensibilem in ratione sua, quamvis claudat materiam intelligibilem, ut dicitur in 7 *Metaphysica*. Unde ex hoc quidam decepti fuerunt, ut crederent dimensiones esse substantiam rerum sensibilium; quia remotis qualitatibus nihil sensibile remanere videbant nisi quantitatem, quae tamen secundum esse suum dependet a substantia, sicut et alia accidentia. Virtute autem divina confertur dimensionibus quae fuerunt panis, ut sine subjecto subsistant in hoc sacramento, quod est prima proprietas substantiae; et per consequens datur eis ut sustineant alia accidentia, sicut et sustinebant quando substantia eis suberat; et sic alia accidentia sunt in dimensionibus sicut in subjecto, ipsae vero dimensiones non sunt in subjecto.

AD PRIMUM ergo dicendum, quod prima accidentia consequentia substantiam sunt quantitas et qualitas; et haec duo proportionantur duobus principiis essentialibus substantiae, scilicet formae et materiae[24] unde magnum et parvum Plato posuit differentias materiae; sed qualitas ex parte formae. Et quia materia est subjectum primum quod non est in alio, forma autem est in alio, scilicet materia; ideo magis appropinquat ad hoc quod est non esse in alio, quantitas quam qualitas, et per consequens quam alia accidentia.

AD SECUNDUM dicendum, quod quantitas dimensiva secundum suam rationem non dependet a materia sensibili, quamvis dependeat secundum suum esse;

matter does not enter into their definition, if the dimensions of the bread are again in the air as in a subject, it follows that two accidents of the same species are in the same subject; which is for contradictories to be simultaneously true, for the numbering of accidents of the same species is only by the subject; and thus if the subject is one, it follows that those accidents are many and not many. It is also clear that air is not susceptible to accidents like these, namely, firmness, determinate shape, and others like this that appear there.

And so it should be said that the accidents are there without a subject; for it cannot be said that they are in the body of Christ as their subject. But it should be known that it belongs to bodily substance to be the subject of accidents by its own matter, to which it first belongs to be subject to another. Now the first disposition of matter is quantity; for its being divided or being undivided depends upon quantity, as does its oneness or multiplicity, which are the first things consequent on being; and because of this they are dispositions of all matter, not just this or that matter alone. And for this reason all other accidents are founded on substance through the mediation of quantity, and quantity is prior to them naturally; and so it does not include sensible matter in its definition, although it includes intelligible matter, as is said in *Metaphysics* 7.[23] Hence certain people were deceived by this, so that they believed the dimensions to be the substance of sensible things; for once qualities have been removed, nothing sensible seemed to remain except quantity, which nevertheless according to its being depends on substance, just like all the other accidents. But by divine power it is conferred on the dimensions that were the bread's that in this sacrament they subsist without a subject, which is the first property of substance. And as a result it is given to them to support other accidents, just as they did when a substance was underlying them; and this is how other accidents are in the dimensions as in a subject, but those dimensions themselves are not in a subject.

REPLY OBJ. 1: The first accidents consequent on substance are quantity and quality; and these two are proportionate to the two essential principles of substance, namely, form and matter; for quantity corresponds to matter, (hence Plato posited large and small as differences of matter); but quality is on the part of the form. And since matter is the first subject that is not in something else, but form is in something else, namely, matter, this is why quantity approaches more closely than quality to what is not being in something else, and consequently more than the other accidents.

REPLY OBJ. 2: Dimensive quantity as regards it definition does not depend on sensible matter, although it does depend on it as regards its being. And so in predicates and

---

23. Aristotle, *Metaphysics*, Bk. 7, ch. 10 (1036a8–9).
24. *materiae unde.—materiae quia quantitas respondet materiae unde* PLE.

ideo in praedicando et subjiciendo accipit modum substantiae et modum accidentis; unde lineam dicimus et quantitatem et quantam, et magnitudinem et magnam; et ideo cum sint ibi dimensiones sine substantia, non tantum videt sensus quantitatem, sed etiam quantum. De aliis autem accidentibus planum est quod est ibi aliquid album, quia albedo est ibi in subjecto.

AD TERTIUM dicendum, quod de ratione individui duo sunt: scilicet quod sit ens actu vel in se vel in alio; et quod sit divisum ab aliis quae sunt vel possunt esse in eadem specie, in se indivisum existens; et ideo primum individuationis principium est materia, qua acquiritur esse in actu cuilibet tali formae sive substantiali sive accidentali; et secundarium principium individuationis est dimensio, quia ex ipsa habet materia quod dividatur; unde in carentibus dimensione impossibile est aliam esse divisionem nisi per formam, quae facit diversitatem speciei; et propter hoc in angelis sunt tot species quot individua; quia cum sint formae sive quidditates subsistentes ex seipsis, habent esse in actu et distinctionem; et ideo non indigent ad sui individuationem neque materia neque dimensione. Si ergo quantitas sine materia haberet esse actu, per se haberet individuationem, quia per se habet divisionem²⁵ illam secundum quam dividitur materia; et sic una pars differret ab alia non specie, sed numero, secundum ordinem qui attenditur in situ partium; et similiter una linea ab alia differret numero, dummodo acciperetur in diverso situ. Quia ergo in hoc sacramento ponimus dimensiones per se subsistere, constat quod ex seipsis individuantur, et per ea alia accidentia quae in eis fundantur.

AD QUARTUM dicendum, quod illud quod est intellectus vel intellectum in actu, secundum philosophos, oportet esse separatum non solum a materia, sed etiam a conditionibus materiae individuantibus; et hoc non est in proposito, ut ex dictis patet.

AD QUINTUM dicendum, quod cum ista accidentia habeant esse et essentias proprias, et eorum essentia non sit eorum esse, constat quod aliud est in eis esse et quod est; et ita habent compositionem illam quae in angelis invenitur, et ulterius compositionem ex partibus quantitatis, quae in angelis non invenitur; et sic magis recedunt a divina simplicitate.

AD SEXTUM dicendum, quod sicut subjectum quod ponitur in definitione aliorum accidentium, non est de essentia accidentis; ita etiam materia, quae ponitur in definitione raritatis et densitatis, non est de essentia eorum; non enim est densitas materia multa existens sub parvis dimensionibus, sed proprietas quaedam conse-

subjects of sentences it takes the mode of substance and the mode of accident; which is why we call a line both a quantity and how much, both a magnitude and large. And so since dimensions exist there without substance, the senses do not only see quantity, but also an amount. But it is plain with respect to the other accidents that there is something white there, for whiteness is there in a subject.

REPLY OBJ. 3: There are two things in the concept of 'individual': namely, that there is a being in act, whether in itself or in another; and that it is divided from others that do or can exist in the same species, existing undivided in itself. And thus the first principle of individuation is matter, by which it acquires being in act for any such form whether substantial or accidental; and the secondary principle of individuation is dimension, for matter is able to be divided by it. And this is why it is impossible in things that lack dimension for there to be another division except by form, which makes the difference of species. And because of this among the angels there are as many species as individuals, for since they are forms or subsistent whatnesses from themselves, they have being in act and distinction; and so they do not need matter or dimension for their individuation. Therefore, if quantity without matter had being in act, it would have individuation through itself, for it has through itself that dimension according to which matter is divided. And so one part would differ from another not in species but in number, according to the order that is found in the position of the parts. And similarly one line would differ from another in number as long as it were taken in a different position. Therefore because in this sacrament we hold that dimensions subsist by themselves, it is clear that they are individuated by themselves, and the other accidents that are founded in them are individuated by them.

REPLY OBJ. 4: What is understanding or understood in act, according to philosophers, must be separated not only from matter but also from the individuating conditions of matter; and this is not the case here, as is clear from what has been said.

REPLY OBJ. 5: Since those accidents have being and proper essences, and their essence is not their being, it is clear that being and 'what it is' differ in them. And so they have that composition that is found in the angels, and further composition on the part of quantity, which is not found in the angels; and this is how they are more distant from divine simplicity.

REPLY OBJ. 6: Just as the subject that is included in the definition of other accidents is not of the accident's essence, so also matter, which is included in the definition of rarity and density, is not of their essence. For density is not more matter existing under small dimensions, but a certain property consequent on the fact that matter is so arranged; and

---

25. *divisionem.—dimensionem* PLE.

quens ex hoc quod materia sic se habet; unde talem proprietatem Deus potest facere, etiam si materia non esset.

thus God can make such a property, even if matter did not exist.

ARTICLE 2

About the operation of those accidents

Quaestiuncula 1

AD SECUNDUM SIC PROCEDITUR. Videtur quod accidentia quae remanent in hoc sacramento, non possunt immutare aliquid extrinsecum. Illa enim agunt et patiuntur ad invicem quae communicant in materia, ut dicitur in 1 *de Generat.* Sed accidentia illa non communicant in materia cum corporibus exterioribus. Ergo non possunt ea immutare.

PRAETEREA, actio naturalis requirit contactum naturalem, ut patet in 1 *de Generat.* Sed mathematicis, idest dimensionibus separatis, non convenit tactus physicus, sed mathematicus tantum, sicut et locus, ut ibidem dicitur. Ergo cum in hoc sacramento sint dimensiones separatae, in quibus alia accidentia fundantur, ut dictum est, videtur quod non possint agere in aliquid extrinsecum.

PRAETEREA, passum, quamvis in principio sit contrarium, tamen in fine est simile. Sed si corpora exteriora immutarentur, ipsa jam immutata non essent formae tantum, sed formae in materia. Ergo non possunt immutari a dimensionibus quae sunt formae tantum.

SED CONTRA, nihil sentitur nisi quod immutat sensum. Sed hujusmodi accidentia sentiuntur. Ergo immutant.

PRAETEREA, omne quod habet esse, habet agere aliquo modo: quia nulla res destituitur propria operatione. Sed hujusmodi accidentia habent esse. Ergo possunt agere.

OBJ. 1: It seems that the accidents that remain in this sacrament cannot change something outside them.[26] For those things act on each other that share in matter, as is said in *On the Generation of Animals* 1.[27] But those accidents do not share in matter with external bodies. Therefore, they cannot change them.

OBJ. 2: Furthermore, natural action requires natural contact, as is clear in *On the Generation of Animals* 1.[28] But physical touch does not apply to mathematicals, i.e., separated dimensions, but only mathematical touch, just as also place, as it says in the same text. Therefore, since in this sacrament there are separated dimensions on which the other accidents are founded, as was said, it seems that they cannot act on anything extrinsic.

OBJ. 3: Furthermore, what is affected, although it is contrary in the beginning, nevertheless in the end is the same. But if external bodies were changed, once they were changed they would not be forms alone but forms in matter. Therefore, they cannot be changed by dimensions that are forms alone.

ON THE CONTRARY, nothing is sensed without changing the senses. But accidents of this sort are sensed. Therefore, they change things.

FURTHERMORE, everything that has being can act in some way: for no thing is left without its proper operation. But these accidents have being. Therefore, they can act.

Quaestiuncula 2

ULTERIUS. Videtur quod non possint aliquid extrinsecum immutare substantialiter. Generans enim debet esse simile generato. Sed omne generatum est compositum ex materia et forma. Cum ergo accidentia illa sint formae tantum, non possunt immutare generatum aliquid extra se. Et hac ratione utitur Philosophus in 7 *Metaphysica* contra Platonem, qui ponebat formas separatas esse causas generationis sensibilium.

OBJ. 1: Moreover, it seems that these accidents cannot substantially change anything extrinsic.[29] For what generates must be like what is generated. But every generated thing is composed of form and matter. Therefore, since these accidents are only forms, they cannot change something generated outside themselves. And the Philosopher uses this reasoning in the *Metaphysics* 7,[30] against Plato, who claimed that separated forms were the causes of sensible objects being generated.

---

26. Parallels: *ST* III, q. 77, a. 3; *Resp. 35 ad Lector. Venetum.*
27. Aristotle, *On the Generation of Animals*, Bk. 1, ch. 6 (322b13).
28. Ibid., 322b22.
29. Parallels: *ST* III, q. 77, a. 3; *Resp. 35 ad Lector. Venetum.*
30. Aristotle, *Metaphysics*, Bk. 7, ch. 8 (1033b20ff.).

PRAETEREA, nihil agit ultra suam speciem, sed citra quandoque: quia effectus non est nobilior causa. Sed substantia est nobilior omni accidente. Ergo illa accidentia non possunt aliquam substantiam generare.

SED CONTRA, species istae habent eamdem virtutem quam habebant ante transubstantiationem: quia nihil est eis ablatum, sed additum. Sed ante transubstantiationem poterant aliquid substantialiter immutare. Ergo et post.

OBJ. 2: Furthermore, nothing acts outside its own species, but always within it: for the effect is not nobler than the cause. But substance is nobler than any accident. Therefore, these accidents cannot generate any substance.

ON THE CONTRARY, these species have the same power that they had before transubstantiation, for nothing is taken away from them, only added. But before transubstantiation, they could change something substantially. Therefore, they also can afterward.

Quaestiuncula 3

ULTERIUS. Videtur quod ista accidentia nullo modo possint corrumpi. Quia ista accidentia sunt formae tantum. Sed forma est invariabili essentia consistens, ut dicitur in *Lib. Sex Principiorum*. Ergo hujusmodi species non corrumpuntur.

PRAETEREA, omnis res per se subsistens sine materia, est incorruptibilis: quia materia est corruptionis principium, sicut patet in angelis et animabus. Sed hujusmodi species sunt formae sine materia subsistentes. Ergo sunt incorruptibiles.

PRAETEREA, si corrumpuntur, aut corruptio ista est naturalis, aut miraculosa. Naturalis non: quia sicut nihil generatur naturaliter nisi compositum, ita nihil corrumpitur nisi compositum naturaliter. Similiter neque miraculosa: quia sic sola Dei virtute fieret: Deus autem, secundum Augustinum, non est causa tendendi in non esse. Ergo nullo modo corrumpitur.

SED CONTRA, quamdiu sunt accidentia sensibilia sentiri possunt. Sed quandoque desinunt sentiri posse hujusmodi accidentia. Ergo desinunt esse.

PRAETEREA, quamdiu species manent, et corpus Christi manet sub sacramento. Sed corpus Christi quandoque desinit esse sub sacramento. Ergo quandoque desinunt esse species illae.

OBJ. 1: Moreover, it seems that those accidents cannot be corrupted in any way.[31] For those accidents are only forms. But form is something that consists of an invariable essence, as it says in the book of the *Six Principles*.[32] Therefore, species like this can never be corrupted.

OBJ. 2: Furthermore, every thing subsisting on its own without matter is incorruptible: for matter is the principle of corruption, as is seen in the cases of angels and souls. But these species are forms subsisting without matter. Therefore, they are incorruptible.

OBJ. 3: Furthermore, if they are corrupted, either their corruption is natural or miraculous. But it is not natural: for just as only composed things are generated naturally, so also only composed things are naturally corrupted. Likewise, neither is it miraculous: for this would only happen by the power of God, but God, according to Augustine, is not a cause of anything tending toward non-being.[33] Therefore, it does not corrupt in any way.

ON THE CONTRARY, as long as sensible accidents exist, they can be sensed. But at some point accidents like this can no longer be sensed. Therefore, they can stop existing.

FURTHERMORE, as long as the species remain, the body of Christ also remains under the sacrament. But at some point the body of Christ stops existing under the sacrament. Therefore, sometimes those species cease to exist.

Quaestiuncula 4

ULTERIUS. Videtur quod ex eis non possit aliquid generari. Corruptio enim generationi vel factioni opponitur. Sed omne quod non habet materiam partem sui, si fit, oportet quod ex nihilo fiat. Ergo si corrumpitur, oportet quod in nihilum tendat, et nihil ex eo fiat.

PRAETEREA, substantia et accidens magis differunt quam corpus et spiritus. Sed ex corpore non potest fieri

OBJ. 1: Moreover, it seems that nothing can be generated from them.[34] For corruption is opposed to generation or making. But everything that does not have matter as part of it, if it is made, must be made out of nothing. Therefore, if it is corrupted, it must tend toward nothing, and nothing be made from it.

OBJ. 2: Furthermore, substance and accident are more different than body and spirit. But spirit cannot be made

---

31. Parallels: *ST* III, q. 77, a. 4; *SCG* IV, ch. 66; *Resp. 35 ad Lector. Venetum.*
32. Gilbert de la Porrée (Gilbertus Porretanus), *Sex principiis* (ed. Heysse), ch. 1, l. 4, pg. 8.
33. See Augustine, *De diuersis quaestionibus octoginta tribus* (CCSL 44A), q. 21.
34. Parallels: *ST* III, q. 77, a. 5; *SCG* IV, ch. 66; *Quodl.* IX, a. 5, ad 3; *Super I ad Cor.* 11, lec. 4.

spiritus, ut patet in *Lib. de Duabus Naturis*. Ergo ex speciebus illis quae sunt accidentia tantum, non potest substantia aliqua generari.

PRAETEREA, impossibile est ex uno simul et semel multa fieri. Sed si aliquid generatur, in illo est invenire substantiam et accidens. Ergo non potest generari ex accidente tantum.

PRAETEREA, si aliquid generatur, aut illa generatio est naturalis, aut miraculosa. Naturalis non: quia generatum et id ex quo generatur naturaliter conveniunt in materia, ut patet in omnibus generationibus naturalibus; quod hic non potest inveniri. Similiter nec miraculosa: quia quod vermes aliquando inde generentur, vel in cinerem resolvantur, hoc est in irreverentiam tanti sacramenti; quod a Deo non est. Ergo nullo modo aliquid ex hujusmodi speciebus generari potest.

SED CONTRA est, quod sensibiliter apparet, si diu reserventur, paulatim in aliud mutari.

PRAETEREA, Innocentius dicit: *in quo similitudo deficeret, in eo sacramentum non esset, sed ibi se proderet, et locum fidei auferret*. Ergo oportet esse omnimodam similitudinem specierum ad substantiam panis. Sed ex substantia panis poterat aliquid generari. Ergo et ex speciebus ibi remanentibus.

from a body, as is clear in the book *On the Two Natures*.[35] Therefore, from those species that are accidents alone, no substance can be generated.

OBJ. 3: Furthermore, it is impossible for many things to be made out of one thing at one and the same time. But if anything is generated, it means that substance and accident are found in it. Therefore, it cannot be generated by accident alone.

OBJ. 4: Furthermore, if anything is generated, either that generation is natural or miraculous. But it is not natural, for the thing generated and what it is generated from naturally share in matter, as is clear in all natural generating; but that cannot be found here. Likewise, it is not miraculous: for the fact that worms are sometimes generated from these accidents, or they crumble into dust, shows irreverence for such a great sacrament, which is not from God. Therefore, in no way can anything be generated from accidents[36] like this.

ON THE CONTRARY, what appears sensibly, if it is kept for a long time, will gradually change into something else.

FURTHERMORE, Innocent says, *in anything where a likeness would be lacking, the sacrament would not exist, but it would betray itself and steal the place of faith*.[37] Therefore, the species must bear a likeness to the substance of bread in every way. But something can be generated from the substance of bread. Therefore, the same is true of the species that remain there.

Quaestiuncula 5

ULTERIUS. Videtur quod non possint nutrire. Quia omnis cibus qui nutrit, in corpus transit, et superfluitates ex eo resolvuntur. Sed cibus iste non vadit in corpus, ut Ambrosius in littera dicit. Ergo non nutrit.

PRAETEREA, *ex eisdem nutrimur ex quibus sumus*, ut dicitur in 2 *de Generat*. Sed non sumus ex accidentibus. Ergo ex eis non nutrimur.

PRAETEREA, omne quod nutrit quocumque modo, solvit jejunium. Si ergo species istae nutriunt, solverent jejunium; et sic post sumptionem corporis Christi non posset aliquis communicare; quod falsum est.

SED CONTRA est quod dicitur in Glossa, 1 Corinth. 11, super illud: *alius quidem esurit, alius autem ebrius est*,

OBJ. 1: Moreover, it seems that it cannot nourish.[38] For all food that nourishes changes into the body, and excesses are expelled from it. But this food does not go into the body, as Ambrose says in the text.[39] Therefore, it does not nourish.

OBJ. 2: Furthermore, *we are nourished by the same things of which we are made*, as is said in *On Generation and Corruption* 2.[40] But we are not made from accidents. Therefore, we are not nourished by them.

OBJ. 3: Furthermore, everything that nourishes in some way breaks a fast. But if these species nourish us, then they would break our fast; and then after consuming the body of Christ someone could not receive Communion, which is false.

ON THE CONTRARY, it says in the Gloss on this text: *for one man goes hungry while another is drunk* (1 Cor 11),[41]

35. Boethius, *Liber de persona et duabus naturis contra Eutychen et Nestorium*, ch. 6 (PL 64:1349; Loeb ed., pp. 108–9).

36. *Species* has many meanings, including appearance, form, kind, beauty, and the species that is contrasted with genus. In reference to the Eucharist, Aquinas uses *species* to mean the substance of the body and blood of Christ under the *appearance* or accidents of bread and wine.

37. Innocent III, *De sacro altaris mysterio*, Bk. 4, ch. 16 (PL 217:867).

38. Parallels: *ST* III, q. 77, a. 6; *SCG* IV, ch. 66; *Super I ad Cor*. 11, lec. 4.

39. See Lombard, d. 12, ch. 4, n. 3, citing Ambrose, *De sacramentis* (CSEL 73), Bk. 5, ch. 4, nn. 24–25.

40. Aristotle, *On Generation and Corruption*, Bk. 2, ch. 8 (335a10).

41. See *Glossa ordinaria*, PL 114:539.

quod aliqui sunt inebriati ex usu specierum hujus sacramenti.

PRAETEREA, nihil aufert sitim vel famem, nisi quod nutrit. Sed sensibiliter reperiri potest quod ex potu illo sitis tollitur, praecipue si in multa quantitate sumatur. Ergo nutriunt species illae.

that some people are drunk from using the species of this sacrament.

FURTHERMORE, nothing takes away thirst or hunger except what nourishes. But it can be sensibly experienced that thirst is removed by this drink, particularly if it is taken in great quantity. Therefore, these species nourish.

Quaestiuncula 6

ULTERIUS. Videtur quod nullus liquor possit speciebus illis permisceri. Quia, ut in 1 *de Generat.*, probat Philosophus, accidens non permiscetur substantiae. Sed quilibet liquor substantia quaedam est. Cum ergo illae species sint tantum accidentia, videtur quod nihil possit eis permisceri.

PRAETEREA, sicut hoc sacramentum sub certa forma verborum consecratur, ita et aqua benedicta. Sed si aqua permiscetur aquae benedictae, totum fit benedictum. Si ergo aliquis liquorum permisceri posset vino consecrato, esset totum consecratum; et sic liquor ille transiret in sanguinem Christi sine forma verborum, quod falsum est.

PRAETEREA, humidorum permixtorum efficitur superficies una. Si ergo illis speciebus aliquis liquor admisceatur, efficitur una superficies liquoris advenientis et specierum praeexistentium. Sed superficies liquoris est in subjecto, superficies autem specierum non est in subjecto. Ergo eadem superficies erit in subjecto et non in subjecto; quod est impossibile.

PRAETEREA, corpus Christi non est sub sacramento ex quo sub speciebus illis est alia substantia. Sed si aliquis liquor subtilis, puta vinum vel aqua, admisceatur illis speciebus, cum non contineatur propriis terminis, oportet quod diffluat ad terminos dimensionum sub quibus erat corpus Christi. Ergo desinit esse ibi corpus Christi. Sed quamdiu sunt species illae, non desinit ibi esse corpus Christi. Ergo desinunt ibi esse species: ergo corrumpuntur et non permiscentur.

PRAETEREA, sicut album et nigrum sunt differentiae coloris; ita magnum et parvum sunt differentiae quantitatis, vel circa quantitatem. Sed idem color non est albus et niger. Ergo neque eaedem dimensiones sunt magnae et parvae. Sed addito aliquo liquore dimensiones illae efficiuntur magnae. Ergo non sunt eaedem quae prius; ergo non permiscentur.

OBJ. 1: Moreover, it seems that no liquid could be mixed with those species.[42] For as the Philosopher proves in *On Generation and Corruption* 1, accidents do not mix with substance.[43] But any liquid is a kind of substance. Therefore, since those species are only accidents, it seems that nothing can be mixed with them.

OBJ. 2: Furthermore, just as this sacrament is consecrated under a certain form of words, so also is holy water. But if water is mixed with holy water, it makes all of it holy. Therefore, if any liquid can be mixed with consecrated wine, it would make all of it consecrated; and then that liquid would have changed into the blood of Christ without the form of the words, which is false.

OBJ. 3: Furthermore, wet mixtures form one surface. Therefore, if any liquid were mixed into those species, one surface is made of the added liquid and the pre-existing species. But the surface of a liquid is in a subject, while the surface of the species is not in a subject. Therefore, the same surface will be in a subject and not in a subject, which is impossible.

OBJ. 4: Furthermore, the body of Christ is not under the sacrament by there being another substance under those species. But if some thin liquid, like wine or water, were mixed into those species, since it is not contained under its own boundaries, it is necessary that it flow out to the limits of the dimensions under which the body of Christ existed. Therefore, the body of Christ would cease to be there. But as long as those species exist, the body of Christ does not cease to be there. Therefore, the species would cease to exist there: therefore they would be corrupted and not mixed in.

OBJ. 5: Furthermore, just as white and black are different colors, so large and small are different quantities, or things related to quantity. But the same color is not white and black. Therefore, neither are the same dimensions large and small. But if any liquid were added, those dimensions would be made large. Therefore they are not the same as before; therefore they have not been mixed together.

---

42. Parallels: *ST* III, q. 77, a. 8; *Quodl.* X, q. 1, a. 3.
43. Aristotle, *On Generation and Corruption*, Bk. 1, ch. 10 (327b20–23).

SED CONTRA, secundum Philosophum in 1 *de Generat.*, ea quae sunt divisibilia in minima, sunt bene permiscibilia. Sed ita est de speciebus illis. Ergo, etc.

PRAETEREA, majus est corrumpi quam permisceri. Sed species illae possunt corrumpi. Ergo possunt permisceri.

ON THE CONTRARY, according to the Philosopher in *On Generation and Corruption* 1, things that are divisible into the tiniest parts are very mixable.[44] But this is the case with these species. Therefore, etc.

FURTHERMORE, it is a bigger thing to be corrupted than to be mixed into something. But those species can be corrupted. Therefore, they can also be mixed into something.

Response to Quaestiuncula 1

RESPONDEO dicendum ad primam quaestionem, quod agere non est nisi rei per se subsistentis; et ideo neque materia agit neque forma, sed compositum; quod tamen non agit ratione materiae, sed ratione formae, quae est actus, et actionis principium. Et quia quantitas se tenet ex parte materiae, et qualitas ex parte formae; ideo quantitas non agit nisi mediante qualitate, quae est per se actionis principium; unde qualitates sunt sensibiles primo, quantitates secundo. Quia ergo in sacramento quantitates retinent eumdem modum essendi quem habebant substantia panis existente, ideo habent eumdem modum agendi, ut immutent et agant naturaliter sicut prius. Quantitatis enim, quae alium modum essendi habet, quia non est in subjecto, non est agere nisi mediante qualitate.

AD PRIMUM ergo dicendum, quod materia accidentis est proximum subjectum ejus; proximum autem subjectum qualitatis corporalis est quantitas, ut superficies coloris; et ideo qualitas quae est actionis principium, communicat quodammodo in materia cum his quae sunt extra, quia quantitas hinc inde subesse invenitur.

AD SECUNDUM dicendum, quod mathematici non solum abstrahunt a materia, sed a sensibilibus accidentibus. Et quia dimensiones in hoc sacramento non sunt separatae ab accidentibus sensibilibus; ideo non solum habent tactum metaphoricum sicut mathematica, sed etiam physicum: quia ratione illorum accidentium possunt immutare et immutari.

AD TERTIUM dicendum, quod quantum ad immutationem accidentalem satis simile invenitur hinc inde: quia sicut in sacramento non est albedo separata, sed album quod agit; ita exterius per immutationem non fit albedo, sed aliquod album; et ita, inquantum hujusmodi, passum in fine est simile.

TO THE FIRST QUESTION, I answer that to act only belongs to a thing subsisting on its own; and so neither matter nor form acts, but only a composite, which nevertheless does not act by reason of its matter, but by reason of its form, which is act, and the principle of action. And since quantity holds itself on the part of the matter, and quality on the part of the form, for this reason quantity acts only by means of quality, which is *per se* the principle of action; hence qualities are sensible first, quantities second. Therefore, because in the sacrament quantities retain the same mode of being that they had when the bread's substance existed, for this reason they have the same mode of acting, so that they change and act naturally as before. For the quantity, which has a different mode of being since it is not in a subject, only acts by means of quality.

REPLY OBJ. 1: The matter of an accident is its proximate subject, but the proximate subject of corporeal quality is quantity, like the surface of a color; and so quality which is the principle of action shares in some way in matter with those things that are outside, because on both sides quantity is found to be underlying.

REPLY OBJ. 2: Mathematics abstracts not only from matter but also from sensible accidents. And because the dimensions in this sacrament are not separated from sensible accidents, for this reason they not only have touch in a metaphorical sense, like mathematicals, but also physical touch: for by reason of those accidents they can change and be changed.

REPLY OBJ. 3: As to accidental change it is found to be similar enough on both sides, because just as in this sacrament there is no separate whiteness, but a white thing that acts, so also outwardly by this change whiteness does not come about, but rather something white; and so insofar as it is this kind of thing, what is effected in the end is the same.

Response to Quaestiuncula 2

AD SECUNDAM QUAESTIONEM dicendum, quod in actionibus naturalibus formae substantiales non sunt

TO THE SECOND QUESTION, it should be said that in natural actions substantial forms are not an immediate and

---

44. Aristotle, *On Generation and Corruption*, Bk. 1, ch. 10 (328a35ff.).

immediatum[45] actionis principium, sed agunt mediantibus qualitatibus activis et passivis, sicut propriis instrumentis; ut dicitur in 2 de anima, quod calor naturalis est quo anima agit; et ideo qualitates non solum agunt in virtute propria, sed etiam in virtute formae substantialis. Unde actio earum non solum terminatur ad formam accidentalem, sed etiam ad formam substantialem; et propter hoc generatio est terminus alterationis. Hujusmodi autem virtutem instrumentalem recipiunt eo ipso quo a principiis essentialibus causantur. Unde sicut remotis substantiis remanet accidentibus idem esse secundum speciem virtute divina, ita etiam remanet eis eadem virtus quae et prius; et ideo, sicut ante poterant immutare ad formam substantialem, ita et nunc.

AD PRIMUM ergo dicendum, quod nos non ponimus omnino hujusmodi qualitates separatas, sicut Plato ponebat formas naturales, cum ponamus pro subjecto id quod erat proximum subjectum eorum primo; et ideo non est similis ratio hinc inde. Tamen hic etiam generans non est omnino simile generato: quia generatum est substantia, generans autem non. Sed hoc ideo contingit, quia, ut dictum est, hujusmodi qualitates habent instrumentalem virtutem generandi. Generatum autem non oportet quod assimiletur instrumento, sed principali generanti, ut dicit Commentator in 11 *Metaphysica.*: quia instrumentum non agit virtute sua sed alterius, et illi assimilat, non sibi; unde generatum hic assimilatur substantiae quae prius erat. Plato autem formas separatas non ponebat instrumentalia generantia, sed primas causas generationis et principales.

AD SECUNDUM dicendum, quod propria virtute nihil agit ultra suam speciem: sed virtute alterius, cujus est instrumentum, potest agere ultra speciem suam, sicut serra agit ad formam scamni.

proximate principle of action, but they act by means of active and passive qualities as by their proper instruments; as it says in *On the Soul* 2, natural heat is that by which the soul acts.[46] And so qualities do not act only in their proper power, but also in the power of substantial form. And for this reason their action terminates not only in accidental form, but also in substantial form; and because of this, generation is the terminus of alteration. However, they receive instrumental power of this kind by the very fact of being caused by essential principles. And so just as when the substances are removed the same being remains in the accidents according to species by divine power, so also the same power remains in them that they had previously; and thus just as before they could change a substantial form, so too now.

REPLY OBJ. 1: We do not at all posit separate qualities like this, as Plato posited natural forms, since we posit for the subject what was first their proximate subject; and so it is not the same argument here as there. Nevertheless, what generates here is also not at all similar to what is generated: for what is generated is substance, but what generates is not. But the reason this happens is because, as was said, qualities like this have an instrumental power of generating. But what is generated need not resemble the instrument, but only the chief thing generating, as the Commentator says in *Metaphysics* 11,[47] for an instrument does not act by its own power, but by another's power, and it resembles that thing, not the instrument; which is why the generated here resembles the substance that was formerly there. But Plato did not consider separated forms as things that generate instrumentally, but as first and chief causes of generation.

REPLY OBJ. 2: Nothing acts by its proper power outside its own species; but by the power of another, whose instrument it is, it can act outside its own species, as a saw acts to form a stool.

Response to Quaestiuncula 3

AD TERTIAM QUAESTIONEM dicendum, quod unaquaeque res habet proprium esse suae speciei. Non enim esse in omnibus est unius speciei, sicut nec animalitas est unius speciei in omnibus animalibus, nec humanitas eadem numero in omnibus hominibus, sicut et unaquaeque res habet propriam actionem. Unde sicut in qualitatibus quae remanent in sacramento, remanet actio conformis actioni substantiae prius existentis; ita etiam esse subsistens quod convenit dimensionibus remanentibus, est conforme illi esse quod prius substantia panis habebat. Unde sicut qualitas facit eamdem actionem quam

TO THE THIRD QUESTION, it should be said that each and every thing has being proper to its own species. For being is not of one species in all things, just as neither is animality of one species in all animals, nor is humanity the same in number among all men, just as also each thing has its own proper action. Hence, just as in the qualities that remain in the sacrament there remains an action like the action of the substance that previously existed, so also the subsistent being that shares the dimensions that remain is like that being that the bread's substance formerly had. Hence just as the quality performs the same action that

---

45. *immediatum actionis.—immediatum et proximum actionis* PLE.
46. Aristotle, *On the Soul*, Bk. 2, ch. 4 (416b25–30).
47. Averroes, *Metaphysics*, Bk. 11, text 13.

prius faciebat, substantia panis et vini existente; ita esse, in quo dimensiones subsistunt, tollitur eisdem passionibus quibus antea tolleretur, eadem substantia existente; et propter hoc eodem modo corrumpuntur accidentia remanentia, sicut et prius corrumpi poterant.

Prius autem corrumpi poterant dupliciter. Uno modo manente substantia subjecti, per aliquam accidentalem mutationem: sicut ex parte qualitatum secundum aliquam alterationem vinum saporem vel colorem mutare poterat; et ita color qui prius erat, aut sapor, corrumpebatur; sed quantitas praedicto modo non poterat corrumpi per motum in quantitate, scilicet augmentum, quia vinum et panis non sunt corpora animata, quae possunt esse subjectum augmenti et diminutionis, sed per additionem vel divisionem: quia secundum Philosophum in 3 *Metaphysica*, in additione quantitatis ad quantitatem una quantitas esse incipit duabus esse desinentibus, et e contrario est in divisione. Alio modo per corruptionem substantiae: quae quidem contingit ex transmutatione accidentium, et ex parte qualitatum: quia sicut generatio, ita et corruptio est terminus alterationis; et ex parte quantitatis: quia cum unaquaeque res naturalis habeat quantitatem determinatam, intantum poterit divisio fieri quod species non remanebit.

Unde etiam in hoc sacramento aliquando aliqua alteratione facta in qualitatibus, adhuc manet esse illud dimensionum conforme substantiae praecedenti; et tunc ratione ipsius corruptionis accidentium non desinit esse corpus Christi sub sacramento. Aliquando autem alteratio ad terminum venit, et tunc esse praedictum tollitur, et sic desinit esse sacramentum. Et similiter ex parte quantitatis: quia si fiat divisio in partes tantae quantitatis quae sufficiat ad speciem panis vel vini; sunt quidem aliae dimensiones, quia partes continui, quae erant potentia, fiunt actu; sed esse conforme substantiae praeexistenti manet, et ideo adhuc est sacramentum. Si autem quantitas partium ad hoc non sufficiat, utrumque esse desinet, et dimensio et esse praedictum; et ideo corpus Christi desinit esse sub sacramento.

AD PRIMUM ergo dicendum, quod forma dicitur esse invariabilis, quia non est variationis subjectum; tamen per variationem tollitur, sicut patet in alteratione et augmento; et ita largo modo dicuntur corrumpi, prout omne quod esse desinit, dicitur corrumpi.

AD SECUNDUM dicendum, quod dimensiones, quae sunt proximae dispositiones materiae, retinent in hoc sacramento vicem materiae; et ideo se habent ad esse in quo subsistunt sicut materia ad formam substantialem,

it performed before, when the substance of the bread and wine existed, so the being in which the dimensions subsist is destroyed by the same occurrences that would have destroyed it before, when the same substance existed. And because of this the remaining accidents are corrupted in the same way as they would have been corrupted before.

Now there are two ways they could have been corrupted before. In one way, with the substance of the subject remaining, by a certain accidental change: as according to a certain alteration in the qualities, the wine could change color or flavor; and then the color that had been there before, or the flavor, would have been corrupted. But quantities could not have been corrupted in the way mentioned by a movement in quantity, namely, increase, for wine and bread are not animate bodies that can be the subjects of increase and diminution, except by addition and division. For according to the Philosopher in *Metaphysics* 3,[48] in the addition of one quantity to another, one quantity begins to exist when two cease to exist, and the reverse happens in division. In the other way, by the corruption of the substance, which does indeed happen by the transformation of accidents, either on the part of the qualities, for, like generation, corruption is a terminus of change; or on the part of the quantity: for since each natural thing has a determinate quantity, inasmuch as a division could be made that species will not remain.

And this is why sometimes in this sacrament when a certain alteration is made in the qualities, that being of the dimensions still remains conformed to the former substance; and then by reason of this corruption of accidents, the body of Christ does not cease to exist under the sacrament. But sometimes the change comes to its terminus, and then the being mentioned is destroyed, and that is how the sacrament ceases to exist. And likewise on the part of quantity: for if a division is made into parts of such great amount that it is enough for the appearance of bread or wine, there are indeed other dimensions, for the continuous parts that existed in potency, become actual. But the being remains like the pre-existing substance, and therefore the sacrament still exists. However, if the quantity of the parts is not sufficient for this, both the dimension and the being mentioned cease to exist. And then the body of Christ ceases to exist under the sacrament.

REPLY OBJ. 1: A form is said to be invariable because it is not subject to variation; however, it is destroyed by variation, as is clear in the case of change and increase; and so in a broad way they are said to be corrupted, as everything that ceases to exist can be said to be corrupted.

REPLY OBJ. 2: The dimensions that are the closest dispositions of the matter retain the place of the matter in this sacrament; and so they are related to the being in which they subsist as matter to substantial form, and they are un-

---

48. Aristotle, *Metaphysics*, Bk. 3, ch. 5 (1002b1).

et ipsae subsunt[49] sicut subjectum accidentibus; et hoc modo corruptionis principium esse possunt, sicut et materia esset. Ipsae etiam partes dimensionum, cum sint in potentia, habent quamdam rationem materiae ratione totius dimensionis; et ideo ex parte earum accidit corruptio aliqua in tota dimensione per divisionem.

AD TERTIUM dicendum, quod species sic remanere miraculosum est; sed quod sic remanentes corrumpantur, est naturale; sicut miraculosum est quod caecus visum recipiat; sed quod jam visu recepto videat, est naturale. Remanet enim quidam compositionis modus in accidentibus istis, dum quantitas retinet rationem materiae, et qualitas rationem formae, ut dictum est.

derneath the qualtities like a subject under accidents. And in this way they can be a principle of corruption, just as matter would also be. Also, the parts of the dimensions, since they exist in potency, have a certain character of matter by reason of the whole dimension. And so a certain corruption happens on their part in the whole dimension by division.

REPLY OBJ. 3: It is miraculous for species to remain in this way, but the fact that as they remain they are corrupted, is natural; just as it is miraculous for a blind man to receive his sight, but that he sees once he has received sight, is natural. For a certain mode of composition remains in these accidents, as long as the quantity retains the character of matter, and the qualities retain the character of form, as was said.

Response to Quaestiuncula 4

AD QUARTAM QUAESTIONEM dicendum, quod quidam dicunt, quod quamvis illae species possint corrumpi et putrefieri, tamen ex tali putrefactione vel corruptione non generantur vermes, vel aliquid hujusmodi. Sed hoc nihil est. Constat enim quod accidentia quando corrumpuntur, non hoc modo desinunt ut dispareant omnino, ac si totaliter annihilarentur; sed succedit illis accidentibus aliquid sensibile; et hoc oportet esse de novo generatum. Nec est differentia, quidquid sit illud, utrum sit vermis, vel cinis, vel aliquid hujusmodi; quia similis difficultas est de omnibus.

Et ideo alii dixerunt, quod substantia panis ibi remanet, ex qua materialiter aliqua generari possunt. Sed haec opinio supra improbata est. Et ideo alii dixerunt, quod ex mutua actione accidentium sacramenti ad corpora circumstantia generantur vermes ex aere continente. Sed hoc non videtur esse verum; quia accidentia illa non habent ibi aliam actionem quam haberent si substantia remansisset; sed quando substantia erat, non poterant vermes ex aere generari, vel cinis, per talem actionem; unde nec nunc.

Et praeterea, sensibiliter apparet quod in illo loco ubi fuit corpus Christi, est illud quod generatur; et ibidem alteratio praecedens apparet. Aer autem ante ultimum instans corruptionis specierum non erat in loco illo; quia sic subintrasset dimensiones sub quibus erat corpus Christi; quod est impossibile. Nec etiam movebatur ad locum illum, quia quietus forte manebat. Unde sequitur quod totus motus aeris, et alteratio ipsius et cor-

TO THE FOURTH QUESTION, it should be said that some people say that although those species can be corrupted and spoiled, nevertheless, worms and the like are not generated by this spoiling or corruption. But this is nothing. For it is clear that when the accidents are corrupted, they do not cease in such a way that they disappear altogether, as if they were entirely destroyed, but something sensible replaces those accidents, and this must be something newly generated. Nor does it make a difference what it is—-whether it is worms, or dust, or anything like that—-for there is the same difficulty with all of them.

And so other people have said that the substance of bread remains there, from which other things can be generated materially. But this opinion was disproved above.[50] And so others have said that by the mutual action of the sacrament's accidents and the surrounding bodies worms are generated from the air around. But this does not seem to be true, for those accidents do not have any other action there than they would have if the substance remained; but when the substance existed, it could not generate worms out of the air, or dust, by such an action; and so neither can it now.

And furthermore, it appears to the senses that in the place where the body of Christ existed, something exists that was generated; and the previous change appears in the same place. Now air was not in that place before the last instant of the species' corruption; for then it would have entered under the dimensions that the body of Christ was existing under, which is impossible. Nor was it moved to that place, since perhaps it remained still. And so it follows that

---

49. *subsunt sicut.—subsunt qualitatibus sicut* PLE.
50. See d. 11, q. 1, a. 1, qa. 1.

ruptio, et generatio vermium aut cineris, sit in eodem instanti; quod est impossibile.

Et praeterea idem accideret, si corpus Christi conservaretur inter aliqua corpora solida quae non subintraret aer, et non appareret aliqua mutatio facta in corporibus solidis circumstantibus.

Et praeterea, si corpus Christi in magna quantitate consecratum esset, idem posset accidere; et tanta inspissatio aeris non posset de facili accidere sine sensibili ipsius immutatione.

Et ideo alii dicunt, quod peracto sacramento, redit substantia panis sub speciebus quae prius suberat, et ex illa generantur vermes, vel aliquid hujusmodi. Sed hoc non potest esse. Quamdiu enim est ibi corpus Christi, non redit substantia panis; quia sic esset corpus Christi sub speciebus cum substantia panis; quod est tertia opinio, quae non sustinetur. Quamdiu autem sunt ibi species, manet sub speciebus corpus Christi; unde quamdiu manent species, substantia panis non redit; remotis autem speciebus illis, jam non est ibi substantia panis, sed vermium vel cineris, vel alicujus hujusmodi. Nunquam enim est substantia panis sine speciebus panis; unde substantia panis non potest redire.

Nisi forte dicatur redire quo ad materiam tantum, quia illa eadem materia quae prius erat sub forma panis, postmodum fit sub forma cineris, vel alicujus hujusmodi; et hoc posset stare cum secunda opinione prius tacta quantum ad hoc quod ponebat substantiam panis in praejacentem materiam resolvi; quod stare non potest, ut supra probatum est.

Sed quantum ad aliam partem, quae ponebatur quod annihilaretur, non potest stare; quia quod in nihilum redactum est, non potest iterum idem numero sumi.

Sed quantum ad primam opinionem, quae communiter sustinetur, omnino stare non potest; quia quod conversum est in alterum, non potest redire, nisi alterum in ipsum convertatur; substantia autem panis conversa est in corpus Christi; et haec substantia, scilicet panis, facta est illa, scilicet corporis Christi, ut ex praedictis patet; unde non potest esse quod substantia panis redeat neque quantum ad totum neque quantum ad partem, nisi corpus Christi e converso convertatur in substantiam panis, quod est impossibile. Et ideo impossibile est dicere quod substantia panis redeat neque secundum totum neque secundum partem; si redire proprie sumatur, ut sit idem numero quod redit.

all the air's movement, and its alteration and corruption, and the generation of worms or dust is at the same instant, which is impossible.

And furthermore, the same thing would happen if the body of Christ were conserved among other solid bodies, which air could not enter, and no change would appear to be made in the solid bodies surrounding it.

And furthermore, if the body of Christ were consecrated in great quantity, the same thing could happen; and so much contact with the air could not happen easily without its sensible change.

And therefore others say that when the sacrament has been completed, the bread's substance returns under the appearances that it was under before, and worms are generated from it, or something like that. But this cannot be. For as long as the body of Christ is there, the substance of the bread does not return, for then the body of Christ would exist under the appearances along with the bread's substance; which is the third opinion, which is not supportable. Now as long as the appearances exist there, the body of Christ remains under those appearances; and so as long as the appearances remain, the substance of bread does not return. But once those appearances have been removed, the substance of bread is still not there, but the substance of worms or dust, or other things like this. For the substance of bread never exists without the appearances of bread, and therefore the substance of bread cannot return.

Unless perhaps it were said to return only as to its matter, for that same matter that was previously under the form of bread, afterward comes to be under the form of dust or the like; and this could stand with the second opinion touched on earlier, which held that the substance of the bread is resolved into the underlying matter, which cannot stand, as was proved above.[51]

But as to the other side, which held that it would be annihilated, that cannot stand; for what returns to nothing cannot be taken up again in the same number.

But as to the first opinion, which is commonly upheld, it cannot stand in any way, for what is converted into something else cannot return, unless the other thing is converted back into it. But the substance of bread is converted into the body of Christ, and this substance, namely, the bread's, has become that one, namely, the body of Christ's, as is clear from what has already been said.[52] And therefore it cannot be that the bread's substance returns, whether in whole or in part, unless the body of Christ is converted back into the substance of bread, which is impossible. And so it is impossible to say that the substance of bread returns, whether as a whole or as a part, if "to return" is taken properly so that what returns is the same in number.

---

51. See d. 11, q. 1, a. 2.
52. See ibid.

Si autem materia panis redire dicatur, non quia eadem numero redeat, sed alia ejusdem rationis; tunc oportebit dicere, quod illa alia materia de novo creetur. Et forte hoc intellexerunt qui dixerunt substantiam panis redire; unde satis probabiliter per hunc modum opinio sustineri potest, ut dicatur, quod ad hoc Deus materiam creat, ne sacramentum deprehendatur, et sic fides meritum perdat. Nec tamen materia corporalis in principio creata augetur; quia quantum de materia conversum fuit in substantiam corporis Christi, tantum de materia creatur nunc de novo.

Potest tamen et aliter dici, quod illae species sicut habent ex hoc quod subsistunt, quod possunt agere quidquid poterant substantiis panis et vini existentibus; ita habent ut possint converti in quidquid converti poterant substantiae praeexistentes, quod sic intelligi potest. Sicut enim Commentator dicit in 1 *Physica*, et in Lib. *de Substantia orbis*, in materia generabilium et corruptibilium oportet intelligere dimensiones interminatas ante adventum formae substantialis; alias non posset intelligi divisio materiae, ut in diversis partibus materiae diversae formae substantiales essent. Hujusmodi autem dimensiones post adventum formae substantialis accipiunt esse terminatum et completum. Quidquid autem intelligitur in materia ante adventum formae substantialis, hoc manet idem numero in generato et in eo ex quo generat; quia remoto posteriori oportet remanere prius; dimensiones autem illae interminatae se habent ad genus quantitatis sicut materia ad genus substantiae.

Unde sicut in quolibet completo in genere substantiae est accipere materiam, quae est ens incompletum in genere illo; ita in dimensionibus completis, quae sunt in hoc sacramento, est accipere dimensiones incompletas; et his mediantibus materia panis formam reciperet ejus quod ex pane generaretur, pane non converso in corpus Christi; unde sicut dimensionibus illis est datum ut subsistant et subsint et illi esse quod est conforme esse priori substantiae, et terminationi quantitatis, et omnibus aliis accidentibus; ita etiam datur eis ut possint subesse alteri formae naturali, et aliis accidentibus; quia de natura sua non habent ut subsint tantum accidenti, sed etiam formae substantiali, ut dictum est; et tunc vel ex consequenti adveniet etiam materia propter concomitantiam naturalem formae ad materiam, sicut propter concomitantiam naturalem animae Christi ad corpus, erat anima sub sacramento; et hoc quodammodo redit in primum dictum, ut scilicet materia de novo fiat; vel ipsi dimensioni virtute divina dabitur natura materiae propter pro-

But if the matter of the bread is said to return, not so that it returns the same in number, but as a different matter of the same description, then it will be necessary to say that that different matter would be newly created. And perhaps this is what was meant by those who said the substance of the bread returned; therefore by this mode the opinion can be probably enough upheld, so that it may be said that God creates matter for this, that the sacrament will not be disgraced and so that faith would not lose its merit. But the physical matter created in the beginning is not increased; for as much matter is newly created now as was converted into the substance of the body of Christ.

However, it can also be said otherwise that those species, just as they have from the fact that they subsist that they can do whatever they could have when the substances of bread and wine existed, so they have that they can be converted into whatever the pre-existing substances could have been converted into, which can be understood thus. For as the Commentator says about *Physics* 1, and in his book *On the Substance of the Earth*,[53] in the matter of generable things and corruptible things it is necessary to understand unbounded dimensions before the advent of substantial form; otherwise a division of matter could not be understood such that in different parts of the matter there would be different substantial forms. Now after the advent of substantial form, dimensions like this receive a limited and complete being. But whatever is understood in matter before the advent of substantial form, this remains the same in number in what is generated and in that from which it is generated; for once what comes after is removed, what comes before must remain. Now those unbounded dimensions are related to the genus of quantity as matter is to the genus of substance.

And so just as in any complete thing in the genus of substance one can take matter, which is incomplete being in its genus, so also in the completed dimensions that exist in this sacrament, one can take incomplete dimensions. And by means of these the matter of the bread would receive the form of whatever would be generated from the bread, if the bread had not been converted into the body of Christ. And so just as to these dimensions it was given that they would subsist and exist under both that being that is like the being of the prior substance, and the termination of quantity, and all other accidents; so also it is given to them that they can exist under another natural form, and other accidents. For they do not have from their nature that they exist only under an accident, but also a substantial form, as was said; and then either matter will also come consequently because of the natural concomitance of form with matter, as because of the natural concomitance of Christ's soul with his body, the soul was under the sacrament; and this in a certain way returns to the first thing said, so that namely, matter is made

---

53. Averroes, *Physics*, Bk. 1, text 63; idem, *De substantia orbis*, ch. 1.

pinquitatem ad ipsam, ut sic illud generatum sit compositum ex materia et forma.

AD PRIMUM ergo dicendum, quod secundum penultimam opinionem species illae penitus cedunt in nihil; sed substantia praedicto modo redeunte generatur illud quod succedit. Nec dicitur generari ex speciebus secundum quod ly ex dicit causam materialem, sed solum secundum quod dicit ordinem, ut ex mane fit meridies, idest post. Sed secundum aliam opinionem illud totum demonstratum sensibile in sacramento habebat aliquid (scilicet partem sui) simile materiae, scilicet dimensiones interminatas; et illud non cedit in nihil, sed remanet sicut et remaneret, si substantia panis esset.

AD SECUNDUM dicendum, quod hoc non est remotum quin Deus possit mutare corpus in spiritum; et tamen quantum ad aliquid dimensiones interminatae magis sunt propinquae materiae corporali quam corpus spiritui.

AD TERTIUM dicendum, quod sicut quando aer convertitur in ignem, non dicitur quod materia aeris fiat duo, scilicet materia ignis et forma ignis; sed unum tantum, quod fit scilicet ignis; ita etiam dimensiones illae non dicuntur fieri duo, sed unum tantum, scilicet materia sic dimensionata; et hoc fit divina virtute.

AD QUARTUM dicendum, quod secundum quamlibet positionem oportet ponere aliquid in hac generatione esse miraculosum, et aliquid naturale; reditus enim substantiae, vel creatio materiae, vel conversio dimensionum in materia, est miraculosum; sed quod materia jam existens recipiat talem formam, cujus dispositiones praecesserunt in dimensionibus, hoc est naturale.

anew; or the nature of matter will be given to the dimension itself by divine power because of the closeness to it, so that in this way what is generated is a composite of matter and form.

REPLY OBJ. 1: According to the penultimate opinion those species inwardly pass away into nothing; but by the substance returning in the way mentioned something is generated that takes its place. Nor is it said to be generated out of the species, where the 'out of' means a material cause, but only as it means an order, as noon happens out of morning, which is to say, after. But according to another opinion that sensible whole that was shown to be in the sacrament had something (namely, a part of it) like matter, namely, unbounded dimensions; and that does not pass away into nothing, but remains as it also would remain if it were the substance of bread.

REPLY OBJ. 2: It is not out of the question that God could change a body into a spirit; and yet in a certain regard unbounded dimensions are closer to bodily matter than a body is to a spirit.

REPLY OBJ. 3: Just as when air is converted into fire, it is not said that the matter of the air becomes two things, namely, the matter of fire and the form of fire, but only one thing, namely that it becomes fire; so also, those dimensions are not said to become two things, but only one, namely, matter dimensioned in this way, and this is done by divine power.

REPLY OBJ. 4: According to any position it is necessary to hold that something in this generating is miraculous, and something is natural. For the return of substance, whether the creation of matter, or the conversion of dimensions into matter, is miraculous. But that matter already existing should receive a form like this, whose dispositions preceded in the dimensions, this is natural.

Response to Quaestiuncula 5

AD QUINTAM QUAESTIONEM dicendum, quod quidam dixerunt quod species illae non nutriunt, sed reficiunt et inebriant ex sola immutatione accidentali, sicut aliqui inebriantur odore vini, et reficiuntur et famem amittunt ex sapore et odore. Sed hoc non potest esse; quia talis immutatio quamvis ad horam reficiat, tamen sustentare non potest; quod tamen facerent species illae, si in magna quantitate sumerentur. Et ideo alii dixerunt, quod remanet forma substantialis panis, et illa habet eamdem operationem quam habebat panis, et ideo nutrit sicut panis nutriret. Sed hoc non potest esse; quia operatio formae non est pati, sed agere; nutrimentum autem non nutrit, nisi ex hoc quod convertitur in substantiam

TO THE FIFTH QUESTION, it should be said that some people have said that these species do not nourish us, but refresh and inebriate by accidental change alone, just as some people are inebriated by the odor of wine, and they are refreshed and lose their hunger from the flavor and odor of food. But this cannot be, for a change like this, although it might refresh one for the moment, nevertheless cannot sustain one; which nevertheless those species would do if they were consumed in great quantity. And so others have said that the substantial form of the bread remains and it has the same operation as bread does, and so it nourishes just like bread would. But this cannot be, for the operation of form is not to suffer but to act; however, nourishment

nutriti; et ideo nutrit secundum quod[54] ex eo aliquid generatur; quod non potest dici de forma. Et ideo dicendum est, quod cum generari aliquid ex illis speciebus possit per modum praedictum, eodem modo et nutrire possunt.

AD PRIMUM ergo dicendum, quod hoc quod dicitur, *quod non transit in corpus*, intelligendum est quantum ad rem contentam sub sacramento, scilicet verum corpus Christi, quod non mutatur in manducantem, sed ipsum in se mutat spiritualiter. Sed species in corpus comedentis convertuntur, sicut et in aliquod aliud corpus converti possunt, ut dictum est.

AD SECUNDUM dicendum, quod accidentia manentia in suo esse accidentali non nutriunt, sed eo modo quo in aliud convertuntur, vel aliud sub eis creatur vel redit.

AD TERTIUM dicendum, quod illa nutritio non est omnino secundum ordinem naturae, ut dictum est; et ideo talis manducatio jejunium non solvit.

does not nourish unless it is converted into the substance of what is nourished, and so it nourishes according as it suffers, and according as something is generated from it, which cannot be said about form. And so it should be said that since something is generated from those species by the way mentioned, they can also nourish in the same way.

REPLY OBJ. 1: When it is said that *this does not change into the body*, this is to be understood of the reality contained under the sacrament, namely, the true body of Christ, which is not changed into the one eating it, but changes that person into itself spiritually. But the species are converted into the body of the one eating, just as also they can be converted into some other body, as was said.

REPLY OBJ. 2: The accidents remaining do not nourish in their own accidental being, but in the same way that they are converted into something else; either something else is created under them or returns to them.

REPLY OBJ. 3: That nourishment is not entirely according to the order of nature, as has been said; and so this kind of eating does not break a fast.

Response to Quaestiuncula 6

AD SEXTAM QUAESTIONEM dicendum, quod quidam dicunt, quod quicumque liquor addatur speciebus vini in quantacumque quantitate, statim desinit ibi esse corpus Christi; quia dimensiones illae non manent eaedem, et iterum liquor additus per totum diffunditur. Unde cum corpus Christi non sit sub speciebus cum alio corpore, oportet quod in toto desinat esse corpus Christi.

Sed haec positio non potest stare. Constat enim quod corpus Christi manet quamdiu illa accidentia manent; illa autem accidentia non corrumpuntur aliter quam corrumperetur substantia panis et vini. Constat autem quod ex parvo liquore addito non destrueretur vinum, et ideo nec species vini remanentes. Rationes enim praedictae non cogunt. Primo, quia non quaelibet dimensionum destructio tollit sacramentum; sicut enim additio, ita et divisio facit aliam dimensionem, ut ex dictis patet per Philosophum. Divisio autem non tollit veritatem sacramenti, ut patet in pane qui frangitur; unde nec additio; quia illa varietas dimensionum quam facit talis additio et divisio, est quantum ad determinationem ipsarum, non quantum ad indeterminatum esse earum, secundum quod competit eis subsistere; neque quantum ad esse quo subsistunt conformes substantiae praecedenti. Similiter etiam parvus liquor constat quod non potest diffundi per omnes dimensiones; nisi rarefieret et trans-

TO THE SIXTH QUESTION, it should be said that certain people say that if any liquid is added to the species of wine in any quantity whatsoever, the body of Christ immediately ceases to exist there. For those dimensions do not remain the same, and added liquid is diffused throughout the whole. And so since the body of Christ does not exist under the species with another body, the body of Christ must cease to exist in all of it.

But this position cannot stand. For it is clear that the body of Christ remains as long as those accidents remain; but those accidents are not corrupted in any way other than the substance of bread and wine would be corrupted. But it is clear that wine would not be destroyed by having a little liquid added to it, and so neither would the species of wine that remain. For the arguments given are not compelling. First, because not every destruction of dimensions destroys the sacrament, for just as addition makes new dimensions, so does division, as is evident from what the Philosopher has said. But division does not take away the truth of the sacrament, as is clear in the fact that the bread is broken. Therefore, neither would addition, for the kind of difference in dimensions that an addition or division like this causes, has to do with their very determination, not their indeterminate being according to which it belongs to them to subsist, nor the being by which they subsist like the former substance. In the same way, it is clear that a little liquid cannot

---

54. *quod ex.—quod patitur et secundum quod ex* PLE.

mutaretur in aliam speciem. Unde non oportet quod occupet omnes dimensiones.

Et ideo aliter dicendum, quod hoc modo admiscetur liquor quicumque speciebus illis, sicut admisceretur substantiae vini. Liquor autem additus si esset aequalis quantitatis vel majoris, pertingeret ad omnes dimensiones vini; et sic si esset alterius speciei, faceret aliam speciem liquoris mediam; si autem esset ejusdem speciei, vinum faceret aliud vinum secundum numerum, maxime quantum ad accidentia. Si autem liquor additus esset minoris quantitatis, non posset pertingere ad omnes dimensiones totius vini, sed ad aliquas, et illas immutaret altero dictorum modorum; et forte immutaretur secundum speciem, si esset alterius speciei. Constat autem quod in hoc sacramento non manet corpus Christi nisi quamdiu illae species manent eaedem numero; et ideo si apponatur parvus liquor, corrumpet partem specierum, et sub illa parte desinit esse corpus Christi; non enim est probabile quod una gutta aquae per totum scyphum diffundatur. Si autem addatur in magna quantitate, sic corrumpet species secundum totum; et ita totaliter desinit ibi esse corpus Christi.

AD PRIMUM ergo dicendum, quod Philosophus intelligit de accidente cujus subjectum est substantia, quod ei non permiscetur; sic autem non est in proposito.

AD SECUNDUM dicendum, quod in aqua benedicta non fit aliqua mutatio substantialis ipsius aquae, sicut est in hoc sacramento, sed acquiritur ei virtus aliqua ex benedictione; ideo illa virtus potest pervenire ad aquam additam. Sed in hoc sacramento vinum convertitur substantialiter in aliud virtute verborum; et ideo non oportet quod vinum additum substantialiter etiam convertatur in sacramentum; sed potest esse quod convertatur in vinum virtute accidentium vini quae remanent, ut dictum est.

AD TERTIUM dicendum, quod non est inconveniens unam dimensionem secundum unam partem sui esse in hoc sacramento non in subjecto et aliam esse in subjecto; quia plures partes dimensionis quamvis sint una dimensio in actu, sunt tamen plures in potentia.

AD QUARTUM patet solutio ex dictis.

AD QUINTUM dicendum, quod magnum et parvum consequuntur quantitatem secundum quod ad certam mensuram determinatur. In sacramento autem altaris non oportet remanere dimensiones easdem secundum terminationem eamdem; quia sic divisis speciebus non remanerent eaedem dimensiones, nec per consequens idem sacramentum; sed sufficit ad subsistentiam sacramenti quod remaneant dimensiones eaedem secundum quod interminatae intelliguntur.

be diffused throughout all the dimensions, unless it were thinned out and transformed into another species. Hence it is not necessary that it occupy all the dimensions.

And so it should be said rather that any liquid is mixed with those species in the same way that it would be mixed with the substance of wine. But if the added liquid were of equal or greater amount, it would permeate all the dimensions of the wine; and so if it were of another species, it would make a different third species of liquid. But if it were of the same species, it would make the wine into a different wine in number, especially as to the accidents. But if the liquid added were of lesser amount, it would not permeate the dimensions of all the wine, but only some, and those it would change into a different liquid in the ways mentioned, and it might change according to species if it were of another species. However, it is clear that in this sacrament the body of Christ only remains as long as those species remain the same in number; and so if a little liquid were added, it would corrupt part of the species, and under that part the body of Christ would cease to exist. But it is not probable that one drop of water would be diffused throughout the whole goblet. But if it were added in a large amount, then it would corrupt the species according to the whole, and so the body of Christ would completely cease to exist there.

REPLY OBJ. 1: The Philosopher understands of an accident whose subject is a substance that it is not mixed into it; but this is not the case here.

REPLY OBJ. 2: In holy water no substantial change happens to that water, as is the case in this sacrament, but rather it acquires a certain power from being blessed. And so that power can extend to the added water. But in this sacrament the wine is substantially converted into something else by the power of the words, and so it is not necessary that the added wine also be converted into the sacrament; but it can be that it is converted into wine by virtue of the wine's accidents that remain, as was said.

REPLY OBJ. 3: It is not unfitting for one dimension to be not in a subject in this sacrament according to one of its parts and according to another to be in a subject; for although the many parts of the dimension are one dimension in act, they are nevertheless many in potency.

REPLY OBJ. 4: The solution is clear from what has been said.

REPLY OBJ. 5: Large and small follow quantity according as it is determined to a certain measure. But in the sacrament of the altar it is not necessary for dimensions to remain the same according to the same boundaries, for then the same dimensions would not remain when the species are divided, and consequently it would not be the same sacrament; but it suffices for the subsistence of the sacrament that the dimensions remain the same according as they are understood to be unbounded.

ARTICLE 3

About the breaking which is founded on the accidents[55]

Quaestiuncula 1

AD TERTIUM SIC PROCEDITUR. Videtur quod ipsum verum corpus Christi frangatur in sacramento. Omne enim quod manducatur, masticatur et frangitur. Sed verum corpus Christi manducatur: Joan. 6, 57: *qui manducat carnem meam*, etc. Ergo et frangitur.

PRAETEREA, hoc sacramentum est memoriale Dominicae passionis. Sed in passione ipsum corpus Christi est perforatum clavis et lancea. Ergo in sacramento ipsum corpus Christi frangitur.

PRAETEREA, sicut corpus Christi est totum in qualibet parte specierum, ita forma substantialis. Sed forma substantialis materialis dividitur per accidens per divisionem specierum. Ergo et corpus Christi.

SED CONTRA, quod frangitur, non manet integrum. Sed corpus Christi manet integrum, ut in littera dicitur. Ergo non frangitur.

PRAETEREA, omne corpus frangibile est passibile. Sed corpus Christi est impassibile, cum sit gloriosum. Ergo non frangitur.

OBJ. 1: To the third we proceed thus. It seems that the true body of Christ is broken in the sacrament. For everything that is eaten is chewed and broken. But the true body of Christ is eaten: *who eats my flesh*, etc. (John 6:57). Therefore, it is also broken.

OBJ. 2: Furthermore, this sacrament is a memorial of the Lord's Passion. But in the Passion, the body of Christ itself was pierced by nails and by a lance. Therefore, in the sacrament the body of Christ is broken.

OBJ. 3: Furthermore, just as the body of Christ exists whole in every part of the species, so does the substantial form. But substantial material form is incidentally divided through the division of the species. Therefore, also the body of Christ.

ON THE CONTRARY, what is broken does not remain whole. But the body of Christ remains whole, as is said in the text. Therefore, it is not broken.

FURTHERMORE, every breakable body can suffer. But the body of Christ is impassible, since it is glorified. Therefore, it is not broken.

Quaestiuncula 2

ULTERIUS. Videtur quod nec etiam species frangantur. Signum enim debet respondere signato. Sed species sunt signum corporis Christi. Cum ergo verum corpus Christi non frangatur, nec ipsae species frangentur.

PRAETEREA, secundum Philosophum in 4 *Meteor.*, corporea dicuntur frangibilia et comminuibilia secundum determinatam dispositionem pororum. Sed species illae non habent poros: quia sub omnibus partibus specierum est aequaliter corpus Christi, et sub nulla aliquid aliud. Ergo species illae neque frangi neque comminui possunt.

PRAETEREA, in omni fractione, ea perfecta, aliud est quod continetur sub diversis partibus. Sed omnino est idem quod continetur sub diversis partibus specierum, qualitercumque disponantur. Ergo non proprie dicuntur frangi.

SED CONTRA, Matth. 26, dicitur, quod Dominus *benedixit et fregit*. Sed verba Evangelii non possunt esse fal-

OBJ. 1: Moreover, it seems that neither are the appearances broken. For the sign must correspond to what is represented. But the species are the sign of the body of Christ. Since therefore the true body of Christ is not broken, neither are the species themselves broken.

OBJ. 2: Furthermore, according to the Philosopher in *Meteorology* 4,[56] corporeal things are said to be breakable and crumbleable according to the particular disposition of their pores. But those species do not have pores, for under all the species' parts the body of Christ exists equally, and under no part does anything else exist. Therefore, those species can neither be broken nor crumbled.

OBJ. 3: Furthermore, any time a breaking is completed, the different parts each contain something different. But what is contained under the different parts of the species is entirely the same, no matter how they are disposed. Therefore, they are not properly said to be broken.

ON THE CONTRARY, it is said in Matthew 26:26 that the Lord *blessed it and broke it*. But the words of the Gospel can-

---

55. Parallels: *ST* III, q. 77, a. 7; *SCG* IV, ch. 67; *Super I ad Cor.* 11, lec. 5.
56. Aristotle, *Meteorology*, Bk. 4, ch. 9 (386a14ff.).

sa. Ergo fuit ibi fractio vera. Sed non in corpore Christi, ut probatum est. Ergo in speciebus fuit.

PRAETEREA, magis competit quantitati dividi quam corrumpi, vel in aliud converti. Sed hoc contingit dimensionibus ibi remanentibus, ut ex dictis patet. Ergo et frangi, sive dividi.

not be false. Therefore, there was a true breaking, but not in the body of Christ, as was proved. Therefore, it was in the species.

FURTHERMORE, it belongs to quantity to be divided more than to be corrupted, or to be converted into something else. But this happens to the dimensions that remain there, as is clear from what has been said. Therefore, also to be broken or divided.

Quaestiuncula 3

ULTERIUS. Videtur quod inconvenienter assignetur in littera significatio partium fractionis. Quia partes fractionis fractioni respondent. Sed fractio significat passionem Christi, ut in littera dicitur. Ergo partes fractionis debent significare partes veri corporis Christi, in quas per passionem divisum est corpus ejus.

PRAETEREA, hoc sacramentum est maxime sacramentum unionis. Sed distinctio partium unioni opponitur. Ergo non competit in hoc sacramento significari partes distinctas corporis mystici.

PRAETEREA, hoc non videtur servari secundum communem morem ecclesiae quod aliqua pars usque in finem Missae reservetur. Ergo secundum hoc non debet accipi significatio alicujus partis.

PRAETEREA, Innocentius, et Hugo de s. Victore, dicunt, quod pars extra calicem servata significat beatos; et ita videtur male dicere, quod significat illos qui sunt in sepulcris.

PRAETEREA, beati remedio non indigent. Sed sacramenta ecclesiae in remedium ordinantur. Ergo non debet esse aliqua pars quae beatos significet.

PRAETEREA, sicut est diversitas inter mortuos, ita etiam inter vivos. Sed pro mortuis ponuntur duae partes. Ergo et pro vivis duae poni debent ad minus.

PRAETEREA, sicut membra distinguuntur ab invicem, ita caput distinguitur a membris. Ergo cum sint tres partes ad significandum diversitatem membrorum corporis mystici, deberet addi et quarta ad significandum ipsum caput.

OBJ. 1: Moreover, it seems that the signification of the breaking of the parts is unfittingly assigned in the text. For the parts of the breaking correspond to the breaking. But the breaking signifies the Passion of Christ, as is said in the text. Therefore, the parts of the breaking should signify the parts of the true body of Christ, into which his body was divided by the Passion.

OBJ. 2: Furthermore, this sacrament is the supreme sacrament of union. But the distinction of parts is opposed to union. Therefore, it does not befit this sacrament for the different parts of the mystical body to be signified.

OBJ. 3: Furthermore, this does not seem to be according to the common practice of the Church that a certain part be reserved until the end of Mass. Therefore, the signification of any part should not be taken according to this.

OBJ. 4: Furthermore, Innocent[57] and Hugh of St. Victor[58] say that the part reserved outside the chalice represents the blessed; and so it seems wrong to say that it represents those who are in their graves.

OBJ. 5: Furthermore, the blessed do not need any remedy. But the Church's sacraments are directed to being a remedy. Therefore, there should not be any part that represents the blessed.

OBJ. 6: Furthermore, just as there is a diversity among the dead, so also among the living. But two parts are set down for the dead. Therefore, two parts at least should be set down for the living.

OBJ. 7: Furthermore, just as the members are distinguished from each other, so also the head is distinguished from its members. Therefore, since there are three parts for representing the diversity of the mystical body's members, there would have to be added also a fourth to signify the head.

Response to Quaestiuncula 1

RESPONDEO DICENDUM ad primam quaestionem, quod sicut supra dictum est, corpus Christi non comparatur ad species sub quibus continetur, mediantibus suis

TO THE FIRST QUESTION, I answer that, as was said above, the body of Christ is not related to the species under which it is contained by means of its own dimensions; on

---

57. Innocent III, *De sacra altaris mysterio*, Bk. 6, ch. 3 (PL 217:907).
58. Hugh of St. Victor, *De sacramentis fidei*, Bk. 2, pt. 8, ch. 10 (PL 176:468).

dimensionibus; immo dimensiones ejus sunt ibi quasi ex consequenti; ideo quidquid convenit corpori Christi mediantibus dimensionibus suis, hoc non convenit ei secundum quod est sub sacramento. Cum ergo divisio quantitativa ei convenire non possit nisi mediante dimensione propria, constat quod fractione specierum ipsum corpus ejus non dividitur neque frangitur, etiam si passibile esset, sicut in coena fuit.

AD PRIMUM ergo dicendum, quod in manducatione sunt multa; et fractio sive masticatio, et trajectio in ventrem sive nutritio. Primum autem convenit ipsis speciebus tantum; sed secundum et speciebus continentibus et corpori contento: quia ubi sunt species, est verum corpus Christi. Sed tertium, si loquamur spiritualiter, convenit corpori Christi, si autem corporaliter, speciebus, ut dictum est. Et ideo manducatio aliquo modo competit corpori Christi, sed non fractio, seu divisio.

AD SECUNDUM dicendum, quod quia hoc sacramentum est signum passionis Christi, et non ipsa passio; ideo oportet quod passio quam significat fractio, non sit in corpore Christi, sed in speciebus, quae sunt signum ejus.

AD TERTIUM dicendum, quod forma substantialis materialis aliquo modo habet ordinem ad dimensiones, cum dimensiones interminatae praeintelligantur in materia ante formam substantialem, ut dictum est; sed corpus Christi nequaquam; et ideo non est simile de corpore Christi et illis formis.

the contrary, its dimensions are there somehow as a result. And so whatever applies to the body of Christ by means of its own dimensions does not apply to it according as it is under the sacrament. Therefore, since quantitative division cannot apply to it except by means of its proper dimensions, it is evident that in the breaking of the species, the body itself is neither divided nor broken, even if it were passible, as it was at the Last Supper.

REPLY OBJ. 1: In eating there are many things, both breaking or chewing, as well as swallowing down into the stomach, and nourishing. However, the first belongs to these species alone; but the second applies both to the species containing and to the body contained: for wherever the species are, there is the true body of Christ. But the third, if we are speaking spiritually, applies to the body of Christ, but if we are speaking physically, to the species, as has been said. And so eating does apply to the body of Christ in a certain way, but not breaking or dividing.

REPLY OBJ. 2: Because this sacrament is a sign of Christ's Passion, and not the Passion itself, for this reason the Passion that the breaking signifies must not exist in the body of Christ, but in the species, which are its sign.

REPLY OBJ. 3: Material substantial form has an order to the dimensions in a certain way, since unbounded dimensions are understood in matter before substantial form, as was said; but the body of Christ by no means; and so it is not the same for the body of Christ and those forms.

Response to Quaestiuncula 2

AD SECUNDAM QUAESTIONEM dicendum, quod quidam dixerunt, quod fractio secundum rei veritatem non erat in hoc sacramento. Sed hoc non potest esse: quia fractio importat passionem, sive motum quemdam, et multitudinem ad quam terminatur motus; et utrumque horum est sensibile per se. Sunt enim sensibilia communia, quae contra sensibilia per accidens dividuntur in 2 de Anima; et ita judicium de his pertinet ad sensitivam partem; unde cum sensus judicet fractionem, si non esset fractio, esset falsum judicium; quod non competit in sacramento veritatis. Et ideo alii dixerunt, quod est ibi fractio sine subjecto. Sed hoc non potest dici; quia fractio cum sit quidam motus, secundum rationem suae speciei, requirit terminum a quo et in quem; et ideo oportet ibi esse unum quod in multa dividitur, et hoc est subjectum fractionis. Et praeterea actio vel passio habet magis debile esse quam qualitas; unde cum qualitates in hoc sacramento ponamus in subjecto, multo fortius passionem. Et ideo, cum fractio non possit esse in

TO THE SECOND QUESTION, it should be said that some people said that the breaking, according to the truth of things, did not exist in this sacrament. But this cannot be, because breaking implies something that happens to something else, or a certain motion, and a multitude in which the motion terminates; and either of these is sensible in itself. For there are common sensible objects which are divided against things that are incidentally sensible in *On the Soul* 2;[59] and so the judgment of these things pertains to the sensitive part. And that is why since the senses judge there to be a breaking, if there were not a breaking, it would be a false judgment, which does not befit the sacrament of truth. And therefore others have said that there is a breaking there without a subject. But this cannot be said, for a breaking, since it is a certain motion according to the definition of its species, requires a starting terminus and an ending terminus. And so it is necessary that it be one thing that is divided into many, and this is the subject of the breaking. And furthermore, action and passion have weaker being than

---

59. Aristotle, *On the Soul*, Bk. 2, ch. 6 (418a7ff.).

corpore Christi sicut in subjecto, ut dictum est, oportet quod sit in speciebus.

AD PRIMUM ergo dicendum, quod signum respondet signato quantum ad id quod[60] est: est enim hoc sacramentum signum rememorativum respectu Dominicae passionis.

AD SECUNDUM dicendum, quod sicut densitas manet in hoc sacramento, ita durities, quae est ejus effectus; et propter hoc etiam species illae sonum facere natae sunt, et sic etiam est ibi porositatem invenire.

AD TERTIUM dicendum, quod illud de speciebus quod est in una portione, non est in alia: quia species sunt quae franguntur: corpus autem Christi non frangitur, quia totum remanet sub qualibet parte; et ratio hujus dicta est supra, dist. 10.

quality; and so since we posit qualities to exist in this sacrament in the subject, much more should passion. And so, since breaking cannot be in the body of Christ as in a subject, as was said, it is necessary that it be in the species.

REPLY OBJ. 1: The sign corresponds to what it represents in what it was, but not as to what it is, for this sacrament is a commemorative sign with regard to the Lord's Passion.

REPLY OBJ. 2: Just as density remains in this sacrament, so does hardness, which is its effect; and because of this also those species are bound to make a sound, and this is also how a porousness is found there.

REPLY OBJ. 3: Whatever of the species that exists in one portion is not in the others, for it is the species that are broken. But the body of Christ is not broken since the whole remains under every part, and the reason for this has been said above, in Distinction 10.[61]

Response to Quaestiuncula 3

AD TERTIAM QUAESTIONEM dicendum, quod sicut in hoc sacramento est duplex res sacramenti, scilicet corpus Christi verum et mysticum; ita etiam fractio duo significat, scilicet ipsam divisionem corporis veri, quae facta est in passione, et haec significatio tangitur in littera, et distributionem virtutis redemptionis Christi per diversa membra ecclesiae; et hanc significationem tangit Dionysius in 3 cap. *Eccl. Hierar.* Et secundum hoc accipitur significatio partium secundum diversum membrorum statum. Quia quidam sunt adhuc vivi, et hi significantur per partem quae comeditur: quia ipsi atteruntur diversis poenalitatibus, et sunt in ipso motu, ut incorporentur Christo. Quidam autem sunt mortui: et hi sunt in duplici statu. Quia quidam in plena participatione beatitudinis; et hoc est corpus Christi quod jam surrexit, sicut ipse Christus, et Beata Virgo; et hi significantur per partem in calice missam, quia *illi inebriantur ab ubertate domus Dei.* Quidam autem sunt in expectatione plenae beatitudinis, qui vel stolam animae tantum habent, vel neutram, ut hi qui sunt in Purgatorio; et hi significantur per tertiam partem quae reservatur usque in finem: quia hi perfectam gloriam consequuntur in fine mundi, et interim in speciebus quiescunt.

AD PRIMUM ergo dicendum, quod ipsum corpus Christi verum significat corpus Christi mysticum; unde partes corporis veri significant partes corporis mystici.

TO THE THIRD QUESTION, it should be said that just as in this sacrament there is a twofold reality of the sacrament, namely, the true and the mystical body of Christ, so also the breaking signifies two things, namely the very division of the true body, which happened in his Passion, and this signification is referred to in the text; and the distribution of the power of Christ's redemption through the diverse members of the Church, and Dionysius refers to this signification in Chapter 3 of the *Ecclesiastical Hierarchy.*[62] And according to this the signification of the parts is taken according to the different states of the members. For some people are still living, and these are represented by the part that is eaten; for they are ground by different penalties, and they are in this very motion so that they may be incorporated into Christ. Certain others are dead; and these are in two states. For some are in the full participation of blessedness; and this is the body of Christ that has already risen, like Christ himself and the Blessed Virgin; and these are represented by the part placed into the chalice, for *they are inebriated with the richness of the house of God* (Ps 35:9). But some others are in the expectation of full blessedness, who either have only the soul's garment, or neither, like those who are in purgatory; and these are represented by the third part which is reserved until the end: for these people will receive perfect glory at the end of the world, and meanwhile they rest in appearances.

REPLY OBJ. 1: The true body of Christ itself signifies the mystical body of Christ; hence parts of the true body signify parts of the mystical body.

---

60. *quod est.—quod fuit sed non quantum ad id quod est* PLE.
61. See d. 10, a. 3, qa. 3.
62. Pseudo-Dionysius, *Ecclesiastical Hierarchy*, ch. 3, p. 3, n. 13 (PG 3:443).

AD SECUNDUM dicendum, quod ista unio facta est per passionem Christi; et ideo oportet quod sit in hoc sacramento fractio, quae passionem significet.

AD TERTIUM dicendum, quod talis mos fuit in primitiva ecclesia, qui tamen modo cessavit propter periculum; nihilominus remanet eadem significatio partium.

AD QUARTUM dicendum, quod non est inconveniens per idem diversa significari secundum suas proprietates diversas; unde et calix passionem significat inquantum inebriat; et sic procedit significatio quam ponit Innocentius: quia pars extra calicem significat eos qui sunt extra passionem praesentis miseriae, et pars in calice missa eos qui praedictis passionibus opprimuntur. Sed inquantum potus calicis delectat, significat gaudium aeternitatis; et ita procedit significatio in littera posita, quae continetur sub his versibus: *hostia dividitur in partes. Tincta beatos plene: sicca notat vivos, servata sepultos.*

AD QUINTUM dicendum, quod hoc sacramentum non solum est in remedium, sed etiam in gratiarum actionem; et ideo, quamvis beati non consequantur aliquod remedium in isto sacramento, quia tamen est in gratiarum actionem pro eorum gloria, conveniens fuit ut et ipsi in hoc sacramento significarentur.

AD SEXTUM dicendum, quod omnes vivi indigent hoc sacramento ad remedium, sed non omnes mortui; et ideo pro mortuis ponuntur duae partes, sed pro vivis una tantum. Vel dicendum, quod duae ponuntur pro vivis in hoc saeculo, et alia pro vivis in gloria, qui resurrexerunt; et pro omnibus qui adhuc non resurrexerunt, una tantum.

AD SEPTIMUM dicendum, quod resurrectio membrorum est conformis resurrectioni capitis; quia *reformabit corpus humilitatis nostrae configuratum corpori claritatis suae*; Philip. 3, 21: et ideo eadem parte significatur et caput et membra ei perfecte configurata.

REPLY OBJ. 2: That union happened by Christ's Passion; and so it is necessary that there be a breaking that signifies the Passion in this sacrament.

REPLY OBJ. 3: This kind of practice existed in the early Church, which has now ceased, however, because of the danger; nevertheless the same signification of parts remains.

REPLY OBJ. 4: It is not unfitting if different things are signified by the same thing according to its different properties; hence also the chalice signifies the Passion in that it inebriates, and this is how the signification that Innocent gives proceeds: for the part outside the chalice signifies those who are outside the passion of this present misery, and the part placed in the chalice represents those who are oppressed by the passion or sufferings mentioned. But inasmuch as a drink of the chalice delights, it represents the joy of eternity, and in this way the signification that is set down in the text proceeds, which is contained under these verses: *the host is divided into parts. The dipped part is the fully blessed; the dry part symbolizes the living, the reserved part, those buried.*

REPLY OBJ. 5: This sacrament is not only for a remedy, but also for thanksgiving; and so although the blessed do not seek any remedy in this sacrament, nevertheless, because it is still in thanksgiving for their glory, it was fitting that they too be signified in this sacrament.

REPLY OBJ. 6: All the living need this sacrament as a remedy, but not all the dead; and so two parts are placed for the dead, but for the living, only one. Or it could be said that two parts are set down for the living in this world, and another for those living in glory, who have risen; and for all who have not yet risen, only one.

REPLY OBJ. 7: The resurrection of the members is like the resurrection of the head; because *he shall reform the body of our lowness, made like to the body of his glory* (Phil 3:21); and so by the same part is signified both the head and the members perfectly configured to it.

QUESTION 2

THE EFFECTS OF HOLY COMMUNION

Deinde quaeritur de effectu hujus sacramenti; et circa hoc quaeruntur duo:

primo, de effectu ejus quantum ad consecutionem boni;

secundo, de effectu ejus quantum ad remotionem mali.

Next this sacrament's effect is considered. And concerning this, two questions arise:

first, its effect in bringing about good;

second, its effect in removing evil.

ARTICLE 1

The effect of the Eucharist in bringing about good

Quaestiuncula 1

AD PRIMUM SIC PROCEDITUR. Videtur quod per hoc sacramentum non augeantur virtutes. Quia diversarum causarum diversi sunt effectus. Sed augmentum virtutis est effectus baptismi, et etiam confirmationis, ut supra dictum est. Ergo non est effectus Eucharistiae.

PRAETEREA, per augmentum caritatis ad perfectionem caritatis venitur. Si ergo per hoc sacramentum caritas et aliae virtutes augerentur, toties posset sumi quod homo in hac vita ad perfectam caritatem veniret, et ad summum gradum ipsius; quod non est nisi in patria, ut Augustinus dicit.

PRAETEREA, omnes virtutes simul augentur. Si ergo augmentum virtutum esset effectus hujus sacramenti, non magis deberet poni effectus augmentum caritatis quam aliarum virtutum.

SED CONTRA, nihil spiritualiter perficitur nisi per augmentum virtutum. Sed secundum Dionysium, Eucharistia habet virtutem perfectivam. Ergo effectus ejus est virtutis augmentum.

PRAETEREA, effectus hujus sacramenti est plenitudo gratiae, ut patet in oratione canonis: *quotquot ex hac altaris participatione sumpserimus, omni benedictione caelesti et gratia repleamur.* Sed ad plenitudinem gratiae per augmentum virtutis pervenitur. Ergo idem quod prius.

OBJ. 1: To the first we proceed thus. It seems that virtues are not increased by this sacrament.[63] For different effects come from different causes. But the increase of virtue is an effect of baptism, and also confirmation, as was said above.[64] Therefore, it is not an effect of the Eucharist.

OBJ. 2: Furthermore, by the increase of charity one comes to the perfection of charity. If therefore charity and the other virtues are increased by this sacrament, it could be received so many times that a man might arrive at perfect charity and its highest degree in this life; which only happens in the heavenly fatherland, as Augustine says.[65]

OBJ. 3: Furthermore, all virtues increase together. If therefore the increase of virtues were the effect of this sacrament, the effect could not include a greater increase in charity than in the other virtues.

ON THE CONTRARY, nothing is spiritually perfected without the increase of virtues. But according to Dionysius,[66] the Eucharist has a perfective power. Therefore, its effect is the increase of virtue.

FURTHERMORE, this sacrament's effect is the fullness of grace, as is clear from the prayer in the canon of the Mass: *that as many of us at this altar shall partake and receive, shall be filled with every heavenly blessing and grace.* But one attains the fullness of grace by an increase of virtue. Therefore, the same as before.

---

63. Parallel: *ST* III, q. 79, a. 1.
64. See d. 4, q. 2, a. 2; d. 7, q. 2, a. 2.
65. Augustine, *De perfectione iustitiae hominis* (CSEL 42), ch. 3.
66. Pseudo-Dionysius, *Ecclesiastical Hierarchy*, ch. 3 (PG 3:423).

Quaestiuncula 2

ULTERIUS. Videtur quod hoc sacramentum prosit etiam beatis ad augmentum gloriae. In collecta enim beati Leonis Papae, ut Innocentius dicit, ita dicitur: *annue nobis Domine, ut animae famuli tui Leonis haec prosit oblatio*. Sed constat beatum Leonem in gloria esse. Ergo prodest beatis ad gloriae augmentum.

PRAETEREA, hoc sacramentum offertur etiam pro parvulis decedentibus in innocentia baptismali. Sed constat quod tales ad gloriam transeunt. Ergo prodest etiam hoc sacramentum ad augmentum gloriae.

SED CONTRA, sacramenta ecclesiae non prosunt alicui qui non sit in statu proficiendi. Sed sancti in patria existentes non sunt in statu proficiendi, cum sint in termino profectus. Ergo eis Eucharistia non prodest.

OBJ. 1: Moreover, it seems that this sacrament could also benefit the blessed in the increase of glory. For in the collect of the Mass of blessed Pope Leo, as Innocent says, it is said thus: *favor us, Lord, that this offering may benefit the soul of your servant Leo.*[67] But it is clear that blessed Leo is in glory. Therefore, it benefits the blessed in an increase of glory.

OBJ. 2: Furthermore, this sacrament is offered also for those children who die in baptismal innocence. But it is obvious that they pass on to glory. Therefore, this sacrament also benefits them in an increase of glory.

ON THE CONTRARY, the sacraments of the Church do not benefit anyone who is not in the state of progressing. But the saints in the fatherland are not in the state of progressing, since they are at the terminus of progress. Therefore, the Eucharist does not benefit them.

Quaestiuncula 3

ULTERIUS. Videtur quod effectus hujus sacramenti non possit impediri nisi per peccatum mortale. Quia, sicut Ambrosius in littera dicit, *spiritualiter manducat qui innocentiam ad altare portat*. Sed quicumque sine peccato mortali accedit, portat innocentiam ad altare; quia venialia peccata innocentiam non tollunt. Cum ergo spiritualiter manducans effectum sacramenti percipiat, videtur quod effectus sacramenti non possit impediri nisi per peccatum mortale.

PRAETEREA, baptismus non est nobilius sacramentum quam istud. Sed nihil impedit effectum baptismi nisi peccatum mortale. Ergo nec effectum hujus sacramenti.

PRAETEREA, peccatum veniale non facit fictum. Sed sola fictio impedit sacramentorum effectum. Ergo solum peccatum mortale impedit sacramenti effectum.

SED CONTRA, nullus percipit effectum hujus sacramenti nisi qui accedit sicut accedendum est. Sed aliquis debet accedere ad hoc sacramentum cum diligenti conscientiae suae examinatione, ut patet 1 Corinth. 11. Cum ergo sine peccato mortali possit hoc praetermitti, videtur quod sine peccato mortali possit effectus hujus sacramenti impediri.

PRAETEREA, ad hoc quod aliquis adultus gratiam recipiat, oportet quod se ad gratiam habendam praepa-

OBJ. 1: Moreover, it seems that this sacrament's effect cannot be impeded by anything but mortal sin.[68] For just as Ambrose says in the text, *he eats spiritually who bears his innocence to the altar.*[69] But whoever approaches without mortal sin, bears his innocence to the altar, for venial sins do not destroy innocence. Since, then, whoever receives Communion spiritually receives the sacrament's effect, it seems that the sacrament's effect cannot be impeded by anything but mortal sin.

OBJ. 2: Furthermore, baptism is not a nobler sacrament than this one. But nothing impedes baptism's effect except mortal sin. Therefore, not this sacrament's effect either.

OBJ. 3: Furthermore, venial sin does not make someone a fake. But only false pretenses impede the effects of the sacraments. Therefore, only mortal sin impedes the sacrament's effect.

ON THE CONTRARY, no one receives this sacrament's effect unless he approaches as it should be approached. But someone must approach this sacrament with a careful examination of his conscience, as is clear from 1 Corinthians 11:28. Therefore, since this can be omitted without mortal sin, it seems that without mortal sin the effect of this sacrament can be impeded.

FURTHERMORE, for an adult to receive grace, he must have prepared himself for having grace. But this prepara-

---

67. See the Decretalium Gregorii papae IX compilationis, Bk. 3, title 41, ch. 6, "Quum [cum] Martha," retrieved from http://www.hs-augsburg.de/~harsch/Chronologia/Lspost13/GregoriusIX/gre_3t41.html on January 30, 2015.

68. Parallel: *ST* III, q. 79, a. 8.

69. In the text of Lombard this saying is not attributed to any particular author. The Moos edition gives as its source Ivo of Chartres, *Decretum*, p. 2, ch. 4 (PL 161:137).

raverit. Sed hanc praeparationem contingit sine peccato mortali impediri. Ergo sine peccato mortali contingit impediri effectum hujus sacramenti.

tion may be impeded without mortal sin. Therefore, this sacrament's effect may be impeded without mortal sin.

Response to Quaestiuncula 1

RESPONDEO dicendum ad primam quaestionem, quod proprius effectus cujuslibet sacramenti debet assumi ex similitudine ad materiam illius sacramenti; sicut expurgatio veteris vitae est effectus baptismi per ablutionem aquae significata. Et ideo cum materiale in hoc sacramento sit cibus, oportet quod effectus proprius hujus sacramenti accipiatur secundum similitudinem ad effectum cibi. Cibus autem corporalis primo in cibatum convertitur, et ex tali conversione, deperdita restaurat, et quantitatem auget; sed spiritualis cibus non convertitur in manducantem, sed eum ad se convertit. Unde proprius effectus hujus sacramenti est conversio hominis in Christum, ut dicat cum Apostolo, Galat. 2, 20: *vivo ego, jam non ego; vivit vero in me Christus*; et ad hoc sequuntur duo effectus: augmentum spiritualis quantitatis in augmento virtutum, et restauratio deperditorum in remissione venialium vel reparatione cujuscumque defectus praecedentis.

AD PRIMUM ergo dicendum, quod augmentum dicitur dupliciter. Uno modo communiter, prout invenitur in viventibus et non viventibus, secundum quod quaelibet additio augmentum facit; et hoc modo virtutes augentur per omnia sacramenta quae gratiam inveniunt in subjecto, ex eo quod ipsa de se nata sunt gratiam causare. Alio modo augmentum dicitur proprie, prout est in viventibus ex conjunctione nutrimenti; et talis modus augmenti virtutum est proprius huic sacramento.

AD SECUNDUM dicendum, quod duplex est perfectio caritatis; scilicet viae, et patriae; et quamvis non possit hoc sacramentum existentes in via perducere ad perfectionem patriae propter diversum statum, potest tamen perducere ad perfectionem viae. Per augmentum enim caritatis ad perfectionem patriae in via pervenire non possumus.

AD TERTIUM dicendum, quod caritatis proprium est transformare amantem in amatum, quia ipsa est quae extasim facit, ut Dionysius dicit. Et quia augmentum virtutum in hoc sacramento fit per conversionem manducantis in spiritualem cibum, ideo magis attribuitur huic sacramento caritatis augmentum quam aliarum virtutum.

TO THE FIRST QUESTION, I answer that the proper effect of any sacrament should be gathered from a likeness to the matter of that sacrament; just as the purification of the old life is the effect of baptism, signified by the cleansing of water. And so since the matter in this sacrament is food, the sacrament's proper effect must be taken from a likeness to the effect of food. Now physical food is first converted into what has been fed, and by this conversion it restores what has been lost, and increases quantity. But spiritual food is not converted into the one eating it, but converts him to itself. And this is why the proper effect of this sacrament is a man's conversion into Christ, so that he may say with the Apostle, *I live; not I but Christ lives in me* (Gal 2:20). And for this two effects follow: increase of spiritual quantity in the increase of virtues, and restoration of what has been lost in the remission of venial sins, or the reparation of any previous defects.

REPLY OBJ. 1: Increase can be said in two ways. In one way, commonly, as it is found in living things and non-living things, according to which any addition makes an increase; and in this way the virtues are increased by all the sacraments that find grace in the subject, by the fact that it is their nature to cause grace. In another way, increase is said properly, as it exists in living things by the union of nourishment; and this kind of increase of the virtues is more proper to this sacrament.

REPLY OBJ. 2: There are two kinds of perfection in charity, namely, in this life, and in the fatherland; and although this sacrament cannot bring those who are wayfaring to the perfection of the fatherland because of their difference in state, it can however lead them to the perfection of the wayfarer. For we cannot arrive at the perfection of heaven by an increase in charity while we are in this life.

REPLY OBJ. 3: It is proper to charity for the lover to be transformed into the beloved, for it is charity that brings about ecstasy, as Dionysius says.[70] And since the increase of virtues in this sacrament happens by the eater being converted into his spiritual food, for this reason the increase of charity more than the other virtues is attributed to this sacrament.

---

70. Pseudo-Dionysius, *On the Divine Names*, ch. 4, n. 13 (PG 3:711).

Response to Quaestiuncula 2

AD SECUNDAM QUAESTIONEM dicendum, quod gloria comprehendit sanctorum praemium; quod quidem est duplex; scilicet essentiale gaudium quod de divinitate habent; et accidentale, idest gaudium quod habent de quocumque bono creato. Quantum autem ad praemium essentiale, secundum probabiliorem opinionem, eorum gloria augeri non potest; sed quantum ad praemium accidentale usque ad diem judicii augeri potest; alioquin tunc non augeretur gaudium de gloria corporis; unde de omnibus beneficiis eis gloria accrescit; quia *gaudium est angelis Dei super uno peccatore poenitentiam agente*; Luc. 15, 10; et ita etiam de omnibus quae in Dei honorem fiunt, gaudent, et maxime de his in quibus de eorum gloria Deo gratias agimus. Unde simpliciter loquendo, hoc est quantum ad essentiam gloriae, hoc sacramentum non auget in beatis gloriam; sed secundum quid, scilicet quantum ad accidentale praemium, auget.

AD PRIMUM ergo dicendum, quod sicut Innocentius solvit, ubicumque talis loquendi modus invenitur, ita debet intelligi, ut ad hoc prosit ut a fidelibus magis ac magis glorificetur in terris.

AD SECUNDUM dicendum, quod pro pueris baptizatis Missarum solemnia celebrantur, non quia eis juventur quantum ad remissionem alicujus culpae, vel quantum ad augmentum gloriae, sed propter alias rationes: tum propter solatium vivorum; tum ad ostendendum parvulos ad unitatem corporis mystici pertinere, dum idem modus exequiarum servatur in ipsis et in aliis; tum ad commendandum redemptionis mysterium, quod in hoc sacramento commemoratur, per quod parvuli sine proprio merito salutem consequuntur aeternam.

TO THE SECOND QUESTION, it should be said that glory encompasses the reward of the saints, which is twofold: namely, the essential prize, the joy that they have in the divinity; and the incidental prize, which is the joy that they have in any created good. As to the essential prize, according to the more probable opinion, their glory cannot be increased; but as to the incidental prize, it can be increased up until the day of judgment, otherwise their joy would not be increased on that day with the glory of the body. And this is why glory grows in them from every benefit, for *there is joy among the angels of God over the repentance of one sinner* (Luke 15:10). And thus also they rejoice in everything that is done to honor God, and especially those things whereby we thank God for their glory. And so, simply speaking, with regard to the essence of glory, this sacrament does not increase the glory of the blessed; but in a certain respect, namely, the incidental reward, it does increase it.

REPLY OBJ. 1: As Innocent resolves it, wherever such a mode of speaking is found, it should be understood as benefiting him such that he is glorified by the faithful more and more on earth.

REPLY OBJ. 2: The solemn Masses are celebrated for baptized children, not because they assist them by the remission of any guilt, or as to the increase of their glory, but for other reasons: both for the consolation of the living, and in order to show that little ones belong to the unity of the mystical body, since the same manner of funeral rites is observed for them as for others; and also to remind people of the mystery of redemption, which is commemorated in this sacrament, by which little ones obtain eternal salvation without their own meriting.

Response to Quaestiuncula 3

AD TERTIAM QUAESTIONEM dicendum, quod omnis perfectio acquirenda impeditur per remotionem propriae dispositionis. Sicut autem dispositiones materiales se habent ad perfectionem formae, ita actus se habent ad perfectionem finis; unde cum hoc sacramentum perficiat conjungendo fini, ut supra dictum est; ad hoc quod effectum suum plene habeat in sumente, oportet quod adsit actualis devotio. Et quia interdum absque mortali peccato actualis devotio impediri potest, cum distractiones variae ipsam impediant, et peccata venialia virtutum actum tollant; absque peccato mortali potest effectus hujus sacramenti impediri, ita quod aliquis augmentum gratiae non consequatur; nec tamen reatum peccati mortalis incurret, sed forte reatum venialis peccati, ex hoc quod imparatus accedit.

TO THE THIRD QUESTION, it should be said that every perfection to be acquired is impeded by the removal of its proper disposition. But just as material dispositions are ordered to the perfection of form, so acts are ordered to the perfection of the end. And therefore since this sacrament perfects by uniting to the end, as was said above, in order for it to have its own effect fully in the one who receives it, there must be actual devotion present. And since sometimes actual devotion can be impeded without mortal sin, since various distractions impede it, and venial sins destroy the act of the virtues, this sacrament's effect can be impeded without mortal sin so that someone does not receive the increase of grace; but neither would he have become guilty of mortal sin, but perhaps guilty of venial sin, by the fact that he approaches the sacrament without proper preparation.

Ad primum ergo dicendum, quod innocentiam portans spiritualiter manducat habitu, sed non semper actu; et ad hoc quod effectum sacramenti percipiat, oportet quod actu spiritualiter manducet.

Ad secundum dicendum, quod in baptismo datur primum esse spirituale; et ideo effectus ejus non impeditur nisi per propositum peccati mortalis committendi, quod directe vitae spirituali opponitur. Sed in hoc sacramento fit conjunctio ad finem, quae debet esse per debitam operationem; et ideo defectus talis operationis impedit effectum hujus sacramenti.

Ad tertium dicendum, quod quamvis peccatum veniale non faciat fictum simpliciter, facit tamen fictum quo ad aliquid. Nec tamen dicendum quod omne peccatum veniale impediat effectum hujus sacramenti, sed solum illud quod tollit actualem devotionem quae exigitur in hoc sacramento.

Reply Obj. 1: Someone bearing his innocence eats spiritually in habit, but not always in act. And in order to receive the effect of the sacrament, one must eat spiritually in act.

Reply Obj. 2: In baptism the first spiritual existence is given, and so its effect is not impeded by anything but the intention of committing a mortal sin, which is directly opposed to the spiritual life. But in this sacrament the union with the end happens, which should be by the due operation, and so a defect of this kind of operation impedes the effect of this sacrament.

Reply Obj. 3: Although venial sin does not make one a fake simply, it nevertheless makes one a fake in a certain respect. Nor, however, should it be said that every venial sin impedes the effect of this sacrament, but only one that takes away the actual devotion that is demanded in this sacrament.

ARTICLE 2

The effect of the Eucharist in removing evil

Quaestiuncula 1

AD SECUNDUM SIC PROCEDITUR. Videtur quod virtute hujus sacramenti venialia peccata non dimittantur. Qua enim ratione dimittitur unum, et aliud. Sed omnia non dimittuntur; quia sic aliquis esset frequenter absque omni veniali peccato; quod est contra illud quod dicitur 1 Joan. 1, 8: *si dixerimus quod peccatum non habemus, nosipsos seducimus.* Ergo non delet aliquod peccatum veniale.

PRAETEREA, peccatum non deletur nisi per id quod habet oppositionem ad ipsum. Sed veniale peccatum non habet oppositionem ad gratiam, quam hoc sacramentum confert. Ergo virtute hujus sacramenti venialia non dimittuntur.

PRAETEREA, baptismus, quia dimittit omnia peccata mortalia et venialia, non requirit luctum exteriorem. Si ergo in hoc sacramento venialia peccata dimittantur, non requiritur quod post sumptionem hujus sacramenti aliquis faceret poenitentiam de peccatis venialibus; quod falsum est.

SED CONTRA, Innocentius dicit, quod hoc sacramentum *venialia delet, et cavet mortalia.*

PRAETEREA, ut ex verbis Ambrosii in littera positis accipi potest, hoc sacramentum datur in remedium quotidianae infirmitatis. Sed quotidiana peccata dicuntur venialia. Ergo hoc sacramentum tollit venialia peccata.

OBJ. 1: To the second question we proceed thus. It seems that venial sins are not forgiven by the power of this sacrament.[71] For if one thing is forgiven, by the same reasoning another should be. But all sins are not forgiven, for then someone would be without any venial sin often; which is against what is said: *if we say that we have no sin, we deceive ourselves* (1 John 1:8). Therefore, it does not erase any venial sin.

OBJ. 2: Furthermore, sin is only blotted out by what is opposed to it. But venial sin is not opposed to grace, which this sacrament confers. Therefore, venial sins are not forgiven by the power of this sacrament.

OBJ. 3: Furthermore, baptism, which forgives all sins, mortal and venial, does not require outward sorrow. Therefore, if venial sins were forgiven by this sacrament, it would not be required that after receiving this sacrament someone should do penance for his venial sins, which is false.

ON THE CONTRARY, Innocent says that this sacrament *removes venial sins and guards against mortal ones.*[72]

FURTHERMORE, as can be drawn from the words of Ambrose quoted in the text, this sacrament is given as a remedy for daily infirmity. But daily sins are called venial. Therefore, this sacrament takes away venial sins.

Quaestiuncula 2

ULTERIUS. Videtur quod etiam virtute hujus sacramenti dimittantur mortalia. Dicitur enim in collecta illa: *purificent nos, quaesumus Domine, sacramenta quae sumpsimus*; et mox: *praesta ut hoc tuum sacramentum sit ablutio scelerum.* Sed scelera dicuntur mortalia peccata. Ergo delet peccata mortalia.

PRAETEREA, hoc sacramentum expressius passionem Christi repraesentat quam baptismus. Sed baptismus virtute passionis in eo operantis delet peccata mortalia. Ergo et hoc sacramentum.

OBJ. 1: Moreover, it seems that also mortal sins are forgiven by the power of this sacrament.[73] For it is said in one collect of the Mass: *May the sacraments we receive purify us, we beg, Lord*, and then, *Grant that this your sacrament may be for the cleansing of crimes.*[74] But crimes mean mortal sins. Therefore, it takes away mortal sins.

OBJ. 2: Furthermore, this sacrament represents Christ's Passion more explicitly than baptism. But baptism takes away mortal sins by the power of the Passion working in it. Therefore, so does this sacrament.

---

71. Parallels: *ST* III, q. 79, a. 4; q. 87, a. 3.
72. Innocent III, *De sacro altaris mysterio*, Bk. 4, ch. 44 (PL 217:885).
73. Parallels: above, d. 9, a. 3, qa. 2; *ST* III, q. 79, a. 3.
74. These phrases are found in the third Lenten postcommunion, "for the Living and the Dead," found in missals printed prior to the reduction of orations to one set only.

PRAETEREA, minima gratia sufficit ad delendum omnia mortalia. Sed hoc sacramentum gratiam confert. Ergo mortalia delet.

PRAETEREA, hoc sacramentum magis operatur in sumente quam in alio; alias frustra quis assumeret. Sed offertur sacrificium ecclesiae pro aliquibus impiis ut convertantur, et non frustra. Ergo et in ipso qui sumit, mortalia peccata delet.

SED CONTRA, Augustinus ad renatum: *quis offerat corpus Christi nisi pro his qui sunt membra Christi?* Sed illi qui sunt membra Christi, non habent peccatum mortale. Ergo virtute hujus sacramenti non delentur mortalia.

PRAETEREA, hoc sacramentum non habet aliquem effectum in indigne accedentibus. Sed quicumque accedit cum mortali, indigne accedit. Ergo non percipit effectum hujus sacramenti; et ita non delet mortalia.

OBJ. 3: Furthermore, the slightest grace suffices to take away all mortal sins. But this sacrament confers grace. Therefore, it takes away mortal sins.

OBJ. 4: Furthermore, this sacrament works more in the one receiving it than in another; otherwise, he would receive it in vain. But the sacrifice of the Church is offered for certain sinners that they be converted, and not in vain. Therefore, also in the person who receives it, it removes mortal sins.

ON THE CONTRARY, Augustine says to one reborn: *who offers the body of Christ except on behalf of those who are members of Christ?*[75] But those who are members of Christ do not have mortal sin. Therefore, mortal sins are not blotted out by the power of this sacrament.

FURTHERMORE, this sacrament does not have any effect in those who approach it unworthily. But anyone who approaches it with mortal sin approaches unworthily. Therefore, he does not receive the effect of this sacrament, and so it does not remove mortal sins.

Quaestiuncula 3

ULTERIUS. Videtur quod remittat poenam peccati mortalis. Deus enim pronior est ad miserendum quam ad puniendum, ut dicit Glossa in principio Hier. Sed indigne accedens incurrit reatum poenae mortalis peccati. Ergo digne accedens ab eo absolvitur.

PRAETEREA, hoc sacramentum non minus valet vivis quam mortuis. Sed mortuis valet ad remissionem poenae, quia ad hoc pro eis offertur. Ergo multo magis vivis.

PRAETEREA, veritas est majoris efficaciae quam figura. Sed sacrificia veteris testamenti in satisfactionem pro peccatis mortalibus offerebantur. Ergo multo fortius et hoc, cujus sunt illa figura; et sic remittit mortalium poenam.

SED CONTRA: quicumque non est debitor poenae, statim moriens evolat. Si ergo hoc sacramento poena mortalis peccati dimitteretur, quilibet munitus hoc sacramento ex hac vita decedens evolaret; quod falsum est.

PRAETEREA, satisfactio non exigitur nisi ad dimissionem poenae. Si ergo hoc sacramento dimitteretur poena, omnis alia satisfactio tolleretur; quod est inconveniens.

OBJ. 1: Furthermore, it seems that it remits the punishment for mortal sin.[76] For God is more prone to having mercy than to punishing, as the Gloss on the beginning of the book of Jeremiah says.[77] But someone approaching this sacrament unworthily is culpable for the punishment of mortal sin. Therefore, someone approaching worthily is absolved of it.

OBJ. 2: Furthermore, this sacrament is not less effective for the living than for the dead. But it avails the dead for the remission of punishment, for it is offered for this on their behalf. Therefore, much more for the living.

OBJ. 3: Furthermore, truth is of greater efficacy than figure. But the sacrifices of the Old Testament were offered in satisfaction for mortal sins. Therefore, much stronger is this sacrifice, of which those were the figures. And thus it remits mortal punishment.

ON THE CONTRARY, anyone who does not owe punishment goes straight to heaven when he dies. Therefore, if this sacrament remitted the punishment of mortal sin, anyone departing this life fortified by this sacrament would go straight to heaven, which is false.

FURTHERMORE, satisfaction is only required for the forgiveness of punishment. Therefore, if punishment were forgiven by this sacrament, all other satisfaction would be taken away, which is unfitting.

---

75. Augustine, *De natura et origine animae* [also known as *Ad Renatum* and *De origine animae*], Bk 1, ch. 9, par. 10 (CSEL 60:311).

76. Parallels: above, d. 4, q. 2, a. 1, qa. 2, ad 3; *ST* III, q. 79, a. 5.

77. From Origen's *Homilies on Jeremiah*, Hom. 1 (PG 13:225).

Response to Quaestiuncula 1

RESPONDEO dicendum ad primam quaestionem, quod virtute hujus sacramenti fit quaedam transformatio hominis ad Christum per amorem, ut dictum est, et hic est proprius ejus effectus. Et quia ex fervore caritatis peccata venialia dimittuntur, propter hoc quod dicto fervori contrariantur, ideo ex consequenti, virtute hujus sacramenti, venialia delentur.

AD PRIMUM ergo dicendum, quod tantus potest esse devotionis fervor, quod omnia venialia peccata deleat. Nec est inconveniens quod aliqua hora homo sit absque omni peccato veniali; quamvis hoc diu durare non possit propter difficultatem vitandi peccata venialia. Nec tamen oportet quod semper omnia peccata venialia deleat, sed secundum mensuram devotionis: quia non est proximus effectus ejus deletio venialium, sed ex consequenti, ut ex dictis patet.

AD SECUNDUM dicendum, quod in hoc sacramento non solum confertur gratia habitualis, sed excitatur fervor actualis devotionis; et ideo gratiae hujus sacramenti non solum mortalia, sed etiam venialia opponuntur.

AD TERTIUM dicendum, quod baptismus habet pro principali effectu delere peccatum; et ideo quando non impeditur, delet omnia; sed non est ita in hoc sacramento; et ideo ratio non sequitur.

TO THE FIRST QUESTION, I answer that by the power of this sacrament a certain transformation of the person into Christ is made by love, as was said, and this is its proper effect. And since by the fervor of charity venial sins are forgiven, because of the fact that they are contrary to this fervor, as a result by the power of this sacrament venial sins are wiped away.

REPLY OBJ. 1: The fervor of devotion can be so great that it wipes away all venial sins. Nor is it unfitting that at some moment a man should be free of all venial sin; although this cannot last very long because of the difficulty of avoiding venial sin. Nor, however, is it necessary that all venial sins be erased, but only according to the measure of devotion, for the removal of venial sins is not its proximate effect, but something following on its proximate effect, as is clear from what has been said.

REPLY OBJ. 2: In this sacrament not only is habitual grace conferred, but the fervor of actual devotion is excited. And so the grace of this sacrament is not only opposed to mortal sins, but also to venial ones.

REPLY OBJ. 3: Baptism has for its chief effect the removal of sin; and so when it is not impeded, it removes all of them. But it is not the case in this sacrament, and so the argument does not follow.

Response to Quaestiuncula 2

AD SECUNDAM QUAESTIONEM dicendum, quod effectus sacramenti, ut dictum est, respondet his quae exterius in sacramento geruntur. Exterius autem usus hujus sacramenti est per manducationem, quae non debetur nisi rei viventi; et ideo effectus hujus sacramenti praesupponit vitam in sumente. Et quia peccatum mortale vitam spiritualem tollit, ideo hoc sacramentum non est ad abluenda peccata mortalia in sumentibus, sed illos solum defectus qui cum vita esse possunt.

AD PRIMUM ergo dicendum, quod sicut Innocentius dicit, hujusmodi locutiones sunt impropriae. Dicitur enim hoc sacramentum scelera vel crimina abluere vel tollere, inquantum ea impedit, contra ipsa robur ministrando. Vel dicendum, quod in aliquo potest esse peccatum mortale, qui ejus conscientiam non habet; et talis si devote accedit, veniam consequitur, ut supra, dist. 9, dictum est.

AD SECUNDUM dicendum, quod baptismus non solum exprimit passionem Christi, sed etiam facit baptizatum Christo commori. Et quia corruptio unius est generatio alterius, generatio autem est motus in vitam, et non praesupponit vitam, sed privationem ejus; ideo per

TO THE SECOND QUESTION, it should be said that a sacrament's effect, as was said, corresponds to the outward gestures in the sacrament. Now outwardly this sacrament's use is by eating, which activity is only due to a living thing. And so this sacrament's effect presupposes life in the one receiving it. And since mortal sin destroys spiritual life, for this reason this sacrament is not for washing away mortal sin in those who receive it, but only those defects that can coexist with life.

REPLY OBJ. 1: As Innocent says, speech like this seems improper. For this sacrament is said to take away or cleanse wicked deeds or crimes inasmuch as it impedes them, by administering strength against them. Or it should be said that there can be mortal sin in a person who has no consciousness of it. And if someone like this approaches devoutly, he obtains pardon, as was said above in Distinction 9.[78]

REPLY OBJ. 2: Baptism does not only express Christ's Passion, but it also causes the baptized to die with Christ. And since the corruption of one thing is the generation of another, while generation is a movement into life, and it does not presuppose life but rather its absence, therefore

---

78. See d. 9, q. 1, a. 3, qa. 2.

baptismum possunt peccata mortalia dimitti virtute passionis, non enim per Eucharistiam, per cujus sumptionem homo non significatur commori Christo, sed fructu mortis Christi refici, quod vitam praesupponit.

AD TERTIUM dicendum, quod gratia quam Eucharistia confert, quantum est de se, habet virtutem mortalia delendi. Sed ratione ordinis quem habet ad vitam quam praesupponit, mortalia invenire non potest, et ideo nec ea delere. Si autem inveniat in subjecto, non in conscientia, nihilominus ea delet.

AD QUARTUM dicendum, quod Eucharistia non solum est sacramentum, sed etiam est sacrificium. Inquantum autem est sacramentum, habet effectum in omni vivente, in quo requirit vitam praeexistere. Sed inquantum est sacrificium, habet effectum etiam in aliis, pro quibus offertur, in quibus non praeexigit vitam spiritualem in actu, sed in potentia tantum; et ideo, si eos dispositos inveniat, eis gratiam obtinet virtute illius veri sacrificii a quo omnis gratia in nos influxit; et per consequens peccata mortalia in eis delet, non sicut causa proxima, sed inquantum gratiam contritionis eis impetrat.

ET QUOD in contrarium dicitur, quod non offertur nisi pro membris Christi, intelligendum est pro membris Christi offerri, quando offertur pro aliquibus ut sint membra.

through baptism mortal sins can be forgiven by the power of the Passion, but not through the Eucharist, by whose reception a man is not signified to have died with Christ, but to have been refreshed as a fruit of Christ's death, which presupposes life.

REPLY OBJ. 3: In itself, the grace that the Eucharist confers has the power to remove mortal sins. But by reason of the ordering that it has to life, which it presupposes, it cannot light upon mortal sins, and so neither does it remove them. But if it came upon them in the subject but not in his conscience, it would remove them nevertheless.

REPLY OBJ. 4: The Eucharist is not only a sacrament but also a sacrifice. Now, as it is a sacrament, it has an effect in anyone living, in whom it requires that life pre-exist. But as it is a sacrifice, it has its effect also on others, on whose behalf it is offered, in whom it does not require spiritual life to exist actually, but only potentially. And so if it finds them disposed, it obtains grace for them by virtue of that true sacrifice from which all grace flows into us. And consequently it removes mortal sins in them, not as proximate cause, but inasmuch as it procures the grace of contrition for them.

AND WHAT IS SAID to the contrary, that it is only offered for the members of Christ, is to be understood such that the sacrifice is offered for Christ's members when it is offered for some people so that they might be members.

Response to Quaestiuncula 3

AD TERTIAM QUAESTIONEM dicendum, quod Eucharistia, inquantum est sacramentum, ut dictum est, pro principali effectu habet unionem hominis ad Christum; et ideo per modum sacramenti non aufert nisi ea quae in habente vitam huic unioni opposita invenit. Poena autem peccato mortali debita, quod jam deletum est, non est hujusmodi: ideo inquantum est sacramentum, non habet effectum poenae mortalis dimissionem; sed inquantum est sacrificium, accipit rationem satisfactionis; et secundum hoc in parte vel in toto poenam tollit, sicut et aliae satisfactiones secundum mensuram poenae debitae pro peccato et devotionis qua sacramentum offertur. Nec tamen semper virtute hujus sacramenti tota poena tollitur.

AD PRIMUM ergo dicendum, quod indigne accedens cum conscientia mortalis peccati, mortaliter peccat; et ideo reatum poenae debitae mortali peccato incurrit. Digne autem accedens meretur vitam aeternam, ad quam meritum ordinatur, sicut mortale peccatum ad poenam. Non autem ordinatur meritum directe principaliter ad remissionem poenae; et ideo ratio non procedit.

AD SECUNDUM dicendum, quod non totaliter semper aufertur poena per hoc sacrificium illis qui sunt in

TO THE THIRD QUESTION, it should be said that the Eucharist, insofar as it is a sacrament, as was said, has for its chief effect the union of man with Christ. And so by the mode of sacrament it only takes away those things that it finds opposed to this union in those who have life. However, the punishment due to mortal sin that has already been forgiven is not one of these things. And so, insofar as it is a sacrament it does not have the effect of forgiving mortal sin; but insofar as it is a sacrifice, it has the nature of satisfaction; and according to this it removes punishment partly or completely, just as other satisfactions, according to the measure of both punishment due for sin and the measure of devotion with which the sacrament is offered. Nor, however, is all the punishment always taken away by this sacrament.

REPLY OBJ. 1: Someone approaching unworthily, conscious of mortal sin, sins mortally. And so he is culpable for the punishment due to mortal sin. But someone approaching worthily merits eternal life, to which merit is ordered, just as mortal sin is ordered to punishment. However, merit is not directly or principally ordered to the remission of punishment, and so the argument does not follow.

REPLY OBJ. 2: For those who are in purgatory, punishment is not always completely taken away by this sacrifice,

Purgatorio, nec auferebatur in veteri lege per antiqua sacrificia.

UNDE PATET solutio ad tertium.

nor was it taken away by the ancient sacrifices under the Old Law.

AND BY THIS the solution to the third objection is clear.

QUESTION 3

THE FREQUENCY OF HOLY COMMUNION

Deinde quaeritur de frequentatione hujus sacramenti; et circa hoc quaeruntur duo:
primo, de frequentatione;
secundo, de cessatione.

Next the frequency of this sacrament should be considered; and concerning this, two questions arise:
first, its frequency;
second, abstention from it.

ARTICLE 1

The frequency of Holy Communion[79]

Quaestiuncula 1

AD PRIMUM SIC PROCEDITUR. Videtur quod non debeat homo frequentare hoc sacramentum, sed semel tantum in vita sua sumere. Injuriam enim facit sacramento qui sacramentum iterat. Sed rei digniori minus facienda est injuria. Cum ergo hoc sacramentum sit dignius aliis quibusdam quae non iterantur, videtur quod non nisi semel accipi debeat.

PRAETEREA, apostolus probat, Hebr. 10, ex unitate hostiae vel passionis Christi, unitatem baptismi. Sed hoc sacramentum magis convenit cum passione Christi, inquantum est hostia, quam baptismus. Ergo cum baptismus semel tantum percipiatur, et hoc sacramentum semel tantum debet percipi.

SED CONTRA, *cum frequentatione mysterii crescit nostrae salutis effectus*, ut in collecta dicitur. Sed ad hoc debemus niti ut effectus salutis in nobis crescat. Ergo debemus frequenter sumere.

OBJ. 1: To the first question we proceed thus. It seems that a man should not frequent this sacrament, but only receive it once in his life. For anyone who receives a sacrament over and over does injury to the sacrament. But injury should be done less to a nobler thing. Since therefore this sacrament is nobler than others that are not received over and over, it seems that it should only be received once.

OBJ. 2: Furthermore, the Apostle proves the uniqueness of baptism from the uniqueness of the victim or the Passion of Christ (Heb 10). But this sacrament has more to do with Christ's Passion than baptism, inasmuch as he is the victim. Therefore, since baptism is only received once, this sacrament should also only be received once.

ON THE CONTRARY, *The effect of our salvation grows with frequenting this mystery*, as is said in the collect of the Mass.[80] But we should strive for the effect of salvation to grow in us. Therefore, we should receive this sacrament frequently.

Quaestiuncula 2

ULTERIUS. Videtur quod qualibet die. Ambrosius enim dicit: *iste panis quotidianus est; accipe quotidie quod quotidie tibi prosit.*

OBJ. 1: Moreover, it seems that we should receive it on any day. For Ambrose says: *this bread is our daily bread; receive daily what will benefit you every day.*[81]

---

79. Parallels: *ST* III, q. 80, a. 10; *Super I ad Cor.* 11, lec. 7.

80. Moos refers to the postcommunion for the Sunday within the Octave of Corpus Christi. In the *Missale Romanum* 1962, the prayer appears as the postcommunion for the Fourth Sunday of Advent.

81. Ambrose, *On the Sacraments* (CSEL 73), Bk. 5, ch. 4, n. 25.

PRAETEREA, isto sacramento excitatur fervor caritatis, qua homo Christo unitur. Sed hoc expedit ut quotidie fiat. Ergo quotidie communicandum est.

SED CONTRA est quod Augustinus dicit in Lib. *de Eccl. Dogmat.*: *quotidie Eucharistiam sumere nec laudo nec vitupero.* Ergo non est quotidie communicandum.

OBJ. 2: Furthermore, the fervor of charity is excited in this sacrament, by which a man is united to Christ. But this should happen daily. Therefore, Communion should be received daily.

ON THE CONTRARY, Augustine says in his book *On Church Dogmatics*: *I neither praise nor condemn receiving the Eucharist daily.*[82] Therefore, Communion should not be received daily.

Quaestiuncula 3

ULTERIUS. Videtur quod sit semel in anno communicandum tantum. Quia agnus paschalis signum fuit hujus sacramenti. Sed sumebatur tantum semel in anno. Ergo et hoc sacramentum debet semel in anno tantum percipi.

PRAETEREA, hoc sacramentum est memoriale Dominicae passionis. Sed passionem Domini commemorat ecclesia semel in anno. Ergo tunc tantum debet esse tempus communicandi.

SED CONTRA est quod dicit Fabianus Papa: *et si non pluries, ter saltem in anno communicent homines, scilicet in Pascha, Pentecoste, et natali Domini.*

OBJ. 1: Moreover, it seems that one should receive Communion only once per year. For the paschal lamb was the sign of this sacrament. But it was only consumed once per year. Therefore, this sacrament should also be received only once per year.

OBJ. 2: Furthermore, this sacrament is the memorial of the Lord's Passion. But the Church commemorates the Lord's Passion once a year. Therefore, the time for receiving Communion should be only then.

ON THE CONTRARY, Pope Fabian says: *and if not many times, let men communicate at least three times per year, namely, at Easter, Pentecost, and Christmas.*[83]

Quaestiuncula 4

ULTERIUS. Videtur quod homo possit una die pluries communicare. Quia majus est celebrare quam communicare. Sed sacerdos potest una die celebrare pluries, si necesse sit. Ergo et alius fidelis potest pluries communicare.

PRAETEREA, quotiescumque aegritudo corporalis iteratur, extrema unctio potest iterari. Sed Eucharistia ordinatur contra aegritudinem peccatorum venialium, quae uno die pluries iterantur. Ergo una die potest homo pluries communicare.

SED CONTRA est quod dicitur *de Consecr.*, dist. 1: *sufficiat sacerdoti semel in die Missam celebrare; quia Christus semel passus est, et totum mundum redemit.* Ergo etiam semel tantum in die debet quis communicare.

OBJ. 1: Furthermore, it seems that a person may communicate many times in a day. For it is a bigger thing to celebrate than to receive Communion. But the priest can celebrate many times in one day, if it is necessary. Therefore, any other member of the faithful can also communicate many times.

OBJ. 2: Furthermore, extreme unction can be repeated as many times as physical sickness recurs. But the Eucharist is ordered against the sickness of venial sins, which are repeated many times a day. Therefore, in one day a person may communicate several times.

ON THE CONTRARY, it is said in *On Consecration*, Distinction 1: *Let it suffice for a priest to celebrate Mass once a day, for Christ died once and redeemed the whole world.*[84] Therefore, someone should receive Communion only once per day.

Response to Quaestiuncula 1

RESPONDEO dicendum ad primam quaestionem, quod ea quae in hoc sacramento geruntur, habent similitudinem cum his quae accidunt in corporali nutrimento.

TO THE FIRST QUESTION, I answer that those things that are enacted in this sacrament have a likeness to what happens in physical nourishment. For since a loss of nat-

---

82. Among works once attributed to Augustine: Gennadius Massiliensis, *De ecclesiasticis dogmatibus*, ch. 53 (PL 58:994).
83. Gratian's *Decretals*, Part 3, *De consecratione*, d. 2, ch. 16 (PL 187:1738).
84. Gratian's *Decretals*, Part 3, *De consecratione*, d. 1, ch. 53 (PL 187:1723), citing Alexander II.

Quia enim fit quasi continua deperditio naturalis humiditatis per actionem caloris naturalis et exercitium laboris, ideo oportet frequenter corporalem cibum assumere ad restaurationem deperditi, ne perditio continua mortem inducat. Similiter autem ex concupiscentia innata et occupatione circa exteriora fit deperditio devotionis et fervoris, secundum quae homo in Deum colligitur; unde oportet quod pluries deperdita restaurentur, ne homo totaliter alienetur a Deo.

Ad primum ergo dicendum, quod perfectio hujus sacramenti, ut dictum est, dist. 8, consistit in consecratione materiae, non in usu ipsius; et ideo consecratio non repetitur super eamdem materiam propter reverentiam sacramenti, sed usus potest repeti.

Ad secundum dicendum, quod baptismus repraesentat illam hostiam, secundum quod facit in nobis spiritualem vitam; et quia generatio uniuscujusque non est nisi semel, ideo baptismus non repetitur. Sed Eucharistia repraesentat illam hostiam secundum quod reficit; et ideo oportet quod frequenter sumatur.

ural moisture happens almost constantly by the action of natural heat and the exercise of labor, therefore it is necessary to take physical food often to restore this loss, lest a continual loss should lead to death. In the same way, from innate concupiscence and by the occupation with externals there arises a loss of the devotion and fervor according to which man is recollected unto God; and so it is necessary that these losses be restored many times, lest a man become completely alienated from God.

Reply Obj. 1: This sacrament's perfection, as was said in Distinction 8,[85] consists in the consecration of the matter, not in its use. And so the consecration is not repeated upon the same matter out of reverence for the sacrament, but its use can be repeated.

Reply Obj. 2: Baptism represents that victim, according as he causes spiritual life in us; and since the generation of each thing only happens once, baptism is not repeated. But the Eucharist represents that victim according as he refreshes us; and so it is necessary that it be consumed frequently.

Response to Quaestiuncula 2

Ad secundam quaestionem dicendum, quod in hoc sacramento duo requiruntur ex parte recipientis; scilicet desiderium conjunctionis ad Christum, quod facit amor; et reverentia sacramenti, quae ad donum timoris pertinet. Primum autem incitat ad frequentationem hujus sacramenti quotidianam, sed secundum retrahit. Unde si aliquis experimentaliter cognosceret ex quotidiana sumptione fervorem amoris augeri, et reverentiam non minui, talis deberet quotidie communicare; si autem sentiret per quotidianam frequentationem reverentiam minui, et fervorem non multum augeri, talis deberet interdum abstinere, ut cum majori reverentia et devotione postmodum accederet. Unde quantum ad hoc unusquisque relinquendus est judicio suo; et hoc est quod Augustinus dicit: *Dixit quispiam, non quotidie accipiendam esse Eucharistiam, alius affirmet quotidie sumendam; faciat unusquisque quod secundum fidem suam pie credit esse faciendum*; et probat per exemplum Zachaei et centurionis; quorum unus recipit Dominum gaudens, Luc. 19, alius dicit Matth. 8, 8: *non sum dignus ut intres sub tectum meum*; et uterque misericordiam consecutus est.

Et per hoc patet solutio ad objecta.

To the second question, it should be said that in this sacrament two things are required on the part of the recipient; namely, the desire for union with Christ, which love causes, and reverence for the sacrament, which belongs to the gift of fear. Now the first incites one to frequent this sacrament daily, but the second restrains one from it. Hence if someone experientially noticed that the fervor of his love was increased by daily reception and his reverence was not diminished, this person should receive Communion daily. But if someone perceived that his reverence diminished by daily frequenting, and his fervor was not much increased, this person should sometimes abstain, so that he might later approach with greater reverence and devotion. Hence each person is left to his own judgment in this matter; and this is what Augustine says: *One says that the Eucharist should not be received every day, someone else may approve its daily reception; let each one do what he conscientiously believes should be done according to his own faith*;[86] and he proves this by the example of Zacchaeus and the centurion, one of whom receives the Lord rejoicing (Luke 19:6), while the other says, *I am not worthy that you should enter under my roof* (Matt 8:8); and both obtained mercy.

And by this the answers to the objections are clear.

85. See d. 8, q. 1, q. 1, qa. 1.
86. See Augustine, *Epistle 54*, ch. 3 (CSEL 34.2:162).

Response to Quaestiuncula 3

AD TERTIAM QUAESTIONEM dicendum, quod secundum diversos status fidei diversus mos de hoc inolevit. Nam in primitiva ecclesia, quando vigebat devotio major ex propinquitate passionis Christi, et erat major impugnatio ab infidelibus, quia haec mensa adversus tribulationes ecclesiae praeparatur, quotidie communicandum fidelibus indicebatur; unde Anacletus Papa dicit: *peracta consecratione omnes communicent, qui nolunt ecclesiasticis carere liminibus. Sic enim apostoli statuerunt.* Postmodum indictum fuit ut saltem ter in anno communicarent, ut dictum est, propter solemnitatem illorum dierum. Sed postmodum arctatum est, ut saltem semel in anno, scilicet in Pascha, communicent; et ad hoc etiam multi idonei non inveniuntur. Et quamvis statutum ecclesiae non liceat praeterire, tamen licet pluries communicare. Unde Augustinus laudat omnibus diebus Dominicis communicandum esse; et ita pluries in anno potest communicare quis.

AD PRIMUM ergo dicendum, quod agnus paschalis fuit figura hujus sacramenti ratione passionis Christi, quae semel tantum facta est; et ideo semel tantum in anno sumebatur: sed manna, quod fuit figura hujus sacramenti, inquantum hoc sacramentum est cibus fidelium, quolibet die sumebatur.

AD SECUNDUM dicendum, quod ecclesia tempore passionis recolit ipsam passionem secundum se, et ideo semel in anno tantum recolit, sed in hoc sacramento recolitur passio secundum quod per ipsam reficimur; et quia tali refectione pluries indigemus, ideo pluries hoc modo recolitur Dominica passio.

TO THE THIRD QUESTION, it should be said that according to the different states of the faith, different customs have grown up concerning this. For in the early Church, when devotion thrived more by the recentness of Christ's Passion, and the attack of unbelievers was greater, for this table is prepared against tribulations of the Church, daily Communion was enjoined upon believers. And this is why Pope Anicletus says, *once their consecration is completed, all may receive Communion who do not wish to be without ecclesiastical thresholds. For this is how the apostles established it.*[87] Afterward it was appointed that at least three times per year they should receive Communion, as was said, because of the solemnity of those days. But later it was reduced so that they should communicate at least once per year, namely, at Easter; and even for this many are found to be not fit. And although one is not permitted to ignore the statutes of the Church, nevertheless it is permitted to communicate many times. Hence Augustine[88] praises receiving Communion every Sunday; and so someone can communicate many times a year.

REPLY OBJ. 1: The paschal lamb was the figure of this sacrament by reason of Christ's Passion, which only happened once; and so it was only consumed once per year. But manna, which was the figure of this sacrament inasmuch as this sacrament is the food of the faithful, was consumed on any given day.

REPLY OBJ. 2: The Church at Passiontide remembers the Passion in itself, and so it commemorates it only once per year, but in this sacrament the Passion is commemorated inasmuch as we are renewed by it, and since we need such a renewal many times, the Lord's Passion is commemorated many times in this way.

Response to Quaestiuncula 4

AD QUARTAM QUAESTIONEM dicendum, quod homo non debet pluries in una die communicare, ut saltem quantum ad unam diem repraesentetur unitas Dominicae passionis, et ut quantum ad aliquid reverentia sacramento exhibeatur semel tantum sumendo.

AD PRIMUM ergo dicendum, quod sacerdos est quasi persona publica, et ideo oportet quod non solum pro se, sed etiam pro aliis celebret; et ideo necessitate cogente potest pluries celebrare in die. Sed non est eadem ratio de illis qui non sumunt nisi ratione sui.

AD SECUNDUM dicendum, quod sunt alia remedia quibus peccatum veniale expiari potest; unde non oportet ut ad ea expianda homo pluries in die communicet.

TO THE FOURTH QUESTION, it should be said that a man should not receive Communion many times in a day, so that at least in one day the oneness of the Lord's Passion would be represented, and so that in one respect reverence would be shown the sacrament by receiving once only.

REPLY OBJ. 1: A priest is like a public person, and so it is necessary that he not only celebrate for himself, but also for others; and so when necessity compels him he can celebrate many times in a day. But there is not the same reason for those who only receive Communion for themselves.

REPLY OBJ. 2: There are other remedies by which venial sin can be expiated, and so it is not necessary that someone communicate many times a day to expiate them.

---

87. Gratian's *Decretals*, Part 3, *De consecratione*, d. 2, ch. 10 (PL 187:1735).
88. In the letter cited just above.

ARTICLE 2

Abstention from Holy Communion[89]

Quaestiuncula 1

AD SECUNDUM SIC PROCEDITUR. Videtur quod liceat omnino a communione cessare. Quia nullus tenetur nisi ad ea quae sunt necessitatis. Sed hoc sacramentum, ut supra, dist. 9, dictum est, non est necessitatis. Ergo aliquis potest omnino a sacramenti sumptione cessare.

PRAETEREA, quod fit ad reverentiam Dei, non est peccatum. Sed aliquis potest ex reverentia sacramenti omnino cessare. Ergo si omnino cesset, non est peccatum.

PRAETEREA, Augustinus dicit, quod de sumptione hujus sacramenti debet quilibet facere quod pie credit faciendum esse. Ergo non peccat, si omnino cesset, et putat hoc esse faciendum.

SED CONTRA est quod Innocentius dicit: *cavendum est ne si nimium hujus sacramenti sumptio differatur, mortis periculum incurratur.* Ergo si omnino cessatur, est mortiferum.

PRAETEREA, statutum est ecclesiae, ut saltem semel in anno fideles communicent. Ergo qui omnino cessat, peccat.

OBJ. 1: To the second question we proceed thus. It seems that it is permitted to abstain from holy Communion entirely. For a person is only bound to what is of necessity. But this sacrament, as was said above in Distinction 9,[90] is not of necessity. Therefore, someone can completely abstain from receiving the sacrament.

OBJ. 2: Furthermore, whatever is done in reverence for God is not a sin. But someone can completely abstain out of reverence for the sacrament. Therefore, if he completely abstains, it is not a sin.

OBJ. 3: Furthermore, Augustine says that concerning this sacrament's reception, everyone should do whatever he conscientiously believes should be done.[91] Therefore, he does not sin if he abstains entirely and believes this is to be done.

ON THE CONTRARY, Innocent says: *one must be careful lest the reception of this sacrament be deferred too long, and one incur the danger of death.*[92] Therefore, it is deadly to abstain from it entirely.

FURTHERMORE, it is established by the Church that the faithful should communicate at least once per year. Therefore, whoever abstains entirely, sins.

Quaestiuncula 2

ULTERIUS. Videtur quod ille qui consecrat, possit a communione cessare. Quia ubi est major necessitas, ibi secundum ordinem debitum caritatis est magis subveniendum. Sed potest contingere quod postquam sacerdos consecraverit, aliquis infirmetur ad mortem, et instanter petat corpus Christi in ultima necessitate constitutus. Ergo cum sit hoc sacramentum caritatis, debet sacerdos ipse a communione desistere, et infirmo dare.

PRAETEREA, gravius est peccatum peccato superaddere quam unum simplex peccatum committere. Sed habens conscientiam peccati mortalis peccat consecrando, peccat etiam communicando. Ergo ex quo consecravit, debet saltem a sumptione cessare.

OBJ. 1: Moreover, it seems that someone who consecrates can abstain from holy Communion. For where there is a greater need, more assistance should be brought according to the due order of charity. But it can happen that after a priest has consecrated, someone becomes sickened unto death, and urgently begs the body of Christ in his last necessity. Therefore, since this is the sacrament of charity, the priest himself should abstain from Communion and give it to the sick person.

OBJ. 2: Furthermore, it is a more grave thing to add sin to sin than to commit one single sin. But someone conscious of mortal sin sins by consecrating, and he also sins by communicating. Therefore, by the fact that he has consecrated, he should at least refrain from receiving.

---

89. Parallels: *ST* III, q. 80, a. 11; *Super Ioan.* 6, lec. 7.
90. See d. 9, q. 1, a. 1, qa. 2.
91. In the letter cited just above.
92. Innocent III, *de Sacro altaris mysterio*, Bk. 4, ch. 42 (PL 217:882).

PRAETEREA, communicatio corporis Domini et sanguinis aequaliter debetur omnibus membris Christi. Sed aliis datur corpus Christi sine sanguine. Ergo sacerdos saltem a sumptione sanguinis abstinere potest.

SED CONTRA est quod dicitur *de Consecr.*, dist. 2, cap. relatum, ubi reprobatur eorum error qui volebant consecrare corpus Christi, et non sumere.

PRAETEREA, hoc idem videtur ex verbis Domini, quibus dixit hoc sacramentum instituens: *accipite, et comedite*; Matth. 26, 26.

OBJ. 3: Furthermore, receiving the Lord's body and blood in Communion is equally due to all Christ's members. But to some people the body of Christ is given without the blood. Therefore, the priest can at least refrain from receiving the blood.

ON THE CONTRARY, is what is said in *On Consecration*, Distinction 2, where the error of those who wanted to consecrate the body of Christ but not consume it is rejected.[93]

FURTHERMORE, this same thing is seen by the Lord's words, which he said when he instituted this sacrament: *take and eat* (Matt 26:26).

Quaestiuncula 3

ULTERIUS. Videtur quod laudabilius sit abstinere ab hoc sacramento quam accedere. Quia ad Deum maxime per humilitatem appropinquamus. Sed quod homo ex reverentia sacramenti a communione desistit, humilitatis est. Ergo videtur magis meritorium et fructuosum, quam etiam sumere.

PRAETEREA, caritatis verae est magis Dei gloriam quam commodum proprium quaerere. Sed iste qui abstinet, videtur propter gloriam Dei facere quam revereretur; qui autem sumit, propter proprium commodum facere, quia fructum sacrum quaerit. Ergo illud est perfectioris caritatis, et ita magis meritorium.

SED CONTRA, in aliis sacramentis ei cui licet sacramentum accipere, melius est accipere quam desistere. Sed hoc sacramentum dignius est aliis. Ergo multo melius est homini parato accipere quam ex reverentia desistere.

OBJ. 1: Moreover, it seems that it is more praiseworthy to abstain from this sacrament than to approach it. For we approach God most by humility. But it belongs to humility for a man to desist from Holy Communion out of reverence for the sacrament. Therefore, it seems more meritorious and fruitful than even receiving it.

OBJ. 2: Furthermore, it belongs to true charity to seek more God's glory than one's own benefit. But the person who abstains seems to do it for the sake of God's glory which he reveres; but the one who receives does it for the sake of his own advantage, for he seeks sacred fruit. Therefore, the former belongs to a more perfect charity, and so it is more meritorious.

ON THE CONTRARY, in the other sacraments it is better for anyone who is permitted to receive the sacrament to receive rather than abstain. But this sacrament is more worthy than the others. Therefore, it is much better for a person who has prepared to receive it, than to desist out of reverence.

Response to Quaestiuncula 1

RESPONDEO dicendum ad primam quaestionem, quod nulli licet omnino a communione cessare: quia ecclesia statuit tempus in quo fideles communicare debeant; unde qui omnino desistunt, efficiuntur rei transgressionis praecepti. Institutio autem ecclesiae fuit necessaria: quia enim in quotidiana pugna sumus, vita spiritualis in nobis evanesceret, nisi aliquando cibum vitae sumeremus.

AD PRIMUM ergo dicendum, quod hoc sacramentum de sui institutione prima, quamvis non sit de necessitate salutis, tamen ex institutione ecclesiae necessarium efficitur; et sine hoc etiam necessarium esset non simpliciter, ut sine quo non esset salus, sed ex supposi-

TO THE FIRST QUESTION, I answer that it is not permitted to anyone to abstain from Communion entirely: for the Church has established a time in which the faithful should receive Holy Communion; and so any who desist entirely are made guilty of transgressing a precept. Moreover, the institution of the Church was necessary: for since we are in a daily fight, spiritual life would fade away in us if we did not sometimes receive the food of life.

REPLY OBJ. 1: Although this sacrament is not necessary for salvation by its first institution, nevertheless the institution of the Church has made it necessary; and even without this it would not be necessary simply, so that there would be no salvation without it, but it would be necessary by the

---

93. Gratian's *Decretals*, Part 3, *De consecratione*, d. 2, ch. 11 (PL 187:1735).

tione finis; si scilicet homo in vita spirituali firmus persistere vellet.

AD SECUNDUM dicendum, quod reverentia debita Deo in hoc exhibetur quod homo non se nimis divinis ingerat supra suum modum; sed quod homo omnino se subtrahat, hoc est contemptus, et pusillanimitatis.

AD TERTIUM dicendum, quod verbum Augustini referendum est ad hoc quod quotidie sumatur, vel non; non autem ad hoc quod omnino quis desistat.

supposition of the end: namely, if a person wished to persist steadily in the spiritual life.

REPLY OBJ. 2: The reverence due to God is shown in this, that a man does not force himself into divine matters too much above his own mode; but that man entirely remove himself, this belongs to contempt and cowardice.

REPLY OBJ. 3: Augustine's words refer to receiving every day or not, but not to completely abstaining.

Response to Quaestiuncula 2

AD SECUNDAM QUAESTIONEM dicendum, quod semper ille qui consecrat, debet sumere corpus et sanguinem Christi, nisi impediatur vel per violentiam, vel per mortem, vel per infirmitatem, aut aliquid hujusmodi: cujus ratio potest sumi ex parte ipsius sacramenti, quod in ipsa sumptione complementum suae significationis accipit: quia, ut dicit Augustinus, dum sanguis in ore fidelium de calice funditur, sanguinis effusio de latere Christi designatur: et etiam complementum suae efficaciae, quia ultimum effectum proprium habet in hoc quod sumitur. Ut ergo sacramentum sit perfectum, oportet illum qui sacramentum celebravit, communicare. Potest etiam sumi ratio ex parte ipsius consecrantis: quia cum ipse sit aliis dispensator divinorum, debet primo in participatione divinorum fieri, ut Dionysius dicit in 3 cap. Eccles. Hierar.

AD PRIMUM ergo dicendum, quod in tali casu non oportet quod sacerdos communionem intermittat; sed potest dare infirmo petenti partem hostiae consecratae.

AD SECUNDUM dicendum, quod magis peccaret non sumendo, quia sacrilegium committeret pervertens ritum sacramentorum. Nec tamen est perplexus; quia potest ad Deum converti, et conteri: et tunc sine periculo in tali articulo sumet.

AD TERTIUM dicendum, quod perfectio sacramenti hujus in utroque consistit, ut ex supra dictis patet; et ideo sacerdos celebrans qui alterum tantum sumeret, imperfecte sacramentum perageret; unde reus sacrilegii secundum canones judicatur, de Consec., dist. 2, cap. *comperimus*. Secus est autem de aliis qui non perficiunt sacramentum: quia eis subtrahitur sanguis propter effusionis periculum; unde et sacerdos in parasceve, quando non consecrat, corpus sine sanguine sumit.

TO THE SECOND QUESTION, it should be said that the man who consecrates the body and blood of Christ should always consume them unless he is impeded either by violence or death or illness, or something like that. And the reason for this can be taken on the part of the sacrament itself, whose signification is completed by that very consumption. For, as Augustine says, when the blood is poured from the chalice into the mouth of the faithful, the flow of blood from the side of Christ is indicated;[94] and its efficacy is completed as well, for it has its ultimate proper effect in being consumed. Therefore, so that the sacrament may be perfect, it is necessary that whoever celebrates the sacrament communicates. The reason can also be taken on the part of the man consecrating, for since he is the minister of divine things to others, he must become first in partaking of divine things, as Dionysius says in Chapter 3 of the *Ecclesiastical Hierarchy*.[95]

REPLY OBJ. 1: In such a case it is not necessary that the priest forego Communion; but he can give to the sick person a part of the consecrated host.

REPLY OBJ. 2: He would sin more by not consuming, for he would commit a sacrilege by perverting the rite of the sacraments. Nevertheless, this is not a conundrum, for he can turn to God and repent, and then he would receive in such an instance without danger.

REPLY OBJ. 3: The perfection of this sacrament consists in both things, as is clear from what was said above; and so the celebrating priest who would consume only one or the other would imperfectly carry out the sacrament; and so he is judged culpable for sacrilege according to the canons.[96] But it is different for those who do not consecrate the sacrament, since for them the blood is removed because of the danger of spilling; and so the priest on Good Friday, when he does not consecrate, consumes the body without the blood.

---

94. This may be gathered from Lanfranc's quotations and discussion in *Liber de corpore et sanguine Domini*, ch. 13 (PL 150:423).
95. Pseudo-Dionysius, *Ecclesiastical Hierarchy*, ch. 3, p. 3, n. 14 (PG 3:443).
96. Gratian's *Decretals*, Part 3, *De consecratione*, d. 2, ch. 12 (PL 187:1736).

Response to Quaestiuncula 3

AD TERTIAM QUAESTIONEM dicendum, quod in his quae sunt ex genere suo bona, peccatum non accidit, nisi ex aliquo accidente, dum inordinate explentur; et ideo ea perficere per se bonum est; sed abstinere ab eis non est bonum nisi ratione accidentis alicujus. Unde cum Eucharistiam accipere sit bonum ex genere, assumere eam est bonum per se, abstinere est bonum per accidens, inquantum scilicet timetur ne inordinate sumatur. Et quia quod est per se, praejudicat ei quod est per accidens; ideo simpliciter loquendo, melius est Eucharistiam sumere quam ab ea abstinere; sed in casu aliquo nihil prohibet esse melius abstinere, quando aliquis probabiliter praesumit ex sumptione reverentiam minui. Si autem haec duo comparemus, adhuc invenitur praevalere sumptio sacramenti abstinentiae a sacramento, tum ratione effectus sacramenti, tum ratione praeparationis, quantulacumque sit; tum etiam ratione virtutis elicientis actum: quia sumere videtur esse caritatis, in qua radix meriti consistit; abstinere autem timoris: amor autem timori praevalet.

AD PRIMUM ergo dicendum, quod caritas est quae Deo directe nos conjungit; sed humilitas ad hanc unionem disponit, inquantum hominem Deo subdit; unde meritum magis consistit in caritate quam in humilitate.

AD SECUNDUM dicendum, quod in hoc maxime est gloria Dei et bonitas, quod se creaturis pro captu earum communicat; unde magis videtur ad Dei gloriam pertinere quod aliquis ad communionem accedat quam quod abstineat.

TO THE THIRD QUESTION, it should be said that among things that are good by their genus, a sin does not happen, except sometimes incidentally, when they are fulfilled inordinately; and so to complete them is good in itself, but to abstain from them is not good except by reason of something incidental. And this is why, since receiving the Eucharist is good by its genus, to take it is good per se, and to abstain is good incidentally, namely inasmuch as it is feared that it might be consumed inordinately. And because what is *per se* takes precedence over what is incidental, for this reason simply speaking it is better to consume the Eucharist than to abstain from it. But in a certain case nothing prevents it from being better to abstain, when someone has a probable belief that reverence will be diminished by receiving it. However, if we compare these two things, the reception of the sacrament is found to prevail over abstention from the sacrament, both by reason of the sacrament's effect, and by reason of preparation, however little it may be; and also by reason of the virtue eliciting the act: for receiving seems to belong to charity, in which the root of merit consists; but abstaining belongs to fear. And love prevails over fear.

REPLY OBJ. 1: Charity is what directly unites us to God; but humility disposes us to this union, inasmuch as it places someone under God. And this is why merit consists more in charity than in humility.

REPLY OBJ. 2: The glory and goodness of God is most in this, that he communicates himself to creatures according to their capacity. And so it seems to belong more to the glory of God that someone come to Communion than that he abstain.

Exposition of the text

Sicut et Christus se ostendit, etc. Contra, veritatem non decet aliqua fictio. Ergo non debuit eis aliud ostendere quam quod in ipso erat. Et ideo dicendum, quod Christus eis speciem suam naturalem ostendit, et sensus exterior per eam movebatur; sed propter dubitationem resurrectionis, sensus interioris judicium impediebatur; unde *eum talem inspiciebant exterius*, ut Gregorius dicit *qualis erat apud eos interius*; et ita non erat aliqua deceptio ex parte Christi, sicut non est aliqua deceptio in sacra Scriptura ex hoc quod finguntur figurae angelis et ipsi Deo; non enim ad hoc fit ut in eis intellectus remaneat, sed ut ex his in significata eorum surgat; et ita etiam per speciem illam in qua eis apparuit, voluit eis Dominus interiorem eorum dispositionem significare.

Qui confessus est coram Nicolao Papa, etc. Videtur ex hoc quod haec opinio omnino sit tenenda, quia in principio confessionis hujus dicitur: *consentio Romanae ecclesiae, et apostolicae sedi*. Ergo nulli licet aliter tenere. Et dicendum, quod quia Berengarius negaverat verum corpus Christi in altari esse, coactus fuit hanc confessionem facere; unde non intendit dicere, quod ipsum corpus Christi frangatur, sed quod sub speciebus, in quibus est fractio, verum corpus Christi sit; et in hoc se dicit consentire apostolicae sedi, a contrario errore reversus.

Manet integer in corde tuo. Et intelligendum est quantum ad effectum; non quod corpus ejus menti illabatur, quia hoc solius Dei est.

Ubi est pars corporis, etc. De hoc dictum est supra, dist. 10, qu. unic., art. 3, quaestiunc. 3.

Indignus est qui aliter celebrat. Aliter celebrare dicitur qui non servat materiam vel formam aut ritum debitum ab ecclesia institutum; et debet talis, si ex contemptu faciat, gradus sui periculo subjacere.

Etsi Christus quotidie immoletur, vel semel tantum immolatus sit. Sciendum est, quod omnia illa verba quae important comparationem Judaeorum ad Christum et

Similarly, Christ shows himself to his disciples on the road, etc.[97] Against this, no false pretenses befit the truth. Therefore, he should not have shown anything to them other than what he was in himself. And so it should be said that Christ showed them his own natural appearance, and the external senses were moved by this; but because of doubt about the Resurrection, the judgment of the interior senses was impeded. And this is why *they were seeing him outwardly*, as Gregory says, *as he was with them interiorly*;[98] and so there was no deception on Christ's part, just as there is no deception in sacred Scripture by the fact that figures are contrived for angels and for God himself. For it is not done for the understanding to remain in them, but so that it will rise from them to what they signify. And so also by that appearance in which he appeared to them the Lord wished to signify their inward disposition.

Berengar, who confessed before Pope Nicholas, etc.[99] It seems from this that this opinion is absolutely to be held, for in the beginning of this confession it says, "I consent to the Roman Church, and to the Apostolic See." Therefore, one is not permitted to hold otherwise. And it is to be said that because Berengar denied that the true body of Christ is on the altar, he was forced to make this confession; and so he does not intend to say that the body of Christ itself is broken, but that the true body of Christ exists under the appearances in which the breaking happens. And in this he says that he consents to the Apostolic See, having reverted from the opposing error.

"He remains whole and entire in your heart."[100] And this is to be understood as to its effect, not that his body sinks into your mind, for this only belongs to God.

"Where there is a part of the body,"[101] etc. This was discussed above in Distinction 10, Question 1, Article 3, Subquestion 3.

"He is unworthy, who celebrates the mystery otherwise than Christ gave it."[102] Someone is said to celebrate otherwise who does not preserve the matter and form or the due rite instituted by the Church; and such a person, if he did this out of contempt, should be subject to trial of his position.

And if Christ is immolated every day, or if he was immolated only once.[103] It should be known that all those words that convey the relation of the Jews to Christ and Christ's

---

97. *Sent* IV, 12.2 (67). 2.
98. See Gregory the Great, *Homilies on the Gospels*, Bk. 2, hom. 23 (CCSL 141).
99. *Sent* IV, 12.3 (68). 1.
100. *Sent* IV, 12.3 (68). 3 citing Augustine, *Sermo Mai 129*.
101. *Sent*. IV. 12. 3 (68), 4, attributed to Hilary.
102. *Sent* IV, 12.4 (69). 3 citing ordinary gloss on 1 Cor. 11, 27, from Ambrosiaster on the same place.
103. *Sent* IV, 12.5 (70). 1.

poenam Christi, non dicuntur quotidie fieri. Non enim dicimus quod Christus quotidie crucifigatur et occidatur; quia actus Judaeorum et poena Christi transit. Illa autem quae important comparationem Christi ad Deum patrem, dicuntur quotidie fieri, sicut offerre, sacrificare, et hujusmodi, eo quod hostia illa perpetua est; et hoc modo est semel oblata per Christum, quod quotidie etiam per membra ipsius offerri possit.

In sacramento recordatio illius fit quod factum est semel. Sacerdos enim non solum verbis, sed etiam factis, Christi passionem repraesentat.

Unde et in principio canonis tres cruces facit super illud: *haec dona, haec munera, haec sancta sacrificia illibata,* ad significandum trinam traditionem Christi, scilicet a Deo, Juda, et Judaeis. Secundo autem super illud: *benedictam, adscriptam, ratam* etc. facit tres communiter super utrumque, ad ostendendum quod tribus Christus est venditus, scilicet sacerdotibus, Scribis, et Pharisaeis. Duas autem facit divisim super corpus et sanguinem, ad ostendendum venditorem et venditum. Tertio facit duas super illud: *benedixit et fregit*: unam super corpus, aliam super sanguinem, ad ostendendum quod hoc sacramentum valet ad salutem corporis et animae. Et quia Dominus hoc sacramentum in mortis suae memoriam exercendum mandavit, ideo statim post consecrationem brachiorum extensione crucis effigiem repraesentat. Unde etiam, ut Innocentius dicit, verba consecrationis, quae in fine ponenda essent quasi complementum totius, in medio ponuntur ad historiae ordinem observandum; quia verba canonis ad Eucharistiam consecrandam principaliter pertinent, sed signa ad historiam recolendam. Quarto facit quinque cruces super illud: *hostiam puram* etc. ad repraesentandum quinque plagas. Quinto facit duas super illud: *sacrosanctum filii tui corpus* etc. ad signandum vincula et flagella Christi. Et additur tertia, qua sacerdos seipsum signat super illud: *omni benedictione*; quia Christi vulnera, nostra sunt medicamenta. Vel per has tres cruces significatur triplex oratio, qua Christus orasse legitur Matth. 26, passione imminente. Sexto facit tres super illud: *sanctificas, vivificas, benedicis* etc. ad repraesentandum, quod Judaei ter dixerunt: *crucifige,* verbo crucifigentes Christum, quod fuit tertia hora. Septimo iterum facit tres super illud: *per ipsum, et in ipso, et cum ipso,* ad repraesentandum secundam crucifixionem, qua a militibus hora sexta post trium horarum spatium crucifixus est; vel ad repraesentandum tres ejus cruciatus, scilicet passionis, propassionis, compassionis. Deinde facit duas extra calicem super illud: *est tibi Deo patri omnipotenti in unitate Spiritus Sancti omnis honor et gloria,* ad repraesentandum separationem animae a corpore, quae facta est hora nona; vel

punishment are not said to happen daily. For we do not say that Christ is crucified and killed daily, for the Jews' act and Christ's punishment have passed. But those things that convey the relation of Christ to God the Father are said to happen daily, such as to offer, to sacrifice, and the like, by the fact that that victim is perpetual; and this is how what was offered once by Christ can also be offered daily by his members.

In the sacrament is made a remembrance of what was done once.[104] For a priest represents Christ's Passion not only by words but also by deeds.

And this is also why in the beginning of the Canon of the Mass he makes three crosses when he says: *these gifts, these offerings, these holy and unblemished sacrifices,* to signify the threefold handing-over of Christ, namely, by God, by Judas, and by the Jews. But second when he says: *be pleased, O God, we pray, to bless, acknowledge, and approve,* etc., he makes three crosses over each, to show that Christ was sold to three, namely, the priests, scribes, and pharisees. But he makes two crosses separately above the body and blood, to show the one selling and the one sold. Third, he makes two crosses when he says: *he said the blessing, broke the bread*: one above the body, another above the blood, to show that this sacrament avails to the health of body and soul. And since the Lord commanded this sacrament to be administered in memorial of his death, for this reason immediately after the consecration, he represents the form of the Cross by the extension of his arms. And so also, as Innocent says,[105] the words of consecration, which placed at the end would be like a completion of the whole, are placed in the middle to observe the historical order; for the words of the Canon pertain chiefly to consecrating the Eucharist, but signs pertain to renewing the memory of the story. Fourth, he makes five crosses when he says: *pure victim,* etc. to represent the five wounds. Fifth, he makes two at: *the most holy Body and Blood of your Son,* etc., to signify the chains and scourging of Christ. And a third is added, in which the priest signs himself, at: *every blessing*; for Christ's wounds are our medicine. Or by these three crosses the threefold prayer is signified, which Christ is read to have prayed in Matthew 26, when his Passion was imminent. Sixth, he makes three crosses at: *you sanctify them, fill them with life, bless them,* etc., to represent that the Jews said three times, *crucify him,* crucifying Christ by a word, which was at the third hour. Seventh, again he makes three at: *through him, and with him, and in him,* to represent the second crucifixion, in which he was crucified by the soldiers at the sixth hour after the space of three hours; or to represent the three forms of torture, namely suffering, suffering on behalf of another, and suffering with another. Next he makes two crosses outside the chalice at: *O*

---

104. *Sent* IV, 12.5 (70). 2.
105. Innocent III, *De sacro altaris mysterio*, Bk. 5, ch. 2 (PL 217:888).

propter sanguinem et aquam, quae de latere Christi pro-fluxerunt.

Inclinationes etiam factae a sacerdote, signant Christi obedientiam ad patrem, ex qua mortem sustinuit.

Tacita etiam locutio exprimit consilium Judaeorum mortem Christi machinantium, vel discipulorum, qui palam Christum confiteri non audebant.

Quid autem fractio significet, dictum est.

Quia autem commixtio corporis et sanguinis unionem animae et corporis significat; ideo illa crucis signatio quae fit super illa verba: *pax Domini sit semper vobiscum*, magis pertinet ad resurrectionem, quae virtute Trinitatis et tertia die facta est. Quod autem quinquies se sacerdos ad populum convertit, significat quod Dominus die resurrectionis quinquies se manifestavit: primo Mariae Magdalenae, Joan. ult. secundo Petro, Luc. ult. tertio mulieribus, Matth. ult. quarto discipulis in Emaus, Lucae ultim. quinto discipulis in unum, Joan. ult.

Salutat autem populum septies ad septiformem gratiam Spiritus Sancti ostendendam. *Sine quibus mortalis vita duci non potest*; quia etsi possumus vitare singula, non tamen omnia.

God, almighty Father, in the unity of the Holy Spirit, all glory and honor is yours, to represent the separation of soul from body, which happened at the ninth hour; or because of the blood and water, which flowed forth from Christ's side.

Also, the bows made by the priest represent Christ's obedience to the Father, out of which he underwent death.

Also, the silent speech expresses the counsel of the Jews plotting Christ's death, or of the disciples, who did not dare to confess Christ openly.

Now what the breaking of the bread signifies has been said.[106]

However, since the mingling of body and blood signifies the union of body and soul, for this reason that sign of the Cross that happens at these words: *the peace of the Lord be with you always*, relates more to the Resurrection, which happened on the third day by the power of the Trinity. Moreover, that the priest turns himself to the people five times signifies that the Lord revealed himself five times on the day of the Resurrection: first, to Mary Magdalen (John 20:14); second, to Peter (Luke 24:34); third, to the women (Matt 28:9); fourth, to the disciples in Emmaus (Luke 24:15); fifth, to the disciples together (John 20:19).

But he greets the people seven times to show the sevenfold grace of the Holy Spirit. *Without which mortal life cannot be led*; for even if we are able to avoid individual sins, we still cannot avoid all.

---

106. See this distinction, q. 1, a. 3, qa. 3.

DISTINCTION 13
MINISTER OF THE EUCHARIST

Postquam determinavit Magister de sacramento Eucharistiae, hic determinat de ministris hujus sacramenti; et dividitur in partes duas: in prima determinat propositum; in secunda epilogat, ibi: *de hoc caelesti mysterio aliqua perstrinximus, a Catholicis fideliter tenenda.*

Prima in duas: in prima ostendit quis possit consecrare et dispensare hujusmodi sacramentum; in secunda quis possit sumere, ibi: *illud etiam sane dici potest.*

Prima in duas: in prima inquirit, utrum potestas consecrandi, per peccatum a ministro tollatur; in secunda ostendit quae requiruntur in ministro ad hoc quod sacramentum consecrare possit, ibi: *in hujus autem mysterii expletione sicut formam servare, ita ordinem haberi, scilicet ut sit sacerdos, et intentionem adhiberi oportet.*

Prima in duas: in prima inquirit, utrum malus sacerdos possit consecrare; in secunda, utrum ab ecclesia praecisi, ibi: *illi vero qui excommunicati sunt, vel de haeresi manifeste notati, non videntur hoc sacramentum posse conficere.*

De hoc caelesti mysterio aliqua perstrinximus a Catholicis fideliter tenenda. Hic epilogat; et circa hoc duo facit: primo ponit epilogum; secundo ex incidenti determinat quid faciat haereticum, ibi: *ne autem ignores quid faciat haereticum, vel quid sit haereticus, audi breviter quae inde sancti doctores tradant.*

Hic est duplex quaestio. Prima de ministro consecrante. Secunda de haeresi.

After the Master has examined the sacrament of the Eucharist, here he considers the ministers of this sacrament. And this is divided into two parts: in the first, he defines his aim; in the second, he adds an epilogue, at: *concerning this heavenly mystery we have summarized some things which are to be held faithfully by Catholics.*[1]

The first is in two parts: in the first, he shows who can consecrate and administer this kind of sacrament; in the second, who can receive it, at: *It may also be truly said.*[2]

The first is in two parts: in the first, he inquires whether the power of consecrating is taken away by the sin of the minister; in the second, he shows what things are required in the minister for him to be able to consecrate, at: *In the performance of this mystery, just as it is necessary to preserve the form, so also it is necessary to have the order, that is, that [the celebrant] be a priest, and to have the intention.*[3]

The first is in two parts: in the first, he inquires whether a bad priest can consecrate; in the second, whether those who are cut off from the Church can, at: *but those who are excommunicate, or publicly known to be heretics, do not seem to be able to confect this sacrament.*[4]

Concerning this heavenly mystery we have summarized some things which are to be held faithfully by Catholics.[5] Here he adds an epilogue; and concerning this he does two things: first, he sets down the epilogue; second, he defines what makes a heretic from an incidental, at: *but lest you be ignorant of what makes a heretic, or what a heretic is, hear briefly what the holy doctors have taught on this point.*[6]

Here there are two questions. First, about the consecrating minister. Second, about heresy.

---

1. Peter Lombard, *Sententiae* IV, 13.1 (72). 9.
2. *Sent* IV, 13.1 (72). 8.
3. *Sent* IV, 13.1 (72). 7.
4. *Sent* IV, 13.1 (72). 4.
5. *Sent* IV, 13.1 (72). 9.
6. *Sent* IV, 13.2 (73). 1.

QUESTION 1

THE CONSECRATION OF THE EUCHARIST

Circa primum quaeruntur tria:
primo, quis possit consecrare;
secundo, de ritu consecrandi;
tertio, de dispensatione sacramenti.

Concerning the first, three questions arise:
first, who can consecrate;
second, the rite of consecrating;
third, the administering of this sacrament.

ARTICLE 1

Who can consecrate

Quaestiuncula 1

AD PRIMUM SIC PROCEDITUR. Videtur quod etiam laicus possit consecrare. Consecrare enim sacerdotis est. Sed omnis laicus, si sit bonus, sacerdos est; quia, ut dicit Chrysostomus, *omnis sanctus, sacerdos est*; et omnibus fidelibus dictum est, 1 Petr. 2, 9: *vos estis genus electum, regale sacerdotium*. Ergo bonus laicus potest consecrare.

PRAETEREA, homo non potest consecrare virtute propria, sed virtute Dei. Sed bonus laicus magis est particeps divinae virtutis quam malus sacerdos. Ergo magis potest bonus laicus consecrare quam malus sacerdos.

PRAETEREA, magis est sumere sacramentum quam conficere; quia hoc ad illud ordinatur. Sed bonus laicus potest sumere sacramentum. Ergo et consecrare.

SED CONTRA, hoc sacramentum offertur ad reconciliandum nos Deo, quod est officium mediatoris. Cum ergo sacerdotis tantum sit medium esse inter Deum et populum, soli sacerdotes hoc sacramentum conficere possunt.

PRAETEREA, bonitas virtutis non est manifesta, quia nemo scit utrum sit dignus odio vel amore, Eccle. 9, et praecipue alteri nota esse non potest. Si ergo potestas consecrandi sequatur bonitatem personae, non poterit esse notum quando consecratum sit vere, et quando non; et ita erit deceptio in sacramentis.

OBJ. 1: To the first question we proceed thus. It seems that a lay person can also consecrate.[7] For it belongs to a priest to consecrate. But every lay person, if he is good, is a priest; for as John Chrysostom says, *every holy person is a priest*;[8] and to all the faithful it is said, *you are a chosen people, a royal priesthood* (1 Pet 2:9). Therefore, a good lay person can consecrate.

OBJ. 2: Furthermore, a person cannot consecrate by his own power, but by God's power. But a good lay person is more a partaker of divine power than a bad priest. Therefore, a good lay person can consecrate more than a bad priest.

OBJ. 3: Furthermore, it is a greater thing to receive the sacrament than to consecrate it; for the latter is ordered to the former. But a good lay person can receive the sacrament. Therefore, he can also consecrate it.

ON THE CONTRARY, this sacrament is offered to reconcile us to God, which is the office of a mediator. Therefore, since the priest alone is a medium between God and the people, only priests can consecrate this sacrament.

FURTHERMORE, the goodness of virtue is not obvious, for no one knows whether he is worthy of hatred or love (Eccl 9:1), and this can especially not be known to someone else. Therefore, if the power of consecrating resulted from the goodness of the person, it could not be known when the consecration had truly happened or not. And so there would be deception in the sacraments.

---

7. Parallels: *ST* III, q. 72, a. 2; q. 82, a. 1.
8. John Chrysostom, *Homilies on Matthew*, Hom. 43 (PG 56:876).

Quaestiuncula 2

ULTERIUS. Videtur quod solus episcopus possit consecrare. Quia in qualibet republica principi debetur actus nobilissimus, sicut etiam Commentator dicit in 11 *Metaphysica*. Sed summus in nostra hierarchia est episcopus, ut dicit Dionysius. Ergo cum consecrare sit summus actus nostrae hierarchiae, hic actus sibi soli debebitur.

PRAETEREA, secundum Dionysium, loco cit., perficere est tantum episcopi. Sed secundum ipsum, Eucharistia est perfectivam habens virtutem. Ergo solus episcopus potest consecrare.

PRAETEREA, majus est consecrare corpus Christi quam consecrare altare, vel benedicere virgines. Sed illa reservantur solis episcopis. Ergo multo fortius consecratio corporis Domini.

SED CONTRA est communis usus ecclesiae, et canonum institutio, qui docent potestatem consecrandi et baptizandi episcopis et sacerdotibus esse communem.

OBJ. 1: Moreover, it seems that only a bishop can consecrate.[9] For in any nation the noblest action belongs to the leader, as the Commentator says in *Metaphysics* 11. But the highest one in our hierarchy is the bishop, as Dionysius says.[10] Therefore, since consecrating is the highest action of our hierarchy, this act will be for him alone.

OBJ. 2: Furthermore, according to Dionysius,[11] in the place cited, to perfect belongs to the bishop alone. But according to him, it is the Eucharist that has perfective power. Therefore, only the bishop can consecrate.

OBJ. 3: Furthermore, it is a greater thing to consecrate the body of Christ than to consecrate an altar, or to consecrate virgins. But these are reserved to bishops alone. Therefore, much more should the consecration of the body of Christ be reserved to them.

ON THE CONTRARY, is the Church's common practice, and the institution of the canons, which teach that the power of consecrating and baptizing is common to bishops and priests.

Quaestiuncula 3

ULTERIUS. Videtur quod haeretici et schismatici et excommunicati consecrare non possint. Quia, sicut dicit canon 24, qu. 1, cap. *audivimus, quicumque fuerit ab unitate ecclesiae alienus, exercere potest, consecrare non valet.* Augustinus etiam dicit, quod extra ecclesiam non est locus veri sacrificii. Sed omnes praedicti sunt extra ecclesiam. Ergo non possunt consecrare.

PRAETEREA, hoc sacramentum pollui non potest. Sed secundum Hieronymum, haeretici panem pollutum comedunt. Ergo verum sacrificium[15] non habent; ergo non consecrant.

PRAETEREA, hoc sacramentum est unionis ecclesiae; unde et *communio* dicitur. Sed omnes praedicti hac unione carent. Ergo consecrare non possunt.

SED CONTRA, sacerdos habet potestatem consecrandi ex ipso charactere; sed character manet in ipso haeretico, schismatico, et excommunicato. Ergo possunt consecrare.

OBJ. 1: Moreover, it seems that heretics and schismatics and those excommunicated cannot consecrate.[12] For, as Cause 24, Question 1, says, *we have heard anyone who was estranged from the unity of the Church can assist, but he cannot consecrate.*[13] Augustine also says that outside the Church there is no place of true sacrifice.[14] But all those mentioned are outside the Church. Therefore, they cannot consecrate.

OBJ. 2: Furthermore, this sacrament cannot be polluted. But according to Jerome, heretics eat polluted bread.[16] Therefore, they do not have the true sacrament; therefore, they do not consecrate.

OBJ. 3: Furthermore, this sacrament belongs to the Church's union; hence it is also called *Communion*. But all those mentioned lack this union. Therefore, they cannot consecrate.

ON THE CONTRARY, a priest has the power of consecrating from the character itself; but the character remains in the person of a heretic, schismatic, and someone excommunicated. Therefore, they can consecrate.

---

9. Parallels: *ST* III, q. 72, a. 2; q. 82, a. 1.

10. Pseudo-Dionysius, *Ecclesiastical Hierarchy*, ch. 5, p. 1, n. 5 (PG 3:506).

11. Ibid., n. 6.

12. Parallels: below, exposition of the text; d. 19, q. 1, a. 2, qa. 3, ad 1; *ST* III, q. 74, a. 9, ad 2; q. 82, a. 5; *Quodl.* XII, q. 11, a. 1.

13. Gratian's *Decretals*, Part 2, cause 24, ch. 4 (PL 187:1265).

14. See Augustine, *Contra Cresconium* (CSEL 52), Bk. 2, chs. 12–13.

15. *sacrificium.—sacramentum* PLE.

16. See Jerome, *Commentarii in prophetas minores* (CCSL 76A), *In Aggaeum*, ch. 2.

PRAETEREA, qualitas personae non exigitur nisi ad actum proprium personae. Sed consecratio non est actus personalis ipsius sacerdotis, sed Dei cujus verbis consecrat. Ergo non impeditur propter propriam qualitatem.

FURTHERMORE, the quality of a person is only required for action that is proper to the person. But consecration is not a personal act of the priest himself, but of God, by whose words he consecrates. Therefore, it is not impeded because of a proper quality.

Quaestiuncula 4

ULTERIUS. Videtur quod degradatus non possit consecrare. Nullus enim consecrare potest qui non habet potestatem consecrandi. Sed degradatus non habet potestatem consecrandi, quamvis habeat potestatem baptizandi, ut dicit canon. Ergo non potest consecrare.

PRAETEREA, *ex eisdem fit res et corrumpitur*, secundum Philosophum in 2 *Ethic*. Sed aliquis ex potestate episcopi accipit posse consecrare. Ergo quando ab ipso degradatur, videtur quod hoc posse amittat.

PRAETEREA, habens ordinem sacerdotalem non relinquitur puniendus judicio saeculari. Sed degradatus relinquitur. Ergo non habet ordinem; ergo non potest consecrare.

SED CONTRA, si degradatus reconciliatur, non iterum ordinatur. Ergo ordinem non amisit; ergo consecrare potuit.

PRAETEREA, hoc idem probatur per indelebilitatem characteris, ut supra. Utrum autem malus sacerdos, vel angelus, possit consecrare, eadem ratio est quae et de baptizatione; et ideo quaeruntur supra, dist. 5.

OBJ. 1: Moreover, it seems that someone who has been deprived of office cannot consecrate.[17] For no one can consecrate who does not have the power of consecrating. But one deprived of office does not have the power of consecrating, although he has the power of baptizing, as the canon says.[18] Therefore, he cannot consecrate.

OBJ. 2: Furthermore, *a thing is made and is corrupted out of the same things*, according to the Philosopher in *Ethics* 2.[19] But someone receives the ability to consecrate from the power of the bishop. Therefore, when he is stripped of office by the bishop, it seems that he loses this ability.

OBJ. 3: Furthermore, someone possessing priestly orders is not left to the punishment of secular courts. But someone stripped of his office is left to them. Therefore, he does not have holy orders; and therefore he cannot consecrate.

ON THE CONTRARY, if someone who was stripped of office is reconciled to the Church, he is not ordained again. Therefore, he did not lose holy orders; therefore he was able to consecrate.

FURTHERMORE, the same thing is proved by the indelible nature of the character, as was said above. But whether a bad priest or an angel can consecrate, the reasoning is the same as about baptizing; and so it should be looked for above in Distinction 5.

Quaestiuncula 5

ULTERIUS. Videtur quod Missa mali sacerdotis non minus valeat quam boni. Quia, sicut dicit Augustinus in Lib. *de Corpore Christi, in mysterio corporis et sanguinis Domini nihil a bono majus, nihil a malo minus perficitur sacerdote*.

PRAETEREA, baptismus datus a bono ministro nihil melius valet quam datus a malo. Ergo nec Missa a bono sacerdote vel malo dicta.

OBJ. 1: Moreover, it seems that the Mass of a bad priest is not worth less than that of a good priest.[20] For, as Augustine says in the book *On the Body of Christ, in the mystery of the Lord's body and blood nothing greater is accomplished by a good priest, and nothing less is accomplished by a bad priest*.[21]

OBJ. 2: Furthermore, baptism given by a good minister is no better than that given by a bad one. Therefore, neither is the Mass said by a good or by a bad priest.

---

17. Parallels: *ST* III, q. 82, a. 8; *Quodl*. XII, q. 11, a. 1.
18. Gratian's *Decretals*, Part 2, canon 1, q. 1, ch. 97 (PL 187:525).
19. Aristotle, *Nicomachean Ethics*, Bk. 2, ch. 1 (1104b7).
20. Parallel: *ST* III, q. 82, a. 6.
21. See Lanfranc, *Liber de corpore et sanguine Domini*, ch. 12 (PL 150:1310).

SED CONTRA, melius est quod est fructuosius. Sed Missa boni sacerdotis est fructuosior, quia ejus oratio magis exauditur. Ergo est melior.

ON THE CONTRARY, what is more fruitful is better. But the Mass of a good priest is more fruitful, for his prayer is heard more. Therefore, his Mass is better.

Response to Quaestiuncula 1

RESPONDEO dicendum ad primam quaestionem, quod ordo ecclesiae derivatus est ab ordine caelestis hierarchiae; unde sicut in angelis diversis ordinibus diversi actus debentur, ita et in ecclesia militante ad diversos actus diversi ordines applicantur, sicut etiam et in corpore diversa membra diversa habent officia, cui corpus mysticum similatur, ut patet 1 Corinth. 12. Ordines autem ecclesiae distingui non possunt per diversitatem interioris bonitatis, quia ignota est, et indeterminati sunt gradus ejus. Et quia bonitas vel virtus alicujus non ordinatur ad hoc quod aliquis aliquid possit, sed ad hoc quod bene faciat illud quod potest; habitus enim virtutum non sunt potentia, sicut Philosophus probat; ideo quod unus possit actum quem alius non potest, non contingit ex diversitate bonitatis vel malitiae, sed ex potestate suscepta, quam habet unus, et non alius; et ideo, quia laicus potestatem consecrandi non accipit, sua bonitas quantacumque sit, non juvat eum ad hoc quod consecrare possit.

AD PRIMUM ergo dicendum, quod omnis bonus homo dicitur esse sacerdos mystice, quia scilicet mysticum sacrificium Deo offert seipsum, scilicet *hostiam viventem Deo*, Rom. 12.

AD SECUNDUM dicendum, quod laicus bonus fit particeps Dominicae virtutis ad bene agendum hoc quod poterat prius aliquo modo facere, non autem ad hoc quod possit hoc per virtutem quod prius non poterat.

AD TERTIUM dicendum, quod, quamvis acceptio sacramenti sit major in fructu, tamen consecratio est major in potestate; unde non oportet quod qui potest accipere, possit consecrare.

TO THE FIRST QUESTION, I answer that the Church's orders are derived from the order of the heavenly hierarchy; and so just as among the angels different actions are due to different orders, so also in the Church Militant different orders are applied to different acts, just as also in a body different members have different functions, which the mystical body resembles, as is clear from 1 Corinthians 12. However, the orders of the Church cannot be distinguished by the difference in interior goodness, which is unknown, and its degrees are indeterminate. And so the goodness or virtue of someone is not ordered to his being able to do something, but to his doing well whatever he can do. For the habits of the virtues are not powers, as the Philosopher proves,[22] and that is why the fact that one person is capable of an act that another is not, does not depend on their difference in goodness or badness, but on the power received that one person has and not another; and so, because a lay person does not receive the power of consecrating, however great his goodness may be, it does not help him to be able to consecrate.

REPLY OBJ. 1: Every good person is said to be a priest mystically, because he offers himself as mystical sacrifice to God, namely, *a living victim to God* (Rom 12:1).

REPLY OBJ. 2: A good lay person is made partaker of the Lord's power for accomplishing well what he was able to do in any fashion before, but not for being able to do through this power what he could not do before.

REPLY OBJ. 3: Although receiving the sacrament is greater in its fruit, nevertheless, consecrating it is greater in its power. And this is why it is not necessary that whoever can receive can consecrate.

Response to Quaestiuncula 2

AD SECUNDAM QUAESTIONEM dicendum, quod potestas consecrandi non solum episcopis, sed etiam sacerdotibus collata est; quia ordo sacerdotis est medius inter episcopum et populum. Unde sicut in angelica hierarchia illuminationes ad inferiorem ordinem mediante superiore perveniunt, ita omnia sacramenta quae communiter toti populo dispensantur, per sacerdotes conferuntur; et hujusmodi sunt omnia quae non collocant in aliquo statu vel gradu super alios. Et quia Eucharistia est

TO THE SECOND QUESTION, it should be said that the power of consecrating does not only belong to the bishop, but it is also conferred on the priests. For the order of priest is an intermediate between the bishop and the people. And so, just as in the angelic hierarchy illuminations arrive at inferior orders by means of the superior ones, so all sacraments that are commonly administered to the whole people are conferred by the priests; and these are all the sacraments that do not establish one in any state or degree above oth-

22. Aristotle, *Nicomachean Ethics*, Bk. 2, ch. 4 (1106a6).

hujusmodi, ideo non solum per episcopos, sed etiam per sacerdotes dispensatur et consecratur. Est etiam alia ratio, ut sit frequentior memoria Dominicae passionis, et magis subveniatur vivis et mortuis ex majori frequentia sacramenti.

AD PRIMUM ergo dicendum, quod, licet iste actus sit maximus in se, tamen non est maximus quantum ad constituendum in ordine ecclesiae; quia per sumptionem hujus sacramenti non constituitur aliquis in gradu vel statu altiori inter membra ecclesiae, sicut fit per ordinem; et ideo non oportet quod ille actus solis episcopis reservetur.

AD SECUNDUM dicendum, quod in rebus ordinatis, ita est quod semper inferior participat aliquid de perfectione superioris, ut Dionysius dicit; et hoc modo est in connexione caelestis hierarchiae, ut in 2 Lib., dist. 9, qu. 1, art. 6 dictum est. Et ideo, quia ordo sacerdotis continuus est ordini episcopi, participat etiam aliquid de perfectiva virtute quantum ad illam perfectionem qua quis in seipso perficitur; non autem quantum ad perfectionem qua aliquis in eminentiori gradu constituitur, sicut est in ordine; vel altiori officio, sicut est in confirmatione; et ideo sacerdos participat ab episcopo potestatem consecrandi, non autem confirmandi vel ordinandi. Et quod ipsam habeat quasi participative, Dionysius dicit, quod patet ex hoc quod sacerdos consecrat super altare ab episcopo consecrato, et in vasis consecratis per episcopum, ipse etiam consecratus per episcopum.

AD TERTIUM dicendum, quod illae benedictiones non veniunt in usum totius populi, sed aliquarum excellentium personarum; et ideo solis episcopis reservantur.

ers. And since the Eucharist is one of these, it can be administered and consecrated not only by a bishop but also by a priest. And there is also another reason, so that the memorial of the Lord's Passion might be more frequent, and come more to the aid of the living and the dead by its greater frequency.

REPLY OBJ. 1: Although this act is the greatest in itself, nevertheless it is not the greatest as to establishing one in the Church's order; for by the reception of this sacrament no one is established in a higher level or state among the members of the Church, as happens by holy orders; and so it is not necessary that that act be reserved to the bishops alone.

REPLY OBJ. 2: Among ordered things, the lower always partakes of something of the higher, as Dionysius says;[23] and this is how it is in the relations of the heavenly hierarchy, as was said in Book II, Distinction 9, Question 1, Article 6. And so, since the order of priest is connected with the order of bishop, it also partakes something of its perfective power in the perfection that perfects someone in himself, but not the perfection by which someone is established in a more eminent level, as is the case in holy orders, or in a higher office as it is in confirmation. And so the priest partakes in the power of consecrating from the bishop, but not the power of confirming or ordaining. And Dionysius says that he has this as it were participatively, which is clear from the fact that a priest consecrates upon an altar consecrated by a bishop, and in vessels consecrated by a bishop, and he himself was also consecrated by a bishop.

REPLY OBJ. 3: Those blessings are not available for use by the whole people, but by certain preeminent persons; and so they are reserved to the bishops alone.

Response to Quaestiuncula 3

AD TERTIAM QUAESTIONEM dicendum, quod quidam dixerunt, quod haeretici ab ecclesia praecisi, et similiter excommunicati et schismatici, quia sunt extra unitatem ecclesiae, non possunt consecrare: et hujus opinionis videtur fuisse Magister in littera. Sed quia omne illud quod per consecrationem datur, est perpetuum; ideo, sicut baptismus, qui per consecrationem datur, nunquam amittitur, quantumcumque aliquis in haeresim labatur vel schisma vel excommunicationem; ita nec sacerdotalis ordo aliquo modo amitti potest, ut Augustinus dicit ad Parmenianum. Et quia potestas consecrandi ordinem sacerdotalem consequitur, ut dictum est, ideo haeretici et schismatici et excommunicati consecrant, quamvis ad suam perniciem, dummodo servetur debita forma et materia et intentio, quae etiam in infide-

TO THE THIRD QUESTION, it should be said that certain people have said that heretics who have been cut off from the Church, and likewise the excommunicated and schismatics, since they are outside the unity of the Church, cannot consecrate; and the Master seems to be of this opinion in the text. But since everything that is given through consecration is perpetual, for this reason, just as baptism, which is given through a consecration, is never lost, no matter how much someone falls into heresy or schism or excommunication; so neither can priestly orders be lost in any way, as Augustine says to Parmenianus.[24] And since the power of consecrating results from priestly orders, as was said, for this reason heretics and schismatics and those excommunicated consecrate, although to their own ruin, as long as the due form and matter and intention are pre-

---

23. Pseudo-Dionysius, *Ecclesiastical Hierarchy*, ch. 6, p. 3 (PG 3:534).
24. Augustine, *Contra epistulam Parmeniani* (CSEL 51), Bk. 2, ch. 13.

libus esse possunt, ut supra, dist. 5 de baptismo, dictum est.

AD PRIMUM ergo dicendum, quod verbum canonis intelligendum est quantum ad illos qui debitam formam non servant, vel quantum ad executionem quam amittunt; non enim jus consecrandi habent; et hoc solum posse dicimur in jure, quod juste possumus. Vel loquitur de consecratione qua ordines conferuntur; quia ad damnationem potius quam ad sanctificationem recipientium cedit. Et similiter quod Augustinus dicit, quod extra ecclesiam non est locus veri sacrificii, intelligendum est quantum ad effectum; vel extra ecclesiam, idest extra formam ecclesiae.

AD SECUNDUM dicendum, quod dicitur panis pollutus non in se, sed quia ipsi et seipsos polluunt consecrando et sumendo, et alios qui ab eis sacramenta scienter accipiunt.

AD TERTIUM dicendum, quod inquantum ordinem habet, ad unitatem ecclesiae pertinet, quamvis quantum ad aliud possit ab ecclesia esse praecisus.

served, which can also happen among unbelievers, as was said of baptism above in Distinction 5.[25]

REPLY OBJ. 1: The words of the canon are to be understood about those who do not preserve the due form or about the carrying out that they lose, for they do not have the right to consecrate, and in law we are said to be able to do only what we can do justly. Or it speaks about the consecration by which holy orders are conferred, for it results in the damnation rather than the sanctification of the recipients. And likewise what Augustine says, that outside the Church there is no place of true sacrifice, is to be understood as to the effect; or outside the Church, that is, outside the Church's form.

REPLY OBJ. 2: It is called polluted bread not in itself, but because by consecrating and receiving they pollute themselves and others who knowingly receive the sacraments from them.

REPLY OBJ. 3: Inasmuch as he has holy orders, he belongs to the unity of the Church, although in a certain respect he may be cut off from the Church.

Response to Quaestiuncula 4

AD QUARTAM QUAESTIONEM dicendum, quod degradatus, quia ordinem non amittit, potestatem consecrandi retinet; sed jus consecrandi sibi aufertur; et ideo si consecrat, peccat: tamen consecratum est.

AD PRIMUM ergo dicendum, quod ille canon non loquitur asserendo, sed quasi opponendo, ut ex circumstantia litterae apparet.

AD SECUNDUM dicendum, quod episcopus non dedit ordinem, sed Deus per ministerium episcopi; et Deus posset auferre, sed non episcopus; quia non est constitutus minister auferendi ordinem, sicut conferendi; quia propter efficaciam consecrationis debet esse ordo perpetuus.

AD TERTIUM dicendum, quod non est essentiale ordini sacerdotali, quod judicio saeculari relinqui non possit, sed ex privilegio indultum; et ideo manente ordine degradatus sua culpa hoc privilegium amittit.

TO THE FOURTH QUESTION, it should be said that someone stripped of office, because he does not lose holy orders, retains the power of consecrating. But the right of consecrating is taken away from him; and so if he consecrates, he sins, but it is consecrated nevertheless.

REPLY OBJ. 1: That canon does not speak by way of assertion, but as if by opposition, as is apparent from the context.

REPLY OBJ. 2: The bishop did not give holy orders, but God did through the ministry of the bishop. And God could take it away, but the bishop could not, for he was not constituted a minister of removing holy orders, as he was of conferring them, since orders should be perpetual because of the efficacy of the consecration.

REPLY OBJ. 3: It is not essential to priestly orders that someone not be left to secular judgment, but rather, it is granted by a privilege. And so someone stripped of his office who remains in holy orders loses this privilege by his own fault.

Response to Quaestiuncula 5

AD QUINTAM QUAESTIONEM dicendum, quod de Missa possumus loqui dupliciter: aut quantum ad id quod est essentiale in ea, scilicet corpus Christi; et sic a quocumque dicatur, aequaliter[26] bonum est et virtuo-

TO THE FIFTH QUESTION, it should be said that we can speak about the Mass in two ways: either as to what is essential in it, namely, the body of Christ, and in this way no matter who says it, it is equally good, because the work per-

---

25. See d. 5, q. 2, a. 2.
26. *aequaliter bonum.—aequaliter bona est quia opus operatum aequaliter bonum* PLE.

sum: vel quantum ad id quod est annexum sacramento, et quasi secundarium; et sic Missa boni sacerdotis melior est, quia non solum habet efficaciam ex opere operato, sed ex opere operante: et ideo ceteris paribus melius est audire Missam boni sacerdotis quam mali.

ET PER HOC patet solutio ad utramque partem.

formed is equally good and also powerful; or as to what is attached to the sacrament, and secondary, as it were, and in this way, the Mass of a good priest is better, because it does not only have efficacy by the work itself having been performed, but by the work of the one doing it. And so, all other things being equal, it is better to hear the Mass of a good priest than a bad one.

AND BY THIS the solutions to both sides are clear.

ARTICLE 2

The rite of consecrating

Quaestiuncula 1

AD SECUNDUM SIC PROCEDITUR. Videtur quod liceat sacerdoti omnino a consecratione abstinere. Quia de beato Marco narrat Hieronymus quod sibi pollicem amputaverit, ut sacerdotio reprobus haberetur. Nec hoc fecit nisi indignum se reputans tali sacramento. Ergo videtur quod si omnino a celebratione abstineat ex reverentia Dominici corporis et propriae infirmitatis consideratione aliquis sacerdos, non peccet.

PRAETEREA, sicut sacerdotis officium est consecrare, ita et ligare et solvere. Sed non exigitur ut liget et solvat, nisi habeat curam animarum. Ergo etiam a sacerdote qui non habet populum cui teneatur, non exigitur quod consecret; et ita non peccat omnino abstinendo.

SED CONTRA est quod Ambrosius dicit: *grave est quod ad mensam tuam mundo corde et manibus innocentibus non venimus; sed gravius est, si dum peccatum metuimus, etiam sacrificium non reddamus.* Sed primum est peccatum mortale. Ergo et secundum.

OBJ. 1: To the second we proceed thus. It seems that a priest is permitted to abstain entirely from consecrating.[27] For Jerome tells of blessed Mark that he cut off his own thumb so that he would be considered rejected from the priesthood.[28] Nor did he do this for any reason other than considering himself unworthy of such a sacrament. Therefore, it seems that if some priest abstained from celebration entirely out of reverence for the body of the Lord and consideration of his own weakness, he would not sin.

OBJ. 2: Furthermore, just as the office of a priest is to consecrate, so also it is to bind and loose. But it is not required that he bind and loose unless he has the care of souls. Therefore, it is also not required of a priest who does not have a people to whom he is bound, that he consecrate, and so he does not sin by abstaining entirely.

ON THE CONTRARY, Ambrose says: *it is a grave thing when we do not come to your table with clean heart and innocent hands; but it is a graver thing if while in dread of our sins, we do not even render the sacrifice.*[29] But the first thing is a mortal sin; therefore the second is as well.

Quaestiuncula 2

ULTERIUS. Videtur quod non possint plures simul eamdem hostiam consecrare. Quia plurium agentium sunt plures actiones, maxime quando unusquisque sufficit ad agendum. Sed unus sacerdos tantum potest consecrare. Ergo si plures simul consecrent, sunt plures consecrationes super eamdem hostiam; et ita fit injuria sacramento.

PRAETEREA, unus dicens verba, virtute verborum consecrat. Sed quod factum est, fieri non potest; quia quod est, non fit. Ergo alii nihil faciunt; ergo superfluum est quod dicunt verba.

SED CONTRA est consuetudo quarumdam ecclesiarum, in quibus novi sacerdotes simul episcopo concelebrant.

OBJ. 1: Moreover, it seems that many men cannot consecrate the same host at the same time.[30] For several actions come from several agents, especially when each one is sufficient to act. But one priest can consecrate alone. Therefore, if several priests consecrated at the same time, there would be several consecrations upon the same host; and so injury would be done to the sacrament.

OBJ. 2: Furthermore, one person saying the words consecrates by the power of the words. But what has been done cannot come to be done, for that which is does not come to be. Therefore, the others do nothing, and so the words they say are superfluous.

ON THE CONTRARY, it is the custom of some churches that new priests concelebrate together with the bishop.

---

27. Parallel: *ST* III, q. 82, a. 10.

28. Moos writes in a note: "Thus in the old prologue *On Mark*, erroneously ascribed to Jerome." Note that this story found its way into *The Golden Legend*, of enormous popularity in the Middle Ages: "He [Mark] was bent over in his profound humility, for it was due to his humility that he cut off his thumb, as we are told, in order to be judged unfit for the priesthood" (Ryan ed., 1:243).

29. Not found verbatim in the works of Ambrose. In *ST* III, q. 82, a. 10, Thomas cites the same text as "Ambrose says in a certain prayer . . . "; the editors of Editiones Paulinae send us to Anselm, *Orationes*, n. 33 (PL 158:926).

30. Parallel: *ST* III, q. 82, a. 2.

Quaestiuncula 3

Ulterius. Videtur quod non debeat quotidie Missa in ecclesia celebrari. Quia in Missa recolitur Dominica passio. Sed ecclesia celebrat memoriam Dominicae passionis semel in anno. Ergo non pluries debet in ecclesia Missa dici.

Praeterea, in die parasceves agitur memoria Dominicae passionis, nec tamen tunc consecratio fit. Ergo multo minus deberet fieri in aliis diebus.

Praeterea, aliquibus diebus celebratur hoc sacramentum pluries una die solemniter in ecclesia, sicut patet in festo nativitatis, et multis aliis diebus. Ergo videtur quod aliquando deberet praetermitti.

Sed contra, sacramenta ecclesiae debent magis assiduari quam sacramenta veteris legis. Sed quotidie in veteri lege offerebatur sacrificium. Ergo multo fortius debet in nova lege fieri.

Praeterea, panis hujus sacramenti dicitur *quotidianus*. Sed non nisi quia quotidie consecratur. Ergo quotidie consecrari debet.

Obj. 1: Moreover, it seems that Mass should not be celebrated daily in the Church.[31] For in Mass we call to mind the Lord's Passion. But the Church celebrates the memorial of the Lord's Passion once a year. Therefore, Mass should not be said many times in the Church.

Obj. 2: Furthermore, on Good Friday the memorial of the Lord's Passion is enacted, yet no consecration is done on that day. Therefore, much less should it be done on all the other days.

Obj. 3: Furthermore, on certain days this sacrament is celebrated solemnly several times in the Church, as is seen on the feast of Christmas, and many other days. Therefore, it seems that sometimes it should be omitted.

On the contrary, the sacraments of the Church should be made use of more assiduously than the sacraments of the Old Law. But sacrifice was offered daily under the Old Law. Therefore, much more should it be done in the New Law.

Furthermore, this sacrament's bread is called *daily bread*. But it would not be unless it were consecrated daily. Therefore, it should be consecrated daily.

Quaestiuncula 4

Ulterius. Videtur quod hora vespertina debeat Missa celebrari. Quia Christi actio nostra est instructio. Sed ipse Christus hoc sacramentum fecit in coena hora serotina. Ergo et tali hora deberet fieri.

Praeterea, secundum canones ordines sunt celebrandi circa vespertinam horam. Sed ordines sacri non celebrantur sine Missarum solemniis. Ergo debet Missa vespertina hora celebrari.

Item, videtur quod post mediam noctem; quia tunc dies secundum ecclesiae computum incipit.

Item videtur quod tantum in hora sexta, quia in illa hora Dominus passus est; cujus passionis hoc sacramentum est memoriale.

Obj. 1: Moreover, it seems that Mass should be celebrated in the evening.[32] For Christ's act is our instruction. But Christ himself did this sacrament in the evening at supper. Therefore, it should be done at that hour.

Obj. 2: Furthermore, according to the canons, holy orders are to be celebrated at an evening hour. But sacred orders are not celebrated without a solemn Mass. Therefore, Mass should be celebrated at an evening hour.

Obj. 3: Or else, it seems that it should be after midnight, for that is when the day begins according to the counting of the Church.

Obj. 4: Or else it seems that only at the sixth hour, for in that hour the Lord suffered, and this sacrament is the memorial of his Passion.

Quaestiuncula 5

Ulterius. Videtur quod non oporteat in loco sacro celebrari. Quia sicut hoc sacramentum non est necessitatis, ita nec confirmatio. Sed confirmatio potest conferri in loco non sacro. Ergo et hoc sacramentum non oportet quod in loco sacro conficiatur.

Obj. 1: Moreover, it seems that it does not need to be celebrated in a sacred place.[33] For just as this is not a necessary sacrament, so neither is confirmation. But confirmation can be conferred in a non-sacred place. Therefore, neither does this sacrament need to be celebrated in a sacred space.

---

31. Parallel: *ST* III, q. 83, a. 2.
32. Parallel: *ST* III, q. 83, a. 2.
33. Parallels: below, d. 24, q. 2, a. 2, ad 9; *ST* III, q. 83, a. 3.

ITEM, videtur quod non oporteat esse altare de lapide. Quia sacrificia veteris legis fuerunt sacrificii hujus figura. Sed ad veteris legis sacrificia altare fiebat de lignis sethim, ut patet Exod. 25, et iterum de auro, ut patet 3 Reg. 7, et iterum de terra, ut patet Exod. 26. Ergo et in nova lege non solum de lapide oportet quod fiat.

ITEM, videtur quod in pannis sericis debeat consecrari. Quia panni illi sunt pretiosiores. Ergo ad reverentiam sacramenti magis eis debemus uti.

ITEM, videtur quod in calice de petra possit celebrari. Quia calix significat sepulcrum Christi. Sed illud sepulcrum fuit de petra. Ergo et calix de petra debet fieri.

DE INDUMENTIS autem sacerdotalibus dicetur in tractatu de ordine, dist. 24, qu. 1, art. 3.

OBJ. 2: Or else, it seems that it need not be on an altar of stone. For the sacrifices of the Old Law were a figure of this sacrifice. But the sacrifices of the Old Law were done on an altar of acacia wood, as is seen in Exodus 25:10, and again, an altar of gold, as is seen in 1 Kings 7:48, and again, an altar of earth, as is seen in Exodus 20:24. Therefore, in the New Law it is also not necessary that the altar be made only of stone.

OBJ. 3: Or else, it seems that it should be consecrated in silken cloths. For that cloth is most valuable. Therefore, we should rather use it for the reverence of the sacrament.

OBJ. 4: Or else, it seems that it could be celebrated in a chalice of stone. For the chalice represents Christ's tomb. But that tomb was of stone. Therefore, the chalice too should be made of stone.

THE PRIESTLY VESTMENTS will be discussed in the treatise on holy orders, Distinction 24, Question 1, Article 3.

Quaestiuncula 6

ULTERIUS. Videtur quod aliquo praedictorum omisso non sit consecratio. Quia, sicut dicit Dionysius, *operationes hierarchicae ordinantur secundum divinas leges.* Sed ille qui praetermittit ritum ab ecclesia institutum, non sequitur divinas leges, quae per partes nobis positae sunt. Ergo talis non consecrat, cum consecrare sit actus hierarchicus, quia est actus ordinis.

PRAETEREA, totus ritus sacramenti suam habet significationem. Sed significatio est de essentia sacramenti. Ergo et ritus consecrandi; et ita, si praetermittatur, non erit vera consecratio.

PRAETEREA, actiones spirituales magis sunt ordinatae quam saeculares. Sed si aliqua actio in rebus saecularibus, puta venditio vel emptio vel aliquid hujusmodi, contra statuta principum fiat, pro nulla haberetur. Ergo et si aliquis consecraret contra statutum ecclesiae, consecratio nulla est.

SED CONTRA, ea quae sunt de essentia sacramenti, sunt eadem apud omnes. Sed ritus sacramenti non est idem apud omnes, nec secundum omne tempus. Ergo non est de essentia sacramenti; ergo sine hoc potest fieri consecratio.

PRAETEREA, in baptismo sunt quaedam quae si omittantur, non reputatur sacramentum irritum, quia sunt ad solemnitatem sacramenti. Ergo et hic si omittantur illa quae pertinent ad solemnitatem consecrationis, vere consecratio erit.

OBJ. 1: Moreover, it seems that if any of the aforementioned things are omitted, there will be no consecration.[34] For as Dionysius says, *the operations of the hierarchy are ordered according to divine laws.*[35] But the person who neglects the rite instituted by the Church does not follow divine laws, which were set down for us by its office. Therefore, such a person does not consecrate, since consecrating is a hierarchical act, for it is an act of holy orders.

OBJ. 2: Furthermore, the sacrament's entire rite has its signification. But the signification is essential to the sacrament. Therefore, so is the rite of consecrating; and thus, if it is not observed, there will be no true consecration.

OBJ. 3: Furthermore, spiritual actions are more ordered than secular ones. But if any action in secular matters, like selling or buying or anything like that, were done against what was established by the lawmakers, it would be held as null. Therefore, if anyone consecrated against the Church's statutes, the consecration would also be null.

ON THE CONTRARY, those things that are essential to the sacrament are the same among all people. But the sacrament's rite is not the same among all, nor in every age. Therefore, it is not of the sacrament's essence; therefore the consecration can happen without it.

FURTHERMORE, in baptism there are certain things that, if they were omitted, are not considered to invalidate the sacrament, for they belong to the sacrament's solemnity. Therefore, also here, if things are omitted that belong to the solemnity of the consecration, the consecration will truly exist.

---

34. Parallel: *ST* III, q. 83, a. 3.
35. Pseudo-Dionysius, *Celestial Hierarchy*, ch. 3, n. 2 (PG 3:166).

Response to Quaestiuncula 1

RESPONDEO dicendum ad primam quaestionem, quod secundum quosdam non peccat qui dimittit celebrationem, nisi populum habeat commissum, vel ex obedientia teneatur celebrare. Sed quia secundum Gregorium, *cum crescunt dona, rationes crescunt donorum*; cum sacerdoti sit data potestas nobilissima, reus negligentiae erit, nisi illa utatur ad honorem Dei et salutem suam, et aliorum vivorum et mortuorum, secundum illud 1 Petr. 4, 10: *unusquisque gratiam quam accepit, in alterutrum illam administrantes*. Nisi forte aliquis ex familiari Spiritus Sancti instinctu dimittat, sicut legitur de quodam sancto patre in *Vitis patrum*, qui ordinatus nunquam postea celebravit.

AD PRIMUM ergo dicendum, quod ille qui non habet ordinem, potest ordinem refugere. Sed ille qui habet, tenetur ipsum exequi.

AD SECUNDUM dicendum, quod secundum omnes, alios actus ordinum debet homo non soli Deo, sed etiam proximis; quia actus inferiorum sunt ad ministerium sacerdotis. Alii autem actus sacerdotis, ut ligare et solvere, respiciunt corpus mysticum; similiter etiam docere et baptizare; et ideo qui non tenetur aliis vel subjectione vel praelatione, potest ab illis actibus sine peccato cessare. Sed consecratio est actus dignior, et ordinatus ad corpus Christi verum, nec respicit corpus Christi mysticum nisi ex consequenti; et ideo etiam si nulli homini teneatur, tamen tenetur Deo, ut reddat ei sacrificium acceptum; sacerdotibus enim praeceptum est: *hoc facite in meam commemorationem*.

TO THE FIRST QUESTION, I answer that according to certain people, a man who abstains from celebration of the Eucharist does not sin, unless he has a congregation committed to him, or he is bound to celebrate out of obedience. But since, according to Gregory, *when gifts grow, the reasons for the gifts grow*,[36] and since the noblest power is given to a priest, he will be culpable for negligence unless he uses it for the honor of God and the salvation of himself and others, living and dead, according to the text: *serving one another with whatever gift each of you has received* (1 Pet 4:10). Unless perhaps someone abstains by the intimate prompting of the Holy Spirit, as is read of a certain holy father in the *Lives of the Fathers*, who never celebrated Mass once he was ordained.[37]

REPLY OBJ. 1: Someone who does not have holy orders can refuse holy orders. But someone who has them, is bound to exercise them.

REPLY OBJ. 2: According to everyone, a man owes the other acts of holy orders not only to God, but also to his neighbors. For the acts of the lower orders are for the sake of the priest's ministry. But other acts of the priest, like binding and loosing, regard the mystical body; likewise also teaching and baptizing. And so whoever is not bound to others either by being subject to or by being set over them, can refrain from these acts without sin. But consecration is a worthier act, and it is ordered to the true body of Christ, nor does it regard the mystical body of Christ except as a result. And thus even if he is bound to no man, he is still bound to God, that he render him an acceptable sacrifice; for it is commanded to priests: *do this in memory of me* (Luke 22:19).

Response to Quaestiuncula 2

AD SECUNDAM QUAESTIONEM dicendum, quod secundum morem quarumdam ecclesiarum plures sacerdotes episcopo concelebrant, quando ordinantur; ad repraesentandum, quod quando Dominus hoc sacramentum instituit, et potestatem consecrandi discipulis dedit, eis concoenavit, sicut episcopus simul cum ordinatis presbyteris celebrat.

AD PRIMUM ergo dicendum, quod quia intentio requiritur ad perfectionem sacramentorum, ideo, cum omnes habeant intentionem unam consecrationem faciendi, non est ibi nisi una tantum consecratio.

AD SECUNDUM dicendum, quod sicut Innocentius dicit, omnes celebrantes debent intentionem referre ad

TO THE SECOND QUESTION, it should be said that according to the custom of certain churches, several priests concelebrate with the bishop when they are ordained. This is to represent that when the Lord instituted this sacrament, he also gave the power of consecrating to the disciples when he ate supper with them, just as the bishop celebrates together with the priests he has ordained.

REPLY OBJ. 1: Since intention is required for the perfection of the sacraments, for this reason since all have one intention of performing the consecration, there is only one consecration there.

REPLY OBJ. 2: As Innocent says,[38] all those celebrating should direct their intention to that instant when the

---

36. Gregory the Great, *Homilies on the Gospels*, Bk. 1, homily 9, par. 1 (CCSL 141:58): "Cum enim augentur dona, rationes etiam crescunt donorum."
37. See *De vitis patrum*, Bk. 9, ch. 19 (PL 74:80).
38. Innocent III, *De sacro altaris mysterio*, Bk. 4, ch. 25 (PL 217:873).

illud instans in quo episcopus verba profert; et sic episcopi intentio non defraudatur, nec aliquis ibi facit quod factum est.

bishop utters the words; and in this way the bishop's intention is not spoiled, nor does anyone do something that is already done.

Response to Quaestiuncula 3

AD TERTIAM QUAESTIONEM dicendum, quod secundum Innocentium, quinque de causis quotidie Missa in ecclesia celebratur. Primo, quia oportet semper esse paratam medicinam contra quotidiana peccata. Secundo, ut lignum vitae semper sit in medio paradisi. Tertio, ut nobis quotidie Christus uniatur sacramentaliter, et nos ei spiritualiter. Quarto, ut sit apud nos vigil memoria passionis. Quinto, ut vero agno loco typici quotidie utamur ad vesperam quem Judaei ad vesperam convertendi esurient, secundum illud Psalm. 58, 15: *convertentur ad vesperam, et famem patientur ut canes.*

AD PRIMUM ergo dicendum, quod passio Christi prout in capite contingit, semel tantum in anno repraesentatur in ecclesia; sed prout in nos ejus effectus provenit, quotidie debet repraesentari, quia ejus effectus in nobis continuus est, et sic repraesentatur in hoc sacramento.

AD SECUNDUM dicendum, quod ecclesia volens populum Christianum circa ipsam Dominicam passionem prout in capite nostro fuit, mente occupari, statuit ut illa die non consecraretur corpus Christi. Ne tamen ecclesia omnino sine corpore Christi esset, corpus Christi praecedenti die consecratum et reservatum sumitur; sanguis autem non reservatur propter effusionis periculum. Nec est verum quod quidam dicunt, quod vinum ex immissione partis hostiae in calicem consecratur: quia transubstantiatio non fit sine debita forma verborum; unde post potum illum non liceret eadem die communicare.

AD TERTIUM dicendum, quod omnis nostra actio per Christum perfici debet; et ideo, quando in una die occurrunt vel diversa Dei beneficia commemoranda, de quibus sunt gratiae Deo reddendae, vel etiam plura a Deo impetranda pro salute vivorum et mortuorum; oportet quod pluries Missa in ecclesia celebretur, si adsit facultas; nec ex hoc sequitur quod aliquando debeat intermitti.

TO THE THIRD QUESTION, it should be said that according to Innocent, Mass is celebrated daily in the Church for five reasons. First, because it is always necessary for the medicine to be prepared against daily sins. Second, so that the wood of life may always be in the middle of Paradise. Third, so that every day Christ may be united to us sacramentally, and we to him spiritually. Fourth, so that the memory of the Passion may be kept watchfully among us. Fifth, so that in place of its type we might use that true lamb toward evening, for whom the Jews still to be converted will thirst in the evening, according to the scripture: *they shall return toward evening, and suffer hunger like dogs* (Ps 59 [58]:15).

REPLY OBJ. 1: Christ's Passion as it happened to our Head is only represented once per year in the Church; but as its effects reach to us, it should be represented every day, for its effect in us is continuous, and that is how it is represented in this sacrament.

REPLY OBJ. 2: The Church, desiring the Christian people to meditate on the Lord's Passion itself as it existed in our Head, established that on that day the body of Christ should not be consecrated. But lest the Church should be entirely without the body of Christ, the body of Christ that was consecrated and reserved the day before is received. But the blood is not reserved because of the danger of spilling. Nor is it true what some people say, that the wine is consecrated by dropping a piece of the host into the chalice, for transubstantiation does not happen without the due form of words. And so after it has been drunk, it is not permitted to the priest receive Communion again that day.

REPLY OBJ. 3: All our actions should be perfected by Christ. And this is why when it happens that on a single day either different benefits of God must be commemorated, for which thanks should be rendered to God, or else many things are to be requested from God for the salvation of the living and the dead, it is necessary that several Masses be celebrated in a church, if it has the faculties. Nor does it follow from this that sometimes it should be omitted.

Response to Quaestiuncula 4

AD QUARTAM QUAESTIONEM dicendum, quod communiter loquendo Missa debet dici in die, et non in nocte; quia hoc sacramentum ad tempus gratiae pertinet, quod per diem significatur. Rom. 13, 12: *nox praeces-*

TO THE FOURTH QUESTION, it should be said that commonly speaking, Mass should be said in the daytime, not at night, for this sacrament belongs to the time of grace, which is signified by the day: *the night is far gone, but the day is at*

sit, dies autem appropinquavit. Dies autem judicatur non solum ab ortu solis, sed ex quo incipiunt orituri solis signa manifestari per aliquam aeris illustrationem. Tamen in duabus noctibus Missa decantatur propter privilegium illarum noctium, scilicet in nocte nativitatis, quando Christus natus est, et in nocte resurrectionis circa principium, ut patet ex oratione *Deus qui hanc sacratissimam noctem gloria Dominicae resurrectionis illustras* etc., quamvis hoc non oporteat semper observari. Solemnis autem Missae celebratio tribus horis instituta est fieri; scilicet in tertia diebus festis, in sexta diebus profestis, in nona diebus jejuniorum; quia in Missa recolitur mors Christi, qui quidem hora tertia crucifixus est linguis Judaeorum, hora sexta manibus militum, hora nona expiravit. Sed quando fiunt ordines, Missa potest cantari etiam post nonam, et praecipue in sabbato sancto, quia ordines pertinent ad diem Dominicam; vel etiam ut diligentior fiat praeparatio, differtur quantum differri potest ante prandium; et ideo quando non est dies jejunii, celebratur inter tertiam et sextam, qua hora comeditur communiter; sed in diebus jejunii in nona. Privatae autem Missae possunt dici a mane usque ad tertiam, vel etiam usque ad nonam in diebus jejuniorum.

AD PRIMUM ergo dicendum, quod eadem ratio est quare Christus hora vespertina consecravit, et quare post coenam; unde sicut non oportet quod imitemur eum in secundo, ita nec in primo.

AD SECUNDUM dicendum, quod hoc singulariter est in diebus ordinum ratione jam dicta.

AD TERTIUM dicendum, quod in medio noctis secundum ecclesiam incipit dies naturalis, non autem dies artificialis, in qua solum licet celebrare.

AD QUARTUM dicendum, quod quamvis Christus hora sexta fuerit in cruce positus, tamen sacramentum passionis suae peractum est in aliis horis; et ideo non oportet quod tunc tantum Missa celebretur.

hand (Rom 13:12). But day is not only judged by the rising of the sun, but by the signs that the sunrise is about to begin, by a certain brightening of the air. However, the Mass is sung on two nights because of the privilege of those nights, namely on the night before Christmas, when Christ was born, and around the beginning of the night of the resurrection, as is seen in the prayer, *O God, who make this most sacred night radiant with the glory of the Lord's Resurrection*, etc.[39] although it is not necessary always to observe this. But the celebration of solemn Mass is established to be done at three times of day; namely at the third hour on feast days, at the sixth hour on a ferial day, and at the ninth hour on days of fasting. For in the Mass we call to mind Christ's death, who indeed was crucified at the third hour by the tongues of the Jews, and at the sixth hour by the hands of the soldiers, and at the ninth hour he breathed his last. But when holy orders are done, the Mass can be sung even after the ninth hour, and particularly on Holy Saturday, for holy orders pertain to the Sunday; or also so that the preparation may be more diligently made, it may be deferred as much as possible before lunch. And so when it is not a day of fast, it is celebrated between the third hour and the sixth, when it is common to eat; but on fasting days at the ninth hour. However, private Masses may be said from morning until the third hour, or even until the ninth on days of fast.

REPLY OBJ. 1: Christ consecrated at an evening hour for the same reason that it was also after dinner; and so just as we do not need to imitate him in the second, so neither in the first.

REPLY OBJ. 2: This happens specially on days when holy orders are conferred for the reason already mentioned.

REPLY OBJ. 3: According to the Church the natural day begins at midnight, but not the artificial day in which alone it is licit to celebrate Mass.

REPLY OBJ. 4: Although Christ was placed on the Cross at the sixth hour, nevertheless the sacrament of his Passion is enacted at other times; and so it is not necessary that Mass be celebrated only then.

Response to Quaestiuncula 5

AD QUINTAM QUAESTIONEM dicendum, quod in hoc sacramento continetur ille qui est totius sanctitatis causa; et ideo omnia quae ad consecrationem hujus sacramenti pertinent, etiam consecrata sunt; sicut ipsi sacerdotes consecrantes, et ministri, et vestes, et vasa, et omnia hujusmodi; et ideo etiam debet in altari et in domo consecrata celebrari hoc sacramentum. Si autem necessitas adsit, vel propter destructionem ecclesiarum in aliqua terra, vel in itinere constitutis, licet etiam in locis non consecratis celebrare; dummodo habeant altare

TO THE FIFTH QUESTION, it should be said that in this sacrament is contained the one who is the cause of all holiness; and so everything that relates to this sacrament's consecration should also be consecrated, like the consecrating priests themselves, and the ministers, and vestments, and vessels, and everything like them. And therefore this sacrament should also be celebrated on a consecrated altar in a consecrated house. But if there is a present necessity, either because of destruction of the churches in a certain land, or for people on a journey, it is permitted also to celebrate

39. The Collect for the Easter Vigil.

portatile consecratum, et alia hujusmodi, quae ad consecrationem hujus mysterii requiruntur; alias non licet, nisi episcopo concedente.

AD PRIMUM ergo dicendum, quod confirmationis sacramentum non continet ipsum Christum; et ideo non requiritur loci sanctificatio, sicut in hoc sacramento.

AD SECUNDUM dicendum, quod beatus Silvester instituit quod altare de cetero non nisi lapideum esset. Quia enim altare consecrari debet, oportet esse aliquam rem fortem et non fragilem, sicut est lignum vel terra, de qua fiat altare. Item quia debet esse in ecclesia copia altarium, ut frequentetur hoc mysterium, ideo debet esse materia communis, non autem aurum vel argentum, vel aliquid hujusmodi, quod non de facili possit haberi. In veteri autem lege erat tantum unum altare ad unum tantum effectum deputatum; et ideo nihil oberat, si de auro fieret. Competit etiam lapis ad significationem altaris, quod Christum significat, qui etiam per petram significatur; 1 Corinth. 10, 4: *petra autem erat Christus*. Sed ante tempus Silvestri, propter persecutionem non erat fidelibus certus locus ad manendum; et ideo habebant altare ligneum, quod facile transferretur.

AD TERTIUM dicendum, quod panni in quibus corpus Christi consecratur, repraesentant sindonem mundam qua corpus Christi involutum est; et ideo sicut illa linea fuit, ita non licet nisi in pannis lineis corpus Christi consecrare. Linum etiam competit huic sacramento et propter puritatem, quia ex eo panni candidissimi et facile mundabiles fiunt; et propter multiplicem tunsionem lini qua paratur ad hoc ut ex eo fiat pannus candidus, quae competit ad significandum passionem Christi; unde non decet de pannis sericis corporale et pallas altaris esse, quamvis sint pretiosiores: neque de panno lineo tincto, quamvis sit pulchrior.

AD QUARTUM dicendum, quod secundum statum ecclesiae calix debet esse tantum de auro vel argento vel stagno; non autem de aere vel aurichalco, quia ex fortitudine vini rubiginem generaret, et nauseam provocaret; neque ex vitro vel ex crystallo propter fragilitatem; neque ex ligno propter porositatem, quia imbibit liquorem immissum; neque ex lapide, propter ineptitudinem; non enim oportet quod quantum ad omnia, signa signatis respondeant.

in non-consecrated places, as long as they have a portable consecrated altar and other things like that which are required for the consecration of this mystery. Otherwise it is not permitted unless granted by the bishop.

REPLY OBJ. 1: The sacrament of confirmation does not contain Christ himself; and so the sanctification of place is not required as in this sacrament.

REPLY OBJ. 2: Blessed Sylvester established finally that the altar not be of anything but stone.[40] For since the altar must be consecrated, the altar must be made of something strong and not fragile, like wood or earth. Again, because there must be in the church a great number of altars, so that this mystery may be done frequently, it must be a common material, not gold or silver or anything like that which cannot easily be had. However, in the Old Law there was only one altar designated for only one effect, and so nothing prevented it from being made of gold. Stone also fits with the signification of the altar, which signifies Christ, who is also signified by stone: *but the rock was Christ* (1 Cor 10:4). But before the time of Sylvester, because of the persecution, the faithful did not have a safe place to remain, and so they had a wooden altar which was easily moved.

REPLY OBJ. 3: The cloths in which the body of Christ is consecrated represent the white shroud in which the body of Christ was wrapped. And as it was linen, it is not permitted to consecrate the body of Christ in any cloth but linen. Linen is also suited to this sacrament because of its purity, for the whitest and most easily cleaned cloths are made from it. And because of the repeated beating of the linen by which it is prepared to be made into white cloth, it is suited to signifying Christ's Passion. And so it is not becoming for silken cloths to be the corporal and altar cloth, although they are more precious; nor for dyed linen cloth, although it is more beautiful.

REPLY OBJ. 4: According to the Church's statutes the chalice must be only of gold or silver or pewter; but not of bronze or brass, because from the strength of the wine it could rust, and provoke nausea; nor from glass or crystal because of their fragility; nor from wood because of its porousness, which absorbs the liquid placed in it; nor from stone, because it is clumsy; for it is not necessary that the signs correspond to what they represent in everything.

Response to Quaestiuncula 6

AD SEXTAM QUAESTIONEM dicendum, quod remotis his quae non sunt de essentia rei, nihilominus res

TO THE SIXTH QUESTION, it should be said that once those things that are not essential to a thing are removed,

---

40. In contemporary dictionaries of Christian antiquity, the attribution to Pope Sylvester I (314–335) of a decree mandating stone altars is questioned or rejected outright; however, the use of stone for the construction of altars was widespread by the 4th century, and in the succeeding two centuries became normative, having been prescribed by regional councils.

manet; unde cum hujusmodi ritus quantum ad determinationem horae vel loci vel indumentorum, non sint de essentia sacramenti, sed de solemnitate, si omittantur, nihilominus consecratum est sacrificium, dummodo adsint ea quae sunt de essentia sacramenti, scilicet ordo et intentio ex parte consecrantis, et materia et forma ex parte consecrati. Tamen graviter peccat qui aliter facit, et degradandus esset.

AD PRIMUM ergo dicendum, quod leges divinae quae pertinent ad essentialem institutionem sacramenti, si mutentur, nihil fit, ut si alia materia esset vel forma; secus autem est de legibus quae pertinent ad solemnitatem sacramenti.

AD SECUNDUM dicendum, quod significatio rei sacramentalis est de essentia sacramenti; et hoc sufficienter habetur per materiam; et ideo significatio quae superadditur in aliquo ritu, est de solemnitate, non de essentia sacramenti.

AD TERTIUM dicendum, quod sacramenta originem habent ex institutione divina; et ideo omissio alicujus quod sit ab ecclesia institutum, non potest impedire quin verum sacramentum fiat. Impediret autem, si sacramenta ex institutione ecclesiae efficaciam haberent, sicut actiones saeculares ex statutis[41] ratificantur.

the thing nevertheless remains. And this is why, since the determination of the hour or the place or the vestments in the rites are not essential to the sacrament but to the solemnity, if they are omitted, the sacrament is consecrated nevertheless, as long as those things are present that are essential to the sacrament, namely, the order and intention on the part of the one consecrating, and the matter and form on the part of what is consecrated. Still, the person who does otherwise sins gravely, and should be demoted.

REPLY OBJ. 1: If the divine laws that pertain to the essential institution of a sacrament are changed, nothing happens, as if there were other matter or form. But it is otherwise with the laws that pertain to the solemnity of the sacrament.

REPLY OBJ. 2: The signification of the sacramental reality is of the sacrament's essence. And this is sufficiently possessed by the matter. And so the signification that is added by any of the rites belongs to the solemnity, and not to the sacrament's essence.

REPLY OBJ. 3: The sacraments have their origin from divine institution, and so the omission of anything that was instituted by the Church cannot impede the valid sacrament from happening. But it would impede it if the sacrament had its efficacy from the Church's institution, as secular actions are ratified by statutes of princes.

---

41. *statutis ratificantur.—statutis principum ratificantur* PLE.

ARTICLE 3

The administering of Holy Communion

Quaestiuncula 1

AD TERTIUM SIC PROCEDITUR. Videtur quod laicus potest dispensare corpus Christi. Perfectio enim hujus sacramenti in materiae consecratione consistit, ut supra dictum est, non in usu sacramenti. Sed ordinati, sunt ministri sacramentorum. Ergo etsi consecratio materiae ad solos sacerdotes pertineat, tamen dispensatio debet ad omnes pertinere.

PRAETEREA, ab illis debet dispensari sacramentum qui cum reverentia ipsum tractant. Sed quidam laici sunt majoris reverentiae ad sacramentum quam etiam sacerdotes; et etiam mulieres interdum. Ergo per eos potest hoc sacramentum dispensari.

PRAETEREA, sicut sacerdotis est dispensare corpus Christi, ita et tangere. Sed in aliquo casu licet tangere laico corpus Christi; puta, si videret ipsum in terra jacere, et non esset sacerdos qui tolleret. Ergo et in aliquo casu liceret ei dispensare.

SED CONTRA est quod dicitur *de Consecr.*, dist. 2, cap. pervenit, ubi inhibetur ne etiam infirmis per laicos sacerdotes hoc sacramentum transmittant.

PRAETEREA, ad eosdem pertinet esse ministros ecclesiae, et dispensatores mysteriorum Dei, 1 Cor. 4: *sic nos existimet homo ut ministros Christi, et dispensatores mysteriorum Dei.* Sed laici non sunt ministri ecclesiae. Ergo non debent esse dispensatores sacramentorum.

OBJ. 1: To the third question we proceed thus. It seems that a lay person can administer the body of Christ.[42] For the completion of this sacrament consists in the consecration of the matter, as was said above, not in the sacrament's use. But ordained ministers are the ministers of the sacraments. Therefore, even if the consecration of the matter pertains only to priests, nevertheless the administering should pertain to all.

OBJ. 2: Furthermore, the sacrament should be administered by those who treat it with reverence. But some laymen have greater reverence for the sacrament than even priests; and sometimes even women. Therefore, the sacrament can be administered by them.

OBJ. 3: Furthermore, as it belongs to priests to administer the body of Christ, so also to touch it. But in a certain case it is permitted for a layman to touch the body of Christ, for example, if he saw it lying on the ground, and there were no priest who could pick it up. Therefore, in a certain case he is also allowed to administer it.

ON THE CONTRARY, it is said in *On Consecration*, Distinction 2, that it a priest is restrained even from sending this sacrament to the sick through laymen.[43]

FURTHERMORE, those to whom it belongs to be ministers of the Church are also dispensers of God's mysteries: *let a man so consider us as ministers of Christ and dispensers of God's mysteries* (1 Cor 4). But laymen are not ministers of the Church. Therefore, they should not be dispensers of the sacraments.

Quaestiuncula 2

ULTERIUS. Videtur quod diaconus possit dispensare. Quia beatus Laurentius diaconus fuit. Sibi autem commissa fuit dispensatio Dominici sanguinis, ut patet in legenda sua. Ergo diaconus potest dispensare.

PRAETEREA, dispensatio hujus sacramenti ad populi curationem pertinet. Sed diaconus potest habere curam

OBJ. 1: Moreover, it seems that a deacon can administer it.[44] For blessed Laurence was a deacon. But the administering of the Lord's blood was entrusted to him, as is known from his legend.[45] Therefore, a deacon can administer this sacrament.

OBJ. 2: Furthermore, the administering of this sacrament pertains to the care of the people. But a deacon can

---

42. Parallel: *ST* III, q. 82, a. 3.

43. Gratian's *Decretals*, Part 3, *De consecratione*, d. 2, ch. 29 (PL 187:1743).

44. Parallel: *ST* III, q. 82, a. 3, corp. and ad 1.

45. As is written in *The Golden Legend*, ch. 117, Laurence ran after Sixtus while the latter was being led away to his martyrdom, crying out: "Where are you going, father, without your son? . . . Try me, surely, to see whether you have chosen a minister suitable to have the dispensing of the Lord's Blood entrusted to him!" (Ryan ed., 2:64).

animarum. Ergo et ipse est dispensator hujus sacramenti.

SED CONTRA est quod dicit canon dist. 93: *non oportet diaconum panem dare*, idest corpus Christi.

have care of souls. Therefore, he can also be a minister of this sacrament.

ON THE CONTRARY, it says in Canon Distinction 93: *it is not fitting for the deacon to give the bread*, that is, the body of Christ.[46]

Quaestiuncula 3

ULTERIUS. Videtur quod aliquis possit licite recipere dispensationem sacramenti a fornicario vel excommunicato vel haeretico sacerdote. Augustinus enim dicit: *neque in homine bono, neque in homine malo aliquis sacramenta Dei fugiat*. Ergo potest a quolibet sacerdote hoc sacramentum recipere.

PRAETEREA, virtus divina praevalet malitiae humanae. Sed sacramentum divina virtute continet gratiam, et causat. Ergo quantumcumque sit malus ille qui dederit, vel haereticus, consequitur gratiam qui ab eo sacramentum recipit.

PRAETEREA, iniquitas sacerdotis non potest ipsum corpus Christi inquinare. Sed hoc sacramentum ex ipso opere operato, quod est corpus Christi, gratiam confert. Ergo etiam si aliquis sit excommunicatus vel haereticus, sacramentum ab eo perceptum gratiam confert.

SED CONTRA est quod dicit canon: *nullus Missam audiat sacerdotis quem scit concubinam indubitanter habere*. Ergo peccat qui recipit sacramentum a concubinario sacerdote.

PRAETEREA, nullus debet recipere sacramentum praeter institutionem ecclesiae; quia indignus accederet. Sed aliqui secundum institutionem ecclesiae sunt suspensi. Ergo non licet ab eis sacramenta recipere.

OBJ. 1: Moreover, it seems that someone could licitly receive this sacrament administered by a fornicating priest, or an excommunicated or heretical priest.[47] For Augustine says: *neither in a good man nor in a bad man does anyone escape the sacraments of God*.[48] Therefore, this sacrament can be received from any kind of priest.

OBJ. 2: Furthermore, divine power is stronger than human wickedness. But the sacrament contains and causes grace by divine power. Therefore, no matter how wicked the man who gives it is, or whether he is a heretic, whoever receives the sacrament from him obtains grace.

OBJ. 3: Furthermore, the wickedness of a priest cannot soil the body of Christ itself. But this sacrament, which is the body of Christ, confers grace by the very accomplishment of the action. Therefore, even if someone is excommunicated or a heretic, the sacrament received from him confers grace.

ON THE CONTRARY, the canon says: *no one may hear the Mass of a priest whom he knows without a doubt to keep a concubine*.[49] Therefore, whoever receives the sacrament from a cohabiting priest sins.

FURTHERMORE, no one should receive the sacrament outside the institution of the Church, for he would approach unworthily. But certain people are suspended according to the Church's institution. Therefore, it is not permitted to receive the sacrament from them.

Response to Quaestiuncula 1

RESPONDEO dicendum ad primam quaestionem, quod sicut in corpore naturali sunt quaedam membra principalia, per quae virtutes et operationes vitae a principio vitae ad cetera membra decurrunt; ita et in ecclesia sacerdotes et alii ministri sunt quasi membra principalia quibus mediantibus sacramenta vitae populo dispensari debent; et ita laicis, quantumcumque sanctis, sicut nec consecratio, ita nec dispensatio hujus sacramenti competit.

TO THE FIRST QUESTION, I answer that just as in a natural body there are certain principal members, through which the powers and operations of life pass from the principle of life to the other members, so also in the Church the priests and other ministers are like principal members by whose mediation the sacraments of life should be dispensed to the people. And so, just as consecration is not befitting to laypeople, no matter how holy they are, neither is the administering of this sacrament.

---

46. Gratian's *Decretals*, Part 1, dist. 93, ch. 16 (PL 187:438).

47. Parallels: below, d. 24, q. 1, a. 3, qa. 5, ad 3 & 4; *ST* III, q. 64, a. 9, ad 3; q. 82, a. 9; *Quodl.* XI, q. 8, aa. 1–2.

48. As given in the text of the *Decretals*, Part 2, c. 1, q. 1, ch. 35 (PL 187:498); however, the original text, from Augustine, *Contra epistulam Parmeniani*, Bk. 3, ch. 9, par. 10 (CSEL 52:171): "nemo glorietur nec in homine bono, nemo bona dei fugiat nec in homine malo."

49. Gratian's *Decretals*, Part 1, d. 32, ch. 5 (PL 187:177).

AD PRIMUM ergo dicendum, quod quamvis in essentia sua sacramentum sit perfectum sine usu sacramenti, tamen perfectionem quantum ad effectum sine usu non habet; et ideo etiam usus sacramenti hujus ad dispensationem ministrorum ecclesiae pertinet.

AD SECUNDUM dicendum, quod in hoc sacramento ad reverentiam ipsius non solum exigitur sanctificatio morum, sed etiam sacramentalis sanctificatio: quia et ipse calix in quo sanctitas morum esse non potest, consecratur propter reverentiam sacramenti; et similiter in dispensante hoc sacramentum debet esse utraque sanctificatio; unde et manus sacerdotis unctione sanctificantur, sicut et calix. Et ideo quia laicus hanc sanctitatem non habet, ideo non potest hoc sacramentum dispensare.

AD TERTIUM dicendum, quod sicut baptismum conferre competit sacerdoti ex officio, tamen laicus in casu necessitatis non peccat baptizans; ita tangere corpus Christi ex officio soli sacerdoti competit; sed in casu necessitatis potest et debet corpus Christi tangere, etiam si sit peccator, ut si in aliquo loco immundo jaceret. Sed non est simile de dispensatione sacramenti: quia receptio hujus sacramenti non est necessitatis; unde ei qui non potest sacramentaliter manducare, dicendum est: *crede et manducasti.*

REPLY OBJ. 1: Although in its essence, this sacrament is complete without the sacrament's use, nevertheless, it is not complete as regards its effect without its use. And therefore this sacrament's use also pertains to the administering of the ministers of the Church.

REPLY OBJ. 2: For this sacrament's reverence, not only sanctification of morals is required, but also sacramental sanctification: for even the very chalice, in which there cannot exist holiness of morals, is consecrated out of reverence for the sacrament. And in the same way, in the person administering this sacrament there should be both kinds of sanctification, which is why not only are the priest's hands sanctified by anointing, but also the chalice. And thus, since a layman does not have this sanctity, for this reason he cannot administer this sacrament.

REPLY OBJ. 3: Just as it belongs to the priest to confer baptism by his office, though a layman does not sin by baptizing in an emergency, so also to touch the body of Christ belongs to a priest alone by his office, but in an emergency, for example if it were lying in some unclean place, he can and should touch the body of Christ, even if he is a sinner. But the administering of the sacrament is not the same, for the reception of this sacrament is not of necessity; and so to anyone who cannot eat it sacramentally, it should be said, *believe and you will have eaten.*[50]

Response to Quaestiuncula 2

AD SECUNDAM QUAESTIONEM dicendum, quod dispensatio hujus sacramenti proprie ad sacerdotem pertinet, eo quod ipse repraesentat Christum, qui fuit mediator Dei et hominum; unde cum hoc sacramentum sit ad reconciliandum nos Deo, debet per sacerdotem, qui est mediator inter Deum et populum, dispensari. Sed sicut sacerdos, ut dictum est, participat aliquid de virtute perfectiva, quae est episcopi, ita diaconus participat aliquid de dispensatione hujus sacramenti: competit enim ei ex officio sanguinem Domini dispensare, sed non corpus: quia dispensator corporis oportet quod ipsum corpus tangat, non autem dispensator sanguinis: diacono autem non licet corpus Christi tangere, cum non habeat manus consecratas; et ideo non debet corpus dispensare nisi de mandato presbyteri vel episcopi, vel presbytero longe posito in casu necessitatis. Vel ideo dispensat sanguinem et non corpus, quia per sanguinem significatur redemptionis mysterium, quod a capite Christo in membra diffunditur officio ministrorum; unde et sanguini aqua, quae populum significat, admiscetur; sed incarnatio, quam corpus Christi significat, non est humano ministerio facta.

TO THE SECOND QUESTION, it should be said that the administering of this sacrament properly belongs to the priest by the fact that he represents Christ, who was the mediator of God and men. Hence, since this sacrament is for reconciling us to God, it ought to be administered by a priest, who is the mediator between God and the people. But just as a priest, as was said, participates in something of the perfective power that belongs to a bishop, so also a deacon participates in something of the administering of this sacrament, for it belongs to him by office to dispense the Lord's blood but not his body. For the minister of the body must touch the body, but the minister of the blood need not. However, it is not permitted for a deacon to touch the body of Christ, since he does not have consecrated hands. And so he should not administer the body except by the special command of the priest or bishop, or when the priest is far away in an emergency. Or he administers the blood and not the body for this reason, that the mystery of redemption is signified by the blood, which flows down from Christ the head to his members by the office of his ministers, and so also the water which signifies the people is mixed into the blood. But the Incarnation, which the body of Christ signifies, did not happen by human ministry.

---

50. Augustine, *In Iohannis euangelium tractatus* (CCSL 36), Tract. 26, par. 1.

AD PRIMUM ergo dicendum, quod quamvis fuerit dispensator sanguinis, non tamen legitur fuisse dispensator corporis; unde et adhuc hodie in quibusdam ecclesiis sanguis per diaconum ministris altaris dispensatur.

AD SECUNDUM dicendum, quod diaconus potest habere curam animarum quantum ad ea quae jurisdictionis sunt, sed non quantum ad ea quae sunt ordinis: dispensatio autem sacramentorum ad ordinem pertinet.

REPLY OBJ. 1: Although he was minister of the blood, nevertheless it is not read that he was minister of the body; and so also to this day in any church the blood is administered to the altar servers by a deacon.

REPLY OBJ. 2: A deacon can have the care of souls as to what belongs to legal authority, but not as to those things that belong to priestly orders; and the administering of the sacraments pertains to priestly orders.

Response to Quaestiuncula 3

AD TERTIAM QUAESTIONEM dicendum, quod si aliquis cum peccato ad hoc sacramentum accedit, magis cedit ei in nocumentum quam in profectum. Quicumque autem contra ordinationem ecclesiae accedit, per inobedientiam peccat. Simoniaci autem et schismatici et excommunicati ex statuto ecclesiae a dispensatione hujus sacramenti sunt suspensi: quia sunt extra unitatem ecclesiae, in qua sacramenta conferuntur; et similiter interdictum est concubinariis sacerdotibus propter spiritualitatem maximam quae in hoc sacramento requiritur. Unde si aliquis ab aliquo praedictorum sacramentum suscipiat, peccat, et sic gratiam non consequitur. Tamen differt de fornicariis et aliis praedictis: quia aliis non debet homo communicare in divinis scienter, quantumcumque sint occulti; sed concubinarii sacerdotes non sunt vitandi, nisi sint notorii. Et dicuntur notorii tribus modis: vel propter sententiam, quia convicti sunt; vel per confessionem in jure factam; vel per rei evidentiam, sicut quando est ita manifestum quod nulla potest tergiversatione celari. Ab aliis autem peccatoribus licet sacramenta recipere.

AD PRIMUM ergo dicendum, quod inquantum est malus, non fugitur, sed propter ecclesiae prohibitionem. Vel dicendum, quod Augustinus dicit quod sacramenta non sunt fugienda, quia cognoscendum est etiam ab eis verum perfici sacramentum.

AD SECUNDUM dicendum, quod quamvis sacramentum virtutem suam non amittat, tamen in eo qui indigne accedit contra obedientiam ecclesiae faciens, effectum non habet.

ET SIMILITER dicendum ad tertium.

TO THE THIRD QUESTION, it should be said that if anyone approaches this sacrament with sin, it will be more to his damage than his advancement. But anyone who approaches against the ordering of the Church sins by disobedience. Now simoniacs and schismatics and the excommunicated are suspended from administering this sacrament by the Church's decree: for they are outside the unity of the Church, in which the sacraments are conferred. Likewise it is forbidden to cohabiting priests because of the supreme spirituality that is required in this sacrament. This is why if someone receives the sacrament from one of these, he sins, and so he does not receive grace. Nevertheless, there is a difference between fornicating priests and the others mentioned: for a man should not share with the others in divine things knowingly, however much they are private; but fornicating priests are not to be avoided unless they are notorious. And there are three ways of being called notorious: either because of public opinion, because people are convinced; or by having confessed it in court; or by the obviousness of the matter, as when it is so evident that no one can turn a blind eye to it. But from other sinners it is permitted to receive the sacraments.

REPLY OBJ. 1: He is not fled because he is wicked, but because of the Church's prohibition. Or it could be said that Augustine says that the sacraments are not to be fled, for one must also be recognized that a valid sacrament is consecrated by them.

REPLY OBJ. 2: Although the sacrament does not lose its power, nevertheless in someone who approaches unworthily by acting against obedience to the Church, it does not have its effect.

AND THE SAME THING should be said to the third objection.

QUESTION 2

HERESY

Deinde quaeritur de haeresi; et circa hoc quaeruntur tria:

    primo, quid faciat haereticum;

    secundo, utrum haeresis sit majus peccatum aliis;

    tertio, utrum haeretici sint tolerandi.

Next it should be asked about heresy, and concerning this, three questions arise:

    first, what a heretic does;

    second, whether heresy is a greater sin than others;

    third, whether heretics are to be tolerated.

ARTICLE 1

What a heretic does[51]

AD PRIMUM SIC PROCEDITUR. Videtur quod haeresis non dicat perversitatem fidei. *Haeresis enim*, ut dicit Isidorus, *idem est quod divisio*. Divisio autem unioni opponitur; unio autem fit per caritatem, quia amor est unitiva virtus, ut dicit Dionysius. Ergo haeresis non pertinet ad perversitatem fidei, sed magis ad perversitatem odii.

PRAETEREA, schisma divisionem importat; et ita videntur schismatici haeretici esse. Sed schismatici non semper habent fidei perversitatem. Ergo haeresis non consistit in perversitate fidei.

PRAETEREA, simoniaci non errant in fide. Sed tamen simoniaci sunt haeretici: quia, ut dicit Gregorius in registro: *qui per pecuniam ordinatur, haereticus promovetur*. Ergo haeresis non importat errorem in fide.

PRAETEREA, superstitio religioni opponitur, non fidei. Sed haeresis superstitio dicitur. Ergo non pertinet ad fidei perversitatem, sed magis ad perversitatem religionis.

PRAETEREA, Hieronymus dicit, quod *ex verbis inordinate prolatis incurritur haeresis*. Sed fides non consistit in verbis oris, sed in assensu cordis. Ergo haeresis non dicit perversitatem fidei.

PRAETEREA, multa sunt de his quae ad fidem pertinent, in quibus sunt contrariae opiniones; et sic oportet alteram earum esse falsam; nec tamen aliqua judicatur haeretica. Ergo tota ratio haeresis non consistit in perversitate fidei.

OBJ. 1: To the first we proceed thus. It seems that 'heresy' does not mean a perversion of the faith. For *heresy is the same as division*, as Isidore says.[52] But division is opposed to union. Now union happens by charity, for love is the unitive virtue, as Dionysius says.[53] Therefore, heresy does not pertain to a perversion of the faith, but rather to a perversion of hatred.

OBJ. 2: Furthermore, schism conveys division, and so it seems that schismatics are heretics. But schismatics do not always hold a perversion of the faith. Therefore, heresy does not consist in the perversion of the faith.

OBJ. 3: Furthermore, simoniacs do not err in the faith. But nevertheless simoniacs are heretics, for, as Gregory says in the register: *let anyone who is ordained for money be brought forth as a heretic*.[54] Therefore, heresy does not include error in the faith.

OBJ. 4: Furthermore, superstition is opposed to religion, not to faith. But superstition is called a heresy. Therefore, it does not pertain to the perversion of the faith, but rather to the perversion of religion.

OBJ. 5: Furthermore, Jerome says that *heresy is incurred by words uttered inordinately*.[55] But faith does not consist in words of the mouth, but in the assent of the heart. Therefore, heresy does not mean a perversion of the faith.

OBJ. 6: Furthermore, there are many things relating to the faith in which there are contrary opinions, and so one of them must be false; but nevertheless it is not judged to be heretical. Therefore, heresy's whole nature does not consist in the perversion of the faith.

---

51. Parallels: *ST* II-II, q. 10, a. 5; q. 11, a. 12; q. 104, a. 1, ad 1.

52. In fact, Isidore nowhere says this; Thomas more correctly cites Isidore below, in his response.

53. Pseudo-Dionysius, *On the Divine Names*, ch. 4, n. 15 (PG 3:714).

54. As the Patrologia volume of the *Decretals* indicates in a note, this sentence is not found in Gregory's epistles, although the *Decretals* attribute it to him; see p. 2, cause 1, q. 1, ch. 5 (PL 187:480). Moos, however, refers to Gregory's *Register*, Bk. 9, epist. 106 (PL 77:1029).

55. In the text of Lombard, d. 13, ch. 2; see *Glossa ordinaria* on Hos. 2:16.

PRAETEREA, Judaei habent perversam fidem, nec tamen haeretici dicuntur. Ergo omnis haeresis non consistit in perversitate fidei.

PRAETEREA, multi habent perversam fidem qui non habent novam opinionem, sicut Manichaei. Sed habere novam opinionem est de essentia haeresis, sicut patet per definitionem Augustini. Ergo, etc.

PRAETEREA, multi habent perversam opinionem in iis quae sunt fidei, qui ex hoc nullum commodum temporale sperant. Sed hoc est de essentia haeresis, ut patet per Augustinum. Ergo, etc.

SED CONTRA, haeresis est peccatum. Ergo alicui virtuti opponitur. Sed nulla cognitio inter virtutes computatur nisi fides. Ergo cum haeresis ad cognitionem pertineat, ut ex definitione Augustini patet; ubi supra, videtur quod haeresis sit perversitas fidei.

PRAETEREA, hoc patet ex communi usu loquendi.

RESPONDEO dicendum, quod nomen haeresis Graecum est, et electionem importat secundum Isidorum; unde et haeretica divisiva dicuntur. Et quia in electione fit divisio unius ab altero, electio prohaeresis dicitur, ut patet 9 *Metaphysica* Divisio autem contingit alicui parti per recessum a toto. Prima autem congregatio quae est in hominibus, est per viam cognitionis, quia ex hac omnes aliae oriuntur; unde et haeresis consistit in singulari opinione praeter communem opinionem. Unde et Philosophi qui quasdam positiones habebant praeter communem sententiam aliorum, sectas vel haereses proprias constituebant. Sed quia nullus denominatur ab eo quod inest sibi imperfecte, sed solum quando confirmatur in illo (sicut non dicitur iracundus cui inest passio irae, sed qui passibilis est de facili ab ea; neque qui habet dispositionem dicitur sanus), ideo neque haereticus nominatur nisi qui in singulari opinione firmam habet stabilitatem; unde etiam competit ei nomen haeresis, secundum quod in electionem sonat: quia quod in electione fit, quasi ex habitu firmato procedit. Competit ei etiam nomen haeresis, secundum quod Latinum est, ab haerendo dictum: quia suae opinioni vehementer inhaeret. Et quia congregatio corporis mystici per unitatem verae fidei primo constituitur, ideo haereticus secundum nos dicitur qui a communi fide, quae Catholica dicitur, discedit, contrariae opinioni vehementer inhaerens per electionem.

OBJ. 7: Furthermore, the Jews hold a perversion of the faith, yet they are not called heretics. Therefore, not every heresy consists in the perversion of the faith.

OBJ. 8: Furthermore, many people hold a perversion of the faith who do not hold new opinions, like the Manichees. But to hold a new opinion is essential to heresy, as is clear from Augustine's definition.[56] Therefore, etc.

OBJ. 9: Furthermore, many people hold a perverse opinion in things that belong to the faith who do not hope for any temporal benefit from this. Yet that is essential to heresy, as is clear from Augustine.[57] Therefore, etc.

ON THE CONTRARY, heresy is a sin. Therefore, it is opposed to some virtue. But no knowledge is counted among the virtues except faith. Therefore since heresy belongs to knowledge, as is evident from Augustine's definition cited above, it seems that heresy is a perversion of the faith.

FURTHERMORE, this is clear from the common way of speaking.

I ANSWER THAT, 'heresy' is a Greek word, and it means a choosing, according to Isidore, and this is why heresy is also said to be divisive.[58] And since in choosing, a division is made of one thing from another, choosing is called pro-heresy, as is clear in *Metaphysics* 9.[59] But a division occurs by removing one part from the whole. Now, the first thing that brings people together is a way of knowing, for from that all others arise. And so heresy also consists in holding an individual opinion apart from the common opinion. And for this reason the philosophers who held certain positions outside the common judgment of others established their own sects or 'heresies.'[60] But because no one is named by what is in him incompletely, but only when he is confirmed in it (as a man is not called hot-tempered by having the passion of anger in himself, but by being easily overcome by it, nor is someone called healthy from being merely disposed to it). And so neither is someone called a heretic unless he is firmly entrenched in an individual opinion. And so the name heresy also applies to him according as it means choosing, because what happens in a choosing proceeds from something like a firm habit. The name heresy also applies to him in Latin, as coming from *haerere*, sticking, for he sticks to his own opinion stubbornly. And since the mystical body is first brought together by the unity of the true faith, this is why in our opinion someone is called a heretic who departs from the common faith that is called Catholic, sticking stubbornly to a contrary opinion of his own choosing.

---

56. In the text of Lombard, ch. 2; see Augustine, *De utilitate credendi* (CSEL 25), ch. 1, n. 1.

57. This and the next reference are to the same passage.

58. Isidore writes: "Haeresis Graece ab electione uocatur, quod scilicet unusquisque id sibi eligat quod melius illi esse uidetur, ut philosophi Peripatetici, Academici, et Epicurei et Stoici, uel sicut alii qui peruersum dogma cogitantes arbitrio suo de Ecclesia recesserunt. Inde ergo haeresis, dicta Graeca uoce, ex interpretatione electionis, qua quisque arbitrio suo ad instituenda, siue ad suscipienda quaelibet ipse sibi elegit" (*Etymologiarum siue Originum libri XX* [ed. Lindsay], Bk. 8, ch. 3). Moos "corrects" *electionem* to *divisionem*, as objection 1 also reads. If Moos is correct, Thomas would be misquoting Isidore twice.

59. Aristotle, *Nicomachean Ethics*, Bk. 1, ch. 1 (1094a2).

60. See the Isidore quotation above, which connects the term with the schools of philosophy.

AD PRIMUM ergo dicendum, quod amor facit completam unionem; sed principium unionis est ex cognitione; et ideo divisio quae est in fide, haeresim constituit.

AD SECUNDUM dicendum, quod schisma importat divisionem oppositam caritatis unioni: dicuntur enim schismatici qui concordiam non servant in ecclesiae observantiis, ut ecclesiae praelatis obediant, volentes per se ecclesiam constituere singularem: et isti in principio perversum dogma non habent, sed ab ecclesiae fundamento recedentes in vaniloquium vertuntur, et perversum dogma aliquod confingunt, et sic in fine in haeresim labuntur; unde Hieronymus dicit, quod haeresis et schisma differunt sicut genus et species.

AD TERTIUM dicendum, quod simoniaci quandoque dicuntur per similitudinem haeretici: quia sicut haereticus contra fidem sentit, ita simoniacus operatur ac si contra fidem sentiret, dum pretio sacra vult adipisci vel dare, ac si aestimaret donum Spiritus Sancti pecunia possideri.

AD QUARTUM dicendum, quod fides est primum eorum quae ad religionem requiruntur: quia omnis religio, sive cultus Dei, est quaedam fidei protestatio; et ideo veritas fidei dicitur veritas quae secundum pietatem est, Tit. 1; ideo etiam ea quae haeresis sunt, ad superstitionem pertinent.

AD QUINTUM dicendum, quod fides principaliter consistit in corde et primo, sed secundario in ore: quia *corde creditur ad justitiam, ore confessio fit ad salutem*; Rom. 10, 10; et similiter haeresis principaliter consistit in corde, secundum quod Hilarius dicit: *intellectivae sensus in animo est*, sed *secundario in ore*. Unde Hieronymus dicit, quod *ex verbis inordinate prolatis incurritur haeresis*, non quia haeresis per se in his consistat, sed quia sunt occasio et causa erroris.

AD SEXTUM dicendum, quod in fide sunt aliqua ad quae explicite cognoscenda omnis homo tenetur; unde si in his aliquis errat, infidelis reputatur, et haereticus, si pertinaciam adjungat. Si autem sunt aliqua ad quae explicite credenda homo non tenetur, non efficietur haereticus in his errans; ut si aliquis simplex credat, Jacob patrem fuisse Abrahae, quod est contra veritatem Scripturae quam fides profitetur, quousque hoc sibi innotescat, quod fides ecclesiae contrarium habet: quia non discedit per se loquendo a fide ecclesiae nisi ille qui scit hoc a quo recedit, de fide ecclesiae esse. Et quia quaedam sunt quae in fide ecclesiae implicite continentur, ut conclusiones in principiis; ideo in his diversae opiniones sustinentur, quousque per ecclesiam determinatur quod

REPLY OBJ. 1: Love makes a union complete, but the beginning of union comes out of knowing. And so a division that is in the faith constitutes heresy.

REPLY OBJ. 2: Schism conveys a division opposed to the union of love, for those are called schismatics who do not keep agreement in the Church's observances by obeying the Church's prelates, wanting instead to establish an individual church by themselves. And they do not have a subverted dogma in the beginning, but by withdrawing from the Church's foundation they turn to idle talk, and devise some subverted dogma, and that is how they fall into heresy in the end. And so Jerome says that heresy and schism differ as genus and species.[61]

REPLY OBJ. 3: Simoniacs are sometimes called heretics by their resemblance, for just as a heretic believes against the faith, so a simoniac acts as if he believed against the faith as long as he wants to obtain or give sacred things for a price, as if he thought the gift of the Holy Spirit was possessed by money.

REPLY OBJ. 4: Faith is the first of the things that are required for religion, for every act of religion or worship of God is a certain protestation of faith. And therefore the truth of the faith is called the truth that is according to godliness (cf. Tit 1:1). And so those things that are heresies also pertain to superstition.

REPLY OBJ. 5: Faith subsists principally and first in the heart, but secondarily in the mouth, for *it is believed in the heart for righteousness, and confessed with the mouth for salvation* (Rom 10:10). And in the same way heresy chiefly subsists in the heart, as Hilary says: *the intellect's meaning is in the soul, but secondarily, in the mouth*.[62] Hence Jerome says that *heresy is incurred by words inordinately spoken*, not because heresy consists in them per se, but because they are an occasion and cause of error.

REPLY OBJ. 6: In faith there are certain things that every man is bound to recognize explicitly, and so if someone errs in these things, he is considered an unbeliever, and a heretic, if he adds obstinacy to it. But if there are certain things that a man is not bound to believe explicitly, he is not made a heretic by erring in these things; as if someone simple believes that Jacob was the father of Abraham, which is against the truth of scripture that faith professes, until it becomes known to him that the Church's faith holds the contrary; for no one departs from the Church's faith, speaking essentially, unless it is someone who knows that what he is withdrawing from is the Church's faith. And since there are certain things that are contained implicitly in the Church's faith as conclusions in their principles, this is the reason

---

61. Jerome, *Commentarii in iv epistulas Paulinas, Ad Titum*, ch. 3, 10 (PL 26:598).

62. Moos says this text has not been located in the works of Hilary. One wonders if the following might not have formed a basis: *Tractatus super psalmos* (CCSL 61A), Ps. 118, par. 11: "Sed Dei eloquia in faucibus dulcia sunt, in animam scilicet defluentia et interna penetrantia, non in ore modo cibi placentia, sed illic dulcia ubi cognitionis et prudentiae et intellegentiae sensus est."

aliquid eorum contra fidem ecclesiae est, quia ex eo sequitur aliquid contrarium fidei directe.

AD SEPTIMUM dicendum, quod dividi non convenit nisi parti; et ideo illi qui nunquam fuerunt de fide ecclesiae, non reputantur haeretici, si perversam fidem habeant, ut Judaei vel pagani: quia nunquam fuerunt partes hujus totius quod est ecclesia.

AD OCTAVUM dicendum, quod omnis opinio quae non habet initium a doctrina Christi, quae est fundamentum, nova reputatur, quantumcumque secundum tempus sit antiqua. Vel dicendum, quod Augustinus loquitur quantum ad primos haeresum inventores.

AD NONUM dicendum, quod illi qui haeresim confingunt de novo, constat quod aliquod expectant commodum, saltem principatum: volunt enim habere sequaces. Hoc etiam in omnibus ex superbia procedit, quae est amor propriae excellentiae, quod a communi via discedunt animi levitate aut perversitate.

that different opinions are allowed in them, until it is determined by the Church that one of them is against the Church's faith, because something contrary to the faith follows directly from it.

REPLY OBJ. 7: Being divided only applies to parts; and so those who never were of the Church's faith, like Jews and pagans, are not considered to be heretics, if they hold a perverted faith, for they were never parts of this whole that is the Church.

REPLY OBJ. 8: Every opinion that does not have its start in Christ's teaching, which is the foundation, is considered to be new, no matter how ancient it is in time. Or it could be said that Augustine is speaking about the first inventors of heresy.

REPLY OBJ. 9: It is clear that those who devise new heresies are looking for some benefit, at least domination: for they want to have followers. In all of them this also proceeds from pride, which is the love of one's own excellence, that souls depart from the common path by frivolousness or by stubbornness.

ARTICLE 2

Whether heresy is a greater sin than others[63]

AD SECUNDUM SIC PROCEDITUR. Videtur quod haeresis non sit maximum peccatum. Maxima enim peccata videntur esse principalia peccata: quia illud est maximum in unoquoque genere quod est principale. Sed haeresis non est principale vitium. Ergo non est maximum.

PRAETEREA, secundum Philosophum in 8 *Ethic.*, pessimum opponitur optimo. Sed fides cui opponitur haeresis, non est optima virtutum. Ergo nec haeresis est maximum peccatum.

PRAETEREA, illud quod excusat, non est maximum peccatorum. Sed haeresis vel infidelitas excusat; 1 Tim., 1, 13: *sed misericordiam consecutus sum, quia ignorans feci in incredulitate mea.* Ergo haeresis non est maximum peccatum.

PRAETEREA, secundum mensuram peccati est mensura poenae. Sed secundum Hieronymum, peccatum schismatis est magis punitum quam aliquod aliud peccatum: quia absorpti sunt a terra; ut patet Numer. 16. Ergo haeresis non est maximum peccatum.

PRAETEREA, peccatum in Spiritum Sanctum est gravius ceteris peccatis. Sed haeresis non est hujusmodi. Ergo non est gravissimum.

SED CONTRA, in epistola Clementis dicitur, quod primum locum in poenis habent qui aberrant a Deo. Sed tales sunt haeretici. Ergo, etc.

PRAETEREA, Ambrosius dicit: *gravissime peccas, si ignoras.* Sed haeretici ignorantiam Dei habent. Ergo gravissime peccant.

PRAETEREA, Dionysius dicit, quod *ille qui habet participationem quamdam sacratissimarum consummationum, non est aequalis universaliter indocto, et non participanti aliquam divinarum teletarum,* idest consecrationum.[69] Sed tales sunt haeretici. Ergo alii peccatores non sunt eis aequandi in malo.

RESPONDEO dicendum, quod unumquodque dicitur malum quia nocet. Unde cum haeresis plus noceat quam aliquod aliud peccatum, quia subvertit fundamentum omnium bonorum, sine quo nihil boni remanet; ideo haeresis est ex genere suo maximum peccatorum, quamvis ex accidenti aliquod peccatum possit esse gravius; sicut si multum cresceret contemptus Dei in aliquo

OBJ. 1: To the second we proceed thus. It seems that heresy is not the greatest sin. For the greatest sins seem to be the chief sins: for the greatest thing in any genus is what is principal. But heresy is not chief among vices. Therefore, it is not the greatest.

OBJ. 2: Furthermore, according to the Philosopher in *Ethics* 8,[64] the worst is the opposite of the best. But faith, to which heresy is opposed, is not the best of virtues. Therefore, neither is heresy the greatest sin.

OBJ. 3: Furthermore, what is excusable is not the greatest of sins. But heresy or unbelief is excusable: *but I obtained mercy, because I acted unknowing in my unbelief* (1 Tim 1:13). Therefore, heresy is not the greatest sin.

OBJ. 4: Furthermore, the measure of punishment is according to the measure of the sin. But according to Jerome,[65] the sin of schism is punished more than any other sin: for they are swallowed up by the earth, as is seen in Numbers 16:32. Therefore, heresy is not the greatest sin.

OBJ. 5: Furthermore, the sin against the Holy Spirit is graver than other sins. But heresy is not this kind of sin. Therefore, it is not the most grave.

ON THE CONTRARY, in the letter of Clement it says that those who wander away from God hold the first place in punishments.[66] But such people are heretics. Therefore, etc.

FURTHERMORE, Ambrose says: *you sin most seriously if you do not know.*[67] But heretics have ignorance of God. Therefore, they sin most seriously.

FURTHERMORE, Dionysius says that *that man who has a certain participation of most sacred consummations is not the equal of someone entirely untaught, or of one who does not partake of divine ceremonies,* that is, of sacraments.[68] But this kind of person is a heretic. Therefore, other sinners are not to be equated with them in wickedness.

I ANSWER THAT, anyone who does harm is called wicked. And so since heresy harms more than any other sin, because it subverts the foundation of all goods without which nothing of good remains, this is why heresy is the greatest sin in kind, although some other sin could be more serious incidentally, as for example if contempt of God were to grow more in something that was even a venial sin by its

---

63. Parallels: *ST* II-II, q. 10, a. 3; q. 20, a. 3; q. 34, a. 2, ad 2; q. 39, a. 2, ad 3; *ST* III, q. 80, a. 5; *De malo*, q. 2, a. 10; *Super I ad Tim.* 5, lec. 1.

64. Aristotle, *Nicomachean Ethics*, Bk. 8, ch. 12 (1160b9).

65. In the ancient *Decretals* Jerome was cited as the source, but later editions correctly attribute the statement to Augustine: see PL 187:264 and the source, *De baptismo*, Bk 2, ch. 6, par. 9 (CSEL 51:183).

66. *Epistle of Clement*, n. 7 (PG 2:42).

67. Apparently not from Ambrose, this comment on Romans 2:4 may be found in the *Glossa ordinaria* and the *Glossa Lombardi* (PL 191:1338).

68. Pseudo-Dionysius, *Ecclesiastical Hierarchy*, ch. 3 (PG 3:423).

69. *consecrationum.*—*sacramentorum* PLE.

quod etiam ex genere suo esset veniale. Sed *de eo quod est secundum accidens, non est curandum in arte*, ut Philosophus dicit in 5 *Ethic.*

AD PRIMUM ergo dicendum, quod sicut secundum Philosophum in 7 *Ethic.*, bestialitas ponitur extra numerum aliarum humanarum malitiarum, quia humanum modum transcendit; ita a sanctis ponitur haeresis extra numerum peccatorum, quae in fidelibus inveniuntur, quasi gravius eis; et ideo non computatur inter vitia capitalia, nec inter eorum filias: quia vitia capitalia, secundum Isidorum in Glossa Deuteronom. 7, signantur per septem populos, qui in terra promissionis non remanserunt. Tamen si ad aliquod de septem capitalibus reduci debeat, poterit ad superbiam reduci, ut per definitionem Augustini in littera positam patet.

AD SECUNDUM dicendum, quod verbum Philosophi intelligendum est in his quae non sunt ordinata ad invicem, in quibus destructo uno alterum non destruitur. Sed in ordinatis ad invicem destructio prioris semper est pejor, sive illud sit melius, sive non; quia eo remoto consequentia removentur; sicut aegritudo est pejor quam sanitas.[73]

AD TERTIUM dicendum, quod sicut fides habet aliquid in affectu, ita et haeresis; et quamvis ex illa parte qua habet ignorantiam in intellectu, aliquo modo excusare possit; tamen secundum quod habet duritiam in affectu ad non obediendum primae veritati, nihil prohibet eam esse maximum peccatorum.

AD QUARTUM dicendum, quod quamvis schisma fuerit gravius punitum quantum ad novitatem poenae (quia expediebat ut praelati ecclesiae non contemnerentur), tamen infidelitas est magis punita quantum ad multitudinem punitorum, ut patet Exod. 20.

AD QUINTUM dicendum, quod haeresis, secundum quod pertinaciam importat, species est peccati in Spiritum Sanctum, quia est impugnatio veritatis agnitae.

genus. But *what is incidental is not the concern of an art*, as the Philosopher says in *Ethics* 5.[70]

REPLY OBJ. 1: As the Philosopher says in *Ethics* 7, bestiality is counted outside the number of other human wickednesses, because it goes beyond the human manner.[71] In the same way, the saints count heresy outside the number of sins that are found among the faithful, as more serious than they. And this is why it is not reckoned among the capital vices, nor among their daughter vices, for capital vices, according to Isidore in the Gloss on Deuteronomy 7,[72] are represented by the seven nations that did not remain in the land of promise. Nevertheless if the seven capital vices had to be reduced to one, they could be reduced to pride, as is evident from Augustine's definition included in the text.

REPLY OBJ. 2: The words of the Philosopher are to be understood about matters that are not ordered to each other, where when one is destroyed the other is not destroyed. But among things that are ordered to each other, the destruction of the first is always worse, whether the first is better or not; for once it is removed, its results are removed, just as sickness is worse than unwholesome habits although wholesome living is better than health.

REPLY OBJ. 3: Just as faith is somewhat in the desire, so is heresy; and although it may be excused in a certain way on the part of the ignorance it has in the intellect, nevertheless as it has hardness in the desire for not obeying the first truth, nothing prevents it from being the greatest sin.

REPLY OBJ. 4: Although schism was most gravely punished as to the newness of punishment—for it was expedient so that the Church's prelates would not be held in contempt—nevertheless, infidelity is punished more as to the great number of those punished, as is clear from Exodus 32:28.[74]

REPLY OBJ. 5: Heresy, according as it includes obstinacy, is a species of the sin against the Holy Spirit, for it is an attack on recognized truth.

---

70. Aristotle, *Nicomachean Ethics*, Bk. 5, ch. 11 (1138b1–2).

71. Aristotle, *Nicomachean Ethics*, Bk. 7, ch. 6 (1148b35ff.).

72. See *Glossa ordinaria*, PL 113:459.

73. *quam sanitas.—quam cacexia quamvis euexia sit melior quam sanitas* PLE.

74. The Busa text cites Exodus 20; the Moos text has Exodus 22:35; but neither of these citations can be right. Exodus 32 makes the point Thomas is making.

ARTICLE 3

Whether heretics are to be tolerated[75]

Ad tertium sic proceditur. Videtur quod haeretici sint sustinendi. Nihil enim debet impugnari, nisi quod est contra amicitiam. Sed diversitas opinionum non est contra concordiam amicitiae, ut Philosophus in 9 *Ethic.* innuit. Ergo non sunt impugnandi.

Praeterea, quod est necessarium, non est impediendum. Sed haeresis est necessaria ecclesiae: 1 Corinth. 11, 19: *necesse est haereses esse, ut qui probati sunt, manifesti fiant.* Ergo non sunt impugnandi.

Praeterea, Matth. 13, Dominus praecipit ut zizania permitterentur crescere usque ad messem. Messis autem est finis saeculi. Cum ergo haeretici sint zizania, videtur quod debeant permitti crescere usque ad finem mundi.

Praeterea, nullus sapiens debet niti ad hoc quod consequi non potest. Sed, sicut dicit quaedam Glossa Isai. 7, *quamdiu stabit mundus, sapiens, saecularis, et haereticus sermo dominabuntur.* Ergo non debet ecclesia niti ad haeresum impugnationem.

Praeterea, nullus credit non volens, ut dicit Augustinus. Sed haeretici in fide errant. Ergo non sunt cogendi.

Sed contra, 1 Corinth. 5, apostolus praecepit esse extirpandum vetus fermentum, quia totam massam corrumpit. Sed haeretici ecclesiam maxime corrumpunt. Ergo sunt ab ecclesia exstirpandi.

Praeterea, lupi sunt ab ovibus arcendi pastorum officio, ut patet Joan. 2. Sed haeretici sunt lupi, ut patet Act. 20. Ergo debent extirpari.

Praeterea, vita spiritualis est melior quam corporalis. Sed homicidae extirpantur, quia auferunt hominibus vitam corporalem. Ergo multo amplius haeretici, qui auferunt hominibus vitam spiritualem.

Respondeo dicendum, quod haeresis est infectivum vitium; unde 2 Timoth. 2, 16, dicitur, quod *multum proficiunt ad impietatem, et sermo eorum ut cancer serpit*; et ideo ecclesia eos a consortio fidelium excludit, et praecipue illos qui alios corrumpunt; ut simplices, qui de facili corrumpi possunt, ab eis sint segregati non solum mente, sed etiam corporaliter; unde per ecclesiam incarcerantur et expelluntur. Si autem alios non corrumpe-

Obj. 1: To the third we proceed thus. It seems that heretics should be tolerated. For nothing should be attacked except what is against friendship. But a difference of opinions is not against the harmony of friendship, as the Philosopher implies in *Ethics* 9.[76] Therefore, they are not to be attacked.

Obj. 2: Furthermore, what is necessary is not to be impeded. But heresy is necessary to the Church: *it is necessary for heresies to exist, so that those who are tested may be made manifest* (1 Cor 11:19). Therefore, they are not to be attacked.

Obj. 3: Furthermore, the Lord commanded that weeds be permitted to grow until harvest (cf. Mt 13:30). But the harvest is the end of the ages. Therefore, since heretics are weeds, it seems that they must be permitted to grow until the end of the world.

Obj. 4: Furthermore, no wise man should strive for what cannot ensue. But, as it says in a certain gloss on Isaiah 7, *as long as the world stands, wise speech, secular speech, and heretical speech will dominate.*[77] Therefore, the Church should not strive for the persecution of heretics.

Obj. 5: Furthermore, no one believes without willing, as Augustine says.[78] But heretics err in their faith. Therefore, they are not to be forced.

On the contrary, the Apostle commands that the old leaven be uprooted, for it corrupts the whole mass (cf. 1 Cor 5:6–7). But heretics corrupt the Church the most. Therefore, they are to be rooted out of the Church.

Furthermore, it is the office of pastors to keep wolves away from the sheep, as is clear from John 10:12. But heretics are wolves, as is clear in Acts 20:29. Therefore, they should be rooted out.

Furthermore, spiritual life is better than physical. But murderers are rooted out because they take men's physical lives. Therefore, much more should heretics be, who take men's spiritual lives.

I answer that, heresy is an infectious vice; hence it is said, *they lead much toward ungodliness, and their speech spreads like a cancer* (2 Tim 2:16–17). And so the Church excludes them from the company of the faithful, and particularly those who corrupt others, so that the simple, who can be easily corrupted, are segregated from them not only in mind, but even physically. And this is why they are imprisoned and expelled by the Church. Now, if they did not

---

75. Parallels: *ST* II-II, q. 10, a. 8, ad 1; q. 11, a. 3; *Quodl.* X, q. 7, a. 1; *Super Matt.* 13.
76. Aristotle, *Nicomachean Ethics*, Bk. 9, ch. 6 (1167a24).
77. Jerome, *Commentariorum in Isaiam Prophetam*, Bk. 3, ch. 7 (PL 24:105).
78. Augustine, *In Iohannis euangelium tractatus* (CCSL 36), Tract. 26, par. 2.

rent, possent etiam celari.[79] Sed illi qui sunt firmi in fide, possunt cum eis corpore conversari, ut eos convertant; non tamen in divinis, quia excommunicati sunt. Sed judicio saeculari possunt licite occidi, et a bonis suis spoliari, etsi alios non corrumpant; quia sunt blasphemi in Deum, et fidem falsam observant; unde magis possunt puniri juste isti quam illi qui sunt rei criminis laesae majestatis, et illi qui falsam monetam cudunt.

AD PRIMUM ergo dicendum, quod Philosophus loquitur de opinionibus speculativis tantum. Sed consensus in unitate fidei est principium communionis in caritate; et ideo dissensus in fide excludit amicitiam familiaritatis.

AD SECUNDUM dicendum, quod haeresis dicitur necessaria non per se loquendo, sed per accidens, inquantum ex quolibet malo Deus elicit aliquod bonum; quia secundum Augustinum, ecclesia utitur haereticis ad probationem doctrinae suae, dum scilicet eorum falsa dogmata impugnat.

AD TERTIUM dicendum, quod Dominus ideo praecepit ut zizania non eradicarentur, ne forte simul cum ipsis eradicaretur et triticum; et ideo hoc locum habet in illis de quibus non constat utrum sint haeretici, vel non.

AD QUARTUM dicendum, quod quamvis ecclesia non possit facere quin sint aliqui haeretici, tamen potest singulariter hunc vel illum coercere; sicut etiam omnia peccata venialia vitare non possumus, tamen singula vitare nitimur.

AD QUINTUM dicendum, quod ecclesia non persequitur eos ut per violentiam inducantur ad credendum, sed ne alios corrumpant, et ne tantum peccatum inultum remaneat.

corrupt others, they could also be concealed. But those who are firm in the faith can spend time with them physically so that they might convert them; nevertheless they cannot share in divine things, for they are excommunicated. But they can licitly be killed and despoiled of their goods by the secular authority, even if they do not corrupt others, for they are blaspheming against God, and they keep a false faith. And so they can be justly punished more than those who are guilty of the crime of offending majesty and those who forge false money.

REPLY OBJ. 1: The Philosopher is speaking only of speculative opinions. But consensus in the unity of the faith is the principle of communion in charity, and therefore dissent in the faith excludes the friendship of familiarity.

REPLY OBJ. 2: Heresy is said to be necessary not speaking *per se*, but incidentally, inasmuch as God draws something good out of any evil. For according to Augustine, the Church uses heretics to prove its own faith, namely when it attacks their false dogmas.[80]

REPLY OBJ. 3: The Lord commanded that the weeds not be rooted out for this reason: lest perhaps the wheat should be uprooted at the same time with them. And so, this approach has a place among those about whom it is not clear whether or not they are heretics.

REPLY OBJ. 4: Although the Church cannot make it so that there are no heretics, nevertheless it can repress this or that one individually; just as also we cannot avoid all venial sins, but we can strive to avoid individual ones.

REPLY OBJ. 5: The Church does not prosecute them so that they may be led to believe by violence, but so that they may not corrupt others, and lest so great a sin remain unpunished.

---

79. *celari.—tolerari* PLE.
80. See Augustine, *Confessions* (CCSL 27), Bk. 7, ch. 19.

EXPOSITION OF THE TEXT

Qui intus sunt nomine et sacramento, etsi non vita. Hoc dicit propter schismaticos et haereticos, qui secundum ipsum non possunt consecrare.

Et quid majus corpore et sanguine? Videtur quod corpus mysticum quod significatur per ipsum. Et dicendum, quod in his quae sunt tantum ad significandum, verum est quod signatum praevalet signo, non autem in aliis quae ex consequenti significant. Et ideo dicendum, quod corpus Christi mysticum, si accipiatur cum ipso capite, est melius quam corpus Christi verum, si tamen corpus Christi verum accipiatur sine divinitate cui est unitum; alias non; quia Deus et omnes creaturae non sunt aliquid melius quam Deus tantum. Si autem accipiatur corpus Christi mysticum absque capite, sic corpus Christi verum est nobilius.

Illi vero qui excommunicati sunt, vel de haeresi manifeste notati, non videntur hoc sacramentum posse conficere. Sciendum, quod in hoc opinio Magistri discordat a communi opinione; et ideo contrariae opinioni adhaerendum est.

Missa enim dicitur, eo quod caelestis missus ad consecrandum vivificum corpus adveniat. Praeter hanc rationem nominis assignat Hugo tres alias rationes. Primo, quia Missa dicitur quasi transmissa, eo quod populus fidelis per ministerium sacerdotis, qui mediatoris vice fungitur inter Deum et hominem, preces, vota et oblationes Deo transmittit. Secundo ipsa hostia sacra Missa vocari potest; quia transmissa est prius a patre nobis, ut scilicet nobiscum esset, postea a nobis patri, ut apud patrem pro nobis esset. Tertio Missa ab emittendo dicitur, ut quidam dicunt; quia ut sacerdos hostiam consecrare incipit, per manum diaconi et ostiarii catechumenos et non communicantes foras ecclesiam mittit. Quarta causa ponitur in littera.

Jube ergo haec perferri per manus sancti angeli tui in sublime altare tuum. Angelus sacris mysteriis interesse credendus est, non ut consecret, quia hujusmodi potestatem non habet, sed ut orationes sacerdotis et populi Deo repraesentet, secundum illud Apoc. 8, 4: *ascendit fumus aromatum in conspectu Domini de manu ange-*

Those who are within the Church in name and sacrament, if not in their [way of] life.[81] He says this because of schismatics and heretics, who, according to him, cannot consecrate.

And what could be better than the body and blood of Christ?[82] It seems that the mystical body is, which is signified by it. And it should be said that among things that are only for the sake of signifying, it is true that what is signified is greater than the sign, but not among other things that signify as a result. And so it should be said that the mystical body of Christ, if it is taken with its head, is better than the true body of Christ, but only if the true body of Christ is taken without the divinity to which it is united; otherwise not, for God and all created things are not in the least better than God alone. But if the mystical body of Christ is considered without its head, then the true body of Christ is more noble.

But those who are excommunicate, or publicly known to be heretical, do not seem to be able to confect this sacrament.[83] It should be known that in this opinion of the Master, he disagrees with the common opinion. And so the contrary opinion should be adhered to.

"For the mass is so called because the heavenly messenger comes to consecrate the life-giving body."[84] Besides this reason, Hugh assigns three other reasons.[85] First, that it is called the Mass as something 'transmitted,' by the fact that the faithful people by the ministry of the priest, who performs the role of a mediator between God and man, transmits prayers, vows, and offerings to God. Second, the victim himself can be said to be something sacred that is 'sent,' for he was first sent down by our Father to us, so that he might be with us, and afterward from us to our Father, so that he might be before the Father on our behalf. Third, it is called the Mass from 'dismissal,' as some people say, for as the priest is about to consecrate the host, he sends the catechumens and those not receiving Communion out of the church by the hand of the deacon and the porter. The fourth reason is set down in the text.

Therefore, "command these to be borne by the hands of your holy angels to your altar in heaven."[86] It should be believed that the angels assist at the sacred mysteries, not to consecrate, for none of their kind has the power, but that they may present to God the prayers of the priest and people, as it says, *the smoke of the incense, which are the*

---

81. Peter Lombard, *Sententiae* IV, 13.1 (72). 1.
82. *Sent* IV 13.1 (72). 3.
83. *Sent* IV 13.1 (72). 4.
84. *Sent* IV 13.1 (72). 4 citing Pseudo-Augustine, unidentified.
85. Hugh of St. Victor, *De sacramentis fidei*, Bk. 2, pt. 8, ch. 14 (PL 176:472).
86. *Sent* IV 13.1 (72). 4 citing Roman Canon, after the consecration.

li, quae sunt orationes sanctorum. Petit ergo sacerdos ut *haec*, idest significata per haec, scilicet corpus mysticum, *per manus angeli*, idest ministerio angelorum, perferantur *in altare sublime*, idest in ecclesiam triumphantem, vel in participationem divinitatis plenam; quia Deus ipse altare sublime dicitur; Exod. 20, 26: *non ascendes ad altare meum per gradus*; idest, in Trinitate non facies gradus. Vel per angelum ipse Christus intelligitur, qui est magni consilii angelus, Isai. 9, 6, juxta 70, qui corpus suum mysticum Deo patri conjungit, et ecclesiae triumphanti.

Oblationem ejus consecrare, idest consecratam Deo repraesentare, ut accepta sit in conspectu Dei quantum ad illos qui offerunt; quia quantum ad id quod continetur, semper est Deo accepta.

Non maledicam benedictionibus vestris. Hostiae benedictio non est principaliter a sacerdote, sed a Deo; unde haec auctoritas non est ad propositum.

Et intentionem adhiberi oportet. De intentione idem dicendum est quod supra de baptismo, dist. 6.

Illud etiam sane dici potest, quod a brutis animalibus corpus Christi non sumitur; etsi videatur. Quomodo hoc sit verum, supra, dist. 10, dictum est. Debet autem ille cujus negligentia hoc accidit quod mus species comedat, secundum canones, quadraginta diebus poenitere; et mus si capi potest, comburi debet, et cinis in sacrarium projici. Si autem amissa fuerit hostia, vel pars ejus, ut inveniri non possit, debet viginti duobus diebus poenitere.

Si autem per negligentiam aliquid de sanguine stillaverit in tabulam quae terrae adhaeret, lingua lambetur, et tabula radetur. Si vero non fuerit tabula, terra radetur, et igni comburetur, et cinis in altari condetur; et sacerdos quadraginta diebus poeniteat. Si autem super altare calix stillaverit, sorbeat minister stillam, et tribus diebus poeniteat.

Si super linteum altaris, et ad aliud stilla pervenerit, quatuor diebus poeniteat. Si usque ad tertium linteum, octo diebus poeniteat. Si usque ad quartum, viginti diebus poeniteat, et linteamina quae stilla tetigit, tribus vicibus lavet minister calice subtus posito; et aqua ablutionis sumatur, et juxta altare condatur. Tutum est etiam ut

prayers of the saints, rose up in the sight of the Lord from the hand of the angel (Rev 8:4). Therefore, the priest prays that *these*, that is, what is signified by these, namely, the mystical body, *by the hands of your angel*, that is, the ministry of angels, may be borne *to your altar in heaven*, that is, into the Church Triumphant, or into the full participation of divinity, for God himself is said to be the heavenly altar: *you shall not ascend to my altar by steps* (Exod 20:26); that is, you will not establish levels within the Trinity. Or by 'angel' Christ himself may be understood, who is the angel of great counsel[87] who unites his own mystical body to God the Father, and to the Church Triumphant.

"Would God send his angel . . . to consecrate his offering,"[88] that is, to present what he has consecrated to God, so that it might be accepted in the sight of God for those who offer it; for as to what it contains, it is always acceptable to God.

"I will curse your blessings."[89] The blessing of the host is not chiefly from the priest, but from God; hence this text is not relevant to the case at hand.

And to have the intention.[90] About the intention the same thing may be said as what was said about baptism in Distinction 6.[91]

It may also be truly said that the body of Christ is not received by brute animals, even when they appear to do so.[92] How this is true was said above in Distinction 10.[93] However, the person through whose negligence it happens that a mouse eats the species, according to the canons, must do penance for forty days; and if the mouse can be caught, it should be incinerated and the ashes thrown into the sacrarium. But if the host has been lost, or part of it, so that it cannot be found, he should do twenty-two days of penance.

But if by negligence some of the precious blood should drip onto a board or tile that is affixed to the ground, it should be licked up and the board should be scraped. But if there was no floorboard, the ground should be scraped, and burned in a fire, and the ashes should be buried in the altar, and the priest should do penance for forty days. However, if the chalice spills on the altar, the minister should mop up the spill, and do three days' penance.

If the spill is too much for one altar cloth and requires another, let him do penance for four days. If it takes three altar cloths, let him do penance for eight days. If it takes four, let him do penance for twenty days, and let the minister wash the linens that the spill touched over the chalice three times, and let the washing water be taken up and kept

---

87. As Isaiah 9:6 reads in the LXX.
88. *Sent* IV 13.1 (72). 4 citing Pseudo-Augustine, unidentified.
89. *Sent* IV 13.1 (72). 4 citing Mal. 2,2.
90. *Sent* IV 13.1 (72). 7.
91. See d. 6, q. 1, a. 2, qa. 1.
92. *Sent* IV 13.1 (72). 8.
93. Actually, d. 9, a. 2, qa. 3.

pars illa lintei abscindatur et comburatur, et cinis in altari condatur.

Si autem aliquis per ebrietatem vel voracitatem Eucharistiam vomuerit, quadraginta diebus poeniteat; clerici, vel monachi, sexaginta; episcopus nonaginta. Si autem infirmitatis causa vomuerit, septem diebus poeniteat.

Dicunt autem quidam, quod poena irrogata fuit ad cautelam, ut negligentia magis caveretur; et ideo circumstantiis pensatis potest minui vel addi ad poenam praedictam. Sed tutius est ut praedictam peragat.

Debet autem secundum quosdam illis diebus jejunare, et a communione cessare. Alii vero dicunt, quod his diebus injungenda est poenitentia arbitraria pensatis conditionibus personae et negotii; et hoc probabilius videtur. Et haec de Eucharistia dicta sufficiant.

beside the altar. The safest thing is to cut off and burn that part of the linen, and to bury the ashes under the altar.

But if someone should vomit up the Eucharist by drunkenness or overeating, let him do forty days' penance; clerics or monks should do sixty; a bishop should do ninety. But if someone vomits by reason of illness, he may do seven days' penance.

However, some people say that these penalties were imposed as a caution, so that negligence would be more guarded against. And so, when the circumstances are taken into account, the penalty can be lessened or increased up to the penalty listed above. But the safest thing is that he do the amount mentioned.

Now according to some, he should fast for those days, and abstain from Communion. But others say that for these days the penalties imposed are to be decided based on the conditions of the person and the problem; and this seems more probable. And let these things said about the Eucharist suffice.